W9-AGB-320

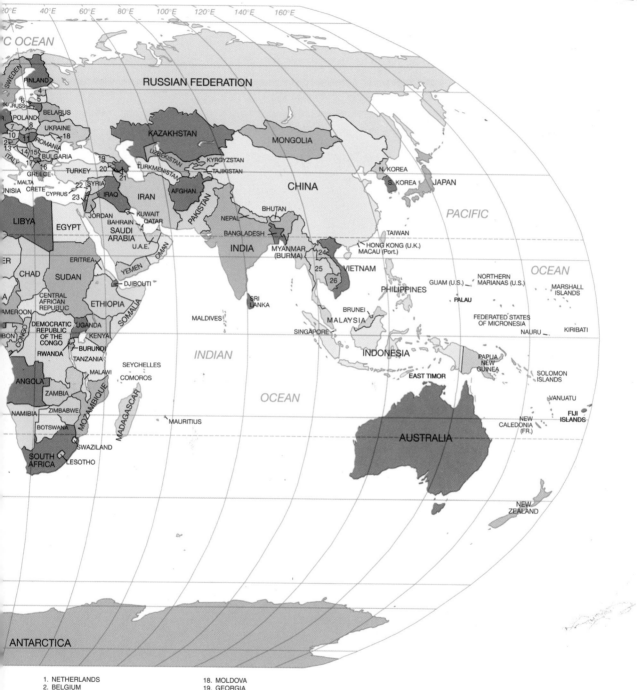

1. NETHERLANDS
2. BELGIUM
3. LUXEMBOURG
4. ESTONIA
5. LATVIA
6. LITHUANIA
7. CZECH REPUBLIC
8. SLOVAKIA
9. SWITZERLAND
10. AUSTRIA
11. HUNGARY
12. SLOVENIA
13. CROATIA
14. BOSNIA AND HERCEGOVINA
15. SERBIA AND MONTENEGRO
16. MACEDONIA
17. ALBANIA

18. MOLDOVA
19. GEORGIA
20. ARMENIA
21. AZERBAIJAN
22. LEBANON
23. ISRAEL
24. LAOS
25. THAILAND
26. CAMBODIA
27. PUERTO RICO (U.S.)
28. ST. KITTS AND NEVIS
29. ANTIGUA AND BARBUDA
30. DOMINICA
31. ST. LUCIA
32. ST. VINCENT AND THE GRENADINES
33. BARBADOS
34. TRINIDAD AND TOBAGO

IMPORTANT:

HERE IS YOUR REGISTRATION CODE TO ACCESS
YOUR PREMIUM McGRAW-HILL ONLINE RESOURCES.

MCGRAW-HILL
ONLINE RESOURCES

For key premium online resources you need THIS CODE to gain access. Once the code is entered, you will be able to use the Web resources for the length of your course.

If your course is using **WebCT** or **Blackboard**, you'll be able to use this code to access the McGraw-Hill content within your instructor's online course.

Access is provided if you have purchased a new book. If the registration code is missing from this book, the registration screen on our Website, and within your WebCT or Blackboard course, will tell you how to obtain your new code.

Registering for McGraw-Hill Online Resources

To gain access to your McGraw-Hill web resources simply follow the steps below:

1. USE YOUR WEB BROWSER TO GO TO: **www.mhhe.com/davidsonnation5**

2. CLICK ON **FIRST TIME USER**.

3. ENTER THE REGISTRATION CODE* PRINTED ON THE TEAR-OFF BOOKMARK ON THE RIGHT.

4. AFTER YOU HAVE ENTERED YOUR REGISTRATION CODE, CLICK **REGISTER**.

5. FOLLOW THE INSTRUCTIONS TO SET-UP YOUR PERSONAL UserID AND PASSWORD.

6. WRITE YOUR UserID AND PASSWORD DOWN FOR FUTURE REFERENCE.
   KEEP IT IN A SAFE PLACE.

TO GAIN ACCESS to the McGraw-Hill content in your instructor's **WebCT** or **Blackboard** course simply log in to the course with the UserID and Password provided by your instructor. Enter the registration code exactly as it appears in the box to the right when prompted by the system. You will only need to use the code the first time you click on McGraw-Hill content.

Thank you, and welcome to your McGraw-Hill online Resources!

Mc Graw Hill **Higher Education**

* YOUR REGISTRATION CODE CAN BE USED ONLY ONCE TO ESTABLISH ACCESS. IT IS NOT TRANSFERABLE.
0-07-299354-5 T/A DAVIDSON, NATION OF NATIONS, 5E

REGISTRATION CODE

2KSW-Q585-BJ7E-DE3Q-LU78

Mc Graw Hill **Higher Education**

Nation of Nations

A Narrative History of the American Republic

Fifth Edition

James West Davidson

William E. Gienapp
Harvard University

Christine Leigh Heyrman
University of Delaware

Mark H. Lytle
Bard College

Michael B. Stoff
University of Texas, Austin

Here is not merely a nation but a teeming nation of nations

Walt Whitman

McGraw Hill

Boston   Burr Ridge, IL   Dubuque, IA   Madison, WI   New York   San Francisco   St. Louis
Bangkok   Bogotá   Caracas   Kuala Lumpur   Lisbon   London   Madrid   Mexico City
Milan   Montreal   New Delhi   Santiago   Seoul   Singapore   Sydney   Taipei   Toronto

The McGraw·Hill Companies

NATION OF NATIONS: A NARRATIVE HISTORY OF THE AMERICAN REPUBLIC

1 2 3 4 5 6 7 8 9 0 DOW/DOW 0 9 8 7 6 5 4

ISBN 0–07–287098–2

Vice president and editor-in-chief: *Emily Barrosse*
Publisher: *Lyn Uhl*
Sponsoring editor: *Steven Drummond*
Development editor: *Kristen Mellitt*
Marketing manager: *Katherine Bates*
Senior Media Producer: *Sean Crowley*
Production editor: *Holly Paulsen*
Manuscript editor: *Joan Pendleton*
Art director: *Jeanne M. Schreiber*

Design manager: *Gino Cieslik*
Cover designer: *Gino Cieslik*
Interior designer: *Maureen McCutcheon*
Art manager: *Robin Mouat*
Art editors: *Cristin Yancy and Emma Ghiselli*
Photo research coordinator: *Nora Agbayani*
Photo researcher: *Deborah Bull and Deborah Anderson, PhotoSearch, Inc.*
Illustrators: *Patty Isaacs*
Production supervisor: *Rich Devitto*

The text was set in 10/12 Berkeley Medium by The GTS Companies, York, PA Campus, and printed on acid-free 45# Publisher's Matte Thin Bulk by R.R. Donnelley, Willard.

Cover images: (left to right) Library of Congress, Prints & Photographs Division [reproduction number LC-USZ62-15887]; © Austrian Archives/Corbis; Library of Congress, Prints & Photographs Division, Edward S. Curtis Collection [reproduction number LC-USZC4-8819]

The credits for this book begin on page C-1, a continuation of the copyright page.

Text Permissions:
Page 268 From Charles A. Johnson, *Frontier Camp Meeting*, copyright 1955, 1985 SMU Press. Reprinted with permission. **813** From Charles P. Kindleberg, *The World in Depression, 1929–1939* (revised ed., 1986), p. 170. Copyright © 1986 The Regents of the University of California. Reprinted by permission from University of California Press. **947, 1063** From Frank Levy, *Dollars and Dreams: The Changing American Income Distribution.* © 1987 Russell Sage Foundation. Used with permission of the Russell Sage Foundation. Reprinted with permission. **1063 (verse)** From "I Am Changing My Name to Chrysler," by Tom Paxton. Copyright © 1980 Pax Music. All rights reserved. Used by permission.

Library of Congress Cataloging-in-Publication Data

Nation of nations : a narrative history of the American republic / James West Davidson ...
  [et al.]. — 5th ed.
    p. cm.
  Includes bibliographical references (p.) and index.
  ISBN 0–07–287098–2 — ISBN 0–07–287099–0 (v. 1 : pbk. : acid-free paper) — ISBN 0–07–287100–8 (v. 2 : pbk. : acid-free paper)
  1. United States—History—Textbooks. I. Davidson, James West.
E178.1.N346   2004
973—dc22   2004052436

www.mhhe.com

William E. Gienapp

1944–2003

Inevitably, contingency brings grief as well as joy. We are saddened to report the passing of our dear friend and co-author, William E. Gienapp. It would be hard to imagine a colleague with greater dedication to his work, nor one who cared more about conveying both the excitement and the rigor of history to those who were not professional historians—as has been attested by so many of his students at the University of Wyoming and at Harvard. Bill had a quiet manner, which sometimes hid (though not for long) his puckish sense of humor and an unstinting generosity. When news of his death was reported, the *Harvard Crimson,* a student newspaper known more for its skepticism than its sentimentality, led with the front-page headline: "Beloved History Professor Gienapp Dies." Bill went the extra mile, whether in searching out primary sources enabling us to assemble a map on the environmental effects of the Lowell Mills, combing innumerable manuscript troves in the preparation of his masterful *Origins of the Republican Party,* or collecting vintage baseball caps from the nineteenth and twentieth centuries to wear (in proper chronological sequence, no less) to his popular course on the social history of baseball. When an illness no one could have predicted struck him down, the profession lost one of its shining examples. His fellow authors miss him dearly.

contents

> **AFTER THE FACT**
> *Historians Reconstruct the Past:*
> Tracking the First Americans   16

Part Two

The Creation of a New Republic   139

Chapter 5

Toward the War for American Independence (1754–1776)   144

Chapter 6

The American People and the American Revolution (1775–1783)   170

Chapter 7

Crisis and Constitution (1776–1789)   196

AFTER THE FACT
Historians Reconstruct the Past:
White and Black Southerners
Worshiping Together   224

Chapter 8

**The Republic Launched
(1789–1801)   228**

Chapter 9

**The Jeffersonian Republic
(1801–1824)   256**

AFTER THE FACT
Historians Reconstruct the Past:

Part Three
The Republic Transformed and Tested   293

Chapter 10
The Opening of America (1815–1850)   298

Chapter 11
The Rise of Democracy (1824–1840)   330

Chapter 12

The Fires of Perfection (1820–1850) 362

Chapter 13

The Old South (1820–1860) 392

AFTER THE FACT
Historians Reconstruct the Past:
What Caused the New York Draft Riots? 525

Chapter 17

Reconstructing the Union (1865–1877) 530

Part Four

The United States in an Industrial Age 561

Chapter 18

The New South and the Trans-Mississippi West (1870–1896) 566

Chapter 19

**The New Industrial Order
(1870–1900) 610**

Chapter 20

**The Rise of an Urban
Order (1870–1900) 642**

Chapter 21

The Political System under Strain (1877–1900)   670

AFTER THE FACT
Historians Reconstruct the Past:
Engendering the Spanish-American War   707

Chapter 22

The Progressive Era (1890–1920)   712

Chapter 26

America's Rise to Globalism (1927–1945)   860

> **AFTER THE FACT**
> *Historians Reconstruct the Past:*
> Did the Atomic Bomb Save Lives?   902

Part Six

The United States in a Nuclear Age   907

Chapter 27

Cold War America (1945–1954)   912

Chapter 28

The Suburban Era (1945–1963)   942

Chapter 29

Civil Rights and the Crisis of Liberalism (1947–1969)   976

AFTER THE FACT
Historians Reconstruct the Past:
The Contested Ground of Collective Memory   1069

Chapter 33

Nation of Nations in a Global Community (1980–2000)   1102

Epilogue

Fighting Terrorism in a Global Age (2000–2003)   1136

list of maps & charts

preface
to the fifth edition

*A*ll good history begins with a good story: that has been the touchstone of *Nation of Nations*. Narrative is embedded in the way we understand the past; hence it will not do simply to compile an encyclopedia of American history and pass it off as a survey.

Yet the narrative keeps changing. A world that has become suddenly and dangerously smaller requires, more than ever, a history that is broader. That conviction has driven our revision for the fifth edition of *Nation of Nations*.

The events following on the heels of September 11, 2001, have underlined the call historians have made over the past decade to view American history within a global context. From its first edition, published in 1990, *Nation of Nations* has taken such an approach, with global essays opening each of the book's six parts to establish an international framework and a global timeline correlating events nationally and worldwide. In the fourth edition, we added global focus sections within chapter narratives and a final chapter ("Nation of Nations in a Global Community") highlighting the ties of the United States to the rest of the world.

Changes to the Fifth Edition

The fifth edition expands on the global coverage that has been so important to our text by adding new narratives that place American history in an international perspective. These narratives are not separate special features. Sometimes only a paragraph in length, sometimes an entire section, they are designed to be an integral part of the text. New material includes

- A section on the Barbary pirates and cultural identities in Chapter 9

- Information comparing debt peonage in the New South with similar circumstances in India, Egypt, and Brazil in Chapter 18
- A section on worldwide recovery from the Great Depression in Chapter 25
- A map on the global spread of the influenza pandemic in autumn 1918 in Chapter 23
- More on global labor migrations in Chapter 26
- A section about Vatican II and American Catholics in Chapter 29

Other important content and pedagogical changes include

- Two new After the Fact essays exploring cultural history topics that have received recent scholarly attention. The new essay in Part Two focuses on Sally Hemings and Thomas Jefferson, and the new essay in Part Four, "Engendering the Spanish-American War," looks at contemporary constructions of gender as the United States went to war with Spain in 1898.
- Updates to Chapter 33, including a new section and map on the election of 2000 and material on recent court cases regarding affirmative action.
- To conclude the book, a new epilogue, "Fighting Terrorism in a Global Age," which includes a chart showing terrorist incidents by region and a map on the war on terror in Afghanistan and Iraq.
- The addition of date ranges to chapter titles, to provide students with more guidance as to the chronology of events.
- An "Interactive Learning" section at the end of every chapter, directing students to relevant materials on the Primary Source Investigator CD-ROM.

- In addition to the Additional Readings feature at the end of each chapter, a full bibliography for the book can be found at www.mhhe.com/davidsonnation5.

Information about Supplements

The supplements listed here accompany *Nation of Nations: A Narrative History of the American Republic,* Fifth Edition. Please contact your local McGraw-Hill representative for details concerning policies, prices, and availability, as some restrictions may apply.

For the Student

- Packaged free with every copy of the book, **Primary Source Investigator CD-ROM** (007295700X) includes hundreds of documents to explore, short documentary movies, interactive maps, and more. Find more information about the CD-ROM where it is packaged in your book.
- Located on the book's Web site (www.mhhe.com/davidsonnation5), the **Student Online Learning Center** offers interactive maps with exercises, extensive Web links, quizzes, counterpoint essays with exercises, a bibliography, and more.

For the Instructor

- A set of **Overhead Transparencies** (0072956976) includes maps and images from the textbook.
- An **Instructor's Resource CD-ROM** (0072456992) provides materials for instructors to use in the classroom, including PowerPoint presentations and electronic versions of the maps in the textbook. An instructor's manual and computerized test bank are also included.
- Located on the book's Web site (www.mhhe.com/davidsonnation5), the **Instructor Online Learning Center** offers PowerPoint presentations, an image bank, an instructor's manual, a bibliography, and more.

Acknowledgments

Wayne Ackerson
Salisbury State University

Robert Alderson
Georgia Perimeter College

Jay Antle
Johnson County Community College

Alan C. Atchison
Southwest Texas State

Eirlys M. Barker
Thomas Nelson Community College

Vince Clark
Johnson County Community College

P. Scott Corbett
Oxnard College

Mary Paige Cubbison
Miami Dade Community College

George Gerdow
Northeastern Illinois University

Ronald Goldberg
Thomas Nelson Community College

Michael Hamilton
Seattle Pacific University

Reid Holland
Midland Technical College

Lisa Hollander
Jefferson College

Carol Keller
San Antonio College

Lawrence Kohl
University of Alabama

Janice M. Leone
Middle Tennessee State University

Daniel Littlefield
University of South Carolina

Susan Matt
Weber State University

Randy D. McBee
Texas Tech University

Robert M. S. McDonald
United States Military Academy

Paul C. Milazzo
Ohio University

Roberto M. Salmón
University of Texas, Pan American

Richard Straw
Radford University

William Woodward
Seattle Pacific University

In addition, friends and colleagues contributed their advice and constructive criticism in ways both small and large. We owe a debt to Myra Armstead, Lawrence A. Cardoso, Dinah Chenven, Christopher Collier, James E. Crisp, R. David Edmunds, George Forgie, Erica Gienapp, Richard John, Virginia Joyner, Philip Kuhn, Stephen E. Maizlish, Drew McCoy, James McPherson, Walter Nugent, Vicki L. Ruiz, Jim Sidbury, David J. Weber, Devra Weber, and John Womack.

The division of labor for this book was determined by our respective fields of scholarship: Christine Heyrman, the colonial era, in which Europeans, Africans, and Indians participated in the making of both a new America and a new republic; William Gienapp, the 90 years in which the young nation first flourished, then foundered on the issues of section and slavery; Michael Stoff, the post–Civil War era, in which industrialization and urbanization brought the nation more centrally into an international system regularly disrupted by depression and war; and Mark Lytle, the modern era, in which Americans finally faced the reality that even the boldest dreams of national greatness are bounded by the finite nature of power and resources both natural and human. Finally, because the need to specialize inevitably imposes limits on any project as broad as this one, our fifth author, James Davidson, served as a general editor and writer, with the intent of fitting individual parts to the whole as well as providing a measure of continuity, style, and overarching purpose. In producing this collaborative effort, all of us have shared the conviction that the best history speaks to a larger audience.

James West Davidson
William E. Gienapp
Christine Leigh Heyrman
Mark H. Lytle
Michael B. Stoff

Global Essay

Each of the book's six parts begins with an essay that sets American events into a global context.

Global Timeline

Each global essay includes a timeline comparing political and social events in the United States with developments elsewhere.

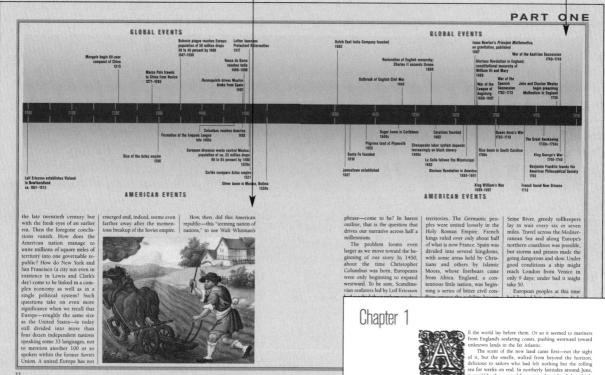

PART ONE

GLOBAL EVENTS

Mongols begin 60-year conquest of China 1215

Marco Polo travels to China from Venice 1271–1295

Bubonic plague reaches Europe; population of 50 million drops 30 to 40 percent by 1400 1347–1500

Luther launches Protestant Reformation 1517

Vasco da Gama reaches India 1498–1500

Reconquista drives Muslim Arabs from Spain 1492

Dutch East India Company founded 1602

Restoration of English monarchy; Charles II ascends throne 1660

Outbreak of English Civil War 1642

Isaac Newton's *Principia Mathematica,* on gravitation, published 1687

Glorious Revolution in England; constitutional monarchy of William III and Mary 1688

War of the League of Augsburg 1688–1697

War of the Spanish Succession 1702–1713

War of the Austrian Succession 1740–1748

John and Charles Wesley begin preaching Methodism in England 1738

AMERICAN EVENTS

Leif Ericsson establishes Vinland in Newfoundland ca. 1001–1015

Rise of the Aztec empire 1300

Formation of the Iroquois League late 1400s

Columbus reaches America 1492

European diseases waste central Mexico; population of ca. 25 million drops 80 to 95 percent by 1600 1520s

Cortés conquers Aztec empire 1521

Silver boom in Mexico, Bolivia 1550s

Jamestown established 1607

Santa Fe founded 1610

Pilgrims land at Plymouth 1620

Sugar boom in Caribbean 1640s

Chesapeake labor system depends increasingly on black slavery 1680s

La Salle follows the Mississippi 1682

Glorious Revolution in America 1688–1691

King William's War 1689–1697

Carolina founded 1663

Rice boom in South Carolina 1700s

Queen Anne's War 1702–1713

French found New Orleans 1718

The Great Awakening 1730s–1750s

King George's War 1740–1748

Benjamin Franklin founds the American Philosophical Society 1743

the late twentieth century but with the fresh eyes of an earlier era. Then the foregone conclusions vanish. How does the American nation manage to unite millions of square miles of territory into one governable republic? How do New York and San Francisco (a city not even in existence in Lewis and Clark's day) come to be linked in a complex economy as well as in a single political system? Such questions take on even more significance when we recall that Europe—roughly the same size as the United States—is today still divided into more than four dozen independent nations speaking some 33 languages, not to mention another 100 or so spoken within the former Soviet Union. A united Europe has not

22

emerged and, indeed, seems even farther away after the momentous breakup of the Soviet empire.

How, then, did this American republic—this "teeming nation of nations," to use Walt Whitman's

phrase—come to be? In barest outline, that is the question that drives our narrative across half a millennium.

The problem looms even larger as we move toward the beginning of our story. In 1450, about the time Christopher Columbus was born, Europeans were only beginning to expand westward. To be sure, Scandinavian seafarers led by Leif Ericsson

territories. The Germanic peoples were united loosely in the Holy Roman Empire. French kings ruled over only about half of what is now France. Spain was divided into several kingdoms, with some areas held by Christians and others by Islamic Moors, whose forebears came from Africa. England, a contentious little nation, was beginning a series of bitter civil con-

Seine River, greedy tollkeepers lay in wait every six or seven miles. Travel across the Mediterranean Sea and along Europe's northern coastlines was possible, but storms and pirates made the going dangerous and slow. Under good conditions a ship might reach London from Venice in only 9 days; under bad it might take 50.

European peoples at this time

Chapter 1

A ll the world lay before them. Or so it seemed to mariners from England's seafaring coasts, pushing westward toward unknown lands in the far Atlantic.

The scent of the new land came first—not the sight of it, but the smells, wafted from beyond the horizon, delicious to sailors who had felt nothing but the rolling sea for weeks on end. In northerly latitudes around June, it would be the scent of fir trees or the sight of shore birds wheeling about the masts. Straightaway the captain would call for a lead to be thrown overboard to sound the depths. At its end was a hollowed-out socket with a bit of tallow in it, so some of the sea bottom would stick when the lead was hauled up. Even out of sight of land, a good sailing master could tell where he was by what came up—"oosy sand" or perhaps "soft worms" or "popple-stones as big as beans." If the ship was approaching unknown shores, the captain would hope to sight land early in the day, allowing time to work cautiously toward an untried harbor on uncharted tides.

Since the time of King Arthur, the English living along the rugged southwestern coasts of Devon and Cornwall had followed the sea. From the wharves of England's West Country seaports like Bristol, ships headed west and north to Ireland, bringing back animal hides as well as timber for houses and barrels. Or they turned south, fetching wines from France and olive oil or figs and raisins from the Spanish and Portuguese coasts. In return, West Country ports offered woven woolen cloth and codfish, caught wherever the best prospects beckoned.

Through much of the fifteenth century the search for cod drew West Country sailors north and west, toward Iceland. In the 1480s and 1490s, however, a few English tried their luck farther west. Old maps, after all, claimed that the bountiful *Hy-Brasil*—Gaelic for "Isle of the Blessed"—lay somewhere west of Ireland. These western ventures returned with little to show for their daring until the coming of an Italian named Giovanni Caboto, called John Cabot by the English. Cabot, who hailed from Venice, obtained the blessing of King Henry VII to hunt for unknown lands. From the port of Bristol his lone ship set out to the west in the spring of 1497.

Cabot discovers Newfoundland

This time the return voyage brought news of a "new-found" island where the trees were tall enough to make fine masts and the codfish were plentiful. After returning to Bristol, Cabot marched off to London to inform His Majesty; received 10 pounds as his reward, and with the proceeds dressed himself in dashing silks. The multitudes of London flocked after him, wondering over "the Admiral;" then Cabot returned triumphantly to Bristol to undertake a more ambitious search for a northwest passage to Asia. He set sail with five ships in 1498 and was never heard from again.

26

Old World, New Worlds

1400–1600

preview • In the century after 1492, Europeans expanded boldly and often ruthlessly into the Americas, thanks to a combination of technological advances in sailing and firearms, the rise of new trading networks, and stronger, more centralized governments. Spain established a vast and profitable empire but at fearful human cost. A diverse Mesoamerican population of some 20 million was reduced to only 2 million through warfare, European diseases, and exploitation.

Preview

A preview introduces each chapter's main themes.

AFTER THE FACT
Historians Reconstruct the Past

Sally Hemings and Thomas Jefferson

The rumors began in Albemarle County, Virginia, more than two hundred years ago; they came to the notice of a journalist by the name of James Callender. A writer for hire, Callender had once lent his pen to the Republicans, but turned from friend into foe when the party failed to reward him with a political appointment. When his story splashed onto the pages of the *Recorder*, a Richmond newspaper, the trickle of rumor turned into a torrent of scandal. Callender alleged that Thomas Jefferson, during his years in Paris as the American minister, had contracted a liaison with one of his own slaves. The woman was the president's mistress even now, he insisted, in 1802. She was kept at Monticello, and Jefferson had fathered children with her. Her name was Sally Hemings.

Solid information about Sally Hemings is scarce. She was one of six children, we know, born to Betty Hemings and her white master, John Wayles, a Virginia planter whose white daughter, Martha Wayles Skelton, married Jefferson in 1772. We know that Betty Hemings was the child of an African woman and an English sailor, which means Betty's children with Wayles, Sally among them, were quadroons—light-skinned men and women whose ancestry was one-quarter African. We know that Sally accompanied one of Jefferson's daughters to Paris as her maid in 1787 and that, upon returning to Virginia a few years later, she performed domestic work at Monticello. We know that she had six children and that the four who survived to adulthood escaped from slavery into freedom: Jefferson assisted her two eldest children, Beverly and Harriet, in leaving Monticello in 1822, and her two younger children, Madison and Eston, were freed by Jefferson's will in 1827. We know that shortly after Jefferson's death, his daughter, Martha Jefferson Randolph, freed Sally Hemings and that she lived with her two younger sons in Charlottesville until her own death in 1835.

We know, too, that Jefferson's white descendants stoutly denied (and, to this day, some still deny) any familial connection with the descendants of Sally Hemings. Even though Callender's scandal

Jefferson owned 5000 acres of land in Albemarle County, Virginia, his "home farm" of Monticello and three "quarter farms"—Lego, Tufton, and Shadwell. Sally Hemings and her children lived at the Monticello plantation.

quickly subsided, doing Jefferson no lasting political damage, his white grandchildren were still explaining away the accusations half a century later. In the 1850s, Jefferson's granddaughter, Ellen Coolidge Randolph, claimed that her brother, Thomas Jefferson Randolph, had told her that one of Jefferson's nephews, Samuel Carr, fathered Hemings's children. In the 1860s, Henry Randall, an early biographer of Jefferson, recalled a conversation with Thomas Jefferson Randolph in the 1850s in which he attributed paternity to another nephew, Samuel's brother Peter Carr.

Until the end of the twentieth century, most scholars resolved the discrepancy of this dual claim by suggesting that one of the Carr nephews had fathered Sally Hemings's children. And all of Jefferson's most eminent twentieth-century biographers—Douglas Adair, Dumas Malone, John Chester Miller, and Joseph J. Ellis—contended that a man of Jefferson's character and convictions could not have engaged in a liaison with a slave woman. After all, Jefferson was a Virginia gentleman and an American philosophe who believed that reason should rule over passion; he was also an eloquent apostle of equality and democracy and an outspoken critic of the tyrannical power of masters over slaves. And despite his opposition to slavery, Jefferson argued in his *Notes on the State of Virginia* (1785) for the likelihood that peoples of African descent were inferior intellectually and artistically to those of European descent. Because of that conviction, he warned of the dire consequences that would attend the mixing of the races.

The official version of events did not go unchallenged. Madison Hemings, a skilled carpenter who, a year after his mother's death, moved from Virginia to southern Ohio, publicly related an oral tradition repeated among his family. When interviewed by a Pike County, Ohio, newspaper in 1873, Madison reported that his mother had been Thomas Jefferson's "concubine" and that Jefferson had fathered all of her children. Even so, nearly a century passed before Madison Hemings's claims won wider attention. In 1968, the historian Winthrop Jordan noted that Sally Hemings's pregnancies coincided with Jefferson's stays at Monticello. In 1975, Fawn Brodie's best-selling "intimate history" of Jefferson portrayed his relationship with Sally Hemings as an enduring love affair; four years later, the African American novelist Barbara Chase-Rimboud set Brodie's findings to fiction.

This view of Monticello was painted shortly after Jefferson's death. It portrays his white descendants surrounded by a serene landscape.

288

289

After the Fact: Historians Reconstruct the Past

The book includes eight essays that demonstrate the methods used by historians to analyze a variety of sources, ranging from typescript drafts of presidential memoirs or handwritten notations in church records to military casualty estimates, public monuments, and even climate data derived from the analysis of tree rings.

Global Coverage

A section of the narrative in each chapter discusses American history from a global perspective, showing that the United States did not develop in a geographic or cultural vacuum and that the broad forces shaping it also influenced other nations.

---

34   Part One **The Creation of a New America**

keep pace with the "Price Revolution," landlords raised rents, adding to the burden of the peasantry.

To Europe's hopeful and desperate alike, this climate of disorder and uncertainty led to dreams that the New World would provide an opportunity to renew the Old. As Columbus wrote eagerly of Hispaniola: "This island and all others are very fertile to a limitless degree. . . . There are very large tracts of cultivated land. . . . In the interior there are mines and metals." Columbus and many other Europeans expected that the Americas would provide land for the landless, work for the unemployed, and wealth beyond the wildest dreams of the daring.

The Conditions of Colonization

Sixteenth-century Europeans sought to colonize the Americas, not merely to escape from scarcity and disruption at home. They were also propelled across the Atlantic by dynamic changes in their society. Revolutions in technology, economics, and politics made overseas settlement practical and attractive to seekers of profit and power.

Expansion of trade and capital

The improvements in navigation and sailing also fostered an expansion of trade. By the late fifteenth century Europe's merchants and bankers had devised more efficient ways of transferring money and establishing credit in order to support commerce across longer distances. And although rising prices and rents pinched Europe's peasantry, that same inflation enriched those who had goods to sell, money to lend, and land to rent. Wealth flowed into the coffers of sixteenth-century traders, financiers, and landlords, creating a pool of capital that those investors could plow into colonial development. Both the commercial networks and the private fortunes needed to sustain overseas trade and settlement were in place by the time of Columbus's discovery.

Political centralization

The direction of Europe's political development also paved the path for American colonization. After 1450 strong monarchs in Europe steadily enlarged the sphere of royal power at the expense of warrior lords. Henry VII, the founder of England's Tudor dynasty, Francis I of France, and Ferdinand and Isabella of Spain began the trend, forging modern nation-states by extending their political control over more territory, people, and resources. Those larger, more centrally organized states were able to marshal the resources necessary to support colonial outposts and to sustain the professional armies and navies capable of protecting empires abroad.

Europeans, Chinese, and Aztecs on the Eve of Contact

It was the growing power of monarchs as well as commercial and technological development that allowed early modern Europeans to establish permanent settlements—even empires—in another world lying an ocean away. But that conclusion raises an intriguing question: why didn't China, the most advanced civilization of the early modern world, engage in expansion and colonization? Or for that matter, if events had fallen out a little differently, why didn't the Aztecs discover and colonize Europe?

The Chinese undoubtedly possessed the capability to navigate the world's oceans and to establish overseas settlements. A succession of Ming dynasty emperors and their efficient bureaucrats marshaled China's resources to develop a thriving shipbuilding industry and trade with ports throughout southeast Asia and India. By the opening of the fifteenth century, the Chinese seemed poised for even greater maritime exploits. Seven times between 1405 and 1433, China's "treasure

Daily Lives

POPULAR ENTERTAINMENT
Exploring the Wondrous World

In 1786 Charles Willson Peale, painter and jack-of-all-trades, opened a museum of natural history in his home on Lombard Street in Philadelphia. Americans had always been fascinated by freaks of nature and "remarkable providences" (see Daily Lives, "A World of Wonders and Witchcraft," on pages 94–95). But unlike seventeenth-century colonials, Peale was not searching for signs of the supernatural in everyday life. A student of the Enlightenment, Peale intended his museum to be "a school of useful knowledge" that would attract men and women of all ages and social ranks. By studying natural history, Peale believed, citizens would gain an understanding of themselves, their country, and the world and thereby help sustain civilization in the United States. The sign over the door read, "Whoso would learn wisdom, let him enter here!"

Inside, the visitor found a wide assortment of items from around the world. Peale displayed nearly a hundred paintings he had completed of leading Americans, stuffed birds and animals, busts of famous scientists, cases of minerals, and wax figures representing the races of the world. Among the technological innovations that were showcased, a machine called a *physiognotrace* produced precise silhouettes. Moses Williams, a former slave, operated the machine and did a thriving business, selling 8880 profiles in the first year. Peale's backyard soon contained a zoo with a bewildering assortment of animals, including two grizzly bear cubs, an eagle, numerous snakes, monkeys, and a hyena. Prominent acquaintances such as Benjamin Franklin, George Washington, and Thomas Jefferson sent specimens, and the collection eventually totaled some 100,000 items.

Peale's most famous exhibit was a skeleton of a mastodon (he misnamed it a mammoth, thereby adding a synonym for *huge* to the American vocabulary). Assembled from several digs he had conducted with great publicity in upstate New York, it stood 11 feet high at the shoulder and was the first complete mastodon skeleton ever mounted. Billed "the ninth wonder of the world," it was

In this self-portrait, Charles Willson Peale lifts a curtain to reveal the famous Long Room of his museum. Partially visible on the right behind Peale is the great mastodon skeleton, at which a woman gazes in awe, while in the rear a father instructs his son on the wonders of nature.

housed in a special "Mammoth Room" that required a separate admission fee.

In gathering and mounting his specimens, Peale sought "to bring into one view a world in miniature." He carefully labeled plants, animals, insects, and birds and arranged them according to accepted scientific classifications. He also pioneered the grouping of animals in their natural habitat. Stuffed tigers and deer stood on a plaster mountainside, while below, a glass pond was filled with fish, reptiles, and birds. For the safety of visitors who could not resist handling the exhibits, the birds, whose feathers were covered with arsenic, were eventually put in glass-fronted cases with painted habitats behind them.

Peale refused to indulge the popular taste for spectacles and freaks. He hesitated before accepting a five-legged cow with two tails, fearing it would lower the institution's dignity and compromise its serious purpose. He declined to display a blue sash belonging to George Washington because it had no educational value, and only after Peale's death was it exhibited. He put curiosities away in cabinets and showed them only on request.

Peale's museum was an expression of its founder's republican ideals of order, stability, and harmony. It was, in his mind, an institute of eternal laws, laid bare for the masses to see and understand. Peale hoped the museum would instill civic responsibility in its patrons, and he often told the story of how two hostile Indian chiefs, meeting by accident in the museum, were so impressed with its harmony that they agreed to sign a peace treaty.

The museum attracted thousands of curious customers and prospered in its early years. It was one of the major attractions in Philadelphia and became famous throughout the nation. Yet Peale's vast collection soon overwhelmed his scientific classification scheme, and his grandiose plans always outran his funds and soon his space as well. Refusing to slow his collection efforts, Peale moved his museum in 1794 to Philosophical Hall, and then in 1802 he took over the second floor of Independence Hall.

Before he retired in 1810, Peale tried vainly to interest the national government in acquiring his collection and creating a national museum. Under the direction of his son, the museum struggled on, but it was unable to satisfy the growing popular appetite for showmanship rather than education. The museum finally closed its doors in 1850, but during the Republic's formative years it offered thousands of Americans a unique opportunity, as the ticket of admission promised, to "explore the wondrous world."

250

limits and threatened the liberties of citizens, states had the right to interpose their authority.

But Jefferson and Madison were not ready to rend a union that had so recently been forged. The two men intended for the Virginia and Kentucky resolutions only to rally public opinion to the Republican cause. They opposed any effort to resist federal authority by force. Furthermore, other states openly rejected the doctrine of "interposition." During the last year of the Adams administration, the Alien and Sedition Acts quietly expired. Once in power, the Republicans repealed the Naturalization Act.

The Election of 1800

With a naval war raging on the high seas and the Alien and Sedition Acts sparking debate at home, Adams suddenly shocked his party by negotiating a peace treaty with France. It was a courageous act, for Adams not only split his party in two but also ruined his own chances for reelection by driving Hamilton's pro-British wing of the party into open opposition. The nation benefited, however, for France signed a peace treaty ending its undeclared war. Adams, who bristled with pride and independence, termed this act "the most disinterested, the most determined and the most successful of my whole life."

251

Daily Lives

Every chapter contains an essay focusing on one of five themes that give insight into the lives of ordinary Americans: clothing and fashion; time and travel; food, drink, and drugs; public space/private space; and popular entertainment.

Marginal Headings

Succinct notes in the margins highlight key terms and concepts.

---

542 Part Three **The Republic Transformed and Tested**

From the beginning of Reconstruction, African Americans demanded the right to vote as free citizens. The Fifteenth Amendment, ratified in 1870, secured that right for black males. In New York, black citizens paraded in support of Ulysses Grant for president. Parades played a central role in campaigning: this parade exhibits the usual banners, flags, costumes, and a band. Blacks in both the North and the South voted solidly for the Republican party as the party of Lincoln and emancipation, although white violence in the South increasingly reduced black turnout.

The New State Governments

New state constitutions

The new southern state constitutions enacted several significant reforms. They put in place fairer systems of legislative representation, allowed voters to elect many officials who before had been appointed, and abolished property requirements for officeholding. In South Carolina, for the first time, voters were allowed to vote for the president, governor, and other state officers.* The Radical state governments also assumed some responsibility for social welfare and established the first statewide systems of public schools in the South. Although the Fourteenth Amendment prevented high Confederate officials from holding office, only Alabama and Arkansas temporarily forbade some ex-Confederates to vote.

Race and social equality

All the new constitutions proclaimed the principle of equality and granted black adult males the right to vote. On social relations they were much more cautious. No state outlawed segregation, and South Carolina and Louisiana were the only states that required integration in public schools (a mandate that was almost universally ignored). Sensitive to status, mulattoes pushed for prohibition of social discrimination, but white Republicans refused to adopt such a radical policy.

Economic Issues and Corruption

The war left the southern economy in ruins, and problems of economic reconstruction were as difficult as those of politics. The new Republican governments encouraged industrial development by providing subsidies, loans, and even

---

*Previously, presidential electors as well as the governor had been chosen by the South Carolina legislature.

---

xxvi

Summary

A bulleted summary reinforces each chapter's main points.

Interactive Learning

Lists at the end of every chapter direct students to relevant interactive maps, short documentary movies, and primary source materials located on the Primary Source Investigator CD-ROM.

Additional Reading

Annotated references to both classic studies and recent scholarship encourage further pursuit of the topics and events covered in the chapter.

Significant Events

A chronology at the end of each chapter shows the temporal relationship among important events.

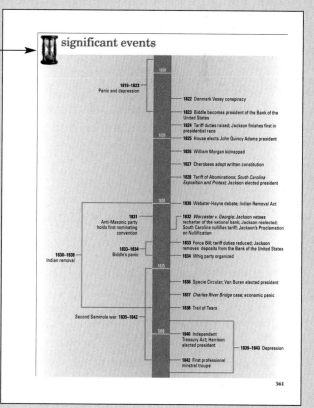

Printer Ornaments and Initial Blocks

History records change over time in countless ways. The flow of history is reflected not only in the narrative of this text but in the decorative types used in its design.

  Over the years printers have used ornamental designs to enliven their texts. Each chapter of *Nation of Nations* incorporates an ornament created during the period being written about. Often these ornaments are from printers' specimen books, produced by type manufacturers so printers could buy such designs. In other chapters the ornaments are taken from printed material of the era.

The initial blocks—the large decorative initials beginning the first word of every chapter—are drawn from type styles popular during the era covered by each of the book's six parts.

 Part 1 uses hand-engraved initials of the sort imported from England and Europe by colonial printers in the seventeenth and eighteenth centuries.

 Part 2 displays mortised initial blocks. These ornaments had holes cut in the middle of the design so a printer could insert the initial of choice. These holes provided greater flexibility when the supply of ornaments was limited.

T Part 3 features initial blocks cut from wood, an approach common in the early and middle nineteenth century. This design, Roman X Condensed, allowed more letters to be squeezed into a limited space.

T Part 4 makes use of a more ornamental initial block common in the late nineteenth and early twentieth centuries. Some Victorian designs became quite ornate. This font, a style that is relatively reserved, is Latin Condensed.

T Part 5 illustrates an initial block whose clean lines reflect the Art Deco movement of the 1920s and 1930s. Printers of the New Era turned away from the often-flowery nineteenth-century styles. This font is Beverly Hills.

7 Part 6 features an informal style, Brush Script Regular. First introduced during World War II, this typeface reflects the more casual culture that blossomed during the postwar era.

about the authors

James West Davidson received his Ph.D. from Yale University. A historian who has pursued a full-time writing career, he is the author of numerous books, among them *After the Fact: The Art of Historical Detection* (with Mark H. Lytle), *The Logic of Millennial Thought: Eighteenth-Century New England,* and *Great Heart: The History of a Labrador Adventure* (with John Rugge). He is coeditor, with Michael Stoff, of the *Oxford New Narratives in American History* and is at work on a study of Ida B. Wells for the series.

William E. Gienapp has a Ph.D. from the University of California, Berkeley and taught at the University of Wyoming before going to Harvard University, where he was Professor of History until his death in 2003. In 1988 he received the Avery O. Craven Award for his book *The Origins of the Republican Party, 1852–1856.* He edited *The Civil War and Reconstruction: A Documentary Collection,* and most recently published *Abraham Lincoln and Civil War America* and a companion volume, *This Fiery Trial: The Speeches and Writings of Abraham Lincoln.*

Christine Leigh Heyrman is Professor of History at the University of Delaware. She received a Ph.D. in American Studies from Yale University and is the author of *Commerce and Culture: The Maritime Communities of Colonial Massachusetts, 1690–1750.* Her book *Southern Cross: The Beginnings of the Bible Belt* was awarded the Bancroft Prize in 1998.

Mark H. Lytle, who received a Ph.D. from Yale University, is Professor of History and Environmental Studies and Chair of the History Program at Bard College. He was recently reappointed Mary Ball Washington Professor of History at University College, Dublin, in Ireland. His publications include *The Origins of the Iranian-American Alliance, 1941–1953, After the Fact: The Art of Historical Detection* (with James West Davidson), and "An Environmental Approach to American Diplomatic History" in *Diplomatic History.* His most recent book, *The Uncivil War: America in the Vietnam Era,* will be published in 2005, and he is completing a biography of Rachel Carson.

Michael B. Stoff is Associate Professor of History at the University of Texas at Austin. The recipient of a Ph.D. from Yale University, he has received many teaching awards, most recently the Friars' Centennial Teaching Excellence Award. He is the author of *Oil, War, and American Security: The Search for a National Policy on Foreign Oil, 1941–1947* and coeditor (with Jonathan Fanton and R. Hal Williams) of *The Manhattan Project: A Documentary Introduction to the Atomic Age.* He is currently working on a brief narrative of the bombing of Nagasaki.

introduction

History is both a discipline of rigor, bound by rules and scholarly methods, and something more: the unique, compelling, even strange way in which we humans define ourselves. We are all the sum of the tales of thousands of people, great and small, whose actions have etched their lines upon us. History supplies our very identity—a sense of the social groups to which we belong, whether family, ethnic group, race, class, or gender. It reveals to us the foundations of our deepest religious beliefs and traces the roots of our economic and political systems. It explores how we celebrate and grieve, how we sing the songs we sing, how we weather the illnesses to which time and chance subject us. It commands our attention for all these good reasons and for no good reason at all, other than a fascination with the way the myriad tales play out. Strange that we should come to care about a host of men and women so many centuries gone, some with names eminent and familiar, others unknown but for a chance scrap of information left behind in an obscure letter.

Yet we do care. We care about Sir Humphrey Gilbert, "devoured and swallowed up of the Sea" one black Atlantic night in 1583; we care about George Washington at Kips Bay, red with fury as he takes a riding crop to his retreating soldiers. We care about Octave Johnson, a slave fleeing through Louisiana swamps trying to decide whether to stand and fight the approaching hounds or take his chances with the bayou alligators; we care about Clara Barton, her nurse's skirts so heavy with blood from the wounded, that she must wring them out before tending to the next soldier. We are drawn to the fate of Chinese laborers, chipping away at the Sierras' looming granite; of a Georgian named Tom Watson seeking to forge a colorblind political alliance; and of desperate immigrant mothers, kerosene lamps in hand, storming Brooklyn butcher shops that had again raised prices. We follow, with a mix of awe and amusement, the fortunes of the quirky Henry Ford ("Everybody wants to be somewhere he ain't"), turning out identical automobiles, insisting his factory workers wear identical expressions ("Fordization of the Face").

We trace the career of young Thurgood Marshall, crisscrossing the South in his own "little old beat-up '29 Ford," typing legal briefs in the back seat, trying to get black teachers to sue for equal pay, hoping to get his people somewhere they weren't. The list could go on and on, spilling out as it did in Walt Whitman's *Leaves of Grass*: "A southerner soon as a northerner, a planter nonchalant and hospitable, / A Yankee bound my own way . . . a Hoosier, a Badger, a Buckeye, a Louisianian or Georgian. . . ." Whitman embraced and celebrated them all, inseparable strands of what made him an American and what made him human:

> In all people I see myself, none more and not one
> a barleycorn less; And the good or bad I say of
> myself, I say of them.

To encompass so expansive an America, Whitman turned to poetry; historians have traditionally chosen *narrative* as their means of giving life to the past. That mode of explanation permits them to interweave the strands of economic, political, and social history in a coherent chronological framework. By choosing narrative, historians affirm the multicausal nature of historical explanation—the insistence that events be portrayed in context. By choosing narrative, they are also acknowledging that, although long-term economic and social trends shape societies in significant ways, events often take on a logic (or an illogic) of their own, jostling one another, being deflected by unpredictable personal decisions, sudden deaths, natural catastrophes, and chance. There are literary reasons, too, for preferring a narrative approach, because it supplies a dramatic force usually missing from more structural analyses of the past.

In some ways, surveys such as this text are the natural antithesis of narrative history. They strive, by definition, to be comprehensive: to furnish a broad, orderly exposition of their chosen field. Yet to cover so much ground in so limited a space necessarily deprives readers of the context of more detailed accounts. Then, too, the resurgence of social history—with its concern for class and race, patterns of rural and urban life, the spread of market and industrial economies—lends itself to more analytic, less chronological treatments. The challenge facing historians is to incorporate these areas of research without losing the story's narrative drive or the chronological flow that orients readers to the more familiar events of our past.

With the cold war of the past half-century at an end, there has been increased attention to the worldwide breakdown of so many nonmarket economies and, by inference, to the greater success of the market societies of the United States and other capitalist nations. As our own narrative makes clear, American society and politics have indeed come together centrally in the marketplace. What Americans produce, how and where they produce it, and the desire to buy cheap and sell dear have been defining elements in every era. That market orientation has created unparalleled abundance and reinforced striking inequalities, not the least a society in which, for two centuries, human beings themselves were bought and sold. It has made Americans powerfully provincial in protecting local interests and internationally adventurous in seeking to expand wealth and opportunity.

It goes without saying that Americans have not always produced wisely or well. The insistent drive toward material plenty has levied a heavy tax on the global environment. Too often quantity has substituted for quality, whether we talk of cars, education, or culture. When markets flourish, the nation abounds with confidence that any problem, no matter how intractable, can be solved. When markets fail, however, the fault lines of our political and social systems become all too evident.

In the end, then, it is impossible to separate the marketplace of boom and bust and the world of ordinary Americans from the corridors of political maneuvering or the ceremonial pomp of an inauguration. To treat political and social history as distinct spheres is counterproductive. The primary question of this narrative—how the fledgling, often tumultuous confederation of "these United States" managed to transform itself into an enduring republic—is not only political but necessarily social. In order to survive, a republic must resolve conflicts between citizens of different geographic regions and economic classes, of diverse racial and ethnic origins, of competing religions and ideologies. The resolution of these conflicts has produced tragic consequences, perhaps, as often as noble ones. But tragic or noble, the destiny of these states cannot be understood without comprehending both the social and the political dimensions of the story.

primary source investigator CD-ROM

History comes alive through narrative; but the building blocks of that narrative are primary sources. McGraw-Hill's Primary Source Investigator (PSI) CD-ROM provides instant access to hundreds of the most important and interesting documents, images, artifacts, audio recordings, and videos from our past. You can browse the collection across time, source types, subjects, historical questions, textbook chapters, or your own custom search terms. Clicking on a source opens it in our Source Window, packed with annotations, investigative tools, transcripts, and interactive questions for deeper analysis.

As close companions to the primary sources, original secondary sources are also included on the PSI: 5- to 8-minute documentaries and interactive maps complete with underlying statistical data. Together these features weave a rich historical narrative or argument on topics that are difficult to fully grasp from primary sources alone. Each secondary source also provides links back to related primary sources, enabling you to test a secondary source's argument against the historical record.

While examining any of these sources you can use our notebook feature to take notes, bookmark key sources, and save or print copies of all the sources for use outside the archive. After researching a particular theme or time period, you can use our argument-outlining tool to walk you through the steps of composing a historical essay or presentation.

Through its browsing and inspection tools, Primary Source Investigator helps you practice the art of historical detection using a real archive of historical sources. This process of historical investigation follows three basic steps:

- *Ask*   Use our browsing panels to search and filter the sources.
- *Research*   Use the Source Window to examine sources in detail and the Notebook to record your insights.
- *Argue*   Practice outlining historical arguments based on archival sources.

Nation of Nations

Prologue

T he land that they made their own became the hearth of civilization in the Americas. It was a fitting tribute to their ancestors who, thousands of years earlier, had discovered and colonized a truly new world, one in which no human beings had ever lived. No less bold, their descendants created cultures that rank among the most brilliant in all the ancient world. They invented farming, built the first cities, and developed complex ways of organizing society, government, and religious worship. They devised precise calendars and elegant hieroglyphic systems of writing. They crafted useful tools and fashioned beautiful works of art.

These were the peoples of ancient Mesoamerica during the first millennium C.E.*—some living on the Yucatán Peninsula, some along the gulf coast of Mexico, others in the highlands of central Mexico, and still others on the narrow strip of land from Guatemala to Panama. What the Greeks and Romans of antiquity were to Europe, the earliest settlers of Mesoamerica were to their side of the Atlantic—the founders of classical civilizations, empires whose cultural influence left a profound impression on other peoples, including those living hundreds of miles to the north.

Settling and Civilizing the Americas

preview • The civilizations that arose in the Americas during the first millennium C.E. rivaled the classical civilizations of the ancient world. Mesoamerica was the hearth of these vibrant cultures–cultures whose influence reached far into North America. Yet just as Greek and Roman civilizations declined, so did many Mesoamerican cultures–until the Aztecs of the fifteenth century flourished, seemingly on the brink of projecting their power and influence over even vaster distances.

Peopling the Continents

Hunters cross the
Bering Strait

Like all of the Western Hemisphere's first human inhabitants, the ancestors of these ancient Mesoamericans came from northeastern Asia. At least 15,000 years ago during the most recent Ice Age, they crossed the Bering Strait, then a narrow bridge of land connecting Siberia to Alaska. Gradually these Stone Age wanderers filtered southward, some following the Pacific coastline in small boats, but most making their way down a narrow, glacier-free corridor along the eastern base of the Rocky Mountains and onto the northern Great Plains. There they found a bountiful supply of big-game animals, including their quarry of choice—enormous woolly mammoths and mastodons whose carcasses supplied their bands not only with meat but also with skins for clothing, tusks and bones for fashioning spear points, and oil for light. With the passage of generations, some of the nomads pressed farther south and east, and within a few thousand years, the descendants of these Stone Age Siberians, people whom Columbus would wishfully dub "Indians," had spread throughout the length and breadth of the Americas.

---

*Common Era, equivalent to the Christian Era or A.D.; B.C.E. is Before the Common Era, equivalent to B.C.

Legend:

- Bering Strait land bridge
- Extent of ice cap during most recent glaciation
- Adena cultural distribution
- Hopewell cultural distribution
- Mississippian Core Area
- Primary Mississippian influence
- Secondary Mississippian influence
- Approximate Southwestern cultural boundaries
- ➤ Possible migration routes of early Indians
- ◇ Adena/Hopewell Site
- ■ Mississippian Site
- ○ Mayan Site
- ○ Olmec Site
- ● Southwestern Sites

ANASAZI
Mesa Verde
Canyon de Chelly
PATAYAN
Chaco Canyon
SINAGUA
HOHOKAM
MOGOLLON
Poverty Point
Mississippi R.
Missouri R.
Ohio R.
Teotihuacán

Early Peoples of North America
Migration routes across the Bering Strait from Asia were taken by peoples whose descendants created the major civilizations of ancient Americans. The influence of Meso-america is most striking among the cultures of the Southwest and the Mississippians.

As the new world of the Americas was settled, it was also changing dramatically. The last Ice Age literally melted away as warmer global temperatures freed the great reservoirs of water once locked in glaciers. A rise in sea levels inundated the Bering Strait, cutting off migration over the land bridge, and as meltwater flooded the land, new lakes filled and new rivers flowed. The emergence of new climates, waterways, environments, and ecosystems made for an ever greater diversity among the human beings who ranged across those increasingly varied landscapes. The first human inhabitants of the Americas had fed, clothed, warmed, and armed themselves by hunting mammoths and mastodons, animals that did not survive the end of the Ice Age. As the glaciers receded, later generations adapted to changing conditions.

Diversified societies

So it was that distinctive regional cultures developed among the peoples in different parts of the Americas—sometime between 10,000 and 2500 years ago. Those who remained in the Great Plains turned to hunting herds of bison; those in the deserts of the Great Basin foraged seeds and edible plants; those in the Pacific Northwest relied mainly on fishing; and those east of the Mississippi, besides fishing and gathering, tracked deer and bear and trapped smaller game animals and birds. Over these same centuries, each tribe developed its own language, social organization, government, and religious beliefs and practices. Cultural unity gave way to cultural variety.

Cultures of Ancient Mexico

Of all these early regional cultures, those that proved most crucial to the evolution of ancient North America lay to the south, within the slim crescent of land connecting North and South America. It was in Mesoamerica, about 9000 years ago, that agriculture began in the Western Hemisphere. Here farmers first tilled American soil, growing maize (Indian corn, its ears originally only about the size of a human finger) and slowly learning to cultivate other crops such as beans, squashes, tomatoes, and chilis.

Olmec city-building

About 1500 B.C.E., the peoples who had been working the soil many thousands of years began to turn their once-tiny farming villages into larger societies, into richer and more advanced cultures. As the abundant food supply steadily expanded their populations, new groups emerged who specialized in certain kinds of work. While some people continued to labor on the land, others became craftworkers and merchants, architects and artists, warriors and priests. Their built environment reflected that social change as humble villages expanded into skillfully planned urban sites that were centers of trade, government, artistic display, and religious ceremony. Their inhabitants constructed large plazas and pyramidal structures, erected stone-carved altars and enormous heads chiseled from basalt. That was the singular achievement of the ancient people known as the Olmecs, the first city-builders in the Americas.

The Olmec cultural influence gradually spread throughout Mesoamerica, perhaps as a result of their trade with neighboring peoples. By about 100 B.C.E., the Olmecs' example had inspired the flowering of Teotihuacán from a small town in central Mexico into a metropolis of towering pyramids, bustling marketplaces, palaces decorated with mural paintings that housed an elite of warriors and priests, schools for their children, and sprawling suburbs where the commoners lived. At its height, around 650 C.E., Teotihuacán spanned 15 square miles and its population was larger than that of ancient Rome.

Mayan civilization

More impressive still was the achievement of the Mayas, who benefited from their contacts with both the Olmecs and Teotihuacán. In the lowland jungles of Mesoamerica they built cities filled with palaces, bridges, aqueducts, baths, astronomical observatories, and pyramids topped with temples. Their priests developed a written language, their mathematicians discovered the zero, and their astronomers devised a calendar more accurate than any then existing. In its glory, between the third and ninth century C.E., the Mayan empire boasted some 50 urban centers scattered throughout the Yucatán Peninsula, Belize, Guatemala, and Honduras.

But neither the earliest urban centers of the Olmecs, nor the glittering city-state of Teotihuacán, nor even the fabulous kingdom of the Mayas survived. Like the ancient civilizations of Greece and Rome, they thrived for many centuries and then fell. The reasons for their collapse remain one of the past's mysteries. Military attack may have brought about their ruin, or perhaps the pressure of their large population on the resources of surrounding fields and forests caused drastic changes in the ecology and environment. Whatever catastrophes caused their downfall, which occurred between about 650 and 950 C.E., those who survived fled the ruins. Some migrated elsewhere in Mesoamerica or to South America or even to the islands of the Caribbean. But others—possibly many others—moved north into the Southwest and Southeast of the present-day United States. After all, Mesoamerican merchants had been exchanging ideas as well as goods with the peoples living in those regions for many centuries.

The clay figure of an ancient Mayan ballplayer doubles as a whistle. The popularity of ball games spread from Mesoamerica into the southwestern regions of the present-day United States.

Cultures of the Southwest

By whatever means it was transmitted, Mesoamerican influence powerfully affected those tribes who had settled in the sagebrush deserts beneath the Southwest's vast canopy of sky. Farming had spread to this northernmost frontier of Mesoamerica by about 1000 B.C.E., and its most successful ancient practitioners in the region were the Mogollon and Hohokam peoples, two cultures that flourished in southern Arizona and New Mexico during the first millennium C.E. Both clustered their subterranean, dirt-roofed dwellings known as pit houses near streams, which allowed them to adopt the systems of irrigation as well as the maize cultivation of central Mexico. The Hohokam, who had originally emigrated from the south, even modeled their platform mounds and ball-playing courts on those of Mexico.

Mogollon and Hohokam peoples

Their neighbors to the north, in what is now known as the Four Corners of Arizona, Colorado, New Mexico, and Utah, were the Anasazi, a name given them by later tribes in the region that means "the ancient ones." The Anasazi devised an even more productive agriculture, and this prosperity allowed the growing number of their people to turn their energies toward more than mere survival. Their most stunning achievements were villages of cliff dwellings—apartment-like structures up to four stories high and containing hundreds of rooms, carved out of the rock at places like Mesa Verde (Colorado) and Canyon de Chelly (Arizona). More than 100 towns in Chaco Canyon (New Mexico), the largest center of Anasazi settlement, were linked by miles of wide, straight roads.

The Anasazi

Besides their impressive dwellings, the Anasazi filled their towns with religious shrines, astronomical observatories, and stations for sending signals to other villages. Their craftworkers fashioned exquisitely woven baskets and pottery painted with black and white geometric designs as well as turquoise jewelry that they traded to central Mexico. For more than a thousand years, Anasazi civilization prospered, reaching its zenith between about 900 and 1100 C.E. During those three centuries, the population grew to approximately 30,000 spread over 50,000 square miles, a total area larger than present-day California.

This artist's depiction of Pueblo Bonita, one of the nine Great House complexes of Chaco Canyon, suggests the sophistication of Anasazi architecture. By the end of the eleventh century, Pueblo Bonita stood four stories high at the rear and contained 800 rooms as well as many towers and terraces and a large central plaza.

Cultures of the Eastern Woodlands

Mesoamerican influence spread less evenly among the peoples who ranged across the Eastern Woodlands of North America, the region lying east of the Mississippi and south of the Subarctic belt of lower Canada. The environments that became most densely settled were its major river valleys (of the Mississippi, Ohio, Tennessee, and Cumberland), the shores of the Great Lakes, and the coast of the Atlantic. Everywhere the earliest inhabitants depended on a combination of fishing, gathering, and hunting—mainly deer, but also bear, raccoon, and a variety of birds. Around 2000 B.C.E., some groups in the temperate, fertile Southeast began growing the gourds and pumpkins first cultivated by Mesoamerican farmers, and later they also adopted the cultivation of maize. But unlike the ancient peoples of the Southwest, most Eastern Woodland tribes continued to rely for their subsistence primarily on animals, fish, and nuts, all of which were abundant enough to meet their needs and even to expand their numbers.

Indeed, some of the most striking cultural achievements of the ancient Eastern Woodlands were the work of peoples who did not practice agriculture but instead depended exclusively on hunting and gathering. About 1000 B.C.E., those who lived in a place now known as Poverty Point in northeastern Louisiana fashioned spectacular earthworks—six semicircular rings that rose nine feet in height and covered more than half a mile in diameter. While these structures might have been sites for studying the planets and stars, other mounds—hundreds built about 2000 years ago by the Adena and Hopewell cultures of the Ohio and Mississippi valleys—served as the burial places of their leading men and women. Alongside the corpses mourners heaped their richest goods—headdresses of antlers, necklaces of copper, troves of shells and pearls—rare and precious items imported from as far north as Canada, as far west as Wyoming, and as far east as Florida. All these mounds attest powerfully not only to the skill and sheer numbers of their builders, but also to the complexity of these ancient societies, their elaborate religious practices, and the wide scope of their trading networks.

Adena and Hopewell cultures

Mississippian culture

Even so, the most magnificent culture of the ancient Eastern Woodlands, the Mississippian, owed much of its prominence to farming. By the twelfth century C.E.,

An artist's reconstruction of the city of Cahokia, c. 1100 C.E., the hearth of Mississippian culture. Note how tiny the human figures are compared to the massive proportions of the temples.

these peoples had emerged as the premier city-builders of North America, and their towns radiated for hundreds of miles in every direction from the hub of their trading network at Cahokia, a port city of more than 20,000 located directly across from present-day St. Louis at the confluence of the Missouri and the Mississippi rivers. Cahokia's many broad plazas swarmed with farmers hawking their corn, squash, and beans and with craftworkers and merchants displaying their wares. But what commanded every eye were the structures surrounding the plazas—more than 100 flat-topped pyramidal mounds crowned by religious temples and the palaces of rulers. This shape distinguished Mississippian mounds from earlier ones in North America, which were circular or elliptical, but it made the mounds remarkably similar to those in ancient Mesoamerica. It is highly likely, then, that either by traders or emigrants, Mesoamerican influences were carried far into this interior region of North America, shaping these peoples' agriculture, architecture, social structure, and religious ceremonies.

Beyond the Mesoamerican Sphere

The maize cultivation pioneered in Mexico made its earliest and deepest impression on the ancient societies of southwestern and southeastern North America. Most other groups on the continent, farther from the sphere of Mesoamerican influence, remained hunters and gatherers, following the ancestral ways of many generations.

Cultures of the Great Plains

The sole exception could be found in the farming villages of the Great Plains, a sweeping swath of rich prairie drained by the Missouri River and situated between the Eastern Woodlands and the Great Basin. Tribes like the Hidatsa, the Mandan, and the Pawnee finally settled along the tree-lined rivers and streams of this region and cultivated corn, beans, squash, and sunflowers, a food supply that they supplemented by hunting.

Migratory peoples

But the other peoples of the Plains—Teton Sioux, Blackfeet, Comanche, Cheyenne, and Crow in the North and Apache in the South—migrated with the seasons and relied for their survival almost entirely on hunting buffalo. Like all Plains tribes, they pursued game on foot, for the horses that had once roamed the Americas became extinct after the last Ice Age. Usually, large groups of men worked together to drive the buffalos over cliffs or to trap them in corrals. The only major change in that Plains culture took place around 550 C.E., when the bow and arrow replaced the spear, which had been the hunters' favored weapon for some 10,000 years.

Cultures of the Great Basin

Some peoples west of the Great Plains also kept to older ways of subsistence. Among them were the Utes, Shoshones, and Paiutes of the Great Basin, which includes present-day Nevada and Utah, eastern California, and western Wyoming and Colorado. These tribes scoured their stark, arid landscape for the limited supplies of food it yielded, moving with each passing season to make the most of their environment. Men tracked elk and antelope and trapped smaller animals, birds, even toads, rattlesnakes, and insects. But the staples of their diet were edible seeds, nuts, and plants, which women gathered and stored in woven baskets to consume in times of scarcity. Families occasionally hunted together or wintered in common quarters, but because the desert heat and soil defied farming, these bands usually numbered no more than about 50 people.

Cultures of the Subarctic and Arctic

This ornately carved and painted house post once supported the main beams of a dwelling belonging to a Kwakiutl whaler in the Pacific Northwest. A man of wealth and high rank, he has a whale painted on his chest and copper ornaments on his arms. Two smaller figures, in shadow by the whaler's knees, each support one end of a plank seat. These were his household slaves, most likely children captured in an attack on rival tribes.

Most of present-day Canada and Alaska were equally inhospitable to agriculture. In the farthest northern reaches—a treeless belt of Arctic tundra—temperatures fell below freezing for eight or nine months of the year; likewise, immediately to the south the Subarctic, although densely forested, had only about 100 frost-free days each year. As a result, the peoples of both regions survived by fishing and hunting. The Inuits, or Eskimos, of northern Alaska harvested whales from their umiaks, boats that could bear more than a ton and that were made by stretching walrus skin over a driftwood frame. In the central Arctic, they tracked seals. The inhabitants of the Subarctic, both Algonquian-speaking peoples in the East and the Athapaskan speakers of the West, moved from their summer fishing camps to berry patches in the fall to moose and caribou hunting grounds in the winter.

Whether on the Great Plains, in the Great Basin, or in the Arctic, most societies of hunters and gatherers were smaller than those that relied entirely or in part on agriculture. These nomadic groups also tended to be simpler in their social structure, their political organization, and their modes of religious worship. Typically, families were roughly equal in wealth and prestige, and governing authority lay with either the male family head or the most expert hunter of a small band. Shamans—any person claiming special spiritual powers—enlisted the supernatural to assist individuals. But there are important exceptions to that pattern—not only the Adena and Hopewell cultures of the ancient Eastern Woodlands but, even more dramatically, the seafaring cultures of the Pacific Northwest.

Cultures of the Pacific Northwest

The rugged stretch of coast from the southern banks of present-day British Columbia to northern California has always been an extraordinarily rich natural environment. Its mild climate and abundant rainfall yield forests lush with plants and game; its bays and rivers teem with salmon and halibut, its oceans with whales and porpoises, and its rocky beaches with seals, otters, abalone, mussels, and clams. To survive, even to prosper, in such a place, there was no need to till the soil, only to reap the foods nature provided. In that work, the peoples of the Pacific Northwest excelled—the Nootkan and the Makah, the Tlingit, Tshimshian, and Kwakiutls. From their villages on the banks of rivers, the shores of bays, and the beaches of low-lying offshore islands, they speared or netted salmon, trapped sea mammals, gathered shellfish, and launched canoes. The largest of these craft, from which they harpooned whales, measured 45 feet bow to stern and nearly 6 feet wide.

By the fifteenth century these fecund lands supported a population of perhaps 130,000. They also permitted a culture with the leisure time needed to create works of art as well as an elaborate social and ceremonial life. The peoples of the Northwest built houses and canoes from red cedar; carved bowls and dishes from red alder; crafted paddles and harpoon shafts, bows, and clubs from Pacific yew; wove baskets from bark and blankets from mountain goat wool. They evolved a society of sharp distinctions between nobles, commoners, and slaves, the latter being mainly women and children captured in raids on other villages. Those who were free devoted their lives to accumulating and then distributing their wealth among other villagers in elaborate potlatch ceremonies in order to confirm or enhance their social prestige.

Social and ceremonial distinctions

North America and the Caribbean on the Eve of European Invasion

Over many generations, cultural patterns changed little for those peoples who learned to adapt to whatever their environments granted or withheld in the Pacific Northwest, Arctic and Subarctic, Great Basin, and Great Plains. And little would change until they encountered Europeans.

But for many others who lived elsewhere in North America, the centuries immediately preceding the arrival of Columbus marked a period of cataclysmic decline. During those centuries, the continent's most impressive civilizations collapsed as suddenly and mysteriously as had the Olmecs and Mayas of Mesoamerica. In the Southwest, the Mogollon culture went into eclipse around the twelfth century, the Hohokam and the Anasazi by about the fourteenth century. In the Eastern Woodlands, the story was strikingly similar: the Adena and Hopewell cultures as well as that of the Mississippians had faded by the fourteenth century.

Sudden declines

There is no shortage of speculation about what brought down North America's most impressive ancient civilizations—drought, warfare, and epidemic disease head the list of possible causes. But as yet, there is no way of knowing why so many cultures that had attained such heights declined and fell—and did so in rapid succession within the span of a few centuries. Nor is there any way of knowing at present why many other North American cultures, some built on the ruins of these earlier civilizations, endured and even flourished, up to and beyond their first encounters with the invading Europeans.

Enduring Cultures

Pueblos

Among the survivors were the Pueblos, the heirs of the artistic and architectural traditions of the Anasazi and their predecessors in the Southwest. The Pueblos were sedentary farmers who lived in permanent villages, growing crops of corn, beans, squash, and cotton. Like most agricultural peoples, they called on their gods to bring rain and good harvests, ceremonies that the Pueblos conducted in kivas, underground circular dwellings that resemble the pit houses of the earlier Mogollons and Hohokams. And to ensure their safety, the Pueblos situated their villages atop high, steep mesas. That was their best defense against attacks by Athapaskan-speaking tribes, mainly the Apache and the Navajo, hunters and gatherers from western Canada and Alaska who entered the Southwest around 1300 C.E.

Muskogean peoples

In the Eastern Woodlands, the Mississippian heritage passed to various Muskogean tribes, the dominant group in the Southeast by the fifteenth century. That legacy was preserved best by the Natchez of the lower Mississippi valley, who adopted both the temple mound–building tradition and the rigid social distinctions of that earlier civilization. Below the chief, or "Great Sun," of the Natchez stood a hereditary nobility of lesser "Suns" who demanded respect from the lowly "Stinkards," the common people.

Iroquois

By the fifteenth century, agriculture had come to figure prominently not only among the Muskogean peoples but also among the Iroquois, the second major tribal group of the Eastern Woodlands. They were concentrated in present-day upstate New York and Pennsylvania as well as in the hill country of the Carolinas and Georgia. Like the Muskogean tribes, the Iroquois lived in permanent villages. The distinctive feature of their architecture was not the temple mound but rather the longhouse (some stretching up to 100 feet in length) that might shelter as many as 10 families.

An artist traveling with the English explorer Francis Drake (probably in the 1590s) painted this Indian tending a tropical Caribbean garden. Maize corn flourishes (right) as well as beans on two poles, while a papaya tree can be seen (upper left) as well as a manioc shrub (middle left) and gourds (lower left). Many of these crops—corn and manioc especially—eventually became important staples in diets around the globe.

Indians of North and Central America circa 1500

The Algonquins were the third major group of Eastern Woodlands people. **Algonquins**
They lived along the Atlantic seaboard and the Great Lakes in bands smaller than
those of either the Muskogeans or the Iroquois. By the fifteenth century, the coastal
tribes from southern New England to Virginia had adopted agriculture to
supplement their diets, but those in the colder northern climates with shorter
growing seasons depended entirely on hunting, fishing, and gathering plants like
wild rice.

Cultures of equal and even greater resources persisted and flourished during **Caribbean cultures**
the fifteenth century in the Caribbean, particularly on the Greater Antilles—the

islands of present-day Cuba, Haiti, Jamaica, and Puerto Rico. Although the earliest inhabitants of the ancient Caribbean, the Ciboneys, probably came from the Florida peninsula, it was the Arawaks, later emigrants from northern South America, who expanded throughout the Greater Antilles and the Bahamas. Through a canoe-borne commerce dating at least from the time of the Mayan empire, the Arawaks established close ties with Mesoamerica. They modeled not only their agriculture but also their society and government on the example of Central America's most glittering civilizations. Arawak chiefs known as caciques, along with a small number of noble families, ruled island tribes, controlling the production and distribution of food and tools and exacting tribute from the great mass of commoners, farmers, and fisherfolk. Attending to these elites were the poorest Arawak peoples—servants who bedecked their masters and mistresses in brilliant diadems of feathers, fine woven textiles, and gold nose and ear pieces and then shouldered the litters from which the rulers paraded their finery.

Cultural diversity of North America

Thus, by the end of the fifteenth century, tremendous cultural diversity characterized North America. Its peoples numbered about 4.5 million—with another 4 million living on the islands of the Caribbean—and they were spread among more than 350 societies speaking nearly as many distinct languages. (The total precontact population for all of the Americas is estimated at between 57 and 112 million.) Some relied entirely on farming; others on hunting, fishing, and gathering; still others on a combination of the two. Some, like the Natchez and the Iroquois, practiced matrilineal forms of kinship, in which women owned land, tools, and even children. Among others, like the Algonquins, patrilineal kinship prevailed, and all property and prestige descended in the male line. Some societies, like those of the Great Plains and the Great Basin in the West, the Inuit in the Arctic, and the Iroquois and Algonquins in the East, were roughly egalitarian, while others, like many in the Caribbean and the Pacific Northwest, were rigidly divided into nobles and commoners and servants or slaves. Some, like the Natchez and the Arawaks, were ruled by powerful chiefs; others, like the Algonquins and the Pueblos, by councils of village elders or heads of family clans; still others in the Great Basin, the Great Plains, and the far North, by the most skillful hunter or the most powerful shaman in their band. Those people who relied on hunting practiced religions that celebrated their kinship with animals and solicited their aid as guardian spirits, while predominantly agricultural peoples sought the assistance of their gods to make the rain fall and the crops ripen.

The Rise of the Aztec Empire

Already rich in a long history of human achievement, of which its diversity stood as one legacy, late-fifteenth-century North America might also have been a world poised on the brink of a cultural renaissance. For even as many of its people were rebuilding on the ruins of earlier civilizations, a new empire to the south, one more stunning in its sheer scope and magnificence than any of its predecessors in Mesoamerica, was taking shape.

In the middle of the thirteenth century, the Aztecs, a people who originally lived on Mesoamerica's northern frontiers, swept into central Mexico. By the end of the fifteenth century, they ruled over a vast empire from their capital at Tenochtitlán, an island metropolis of at least a quarter of a million people. At its center lay a large plaza bordered by sumptuous palaces and the Great Temple of the Sun. Beyond stood three broad causeways connecting the island to the mainland, many other tall temples adorned with brightly painted carved images of the gods, zoological and botanical gardens, and well-stocked marketplaces. Through Tenochtitlán's canals flowed gold, silver, exotic feathers and jewels, cocoa, and millions of pounds of maize—all trade goods and tribute from the several million other Mexican peoples subjugated by the Aztecs.

Unsurpassed in power and wealth, technological and artistic attainments, theirs was also a highly stratified society. The Aztec ruler, or Chief Speaker, shared governing power with the aristocrats who monopolized all positions of religious, military, and political leadership, while the commoners—merchants, farmers, and craftworkers—performed all manual labor. There were slaves as well, some captives taken in war, others from the ranks of commoners forced by poverty to sell themselves or their children.

It is tantalizing to imagine what might have happened. What if Aztec civilization had continued to flourish and expand, to export its influence by trade or migration into the sixteenth century and beyond? Would the Aztecs have emerged as the Olmecs and Mayas of a later age—an empire that projected its power and influence over vast distances and millions of people? Would their civilization have become a new cultural hearth, one that shaped, once again, the destiny of North America?

There is no way of knowing, because the grandeur of the Aztecs did not outlast the opening of the sixteenth century. Instead, a reversal of historical fortunes took place, one as sudden as it was startling. The Aztecs, themselves unexpected invaders from the north who fashioned Mesoamerica's most glorious civilization, were conquered by yet another group of invaders, still more unexpected, from the west.

Aztec merchants, or pochtecas, spoke many languages and traveled on foot great distances throughout Mesoamerica and parts of North America. The one shown (above, left) carries a cane and bears a sack of trade goods (topped off by a parrot). The pochtecas' patron god, Yacatecuhtli, is often portrayed with a long nose and most likely is the same deity depicted by the shell and copper masks (inset) found at many sites of ancient Mississippian culture.

prologue summary

During the thousands of years after bands of Siberian nomads migrated across the Bering Strait to Alaska, their descendants spread throughout the Americas, creating civilizations that rivaled those of ancient Europe, Asia, and Africa.

- Around 1500 B.C.E. Mesoamerica emerged as the hearth of classical civilization in the Western Hemisphere, a process started by the Olmecs and brought to its height by the Mayans.

  – These Central American peoples devised complex ways of organizing society, government, and religious worship and built cities remarkable for their art, architecture, and trade.

  – Both commerce and migration spread cultural influences throughout the hemisphere, notably to the islands of the Caribbean basin and to North America, an influence that endured long after these empires declined.

- Mesoamerican cultures influenced the Mogollons, the Hohokams, and the Anasazi of the Southwest as well as the Mississippians and other peoples living in the southern portion of the Eastern Woodlands.

  – Such influences included not only the practice of agriculture but also elements of Mesoamerican architecture, social structure, and religious worship.

- Inhabitants of the Great Plains, the Great Basin, the Arctic, and the Subarctic evolved their own diverse cultures distinct from the Mesoamerican, relying for subsistence on fishing, hunting, and gathering.

- Peoples of the Pacific Northwest boasted large populations and prosperous economies as well as an elaborate social, ceremonial, and artistic life.

- By the end of the fifteenth century, many of North America's most impressive early civilizations had collapsed.

  – Yet these cultures influenced those that succeeded them, including the Pueblos of the Southwest; the Muskogean, Iroquois, and Algonquin tribes of the Eastern Woodlands; and the Arawaks of the Caribbean basin.

- The worlds of these diverse peoples may have been poised on the brink of a cultural renaissance, because the Aztec civilization began growing rapidly beginning in the fourteenth century.

additional reading

The best descriptions of ancient American civilizations are offered by Brian M. Fagan, *Kingdoms of Gold, Kingdoms of Jade: The Americas before Columbus* (1991); and Jesse D. Jennings, ed., *Ancient North America* (1983). Francis Jennings, *The Founders of America* (1993), provides provocative coverage of the same topic, while Roger G. Kennedy, *Hidden Cities: The Discovery and Loss of Ancient North American Civilization* (1994), gives a fascinating account of how white Americans responded to encountering the ruins of ancient American cultures.

For native civilizations throughout the Americas in the fifteenth century, the best brief treatment is Alvin M. Josephy, ed., *America in 1492* (1992); On the Aztec empire specifically see Inga Clendinnen, *Aztecs: An Interpretation* (1991); and Brian M. Fagan, *The Aztecs* (1984). For exhaustive surveys of all regional cultures in North America, consult Alice B. Kehoe, *North American Indians* (1992); and William C. Sturtevant, general editor, *Handbook of North American Indians*, 20 volumes projected (1978–); Carl Waldman, *Atlas of the North American Indian* (1985), is also an excellent source of information, offering much more than good maps.

significant events

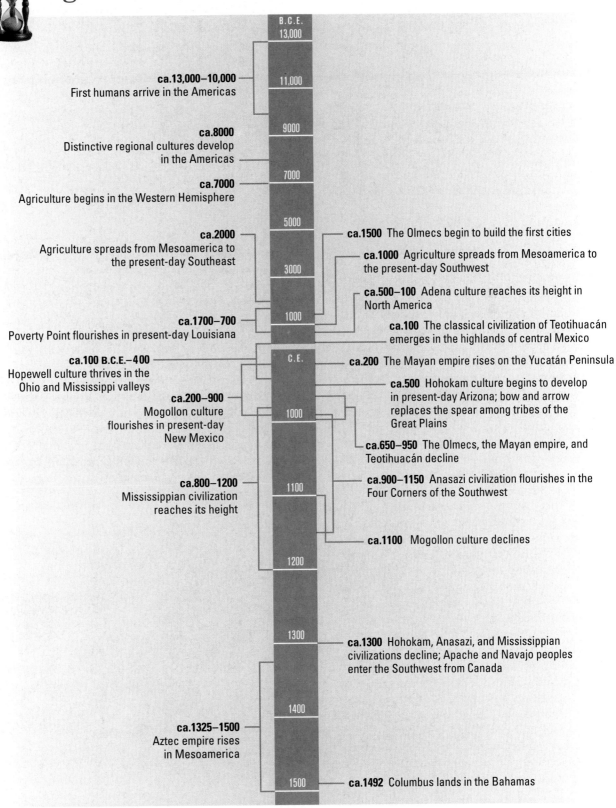

B.C.E.
13,000

ca.13,000–10,000
First humans arrive in the Americas

11,000

9000

ca.8000
Distinctive regional cultures develop
in the Americas

7000

ca.7000
Agriculture begins in the Western Hemisphere

5000

ca.2000
Agriculture spreads from Mesoamerica to
the present-day Southeast

3000

ca.1500 The Olmecs begin to build the first cities

ca.1000 Agriculture spreads from Mesoamerica to
the present-day Southwest

ca.500–100 Adena culture reaches its height in
North America

1000

ca.1700–700
Poverty Point flourishes in present-day Louisiana

ca.100 The classical civilization of Teotihuacán
emerges in the highlands of central Mexico

ca.100 B.C.E.–400
Hopewell culture thrives in the
Ohio and Mississippi valleys

C.E.

ca.200 The Mayan empire rises on the Yucatán Peninsula

ca.200–900
Mogollon culture
flourishes in present-day
New Mexico

ca.500 Hohokam culture begins to develop
in present-day Arizona; bow and arrow
replaces the spear among tribes of the
Great Plains

1000

ca.650–950 The Olmecs, the Mayan empire, and
Teotihuacán decline

ca.900–1150 Anasazi civilization flourishes in the
Four Corners of the Southwest

ca.800–1200
Mississippian civilization
reaches its height

1100

ca.1100 Mogollon culture declines

1200

1300

ca.1300 Hohokam, Anasazi, and Mississippian
civilizations decline; Apache and Navajo peoples
enter the Southwest from Canada

1400

ca.1325–1500
Aztec empire rises
in Mesoamerica

1500

ca.1492 Columbus lands in the Bahamas

Tracking the First Americans

Sometimes the most ordinary circumstances end in the most extraordinary discoveries. One of those times was a morning in 1908 when George McJunkin, an African American cowboy scanning the range near Folsom, New Mexico, for stray cattle dropped his gaze into a dry gully and spotted some large bones poking through the soil. Intrigued, he began digging and found a stone spear point lodged in the skeleton. He carried the lot back to his ranch, where they remained for the next seventeen years. Then McJunkin's curiosities somehow came to the attention of archaeologists, who identified the bones as those of a long-extinct form of bison that had ranged throughout the Southwest at least ten thousand years earlier. They realized, too, that only a spear-wielding human could have killed the bison.

That discovery rocked the scientific community, which for the previous century had confidently declared that Indians had first arrived in the Americas only about 4000 years ago. Shortly thereafter, in 1932, another shock wave followed when some amateur collectors digging at Clovis, New Mexico, unearthed bones and spearheads suspected to be even older. Finally, in 1949, scientists established the great antiquity of both finds by using "radiocarbon dating," a method for measuring decay rates of the radioactive isotope of carbon, which exists in organic matter like bone and starts to break down immediately after an organism dies. Tests revealed that the Indians whose hunting grounds were now called Folsom and Clovis had been turning bison into bones between 10,800 and 11,500 years ago.

Those conclusions pointedly raised the question of exactly how much earlier the first American an-

cestors of such hunters had come to the New World. This tantalizing mystery puzzles (and divides) archaeologists and anthropologists, geologists and historians, right down to the present. Such men and women devote their lives to the hard work of digging in remote sites or exploring the ocean's floor, to the harder work of analyzing their finds in laboratories, and to the hardest work of all—trying to make sense of what it all means. Their efforts have yielded much new evidence and increasingly sophisticated techniques for understanding its significance, but many important questions still remain unanswered.

Even so, almost all of them agree on a number of points. First, whoever the first inhabitants of the New World were, they came, originally, from the

Arrowheads known as Clovis points found with the skeleton of a mammoth.

whose more limited skills had restricted their settlements to the tropical and temperate parts of the world.

The new species multiplied rapidly, and the pressure of its growing population pushed many into settling in less hospitable regions—including the Arctic frontier of Siberia in northeastern Asia. Indeed, a third point of general agreement among scholars is that the descendants of these migrants to Siberia continued the wandering ways of their ancestors and somehow, at some time, wandered into North America by way of Alaska. The research of physical anthropologists documents key biological similarities between Siberians and American Indians. Both groups share not only certain genetic variants that suggest their descent from common ancient ancestors but also distinctive formations of the roots and crowns of their teeth known as sinodonty.

But how did Asians get to Alaska—a region now separated from Siberia by fifty miles of ocean known as the Bering Strait? It is not impossible that they sailed across, for some *Homo sapiens sapiens* could build boats sturdy enough to navigate short stretches of open ocean. Archaeologists have discovered that Southeast Asians floated across 55 miles of ocean on rafts to reach Australia some

Old World: scientists have found no fossil remains to support the view that human beings evolved into modern men and women in the Americas. Second, these first Americans were almost certainly fully evolved human beings, known as *Homo sapiens sapiens*—not their less-developed forerunners, the Neanderthals, or even earlier ancestors. These *Homo sapiens sapiens* excelled at surviving anywhere, armed as they were with the intellectual ability to plan and project and the technology to sew warm clothing and to store food. About 35,000 years ago, these resourceful adapters came to predominate, edging out the Neanderthals,

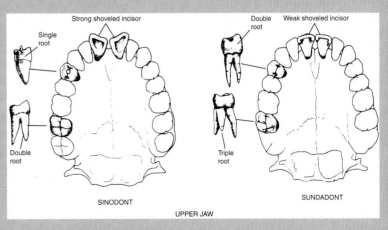

SINODONT
SUNDADONT
UPPER JAW

35,000 years ago. Could their contemporaries in northeast Asia, using bark canoes, have made a voyage of similar length over the Bering Strait? Not impossible, scientists conclude, but not likely either, if only because navigating calm, tropical waters of the southern Pacific is far less difficult than mastering the Bering Strait, which even in summer is choked with ice floes. Such an undertaking would have been even more daunting to the earliest Siberians, who, as anthropologists have discovered, were land-based hunters, not seafaring folk.

So most scientists now believe that Siberians did not sail to the New World: instead, they walked. They were able to do that because the Bering Strait is not a timeless feature of Arctic geography. On the contrary, geologists have discovered, submerged far below the Bering Strait lie traces of a landmass that once connected Siberia to Alaska. Even in the late nineteenth century, some naturalists suspected that such a land bridge had once existed after noting that the vegetation and wildlife of Siberia were nearly identical to those in Alaska. By the 1930s, scientists had enough information to speculate that what turned a waterway into an exposed, inhabitable lowland plain was the coldest phase of the last Ice Age, which began about 30,000 years earlier when plunging temperatures caused the world's oceans to drop in depth by freezing great expanses of seawater into sheets of ice. Those climatic changes formed "Beringia," a land bridge between Siberia and Alaska that existed from about 25,000 B.P. (before the present) until about 15,000 B.P. During those millennia, most scientists now believe, Siberians gradually settled the

Indians of North America, ca. 1490 Dr. James Chatters, an anthropologist, found a skull approximately 9300 years old along the Columbia River in 1996. The skull's Eurasian features suggest that at least some migrants over the Bering Strait may also have been of European stock.

length of this link to the Americas. Thereafter, when temperatures began to warm again and the seas rose and closed over Beringia, some of its inhabitants strayed into Alaska.

But even today, some scientists doubt this account. True, no one has yet discovered an archaeological site in Alaska—or anywhere else in the Americas—that can be positively dated to earlier than about 15,000 B.P. Yet a few archaeologists working mainly in South America claim to have found artifacts in rock shelters dating to 30,000 B.P. Many others argue that such "finds" are the result of not human manufacture but natural processes like erosion. Then, too, those scientists who take the position that the first Americans arrived 30,000 years ago or even earlier—before the existence of the Beringia land bridge—must prove the improbable: that Siberians crossed into Alaska by sailing across the Bering Strait.

A recent discovery in the state of Washington is also prompting scientists to wonder whether the first inhabitants of the Americas might have included peoples other than Asians. In 1996, the sheriff of a small desert town, puzzled by a half-buried human skeleton found along the shores of the Columbia River, showed the bones to an anthropologist, James Chatters. Like McJunkin's find of almost a century earlier, this skeleton encased a stone spear point, and radiocarbon dating revealed it to be nearly as old (9300 years) as the Folsom bones. Also like McJunkin's specimen, this one has sparked debate within the scientific community. Chatters and others who measured the skull discovered that it was far narrower than any Indian skull of similar antiquity. They concluded—astonishingly—that the Kennewick Man, as he came to be known, was Caucasoid in appearance. Within the past thirty years, other ancient skull remains with Caucasian features have been found, but none so well preserved as the Columbia River specimen, which even has some teeth intact. It appeared to be the strongest evidence that in addition to the Siberian migrations, some people of European stock may have somehow crossed to the Americas.

But more recent comparisons of the skull with all other known ethnic groups led a panel of scientists to conclude that the Kennewick Man is not a distant relative either of present-day Indians or of Caucasians. The closest resemblance is to the Ainu people of Japan's Sakhalin Islands and to Polynesians of the South Pacific. If such a link were established, it would strengthen the hypothesis that some of the earliest Americans reached the continent by boat, either hopscotching along the Bering Strait or even sailing across the Pacific. Both the Ainu and the Polynesians were maritime peoples.

For their part, many Indians still living along the Columbia River reject all scientific explanations of their origins in favor of religious accounts—tribal creation myths which proclaim that their people have always lived in the Americas. Angered by the conduct of earlier anthropologists, who freely dug up Indian grave sites, they have demanded the right to rebury the skeleton under the terms of the Native American Graves Protection and Repatriation Act of 1990.

So the debates about America's first colonizers continue, and if recent history is any guide, so too will the discoveries. This part of the past, like every other, holds in store many surprises for those in the present determined to probe its secrets.

BIBLIOGRAPHY Keeping up with recent discoveries in this field poses many challenges. New discoveries turn up frequently, and most reports of those findings are written in a highly technical language. Fortunately, a few well-written books provide a guide to both the early Asian migration to and throughout the Americas and the evolution of scholarly debate. Brian M. Fagan, *The Great Journey* (London, 1987), is lucid, and the same author has more recently written a more detailed textbook on both ancient Native American archaeology and history, *Ancient North America* (1991). A less comprehensive but elegantly written treatment of these topics is William MacLeish's *The Day before America* (1994). Students seeking more advanced and specialized information should consult Stuart J. Fiedel, *Prehistory of the Americas* (2d ed., Cambridge, 1992). Bear in mind, too, that the science section of each Tuesday's *New York Times* regularly features articles on the ongoing research of archaeologists, anthropologists, and geologists. For the report on the Columbia River skeleton, see *The New York Times* for September 30, 1996, A12, and October 16, 1999, A12.

THE CREATION OF A NEW AMERICA

After 1492 the first Americans were no longer alone. In that year—a full 500 years ago—the civilizations of Europe and Africa first made sustained contact with those of North America. The transformations arising out of that event have been astonishing. To gain a rough sense of the scale involved, in both time and space, it is worth looking briefly not at the moment of first contact but at a vista to be glimpsed nearer the midpoint of our story: with Meriwether Lewis and William Clark in August 1805, atop the continental divide. The two men, on orders from President Thomas Jefferson, had been sent on the first American exploratory mission to report on the lands west of the Mississippi. From Lewis and Clark's vantage point, high in the Rocky Mountains, what can we see?

At first glance we see largely what we expect: a seemingly endless land stretching from sea to sea. But living as we do in the twenty-first century, we tend to take for granted that the country spread before us will be united under a single national government. Only hindsight makes this proposition seem natural. In 1800 the sheer size of the land made the notion of political unity difficult to grasp, for the United States themselves remained a group of colonies only recently unified. And the lands west of the Mississippi were still controlled primarily by scores of independent Indian nations.

The methods that Lewis and Clark used to communicate underscore the wide variety of North American cultures that we have already surveyed. With no common language spanning the territory, speech making for the voyagers became a series of translations that reflected the route over which the party had traveled. In present-day Idaho, Clark addressed the Tushepaw tribe in English. His speech was translated into French by a trapper in the party; then a second trapper translated into Minataree, a language that his Indian wife, Sacajawea, understood. Sacajawea, the only female member of the party, had grown up farther west with the Shoshone, so she in turn translated the Minataree into Shoshone, which a boy from the Tushepaw nation understood. He translated the Shoshone into his own people's tongue.

If the territory that Lewis and Clark crossed seemed a patchwork of governments and cultures, the young "United States" appeared nearly as heterogeneous. Dutch-speaking patroons could be found along New York's Hudson River, Welsh and German farmers along Pennsylvania's Lancaster Pike, Swedes in Delaware, Gaelic-speaking Scots scattered through the Appalachian backcountry, African Americans speaking the Gullah dialect along the Carolina coast. In 1800 many of these settlers knew more about their homelands in Europe or Africa than they did about other regions of North America.

Thus our first task in studying the American past becomes one of translation. We must view events not with the jaded eyes of

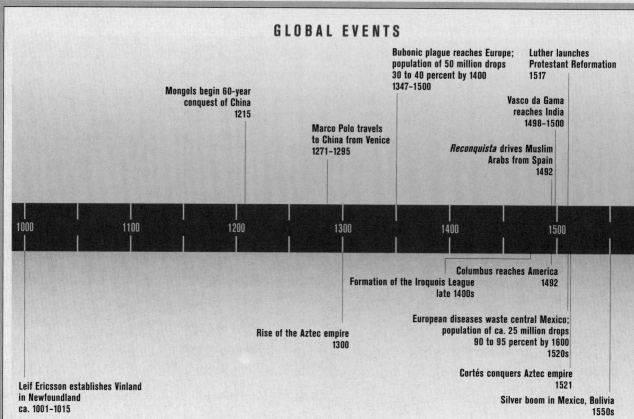

GLOBAL EVENTS

Bubonic plague reaches Europe; population of 50 million drops 30 to 40 percent by 1400
1347–1500

Luther launches Protestant Reformation
1517

Mongols begin 60-year conquest of China
1215

Vasco da Gama reaches India
1498–1500

Marco Polo travels to China from Venice
1271–1295

Reconquista **drives Muslim Arabs from Spain**
1492

1000 1100 1200 1300 1400 1500

Columbus reaches America
1492

Formation of the Iroquois League
late 1400s

European diseases waste central Mexico; population of ca. 25 million drops 90 to 95 percent by 1600
1520s

Rise of the Aztec empire
1300

Cortés conquers Aztec empire
1521

Leif Ericsson establishes Vinland in Newfoundland
ca. 1001–1015

Silver boom in Mexico, Bolivia
1550s

AMERICAN EVENTS

the late twentieth century but with the fresh eyes of an earlier era. Then the foregone conclusions vanish. How does the American nation manage to unite millions of square miles of territory into one governable republic? How do New York and San Francisco (a city not even in existence in Lewis and Clark's day) come to be linked in a complex economy as well as in a single political system? Such questions take on even more significance when we recall that Europe—roughly the same size as the United States—is today still divided into more than four dozen independent nations speaking some 33 languages, not to mention another 100 or so spoken within the former Soviet Union. A united Europe has not

emerged and, indeed, seems even farther away after the momentous breakup of the Soviet empire.

How, then, did this American republic—this "teeming nation of nations," to use Walt Whitman's

PART ONE

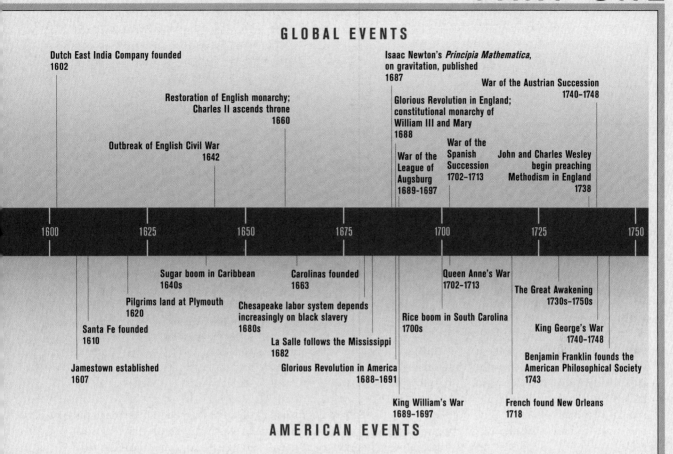

GLOBAL EVENTS

Dutch East India Company founded
1602

Isaac Newton's *Principia Mathematica*,
on gravitation, published
1687

War of the Austrian Succession
1740–1748

Restoration of English monarchy;
Charles II ascends throne
1660

Glorious Revolution in England;
constitutional monarchy of
William III and Mary
1688

Outbreak of English Civil War
1642

War of the
League of
Augsburg
1689–1697

War of the
Spanish
Succession
1702–1713

John and Charles Wesley
begin preaching
Methodism in England
1738

1600   1625   1650   1675   1700   1725   1750

Sugar boom in Caribbean
1640s

Carolinas founded
1663

Queen Anne's War
1702–1713

The Great Awakening
1730s–1750s

Pilgrims land at Plymouth
1620

Chesapeake labor system depends
increasingly on black slavery
1680s

Rice boom in South Carolina
1700s

King George's War
1740–1748

Santa Fe founded
1610

La Salle follows the Mississippi
1682

Benjamin Franklin founds the
American Philosophical Society
1743

Jamestown established
1607

Glorious Revolution in America
1688–1691

King William's War
1689–1697

French found New Orleans
1718

AMERICAN EVENTS

phrase—come to be? In barest outline, that is the question that drives our narrative across half a millennium.

The problem looms even larger as we move toward the beginning of our story. In 1450, about the time Christopher Columbus was born, Europeans were only beginning to expand westward. To be sure, Scandinavian seafarers led by Leif Ericsson had reached the northern reaches of the Americas, planting a settlement in Newfoundland around 1000 C.E. But news of Vinland, as Leif called his colony, never reached most of Europe. The site was soon abandoned and forgotten. In Columbus's day localism still held sway. Italy was divided into five major states and an equal number of smaller

territories. The Germanic peoples were united loosely in the Holy Roman Empire. French kings ruled over only about half of what is now France. Spain was divided into several kingdoms, with some areas held by Christians and others by Islamic Moors, whose forebears came from Africa. England, a contentious little nation, was beginning a series of bitter civil conflicts among the nobility, known eventually as the Wars of the Roses.

Localism was also evident in the patterns of European trade. Goods moving overland were usually carried by wheeled carts or pack animals over rutted paths. Along rivers and canals, lords repeatedly taxed boats that crossed their territories. On the

Seine River, greedy tollkeepers lay in wait every six or seven miles. Travel across the Mediterranean Sea and along Europe's northern coastlines was possible, but storms and pirates made the going dangerous and slow. Under good conditions a ship might reach London from Venice in only 9 days; under bad it might take 50.

European peoples at this time had limited but continuous dealings with Africa, mostly along the Mediterranean Sea. There, North African culture had been shaped since the seventh century by the religion of Islam, whose influence spread as well into Spain. Below the Sahara desert the Bantu, an agricultural people, had migrated over the course of 2000 years from their West African homeland to

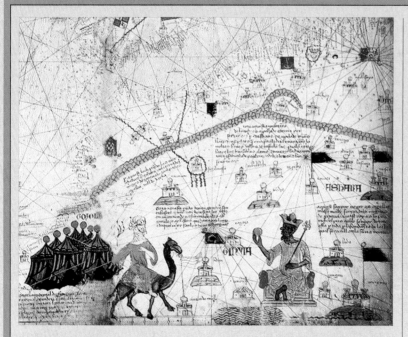

establish societies throughout the continent. The tempo of these migrations increased as the Bantu learned to produce iron and—equally important—introduced bananas into their diet after the plants were imported to Africa and Asia around 300 to 500 C.E. As a result, the sub-Saharan African population rose sharply from around 11 million at the beginning of the first millennium C.E. to more than 22 million at the end of it.

Traditionally, Bantu agricultural societies governed themselves through family and kinship groups, clustered in villages of around a hundred people and linked with nearby villages in a district. But larger political states developed in response to the arrival of Muslim trading caravans penetrating the Sahara desert beginning around 800 C.E. The first was Ghana, a kingdom that flourished in the eleventh and twelfth centuries. It was followed in the thirteenth century by the even larger Mali empire. Mali's princes controlled almost all the considerable trade in gold, ivory, and slaves, sending and receiving desert caravans that boasted as many as 25,000 camels. Yet Mali too was split by factions from within and military challenges from without. By the 1490s the Songhai empire had replaced Mali as the most important centralized kingdom in West Africa.

In 1490 these three worlds—Europe, Africa, the Americas—remained largely separate from one another. Europe's fleeting encounter with North America had long been forgotten; the empires of interior Africa remained unvisited by Europeans and largely unknown. Only Portugal had begun to explore the West African coast by sea. Yet currents of change would soon bring these three worlds together in vibrant and creative as well as violent and chaotic ways. What social and economic forces spurred so many Europeans—desperate and opportunistic, high-minded and idealistic—to turn west to the Americas in pursuit of their dreams? How did the civilizations of North and South America react to the European invaders? And not least, how did the mix of cultures from Africa, Europe, and North America come together to create what was truly a new America, in which some of the most independent-minded individuals prospered in provinces that exhibited some of the harshest examples of human slavery? These are among the questions we seek to answer as our narrative unfolds.

Chapter 1

A ll the world lay before them. Or so it seemed to mariners from England's seafaring coasts, pushing westward toward unknown lands in the far Atlantic.

The scent of the new land came first—not the sight of it, but the smells, wafted from beyond the horizon, delicious to sailors who had felt nothing but the rolling sea for weeks on end. In northerly latitudes around June, it would be the scent of fir trees or the sight of shore birds wheeling about the masts. Straightaway the captain would call for a lead to be thrown overboard to sound the depths. At its end was a hollowed-out socket with a bit of tallow in it, so some of the sea bottom would stick when the lead was hauled up. Even out of sight of land, a good sailing master could tell where he was by what came up—"oosy sand" or perhaps "soft worms" or "popple-stones as big as beans." If the ship was approaching unknown shores, the captain would hope to sight land early in the day, allowing time to work cautiously toward an untried harbor on uncharted tides.

Old World, New Worlds
1400–1600

preview • In the century after 1492, Europeans expanded boldly and often ruthlessly into the Americas, thanks to a combination of technological advances in sailing and firearms, the rise of new trading networks, and stronger, more centralized governments. Spain established a vast and profitable empire but at fearful human cost. A diverse Mesoamerican population of some 20 million was reduced to only 2 million through warfare, European diseases, and exploitation.

Since the time of King Arthur, the English living along the rugged southwestern coasts of Devon and Cornwall had followed the sea. From the wharves of England's West Country seaports like Bristol, ships headed west and north to Ireland, bringing back animal hides as well as timber for houses and barrels. Or they turned south, fetching wines from France and olive oil or figs and raisins from the Spanish and Portuguese coasts. In return, West Country ports offered woven woolen cloth and codfish, caught wherever the best prospects beckoned.

Through much of the fifteenth century the search for cod drew West Country sailors north and west, toward Iceland. In the 1480s and 1490s, however, a few English tried their luck farther west. Old maps, after all, claimed that the bountiful *Hy-Brasil*—Gaelic for "Isle of the Blessed"—lay somewhere west of Ireland. These western ventures returned with little to show for their daring until the coming of an Italian named Giovanni Caboto, called John Cabot by the English. Cabot, who hailed from Venice, obtained the blessing of King Henry VII to hunt for unknown lands. From the port of Bristol his lone ship set out to the west in the spring of 1497.

Cabot discovers Newfoundland

This time the return voyage brought news of a "new-found" island where the trees were tall enough to make fine masts and the codfish were plentiful. After returning to Bristol, Cabot marched off to London to inform His Majesty, received 10 pounds as his reward, and with the proceeds dressed himself in dashing silks. The multitudes of London flocked after him, wondering over "the Admiral"; then Cabot returned triumphantly to Bristol to undertake a more ambitious search for a northwest passage to Asia. He set sail with five ships in 1498 and was never heard from again.

During the sixteenth century, West Country fisherfolk from England sailed from harbors like Plymouth, shown here. Such seaports were small; the fortifications dotting the coastline and a wall around the town itself were used to defend against invaders.

The fishing season

By the 1550s Cabot's island, now known as Newfoundland, attracted 400 vessels annually, fishermen not only from England but also from France, Portugal, and Spain. The trip was not easy. Individual merchants or a few partners outfitted small ships with provisions, fishing boats, and guns to ward off sea-roving pirates. As early in the season as they dared, crews of 10 or 20 would catch the spring easterlies, watching as familiar roofs and primitive lighthouses burning smoky coal sank beneath the horizon.

Weeks after setting sail the sailors sighted Newfoundland's fog-shrouded beaches. Seals and walruses played along the rocks offshore, and the encircling sea teemed with cod and flounder, salmon and herring. Throughout the summer men launched little boats from each harbor and fished offshore all day and into the night. With lines and nets and baskets weighted with stones, they scooped fish from the sea and then dried and salted the catch on the beach. In odd hours, sailors traded with the native Indians, who shared their summer fishing grounds and the skins of fox and deer.

The harbor of present-day St. John's, Newfoundland, served as the informal hub of the North Atlantic fishery. Portuguese, English, and French vessels all dropped anchor there, either to take on supplies in the spring or to prepare for the homeward voyage in autumn. Besides trading, there was much talking, for these seafarers knew as much as anyone about the new world of wonders that was opening to Europeans. They were acquainted with names like Cristoforo Colombo, the Italian from Genoa whom Cabot might have known as a boy. They listened to Portuguese tales of sailing around the Horn of Africa in pursuit of spices and to stories of Indian empires to the south, rich in gold and silver that Spanish treasure ships were bringing home.

Indeed, Newfoundland was one of the few places in the world where so many ordinary folk of different nations could gather and talk, crammed aboard dank

Principal Routes of European Exploration

ships moored in St. John's harbor, huddled before blazing fires on its beaches, or crowded into smoky makeshift taverns. When the ships sailed home in autumn, the tales went with them, repeated in the tiniest coastal villages by those pleased to have cheated death and the sea one more time. Eager to fish, talk, trade, and take profits, West Country mariners were almost giddy at the prospect of Europe's expanding horizons.

The Meeting of Europe, Africa, and America

Most seafarers who fished the waters of Newfoundland's Grand Banks remain unknown today. Yet it is well to begin with these ordinary fisherfolk, for the European discovery of the Americas cannot be looked upon simply as the voyages of a few bold explorers. Adventurers like Christopher Columbus and John Cabot were only the most visible representatives of a much larger expansion of European peoples and culture that began in the 1450s. That expansion arose out of a series of gradual but telling changes in the fabric of European society—changes that were reflected in the lives of ordinary seafarers as much as in the careers of explorers decked out in flaming silks.

Some of these changes were technological, arising out of advances in the arts of navigating and shipbuilding and the use of gunpowder. Some were economic, involving the development of trade networks like those linking Bristol with ports in Iceland and Spain. Some were demographic, bringing about a rise in Europe's population after a devastating century of plague. Other changes were religious, adding a dimension of devout belief to the political rivalries that fueled discoveries in the Americas. Yet others were political, making it possible for kingdoms to centralize and extend their influence across the ocean. Portugal, Spain, France, and England—all possessing coasts along the Atlantic—led the way in exploration, spurred on by Italian "admirals" like Caboto and Colombo, Spanish "conquistadors" like Hernando Cortés and Francisco Pizarro, and English sea dogs like Humphrey Gilbert and Walter Raleigh. Ordinary folk rode these currents too. The great and the small alike were propelled by forces that were remolding the face of Europe.

Changes in European society

The Portuguese Wave

In 1450 all the world known to western Europeans was Asia and Africa. Most sailors traveled only along the coast of western Europe, following the shores between Norway and the southern tip of Spain, seldom daring to lose sight of land. Beginning in the fifteenth century, bolder seafarers groped down the coast of western Africa, half expecting to be boiled alive in the Atlantic as they approached the equator. Europeans had traded with Asia through the Muslims of the eastern Mediterranean and across an overland route called the "Silk Road." But they had only vague notions about "the Indies"—China and Japan, the Spice Islands, and the lands lying between Thailand and India. What little they knew, they had learned mainly from Marco Polo, whose account of his travels in the East was not published until 1477, more than 150 years after his death.

But a revolution in European geography began in the middle decades of the fifteenth century, as widening networks of travel and trade connected Europeans to civilizations beyond western Europe. The Portuguese took the lead, encouraged by Prince Henry, known as the Navigator. The devout Henry, a member of

Revolution in geography

Portugal's royal family, had heard tales of Prester John, a Catholic priest rumored to rule a Christian kingdom somewhere beyond the Muslim kingdoms of Africa and Asia. Henry dreamed of joining forces with Prester John and trapping the Muslims in a vise. To that end, he helped finance a series of expeditions down the coast of West Africa. He founded an informal school of navigation on the Portuguese coast, supplying shipmasters with information about wind and currents, as well as navigational charts.

Portuguese merchants, who may or may not have believed in Prester John, never doubted that there was money to be made in Africa. They invested in Prince Henry's voyages in return for trading monopolies of ivory and slaves, grain and gold. A few may have hoped that the voyages down the coast of West Africa would lead to a direct sea route to the Orient. By discovering such a route, Portugal would be able to cut out the Muslim merchants who funneled all the Asian trade in silks, spices, dyes, drugs, and perfumes through Mediterranean ports.

The Portuguese focus on Africa and Asia

While Portugal's merchants were establishing trading posts along the west coast of Africa, its mariners were discovering islands in the Atlantic: the Canaries, Madeira, and the Azores. Settlers planted sugarcane and imported slaves from Africa to work their fields. The Portuguese might have pressed even farther west but for the daring of Bartholomeu Dias. In 1488 Dias rounded the Cape of Good Hope on the southern tip of Africa, sailing far enough up that continent's eastern coast to claim discovery of a sea route to India. Ten years later Vasco da Gama reached India itself, and Portuguese interests ultimately extended to Indochina and China. With the trade of Africa and Asia to occupy them, they showed less interest in exploring the Atlantic.

By 1500, all of seafaring Europe sought the services of Portuguese pilots, prizing their superior maps and skills with the quadrant. That instrument made it possible to determine latitude fairly accurately, allowing ships to plot their position after months out of the sight of land. The Portuguese had also pioneered the caravel, a lighter, more maneuverable ship that could sail better against contrary winds and in rough seas. More seaworthy than the lumbering galleys of the Middle Ages, caravels combined longer, narrower hulls—a shape built for speed—with triangular lateen sails, which allowed for more flexible steering.

This stately ivory mask made by an African artist in the early sixteenth century for the Court of Benin (present-day Nigeria) is adorned with 10 bearded heads of white men, representing Portuguese explorers and traders who had first arrived in Benin in 1472.

Despite its focus on the Indies, Portugal continued to dominate trade along Africa's west coast. And the farther south the Portuguese extended their influence along the Atlantic rim of sub-Saharan Africa, the more likely they were to meet with native peoples who had had no earlier encounters with Europeans and, indeed, had no knowledge of the existence of other continents. On catching their first sight of a Portuguese expedition in 1455, the inhabitants of one village on the Senegal River marveled at the strangers' clothing and their white skin. As an Italian member of that expedition recounted, some Africans "rubbed me with their spittle to discover whether my whiteness was dye or flesh." Equally astonishing were the Portuguese ships and weapons, especially their deadly cannon and muskets. While some Africans concluded that these white newcomers must surely be either wizards or cannibals, dangerous men who should be either shunned or killed, others eagerly enlisted Europeans as military allies and trading partners, hoping to gain both power and practical knowledge.

This African fortune-teller reads the palm of her white client in this seventeenth-century painting by a Franco-Flemish artist, Nicolas Regnier. In early modern Europe, class and religion were more important in defining social divisions than color and ethnicity. Slaves, servants, and free workers of all races often worked and socialized together.

The debate among West Africans about whether to resist or accommodate the new European presence grew sharper as the interest of Portuguese traders in purchasing slaves increased. Before the end of the fifteenth century, most slaves in Europe were white, but among slaves of color, whether black or of mixed race (mulattoes), most were Muslims of North African ancestry and their numbers were concentrated in the Mediterranean. After the 1480s, however, darker-skinned, non-Muslim men and women from all along the west coast of Africa began to appear in greater numbers among the ranks of slaves and servants, as well as among craftworkers and musicians everywhere in western Europe, even as far north as the Netherlands and England. Their presence was most pronounced in Portugal and Spain: by the middle of the sixteenth century, people of African descent accounted for 10 percent of the population of Lisbon, Portugal's capital city.

Even so, the slave trade to the Atlantic islands and western Europe opened by the Portuguese at the end of the fifteenth century was small in scale compared with what was to come. The Atlantic slave trade did not take its full toll on Africa until Spain had made a much greater mark on the Americas.

The Spanish and Columbus

From among the international community of seafarers and pilots, it was a sailor from Genoa, Cristoforo Colombo, who led the Spanish to the Americas. Columbus (the Latinized version of his name survives) had knocked about in a number of harbors, picking up valuable navigation skills by sailing Portugal's merchant ships to Madeira, West Africa, and the North Atlantic. In the Irish port of Galway, Columbus saw two boats drift into the harbor, bearing the dead bodies of "a man and a woman of extraordinary appearance." Most likely they were Lapps or Finns, the victims of a shipwreck. But everyone in Galway, including Columbus, assumed that they were Chinese, "blown across" the Atlantic.

His experiences convinced Columbus that the quickest route to the Indies lay west, across the Atlantic—and that his destiny was to prove it. Perhaps a mere 4500 miles, he reckoned, separated Europe from Japan. His wishful estimate raised eyebrows whenever Columbus asked European monarchs for the money to meet his destiny. Most educated Europeans agreed that the world was round, but they also believed that the Atlantic barrier between themselves and Asia was far wider than Columbus allowed and that it was impossible to navigate. The kings of England, France, and Portugal dismissed him as a crackpot.

The *reconquista*

Almost a decade of rejection had grayed Columbus's red hair when Spain's monarchs, Ferdinand and Isabella, finally agreed to subsidize his expedition in 1492. For the past 20 years they had worked to drive the Muslims out of their last stronghold on the Iberian peninsula, the Moorish kingdom of Granada. In 1492 they completed this *reconquista,* or battle of reconquest, expelling many Jews as well. Yet the Portuguese, by breaking the Muslim stranglehold on trade with Asia, had taken the lead in the competition to smite the Islamic powers. Ferdinand and Isabella were so desperate to even the score with Portugal that jealousy overcame common sense: they agreed to take a risk on Columbus.

Columbus's first voyage across the Atlantic could only have confirmed his conviction that he was destiny's darling. His three ships, no bigger than fishing vessels that sailed to Newfoundland, plied their course over placid seas, south from Seville to the Canary Islands and then due west. A little more than two months after leaving Spain, on October 11, branches, leaves, and flowers floated by their hulls, signals that land lay near. Just after midnight, a sailor spied cliffs shining white in the moonlight. On the morning of October 12, the *Niña,* the *Pinta*, and the *Santa Maria* set anchor in a shallow sapphire bay, and their crews knelt on the white coral beach. Columbus christened the place San Salvador (Holy Savior).

Like many men of destiny, Columbus did not recognize his true destination. At first he confused his actual location, the Bahamas, with an island off the coast of Japan. He coasted along Cuba and Hispaniola (Haiti), expecting at any moment to catch sight of gold-roofed Japanese temples or to happen upon a fleet of Chinese junks. He encountered instead a gentle, generous people who knew nothing of the Great Khan but who showed him their islands. Columbus's journals note that they wore little clothing (see Daily Lives: "Barbaric" Dress—Indian and European, pages 46–47), but they did wear jewelry—tiny pendants of gold suspended from the nose. He dubbed the Arawak people "Indians"—inhabitants of the Indies.

The four voyages of Columbus

Columbus crossed the Atlantic three more times between 1493 and 1504. On his second voyage he established a permanent colony at Hispaniola and explored other Caribbean islands. On his third voyage he reached Venezuela on the continent of South America, and on his last sailing he made landfalls throughout Central America. Everywhere he looked for proof that these lands formed part of Asia.

Columbus died rich in titles, treasure, and tales—everything but recognition. During the last decade of his life, most Spaniards no longer believed that Columbus had discovered the Indies or anyplace else of significance. And shortly after his death in 1506, another Italian stamped his own name on the New World. Amerigo Vespucci, a Florentine banker with a flair for self-promotion, cruised the coast of Brazil in 1501 and again in 1503. His sensational report of his travels misled a German mapmaker into crediting Vespucci with discovering the barrier between Europe and Asia, and so naming it "America."

Europe in the age of discovery was a world graced by the courage of explorers like Columbus and the genius of

The European Background of American Colonization

artists like Michelangelo. It was also a world riddled with war, disease, and uncertainty. In 1450 the continent was still recovering from the ravages of the Black Death, an epidemic of the bubonic plague. Under such vibrant, often chaotic conditions, a sense of crisis was mixed with a sense of possibility. Indeed, it was this blend of desperation and ambition that made the newly discovered Americas so attractive to Europeans. Here were strange and distant lands like the island paradises spoken of in legends, like that of the fabled kingdom of Atlantis. Here were opportunities and riches for the daring to grasp. Here were salvation and security for those escaping a world full of violence and sin or oppressed by disease and poverty.

Life and Death in Early Modern Europe

During the fourteenth and the fifteenth centuries 90 percent of Europe's people, widely dispersed in small villages, made their living from the land. But warfare, poor transportation, and low grain yields all created food shortages, and undernourishment produced a population prone to disease. Under these circumstances life was nasty, brutish, and usually short. One-quarter of all children died in the first year of life. People who reached the ripe age of 40 counted themselves fortunate.

It was also a world of sharp inequalities, where nobles and aristocrats enjoyed several hundred times the income of peasants or craftworkers. It was a world with no strong, centralized political authority, where kings were weak and warrior lords held sway over small towns and tiny fiefdoms. It was a world of hierarchy and dependence, where the upper classes provided land and protection for the lower orders. It was a

St. Sebastian Interceding for the Plague-Stricken City captures the desperation of Europeans during an outbreak of the Black Death. At the top, St. Sebastian, a Christian martyr, intercedes with God to end the suffering. This skull pendant, dating from the 1600s, opens to reveal a skeleton in a coffin. The popularity of this jewelry points up how deeply early modern Europeans were preoccupied with death.

world of violence and sudden death, where homicide, robbery, and rape occurred with brutal frequency. It was a world where security and order of any kind seemed so fragile that most people clung to tradition and feared change.

Into that world in 1347 came the Black Death. In only four years that plague swept away one-third of Europe's population, disrupting both agriculture and commerce. For the next century, recurring outbreaks created additional social disruption and economic depression. Yet the sudden drop in population restored the balance between people and resources. Survivors of the Black Death found that the relative scarcity of workers and consumers made for better wages, lower prices, and more land.

But by the time Columbus reached America, nearly 150 years after the outbreak of the Black Death, Europe again confronted its old problem. Too many people were again competing for a limited supply of food and land. Throughout the sixteenth century diets became poorer, land and work less available, crime and beggary more common. Inflation compounded these problems when prices doubled at the end of the fifteenth century and then quadrupled between 1520 and 1590. To keep pace with the "Price Revolution," landlords raised rents, adding to the burden of the peasantry.

To Europe's hopeful and desperate alike, this climate of disorder and uncertainty led to dreams that the New World would provide an opportunity to renew the Old. As Columbus wrote eagerly of Hispaniola: "This island and all others are very fertile to a limitless degree. . . . There are very large tracts of cultivated land. . . . In the interior there are mines and metals." Columbus and many other Europeans expected that the Americas would provide land for the landless, work for the unemployed, and wealth beyond the wildest dreams of the daring.

The Conditions of Colonization

Sixteenth-century Europeans sought to colonize the Americas, not merely to escape from scarcity and disruption at home. They were also propelled across the Atlantic by dynamic changes in their society. Revolutions in technology, economics, and politics made overseas settlement practical and attractive to seekers of profit and power.

Expansion of trade and capital

The improvements in navigation and sailing also fostered an expansion of trade. By the late fifteenth century Europe's merchants and bankers had devised more efficient ways of transferring money and establishing credit in order to support commerce across longer distances. And although rising prices and rents pinched Europe's peasantry, that same inflation enriched those who had goods to sell, money to lend, and land to rent. Wealth flowed into the coffers of sixteenth-century traders, financiers, and landlords, creating a pool of capital that those investors could plow into colonial development. Both the commercial networks and the private fortunes needed to sustain overseas trade and settlement were in place by the time of Columbus's discovery.

Political centralization

The direction of Europe's political development also paved the path for American colonization. After 1450 strong monarchs in Europe steadily enlarged the sphere of royal power at the expense of warrior lords. Henry VII, the founder of England's Tudor dynasty, Francis I of France, and Ferdinand and Isabella of Spain began the trend, forging modern nation-states by extending their political control over more territory, people, and resources. Those larger, more centrally organized states were able to marshal the resources necessary to support colonial outposts and to sustain the professional armies and navies capable of protecting empires abroad.

Europeans, Chinese, and Aztecs on the Eve of Contact

It was the growing power of monarchs as well as commercial and technological development that allowed early modern Europeans to establish permanent settlements—even empires—in another world lying an ocean away. But that conclusion raises an intriguing question: why didn't China, the most advanced civilization of the early modern world, engage in expansion and colonization? Or for that matter, if events had fallen out a little differently, why didn't the Aztecs discover and colonize Europe?

The Chinese undoubtedly possessed the capability to navigate the world's oceans and to establish overseas settlements. A succession of Ming dynasty emperors and their efficient bureaucrats marshaled China's resources to develop a thriving shipbuilding industry and trade with ports throughout southeast Asia and India. By the opening of the fifteenth century, the Chinese seemed poised for even greater maritime exploits. Seven times between 1405 and 1433, China's "treasure fleet"—300 ships manned by 28,000 sailors and commanded by Zheng He (pronounced "Jung Huh")—unfurled their red silk sails off the south China coast and sailed as far as the kingdoms of eastern Africa. The treasure fleet's largest craft were nine-masted junks measuring 400 feet long that boasted multiple decks and luxury cabins with balconies. In contrast, when Columbus's three ships set sail to find the Indies, the biggest was a mere 85 feet long, and the crew aboard all three totaled just 90 men.

Zheng He could have been another Columbus, given the resources available to him. But the Chinese had little incentive either to seek out the world's trade or to conquer and colonize new territories. Unlike western Europeans, they faced no shortages of land or food, and they led the world in producing luxury goods. On the other hand, China faced the threat of attack from the Mongols on its northwestern border—a threat so pressing that in 1433 the Ming emperor mobilized all the country's wealth and warriors to fend it off. Thus ended the great era of Chinese maritime expansion. All foreign trade was suspended, and Zheng He's treasure fleet, which would remain the world's most impressive navy until the beginning of the twentieth century, rotted away in the ports of southern China.

Why China did not explore farther

As for the Aztecs, their cultural development paralleled that of early modern Europe in many ways. Both societies were predominantly rural, with most inhabitants living in small villages and engaging in agriculture. In both places, merchants and specialized craftworkers clustered in cities, organized themselves into guilds, and clamored for protection from the government. Aztec noble and priestly classes, like those in Europe, took the lead in politics and religion, demanding tribute from the common people. Finally, both societies were robustly expansionist, bent on bringing new lands and peoples under their control.

Yet despite their formidable talents, the Aztecs lacked the knowledge of ocean navigation. Equally important, Aztec rulers had not established their sovereign authority over powerful nobles. The absence of a strong, centralized power made it impossible for the Aztecs to launch a more ambitious expansion. Although their armies put down disturbances in conquered territories and protected trade routes, the Aztecs had not developed the resources to impose their way of life on other places. Instead, conquered city-states within the Aztec empire retained their distinctive languages and customs—and bitterly resented Aztec rule. The result was an empire vulnerable to division from within and to attack from abroad.

Barriers to Aztec colonization

Spain's Empire in the New World

By the reckoning of the Aztecs it was the year 12-House—a time, they believed, when the fate of the whole world hung by a thread. According to their calendar, a 52-year cycle had come to an end. Now the gods might extinguish the sun with a flood or a great wind. The end of this particular cycle had been marked with a chilling omen. In one of the canals, fishermen caught a bird "the color of ashes" with a strange mirror in the crown of its head. They brought the creature to their ruler, Moctezuma II, who looked in the mirror and saw ranks of men mounted on animals resembling deer and moving across a plain.

Two years later, the Aztecs' worst fears were fulfilled. Dust rose in whirlwinds on the roads from the hooves of horses and the boots of men in battle array. "It was as if the earth trembled beneath them, or as if the world were spinning . . . as it spins during a fit of vertigo," one Aztec scribe recorded. This was no image in a magic mirror: Hernando Cortés and his army of Spaniards were marching on Tenochtitlán. By Cortés's calculations, it was A.D. 1519.

Spanish Conquest

To Cortés and the other Spanish explorers who had followed Columbus across the Atlantic, a new and remarkable world was opening. By 1513 the Spanish had explored and mastered the Caribbean basin. Also in 1513, Vasco Núñez de Balboa crossed the Isthmus of Panama and glimpsed the Pacific Ocean. North and South America were revealed as continents of vast size, separated from Asia by another ocean. And Ferdinand Magellan finally did reach the Orient by sailing west across the immense Pacific. After his death in the Philippines in 1521, Magellan's shipmates completed the first circumnavigation of the globe.

From their bases in the islands of the Caribbean, the Spanish pressed outward. To the north they met mostly with disappointment. Juan Ponce de León vainly scoured the shores of the Florida peninsula for the fabled "Fountain of Youth" as well as Indian populations he might enslave to work the gold mines of the Caribbean. Several decades later, Hernando de Soto plundered his way through Florida and into the southeastern interior as far west as the Mississippi River. Between 1540 and 1542 Francisco Vásquez de Coronado moved through Arizona, New Mexico, Texas, Oklahoma, and Kansas. But reports of fantastic cities of gold proved to be merely the stuff of dreams.

During these same decades, however, the Spanish found golden opportunities elsewhere. Those who had first rushed to Hispaniola immediately started scouring the island for gold—and enslaving Indians to work the mines. As for Cortés, when Moctezuma's ambassadors met him on the road to Tenochtitlán in 1519 and attempted to appease him with gold ornaments and other gifts, an Indian witness recorded, "the Spaniards . . . picked up the gold and fingered it like monkeys. . . . Their bodies swelled with greed." For nearly half a year Cortés dominated the indecisive Moctezuma by imprisoning him in his own capital. The Aztecs drove the Spanish out after Moctezuma's death, but Cortés returned with reinforcements, set siege to Tenochtitlán, and in 1521 conquered it. The Aztec empire lay in ruins.

Role of the Conquistadors

To the conquistadors—a motley lot of minor nobles, landless gentlemen, and professional soldiers—the newfound land seemed more than a golden opportunity. They resented the Spanish monarchy's growing strength at home and aimed to re-create in the New World a much older world of their own dreaming. Like medieval knights, Cortés and other conquistadors hoped to establish themselves as a powerful nobility that would enjoy virtual independence from the Spanish Crown an ocean away.

For a time the conquistadors succeeded. By the 1540s Cortés and just 1500 men had taken all of Mexico and the southwestern portion of North America. During the 1530s the ruthless Pizarro brothers and an even smaller band of conquistadors sailed along South America's Pacific coast and overthrew the Incas in Peru, an Andean civilization as impressive as that of the Aztecs. They also laid claim to Ecuador, Chile, Argentina, and Bolivia.

How did a handful of gentlemen heading a rabble of soldiers, seamen, and criminals bring down sophisticated Indian empires in the span of a generation? To begin with, the Spanish enjoyed the edge of surprise and technological superiority. The sight of ships and the explosion of guns at first terrified the Indians, as did men on horseback whom some Indians, at first, took to be single creatures.

Both the Aztecs and the Spanish tried to understand the new in terms of the familiar. Hence an Aztec artist portrayed Cortés as an Indian with strange clothes and stranger beard (left), while a European artist depicted Moctezuma in the style of a Greco-Roman warrior (right).

The only domesticated animals known to the Aztecs were small dogs; the Spanish provided them with their first glimpse of horses and, later, cattle, sheep, oxen, pigs, goats, donkeys, mules, and chickens.

What delivered a more lasting shock to Indian civilizations was exposure to European infections. Smallpox, influenza, typhus, and measles, disease strains against which the Indians had developed no biological resistance, ravaged entire villages and tribes. Tenochtitlán surrendered to Cortés after a siege of 85 days, during which many died from starvation but many more died of smallpox contracted from the Spanish. When the Spanish finally entered the conquered city, "the streets, squares, houses, and courts were filled with bodies, so that it was almost impossible to pass. Even Cortés was sick from the stench in his nostrils."

An equally important factor in the swift conquest was the political disunity within Indian empires. The Aztecs and Incas had subdued the native Indian populations of Mexico and Peru only 100 years before the Spanish invasion. Resentment at Aztec and Inca rule brought the conquistadors eager allies among the subject Indian tribes. But by aiding the Spanish overthrow of the Aztecs and the Incas, the native Indians only substituted one set of overlords for another.

Spanish Colonization

The conquistadors did not long enjoy their mastery in the Americas. The Spanish monarchs, who had just tamed an aristocracy at home, were not about to allow a colonial nobility to arise across the Atlantic. The Crown bribed the conquistadors into retirement—or was saved the expense when men like the Pizarro brothers were assassinated by their own followers. The task of governing Spain's new

Royal control replaces the conquistadors

colonies passed from the conquistadors to a small army of officials, soldiers, lawyers, and Catholic bishops, all appointed by the Crown, reporting to the Crown, and loyal to the Crown. Headquartered in urban centers like Mexico City (formerly Tenochtitlán), an elaborate, centralized bureaucracy administered the Spanish empire, regulating nearly every aspect of economic and social life.

Few Spaniards besides imperial officials settled in the Americas. By 1600 only about 5 percent of the colonial population was of Spanish descent, the other 95 percent being either Indian or African. Even by 1800 only 300,000 Spanish immigrants had come to Central and South America. Indians remained on the lands that they had farmed under the Aztecs and the Incas, now paying Spanish overlords their taxes and producing livestock for export. The Indians were not enslaved outright, but the Spanish compelled them to provide yearly tributes of food and other goods, a system known as *encomienda*. The Spanish also established sugar plantations in the West Indies; these were worked by black slaves who were being imported from Africa in large numbers by 1520.

Discovery of silver

Spain's colonies returned even more spectacular profits to the mother country after 1540, when silver deposits were discovered in both Mexico and Peru. Silver mining developed into a large-scale capitalist enterprise requiring substantial investment. European investors and Spanish immigrants who had profited from cattle raising and sugar planting poured their capital into equipment that would

Spanish America, ca. 1600 By 1600, Spain was extracting large amounts of gold and silver from Central and South America, as well as profits from sugar plantations in the Caribbean. Each year Spanish treasure ships ferried bullion from mines such as the one at Potosí to the Isthmus of Panama, where it was transported by land to the Caribbean coast, and from there to Spain. An expedition from Acapulco sailed annually to the Philippines as well, returning with Asian spices and other trade goods.

mine the silver deposits more efficiently: stamp mills, water-powered crushing equipment, and pumps. To provide workers, the Spanish government introduced another form of forced labor, known as *repartimiento*. Whole villages of Indians were pressed into service in the mines, joining black slaves and free white workers employed there.

In the last decades of the sixteenth century the economies of Mexico and Peru revolved solely around the mines. By 1570 the town of Potosí, the site of a veritable mountain of silver, had become larger than any city in either Spain or its American empire, with a population of 120,000. Local farmers who supplied mining centers with food and Spanish merchants in Seville who exported European goods to Potosí profited handsomely. So, too, did the Spanish Crown, which claimed one-fifth of the silver extracted. All told, between 1500 and 1600 some 16,000 tons were exported from Spanish America to Europe.

The Effects of Colonial Growth

Its American riches made Spain the dominant power in Europe. But that dominance was purchased at a fearful human cost. Devastated by warfare, disease, and exploitation, the Indians of the Caribbean were virtually wiped out within a century. In Mesoamerica, a native population of 20 million was reduced to 2 million.

Only a few of the Spanish spoke out against the exploitation of the natives. Among them was Bartolomé de Las Casas, a Spanish priest who became a bishop in southern Mexico. His writings, reprinted in many translations and illustrated with gruesome drawings, circulated throughout Europe, becoming the basis of the "Black Legend" of Spanish oppression in the Americas.

Most Spaniards did not share Las Casas's scruples. They justified their conquest by claiming that they had "delivered" the Indians from Aztec and Inca tyranny and replaced native "barbarism" and "paganism" with European civilization and Christianity. The sheer size of the Spanish conquest fostered a heady sense of superiority. By the beginning of the seventeenth century Spain's dominions in the Americas spanned 8000 miles, stretching from Baja California to the Straits of Magellan at South America's southern tip. The prevailing mood was captured by the portrait of a Spanish soldier that adorns the frontispiece of his book about the West Indies. He stands with one hand on his sword and the other holding a pair of compasses on top of a globe. Beneath is inscribed the motto "By compasses and the sword / More and more and more and more."

For most of the sixteenth century, Spain met with little interference in the Americas from rival European nations. One reason was religious upheaval in Europe. During the second decade of the sixteenth century—the same decade in which Cortés laid siege to Tenochtitlán—religious changes of enormous significance began in Europe. That revolution in Christianity, known as the Protestant Reformation, would figure as a crucial force in shaping the later history of the Americas.

The Reformation in Europe

Backdrop to Reform

During the Middle Ages, the Roman Catholic church defined what it meant to be a Christian in western Europe. Like other institutions of medieval society the

Catholic church was a hierarchy. At the top was the pope in Rome, and under him were the descending ranks of other church officials—cardinals, archbishops, bishops. At the bottom of the Catholic hierarchy were parish priests, each serving his own village, as well as monks and nuns living in monasteries and convents. But medieval popes were weak, and their power was felt little in the lives of most Europeans. Like political units of the era, religious institutions of the Middle Ages were local and decentralized.

Rise of the papacy

Between about 1100 and 1500, as the monarchs of Europe were growing more powerful, so too were the popes. As the papacy grew in wealth and power, a larger bureaucracy of church officials emerged. The Catholic church acquired land throughout Europe and added to its income through tithing (collecting taxes from church members) and by collecting fees from those appointed to church offices. In the thirteenth century, church officials also began to sell "indulgences." For ordinary believers who expected to spend time after death purging their sins in purgatory, the purchase of an indulgence promised to shorten that punishment by drawing on a "treasury of merit" amassed by the good works of Christ and the saints.

By the fifteenth century the Catholic church and the papacy had become enormously powerful but increasingly indifferent to popular religious concerns. Church officials meddled in secular politics. Popes and bishops flaunted their wealth, while poorly educated parish priests neglected their pastoral duties. At the same time, popular demands for religious assurance grew increasingly intense. The concern for salvation swelled in response to the disorienting changes sweeping the continent during the fifteenth and sixteenth centuries—the widening gulf between rich and poor, the rise in prices, and the discovery of America.

The Teachings of Martin Luther

Into this climate of heightened spirituality stepped Martin Luther, who abandoned studying the law to enter a monastery. Like many of his contemporaries, Luther was consumed by fears over his eternal fate. He was convinced that he was damned, and he could not find any consolation in the Catholic church. Catholic doctrine taught that a person could be saved by faith in God and by his or her own good works—by leading a virtuous life, observing the sacraments (such as baptism, the Mass, and penance), making pilgrimages to holy places, and praying to Christ and the saints. Because Luther believed that human nature was innately evil, he despaired of being able to lead a life that "merited" salvation. If men and women are so bad, he reasoned, how could they ever win their way to heaven with good works?

Justification by faith alone

Luther finally broke through his despair by reading the Bible. It convinced him that God did not require fallen humankind to earn salvation. Salvation, he concluded, came by faith alone, the "free gift" of God to undeserving sinners. The ability to live a good life could not be the *cause* of salvation but its *consequence*: once men and women believed that they had saving faith, moral behavior was possible. Luther elaborated that idea, known as "justification by faith alone," between 1513 and 1517.

Luther was ordained a priest and then assigned to teach at a university in Wittenberg, Germany. Still, he became increasingly critical of the Catholic church as an institution. In 1517 he posted on the door of a local church 95 theses attacking the Catholic hierarchy for selling salvation in the form of indulgences.

In early modern Europe, the uncertainties of religious war and economic upheaval created a pervasive social and spiritual unease, reflected in both these engravings. A contemporary of Martin Luther portrayed St. Anthony (left) being tormented by a host of demons. Their bizarre and twisted shapes bear a notable resemblance to the sea monsters (right) menacing the oceans leading to the newly discovered worlds of Asia and the Americas.

The novelty of this attack was not Luther's open break with Catholic teaching. Challenges to the church had cropped up throughout the Middle Ages. What was new was the passion and force behind Luther's attacks. Using the blunt, earthy Germanic tongue, he expressed the anxieties of many devout laypeople and their outrage at the church hierarchy's neglect. The "gross, ignorant asses and knaves at Rome," he warned, should keep their distance from Germany, or else "jump into the Rhine or the nearest river, and take . . . a cold bath."

The pope and his representatives in Germany at first tried to silence Martin Luther, then excommunicated him. But opposition only pushed Luther toward more radical positions. He asserted that the church and its officials were not infallible; only the Scriptures were without error. Every person, he said, should read and interpret the Bible for himself or herself. In an even more direct assault on church authority, he advanced an idea known as "the priesthood of all believers." Catholic doctrine held that salvation came only through the church and its clergy, a privileged group that possessed special access to God. Luther asserted that every person had the power claimed by priests.

Although Luther had not intended to start a schism within Catholicism, independent Lutheran churches were forming in Germany by the 1520s. And during the 1530s, Luther's ideas spread throughout Europe, where they were eagerly taken up by other reformers.

The Contribution of John Calvin

The most influential of Luther's successors was John Calvin, a French lawyer turned theologian. Calvin agreed with Luther that men and women could not merit their salvation. But while Luther's God was a loving deity who extended his mercy

John Calvin promoted an activist theology.

to sinful humankind, Calvin conceived of God as an awesome sovereign, all-knowing and all-powerful, the controlling force in human history who would ultimately triumph over Satan. To bring about that final victory, Calvin believed, God had selected certain people as his agents for ushering in his heavenly kingdom. These people—"the saints," or "the elect"—had been "predestined" by God for eternal salvation in heaven.

The elect

Calvin's emphasis on predestination led him to another distinctively Protestant notion—the doctrine of calling. How could a person learn whether he or she belonged to the elect who were saved? Calvin answered: strive to behave like a saint. God expected his elect to serve the good of society by unrelenting work in a "calling," or occupation, in the world. In place of the Catholic belief in the importance of good works, Calvin emphasized the goodness of work itself. Success in attaining discipline and self-control, in bringing order into one's own life and the entire society, revealed that a person might be among the elect.

Calvin fashioned a religion to change the world. Whereas Luther believed that Christians should accept the existing social order, Calvin called on Christians to become activists, reshaping society and government to conform with God's laws laid down in the Bible. He wanted all of Europe to become like Geneva, the Swiss city that he had converted into a holy commonwealth in which the elect regulated the behavior and morals of everyone else. And unlike Luther, who wrote primarily for a German audience, Calvin addressed his most important book, *The Institutes of the Christian Religion* (1536), to Christians throughout Europe. Reformers from every country flocked to Geneva to learn more about Calvin's ideas.

The English Reformation

While the Reformation went forward in Europe, King Henry VIII of England was striving for a goal more modest than those of Luther and Calvin. He wanted only to produce a male heir to carry on the Tudor dynasty. When his wife, Catherine of Aragon, gave birth to a daughter, Mary, Henry decided to do something less modest. He set out to get his marriage to Catherine annulled by the pope. This move angered Catherine's nephew, the king of Spain, who persuaded the pope to refuse. Defiantly, Henry went ahead with the divorce and married his mistress, Anne Boleyn.

Henry VIII breaks
with Rome

Henry then widened this breach with Rome by making himself, and not the pope, the head of the Church of England. In 1534 Parliament formalized the relationship with the Act of Supremacy. But Henry, who fancied himself a theologian, had no fondness for Protestant doctrine. Under his leadership the Church of England remained essentially Catholic in its teachings and rituals.

England's Protestants gained ground during the six-year reign of Edward VI but then found themselves persecuted when his Catholic half sister, Mary, became queen in 1553. Five years later the situation turned again, when Elizabeth (Anne Boleyn's daughter) took the throne, proclaiming herself the defender of Protestantism.

Still, Elizabeth was no radical Calvinist. A vocal minority of her subjects were reformers of that stripe, calling for the English church to purge itself of bishops, elaborate ceremonies, and other Catholic "impurities." Because of the austerity and zeal of such Calvinist radicals, their opponents proclaimed them "Puritans."

English Puritans

The Protestant Reformation shattered the unity of Christendom in western Europe. Spain, Ireland, and Italy remained firmly Catholic. England, France, Scotland, the Netherlands, and Switzerland developed either dominant or substantial Calvinist constituencies. Much of Germany and Scandinavia opted for Lutheranism. As these religious groups competed for political power and the loyalties of believers, brutal wars racked sixteenth-century Europe. Protestants and Catholics slaughtered each other in the name of Christianity.

In 1562 Queen Elizabeth gave her blessing to an English army that set sail **England's Entry into America** for France to aid Calvinists there being suppressed by the government. Perhaps the most dashing of the army's captains was a red-faced and robust West Country gentleman, Sir Humphrey Gilbert. "There is not a vallianter man that liveth," the Earl of Warwick assured the queen.

Like so many West Country boys in search of honor and fortune, Gilbert was eager to seize the main chance. In the early 1560s, that chance seemed to be fighting for the Protestant cause in France. Gilbert's stepfather, the seafarer Walter Raleigh, had done a good deal of his own seizing, mostly from Spanish silver ships along the South American coast. Like the conquistadors, Raleigh wanted more. He merely decided he could get more a bit more easily if he let Spain dig and refine the silver first.

If France had not beckoned, Humphrey Gilbert would surely have been happy to harass the Spanish too, along with his stepbrother, the young Walter Raleigh (named after his plundering father). But as Gilbert and young Raleigh came of age, they began to consider more ambitious schemes than the mere plundering of treasure. They looked to conquer Spain's empire—or, at least, to carve out for England a rival empire of its own. During the late 1570s and 1580s, when Queen Elizabeth felt confident enough to challenge Spain in the Americas, Gilbert and Raleigh were ready to lead the way.

Ambitious West Country gentlemen

The English Colonization of Ireland

During the 1560s, however, England was too deeply distracted by religious and political turmoil to pursue dreams of glory across the Atlantic. For Elizabeth, privateers like the senior Walter Raleigh stirred up more trouble than they were worth. Spain, after all, was England's ally against a common rival, France. And the Netherlands, which was then controlled by Spain, imported a good deal of English cloth. Elizabeth had good reason to pursue a policy that would soothe Spain, not offend it.

Reasons for England to soothe Spain

The queen also worried about Catholic Ireland to the west. She feared that the French or the Spanish might use the island as a base for invading England. Beginning in 1565 Elizabeth encouraged a number of her subjects, mainly gentlemen and aristocrats from the West Country, to sponsor private ventures for subduing the native Irish and settling English families on Irish land. Among the gentlemen eager to win fame and fortune were Humphrey Gilbert and Walter Raleigh.

The English invaders of Ireland, almost all ardent Protestants, regarded the native Catholic inhabitants as superstitious, pagan savages. "They blaspheme, they murder, commit whoredome," complained one Englishman, "hold no wedlocke, ravish, steal and commit all abomination without scruple." Thus the English found it easy enough to justify their conquest. They proclaimed it their duty to teach the Irish the discipline of hard work, the rule of law, and the truth of Christianity. And

English repression of the Irish

Martin Frobisher, his face frozen in a glare and a horse pistol fixed in his fist, exemplified the ruthless ambition of England's West Country adventurers.

Joint stock companies

while the Irish were learning civilized ways, they would not be allowed to buy land or hold office or serve on juries or give testimony in courts or learn a trade or bear arms.

When the Irish rebelled at that program of "liberation," the English ruthlessly repressed native resistance, slaughtering not only combatants but civilians as well. Most English in Ireland, like most Spaniards in America, believed that native peoples who resisted civilization and Christianity should be subdued at any cost. No scruples stopped Humphrey Gilbert, in an insurgent country, from planting the path to his camp with the severed heads of Irish rebels.

England's efforts to settle and subdue Ireland would serve as a rough model for later efforts at colonization. The approach was essentially military, like that of the conquistadors. More ominously, it sanctioned the savage repression of any "inferior race." Not only Gilbert but also Raleigh and many other West Country gentry soon turned their attention toward North America. "Neither reputation, or profytt is to be wonne" in Ireland, concluded Gilbert. They wanted more.

Renewed Interest in the Americas

After hard service in France and Ireland, Gilbert and Raleigh returned to England. Elizabeth's court buzzed with gossip of their boasting and pride, "which exceedeth [that] of all men alive." Her cautious bureaucrats, who had been enlarging royal power, considered the two swaggering gentlemen insufferable if not downright dangerous, much as the Spanish officials distrusted their conquistadors. Still, England was becoming more receptive to the schemes of such hotheaded warrior lords for challenging Spain overseas. English Protestantism, English nationalism, and English economic interests all came together to increase support for English exploration and colonization.

The turning point for the English came during the 1570s when Calvinist Dutch in the Netherlands rebelled against their rule by Catholic Spain. The Spanish retaliated savagely by sacking the city of Antwerp, which was England's major European market for cloth. Forced to look elsewhere for markets and investment opportunities, merchants combined in joint stock companies to develop a trade with Africa, Russia, the East Indies, and the Mediterranean. These private corporations, in which many shareholders pooled small amounts of capital, also began to plow money into Atlantic privateering voyages. They pressed Elizabeth to unleash England's sea rovers on Spain's silver ships.

Joining English merchants in the new interest in overseas exploration were gentry families. The high birthrate among England's upper classes throughout the sixteenth century had produced a surplus of younger sons, who stood to inherit no share of family estates. The shortage of land for their sons at home stirred up support among the gentry for England to claim territory across the Atlantic.

With the backing of England's leading merchants and gentry, Elizabeth now needed little encouragement to adopt a more belligerent stance toward Spain. But she got more encouragement from Spain itself, which made no secret of wanting to restore England to Catholicism, by armed invasion if necessary. Elizabeth was not yet prepared to provoke open warfare with Spain, but she watched with interest the exploits of a new generation of English explorers in North America.

The Failures of Frobisher and Gilbert

The adventurer who first caught the queen's eye was Martin Frobisher, the veteran of slaving voyages to West Africa, privateering raids in the Atlantic, fighting in Ireland, and other unsavory enterprises. In 1576 he sailed on another search for a Northwest Passage to Asia.

After sailing north of Labrador, Frobisher returned to England with an Eskimo (plucked, kayak and all, from the Atlantic) and a shiny black stone that seemed to be gold ore. With royal backing, Frobisher made two more voyages to his "New Peru" in 1577 and 1578, hauling back nearly 2000 tons of black rock. Closer inspection revealed all the rock to be fool's gold, and Frobisher's reputation fell under a cloud.

Because Humphrey Gilbert had refused to invest in this fiasco, Frobisher's disgrace became Gilbert's opportunity. In 1578 Elizabeth granted Gilbert a vague patent—the first English colonial charter—to explore, occupy, and govern any territory in America "not actually possessed of any Christian prince or people." That charter, ignoring the Indian possession of North America, made Gilbert lord and proprietor of all the land lying between Florida and Labrador.

Gilbert pictured himself and his heirs as manorial lords of a colony filled with loyal tenant farmers paying rents in return for protection. In a sense his dreams resembled those of Spain's conquistadors: to re-create an older, nearly feudal world that would remain largely free of royal control. Yet Gilbert's vision also looked forward to a utopian society. He planned to encourage England's poor to emigrate by providing them free land and a government "to be chosen by consent of the people."

Gilbert's colonial plans

In the end, the dreams foundered in a stormy present. Gilbert set sail in June 1583, but a late start forced him to turn back before he could scout the North American coast. Then his two ships met with foul weather. Gilbert, with characteristic bravado, sat on the deck of the smaller *Squirrel*, reading a book. "We are as neere to Heaven by sea as by land," he shouted across the heaving swells. The men aboard the *Golden Hind* recognized the words of Thomas More, whose *Utopia*—a dialogue about an ideal society in the New World—Gilbert held in his hand. Gilbert was nearer to heaven than he hoped. Around midnight, the crew of the *Golden Hind* saw the lights of the *Squirrel* extinguished and the ship "devoured and swallowed up by the sea."

Raleigh's Roanoke Venture

Raleigh had been eager to accompany his stepbrother's ill-fated expedition, but Elizabeth's many favors made it hard for him to leave. He was dining on food from palace kitchens, sleeping in a bed adorned with green velvet and spangled plumes of white feathers. Still, Raleigh was restless—and envious when another West Country adventurer, Sir Francis Drake, returned from circumnavigating the globe in 1580, his ships heavy with Spanish plunder.

Raleigh's ambitions led him to Richard Hakluyt, a clergyman with a passion for spreading knowledge of overseas discoveries. At Raleigh's request, Hakluyt wrote an eloquent plea to Elizabeth for the English settlement of America, titled *A Discourse Concerning Westerne Planting*. The temperate and fertile lands of North America, Hakluyt argued, would provide a perfect base from which to harry the Spanish, search for a Northwest Passage, and extend the influence of Protestantism. He also stressed the advantages of colonies as sources of new commodities, as markets for English goods, and as havens for the poor and unemployed.

Hakluyt publicizes America

Daily Lives

CLOTHING AND FASHION

"Barbaric" Dress—Indian and European

It was remarkable to sixteenth-century Europeans how many things seemed to be missing from Indian culture. Even more remarkable, the Indians themselves did not seem to notice. Michel de Montaigne, a French philosopher who had never been to America but liked to talk with explorers and read their accounts, managed to compile quite a list. According to Montaigne, Indians had "no kind of traffic [trade], no knowledge of letters, no intelligence of numbers, no name of magistrate, nor of politics, no use of service [servants], of riches, or of poverty, no contracts, no successions, no partitions, no occupation but idle, no apparel but natural. . . ." When other Europeans, with and without experience in America, made similar lists, they never failed to mention that last crucial item missing in Indian culture—clothing. Even Europeans who never traveled beyond their villages associated America's inhabitants with nakedness, for woodcuts, engravings, and paintings showed native peoples either entirely nude or clad in skimpy loincloths or grass skirts.

Europeans interpreted the simplicity of Indian dress in two different ways. Some saw the lack of clothing as evidence of "barbarism." André Thevet, a shocked French visitor to Brazil in 1557, voiced this point of view when he attributed nakedness to simple lust. If the Indians could weave hammocks, he sniffed, why not shirts? But other Europeans viewed unashamed nakedness as the Indians' badge of innocence. As remnants of a bygone "golden age," they believed, Indians needed clothing no more than government, laws, regular employment, or other corruptions of civilization.

In fact, Indians were no more "naked" than they were without trade, politics, employment, or religion. While the simplest tribes of the Caribbean and Brazil wore little, the members of more advanced Indian cultures in Central and North America clothed themselves with animal pelts sewn into mantles and robes, breechclouts, leggings, and moccasins. They wrought bird feathers into headdresses and ear decorations and fashioned reptile skins into belts and pouches. Even more formidably clad were the Eskimos of the far North, who dressed head to foot in sealskin suits with waterproofed seams, turning the furry side inward for warmth in the winter and outward in the summer.

By the late sixteenth century, Europeans, and especially the English, were paying more heed

Columbus meeting the natives on Hispaniola

Raleigh's chance to settle American lands finally came in 1584, when Elizabeth granted him a patent nearly identical to that of Gilbert. By the summer Raleigh had sent Philip Amadas and Arthur Barlowe across the Atlantic, their two small ships coasting the Outer Banks of present-day North Carolina. Amadas and Barlowe established cordial relations with the Roanoke tribe, ruled by a "werowance," or chief, named Wingina. The enthusiastic Hakluyt promptly envisioned a colony that would become the Mexico of England, full of plantations producing sugar and silk and mountains yielding gold. Elizabeth knighted Raleigh and allowed him to name the new land "Virginia," after his virgin queen. The following summer a full-scale expedition returned to Roanoke Island.

to what the Indians wore, hoping to assure prospective colonists that the natives would not affront European standards of modesty. Captain John Smith, for example, left descriptions of the attire of Virginia's tribes, noting in a telling comparison that "the better sort use large mantels of deare skins not much differing in fashion from the Irish mantels." Even more reassuringly, Smith added, "The women are alwaies covered about their midles with a skin and very shamefast [ashamed] to be seen bare."

If natives struck whites as starkly underdressed, Europeans seemed, by the Indians' standards, grotesquely overdressed. Indeed, European fashion was ill suited to the environment between the Chesapeake and the Caribbean. Elizabethan gentlemen strutted in silk stockings attached with garters to padded, puffed knee breeches, topped by long-sleeved shirts and tight quilted jackets called "doublets." Men of lesser status wore coarse woolen hose, canvas breeches, shirts, and fitted vests known as "jerkins"; when at work, they donned aprons of dressed leather. Women wore gowns with long, full skirts, low-cut bodices, aprons, and hosiery held up by garters. Ladies went about in silk and wore hoods and mantles to ward off the sun, while the rest dressed in flannels or canvas and covered their heads with linen caps or coifs. Both sexes favored long hair, and men sported mustaches and beards.

Such fashions complicated life in the American environment, especially since heavy clothing and even shoes rotted rapidly from sweat and humidity. The pungent aroma of Europeans also compounded the discomfort of natives who came in contact with them. For despite sweltering heat, the whites who swaddled themselves in woolens and brocades also disdained regular bathing and regarded Indian devotion to daily washing as another uncivilized oddity.

It would have been natural for Indians to wonder why the barbaric newcomers did not adapt their dress to a new setting. The answer may be that for Europeans—entering an alien environment inhabited by peoples whom they identified as "naked savages"—the psychological risk of shedding familiar apparel was simply too great. However inappropriate or even unhealthy, heavy, elaborate dress afforded the comfort of familiarity and distinguished "civilized" newcomer from "savage" native in America.

Raleigh apparently aimed to establish on Roanoke a mining camp and a military garrison modeled on Frobisher's venture of the 1570s. In a stroke of genius, he included in the company of 108 men a scientist, Thomas Hariot, to study the country's natural resources and an artist, John White, to make drawings of the Virginia Indians. *A Briefe and True Reporte of the New Found Land of Virginia* (1588), written by Hariot and illustrated by White, served as one of the principal sources about North America and its Indian inhabitants for more than a century. Far less inspired was Raleigh's choice to lead the expedition—two veterans of the Irish campaigns, Sir Richard Grenville and Ralph Lane. Even his fellow conquistadors in Ireland considered Lane proud and greedy. As for Grenville, he was given to

The first colony at Roanoke

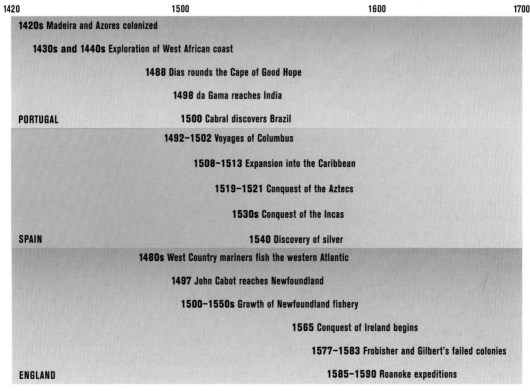

European Exploration: Fifteenth and Sixteenth Centuries

breaking wineglasses between his teeth and then swallowing the shards to show that he could stand the sight of blood, even his own.

The bullying ways of both men quickly alienated the natives of Roanoke. After a year, in response to rumors of an imminent Indian attack, Lane and his men attacked Wingina's main village and killed him. All that averted an Indian counterattack was the arrival of Drake and Frobisher, fresh from freebooting up and down the Caribbean. The settlement's 102 survivors piled onto the pirate ships and put an ocean between themselves and the avenging Roanokes.

A Second Attempt

Undaunted, Raleigh organized a second expedition to plant a colony farther north, in the Chesapeake Bay. He now projected an agricultural community modeled on Humphrey Gilbert's manorial dreams. He recruited 119 men, women, and children, members of the English middle class, and granted each person an estate of 500 acres. He also appointed as governor the artist John White, who brought along a suit of armor for ceremonial occasions.

From the moment of first landfall in July 1587, everything went wrong. The expedition's pilot, Simon Ferdinando, insisted on putting off the colonists at Roanoke Island rather than the Chesapeake. Even before Ferdinando weighed anchor, the settlers were skirmishing with the local Indians. Sensing that the situation on Roanoke could quickly become desperate, White sailed back with Ferdinando, hoping to bring reinforcements.

But White returned home in 1588 just as the massive Spanish navy, the Armada, was marshaling for an assault on England. Elizabeth was enlisting every seaworthy ship and able-bodied sailor in her realm to stave off invasion. Spain's Armada was defeated, but Raleigh left the Roanoke colonists to shift for themselves. When White finally returned to Roanoke Island in 1590, he found only an empty fort and a few cottages in a clearing. The sole clue to the colony's fate was carved on a post: CROATOAN. It was the name of a nearby island off Cape Hatteras.

Had the Roanoke colonists fled to Croatoan for safety? Had they moved to the mainland and joined Indian tribes in the interior? Had they been killed by Wingina's people? The fate of the "lost colony" remains a mystery. White sailed back to England, leaving behind the little cluster of cottages, which would soon be overgrown with vines, and his suit of armor, which was already "almost eaten through with rust."

All the world lay before them. Or so it had seemed to the young men from England's West Country who dreamed of gold and glory, conquest and colonization. Portugal had sent slave and gold traders to Africa, as well as merchants to trade with the rich civilizations of the Indies. Spanish conquerors like Cortés had toppled Indian empires and brought home silver. But England's would-be conquistadors had met only with frustration. In 1600, more than a century after Columbus's first crossing, not a single English settlement existed anywhere in the Americas. The Atlantic had swallowed up Gilbert and his hopes for a manorial utopia; Roanoke lay in ruins.

What was left of the freebooting world of West Country adventurers? Raleigh, his ambition unquenchable, sailed to South America in quest of a rich city named El Dorado. In 1603, however, Elizabeth's death brought to the English throne her cousin James I, the founder of the Stuart dynasty. The new king arrested the old queen's favorite for treason and left him to languish 15 years in the Tower of London. Set free in 1618 at the age of 64, Raleigh returned to South America, his lust for El Dorado undiminished. Along the way he plundered some Spanish silver ships, defying James's orders. It was a fatal mistake, for England had made peace with Spain. Raleigh lost his head.

James I did not want to harry the king of Spain; he wanted to imitate him. The Stuarts were even more determined than the Tudors to enlarge the sphere of royal power. There would be no room in America for a warrior nobility of conquistadors, no room for a feudal fiefdom ruled by the likes of Raleigh or Gilbert. Instead, there would be English colonies in America like the new outpost of Jamestown, planted on the Chesapeake Bay in Virginia in 1607. There would be profitable plantations and other bold enterprises, enriching English royalty and managed by loyal, efficient bureaucrats. Settling America would strengthen English monarchs, paving their path to greater power, just as the dominions of Mexico and Peru had enlarged the authority of the Spanish Crown. America would be the making of kings and queens.

Or would it? For some Europeans, weary of freebooting conquistadors and sea rovers, the order and security that Crown rule and centralized states promoted in western Europe would be enough. But others, the desperate and idealistic men and women who sailed to the world that lay before them, would want more.

chapter summary

During the late fifteenth century, Europeans made their first contact with North and South America, where native cultures were numerous and diverse.

- A combination of technological advances, the rise of new trade networks and techniques, and increased political centralization made Europe's expansion overseas possible.

- The pressure of Europe's growing population on its limited resources of land and food made expansion overseas essential.

- Spain took the lead in exploring and colonizing the Americas, consolidating a vast and profitable empire of its own in the place of Aztec and Inca civilizations.

- Both divisions within Indian empires and the devastating effects of European diseases made Spanish conquest possible.

- England, fearful of Spain's power, did not turn its attention to exploration and colonization until the 1570s and 1580s.

- England's merchants and gentry in search of new markets and land lent support to colonizing ventures, although early efforts, such as those at Roanoke, failed.

interactive learning

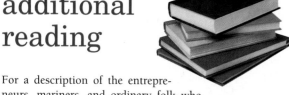

The Primary Source Investigator CD-ROM offers the following materials related to this chapter:

- Interactive maps: **Early Native Peoples in the Era of European Contact** (M1) and **The Atlantic World, 1400–1850** (M2)

- A collection of primary sources, including several that allow investigation of Native American cultures before the arrival of Columbus: an Iroquois creation story that describes the origins of the world, an engraving that depicts an Indian marketplace circa 1500, and early paintings of Native American fishing techniques made by explorers traveling along the eastern coast of North America. Others provide insight into the mind-set of medieval Europeans on the eve of their great expansion into the Atlantic World: a medieval world map, a strikingly more modern Portuguese map showing a water route to Asia around Africa, and several of the key inventions that made trans-Atlantic navigation possible.

additional reading

For a description of the entrepreneurs, mariners, and ordinary folk who participated in the era of exploration and discovery, see Kenneth R. Andrews, *Trade, Plunder, and Settlement: Maritime Enterprise and the Genesis of the British Empire, 1480–1630* (1985); as well as James Lang, *Conquest and Commerce; Spain and England in the Americas* (1975). Alfred Crosby Jr. provides a fascinating account of the biological and ecological effects of contact between Native Americans and Europeans in *The Columbian Exchange* (1972). M. Leon Portilla's *The Broken Spears* (1962) is a vivid account of Cortés's conquest seen through Aztec eyes, while the Spanish perspective is supplied by Bernal Diaz, *The Conquest of New Spain*, trans. J. M. Cohen (1963). The best scholarly overviews of the Spanish invasion and its American empire are Hugh Thomas, *Conquest: Montezuma, Cortes, and the Fall of Old Mexico* (1993); and James Lockhart, *The Nahuas after Conquest: A Social and Cultural History of the Indians of Central Mexico, Sixteenth through Eighteenth Centuries* (1992).

For a good introduction to the Reformation, see Owen Chadwick, *The Reformation* (1964). For early English attempts at colonization, in both Ireland and the Americas, consult the works of Nicholas Canny in the Bibliography. David Beers Quinn, *Set Fair for Roanoke* (1985), contains tantalizing speculation about what happened to the lost colony at Roanoke, and the best overview of English society in this period remains Wallace Notestein, *The English People on the Eve of Colonization, 1603–1630* (1954).

significant events

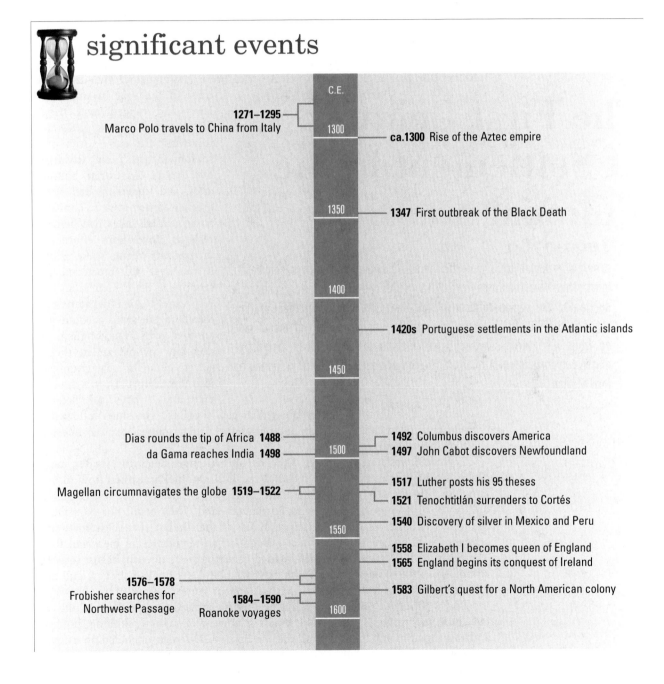

1271–1295 Marco Polo travels to China from Italy	
	C.E.
	1300
	ca.1300 Rise of the Aztec empire
	1350 — **1347** First outbreak of the Black Death
	1400
	1420s Portuguese settlements in the Atlantic islands
	1450
Dias rounds the tip of Africa **1488**	**1492** Columbus discovers America
da Gama reaches India **1498**	1500 — **1497** John Cabot discovers Newfoundland
	1517 Luther posts his 95 theses
Magellan circumnavigates the globe **1519–1522**	**1521** Tenochtitlán surrenders to Cortés
	1540 Discovery of silver in Mexico and Peru
	1550
	1558 Elizabeth I becomes queen of England
	1565 England begins its conquest of Ireland
1576–1578 Frobisher searches for Northwest Passage	**1583** Gilbert's quest for a North American colony
1584–1590 Roanoke voyages	1600

Chapter 2

In the year 1617, as Europeans counted time, on a bay they called the Chesapeake, in a land they named Virginia, an old Indian chief surveyed his domain. It had all worked according to plan, and Powhatan, leader of the Pamunkeys, had laid his plans carefully. While in his prime, the tall, robust man had drawn some 30 smaller tribes along the Virginia coast into a powerful confederacy. As tribute for his protection and leadership, Powhatan collected food, furs, and skins. He installed his relatives as these tribes' new leaders and as his new vassals.

By 1607 Powhatan's confederacy numbered nearly 9000, a political alliance that had overcome formidable obstacles. The natives of Virginia, like the peoples who inhabited the length of eastern North America, were seminomadic. They lived for most of the year in small villages and ranged over tribal hunting and fishing grounds, following the game from one season to the next. Rivalries over trade, territorial boundaries, and leadership had often erupted into armed conflict. Some coastal tribes had fiercely resisted Powhatan's efforts to incorporate them; some tribes to the west still threatened the security of his confederacy.

The First Century of Settlement in the Colonial South

1600–1750

preview • Instability and conflict wracked England's southern colonies for most of the seventeenth century. But by 1720, one-crop plantation economies dominated the region–tobacco in the Chesapeake, rice in the Carolinas, sugar in the Caribbean. In the process, the original system of labor, based on white indentured servitude, gave way to the slave labor fueled by a massive importation of Africans. Spain too extended its empire in Florida and New Mexico.

After 1607 Powhatan was forced to take into account yet another tribe. The English, as this new people called themselves, came by sea, crammed into three ships. They were 100 men and 4 boys, all clad in heavy, outlandish clothing, many dressed in gaudy colors. The ships followed a river deep into Powhatan's territory and built a fort on a swampy, mosquito-infested site that they called Jamestown.

Powhatan was not frightened. The English had larger boats and louder, more deadly weapons than his people did. But the Indians quickly learned how to use guns, and they vastly outnumbered the English, an inferior race who seemed unlikely to live long and prosper in Powhatan's land. They could not even manage to feed themselves from the rich resources of the Chesapeake. With bows and arrows, spears and nets, Indian men brought in an abundance of meat and fish. The fields tended by Indian women yielded generous crops of corn, beans, squash, and melon, and edible nuts and fruits grew wild. Still the English starved, and not just during the first few months of their settlement but for several years afterward.

Powhatan could understand why the English refused to grow food. Cultivating crops was women's work—like building houses; or making clothing, pottery, and baskets; or caring for children. And the English settlement included no women until two arrived in the fall of 1608. Yet even after more women came, the English still starved, and they expected—no, they demanded—that the Indians supply them with food.

Most incredible to Powhatan was that the inferior English considered themselves a superior people. They boasted constantly about the power of their god—they had only one—and denounced the Indians' "devil-worship" of "false gods." The English also boasted without end about the power of their king, James I, who expected Powhatan to become his vassal. The English had even planned a "coronation" to crown Powhatan as a "subject king." He had not been impressed. "If your king has sent me presents," he responded, "I also am a king, and this is my land. . . . Your father is to come to me, not I to him." In the end the English did come to Powhatan, only to find what "a fowle trouble there was to make him kneele to receave his crowne. . . . [he] indured so many perswasions, examples and instructions as tired them all. At last by leaning hard on his shoulders, he a little stooped, and . . . put the Crowne on his head."

It was inconceivable to Powhatan that he should willingly bow before this King James, the ruler of so savage a race. When the Indians made war, they killed the male warriors of rival tribes but adopted their women and children. But when Powhatan's people withheld food or defended their land from these invaders, the English retaliated by murdering Indian women and children. To make matters worse, the English could not even keep order within their own tribe. Too many of them wanted to be chiefs, and they squabbled constantly among themselves.

Captain John Smith

Only one man, a brash fellow called Captain John Smith, had briefly been able to bring order to the English settlement. Powhatan granted him a grudging respect, though he boasted so much that even other English seemed modest by comparison. Smith bragged endlessly of his earlier exploits across the ocean, where he had fought as a soldier of fortune. He told wonderful tales of his irresistible appeal to beautiful women who had rescued him from harrowing perils. A rough man, he bullied the Indians for food and would have enslaved them if it had been in his power. Even so, Smith took a genuine interest in Indian ways.

But Smith returned to England in 1609 after being injured when some of the white people's gunpowder blew up by mistake. Thereafter the English returned to squabbling and starving. Small wonder that some English had deserted their settlement to live among Powhatan's people. Anyone could see the superiority of Indian culture to English ways.

Powhatan's strategy

The temptation to wipe out the helpless, troublesome, arrogant tribe of English—or simply to let them starve to death—had been almost overwhelming. But Powhatan allowed the English to survive because he had decided that even these barbaric people had their uses. English labor, English trading goods, and, most important, English guns would help him quell resistance within his confederacy and subdue his Indian rivals to the west. In 1614 Powhatan cemented his claim

When the English attempted to crown Powhatan as a subject king, he may have sent King James I this cloak as a reciprocal present. Made from four tanned deerskins, the mantle is decorated with many small marine shells sewn into designs. In addition to human and animal figures, the cloak has 34 roundlets that may represent the Indian districts under Powhatan's control.

No stranger to self-promotion, Captain John Smith included this portrait of himself and verses celebrating his ennobling exploits at the beginning of his *Description of New England* (1616). As the military armor and knightly bearing suggest (note Smith on horseback, lower right), the outspoken captain stood in the tradition of West Country adventurers and Spanish conquistadors.

Thefe are the Lines that fhew thy Face but thofe
That fhew thy Grace and Glory, brighter bee
Thy Faire-Difcoueries and Fowle-Ouerthrowes
Of Salvages, much Ciuilliz'd by thee
Beft fhew thy Spirit and to it Glory Wyn;
So thou art Braffe without but Golde within.

on the English and their weapons with the marriage between his favorite child, Pocahontas, and a white settler, John Rolfe.

By 1617 events had vindicated Powhatan's strategy of tolerating the English. His empire flourished, ready to be passed on to his brother, Opechancanough. Powhatan's people still outnumbered the English, who seldom starved outright now but continued to fight among themselves and sicken and die. Only one thing had changed in the Chesapeake by 1617: the English were clearing woodland along the rivers and planting tobacco.

That was the doing of Powhatan's son-in-law, Rolfe, a man as strange as the rest of his tribe, all of them eager to store up wealth and worldly goods. Rolfe had been obsessed with finding a crop that could be grown in Virginia and then sold for gain across the sea. When he succeeded by growing tobacco, other English followed his lead. Odder still, not women but men tended the tobacco fields. Here was more evidence of English inferiority. Men wasted long hours laboring when they might supply their needs with far less effort.

In 1617 Powhatan, ruler of the Pamunkeys, surveyed his empire, and sometime in that year, he looked no longer. He had lived long enough to see the tobacco fields lining the riverbanks, straddling the charred stumps of felled trees. But he died believing that he had bent the English to his purposes—died before those stinking tobacco weeds spread over the length of his land and sent his hard-won empire up in smoke.

English Society on the Chesapeake

While the chief of the Chesapeake was expanding his dominions and consolidating his power, the king of England was doing the same. Just as Spain had begun to profit from the riches of silver mines and sugar plantations, James I of England hoped that the wealth and power of his kingdom would grow as English colonists settled the American coasts north of Spain's empire. The first newcomers clustered along the many bays of the Chesapeake, as well as in a few island outposts of the Caribbean. A generation later, during the 1670s and 1680s, colonists from the Caribbean hopscotched to the mainland to found colonies along the Carolina coast. As the English struggled to put down roots, the ambitions of merchants and planters and kings clashed with the conflicting goals of Indian leaders like Powhatan.

Instability of the southern colonies

The result was a chaotic and deadly landscape. During much of the seventeenth century, ambitious colonists scrambled to control the land and the labor needed to secure profits from tobacco, sugar, and rice. Only after decades of uncertainty, violence, and high mortality did the colonies along the southern Atlantic crescent begin to prosper. Even then, stability was bought at a high price. In order to supply the workers so desperately sought by plantation owners, English colonists introduced the institution of slavery.

The Mercantilist Impulse

As European powers began establishing permanent colonies in America, they were putting into practice a theory about how best to attain national wealth and influence. That idea, which guided Europe's commercial expansion for 200 years, was named "mercantilism" by the eighteenth-century economist Adam Smith. Mercantilists called for the state to regulate and protect industry and commerce. Their primary objective was to enrich the nation by fostering a favorable balance of trade. Once the value of exports exceeded the cost of imports, they theorized, gold and silver would flow into home ports.

Mercantilism

If a nation could make do without any imports from other countries, so much the better, and it was here that the idea of colonies entered the mercantilist scheme. Colonial producers would supply raw materials that the mother country could not produce, while colonial consumers swelled demand for the finished goods and financial services that the mother country could provide. Convinced that colonies would enhance national self-sufficiency, mercantilists urged states to sponsor overseas settlements.

Mercantilist notions appealed to Europe's monarchs. A thriving trade meant that more taxes and customs duties would fill royal coffers, increasing royal power. That logic led James I to lend his approval to the private venture that brought the first white settlers to the Chesapeake.

The Virginia Company

In 1606 the king granted a charter to a number of English merchants, gentlemen, and aristocrats, incorporating them as the Virginia Company of London. The members of the new joint stock company sold stock in their venture to English investors, as well as awarding a share to those willing to settle in Virginia at their own expense. With the proceeds from the sale of stock, the company planned to send to Virginia hundreds of poor and unemployed people as well as scores of skilled craftworkers. These laborers were to serve the company for seven years in return for their passage, pooling their efforts to produce any commodities that would return a profit to stockholders. If gold mines like Spain's could not be found, perhaps North America would yield other valuable commodities—furs, pitch, tar, or lumber. In the spring of 1607 the first expedition dispatched by the Virginia Company, 104 men and boys, founded Jamestown.

Making the first of many mistakes, Jamestown's settlers pitched their fort on an inland peninsula in order to prevent a surprise attack from the Spanish. Unfortunately, the marshy, thickly wooded site served as an ideal breeding ground for malaria. The Virginia Company settlers, weakened by bouts of malaria and then beset by dysentery, typhoid, and yellow fever, died by the scores.

Jamestown's problems

Even before sickness took its toll, many of Jamestown's first settlers had little taste for labor. The gentlemen of the expedition expected to lead rather than to work, while most other members of the early colonizing parties were gentlemen's servants and craftworkers who knew nothing about growing crops. The settlers resorted to bullying Powhatan's people for food. Many colonists suffered from malnutrition, which heightened their susceptibility to disease. Only 60 of Jamestown's 500 inhabitants lived through the winter of 1609–1610, known as the "starving time." Some desperate colonists unearthed and ate corpses; one settler even butchered his wife.

In Jamestown's early years its military orientation was clear. The fort's heavy palisades and its strategic location upriver and some distance inland underscore the colonists' concern for defense—as does the imposing figure of Powhatan seated at the right.

Reports of starvation and staggering death rates stiffened the Virginia Company's resolve: in 1611 it imposed on the colonists what amounted to martial law. Company officials in Virginia organized the settlers into work gangs and severely punished the lazy and the disorderly. Still the company failed to turn a profit. And after 1617, skirmishes with the Indians became more brutal and frequent as rows of tobacco plants steadily invaded tribal lands.

Reform and a Boom in Tobacco

Key reforms

Desperate to salvage their investment, Virginia Company managers in 1618 set in place sweeping reforms. To attract more capital and colonists, the company established a "headright" system for granting land to individuals. Those already settled in the colony received 100 acres apiece. New settlers each received 50 acres, and anyone who paid the passage of other immigrants to Virginia—either family members or servants—received 50 acres per "head." The company also abolished martial law, allowing the planters to elect a representative assembly. Along with a governor and an advisory council appointed by the company, the House of Burgesses had the authority to make laws for the colony. It met for the first time in 1619, beginning what would become a strong tradition of representative government in the English colonies.

The new measures met with immediate success. The free and unfree laborers who poured into Virginia during the 1620s made up the first wave of an English migration to the Chesapeake that numbered between 130,000 and 150,000 over the seventeenth century. Drawn from the ranks of ordinary English working people, the

The Smokers (left), painted by Adriaen Brouwer, a seventeenth-century Dutch artist, suggests that the use of tobacco was both popular and disreputable. Native American peoples such as the Mayan (right) had been cultivating and smoking tobacco long before the arrival of Europeans.

immigrants were largely men, outnumbering women by six to one. Most were young, ranging in age from 15 to 24. Because of their youth, most lacked skills or wealth.

Some of those who came to the Chesapeake as free immigrants prospered, lured by the chance to make a fortune in tobacco. During the 1620s Virginia's tobacco economy took off. As demand soared and prices peaked in European markets, colonists with an eye for profit planted every inch of their farms in tobacco and reaped windfalls. But for the vast majority of settlers—and, specifically, the three-quarters of all immigrants who arrived in the Chesapeake as indentured servants—the future was far grimmer.

Indentured servants

For most of the new servants, the crossing to Virginia was simply the last of many moves made in the hope of finding work. Although England's population had been rising since the middle of the fifteenth century, the demand for farm laborers was falling because many landowners were converting croplands into pastures for sheep. The search for work pushed young men and women out of their villages, sending them through the countryside and then into the cities. Down and out in London, Bristol, or Liverpool, some decided to make their next move across the Atlantic and signed indentures. Pamphlets promoting immigration promised abundant land and quick riches once servants had finished their terms of four to seven years.

Even the most skeptical immigrants were shocked at what they found. The death rate in Virginia during the 1620s was higher than that of England during times of epidemic disease. The life expectancy for Chesapeake men who reached the age of 20 was a mere 48 years; for women it was lower still. Servants fared worst of all, because malnutrition, overwork, and abuse made them vulnerable to disease. As masters scrambled to make quick profits, they extracted the maximum amount of work before death carried off their laborers. An estimated 40 percent of servants did not survive to the end of their indentured terms.

War with the confederacy

The expanding cultivation of tobacco also claimed many lives by putting unbearable pressure on Indian land. After Powhatan's death in 1617, leadership of the confederacy passed to Opechancanough, who watched, year after year, as the tobacco mania grew. In March 1622 he coordinated a sweeping attack on white settlements that killed about one-fifth of Virginia's white population. Swift English retaliation wiped out whole tribes and cut down an entire generation of young Indian men.

News of the Indian war jolted English investors into determining the true state of their Virginia venture. It came to light that, despite the tobacco boom, the Virginia Company was plunging toward bankruptcy. Nor was that the worst news. Stockholders discovered that more than 3000 immigrants had not survived the brutal conditions of Chesapeake life. An investigation by James I brought out the grisly truth, causing the king to dissolve the Virginia Company and take control of the colony himself in 1624. Henceforth Virginia would be governed as a royal colony.

Settling Down in the Chesapeake

During the 1630s and 1640s the fever of the tobacco boom broke, and a more settled social and political life emerged in Virginia. The settlers who had become wealthy by exploiting servant labor now began to acquire political power. They established local bases of influence in Virginia's counties, serving as justices of the peace and sheriffs, maintaining roads and bridges, collecting taxes, and supervising local elections. They organized all able-bodied adult males into militias for local defense and sat on vestries, the governing bodies of local Anglican parishes, hiring the handful of clergy who came to Virginia and providing for the neighborhood poor.

The biggest tobacco planters of each county also dominated colony politics. Even though King James had replaced the Virginia Company's government with his own royal administration, the colony's elected assembly continued making laws for the colony. Along with the council (the upper house of the legislature), the assembly resisted interference in Virginia's affairs from the royal governor, the king's representative.

Decline in mortality rates

The colony's growing stability was reflected in improved conditions for less powerful Virginians. Although servants still streamed into the colony, the price of tobacco leveled off. That meant planters were less likely to drive their servants to death in search of overnight fortunes. As tobacco became less profitable, planters raised more corn and cattle, and mortality rates declined as food supplies rose. Freed servants who survived their indentures usually worked a few more years as hired hands or tenant farmers. In doing so, most managed to save enough money to buy their own land and become independent planters. For women who survived servitude, prospects were even better. With wives at a premium, single women stood a good chance of improving their status by marriage. Even so, high mortality rates still fractured families: one out of every four children born in the Chesapeake did not survive to maturity, and among those children who reached their eighteenth birthday, one-third had lost both parents to death.

By 1650 Virginia could boast about 15,000 inhabitants, although much of that increase resulted from servants and free immigrants arriving in the colony every year. But Virginians looking to expand into more northerly bays of the Chesapeake found their way blocked by a newer English colony.

The Founding of Maryland and the Renewal of Indian Wars

Unlike Virginia, which was first settled by a private corporation and later converted into a royal colony, Maryland was founded by a single aristocratic family, the Calverts. Indeed, it was the first of several such "proprietary" colonies given by English monarchs to loyal followers. Thus in 1632, Maryland became the private preserve of the Calverts. They held absolute authority to dispose of 10 million acres of land, administer justice, and establish a civil government. All these powers they exercised, granting estates, or "manors," to their friends and dividing other holdings into smaller farms for ordinary immigrants. From all these "tenants"—that is, every settler in the colony—the Calverts collected "quitrents" every year, fees for use of the land. The Calverts appointed a governor and a council to oversee their own interests while allowing the largest landowners to dispense local justice in manorial courts and make laws for the entire colony in a representative assembly.

Proprietary colonies

Virginians liked nothing at all about Maryland. To begin with, the Calvert family was Catholic and had extended complete religious freedom to all Christians, making Maryland a haven for Catholics. Worse than that, the Marylanders were a source of economic competition. Two thousand inhabitants had settled on Calvert holdings by 1640, virtually all of them planting tobacco on land coveted by the Virginians.

Another obstacle to Virginia's expansion was the remnant of the Powhatan confederacy, still determined to repel white invaders. Opechancanough led a new generation of Indians into battle in 1644 against the encroaching Virginia planters. The hostilities inflicted as many casualties on both sides as the fighting did in 1622.

Changes in English Policy in the Chesapeake

Throughout the 1630s and 1640s colonial affairs drew little concern from royal officials. England itself had become engulfed first by a political crisis and then by a civil war.

The conflict grew out of efforts by both James I and Charles I (who succeeded his father in 1625) to expand their royal power and rule the nation without the nuisance of having to consult Parliament. When Parliament condemned Charles for usurping its power to raise money, he simply dissolved that body in 1629. But when the Scots invaded England in 1639, Charles found he could raise funds to pay for an army only by calling Parliament back into session. By then, many of the merchants and landed gentlemen who were members were beginning to believe that the Stuart kings might be more trouble than they were worth. In 1642 Parliament and its Puritan allies squared off against Charles I and his royalist supporters, defeating them in battle; and in 1649 they beheaded the king. England became a republic ruled by Oliver Cromwell, the man who had led Parliament's army.

The English Civil War

In truth, Cromwell's "republic" more accurately resembled a military dictatorship. After his death, most English were happy to see their throne restored in 1660 to Charles II, the son of the beheaded king. And the new king was determined to ensure that not only his subjects at home but also his American colonies abroad contributed to England's prosperity. His colonial policy was reflected in a series of regulations known as the Navigation Acts.

The first, passed by Parliament in 1660, gave England and English colonial merchants a monopoly on the shipping and marketing of all colonial goods. It also ordered that the colonies could export certain "enumerated commodities" only to

Oliver Cromwell

Colonies of the Chesapeake
Settlements in Virginia and Maryland spread out along the many bays of the Chesapeake, where tobacco could easily be loaded from plantation wharves. The "fall line" on rivers, dividing Tidewater and Piedmont regions, determined the extent of commercial agriculture, since ships could not pick up exports beyond that point.

England or other British ports. These goods included sugar, tobacco, cotton, ginger, and indigo (a blue dye). In 1663 Parliament added another regulation, giving British merchants a virtual monopoly on the sale of European manufactured goods to Americans by requiring that most imports going to the colonies pass through England. In 1673 a third Navigation Act placed duties on the coastal trade of the American colonies and provided for customs officials to collect tariffs and enforce commercial regulations.

Parliament later made minor modifications in the Navigation Acts, adding other exports such as rice to the category of enumerated commodities, prohibiting the colonies from exporting certain textiles or hats, and offering incentives to encourage colonists to produce indigo and iron. All these regulations were mercantilistic. That is, they were designed to ensure that England—and no foreign nations or their merchants—would profit from colonial production and trade.

The regulations of trade put in place by # Chesapeake Society in Crisis
Restoration kings Charles II and James
II and their Parliaments had a decisive impact on colonials. Chesapeake planters chafed under the Navigation Acts. They were accustomed to conducting their affairs as they pleased—and they were often pleased to trade with the Dutch. What was worse, the new restrictions came at the same time as a downturn in tobacco prices. In the effort to consolidate its empire, England unintentionally worsened the economic and social difficulties of Chesapeake society.

The Conditions of Unrest

The Chesapeake colonies were heading for trouble partly because of their success. As inhabitants had started to live longer, more servants survived their terms of service. Once free, they set up as independent tobacco planters. More planters meant more production, and overproduction sent the price of tobacco plummeting, especially between 1660 and 1680. To maintain their advantage, the biggest planters bought up all the prime property along the coast, forcing newly freed servants to become tenants or to settle on unclaimed land in the interior. Either way, poorer men lost. Depending on bigger planters for land and credit made the small farmers vulnerable to debt. Moving to the frontier made them vulnerable to Indian attack.

> Diminishing opportunities

The slim resources of small planters were stretched even thinner, not only from county taxes but also from export duties on tobacco paid under the Navigation Acts. During the hard times after 1660, many small planters fell deeply into debt, and some were forced back into servitude. By 1676 one-quarter of Virginia's free white men were landless. Many former servants were unable to gain a foothold even as tenants.

Diminishing opportunity in the 1660s and 1670s provided the tinder for unrest in Virginia. As the discontent of poor men mounted, so did the worries of big planters. The assembly of the colony lengthened terms of servitude, hoping to limit the number of servants entering the free population. It curbed the political rights of landless men, hoping to stifle opposition by depriving them of the vote. But these measures only set off a spate of mutinies among servants and protests over rising taxes among small planters.

Bacon's Rebellion and Coode's Rebellion

Those tensions came to a head in 1676 when civil war erupted. The immediate catalyst of the rebellion was renewed skirmishing between whites expanding westward and Indians. Virginia's royal governor, William Berkeley, favored building forts to contain the Indian threat, but frontier farmers opposed his plan as an expensive and ineffective way to defend their scattered plantations. As they clamored for an expedition to punish the Indians, Nathaniel Bacon stepped forward to lead it.

Wealthy and well connected, Bacon had arrived recently from England, expecting to receive every favor from the governor—including permission to trade with the Indians from his frontier plantation. But Berkeley and a few select friends already held a monopoly on the Indian trade. When they declined to include Bacon, he took up the cause of his poorer frontier neighbors against their common enemy, the governor. Other recent, well-to-do immigrants who resented being excluded from Berkeley's circle of power and patronage also joined Bacon.

> Nathaniel Bacon

In the summer of 1676 Bacon marched into Jamestown with a body of armed men and bullied the assembly into approving his expedition to kill Indians. While

Bacon carried out that grisly business, slaughtering friendly as well as hostile tribes, Berkeley rallied his supporters and declared Bacon a rebel. Bacon retaliated by turning his forces against those led by the governor. Both sides sought allies by offering freedom to servants and slaves willing to join their ranks. Many were willing: for months the followers of Bacon and Berkeley plundered one another's plantations. In September 1676 Bacon reduced Jamestown itself to a mound of ashes. It was only his death from dysentery a month later that snuffed out the rebellion.

Political upheaval also shook Maryland, where colonists had long resented the sway of the Calvert family. As proprietors, the Calverts and their favorites monopolized political offices, just as Berkeley's circle had in Virginia. Well-to-do planters wanted a share of the Calverts' power. Smaller farmers, like those in Virginia, wanted a less expensive and more representative government. Compounding the tensions were religious differences: the Calverts and their friends were Catholic, but other colonists, including Maryland's most successful planters, were Protestant.

The unrest among Maryland's discontented planters peaked in July 1689. A former member of the assembly, John Coode, gathered an army, captured the proprietary governor, and then took grievances to authorities in England. There Coode received a sympathetic hearing. The Calverts' charter was revoked and not restored until 1715, by which time the family had become Protestant.

Growing stability

After 1690 rich planters in both Chesapeake colonies fought among themselves less and cooperated more. In Virginia older leaders and newer arrivals divided the spoils of political office. In Maryland Protestants and Catholics shared power and privilege. Those arrangements ensured that no future Bacon or Coode would mobilize restless gentlemen against the government. By acting together in legislative assemblies, the planter elite managed to curb the power of royal and proprietary governors for decades.

But the greater unity among the Chesapeake's leading families did little to ease that region's most fundamental problem. That was the sharp inequality of white society. The gulf between rich and poor planters, which had been etched ever more deeply by the troubled tobacco economy, persisted long after the rebellions of Bacon and Coode. All that saved white society in the Chesapeake from renewed crisis and conflict was the growth of black slavery.

From Servitude to Slavery

Like the tobacco plants that spread across Powhatan's land, a labor system based on slavery had not figured in the first plans for the Chesapeake. Both early promoters and planters preferred buying English servants to importing alien African slaves. Black slaves, because they served for life, were more expensive than white workers, who served only for several years. Because neither white nor black emigrants lived long, cheaper servant labor was the logical choice. The black population of the Chesapeake remained small for most of the seventeenth century, comprising just 5 percent of all inhabitants in 1675.

The lives of servants and slaves

Africans had arrived in Virginia by 1619, most likely brought by the Dutch, who dominated the slave trade until the middle of the eighteenth century. The lives of those newcomers resembled the lot of white servants, with whom they shared harsh work routines and living conditions. White and black bound laborers socialized with each other and formed sexual liaisons. They conspired to steal from their masters and ran away together; if caught, they endured similar punishments. There was more common ground: many of the first black settlers did not arrive directly from Africa but came from the Caribbean, where some had learned English and had adopted Christian beliefs. And not all were slaves: some were indentured servants, and a handful were free.

A number of changes after 1680 caused planters to invest more heavily in slaves than in servants. First, declining mortality rates in the Chesapeake made slaves the more profitable investment. Although slaves were more expensive than servants, planters could now expect to get many years of work from their bondspeople. Equally important, masters would have title to the children that slaves would now live long enough to have. At the same time, the influx of white servants was falling off just as the pool of available black labor was expanding. When the Royal African Company lost its monopoly on the English slave trade in 1698, other merchants entered the market. The number of Africans sold by British dealers swelled to 20,000 annually.

Africa and the Atlantic Slave Trade

But rising demand from the Chesapeake for slaves—and later, from all the colonies of mainland North America—played only a part in spurring growth of the Atlantic slave trade. Rather, it was the spread of plantation economies in the Caribbean and South America that created and sustained the traffic in human beings. Between the mid–fifteenth and the late nineteenth centuries, perhaps as many as 13 million men, women, and children crossed the Atlantic as slaves—a number not equaled by voluntary European migrants to the Americas until as late as the 1880s. For a century after Columbus's arrival, the traffic in slaves to the Americas had numbered a few thousand annually. But as sugar cultivation steadily prospered after 1600, slave imports rose to 19,000 a year during the seventeenth century and mushroomed to 60,000 a year in the eighteenth century. All told, as many as 21 million people were captured in West Africa between 1700 and 1850: some 9 million among them entered the Americas as slaves, but millions died before or during the Atlantic crossing, and as many as 7 million remained slaves in Africa.

The rapid growth of the Atlantic slave trade transformed not only the Americas but also Africa. Slavery became more widespread within West African society, and slave trading more central to its domestic and international commerce. Most important, the African merchants and political leaders most deeply invested in the slave trade used their profits for political advantage—to build new chiefdoms and states. Their ambitions and the greed of European slave dealers drew an increasingly large number of Africans, particularly people living in the interior, into slavery's web. By the late seventeenth century, Africans being sold into slavery were no longer only those who had put themselves at risk by committing crimes, running into debt, or voicing unpopular political and religious views. The larger number were instead captives taken by soldiers or kidnappers in raids launched specifically to acquire prisoners for the slave trade. During the decades after 1680, captives coming directly from Africa made up more than 80 percent of all new slaves entering the Chesapeake and the rest of mainland North America. Many were shipped from the coast of Africa that Portuguese explorers had first probed, between the Senegal and Niger rivers, and most of the rest from Angola, farther south.

Seized by other Africans, captives were yoked together at the neck and marched hundreds of miles through the interior to coastal forts or other outposts along the Atlantic. There, they were penned in hundreds of prisons, in lots of anywhere from twenty or thirty to more than a thousand. They might be forced to wait for slaving vessels in French *captiveries* below the fine houses of traders on the island of Goree, or herded into "outfactories" on the Banana Islands upstream

Effect of the slave trade on Africa

African Transatlantic Slave Trade, 1450–1760 Toward the end of the seventeenth century, Chesapeake and Carolina planters began importing increasing numbers of slaves. In Africa, the center of that trade lay along a mountainous region known as the Gold Coast, where more than a hundred European trading posts and forts funneled the trade. Unlike most of the rest of West Africa's shoreline, the Gold Coast had very little dense rain forest. Despite the heavy trade, only about 4 percent of the total transatlantic slave trade went to North America.

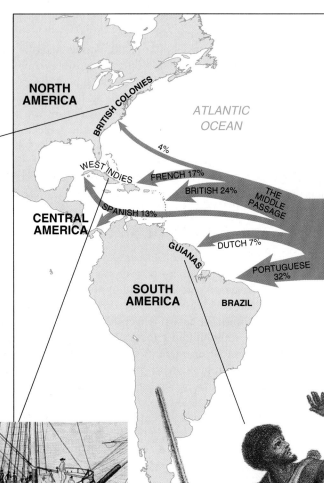

NORTH AMERICA

BRITISH COLONIES

ATLANTIC OCEAN

WEST INDIES

FRENCH 17%

4%

BRITISH 24%

THE MIDDLE PASSAGE

SPANISH 13%

CENTRAL AMERICA

GUIANAS

DUTCH 7%

SOUTH AMERICA

BRAZIL

PORTUGUESE 32%

Slaves were often bought and sold on the decks of the ship they traveled on, as in this painting from the 1770s (lower left). Note that the ship has put up a barricade (left side of the illustration) to keep slaves separate from the rest of the ship while the selling is proceeding. Africans found themselves in a variety of conditions in the Americas. Most toiled on plantations. Some, however, like these "watermen" along the James River in Virginia (upper left), claimed more independence. Still others ran away to maroon communities in the interior. This armed Maroon (a runaway slave; lower right) is from Dutch Guiana, where conditions on the plantations were particularly harsh.

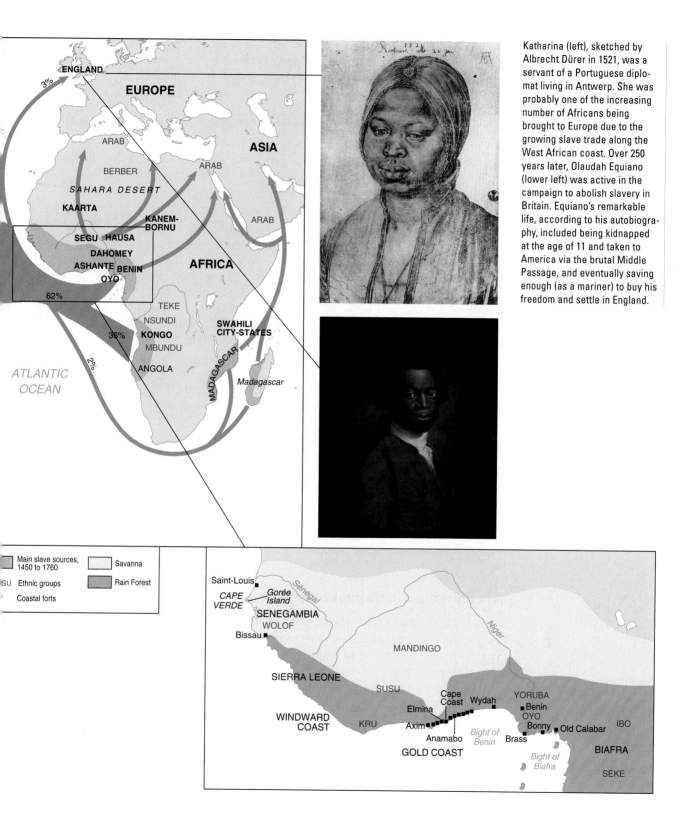

Katharina (left), sketched by Albrecht Dürer in 1521, was a servant of a Portuguese diplomat living in Antwerp. She was probably one of the increasing number of Africans being brought to Europe due to the growing slave trade along the West African coast. Over 250 years later, Olaudah Equiano (lower left) was active in the campaign to abolish slavery in Britain. Equiano's remarkable life, according to his autobiography, included being kidnapped at the age of 11 and taken to America via the brutal Middle Passage, and eventually saving enough (as a mariner) to buy his freedom and settle in England.

ENGLAND
3%
EUROPE
ASIA
ARAB
BERBER
ARAB
SAHARA DESERT
KAARTA
ARAB
KANEM-BORNU
SEGU HAUSA
DAHOMEY
ASHANTE BENIN
OYO
AFRICA
62%
TEKE
NSUNDI
SWAHILI CITY-STATES
KONGO
MBUNDU
36%
MADAGASCAR
ANGOLA
Madagascar
ATLANTIC OCEAN
2%

Main slave sources, 1450 to 1760
SU   Ethnic groups
Coastal forts
Savanna
Rain Forest

Saint-Louis
Senegal
CAPE VERDE
Gorée Island
SENEGAMBIA
WOLOF
Bissau
MANDINGO
Niger
SIERRA LEONE
SUSU
Cape Coast   Wydah
YORUBA
Elmina   Benin
WINDWARD COAST
KRU   Axim   OYO
Anamabo   Bonny   Old Calabar
Brass
IBO
GOLD COAST
Bight of Benin
Bight of Biafra
BIAFRA
SEKE

65

on the Sierra Leone River, or perhaps marched into the gloomy underground slave-holds at the English fort at Cape Coast. Farther south, captives were held in marshy, fever-ridden lowlands along the Bight of Benin, waiting for a slaver to drop anchor. One African, Ottobah Cugoano, recalled finally being taken aboard ship:

> There was nothing to be heard but the rattling of chains, smacking of whips, and the groans and cries of our fellow-men. Some would not stir from the ground, when they were lashed and beat in the most horrible manner. . . . And when we found ourselves at last taken away, death was more preferable than life, and a plan was concerted amongst us that we might burn and blow up the ship and to perish altogether in the flames.

Middle Passage

Worse than the imprisonment was the voyage itself: the so-called Middle Passage, a journey of 5000 miles across the Atlantic to America. As many as 200 black men, women, and children were packed belowdecks, squeezed onto platforms built in tiers spaced so close that sitting upright was impossible. It was difficult to know whether the days or the nights were more hellish. Slaves were taken out and forced to exercise for their health for a few hours each day; the rest of the day, the sun beat down and the heat below the decks was "so excessive," one voyager recalled, that the doctors who went below to examine slaves "would faint away, and the candles would not burn." At night, the slaves "were often heard making a howling melancholy kind of noise, something expressive of extreme anguish," noted a doctor aboard another ship. When he made inquiries, he discovered it was because the slaves, in sleeping, had dreamed "they were back in their own country again, amongst their families and friends" and "when they woke up to find themselves in reality on a slave ship they began to bay and shriek."

After the numb, exhausted survivors of the Middle Passage reached American ports, they faced more challenges to staying alive. The first year in the colonies was the most deadly for new, unseasoned slaves. The sickle cell genetic trait gave blacks a greater immunity than white Europeans had to malaria, but slaves were highly susceptible to respiratory infections. One-quarter of all Africans died during their first year in the Chesapeake, and among Carolina and Caribbean slaves, mortality rates were even higher. In addition to the new disease environment, Africans were forced to adapt to lives without freedom in a wholly unfamiliar country and culture.

A Changing Chesapeake Society

Exchanging a labor system based on servitude for one based on slavery transformed the character of Chesapeake society. Most obviously, the number of black Virginians rose sharply. By 1740, 40 percent of all Virginians were black, and most of those were African-born. Unlike black men and women who had arrived earlier, these new inhabitants had little familiarity with English language and culture. This larger, more distinctively African community was also locked into a slave system that was becoming ever more rigid and demeaning. By the late decades of the seventeenth century, laws were in place making it more difficult for masters to free slaves. Other legislation systematically separated the races by prohibiting free black settlers from owning white servants and outlawing interracial marriages and sexual relationships. The legal code encouraged white contempt for black Virginians in a variety of other ways. While masters were prohibited from whipping their white servants on the bare back, slaves had no such protection. And "any Negro that shall presume to strike any white" was to receive 30 lashes for that rash act.

The new laws both reflected and encouraged racism among white colonists of all classes. Deepening racial hatred, in turn, made it unlikely that poor white planters, tenants, and servants would ever join with poor black slaves to challenge the privilege of great planters. Instead of identifying with the plight of the slaves, the Chesapeake's poorer white residents considered black Virginians their natural inferiors. They could pride themselves on sharing with wealthy white gentlemen the same skin color and on being their equals in the eyes of the law.

The leaders of the Chesapeake colonies cultivated unity among white inhabitants by improving economic prospects for freed servants and lesser planters. The Virginia assembly made provisions for freed servants to get a better start as independent farmers. It lowered taxes, allowing small planters to keep more of their earnings. New laws also gave most white male Virginians a vote in elections, allowing them an outlet to express their grievances. Economic trends toward the end of the seventeenth century contributed to the greater prosperity of small planters, because tobacco prices rose slightly and then stabilized. As a result of Bacon's savage campaign against the Virginia Indians, new land on the frontier became available. Even the domestic lives of ordinary people became more secure as mortality rates declined and the numbers of men and women in the white population evened out. As a result, virtually all men were now able to marry, and families were fragmented less often by the premature deaths of spouses and parents.

After 1700 the Chesapeake evolved into a more stable society. Gone were the bands of wild, landless, young bachelors one step ahead of the law, the small body of struggling lesser planters one step ahead of ruin, and the great mass of exploited servants one step away from rebellion. Virginia and Maryland became colonies of farming families, most of them small planters who owned between 50 and 200 acres. These families held no slaves, or at most two or three. And they accepted, usually without question, the social and political leadership of their acknowledged "superiors," great planters who styled themselves the "gentry."

The Chesapeake Gentry

The new Chesapeake gentry were the sons of well-to-do London merchant families, many of whom had intermarried with England's landed gentry. For both landed gentry and merchants, Virginia offered new prospects for land and commercial wealth. Enterprising fathers sent their sons to the Chesapeake between 1640 and 1670 to establish family interests in America by creating vast plantations. This new colonial generation of merchant-gentlemen did not plunge into the feverish gambling and exploitation practiced by the first planters along the Chesapeake. Instead, they and their coolly calculating descendants achieved status and power by shrewdly using their capital and influence and by skillfully managing their family estates.

The gentry's fortunes rested in part on the cultivation of tobacco on thousands of acres by hundreds of slaves. But the leading planters made even more money by marketing the tobacco of their humbler neighbors, selling them manufactured goods, supplying them with medical and legal services, lending money, and hiring out slaves. Unlike the rough-hewn barons of the early tobacco boom, the gentry

George Booth, the son of a wealthy planter family in Gloucester County, Virginia, was being raised for mastery. The young man's self-assured stance, the bow and arrows, the dog at his feet clutching the kill, the classical busts of women flanking his figure, and his family estate in the distance all suggest the gentry's concern for controlling the natural and social worlds.

did not owe their wealth to wringing work from poor whites. Instead they amassed great estates by wringing work from black slaves while converting their white "inferiors" into modestly prosperous small planters and paying clients.

But the gentry wanted more than money: they wanted the respect of lesser whites. On election days, when all the voters in the county assembled, each approached in his turn the gentleman candidate he preferred, publicly announced his vote, and sometimes made a brief, flattering speech about his choice. At militia musters, when every able-bodied man in the county over the age of 16 gathered, gentlemen officers led the military drills. On court days, defendants and plaintiffs testified before gentlemen justices of the peace, bedecked in wigs and robes and seated on raised benches. And every Sunday, when many in the county came to worship at the Anglican chapel, families filed soberly into the church in order of their social rank, with the gentlemen vestry heading the procession. The courthouse and church, the tavern and training field—all served as theaters in which the new Chesapeake gentry dramatized their superiority and lesser men deferred.

The plantation societies of Virginia and Maryland remained as unequal after 1700 as they had been a century earlier. Indeed, they were even more unequal because the rise of slavery sharpened economic distinctions within the white population. Those who owned slaves enjoyed a decided economic edge over those who did not. But while extreme economic inequality persisted, social tension between richer and poorer white settlers lessened. As racism unified all classes within white society and as economic and political gains eased discontent among small planters, the changing character of the Chesapeake's leaders also reduced social friction. The unscrupulous scoundrels who once dominated society had been replaced by gentlemen-planters who fancied themselves the "fathers" of their plantations and neighborhoods.

From the Caribbean to the Carolinas

During the same decade that the English invaded Powhatan's land, they began to colonize the Caribbean. A century earlier, Columbus had charted the route: ships picked up the trade winds off Madeira and the Canary Islands and headed west across the Atlantic to paradise. At journey's end the surf broke over shores rimmed with white sand beaches that rose sharply to coral terraces, then to broad plateaus or mountain peaks shrouded in rain forests.

Transformation of the Caribbean

Paradise was lost to the Indians of the Caribbean, or at least to those few remaining alive. European diseases, combined with Spanish exploitation, had eliminated virtually all the natives of Hispaniola by the 1520s. Over the next century the natives of Cuba, Puerto Rico, the Bahamas, the Lesser Antilles, and Jamaica would likewise be decimated. And the "paradise" that remained was filled with plants and animals that would have been strange to natives only a century earlier. Hogs and cattle, now wild, had been imported by Europeans, as had figs, oranges, pomegranates, and African yams. That ecological migration of flora and fauna would continue to transform the Americas in the century to come.

Paradise was lost to the English as well. At first they came to the Caribbean intending not to colonize but to steal from the Spanish. Even after 1604 when some English settled on the islands, few intended to stay. Yet not only did the English establish permanent plantation colonies in the West Indies, but their Caribbean settlements also became the jumping-off points for a new colony on the North American mainland—South Carolina. Because of the strong West Indian influence, South Carolina developed a social order in some ways distinct from that of the Chesapeake. Yet in other ways, the development of the Carolinas paralleled Virginia and Maryland's path from violence, high mortality, and uncertainty toward relative stability.

Paradise Lost

The English had traded and battled with the Spanish in the Caribbean since the 1560s. From those island bases English buccaneers conducted an illegal trade with Spanish settlements, sacked the coastal towns, and plundered silver ships bound for Seville. Weakened by decades of warfare, Spain could not hold the West Indies. The Dutch drove a wedge into Caribbean trade routes, and the French and the English began to colonize the islands.

In the 40 years after 1604, some 30,000 immigrants from the British Isles planted crude frontier outposts on St. Kitts, Barbados, Nevis, Montserrat, and Antigua. The settlers—some free, many others indentured servants, and almost all young men—devoted themselves to working as little as possible, drinking as much as possible, and returning to England as soon as possible. They cultivated for export a poor quality of tobacco, which returned just enough profit to maintain straggling settlements of small farms.

Then, nearly overnight, sugar cultivation transformed the Caribbean. In the 1640s Barbados planters learned from the Dutch how to process sugarcane. The Dutch also supplied African slaves to work the cane fields and marketed the sugar for high prices in the Netherlands. Sugar plantations and slave labor rapidly spread to other English and French islands as Europeans developed an insatiable sweet tooth for the once scarce commodity. Caribbean sugar made more money for England than the total volume of commodities exported by all the mainland American colonies.

Caribbean sugar

In 1650, when this map of Barbados was drawn, the sugar boom was only beginning. Most of the settlements lie on the leeward side of the island, away from the prevailing winds. The map's drawings indicate that, already, escaped slaves (upper left) were being hunted down in their mountain hideaways. Hogs (two are shown) ran wild everywhere on the island. They were an import from Europe that in a few short years had multiplied more rapidly than the humans who brought them.

Even though its great planters became the richest people in English America, they could not have confused the West Indies with paradise. Throughout the seventeenth century, disease took a fearful toll, and island populations grew only because of immigration. In the scramble for land, small farmers were pushed onto tiny plots that barely allowed them to survive.

Slavery in the Caribbean

The desperation of bound laborers posed another threat. After the Caribbean's conversion to cultivating sugar, black slaves gradually replaced white indentured servants in the cane fields. By the beginning of the eighteenth century, black inhabitants outnumbered white residents by four to one. Fear of servant mutinies and slave rebellions frayed the nerves of island masters. They tried to contain the danger by imposing harsh slave codes and inflicting brutal punishments on white and black laborers alike. But planters lived under a constant state of siege. One visitor to Barbados observed that whites fortified their homes with parapets from which they could pour scalding water on attacking servants and slaves. During the first century of settlement, seven major slave uprisings shook the English islands.

As more people, both white and black, squeezed onto the islands, some settlers looked for a way out. With all the land in use, the Caribbean no longer offered opportunity to freed servants or even planters' sons. It was then that the West Indies started to shape the history of the American South.

The Founding of the Carolinas

The colonization of the Carolinas began with the schemes of Virginia's royal governor, William Berkeley, and Sir John Colleton, a supporter of Charles I who had been exiled to the Caribbean at the end of England's civil war. Colleton saw that the Caribbean had a surplus of white settlers, and Berkeley knew that Virginians needed room to expand as well. Together the two men set their sights on the area south of Virginia. Along with a number of other aristocrats, they convinced Charles II to make them joint proprietors in 1663 of a place they called the Carolinas, in honor of the king.

North Carolina

A few hardy souls from Virginia had already squatted around Albemarle Sound in the northern part of the Carolina grant. The proprietors provided them with a governor and a representative assembly. About 40 years later, in 1701, they set off North Carolina as a separate colony. The desolate region quickly proved a disappointment. Lacking good harbors and navigable rivers, the colony had no convenient way of marketing its produce. North Carolina remained a poor colony, its sparse population engaged in general farming and the production of masts, pitch, tar, and turpentine.

South Carolina

The southern portion of the Carolina grant held far more promise, especially in the eyes of one of its proprietors, Sir Anthony Ashley Cooper, earl of Shaftesbury. In 1669 he sponsored an expedition of a few hundred English and Barbadian immigrants, who planted the first permanent settlement in South Carolina. By 1680 the colonists had established the center of economic, social, and political life at the confluence of the Ashley and the Cooper rivers, naming the site Charles Town (later Charleston) after the king.

Cooper had big plans for his Carolina colony. Charleston stood at the hub of a network of river routes, allowing for easy development of the region's commercial potential. Because the proprietors were offering liberal land grants and had promised religious toleration and a representative government, settlers would flock to the colony. These new inhabitants would enrich the proprietors by paying quitrents, a halfpenny per acre annually.

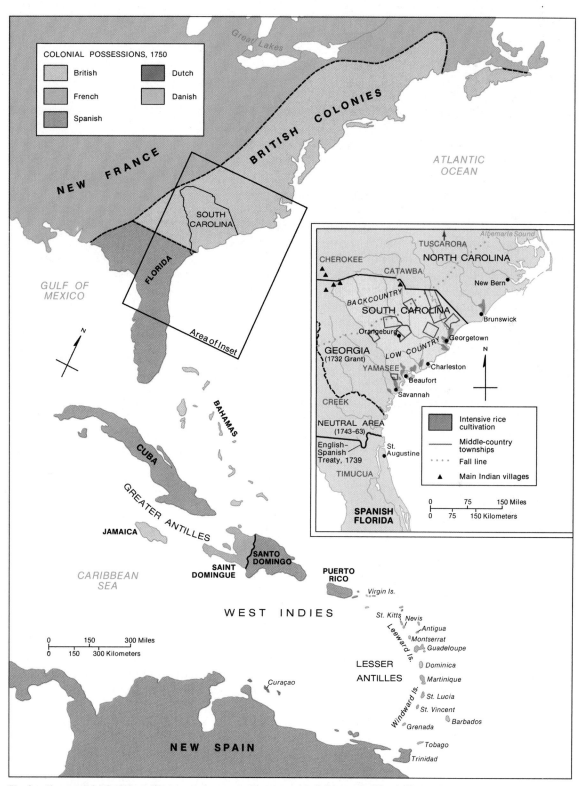

COLONIAL POSSESSIONS, 1750

- British
- French
- Spanish
- Dutch
- Danish

NEW FRANCE

BRITISH COLONIES

ATLANTIC OCEAN

SOUTH CAROLINA

FLORIDA

GULF OF MEXICO

Area of Inset

N

BAHAMAS

CUBA

GREATER ANTILLES

JAMAICA

SANTO DOMINGO

SAINT DOMINGUE

PUERTO RICO

CARIBBEAN SEA

Virgin Is.

WEST INDIES

St. Kitts Nevis

Antigua

Leeward Is. Montserrat

Guadeloupe

LESSER ANTILLES

Dominica

Martinique

St. Lucia

Windward Is. St. Vincent

Barbados

Grenada

Curaçao

Tobago

Trinidad

NEW SPAIN

0   150   300 Miles
0   150   300 Kilometers

Inset map:

Great Lakes

Albemarle Sound

TUSCARORA

CHEROKEE   NORTH CAROLINA

CATAWBA

New Bern

BACKCOUNTRY

SOUTH CAROLINA

Brunswick

Orangeburg

Georgetown

LOW COUNTRY

GEORGIA (1732 Grant)

Charleston

YAMASEE

Beaufort

Savannah

CREEK

N

NEUTRAL AREA (1743-63)

English–Spanish Treaty, 1739

St. Augustine

TIMUCUA

- Intensive rice cultivation
- Middle-country townships
- Fall line
- ▲ Main Indian villages

SPANISH FLORIDA

0   75   150 Miles
0   75   150 Kilometers

The Carolinas and the Caribbean The map underscores the geographic link between West Indian and Carolina settlements. Emigrants from Barbados dominated politics in early South Carolina, while Carolinians provided foodstuffs, grain, and cattle to the West Indies. As South Carolinians began growing rice, Caribbean slave ships found it an easy sail north and west to unload their cargoes in Charleston.

Daily Lives

FOOD/DRINK/ DRUGS

A Taste for Sugar

It is said that shortly before his death in 735 C.E., the Venerable Bede, an English abbot, bequeathed a precious treasure to his brother monks. It consisted of a cache of spices, including a little stock of sugar. What separated Bede's world, in which sugar was a costly luxury, from twentieth-century Americans' world of ever-present sweetness was the discovery of America and the establishment of plantation economies in the Caribbean and Brazil.

Europeans first learned of sugar during an earlier surge of expansion—the Arab conquests in the Mediterranean, North Africa, and Spain during the seventh and eighth centuries. From then until the fourteenth century, Europe's merchants imported small quanti-

ties of sugar at great expense from Arab plantations as well as from distant Persia and India, countries that had produced sugar since 500 C.E.

Throughout the Middle Ages and the early modern era, only the royal and the rich of Europe could indulge their desire for sugar, and even those classes partook sparingly. Europeans classified sugar as a spice, like the equally scarce and exotic pepper, nutmeg, ginger, and saffron. Nobility valued sugar as a medicine for sore throats, stomach disorders, and infertility. It was also used as a remedy for the Black Death and tooth decay. The cooks of castle kitchens seasoned food and sauces with a pinch of sugar or sprinkled it on meat, fish, fowl, and fruit to preserve freshness— or to conceal rot. Only on great occasions did the confectioners of noble families splurge, fashioning for courtly feasts great baked sugar sculptures of knights and kings, horses and apes, called "subtleties."

The Sugar Mill.

Once harvested, sugarcane in the West Indies was crushed, as in this sugar mill. The juice was collected and channeled to the sugar works, where it was concentrated through boiling and evaporation. This neat diagrammatic picture belies the harsh conditions of labor and the high mortality that slaves experienced: sweetness came at a steep price.

The Fundamental Constitutions

Such plans were big enough to satisfy most of the Carolina proprietors, who regarded their venture simply as land speculation. But Cooper, like others before him, hoped to create an ideal society in America. Cooper's utopia was one in which a few landed aristocrats and gentlemen would rule with the consent of many smaller property holders. With his personal secretary, John Locke, Cooper drew up an intricate scheme of government, the Fundamental Constitutions. The design provided Carolina with a proprietary governor and a hereditary nobility who, as a Council of Lords, would recommend all laws to a Parliament elected by lesser landowners.

The Fundamental Constitutions met the same fate as other lordly dreams for America. Instead of peacefully observing its provisions, Carolinians plunged into the political wrangling that had plagued Maryland's proprietary rule. Assemblies resisted the sweeping powers granted to the proprietary governors. Ordinary settlers protested against paying quitrents claimed by the proprietors. Political unrest in North Carolina triggered three rebellions between 1677 and 1711. In South Carolina opposition to the proprietors gathered strength more slowly but finally exploded with equal force.

For the rest of Europe, life was not as sweet. While the rich and royal savored sugary treats, the diets of ordinary people ran to monotonous, meager starches. The staff of everyday life consisted of bread, peas, beans, and, in good years, a little milk, butter, and cheese. The occasional pig slaughtered, rabbit trapped, or fish caught supplied stray protein for the poor.

That pattern of consumption started to change as Europeans turned to African slave labor to grow sugar for them. Madeira and the Canary Islands became more than stepping-stones across the Atlantic for Spain and Portugal. The sugar plantations established there were a foretaste of veritable sugar factories created in the Caribbean colonies of England and France.

By the sixteenth and seventeenth centuries, Europe's merchant classes could imitate elite patterns of eating by pouring sugar into pastries and puddings. And by the middle of the eighteenth century, an increasingly large and inexpensive supply from the Caribbean was making sugar essential to the poorest Europeans. Among England's laboring classes, another colonial import—Indian tea, laced heavily with sugar—began to accompany an otherwise cold supper of bread. Sweet tea and bread constituted the entire diet of those at the bottom of English society. Cheaper, warmer, and more stimulating than milk or beer (its prime competitors), sugared tea won the loyalty of England's mass market and ranked as the non-alcoholic beverage of national choice. By the nineteenth century, English working families were also combining sugar and starch by pouring treacle (molasses) over porridge and spreading jams or marmalades on their bread.

Europe and America affected each other in many ways, but diet figured among the more fundamental conditions of life altered by colonization. More than coffee, chocolate, rum, or tobacco— indeed, more than any of the other "drug foods" produced by the colonies except tea—sugar provided a major addition to the diet of the English and other Europeans.

Even though sugar changed gradually from a scarce, coveted luxury to a mass-marketed basic foodstuff, its association with power persisted. But by the eighteenth century, it was no longer the *consumption* of sugar that bestowed status. On the contrary, as sweeteners found their way into the barest cupboards, the rich and royal probably used less sugar than the poor and powerless. Instead, after 1700 it was the *production* of sugar that conferred power. Planters who grew it, merchants who shipped and sold it, industrialists who refined it, and politicians who taxed it discovered in sugar sources of profit and distinction less perishable than the subtleties of noble banquets or the legacy of the Venerable Bede.

Early Instability

Immigrants from Barbados, the most numerous among the early settlers, came quickly to dominate South Carolina politics. Just as quickly, they objected to proprietary power. To offset the influence of the Barbadians, most of whom were Anglican, the proprietors encouraged the migration of French Huguenots and English Presbyterians and Baptists. The stream of newcomers only heightened tensions, splitting South Carolinians into two camps with competing political and religious loyalties.

Meanwhile, settlers spread out along the coastal plain. Searching for a profitable export, the first colonists raised grains and cattle, foodstuffs that they exported to the West Indies. South Carolinians also developed a large trade in deerskins with coastal tribes like the Yamasee and the Creeks and Catawbas of the interior. More numerous than the Indians of the Chesapeake and even more deeply divided, the Carolina tribes competed to become the favored clients of white traders. Southeastern Indian economies quickly became dependent on English guns, rum, and clothing. To repay their debts to white traders, Indians enslaved

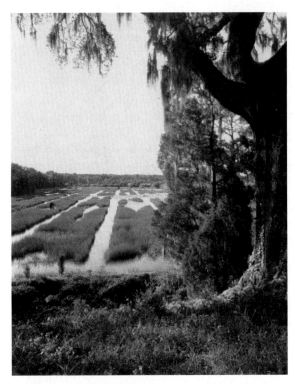

Mulberry Plantation in South Carolina was first carved from coastal swamps in 1714. This photograph from 1935 suggests the way that the landscape may have looked. Stands of live oak draped with Spanish moss ringed the paddy fields, where African slaves skilled in rice cultivation oversaw the difficult and arduous task of properly irrigating the crop.

Yamasee War

The end of proprietary rule

and sold to white buyers large numbers of men, women, and children taken in wars waged against rival tribes.

Provisions, deerskins, and Indian slaves proved less profitable for South Carolinians than did rice, which became the colony's cash crop by the opening of the eighteenth century. Constant demand for rice in Europe made South Carolina the richest colony and South Carolina planters the richest people on the mainland of North America.

Unfortunately, South Carolina's swampy coast, so perfectly suited to growing rice, was less suited for human habitation. Weakened by chronic malaria, settlers died in epic numbers from yellow fever, smallpox, and respiratory infections. The white population grew slowly, through immigration rather than natural increase, and numbered a mere 10,000 by 1730.

Early South Carolinians had little in common but the harsh conditions of frontier existence. Most colonists lived on isolated plantations; early deaths fragmented families and neighborhoods. Immigration after 1700 only intensified the colony's ethnic and religious diversity, adding Swiss and German Lutherans, Scots-Irish Presbyterians, Welsh Baptists, and Spanish Jews. The colony's only courts were in Charleston; churches and clergy of any denomination were scarce. On those rare occasions when early Carolinians came together, they gathered at Charleston to escape the pestilential air of their plantations, to sue each other for debt and haggle over prices, or to fight over religious differences and proprietary politics.

White, Red, and Black: The Search for Order

By the opening decades of the eighteenth century, South Carolina seemed as strife-torn and unstable as the early Chesapeake colonies. In addition to internal tensions, external dangers threatened the very life of the Carolina settlements. The Spanish were rattling their sabers in Florida, the French were filtering into the Gulf region, and pirates were lurking along the North Carolina coast.

Most menacing were the Indians, and in 1715 they struck. The Yamasee of the coast allied themselves with the Creeks farther inland and launched a series of assaults that nearly pushed white Carolinians into the sea. All that saved the colony was an alliance with the Cherokee, another interior tribe who, in return for trading privileges, mounted a counterattack against their Indian rivals.

As colonists reeled from the Yamasee War, opposition mounted against the proprietors, who had done nothing to protect their vulnerable colony. Military expenses had also forced Carolinians to fall into greater debt, to pay higher taxes, and to struggle with an inflated currency that month by month was worth less. Even Presbyterians, Baptists, and Huguenots, who had once defended the proprietors, shifted their sympathies because they disapproved of more recent attempts to establish the Church of England as South Carolina's official religion. During the 1720s, mass meetings and riots so disrupted government that it all but ground to a halt. Finally, in 1729, the Crown formally established royal government; by 1730 economic recovery had done much to ease the strife. Even more important in bringing greater political stability, the white colonists of South Carolina came to realize that they must unite if they were to counter the Spanish in Florida and the French and their Indian allies to the southwest.

The growing black population gave white Carolinians another reason to maintain a united front. During the first decades of settlement, frontier conditions and the scarcity of labor had forced masters to allow enslaved Africans greater freedom within bondage. White and black laborers shared chores on small farms. On stock-raising plantations, called "cowpens," black cowboys ranged freely over the countryside. Black contributions to the defense of the colony also reinforced racial interdependence and muted white domination. Whenever the Spanish, the French, or the Indians threatened, black Carolinians were enlisted in the militia.

Slavery in South Carolina

White Carolinians depended on black labor even more after turning to rice as their cash crop. In fact, planters began to import slaves in larger numbers because of West African skill in rice cultivation. But whites harbored deepening fears of the black workers whose labor built planter fortunes. As early as 1708 black men and women had become a majority in the colony, and by 1730 they outnumbered white settlers by two to one. Like Caribbean planters, white Carolinians put into effect strict slave codes that converted their colony into an armed camp and snuffed out the freedoms that black settlers had enjoyed earlier.

The ever-present threat of revolt on the part of the black majority gave all white South Carolinians an incentive to cooperate, whatever their religion, politics, or ethnic background. To be sure, the colony's high death rates and cultural differences persisted, while local government and churches remained weak. Yet against all these odds, white South Carolinians prospered and political peace prevailed after 1730. Any course except harmony would have exacted too high a price.

The Founding of Georgia

After 1730 South Carolinians could take comfort not only from their new prosperity and new political harmony but also from the founding of a new colony on their southern border. South Carolinians liked Georgia a great deal more than the Virginians had liked Maryland, for the colony formed a defensive buffer between British North America and Spanish Florida.

Enhancing the military security of South Carolina was only one reason for the founding of Georgia. More important to General James Oglethorpe and other idealistic English gentlemen was the aim of aiding the "worthy poor" by providing them with land, employment, and a new start. They envisioned a colony of hardworking small farmers who would produce silk and wine, sparing England the need to import those commodities. That dream seemed within reach when George II made Oglethorpe and his friends the trustees of the new colony in 1732, granting them a charter for 21 years. At the end of that time Georgia would revert to royal control.

James Oglethorpe

The trustees did not, as legend has it, empty England's debtors' prisons to populate Georgia. They freed few debtors but recruited from every country in Europe paupers who seemed willing to work hard—and who professed Protestantism. They paid their passage and provided each with 50 acres of land, tools, and a year's worth of supplies. Settlers who could pay their own way were encouraged to come by granting them larger tracts of land. Much to the trustees' dismay, that generous offer was taken up not only by many hoped-for Protestants but also by several hundred Ashkenazim (German Jews) and Sephardim (Spanish and Portuguese Jews), who established a thriving community in early Savannah.

The trustees were determined to ensure that Georgia became a small farmers' utopia. Rather than selling land, the trustees gave it away, but none of the colony's

The Yuchi were neighbors of one of Georgia's early settlements, and one of the newly emigrated German colonists painted this watercolor of a Yuchi celebration. Judging from the guns hanging at the back of the shelter, these Indians were already trading with white settlers in the area.

settlers could own more than 500 acres. The trustees also outlawed slavery and hard liquor in order to cultivate habits of industry and sustain equality among whites. This design for a virtuous and egalitarian utopia was greeted with little enthusiasm by Georgians. They pressed for a free market in land and argued that the colony could never prosper until the trustees revoked their ban on slavery. Because the trustees had provided for no elective assembly, settlers could express their discontent only by moving to South Carolina—which many did during the early decades.

Utopian designs

As mounting opposition threatened to depopulate the colony, the trustees caved in. They revoked their restrictions on land, slavery, and liquor a few years before the king assumed control of the colony in 1752. Under royal control, Georgia continued to develop an ethnically and religiously diverse society, similar to that of South Carolina. Similarly, its economy was based on rice cultivation and the Indian trade.

Similarities among the plantation colonies

Although South Carolina and the English West Indies were both more opulent and more embattled societies than Virginia and Maryland, the plantation colonies stretching from the Chesapeake to the Caribbean had much in common. Everywhere planters depended on a single staple crop, which brought both wealth and political power to those commanding the most land and the most labor. Everywhere the biggest planters relied for their success on the very people whom they deeply feared—enslaved African Americans. Everywhere, that fear was reflected in the development of repressive slave codes and the spread of racism throughout all classes of white society.

The Spanish Borderlands

When the English founded Jamestown, Spanish settlement in the present-day United States consisted of one feeble fort in southeastern Florida and a single outpost in New Mexico. Hoping both to intimidate privateers who preyed on silver ships and to assert their sovereign claim to the Americas, Spain had established St. Augustine on the Florida coast in 1565. But for decades the place remained a squalid garrison town of a few hundred soldiers and settlers beleaguered by

St. Augustine and Santa Fe

hurricanes, pirates, and Indians. Meanwhile, the Spanish planted a straggling settlement under azure skies and spectacular mesas near present-day Santa Fe in 1598. Their fervent desire was to create colonies in the Southwest that would prove more richly profitable than even those in Central and South America.

Defending both outposts proved so great a drain on royal resources that the Spanish government considered abandoning its precarious footholds in North America. Only the pleas of Catholic missionaries, who hoped to convert the native peoples, persuaded the Crown to sustain its support. But even by 1700, St. Augustine could boast only about 1500 souls, an assortment of Spaniards, black slaves, and Hispanicized Indians. New Mexico's colonial population amounted to fewer than 3000 Spanish ranchers, soldiers, and clergy scattered among the haciendas (cattle and sheep ranches), presidios (military garrisons), and Catholic missions along the Rio Grande. There, the native Pueblo Indians numbered some 30,000.

Still, during these years the Catholic clergy remained active, creating mission communities designed to incorporate native tribes into colonial society. In New Mexico, Franciscan friars supervised Pueblo women (who traditionally built their people's adobe homes) in the construction of more than 30 missions. By 1675 in Florida, perhaps 10,000 Indians were living in 35 villages in which the friars came to stay. Although the new churches were built with native materials, their rectangular forms contrasted sharply with the circular public halls preferred by the Indians of both New Mexico and Florida. Like the curves of a circle interrupted by the right angles of a square, Spanish and Indian cultures coexisted uneasily.

Mission communities

Unlike the English, the Spanish projected a place in their colonies for the Indians. Homes, workshops, granaries, and stables clustered around the church. The missionaries taught Indians European agricultural techniques and crafts. At mission schools, adults as well as children learned to say prayers, sing Christian hymns, and speak Spanish. In 1675, when the bishop of Cuba toured Florida's missions, he spoke enthusiastically of converts who embraced "with devotion the mysteries of our holy faith."

The Indians were selective, however, in the European "mysteries" they chose to adopt. Some natives regarded the friars' presence simply as a means of protecting themselves against the harsher treatment of Spanish soldiers and ranchers. Other Indians used the Spanish presence to give them the upper hand in dealing with rival tribes, just as Powhatan had used white Virginians to further his own designs. And in their religious ceremonies, many natives simply placed Jesus, Mary, and Christian saints beside the other deities they honored. They continued their own religious devotions, much to the frustration of the friars.

Indian and Spanish cultures bumped up against each other in material ways as well. When the Spanish at St. Augustine found the climate unsuitable for growing wheat, olives, and grapes, they turned to Indian maize, beans, and squash. Indians adopted domesticated animals from Europe—horses, cattle, sheep, mules, and donkeys. Watermelons and peach trees, brought to the Atlantic coast by the Spanish, spread quickly along Indian trade routes, often ahead of Europeans themselves.

To their dismay, Indians discovered that in the long run, becoming "civilized" usually meant learning to work for Spanish masters as docile servants. The labor was harsh enough to send many to an early death. European diseases, too, took a gruesome toll among mission Indians. As the population dropped sharply, the demand by Spanish colonists rose for increasingly scarce Indian labor. In theory, Spanish laws protected Indians from ruthless exploitation, but soldiers and settlers illegally forced natives to tend herds, till fields, and haul heavy loads. In New Mexico, captured Indians were sent south to be sold as slaves in the mines of New Spain.

This Native American drawing on a canyon wall in present-day Arizona represents the progress of the Spanish into the Southwest. The prominence of horses underscores their novelty to the Indians, an initial advantage enjoyed by the invaders. "The most essential thing in new lands is horses," one of Coronado's men emphasized. "They instill the greatest fear in the enemy and make the Indians respect the leaders of the army." Many Indian peoples soon put the horse to their own uses, however, and even outshone the Spanish in their riding skills.

As the abuses increased, so did the resentment. Indians regularly fled the mission settlements; others made life miserable for their "benefactors." One padre at Taos Pueblo was served corn tortillas laced with urine and mouse meat. From beyond Spanish lines, the Apache used the horses introduced from Europe to rustle Spanish cattle. On occasion discontent and anger ignited major insurrections. The most successful was the Pueblo Revolt of 1680, which drove the Spanish out of New Mexico for more than a decade. Popé, an Indian spiritual leader in Taos, coordinated an uprising of several Pueblo tribes that vented the full force of their hatred of Spanish rule. They killed 400 people in outlying haciendas and burned the Spanish-style houses and churches to the ground. The attack wiped out one-fifth of the Spanish population of 2500 and sent survivors scurrying for refuge down Dead Man's Road to El Paso, Texas.

Despite native opposition, the Spanish persisted, especially because they saw their European rivals making headway in North America. By the end of the seventeenth century, English settlements in South Carolina were well entrenched, which prompted the Spanish in Florida to offer freedom to any escaped slaves willing to defend the colony and convert to Catholicism. The black fugitives established a fortified settlement north of St. Augustine, Gracia Real de Santa Teresa de Mose, which served as a barrier against English attacks and as a base for raiding Carolina's plantations. Meanwhile the French were building forts at Biloxi and Mobile near the mouth of the Mississippi River, signaling their designs on the Gulf of Mexico. As a counterweight, the Spanish added a second military outpost in Florida at Pensacola and founded several missions in present-day Texas. And after 1769, to secure their claims to the Pacific coast from England and Russia, Spanish soldiers and missionaries began colonizing California. Led by the Franciscan friar Junípero Serra, they established 20 communities along the Pacific coastal plain.

Empire . . . utopia . . . independence. . . . For more than a century after the founding of Jamestown in 1607, those dreams inspired the inhabitants of the Chesapeake, the Carolinas and Georgia, the Caribbean, and the Spanish borderlands. The regions served as staging grounds where kings and commoners, free and unfree, men and women, red, white, and black played out their hopes. Most met only disappointment and many met disaster in the painful decades before the new colonies achieved a measure of stability.

The dream of an expanding empire faltered for the Spanish, who found no new El Dorado in the Southwest. The dream of empire failed, too, when James I and Charles I, England's early Stuart kings, found their power checked by Parliament. And the dream foundered fatally for Powhatan's successors, who were unable to resist both white diseases and land-hungry tobacco planters.

English lords had dreamed of establishing feudal utopias in America. But proprietors like the Calvert family in Maryland and Cooper in the Carolinas found themselves hounded by frontier planters and farmers who sought economic and political power. Georgia's trustees struggled in vain to nurture their dream of a utopia for the poor. The dream of a Spanish Catholic utopia brought by missionaries to the American Southwest dimmed with Indian resistance.

The dream of independence proved the most deceptive of all, especially for the inhabitants of England's colonies. Just a bare majority of the white servant immigrants to the Chesapeake survived to enjoy freedom. The rest were struck down by disease or worn down at the hands of tobacco barons eager for profit. Not only in the Chesapeake but also in the Caribbean and the Carolinas, real independence eluded the English planters. Poorer people—dependent on richer people for land and leadership—deferred to them at church and on election days and depended on them to buy crops or to extend credit. Even the richest planters were dependent on the English and Scottish merchants who supplied them with credit and marketed their crops, as well as on the English officials who made colonial policy.

And everywhere in the American South and Southwest, white people's lingering dreams were realized only through the labor of the least free members of colonial America. In the Southwest the Spanish made servants of the Indians. Along the southern Atlantic coast and in the Caribbean, English plantation owners (like the Spanish before them) turned for labor to the African slave trade. Only after slavery became firmly established as a social and legal institution did England's southern colonies begin to settle down and grow: during the late seventeenth century for the Chesapeake region and the early eighteenth for the Carolinas. That stubborn reality would haunt Americans of all colors who continued to dream of freedom and independence.

chapter summary

During the seventeenth century, plantation economies based on slavery gradually developed throughout the American South.

- Native peoples everywhere in the American South resisted white settlement, but their populations were drastically reduced by warfare, disease, and enslavement.

- Thriving monocultures were established throughout the region—tobacco in the Chesapeake, rice in the Carolinas, and sugar in the Caribbean.

- African slavery emerged as the dominant labor system in all the southern colonies.

- Instability and conflict characterized the southern colonies for most of the first century of their existence.

- As the English colonies took shape, the Spanish extended their empire in Florida and New Mexico, establishing military garrisons, missions, and cattle ranches.

interactive learning

The Primary Source Investigator CD-ROM offers the following materials related to this chapter:

- Interactive maps: **The Atlantic World, 1400–1850** (M2) and **Growth of the Colonies, 1610–1690** (M3)

- A collection of primary sources on the English colonization of North America, such as an engraving that

illustrates the dress and customs of Native Americans living near Jamestown, letters and documents about the peace resulting from the marriage of Pocahontas and John Rolfe, and the terrible collapse of that peace captured in a contemporary engraving of the Indian massacre of Jamestown settlers. Also included are several sources on the origins of slavery in America: a document that presents one of the earliest restrictive slave codes in the British colonies, images of Portuguese slave trading forts on the coast of West Africa, and a sobering diagram of the human cargo holds of that era's slave-trading ships.

additional reading

The best treatment of early Virginia is Edmund S. Morgan, *American Slavery, American Freedom* (1975). A more intimate portrait of an early Virginia community can be found in Darrett and Anita Rutman's study of Middlesex County, *A Place in Time* (1984). Karen Kupperman offers an excellent overview of relations between whites and Indians not only in the early South but throughout North America in *Settling with the Indians* (1980), while James Merrell sensitively explores the impact of white contact on a single southern tribe in *The Indians' New World* (1989). Two other notable treatments of slavery

and race relations in Britain's southern colonies are Richard Dunn's study of the Caribbean, *Sugar and Slaves* (1972), and Peter Wood's work on South Carolina, *Black Majority* (1974). And for the Spanish borderlands, see David J. Weber, *The Spanish Frontier in North America* (1992).

The Chesapeake has always drawn more notice from early American historians than South Carolina has, but in recent years some important studies have redressed that neglect. The best overview of that colony's development remains Robert Weir, *Colonial South Carolina* (1982); for fine explorations of more specialized topics, see Daniel C. Littlefield, *Rice and Slaves* (1981); Peter Colclanis, *The Shadow of a Dream* (1989); and Timothy Silver, *A New Face on the Countryside* (1990). For a fuller list of readings, see the Bibliography at www.mhhe.com/davidsonnation5.

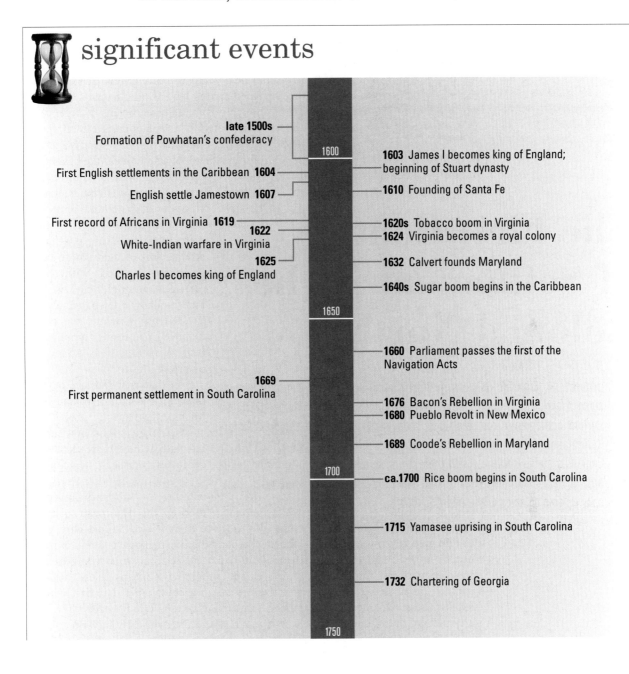

significant events

late 1500s
Formation of Powhatan's confederacy

1603 James I becomes king of England; beginning of Stuart dynasty

First English settlements in the Caribbean **1604**

English settle Jamestown **1607**

1610 Founding of Santa Fe

First record of Africans in Virginia **1619**

1622
White-Indian warfare in Virginia

1620s Tobacco boom in Virginia
1624 Virginia becomes a royal colony

1625
Charles I becomes king of England

1632 Calvert founds Maryland

1640s Sugar boom begins in the Caribbean

1660 Parliament passes the first of the Navigation Acts

1669
First permanent settlement in South Carolina

1676 Bacon's Rebellion in Virginia
1680 Pueblo Revolt in New Mexico

1689 Coode's Rebellion in Maryland

ca.1700 Rice boom begins in South Carolina

1715 Yamasee uprising in South Carolina

1732 Chartering of Georgia

1600
1650
1700
1750

hey came to her one night while she slept. Into her dreams drifted a small island, and on the island were tall trees and living creatures, one of them wearing the fur of a white rabbit. When she told of her vision, no one took her seriously, not even the wise men among her people, shamans and conjurers whose business it was to interpret dreams. No one, that is, until two days later, when the island appeared to all, floating toward shore. On the island, as she had seen, were tall trees, and on their branches—bears. Or creatures that looked so much like bears that the men grabbed their weapons and raced to the beach, eager for the good hunt sent by the gods. They were disappointed. The island was not an island at all but a strange wooden ship planted with the trunks of trees. And the bears were not bears at all but a strange sort of men whose bodies were covered with hair. Strangest among them, as she had somehow known, was a man dressed all in white. He commanded great respect among the bearlike men as their "shaman," or priest.

The First Century of Settlement in the Colonial North

1600–1700

preview • Europe's religious rivalries shaped seventeenth-century colonies along America's northern rim: the Protestant Reformation stamped English Puritan settlements from Maine to Long Island, and the Catholic Counter-Reformation encouraged the less numerous settlers of French Canada. New England's stable societies, with their strong family bonds and growing tradition of self-government, contrasted with the more prosperous and ethnically diverse colonies of the mid-Atlantic.

In that way, foretold by the dreams of a young woman, the Micmac Indians in 1869 recounted their tribe's first meeting with whites more than two centuries earlier. Uncannily, the traditions of other northern tribes record similar dreams predicting the European arrival: "large canoes with great white wings like those of a giant bird," filled with pale bearded men bearing "long black tubes." Perhaps the dreamers gave shape in their sleep to stories heard from other tribes who had actually seen white strangers and ships. Or perhaps, long before they ever encountered Europeans, these Indians imagined them, just as Europeans fantasized about a new world. The first whites seen by those tribes might have been English or Dutch. But probably, like the party met by the Micmacs, they were French, the most avid early adventurers in the northern reaches of the Americas.

Cartier and Champlain

For the time being, few French had dreams of their own about settling in the Americas. Jacques Cartier looked for a Northwest Passage to Asia in 1535 and instead discovered the St. Lawrence River. But not until 1605 did the French plant a permanent colony, at Port Royal in Acadia (Nova Scotia). Three years later, Samuel de Champlain shifted French interests to the St. Lawrence valley, where he founded Quebec. His plan was to follow the network of rivers and lakes leading from Quebec into the interior, exploring the continent for furs and a passage to the Pacific.

Over the next several decades the handful of soldiers, traders, and missionaries who came to New France established friendly relations with tribes of expert fishers and hunters. There were the Algonquin and Montagnais of the St. Lawrence valley; and in the fertile meadows and rich forests around Georgian Bay there was Huronia, a nation 25,000 strong. In return for French goods, these peoples traded

Converts of the French Jesuits, these women of the Caughnawaga tribe (right) are kneeling before a statue of the Virgin Mary, taking vows of celibacy. One cuts her hair, a symbol of banishing pride, in imitation of the practice of Catholic nuns like Marguerite Bourgeoys (left), who founded a religious community dedicated to the education of young girls. Women as well as men in religious orders dedicated their lives to missionary work in Canada.

beaver, otter, and raccoon they had trapped. The furs went to make fashionable European hats, while mink and marten were sent to adorn the robes of high-ranking European officials and churchmen. The French had a name for what New France had become by 1630—a *comptoir*, a storehouse for the skins of dead animals, not a proper colony.

That began to change when other French with their own dreams took responsibility for Canada. Louis XIII and his chief minister, Cardinal Richelieu, hoped that American wealth might be the making of France and its monarchs. In the 1630s they granted large tracts of land and a trading monopoly to a group of private investors, the Company of the Hundred Associates. The Associates brought a few thousand French farmers across the Atlantic and scattered them over 200 miles of company lands along the St. Lawrence.

Religious zeal, as much as the hope of profit, spurred France's renewed interest in colonization. Throughout Europe the Catholic church was enjoying a revival of religious piety as a result of the Counter-Reformation, an effort to correct those abuses that had prompted the Protestant Reformation. To reclaim members lost to Protestantism, the Counter-Reformation also launched an aggressive campaign of repression in Europe and missionary work abroad. In France the Catholic majority persecuted Protestant Huguenots and targeted Canada as a field for harvesting Indian converts.

The shock troops of these missions, not only in the Americas but also in India and Japan, were the Jesuits, members of the Society of Jesus. With Richelieu's encouragement Jesuit missionaries streamed into Canada to assist other French settlers in bringing the Indians the "right" kind of Christianity. At first, it seemed unlikely that the Jesuits would shake the Indians' strong belief in the superiority of their own cultures. In Indian eyes these spiritual soldiers were a joke—men encumbered by their

The Jesuits

effeminate robes, deformed by their "very ugly" beards, and forbidden physical pleasure by their vow of celibacy. The Jesuits were also a nuisance. Not content to preach at French settlements and Indian villages, they undertook "flying" missions to the nomadic tribes, tagging along with Indian trappers. Once in the wilderness the Jesuits were a disaster—tangling in their snowshoes as they tried to surmount wintry drifts, trying for a first and last time to stand in canoes, refusing to carry any weapons, and sponging off the Indians for food and shelter.

Some Indians gradually formed a better opinion of the French and their priests. French traders, known as *coureurs de bois,* and their soldiers often adopted the native way of life and married Indian women. More to the point, the French were still relatively few. Interested primarily in trade, they had no designs on Indian land. The Jesuits, too, won acceptance among some tribes. Their lack of interest in Indian land, furs, and women made them a novelty among white men, while their greater immunity to the diseases that killed many Indians confirmed their claims to superior power. And once the Jesuits mastered the native languages, they showed a talent for smooth talk that the Indians, who prized oratory, greatly admired.

Jesuit persistence slowly paid off. Christian factions formed in many tribes, especially those in which shamans or important families embraced the new religion. Part of the Jesuits' appeal was that they accepted and even appreciated much of Indian culture. The Jesuits never wavered in their zeal to replace Indian religions with Catholicism, but they did not try to transform the Indians into French men and women. If the natives chose to become Catholics in their religion while retaining the rest of their culture, it was all to the good—a good deal better than their becoming English and Protestant.

Throughout the seventeenth century, the French in North America remained relatively few. Instead, it was English Protestants who established the most populous settlements along the north Atlantic coast, challenging Indian dreams with religious visions of their own. Just as Jesuit crusaders of the Counter-Reformation shaped the culture of New France, so the zealous followers of John Calvin left their unmistakable imprint on New England.

The Founding of New England

The English regarded the northern part of North America as a place in which only the mad French could see possibility. English fisherfolk who strayed from Newfoundland to the coast of Acadia and New England carried home descriptions of the long, lonely coast, rockbound and rugged. Long winters of numbing cold melted into short summers of steamy heat. There were no minerals to mine, no crops suitable for export, no large native population available for enslaving. The Chesapeake, with its temperate climate and long growing season, seemed a much likelier spot.

But by 1620, worsening conditions at home instilled in some English men and women the mixture of desperation and idealism needed to settle an uninviting, unknown world. Religious differences among English Protestants became a matter of sharper controversy during the seventeenth century. Along with the religious crisis came mounting political tensions and continuing problems of unemployment and recession. Times were bad—so bad that the anticipation of worse times to come swept men and women to the shores of New England.

The Puritan Movement

The settlement of New England started with a king who chose his enemies unwisely. James I, shortly after succeeding Elizabeth I in 1603, vowed to purge England of all radical Protestant reformers. The radicals James had in mind were the Puritans, most of whom were either Presbyterians or Congregationalists. Although both groups of Puritan reformers embraced Calvin's ideas, they differed on the best form of church organization. Individual Presbyterian churches (or congregations) were guided by higher governing bodies of ministers and laypersons. Congregationalists, on the other hand, believed that each congregation should conduct its own affairs independently, answering to no other authority.

Presbyterians and Congregationalists

King James angered not only the Puritans but also members of Parliament, who objected to his attempts to levy taxes without their consent. The hostility of both Parliament and the Puritans did not bode well for James's reign. In Parliament he faced influential landowners and merchants who were convinced that the law was on their side. And in the Puritans he faced determined zealots who were convinced that God was on their side.

Like all Christians, Protestant and Catholic, the Puritans believed that God was all-knowing and all-powerful. And like all Calvinists, the Puritans emphasized that idea of divine sovereignty known as predestination. At the center of their thinking was the belief that God had ordained the outcome of history, including the eternal fate of every human being. The Puritans found comfort in their belief in predestination because it provided their lives with meaning and purpose. They felt assured that a sovereign God was directing the fate of individuals, nations, and all of creation. The Puritans strove to play their parts in that divine drama of history and to discover in their performances some signs of personal salvation.

Predestination

The divine plan, as the Puritans understood it, called for reforming both church and society along the lines laid down by John Calvin. It seemed to the Puritans that England's government hampered rather than promoted religious purity and social order. It tolerated drunkenness, theatergoing, gambling, extravagance, public swearing, and Sabbath breaking. It permitted popular recreations rooted in pagan custom and superstition—sports like bear baiting and maypole dancing and festivals like the celebration of Christmas and saints' days.

What was worse, the state had not done enough to purify the English church of the "corruptions" of Roman Catholicism. The Church of England counted as its members everyone in the nation, saint and sinner alike. To the Puritans, belonging to a church was no birthright. They wished to limit membership and the privileges of baptism and communion to godly men and women. The Puritans also deplored the hierarchy of bishops and archbishops in the Church of England, as well as its elaborate ceremonies in which priests wore ornate vestments. Too many Anglican clergy were "dumb dogges" in Puritan eyes, too poorly educated to instruct church-goers in the truths of Scripture or to deliver a decent sermon. In reformer John Foxe's vision of good and evil (page 86), Anglican priests on the right side of the drawing are shown in vestments and headdresses worshiping Satan before an altar. Anglican worshipers (bottom right) superstitiously count rosary beads and follow a priestly procession like so many dumb sheep. In contrast, Puritan worshipers (bottom left) conspicuously hold their Bibles and attend only to the word of God.

Puritan calls for reform

Because English monarchs had refused to take stronger measures to reform church and society, the Puritans became their outspoken critics. Elizabeth I had tolerated this opposition, but James I would not endure it and intended to rid England of these radicals. With some of the Puritans, known as the Separatists, he seemed to succeed.

John Foxe's *Actes and Monuments* (1563), a book revered by the Puritan founders of New England, arrayed the forces of righteousness (left side of the page) against a host of devils, priests, and their sheeplike followers within the Church of England at right. Under the Catholic Queen Mary, Protestants were regarded as heretics and some were burned at the stake (middle left).

The Pilgrim Settlement at Plymouth Colony

The Separatists were devout Congregationalists who concluded that the Church of England was too corrupt to be reformed. They abandoned Anglican worship and met secretly in small congregations. From their first appearance in England during the 1570s, the Separatists suffered persecution from the government—fines, imprisonment, and, in a few cases, execution. Always a tiny minority within the Puritan movement, the Separatists were people from humble backgrounds: craft-workers and farmers without the influence to challenge the state. By 1608 some had become so discouraged that they migrated to Holland, where the Dutch government permitted complete freedom of religion. But when their children began to adopt Dutch customs and other religions, some Separatists decided to move again, this time to Virginia.

It can only be imagined what fate would have befallen the unworldly Sepa-ratists had they actually settled in the Chesapeake during the tobacco boom. But a series of mistakes—including an error in charting the course of their ship, the *Mayflower*—landed the little band in New England instead. In November 1620, some 88 Separatist "Pilgrims" set anchor at a place they called Plymouth on the coast of present-day southeastern Massachusetts. They were sick with scurvy, weak from malnutrition, and shaken by a shipboard mutiny, and neither the site nor the season invited settlement. As one of their leaders, William Bradford, later re-membered:

Early difficulties

> For summer being done, all things stand upon them with a weatherbeaten face,
> and the whole country, full of woods and thickets represented a savage hue. If they
> looked behind them, there was the mighty ocean which they had passed and was
> now as a main bar and gulf to separate them from all the civil parts of the world.

For some, the shock was too great. Dorothy Bradford, William's wife, is said to have fallen overboard from the *Mayflower* as it lay anchored off Plymouth. It is more likely that she jumped to her death.

Few Pilgrims could have foreseen founding the first permanent white settle-ment in New England, and many did not live long enough to enjoy the distinc-tion. They had arrived too late to plant crops and had failed to bring an adequate supply of food. By the spring of 1621, half the immigrants had died. English merchants who had financed the *Mayflower* voyage failed to send supplies to the struggling colony.

Plymouth might have become another doomed colony had the Pilgrims not received better treatment from native inhabitants than they did from their English backers. Samoset and Squanto, two Indians who had learned to speak English from visiting fishermen, introduced the settlers to native strains of corn. They also arranged a treaty between the Pilgrims and the region's main tribe, the Wampanoags.

The Pilgrims also set up a government for their colony, the framework of which was the Mayflower Compact. That agreement provided for a governor and several assistants to advise him, all to be elected annually by Plymouth's adult males. In the eyes of English law, the Plymouth settlers had no clear basis for their land claims or their government, for they had neither a royal charter nor approval from the Crown. But English authorities, distracted by problems closer to home, left the tiny colony of farmers alone.

The Mayflower Compact

The Puritan Settlement at Massachusetts Bay

Among the Crown's distractions were two groups of Puritans more numerous and influential than the gentle Pilgrims. They included both the Presbyterians and the majority of Congregationalists who, unlike the Pilgrim Separatists, still considered the Church of England capable of being reformed. But the 1620s brought these Puritans only fresh discouragements. In 1625 Charles I inherited his father's throne and all his enemies. When Parliament attempted to limit the king's power, Charles

Early New England Despite some variety among emigrants to New England, the region remained relatively homogeneous and stable, with everyday life centered in small towns like Sudbury (located to the west of Boston). Most families lived close to one another in houses clustered around the meetinghouse, in contrast to the decentralized plantations of the South. The privately held farm lots were mixed together as well, so that neighbors worked and lived in close contact with one another.

simply dissolved it, in 1629, and proceeded to rule without it. When Puritans pressed for reform, he supported a host of measures proposed by his archbishop, William Laud, for purging England's parishes of ministers with Puritan leanings.

This persecution swelled a second wave of Puritan migration that also drew from the ranks of Congregationalists. Unlike the humble Separatists, these emigrants included merchants, landed gentlemen, and lawyers who organized the Massachusetts Bay Company in 1629. Those able Puritan leaders aimed to build a better society in America, an example to the rest of the world. Unlike the Separatists, they had a strong sense of mission and destiny. They were not abandoning the English church, they insisted, but merely regrouping for another assault on corruption from across the Atlantic. They began organizing a mass migration to Massachusetts Bay that had the efficiency of a military maneuver and the martial spirit of a crusade. One of the immigrants, Edward Johnson, described his fellows as "Soldiers of Jesus Christ," who "for England's sake . . . are going from England to pray without ceasing for England."

Despite the company's Puritan leanings, it somehow obtained a royal charter confirming its title to most of present-day Massachusetts and New Hampshire. Advance parties in 1629 established the town of Salem on the coast well north of Plymouth. In 1630 the company's first governor, John Winthrop, sailed from England with a dozen other company stockholders and a fleet of men and women committed to the Puritan cause. Winthrop, a landed gentleman, was both a tough-minded lawyer and a visionary determined to set an example for the world. "We shall be as a city on a hill," he told his fellow passengers during the crossing on the ship *Arbella*.

Once established in the Bay Colony, Winthrop and the other stockholders transformed the charter for their trading company into the framework of govern-ment for a colony. The company's governor became the colony's chief executive, and the company's other officers became the governor's assistants. The charter pro-vided for annual elections of the governor and his assistants by company stock-holders, known as the freemen. But to create a broad base of support for the new government, Winthrop and his assistants expanded the freemanship in 1631 to include every adult male church member.

Establishing the colony's government

The governor, his assistants, and the freemen together made up the General Court of the colony, which passed all laws, levied taxes, established courts, and made war and peace. In 1634 the whole body of the freemen stopped meeting and instead each town elected representatives or deputies to the General Court. Ten years later, the deputies formed themselves into the lower house of the Bay Colony legislature, and the assistants formed the upper house. By refashioning a company charter into a civil constitution, Massachusetts Bay Puritans gained full control of their future, fulfilling their dream of shaping society, church, and state to their liking.

New England Communities

Contrary to expectations, New England proved more hospitable to the English than did the Chesapeake. The character of the migration itself gave New England settlers an advantage, for most arrived in family groups—not as young, single, indentured servants of the sort whose discontents unsettled Virginia society. The heads of New England's first households were typically free men—farmers, artisans, and merchants. Most were skilled and literate. Since husbands usually migrated with their wives and children, the ratio of men to women within the population was fairly evenly balanced.

Most immigrants, some 21,000, came in a cluster between 1630 and 1642. Thereafter new arrivals tapered off because of the outbreak of the English Civil War. This relatively rapid settlement fostered solidarity because immigrants shared a common past of persecution and a strong desire to create an ordered society modeled on Scripture.

The "Great Migration"

Stability and Order in Early New England

Puritan emigrants and their descendants thrived in New England's bracing but healthy climate. The first generation of colonists lived to an average age of 70, nearly twice as long as Virginians and 10 years longer than English men and women. With 90 percent of all children reaching adulthood, the typical family con-sisted of seven or eight children who came to maturity. Because of low death rates and high birthrates, the number of New Englanders doubled about every 27 years—while the populations of Europe and the Chesapeake barely reproduced themselves.

Long-lived New Englanders

By 1700, New England and the Chesapeake both had populations of approximately 100,000. But whereas the southern population grew because of continuing immigration, New England's expanded through natural increase.

As immigrants arrived in the Bay Colony after 1630, they carved out an arc of small villages around Massachusetts Bay. Within a decade settlers pressed into Connecticut, Rhode Island, and New Hampshire. Connecticut and Rhode Island received separate charters from Charles II in the 1660s, guaranteeing their residents the rights to land and government. New Hampshire, to which Massachusetts laid claim in the 1640s, did not become a separate colony until 1679. The handful of hardy souls settled along the coast of present-day Maine had also accepted the Massachusetts Bay Colony's authority.

Patterns of settlement

Early New Englanders planted most of their settlements with an eye to stability and order. Unlike the Virginians, who scattered across the Chesapeake to isolated plantations, most New Englanders established tightly knit communities like those they had left behind in England. In fact, migrating families from the same village or congregation back in England often petitioned the colony government for a tract of land to found their own new town. All prospective adult townsmen initially owned in common this free grant of land, along with the right to set up a local government. Townsmen gradually parceled out among themselves the land granted by the colony. Each family received a lot for a house along with about 150 acres of land in nearby fields. Farmers left many of their acres uncultivated as a legacy for future generations, for most had only the labor of their own families to work their land. While the Chesapeake abounded with servants and tenant farmers, almost every adult male in rural New England owned property.

The economy that supported most of New England's families and towns offered few chances for anyone to get rich. Farmers could coax a yield of food crops sufficient to feed their families, but the stony soil and long winters could not support cash crops like tobacco, rice, or sugar. With no resources for commercial agriculture, New England farmers also had no incentive to import large numbers of servants and slaves or to create large plantations.

Strong family institutions contributed to New England's order and stability. While the early deaths of parents regularly splintered Chesapeake families, two adult generations were often on hand to encourage order within New England households. Husbands and fathers exacted submission from wives and strict obedience from children. Land gave New England's long-lived fathers great authority over even their grown children, for sons and daughters relied on paternal legacies of farms in order to marry and establish their own families.

Hierarchy in village leadership

New Englanders also created, quite deliberately, a distinctive village leadership. Few members of the English upper class migrated to New England, but the Puritan colonists, like most other seventeenth-century English, believed that a stable society depended on some degree of inequality. Each town favored certain families in its land distribution, awarding them a little more than the average allotment. The heads of such families were often ministers or other men with university educations or artisans with skills useful to the community. Such men became the "town fathers" and took the lead in directing local affairs. The trust that most New Englanders invested in their leaders contrasts sharply with the attitudes of early Virginians, who constantly challenged the authority of their elites.

Congregational Church Order

Equally important in preserving local order was the church. Most settlers formed churches as quickly as they founded towns, and each congregation ran its own affairs, hiring and dismissing ministers, admitting and disciplining members.

Membership in New England's Congregational churches was voluntary, but it was not available for the asking. Those wishing to join had to satisfy the church that they had experienced "conversion." Puritans understood conversion to mean a turning of the heart and soul toward God, a spiritual rebirth that was reflected by a pious and disciplined life. In New England, believers who could credibly relate their conversions to the minister and other church members gained admission to membership. Most early New Englanders sought and received church membership, a status that entitled them to receive communion and to have their children baptized. Widespread membership also enabled the churches to oversee public morality. Although the churches of New England could not inflict corporal punishment or fines on their members, as church courts did in England, Puritan churches could and did censure and expel wayward members for misbehavior.

Church membership

Everywhere in New England except Rhode Island, civil laws obliged everyone to attend worship services on the Sabbath and to pay taxes to support Congregationalist ministers. Although the separation between church and state was incomplete, it had progressed further in New England than in most nations of Europe. New England ministers did not serve as officers in the civil government, and the Congregational churches owned no property. In contrast, Catholic and Anglican church officials wielded real temporal power in European states, and the churches held extensive tracts of land.

Separation of church and state

The interior of the Old Ship Meetinghouse, built in Hingham, Massachusetts, in 1681, expresses the importance of hierarchy among New England Puritans. Families with wealth and influence enjoyed the comfort of enclosed wooden pews on the ground floor, while those with slimmer means sat on rows of benches on the second-floor gallery. The raised pulpit at the front of the meetinghouse bespeaks the congregation's respect for the authority and learning of the clergy.

Colonial Governments

The last institution fostering order in daily life was the town meeting, the basis of local self-government. In every New England village, all white, male adult inhabitants met regularly at the meetinghouse to decide matters of local importance. Nearly all of them could vote for town officials. The town fathers generally set the meeting's agenda and offered advice, but the unanimous consent of townsmen determined all decisions. Reaching consensus was a practical necessity because the town fathers had no means of enforcing unpopular decisions.

Colony governments in early New England also evolved into representative and responsive institutions. Typically the central government of each colony, like the General Court of Massachusetts Bay, consisted of a governor and a bicameral legislature, including an upper house, or council, and a lower house, or assembly. All officials were elected annually by the freemen—white adult men entitled to vote in colony elections. Voting qualifications varied, but the number of men enfranchised made up a much broader segment of society than that in seventeenth-century England.

Communities in Conflict

Not every community in early New England was a small, self-sufficient farming village in which strong families, town fathers, and watchful churches pursued the ideals of Puritanism. Along the edges of settlement, several towns departed dramatically from the usual patterns.

Commerce and "company towns"

One such outpost was Marblehead, a fishing port on the Massachusetts coast settled by immigrant fisherfolk from every port in the British Isles. Most eked out a bare existence as suppliers and employees of Boston merchants, who managed Marblehead's fishery. Single men dominated the population, and their brawls and drunken cavorting often spilled out of the town's many taverns onto the streets. Local government remained weak for most of the seventeenth century, and inhabitants managed to avoid founding a local church for 50 years.

Similar problems plagued Springfield, Massachusetts, in the fertile Connecticut River valley. A single powerful family, the Pynchons, founded the town as a center of the fur trade and later developed a thriving commercial agriculture. Here, too, profit-minded merchants dominated local life and exploited the labor of most inhabitants—an assortment of Scottish convicts and English indentured servants.

The rest of Massachusetts tolerated chaotic "company towns" like Marblehead and Springfield because their inhabitants produced what few commodities New England could trade to the rest of the world. Marblehead's fish found a ready market in Catholic Spain and Portugal; Springfield's grain and livestock commanded a good price among Caribbean planters. In exchange, New Englanders acquired wine, sugar, molasses, textiles, and iron goods—commodities that they needed but could not produce.

Conflict over religious differences

More commonly, conflicts in New England towns were likely to arise over religious differences. Although most New Englanders called themselves Puritans and Congregationalists, the very fervency of their convictions often led them to disagree about how best to carry out the teachings of the Bible and the ideas of John Calvin. The Puritans of Plymouth Colony, for example, believed that religious purity required renouncing the Church of England, while those of the Bay Colony clung to the hope of reforming the Anglican church from within.

Even within Massachusetts Bay, Puritans differed among themselves about how to organize their churches. During the first decades of settlement, those differences led to the founding of new colonies in New England. In 1636 Thomas Hooker, the minister of Cambridge, Massachusetts, led part of his congregation to Connecticut, where they established the first English settlement. Somewhat more liberal than other Bay Puritans, Hooker favored more lenient standards for church membership. He also opposed the Bay's policy of limiting voting in colony elections to church members. In contrast, New Haven (a separate colony until it became part of Connecticut in 1662) was begun in 1638 by strict Congregationalists who found Massachusetts too liberal. Massachusetts recognized its southern neighbors, including Separatist Plymouth, as colonies within the Puritan fold, respectable suburbs of Winthrop's city on a hill.

Heretics

The same could not be said of Rhode Island, for that little colony on Narragansett Bay began as a ghetto for heretics. While voluntary migration formed Connecticut and New Haven, enforced exile filled Rhode Island with men and women whose radical ideas unsettled the rest of Massachusetts.

Roger Williams, Rhode Island's founder, had come to New England in 1631, serving as a respected minister of Salem. But soon Williams announced that he was a Separatist, like the Pilgrims of Plymouth. He encouraged the Bay Colony to break all ties to the corrupt Church of England. He also urged a more complete separation of church and state than most New Englanders were prepared to accept, and later in his career he endorsed full religious toleration. Finally, Williams denounced the Bay's charter—the legal document that justified Massachusetts's existence—on the grounds that the king had no right to grant land that he had not purchased from the Indians. When Williams made bold to suggest that Massachusetts actually inform the king of his mistake, angry authorities prepared to deport him. Instead Williams fled the colony in the dead of winter to live with the Indians. In 1636, he became the founder and first citizen of Providence, later to be part of Rhode Island.

Roger Williams

Another charismatic heretic from Massachusetts arrived soon after. Anne Hutchinson, a skilled midwife and the spouse of a wealthy merchant, came to Boston in 1634. Enthusiasm for her minister, John Cotton, started her on a course of explaining his sermons to gatherings of her neighbors—and then to elaborating ideas of her own in which many of the Bay's leaders detected the dangerous heresy of antinomianism.

Anne Hutchinson

The Bay Puritans, like all Calvinists, denied that men and women could "earn" salvation simply by obeying God's laws. They held that salvation came through divine grace, not human actions. But many Puritans believed that the ability to lead an upright life was a natural consequence of being saved. A minority in the Puritan movement, including Anne Hutchinson, rejected that notion. Hutchinson contended that outward obedience to God's laws indicated nothing whatsoever about the inward state of the soul. She was certain that those predestined for salvation knew it intuitively and could recognize the same grace in others.

When most of the Bay Colony's ministers rejected her views, Anne Hutchinson denounced them. Her attack on the clergy, along with the popularity of her preaching

Daily Lives

POPULAR ENTERTAINMENT

A World of Wonders and Witchcraft

Early in the 1680s the Reverend Increase Mather, a learned and devout Boston minister, was putting the finishing touches on a book. It would be a plump volume when published, its pages packed with remarkable occurrences that had taken place during the first 50 years of New England's settlement. Those occurrences dealt not with politics, nor even with the churches, but rather with "wonders"—interventions of the supernatural in the normal order of things. Ministers throughout New England contributed accounts of such wonders to Mather's book. Reverend John Higginson of Salem told of a "Conjuring Book," which filled readers with "a strange kind of Horror" and caused their hair to stand on end. From Newbury, Massachusetts, Reverend Joshua Moodey reported a house inhabited by evil spirits and a "monstrous birth." From Connecticut came the story of a phantom ship sighted sailing into New Haven harbor that suddenly disappeared. Other ministers related cases of bewitchment, appearances of the devil, and dire events forecast by comets, eclipses, earthquakes, and rainbows.

Mather's book of wonders became one of many available to New England readers—a numerous group, for literacy was almost universal. Accounts of marvelous events poured from presses in England, the Continent, and the colonies. Some were splashed across a single sheet by literary hacks; others, like Mather's book, filled the fat volumes written by learned men. The authors drew their reports of visions and voices, untimely deaths and natural disasters from ancient and early Christian authors, medieval chronicles, the Bible, and local lore collected by contemporaries, like Mather's network of New England ministers.

Most seventeenth-century New Englanders preferred to read religious books: the Bible, psalmbooks, sermons, stories of the sufferings of Protestant martyrs, and accounts of the battles against temptation waged by ordinary people. Even so, authors like Increase Mather recognized that a wider audience might be reached by volumes blending godly messages with sensational topics. Ministers recounted wonders to make the religious argument that the world was shot through with mystery and miracle and that men and women were at the mercy of God's will and the devil's wiles. At the same time, these books titillated readers with accounts of witches, apparitions, and freaks

Witchcraft trials and executions took place throughout Europe in the sixteenth and seventeenth centuries, occurring far more frequently and claiming many more victims than in colonial America. But, as this engraving of an English hanging of witches indicates, women composed a majority of those charged and executed on both sides of the Atlantic.

among many important merchant families, prompted the Bay Colony government to expel Hutchinson and her followers for sedition in 1638. She settled briefly in Rhode Island before moving on to Long Island, where she died in an Indian attack.

Colony leaders were especially critical of Hutchinson because she was a woman, and they believed that women should remain less assertive of their beliefs. In later religious controversies, the devil of dissent assumed the shape of a woman as well. The Quakers, one of the most radical religious groups produced by the Protestant Reformation in England, sent Ann Austin and Mary Fisher as their first missionaries to the Bay. Women were among the most active early converts, and one of them, Mary Dyer, was hanged for her persistence, along with three Quaker men, in 1656. Like the antinomians, the Quakers attached great

Quakers of New England

of nature. Published narratives of New Englanders taken captive by the Indians and the confessions of convicted murderers combined the same mixture of religion and sensationalism. The pious message that God prevailed over Satan and his servants was mixed with lurid depictions of violence and evildoing.

Knowing what early New Englanders liked to read offers a glimpse not only of their entertainments but of their inner world. Especially significant was their enduring fascination with wonders, which were believed to be true both by learned folks and by humble farmers and their wives. The popularity of wonder lore is powerful proof that all New Englanders inhabited an enchanted universe. Their world brimmed with invisible forces and supernatural beings that could interrupt the order of nature.

That widely shared belief made witchcraft a crime punishable by death and allowed for the unfolding of the notorious witchcraft trials in Salem Village. There, in the early months of 1692, a group of adolescent girls used the white of a raw egg suspended in a glass of water as a kind of crude crystal ball to divine what sorts of men their future husbands might be. Somehow, the seance went sour and the frightened adolescents began behaving in ways that other villagers took to be signs of bewitchment. Crying out in pain and terror, the afflicted women claimed to see taunting specters of witches, whom they recognized as fellow villagers. In the hysteria that ensued, hundreds of accusations of witchcraft led to the trial and execution of 20 innocent men and women. Only when Increase Mather and 14 other Massachusetts ministers publicly warned against the trials' excesses did the hangings stop.

Many historians have tried to explain the deeper causes behind the Salem episode. Some point to the Puritan mistrust of independent women, others to the bitter rivalries among Salem Village families. Still others have noted ties between accused witches and heretical groups like the Quakers. Whatever the source of Salem's particular troubles, the witchcraft charges there and elsewhere in seventeenth-century New England were rooted in the widespread belief in a world of wonders, at once terrible and fascinating.

significance to an inward state of grace, called the "Light Within." Through that inner light, the Quakers claimed, God revealed his will directly to believers, enabling men and women to attain spiritual perfection. Because they held that everyone had immediate access to God, the Quakers also dispensed with a clergy and the sacraments.

Goodwives and Witches

If Anne Hutchinson and Mary Dyer had been men, their ideas would still have been deemed heretical. On the other hand, if these women had been men, they might have found other ways to express their intelligence and magnetism. But life

95

The artist who sketched this Quaker meeting called attention to one of that sect's most controversial practices by placing a woman at the center of his composition. Women were allowed to speak in Quaker worship services and to preach and proselytize at public gatherings of non-Quakers. The Puritans roundly condemned this liberty as contrary to the teachings of St. Paul.

in colonial New England offered women, especially married women, little scope for their talents.

Most adult women were hardworking farm wives who cared for large households of children. Between marriage and middle age, most New England wives were pregnant except when breast-feeding. When they were not nursing or minding children, mothers were producing and preparing much of what was consumed and worn by their families. They planted vegetable gardens and pruned fruit trees, salted beef and pork and pressed cider, milked cows and churned butter, kept bees and tended poultry, cooked and baked, washed and ironed, spun, wove, and sewed. While husbands and sons engaged in farm work that changed with the seasons, took trips to taverns and mills, and went off to hunt or fish, housebound wives and daughters were locked into a humdrum routine with little time for themselves.

Legal barriers for women

Women suffered legal disadvantages as well. English common law and colonial legal codes accorded married women no control over property. Wives could not sue or be sued, they could not make contracts, and they surrendered to their husbands any property that they possessed before marriage. Divorce was almost impossible to obtain until the late eighteenth century. Only widows and a few single women had the same property rights as men, but they could not vote in colony elections.

The one arena in which women could attain something approaching equal standing with men was the churches. Women wielded their greatest influence among the Quakers. They could speak in Quaker meetings, preach as missionaries, and oversee the behavior of other female members in "women's meetings." Puritan women could not become ministers, but after the 1660s they made up the majority of church members. In some churches membership enabled them to vote for ministerial candidates and to voice opinions about admitting and disciplining members. Puritan doctrine itself rejected the medieval Catholic suspicion of women as "a necessary evil," seeing them instead as "a necessary good." Even so, the Puritan ideal of the virtuous woman was a chaste, submissive "helpmeet," a wife and mother who served God by serving men.

Communities sometimes responded to assertive women with accusations of witchcraft. Like most early modern Europeans, New Englanders believed in wizards and witches, men and women who were said to acquire supernatural powers by signing a compact with Satan. A total of 344 New Englanders were charged with witchcraft during the first century of settlement, with the notorious Salem Village episode of 1692 producing the largest outpouring of accusations and 20 executions. More than three-quarters of all accused witches were women, usually middle-aged and older, and most of those accused were regarded as unduly independent. Before they were charged with witchcraft, many had been suspected of heretical religious beliefs, others of sexual impropriety. Still others had inherited or stood to inherit property.

Witchcraft

Salem witchcraft crisis of 1692

Whites and Indians in Early New England

Most white settlers in New England, like those in the Chesapeake, condemned the "savagery" and "superstition" of the Indians around them. Unlike the French, however, the Puritans made only a few efforts to spread their faith to the Indians.

In truth, the "godly" New Englanders had more in common with the natives in the region than they might have cared to admit. Perhaps 100,000 Algonquin men and women lived in the area reaching from the Kennebec River in Maine to Cape Cod. Like the Puritans, they relied for food on fishing in spring and summer, hunting in winter, cultivating and harvesting food crops in spring and fall. And, to an even greater degree than among white settlers, Indian political authority was local. Within each village, a single leader known as the "sachem" or "sagamore" directed economic life, administered justice, and negotiated with other tribes and English settlers. As with New England's town fathers, a sachem's power depended on keeping the trust and consent of his people.

Similarities between Puritans and Indians

The Indians of New England shared one other characteristic with all Europeans: they quarreled frequently with neighboring nations. The antagonism among the English, Spanish, Dutch, and French was matched by the hostilities among the Abenaki, Pawtucket, Massachusett, Narragansett, and Wampanoag tribes of the north Atlantic coast. Rivalries kept different tribes from forging an effective defense against white colonials. New England settlers, like those in the Chesapeake, exploited Indian disunity.

The first New England natives to put up a strong resistance to Europeans were the Pequots, whom white settlers encountered when they began to push into Connecticut. Had the Pequots allied with their neighbors, the Narragansetts, they could have retarded English expansion. But the Narragansetts, bitter enemies of the Pequots, allied with the English instead. Together they virtually destroyed the Pequots in 1637. Then, in 1643, the English turned against their former allies; they joined forces with the Narragansetts' rivals, the Mohegans, and intimidated the Narragansetts into ceding much of their territory. Only a few whites objected to those ruthless policies, among them Roger Williams. "God Land," he warned one Connecticut leader, "will be (as it now is) as great a God with us English as God Gold was with the Spanish."

War

Playing one tribe off against another finally left the Wampanoags of Plymouth the only coastal tribe capable of resisting Puritan expansion. In 1675, their sachem Metacomet, whom the English called King Philip, organized an uprising that devastated white frontier settlements. By the spring of 1676, Metacomet's forces were closing in on the coast, raiding towns that lay within 20 miles of Boston.

Faced with shortages of food and ammunition, Metacomet called for assistance from the Abenaki, a powerful Maine tribe, and from the Iroquois of New York. But those tribes withheld their support, not wishing to jeopardize their trade with the English. In the summer of 1676 Metacomet met his death in battle, and the Indian offensive collapsed. In seventeenth-century New England, as in the Chesapeake, the clash between Indians and white settlers threatened the very survival of both groups. Perhaps 20,000 whites and Indians lost their lives in Metacomet's War.

Effect of Old World diseases

Even if the natives of New England had been able to unify against whites, they still would have had no defense against another deadly enemy—disease. Like all the Indians of the precolonial Americas, those in New England had been singularly free of the illnesses such as chicken pox and measles that most Europeans experienced in childhood. They were free, too, of the deadly epidemics that beset the Old World—smallpox, influenza, plague, malaria, yellow fever, and tuberculosis. But the absence of those pathogens in the pre-Columbian environment also meant that native Americans had built up no acquired immunity. For that reason, European microbes devastated Indian populations throughout the Americas. In New England, the total number of native Americans plummeted from 70,000 to fewer than 12,000 during the first 75 years of the seventeenth century.

The Mid-Atlantic Colonies

The inhabitants of the mid-Atlantic colonies—New York, New Jersey, Pennsylvania, and Delaware—enjoyed more secure lives than most southern colonials. But they lacked the common bonds that lent stability to early New England. Instead, throughout the mid-Atlantic region a variety of ethnic and religious groups vied for wealth from farming and the fur trade and contended bitterly against governments that commanded little popular support.

The Founding of New Netherlands

New York was settled in 1624 as New Netherlands, an outpost of the Dutch West India Company. Far more impressed with the commercial potential of Africa and South America, the company limited its investment in North America to a few fur-trading posts along the Hudson, Connecticut, and Delaware rivers.

Ethnic and religious diversity

Intent only on trade, the Dutch had little desire to plant permanent colonies abroad because they enjoyed prosperity and religious freedom at home. Most of New Netherlands' few settlers clustered in the village of New Amsterdam on Manhattan Island at the mouth of the Hudson. One hundred and fifty miles upriver lay a fur-trading outpost, Fort Orange (Albany), and by the 1660s a few other farming villages dotted the west end of Long Island, upper Manhattan Island, Staten Island, and the lower Hudson valley. In all, there were fewer than 9000 New Netherlanders—a mixture of Dutch, Belgians, French, English, Portuguese, Swedes, Finns, and Africans. The first blacks had arrived in 1626, imported as slaves; some later became free, intermarried with whites, and even owned white indentured servants.

This ethnic diversity ensured a variety of religions. Although the Dutch Reformed church predominated, other early New Netherlanders included Lutherans, Quakers, and Catholics. There were Jews as well, refugees from Portuguese Brazil, who were required by law to live in a ghetto in New Amsterdam. Yet another religious group kept to themselves by choice: New England Congregationalists. Drawn by promises of cheap land and self-government, they planted farming communities on eastern Long Island during the 1640s.

New Amsterdam (later New York City) in about 1626. Despite having this outpost in New Netherlands, the Dutch had far more interest in vying with the Portuguese for control of commerce with the Far East than in competing with the English for the fur trade in North America.

New Netherlanders knew that their cultural differences hampered the prospects for a stable social and political life. The Dutch West India Company made matters worse by appointing corrupt, dictatorial governors who ruled without an elective assembly. The company also provided little protection for its outlying settlers; when it did attack neighboring Indian nations, it did so savagely, triggering terrible retaliations. By the time the company went bankrupt in 1654, it had virtually abandoned its American colony.

New Englanders on Long Island, who had insisted on a free hand in governing their own villages, now began to demand a voice in running the colony as well. By the 1660s they were openly challenging Dutch rule and calling for English conquest of the colony.

English Rule in New York

Taking advantage of the disarray in New Netherlands, Charles II ignored Dutch claims in North America and granted his brother, James, the Duke of York, a proprietary charter there. It granted James all of New Netherlands to Delaware Bay as well as Maine, Martha's Vineyard, and Nantucket Island. In 1664 James sent an invading fleet, whose mere arrival caused the Dutch to surrender.

English management of the new colony, renamed New York, did little to ease ethnic tensions or promote political harmony. The Dutch resented English rule, and only after a generation of intermarriage and acculturation did that resentment fade. James also failed to win friends among Long Island's New Englanders. He grudgingly gave in to their demand for an elective assembly in 1683 but rejected its first act, the Charter of Liberties, which would have guaranteed basic political rights. The chronic political strife discouraged prospective settlers. By 1698 the colony numbered only 18,000 inhabitants, and New York City, the former New Amsterdam, was an overgrown village of a few thousand.

The League of the Iroquois

While New York's colonists wrangled, many of its native Indians succumbed to the same pressures that shattered the natives of New England and the Chesapeake. Only one tribe of Indians in New York's interior, the Iroquois nation, actually gained greater strength from its contacts with whites.

The Indian trade

Like the tribes of South Carolina, the Indians of northern New York became important suppliers of furs to white traders. As in the Carolinas, powerful tribes dominated the interior, far outnumbering white settlers. The handful of Dutch and, later, English traders had every reason to keep peace with the Indians. But the fur trade heightened tensions among interior tribes. At first the Mahicans had supplied furs to the Dutch. But by 1625 the game in their territory had been exhausted, and the Dutch had taken their business to the Iroquois. When the Iroquois faced the same extinction of fur-bearing animals in the 1640s, they found a solution. With Dutch encouragement and Dutch guns, the Iroquois virtually wiped out the neighboring Huron nation and seized their hunting grounds.

The destruction of the Huron made the Iroquois the undisputed power on the northern frontier. More successfully than Powhatan's confederacy in the Chesapeake, the League of the Iroquois welded different tribes into a coherent political unit. This union of the Five Nations (to become six after the Tuscaroras joined them in 1712) included the Mohawk, Oneida, Onondaga, Cayuga, and Seneca tribes and stretched from the lands around the upper Hudson in the east to the Genesee River in the west. Political strength enabled the Iroquois to deal effectively with their Algonquin rivals in New England as well as European newcomers. As the favored clients of the Dutch and, later, the English, they became opponents of the French.

Iroquois women

The League's strength rested on a remarkable form of political and social organization, one in which men and women shared authority. The most powerful women anywhere in colonial North America were the matriarchs of the Iroquois. Matrilineal kinship formed the basis of Iroquois society, as it did among the Pueblos of the Southwest. When men married, they joined their wives' families, households over

Many French colonials showed an abiding interest in and respect for Native American culture. Among them was George Heriot, an eighteenth-century Quebec-based painter, who produced a series of watercolor sketches of Iroquois ceremonies, including this portrayal of a calumet (or peace-pipe) dance.

which the eldest female member presided. But unlike Pueblo women, Iroquois matriarchs wielded political influence as well. The most senior Iroquois women selected the confederation's council of chiefs, advised them, and "dehorned"—removed from office—those deemed unfit. Throughout the eighteenth century, the League of the Iroquois would continue to figure as a major force in North America.

The Founding of New Jersey

New Jersey took shape in the shadow of its stronger neighbors to the north. Its inhabitants were less united and powerful than the Iroquois, less wealthy and influential than New Yorkers, and less like-minded and self-governing than New Englanders.

Confusion attended New Jersey's beginnings. The lands lying west of the Hudson and east of the Delaware River had been part of the Duke of York's proprietary grant. But in 1664 he gave about 5 million of these acres to Lord Berkeley and Sir George Carteret, two of his favorites who were already involved in the proprietary colonies of the Carolinas. New Jersey's new owners guaranteed settlers land, religious freedom, and a representative assembly in exchange for a small quitrent, an annual fee for the use of the land. The proprietors' terms promptly drew Puritan settlers from New Haven, Connecticut. At the same time, unaware that James had already given New Jersey to Berkeley and Carteret, New York's Governor Richard Nicolls granted Long Island Puritans land there.

More complications ensued when Berkeley and Carteret decided to divide New Jersey into east and west and sell both halves to Quaker investors—a prospect that outraged New Jersey's Puritans. Although some English Quakers migrated to West Jersey, the investors quickly decided that two Jerseys were less desirable than one Pennsylvania and resold both East and West Jersey to speculators. In the end the Jerseys became a patchwork of religious and ethnic groups. Settlers who shared a common religion or national origin formed communities and established small family farms. When the Crown finally reunited east and west as a single royal colony in 1702, New Jersey was overshadowed by settlements not only to the north but now, also, to the south and west.

Quaker Odysseys

Religious and political idealism similar to that of the Puritans inspired the settlement of Pennsylvania, making it an oddity among the mid-Atlantic colonies. The oddity began with an improbable founder, William Penn. Young Penn devoted his early years to disappointing his distinguished father, Sir William Penn, an admiral in the Royal Navy. Several years after being expelled from college, he finally chose a career that may have made the admiral yearn for mere disappointment: young Penn undertook a lifelong commitment to put into practice Quaker teachings. By the 1670s he had emerged as an acknowledged leader of the Society of Friends, as the Quakers formally called themselves.

The Quakers behaved in ways and believed in ideas that most people regarded as odd. They dressed in a deliberately plain and severe manner. They withheld from their social superiors the customary marks of respect, such as bowing, kneeling, and removing their hats. They refused to swear oaths or to make war. They allowed   Quaker beliefs
women public roles of religious leadership. That pattern of behavior reflected their egalitarian ideals, the belief that all men and women shared equally in the "Light Within." Some 40,000 English merchants, artisans, and farmers embraced Quakerism by 1660, and many suffered fines, imprisonment, and corporal punishment.

Since the English upper class has always prized eccentricity among its members, it is not surprising that Penn, despite his Quakerism, remained a favorite of Charles II. More surprising is that the king's favor took the extravagant form of presenting Penn in 1681 with all the land between New Jersey and Maryland. Perhaps the king was repaying Penn for the large sum that his father had lent the Stuarts. Or perhaps the king was hoping to export England's Quakers to an American colony governed by his trusted personal friend.

Penn envisioned that his proprietary colony would provide a refuge for Quakers while producing quitrents for himself. To publicize his settlement, he distributed pamphlets praising its attractions throughout the British Isles and Europe. The response was overwhelming: by 1700 its population stood at 21,000. The only early migration of equal magnitude was the Puritan colonization of New England.

Patterns of Settlement

Perhaps half of Pennsylvania's settlers arrived as indentured servants, while the families of free farmers and artisans made up the rest. The majority were Quakers from Britain, Holland, and Germany, but the colonists also included Catholics, Lutherans, Baptists, Anglicans, and Presbyterians. In 1682 when Penn purchased and annexed the Three Lower Counties (later the colony of Delaware), his settlement included the Dutch, Swedes, and Finns living there, about 1000 people.

Quakers from other colonies—West Jersey, Maryland, and New England—also flocked to the new homeland. Those experienced settlers brought skills and connections that contributed to Pennsylvania's rapid economic growth. Farmers sowed their rich lands into a sea of wheat, which merchants exported to the Caribbean. The center of the colony's trade was Philadelphia, a superb natural harbor situated at the confluence of the Delaware and Schuylkill rivers.

In contrast to New England's landscape of villages, the Pennsylvania countryside beyond Philadelphia was dotted with dispersed farmsteads. Commercial

The tidy, productive farmsteads of the Pennsylvania countryside were the basis of that colony's prosperity during the eighteenth century. Their produce fueled the growth of Philadelphia and sustained the expansion of sugar plantations on England's Caribbean islands.

agriculture required larger farms, which kept settlers at greater distances from one another. As a result, the county rather than the town became the basic unit of local government in Pennsylvania.

Another reason that farmers did not need to cluster their homes within a central village was that the coastal Indians, the Lenni Lenapes (also called Delawares by the English), posed no threat. Thanks to two of the odder Quaker beliefs—their commitment to pacifism and their conviction that the Indians rightfully owned their land—peace prevailed between native inhabitants and newcomers. Before Penn sold any land to white settlers, he purchased it from the Indians. He also prohibited the sale of alcohol to the tribe, strictly regulated the fur trade, and learned the language of the Lenni Lenapes. "Not a language spoken in Europe," he remarked, "hath words of more sweetness in Accent and Emphasis than theirs."

Quakers and Indians

"Our Wildernesse flourishes as a Garden," Penn declared late in 1683, and in fact, his colony lived up to its promises. New arrivals readily acquired good land on liberal terms, while Penn's Frame of Government instituted a representative assembly and guaranteed all inhabitants the basic English civil liberties and complete freedom of worship.

Quakers and Politics

Even so, Penn's colony suffered constant political strife. Rich investors whom he had rewarded with large tracts of land and trade monopolies dominated the council, which held the sole power to initiate legislation. That power and Penn's own claims as proprietor set the stage for controversy. Members of the representative assembly battled for the right to initiate legislation. Farmers opposed Penn's efforts to collect quitrents. The Three Lower Counties agitated for separation, their inhabitants feeling no loyalty to Penn or Quakerism.

Penn finally bought peace at the price of approving a complete revision of his original Frame of Government. In 1701 the Charter of Privileges, Pennsylvania's new constitution, stripped the council of its legislative power, leaving it only the role of advising the governor. The charter also limited Penn's privileges as proprietor to the ownership of ungranted land and the power to veto legislation. Thereafter an elective unicameral assembly, the only single-house legislature in the colonies, dominated Pennsylvania's government.

Penn's compromises

As Pennsylvania prospered, Philadelphia became the commercial and cultural center of England's North American empire. Gradually the interior of Pennsylvania filled with immigrants—mainly Germans and Scots-Irish—who harbored no "odd" ideas about Indian rights, and the Lenni Lenapes and other tribes were bullied into moving farther west. As for William Penn, he returned to England and spent time in a debtors' prison after being defrauded by his unscrupulous colonial agents. He died in 1718, an ocean away from his American utopia.

Adjustment to Empire

In the year 1685, from the city of London, a new English king surveyed his American domains. The former Duke of York, now James II, had hoped that America might contribute to the making of kings and queens. Like earlier Stuart monarchs, James hoped to ride to absolute power on a wave of colonial wealth, just as Spain's monarchs had during the previous century. To encourage colonial settlement, Stuart kings had chartered the private trading companies of Virginia, Plymouth,

England, in an effort to regulate colonial trade, required all ships bound from America to pass through British ports and pay customs duties. Places like Plymouth, Liverpool, and Bristol (shown here) thrived as a result. Contrast this large, bustling commercial center with the modest size of Plymouth 200 years earlier (illustration, page 27).

and Massachusetts Bay. They had rewarded their aristocratic favorites with huge tracts of land—Maryland, the Carolinas, New York, New Jersey, and Pennsylvania.

Yet to what end? Although North America now abounded in places named in honor of English monarchs, the colonies themselves lacked any strong ties to the English state. In only three colonies—New Hampshire, New York, and Virginia—did England exercise direct control through royally appointed governors and councils. Until Parliament passed the first Navigation Acts in 1660, England had not even set in place a coherent policy for regulating colonial trade. Even more disheartening, ungrateful colonists were resisting their duty to enrich the English state and the Stuarts. While Chesapeake planters grumbled over the customs duties levied on tobacco, New Englanders, the worst of the lot, ignored the Navigation Acts altogether and traded openly with the Dutch. New Yorkers were turning out just as badly, as James, the first proprietor of that colony, recalled all too well. Even in recently settled colonies like New Jersey, the Carolinas, and Pennsylvania, the stirrings of opposition to royally appointed proprietors did not bode well.

Control over the colonies tightened

What was needed, in James's view, was an assertion of royal authority over America, starting with Massachusetts. His brother, Charles II, had laid the groundwork in 1673 by persuading Parliament to authorize the placement of customs agents in colonial ports to suppress illegal trade. Charles also formed the Lords of Trade and Plantations, a committee to oversee colonial affairs. When reports of defiance continued to surface, the king delivered the decisive blow: an English court in 1684 revoked Massachusetts' original charter, leaving the Bay Colony without a legal basis for its claim to self-government.

The Dominion of New England

Charles died the following year, leaving James II to finish the job of reorganization. In 1686, at the king's urging, the Lords of Trade consolidated the colonies of Connecticut, Plymouth, Massachusetts Bay, Rhode Island, and New Hampshire into a single entity to be ruled by a royal governor and a royally appointed council. By 1688 James had added New York and New Jersey to that domain, now called the

Dominion of New England. Showing the typical Stuart distaste for representative government, James also abolished all northern colonial assemblies. The king's aim to centralize authority over such a large territory made the Dominion not only a royal dream but a radical experiment in English colonial administration.

Sir Edmund Andros, a tough professional soldier sent to Boston as the Dominion's royal governor, quickly came to rival his king for the title of most unpopular man north of Pennsylvania. Andros set in force policies that outraged every segment of New England society. He strictly enforced the Navigation Acts, which slowed down commerce and infuriated merchants and workers in the maritime trades. He commandeered a Boston meetinghouse for Anglican worship and immediately angered devout Congregationalists. He abolished all titles to land granted under the old charter, alarming farmers and speculators. He imposed arbitrary taxes, censored the press, and forbade all town meetings, thereby alienating almost everyone.

Edmund Andros

The Aftershocks of the Glorious Revolution

About the same time that northern colonials were reaching the end of their patience with Andros, the English decided they had taken enough from his royal master. James II had revealed himself to be yet another Stuart who tried to dispense with Parliament and who had embraced Catholicism besides. As it had before with Charles I, Parliament dispensed with the king. In a quick, bloodless coup d'état known as the Glorious Revolution, Parliament forced James into exile in 1688. In his place it elevated to the throne of England his daughter, Mary, and her Dutch husband, William of Orange. Mary was a distinctly better sort of Stuart. A staunch Protestant, she agreed to rule with Parliament.

The deposing of James II proved so popular among New Englanders that even before Parliament had officially proclaimed William and Mary king and queen, Boston's militia seized Governor Andros and sent him home in April 1689. William and Mary officially dismembered the Dominion and reinstated representative assemblies everywhere in the northern colonies. Connecticut and Rhode Island were restored their old charters, but Massachusetts received a new charter in 1691. Under its terms Massachusetts, Plymouth, and present-day Maine were combined into a single royal colony headed by a governor appointed by the Crown rather than elected by the people. The charter also made property ownership rather than church membership the basis of voting rights and imposed religious toleration.

The Dominion overthrown

Leisler's Rebellion

The new charter did not satisfy all New Englanders, but they soon adjusted to the political realities of royal rule. In contrast, the violent political infighting that plagued New York mirrored that colony's instability.

Word of revolution in England and rebellion in Massachusetts roused New Yorkers into armed opposition in May 1689. Declaring their loyalty to William and Mary, the New York City militia forced from office Andros's second-in-command, the Dominion's lieutenant governor. In his place they installed one of their own leaders, Jacob Leisler, a German merchant.

Because James II had won few friends in New York, the rebellion met no opposition. But Leisler could not win commanding support for his authority. Although Protestant Dutch farmers, artisans, and small shopkeepers stood by him, the leaders of the colony—an intermarried elite of English and Dutch merchants—considered Leisler an upstart who threatened their own influence. After royal rule was restored to New York in 1691, a jury composed of Englishmen convicted Leisler and his son-in-law, Jacob Milburne, of treason. Their executions guaranteed a long life to the bitter political rivalries that Leisler's Rebellion had fueled in New York.

Royal Authority in America in 1700

Closer regulation of trade

In the wake of upheaval at home and in North America, England focused its imperial policy on reaping maximum profit from the colonial trade. In 1696 Parliament enlarged the number of customs officials stationed in each colony to enforce the Navigation Acts. To help prosecute smugglers, Parliament established colonial vice-admiralty courts, tribunals without juries presided over by royally appointed justices. To keep current on all colonial matters, the king appointed a new Board of Trade to replace the old Lords of Trade. The new enforcement procedures generally succeeded in discouraging smuggling and channeling colonial trade through England.

That was enough for England and its monarchs for half a century thereafter. English kings and queens gave up any dreams of imposing the kind of centralized administration of colonial life that James II had attempted in his Dominion of New England. To be sure, royal control had increased over the previous half century. By 1700 royal governments had been established in Virginia, New York, Massachusetts, and New Hampshire. New Jersey, the Carolinas, and Georgia would shortly be added to the list. Royal rule meant that the monarch appointed governors and (everywhere except Massachusetts) also appointed their councils. Royally appointed councils could veto any law passed by a colony's representative assembly, royally appointed governors could veto any law passed by both houses, and the Crown could veto any law passed by both houses and approved by the governor.

The limits of royal power

Despite the ability to veto, the sway of royal power remained more apparent than real after 1700. The Glorious Revolution asserted once and for all that Parliament's authority—rule by the legislative branch of government—would be supreme in the governing of England. In the colonies members of representative assemblies grew more skilled at dealing with royal governors and more protective of their rights. They guarded most jealously their strongest lever of power—the right of the lower houses to levy taxes.

The political reality of the assemblies' power reflected a social reality as well. No longer mere outposts along the Atlantic, the colonies of 1700 were becoming more firmly rooted societies. Their laws and traditions were based not only on what they had brought from England but also on the conditions of life in America. That social reality had already blocked Stuart ambitions to shape the future of North America, just as it had thwarted the designs of lordly proprietors and the dreams of religious reformers.

Still, the dream of empire would revive among England's rulers in the middle of the eighteenth century—in part because the same dream had never died among the rulers of France. By 1663, Louis XIV had decided that kings could succeed where the enterprise of private French traders had failed: he placed New France under royal rule. Thereafter France's fortunes in America steadily improved. Soldiers strengthened Canada's defenses, colonists and traders expanded the scope of French influence, and the Jesuits made more converts among the tribes of the interior. Under the Sun King, as Louis was known to admiring courtiers, royal rule became absolute, and the hopes for empire grew absolutely. Louis and his heirs would continue their plans for the making of France by contending for empire with the English, both in the Old World and in the New.

chapter summary

While the Catholic Counter-Reformation encouraged the French colonization of Canada, the Protestant Reformation in England spurred the settlement of New England and Pennsylvania.

- During the seventeenth century, the French slowly established a fur trade, agricultural communities, and religious institutions in Canada.

- Over the same period, English Puritans planted more populous settlements between Maine and Long Island.

- The migration of family groups and a rough equality of wealth lent stability to early New England society, reinforced by the settlers' shared commitment to Puritanism and a strong tradition of self-government.

- The mid-Atlantic colonies also enjoyed a rapid growth of people and wealth, but political wrangling as well as ethnic and religious diversity made for a higher level of social conflict.

- Whereas New Englanders attempted to subdue native peoples, white settlers in the mid-Atlantic colonies enjoyed more harmonious relations with local Indian tribes.

- The efforts of the later Stuart kings to centralize England's empire ended with the Glorious Revolution in 1688, which greatly reduced tensions between the colonies and the parent country.

interactive learning

The Primary Source Investigator CD-ROM offers the following materials related to this chapter:

- Interactive maps: **The Atlantic World, 1400–1850** (M2) and **Salem Witchcraft** (M4)

- A short documentary movie on the Salem witchcraft crisis of 1692 (D1)

- A collection of primary sources about the development of the English colonies from hardscrabble outposts into thriving and complex societies: models of a colonial dwelling, an image of a New England garrison home, a poem describing life in servitude, and plans and maps of colonial urban centers. The expansion of European settlement did not come without resistance from Native Americans, and several sources shed light on those ever-deepening cultural tensions: an engraving of a Pequot village being destroyed by English colonists, a legal agreement between Indians and colonists, and Puritan William Bradford's remarks on the wilderness. A number of other sources examine the Salem witchcraft crisis.

additional reading

James Axtell, *The Invasion Within* (1985), offers a readable and fascinating account of relations between northern Indian tribes and French and English colonials. The best introductions to Puritanism are still Francis Bremer, *The Puritan Experiment* (1976); and Edmund S. Morgan, *The Puritan Dilemma* (1958), but David Hall, *Worlds of Wonder, Days of Judgment* (1989), provides the best coverage of the religious experiences and supernatural beliefs of ordinary New Englanders.

There are many studies of individual New England communities, but the classic account of local political and social life remains Kenneth Lockridge, *A New England Town* (1970). Family life and women's experience in the early northern colonies are ably described by Laurel Ulrich, *Good Wives* (1982), and by Barry Levy's provocative study of Pennsylvania, *Quakers and the American Family* (1988). David Lovejoy, *The Glorious Revolution in America* (1972), provides a useful overview of that event, but the most thoughtful assessment of British imperial policy in the late seventeenth century is Richard R. Johnson, *Adjustment to Empire* (1981). For a fuller list of readings, see the Bibliography at www.mhhe.com/davidsonnation5.

The ethnic and religious diversity of the mid-Atlantic region offers an intriguing and instructive contrast to the relative homogeneity of early New England. Among the recent studies that render memorable portraits of those complex societies in early New York are Donna Merwick, *Possessing Albany, 1630–1710* (1990), and Joyce Goodfriend, *Before the Melting Pot* (1991). For Pennsylvania, see the fine overview of Joseph Illick, *Colonial Pennsylvania* (1976), and the topical essays in Richard Dunn and Mary Maples Dunn, eds., *The World of William Penn* (1986). For a fuller list of readings, see the Bibliography at www.mhhe.com/davidson5.

significant events

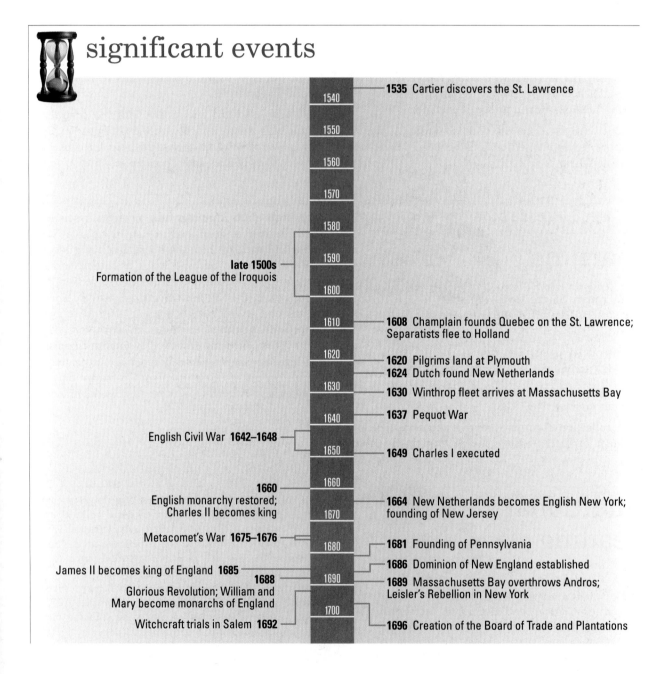

1535 Cartier discovers the St. Lawrence

late 1500s
Formation of the League of the Iroquois

1608 Champlain founds Quebec on the St. Lawrence; Separatists flee to Holland

1620 Pilgrims land at Plymouth
1624 Dutch found New Netherlands
1630 Winthrop fleet arrives at Massachusetts Bay

1637 Pequot War

English Civil War **1642–1648**

1649 Charles I executed

1660
English monarchy restored;
Charles II becomes king

1664 New Netherlands becomes English New York; founding of New Jersey

Metacomet's War **1675–1676**

1681 Founding of Pennsylvania

James II becomes king of England **1685**

1686 Dominion of New England established

1688
Glorious Revolution; William and Mary become monarchs of England

1689 Massachusetts Bay overthrows Andros; Leisler's Rebellion in New York

Witchcraft trials in Salem **1692**

1696 Creation of the Board of Trade and Plantations

Chapter 4

bout 150 Iroquois sat facing the colonial commissioners in Albany, New York, on the morning of June 29, 1754. In front of the governor's house, servants had set up rows of long wooden planks upon which the delegates from the Six Nations of the Iroquois now sat. The commissioners themselves, 25 in all, were not about to make do with planks; each had his own chair. They represented seven colonies, from Massachusetts Bay in the north to Maryland in the south.

Governor James DeLancey of New York stood and read a proclamation of welcome, pledging to "brighten the Chain of Friendship" between the Iroquois and the English. As each paragraph of the governor's speech was translated, the Iroquois were presented with a decorative belt, to which they responded with a ceremonial "Yo-heigh-eigh," shouted in unison. The noise unsettled those colonials attuned to the subtleties of Iroquois diplomacy. Normally, each nation voiced its agreement individually: six Yo-heigh-eighs coming one after another. By mixing them together, noted one observer, the delegates "had a mind to disguise that all the Nations did not universally give their hearty assent" to uniting with the English.

Unity—and not merely the unity of the Iroquois—was much on the mind of one commissioner from Philadelphia. Several chairs to the left of Governor DeLancey sat the most influential member of the Pennsylvania delegation, Benjamin Franklin. He knew that the question of whether the Iroquois would unite in an alliance with British America was only half the issue for this gathering at Albany. Equally important was whether the British colonies themselves could unite to deal effectively with France's threat throughout North America. Franklin had a plan for bringing the colonies together, but whether they would pay any notice remained an open question.

The Mosaic of Eighteenth-Century America

1689–1771

preview • British colonials were such a diverse, contentious lot that any hope of political union seemed utterly impractical. The most bitter conflicts sprang from sectional disputes between the established East and the back-country West. The South became more embattled too, as resistance increased among enslaved African Americans. Yet despite such disagreements, a majority of white colonials took pride in their English traditions and in membership in a powerful empire.

Rivalry between France and England

In a sense that plan grew out of a lifetime of experience, for the imperial rivalry between England and France had begun well before Franklin's birth and had flared, on and off, throughout his adult years. In 1689 England had joined the Netherlands and the League of Augsburg (several German-speaking states) in a war against France. While the main struggle raged on the continent of Europe, French and English colonials, joined by their Indian allies, skirmished in what was known as King William's War. Peace returned in 1697, but only until 1702, when the Anglo-French struggle resumed again, four years before Franklin was born. It continued throughout his boyhood, until 1713.

For a quarter of a century thereafter, the two nations waged a kind of cold war, competing for position and influence. At stake was not so much control over people or even territory as control over trade. In North America, France and

In the mid–eighteenth century, Philadelphia became the largest city in the colonies and the second largest in all the British empire. Its busy harbor served not only as a commercial hub but also as the disembarkation point for thousands of immigrants.

England vied for access to the sugar islands of the Caribbean, a monopoly on supplying manufactured goods to New Spain, and title to the fur trade. The British had the advantage of numbers: nearly 400,000 subjects in the colonies in 1720, compared with only about 25,000 French spread along a thin line of fishing stations and fur-trading posts. Yet the French steadily strengthened their chain of forts, stretching from the mouth of the Mississippi north through the Illinois country and into Canada. The forts helped channel the flow of furs from the Great Lakes and the Mississippi River valley into Canada, thus keeping them out of the clutches of English traders. And the forts neatly encircled England's colonies, confining their settlement to the eastern seaboard.

When fighting again engulfed Europe and the colonies in 1744, the results were inconclusive. King George's War, as the colonials dubbed it, ended four years later, but peace did nothing to diminish the old rivalry. As English traders and settlers filtered steadily into the Ohio River valley, the French built a new line of forts in 1752, from south of Lake Erie to the Ohio River. Two years later they erected Fort Duquesne at the strategic forks of the Ohio, flush against the border of Franklin's Pennsylvania. That startled Pennsylvania and other colonies into sending commissioners to Albany in 1754 to coordinate efforts to deal with the worsening crisis. Franklin put the message plainly in his newspaper, the *Pennsylvania Gazette,* in a cartoon of a snake cut into segments. It was inscribed "Join, or Die."

Throughout those years of imperial maneuvering, the Iroquois League maintained a cool neutrality. The Six Nations had become uneasy at the prospect of a North America without the French. Without French competition for Indian furs, what would spur British colonials to offer fair prices and trade goods of high quality? Without the arc of French settlement encircling the British American colonies, what would halt the westward spread of white settlement? Increasingly, too, the Iroquois were impressed by the show of French military might.

For the time being, the commissioners at Albany could do little to satisfy Iroquois doubts except lavish as much hospitality as their budgets would allow. In the end the Iroquois made vague promises of loyalty and then hauled away 30 wagons full of presents.

The Albany Plan of Union

But would the colonies themselves unite? On the way to the Albany Congress Franklin had sketched out a framework for colonial cooperation. He proposed establishing "one general government" for British North America—a federal council composed of representatives from each colony, presided over by a president-general appointed by the Crown. The council would assume all responsibility for colonial defense and Indian policy, building forts and patrolling harbors with taxes levied on all Americans. The commissioners were bold enough to accept the plan, alarmed by the wavering Iroquois and the looming French threat.

But the union born at Albany was smothered by the jealous colonies, who were unwilling to sing "yo-heigh-eigh" either in unison or separately. Not a single assembly approved the Albany Plan of Union. And no American legislature was ready to surrender its cherished right to tax inhabitants of its own colony—not to a federal council or to any other body. "Everyone cries, a union is necessary," Franklin wrote Governor Shirley of Massachusetts in disgust; "but when they come to the manner and form of the union, their weak noodles are perfectly distracted." If the Albany Congress proved one thing, it was that American colonials were hopelessly divided.

Forces of Division

Franklin, of course, should have known better than to hope for an intercolonial union. A practical man not given to idle dreams, he recognized the many forces of division at work in America. He knew that the colonies were divided by ethnic and regional differences as well as racial and religious prejudices. Year after year small wooden ships brought a bewildering variety of immigrants to American seaports—especially Philadelphia, where Franklin had lived since 1723. From his efforts to reorganize the post office Franklin knew, too, that Americans were separated by vast distances, poor transportation, and slow communications. He knew how suspicious the frontier districts remained of seaboard communities and how the eastern seaboard disdained the backcountry. Taken all in all, the British settlements in America were, in the eighteenth century, a diverse and divided lot.

Immigration and Natural Increase

One of the largest immigrant groups—250,000 black men, women, and children—had come to the colonies from Africa not by choice but in chains. White arrivals included many English immigrants but also a quarter of a million Scots-Irish, the descendants of seventeenth-century Scots who had regretted settling in northern Ireland; perhaps 135,000 Germans; and a sprinkling of Swiss, Swedes, Highland Scots, and Spanish Jews. Most non-English white immigrants were fleeing lives torn by famine, warfare, and religious persecution. All the voyagers, English and non-English, risked the hazardous Atlantic crossing (see Daily Lives, pages 114–115). Many had paid for passage by signing indentures to work as servants in America.

High birthrate

The immigrants and slaves who arrived in the colonies between 1700 and 1775 swelled an American population that was already growing dramatically from natural increase. The birthrate in eighteenth-century America was triple what it is today. Most women bore between five and eight children, and most children survived to maturity. Indeed, the social and political consequences of this population explosion so intrigued Franklin that he wrote an essay on the subject in 1751. He recognized that ethnic and religious diversity, coupled with the hectic pace of westward expansion after 1700, made it hard for colonials to share any common identity. Far from fostering political union, almost every aspect of social development set Americans at odds with one another.

The Settlement of the Backcountry

To white immigrants from Europe weary of war or worn by want, the seaboard's established communities must have seemed havens of order and stability. But by the beginning of the eighteenth century, even the children of longtime settlers could not acquire land along the coast. In older New England towns, three and four generations were putting pressure on a limited supply of land, while wasteful farming practices had depleted the soil of its fertility. Farther south, earlier settlers had already snatched up the farmland of Philadelphia's outlying counties, the prime Chesapeake tobacco property, and low-country rice swamps.

With older rural communities offering few opportunities to either native-born or newly arrived white families, both groups were forced to create new communities on the frontier. The peopling of New England's frontier—Maine, New Hampshire, and Vermont—was left mainly to the descendants of old Yankee families. Better opportunities for new immigrants to acquire land at cheaper prices lay south of New York. By the 1720s German and Scots-Irish immigrants as well as native-born settlers were pouring into western Pennsylvania. Some settled permanently, but others streamed southward into the backcountry of Virginia and the Carolinas, where they encountered native-born southerners pressing westward.

This log cabin, built in the North Carolina backcountry in 1782, would have been dark inside, given its lack of windows. The spaces between the logs in such cabins were usually chinked with thin stones or wedges of wood and then daubed with mortar.

Daily Lives

TIME AND TRAVEL
Transatlantic Trials

A mountain of water swelled from the Atlantic, towered over the *Jamaica Packet,* then toppled onto the small wooden passenger ship. The impact hurled Janet Schaw and her maid about their cabin like rag dolls. As seawater surged in, the two women struggled to grasp something, anything, to keep from drowning. The ship pitched wildly, "one moment mounted to the clouds and whirled on the pointed wave," the next plunging prow first into the heaving ocean. Four sailors lashed to the helm fought for control, while the rest of the crew worked with their hands "torn to pieces by the wet ropes." The ship's provisions—hogsheads of water, coops of chickens, and barrels of salted meat—snapped from their fastenings and careened across the deck before bouncing overboard.

For more than two days the *Jamaica Packet* hurtled in the gale's grip. Then its foremast splintered, and the ship flipped onto its side. Passengers, crew, and furniture crashed "heels over head to the side the vessel had laid down on." Schaw found herself "swimming amongst joint-stools, chests, [and] tables" in her cabin and listening to the sound of "our sails fluttering into rags." It would have been the end of the *Jamaica Packet* if, at that moment, its masts had not washed overboard. With the weight of the masts gone, the ship righted itself.

Schaw, "a lady of quality," as she described herself, was traveling by the finest accommodations from Great Britain to America in the age of sail. For those passengers who could not pay for a private cabin on the *Jamaica Packet,* the storm was worse. Twenty-two or more indentured servants from Scotland in that year of 1774 were bound aboard ship for the West Indies. Those impoverished families of farmers and fisherfolk had agreed with British merchants to work for American masters in return for the costs of passage. Like thousands of others who came to America in the eighteenth century, they were consigned to steerage, the between-decks area or "upper hold."

Perhaps four to five feet high, that space was crowded with narrow wooden bunks arranged in tiers about two feet apart. It was impossible for most people to stand in steerage or to sit up in a bunk, where as many as four people huddled together at night. Sanitary facilities consisted of a few wooden buckets filled with seawater; candles and fish-oil lanterns supplied the only light. The sole source of air was the hatch opening onto the deck.

Isolation of the backcountry

Backcountry settlers endured greater isolation than did other colonials. From many farmsteads it was a day's ride to the nearest courthouse; taverns and churches were often just as distant. Isolation hindered the formation of strong social bonds, as did the rapid rate at which people came to and left western communities. Many families pulled up stakes three or four times before settling permanently. Houses reflected that transience: most families crowded into one-room shacks walled with mud, turf, or crude logs.

The backcountry meant economic isolation as well. Large portions of the interior were cut off from water transport because they were located above the fall line, where rivers flowing to the Atlantic became unnavigable. By 1755 several crude wagon roads linked western Pennsylvania and Virginia to towns farther east, including Philadelphia, but transporting crops and driving livestock overland proved prohibitively expensive. Cut off from outside markets, farmers grew only enough to feed their households. Most backcountry inhabitants could not afford to invest in a slave or even a servant, so they relied on family labor alone to cultivate a small fraction of their farms' total acreage. Those conditions made the frontier, more than anywhere else in America, a society of equals.

When the storm struck, the hatch was fastened tightly to keep the holds from filling with water. But as waves dashed over the decks, water streamed into steerage, forcing its occupants to stand, clutching their children to keep them from being crushed or suffocated as the storm tumbled everyone from one side of their dark, watery prison to the other. For nine days they stood in water, without a fire or any food except raw potatoes and moldy biscuits. And they were without light or fresh air, except for one young man and his pregnant wife. During the storm the woman miscarried, and her "absolutely distracted" husband, Schaw reported, somehow forced open the hatch and carried her up to the deck, reviving the unconscious woman and saving her life. When at last the servants were allowed to come up on deck, they discovered that all their belongings had been swept overboard.

What followed the servants up to the deck, to the horror of all, was a stench "sufficient to raise a plague aboard." But the luck of the *Jamaica Packet* held, for it escaped not only shipwreck but epidemic disease. Passengers on other transatlantic voyages were not so fortunate. Throughout the eighteenth century notices of ships "lost at sea" or of passengers who slipped overboard in storms filled colonial newspapers. Outbreaks of epidemic disease—smallpox, influenza, typhus, and diphtheria—were common. Although there are no reliable statistics for shipboard mortality during the eighteenth century, estimates range from 3 percent of all passengers to as high as 10 to 15 percent, a rate nearly comparable to that for slave ships during the Middle Passage across the Atlantic.

For all who ventured abroad, transatlantic travel was tedious and dirty at best, hazardous and horrific at worst. Those who risked the crossing routinely made out wills and sought the prayers of loved ones. But disease and danger at sea took the greatest toll from the poor, indentured servants and convict laborers who made up the majority of eighteenth-century emigrants.

What the frontier gained in equality it may have lost in stability. In the backcountry there were no southern gentlemen or northern town fathers to supply continuous, experienced local leadership. There was only a handful of farmers in each county set above their neighbors by owning a few extra acres or a single slave. To these inexperienced and poorly educated men fell the tasks of overseeing public order as justices of the peace or officers in the local militia or representatives to colonial assemblies. It was hard for those with so little authority over their fellows to police sprawling backcountry communities; not surprisingly, coarse and aggressive behavior dominated frontier life. Backcountry men and women mated out of wedlock, swore in public, drank to excess, and brawled at any provocation.

Nor were the churches much help in promoting law and order. Building churches lay beyond the means of many frontier communities, and few ministers were willing to endure the rigors of preaching from one backcountry neighborhood to another. While churches loomed large in the lives of Americans on the coast, most western families, although often deeply pious, had only occasional contact with organized religion.

Frontier women

Hard work dominated the lives of backcountry settlers. Besides doing the usual chores of farm women, western wives and daughters joined male family members in the fields. One traveler from the East expressed his astonishment at seeing German women in western Pennsylvania "at work abroad on the Farm mowing, Hoeing, Loading Dung into a Cart." Perhaps even more difficult to endure than the hard labor was the loneliness of many women's lives. The reactions of women to being resettled on the frontier can be imagined from the promise that one Scottish husband offered his wife: "We would get all these trees cut down . . . [so] that we would see from house to house."

Social Conflict on the Frontier

Despite the discomforts of frontier life, cheap land lured many families to the West. Benjamin Franklin had observed the hordes of Scots-Irish and German immigrants lingering in Philadelphia just long enough to scrape together the purchase price of a frontier farm. From Franklin's point of view, the backcountry performed a valuable service by siphoning off surplus people from congested eastern settlements. But he knew, too, that the frontier was an American Pandora's box. Once opened, the West unleashed discord, especially between the eastern seaboard and the backcountry.

The Paxton Boys

In Pennsylvania, Franklin himself mediated one such contest between East and West. In 1763 a band of Scots-Irish farmers known as "the Paxton Boys" protested the government's inadequate protection of frontier settlers by killing a number of Indians.

This cartoon supported the Paxton Boys by branding Quakers as treacherously sympathetic to frontier Indians. One Quaker, on the left, eagerly supplies Indians with tomahawks, while on the right another makes sexual advances to an Indian woman. Meanwhile Benjamin Franklin, center, offers a sack of money to buy off hostile Indians.

Then the Paxton Boys took their protests and their guns to Philadelphia, marching as far as Lancaster before Franklin intervened and promised redress of their grievances.

Strife between East and West was even deadlier and more enduring in North and South Carolina. In both colonies legislatures dominated by coastal planters refused to grant inland settlers equitable political representation or even basic legal institutions. In response to those injustices, two protest movements emerged in the Carolina interior, each known as the Regulation.

Farmers in the South Carolina backcountry organized their Regulation in the 1760s, after that colony's assembly refused to set up courts in the backcountry. Westerners were desperate for protection from outlaws who stole livestock, kidnapped and raped women, and tortured and murdered men. In the absence of courts the Regulators acted as vigilantes, meting out their own brand of grisly frontier justice against these criminals. Regulator threats to march on Charleston itself finally panicked eastern political leaders into extending the court system, but bitter memories lingered among westerners.

Regulation movements

Western North Carolinians organized their Regulation to protest not the absence of a legal system but the corruption of local government. Lawyers and merchants, backed by wealthy eastern planters, moved into the western parts of that colony and seized control of politics. Then they used those local offices to exploit frontier settlers, charging exorbitant fees for legal services, imposing high taxes, and manipulating debt laws. Western farmers responded to these abuses with the Regulation: they seized county courts and finally squared off against an eastern militia led by the governor. Easterners crushed the Regulators at the Battle of Alamance in 1771 but left frontier North Carolinians with an enduring hostility to the seaboard.

Ethnic differences heightened sectional tensions between East and West. People of English descent predominated along the Atlantic coast, whereas Germans, Scots-Irish, and other white minorities were concentrated in the interior. Many English colonials regarded these new immigrants as culturally inferior and politically subversive. Charles Woodmason, an Anglican missionary in the Carolina backcountry, lamented the arrival of "5 or 6000 Ignorant, mean, worthless, beggarly Irish Presbyterians, the Scum of the Earth, the Refuse of Mankind," who "delighted in a low, lazy, sluttish, heathenish, hellish life."

Ethnic conflicts

German immigrants were generally credited with having steadier work habits, as well as higher standards of sexual morality and personal hygiene. But like the clannish Scots-Irish, the Germans preferred to live, trade, and worship among themselves. By 1751 Franklin was warning that the Germans would retain their separate language and customs: the Pennsylvania English would be overrun by "the Palatine Boors."

Boundary Disputes and Tenant Wars

The settlement of the frontier also triggered disputes between colonies over their boundaries. At the root of the confusion were the old colonial charters and their vague definitions of western borders that allowed groups of settlers and speculators from different colonies to claim the same tract of land. The most serious of these border wars pitted New York against farmers from New England who had settled in present-day Vermont: Ethan Allen and the Green Mountain Boys. In the 1760s, New York, backed by the Crown, claimed land that Allen and his friends had already purchased from New Hampshire. When New York tried to extend its rule over Vermont, Allen led a successful guerrilla resistance, harassing Yorker settlers and officials, occupying Yorker courthouses, and setting up a competing judicial system in the Green Mountains.

Green Mountain Boys

Patterns of Settlement in the Eighteenth Century The French, English, and Indian nations all jockeyed for power and position across North America during the eighteenth century. The French expanded their fur trade through the interior while English settlement at midcentury began to press the barrier of the Appalachians. Many non-English settlers spilled into the backcountry: the Scots-Irish and Germans followed the Great Wagon Road through the western parts of the middle colonies and southern colonies while the Dutch and Germans moved up the Hudson River valley. Albany, where Franklin journeyed in 1754 for the Albany Congress, was one natural pivotal point in the rivalry—a place where Iroquois, French, and English interests converged.

The spread of settlement also set the stage for mass revolts by tenants in those areas where proprietors controlled vast amounts of land. In eastern New Jersey, proprietors insisted that squatters pay quitrents on land that had become increasingly populated and therefore more valuable. When the squatters, many of them migrants from New England, refused to pay rents, buy the land, or move, the proprietors began evictions, touching off riots in the 1740s. Tenant unrest also raged in New York's Hudson River valley. In the 1680s the royal governor had granted several prominent merchant families large estates in that region. By the middle of the eighteenth century, there were about 30 manors around New York City and Albany, totaling some 2 million acres and worked by several thousand tenants. Newcomers from New England, however, demanded to own land and preached their ideas to Dutch and German tenants. Armed insurrection exploded in 1757 and again, more violently, in 1766. Tenants refused to pay rents, formed mobs, and stormed the homes of landlords.

Eighteenth-Century Seaports

While most Americans on the move settled on the frontier, others swelled the populations of colonial cities. By present-day standards such cities were small, harboring from 8000 to 22,000 citizens by 1750. The scale of seaports remained intimate, too: all of New York City was clustered at the southern tip of Manhattan Island, and the length of Boston or Charleston could be walked in less than half an hour.

All major colonial cities were seaports, their waterfronts fringed with wharves and shipyards. A jumble of shops, taverns, and homes crowded their streets; the spires of churches studded their skylines. By the 1750s, the grandest and most populous was Philadelphia, which boasted straight, neatly paved streets, flagstone sidewalks, and three-story brick buildings. Older cities like Boston and New York had a more medieval aspect: most of their dwellings and shops were wooden structures with tiny windows and low ceilings, rising no higher than two stories to steeply pitched roofs. The narrow cobblestone streets of Boston and New York also challenged pedestrians, who competed for space with livestock being driven to the butcher, roaming herds of swine and packs of dogs, clattering carts, carriages, and horses.

The commercial classes

Commerce, the lifeblood of seaport economies, was managed by merchants who tapped the wealth of surrounding regions. Traders in New York and Philadelphia shipped the Hudson and Delaware valleys' surplus of grain and livestock to the West Indies. Boston's merchants sent fish to the Caribbean and Catholic Europe, masts to England, and rum to West Africa. Charlestonians exported indigo to English dyemakers and rice to southern Europe. Other merchants specialized in the import trade, selling luxuries and manufactured goods produced in England—fine fabrics, ceramics, tea, and farming implements. Wealth brought many merchants political power: they dominated city governments and shared power in colonial assemblies with lawyers and the largest farmers and planters.

Skilled craftworkers or artisans made up the middling classes of colonial cities. The households of master craftworkers usually included a few younger and less skilled journeymen working in other artisans' shops. Unskilled boy apprentices not only worked but also lived under the watchful eye of their masters. No large-scale domestic industry produced goods for a mass market: instead craft shops filled orders for specific items placed by individual purchasers. Some artisans specialized in the maritime trades as shipbuilders, blacksmiths, and sailmakers. Others, like butchers, millers, and distillers,

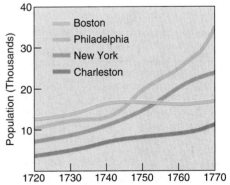

Estimated Population of Colonial Cities, 1720–1770 Although Boston's population remained stable after 1740, it was surpassed due to the sharp growth of New York and, especially, Philadelphia.

Estimated Population by Region, 1720–1760

processed and packed raw materials for export. Still others served the basic needs of city dwellers—the men and, occasionally, women who baked bread, mended shoes, combed and powdered wigs, and tended shops and taverns.

On the lowest rung of a seaport's social hierarchy were free and bound workers. Free laborers were mainly young white men and women—journeyman artisans, sailors, fishermen, domestic workers, seamstresses, and prostitutes. The ranks of unfree workers included apprentices and indentured servants doing menial labor in shops and on the docks.

Black men and women also made up a substantial part of the bound labor force of colonial seaports, not only in southern Charleston but in northern cities as well. Although the vast majority of slaves imported from Africa were destined for southern plantations, a smaller number were sold to urban merchants and craftworkers. Laboring as porters at the docks, as assistants in craft shops, or as servants in wealthy households, black residents made up almost 20 percent of the population in New York City and 10 percent in Boston and Philadelphia.

The character of slavery in northern seaports changed decisively during the mid–eighteenth century. When wars raging in Europe reduced the supply of white indentured servants, colonial cities imported a larger number of Africans. In the two decades after 1730, one-third of all immigrants arriving in New York harbor were black; by 1760, blacks constituted more than three-quarters of all bound laborers in Philadelphia. The preference for importing African men upset what had been an equal balance of black men and women in colonial seaports, making it difficult for the newcomers to establish families. Slaves from Africa also lacked immunity to American diseases, and many did not survive their first winter: the death rate among urban blacks was double that for whites.

But the survivors brought to urban black culture a new awareness of a common West African past. The influence of African traditions appeared most vividly in an annual event known as "Negro election day," celebrated in northern seaports.

Ashley Bowen, an eighteenth-century New Englander, made a drawing to commemorate his courtship of Dorothy Chadwick. Although she refused him at first (He: "Will thee consent to be my bride"; She: "Sir, I have not that Desire."), Bowen finally prevailed. Ashley's self-portrait, dominating both the sketch and the diminutive Dorothy, underscores colonial views of the relative status of men and women.

During the festival, similar to ones held in West Africa, some black men and women paraded in their masters' clothes or mounted on their horses. An election followed to choose black kings, governors, and judges who then held court and settled minor disputes among white and black members of the community. Negro election day did not challenge the established racial order with its temporary reversal of roles, but it did allow the black communities of seaports to honor their own leaders.

The availability of domestic workers, both black and white, made for leisured lives among women from wealthy white families. Even those city women who could not afford household help spent less time on domestic work than did farming wives and daughters. Although some housewives grew vegetables in backyard gardens or kept a few chickens, large markets stocked by outlying farmers supplied most of the food for urban families.

Women in cities

For women who had to support themselves, seaports offered a number of employments. Young single women from poorer families worked in wealthier households as maids, cooks, laundresses, seamstresses, or nurses. The highest-paying occupations for women, midwifery and dressmaking, both required long apprenticeships and expert skills. The wives of artisans and traders sometimes assisted their husbands and, as widows, often continued to manage groceries, taverns, and print shops. But most women were confined to caring for households, husbands, and children; fewer than 1 out of every 10 women in seaports worked outside their own homes.

Urban diversions and hazards

All seaport dwellers—perhaps 1 out of every 20 Americans—enjoyed a more stimulating environment than other colonials did. The wealthiest could attend an occasional ball or concert; those living in New York or Charleston might even see a play performed by touring English actors. The middling classes could converse with other tradespeople at private social clubs and fraternal societies. Men of every class found diversion in drink and cockfighting. Crowds of men, women, and children swarmed to tavern exhibitions of trained dogs and horses or the spectacular waxworks of one John Dyer, featuring "a lively Representation of Margaret, Countess of Herrinburg, who had 365 Children at one Birth."

But city dwellers, then as now, paid a price for their pleasures. Commerce was riddled with risk: ships sank and wars disrupted trade. When such disasters struck, the lower classes suffered most. The ups and downs of seaport economies, combined with the influx of immigrants, swelled the ranks of the poor in all cities by the mid–eighteenth century. Although the major seaports established workhouses to employ the able-bodied poor, city governments continued to aid most of the dependent with small subsidies of money, food, and firewood. Furthermore, epidemics and catastrophic fires occurred with greater frequency and produced higher mortality rates in congested seaports than in the countryside.

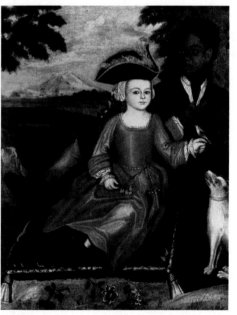

During the eighteenth century in both England and America, portraits of prominent white families and individuals sometimes included black slaves who served wealthy households. This portrait depicts a young child of New York's Van Rensselaer family and foretells his future mastery of both the young black male slave and, in the background, a fine estate in the Hudson River valley.

Social Conflict in Seaports

The swelling of seaport populations, like the movement of whites to the West, often churned up trouble. English, Scots-Irish, Germans, Swiss, Dutch, French, and Spanish jostled uneasily against one another in the close quarters of Philadelphia and New York. To make matters worse, religious differences heightened ethnic divisions. Jewish funerals in New York, for example, drew crowds of hostile and curious Protestants, who heckled the mourners.

Class resentment also stirred unrest. Some merchant families flaunted their wealth, building imposing town mansions and dressing in the finest imported fashions. During hard times, symbols of merchant wealth like expensive coaches and full warehouses became targets of mob vandalism. Crowds also gathered to intimidate and punish other groups who provoked popular hostility—unresponsive politicians, prostitutes, and "press gangs." Impressment, attempts to force colonials to serve in the British navy, triggered some of the most violent urban riots.

Slave Societies in the Eighteenth-Century South

Far starker than the inequalities and divisions among seaport dwellers were those between white and black in the South. By 1775 one out of every five Americans was of African ancestry, and more than 90 percent of all black Americans lived in the South, most along the seaboard. Here, on tobacco and rice plantations, slaves fashioned a distinctive African American society and culture. But they were able to build stable families and communities only late in the eighteenth century and against enormous odds.

The Chesapeake versus the Lower South

Whether a slave was auctioned off to the Chesapeake or to the Lower South shaped his or her future in important ways. Slaves in the low country of South Carolina and Georgia lived on large plantations with as many as 50 other black workers, about half of whom were African-born. They had infrequent contact with

Distribution of the American Population, 1775 The African American population expanded dramatically during the eighteenth century, especially in the southern colonies. The high volume of slave imports accounts for most of the growth in the first half of the century, but natural increase was responsible for the rising black population during later decades.

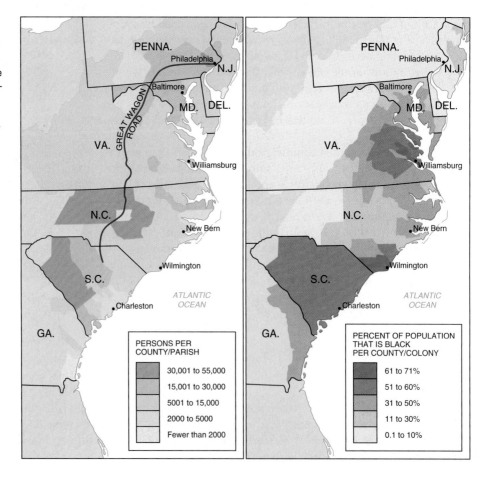

either their masters or the rest of the sparse white population. "They are as 'twere, a Nation within a Nation," observed Francis LeJau, an Anglican priest in the low country. And their work was arduous, for rice required constant cultivation. Black laborers tended young plants and hoed fields in the sweltering summer heat of the mosquito-infested lowlands. During the winter and early spring, they built dams and canals to regulate the flow of water into the rice fields. But the use of the "task system" rather than gang labor widened the window of freedom within slavery. When a slave had completed his assigned task for the day, one planter explained, "his master feels no right to call upon him."

Many Chesapeake slaves, like those in the Lower South, were African-born, but most lived on smaller plantations with fewer than 20 fellow slaves. Less densely concentrated than in the low country, Chesapeake slaves also had more contact with whites. Unlike Carolina's absentee owners, who left white overseers and black drivers to run their plantations, Chesapeake masters actively managed their estates and subjected their slaves to closer scrutiny.

The Slave Family and Community

The four decades following 1700 marked the heaviest years of slave importation into the Chesapeake and Carolina regions. Those Africans had survived the trauma of captivity, the Middle Passage, and sale at slave auctions only to be thrust into a bewildering new world: a sea of unfamiliar faces, a clamor of different languages, a host of demands from men and women who called themselves masters.

The newcomers also had to adjust to their fellow slaves. The "new Negroes" hailed from a number of diverse West African tribes, each with a separate language or dialect and distinctive cultures and kinship systems. Often, they had little in common with one another and even less in common with the American-born black minority. Native-born African Americans enjoyed better health, command of English, and experience in dealing with whites. They were also more likely to enjoy a family life, for their advantages probably made them the preferred partners of black women, who were outnumbered two to one by black men. And since immigrant women waited two or three years before marrying, some immigrant men died before they could find a wife, and many never married. Africans resented native-born men as rivals in the competition for wives, and some immigrants held in particular contempt native converts to Christianity.

African slaves versus American-born slaves

After the middle of the eighteenth century, a number of changes fostered the growth of black families and the vitality of slave communities. As slave importations began to taper off, the rate of natural reproduction among blacks started to climb. As the proportion of new Africans dropped and the number of native-born black Americans grew, the ratio of men to women in the slave community became more equal. Those changes and the appearance of more large plantations, even in the Chesapeake, created more opportunities for black men and women to find partners and form families. Elaborate kinship networks gradually developed, often extending over several plantations in a single neighborhood. And as the immigrant generations were replaced by native-born offspring, earlier sources of tension and division within the slave community disappeared.

Even so, black families remained vulnerable. If a planter fell on hard times, members of black families might be sold off to different buyers to meet his debts. When an owner died, black spouses, parents, and children might be divided among surviving heirs. Even under the best circumstances, fathers might be hired out to other planters for long periods or sent to work in distant quarters. The migration

The Old Plantation affords a rare glimpse of life in the slave quarters. At this festive gathering, both men and women dance to the music of a molo (a stringed instrument similar to a banjo) and drums. Below is a gudugudu drum, an instrument common throughout West Africa and similar to the drum depicted (far right) in the painting.

of slaveholders from the coast to the interior also disrupted black efforts to fashion domestic and communal bonds. Between 1755 and 1782, masters on the move resettled fully one-third of all adult African Americans living in Tidewater, Virginia. Most slaves forced to journey west were men and women in their teens and early twenties, who had to begin again the long process of establishing families and neighborhood networks far from kin and friends.

Black families struggling with terrible uncertainties were sustained by the distinctive African American culture evolving in the slave community. The high percentage of native Africans among the eighteenth-century American black population made it easier for slaves to retain the ways of their lost homeland. Christianity won few converts, in part because white masters feared that baptizing slaves might make them more rebellious but also because African Americans preferred their traditional religions. African influence appeared as well in the slaves' agricultural skills and practices, folktales, music, and dances.

Slavery and Colonial Society in French Louisiana

The experience of Africans unfolded differently in the lower Mississippi Valley, France's southernmost outpost in eighteenth-century North America. Louisiana's earliest colonial settlements were begun by a few thousand French soldiers, indentured servants, and free settlers who had straggled down from Canada, and by immigrants who came from France and Germany. When they founded New Orleans in 1718 the colonists, hoping to create prosperous plantations in the surrounding Mississippi delta, immediately clamored for bound laborers. A year later, French authorities bent to their demands, and the Company of the Indies, which managed France's slave trade, brought nearly 6000 slaves, overwhelmingly men, directly from Africa to Louisiana. Yet even with this influx of new laborers, the search for a cash crop eluded white planters, whose tobacco and, later, indigo proved inferior to the varieties exported from Britain's colonies.

Louisiana's socially mixed society is evident from this market scene: the buyers and sellers include Indians as well as colonials of French, Spanish, and African descent.

Instead of proving the formula for economic success, the sudden influx of Africans challenged French control. In 1729, with blacks already constituting a majority of the population, some newly arrived slaves joined forces with the Natchez Indians, who feared the expansion of white settlement. Their rebellion, the Natchez Revolt, left 200 French planters dead—more than 10 percent of the European population of Louisiana. The French retaliated in a devastating counterattack, enlisting both the Choctaw Indians, who were rivals of the Natchez, and other enslaved blacks, who were promised freedom in return for their support.

Natchez Revolt

The planters' costly victory persuaded French authorities to stop importing slaves into Louisiana, which helped to ensure that the colony did not develop a plantation economy until the end of the eighteenth century, when the cotton boom transformed its culture. In the meantime, blacks continued to make up a majority of all Louisianans, and by the middle of the eighteenth century, nearly all were native-born. The vast majority were slaves, but their work routines—tending cattle, cutting timber, producing naval stores, manning boats—afforded them greater freedom of movement than most slaves enjoyed elsewhere in the American South. They were also encouraged to market the produce of their gardens, hunts, and handicrafts, which became the basis of a thriving trade with both white settlers and the dwindling numbers of Native Americans. But the greatest prize—freedom—was awarded those black men who served in the French militia, defending the colony from the English and Indians as well as capturing slave runaways. The descendants of these black militiamen would become the core of Louisiana's free black community.

Greater freedom for blacks in Louisiana

Slave Resistance in Eighteenth-Century British North America

British North America had no comparable group of black soldiers, but it also had no shortage of African Americans who both resisted captivity and developed strategies for survival. Among newly arrived Africans, collective attempts at escape were most common. Groups of slaves, often made up of newcomers from the same tribe, fled inland and formed "Maroon" communities of runaways. These efforts were usually unsuccessful because the Maroon settlements were large enough to be easily detected.

More acculturated blacks adopted subtler ways of subverting slavery. Domestics and field hands alike faked illness, feigned stupidity and laziness, broke tools, pilfered from storehouses, hid in the woods for weeks at a time, or simply took off to visit other plantations. Other slaves, usually escaping bondage as solitary individuals, found a new life as craftworkers, dock laborers, or sailors in the relative anonymity of colonial seaports.

The Stono Rebellion

More infrequently, black rebellion took direct and violent form. Whites in communities with large numbers of blacks lived in gnawing dread of arson, poisoning, and insurrection. Four slave conspiracies were reported in Virginia during the first half of the eighteenth century. In South Carolina, more than two decades of abortive uprisings and insurrection scares culminated in the Stono Rebellion of 1739, the largest slave revolt of the colonial period. Nearly 100 African Americans, led by a slave named Jemmy, seized arms from a store in the coastal district of Stono and killed several white neighbors before they were caught and killed by the white militia.

But throughout the eighteenth century, slave rebellions occurred far less frequently on the mainland of North America than in the Caribbean or Brazil. Whites outnumbered blacks in all of Britain's mainland colonies except South Carolina, and only there did rebels have a haven for a quick escape—Spanish Florida. Faced with those odds, most slaves reasoned that the risks of rebellion outweighed the prospects for success—and most sought opportunities for greater personal freedom within the slave system itself.

Despite the growing rebelliousness of black slaves, southern planters continued to import Africans throughout the eighteenth century. The practice mystified Franklin, revealing at least one gap in his knowledge—the crucial importance of slavery in the southern economy. But unlike some of his Quaker neighbors in Pennsylvania, who were beginning to object to slavery on moral and humanitarian grounds, Franklin's reservations—like his opposition to German immigration—were overtly racist. "Why increase the sons of Africa by planting them in America," he asked, "where we have so fair an opportunity, by excluding all blacks and tawnys, of increasing the lovely white and red?"

Enlightenment and Awakening in America

The differences among eighteenth-century colonials resulted in more than clashes between regions, races, classes, and ethnic groups. Those differences also made for diversity in the ways that Americans thought and believed. City dwellers were more attuned to European culture than were people living in small villages or on the frontier. White males from well-to-do families of English ancestry were far more likely to receive college educations than were those from poorer or immigrant households. White women of every class and background were excluded from higher education, and slaves received no formal education at all. Where they lived, how well they lived, whether they were male or female, native-born or immigrant, slave or free—all these variables fostered among colonials distinctive worldviews, differing attitudes and assumptions about the individual's relationship to nature, society, and God.

The Enlightenment in America

The diversity of colonials' inner lives became even more pronounced during the eighteenth century because of the Enlightenment, an intellectual movement that started in Europe during the seventeenth century. The leading figures of the Enlightenment, the philosophes, stressed the power of human reason to promote progress by revealing the laws that governed both nature and society. In the American colonies the Enlightenment influenced some curious artisans in major seaports and some wealthy merchants, lawyers, and landowners with the leisure and education to read the latest books from Europe.

Like many devotees of the Enlightenment, Franklin was most impressed by its emphasis on useful knowledge and experimentation. He pondered air currents and then invented a stove that heated houses more efficiently. He toyed with electricity and then invented lightning rods to protect buildings in thunderstorms. Other amateur colonial scientists constructed simple telescopes, classified animal species native to North America, or sought to explain epidemics in terms of natural causes.

Higher education helped spread Enlightenment ideas among young colonials from affluent families. Although many Americans were still educated at English universities, six colleges had been established in the colonies by 1763. The founders of some of these institutions, such as Harvard (1636) and Yale (1701), had intended them primarily to train ministers, but by the eighteenth century their graduates included lawyers, merchants, doctors, and scientists. Most offered courses in mathematics and the natural sciences that taught students algebra and such advanced theories as Copernican astronomy and Newtonian physics.

Some clergy educated at American colleges were touched by the Enlightenment, adopting a more liberal theology that stressed the reasonableness of Christian beliefs. By the middle of the eighteenth century this "rational Christianity" commanded a small following among colonials, usually Anglicans or liberal Congregationalists. Their God was not the Calvinists' awesome deity but a benevolent creator who offered salvation to all, not just to a small, predestined elite. They believed that God's greatest gift to humankind was reason, which enabled all human beings to follow the moral teachings of Jesus. They muted the Calvinist emphasis on human sinfulness and the need for a soul-shattering conversion.

Rational versus traditional Christianity

Enlightenment philosophy and rational Christianity did not affect the outlook of most colonials. By the middle of the eighteenth century, more than half of all white men (and a smaller percentage of white women) were literate, but most colonial readers were not equipped to tackle the learned writings of Enlightenment philosophes. As a result, the outlook of most colonials contrasted sharply with that of the cosmopolitan few. The great majority of Americans still looked for ultimate truth in biblical revelation rather than human reason and explained the workings of the world in terms of divine providence rather than natural law.

Widespread attachment to traditional Christian beliefs was strengthened by the hundreds of new churches built during the first half of the eighteenth century. Church attendance ran highest in the northern colonies, where some 80 percent of the population turned out for public worship on the Sabbath. In the South, because of the greater distances involved and the shortage of clergy, about half of all colonials regularly attended Sunday services.

Despite the prevalence of traditional religious beliefs, many ministers expressed concern about the dangerous influence of rational Christianity. They also worried that the lack of churches might tempt many frontier families to abandon Christianity altogether. Exaggerated as these fears may have been, the consequence was a major religious revival that swept the colonies during the middle decades of the eighteenth century.

The First Great Awakening

The Great Awakening, as the revival came to be called, deepened the influence of older forms of Protestant Christianity and, specifically, Calvinism throughout British America. Participation in the revival was the only experience that a large number of people everywhere in the colonies had in common.

George Whitefield drew critics as well as admirers in both England and America. In this satirical English cartoon, he is depicted as a moneygrubbing evangelist who uncharitably condemns other ministers. His audience, which consists mainly of women, is taken in by his pose of sanctity and his youthful good looks.

The first stirrings of revival appeared in the 1730s among Presbyterians and Congregationalists in the Middle Colonies and New England. Many ministers in these churches preached an "evangelical" message, emphasizing the need for individuals to experience "a new birth" through religious conversion. Among them was Jonathan Edwards, the pastor of a Congregational church in Northampton, Massachusetts. Edwards's preaching combined moving descriptions of God's grace with terrifying portrayals of eternal damnation. "The God that holds you over the pit of hell, much as one holds a spider or some loathsome insect over the fire, abhors you and is dreadfully provoked," he declaimed to one congregation. "There is no other reason to be given, why you have not dropped into hell since you arise in the morning, but that God's hand has held you up."

These local revivals of the 1730s were mere tremors compared to the earthquake of religious enthusiasm that shook the colonies with the arrival in the fall of 1739 of George Whitefield. This handsome, cross-eyed "boy preacher" from England electrified crowds from Georgia to New Hampshire during his two-year tour of the colonies. He and his many imitators among colonial ministers turned the church into a theater, enlivening sermons with dramatic gestures, flowing tears, and gruesome depictions of hell's torments. The drama of such performances appealed to people of all classes, ethnic groups, and races. By the time Whitefield sailed back to England in 1741, thousands of awakened souls were joining older churches or forming new ones.

The Aftermath of the Great Awakening

Whitefield also left behind a raging storm of controversy. Many "awakened" church members now openly criticized their ministers as cold, unconverted, and uninspiring. To supply the missing fire, some laymen—"and even Women and Common Negroes"—took to "exhorting" any audience willing to listen. The most popular ministers became "itinerants," traveling like Whitefield from one town to another. Throughout the colonies the more rationalist and moderate clergy questioned the unrestrained emotionalism and the disorder that attended the gatherings of lay exhorters and itinerants.

Religious divisions

Although Americans had been fighting over religion well before the Great Awakening, the new revivals left colonials even more divided along religious lines. The largest single group of churchgoers in the northern colonies remained within the Congregational and Presbyterian denominations. But both these groups split into factions that either supported or condemned the revivals. Some conservative Presbyterians and Congregationalists, disgusted with the disorder, defected to the Quakers and the Anglicans, who had shunned the revival. On the other hand, the most radical converts joined forces with the warmest champions of the Awakening, the Baptists.

Evangelicalism on the frontier

While northern churches splintered and bickered, the fires of revivalism spread to the South and its backcountry. From the mid-1740s until the 1770s, scores of new Presbyterian and Baptist churches were formed, but conflict often accompanied religious zeal. Ardent Presbyterians in the Carolina backcountry disrupted Anglican worship by loosing packs of dogs in local chapels. In northern Virginia, Anglicans took the offensive against the Baptists, whose strict moral code sounded a silent reproach to the hard-drinking, high-stepping, horse-racing, slaveholding gentry. County officials, prodded by resentful Anglican parsons, harassed, fined, and imprisoned Baptist ministers.

While the West was turning toward evangelical Calvinism, the most powerful people on the southeastern coast remained Anglican and, in the Middle Colonies, Quaker. As a result, the seaboard and the backcountry often found themselves quarreling over religious as well as political and ethnic issues. Inevitably, civil governments were drawn into the fight. In colonies in which one denomination received state support, other churches lobbied legislatures for disestablishment, an end to the favored status of Congregationalism in Connecticut and Massachusetts and of Anglicanism in the southern colonies.

And so a diverse lot of Americans found themselves continually at odds with one another. Because of differences in religion and education, colonials quarreled over whether rational Christianity enlightened the world or emotional revivalists destroyed its order. Because of ethnic and racial tensions, Spanish Jews found themselves persecuted, and African Americans searched for ways to resist their white masters. Because of westward expansion, Carolina Regulators waged war against coastal planters while colonial legislatures from Massachusetts to Virginia quarreled over western boundaries.

Colonial diversity: a summary

Benjamin Franklin, a man who made it his business to know, surely understood the depth of those divisions as he made his way toward the Albany Congress in the spring of 1754. He himself had brooded over the boatloads of non-English newcomers. He had lived in two booming seaports and felt the explosive force of the frontier. He personified the Enlightenment—and he had heard George Whitefield himself preach from the steps of the Philadelphia courthouse.

Why, then, could Franklin, who knew how little held the colonials together, sustain his hopes for political unity? The answer may be that even in 1754, the majority of colonials were of English descent. And these free, white Americans liked being English. That much they had in common.

Most Americans prided themselves on being English. When colonials named their towns and counties, they named them after places in their parent country. When colonials established governments, they turned to England for their political models. They frequently claimed "the liberties of freeborn Englishmen" as their birthright. Even in diet, dress, furniture, architecture, and literature, colonists adopted English standards of taste.

Anglo-American Worlds of the Eighteenth Century

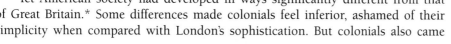

Yet American society had developed in ways significantly different from that of Great Britain.* Some differences made colonials feel inferior, ashamed of their simplicity when compared with London's sophistication. But colonials also came

---

*When England and Scotland were unified in 1707, the nation as a whole became known officially as Great Britain; its citizens, as British.

Coffeehouses such as this establishment in London were favorite gathering places for eighteenth-century Americans visiting Britain. Here merchants and mariners, ministers and students, lobbyists and tourists warmed themselves, read newspapers, and exchanged gossip about commerce, politics, and social life.

to appreciate the greater equality of their society and the more representative character of their governments. If it was good to be English, it was better still to be English in America.

English Economic and Social Development

The differences between England and America began with their economies. Large financial institutions like the Bank of England and influential corporations like the East India Company were driving England's commercial development. A growing number of textile factories and mines were deepening its industrial development. Although most English men and women worked at agriculture, it, too, had become a business. Members of the gentry rented their estates to tenants, members of the rural middle class. In turn, these tenants hired men and women from the swollen ranks of England's landless to perform the actual farm labor. In contrast, most colonial farmers owned their land, and most family farms were a few hundred acres. The scale of commerce and manufacturing was equally modest, limited by the preference of colonials to farm instead.

England's more developed economy fostered the growth of cities, especially London, a teeming colossus of 675,000 in 1750. In contrast, 90 percent of all eighteenth-century colonials lived in towns of fewer than 2000.

The Consumer Revolution

But in another respect, England's more advanced economy drew the colonies and the parent country together, as a consumer revolution transformed the everyday lives of people on both sides of the Atlantic. By the beginning of the eighteenth century, small manufacturers throughout England were producing a newly large and enticing array of consumer goods—fine textiles and hats, ceramics and glassware, carpets and furniture. Americans proved as eager as Britons to acquire these commodities—so eager that the per capita consumption of imported manufactures among colonials rose 120 percent between 1750 and 1773. Only the wealthy could afford goods of the highest quality, but people of all classes demanded and indulged in small luxuries like a tin of tea, a pair of gloves, or a bar of Irish soap. In both England and its colonies, the spare and simple material life of earlier centuries was giving way to a new order in which even people of ordinary means owned a wider variety of things.

This tea caddy, owned by a Massachusetts colonial, was a new consumer luxury, as was the tea it held.

Inequality in England and America

Then there were people of no means, and in England, they were legion. London seethed with filth, crime, and desperate poverty. The poor and the unemployed as well as pickpockets and prostitutes crowded into its gin-soaked slums, taverns, and brothels. The contrast between the luxuries enjoyed by a wealthy few Londoners and the misery of the many disquieted colonial observers. Ebenezer Hazard, an American Quaker, knew for certain that he was not in Philadelphia, but instead in "a Sink of Sin."

Class distinctions

The opportunities for great wealth provided by England's more developed economy created deep class distinctions, as did the inherited privileges of its aristocracy. The members of the upper class, the landed aristocracy and gentry, made up less than 2 percent of England's population but owned 70 percent of its land. By right of birth, English aristocrats claimed membership in the House of Lords; by custom, certain powerful gentry families dominated the other branch of Parliament, the House of Commons. England's titled gentlemen shared power and wealth and often family ties with the rich men of the city—major merchants, successful lawyers, and lucky financiers. They too exerted political influence through the House of Commons.

The colonies had their own prominent families but no titled ruling class holding political privilege by hereditary right. And even the wealthiest colonial families lived in far less magnificence than did their English counterparts. Probably the finest mansion in eighteenth-century America, William Byrd's Westover plantation, was scarcely a tenth the size of the Marquis of Rockingham's country house, which was longer than two football fields.

If England's upper classes lived more splendidly, its lower classes were larger and worse off than those in the colonies. Less than a third of England's inhabitants belonged to the "middling sort" of traders, professionals, artisans, and tenant farmers. More than two-thirds struggled for survival at the bottom of society. In contrast, the colonial middle class counted for nearly three-quarters of the white population. With land cheap, labor scarce, and wages for both urban and rural workers 100 percent higher in America than in England, it was much easier for colonials to accumulate savings and then buy a farm of their own.

Ambivalent Americans

Colonials were both fascinated and repelled by English society. Benjamin Rush, a Philadelphia physician, felt in the House of Lords as if he "walked on sacred ground." He begged his guide for permission to sit on the throne therein, and then sat "for a considerable time." Other colonials gushed over the grandeur of aristocratic estates and imported suits of livery for their servants, tea services for their wives, and wallpaper for their drawing rooms. They exported their sons to Britain for college educations at Oxford and Cambridge, medical school at

This portrait of John Stuart, the third Earl of Bute (1713–1792), wearing the ceremonial robes of the House of Lords, epitomizes the opulence of Britain's ruling class in the eighteenth century.

Edinburgh, and legal training at London's Inns of Court.

But the aping of English ways made colonials uneasy, too. One Philadelphia Quaker ordered an elegant English coach complete with coat of arms—but then reconsidered and removed the crest. Second thoughts also plagued colonial parents when sons educated in England came home wearing dandified silks, affecting foppish manners, and spouting fashionable slang—"Split me, Madam!" "By Gad!" and "Dam me!" Such behavior mirrored the bad habits of some English gentlemen, whose large incomes from renting land encouraged idleness and extravagance.

Colonials recognized that England's ruling classes purchased their luxury and leisure at the cost of the rest of the nation. In his *Autobiography*, Benjamin Franklin painted a devastating portrait of the degraded lives of his fellow workers in a London printshop, who drowned their disappointments by drinking throughout the workday, even more excessively on the Sabbath, and then faithfully observing the holiday of "St. Monday's" to nurse their hangovers. Like Franklin, many colonials believed that gross inequalities of wealth would endanger liberty. They regarded the idle among England's rich and poor alike as ominous signs of a degenerate nation.

Politics in England and America

England's balanced constitution

Colonials were also of two minds about England's government. While they praised the English constitution as the basis of all liberties, they were alarmed by the actual workings of English politics. In theory, England's "balanced constitution" was designed to give every order of English society some voice in the workings of government. While the Crown represented the monarchy and the House of Lords the aristocracy, the House of Commons represented the democracy, the people of England. In fact, the monarch's executive ministers had become dominant by creating support for their policies in Parliament through patronage—or, put more bluntly, bribery.

Tools for "managing" Parliament

Over the course of the eighteenth century, a large executive bureaucracy had evolved in order to enforce laws, collect taxes, and wage the nearly constant wars in Europe and America. The power to appoint all military and treasury officials, customs and tax collectors, judges and justices of the peace lay with the monarch and his or her ministers. By the middle of the eighteenth century, almost half of all members of Parliament held such Crown offices or government contracts. Royal patronage was also used to manipulate parliamentary elections. The executive branch used money or liquor to bribe local voters into selecting their candidates. The small size of England's electorate fostered executive influence. Perhaps one-fourth of all adult males could vote, and many electoral districts were not adjusted to keep pace with population growth and resettlement. The notorious "rotten boroughs" each elected

This satirical rendering of an English election, by the English artist William Hogarth, mirrored the reservations of many Americans about the political culture of the mother country. The man seated in the foreground of the jostling crowd represents Hogarth's dark view of the typical English voter: much incapacitated by drink, he is being told for whom to vote by the man standing and whispering in his ear. In the background, the overturned carriage suggests that political corruption threatens the stability of England.

a member of Parliament to represent fewer than 500 easily bribable voters, while some large cities like Manchester and Leeds, newly populous because of industrial growth, had no representation in Parliament at all.

Americans liked to think that their colonial governments mirrored the ideal English constitution. In terms of formal structure, there were similarities. Most colonies had a royal governor who represented the monarch in America and a bicameral (two-house) legislature made up of a lower house (the assembly) and an upper house (or council). The democratically elected assembly, like the House of Commons, stood for popular interests, while the council, some of which were elected and others appointed, more roughly approximated the House of Lords.

But these formal similarities masked real differences between English and colonial governments. On the face of it, royal governors had much more power than the English Crown. Unlike kings and queens, royal governors could veto laws passed by assemblies; they could dissolve those bodies at will; they could create courts and dismiss judges. However, governors who asserted their full powers quickly met opposition from their assemblies, who objected that such overwhelming authority endangered popular liberty. In any showdown with their assemblies, most royal governors had to give way, for they lacked the government offices and contracts that bought loyalty. The colonial legislatures possessed additional leverage, since all of them retained the sole authority to levy taxes.

Even if the governors had enjoyed greater patronage powers, their efforts to influence colonial legislatures would have been frustrated by the sheer size of the American electorate. There were too many voters in America to bribe. More than half and possibly as many as 70 percent of all white adult colonial men were enfranchised. Property requirements were the same in America as in England, but widespread ownership of land in the colonies allowed most men to meet the qualifications easily.

The colonial electorate was also more watchful. Representatives were required to reside in the districts that they served, and a few even received binding instructions

Colonial governments

from their constituents about how to vote. Representation was also apportioned according to population far more equitably than in England. Because they were so closely tied to their constituents' wishes, colonial legislators were far less likely than members of Parliament to be swayed by executive pressure.

Most Americans were as pleased with their inexpensive and representative colonial governments as they were horrified by the conduct of politics in England. John Dickinson, a young Pennsylvanian training as a lawyer in London, was scandalized by a parliamentary election he witnessed in 1754. The king and his ministers had spent over 100,000 pounds sterling to buy support for their candidates, he wrote his father, and "if a man cannot be brought to vote as he is desired, he is made dead drunk and kept in that state, never heard of by his family and friends, till all is over and he can do no harm."

The Imperial System before 1760

Colonials like Dickinson thought long and hard about the condition of England's society and politics. Meanwhile, the English thought about their colonies little, understood them less, and wished neither to think about them more nor to understand them better. It would be hard to exaggerate just how insignificant North America was in the English scheme of things. Those few Britons who thought about America at all believed that colonials resembled the "savage" Indians more than the "civilized" English. As a London acquaintance remarked to Thomas Hancock, it was a pity Mrs. Hancock had to remain in Boston when he could "take her to England and make her happy with Christians."

The same indifference contributed to England's haphazard administration of its colonies. The Board of Trade and Plantations, created from the Lords of Trade in 1696, gathered information about Atlantic trading and fishing, reviewed laws and petitions drawn up by colonial assemblies, and exchanged letters and instructions with royal governors. But the Board of Trade was only an advisory body, reporting to the king's ministers and passing on information to other government agencies.

Real authority over the colonies was divided among an array of other agencies. The Treasury oversaw customs and gathered other royal revenues; the Admiralty Board enforced regulations of trade; the War Office orchestrated colonial defense. But these departments spent most of their hours handling more pressing responsibilities. Colonial affairs stood at the bottom of their agendas. Most British officials in America seemed equally indifferent. Often enough, they had been awarded their jobs in return for political support, not in recognition of administrative ability.

The branch of England's government most indifferent to America was Parliament. Aside from passing an occasional law to regulate trade, restrict manufacturing, or direct monetary policy, Parliament made no effort to assert its authority in America. Its members assumed that Parliament's sovereignty extended over the entire empire, and nothing had occurred to make them think otherwise.

The benefits of benign neglect

For the colonies, this chaotic and inefficient system of colonial administration worked well enough. The very weakness of imperial oversight left Americans with a great deal of freedom. Even England's regulation of trade rested lightly on the shoulders of most Americans. Southern planters were obliged to send their rice, indigo, and tobacco to Britain only, but they enjoyed favorable credit terms and knowledgeable marketing from English merchants. Colonials were prohibited from finishing iron products and exporting hats and textiles, but they had scant interest in developing domestic industries. Americans were required to import all manufactured goods through England, but by doing so, they acquired high-quality goods

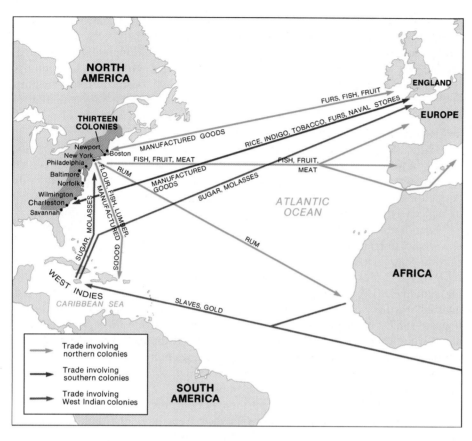

Overseas Trade Networks Commercial ties to Spain and Portugal, Africa, and the Caribbean sustained the growth of both seaports and commercial farming regions on the British North American mainland and enabled colonials to purchase an increasing volume of finished goods from England. The proceeds from exports in foodstuffs and lumber to the West Indies and trade in fish to Spain and Portugal enabled northern merchants and farmers to buy hardware and clothing from the mother country. Southern planters financed their consumption of English imports and their investment in African slaves with the profits from the sale of tobacco, rice, and indigo abroad.

at low prices. At little sacrifice, most Americans obeyed imperial regulations. Only sugar, molasses, and tea were routinely smuggled.

Following this policy of benign neglect the British empire muddled on to the satisfaction of most people on both sides of the Atlantic. Economic growth and political autonomy allowed most Americans to like being English, despite their misgivings about their parent nation. The beauty of it was that Americans could be English in America, enjoying greater economic opportunity and political equality. If imperial arrangements had remained as they were in 1754, the empire might have muddled on indefinitely. But because of the French and the Indians on the American frontier, the British empire began to change. And those changes made it increasingly hard for Americans to be English in America.

In the late spring of 1754, while Benjamin Franklin dreamed of unifying # Toward the Seven Years' War

Americans, a young Virginian dreamed of military glory. As Franklin rode toward Albany, the young man, an inexperienced officer, led his company of Virginia militia toward Fort Duquesne, the French stronghold on the forks of the Ohio.

Less than a year earlier, the king's ministers had advised royal governors in America to halt the French advance into the Ohio country. The Virginia government organized an expedition against Fort Duquesne, placing at its head the young man who combined an imposing physique with the self-possession of an English gentleman. He wanted, more than anything, to become an officer in the regular British army.

Washington at Fort Necessity

But events in the Ohio country during that spring and summer did not go George Washington's way. French soldiers easily captured Fort Necessity, his crude outpost near Fort Duquesne. In early July, as the Albany Congress was debating, Washington was surrendering to a French force in the Pennsylvania backcountry and beating a retreat back to Virginia. By the end of 1754, Washington had resigned his militia command and retired to his plantation at Mount Vernon. The disaster at Fort Necessity had dashed his dreams of martial glory and a regular army commission. He had no future as a soldier.

With the rout of Washington and his troops, the French grew bolder and the Indians more restless. The renewal of war between England and France was certain by the beginning of 1755. This time the contest between the two powers would decide the question of sovereignty over North America. That, at least, was the dream of William Pitt, who was about to become the most powerful man in England.

The ambitions of William Pitt

Even by the standards of English politicians, William Pitt was an odd character. Subject to bouts of illness and depression and loathed for his opportunism and egotism, Pitt surmounted every challenge, buoyed by a strong sense of destiny—his own and that of England. He believed that England must seize the world's trade, for trade meant wealth and wealth meant power. As early as the 1730s, Pitt recognized that the only obstacle between England and its destiny was France—and that the contest between the two for world supremacy would be decided in America. During King George's War, Pitt had mesmerized the House of Commons and the nation with his spellbinding oratory about England's imperial destiny. But the mounting cost of fighting prompted the government to accept peace with France in 1748. In frustration Pitt retired from public life.

But while Pitt sulked in his library, the rivalry for the American frontier moved toward a showdown. The French pressed their front lines eastward; the English pushed for land westward; the Indians maneuvered for position. Heartened by the news from America, Pitt clung to his dream of English commercial dominion and French defeat. By the late spring of 1754, as Benjamin Franklin and George Washington rode toward their defeats, William Pitt knew that he would have his war with France and his way with the world.

Other dreams would wait longer for fulfillment. The Albany Congress had demonstrated that a few Americans like Franklin had seen beyond the diversity of a divided colonial world to the possibility of union, however unaccustomed and untried. But it would take another war, one that restructured an empire, before some Americans saw in themselves a likeness that was not English.

chapter summary

Over the course of the eighteenth century, British North Americans grew increasingly diverse, which made the prospect of any future colonial political union appear remote.

- Differences became more pronounced among whites because of the immigration of larger numbers of non-English settlers, the spread of settlement to the backcountry, and the growth of major seaports.

- Although disorder was not uncommon either on the frontier or in cities, the most serious social and political conflict drew its strength from sectional controversies between East and West.

- The South became more embattled, too, as a result of the massive importation of slaves directly from Africa during the first half of the eighteenth century and a rising tide of black resistance to slavery.

- After about 1750 the growth of a native-born population strengthened black communal and family life.

- Religious conflict among colonials was intensified by the spread of Enlightenment ideas and the influence of the first Great Awakening.

- Despite their many differences, a majority of white colonials took pride in their common English ancestry and in belonging to a powerful empire.

interactive learning

The Primary Source Investigator CD-ROM offers the following materials related to this chapter:

- Interactive maps: **The Atlantic World, 1400–1850 (M2)** and **The Settlement of Colonial America, 1700–1763 (M5)**

- A collection of primary sources exploring the development of the British empire in North America,

such as a diagram of a slave ship, an image of a homespun garment, and a sermon from the famous itinerant preacher George Whitefield. Several sources illustrate the consequences of widespread slavery, including a poem by African American Phyllis Wheatley and a minister's description of racial slavery. In addition, several sources demonstrate how imperial expansion sparked internal problems: disputes with colonial governments and the Carolina Regulators movement, a portrait of the Iroquois go-between Mary Brant, and a political cartoon from Benjamin Franklin on the difficulties of uniting the colonies.

additional reading

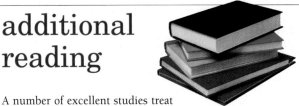

A number of excellent studies treat broad aspects of American development during the later colonial period. For a comprehensive treatment of economic development, see John McCusker and Russell Menard, *The Economy of British America, 1607–1787* (1985). For the evolution of political institutions, consult Bernard Bailyn, *The Origins of American Politics* (1968). On the subject of religious change, the book to read is Patricia Bonomi, *Under the Cope of Heaven* (1986). For family life, consult Philip Greven's *The Protestant Temperament* (1977). The best studies of the frontier are Charles Grant's work on western Connecticut, *Democracy in the Frontier Town of Kent*

(1961), and Rachel Klein's account of the South Carolina backcountry, *The Unification of a Slave State* (1990). The evolution of major seaports is exhaustively chronicled in Gary Nash's *Urban Crucible* (1979), while relations between blacks and whites in the South are ably described by Allan Kulikoff, *Tobacco and Slaves* (1987); Rhys Isaac, *The Transformation of Virginia, 1740–1790* (1982); and Mechal Sobel, *The World They Made Together* (1987).

Understanding the impact of immigration and ethnic diversity is essential to appreciating the dynamism of eighteenth-century colonial society. Some especially vivid accounts include Bernard Bailyn, *Voyagers to the West* (1986); Bernard Bailyn and Philip D. Morgan, eds., *Strangers within the Realm* (1991); and Ira Berlin, "Time, Space, and the Evolution of Afro-American Society in British Mainland North America," *American Historical Review*, 85 (1980), 44–78. For a fuller list of readings, see the Bibliography at www.mhhe.com/davidsonnation5.

significant events

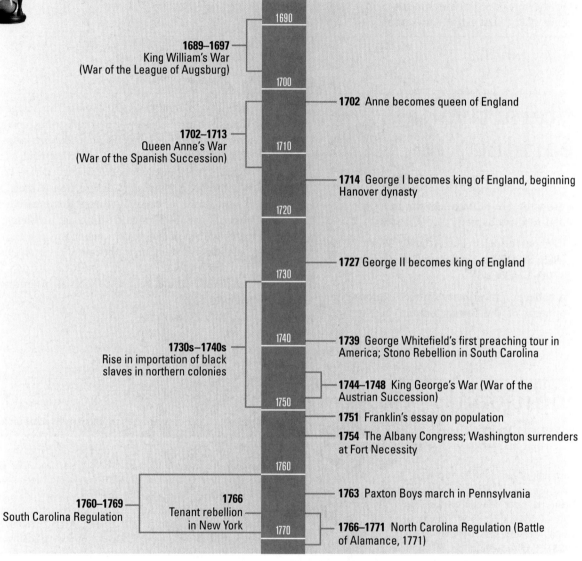

1689–1697
King William's War
(War of the League of Augsburg)

1690

1700

1702 Anne becomes queen of England

1702–1713
Queen Anne's War
(War of the Spanish Succession)

1710

1714 George I becomes king of England, beginning Hanover dynasty

1720

1727 George II becomes king of England

1730

1740

1739 George Whitefield's first preaching tour in America; Stono Rebellion in South Carolina

1730s–1740s
Rise in importation of black slaves in northern colonies

1744–1748 King George's War (War of the Austrian Succession)

1750

1751 Franklin's essay on population

1754 The Albany Congress; Washington surrenders at Fort Necessity

1760

1763 Paxton Boys march in Pennsylvania

1760–1769
South Carolina Regulation

1766
Tenant rebellion in New York

1770

1766–1771 North Carolina Regulation (Battle of Alamance, 1771)

THE CREATION OF A NEW REPUBLIC

As the shrewd Benjamin Franklin had observed in 1751, the population of British North America was doubling approximately every 25 years. This astonishing rate was quite possibly the fastest in the world at the time. Even so, the North American surge was merely one part of a more general global rise in population during the second half of the eighteenth century. In sheer numbers China led the way. Its population of 150 million in 1700 had doubled to more than 313 million by the end of the century. Europe's total rose from about 118 million in 1700 to about 187 million a century later, the greatest growth coming on its eastern and western flanks, in Great Britain and Russia. African and Indian populations seem to have increased as well, although historians have analyzed trends there less closely.

This worldwide rise, unprecedented in previous history, occurred for a variety of reasons. Climate may have been one. In Europe, at least, warmer and drier seasons produced generally better harvests. (The population of the already dry Middle East seems not to have expanded, and that region may have been hurt by the climate changes.) Furthermore, health and nutrition improved globally with the spread of Native American crops. Irish farmers discovered that a single acre planted with the lowly American potato could support an entire family. The tomato added crucial vitamins to the Mediterranean diet, while maize provided more calories per acre than any European or African

grain. In China the American sweet potato thrived in hilly regions where rice would not grow.

Not only plants but diseases were carried back and forth by European ships. As we have seen, contact between previously isolated peoples produced extreme mortality from epidemics, enabling invaders like Hernando Cortés to conquer populous civilizations. Similarly, the Pilgrims unwittingly blessed divine providence for allowing them to take over deserted fields that had been cleared and farmed by Indians only recently struck down by disease. By 1800 the more globally isolated peoples, such as the inhabitants of Australia or the North American plains, remained at risk. But after more than two centuries of sustained contact, Indians developed increased biological resistance to European and African illnesses. The frequent circulation of diseases worldwide led to a more stable environment in which populations began to swell.

During the years that Europeans explored the Atlantic frontiers of North and South America, Slavic and Romanian pioneers were moving eastward into the Eurasian steppes. There they turned sparsely settled pastoral lands into feudal manors and farms. In northern forests unsuitable for farming, Russian fur traders advanced eastward across Siberia until they reached the Pacific in the 1630s. By the 1780s Russian pioneers had pushed into Alaska and down the Pacific American coast, bumping up against western Europeans who were harvesting furs from Canada's forests and streams.

Russian fur traders reach the Pacific Coast

Denis Diderot's *Encyclopedia* published, popularizing the ideas of the Enlightenment 1751–1752

Beginning of global population rise

| 1630 | 1670 | 1740s–1750 | ca. 1750 |

English found Hudson's Bay Company, rival for French fur trade

English and French increase penetration of Ohio valley

1751 Franklin publishes essay on population

AMERICAN EVENTS

Both flanks of this European thrust often depended on forced labor, especially in agricultural settings. As we have seen, the institution of slavery in North America became increasingly restrictive over the course of the seventeenth century. Furthermore, the number of slaves imported to North America paled when compared to the thousands shipped by the Portuguese to the slave markets of Rio de Janeiro. Similarly, the plight of serfs worsened from 1500 to 1650, as the demand for labor increased in eastern Europe. In 1574 Polish nobles received the right to punish their serfs entirely as they pleased—including execution if they chose. By 1603, Russian peasants were routinely sold along with the land they worked.

The eighteenth-century Enlightenment penetrated eastern Europe too, as it had the urban centers of North America. Russia's Peter the Great absorbed many ideas when he traveled, sometimes incognito, to England and western Europe. As czar (1689–1725), he attempted to put them to use in westernizing Russia. Catherine the Great was even more influenced by the artistic currents of the Enlightenment. During her reign (1762–1796), she imported Western architects, sculptors, and musicians to grace her court.

But Catherine's limits to toleration were made brutally clear in 1773. The same year that a group of rowdy Americans were dumping tea into Boston harbor, a Cossack soldier named Emelian Pugachev launched a peasant rebellion. Grandly proclaiming himself emperor, Pugachev issued

decrees abolishing serfdom and taxes. Serfs in the Ural and Volga river valleys flocked to his ragtag army. Catherine ruthlessly imprisoned Pugachev (shown here jailed and chained) and then

GLOBAL EVENTS

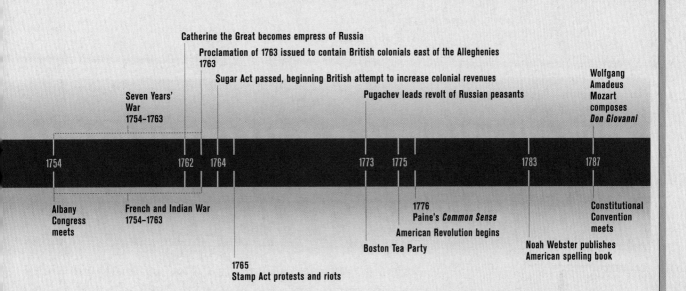

Catherine the Great becomes empress of Russia

Proclamation of 1763 issued to contain British colonials east of the Alleghenies
1763

Sugar Act passed, beginning British attempt to increase colonial revenues

Pugachev leads revolt of Russian peasants

Seven Years' War
1754–1763

Wolfgang Amadeus Mozart composes *Don Giovanni*

1754   1762   1764   1773   1775   1783   1787

Albany Congress meets

French and Indian War
1754–1763

1776
Paine's *Common Sense*

American Revolution begins

Boston Tea Party

Constitutional Convention meets

Noah Webster publishes American spelling book

1765
Stamp Act protests and riots

AMERICAN EVENTS

executed him and scattered his followers. In 1775 she granted Russian nobles even more absolute control over their serfs.

To make the obvious comparison—between a failed Russian revolution for liberty and the triumph of American colonials—would be too smug. Liberty-loving American merchants like John Hancock and genteel tobacco planters like George Washington were hardly in the position of serfs. A more appropriate link might be made between Russian serfs and American slaves, since both groups supplied the forced labor along the frontiers of European expansion. But the slaves, whose African homelands lay thousands of miles away, found the odds of a successful rebellion just as difficult as Russian serfs

did. Ironically, white Americans may have been able to fight so vigorously for their liberties precisely because they had made revolt by a class of forced laborers so difficult.

Americans rebelled in 1775 not out of a serf's desperation; quite the opposite. The Seven Years' War ended in 1763 with the French driven from North America and British colonials thriving, thanks to a wartime boom. Thomas Mayhew, a respected Boston minister, voiced the opinion of many when he envisioned a glorious empire spreading across the continent in the century to come. "I do not mean an independent one," he added carefully, but in 1763 the qualification was hardly necessary. Most white Americans were quite pleased with the prospect

of being English. With the significant exception of the slave class, the distance between the poorest and richest individuals was smaller in America than it was anywhere in Europe. And the British tradition of representative government ensured a broader involvement of citizens in colonial government. Thus, an American Revolution was hardly inevitable in 1776. Most certainly one did not appear likely in 1763. The timing of the break with Great Britain was the result of specific decisions made on both sides of the Atlantic.

America's isolated position on the edge of European expansion certainly created conditions that made separation likely at some point. Most colonials, used to relative social equality among white Americans, blanched at what

GLOBAL EVENTS

Napoleon comes to power in France

Great Britain and France resume war

Congress of Vienna meets to bring political stability to Europe

Napoleon defeated at Waterloo 1815

French Revolution begins

King George III dies

| 1789 | 1797 | 1799 | 1801 | 1803 | 1809 | 1814 | 1817 | 1820 | 1823 | 1825 |
| WASHINGTON | ADAMS | | JEFFERSON | | MADISON | | MONROE | | | ADAMS |

First presidential inauguration

Monroe Doctrine proclaimed

1815 Jackson defeats British at New Orleans

Treaty of Ghent ends War of 1812

Tecumseh organizes Pan-Indian confederacy

First peaceful transfer of power between rival parties

AMERICAN EVENTS

they saw as English luxury and corruption. English governing elites, when they bothered to notice Americans, usually found them provincial and naive. Under different circumstances the move for independence might have come in 1800, or even 1867, as it did for Canada. But the break came earlier. American colonials, who in 1763 liked being English and gloried in the British empire, gradually came to think of themselves as independent Americans, subject neither to a British monarch nor to Parliament.

mericans liked being English. They had liked being English from the beginning of colonial settlement, but they liked it more than ever for a few years after 1759. One wonderful day during those years—September 16, 1762—Bostonians turned out to celebrate belonging to the British empire. Soldiers mustered on the Common; bells pealed from the steeples of local churches; the charge of guns fired from the battery resounded through towns; strains of orchestra music from an outdoor concert floated through the city's crowded streets and narrow alleys. When darkness fell and bonfires illuminated the city, Bostonians consumed "a vast quantity of liquor," drinking "loyal healths" to their young king, George III, and in celebration of Britain's victory in the Seven Years' War.

When the great news of that triumph reached the North American mainland in the fall of 1762, similar celebrations broke out all over the colonies. And with good reason. France's empire in America, which only a few years earlier had appeared so formidable, was now vanquished. Great Britain had become master of Canada, thanks to the joint efforts of British and American colonial troops. In 1763 the Treaty of Paris ratified their victories, making Britain the largest and most powerful empire in the Western world. Americans were among His Majesty's proudest subjects.

Thirteen years after the celebration of 1762, Boston was a different place. Pride in belonging to the empire had shriveled to shrill charges that England conspired to enslave its colonies. Massachusetts led the way, drawing other colonies deep into resistance. Bostonians initiated many of the petitions and resolves against British authority. When words did not work, they ignited riots, harassed British officials, baited British troops, and destroyed British property. In 1775, they were laying plans for rebellion against the British empire.

Toward the War for American Independence

1754–1776

preview • Parliament passed the Sugar Act, Stamp Act, and other measures of the early 1760s in hopes of binding the American colonies more closely to the empire. Instead, once-loyal Americans became convinced that their constitutional rights were being violated: the right to consent to taxes, the right to a trial by jury, and the freedom from standing armies. With the passage of the harsh Coercive Acts of 1774, a break with Britain was not long in coming.

A process of disillusionment

An ironic fate overtook that generation of Americans who loved being English, boasted of their rights as Britons, and celebrated their membership in the all-conquering empire. That very pride drove colonials into rebellion, for the men who ran the British empire after 1763 would not allow Americans to be English. Even before the Seven Years' War, some colonials saw that diverging paths of social and political development made them different from the English. After the Seven Years' War, events demonstrated to even more colonials that they were not considered the political equals of the English who lived in England. As their disillusionment with the empire deepened, British North Americans from Massachusetts to Georgia slowly discovered a new identity as Americans and declared their independence from being English.

"To have a standing army!" wrote one Bostonian in 1768. "Good God! What can be worse to a people who have tasted the sweets of liberty! Things are come to an unhappy crisis!" Paul Revere engraved this print of British redcoats arriving in Boston.

The Seven Years' War, which actually lasted nine years, pitted Britain and its

The Seven Years' War

ally, Prussia, against France, in league with Austria and Spain. The battle raged from 1754 until 1763, ranging over the continent of Europe, the coast of West Africa, India, the Philippines, the Caribbean, and North America.

The Years of Defeat

The war started in 1754 when Virginia sent George Washington and a company of militia into the Ohio River valley to halt French penetration into the area (pages 135–136). Washington's surrender at Fort Necessity only stiffened Britain's resolve to assert its own claims to the Ohio country. In the summer of 1755, as two British regiments led by Major General Edward Braddock approached the French outpost at Fort Duquesne on the forks of the Ohio, they were ambushed and cut to pieces by a party of French and Indians. Washington led the mortally wounded Braddock and the remnants of his army in a retreat.

Braddock's defeat

During the summer of Braddock's defeat, New Englanders fared somewhat better against French forces in Nova Scotia and deported 6000 farmers from that region. The Acadians, as they were known, professed to be neutral in the war between France and Britain. But their ancestors had been French, and the English worried that neighboring Quebec might still persuade them to rebel. Thus the Acadians had their land confiscated, and they were dispersed throughout the colonies.

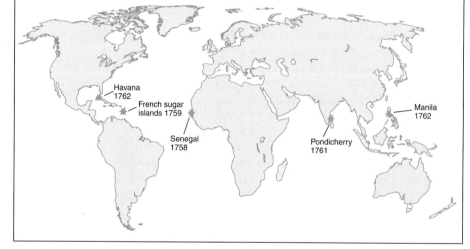

The Seven Years' War After Washington's surrender and Braddock's defeat in the Pennsylvania backcountry, the British and French waged their final contest for supremacy in North America in northern New York and Canada. But the rivalry for empire between France and Britain was worldwide, with naval superiority providing the needed edge to Britain. The British navy isolated French forces in India, winning a victory at Pondicherry, while English offensives captured the French sugar islands in the Caribbean and French trading posts along the West African coast. When Spain entered the war on the side of France, British fleets captured both Havana and the strategic port of Manila in the Philippines.

Still, deporting farmers did little to help win a war. During the opening years of the conflict, Britain mismanaged its forces disastrously. When England and France formally declared war in May 1756, John Campbell, the Earl of Loudoun, took command of the North American theater. American soldiers and colonial assemblies alike hated Lord Loudoun. They balked at his efforts to take command over colonial troops and dragged their heels at his demands for men and supplies. Meanwhile, the French appointed an effective new commanding general of their forces in Canada, Louis Joseph, the marquis de Montcalm. Montcalm drove southward, capturing key British forts and threatening the security of both New York and New England. While he prospered in America, the British were also taking a beating from the French in Europe and in India.

During the years when the French seemed unstoppable, the British looked for help from the strongest tribes of the interior—the Iroquois in the North and the Creek, Choctaw, and Cherokee in the South. Instead, Benjamin Franklin's worst fears were realized: most tribes adopted neutrality or joined the French. As France seemed certain to carry the continent, Indian attacks on English frontier settlements increased.

The Years of Victory

As British fortunes worsened throughout 1756 and 1757, William Pitt resumed his political career and took personal control over the war in his usual bold way. "I know that I can save this country and that no one else can," he announced. Leaving the fighting in Europe to the Prussians, Pitt focused the full strength of the British military on beating the French in America. Pitt also renewed colonial support for the war effort by replacing Lord Loudoun and giving his successor far more limited authority over colonial troops. And Pitt sent requests for men and money directly to each colonial assembly—accompanied by promises of reimbursement in gold and silver.

William Pitt turns the tide

With Pitt now in control, the tide of battle turned. In July of 1758, the British gained control of the St. Lawrence River when the French fortress at Louisbourg fell before the combined force of the Royal Navy and British and colonial troops. In August, a force of New Englanders strangled France's frontier defenses by capturing Fort Frontenac, thereby isolating French forts lining the Great Lakes and the Ohio valley. The Indians, seeing the French routed from the interior, switched their allegiance to the English.

The British succeeded even more brilliantly in 1759. In Canada, Brigadier General James Wolfe gambled on a daring stratagem and won Quebec from Montcalm. Under the cover of darkness, naval squadrons landed Wolfe's men beneath the city's steep bluffs, where they scaled the heights to a plateau known as the Plains of Abraham. Montcalm might have won by holding out behind the walls of his fortress and awaiting reinforcements. Instead, he matched Wolfe's recklessness and offered battle. Five days later both Wolfe and Montcalm lay dead, along with 1400 French soldiers and 600 British and American troops. Quebec had fallen to the British. A year later the French surrender of Montreal ended the fighting in North America, although it continued elsewhere in the world for another two years.

Wolfe and Montcalm battle for Quebec

The Treaty of Paris, signed in February 1763, ended the French presence on the continent of North America. The terms confirmed British title to all French territory east of the Mississippi as well as to Spanish Florida. (Spain had made the last-minute mistake of entering the war, against Britain, in 1762.) France ceded to its ally Spain all of its land lying west of the Mississippi and the port of New Orleans.

Postwar Expectations

Britain's victory gave rise to great expectations among Americans. The end of the war, they were sure, meant the end of high taxes. The terms of the peace, they were confident, meant that the fertile lands of the Ohio valley would be thrown open to English settlement. The prosperity of the war years alone made for a mood of optimism. British military spending and William Pitt's subsidies had made

Colonial pride and optimism

The British navy bombarded Quebec in a vain attempt to compel surrender. Both sides were struck by the devastation of the city, with many of its buildings razed to smoldering shells, which presaged the end of France's empire in North America.

English resentments

money for farmers, merchants, artisans, and anyone else who had anything to do with supplying the army or navy. Colonials also took pride in their contributions of troops and money to the winning of the war. In view of that support, Americans expected to be given more consideration within the British empire. Now, as one anonymous pamphleteer put it, Americans would "not be thought presumptuous, if they consider[ed] themselves upon an equal footing" with English in the parent country.

But most imperial officials in America thought that if Americans took pride in being English, they had done a poor job of showing it. British statesmen complained that colonial assemblies had been tightfisted when it came to supplying the army. British commanders charged that colonial troops had been lily-livered when it came to fighting the French. Such charges were unjust, but they stuck in the minds of many Britons, who concluded that the Americans were selfish and self-interested, unconcerned with the welfare of the empire as a whole. Britain had accumulated a huge national debt that would saddle the nation with high taxes for years to come. To make matters worse, some Britons suspected that, with the French removed from North America, the colonies would move toward independence. As early as 1755, Josiah Tucker, a respected English economist, had warned that "to drive the French out of all North America would be the most fatal step we could take." Ironically, independence entered the minds of some observers in England long before it was ever entertained by Americans.

Americans in 1763 were not, in truth, revolutionaries in the making. They were loyal British subjects in the flush of postwar patriotism. Americans in 1763,

1763

Greenland

ATLANTIC OCEAN

UNEXPLORED

Newfoundland

QUEBEC

NOVA SCOTIA

Montreal

PACIFIC OCEAN

Great Lakes

LOUISIANA

Missouri R.

THIRTEEN COLONIES

Mississippi R.   Ohio R.

Rio Grande

FLORIDA

1750

NEW SPAIN

GULF OF MEXICO

Bahamas   WEST INDIES

Cuba   Hispaniola

CARIBBEAN SEA

British   Russian

French   Dutch

Spanish   Proclamation Line of 1763

European Claims in North America, 1750 and 1763 The British victory in the Seven Years' War secured Great Britain's title to a large portion of present-day United States and Canada. Colonials hoped to settle the newly won territory, but politicians in London intended to restrict westward movement with the Proclamation of 1763.

deeply divided among themselves, were not even "Americans." But most postwar English colonials did expect to enjoy a more equal status in the empire. And most Britons had no inclination to accord them that equality. The differing expectations of the colonies' place in the empire poised the postwar generation for crisis.

It was common sense. Great Britain had waged a costly war to secure its

The Imperial Crisis

empire in America; now it needed to consolidate those gains. The empire's North American territory needed to be protected, its administration tightened, and its colonies made as profitable as possible to the parent nation. In other words, the

The Appalachian Frontier, 1750–1775 Made bold by the presence of British forts and soldiers, land-hungry colonials spilled into the West through the Cumberland Gap, a notch in the chain of mountains stretching the length of the North American interior. Only Indians and some white hunters knew of the Cumberland Gap before it was scouted in 1750 by Dr. Thomas Walker and a party of Virginians on behalf of a company of land speculators. In 1763, Indians led by Pontiac seized eight British forts before troops under Colonel Henry Bouquet stopped the offensive at Bushy Run, Pennsylvania. In 1775 Daniel Boone took the first large party of pioneers through the Cumberland Gap and established a fort at Boonesborough in present-day Kentucky.

empire needed to be centralized. That conclusion dictated Britain's decision to leave a standing army of several thousand troops in America after the Seven Years' War. The British army would prevent France from trying to regain its lost territory.

New Troubles on the Frontier

Keeping troops in North America made sense to the British because of the Indians, as well. With the French gone, English traders, speculators, and settlers would swarm into the West. Without the French as trading partners, Indian tribes were in a weaker position to deal with the British. No longer could they count on a steady supply of arms and ammunition from European rivals competing for their furs. The Indians were edgy, expecting the worst, and the British were worried.

Events bore out British fears. In the early 1760s a Lenni Lenape prophet, Neolin, began advising the tribes to return to their native ways and resist the spread of white settlement. Pontiac, an Ottawa chief, embraced Neolin's message of renaissance and rebellion. Other interior tribes joined Pontiac's offensive, and during the summer of 1763 they captured all the British outposts west of Pittsburgh. British troops and American militia finally smothered Pontiac's Rebellion.

Pontiac's Rebellion

Thereafter British administrators discovered another use for troops in America—to enforce the newly issued Proclamation of 1763. That order, issued by England's Board of Trade, prohibited white settlement past the crest of the Appalachian Mountains. Restricting westward movement might ease Indian fears, the British hoped, and so stave off future conflicts. It might also keep the colonials confined to the seaboard, where they were more easily subject to the control of the empire.

Proclamation of 1763

George Grenville's New Measures

A final reason for keeping troops in the colonies occurred to the British by 1764: an armed presence could enforce American acceptance of other new and sensible measures for tightening the empire. Those measures were the solutions of George Grenville, the first lord of the treasury, to the financial problems facing England after the Seven Years' War.

Britain's national debt had doubled in the decade after 1754. Adding to that burden was the drain of supporting troops in the colonies. As matters stood, heavy taxes were already triggering protests among hard-pressed Britons. Americans, in contrast, paid comparatively low taxes to their colonial governments and little in trade duties to the empire. Indeed, Grenville discovered that the colonial customs service paid out four times more in salaries to its collectors than it gathered in duties and was thereby operating at a net loss.

The income from customs duties was slim because colonial merchants evaded the Molasses Act of 1733. That tariff imposed a hefty duty of six pence on every gallon of molasses imported from the French and Dutch sugar islands. Parliament had designed the duty to encourage colonists to consume more British molasses, which carried a higher price but came duty-free. New England merchants, who distilled molasses into rum and then traded it to the southern colonies and to West Africa, claimed that the British sugar islands could not satisfy the demands of their distilleries. Regrettably, the merchants were forced to import more molasses from the French and Dutch. More regrettably, to keep their costs low and the price of their rum competitive, they had to bribe British customs officials. With the going rate for bribes ranging from a halfpenny to a penny and a half per gallon, the whole

Molasses Act of 1733

regrettable arrangement made handsome profits for both merchants and customs inspectors.

George Grenville reasoned that if Americans could pay out a little under the table to protect an illegal trade, they would willingly pay a little more to go legitimate. Parliament agreed. In April 1764 it passed the Revenue Act, commonly called the Sugar Act. The legislation actually lowered the duty on foreign molasses from six to three pence a gallon. This time, however, Grenville intended to enforce the new duty and to crack down on smugglers. To do so, the Sugar Act required shipmasters to submit papers listing every item in their cargoes when entering or clearing colonial ports. Even common sailors had to declare the contents of their sea chests. Those caught on the wrong side of the law were to be tried in admiralty courts, where verdicts were handed down by royally appointed judges rather than colonial juries more likely to sympathize with their fellow citizens.

By tightening customs enforcement, Grenville hoped to raise more revenue from the American trade. Unlike the earlier Navigation Acts, which imposed duties mainly to regulate trade, the Sugar Act's duties were intended mainly to yield revenue. Even so, Grenville regarded his demands as modest: he did not expect colonials to help reduce England's national debt or even to cover the entire cost of their defense.

Grenville made other modest proposals, all approved by Parliament. There was the Currency Act of 1764, which prohibited the colonies from making their paper money legal tender. That prevented Americans from paying their debts to British traders in currency that had fallen to less than its face value. There was the Quartering Act of 1765, which obliged any colony in which troops were stationed to provide them with suitable accommodations. That contributed to the cost of keeping British forces in America. Finally, in March of 1765, Parliament passed the Stamp Act.

The Stamp Act placed taxes on legal documents, customs papers, newspapers, almanacs, college diplomas, playing cards, and dice. After November 1, 1765, all these items had to bear a stamp signifying that their possessor had paid the tax. Violators of the Stamp Act, like those disobeying the Sugar Act, were to be tried without juries in admiralty courts. The English had been paying a similar tax for nearly a century, so it seemed to Grenville and Parliament that colonials could have no objections.

Every packet boat from London that brought news of Parliament passing another one of Grenville's measures dampened postwar optimism. For all of the differences between the colonies and England, Americans still held much in common with the English. Those shared ideas included firm beliefs about why the British constitution, British customs, and British history all served to protect liberty and the rights of the empire's freeborn citizens. For that reason the new measures, which seemed like common sense to Grenville and Parliament, did not make sense at all to Americans.

The Beginning of Colonial Resistance

Like other Britons, colonials in America accepted a maxim laid down by the English philosopher John Locke: property guaranteed liberty. Property, in this view, was not merely real estate, or wealth, or material possessions. It was the source of strength for every individual, providing the freedom to think and act independently. Protecting the individual's right to own property was the main responsibility of government, for if personal property was not sacred, then neither was personal liberty.

It followed from this close connection between property, power, and liberty that no people should be taxed without their consent or that of their elected

Sugar Act

Currency and Quartering Acts

Stamp Act

Locke on property and liberty

representatives. The power to tax was the power to destroy by depriving a person of property. Yet both the Sugar Act and the Stamp Act were taxes passed by members of Parliament, none of whom had been elected by colonials.

Like the English, colonials also prized the right of trial by jury as one of their basic constitutional liberties. Yet both the Sugar Act and the Stamp Act would prosecute offenders in the admiralty courts, not in local courts, thus depriving colonials of the freedom claimed by all other English men and women.

The concern for protecting individual liberties was only one of the convictions shaping the colonies' response to Britain's new policies. Equally important was their deep suspicion of power itself, a preoccupation that colonials shared with a minority of radical English thinkers. These radicals were known by a variety of names: the Country Party, the Commonwealthmen, and the Opposition. They drew their inspiration from the ancient tradition of classical republicanism, which held that representative government safeguarded liberty more reliably than either monarchy or oligarchy did. Underlying that judgment was the belief that human beings were driven by passion and insatiable ambition. One person (a monarch), or even a few people (an oligarchy), could not be entrusted with governing, because they would inevitably become corrupted by power and turn into tyrants. Even in representative governments, the people were obliged to watch those in power at all times. The price of liberty was eternal vigilance.

Visual imagery brought home the urgency of resistance to Americans who could not read political pamphlets or radical newspapers. This detail from an engraving by Paul Revere includes a liberty tree, from which is hung an effigy of the Boston stamp distributor, and a beast busily destroying the Magna Carta while trampling American colonials. The date on the tree, August 14, 1765, marked the first Stamp Act riot in Boston.

The Opposition believed that the people of England were not watching their rulers closely enough. During the first half of the eighteenth century, they argued, the entire executive branch of England's government—monarchs and their ministers—had been corrupted by their appetite for power. Proof of their ambition was the executive bureaucracy of civil officials and standing armies that steadily grew larger, interfered more with citizens' lives, and drained increasing amounts of money from taxpayers. Even more alarming, in the Opposition's view, the executive branch's bribery of members of Parliament was corrupting the representative branch of England's government. They warned that a sinister conspiracy originating in the executive branch of government threatened English liberty.

Opposition thinkers commanded little attention in England, where they were dismissed as a discontented radical fringe. But they were revered by political leaders in the American colonies. Especially popular were John Trenchard, a lawyer, and Thomas Gordon, a schoolteacher, who collaborated on a series of scathing essays against the political establishment. Too many "unhappy nations have lost that precious jewel *liberty*," Trenchard warned, because they "have permitted a standing army to be kept amongst them." Why, colonials worried, did Britain insist on keeping troops in America, just when Parliament was putting in place new taxes that had never been approved by American legislatures? Events seemed to confirm all too well the Opposition's description of how powerful rulers turned themselves into tyrants and reduced the people whom they ruled to slaves.

In sum, Grenville's new measures led some colonials to suspect that ambitious men ruling England might be conspiring against American liberties. At the very least, the new measures implied that colonials were not the political equals of the English living in England. They were not entitled to taxation by consent or to trial by jury. To be treated like second-class citizens wounded colonials' pride and mocked their postwar expectations. The heady dreams of the role that the colonies would play in the British empire evaporated, leaving behind the bitter dregs of disappointment.

Impact of postwar recession

Britain's determination to centralize its empire after 1763 was a disaster of timing, not just psychologically but also economically. By then, the colonies were in the throes of a recession. The boom produced in America by government spending during the war had collapsed once subsidies were withdrawn. Colonial merchants were left with stocks full of imported goods gathering dust on their shelves. Farmers lost the brisk and profitable market of the army.

Colonial response to the Sugar Act reflected the painful postwar readjustments. New England merchants led the opposition, objecting to the Sugar Act principally on economic grounds. But with the passage of the Stamp Act, the terms of the imperial debate widened, and resistance intensified within all the colonies. The Stamp Act hit all colonials, not just New England merchants. It took money from the pockets of anyone who made a will, filed a deed, traded out of a colonial port, bought a newspaper, consulted an almanac, graduated from college, took a chance at dice, or played cards. More important, the Stamp Act served notice that Parliament possessed the rightful authority to tax the colonies directly and for the sole purpose of raising revenue.

Riots and Resolves

That unprecedented assertion provoked an unprecedented development: the first display of colonial unity. A nearly unanimous chorus of outrage greeted Parliament's claim that it could tax the colonies. During the spring and summer of 1765, American assemblies passed resolves denying Parliament that authority. The right to tax Americans belonged to colonial assemblies alone, they argued, by the law of nature and by the liberties guaranteed in colonial charters and in the British constitution.

Virginia's assembly, the House of Burgesses, took the lead in protesting the Stamp Act, prodded by Patrick Henry. Just 29 years old in 1765, Henry had tried his hand at planting in western Virginia before recognizing his real talent—demagoguery. Blessed with the eloquence of an evangelical preacher, the dashing charm of a southern gentleman, and a mind uncluttered by much learning, Henry parlayed his popularity as a smooth-talking lawyer into a place among the Burgesses. He took his seat just 10 days before introducing the Virginia Resolves against the Stamp Act.

Patrick Henry's resolves

This idealized likeness of Patrick Henry, by the American artist Thomas Sully, conveys the subject's intensity. Henry's eloquence and passion as an orator made a vivid impression on his contemporaries.

The Burgesses passed Henry's resolutions upholding their exclusive right to tax Virginians. They stopped short of adopting those resolves that called for outright resistance to the Stamp Act. When news of Virginia's stand spread to the rest of the colonies, other assemblies followed suit, affirming that the sole right to tax Americans resided in their elected representatives. But some colonial newspapers deliberately printed a different story—that the Burgesses had approved all of Henry's resolves, including one that sanctioned disobedience to any parliamentary tax. That prompted a few assemblies to endorse resistance. In October 1765 delegates from nine colonies convened in New York, where they prepared a joint statement of the American position and petitioned the king and Parliament to repeal both the Sugar Act and the Stamp Act.

Meanwhile, colonial leaders turned to the press to arouse popular opposition to the Stamp Act. Disposed by the writings of the English Opposition to think of politics in conspiratorial terms, they warned that Grenville and the king's other ministers schemed to deprive the colonies of their liberties by unlawfully taxing their property. The Stamp Act was only the first step in a sinister plan to enslave Americans.

Whether or not dark fears of a ministerial conspiracy haunted most colonials in 1765, many resisted the Stamp Act. The merchants of Boston, New York, and Philadelphia agreed to stop importing English goods in order to pressure British traders to lobby for repeal. In every colony, organizations emerged to ensure that the Stamp Act, if not repealed, would never be enforced.

The new resistance groups, which styled themselves the "Sons of Liberty," consisted of traders, lawyers, and prosperous artisans. With great success, they organized the lower classes of seaports in opposition to the Stamp Act. The sailors, dockworkers, poor artisans, apprentices, and servants who poured into the streets resembled mobs that had been organized from time to time earlier in the century. Previous riots against houses of prostitution, merchants who hoarded goods, or supporters of smallpox inoculation had not been spontaneous, uncontrolled outbursts. Crowds chose their targets and their tactics carefully and then carried out the communal will with little violence.

Sons of Liberty

In every colonial city, the mobs of 1765 burnt the stamp distributors in effigy, insulted them on the streets, demolished their offices, and attacked their homes. One hot night in August 1765, a mob went further than the Sons of Liberty had planned. They vandalized the stately mansion of Thomas Hutchinson, the unpopular lieutenant governor of Massachusetts and the brother-in-law of the colony's stamp distributor. By morning Hutchinson's home had been all but leveled. The destruction stunned Bostonians, especially the Sons of Liberty, who resisted Britain in the name of protecting private property. Thereafter they took care to keep crowds under tighter control. In most cases, the mere show of popular force was sufficient: by the first of November, the day that the Stamp Act took effect, most of the stamp distributors had resigned.

Repeal of the Stamp Act

Meanwhile, the repeal of the Stamp Act was already in the works back in England. The man who came—unintentionally—to America's relief was George III. The young king was a good man, industrious and devoted to the empire, but he was also immature and not particularly bright. Insecurity made the young king an irksome master, and he ran through ministers rapidly. By the end of 1765, George had dismissed Grenville for reasons unrelated to the uproar in America and appointed a new first minister, the Marquis of Rockingham. Rockingham had opposed the Stamp Act from the outset, and he had no desire to enforce it. He received support from London merchants, who were beginning to feel the pinch of the American nonimportation campaign, and secured repeal of the Stamp Act in March 1766.

The Stamp Act controversy demonstrated to colonials how similar in political outlook they were to one another and how different they were from the British. Americans had found that they shared the same assumptions about the meaning of representation. To counter colonial objections to the Stamp Act, Grenville and his supporters had claimed that Americans *were* represented in Parliament, even though they had elected none of its members. Americans were virtually represented, Grenville insisted, for each member of Parliament stood for the interests of the whole empire, not just those of the particular constituency that had elected him.

Virtual versus actual representation

Colonials could see no virtue in the theory of virtual representation. After all, the circumstances and interests of colonials, living an ocean away, were so different from those of Britons. The newly recognized consensus among Americans was that colonials could be truly represented only by those whom they had elected. Their view, known as actual representation, emphasized that elected officials were directly accountable to their constituents.

Americans also had discovered that they agreed about the extent of Parliament's authority over the colonies: it stopped at the right to tax. Colonials conceded Parliament's right to legislate and to regulate trade for the good of the whole empire. But taxation, in their view, was the free gift of the people through their representatives—who were not sitting in Parliament.

Declaratory Act

Members of Parliament had brushed aside colonial petitions and resolves, all but ignoring their constitutional argument. To make its own authority perfectly clear, Parliament accompanied the repeal of the Stamp Act with a Declaratory Act, asserting that it had the power to make laws for the colonies "in all cases whatsoever." In fact, the Declaratory Act clarified nothing. Did Parliament understand the power of legislation to include the power of taxation?

This 1766 porcelain of *Lord Chatham and America* attests to the popularity of William Pitt, Earl of Chatham, among Americans who resisted the Stamp Act. The artist's representation of "America" as a black kneeling in gratitude echoes the colonists' association of taxation with slavery.

The Townshend Acts

In the summer of 1766 George III—again inadvertently—gave the colonies what should have been an advantage by changing ministers again. The king replaced Rockingham with William Pitt, who enjoyed great favor among colonials for his leadership during the Seven Years' War and for his opposition to the Stamp Act. Almost alone among British politicians, Pitt had grasped and approved the colonists' constitutional objections to taxation. During Parliament's debate over repeal of the Stamp Act, Grenville asked sarcastically, "Tell me when the colonies were emancipated?" Pitt immediately shot back, "I desire to know when they were made slaves!"

If the man who believed that Americans were "the sons not the bastards of England" had been well enough to govern, matters between Great Britain and the colonies might have turned out differently. But almost immediately after Pitt took office, his health collapsed, and power passed into the hands of Charles Townshend, the chancellor of the exchequer, who wished only to raise more revenue from the Americans. In 1767 he persuaded Parliament to tax the lead, paint, paper, glass, and tea that Americans imported from Britain.

In addition, Townshend was determined to curb the power of the upstart American assemblies. To set a bold example, he singled out for punishment the New York legislature, which was refusing to comply with provisions of the Quartering Act of 1765. The troops that were left on the western frontier after the Seven Years' War had been pulled back into colonial seaports in 1766. In part their movement was meant to economize on costs, but royal officials also hoped the troops' presence would help quiet agitation over the Stamp Act. When the largest contingent came to New York, that colony's assembly protested, claiming that the cost of quartering the troops constituted a form of indirect taxation. But Townshend was determined, and Parliament backed him, suspending the New York assembly in 1767 until it agreed to obey the Quartering Act.

Townshend also dipped into the revenue from his new tariffs in order to make royal officials less dependent on the assemblies. Governors and other officers like customs collectors and judges had previously received their salaries from colonial legislatures. The assemblies lost that crucial leverage when Townshend used the revenues to pay those bureaucrats directly. Finally, in order to ensure more effective enforcement of all the duties on imports, Townshend created an American Board of Customs Commissioners, who appointed a small army of new customs collectors. He also established three new vice-admiralty courts in Boston, New York, and Charleston to bring smugglers to justice.

The Resistance Organizes

In Townshend's efforts to centralize the administration of the British empire, Americans saw new evidence that they were not being treated like the English. In newspapers and pamphlets colonial leaders repeated their earlier arguments against taxation. The most widely read publication, "A Letter from a Farmer in Pennsylvania," was the work of John Dickinson—who was, in fact, a Philadelphia lawyer. He urged Americans to protest the Townshend duties with a show of superior virtue—hard work, thrift, simplicity, and home manufacturing. By consuming fewer imported English luxuries, Dickinson argued, Americans would advance the cause of repeal.

John Dickinson and Samuel Adams

As Dickinson's star rose over Philadelphia, the Townshend Acts also shaped the destiny of another man, farther north. By the 1760s Samuel Adams was a leader in the Massachusetts assembly. In some ways his rise had been unlikely. Adams's earlier ventures as a merchant ended in bankruptcy; his stint as a tax collector left all of Boston in the red. But he proved a consummate political organizer and agitator, a man who knew how to exploit every advantage. First his enemies and later his friends claimed that Adams had decided on independence for America as early as 1768. In that year he persuaded the assembly to send to other colonial legislatures a circular letter condemning the Townshend Acts and calling for a united American resistance.

As John Dickinson and Samuel Adams whipped up public outrage, the Sons of Liberty again organized the opposition in the streets. Customs officials, like the stamp distributors before them, became targets of popular hatred. But the customs collectors gave as good as they got. Using the flimsiest excuses, they seized American vessels for violating royal regulations. With cold insolence they shook down American merchants for what amounted to protection money. The racketeering in the customs service brought tensions in Boston to a flash point in June 1768 after officials seized and condemned the *Liberty,* a sloop belonging to one of the city's biggest merchants, John Hancock. Several thousand Bostonians vented their anger in a night of rioting, searching out and roughing up customs officials.

The new secretary of state for the colonies, Lord Hillsborough, responded to the *Liberty* riot by sending two regiments of troops to Boston. In the fall of 1768 the redcoats, like a conquering army, paraded into town under the cover of warships lying off the harbor. (See Paul Revere's illustration on page 145.) In the months that followed, citizens bristled when challenged on the streets by armed soldiers. Even more disturbing to Bostonians was the execution of British military justice on the Common. British soldiers were whipped savagely for breaking military discipline, and desertion was punished by execution.

John Dickinson, a moderate who defended American rights but hoped for reconciliation

Daily Lives

PRIVATE SPACE/ PUBLIC SPACE
Street Theater

On the first night of November 1765 the narrow, winding streets of New York glowed with unaccustomed light. The Stamp Act was to have taken effect on that date, but the colony's stampmaster had long since resigned his office. What had frightened him into resignation could be seen in the moving shadows of men, women, and children, hundreds of them. The flaring torches and flickering candles that they carried aloft through the city's crooked byways cast on storefronts and doorways dark images of a crowd protesting the "death of Liberty."

Bringing up the rear of the procession was a seaman, bearing atop his head an old chair in which was seated a paper effigy. It represented Cadwallader Colden, "the most hated man in the province," and as New York's temporary governor, the local representative of British authority. The crowd marched to the center of town, shouting insults at Colden's figure and peppering it with pistol shots. When some of the marchers decided that their effigy should evoke the Roman Catholic pope, the chief symbol of tyrannical power to colonial Americans, they broke into Colden's stable and stole his fine coach for a proper papal throne. A second group joined the crowd, bearing their own piece of portable political theater—a gallows illuminated with two lanterns. Hanging from the gallows were effigies of Colden and the devil, the "grand Deceiver of Mankind." The entire assembly climaxed the evening by burning the effigies in a bonfire and then vandalizing the homes of several Stamp Act supporters.

Similar protests had been staged in seaports all over the colonies, following Boston's rioting against the Stamp Act. Some crowds held mock trials of unpopular British officials and then tarred and feathered, beat, hung, or burned their effigies. Other crowds enacted mock funerals, parading effigies in carts or coffins to the accompaniment of tolling church bells. Certain symbols appeared repeatedly: devils and gallows, lanterns and the paraphernalia of papal authority. The "people-out-of-doors," as such crowds were called in the eighteenth century, were making their views known—and their collective power felt.

The frequency and the political focus of street protests were new

A Pope's Day parade in mid-eighteenth-century Boston. Dressed as the devil's imps, boys accompany a cart bearing an effigy of the pope.

The *Liberty* riot and the arrival of British troops in Boston pushed colonial assemblies to coordinate their resistance more closely. Most legislatures endorsed the Massachusetts circular letter sent to them by Samuel Adams. They promptly adopted agreements not to import or to consume British goods. The reluctance among some merchants to revive nonimportation in 1767 gave way to greater enthusiasm by 1768, and by early 1769, such agreements were in effect throughout the colonies.

The Stamp Act crisis had also called forth intercolonial cooperation and tactics like nonimportation. But the protests against the Townshend Acts raised the stakes by creating new institutions to carry forward the resistance. Subscribers to the nonimportation agreements established "committees of inspection" to enforce to the decade preceding the Revolution. Still, the actions taken resembled those of earlier colonial crowds in their direction and restraint.

Equally striking, the resistance after 1765 drew on rituals and symbols surrounding traditional forms of protest, punishment, and celebration. For centuries before the Revolution, for example, crowds on both sides of the Atlantic had meted out to prostitutes, adulterers, or henpecked husbands punishments known in England as "rough music." After being tarred and feathered, the targets of rough music were often ridden "skimmington": placed on the back of a donkey, pelted with mud and dung, and driven through the streets to the accompaniment of hooting laughter and beating drums.

An even more important inspiration for resistance rituals came from Pope's Day, an elaborate annual outdoor celebration of anti-Catholic sentiment that started in Boston early in the eighteenth century. Craftworkers and apprentices from both the North End and the South End of town fashioned a cart bearing a lantern, effigies of the pope and the devil, and signs reading "The devil take the pope" and "North [or South] End Forever." Local boys with blackened faces and jester's caps played the part of the "devil's imps," taunting the pope's effigy as laboring people from both ends of town paraded their carts through the streets. Each group tried to destroy the other's creation before the final bonfire at the end of the evening.

As colonials adopted the symbols of the past for their street theater of political resistance, the borrowing took an odd twist. Pope's Day, the model for later protests, was in fact a colonial adaptation of an English celebration of monarchy, Guy Fawkes Day. In 1605 Fawkes, a Catholic, had been foiled in his attempt to assassinate James I, a failure that the English annually commemorated with a parade ending with burning the conspirator in effigy. In colonial America an effigy of the pope took the place of the Catholic Fawkes; in resistance rituals after 1765 hated British officials took the place of the pope. Beginning in 1776 Americans celebrated public readings of the Declaration by parading, burning, and burying effigies of George III. Strangely enough, Americans had converted symbols and ceremonies designed to honor monarchy to represent the killing of a king.

the ban on trade with Britain. The committees publicly denounced merchants who continued to import, vandalized their warehouses, forced them to stand under the gallows, and sometimes resorted to tar and feathers.

After 1768 the resistance also brought a broader range of colonials into the politics of protest. Artisans, who recognized that nonimportation would spur domestic manufacturing, began to organize as independent political groups. In many towns, women took an active part in opposing the Townshend duties. The "Daughters of Liberty" took to heart John Dickinson's advice: they wore homespun clothing instead of English finery, served coffee instead of tea, and boycotted shops selling British goods.

The International Sons of Liberty

The resistance after 1768 grew broader in another sense as well. Many of its supporters in the American colonies felt a new sense of kinship with freedom fighters throughout Europe and increasingly regarded themselves as part of a transatlantic network of the friends of liberty. They eagerly read about the doings of men like Charles Lucas, an Irish newspaper editor and member of the Irish Parliament, and John Wilkes, a London journalist and a leading politician of the Opposition, both of whom charged the king's ministers with corrupting the political life of the British Isles. The triumphs and setbacks of those combating tyrannical regimes even in distant Poland and Turkey engaged colonial sympathies. But perhaps the cause abroad that proved dearest to the hearts of liberty's friends in America during the late 1760s was the fate of Corsica.

Colonials follow Paoli's struggle

For years, the state of Genoa had been trying to impose its rule on this tiny island off the coast of Italy. Led by Pascal Paoli, the Corsicans had for decades waged what one New York newspaper touted as a "glorious struggle" against Genoese rule, an insurgency "interesting to every friend of liberty." In 1768, Genoa sold its title to the island to France, prompting many in the British Empire to hope that England would rally to defend Corsica's freedom, if only to keep France from seizing this strategic point in the Mediterranean. But British statesmen had no intention of going to war with France over mere Corsica, and when French troops routed his rebel army, Paoli fled to exile in England in 1769. To add insult to injury, Paoli, once lionized by the colonial resistance as "the greatest man of earth," snubbed Opposition leaders like John Wilkes, hobnobbed with the likes of the Duke of Grafton, the minister of the treasury, and even accepted a pension of 1,000 pounds a year from George III.

The moral of this sad story, one closely followed by the readers of colonial newspapers, was that the British ministry's corruption pervaded not only the empire, but all of Europe. Merely by doing nothing, the king's ministers had snuffed out the Corsican resistance. And by doling a mere thousand pounds annually, they had bought the compliance of its leader, the great Paoli himself. In the fate of Corsica and its sons of liberty, many colonials saw the threat that ambitious men posed to popular liberty—and a disturbing portent for America's future.

The Boston Massacre

A British grenadier

Meanwhile, the situation in Boston deteriorated steadily. British troops found themselves regularly cursed by citizens and occasionally pelted with stones, dirt, and human excrement. The British regulars were particularly unpopular among Boston's laboring classes because they competed with them for jobs. Off-duty soldiers moonlighted as maritime laborers, and they sold their services at cheaper rates than the wages paid to locals. By 1769, brawls between British regulars and waterfront workers broke out with unsettling frequency.

With some 4000 redcoats enduring daily contact with some 15,000 Bostonians under the sway of Samuel Adams, what happened on the night of March 5, 1770, was nearly inevitable. A crowd gathered around the customshouse for the sport of heckling its guard of 10 soldiers. The redcoats panicked and fended off insults and snowballs with live fire, hitting 11 rioters and killing 5. Adams and other propagandists seized upon the incident. Labeling the bloodshed "the Boston Massacre," they publicized that "atrocity" throughout the colonies. The radical *Boston Gazette* framed its account in an eye-catching black-bordered edition headed with a drawing of five coffins.

While Townshend's policies spurred the resistance in America, the obvious finally dawned on Parliament. They recognized that Townshend's duties only discouraged sales to colonials and encouraged them to manufacture at home. The argument for repeal was overwhelming, and the way had been cleared by the unexpected death of Townshend shortly after Parliament adopted his proposals. In 1770 his successor, Lord North, convinced Parliament to repeal all the Townshend duties except the one on tea, allowing that tax to stand as a source of revenue and as a symbol of Parliament's authority.

Resistance Revived

Repeal of the Townshend duties took the wind from the sails of American resistance for more than two years. But the controversy between England and the colonies had not been resolved. Colonials still paid taxes on molasses and tea, taxes to which they had not consented. They were still subject to trial in admiralty courts, which operated without juries. They still lived with a standing army in their midst. Beneath the banked fires of protest smoldered the live embers of Americans' political inequality. Any shift in the wind could fan those embers into flames.

While the new political activism of some American women often amused male leaders of the resistance, it inspired the scorn of some partisans of British authority. When the women of Edenton, North Carolina, renounced imported tea, this British cartoon mocked them.

The wind did shift, quite literally, on Narragansett Bay in 1772, running aground the *Gaspee,* a British naval schooner in hot pursuit of Rhode Island smugglers. Residents of nearby Providence quickly celebrated the *Gaspee*'s misfortune with a bonfire built on the ship's deck. Outraged British officials sent a special commission to look into the matter, intending once again to bypass the established colonial court system. The arrival of the *Gaspee* Commission reignited the imperial crisis, and in America, once again, resistance flared.

It did so through an ingenious mechanism, the committees of correspondence. Established in all the colonies by their assemblies, the committees drew up statements of American rights and grievances, distributed those documents within and among the colonies, and solicited responses from towns and counties. The brainchild of Samuel Adams, the committee structure formed a new communications network, one that fostered an intercolonial agreement on resistance to British measures. The strategy succeeded, and not only among colonies. The committees spread the scope of the resistance from colonial seaports into rural areas, engaging farmers and other country folk in the opposition to Britain.

Committees of correspondence

The committees had much to talk about when Parliament passed the Tea Act in 1773. The law was an effort to bail out the bankrupt East India Company by granting that corporation a monopoly on the tea trade to Americans. Because the company could use agents to sell its product directly, cutting out the middlemen, it could offer a lower price than that charged by colonial merchants. Thus, although the Tea Act would hurt American merchants, it promised to make tea cheaper for ordinary Americans. Still, many colonials saw the act as Parliament's attempt to trick them into accepting its authority to tax the colonies. They set out to deny that power once and for all.

In early winter of 1773 the tempest over the Tea Act peaked in Boston, with popular leaders calling for the cargoes to be returned immediately to England. On the evening of December 16, thousands of Bostonians, as well as farmers from the surrounding countryside, packed into the Old South Meetinghouse. Some members of the audience knew what Samuel Adams had on the evening's agenda, and they awaited their cue. It came when Adams told the meeting that they could do nothing more to save their country. War whoops rang through the meetinghouse, the crowd spilled onto the streets and out to the waterfront, and the Boston Tea Party commenced. From the throng emerged 50 men dressed as Indians to disguise their identities. The party boarded three vessels docked off Griffin's Wharf, broke open casks containing 90,000 pounds of tea, and brewed a beverage worth 10,000 pounds sterling in Boston harbor.

The Empire Strikes Back

The Boston Tea Party proved to British satisfaction that the colonies aimed at independence. Lord North's assessment was grim: "We are now to dispute whether we have, or have not, any authority in that country." To reassert its authority, Parliament passed the Coercive Acts, dubbed in the colonies the "Intolerable Acts." The first of these came in March 1774, two months after hearing of the Tea Party, when Parliament passed the Boston Port Bill, closing that harbor to all oceangoing traffic until such time as the king saw fit to reopen it. And George, Parliament announced, would not see fit until colonials paid the East India Company for their losses.

During the next three months, Parliament approved three other "intolerable" laws designed to punish Massachusetts. The Massachusetts Government Act handed over the colony's government to royal officials. Even convening town meetings would require royal permission. The Impartial Administration of Justice Act permitted any royal official accused of a crime in Massachusetts to be tried in England or in another colony. The Quartering Act allowed the housing of British troops in private homes—not only in Massachusetts but in all the colonies.

Many colonials saw the Coercive Acts as proof of a plot to enslave the colonies. In truth, the taxes and duties, laws and regulations of the past decade *were* part of a deliberate design—a commonsensical plan to centralize the administration of the British empire. But those efforts by the king's ministers and Parliament to run the colonies more efficiently and profitably were viewed by more and more Americans as a sinister conspiracy against their liberties.

For colonials, the study of history confirmed that interpretation, especially their reading of the histories written by the English Opposition. The Opposition's favorite historical subject was the downfall of republics, whether those of ancient Greece and Rome or more recent republican governments in Venice and Denmark. The lesson of their histories was always the same: power overwhelmed liberty. Those who had power would always seek more, and ambitious politicians would always pursue the same strategies to replace representative government and popular freedom with tyranny. In all places and at all times in the past, the Opposition warned, the conspiracy against liberty unfolded in predictable stages.

First, the people of a republic were impoverished by costly wars—something the colonists could well appreciate after the Seven Years' War. Then the government loaded the people with taxes to pay for those wars—as in the case of the Sugar Act or the Stamp Act or the Townshend duties. Next the government stationed a standing army in the country, pretending to protect the people but actually lending military force to those in power. And, of course, troops had been unloaded in Boston harbor, were quartered in New York, and were making trouble wherever they appeared. Then wicked men were favored with public offices and

Coercive Acts

Fear of conspiracy

patronage to secure their loyalty and support for the foes of liberty. And how else could one describe the royal governors, customs collectors, and judges who now received salaries from the revenues of the Townshend duties? Those in power also deliberately promoted luxury, idleness, and extravagance to weaken the moral fiber of the people—like the consumption encouraged by the low prices ensured by the Tea Act. Finally, those in power attempted to provoke the people to violent action in order to justify new oppression.

Week after week in the spring of 1774, reports of legislative outrages came across the waters. Shortly after approving the Coercive Acts, Parliament passed the Quebec Act, which established a permanent government in what had been French Canada. Ominously, it included no representative assembly. Equally ominous to Protestant colonials, the Quebec Act officially recognized the Roman Catholic church and extended the bounds of the province to include all land between the Mississippi and Ohio rivers. Suddenly New York, Pennsylvania, and Virginia found themselves bordering a British colony whose subjects had no voice in their own government.

Quebec Act

With the passage of the Coercive Acts, many more colonials came to believe not only that ambitious men plotted to enslave the colonies but also that those conspirators included almost all British political leaders. At the time of the Stamp Act and again during the agitation against the Townshend Acts, most colonials had confined their suspicions to the king's ministers. By 1774 members of Parliament were also implicated in that conspiracy—and a few radicals were wondering aloud about George III.

As alarm deepened in the wake of the Coercive Acts, one colony after another called for an intercolonial congress—like the one that had met during the Stamp Act crisis—to determine the best way to defend their freedom. But many also remained unsettled about where the logic of their actions seemed to be taking them: toward a denial that they were any longer English.

First Continental Congress called

Toward the Revolution

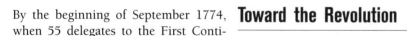

By the beginning of September 1774, when 55 delegates to the First Continental Congress gathered in Philadelphia, the news from Massachusetts was bad. The colony verged on anarchy, it was reported, as its inhabitants resisted the enforcement of the Massachusetts Government Act.

In the midst of this atmosphere of crisis, the members of Congress also had to take one another's measure. Many of the delegates had not traveled outside their own colonies. (All but Georgia sent representatives.) Although the delegates encountered a great deal of diversity, they quickly discovered that they esteemed the same traits of character, attributes that they called "civic virtue." These traits included simplicity and self-reliance, industry and thrift, and above all, an unselfish commitment to the public good. Most members of the Congress also shared a common mistrust of England, associating the mother country with vice, extravagance, and corruption.

Still, the delegates had some misgivings about those from other colonies. Massachusetts in particular brought with it a reputation—well deserved, considering that Samuel Adams was along—for radical action and a willingness to use force to accomplish its ends.

Samuel Adams, a radical who masterminded colonial resistance tactics

The First Continental Congress

As the delegates settled down to business, their aim was to reach agreement on three key points. How were they to justify the rights they claimed as American colonials? What were the limits of Parliament's power? And what were the proper tactics for resisting the Coercive Acts? Congress quickly agreed on the first point. The delegates affirmed that the law of nature, the colonial charters, and the British constitution provided the foundations of American liberties. This position was what most colonials had argued since 1765. On the two other issues, Congress charted a middle course between the demands of radicals and the reservations of conservatives.

Since the time of the Stamp Act, most colonials had insisted that Parliament had no authority to tax the colonies. But later events had demonstrated that Parliament could undermine colonial liberties by legislation as well as by taxation. The suspension of the New York legislature, the *Gaspee* Commission, and the Coercive Acts all fell into this category. Given those experiences, the delegates adopted a Declaration of Rights and Grievances on October 14, 1774, asserting the right of the colonies to tax and legislate for themselves. The Declaration of Rights thus limited Parliament's power over Americans more strictly than colonials had a decade earlier.

Joseph Galloway's plan

By denying Parliament's power to make laws for the colonies, the Continental Congress blocked efforts of the most conservative delegates to reach an accommodation with England. Their leading advocate, Joseph Galloway of Pennsylvania, proposed a plan of union with Britain similar to the one set forth by the Albany Congress in 1754. Under it, a grand council of the colonies would handle all common concerns, with any laws it passed subject to review and veto by Parliament. For its part, Parliament would have to submit for the grand council's approval any acts it passed affecting America. A majority of delegates judged that Galloway's proposal left Parliament too much leeway in legislating for colonials, and they rejected his plan.

Although the Congress denied Parliament the right to impose taxes or to make laws, delegates stopped short of declaring that it had no authority at all in the colonies. They approved Parliament's regulation of trade, but only because of the interdependent economy of the empire. And although some radical pamphleteers were attacking the king for plotting against American liberties, Congress acknowledged the continuing allegiance of the colonies to George III. In other words, the delegates called for a return to the situation that had existed in the empire before 1763, with Parliament regulating trade and the colonies exercising all powers of taxation and legislation.

The Association

On the question of resistance, Congress satisfied the desires of its most radical delegates by drawing up the Continental Association, an agreement to cease all trade with Britain until the Coercive Acts were repealed. They agreed that their fellow citizens would immediately stop drinking East India Company tea and that by December 1, 1774, merchants would no longer import goods of any sort from Britain. A ban on the export of American produce to Britain and the West Indies would go into effect a year later, during September 1775—the lag being a concession to southern rice and tobacco planters, who wanted to market crops already planted.

Revere and the Suffolk Resolves

The Association provided for the total cessation of trade, but Samuel Adams and other radicals wanted bolder action. They received help from Paul Revere, a Boston silversmith who had long provided newspapers with many lurid engravings showing British abuses. On September 16, Revere galloped into Philadelphia bearing a copy of resolves drawn up by Bostonians and other residents of Suffolk

County. The Suffolk Resolves, as they were called, branded the Coercive Acts as unconstitutional and called for civil disobedience to protest them. Congress endorsed the resolves, as Adams had hoped. But it would not approve another part of the radicals' agenda—preparing for war by authorizing proposals to strengthen and arm colonial militias.

Thus the First Continental Congress steered a middle course. Although determined to bring about repeal of the Coercive Acts, it held firm in resisting any revolutionary course of action. If British officials had responded to its recommendations and restored the status quo of 1763, the war for independence might have been postponed—perhaps indefinitely. On the other hand, even though the Congress did not go to the extremes urged by the radicals, its decisions drew colonials farther down the road to independence.

The Last Days of the British Empire in America

Most colonials applauded the achievements of the First Continental Congress. They expected that the Association would bring about a speedy repeal of the Coercive Acts. But fear that the colonies were moving toward a break with Britain led others to denounce the doings of the Congress. Conservatives were convinced that if independence was declared, chaos would ensue. Colonials, they argued, would quarrel over land claims and sectional tensions and religious differences, as they had so often in the recent past. Without Britain to referee such disputes, they feared, the result would be civil war, followed by anarchy.

The man in America with the least liking for the Continental Congress sat in the hottest seat in the colonies, that of the governor of Massachusetts. General Thomas Gage now watched as royal authority crumbled in Massachusetts and the rebellion spread to other colonies. In June 1774 a desperate Gage dissolved the Massachusetts legislature, only to see it re-form, on its own, into a Provincial Congress. That new body assumed the government of the colony in October and began arming the militia. Gage then started to fortify Boston and pleaded for more troops—only to find his fortifications damaged by saboteurs and his requests for reinforcements ignored by Britain.

Thomas Gage in Boston

Outside Boston, royal authority fared no better. Farmers in western Massachusetts forcibly closed the county courts, turning out royally appointed justices and establishing their own tribunals. Popularly elected committees of inspection charged with enforcing the Association took over towns everywhere in Massachusetts, not only restricting trade but also regulating every aspect of local life. The committees called upon townspeople to display civic virtue by renouncing "effeminate" English luxuries like tea and fine clothing and "corrupt" leisure activities like dancing, gambling, and racing. The committees also assigned spies to report on any citizen unfriendly to the resistance. "Enemies of American liberty" risked being roundly condemned in public or beaten and pelted with mud and dung by hooting, raucous mobs.

Collapse of royal authority

Throughout the colonies a similar process was under way. During the winter and early spring of 1775, provincial congresses, county conventions, and local committees of inspection were emerging as revolutionary governments, replacing royal authority at every level. As the spectacle unfolded before General Gage, he concluded that only force could subdue the colonies. It would take more than he had at his command, but reinforcements might be on the way. In February of 1775, Parliament had approved an address to the king declaring that the colonies were in rebellion.

The Fighting Begins

As spring came to Boston, the city waited. A band of artisans, organized as spies and express riders by Paul Revere, watched General Gage and waited for him to act. Gage waited for reinforcements from Lord North and watched the hostile town. On April 14 word from North finally arrived: Gage was to seize the leaders of the Provincial Congress. That would behead the rebellion, North said. Gage knew better than to believe North—but he also knew that he had to do something.

On the night of April 18 the sexton of Boston's Christ Church hung two lamps from its steeple. It was a signal that British troops had moved out of Boston and were marching toward the arms and ammunition stored by the Provincial Congress in Concord. As the lamps flashed the signal, Revere and a comrade, William Dawes, rode out to arouse the countryside.

Lexington and Concord

When the news of a British march reached Lexington, its Minuteman militia of about 70 farmers, chilled and sleepy, mustered on the Green at the center of the small rural town. Lexington Green lay directly on the road to Concord. At about four in the morning 700 British troops massed on the Green, and their commander, Major John Pitcairn, ordered the Lexington militia to disperse. The townsmen, outnumbered and overawed, began to obey. Then a shot rang out—whether the British or the Americans fired first is unknown—and then two volleys burst from the ranks of the redcoats. With a cheer the British set off for Concord, five miles distant, leaving eight Americans dead on Lexington Green.

By dawn, hundreds of Minutemen from nearby towns were surging into Concord. The British entered at about seven in the morning and moved, unopposed, toward their target, a house lying across the bridge that spanned the Concord River. While three companies of British soldiers searched for American guns and ammunition, three others, posted on the bridge itself, had the misfortune to find those American arms—borne by the rebels and being fired with deadly accuracy. By noon, the British were retreating to Boston.

An unknown artist depicted the arrival of British troops in Concord, Massachusetts, just before their fateful encounter with the Minutemen on the North Bridge.

The narrow road from Concord to Boston's outskirts became a corridor of carnage. Pursuing Americans fired on the column of fleeing redcoats from the cover of fences and forests. By the end of April 19, the British had sustained 273 casualties; the Americans, 95. It was only the beginning. By evening of the next day, some 20,000 New England militia had converged on Boston for a long siege.

Common Sense

The bloodshed at Lexington Green and Concord's North Bridge committed colonials to a course of rebellion—and independence. That was the conclusion drawn by Thomas Paine, who urged other Americans to do the same.

Paine himself was hardly an American at all. He was born in England, first apprenticed as a corsetmaker, appointed later a tax collector, and fated finally to become midwife to the age of republican revolutions. Paine came to Philadelphia late in 1774, set up as a journalist, and made the American cause his own. "Where liberty is, there is my country," he declared. In January 1776 he wrote a pamphlet to inform colonials of their identity as a distinct people and their destiny as a nation. *Common Sense* enjoyed tremendous popularity and wide circulation, selling 120,000 copies within three months of its publication.

After Lexington and Concord, Paine wrote, as the imperial crisis passed "from argument to arms, a new era for politics is struck—a new method of thinking has arisen." That new era of politics for Paine was the age of republicanism. He denounced monarchy as a foolish and dangerous form of government, one that violated the dictates of reason as well as the word of the Bible. By ridicule and remorseless argument, he severed the ties of colonial allegiance to the king. *Common Sense* scorned George III as "the Royal Brute of Britain," who had enslaved the chosen people of the new age—the Americans.

Thomas Paine argues for independence

Nor did Paine stop there. He rejected the idea that colonials were or should want to be English. The colonies occupied a huge continent an ocean away from the tiny British Isles—clear proof that nature itself had fashioned America for independence. England lay locked in Europe, doomed to the corruption of an Old World. America had been discovered anew to become an "asylum of liberty."

Many Americans had liked being English, but being English hadn't worked. Perhaps that is another way of saying that over the course of nearly two centuries colonial society and politics had evolved in such a way that the identity between the Americans and the English no longer fit. By the end of the Seven Years' War, the colonies had established political institutions that made the rights of "freeborn Britons" more available to ordinary citizens in America than in the nation that had created those liberties. Perhaps, then, most Americans had succeeded *too* well at becoming English, regarding themselves as political equals entitled to basic constitutional freedoms. In the space of less than a generation, the logic of events made clear that despite all that the English and Americans shared, in the distribution of political power they were fundamentally at odds. And the call to arms at Lexington and Concord made retreat impossible.

Thomas Paine, author of
Common Sense

On that point Paine was clear. It was the destiny of Americans to be republicans, not monarchists. It was the destiny of Americans to be independent, not subject to British dominion. It was the destiny of Americans to be American, not English. That, according to Thomas Paine, was common sense.

chapter summary

Resistance to British authority grew slowly but steadily in the American colonies during the period following the Seven Years' War.

- The new measures passed by Parliament in the early 1760s—the Proclamation of 1763, the Sugar Act, the Stamp Act, the Currency Act, and the Quartering Act—were all designed to bind the colonies more closely to the empire.

- These new measures deflated American expectations of a more equal status in the empire and also violated what Americans understood to be their constitutional and political liberties—the right to consent to taxation, the right to trial by jury, and the freedom from standing armies.

- Although Parliament repealed the Stamp Act, it reasserted its authority to tax Americans by passing the Townshend Acts in 1767.

- With the passage of the Coercive Acts in 1774, many Americans concluded that all British actions in the past decade were part of a deliberate plot to enslave Americans by depriving them of property and liberty.

- When the First Continental Congress convened in September 1774, delegates resisted both radical demands to mobilize for war and conservative appeals to reach an accommodation.

- The First Continental Congress denied Parliament any authority in the colonies except the right to regulate trade; it also drew up the Continental Association, an agreement to cease all trade with Britain until the Coercive Acts were repealed.

- When General Thomas Gage sent troops from Boston in April 1775 to seize arms being stored at Concord, the first battle of the Revolution took place.

interactive learning

The Primary Source Investigator CD-ROM offers the following materials related to this chapter:

- Interactive maps: **The Atlantic World, 1400–1850** (M2) and **The Settlement of Colonial America, 1700–1763** (M5)

- A collection of primary sources examining the age of the American Revolution, including the imperial acts that outraged American colonists, a selection from Thomas Paine's seminal work *Common Sense,* and a gazette article describing the Boston Massacre.

additional reading

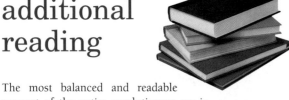

The most balanced and readable account of the entire revolutionary era is still Edmund S. Morgan, *The Birth of the Republic* (1956). His study entitled *The Stamp Act Crisis* (1953), coauthored with Helen M. Morgan, remains the clearest and most vivid description of the issues, events, and people involved in that defining moment of the imperial crisis. Good coverage of later developments can be found in Pauline Maier, *From Resistance to Revolution* (1972). To understand the impact of the Seven Years' War on the attitudes toward Britain among ordinary men in Massachusetts, consult Fred Anderson's excellent *A People's Army* (1984); two equally imaginative interpretations of how the logic of resistance took shape among colonials are Timothy Breen, *Tobacco Culture* (1985); and Robert A. Gross, *The Minutemen and Their World* (1976). Bernard Bailyn, *The Ideological Origins of the American Revolution* (1967), demonstrates the influence of the English opposition in the evolution of colonial political thought. The most important book on British politics in this period is John Brewer, *Party Ideology*

and Popular Politics at the Accession of George III (1976), but for a lively treatment of the monarchy, see J. H. Plumb, *The First Four Georges* (1956).

Biographies shed light on not only their subjects but also the times in which they lived. Some of the best biographies chronicle the careers of eighteenth-century Americans who led—or opposed—the resistance to Britain. For the rebels, see Richard R. Beeman, *Patrick Henry* (1974); Eric Foner, *Tom Paine and Revolutionary America* (1976); Pauline Maier, *The Old Revolutionaries* (1980); and Dumas Malone, *Jefferson the Virginian* (1948). For sympathetic treatment of one American loyalist, see Bernard Bailyn, *The Ordeal of Thomas Hutchinson* (1974). For a fuller list of readings, see the Bibliography at www.mhhe.com/davidsonnation5.

significant events

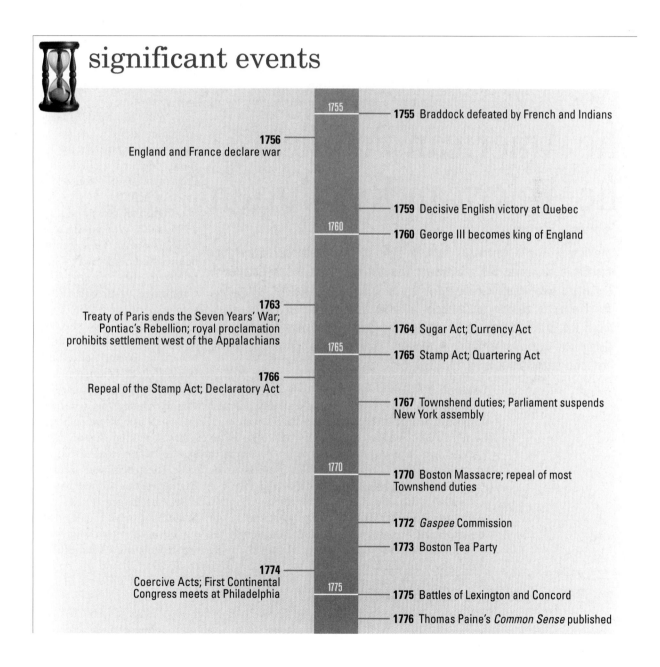

1755 Braddock defeated by French and Indians

1756 England and France declare war

1759 Decisive English victory at Quebec

1760 George III becomes king of England

1763 Treaty of Paris ends the Seven Years' War; Pontiac's Rebellion; royal proclamation prohibits settlement west of the Appalachians

1764 Sugar Act; Currency Act

1765 Stamp Act; Quartering Act

1766 Repeal of the Stamp Act; Declaratory Act

1767 Townshend duties; Parliament suspends New York assembly

1770 Boston Massacre; repeal of most Townshend duties

1772 *Gaspee* Commission

1773 Boston Tea Party

1774 Coercive Acts; First Continental Congress meets at Philadelphia

1775 Battles of Lexington and Concord

1776 Thomas Paine's *Common Sense* published

Chapter 6

F rom a high place somewhere in the city—Beacon Hill, perhaps, or Copse Hill—General Thomas Gage looked down on Boston. Through a spyglass his gaze traveled over the church belfries and steeples, the roofs of brick and white frame houses. Finally he fixed his sights on a figure far in the distance across the Charles River. The man was perched atop a crude fortification on Breed's Hill, an elevation lying just below Bunker Hill on the Charlestown peninsula. Gage took the measure of his enemy: an older man, past middle age, a sword swinging beneath his homespun coat, a broad-brimmed hat shading his eyes. As he passed the spyglass to his ally, an American loyalist, Gage asked Abijah Willard if he knew the man on the fort. Willard peered across the Charles and identified his own brother-in-law, Colonel William Prescott. A veteran of the Seven Years' War, Prescott was now a leader in the rebel army laying siege to Boston.

The American People & The American Revolution

1775–1783

preview • Would Americans actually fight for independence? Even after the Battle of Bunker Hill, the answer was not clear. But British victories in the North were countered by an American triumph at Saratoga, convincing the French to commit to a crucial alliance with the United States. Then, when the British attempted to conquer the South, they were foiled by the Continental Army under Nathanael Greene. Their surrender to Washington at Yorktown astonished most of Europe.

"Will he fight?" Gage wondered aloud.

"I cannot answer for his men," Willard replied, "but Prescott will fight you to the gates of hell."

Fight they did on June 17, 1775, both William Prescott and his men. The evening before, three regiments had followed the colonel from Cambridge to Breed's Hill— soldiers drawn from the thousands of militia who had swarmed to surround British-occupied Boston after the bloodshed at Lexington and

Battle of Bunker Hill

Concord. All through the night, they dug deep trenches and built up high earthen walls atop the hill. At the first light of day, a British warship spotted the new rebel outpost and opened fire. By noon barges were ferrying British troops under Major General William Howe across the half mile of river that separated Boston from Charlestown. The 1600 raw rebel troops tensed at the sight of scarlet-coated soldiers streaming ashore, glittering bayonets grasped at the ready. The rebels were farmers and artisans, not professional soldiers, and they were frightened out of their wits.

But Prescott and his men held their ground. The British charged Breed's Hill twice, and Howe watched in horror as streams of fire felled his troops. Finally, during the third British frontal assault, the rebels ran out of ammunition and were forced to withdraw. Redcoats poured into the rebel fort, bayoneting its handful of remaining defenders. By nightfall the British had taken Breed's Hill and the rest of the Charlestown peninsula. They had bought a dark triumph at the cost of 228 dead and 800 wounded.

The cost came high in loyalties as well. The fighting on Breed's Hill fed the hatred of Britain that had been building since April. Throughout America, preparations for war intensified: militia in every colony mustered; communities stockpiled arms and ammunition. Around Charlestown civilians fled the countryside, abandoning homes and shops set afire by the British shelling of Breed's Hill. "The roads filled with frightened women and children, some in carts with their tattered

Eleven years after the event, the American artist John Trumbull painted *Battle of Bunker's Hill* (1786), a canvas executed in the currently fashionable mode of grand historical painting, designed to commemorate (and elevate) an occasion of note.

furniture, others on foot fleeing into the woods," recalled Hannah Winthrop, one of their number.

The bloody, indecisive fight on the Charlestown peninsula known as the Battle of Bunker Hill actually took place on Breed's Hill. And the exchange between Thomas Gage and Abijah Willard that is said to have preceded the battle may not have taken place at all. But the story has persisted in the folklore of the American Revolution. Whether it really happened or not, the conversation between Gage and Willard raised the question that both sides wanted answered. Were Americans willing to fight for independence from British rule? It was one thing, after all, to oppose the British ministry's policy of taxation. It was another to support a rebellion for which the ultimate price of failure was hanging for treason. And it was another matter entirely for men to wait nervously atop a hill as the seasoned troops of their own "mother country" marched toward them with the intent to kill.

Will they fight? This Pennsylvania regimental flag gives one reason why some did.

Indeed, the question "will they fight?" was revolutionary shorthand for a host of other questions concerning how ordinary Americans would react to the tug of loyalties between long-established colonial governments and a long-revered parent nation and monarch. For slaves, the question revolved around their allegiance to masters who spoke of liberty or to their masters' enemies who promised liberation. For those who led the rebels, it was a question of strengthening the resolve of the undecided, coordinating resistance, instilling discipline—translating the *will* to fight into the ability to do so. And for those who believed the rebellion was a madness whipped up by artful politicians, it was a question of whether to remain silent or risk speaking out, whether to take up arms for the king or flee. All these

Americans react to the Revolution

questions were raised, of necessity, by the act of revolution. But the barrel of a rifle shortened them to a single, pointed question: will you fight?

The Decision for Independence

The delegates to the Second Continental Congress gathered at Philadelphia on May 10, 1775, just one month after the battles at Lexington and Concord. They had to determine whether independence or reconciliation offered the best way to protect the liberties of their colonies.

For a brash, ambitious lawyer from Braintree, Massachusetts, British abuses dictated only one course. "The Cancer [of official corruption] is too deeply rooted," wrote John Adams, "and too far spread to be cured by anything short of cutting it out entire." Yet during the spring and summer of 1775, even strong advocates of independence did not openly seek a separation from Britain. If the radicals' objective of independence was ever to be achieved, greater agreement among Americans had to be attained. Moderates and conservatives harbored deep misgivings about independence: they had to be brought along slowly.

The Second Continental Congress

To bring them along, Congress adopted the "Olive Branch Petition" in July 1775. Drawn up by Pennsylvania's John Dickinson, the document affirmed American loyalty to George III and asked the king to disavow the policies of his principal ministers. At the same time Congress issued a declaration denying that the colonies aimed at independence. Yet, less than a month earlier, Congress had authorized the creation of a rebel military force, the Continental Army, and had issued paper money to pay for the troops.

Aggressive British response

A Congress that sued for peace while preparing for war was a puzzle that British politicians—least of all, Lord George Germain—did not even try to understand. A tough-minded statesman now charged with overseeing colonial affairs, Germain was determined to subdue the rebellion by force. George III proved just as stubborn: he refused to receive the Olive Branch Petition. By the end of that year Parliament had shut down all trade with the colonies and had ordered the Royal Navy to seize colonial merchant ships on the high seas. In November 1775 Virginia's royal governor, Lord Dunmore, offered freedom to any slaves who would join the British. During January of the next year, he ordered the shelling of Norfolk, Virginia, reducing that town to a smoldering rubble.

British belligerence withered the cause of reconciliation within Congress and the colonies. Support for independence gained more momentum from the overwhelming reception of *Common Sense* in January 1776. Radicals in Congress realized that the future was theirs and were ready to act. In April 1776 the delegates opened American trade to every nation in the world except Great Britain; a month later Congress advised the colonies to establish new state governments. And on June 7 Virginia's Richard Henry Lee offered the motion "that these United Colonies are, and of right ought to be, free and independent States . . . and that all political connection between them and the State of Great Britain is, and ought to be, totally dissolved."

The Declaration

Congress postponed a final vote on Lee's motion until July. Some opposition still lingered among delegates from the middle colonies, and a committee appointed to write a declaration of independence needed time to complete its work. That committee included some of the leading delegates in Congress: John Adams, Benjamin Franklin, Connecticut's Roger Sherman, and New York's Robert Livingston. But the man who did most of the drafting was a young planter and lawyer from western Virginia.

Thomas Jefferson was just 33 years old in the summer of 1776 when he withdrew to his lodgings on the outskirts of Philadelphia, pulled a portable writing desk onto his lap, and wrote the statement that would explain American independence to a "candid world." In the document's brief opening section, Jefferson set forth a general justification of revolution that invoked the "self-evident truths" of human equality and "unalienable rights" to "life, liberty, and the pursuit of happiness." These natural rights had been "endowed" to all persons "by their Creator," the Declaration pointed out; thus there was no need to appeal to the narrower claim of the "rights of Englishmen."

While the first part of the Declaration served notice that Americans no longer considered themselves English, its second and longer section denied England any authority in the colonies. In its detailed history of American grievances against the British empire, the Declaration referred only once to Parliament. Instead, it blamed George III for a "long train of abuses and usurpations" designed to achieve "absolute despotism." Unlike *Common Sense,* the Declaration denounced only the reigning king of England; it did not attack the institution of monarchy itself. But like *Common Sense,* the Declaration affirmed that government originated in the consent of the governed and upheld the right of the people to overthrow oppressive rule.

Later generations have debated what Jefferson meant by the "pursuit of happiness" and whether he had either women or black Americans in mind when he wrote the famous phrase "all men are created equal." His own contemporaries in Congress did not pause to consider those questions and surely would have found themselves divided if they had. No matter. By firmly grounding the Declaration on the natural rights due all people, Jefferson placed equality at the center of the new nation's identity, setting the framework for a debate that would continue over the next two centuries. Congress adopted the Declaration of Independence on July 4, 1776.

Thomas Jefferson

Blaming George III

This painting, which commemorated the signing of the Declaration of Independence, shows Benjamin Franklin (seated center), obviously weighing the consequences of the action he and his colleagues are about to undertake. John Hancock, the president of the Congress, is reported to have remarked, "We must be unanimous; there must be no pulling different ways; we must all hang together." Franklin is said to have rejoined, "Yes, we must indeed all hang together, or most assuredly, we shall all hang separately."

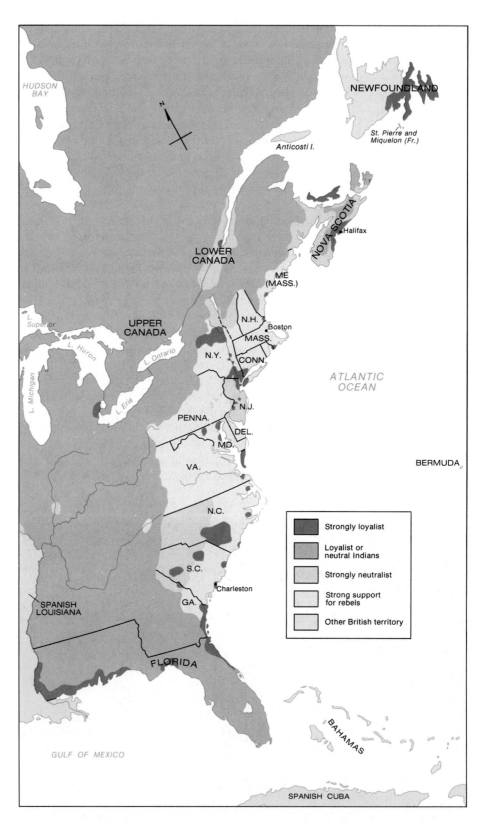

Patterns of Allegiance While most New Englanders rallied behind the rebel cause, support for the Revolution was not as widespread in the middle colonies and southern colonies.

HUDSON BAY

NEWFOUNDLAND

St. Pierre and Miquelon (Fr.)

Anticosti I.

NOVA SCOTIA

Halifax

LOWER CANADA

ME (MASS.)

L. Superior

UPPER CANADA

N.H.

Boston

L. Huron

MASS.

L. Michigan

L. Ontario

N.Y.

CONN.

L. Erie

ATLANTIC OCEAN

N.J.

PENNA.

DEL.

MD.

BERMUDA

VA.

N.C.

Strongly loyalist

Loyalist or neutral Indians

S.C.

Strongly neutralist

Charleston

Strong support for rebels

SPANISH LOUISIANA

GA.

Other British territory

FLORIDA

BAHAMAS

GULF OF MEXICO

SPANISH CUBA

American Loyalists

But the sentiment for independence was not universal. Americans who would not back the rebellion, supporters of the king and Parliament, numbered perhaps one-fifth of the population in 1775. While they proclaimed themselves "loyalists," their rebel opponents dubbed them "tories"—"a thing whose head is in England, whose body is in America, and whose neck ought to be stretched." That division made the Revolution a conflict pitting Americans against one another as well as the British. In truth, the war for independence was the first American civil war.

Predictably, the king and Parliament commanded the strongest support in colonies that had been wracked by internal strife earlier in the eighteenth century. In New York, New Jersey, Pennsylvania, and the Carolinas, not only did memories of old struggles sharpen worries of future upheaval, but old enemies often took different sides in the Revolution. The Carolina backcountry emerged as a stronghold of loyalist sentiment because of influential local men who cast their lot with Britain. To win support against Carolina's rebels, whose ranks included most wealthy coastal planters, western loyalist leaders played on ordinary settlers' resentments of privileged easterners. Grievances dating back to the 1760s also influenced the revolutionary allegiances of former land rioters of New York and New Jersey. If their old landlord opponents opted for the rebel cause, the tenants took up loyalism.

Other influences also fostered allegiance to Britain. Government officials who owed their jobs to the empire, major city merchants who depended on British trade, and Anglicans living outside the South retained strong ties to the parent country. Loyalists were also disproportionately represented among recent emigrants from the British Isles. The inhabitants of Georgia, the newest colony, inclined toward the king, as did the Highland Scots, many of whom had arrived in the colonies as soldiers during the Seven Years' War or had worked for a short time in the southern backcountry as tobacco merchants and Indian traders.

In any case, although a substantial minority, loyalists never became numerous enough anywhere to pose a serious menace to the Revolution. A more formidable threat was posed by the British army. And the greatest threat of all was posed by those very Americans who claimed that they wanted independence. For the question remained: would they fight?

Sources of loyalist support

The Fighting in the North

In the summer of 1775 Americans who wished to remain neutral probably outnumbered either loyalists or rebels. From the standpoint of mere survival, staying neutral made more sense than fighting for independence. Even the most ardent advocates of American rights had reason to harbor doubts, given the odds against the rebel colonists defeating the armed forces of the British empire.

Perhaps no friend of American liberty saw more clearly how slim the chances of a rebel victory were than George Washington. But Washington's principles, and his sense of honor, prevailed. June of 1775 found him, then 43 years old, attending the deliberations of the Second Continental Congress and dressed—a bit conspicuously—in his officer's uniform. The other delegates listened closely to his opinions on military matters, for Washington was the most celebrated American veteran of the Seven Years' War who remained young enough to lead a campaign. Better still, as a southerner he could bring his region into what thus far had

George Washington, general

George Washington

"Regulars" versus
the militia

remained mostly New England's fight. Congress readily appointed him commander in chief of a newly created Continental Army.

The Two Armies at Bay

Thus did Washington find himself, only a month later, looking to bring some order to the rebel forces massing around Boston. He knew he faced a formidable foe.

Highly trained, ably led, and efficiently equipped, the king's troops were seasoned professionals. Rank-and-file soldiers, men drawn mainly from the bottom of British society, were drilled rigorously and disciplined (often savagely) by an aristocratic officer corps. At the height of the campaign in America, reinforcements brought the number of British troops to 50,000, strengthened by some 30,000 Hessian mercenaries from Germany and the support of half the ships in the British navy, the largest in the world.

Washington was more modest about the army under his command, and he had much to be modest about. At first Congress recruited his fighting force of 16,600 rebel "regulars," the Continental Army, from the ranks of local New England militia bands. Although enlistments swelled briefly during the patriotic enthusiasm of 1775, for the rest of the war Washington's Continentals suffered chronic shortages of men and supplies. Even strong supporters of the Revolution hesitated to join the regular army, with its low pay and strict discipline and the constant threat of disease and danger. Most men preferred to fight instead as members of local militia units, the "irregular" troops who turned out to support the regular army whenever British forces came close to their neighborhoods.

The general reluctance to join the Continental Army created a host of difficulties for its commander and for Congress. Washington wanted and needed an army whose size and military capability could be counted on in long campaigns. He could not create an effective fighting force out of civilians who mustered occasionally with the militia or enlisted for short stints in the Continental Army. Washington's desire for a professional military establishment clashed with the preferences of most republican leaders. They feared standing armies and idealized "citizen-soldiers"—men of selfless civic virtue who volunteered whenever needed—as the backbone of the common defense. "Oh, that I was a soldier," chubby John Adams fantasized in 1775. "Everyone must and will and shall be a soldier."

But everyone did not become a soldier, and the dwindling number of volunteers gradually overcame republican fears of standing armies. In September 1776 Congress set terms in the Continental Army at a minimum of three years or for the duration of the war and assigned each state to raise a certain number of troops. They offered every man who enlisted in the army a cash bounty and a yearly clothing issue; enlistees for the duration were offered 100 acres of land as well. Still the problem of recruitment persisted. Less than a year later, Congress recommended that the states adopt a draft, but Congress had no authority to compel the states to meet their troop quotas.

Even in the summer of 1775, before enlistments fell off, Washington was worried. As his Continentals laid siege to British-occupied Boston, he measured them against the adversary and found them wanting. Inexperienced officers provided no real leadership, and the men under their command shirked the most basic responsibilities of soldiers. They slipped away from camp at night; they left sentry duty before being relieved; they took potshots at the British; they tolerated filthy conditions in their camps.

While Washington strove to impose discipline on his Continentals, he also attempted, without success, to rid himself of "the Women of the Army." When American men went off to fight, their wives usually stayed at home. To women then fell the sole responsibility for running farms and businesses, raising children, and keeping households together. They helped to supply the troops by sewing clothing, making blankets, and saving rags and lead weights for bandages and bullets. Other women on the home front organized relief for the widows and orphans of soldiers and protests against merchants who hoarded scarce commodities.

But the wives of poor men who joined the army were often left with no means to support their families. Thousands of such women—1 for every 15 soldiers—drifted after the troops. In return for half-rations, they cooked and washed for the soldiers; and after battles, they nursed the wounded, buried the dead, and scavenged the field for clothing and equipment. An even larger number of women accompanied the redcoats: their presence was the only thing that Washington did not admire about the British army and could barely tolerate in his own. But the services that they performed were indispensable, and women followed the troops throughout the war.

Women of the Army

Laying Strategies

At the same time that he tried to discipline the Continentals, Washington designed a defensive strategy to compensate for their weakness. To avoid exposing raw rebel troops on "open ground against their Superiors in number and Discipline," he planned to fight the British from strong fortifications. With that aim in mind, in March 1776, Washington barricaded his army on Dorchester Heights, an elevation commanding Boston harbor from the south. That maneuver, which allowed American artillery to fire on enemy warships, confirmed a decision already made by the British to evacuate their entire army from Boston and sail for Halifax, Nova Scotia.

Britain had hoped to reclaim its colonies with a strategy of strangling the resistance in Massachusetts. But by the spring of 1776 it saw clearly that more was required than a show of force against New England. Instead Britain's leaders chose to wage a conventional war in America, capturing major cities and crushing the Continental forces in a decisive battle. Military victory, the British believed, would enable them to restore political control and reestablish imperial authority.

British assumptions

The first target was New York City. General William Howe and Lord George Germain, the British officials now charged with overseeing the war, chose that seaport for its central location and—they hoped—its large loyalist population. They planned for Howe's army to move from New York City up the Hudson River, meeting ultimately with British troops under General Sir Guy Carleton coming south from Canada. Either the British drive would lure Washington into a major engagement, crushing the Continentals, or, if unopposed, the British offensive would cut America in two, smothering resistance to the south by isolating New England.

Unfortunately for the British, the strategy was sounder than the men placed in charge of executing it. General Howe took to extremes the conventional wisdom of eighteenth-century European warfare, which aimed as much at avoiding heavy casualties as at winning victories against the enemy. Concern for preserving troops addicted Howe to caution, when daring more would have carried the day. Howe's brother, Admiral Lord Richard Howe, the head of naval operations in America, also stopped short of pressing the British advantage, owing to his personal desire for reconciliation. The reluctance of the Howe brothers to fight became the formula for British frustration in the two years that followed.

Howe brothers

Daily Lives

CLOTHING AND FASHION

Radical Chic and the Revolutionary Generation

Women and men of revolutionary America sought to invest themselves with virtue as they escaped British "corruption." The most zealous partisans of colonial rights took that "investiture" to a literal extreme: they made and wore particular clothing as an emblem of political commitment. In the 1760s "homespun," any coarse cloth made in America, became a badge of opposition to British colonial policy.

Clothes sewn from domestic textiles identified the men and women who wore them as friends of liberty, freed from the vanity of British fashion and the humiliating dependence on British imports. As early as 1766 the radical press called for increased domestic industry to offset American reliance on English cloth. It aimed its pleas particularly at the women who managed colonial households.

By 1769 radical propaganda had produced a new ritual of American resistance, the patriotic spinning competition. Wives and daughters from some of the wealthiest and most prominent families, women who had heretofore vied to outdo each other in acquiring the latest English finery, were the featured players in this new form of political theater. Its setting was usually the home of a local minister, where, early in the morning, "respectable" young ladies, all dressed in homespun, assembled with their spinning wheels. They spent the day spinning furiously, stopping only to sustain themselves with "American produce . . . which was more agreeable to them than any foreign Dainties and Delicacies" and to drink herbal tea. At the end of the day the minister accepted their homespun and delivered an edifying sermon to all present. That was a large group, often including from 20 to 100 "respectable" female spinners as well as hundreds of other townsfolk who had come to watch the competition or to provide food and entertainment.

Women reveled in the new attention and value that the male resistance movement and the

Hunting shirts like the one worn by this rifleman (second from right) captured the imagination of the French army officer in America who made these watercolor sketches of revolutionary soldiers. The enlistment of blacks (infantryman at the far left) drew his attention as well.

The Campaigns in New York and New Jersey

However cautiously, British forces landed on Staten Island in New York harbor during July 1776. The Continentals marched from Boston and fortified Brooklyn Heights on Long Island, the key to the defenses of New York City on Manhattan Island. By mid-August, 32,000 British troops, including 8000 Hessians, the largest expeditionary force of the eighteenth century, faced Washington's army of 23,000.

British capture New York City

At dawn on August 22 the Howe brothers moved on Long Island and easily pushed the rebel army back across the East River to Manhattan. After lingering on Long Island for a month, the Howes again lurched into action, ferrying their forces to Kip's Bay, just a few miles south of Harlem. When the British landed, the handful of rebel defenders at Kip's Bay fled—straight into the towering wrath of Washington, who happened on the scene during the rout. For once the general radical press now attached to a common and humdrum domestic task. By the beginning of 1769 New England newspapers were highlighting spinning bees and their female participants, sometimes termed the "Daughters of Liberty." Front pages overflowed with praise of female patriotism: "The industry and frugality of American ladies must exalt their character in the Eyes of the World and serve to show how greatly they are contributing to bring about the political salvation of a whole Continent."

Spinning competitions and the vogue of wearing homespun served two political purposes. First, the bees actively enlisted American women in the struggle against Britain. Wives and daughters from families of every rank were made to feel that they could play an important role in the resistance by imitating the elite women showcased in public spinning spectacles. Every woman could display her devotion to liberty by encouraging industry and frugality in her own household. Many women took pride in the new political importance that radical propaganda attributed to domestic pursuits. Writing to her English cousin, Charity Clarke of New York City cast herself as one of America's "fighting army of amazones . . . armed with spinning wheels."

Spinning bees and "dressing down" in homespun also contributed to the solidarity of the resistance by narrowing the visible distance between rich and poor Americans. In accounts of spinning competitions, the radical press emphasized that even the daughters of the elite sacrificed for the cause of resistance by embracing domestic economy and simplicity.

And what genteel women wove, leading men wore. On public occasions throughout the revolutionary crisis, radical leaders appeared in homespun, displaying both their patriotic virtue and their identification with poorer Americans who could not afford British finery. When they returned to their home counties to muster local militia companies, many southern gentlemen adopted homespun "hunting shirts," long, loose, full-sleeved frocks that reached past the thigh. This dress of the frontier united the gentry with ordinary men of the backcountry while declaring their superiority to the corrupt mother country.

lost his habitual self-restraint, flogged both officers and men with his riding crop, and came close to being captured himself. But the Howes remained reluctant to hit hard, letting Washington's army escape from Manhattan to Westchester County.

Throughout the fall of 1776 General Howe's forces followed as Washington's fled southward into New Jersey. By mid-November, as the British advance picked up speed, the rebels stepped up their retreat and crossed the Delaware River into Pennsylvania on December 7. There Howe stopped, pulling back most of his army to winter in New York City and leaving the Hessians to hold the British line of advance along the New Jersey side of the Delaware River.

Although the retreat through New York and New Jersey had shriveled rebel strength to only 3000 men, Washington decided that the campaign of 1776 was not over. On a snowy Christmas night, the Continentals floated back across the Delaware, picked their way across roads iced with sleet and finally slid into

Rebel victories at Trenton and Princeton

At the Battle of Princeton, British troops bayoneted the rebel general Hugh Mercer, an assault later commemorated in this painting by George Washington Parke Custis, the adopted step-grandson of George Washington. This rendering draws attention not only to Mercer's courage but also to the savagery of the redcoats, both of which helped the rebels gain civilian support.

Hessian-held Trenton at eight in the morning. One thousand German soldiers, still recovering from their spirited Christmas celebration and caught completely by surprise, quickly surrendered. Washington's luck held when, on January 3, 1777, the Continentals defeated British troops on the outskirts of Princeton, New Jersey.

During the winter of 1776–1777 the British lost more than battles: they alienated the very civilians whose loyalties they had hoped to ensure. In New York City the presence of the main body of the British army brought shortages of food and housing and caused constant friction between soldiers and city dwellers. In the New Jersey countryside still held by the Hessians, the situation was more desperate. Forced to live off the land, the Germans aroused resentment among local farmers by seizing "hay, oats, Indian corn, cattle, and horses, which were never or but very seldom paid for," as one loyalist admitted. The Hessians ransacked and destroyed homes and churches; they kidnapped and raped young women.

Many neutrals and loyalists who had had enough of the king's soldiers now took their allegiance elsewhere. Bands of militia on Long Island, along the Hudson River, and all over New Jersey rallied to support the Continentals.

Capturing Philadelphia

In the summer of 1777 General Howe still hoped to entice the Continentals into a decisive engagement or to seize a major seaport and its surrounding countryside. But he had now decided to goad the Americans into battle by capturing Philadelphia.

The Fighting in the North, 1775–1777 After the British withdrew from Boston in 1775, they launched an attack on New York City the following year. Washington was forced to retreat northward, then across the Hudson and south into New Jersey and Pennsylvania, before surprising the British at Trenton and Princeton. Burgoyne's surrender at Saratoga in 1777 marked a turning point in the war.

Rather than risk his army on a march through hostile New Jersey, he approached the rebel capital by sea. In early August the redcoats disembarked on the Maryland shore and headed for Philadelphia, 50 miles away. Washington had hoped to stay on the strategic defensive, holding his smaller army together and harassing the enemy but avoiding full-scale battles. Howe's march on Philadelphia made that impossible: Washington's army hurried south from New Jersey to protect the new nation's capital. Washington engaged Howe twice: in September at Brandywine Creek and in October in an early dawn attack at Germantown, but both times the rebels were beaten back. He had been unable to prevent the British occupation of Philadelphia.

Still, the rebels could take satisfaction from the troubles that beset the British even in victory. In Philadelphia, as in New York, British occupation jacked up

Brandywine and Germantown

demand and prices for food, fuel, and housing. While inflation hit hardest at the poor, the wealthy resented British officers who became their uninvited house guests. Philadelphians complained of redcoats looting their shops, trampling their gardens, and harassing them on the streets. Elizabeth Drinker, the wife of a Quaker merchant, confided in her diary that "I often feel afraid to go to bed."

Even worse, the British march through Maryland and Pennsylvania had outraged civilians, who fled before the army and then returned to find their homes and barns bare, their crops and livestock gone. Everywhere Howe's men went in the mid-Atlantic, they left in their wake Americans with compelling reasons to support the rebels. Worst of all, just days after Howe marched his occupying army into Philadelphia in the fall of 1777, another British commander in North America was surrendering his entire army to rebel forces at Saratoga, New York.

Disaster at Saratoga

The calamity that befell the British at Saratoga was the doing of a glorymongering general, John "Gentleman Johnny" Burgoyne. After his superior officer, Sir Guy Carleton, bungled a drive into New York during the summer of 1776, Burgoyne won approval to command another attack from Canada. At the end of June 1777 he set out from Quebec with a force of 9500 redcoats, 2000 women and children, and an elaborate baggage train that included the commander's silver dining service, his dress uniforms, and numerous cases of his favorite champagne. As Burgoyne's huge entourage lumbered southward, it was slowed by a rough, winding road that was broken by boulders, felled trees, and ramshackle bridges that swayed over yawning ravines. Meanwhile, a handful of Continentals and a horde of New England militia assembled several miles below Saratoga at Bemis Heights under the command of General Horatio Gates.

Burgoyne surrenders at Saratoga

On September 19 Gates's rebel scouts, nested high in the trees on Bemis Heights, spied the glittering bayonets of Burgoyne's approaching force. Benedict Arnold, a brave young officer, led several thousand rebels into the surrounding woods, meeting Burgoyne's men in a clearing at Freeman's Farm. At the end of the day British reinforcements finally pushed the rebels back from a battlefield piled high with the bodies of soldiers from both sides. Burgoyne tried to flee back to Canada but got no farther than Saratoga, where he surrendered his army to Gates on October 17.

Saratoga changed everything. Burgoyne had not just been nipped in a skirmish; he had lost his entire army. The triumph was enough to convince Britain's old rival France that, with a little help, the Americans might well reap the fruits of victory.

The Turning Point

France had been waiting for revenge against Britain since its humiliating defeat in the Seven Years' War. Over the previous decade, as France's agents in America sent home reports of a rebellion brewing, a scheme for evening the score had been taking shape in the mind of the French foreign minister, Charles Gravier de Vergennes. He reckoned that France might turn discontented colonials into willing allies against Britain.

The American Revolution Becomes a Global War

Vergennes approached the Americans cautiously. He wanted to make certain that the rift between Britain and its colonies would not be reconciled and that the rebels in America stood a fighting chance. Although France had been secretly supplying the Continental Army with guns and ammunition since the spring of 1776, Vergennes would go no further than covert assistance.

Congress approached its former French enemies with equal caution. Would France, the leading Catholic monarchy in Europe, make common cause with the republican rebels? A few years earlier American colonials had fought against the French in Canada. Only recently they had renounced a king. For centuries they had overwhelmingly adhered to Protestantism.

The string of defeats dealt the Continental Army during 1776 convinced Congress that they needed the French enough to accept both the contradictions and the costs of such an alliance. In November Congress appointed a three-member commission to negotiate not only aid from France but also a formal alliance. Its senior member was Benjamin Franklin, who enchanted all of Paris when he arrived in town sporting a simple fur cap and a pair of spectacles (something no fashionable Frenchman wore in public). Hailed as a homespun sage, Franklin played the role of American innocent to the hilt and watched as admiring Parisians stamped his face on everything from the top of commemorative snuffboxes to the bottom of porcelain chamber pots.

Still, Franklin understood that mere popularity could not produce the alliance sought by Congress. It was only news that Britain had surrendered an entire army at Saratoga that finally convinced Vergennes that the rebels could actually win. In February 1778 France signed a treaty of commerce and friendship and a treaty of alliance, which Congress approved in May. Under the terms of the treaties, both parties agreed to accept nothing short of independence for America. France pledged to renounce all future claims in continental North America and to give back any territory captured in the war. The alliance left the British no choice other than to declare war on France. Less than a year later Spain joined France, hoping to recover territory lost to England in earlier wars.

The French public's infatuation with Benjamin Franklin knew no bounds. They particularly delighted in his rustic dress and styled him a representative of "frontier" America. He appears in this guise on a snuffbox along with two revered French philosophers, Voltaire and Rousseau.

Winding Down the War in the North

The Revolution widened into a global war after 1778. Preparing to fight France and Spain dictated a new British strategy in America. No longer could the British concentrate on crushing the Continental Army. Instead they would disperse their forces to fend off challenges all over the world. In May Sir Henry Clinton replaced William Howe as commander in chief and received orders to withdraw from Philadelphia to New York City. There, and in Newport, Rhode Island, Clinton was to maintain defensive bases for harrying northern coastal towns.

Only 18 miles outside of Philadelphia, at Valley Forge, Washington and his Continentals were assessing their own situation. Some 11,000 rebel soldiers had passed a harrowing winter in that isolated spot, starving for want of food, freezing for lack of clothing, huddling in miserable huts, and hating the British who lay so close and yet so comfortably in Philadelphia. The army also cursed their fellow citizens, for the misery of the soldiers resulted from congressional weakness and disorganization and from civilian corruption and indifference. Congress lacked both money to pay and maintain the army and an efficient system for dispensing provisions to the troops. Most farmers and merchants preferred to supply the British, who could pay handsomely, than to do business with a financially strapped Congress and the Continentals. What little did reach the army often was food too rancid to eat or clothing too rotten to wear. Perhaps 2500 perished at Valley Forge, the victims of cold, hunger, and disease.

The soldiers in this 1777 illustration condemn civilian neglect and the profiteering of private contractors who supplied the Continental Army. Such grievances would provoke mutinies within the army before the end of the fighting.

First Soldier: "Keep up courage, my boys, we will soon bring those villains to terms."

Second Soldier: "These d[amne]d Extortioners are the worst enemies to the country."

Third Soldier: "I serve my country for sixteen pence a day, pinched with cold."

Army uprisings

Why did civilians who supported the rebel cause allow the army to suffer? Probably because by the winter of 1777, the Continentals came mainly from social classes that received little consideration at any time. The respectable, propertied farmers and artisans who had laid siege to Boston in 1775 had stopped enlisting. Serving in their stead were single men in their teens and early twenties, some who joined the army out of desperation, others who were drafted, still others who were hired as substitutes for the more affluent. The landless sons of farmers, unemployed laborers, drifters, petty criminals, vagrants, indentured servants, slaves, even captured British and Hessian soldiers—all men with no other means and no other choice—were swept into the Continental Army. The social composition of the rebel rank and file had come to resemble that of the British army. It is the great irony of the Revolution: a war to protect liberty and property was waged by those Americans who were poorest and least free.

The beginning of spring in 1778 brought a reprieve. Supplies arrived at Valley Forge, and so did a fellow calling himself Baron von Steuben, a penniless Prussian soldier of fortune. Although Washington's men had shown spirit and resilience ever since Trenton, they still lacked discipline and training. Those defects and more von Steuben began to remedy. Barking orders and spewing curses in German and French, the baron (and his translators) drilled the rebel regiments to march in formation and to handle their bayonets like proper Prussian soldiers. By the summer of 1778, morale had rebounded as professional pride fused solidarity among Continental ranks in the crucible of Valley Forge.

Spoiling for action after their long winter, Washington's army, now numbering nearly 13,500, set out to harass Clinton's army as it marched overland from Philadelphia to New York. The Continentals caught up with the British force on June 28 at Monmouth Courthouse, where a long, confused battle ended in a draw. After both armies retired for the night, Clinton's forces slipped away to safety in New York City. Washington pursued, longing to launch an all-out assault on New York City, but he lacked the necessary numbers.

While Washington waited outside New York City, his army started to come apart. During the two hard winters that followed, resentments mounted among the rank and file over spoiled food, inadequate clothing, and arrears in pay. The army retaliated with mutinies. Between 1779 and 1780 officers managed to quell uprisings in three New England regiments. But in January 1781 both the Pennsylvania and New Jersey lines mutinied outright and marched on Philadelphia, where Congress had reconvened. Order returned only after Congress promised back pay and provisions and Washington put two ringleaders in front of a firing squad.

War in the West

Trouble also loomed on the western frontier. There both the British and the rebels sought support from the Indians because the most powerful tribes determined the balance of power. Most of the tribes remained neutral, but those tribes who took sides most often joined the British, who had tried to stem the tide of colonials taking Indian lands.

While George Rogers Clark and his few hundred rebel troops helped contain British and Indian raids in the Old Northwest, General John Sullivan led an expedition against the Iroquois in upstate New York. Loyalists under Major John Butler and Iroquois fighters under a Mohawk chief, Thayendanegea (called Joseph Brant by the English), had conducted a series of raids along the New York and Pennsylvania frontiers. Sullivan's expedition routed the marauders and burned more than 40 Indian villages.

The Home Front in the North

Although in 1779 most northern civilians on the seaboard enjoyed a respite from the war, the devastation lingered. Since the outbreak of the fighting at Lexington and Concord, every rumor of approaching enemy troops had pitched the inhabitants of imperiled neighborhoods into a panic. Refugees on foot and in hastily packed carts filled the roads, fleeing the advancing armies. Those who remained to protect their homes and property might be caught in the crossfire of contending forces or cut off from supplies of food and firewood. Loyalists who remained in areas occupied by rebel troops faced harassment, imprisonment, or the confiscation of their property. Rebel sympathizers met similar fates in regions held by the British. Disease, however, disregarded political allegiances: military camps and occupied towns spawned epidemics of dysentery and smallpox that devastated civilians as well as soldiers, rebels and loyalists alike.

While plundering armies destroyed civilian property wherever they marched, military demands disrupted family economies throughout the northern countryside. The seasons of intense fighting drew men off into military service just when their labor was most needed on family farms. Wives and daughters were left to assume the work of husbands and sons while coping with loneliness, anxiety, and grief. Often enough, the disruptions, flight, and loss of family members left lasting scars. Two years after she fled before Burgoyne's advance into upstate New York, Ann Eliza Bleecker confessed to a friend, "Alas! the wilderness is within: I muse so long on the dead until I am unfit for the company of the living."

Women and the war

Despite these hardships, many women vigorously supported the revolutionary cause in a variety of ways. The Daughters of Liberty joined in harassing opponents to the rebel cause. One outspoken loyalist found himself surrounded by angry women who stripped off his shirt, covered him with molasses, and plastered him with flower petals. In more genteel fashion, groups of well-to-do women collected not only money but medicines, food, and pewter to melt for bullets.

Women's perspectives on the War for Independence

Between the autumn of 1778 and the summer of 1781, while Washington and 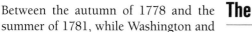 **The Struggle in the South** his restless army waited outside New York City, the British opened another theater in the American war. Despite their armed presence in the North, the British had come to believe that their most vital aim was to regain their colonies in the mainland South. The Chesapeake and the Carolinas were more profitable to the empire and more strategically important, being so much closer to rich British sugar islands in the West Indies. That new "southern strategy" prompted Clinton to dispatch forces

Britain's southern strategy

to the Caribbean and Florida. In addition, the British laid plans for a new offensive drive into the Carolinas and Virginia.

English politicians and generals believed that the war could be won in the South. Loyalists were numerous, they believed, especially in the backcountry. Resentment of the seaboard, a rebel stronghold, would breed readiness among frontier folk to take up arms for the king at the first show of British force. And southern rebels—especially the vulnerable planters along the coast—could not afford to turn their guns away from their slaves. So, at least, the British theorized. All that was needed, they concluded, was for the British army to establish a beachhead in the South and then, in league with loyalists, drive northward, pacifying the population while pressing up the coast.

The Siege of Charleston

The southern strategy worked well for a short time in a small place. In November 1778 Clinton sent 3500 troops to Savannah, Georgia. The resistance in the tiny colony quickly collapsed, and a large number of loyalists turned out to help the British. Encouraged by that success, the British moved on to South Carolina.

During the last days of 1779, an expedition under Clinton himself set sail from New York City. Landing off the Georgia coast, his troops mucked through malarial swamps to the peninsula lying between the Ashley and Cooper rivers. At the tip of that neck of land stood Charleston, and the British began to lay siege. By then, an unseasonably warm spring had set in, making the area a heaven for mosquitoes and a hell for human beings. Sweltering and swatting, redcoats weighted down in their woolen uniforms inched their siege works toward the city. By early May Clinton's army had closed in, and British shelling was setting fire to houses within the city. On May 12 Charleston surrendered.

Clinton sailed back to New York at the end of June 1780, leaving behind 8300 redcoats to carry the British offensive northward to Virginia. The man charged with leading that campaign was his ambitious and able subordinate, Charles, Lord Cornwallis.

The Partisan Struggle in the South

Cornwallis's task in the Carolinas was complicated by the bitter animosity between rebels and loyalists there. Many Carolinians had taken sides years before Clinton's conquest of Charleston. In the summer and fall of 1775 the supporters of Congress and the new South Carolina revolutionary government mobbed, tortured, and imprisoned supporters of the king in the backcountry. These attacks only hardened loyalist resolve: roving bands seized ammunition, broke their leaders out of jail, and besieged rebel outposts. But within a matter of months, a combined force of rebel militias from the coast and the frontier managed to defeat loyalist forces in the backcountry.

Rebels and loyalists battle for the backcountry

With the fall of Charleston in 1780, the loyalist movement on the frontier returned to life. Out of loyalist vengefulness and rebel desperation issued the brutal civil war that seared the southern backcountry after 1780. Neighbors and even families fought and killed each other as members of roaming rebel and tory militias. The intensity of partisan warfare in the backcountry produced unprecedented destruction. Loyalist militia plundered plantations and assaulted local women; rebel militias whipped suspected British supporters and burned their farms; both sides committed brutal assassinations and tortured prisoners. All of society, observed one minister, "seems to be at an end. Every person keeps close on his own plantation. Robberies and murders are often committed on the public roads. . . . Poverty, want, and hardship appear in almost every countenance."

Cornwallis, when confronted with the chaos, erred fatally. He did nothing to stop his loyalist allies or his own troops from mistreating civilians. A Carolina loyalist admitted that "the lower sort of People, who were in many parts originally attached to the British Government, have suffered so severely . . . that Great Britain has now a hundred enemies, where it had one before." Although rebels and loyalists alike plundered and terrorized the backcountry, Cornwallis's forces bore more of the blame and suffered the consequences.

A growing number of civilians outraged by the behavior of the king's troops cast their lot with the rebels. That upsurge of popular support enabled Francis Marion, the "Swamp Fox," and his band of white and black raiders to cut British lines of communication between Charleston and the interior. It swelled another rebel militia led by "the Gamecock," Thomas Sumter, who bloodied loyalist forces throughout the central part of South Carolina. It mobilized the "over-the-mountain men," a rebel militia in western Carolina who claimed victory at the Battle of Kings Mountain in October 1780. By the end of 1780, these successes had persuaded most civilians that only the rebels could restore order.

If rebel fortunes prospered in the partisan struggle, they faltered in the conventional warfare being waged at the same time in the South. In August of 1780 the Continentals commanded by Horatio Gates lost a major engagement to the British force at Camden, South Carolina. In the fall of 1780 Congress replaced Gates with Washington's candidate for the southern command, Nathanael Greene, an energetic 38-year-old Rhode Islander and a veteran of the northern campaigns.

British victory at Camden

Greene Takes Command

Greene bore out Washington's confidence by grasping the military situation in the South. He understood the needs of his 1400 hungry, ragged, and demoralized troops and instructed von Steuben to lobby Virginia for food and clothing. He understood the importance of the rebel militias and sent Lieutenant Colonel Henry "Lighthorse Harry" Lee to assist Marion's raids. He understood the weariness of southern civilians and prevented his men from plundering the countryside.

Above all, Greene understood that his forces could never hold the field against the whole British army. That led him to break the first rule of conventional warfare: he divided his army. In December 1780 he dispatched to western South Carolina a detachment of 600 men under the command of Brigadier General Daniel Morgan of Virginia.

General Nathanael Greene

Back at the British camp, Cornwallis worried that Morgan and his rebels, if left unchecked, might rally the entire backcountry against the British. On the other hand, Cornwallis reckoned that he could not commit his entire army to the pursuit of Morgan's men, for then Greene and his troops might retake Charleston. The only solution, unconventional to be sure, was for Cornwallis to divide *his* army. That he did, sending Lieutenant Colonel Banastre Tarleton and 1100 men west after Morgan. Cornwallis had played right into Greene's hands: the rebel troops might be able to defeat a British army split into two pieces. For two weeks Morgan led Tarleton's troops on a breakneck chase across the Carolina countryside. In January 1781 at an open meadow called Cowpens, Morgan routed Tarleton's force.

Cowpens

The Fighting in the South, 1780–1781 In December 1780 Nathanael Greene made the crucial decision to split his army, sending Daniel Morgan west, where he defeated the pursuing Banastre Tarleton at Cowpens. Meanwhile Greene regrouped and replenished at Cheraw, keeping Cornwallis off balance with a raid (dotted line) toward Charleston and the coast. Then, with Cornwallis in hot pursuit, Greene and Morgan rejoined at Salisbury, retreating into Virginia. Cornwallis was worn down in this vain pursuit and lost three-quarters of the troops he began with before finally abandoning the Carolina campaign.

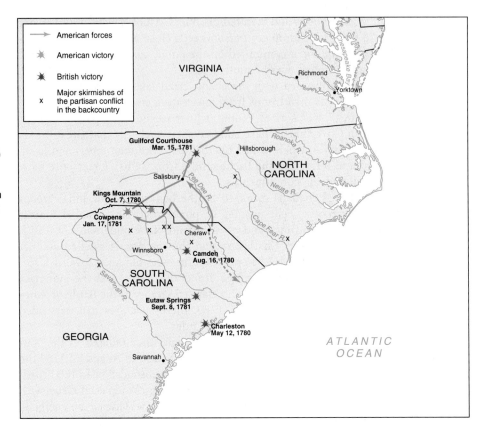

Value of the militia

Now Cornwallis took up the chase. Morgan and Greene joined forces and agreed to keep going north until the British army wore out. Cornwallis finally stopped at Hillsboro, North Carolina, but few local loyalists responded to his call for reinforcements. To ensure that loyalist ranks remained thin, Greene decided to make a show of force near the tiny village of Guilford Courthouse. On a brisk March day the two sides joined battle, each sustaining severe casualties before Greene was forced to retreat. But the high cost of victory convinced Cornwallis that he could not put down the rebellion in the Carolinas. "I am quite tired of marching about the country in quest of adventures," he informed Clinton.

Although Nathanael Greene's command provided the Continentals with effective leadership in the South, it was the resilience of rebel militia that thwarted the British offensive in the Carolinas. Many Continental Army officers complained about the militia's lack of discipline, its habit of melting away when homesickness set in or harvest approached, and its record of cowardice under fire in conventional engagements. But when set the task of ambushing supply trains and dispatch riders, harrying bands of local loyalists, or making forays against isolated British outposts, the militia came through. Many southern civilians refused to join the British or to provide the redcoats with food and information because they knew that once the British army left their neighborhoods, the rebel militia would always be back. The Continental Army in the South lost many conventional battles, but the militia kept the British from restoring political control over the backcountry.

African Americans in the Age of Revolution

The British also lost in the Carolinas because they did not seek greater support from those southerners who would have fought for liberty *with* the British—African American slaves.

Black Americans, virtually all in bondage, made up one-third of the population between Delaware and Georgia. Since the beginning of the resistance to Britain, white southerners had worried that the watchwords of *liberty* and *equality* would spread to the slave quarters. Gripped by the fear of slave rebellion, southern revolutionaries began to take precautions. Marylanders disarmed black inhabitants and issued extra guns to the white militia. Charlestonians hanged and then burned the body of Thomas Jeremiah, a free black who was convicted of spreading the word to others that the British "were come to help the poor Negroes."

Southern whites fully expected the British to turn slave rebelliousness to their strategic advantage. As early as 1775, Virginia's royal governor, Lord Dunmore, confirmed white fears by offering to free any slave who joined the British. When Clinton invaded the South in 1779, he renewed that offer. According to Janet Schaw, an English woman visiting her brother's North Carolina plantation, her brother's neighbors had heard that loyalists were "promising every Negro that would murder his master and family he should have his Master's plantation" and that "the Negroes have got it amongst them and believe it to be true."

> White fears of rebellion

But in Britain there was overwhelming opposition to organizing support among African Americans. British leaders dismissed Dunmore's ambitious scheme to raise a black army of 10,000 and another plan to create a sanctuary for black loyalists on the southeastern coast. Turning slaves against masters, they recognized, was not the way to conciliate southern whites.

Even so, southern fears of insurrection made the rebels reluctant to enlist black Americans as soldiers. At first, Congress barred African Americans from the Continental Army. But as the rebels became more desperate for manpower, policy changed. Northern states actively encouraged black enlistments, and in the Upper

Rebel Americans were able to hold the southern backcountry because of the determination of militias such as the one depicted in this detail of a nineteenth-century painting. Francis Marion's company was unusual among southern militias because it included blacks.

South, some states allowed free men of color to join the army or permitted slaves to substitute for their masters.

African American quests for liberty

Slaves themselves sought freedom from whichever side seemed most likely to grant it. In 1775 more than 800 took up Dunmore's offer and deserted their masters, and thousands more flocked to Clinton's forces after the fall of Charleston. For many runaways the hope of liberation proved an illusion. Although some served the British army as laborers, spies, and soldiers, many died of disease in army camps or were sold back into slavery in the West Indies. An estimated 5000 black soldiers served in the revolutionary army in the hope of gaining freedom. In addition, the number of runaways to the North soared during the Revolution. All told, some 55,000 slaves fled to freedom, some escaping behind British lines, others into the North.

The slave revolts so dreaded by southern whites never materialized. Possibly the boldest slaves were drawn off into the armies; possibly greater white precautions discouraged schemes for black rebellions. In South Carolina, where the potential for revolt was greatest, most slaves chose to remain on plantations rather than risk a collective resistance and escape in the midst of the fierce partisan warfare.

The World Turned Upside Down

Despite his losses in the Carolinas, Cornwallis still believed that he could score a decisive victory against the Continental Army. The theater he chose for that showdown was the Chesapeake. During the spring of 1781, he had marched his army to the Virginia coast and joined forces with the hero of Saratoga and newly turned loyalist, Benedict Arnold. Embarrassed by debt and disgusted by Congress's shabby treatment of the Continental Army, Arnold had started exchanging rebel secrets for British money in 1779 before defecting outright in the fall of 1780. By June of 1781 Arnold and Cornwallis were fortifying a site on the tip of the peninsula formed by the York and James rivers, a place called Yorktown.

Meanwhile, Washington and his French ally, the comte de Rochambeau, met in Connecticut to plan a major attack. Rochambeau urged a coordinated land-sea assault on the Virginia coast. Washington insisted instead on a full-scale offensive against New York City. Just when the rebel commander was about to have his way, word arrived that a French fleet under the comte de Grasse was sailing for the Chesapeake to blockade Cornwallis by sea. Washington's Continentals headed south.

On September 30, 1780, a wagon bearing this two-faced effigy was drawn through the streets of Philadelphia. The effigy represents Benedict Arnold, who sits between a gallows and the devil. Note the similarities between this piece of street theater and the demonstrations mounted on Pope's Day several decades earlier, shown on page 158.

Surrender at Yorktown

By the end of September, 7800 Frenchmen, 5700 Continentals, and 3200 militia had sandwiched Yorktown between the devil of an allied army and the deep blue sea of French warships. "If you cannot relieve me very soon," Cornwallis wrote to Clinton, "you must expect to hear the worst." The British navy did arrive—but seven days after Cornwallis surrendered to the rebels on October 19, 1781. When Germain carried the news from Yorktown to the king's first minister, Lord North replied, "Oh, God, it is over." Then North resigned, Germain resigned, and even George III murmured something about abdicating.

It need not have ended at Yorktown, but timing made all the difference. At the end of 1781 and early in 1782, the British army received setbacks in the other theaters of the war: India, the West Indies, and Florida. The French and the Spanish were everywhere in Europe as well, gathering in the English Channel, planning a major offensive against Gibraltar. The cost of the fighting was already enormous. British leaders recognized that the rest of the empire was at stake and set about cutting their losses in America.

The Treaty of Paris, signed on September 3, 1783, was a diplomatic triumph for the American negotiators: Benjamin Franklin, John Adams, and John Jay. They dangled before Britain the possibility that a generous settlement might weaken American ties to France. The British jumped at the bait. They recognized the independence of the United States and agreed to ample boundaries for the new nation: the Mississippi River on the west, the 31st parallel on the south, and the present border of Canada on the north. American negotiators then persuaded a skeptical France to approve the treaty by arguing that, as allies, they were bound to present a united front to the British. When the French finally persuaded Spain, the third member of the alliance, to reduce its demands on Britain for territorial concessions, the treaty became an accomplished fact. The Spanish settled for Florida and Minorca, an island in the Mediterranean.

Treaty of Paris

The Significance of a Revolution

If the Treaty of Paris marked both the end of a war and the recognition of a new nation, the surrender at Yorktown captured the significance of a revolution. Those present at Yorktown on that clear autumn afternoon in 1781 watched as the British second in command to Cornwallis (who had sent word that he was "indisposed") surrendered his superior's sword. He offered the sword first, in a face-saving gesture, to the French commander, Rochambeau, who politely refused and pointed to Washington. But the American commander in chief, out of a mixture of military protocol, nationalistic pride, and perhaps even wit, pointed to *his* second in command, Benjamin Lincoln.

Some witnesses recalled that British musicians arrayed on the Yorktown green played "The World Turned Upside Down." Their recollections may have been faulty, but the story has persisted as part of the folklore of the American Revolution—and for good reasons. The world had, it seemed, turned upside down with the coming of American independence. The colonial rebels shocked the British with their answer to the question: would they fight?

The answer had been yes—but on their own terms. By 1777 most propertied Americans avoided fighting in the Continental Army. Yet whenever the war reached their homes, farms, and businesses, many Americans gave their allegiance to the new nation by turning out with rifles or supplying homespun clothing, food, or

Citizen-soldiers fight on their own terms

The world turned upside down: the British lay down their arms at Yorktown.

ammunition. They rallied around Washington in New Jersey, Gates in upstate New York, Greene in the Carolinas. Middle-class American men fought, some from idealism, others out of self-interest, but always on their own terms, as members of the militia. These citizen-soldiers turned the world upside down by defeating professional armies.

Of course, the militia did not bear the brunt of the fighting. That responsibility fell to the Continental Army, which by 1777 drew its strength from the poorest ranks of American society. Yet even the Continentals, for all their desperation, managed to fight on their own terms. Some asserted their rights by raising mutinies, until Congress redressed their grievances. All of them, as the Baron von Steuben observed, behaved differently than European soldiers. Americans followed orders only if the logic of commands was explained to them. The Continentals, held in contempt by most Americans, turned the world upside down by sensing their power and asserting their measure of personal independence.

Thus did a revolutionary generation turn the world upside down. Descended from desperate, idealistic, and self-interested men and women who settled colonies named for kings and queens—ruled by kings and queens who aimed to increase the wealth and power of their dynasties and their nations—these Americans rebelled against a king. They wanted more than a monarch. But what more did they want? What awaited in a world turned upside down by republican revolutionaries?

chapter summary

The American Revolution brought independence to Britain's former colonies after an armed struggle that began in 1775 and concluded with the Treaty of Paris in 1783.

- When the Second Continental Congress convened in the spring of 1775, many of the delegates still hoped for reconciliation—even as they approved the creation of the Continental Army.

- The Second Continental Congress adopted the Declaration of Independence on July 4, 1776, hoping that they could count on a majority of Americans to support the Revolution.

- The British scored a string of victories in the North throughout 1776 and 1777, capturing both New York and Philadelphia.

- The British suffered a disastrous defeat at the Battle of Saratoga in early 1778, which prompted France to openly ally with the American rebels soon thereafter.

- By 1780 Britain aimed to win the war by claiming the South, and captured both Savannah, Georgia, and Charleston, South Carolina.

- The Continental Army in the South, led by Nathanael Greene, foiled the British strategy, and Cornwallis surrendered to Washington after the Battle of Yorktown in 1781.

- Except during the first year of fighting, the rank and file of the Continental Army were drawn from the poorest Americans, whose needs for food, clothing, and shelter were neglected by the Continental Congress.

interactive learning

The Primary Source Investigator CD-ROM offers the following materials related to this chapter:

- Interactive map: **The American Revolution, 1775–1781** (M6)

- A short documentary movie on women's perspectives on the War for Independence (D2)

- A collection of primary sources concerning the colonies' struggle for independence, including several drafts of the Declaration of Independence, paintings memorializing fallen heroes, and Thomas Paine's *common sense*. Other sources illustrate the important role of African Americans and Native Americans in the American Revolution, including Lord Dunmore's proclamation freeing slaves in Virginia to fight on the side of the British empire. Still others explore the role of women in the American Revolution, such as Molly Pitcher's recollection of her experiences in the Continental Army and a letter from Abigail Adams to John Adams.

additional reading

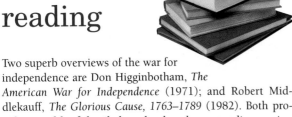

Two superb overviews of the war for independence are Don Higginbotham, *The American War for Independence* (1971); and Robert Middlekauff, *The Glorious Cause, 1763–1789* (1982). Both provide a wealth of detail about battles, the contending armies, and the roles of the militia and the civilian population. Two particularly thoughtful accounts of the relationship between the war and American society are Charles Royster, *A Revolutionary People at War* (1979); and John Shy, *A People Numerous and Armed* (1976). Sylvia Frey offers a fine account of African Americans throughout the years of revolutionary crisis in *Water from the Rock* (1991), and the role of women in wartime America is treated most comprehensively by Mary Beth Norton, *Liberty's Daughters* (1980). An intimate account of the impact of the war on one Connecticut family is Joy Day Buel and Richard Buel Jr., *The Way of Duty* (1984).

Many excellent studies probe the impact of the American Revolution on the institution of slavery and the lives of African Americans. Among the best are Ira Berlin and Ronald Hoffman, eds., *Slavery and Freedom in the Age of the American Revolution* (1983); David Brion Davis, *The Problem of Slavery in the Age of Revolution* (1975); and Gary B. Nash, *Race and Revolution* (1990). For a fuller list of readings, see the Bibliography at www.mhhe.com/davidsonnation5.

significant events

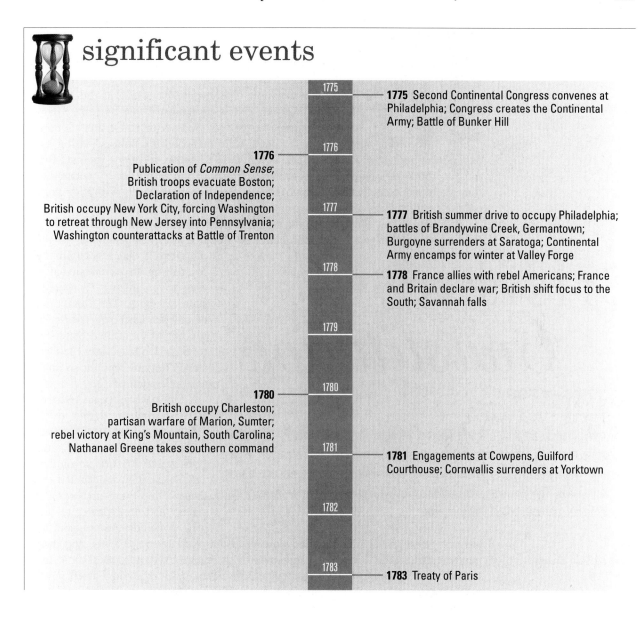

1775 Second Continental Congress convenes at Philadelphia; Congress creates the Continental Army; Battle of Bunker Hill

1776
Publication of *Common Sense*;
British troops evacuate Boston;
Declaration of Independence;
British occupy New York City, forcing Washington
to retreat through New Jersey into Pennsylvania;
Washington counterattacks at Battle of Trenton

1777 British summer drive to occupy Philadelphia; battles of Brandywine Creek, Germantown; Burgoyne surrenders at Saratoga; Continental Army encamps for winter at Valley Forge

1778 France allies with rebel Americans; France and Britain declare war; British shift focus to the South; Savannah falls

1780
British occupy Charleston;
partisan warfare of Marion, Sumter;
rebel victory at King's Mountain, South Carolina;
Nathanael Greene takes southern command

1781 Engagements at Cowpens, Guilford Courthouse; Cornwallis surrenders at Yorktown

1783 Treaty of Paris

Chapter 7

"I am not a Virginian, but an American," Patrick Henry declared in the Virginia House of Burgesses. Most likely he was lying. Certainly no one listening took him seriously, for the newly independent colonists did not identify themselves as members of a nation. They would have said, as did Thomas Jefferson, "Virginia, Sir, is my country." Or as John Adams wrote to another native son, "Massachusetts is our country." Jefferson and Adams were men of wide political vision and experience: both were leaders in the Continental Congress and more inclined than most to think nationally. But like other members of the revolutionary generation, they identified deeply with their home states and even more deeply with their home counties and towns.

It followed that allegiance to the states, not the Union, determined the shape of the first republican political experiments. For a decade after independence, the revolutionaries were less committed to creating an American nation than to organizing 13 separate state republics. The Declaration of Independence referred explicitly not to *the* United States but to *these* United States. It envisioned not one republic so much as a federation of 13.

Crisis & *Constitution*

1776–1789

preview • For a decade after independence, American revolutionaries were less committed to creating a single national republic than to organizing 13 separate state republics, united only loosely under the Articles of Confederation. By the mid-1780s, however, the weakness of the Confederation seemed evident to many Americans. The Constitutional Convention of 1787 produced a new frame of government that was truly national in scope.

Only when peace was restored during the decade of the 1780s were Americans forced to face some unanswered questions raised by their revolution. The Declaration proclaimed that these "free and independent states" had "full power to levy war, conclude peace, contract alliances, establish commerce." Did that mean that New Jersey, as a free and independent state, could sign a trade agreement with France, excluding the other states? If the United States was to be more than a loose federation, how could it assert power on a national scale? Similarly, American borderlands to the west presented problems. If these territories were settled by Americans, would they eventually join the United States? Go their own ways as independent nations? Become new colonies of Spain or England?

How close a union?

Such problems were more than political; they were rooted in social realities. For a political union to succeed, the inhabitants of 13 separate states had to start thinking of themselves as Americans. When it came right down to it, what united a Vermont farmer working his rocky fields and a South Carolina gentleman presiding over a vast rice plantation? What bonds existed between a Kentuckian rafting the Ohio River and a Salem merchant sailing to China for porcelain?

And in a society in which all citizens were said to be "created equal," the inevitable social inequalities had to be confronted. How could women participate in the Revolution's bid for freedom if they were not free to vote or to hold property? How could black Americans feel a bond with white Americans when so often the

The portraits of Captain and Mrs. Samuel Chandler, a New England couple, project the virtuous rectitude of the new republican era. Husband and wife share the same direct, disarming gaze, a mixture of wariness and resolution.

only existing bonds had been forged with chains? To these questions there were no final answers in 1781. And as the decade progressed, the sense of crisis deepened. Americans worried that factions and selfish interest groups would pull "these" United States apart. The new republican union, which spread out over so many miles, constituted a truly unprecedented venture. A good deal of experimenting would be needed if it was to succeed.

Republican Experiments

After independence was declared in July 1776, many of America's best political minds turned to drawing up constitutions for their individual states. Thomas Jefferson deserted the Continental Congress, leaving the conduct of the war and national affairs to other men, for the more important business of creating Virginia's new government.

In truth, the state constitutions were crucial republican experiments, the first efforts at establishing a government of and by the people. All the revolutionaries agreed that the people—not a king or a few privileged aristocrats—should rule. Yet they were equally certain that republican governments were best suited to small territories. They believed that the new United States was too sprawling and its people too diverse to be safely consolidated into a single national republic. They feared, too, that the government of a large republic would inevitably grow indifferent to popular concerns, being distant from many of its citizens. Without being under the watchful eye of the people, representatives would become less accountable to the electorate and turn tyrannical. A federation of small state republics, they reasoned, would stand a far better chance of enduring.

Belief in the need for small republics

The State Constitutions

The new state constitutions retained the basic form of their old colonial governments, all except Georgia and Pennsylvania providing for a governor and a bicameral legislature. But while most states did not alter the basic structure of their governments, they changed dramatically the balance of power among the different branches of government.

Curbing executive power

From the republican perspective in 1776, the greatest problem of any government lay in curbing executive power. What had driven Americans into rebellion was the abuse of authority by the king and his appointed officials. To ensure that the executive could never again threaten popular liberty, the new states either accorded almost no power to their governors or abolished that office entirely. The governors had no authority to convene or dissolve the legislatures. They could not veto the legislatures' laws, grant land, or erect courts. Most important from the republican point of view, governors had few powers to appoint other state officials. All these limits were designed to deprive the executive of any patronage or other form of influence over the legislature. By reducing the governors' power, Americans hoped to preserve their states from the corruption that they deplored in British political life.

Strengthening legislative powers

What the state governors lost, the legislatures gained. Sam Adams, the Boston rebel leader, expressed the political consensus when he declared that "every legislature of every colony ought to be the sovereign and uncontrollable Power within its own limits of territory." To ensure that those powerful legislatures truly represented the will of the people, the new state constitutions called for annual elections and required candidates for the legislature to live in the districts they represented. Many states even asserted the right of voters to instruct the men elected to office how to vote on specific issues. Although no state granted universal manhood suffrage, most reduced the amount of property required of qualified voters. Finally, state supreme courts were also either elected by the legislatures or appointed by elected governors.

Americans responded to independence with rituals of "killing the king," like the one enacted by this New York crowd in 1776 as it pulls down a statue of George III. Americans also expressed their mistrust of monarchs and their ministers by establishing new state governments with weak executive branches.

By investing all power in popular assemblies, Americans abandoned the British system of mixed government. In one sense, that change was fairly democratic. A majority of voters within a state could do whatever they wanted, unchecked by governors or courts. On the other hand, the arrangement opened the door for legislatures to turn as tyrannical as governors. The revolutionaries brushed that prospect aside: republican theory assured them that the people possessed a generous share of civic virtue, the capacity for selfless pursuit of the general welfare.

In an equally momentous change, the revolutionaries insisted on written state constitutions. Whenever government appeared to exceed the limits of its authority, Americans wanted to have at hand the written contract between rulers and ruled. When eighteenth-century Britons used the word *constitution,* they meant the existing arrangement of government—not an actual document but a collection of parliamentary laws, customs, and precedents. But Americans believed that a constitution should be a written code that stood apart from and above government, a yardstick against which the people measured the performance of their rulers. After all, they reasoned, if Britain's constitution had been written down, available for all to consult, would American rights have been violated?

Written constitutions

From Congress to Confederation

While Americans lavished attention on their state constitutions, the national government nearly languished during the decade after 1776. With the coming of independence, the Second Continental Congress conducted the common business of the federated states. It created and maintained the Continental Army, issued currency, and negotiated with foreign powers.

But while Congress acted as a central government by common consent, it lacked any legal basis for its authority. To redress that need, in July 1776 Congress appointed a committee to draft a constitution for a national government. The more urgent business of waging and paying for the war made for delay, as did the consuming interest in framing state constitutions. Congress finally approved the first national constitution in November 1777, but it took four more years for all the states to ratify these Articles of Confederation.

The Articles of Confederation provided for a government by a national legislature—essentially a continuation of the Second Continental Congress. That body had the authority to declare war and make peace, conduct diplomacy, regulate Indian affairs, appoint military and naval officers, and requisition men from the states. In affairs of finance it could coin money and issue paper currency. Extensive as these responsibilities were, Congress could not levy taxes or even regulate trade. The crucial power of the purse rested entirely with the states, as did the final power to make and execute laws. Even worse, the national government had no distinct executive branch. Congressional committees, constantly changing in their membership, not only had to make laws but had to administer and enforce them as well. With no executive to carry out the policies of finance, war, and foreign policy, the federal government's influence was extremely limited.

Articles of Confederation

Those weaknesses of the federal government appear more evident in hindsight. For Congress in 1777 it was no easy task to frame a new government in the midst of a war. Besides that distraction, most American leaders of the 1770s had given little thought to federalism, the organization of a United States. Political leaders had not yet recognized the need for dividing power between the states and the national government. With the new nation in the midst of a military crisis, Congress assumed—correctly in most cases—that the states did not have to be forced to contribute men and money to the common defense. To have given significant powers to the national government would only have aroused opposition among the states, each jealous of its independence. Creating a strong national government would also have antagonized many Americans, who after all had just rebelled against the distant, centralized authority of Britain's king and Parliament.

Guided by republican political theory and by their colonial experience, American revolutionaries created a loose confederation of 13 independent state republics under a nearly powerless national government. They succeeded so well that the United States almost failed to survive the first decade of its independence. The problem was that republican theory and lessons from the colonial past were not always useful guides to postwar realities. Only when events forced Americans to think nationally did they begin to consider the possibility of reinventing "these United States"—this time under the yoke of a truly federal republic.

The Temptations of Peace

The surrender of Cornwallis at Yorktown in 1781 marked the end of military crisis in America. But as the threat from Britain receded, so did the source of American unity. The many differences among Americans, most of which lay submerged during the struggle for independence, surfaced in full force. Those domestic divisions, combined with challenges to the new nation from Britain and Spain, created conflicts that neither the states nor the national government proved equal to handling.

The Temptations of the West

The greatest opportunities and the greatest problems for postwar Americans awaited in the rapidly expanding West. With the boundary of the new United States now set at the Mississippi River, more settlers spilled across the Appalachians, planting farmsteads and raw frontier towns throughout Ohio, Kentucky, and Tennessee. By 1790 places that had been almost uninhabited by whites in 1760 held more than 2.25 million people, one-third of the nation's population.

After the Revolution, as before, western settlement fostered intense conflict. American claims that its territory stretched all the way to the Mississippi were by no means taken for granted by European and Indian powers. The West also confronted Americans with questions about their own national identity. Would the newly settled territories enter the nation as states on an equal footing with the original 13 states? Would they be ruled as dependent colonies? Could the federal government reconcile conflicting interests, cultures, and traditions over so great an area? The fate of the West, in other words, constituted a crucial test of whether "these" United States could grow and still remain united.

Foreign Intrigues

Both the British from their base in Canada and the Spanish in Florida and Louisiana hoped to chisel away at American borders. Their considerable success in the 1780s exposed the weakness of Confederation diplomacy.

Before the ink was dry on the Treaty of Paris, Britain's ministers were secretly instructing Canadians to maintain their forts and trading posts inside the United States' northwestern frontier. They reckoned—correctly—that with the Continental Army disbanded, the Confederation could not force the British to withdraw.

The British also made mischief along the Confederation's northern borders, mainly with Vermont. For decades, Ethan Allen and his Green Mountain Boys had waged a war of nerves with neighboring New York, which claimed Vermont as part of its territory. After the Revolution the Vermonters petitioned Congress for statehood, demanding independence of both New York and New Hampshire. When Congress dragged its feet, the British tried to woo Vermont into their empire as a province of Canada. That flirtation with the British pressured Congress into granting Vermont statehood in 1791.

The loyalty of the southwestern frontier was even less certain. By 1790 more than 100,000 settlers had poured through the Cumberland Gap to reach Kentucky and Tennessee. Along with the farmers came speculators, who bought up large tracts of land from the Indians. But the commercial possibilities of the region depended entirely on access to the Mississippi and the port of New Orleans, since it was far too costly to ship southwestern produce over the rough trails east across the Appalachians. And the Mississippi route was still dominated by the Spanish, who controlled Louisiana as well as forts along western Mississippi shores as far north as St. Louis. The Spanish, seeing their opportunity, closed the Mississippi to American navigation in 1784. That action prompted serious talk among southwesterners about seceding from the United States and joining Spain's empire.

Spanish designs on the Southwest

The Spanish also tried to strengthen their hold on North America by making common cause with the Indians. Of particular concern to both groups was protecting Florida, which had reverted to Spain's possession, from the encroachment of American settlers filtering south from Georgia. Florida's governor alerted his superiors back in Spain to the threat posed by those backwoods folk who were "nomadic like Arabs and . . . distinguished from savages only in their color, language, and the superiority of their depraved cunning and untrustworthiness." So Spanish colonial officials responded eagerly to the overtures of Alexander McGillivray, a young Indian leader whose mother was of French-Creek descent and whose father was a Scots trader. His efforts brought about a treaty of alliance between the Creeks and

Rivalries flared along the southwestern frontier of the United States as Spain vied to win the allegiance of Indians by supplying them with British trade goods. The Indians welcomed such goods (note the shovel, at left, the plow, center, and European clothing worn by some of the Indians). Here a white man, probably the American Indian agent Benjamin Hawkins, visits an Indian village during the 1790s.

the Spanish in 1784, quickly followed by similar alliances with the Choctaws and the Chickasaws. What cemented such treaties were the trade goods that the Spanish agreed to supply the tribes, for, as McGillivray explained, "Indians will attach themselves to and serve them best who supply their necessities." Securing European gunpowder and guns had become essential to southeastern Indians, because their entire economies now revolved around hunting and selling deerskins to white traders. So eager were the Spanish to "serve" the Indians in that matter that they even permitted British merchants, who could command a steady supply of manufactured goods, to monopolize the Indian trade. The largest dealers, William Panton and John Leslie, two loyalists who had fled to Florida in the wake of the Revolution, developed a trading network with southeastern tribes that reached all the way to the Mississippi by the 1790s. This flood of British merchandise sustained the alliance between the Spanish and the Indians, while British guns enabled the Creeks to defend their hunting territory from American invaders.

Disputes among the States

As if foreign intrigues were not divisive enough, the states continued to argue among themselves over western land claims. The old royal charters for some colonies had extended their boundaries all the way to the Mississippi and beyond. (See the map

Western Land Claims, 1782–1802 The Confederation's settlement of conflicting western land claims was an achievement essential to the consolidation of political union. Some states asserted that their original charters extended their western borders to the Mississippi River. A few states, like Virginia, claimed western borders on the Pacific Ocean.

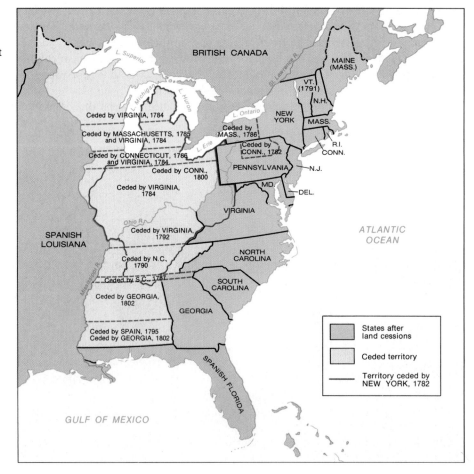

on pg. 202.) But the charters were often vague, granting both Massachusetts and Virginia, for example, undisputed possession of present-day Wisconsin. In contrast, other charters limited state boundaries to within a few hundred miles of the Atlantic coast. "Landed" states like Virginia wanted to secure control over the large territory granted them by their charters. "Landless" states (which included Maryland, Delaware, Pennsylvania, Rhode Island, and New Jersey) called on Congress to restrict the boundaries of landed states and to convert western lands into a domain administered by the Confederation.

Landed versus landless states

The landless states argued that the landed states enjoyed an unfair advantage from the money they could raise selling their western claims. That revenue would allow landed states to reduce taxes, and lower taxes would lure settlers from the landless states. Meanwhile, landless states would have to raise taxes to make up for the departed taxpayers, causing even more residents to leave. Speculators were also eager to see Congress control the western lands. Before the Revolution, many prominent citizens of landless Pennsylvania, Maryland, and New Jersey had purchased tracts in the West from Indians. These speculators now joined forces with the political leaders of the landless states to lobby for congressional ownership of all western lands—except those tracts that they had already purchased from the Indians.

The landless states lost the opening round in the contest over ownership of the West. The Articles of Confederation acknowledged the old charter claims of the landed states. Then Maryland, one of the smallest landless states, retaliated by refusing to ratify the Articles. Since every state had to approve the Articles before they were formally accepted, the fate of the United States hung in the balance. One by one the landed states relented. The last holdout, Virginia, in January 1781 ceded its charter rights to land north of the Ohio River. In a moment of uncharacteristic modesty, the Virginians conceded that they might have trouble extending a republican government over the entire territory allotted them in their charter—a substantial portion of the North American continent. Once Virginia ceded, Maryland ratified the Articles in February 1781, four long years after Congress had first approved them.

The More Democratic West

More bitterly disputed than western land claims was the issue concerning the sort of men westerners elected to political office. The state legislatures of the 1780s were both larger and more democratic in their membership than the old colonial assemblies. Before the Revolution no more than a fifth of the men serving in the assemblies were middle-class farmers or artisans. Government was almost exclusively the domain of the wealthiest merchants, lawyers, and planters. After the Revolution twice as many state legislators were men of moderate wealth. The shift was more marked in the North, where middle-class men predominated among representatives. But in every state, some men of modest means, humble background, and little formal education attained political power.

State legislatures became more democratic in their membership mainly because as backcountry districts grew, so too did the number of their representatives. Since western districts tended to be less developed economically and culturally, their leading men were less rich and cultivated than the eastern seaboard elite. Wealthy, well-educated gentlemen thus became a much smaller and less powerful group within the legislatures because of greater western representation and influence.

Changing composition of state legislatures

But many republican gentlemen, while endorsing government by popular consent, doubted whether ordinary people were fit to rule. The problem, they contended, was that the new western legislators concerned themselves only with the

This sketch of a new cleared farm idealizes many aspects of life on the late-eighteenth-century frontier. Although western farmers first sought to "improve" their acreage by felling trees, as the stumps dotting the landscape indicate, their dwellings were far less substantial than those depicted in the background above. And while Indians sometimes guided parties of white surveyors and settlers into the West, as shown in the foreground, Indians more often resisted white encroachment. For that reason, dogs, here perched placidly in canoes, were trained to alert their white masters to the approach of Indians.

narrow interests of their constituents, not with the good of the whole state. As Ezra Stiles, the president of Yale College, observed, the new breed of politicians were those with "the all-prevailing popular talent of coaxing and flattering," who "whenever a bill is read in the legislature . . . instantly thinks how it will affect his constituents." And if state legislatures could not rise above petty bickering and narrow self-interest, how long would it be before civic virtue and a concern for the general welfare simply withered away?

The Northwest Territory

Such fears of "democratic excess" also influenced policy when Congress finally came to decide what to do with the Northwest Territory. Carved out of the land ceded by the states to the national government, the Northwest Territory comprised the present-day states of Ohio, Indiana, Illinois, Michigan, and Wisconsin. With so many white settlers moving into these lands, Congress was faced with a crucial test of its federal system. If an orderly way could not be devised to expand the confederation of states beyond the original 13 colonies, the new territories might well become independent countries or even colonies of Spain or Britain. Congress dealt with the issue of expansion by adopting three ordinances.

Jefferson's plan for the Northwest

The first, drafted by Thomas Jefferson in 1784, divided the Northwest Territory into 10 states, each to be admitted to the Union on equal terms as soon as its population equaled that in any of the existing states. In the meantime, Jefferson provided for democratic self-government of the territory by all free adult males. A second ordinance of 1785 set up an efficient mechanism for dividing and selling public lands. The Northwest Territory was surveyed into townships six miles square. Each township was then divided into 36 lots of one square mile, or 640 acres.

Congress waited in vain for buyers to flock to the land offices it established. The cost of even a single lot—$640—was too steep for most farmers. Disappointed by the shortage of buyers and desperate for money, Congress finally accepted a proposition submitted by a private company of land speculators who offered to buy

THE SEVEN RANGES
First Area Survey

Seventh Range | Sixth Range | Fifth Range | Fourth Range | Third Range | Second Range | First Range

VIRGINIA
PENNSYLVANIA

Ohio River

BRITISH
CANADA

Lake Superior

Mississippi River

WIS.

Lake Michigan

MICH.

Lake Huron

Lake Erie

NORTHWEST
TERRITORY

OHIO

PA.

ILL. | IND. | Cincinnati

Ohio River

VIRGINIA

KENTUCKY

The Ordinance of 1785 Surveyors entered the Northwest Territory in September of 1785, imposing on the land regular grids of six square miles to define new townships, as shown on this range map of a portion of Ohio. Farmers purchased blocks of land within townships, each one mile square, from the federal government or from land speculators. This pattern was followed in mapping and settling public lands all the way to the Pacific coast.

6 Miles

31	30	19	18	7	6
32	29	20	17	8	5
33	28	21	16	9	4
34	27	22	15	10	3
35	26	23	14	11	2
36	25	24	13	12	1

Detail of township

Section 16 reserved
for schools.

←—1 mile—→

1/2 section

1/4 | 1/8

1/16

Detail of section
(640 acres)

some 6 million acres in present-day southeastern Ohio. That several members of Congress numbered among the company's stockholders no doubt added to enthusiasm for the deal.

The transaction concluded, Congress calmed the speculators' worries that incoming settlers might enjoy too much self-government by scrapping Jefferson's democratic design and substituting the Northwest Ordinance of 1787. That ordinance provided for a period in which Congress held sway in the territory through its appointees—a governor, a secretary, and three judges. When the population reached 5000 free adult males, a legislature was to be established, although its laws required the governor's approval. A representative could sit in Congress but had no vote. When the population reached 60,000, the inhabitants might apply for statehood, and the whole Northwest Territory was to be divided into not less than three or more than five states. The ordinance also guaranteed basic rights—freedom of religion and trial by jury—and provided for the support of public education.

Congress's plan completely ignored the rights of the Shawnee, Chippewa, and other Indian peoples who lived in the region. And in terms of Jefferson's democratic ideals for white inhabitants, the ordinance of 1787 also fell short. Still, Congress had succeeded in extending republican government to the West and incorporating the frontier into the new nation. Congress also outlawed slavery throughout the territory.

Northwest Ordinance

That decision had an unexpected, almost ironic consequence. The Northwest Ordinance went a long way toward establishing a federal system that would minimize tensions between the East and the West, a major source of postwar conflict. The Republic now had a peaceful, orderly way to expand its federation of states. Yet by limiting the spread of slavery in the northern states, Congress deepened the critical social and economic differences between North and South, evident already in the 1780s.

Slavery and Sectionalism

When white Americans declared their independence, they owned nearly half a million black Americans. African Americans of the revolutionary generation, most of them enslaved, constituted 20 percent of the total population of the colonies in 1775, and nearly 90 percent of them lived in the South. Yet few political leaders directly confronted the issue of whether slavery should be permitted to exist in a truly republican society.

Republicanism and slavery

When political discussion did stray toward the subject of slavery, southerners—especially ardent republicans—bristled defensively. Theirs was a difficult position, riddled with contradictions. On the one hand, they had condemned parliamentary taxation as tantamount to political "slavery" and had rebelled, declaring that all men were "created equal." On the other hand, enslaved African Americans formed the basis of the South's plantation economy. To surrender slavery, southerners believed, would be to usher in economic ruin.

Some planters in the Upper South resolved the dilemma by freeing their slaves. Such decisions were made easier by changing economic conditions in the Chesapeake. As planters shifted from tobacco toward wheat, a crop demanding a good deal less labor, Virginia and Maryland liberalized their manumission statutes, laws providing for freeing slaves. Between 1776 and 1789, most southern states also joined the North in prohibiting the importation of slaves, and a few antislavery societies appeared in the Upper South. But no southern state legally abolished slavery. Masters defended their right to hold human property in the name of republicanism.

Eighteenth-century republicans regarded property as crucial, for it provided a man and his family with security, status, and wealth. More important, it provided a measure of independence: to be able to act freely, without fear or favor of others. People without property were dangerous, republicans believed, because the poor could never be politically independent. Southern defenders of slavery thus argued that free, propertyless black people would pose a political threat to the liberty of propertied white citizens. Subordinating the human rights of blacks to the property rights of whites, southern republicans reached the paradoxical conclusion that their freedom depended on keeping African Americans in bondage.

The North followed a different course. Because its economy depended far less on slave labor, black emancipation did not run counter to powerful economic interests. Antislavery societies, the first founded by the Quakers in 1775, spread throughout the northern states during the next quarter century. Over the same period the legislatures of most northern states provided for the immediate or gradual abolition of slavery. Freedom for most northern African Americans came slowly, but by 1830 there were fewer than 3000 slaves out of a total northern black population of 125,000.

The Revolution, which had been fought for liberty and equality, did little to change the status of most black Americans. By 1800 more enslaved African

Negro Methodists Holding a Meeting in a Philadelphia Alley evokes the vibrancy of African American religious life in the city that became a haven for free blacks. The artist, until recently believed to be a visiting Russian, Pavel Petrovich Svinin, is now thought to be the American John Lewis Krimmel.

Americans lived in the United States than had lived there in 1776. Slavery continued to grow in the Lower South as the rice culture of the Carolinas and Georgia expanded and as the new cotton culture spread westward.

Still, a larger number of slaves than ever before became free during the war and in the following decades, whether through military service, successful escape, manumission, or gradual emancipation. All these developments fostered the growth of free black communities, especially in the Upper South and in northern cities. By 1810 free African Americans made up 10 percent of the total population of Maryland and Virginia. The composition of the postwar free community changed as well. Before independence most free blacks had been either mulattoes—the offspring of interracial unions—or former slaves too sick or aged to have value as laborers. In contrast, the free population of the 1780s became darker skinned, younger, and healthier. This group injected new vitality into black communal life, organizing independent schools, churches, and mutual benefit societies for the growing number of "free people of color."

Growth of the free black community

After the Revolution slavery ceased to be a national institution. It became the "peculiar institution" of a single region, the American South. The isolation of slavery in one section set North and South on radically different courses of social development, sharpening economic and political divisions.

Free black sailors

Wartime Economic Disruption

With the outbreak of the Revolution, Americans had suffered an immediate economic loss. Formerly, Britain had supplied manufactured goods, markets for American exports, and credit that enabled commerce to flourish. The war changed all that. Hardest hit were southern planters, who had to seek new customers for their tobacco, cotton, and rice as well as find new sources of capital to finance production. Northerners too faced difficulties, for their major seaports were occupied for a time by British troops, whose presence disrupted commercial activity.

Public and private debt

Matters did not improve with the coming of peace. France and Britain flooded the new states with their manufactures, and postwar Americans, eager for luxuries, indulged in a most unrepublican spending spree. The flurry of buying left some American merchants and consumers as deeply in debt as their governments. When loans from private citizens and foreign creditors like France proved insufficient to finance the fighting, both Congress and the states printed paper money—a whopping total of $400 million. The paper currency was backed only by the government's promise to redeem the bills with money from future taxes, because legislatures balked at the unpopular alternative of levying taxes during the war. For the bills to be redeemed, the United States had to survive, so by the end of 1776, when Continental forces sustained a series of defeats, paper money started to depreciate dramatically. By 1781 it was virtually without value, and Americans coined the expression "not worth a Continental."

Postwar inflation

The printing of paper money, combined with a wartime shortage of goods, triggered an inflationary spiral. As goods became scarcer and scarcer, they cost more and more worthless dollars. In this spiral, creditors were gouged by debtors, who paid them back with depreciated currency. At the same time soaring prices for food and manufactured goods eroded the buying power of wage earners and small farmers. And the end of the war brought on demands for prompt repayment from the new nation's foreign creditors as well as from soldiers seeking back pay and pensions.

Congress could do nothing. With no power to regulate trade, it could neither dam the stream of imported goods rushing into the states nor stanch the flow of gold and silver to Europe to pay for these items. With no power to prohibit the states from issuing paper money, it could not halt depreciation. With no power to regulate wages or prices, it could not curb inflation. With no power to tax, it could not reduce the public debt. Efforts to grant Congress greater powers met with determined resistance from the states. They refused Congress any revenue of its own, fearing the first steps toward "arbitrary" government.

Political divisions over economic policy

Within states, too, economic problems aroused discord. Some major merchants, creditors, and large commercial farmers had profited handsomely during the war by selling supplies to the American, British, and French armies at high prices or by preying on enemy vessels as privateers. Eager to protect their windfall, they lobbied state legislatures for an end to inflationary monetary policies. They pushed for the passage of high taxes to pay wartime debts, a paper currency that was backed up with gold and silver, and an active policy to encourage foreign trade.

Less affluent men fought back, pressing legislatures for programs that met their needs. Western farmers, often in debt, urged the states to print more paper money and to pass laws lowering taxes and postponing the foreclosure of mortgages. Artisans opposed merchants by calling for protection from low-priced foreign imports that competed with the goods they produced. They set themselves against farmers as well by demanding price regulation of the farm products they consumed. In the continuing struggle, the state legislatures became the battleground of competing economic factions, each bent on gaining its own particular advantage.

As the 1780s wore on, conflicts mounted. As long as the individual states remained sovereign, the Confederation was crippled—unable to conduct foreign affairs effectively, unable to set coherent economic policy, unable to deal with discontent in the West. Equally dismaying was the discovery that many Americans, instead of being selflessly concerned for the public good, selfishly pursued their private interests.

The war for independence transformed **Republican Society**
not only America's government and econ-
omy but also its society and culture. Inspired by the Declaration's ideal of equality, some Americans rejected the subordinate position assigned to them under the old colonial order. Westerners, newly wealthy entrepreneurs, urban artisans, and women all claimed greater freedom, power, and recognition. The authority of the traditional leaders of government, society, and the family came under a new scrutiny; the impulse to defer to social superiors became less automatic. The new assertiveness demonstrated how deeply egalitarian assumptions were taking root in American culture.

The New Men of the Revolution

The Revolution gave rise to a new sense of social identity and a new set of ambitions among several groups of men who had once accepted a humbler status. The more democratic society of the frontier emboldened westerners to believe themselves the equals of easterners. As one Kentuckian explained to James Madison, the western migrants "must make a very different mass from one which is composed of men born and raised on the same spot. . . . They see none about them to whom or to whose families they have been accustomed to think themselves inferior."

Gilbert Stuart's *The Skater* captures one American gentleman's characteristic sense of mastery over himself, nature, and society. But the Revolution instilled in many people of humbler status a new sense of pride and potential. Typical of such groups were New York's Society of Pewterers, whose banner proclaimed them "solid and pure"—the equals of those gentlemen who prided themselves on being society's "natural leaders."

The war also offered opportunities to aspiring entrepreneurs everywhere, and often they were not the same men who had prospered before the war. At a stroke, independence swept away the political prominence of loyalists, whose ranks included an especially high number of government officials, large landowners, and major merchants. And while loyalists found their properties confiscated by revolutionary governments, other Americans grew rich. Many northern merchants gained newfound wealth from privateering or military contracts. Commercial farmers in the mid-Atlantic states prospered from the high food prices caused by wartime scarcity and army demand.

The Revolution effected no dramatic redistribution of wealth. Indeed, the gap between rich and poor increased during the 1780s. But those families newly enriched by the Revolution came to demand and receive greater social recognition and political influence. The republican ideal of "an aristocracy of merit" justified their ambitions.

Urban artisans

City craftworkers pushed for recognition too. Their experience in organizing boycotts against British goods during the imperial crisis gave artisans a greater taste of politics. With the Revolution accomplished, they clamored for men of their own kind to represent them in government. Their assertiveness came as a rude shock to gentlemen like South Carolina's William Henry Drayton, who balked at sharing power with men "who never were in a way to study" anything except "how to cut up a beast in the market to the best advantage, to cobble an old shoe in the neatest manner, or to build a necessary house."

While master craftworkers competed for political office, the laborers who worked for them also exhibited a new sense of independence. As domestic manufacturing expanded after the Revolution, journeymen and even apprentices moved out of their masters' households and away from the supervision of their masters. Recognizing that their interests were often distinct from those of masters, journeymen formed new organizations to secure higher wages. Between 1786 and 1816 skilled urban laborers organized the first major strikes in American history.

The New Women of the Revolution

Not long after the fighting with Britain had broken out, Margaret Livingston of New York wrote to her sister Catherine, "You know that our Sex are doomed to be obedient in every stage of life so that we shant be great gainers by this contest." By war's end, however, Eliza Wilkinson from rural South Carolina was complaining boldly to a woman friend: "The men say we have no business with political matters . . . it's not our sphere. . . . [But] I won't have it thought that because we are the weaker Sex (as to bodily strength my dear) we are Capable of nothing more, than minding the Dairy . . . surely we may have enough sense to give our Opinions."

What separated Margaret Livingston's resignation from Eliza Wilkinson's assertion of personal worth and independence was the Revolution. Eliza Wilkinson had managed her parents' plantation during the war and defended it from British marauders. Other women discovered similar reserves of skill and resourcefulness. When soldiers returned home, some were surprised to find their wives and daughters, who had been running family farms and businesses, less submissive and more self-confident.

Exclusion of women from politics

But American men had not fought a revolution for the equality of American women. In fact, male revolutionaries gave no thought whatsoever to the role of women in the new nation, assuming that those of the "weaker sex" were incapable of making informed and independent political decisions. Most women of the revolutionary generation agreed that the proper female domain was the home, not the public arena of politics. Still, the currents of the Revolution occasionally left gaps that allowed women to display their keen political interests. When a loosely worded provision in the New Jersey state constitution gave the vote to "all free inhabitants" owning a specified amount of property, white widows and single women went to the polls. Only in 1807 did the state legislature close the loophole.

Mary Wollstonecraft's *Vindication*

In the wake of the Revolution there also appeared in England a book that would become a classic text of modern feminism, Mary Wollstonecraft's *A Vindication of the Rights of Women* (1792). Attracting a wide, if not widely approving, readership in America as well, it called not only for laws to guarantee women civil and political equality but also for educational reforms to ensure their social and economic equality.

Like many young, single English women with more wit than fortune, Wollstonecraft started her working life as a governess and a school's headmistress. Then she turned to writing for her livelihood, producing book reviews, translations, a novel, and a treatise on women's education before dashing off *Vindication* in six short months. She charged that men deliberately conspired to keep women in "a state of perpetual childhood" by giving them inferior, frivolous educations. That encouraged young girls to fixate on fashion and flirtation and made them "only anxious to inspire love, when they ought to cherish a nobler ambition, and by their abilities and virtues exact respect." Girls, she proposed, should receive the same education as boys, including training that would prepare them for careers in medicine, politics, and business. No woman should have to pin her hopes for

Contrast the portrait of Mary Wollstonecraft rendered just before her death in 1797 with a strikingly masculinized rendering in a book published in the United States in 1809, which placed her in the company of "actresses, adventurers, authoresses, fortunetellers, gipsies, dwarfs, swindlers, and vagrants."

financial security on making a good marriage, Wollstonecraft argued. On the contrary, well-educated and resourceful women capable of supporting themselves would make the best wives and mothers, assets to the family and the nation.

Vindication might have been written in gunpowder rather than ink, given the reaction it aroused on both sides of the Atlantic. Even so, Wollstonecraft at first won many defenders among both men and women, who sometimes publicly and more often privately expressed their agreement with her views. This favorable reception ended abruptly after her death in childbirth in 1797, when a memoir written by her husband revealed that she had lived out of wedlock with him—and before him, with another lover. Even so, Wollstonecraft's views found some admirers in America. Among them were Aaron Burr, the future vice president, who dubbed *Vindication* "a work of genius" and promised to read it aloud to his wife, and the Philadelphia Quaker Elizabeth Drinker, who confided to her diary that "In very many of her sentiments, she . . . *speaks my mind.*"

Republican Motherhood and Education

Wollstonecraft's ideas also lent support to the leading educational reformers in the revolutionary generation. Her sentiments echo in the writings of Judith Sargent Murray, a New Englander who urged the cultivation of women's minds to encourage self-respect and celebrated "excellency in our sex." Her fellow reformer, the Philadelphian Benjamin Rush, agreed that only educated and independent-minded women could raise the informed and self-reliant citizens that a republican government required. Their view, known as "republican motherhood," contributed to the most dramatic change in the lives of women after the war—the spread of female literacy.

Improved schooling and literacy rates

Between 1780 and 1830 the number of American colleges and secondary academies rose dramatically, and some of these new institutions were devoted to educating women. Not only did the number of schools for women increase, but these schools also offered a solid academic curriculum. By 1850—for the first time in American history—there were as many literate women as there were men. To counter popular prejudices, the defenders of female education contended that schooling for women would produce the ideal republican mother.

Women's legal status

The Revolution also prompted some states to reform their marriage laws, making divorce somewhat easier, although it remained extremely rare. But while women won greater freedom to divorce, courts became less concerned with enforcing a widow's traditional legal claim to one-third of her spouse's real estate. And married women still could not sue or be sued, make wills or contracts, or buy and sell property. Any wages that they earned went to their husbands; so did all personal property that wives brought into a marriage; so did the rents and profits of any real estate they owned. Despite the high ideals of republican motherhood, most women remained confined to the domestic sphere of the home and deprived of the most basic legal and political rights.

The Attack on Aristocracy

Why wasn't the American Revolution more revolutionary? Independence secured the full political equality of white men who owned property, but women were still deprived of political rights, African Americans of human rights. Why did the revolutionaries stop short of extending equality to the most unequal groups in American society—and with so little sense that they were being inconsistent?

In part, the lack of concern was rooted in republican ideas themselves. Republican ideology viewed property as the key to independence and power. Lacking property, women and black Americans were easily consigned to the custody of husbands and masters. Then, too, prejudice played its part: the perception of women and blacks as naturally inferior beings.

Republican view of equality

But revolutionary leaders also failed to press for greater equality because they conceived their crusade in terms of eliminating the evils of a European past dominated by kings and aristocrats. They believed that the great obstacle to equality was monarchy—kings and queens who bestowed hereditary honors and political office on favored individuals and granted legal privileges and monopolies to favored churches and businesses. These artificial inequalities posed the real threat to liberty, most republicans concluded. In other words, the men of the Revolution were intent on attaining equality by leveling off the top of society. It did not occur to most republicans that the cause of equality could also be served by raising up the bottom—by attacking the laws and prejudices that kept African Americans enslaved and women dependent.

The most significant reform of the republican campaign against artificial privilege was the dismantling of state-supported churches. Most states had a religious establishment. In New York and the South, it was the Anglican church; in New England, the Congregational church. Since the 1740s, dissenters who did not worship at state churches had protested laws that taxed all citizens to support the clergy of established denominations. After the Revolution dissenters argued that equality required ending such privileges. As more dissenters became voters, state legislators gradually abolished state support for Anglican and Congregational churches.

Disestablishment

Not only in religious life but in all aspects of their culture, Americans rejected inequalities associated with a monarchical past. In that spirit reformers attacked the Society of Cincinnati, a group organized by former officers of the Continental Army in 1783. The society, which was merely a social club for veterans, was forced to disband for its policy of passing on its membership rights to eldest sons. In this way, critics charged, the Cincinnati was creating artificial distinctions and perpetuating a hereditary warrior nobility.

Society of Cincinnati

Today, many of the republican efforts at reform seem misdirected. While only a handful of revolutionaries worked for the education of women and the emancipation of slaves, enormous zeal went into fighting threats from a monarchical past that had never existed in America. Yet the threat from kings and aristocrats was real to the revolutionaries—and indeed remained real in many parts of Europe. Their determination to sweep away every shred of formal privilege ensured that these forms of inequality never took root in America. And if eighteenth-century Americans did not extend equality to women and racial minorities, it was a failure that they shared with later revolutionary movements that promised more.

From Confederation to Constitutions

While Americans in many walks of life sought to realize the republican commitment to equality, leaders in Congress wrestled with the problem of preserving the nation itself. With the new republic slowly rending itself to pieces, some political leaders concluded that neither the Confederation nor the state legislatures were able to remedy the basic difficulties facing the nation. But how could the states be convinced to surrender their sovereign powers? The answer came in the wake of two events—one foreign, one domestic—that lent momentum to the cause of strengthening the central government.

Daily Lives

FOOD/DRINK/DRUGS

The Spirits of Independence

If God had intended man to drink water, Ben Franklin remarked, he would not have made him with an elbow capable of raising a wineglass. Colonials from all across America agreed with Franklin on the virtues of drink. The ruddy glow of colonial cheeks (still visible in the portraits hung in museums) reflected not only good health and ardent republican virtue but also substantial daily doses of alcohol. Colonials consumed about twice as much alcohol as Americans today, though in different forms. Beer was not popular, the only sort consumed being a weak, homemade "small beer" containing about one percent alcohol. Only the wealthy, like Franklin, could afford imported Madeira and port wines. On the other hand, the produce of apple orchards allowed Americans northward from Virginia to drink their fill of hard cider. Far and away the most popular distilled liquor was rum, a potent 90 proof beverage (45 percent alcohol) that they sipped straight or mixed with water and sugar to make "toddies."

Special occasions were particularly convivial. The liquor flowed freely at ministerial ordinations in New England towns, at court days in the South, at house-raisings, corn-huskings, and quilting bees on the frontier, and at weddings, elections, and militia musters everywhere in the colonies. But Americans did not confine their drinking to occasional celebrations. Some, like John Adams, started the day with a tankard of hard cider. Others, merchants and craftworkers, broke the boredom of late mornings and early afternoons by sending the youngest apprentice in the shop out for spirits. Laborers in seaport docks and shipyards, fishermen and sailors at sea, and farm workers in the countryside commonly received a daily allotment of liquor as part of their wages. And at night, men of every class enjoyed a solitary glass at home or a sociable one at a local tavern.

Socialization into the drinking culture started in childhood. Parents permitted youngsters to sip the sweet dregs of a glass of rum, and when young men entered their teens, they joined their fathers at the tavern. Women drank too, although more often at home, and they sometimes explained their use of distilled liquor as serving some "medicinal" purpose. Slaves got around laws restricting their consumption of alcohol by stealing from masters or bartering with white peddlers.

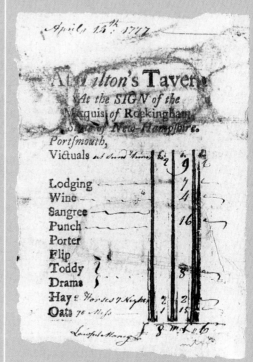

This tavern bill from New Hampshire indicates that in 1777 whiskey was still too rare to be listed.

The Jay-Gardoqui Treaty

The international episode that threatened to leave the Confederation in shambles was a debate over a proposed treaty with Spain. In 1785 southwesterners still could not legally navigate the Mississippi and were still threatening to secede from the union and annex their territory to Spain's American empire. To shore up southwestern loyalties, Congress instructed its secretary of foreign affairs, John Jay, to negotiate an agreement with Spain preserving American rights to navigate on the Mississippi River. But the Spanish emissary, Don Diego de Gardoqui, sweet-talked Jay into accepting a treaty by which the United States would give up all rights to the Mississippi for 25 years. In return, Spain agreed to grant trading privileges to American merchants.

Jay, a New Yorker, knew more than a few northern merchants who were eager to open new markets. But when the proposed treaty became public knowledge,

Until the middle of the eighteenth century, most colonials (and Europeans) considered spirits a source of physical strength and an essential supplement to their diet, as well as a remedy for colds, fevers, snakebite, and, ironically, depression. They did not condone public drunkenness, but they saw nothing amiss in the regular use of alcohol or even in occasional intoxication.

The easy acceptance of drinking prevailed for most of the colonial period for two reasons. First, until about the 1760s, frequent access to the strongest spirits, rum, lay beyond the means of most Americans. Second, the leaders of local communities were able to oversee most public drinking and to keep disorder to a minimum. But by the middle of the eighteenth century, some Americans developed misgivings about the drinking culture. Increased production and importation led the price of rum to drop so sharply that an ordinary laborer could earn enough in a day to stay "drunk as a lord" for the rest of the week. Taverns proliferated, making it impossible for community leaders to monitor the popular consumption of alcohol.

The new concern that the drinking of rum fostered crime and social disruption prompted the first steps toward temperance reform. By the 1770s, Quakers like Anthony Benezet were urging that alcohol, like slavery, was an "unrepublican vice," for both forms of bondage deprived their victims of liberty and the capacity for rationality and self-control. Some members of the medical profession, most notably Benjamin Rush, also joined early temperance ranks.

Although the advocates of more moderate consumption won support among some educated elites, most Americans altered their drinking habits by consuming *more* hard liquor. Rum, the liquor of choice before the Revolution, lost much of its ground to a new rival, whiskey. Whiskey was democratic and cheap, for it could be made in the lowliest backcountry farmhouse. It was patriotic, since it did not depend on imports from the Caribbean. Gradually these "spirits of independence" supplanted rum not only in the frontier West but also in the urban East. Consumption of alcohol was on a steady rise that would finally result, half a century after the Revolution, in louder calls for temperance reform.

southwesterners denounced it as nothing short of betrayal. The treaty was never ratified, but the hostility stirred up during the debate revealed the strength of sectional feelings.

Shays's Rebellion

On the heels of this humiliation by Spain came an internal conflict that challenged the notion that individual states could maintain order in their own territories. The trouble erupted in western Massachusetts, where many small farmers were close to ruin. By 1786 farm wages and prices had fallen sharply and farmers were selling little produce. Yet they still had to pay mortgages on their farms and other debts. In 1786 the lower house of the Massachusetts legislature obliged the farmers with a package of relief measures. But creditors in eastern Massachusetts, determined to safeguard their own investments, persuaded the upper house to defeat the measures.

In the summer of 1786 western farmers responded, demanding that the upper house of the legislature be abolished and that the relief measures go into effect. That autumn 2000 farmers rose in armed rebellion, led by Captain Daniel Shays, a veteran of the Revolution. They closed the county courts to halt creditors from foreclosing on their farms and marched on the federal arsenal at Springfield. The state militia quelled the uprising by February 1787, but the insurrection left many in Massachusetts and the rest of the country thoroughly shaken.

Response to agrarian unrest

Alarmed conservatives saw Shays's Rebellion as the consequence of radical democracy. "The natural effects of pure democracy are already produced among us," lamented one republican gentleman; "it is a war against virtue, talents, and property carried on by the dregs and scum of mankind." He was wrong. The rebels with Daniel Shays were no impoverished rabble. They were reputable members of western communities who wanted their property protected and believed that government existed to provide that protection. The Massachusetts state legislature had been unable to safeguard the property of farmers from the inroads of recession or to protect the property of creditors from the armed debtors who closed the courts. It had failed, in other words, to fulfill the most basic aim of republican government.

What if such violent tactics spread? Other states with discontented debtors feared what the example of western Massachusetts might mean for the future of the Confederation itself. But by 1786 Shays's Rebellion supplied only the sharpest jolt to a movement for reform that was already under way. Even before the rebellion, a group of Virginians had proposed a meeting of the states to adopt a uniform system of commercial regulations. Once assembled at Annapolis in September 1786, the delegates from five states agreed to a more ambitious undertaking. They called for a second, broader meeting in Philadelphia, which Congress approved, for the "express purpose of revising the Articles of Confederation."

Framing a Federal Constitution

It was the wettest spring anyone could remember. The 55 men who traveled over muddy roads to Philadelphia in May 1787 arrived drenched and bespattered. Fortunately, most of the travelers were men in their thirties and forties, young enough to survive a good soaking. Since most were gentlemen of some means—planters, merchants, and lawyers with powdered wigs and prosperous paunches—they could recover from the rigors of their journey in the best accommodations offered by America's largest city.

The delegates came from all the states except Rhode Island. The rest of New England supplied shrewd backroom politicians—Roger Sherman and Oliver Ellsworth from Connecticut and Rufus King and Elbridge Gerry, Massachusetts men who had learned a trick or two from Sam Adams. The middle states marshaled much of the intellectual might: two Philadelphia lawyers, John Dickinson and James Wilson; one Philadelphia financier, Robert Morris; and the aristocratic Gouverneur Morris. From New York there was Alexander Hamilton, the mercurial and ambitious young protégé of Washington. South Carolina provided fiery orators Charles Pinckney and John Rutledge.

It was "an assembly of the demi-gods," gushed Thomas Jefferson, who, along with John Adams, was serving as a diplomat in Europe when the convention met. In fact, the only delegate who looked even remotely divine was the convention's presiding deity. Towering a full half foot taller than most of his colleagues, George Washington displayed his usual self-possession from a chair elevated on the speaker's platform in the Pennsylvania State House, where the delegates met. At first glance, the delegate of least commanding presence was Washington's fellow Virginian, James Madison. Short and slightly built, the 36-year-old Madison had no profession except hypochondria; he read a great deal and dressed in black. But he was an astute politician and a brilliant political thinker who, more than anyone else, shaped the framing of the federal Constitution.

The delegates from 12 different states had two things in common. They were all men of considerable political experience, and they all recognized the need for a stronger national union. So when the Virginia delegation introduced Madison's outline for a new central government, the convention was ready to listen.

The Virginia and New Jersey Plans

What Madison had in mind was a truly national republic, not a confederation of independent states. His "Virginia Plan" proposed a central government with three branches: legislative, executive, and judicial. Furthermore, the legislative branch, Congress, would possess the power to veto all state legislation. In place of the Confederation's single assembly, Madison substituted a bicameral legislature, with a lower house elected directly by the people and an upper house chosen by the lower, from nominations made by state legislatures. Representatives to both houses would be apportioned according to population—a change from practice under the Articles, in which each state had a single vote in Congress. Madison also revised the structure of government that had existed under the Articles by adding an executive, who would be elected by Congress, and an independent federal judiciary.

James Madison, the scholar and statesman whose ideas and political skill shaped the Constitution

After two weeks of debate over the Virginia Plan, William Paterson, a lawyer from New Jersey, presented a less radical counterproposal. Although his "New Jersey Plan" increased Congress's power to tax and to regulate trade, it kept the national government as a unicameral assembly, with each state receiving one vote in Congress under the policy of equal representation. The delegates took just four days to reject Paterson's plan. Most endorsed Madison's design for a stronger central government.

Paterson's New Jersey Plan

Even so, the issue of apportioning representation continued to divide the delegates. While smaller states pressed for each state having an equal vote in Congress, larger states backed Madison's provision for basing representation on population. Underlying the dispute over representation was an even deeper rivalry between southern and northern states. While northern and southern populations were nearly equal in the 1780s, and the South's population was growing more rapidly, the northern states were more numerous. Giving the states equal votes would put the South at a disadvantage. Southerners feared being outvoted in Congress by the northern states and felt that only proportional representation would protect the interests of their section.

That division turned into a deadlock as the wet spring burned off into a blazing summer. Delegates suffered the daily torture of staring at a large sun painted on the speaker's chair occupied by Washington. The stifling heat was made even worse because the windows remained shut to keep any news of the proceedings from drifting out into the Philadelphia streets.

The Deadlock Broken

Finally, as the heat wave broke, so did the political stalemate. On July 2 a committee headed by Benjamin Franklin suggested a compromise. States would be equally represented in the upper house of Congress, each state legislature appointing two senators to six-year terms. That satisfied the smaller states. In the lower

Compromise over representation

house of Congress, which alone could initiate money bills, representation was to be apportioned according to population. Every 30,000 inhabitants would elect one representative for a two-year term. A slave was to count as three-fifths of a free person in the calculation of population, and the slave trade was to continue until 1808. That satisfied the larger states and the South.

By the end of August the convention was prepared to approve the final draft of the Constitution. The delegates agreed that the executive, now called the president, would be chosen every four years. Direct election seemed out of the question—after all, how could citizens in South Carolina know anything about a presidential candidate who happened to live in distant Massachusetts, or vice versa? But if voters instead chose presidential electors, those eminent men would likely have been involved in national politics, have known the candidates personally, and be prepared to vote wisely. Thus the Electoral College was established, with each state's total number of senators and representatives determining its share of electoral votes.

An array of other powers ensured that the executive would remain independent and strong. He would have command over the armed forces, authority to conduct diplomatic relations, responsibility to nominate judges and officials in the executive branch, and the power to veto congressional legislation. Just as the executive branch was made independent, so too the federal judiciary was separated from the other two branches of government. Madison believed that this clear separation of powers was essential to a balanced republican government.

Madison's only real defeat came when the convention refused to give Congress veto power over state legislation. Still, the new bicameral national legislature enjoyed much broader authority than Congress had under the Confederation, including the power to tax and to regulate commerce. The Constitution also limited the powers of state legislatures, prohibiting them from levying duties on trade, coining money or issuing paper currency, and conducting foreign relations. The Constitution and the acts passed by Congress were declared the supreme law of the land, taking precedence over any legislation passed by the states. And changing the Constitution would not be easy. Amendments could be proposed only by a two-thirds vote of both houses of Congress or in a convention requested by two-thirds of the state legislatures. Ratification of amendments required approval by three-quarters of the states.

On September 17, 1787, thirty-nine of the forty-two delegates remaining in Philadelphia signed the Constitution. It was fortunate that the signatories included

Electoral College

Separation of powers

Amending the Constitution

As the Constitution is signed, Benjamin Franklin (second from left) looks on; Washington presides. "The business being closed," Washington wrote, "the members adjourned to the City Tavern, dined together and took cordial leave of each other."

so many lawyers, for the summer's proceedings had been of such dubious legality that many skilled attorneys would be needed to make them seem otherwise. Charged only to revise the Articles, the delegates had instead written a completely new frame of government. And to speed up ratification, the convention decided that the Constitution would go into effect after only nine states had approved it, overlooking the fact that even a revision of the Articles would have required the assent of all state legislatures. They further declared that the people themselves—not the state legislatures—would pass judgment on the Constitution in special ratifying conventions. To serve final notice that the new central government was a republic of the people and not merely another confederation of states, Gouverneur Morris of Pennsylvania hit on a happy turn of phrase to introduce the Constitution. "We the People," the document begins, "in Order to form a more perfect Union . . ."

Ratification

With grave misgivings on the part of many, the states called for conventions to decide whether to ratify the new Constitution. Those Americans with the gravest misgivings—the Anti-Federalists as they came to be called—voiced familiar republican fears. Older and less cosmopolitan than their Federalist opponents, the Anti-Federalists drew upon their memories of the struggle with England to frame their criticisms of the Constitution. Expanding the power of the central government at the expense of the states, they warned, would lead to corrupt and arbitrary rule by new aristocrats. Extending a republic over a large territory, they cautioned, would separate national legislators from the interests and close oversight of their constituents.

The Anti-Federalists

Madison responded to these objections in *The Federalist Papers,* a series of 85 essays written with Alexander Hamilton and John Jay during the winter of 1787–1788. He countered Anti-Federalist concerns over the centralization of power by pointing out that each separate branch of the national government would keep the others within the limits of their legal authority. That mechanism of checks and balances would prevent the executive from oppressing the people while preventing the people from oppressing themselves.

The Federalist Papers

To answer Anti-Federalist objections to a national republic, Madison drew on the ideas of an English philosopher, David Hume. In his famous tenth essay in *The Federalist Papers,* Madison argued that in a great republic, "the Society becomes broken into a greater variety of interests, of pursuits, of passions, which check each other." The larger the territory, the more likely it was to contain multiple political interests and parties, so that no single faction could dominate. Instead, each would cancel out the others.

The one Anti-Federalist criticism Madison could not get around was the absence of a national bill of rights. Opponents insisted on an explicit statement of rights to secure the freedoms of individuals and minorities from being violated by the federal government. Madison finally promised to place a bill of rights before Congress immediately after the Constitution was ratified.

Bill of Rights

Throughout the early months of 1788, Anti-Federalists continued their opposition. But they lacked the articulate and influential leadership that rallied behind the Constitution and commanded greater access to the public press. In the end, too, Anti-Federalist fears of centralized power proved less compelling than Federalist prophecies of the chaos that would follow if the Constitution was not adopted.

Ratification of the Constitution

State	Date	Vote For	Vote Against
Delaware	December 8, 1787	30	9
Pennsylvania	December 12, 1787	46	23
New Jersey	December 18, 1787	38	0
Georgia	January 2, 1788	26	0
Connecticut	January 9, 1788	128	40
Massachusetts	February 16, 1788	187	168
Maryland	April 26, 1788	63	11
South Carolina	May 23, 1788	149	73
New Hampshire	June 21, 1788	57	47
Virginia	June 25, 1788	89	79
New York	July 26, 1788	30	27
North Carolina	November 21, 1789	194	77
Rhode Island	May 29, 1790	34	32

By the end of July 1788 all but two states had voted in favor of ratification. The last holdout—Rhode Island, to no one's surprise—finally came aboard in May 1790, after Madison had carried through on his pledge to submit a bill of rights to the new Congress. Indeed, these 10 amendments proved to be the Anti-Federalists' most impressive legacy.

Changing Revolutionary Ideals

Within the life span of a single generation, Americans had declared their independence twice. In many ways the political freedom claimed from Britain in 1776 was less remarkable than the intellectual freedom that Americans achieved by agreeing to the Constitution. The Constitution represented both a triumph of imagination and common sense and a rejection of some older, long-cherished republican beliefs.

Rejected republican beliefs

Americans thought long and hard before changing their minds, but many did. Committed at first to limiting executive power by making legislatures supreme, they at last ratified a constitution that provided for an independent executive and a balanced government. Committed at first to preserving the sovereignty of the states, they at last established a national government with authority independent of the states. Committed at first to the proposition that a national republic was impossible, they at last created an impossibility that still endures.

Behavior shaped by interest rather than virtue

What, then, became of the last tenet of the old republican creed—the belief that civic virtue would sustain popular liberty? The hard lessons of the war and the crises of the 1780s withered confidence in the capacity of Americans to sacrifice their private interests for the public welfare. Many came to share Washington's sober view that "the few . . . who act upon Principles of disinterestedness are, comparatively speaking, no more than a drop in the Ocean." The Constitution reflected the new recognition that interest rather than virtue shaped the behavior of most people most of the time and that the clash of diverse interest groups would remain a constant of public life.

Yet Madison and many other Federalists did not believe that the competition between private interests would somehow result in policies fostering public welfare. That goal would be met instead by the new national government acting as "a disinterested and dispassionate umpire in disputes between different passions and interests in the State." The Federalists looked to the national government to fulfill that role because they trusted that a large republic, with its millions of citizens, would yield more of that scarce resource—disinterested gentlemen dedicated to serving the public good. Such gentlemen, in Madison's words, "whose enlightened views and virtuous sentiments render them superior to local prejudices," would fill the small number of national offices.

Not all the old revolutionaries agreed. Anti-Federalists drawn from the ranks of ordinary Americans still believed that common people were more virtuous and gentlemen more interested than the Federalists allowed. "These lawyers and men of learning, and moneyed men, that talk so finely," complained one Anti-Federalist, would "get all the power and all of the money into their own hands, and then they will swallow up all us little folks." Instead of being dominated by enlightened gentlemen, the national government should be composed of representatives from every social class and occupational group.

The narrow majorities by which the Constitution was ratified reflected the continuing influence of such sentiments, as well as fear that the states were surrendering too much power. That fear made Patrick Henry so ardent an Anti-Federalist that he refused to attend the Constitutional Convention in 1787, saying that he "smelt a rat." "I am not a Virginian, but an American," Henry had once declared. Most likely he was lying. Or perhaps Patrick Henry, a southerner and a slaveholder, could see his way clear to being an "American" only as long as sovereignty remained firmly in the hands of the individual states. Henry's convictions, 70 years hence, would rise again to haunt the Union.

chapter summary

Leading Americans would give more thought to federalism, the organization of a United States, as the events of the postrevolutionary period revealed the weaknesses of the state and national governments.

- For a decade after independence, the revolutionaries were less committed to creating a single national republic than to organizing 13 separate state republics, each dominated by popularly elected legislatures.

- The Articles of Confederation provided for a government by a national legislature but left the crucial power of the purse, as well as all final power to make and execute laws, entirely to the states.

- Many conflicts in the new republic were occasioned by westward expansion, which created both international difficulties with Britain and Spain and internal tensions over the democratization of state legislatures.

- In the wake of the Revolution, ordinary Americans struggled to define republican society; workers began to organize, some women claimed a right to greater political, legal, and educational opportunities, and religious dissenters called for disestablishment.

- In the mid-1780s the political crisis of the Confederation came to a head, prompted by the controversy over the Jay-Gardoqui Treaty and Shays's Rebellion.

- The Constitutional Convention of 1787 produced an entirely new frame of government that established a truly national republic and provided for a separation of powers among a judiciary, a bicameral legislature, and a strong executive.

- The Anti-Federalists, opponents of the Constitution, softened their objections when promised a bill of rights after ratification, which was accomplished by 1789.

interactive learning

The Primary Source Investigator CD-ROM offers the following materials related to this chapter:

- A short documentary movie on free black sailors (D4)

- A collection of primary sources allowing exploration of the founding of the United States, including the Northwest Ordinance, several arguments from the Federalist Papers, and the Virginia Constitution. Other sources include paintings illustrating key moments in the founding of the nation, and the originals of America's most important founding documents, including the Constitution and the Declaration of Independence. Other documents explore the effects of the Revolution on Native Americans and western lands.

additional reading

Gordon Wood's two books, *The Creation of the American Republic* (1969) and *The Radicalism of the American Revolution* (1992), tell a compelling story about the transformation of American society, culture, and politics in the latter half of the eighteenth century. Forrest MacDonald's accounts of the Confederation period and the Constitution, *E Pluribus Unum* (1965) and *Novus Ordo Seclorum* (1985), are also excellent, as is Linda Kerber's study of the relevance of republicanism for American women, *Women of the Republic* (1980). The liveliest account of the framing of the Constitution is still Clinton Rossiter, *1787: The Grand Convention* (1973), while the best single introduction to the Anti-Federalists remains Cecilia Kenyon's "Men of Little Faith: The Anti-Federalists and the Nature of Representative Government," *William and Mary Quarterly,* 12 (1955).

Historians are developing a new and deeper appreciation for the ways in which the Revolutionary era transformed society and politics in the early republic, particularly in the North. For a vivid sense of how that change affected a single community in western Massachusetts, see John Brooke, *The Heart of the Commonwealth* (1991), and, for a fascinating tale of how the Revolution made one ordinary man's life extraordinary, see Alan Taylor, *William Cooper's Town* (1995). Probably the best single account of how the Revolution's legacy affected one African American community in the North is Shane White, *Somewhat More Independent* (1991). For a fuller list of readings, see the Bibliography at www.mhhe.com/davidsonnation5.

significant events

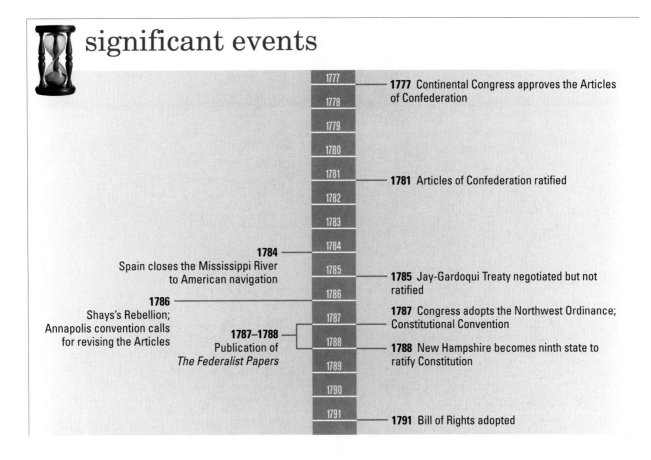

	1777 Continental Congress approves the Articles of Confederation
	1781 Articles of Confederation ratified
1784 Spain closes the Mississippi River to American navigation	
	1785 Jay-Gardoqui Treaty negotiated but not ratified
1786 Shays's Rebellion; Annapolis convention calls for revising the Articles	**1787** Congress adopts the Northwest Ordinance; Constitutional Convention
1787–1788 Publication of *The Federalist Papers*	**1788** New Hampshire becomes ninth state to ratify Constitution
	1791 Bill of Rights adopted

AFTER THE FACT
Historians Reconstruct the Past

White and Black Southerners Worshiping Together

During the 50 years before 1800, evangelicals introduced southerners to new ways of being religious. Those attending their worship services were men and women drawn into the earliest southern Baptist, Methodist, and Presbyterian churches by the First Great Awakening and other local revivals that followed in its wake. Some of these early services were held in private homes, others in crudely constructed churches, and still others in open fields. In such settings, evangelical preachers stressed the importance of being "reborn" by faith in Jesus Christ—and some southerners responded. They wept and confessed their sins; they encouraged one another with hopeful words and warm embraces. Those who came to such gatherings engaged in the most intimate kind of sharing and self-revelation.

But what made these services even more extraordinary is that some who participated were white, and some were black. These religious fellowships were truly biracial, and so they remained until after the Civil War. That remarkable fact has intrigued historians. Evangelical churches were one of the few southern institutions that brought blacks and whites together rather than keeping them apart. How did members behave toward each other daily? Were born-again converts from both races treated equally? How was authority within such churches distributed among black and white members?

The questions are tantalizing, but the answers by no means easy to come by. Some letters and diaries survive from the last half of the eighteenth century, among them the daily journals and correspondence of ministers. A few preachers even published autobiographies of their experiences. But even more valuable information can be gathered from what might seem at first a rather drab source. There are scores of church records dating from this period, most of them kept by Virginia Baptists. The members of each Baptist church elected a clerk, always a white male "brother," whose duty it was to record all the business transacted at their monthly meetings, often in a ledger-sized bound volume called the "church book." Church books provide an insight into relations between whites and blacks in part because their clerks are *not* consciously trying to write about race relations. They are simply recording the everyday business of churches, week in, week out.

Sometimes practical concerns dominated the meeting. Should the church building be repaired? Who among the brethren will be permitted to preach? (Many Baptist churches boasted several preachers besides the pastor.) On other occasions, members debated about what the Bible taught was the holiest way to govern their churches. But at most meetings, members fixed their attention on admitting new converts to their fellowship and "disciplining" older members suspected of sexual misconduct or theft, slander or swearing, drinking or fighting. Church clerks duly noted all those accepted as new members, as well as the names of wayward brothers and sisters—and whether they were merely scolded for their faults or expelled.

Such records offer the most direct and vivid sense of African Americans' presence and participation in early evangelical churches. First, they show that blacks made up a substantial minority—perhaps one-fifth to one-quarter—of the members in most churches. In a few, they constituted a majority. Many churches, too, authorized at least one African American brother to preach, sometimes permitting him that "liberty" only among other blacks but in other instances allowing him to address racially mixed gatherings. There were even a few predominantly white churches in early Virginia that black preachers served as pastors.

In some churches, too, black men and, more rarely, black women were permitted to vote in meetings; and in all, African American members could participate in deliberations and give testimony in discipline cases. Indeed, there are several instances of masters being disciplined after slave members complained of being abused. Black members, too, were sometimes charged with wrongdoing,

but white men were far more likely than any other group of members to be hauled before the church for reported misdeeds. In short, evangelical churches like these Baptist fellowships were among the most racially egalitarian institutions in early southern society. They offered African Americans unusual opportunities to hold positions of authority, to voice their opinions, and to gain leverage over their masters.

Churchbook record: "Names of Black Members"

Note the treatment of black names.

Yet these same church records also reveal the limits of racial equality among early evangelicals. Like all evidence mined by historians, the sources yield data that are sometimes complex and contradictory.

Records of those meetings at which members discussed the mundane matter of church repair reveal, for example, that the Baptists segregated seating at public worship. African Americans were consigned to the least choice spots at the back of the church or in "sheds" attached to the side. Moreover, when white members filled every available seat, black members were ordered outdoors to listen from underneath open windows. The attitude that such practices convey—that whites regarded African Americans as "second-class" members—is also suggested by the manner in which many clerks recorded new church members. While they always entered the full names of white converts, new African American members were usually listed last and often collectively as "several Negroes."

Church discussions about who might preach also show a growing concern on the part of white members to restrict the activities of black preachers. Increasingly after 1750 those allowed that "liberty"

"Uncle Jack," shown in this 1849 engraving, preaches informally to a white congregation. He began his career as a minister in the 1790s and continued until 1832.

were given ever stricter instructions about whom they might preach to, at which times, and from what texts of the Bible. At meetings in which the rules of conducting church business were discussed, white members also began to express concern about whether African American members should be allowed to vote. Most churches revoked that right before the end of the eighteenth century. Tracing how churches dealt with black members accused of misbehavior suggests a similar anxiety among white members, which increased over time. Although African Americans continued to make up only a tiny minority of church members suspected of misbehavior, those convicted of wrongdoing were far more likely than white members to be expelled rather than to receive a milder punishment.

In other words, a closer inspection of church records suggests that white evangelicals drifted toward more racially restrictive policies over the latter half of the eighteenth century. Why? The numbers in the church books are suggestive. After the Revolution, increasing numbers of African Americans were entering Baptist (and other evangelical) churches. As the percentage of black members rose, white evangelicals feared that the "freedoms" given to black worshipers might detract from the church's ability to win converts among slaveholders.

Clearly, evangelicals were winning converts among African Americans. Yet other evidence suggests that black members were left unsatisfied by their treatment in white churches. The diaries and letters of white evangelicals reveal that many black members of biracial churches had also begun conducting their own separate devotions. Even by the 1790s, African American Christians were meeting nightly in the slave quarters to pray, sing, and hear the sermons of black preachers. Such "shadow churches" served as the crucible of Afro-Christianity, a melding of evangelical Protestant and West African religious traditions. John Antrobus's painting *Plantation Burial* (page 227, also on page 393) reflects the situation that prevailed by the mid–nineteenth century. Although blacks attended white services in greater numbers, their most vital worship often took place elsewhere. White masters and preachers were like the shadowy couple Antrobus painted on the right: divorced from the Christian worship of their slaves.

BIBLIOGRAPHY Historians disagree about the extent to which early evangelical churches were egalitarian. The strongest arguments in favor are presented by Mechal Sobel, *The World They Made Together* (1987); the most forceful challenge to Sobel is Jewel Spangler, "Salvation Was Not Liberty: Baptists and Slavery in Revolutionary Virginia," *American Baptist Quarterly*, 13 (1994). Other studies that treat the dynamics of these early biracial churches and the experience of the first black southern evangelicals are Albert J. Raboteau, *Slave Religion* (1978), the best introduction to this subject; Sylvia R. Frey, *Water from the Rock* (1991), which usefully updates Raboteau; and, most recently, Christine Leigh Heyrman, *Southern Cross* (1997). The evolving views of race and slavery among early white evangelicals is thoughtfully analyzed in James Essig, *The Bonds of Wickedness* (1982), while the most eloquent descriptions of Afro-Christianity in the slave quarters appear in Eugene Genovese, *Roll, Jordan, Roll* (1972) and Lawrence Levine, *Black Culture and Black Consciousness* (1977).

Chapter 8

One spring evening in 1794 General John Neville was riding home from Pittsburgh with his wife and granddaughter. While going up a hill his wife's saddle started to slip, so Neville dismounted to tighten the girth. As he adjusted the strap, he heard the clip-clop of approaching horses. A rider galloped up and in a gruff voice asked, "Are you Neville the excise officer?"

"Yes," Neville replied, without turning around.

"Then I must give you a whipping!" cried the rider as he leaped from his horse. He grabbed the startled Neville by the hair and lunged at his throat, and the two began tussling. Breaking free, Neville finally managed to knock the man down and subdue him. He recognized his assailant as Jacob Long, a local farmer. After Long fled, the badly shaken Neville resumed his journey.

John Neville was not accustomed to such treatment. As one of the wealthiest men in the area, Neville expected respect from those of lower social rank. And he had received it—at least he had until becoming embroiled in a controversy over the new "whiskey tax" on distilled spirits. In a frontier district like western Pennsylvania, farmers regularly distilled their grain into whiskey for barter and sale. Not surprisingly, the excise tax, passed by Congress in 1791, was notoriously unpopular. Still, Neville had accepted an appointment to be one of the tax's regional inspectors. For three years he had endured threats as he tried to enforce the law, but this roadside assault clearly indicated that popular hostility was rising.

The REPUBLIC LAUNCHED

1789–1801

preview • In 1789 Americans could be divided into those who were rural, largely self-sufficient farmers and those tied more closely to the world of commerce. Politics in the early republic was rooted in this fundamental social division. Hamilton's Federalists, active in the commercial markets, believed in order, hierarchy, and an active central government. Jefferson's Republicans, champions of the self-sufficient farmer, feared aristocracy and wealth and wanted a less active government.

As spring turned to summer, the grain ripened, and so did the people's anger. In mid-July, a federal marshal arrived to serve summonses to a number of farmer-distillers who had not paid taxes. One, William Miller, squinted at the paper and was amazed to find the government ordering him to set aside "all manner of business and excuses" and appear in court—hundreds of miles away in Philadelphia—in little more than a month. Even worse, the papers claimed he owed $250.

And there, next to this unknown federal marshal, stood the stiff-backed, unyielding John Neville.

"I felt myself mad with passion," recalled Miller. "I thought $250 would ruin me; and . . . I felt my blood boil at seeing General Neville along to pilot the sheriff to my very door." Meanwhile word of the marshal's presence brought 30 or 40 laborers swarming from a nearby field. Armed with muskets and pitchforks, they were both angry and well liquored. When a shot rang out, Neville and the marshal beat a hasty retreat.

Within hours, news of Neville's doings spread to a nearby militia company. Enraged by what they considered this latest trampling on individual liberty, the militia marched to Neville's estate, Bower Hill, the next morning. A battle ensued, and the general, aided by his slaves, beat back the attackers. A larger group,

Frontier farmers in Pennsylvania tar and feather a federal tax collector during the Whiskey Rebellion. The political violence of the 1790s led Americans to wonder whether the new government would succeed in uniting a socially diverse nation.

numbering 500 to 700, returned the following day to find Neville fled and his home garrisoned by a group of soldiers from nearby Fort Pitt. The mob burned down most of the outbuildings and, after the soldiers surrendered, torched Neville's well-furnished home.

Throughout the region that summer, marauding bands roamed the countryside, burning homes, banishing individuals, and attacking tax collectors and other enemies. To many citizens who learned of the disturbances, such echoes of the revolutionary 1760s and 1770s were deeply distressing. In the space of only 15 years, Americans had already overturned two governments: England's colonial administration and the Articles of Confederation. As the aged Benjamin Franklin remarked in 1788, although Americans were quite skilled at overthrowing governments, it remained to be seen whether they were any good at sustaining them. Now, Franklin's warning seemed prophetic.

Yet Federalists—supporters of the Constitution—had recognized from the beginning how risky it was to unite a territory as large as the United States' 890,000 square miles. Yankee merchants living along Boston wharves had economic interests and cultural traditions quite different from those of backcountry farmers who raised hogs, tended a few acres of corn, and distilled whiskey. Even among farmers, there was a world of difference between a South Carolina planter who shipped tons of rice to European markets and a New Hampshire family whose stony fields yielded barely enough to survive. Could the new government established by the Constitution provide a framework strong enough to unite such a socially diverse nation?

1789: A Social Portrait

When the Constitution went into effect, the United States stretched from the Atlantic Ocean to the Mississippi River. The first federal census, compiled in 1790, counted approximately 4 million people, divided about evenly between the northern and southern states. The Republic's population was overwhelmingly concentrated along the eastern seaboard. Only about 100,000 settlers lived beyond the Appalachians in the Tennessee and Kentucky territories, which were soon to become states. In limited parts of this region, commercial agriculture based on slavery had begun to take root. But full-scale operations could not develop in the trans-Appalachian West as long as Spain controlled the mouth of the Mississippi River. The area north of the Ohio River was virtually unsettled by whites.

Within the Republic's boundaries were two major racial groups that lacked effective political influence: African Americans and Indians. In 1790 black Americans numbered 750,000, almost one-fifth the total population. More than 90 percent lived in the southern states from Maryland to Georgia; most were slaves who worked on tobacco and rice plantations. But there were free blacks as well, their numbers increased by the ideals of the Revolution. Indeed, the free black population in 1790 was larger, relative to the total African American population, than it would be at any other time before the Civil War. The census did not count the number of Indians living east of the Mississippi. North of the Ohio, the powerful Miami Confederacy discouraged settlement, while to the south, five strong, well-organized tribes—the Creeks, Cherokees, Chickasaws, Choctaws, and Seminoles—dominated the region from the Appalachians to the Mississippi River.

Population growth   That situation would change, however, as the white population continued to double approximately every 22 years. Immigration contributed only a small part to this astonishing growth. On average, fewer than 10,000 Europeans arrived annually between 1790 and 1820. The primary cause was natural increase, since, on average, American white women gave birth to nearly eight children. As a consequence, the United States had an unusually youthful population: in 1790 almost half of all white Americans were under 16 years old.* The age at first marriage was about 25 for men, 24 for women; but it was significantly lower in newly settled areas (on average perhaps 21 for males and younger for females), which contributed to the high birthrate.

This youthful, growing population remained overwhelmingly rural. Only 24 towns and cities boasted 2500 or more residents, and 19 out of 20 Americans lived outside them. In fact, in 1800 more than 80 percent of American families were engaged in agriculture. In such a rural environment the movement of people, goods, and information was slow. Few individuals used the expensive postal system, and most **Poor transportation**   roads were still little more than dirt paths hacked through the forest, with stumps cut off at 16 inches (so axles would just clear them) and large trees sometimes left in the roadway. The roads were choked with dust during dry spells and overflowed with mud when it rained. In 1790 the country had 92 newspapers, published weekly or semiweekly, mostly in towns and cities along major avenues of transportation. Americans off the beaten path only occasionally heard news of the outside world.

---

*Because the 1790 census did not include significant data on the black population, many of the statistical figures quoted for this era apply only to white Americans.

Life in isolated regions contrasted markedly with that in bustling urban centers like New York and Philadelphia. But the most basic division in American society was not between the cities and the countryside, important as that was. What would divide Americans most broadly over the coming decades was the contrast between semisubsistence and commercial ways of life. Semisubsistence farmers lived on the produce of their own land and labor. Americans in the commercial economy were tied more closely to the larger markets of a far-flung world. As the United States began its life under the new federal union, the distinction between a semisubsistence economy and a commercial economy was a crucial one.

The Semisubsistence Economy of Crèvecoeur's America

Most rural white Americans lived off the produce of their own land in a barter economy. It was this world that a French writer, Hector St. John de Crèvecoeur, described so well.

Crèvecoeur arrived in the British colonies in 1759 and almost immediately began wandering: riding over the rutted roads that led to the farms of New England and New York, fording the streams between the scattered settlements of Ohio and Kentucky, knocking the dust of Virginia off his clothes, stopping to talk at taverns along the roads to Philadelphia, and finally settling for a number of years as a farmer in the Hudson River valley. He published in 1783 his *Letters from an American Farmer,* asking in them the question that had so often occurred to him: "What then is the American, this new man?"

For Crèvecoeur what distinguished American society was the widespread equality of its people, especially the rural farmers. Americans were hostile to social pretensions and anything that smacked of aristocratic privilege. Furthermore, the conditions of the country promoted equality. Land was abundant and widely distributed, citizens lived decently, and the population was not divided into the wealthy few and the desperate many. (Like most of his contemporaries, Crèvecoeur glided

Equality

Work in semisubsistence rural families was done by both sexes and often involved cooperation among neighbors. While a woman milks the cow, a group of men assist in the difficult labor of burning felled trees and plowing a new field with an eight-ox team.

rather quickly over the plight of black slaves.) "We are the most perfect society now existing in the world," he boasted.

Although Crèvecoeur waxed romantic about the conditions of American life, he painted a reasonably accurate portrait of most of the interior of the northern states and the backcountry of the South. Wealth in those areas, while not distributed equally, was spread fairly broadly. And subsistence remained the goal of most white families. "The great effort was for every farmer to produce anything he required within his own family," one European visitor noted. In such an economy women played a key role. Wives and daughters had to be skilled in making articles such as candles, soap, clothing, and hats, since the cost of buying such items was steep.

Barter economy

With labor scarce and expensive, farmers also depended on the help of their neighbors in clearing fields, building homes, and harvesting crops. If a farm family produced a small surplus, they usually exchanged it locally rather than selling it for cash in a distant market. In this barter economy money was seldom seen and was used primarily to pay taxes and purchase imported goods. "Instead of money going incessantly backwards and forwards into the same hands," a French traveler recorded, residents in the countryside "supply their needs . . . by direct reciprocal exchanges. . . . They write down what they give and receive on both sides and at the end of the year they settle a large variety of exchanges with a very small quantity of coin."

Indian economies were also based primarily on subsistence. In the division of labor women raised crops, while men fished or hunted—not only for meat but also for skins to make clothing. Indians did not domesticate cattle, sheep, or pigs, but they managed and "harvested" deer by burning the surrounding forests once or twice a year to produce an environment free of underbrush, full of large, well-spaced trees and open meadows. Because Indians followed game more seasonally than did white settlers, their villages were moved to several different locations over the course of a year. But both whites and Indians in a semisubsistence economy moved periodically to new fields after the old ones were exhausted. Indians exhausted agricultural lands less quickly because they planted beans, corn, and squash in the same field, a technique that better conserved soil nutrients.

Despite the popular image of both the independent "noble savage" and the self-reliant yeoman farmer, virtually no one in the backcountry operated within a truly subsistence economy. Although farmers tried to grow most of the food their families ate, they normally bought salt, sugar, and coffee, and they often traded with their neighbors for food and other items. In addition, necessities such as iron, glass, lead, and gunpowder had to be purchased, usually at a country store, and many farmers hired artisans to make items such as shoes and to weave cloth. Similarly, Indians quickly became enmeshed in the wider world of European commerce, exchanging furs for iron tools or clothing and ornamental materials.

The Commercial Economy of Franklin's America

Outside the backcountry, Americans were tied much more closely to a commercial economy. Here, merchants, artisans, and even farmers did not subsist on what they produced but instead sold goods or services in a wider market and lived on their earnings. Cities and towns, of course, played a key part in the commercial economy. But so did the agricultural regions near the seaboard and along navigable rivers.

For commerce to flourish, goods had to move from producers to market cheaply enough to reap profits. Water offered the only cost-effective transportation over any distance; indeed, it cost as much to ship goods a mere 30 miles over primitive roads as to ship by boat 3000 miles across the Atlantic to London.

Cost-effective transportation was available to the planters of the Tidewater South, and city merchants used their access to the sea to establish trading ties to the West Indies and Europe. But urban artisans and workers were also linked to this market economy, as were many farm families in the Hudson valley, southeastern Pennsylvania, and southern New England. Where transportation was limited or prohibitively expensive, farmers had no incentive to increase production, and an economy of barter and semisubsistence persisted.

Commercial society differed from Crèvecoeur's world in another important way: its wealth was less equally distributed. By 1790, the richest 10 percent of Americans living in cities and in the plantation districts of the Tidewater South owned about 50 percent of the wealth. In the backcountry the top 10 percent was likely to own 25 to 35 percent of the wealth.

Inequality of wealth

Crèvecoeur argued that the American belief in equality sustained this society of small farm families, bound together in a community of relative equals. But he failed to see how much that equality rested on isolation. Without access to market, one could aspire only so high. Where the market economy operated more fully, however, Americans were more acquisitive and materialistic. Europeans were struck by Americans' desire for wealth. "Man here weighs everything, calculates everything, and sacrifices everything to his interest," one foreign visitor reported. Although semisubsistence farm families were eager to rise in life and acquire material goods, only those in the commercial economy could realistically pursue these dreams.

The man who gained international renown as a self-made citizen of commercial America was Benjamin Franklin. In his writings and in the example of his own life, Franklin offered a vision of the new nation that contrasted with Crèvecoeur's ideal of a subsistence America. Franklin had arrived in Philadelphia as a runaway apprentice who by hard work and talent rose to be one of the leading citizens of his adopted city. The preface to Franklin's popular *Poor Richard's Almanack,* as well as his countless essays, spelled out simple maxims for Americans seeking the upward path. "The way to wealth is as plain as the way to market," he noted. "It depends chiefly on two words, industry and frugality." Those anxious to succeed

Commercial values

Philadelphia was the largest and most prosperous city in the country in 1789. Its growth fueled the development of commercial agriculture in the surrounding countryside, as more and more farmers hauled their surplus to town for sale in the city's busy markets. In this scene, both men and women buy fresh foods on the streets. Indians, pictured here, also participated in the commercial economy.

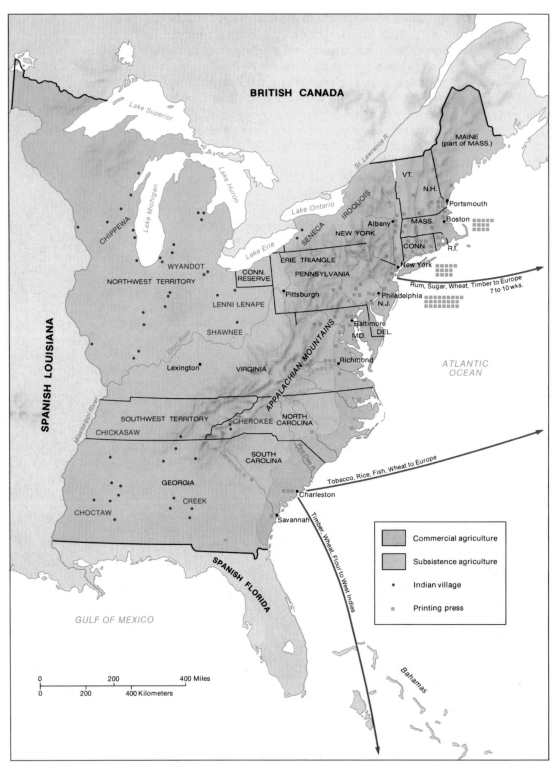

Semisubsistence and Commercial America, 1790 To prosper, a commercial economy demanded relatively cheap transportation to move goods. Thus in 1790 American commerce was confined largely to settled areas along the coast and to navigable rivers below the fall line. Because commerce depended on an efficient flow of information and goods, newspapers flourished in these areas.

should "remember that time is money." The kind of success he preached depended on taking advantage of commerce and a wider market. As a printer, Franklin was able to lead a life of acquisition and social mobility because he could distribute his almanacs and newspapers to ever-greater audiences.

The ethics of Franklin's marketplace, which looked forward to the opening up of opportunity in American society, threatened to destroy Crèvecoeur's egalitarian America. At the time of Franklin's death in 1790, the ideal that Crèvecoeur had so eloquently described still held sway across much of America. But the political debate of the 1790s showed clearly that Franklin's world of commerce and markets was slowly transforming the nation.

The Constitution and Commerce

In many ways the fight over ratification of the Constitution represented a struggle between the commercial and the subsistence-oriented elements of American society. Urban merchants and workers as well as commercial farmers and planters generally rallied behind the Constitution. They took a broader, more cosmopolitan view of the nation's future, and they had a more favorable view of government power. Franklin, predictably, supported the Constitution. So did Madison and Washington, both planters whose wealth depended on trade and commerce.

Americans who remained a part of the semisubsistence barter economy tended to oppose the Constitution. More provincial in outlook, they feared concentrated power, were suspicious of cities and commercial institutions, opposed aristocracy and special privilege, and in general just wanted to be left alone. They were a majority of the population, but they were not easily mobilized, lacked prestigious leaders, and did not have the access to communication that their opponents enjoyed. In defeat they remained suspicious that a powerful government would tax them to benefit the commercial sectors of the economy.

And so in 1789 the United States embarked on its new national course, with two rival visions of the direction that the fledgling Republic should take. Which vision would prevail—a question that was as much social as it was political— increasingly divided the generation of revolutionary leaders during the 1790s.

The New Government

Whatever the Republic was to become, Americans agreed that George Washington personified it. When the first Electoral College cast its votes, Washington was unanimously elected, the only president in history so honored. John Adams became vice president.

The Federalists—supporters of the Constitution—called the new government "the great experiment." They were intensely aware that throughout history democratic republics had in the end degenerated into quarreling factions, as with the city-states of ancient Greece, or ushered in dictatorships, as had happened in Cromwell's England. No republic—not England, or Rome, or the Swiss city-states— had stretched over a territory as large as the United States. Loyalty to the new Republic, with its untried form of government and diversity of peoples and interests, rested to a great degree on the trust and respect Americans gave Washington.

Failure of past republics

Washington's Character

Time has transformed Washington from a man into a monument: remote and unknowable, stiff, unbowing, impenetrable. Even during his own life, he had no close

Washington's trip from Virginia to New York City to assume the presidency was a triumphant procession as Americans enthusiastically greeted him with cheers and even flowers strewn along his path.

friends in public life and discouraged familiarity. "I could never be on familiar terms with the General—a man so cold, so cautious," one foreigner testified after visiting Mount Vernon. Washington learned with age to control his temper and tried to endure criticism patiently, yet he bitterly resented it. In an age of brilliant political thinkers, Washington was intellectually cautious and deliberate. As president he usually asked for written advice and made his decision only after weighing the options carefully.

The president also provoked criticism by the pomp with which he conducted the government. Washington, who was one of the richest men in America, enjoyed the luxuries that wealth brought. Critics complained about his formal public receptions, the large number of servants, and the coach emblazoned with his coat of arms—all aristocratic habits. Still, as much as Washington craved honor and military fame, he did not hunger for power and accepted the office of the presidency only reluctantly.

Organizing the Government

Washington realized that as the first occupant of the executive office, everything he did was fraught with significance. "I walk on untrodden ground," he commented. "There is scarcely any part of my conduct which may not hereafter be drawn into precedent."

The cabinet

The Constitution made no mention of a cabinet. Yet the drafters of the Constitution, aware of the experience of the Continental Congress under the Articles of Confederation, clearly assumed that the president would have some system of advisers. Congress authorized the creation of four departments—War, Treasury, State, and Attorney General—whose heads were to be appointed with the consent of the Senate. Washington's most important choices were Alexander Hamilton as secretary of the treasury and Thomas Jefferson to head the State Department. At first the president did not meet regularly with his advisers as a group, but the idea of a cabinet that met to discuss policy matters eventually evolved. Washington gradually excluded Adams from cabinet discussions, and any meaningful role for the vice president, whose duties were largely undefined by the Constitution, soon disappeared.

The Constitution created a federal Supreme Court but beyond that was silent about the court system. The Judiciary Act of 1789 set the size of the Supreme Court at 6 members; it also established 13 federal district courts and 3 circuit courts of appeal. Supreme Court justices spent much of their time serving on these circuit courts, a distasteful duty whose long hours "riding the circuit" caused one justice to grumble that Congress had made him a "traveling postboy." The Judiciary Act made it clear that federal courts had the right to review decisions of the state courts and specified cases over which the Supreme Court would have original jurisdiction. Washington appointed John Jay of New York, a staunch Federalist, as the first chief justice.

Federal judiciary

The Bill of Rights

Congress also confronted the demand for a bill of rights, which had become an issue during the debate over ratification. At that time, nearly 200 amendments had been put forward in one form or another. Supporters of the Constitution were particularly alarmed over proposals to restrict the federal power to tax. As leader of the Federalist forces in the House of Representatives, James Madison moved to head off any large-scale changes that would weaken federal power by submitting a bill of rights that focused on civil liberties.

Ultimately Congress sent 12 amendments to the states. By December 1791, 10 had been ratified and incorporated into the Constitution.* Their passage by Congress helped persuade North Carolina (1789) and Rhode Island (1790), the two holdouts, to join the Union. At the same time, the advocates of strong federal power, such as Hamilton, were relieved that "the structure of the government, and the mass and distribution of its powers," remained unchanged.

These first 10 amendments, known as the Bill of Rights, were destined to be of crucial importance in defining personal liberty in the United States. Among the rights guaranteed were freedom of religion, the press, and speech, as well as the right to assemble and petition and the right to bear arms. The amendments also established clear procedural safeguards, including the right to a trial by jury and protection against illegal searches and seizures. They prohibited excessive bail, cruel and unusual punishment, and the quartering of troops in private homes. The last two amendments were intended to calm fears about the federal government having unlimited power. Madison was careful, however, to phrase these particular amendments in very general terms. At the same time, an attempt in Congress to apply these same guarantees to state governments failed, and almost a century would pass before Congress moved, during Reconstruction, to prevent states from interfering with certain basic rights.

Protected rights

Hamilton's Financial Program

Before adjourning, Congress called on Alexander Hamilton, as secretary of the treasury, to prepare a report on the nation's finances. Hamilton undertook the assignment eagerly, for he did not intend to be a minor figure in the new administration.

Hamilton never forgot that he was a self-made man. His father was a Scottish merchant of noble birth, but his parents never married, and his father soon

---

*Of the two proposed amendments that were not initially approved, one was ratified in 1992 as the Twenty-seventh Amendment. It stipulates that there must be an intervening election before a congressional pay raise goes into effect.

Hamilton's character

abandoned the family. Hamilton grew up on the islands of the West Indies, scarred by the stigmas of poverty and illegitimacy. To compensate, he was driven constantly to seek respectability and money. He served as a military aide to Washington during the Revolution, and marriage to the daughter of a wealthy New York politician gave him influential connections he could draw on in his political career. Nevertheless, his haughty manner, jealousy, and penchant for intrigue made him many enemies. He was a brilliant thinker, yet he felt out of place in the increasingly democratic society emerging around him. "All communities divide themselves into the few and the many," he declared. "The first are rich and wellborn, the other the mass of the people. . . . The people are turbulent and changing; they seldom judge or determine right."

While Hamilton was not a monarchist, his experience in the army, which impressed on him the necessity of a vigorous government, made him more inclined than most of his colleagues to use force. Convinced that human nature was fundamentally selfish, Hamilton believed that the government needed to appeal to the self-interest of the rich and wellborn in order to succeed. "Men," he observed succinctly, "will naturally go to those who pay them best." He took as his model Great Britain, whose greatness he attributed to its system of public finance and its preeminence in commerce and manufacturing. Thus Hamilton set out to achieve two goals. He intended to use federal power to encourage manufacturing and commerce in order to make the United States economically strong and independent of Europe. And he was determined to link the interests of the wealthy with those of the new government.

Neither goal could be achieved until the federal government solved its two most pressing financial problems: revenue and credit. Without revenue it could not be effective. Without credit—the faith of merchants and other nations that the government would repay its debts—it would lack the ability to borrow. Hamilton proposed that all $52 million of the federal debt be paid in full (or funded). He also recommended that the federal government assume responsibility for the remaining $25 million in debts that individual states owed. He intended with these twin policies to put the new federal government on a sound financial footing and enhance its power by increasing its need for revenue and making the wealthy look to the national government, not the states. Hamilton also proposed a series of excise taxes, including a controversial 25 percent levy on whiskey, to help meet government expenses.

Funding and assumption

After heated debate, Congress deadlocked over funding and assumption. Finally, over dinner with Hamilton, Jefferson and Madison of Virginia agreed to support his proposal if, after 10 years in Philadelphia, the permanent seat of government was

Location of the capital

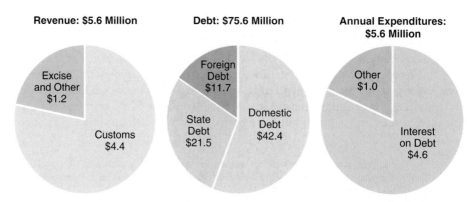

Hamilton's Financial System Under Hamilton's financial system, more than 80 percent of federal revenues went to pay the interest on the national debt. Note that most of the revenue came from tariff duties.

Revenue: $5.6 Million

Excise and Other $1.2

Customs $4.4

Debt: $75.6 Million

Foreign Debt $11.7

State Debt $21.5

Domestic Debt $42.4

Annual Expenditures: $5.6 Million

Other $1.0

Interest on Debt $4.6

located in the South, on the Potomac River between Virginia and Maryland. Aided by this understanding, funding and assumption passed Congress. In 1791 Congress also approved a 20-year charter for the first Bank of the United States. The bank would hold government deposits and issue banknotes that would be received in payment of all debts owed the federal government. Congress proved less receptive to the rest of Hamilton's program, although a limited tariff to encourage manufacturing and several excise taxes, including the one on whiskey, won approval.

Opposition to Hamilton's Program

The passage of Hamilton's program caused a permanent rupture among supporters of the Constitution. Madison, who had collaborated closely with Hamilton in the 1780s, broke with his former ally over funding and assumption. Jefferson finally went over to the opposition when Hamilton announced plans for a national bank. Eventually the two warring factions organized themselves into political parties: the Republicans, led by Jefferson and Madison, and the Federalists, led by Hamilton and Adams.* But the division emerged slowly over several years.

Hamilton's program promoted the commercial sector at the expense of semi-subsistence farmers. Thus it rekindled many of the concerns that had surfaced during the struggle over ratification of the Constitution. The ideology of the Revolution had stressed that republics inevitably contained groups who sought power in order to destroy popular liberties and overthrow the republic. To some Americans,

A study in contrasts, Jefferson and Hamilton increasingly came into conflict in Washington's administration. Despite his aristocratic upbringing, Jefferson (left) was awkward, loose-jointed, reserved, and ill at ease in public. Testifying before a congressional committee, he casually lounged in a chair and spoke in a rambling, nonstop manner. "Yet he scattered information wherever he went," conceded Senator William Maclay of Pennsylvania, "and some even brilliant sentiments sparkled from him." Hamilton (right), though short of stature, cut a dashing figure with his erect bearing, strutting manner, meticulous dress, and carefully powdered hair. Declared the wife of the British ambassador: "I have scarcely ever been more charmed with the vivacity and conversation of any man."

---

*The Republican party of the 1790s, sometimes referred to as the Jeffersonian Republicans, is not to be confused with the modern-day Republican party, which originated in the 1850s.

Fears of a financial aristocracy

Hamilton's program seemed a clear threat to establish a privileged and powerful financial aristocracy—perhaps even a monarchy.

Who, after all, would benefit from the funding proposal? During and after the Revolution, the value of notes issued by the Continental Congress dropped sharply. Speculators had bought up most of these notes for a fraction of their face value from small farmers and workers. If the government ultimately redeemed the debt, speculators would profit accordingly. Equally disturbing, members of Congress had been purchasing the notes before the adoption of Hamilton's program. Nearly half the members of the House owned U.S. securities. Madison urged that only the original holders of the debt be reimbursed in full, but Hamilton rejected this idea, since commercial speculators were precisely the class of people he hoped to bind to the new government.

Similarly, when stock in the Bank of the United States went on sale, speculators snapped up all the shares in an hour. The price of a share skyrocketed from $25 to $300 in two months. Jefferson was appalled by the mania Hamilton's program encouraged. "The spirit of gambling, once it has seized a subject, is incurable," he asserted. "The taylor who has made thousands in one day, tho he has lost them the next, can never again be content with the slow and moderate earnings of his needle."

System of corruption

The national bank struck its critics as a dangerous mimicking of English corruption. Indeed, in Great Britain the Bank of England played a powerful role. Its investments not only helped fuel the economy; its loans to many members of Parliament gave it great political influence. Jefferson warned that the same thing would happen in the United States. English-style corruption seemed to be taking root as "paper men" became rich not by producing anything substantial with their own hard work but by shuffling paper, trading notes, and benefiting from the financial legislation they themselves passed. These fears were heightened because Americans had little experience with banks: only three existed in the country when the Bank of the United States was chartered. One member of Congress expressed a common attitude when he said that he would no more be caught entering a bank than a house of prostitution.

Then, too, banks and commerce were a part of the urban environment that rural Americans so distrusted. Although Hamilton's opponents generally granted that a certain amount of commerce was necessary, they believed that it should remain subordinate. Hamilton's program, in contrast, encouraged manufacturing and urbanization, developments that history had shown to be incompatible with liberty and equality. Moreover, the tariff favored one group in society—manufacturers—at the expense of other groups.

After Congress approved the bank bill, Washington hesitated to sign it. When he consulted his cabinet, Jefferson stressed that the Constitution did not specifically authorize Congress to charter a bank. Both he and Madison upheld the idea of strict construction—that the Constitution should be interpreted narrowly and the federal government restricted to powers expressly delegated to it. Otherwise, the federal government would be the judge of its own powers, and there would be no safeguard against the abuse of power.

Hamilton countered that the Constitution contained implied as well as enumerated powers. He particularly emphasized the clause that permitted Congress to make all laws "necessary and proper" to carry out its duties. A bank would be useful in carrying out the enumerated powers of regulating commerce and maintaining the public credit; therefore, Congress had a right to decide whether to establish one. Because the Constitution could not anticipate all future developments, the government needed flexibility to meet its responsibilities. In the end Washington accepted Hamilton's forceful arguments and signed the bill.

The Specter of Aristocracy

The threat posed by a powerful bank heightened the fears of Hamilton's opponents that an aristocracy was developing in the United States. While Americans did not insist on an equal division of property and wealth, they were hostile to any haughtiness among the upper classes and to Europe's aristocratic traditions. Because Hamilton's program deliberately aided the rich and created a class of citizens whose wealth derived from the federal government, it strengthened these traditional fears. "Money will be put under the direction of government," charged Philip Freneau, a leading Republican editor, "and the government will be put under the direction of money."

Many who opposed Hamilton's financial program had also been against the Constitution, but leadership of the opposition fell to Jefferson and Madison, who had staunchly worked for ratification. Although Jefferson and Madison were planters, well accustomed to the workings of the marketplace, they still distrusted cities and commerce and Hamilton's aristocratic ways.

Economically Hamilton's program was a success. The government's credit was restored, and the national bank ended the inflation of the previous two decades and created a sound currency. At the same time the administration demonstrated that the federal government would not be paralyzed as it had been under the Articles. In addition, Hamilton's theory of implied powers and broad construction gave the nation the flexibility necessary to respond to unanticipated crises.

Hamilton's success

Expansion and Turmoil in the West

In the peace treaty of 1783, Britain ceded to the United States the territory between the Appalachian Mountains and the Mississippi River. Even so, British troops continued to hold the forts in the Northwest and Indian tribes controlled most of this region. To demonstrate the government's effectiveness, Washington moved to extend control over the West.

The Resistance of the Miami

In principle, the United States recognized the rights of Indians to their lands. Furthermore, it had promised that any purchase of Indian land would be made only by treaty and not through private purchases by land companies and individual settlers. Nevertheless, the government was determined to buy out Indian titles in order to promote white settlement.

By 1790 the United States had negotiated purchase of Indian lands in most of Kentucky and about one-quarter of Tennessee. North of the Ohio, however, the Miami Confederacy (composed of eight western tribes headed by the Miami) stoutly refused to sell territory and soundly defeated two American military expeditions. In response, Washington dispatched an army of 2000, commanded by "Mad Anthony" Wayne, an accomplished general and hero of the Revolution, to the Ohio Valley. At the Battle of Fallen Timbers in August 1794 Wayne won a decisive victory, breaking the Indians' hold on the Northwest. In the Treaty of Greenville (1795), he forced the tribes to cede the southern two-thirds of the area between Lake Erie and the Ohio River, thus opening up the Northwest to white settlement.

Treaty of Greenville

The Whiskey Rebellion

Westerners approved of the administration's military policy against the Indians. They were far less pleased that in 1791 Congress had passed a new excise tax on distilled liquors. In the barter economy west of the Appalachians, barrels of whiskey were sometimes used as currency. Furthermore, about the only way farmers could profitably export surplus grain was to distill it and bring the liquor to market. So the whiskey tax brought the question of federal power quite directly to the attention of the ordinary citizen.

Western society

The West during the 1790s was a society in turmoil. Most property owners along the frontier found it hard to make ends meet. In response, a number were forced to sell their land and fell into the ranks of tenant farmers. Thus wealth became more concentrated in the hands of fewer individuals. While the whiskey tax was unpopular in many rural areas, frontier settlers resisted most fiercely, since for them the sale of whiskey made the greatest difference in providing a bit of extra income. Tenant farmers, resentful of the more commercially minded larger landowners of their region, protested loudly too. Many of these poor farmers turned out at mass meetings to condemn the tax and protest against having to support government officials and the burdensome national debt. Beset by economic dislocation, they directed their resentment not just at the authorities but also at wealthy landowners and merchants.

Farmers in the western districts of several states defied federal officials and refused to pay, launching a "whiskey rebellion." The greatest unrest flared in western Pennsylvania, where General Neville was burned out of his home (pages 228–229). That summer an even larger gathering of impoverished farmers threatened to march on Pittsburgh. For rural residents, the city had become a symbol of the corrupt cosmopolitan influences that threatened their liberty. Many in the crowd relished the idea of looting the property of wealthy residents. "I have a bad hat now, but I expect to have a better one soon," shouted one of the mob.

Collapse of resistance

To distant easterners, the Whiskey Rebellion at first appeared serious. Hamilton, who had pushed the whiskey tax in order to demonstrate the power of the new government, saw the matter as a question of authority. "Shall there be government, or no government?" he asked. An alarmed Washington led an army of 13,000 men—larger than he had commanded at Yorktown—into the Pennsylvania countryside to overawe the populace and subdue the rebels. Hamilton soon took charge, but to his disappointment the troops met no organized resistance. "An insurrection was announced and proclaimed and armed against, but could never be found," Jefferson scoffed. Even some of Hamilton's allies conceded that he had overreacted. "Elective rulers can scarcely ever employ the physical force of a democracy," one remarked, "without turning the moral force, or the power of public opinion, against the government."

Pinckney's Treaty

Navigation of the Mississippi

Western unhappiness was also eased somewhat when Washington sent Thomas Pinckney to negotiate a treaty with Spain. That nation still controlled Florida and the mouth of the Mississippi and had never agreed to a northern boundary between its possessions and the United States. Pinckney's Treaty, which the Senate unanimously ratified in 1796, set the 31st parallel as the southern boundary of the United States and granted Americans free navigation of the Mississippi, with the right to deposit goods at New Orleans for reshipment to ports in the East and abroad. No longer could Spain try to detach the western settlements from American control by promising to open the Mississippi to their trade.

The Emergence of Political Parties

Members of the Revolutionary generation fervently hoped that political parties would not take root in the United States. "If I could not go to heaven but with a party, I would not go at all," remarked Jefferson. Influenced by radical English republican thought, American critics condemned parties as narrow interest groups that routinely placed selfishness and party loyalty above a concern for the public good. In fact, many members of Britain's Parliament did in effect sell their votes in return for offices, pensions, and profitable contracts. Yet despite Americans' distrust of such institutions, the United States became the first nation to establish truly popular parties.

Social conditions encouraged the rise of parties. Because property ownership was widespread, the nation had a broad suffrage. Furthermore, during the Revolution legislatures lowered property requirements in many states, increasing the number of voters still further. If party members hoped to hold office, they had to offer a program attractive to the broader voting public. When parties acted as representatives of economic and social interest groups, they became one means by which a large electorate could make its feelings known. In addition, the United States had the highest literacy rate in the world and the largest number of newspapers, further encouraging political interest and participation. Finally, the fact that well-known patriots of the Revolution headed both the Federalists and the Republicans helped defuse the charge that either party was hostile to the Revolution or the Constitution.

Social conditions and parties

Americans and the French Revolution

While domestic issues first split the supporters of the Constitution, it was a crisis in Europe that served to push Americans toward political parties. Americans had hoped that their revolution would spark similar movements for liberty on the European continent, and in fact the American Revolution was only one of a series of revolutions in the late eighteenth century that shook the Western world, the most important of which occurred in France. There a rising population, the growth of a popular press, the failure of reform, the collapse of government finances, and widespread discontent with France's constitutional system sparked a challenge to royal authority that became a mass revolution. Eventually the French revolutionary ideals of "liberty, equality, and fraternity" would spill across the continent, carried by the French army.

When news of the Revolution arrived in the United States in 1789, Americans hailed it as the first stirring of liberty on the European continent. Each new ship from overseas brought exciting news: the Bastille prison had been stormed in July; the new National Assembly had abolished feudal privileges and adopted the Declaration of the Rights of Man. By 1793, however, American enthusiasm for the Revolution had cooled after radical elements instituted a reign of terror, executing the king and queen and many of the nobility. The French republic even outlawed Christianity and substituted the worship of Reason. Finally in 1793 republican France and monarchical England went to war. Americans were deeply divided over whether the United States should continue its old alliance with France or support Great Britain.

The execution of King Louis XVI, by guillotine, left Americans divided over the value of the French Revolution.

Hamilton and his allies viewed the French Revolution as sheer anarchy. Its leaders seemed to be destroying the very institutions that held civilization together: the

Differing views of the Revolution

church, social classes, property, law and order. The United States, Hamilton argued, should renounce the 1778 treaty of alliance with France and side with Britain. "Behold France, an open hell," warned Fisher Ames, a member of Congress from Massachusetts, ". . . still smoking with suffering and crimes, in which we see perhaps our future state." For Jefferson and his followers, the issue was republicanism versus monarchy. France was a sister republic and, despite deplorable excesses, its revolution was spreading the doctrine of liberty. Britain remained repressive and corrupt, presided over by the same tyrannical king who had made war on the colonies. Jefferson argued that the United States should maintain its treaty of alliance with France and insist that, as neutrals, Americans had every right to trade with France as much as with England.

As tempers flared, each faction suspected the worst of the other. To the Jeffersonians, Hamilton and his friends seemed part of a monarchist conspiracy. "The ultimate object of all this," Jefferson said of Hamilton's policies, "is to prepare the way for a change, from the present republican forms of Government, to that of a monarchy." As for the Hamiltonians, they viewed Jefferson and his faction as disciples of French radicals, conspiring to establish mob rule in the United States. Years later, when calm reflection was possible, John Adams conceded that both parties had "excited artificial terrors." But during the 1790s, each side believed that the destiny of the American republic was threatened by events abroad.

Washington's Neutral Course

Washington, for his part, was convinced that in order to prosper, the United States must remain independent of Europe and its unending quarrels and wars. Thus the

France, like Great Britain, put pressure on the United States to abandon its neutrality. The French minister to America, "Citizen" Edmond Genêt, went so far as to have broadsides like this one printed, encouraging Americans to fight for the French republic. Note the appeal to newcomers from Ireland, who were known to dislike the British. Genêt embarrassed even the friends of France like Jefferson, and Washington angrily demanded his recall.

THEY STEER TO LIBERTY'S SHORES

Philadelphia, Auguſt, 1793.

ALL able bodied ſeamen who are willing to engage in the cauſe of Liberty, and in the ſervice of the French Republic, will pleaſe to apply to the French Conſul, at No. 132, North Second-ſtreet.

Particular attention will be paid to the generous and intrepid natives of Ireland, who, it is preſumed, will act like thoſe warlike troops from that oppreſſed country, who took refuge in France about a century ago, and performed prodigies of valor under the old government of that country.

president issued a proclamation of American neutrality and tempered Jefferson's efforts to support France.

Under international law, neutrals could trade with belligerents—nations at war—as long as the trade had existed before the outbreak of hostilities and did not involve war supplies. But both France and Great Britain refused to respect the rights of neutrals in the midst of their desperate struggle. They began intercepting American ships and confiscating cargoes. In addition, Britain, which badly needed manpower to maintain its powerful navy, impressed into service American sailors it suspected of being British subjects. Despite these abuses, Hamilton continued to support a friendly policy toward Britain. He recognized, as did Washington, that the United States was not strong enough to challenge Britain militarily. **Neutral rights**

Moreover, Hamilton's domestic program depended on trade with the British, who purchased 75 percent of America's exports (mostly foodstuffs and naval supplies) as well as providing 90 percent of imports. With Europe torn by war, the demand for American grains rose sharply, driving up the price on the world market. During the decade, American exports nearly quadrupled, and American ships almost completely took over the carrying trade between the United States and Europe. All parts of the commercial economy shared in this unprecedented prosperity, not only merchants but also urban workers and businesspeople, sailors, the shipbuilding industry, and farmers who sold their surplus at high prices.

In addition to violating neutral rights and impressment, Great Britain continued to maintain the western forts it had promised to evacuate in 1783, and it closed the West Indies, a traditional source of trade, to American ships. Washington sent John Jay to Britain as a special minister to negotiate the differences between the two countries. In the end, Jay persuaded the British only to withdraw their troops from the Northwest. With the West Indies still closed to American shipping, Jay's Treaty in essence reinforced the United States' position as an economic satellite of Britain. Only reluctantly did a disappointed Washington submit it to the Senate. **Jay's Treaty**

The treaty debate was extremely bitter. Republicans denounced Jay and hanged him in effigy while a mob stoned Hamilton in the streets. In June 1795 the Senate finally approved Jay's Treaty by a vote of 20 to 10, the bare two-thirds margin required.

The Federalists and Republicans Organize

Thus events in Europe contributed directly to the rise of parties in the United States by stimulating fears over the course of American development. The war, Jefferson commented, "kindled and brought forward the two parties with an ardour which our own interests merely, could never excite." By the mid-1790s both sides were organizing on a national basis. Hamilton took the lead in coordinating the Federalist party, which grew out of the voting bloc in Congress that had enacted his economic program. Increasingly, Washington drew closer to Federalist advisers and policies and became the symbol of the party, although he clung to the vision of a nonpartisan administration and never recognized the extent to which he had become a party leader.

The guiding genius of the opposition movement was Hamilton's onetime colleague James Madison. Jefferson, who resigned as secretary of state at the end of 1793, became the symbolic head of the party, much as Washington headed the Federalists. Even so, Jefferson was unconvinced of the wisdom and necessity of such **Organization of an opposition party** a party and was reluctant to lead it. But Madison acted more vigorously, conferring over strategy and lining up the Republican voting bloc in the House. The disputes over Jay's Treaty and the whiskey tax in 1794 and 1795 gave the Republicans popular issues, and they began organizing on the state and local levels. Unlike the Federalists, who cloaked themselves in Washington's mantle and claimed to uphold the government and the Constitution, the Republicans had to overcome the ingrained idea that an opposition party was seditious and therefore illegitimate. Because of broad support for the Constitution, Republican leaders had to be careful to distinguish between opposing the administration and opposing the Constitution. Indeed, it was by no means clear that an opposition party could arise without threatening the government itself.

As more and more members of Congress allied themselves with one faction or the other, voting became increasingly partisan. In the first two Congresses, party votes occurred mostly on Hamilton's economic program and organization of the government. In the third and fourth Congresses, party questions included foreign affairs and domestic issues, such as the Whiskey Rebellion. By 1796 even minor matters were decided by partisan votes. Gradually, party organization filtered downward to local communities.

The 1796 Election

As long as Washington remained head of the Federalists, they enjoyed an insurmountable advantage. But in 1796 the weary president, stung by the abuse heaped on him by the opposition press, announced he would not accept a third term, thereby setting a two-term precedent that other presidents would follow until Franklin Roosevelt. In his Farewell Address Washington warned against the dangers of parties and urged a return to the earlier nonpartisan system. But that vision had become obsolete: parties were an effective way of expressing the interests of different social and economic groups within the nation. When the Republicans chose Thomas Jefferson to oppose John Adams, the possibility of a nonparty constitutional system ended.

The framers of the Constitution did not anticipate that political parties would run competing candidates for both the presidency and the vice presidency. Thus they provided that, of the candidates running for president, the one with the most electoral votes would win and the one with the second highest number would become vice president. But Hamilton strongly disliked both Adams and Jefferson. Ever the intriguer, he tried to manipulate the electoral vote so that the Federalist vice presidential candidate, Thomas Pinckney of South Carolina, would be elected president. In the ensuing confusion, Adams won with 71 electoral votes, and his rival, Jefferson, gained the vice presidency with 68 votes.

Support for the two parties

The fault line between the two parties reflected basic divisions in American life. Geographically, the Federalists were strongest in New England, with its commercial ties to Great Britain and its powerful tradition of hierarchy and order. Moving farther south, the party became progressively weaker. Of the southernmost states, the Federalists enjoyed significant strength only in aristocratic South Carolina. The Republicans won solid support in semisubsistence areas like the West, where Crèvecoeur's farmers were only weakly involved with commerce. The middle states were closely contested, although the most cosmopolitan and commercially oriented elements remained the core of Federalist strength.

The Republicans won over most of the old Anti-Federalist opponents of the Constitution as well as a number of Americans who had firmly backed the new union. These supporters included some commercial farmers in the North and planters in the South and, increasingly, urban workers and small shopkeepers who were repelled by the aristocratic tone of the Federalists. The Republicans were often led by ambitious men of new wealth who felt excluded by the entrenched Federalist elite. For similar reasons Jefferson attracted the support of immigrants from France and Ireland, who felt culturally excluded, as well as members of religious sects such as the Baptists and Methodists, who resented the power and privileges of New England's established Congregational church.

Federalist and Republican Ideologies

In different ways, each party looked both forward and backward: toward certain traditions of the past as well as toward newer social currents that would shape America in the nineteenth century.

Most Federalists viewed themselves as a kind of natural aristocracy making a last desperate stand against the excesses of democracy. They clung to the notion that the upper class should rule over its social and economic inferiors. In supporting the established social order, most Federalists opposed unbridled individualism. They believed that society's needs were more important than the individual's. In their view, government should regulate individual behavior for the good of society and protect property from the violent and unruly. Pessimistic about human nature, Federalists were almost obsessed by fear of the "mob." In a republic, they argued, government had to restrain popular power.

Federalist ideas

Although the Federalists resolutely opposed the rising tide of democracy and individualism, they were remarkably forward-looking in their economic ideas. They sensed that the United States would become the major economic and military power of their vision only by prospering through commerce and economic development. To that end, they argued, the government ought to use its power actively, to encourage the growth of commerce and manufacturing.

The Republicans, in contrast, looked backward to the traditional Revolutionary fear that government power threatened liberty. Over and over Republicans emphasized the threat of corruption. The Treasury, they warned, was corrupting Congress, the army would enslave the people, and broad construction of the Constitution would make the federal government all-powerful. To them, Federalist attitudes and policies illustrated the corruption eating away at American morals, just as England had become corrupt before 1776.

Republican ideas

Nor did their economic ideals anticipate future American development. For Republicans, agriculture and not commerce stood as the centerpiece of American liberty and virtue. To be sure, leaders like Jefferson and Madison recognized that some commercial activity was necessary, especially to sell America's agricultural surplus abroad. But Jefferson and his followers believed that republican values would be preserved only by limiting commerce and promoting household manufacturing instead of industry. Furthermore, Republicans failed to appreciate the role of financial institutions in promoting economic development. Instead, Republicans focused on the abuses of "paper wealth" and those who manipulated it—speculators, bank directors, and holders of the public debt. Economically, they rejected the forward-looking ideals of urban commerce and industry that would dominate American society in the nineteenth century.

On the other hand, the Jeffersonians were more farsighted in matters of equality and personal liberty. Their faith in the people put them in tune with the emerging egalitarian temper of society. Eagerly they embraced the virtues of individualism, hoping to reduce government to the bare essentials in order to free individuals to develop their potential without interference. And they looked to the West—the land of small farms and a more equal society—as the means to preserve opportunity and American values.

The Presidency of John Adams

As president, John Adams became the nominal head of the Federalists, although in many ways he was out of step with his party. Unlike Hamilton, Adams felt no pressing need to aid the wealthy, nor was he fully committed to Hamilton's commercial-industrial vision. As a crusty revolutionary leader who in the 1780s had served as American minister to England, Adams also opposed any alliance with Britain.

Increasingly Adams and Hamilton clashed over policies and party leadership. Part of the problem stemmed from personalities. Adams was so abrasive and thin-skinned that it was difficult for anyone to get along with him, and Hamilton's intrigues in the 1796 election had not improved relations between the two men. Although Hamilton had resigned from the Treasury Department in 1795, key members of Adams's cabinet regularly turned to the former secretary for advice. Indeed, they opposed Adams so often that the frustrated president sometimes dealt with them, according to Jefferson, "by dashing and trampling his wig on the floor." The feud between the two rivals did not bode well for the Federalist party.

John Adams, who believed that pageantry and pomp were essential to government, aroused fears of monarchy and European corruption by proposing in 1789 that the president's title be "His Highness the President of the United States and Protector of the Rights of the Same." Of distinctly unmilitary bearing, he wore this sword at his inauguration in the vain hope that it would lend dignity. Sarcastic Republicans, noting his paunchy figure, gleefully bestowed a title of their own: "His Rotundity."

The Naval War with France

Adams began his term trying to balance relations with both Great Britain and France. Because the terms of Jay's Treaty were so favorable to the British, the French in retaliation set their navy and privateers to raiding American shipping. To resolve the conflict, Adams dispatched three envoys to France in 1797, but the French foreign minister demanded a bribe before negotiations could even begin. The American representatives refused, and when news of these discussions became public, it was known as the XYZ Affair (because in the official documents the Adams administration substituted the letters X, Y, and Z for the names of the French officials involved). A tremendous outcry ensued.

Confronted with such deeply felt anger, Federalist leaders saw a chance to retain power by exploiting the national emergency and going to war with France. With war fever running high, Congress in 1798 repudiated the French treaty of 1778 and enlarged the army and navy. Republicans suspected that the real purpose of the army was not to fight the French army—none existed in North America—but to crush the opposition party and establish a military despotism. All that remained was for Adams to whip up popular feeling and lead the nation into war.

XYZ Affair

"in such exaggerated and indecent terms as could scarcely be applied . . . to a common pickpocket." By 1797, reported Jefferson sadly, "men who have been intimate all their lives, cross the streets to avoid meeting, and turn their heads another way, lest they should be obliged to touch their hats."

What accounted for this torrent of violence—both real and rhetorical—in the first decade of the Republic? For one thing, Federalists and Republicans alike recognized how fragile a form of government republicanism had proved over the long course of history. Its repeated failure left political leaders uneasy and uncertain about the American experiment. Then, too, the ideology of the American Revolution stressed the need to guard constantly against conspiracies to subvert liberty. All too quickly, turbulent foreign events like the French Revolution heightened domestic suspicions.

In such overheated circumstances, both Republicans and Federalists readily assumed the worst of one another. Neither side grasped that political parties were essential in a democracy to express and resolve peacefully differences among competing social, geographic, and economic interests. Instead, each party considered the other a faction and therefore illegitimate. Each longed to reestablish a one-party system. Not until after 1815 did a political ideology develop that recognized the need for parties.

As John Adams prepared to leave office, he looked back with mixed feelings on the 12 years that the Federalist party had held power. Under Washington's firm leadership and his own, his party had made the Constitution a workable instrument of government. The Federalists had proved that republicanism was compatible with stability and order, and they had established economic policies and principles of foreign affairs that even their opponents would continue. The Union had been strengthened, the Constitution had been accepted, and prosperity had returned.

But most Federalists took no solace in such reflections, for the forces of history seemed to be running against them. As the champions of order and hierarchy, of government by the wellborn, of a society in which social betters guided their

Generating strong popular emotions, elections in the early Republic involved many more voters than ever before. In this detail of an early-nineteenth-century painting by John Lewis Krimmel, party workers bring electors to the Philadelphia polls in carriages while voters argue heatedly about candidates and celebrate.

Ideology of
republicanism

Federalist achievements

respectful inferiors, they had waged one last desperate battle to save their disintegrating world—and had lost. Power had fallen into the hands of the ignorant and unwashed rabble, led by that demagogue Thomas Jefferson. Federalists shared fully the view of the British minister who concluded in 1800 that the entire American political system was "tottering to its foundations."

The great American experiment in republicanism had failed. Of this most Federalists were certain. And surely, if history was any judge, the destruction of liberty and order would soon follow.

chapter summary

Politics in the early Republic was rooted in a fundamental social division between the commercial and semisubsistence areas of the country. Commercially oriented Americans were tied to international trade and depended on the widespread exchange of goods and services, whereas families in the semisubsistence economy produced most of what they consumed and did not buy and sell in an extensive market.

- The first party to organize in the 1790s was the Federalists, led by Alexander Hamilton and George Washington. They were opposed by the Republicans, led by James Madison and Thomas Jefferson.

- Divisions over Hamilton's policies as secretary of the treasury stimulated the formation of rival political parties.

- The commercially minded Federalists believed in order and hierarchy, supported loose construction of the Constitution, and wanted a powerful central government to promote economic growth.

- The Republican party, with its sympathy for agrarian ideals, endorsed strict construction of the Constitution, wanted a less active federal government, and harbored a strong fear of aristocracy.

- The French Revolution and foreign policy also stimulated the formation of parties in the 1790s.

  - The Federalists supported England, and the Jeffersonians supported France.

  - The major events of John Adams's presidency—the XYZ Affair, the naval war, and the Alien and Sedition Acts—were all linked to the debate over foreign policy.

- In the presidential election of 1800, Thomas Jefferson became the first leader of an opposition party to be elected president.

- The Federalists demonstrated that the new government could be a more active force in American society, but their controversial domestic and foreign policies, internal divisions, and open hostility to the masses eventually led to their downfall.

interactive learning

The Primary Source Investigator CD-ROM offers the following materials related to this chapter:

- Interactive map: **Election of 1800** (M7)

- A collection of primary sources exploring the Jeffersonian era and the Revolution of 1800, including the U.S. Constitution and the Treaty of Greenville. Other documents investigate social unrest in the new republic, such as the insightful diaries of Quakers Elizabeth Drinker and John Woolman. Also included are key sources that illuminate the foreign policy of the young United States: Jay's Treaty and the Alien and Sedition Acts.

additional reading

Once the subject of considerable controversy, political developments in this period have attracted less attention from historians in recent years. Much of the scholarship, while older, is nevertheless sound. The most recent overview is Stanley Elkins and Eric McKitrick's massively detailed study, *The Age of Federalism* (1993). James Roger Sharp, *American Politics in the Early Republic* (1993), is a brief, up-to-date survey. Jacob E. Cooke, *Alexander Hamilton* (1982), is a good short biography, while Stephen G. Kurtz, *The Presidency of John Adams* (1957), analyzes the growing split in the party under Adams. Some of the most imaginative work has focused on the ideology of republicanism. Lance Banning, The *Jeffersonian Persuasion* (1978), and Drew R. McCoy, *The Elusive Republic* (1980), are both excellent treatments of the ideology of the Jeffersonians. There is no equivalent study of Federalist ideology. The best account of the Republican party's formation is Noble Cunningham, *The Jeffersonian Republicans* (1963).

Historians are beginning to examine American society in these years. Useful works include Jack Larkin, *The Reshaping of Everyday Life, 1790–1840* (1988); Reginald Horsman, *The Frontier in the Formative Years, 1783–1815* (1970); Howard Rock, *Artisans of the New Republic* (1979); and Laurel Thatcher Ulrich, *A Midwife's Tale* (1990). Crèvecoeur's and Franklin's writings are available in many editions. For a fuller list of readings, see the Bibliography at www.mhhe.com/davidsonnation5.

significant events

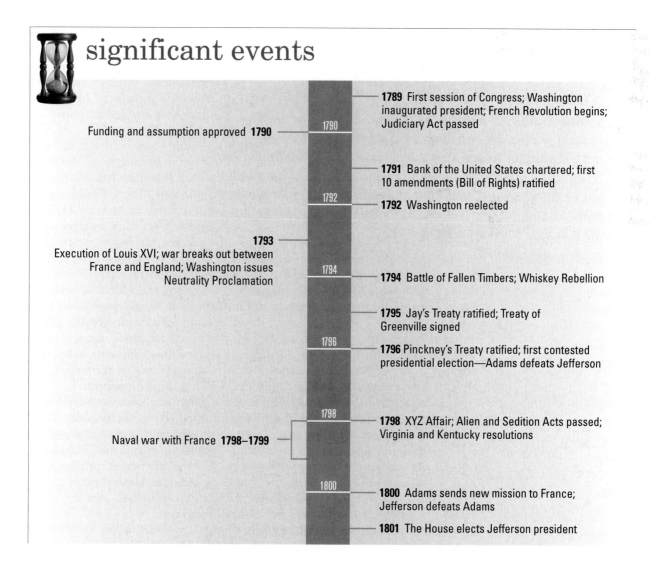

Funding and assumption approved **1790**

1790

1789 First session of Congress; Washington inaugurated president; French Revolution begins; Judiciary Act passed

1791 Bank of the United States chartered; first 10 amendments (Bill of Rights) ratified

1792

1792 Washington reelected

1793 Execution of Louis XVI; war breaks out between France and England; Washington issues Neutrality Proclamation

1794

1794 Battle of Fallen Timbers; Whiskey Rebellion

1795 Jay's Treaty ratified; Treaty of Greenville signed

1796

1796 Pinckney's Treaty ratified; first contested presidential election—Adams defeats Jefferson

1798

1798 XYZ Affair; Alien and Sedition Acts passed; Virginia and Kentucky resolutions

Naval war with France **1798–1799**

1800

1800 Adams sends new mission to France; Jefferson defeats Adams

1801 The House elects Jefferson president

Chapter 9

O n September 29, 1800, following a rather rocky courtship, Margaret Bayard married Samuel H. Smith. Even though Samuel was well educated and from a socially prominent family, Margaret's father consented to the marriage reluctantly, for the Bayards were staunch Federalists and Smith was an ardent Republican. Indeed, Thomas Jefferson had asked Smith, an editor in Philadelphia, to follow the government to Washington, D.C., and establish a Republican newspaper in the new capital. After the wedding, the couple traveled to the new seat of government on the banks of the Potomac River.

When the Smiths arrived in Washington, they found a raw village of 3200 souls. Samuel began publishing the *National Intelligencer,* the first national newspaper in the United States, while Margaret's social charm and keen intelligence made their home a center of Washington society. When she met Jefferson about a month after her arrival, she found herself captivated by his gracious manners, sparkling conversation, and gentlemanly bearing. Whatever remained of her Federalist sympathies vanished, and she became (perhaps as her father feared) a devoted supporter of the Republican leader.

The Jeffersonian Republic

1801–1824

preview • Jefferson supported his agrarian principles by acquiring the Louisiana Territory. But increasingly he abandoned his earlier ideals of limited government in favor of a more active nationalism. Nationalism was also served by the stronger federal courts led by Chief Justice John Marshall and by the expansion of white Americans westward. The growth in national power and pride was not halted, either by a Pan-Indian alliance under Tecumseh or by Great Britain in the War of 1812.

In eager anticipation she went to the Senate on March 4, 1801, to witness Jefferson's inauguration. The chamber was packed, but the members of Congress nonetheless reserved one side for the ladies present. To

Jefferson's inauguration   emphasize the change in attitude of the new administration, the president-elect walked to the Capitol with only a small escort. Absent were the elaborate ceremonies of the years of Federalist rule. Because Jefferson delivered his inaugural address in almost a whisper, few in the assembled crowd heard much of what he said. Then Chief Justice John Marshall, a Virginian but a Federalist whom Jefferson deeply distrusted, administered the oath of office. When the swearing-in was completed, the new president returned to his lodgings at Conrad and McMunn's boardinghouse, where he declined a place of honor and instead took his accustomed seat at the foot of the table. Only several weeks later did he finally move to his official residence.

As Margaret Smith proudly watched the proceedings, she could not help thinking of the most striking feature of this transfer of power: it was peaceful. "The changes of administration," she commented, "which in every government and in every age have most generally been epochs of confusion, villainy and bloodshed, in our happy country take place without any species of distraction, or disorder." After the fierce controversies of the previous decade and the harsh rhetoric of the election of 1800, to see the opposition party take power peacefully—the first such occurrence in the nation's history—was indeed remarkable.

Once in power, Jefferson set out to reshape the government and society into closer harmony with Republican principles. He later referred to his election as "the

We Owe Allegiance to No Crown, by John A. Woodside, reflects the growing nationalism in American life after 1815. Significantly, however, Woodside portrays a sailor and sailing ship, for during these years war on the seas challenged the independence of the United States.

Revolution of 1800," asserting that it "was as real a revolution in the principles of our government as that of 1776 was in its form." That statement is an exaggeration, perhaps. But the rule of the Republican party during the following two decades set the nation on a distinctly more democratic tack. And in working out its relationship with Britain and France, as well as with the Indian nations of the

West, America achieved a sense of its own nationhood that came only with time and with the passing of the Revolutionary generation.

Jefferson in Power

Thomas Jefferson was the first president to be inaugurated in the new capital, Washington, D.C. In 1791 George Washington had commissioned Pierre Charles L'Enfant, a French architect and engineer who had served in the American Revolution, to draw up plans for the new seat of government. L'Enfant designed a city with broad avenues, statues and fountains, parks and plazas, and a central mall. Because the Federalists believed that government was the paramount power in a nation, they had intended that the city would be a new Rome—a cultural, intellectual, and commercial center of the Republic.

The New Capital City

The new city, however, fell far short of this grandiose dream. It was located in a swampy river bottom near the head of navigation on the Potomac, and the surrounding low-lying hills rendered the spot oppressively hot and muggy during the summer. Removed from the thriving commercial centers of the country, the capital had no business or society independent of the government. The streets were filled with tree stumps and became impenetrable seas of mud after a rain. Much of the District was wooded, and virtually all of it remained unoccupied.

When the government moved to its new residence in 1800, the Senate chamber, where Jefferson took the oath of office, was the only part of the Capitol that had been completed. The executive mansion was unfinished as well, although it had been occupied since November, when the Adamses had moved in for the last few months of John Adams's presidency. Except for its classical architecture, the city gave no hint of imitating the great centers of antiquity. A British diplomat grumbled at having to leave Philadelphia, the previous capital, with its bustling commerce, regular communication with the outside world, and lively society, to conduct business in "a mere swamp."

Washington in 1800 barely resembled L'Enfant's grand design. When Jefferson was inaugurated, only one wing of the Capitol was complete, and a primitive Pennsylvania Avenue ran more than a mile through the woods before it connected with the unfinished executive mansion.

Yet the isolated and unimpressive capital reflected the new president's attitude toward government. Distrustful of centralized power of any kind, Jefferson deliberately set out to remake the national government into one of limited scope that touched few people's daily lives. He took as his ideal precisely what the Federalists had striven to avoid—a government, in Hamilton's words, "at a distance and out of sight," which commanded little popular attention.

Jefferson's Character and Philosophy

Jefferson himself reflected that vision of modesty. Even standing nearly 6 feet, 3 inches, the 57-year-old president lacked an imposing presence. He dressed so carelessly in frequently ill-fitting clothes that William Plumer, a New Hampshire Federalist, mistook him for a servant when he called at the executive mansion. Despite his wealth and genteel birth into Virginia society, Jefferson disliked pomp and maintained an image of republican simplicity. His informal manners and habit of conducting business in a frayed coat and slippers dismayed dignitaries who called on him decked out in ribbons and lace.

Jefferson was a product of the Enlightenment, with its faith in the power of human reason to improve society and decipher the universe. While afflicted with occasional bouts of despair, he was on the whole an unshakable optimist. "I steer my bark with Hope in the head," he once declared, "leaving fear astern." An elegant writer but ineffective public speaker, he preferred to accomplish his political business in private conferences or at his renowned dinner parties, where he charmed his guests with his stimulating conversation.

Thomas Jefferson's invitations to dinner may strike readers today as formal, but Jefferson was actually attempting to set a tone of democratic informality. One Federalist did not miss the implication and complained, "It is *Th:Jefferson* not the *President* that invites—& yet were he not the President I presume I should not be invited."

Jefferson considered "the will of the majority" to be "the only sure guardian of the rights of man," which he defined as "life, liberty, and the pursuit of happiness." Although he conceded that the masses might err, he was confident they would soon return to correct principles. His faith in human virtue exceeded that of most of the founding generation, yet in good republican fashion, he feared those in power, even if they had been elected by the people. Government seemed to Jefferson at best a necessary evil.

To Jefferson, agriculture was a morally superior way of life. "Those who labour in the earth are the chosen people of God, if ever he had a chosen people," he wrote in *Notes on the State of Virginia* (1787). Like Crèvecoeur, Jefferson praised rural life for nourishing the honesty, independence, and virtue so essential in a republic. Government would "remain virtuous . . . as long as [the American people] are chiefly agricultural," he assured James Madison. Rather than encouraging large-scale factories, Jefferson wanted to preserve small household manufacturing, which was an essential part of the rural economy. Commerce should exist primarily to sell America's agricultural surplus. He was never able to overcome his earlier belief, rooted in the republican ideology of the Revolution, that cities and commerce promoted speculation, greed, and useless luxury and self-indulgence.

Agrarian values

Although Jefferson asserted that "the tree of liberty must be refreshed from time to time by the blood of patriots and tyrants," his reputation as a radical was undeserved. While he wanted to extend the suffrage to a greater number of Americans, he clung to the traditional republican idea that voters should own property and thus be economically independent. One of the largest slaveholders in the country, he

Jefferson's radicalism exaggerated

increasingly muffled his once-bold condemnation of slavery, and in the last years of his life he reproached critics of the institution who sought to prevent it from expanding westward. Nor did his belief in free speech mean that he had any qualms about state governments punishing political criticism.

Slaveholding aristocrat and apostle of democracy, lofty theorist and pragmatic politician, Jefferson was an exceedingly complex, at times contradictory, personality. But like most politicians, he was flexible in his approach to problems and tried to balance means and ends. And like most leaders, he quickly discovered that he confronted very different problems in power than he had in opposition.

Republican Principles

Limited government

Once Jefferson had settled into the executive mansion, he took steps to return the government to the republican ideals of simplicity and frugality. The states rather than the federal government were "the most competent administrators for our domestic concerns," he asserted in his inaugural address. Ever the individualist, he recommended a government that left people "free to regulate their own pursuits of industry and improvement."

Jefferson also went out of his way to soothe the feelings of defeated Federalists. Acknowledging Hamilton's fiscal policies, he promised to uphold the government's credit and protect commerce as the "handmaiden" of agriculture—both Federalist concerns. Agreeing with Washington, he proposed friendship with all nations and "entangling alliances" with none. Finally, he called on Americans to unite for the common good: "We have called by different names brethren of the same principles. We are all republicans—we are all federalists."

The election of 1800 established the legitimacy of an opposition party in American politics, and Jefferson, in his inaugural address, seemed to endorse the validity of a party system. In reality, however, he hoped to restore one-party rule by winning over moderate and honest Federalists and isolating the party's extremists, whom he still attacked as monarchists.

Jefferson's Economic Policies

But what would Jefferson do about Hamilton's economic program? As he promised in his inaugural address, the new president proceeded to cut spending, reduce the size of the government, and begin paying off the national debt. Unless the debt was paid, he warned Albert Gallatin, his talented secretary of the treasury, "we shall be committed to the English career of debt, corruption and rottenness, closing with revolution." He abolished the internal taxes enacted by the Federalists, including the controversial levy on whiskey, and thus was able to get rid of all tax collectors and inspectors. "What farmer, what mechanic, what laborer, ever sees a tax gatherer in the United States?" boasted Jefferson in 1805. Land sales and the tariff duties would supply the funds needed to run the scaled-down government.

The most serious spending cuts were made in the military branches. Jefferson slashed the army budget in half, decreasing the army to 3000 men. In a national emergency, he reasoned, the militia could defend the country. Jefferson reduced the navy even more, halting work on powerful frigates authorized during the naval war with France and replacing them with a fleet of small gunboats, which captured Jefferson's fancy because they were cheap. In the long term, however, they proved totally inadequate to defend the nation's coasts in war.

By such steps, Jefferson made significant progress toward paying off Hamilton's hated national debt. He lowered it from $83 million to only $57 million by the end of his two terms in office, despite the added financial burden of the Louisiana Purchase (page 263). Still, Jefferson did not entirely dismantle the Federalists' economic program. Funding and assumption could not be reversed—the nation's honor was pledged to paying these debts, and Jefferson fully understood the importance of maintaining the nation's credit. The tariff had to be retained as a source of revenue to meet government expenses. More surprising, Jefferson argued that the national bank should be left to run its course until 1811, when its charter would expire. In reality, he expanded the bank's operations and, in words reminiscent of Hamilton, advocated tying banks and members of the business class to the government by rewarding those who supported the Republican party.

Failure to abolish Hamilton's program

In effect, practical politics had triumphed over agrarian economics. Throughout his presidency, Jefferson often put pragmatic considerations above unyielding principles. As he himself expressed it, "What is practicable must often control what is pure theory."

John Marshall and Judicial Review

Having lost both the presidency and control of Congress in 1800, the Federalists took steps to shore up their power before Jefferson took office. They did so by expanding the size of the federal court system, the one branch of the federal government that they still controlled. The Judiciary Act of 1801 created 6 circuit courts and 16 new judgeships, along with a number of marshals, attorneys, and clerks. Federalists justified these "midnight appointments" (executed by Adams in the last weeks of his term) on the grounds that the expanding nation required a larger judiciary.

Jefferson, however, saw matters differently. "The Federalists, defeated at the polls, have retired into the Judiciary," he fumed, "and from that barricade . . . hope to batter down all the bulwarks of Republicanism." In 1802, by a strict party vote, Congress repealed the 1801 law and eliminated the new courts and their officers.

Among Adams's last-minute appointments was that of William Marbury as justice of the peace for the District of Columbia. When James Madison assumed the office of secretary of state under the new administration, he found a batch of undelivered commissions, including Marbury's. Wishing to appoint loyal Republicans to these posts, Jefferson instructed Madison not to hand over the commissions, whereupon Marbury sued under the Judiciary Act of 1789. Since that act gave the Supreme Court original jurisdiction in cases against federal officials, the case of *Marbury v. Madison* went directly to the Court in 1803.

Marbury v. Madison

Chief Justice John Marshall, a Federalist and one of Adams's late-term appointments, seized on this case to affirm the Court's greatest power, the right to review statutes and interpret the meaning of the Constitution. "It is emphatically the province of and duty of the judicial department to say what the law is," he wrote in upholding the doctrine of judicial review. This idea meant that the Court "must of necessity expound and interpret" the Constitution and the laws when one statute conflicted with another or when a law violated the framework of the Constitution. Marshall found that the section of the Judiciary Act of 1789 that granted the Supreme Court original jurisdiction in the case was unconstitutional. Because the Constitution specified those cases in which the Court had such jurisdiction, they could not be enlarged by statute. *Marbury v. Madison* was so critical to the development of the American constitutional system that it has been called the keystone of the constitutional arch.

John Marshall

Judicial review

Marshall and his colleagues later asserted the power of the Court to review the constitutionality of state laws in *Fletcher v. Peck* (1810) when it struck down a Georgia law. It also brought state courts under the scrutiny of the Supreme Court in *Martin v. Hunter's Lessee* (1816), denying the claim of the Virginia Supreme Court that it was not subject to the authority of the federal judiciary, and in *Cohens v. Virginia* (1821), in which it asserted its right to review decisions of state courts on issues arising under the Constitution. In fact, during his tenure on the bench, Marshall extended judicial review to all acts of government. It took time for the doctrine to be accepted, but since Marshall's time the Supreme Court has successfully defended its position as the final judge of the meaning of the Constitution.

The Jeffersonian Attack on the Judiciary

Having disposed of the bulk of Adams's recent appointments, the Republicans proceeded to attack Federalist judges who had been particularly obnoxious during the party battles of the 1790s. Jefferson argued that impeachment was not limited to criminal acts but was an appropriate political device to remove any judge who proved unacceptable to two-thirds of the Senate. In 1803, after the House had impeached federal district judge John Pickering of New Hampshire, who was both insane and an alcoholic, he was convicted and removed by the Senate.

Encouraged by this success, the administration turned its attention to Associate Justice Samuel Chase of the Supreme Court. An ultra-Federalist, Chase had interpreted the Sedition Act in a blatantly partisan fashion to ensure convictions against Republicans. After the House impeached Chase, a majority of senators voted to convict, but since a two-thirds vote was necessary for removal, Chase was acquitted. In the end, Republicans decided to wait for death and retirement to give them eventual control of the remaining branch of the government through presidential appointments.

Jefferson and Western Expansion

The Federalists feared the West as a threat to social order and stability. Frontiersmen, sneered New Englander Timothy Dwight, were "too idle; too talkative; too passionate . . . and too shiftless to acquire either property or character." Farther south, another observer referred to squatters on western lands as "ragged, dirty, brawling, browbeating monsters, six feet high, whose vocation is robbing, drinking, fighting, and terrifying every peaceable man in the community." Thus when Federalists passed an act in 1796 authorizing the sale of federal land, they viewed it as a revenue measure rather than the means to develop the country and kept the price of land high. It sold for a minimum of $2 an acre, with a required purchase of at least 640 acres, over four times the size of the typical American farm.

Empire of liberty

Jefferson, on the other hand, viewed the West as the means to preserve the values of an agrarian republic. He anticipated that as settled regions of the country became crowded, many rural residents would migrate to the cities in search of work unless cheap land beckoned farther west. America's vast spaces provided land that would last for a thousand generations, he predicted in his inaugural address, enough to transform the United States into "an empire of liberty."

In 1801 the Republican Congress reduced the minimum tract that buyers could purchase to 320 acres and also offered sale on credit. The intention was to encourage rapid settlement of the interior, and in fact, land sales boomed under the new law. Most sales, however, were to speculators and land companies rather than individual settlers. Even so, the West remained strongly Republican. The admission of new western states strengthened Jefferson's party and hastened the decline of the Federalists. From Jefferson's perspective, western expansion was a blessing economically, socially, and politically.

Exploration and Expansion: The Louisiana Purchase The vast, largely uncharted Louisiana Purchase lay well beyond the most densely populated areas of the United States. The Lewis and Clark expedition, along with Lieutenant Zebulon Pike's exploration of the upper Mississippi River and the Southwest, opened the way for westward expansion.

The Louisiana Purchase

Because Spain's colonial empire was disintegrating, Americans were confident that before long they would gain control of Florida and the rest of the Mississippi, either through purchase or by military occupation. This comforting prospect was shattered, however, when Spain ceded Louisiana—the territory lying between the Mississippi River and the Rocky Mountains—to France. Under the leadership of Napoleon Bonaparte, France had become the most powerful nation on the European continent, with the military might to protect its new colony and block American expansion. American anxiety intensified when Spain, while still in control of Louisiana, abruptly revoked Americans' right to navigate the lower Mississippi guaranteed by Pinckney's Treaty. Western farmers, who were suddenly denied access to the sea, angrily protested Spain's high-handed action.

Jefferson dispatched James Monroe to Paris to join Robert Livingston, the American minister, to negotiate the purchase of New Orleans and West Florida from the French and thus secure control of the Mississippi. "There is on the globe one single spot, the [possessor] of which is our natural and habitual enemy," Jefferson reminded them. "It is New Orleans."

Sale of Louisiana

In the meantime, however, Napoleon lost interest in Louisiana. With war looming again in Europe, he needed money, and so in April 1803 he offered to sell not just New Orleans but all of Louisiana to the United States. This proposal flabbergasted Livingston and Monroe. Their instructions said nothing about acquiring all of Louisiana, and they had not been authorized to spend what the French demanded. On the other hand, here was an unprecedented opportunity to expand dramatically the boundaries of the United States. Pressed for an immediate answer, Livingston and Monroe wanted to consult Jefferson but worried that the French might withdraw the offer as suddenly as they had made it. So the American ministers took a deep breath and, after haggling over a few details, agreed to purchase Louisiana for approximately $15 million.

The millions of acres of fertile farmland, untold natural resources, and control of the vital Mississippi River and its tributaries were one of the most extraordinary bargains in the history of the United States. In one fell swoop, the American negotiators had doubled the country's size by adding some 830,000 square miles. "From this day," Livingston asserted, "the United States take their place among the powers of the first rank."

Jefferson's pragmatism

Jefferson, naturally, was immensely pleased at the prospect of acquiring so much territory, which seemed to guarantee the survival of his agrarian republic. At the same time, as someone who favored the doctrine of strict construction, he found the legality of the act deeply troubling. The Constitution, after all, did not specifically authorize the acquisition of territory by treaty. Livingston and Monroe urged haste, however, and in the end, Jefferson sent the treaty to the Senate for ratification, noting privately, "The less we say about constitutional difficulties the better." Once again pragmatism had triumphed over theory.

The purchase of Louisiana was generally popular, and the Senate ratified the treaty 24 to 7. West Florida, which bordered part of the lower Mississippi, remained in Spanish hands, and Jefferson's efforts to acquire this region were unsuccessful. Nevertheless, western commerce could flow down the Mississippi unhindered to the sea. The Louisiana Purchase would rank as the greatest achievement of Jefferson's presidency.

Lewis and Clark

Early in 1803, even before the Louisiana Purchase was completed, Congress secretly appropriated $2500 to send an exploring party up the Missouri River to the Pacific. This expedition was led by Meriwether Lewis, Jefferson's secretary, and William Clark, a younger brother of Revolutionary War hero George Rogers Clark.

Jefferson instructed Lewis and Clark to map the region and make detailed observations of the soil, climate, rivers, minerals, and plant and animal life. They were also to investigate the practicability of an overland route to the Pacific and engage in diplomacy with the Indians along the way. Equally important, by pushing onward to the Pacific, Lewis and Clark would strengthen the American title to Oregon, which several nations claimed but none effectively occupied.

Exploration of the West

In the spring of 1804 Lewis and Clark left St. Louis and headed up the Missouri with 48 men. They laboriously pushed their boats up the Missouri River to present-day North Dakota, where they spent the winter with the Mandan Indians. The next spring, they headed west again. Only with great difficulty did the expedition pass the rugged mountains ahead of the winter snows and then float down first the Snake and then the Columbia River to the Pacific.

After spending a bleak winter in Oregon, vainly awaiting a ship that would take them back, the company returned in 1806 over the Rockies. Having traveled across half the continent in both directions, navigated countless rapids, and conducted nego-tiations with numerous tribes, Lewis and Clark arrived in St. Louis in September, two and a half years after they had departed. The expedition fired the imagination of Amer-icans about the exotic lands of the newly acquired Louisiana Purchase as well as the Pacific Northwest. Lewis and Clark had collected thousands of useful plant and ani-mal specimens, discovered several passes through the Rockies, and produced a remarkably accurate map, their most valuable contribution to western exploration.

Whites and Indians on the Frontier

In February 1803, as American diplo-mats prepared to leave for France in hopes of gaining title to western lands, another delegation was visiting Washing-ton with a similar purpose. Black Hoof, a Shawnee chief from the Ohio River val-ley, asked the secretary of war to issue a deed to the lands that legally belonged to the Shawnees in western Ohio. The deed, said Black Hoof, would ensure that his people could "raise good Grain and cut Hay for our Cattle" and guarantee "that nobody would take advantage" of them. The astonished secretary was not about to give the Shawnee any document that would strengthen their title to land in Ohio. But he did promise to provide some plows and cattle.

Unlike many Shawnees, Black Hoof had decided that the best way to get along with white Americans was to adopt their ways. For a number of years he and his tribe settled along the Auglaize River, built log houses, wore garments like those of whites, cleared land to raise corn, potatoes, cabbage, and turnips, and even planted an apple orchard. But in 1808, after the government refused to pay a Quaker mis-sionary who was providing technical support, Black Hoof's followers became in-creasingly dependent on government payments. Even Black Hoof admitted, "The white people . . . have been our ruin."

The Shawnees along the Auglaize were only one of many Indian tribes forced to make hard choices as white Americans streamed into the fertile lands of the Ohio River valley. In 1790 only about 100,000 whites lived in the West. By 1800 that number had jumped to almost 400,000 and, a decade later, to more than a million. By 1820 more than 2 million whites lived in a region they had first entered only 50 years earlier.

In this backcountry, where white and Indian cultures mixed and often clashed, both peoples experienced the breakdown of traditional cultural systems. White immi-grants pushing into Indian territory often lacked the structures of community such as churches, schools, and legal institutions. But Indian cultures were also severely stressed by the availability of white trade goods and by the more settled agricultural ways of white farmers, with their domesticated animals and fenced-in fields. Above all, Indians had to deal with the unceasing hunger of whites for Indian lands.

Indian attempts at assimilation

The Course of White Settlement

Following the Treaty of Greenville in 1795, white settlers poured into the Ohio Territory by wagon and flatboat. "From what I have seen and heard," one girl wrote while crossing Pennsylvania bound for the West, "I think the State of Ohio will be well fill'd before winter,—Waggons without number, every day go on." The pattern of settlement remained the same: in the first wave came backwoods families who laboriously cleared a few acres of forest by girdling the trees, removing the brush, and planting corn between the dead trunks. Their isolated one-room log cabins were crude, dark, and windowless, with mud stuffed between the chinks; the furniture and utensils were sparse and homemade. Such settlers were mostly squatters without legal title to their land. As a region began to fill up, these restless pioneers usually sold their improvements and headed west again.

Maturing society

Many of the settlers who replaced them were young unmarried men who left crowded regions in the East seeking new opportunities. Their migration, which relieved population pressures back home, contributed to the imbalance of males and females on the frontier. Once established, they quickly married and started families. Like the pioneers before them, most engaged in semisubsistence agriculture. As their numbers increased and a local market developed, they switched to surplus agriculture, growing and making much of what the family needed while selling or exchanging the surplus to obtain essential items. "The woman told me that they spun and wove all the cotton and woolen garments of the family, and knit all the stockings," a visitor to an Ohio farm wrote. "Her husband, though not a shoemaker by trade, made all the shoes. She manufactured all the soap and candles they used." The wife sold butter and chickens to get money to buy coffee, tea, and whiskey.

A Changing Environment

The inrush of new settlers significantly reduced the amount of original forest west of the Appalachian Mountains. Americans, who equated clearing the forest with progress, "have an unconquerable aversion to trees," one observer noted, "and whenever a settlement is made they cut away all before them without mercy; not one is spared; all share the same fate and are involved in the same general havoc." By 1850 they had cleared at least 100 million acres. In newly cleared areas the resulting landscape was often bleak, according to one traveler. "The trees are cut over at the height of three or four feet from the ground and the stumps are left for many years till the roots rot;—the edge of the forest, opened for the first time to the light of the sun looks cold and raw;—the ground rugged and ill-dressed . . . as if nothing could ever be made to spring from it."

Effects of deforestation

This rapid cutting of the forest altered plant and animal life in significant ways. Large animals, such as the deer and bears, became scarce, and the bison soon disappeared east of the Mississippi River. The loss of forest cover, combined with the new plowing of the land, increased the amount of runoff after rains, which lowered the water table and caused many streams to dry up for a good part of the year. At the same time increased runoff made rivers more destructive and floods more common. Clearing the land also produced serious soil erosion, particularly on hillsides, and silted many previously navigable streams and rivers. The climate changed as well: it was hotter in the summer and the winds blew more fiercely, causing erosion in the summer and chilling gusts in the winter.

Deforestation also made the Ohio valley more unhealthy. Malaria was not unknown in the region previously, but the growing population density and the cutting of forests made the disease more common. In clearing the land, settlers often created wasteland with pools of stagnant water from the increased runoff, which became breeding places for mosquitoes that spread the disease. Observers remarked on the greater prevalence of malaria and other summer diseases in the region as the forests came down.

The Second Great Awakening

It was the sparsely settled regions that became famous for a second wave of revivals, known collectively as the Second Great Awakening, that swept across the nation beginning in the late 1790s. Like the first national outpouring of religious enthusiasm

50 years earlier, these revivals were fanned by ministers who traveled the countryside preaching to groups anywhere they could. Beginning in the late 1790s Congregationalists, Presbyterians, and Baptists all participated. The Methodists, however, had the most effective organization for spreading the gospel in remote areas with their system of circuit riders. One competing Presbyterian minister ruefully noted that "into every hovel I entered I learned that the Methodist missionary had been there before me."

News of several revivals in Kentucky in the summer of 1800 quickly spread, and people came from 50 and 100 miles around, camping in makeshift tents and holding services out of doors. This new form of worship, the camp meeting, reached its climax at Cane Ridge, Kentucky, in August 1801. At a time when the largest city in the state had only 2000 people, more than 10,000 gathered for a week to hear dozens of ministers.

Cane Ridge

Men and women earnestly examined their hearts; scoffers came, half-mocking, half-fearful of what they might see. For rural folk accustomed to going to bed soon after dark, the sight of hundreds of campfires flickering throughout the woods far into the night, reinforced by the endless singing, praying, and crying, was a powerful tonic indeed. "The vast sea of human beings seemed to be agitated as if by storm," recalled one skeptic, who himself was converted at Cane Ridge.

> I counted seven ministers all preaching at once. . . . Some of the people were singing, others praying, some crying for mercy in the most piteous accents. . . . At one time I saw at least 500 swept down in a moment as if a battery of a thousand guns had been opened upon them, and then immediately followed shrieks and shouts that rent the very heavens.

Although the clergy at camp meetings were male, women played prominent roles, often pressing husbands to convert. In the overwhelming emotion of the moment, converts might dance, bark, laugh hysterically, or jerk uncontrollably, hair flying, the whole body shaking, as they sought to gain assurance of their salvation. (See Daily Lives, "The Frontier Camp Meeting," pages 268–269.)

Men and women witness the baptism of a female worshiper. A European observer said of such baptisms, "Barefoot and bareheaded, with flowing hair, they step solemnly into the river, while a choir sings." Like camp meetings and revivals, such scenes were an emotional experience for the congregation as well as the converts. Several members kneel in prayer or shout praises to the Lord while the rest of the group gaze with rapt attention.

Daily Lives

PUBLIC SPACE/ PRIVATE SPACE

The Frontier Camp Meeting

The Cane Ridge revival, one of the earliest along the frontier, was a chaotic, disorganized affair. But as western clergy became more experienced with outdoor camp meetings, they standardized the format. About a week in advance, organizers chose a forest clearing, removed nearby underbrush, erected pulpits, and constructed benches. Usually the camp went up near an established church, which provided lodging for the ministers. Since a water supply was essential, camps were located near springs, creeks, or rivers. A good site needed dry ground, shade so worshipers could escape the blazing sun, and pasturage for the horses.

The site might be laid out in a horseshoe, a rectangle, or, most popularly, a broad circle. In each case the tents of the worshipers formed a ring around the outdoor auditorium where services were held. As participants arrived, a supervisor directed drivers where to park wagons, tether animals, and pitch tents. At large meetings, where as many as 200 tents covered the site, tents were set up in several rows with streets in between to allow easy access. To help people find their lodgings, the streets were sometimes even named. This outer perimeter constituted the meeting's private space. Here, beneath tents of sailcloth or even shelters patched together from old blankets and sheets, individuals could withdraw from the larger group to find relative solitude, cook meals in front of campfires, and sleep on rude beds of straw or simply on the ground.

Worshipers were naturally drawn toward the central public space, where they filled bench after bench at the periodic call of a bugle. Rising above the listeners, at one or both ends of the clearing, stood the preachers' pulpit. Sometimes it was merely a 10-foot-square platform on stilts; other times it was more elaborate, with several levels and a roof. Services were held in the open, and neither rain nor thunderstorms would interrupt them. At night, the dancing light and shadows produced by the candles, torches, campfires, and fire altars (earthen-covered platforms) at each corner heightened the feeling of awe.

The democracy of the frontier did not automatically break down customary social constraints. For reasons of authority as well as practicality, the ministers' pulpit rose above the congregation. And the audience itself was segregated: women on one side of the clearing, men on the other. In the South, black worshipers were

CODE
X Cooking fires—illumination also from candles in trees
△ Tents
🛒 Wagons
⊟ Horses
1. Speakers' stand—candles for illumination
2. Earthen covered fire platforms
3. Mourners' bench
4. Blacks' worship area
5. Seats—women's side
6. Seats—men's side
7. Preachers' tent
8. Boarding tent

Source: Adapted from Charles A. Johnson, *The Frontier Camp Meeting: Religion's Harvest Time* (Dallas: SMU Press, 1955), pp. 43 and 47.

African Americans and revivals

In the South, African Americans, including slaves, attended camp meetings and enthusiastically participated in the tumultuous services. Indeed, revivals were a major force in spreading Christianity to African Americans and producing slave conversions. Revivalists' clear and vivid speech, their acceptance of the moral worth of every individual regardless of race, and their emphasis on the conversion experience rather than abstract theology had the same appeal to black listeners, who had little formal schooling, as they did to poorly educated white churchgoers. Blacks worshiped separately from and sometimes together with whites. The revivals also produced black preachers, who exhorted white as well as black audiences. Some slaveholders, especially in eastern plantation districts, worried that camp meetings might foster racial egalitarianism, but revivalists concentrated on bringing slaves to Christ rather than questioning society's institutions. As was the case seated in an area behind the pulpit, where they set up their own camp and conducted separate services.

Since the purpose of camp meetings was to "revive" religion and stir listeners' hearts, several rows of planks were set aside directly in front of the pulpit as an "anxious bench," for those whose souls struggled in the agony of conversion. The design of the space thus focused the attention of both congregation and ministers on the "mourners," who were exhorted and prayed over in hopes that they would receive a new birth in Christ. As camp meetings became increasingly organized, separate mourning tents were set up on the edge of the arena near the anxious benches. (Again, curtains separated the male and female sections, and black participants had their own mourning tents.)

But the social boundaries between public and private, male and female, and even black and white could be broken down. As excitement grew, several services might be held at once, some people praying, others singing, shouting, or listening to ministers who stood on wagons or makeshift platforms of felled trees. And when formal services ended, men and women often continued singing and exhorting in small groups, going into the woods to pray, and searching one another's souls by campfires late into the night. Indeed, the social mixing and spontaneous excitement were great enough that meeting sponsors quickly learned that supervision was necessary to prevent unseemly activities. The nearby forest, the numerous tents, and nightfall all offered temptations for drinking, carousing, or lovemaking. Therefore, official patrols were set up to regularly investigate suspicious activities and to monitor sleeping arrangements.

On the final day white and black worshipers joined together in a singing and marching festival before disbanding to their more humdrum daily routines. Successful camp meetings depended on more than the talents of the clergy and the enthusiasm of participants. In their layout they were carefully planned and regulated communities in the forest, designed to reduce the distance between public and private space and thereby instill a sense of religion into all the activities that took place in the meeting as well as those that would be resumed in the regular world.

with white worshipers, the Baptist and Methodist churches received the bulk of African American converts.

The revivals quickly found critics, who decried the emotionalism and hysteria they produced. For a time Presbyterians and Baptists withdrew from camp meetings, leaving the field to the Methodists. Eventually even the Methodists sought to dampen excessive emotion by restricting admittance and patrolling the meeting grounds.

Revivals like Cane Ridge provided an emotional release from the hard, isolated life on the frontier. Pioneers could momentarily forget the drabness of their lives, the pains and sorrows they endured as they struggled to carve an existence out of the forest. For families with few neighbors, camp meetings offered a chance to participate in a wider social gathering while relieving pent-up emotions. And for those

Attraction of revivals

at the bottom of the social hierarchy, the revivalists' message emphasized an individual's ability to gain personal triumph and salvation regardless of his or her station in life. In the swiftly changing borderlands north and south of the Ohio River, where society seemed constantly in flux, revivals brought a sense of uplift and comfort.

Pressure on Indian Lands and Culture

As white settlers continued to flood into the backcountry, the pressure to acquire Indian lands increased. Jefferson endorsed the policy that Indian tribes would either have to assimilate into American culture by becoming farmers and abandoning their seminomadic hunting or would have to move west of the Mississippi River. There, isolated from white settlement, the Indians could gradually develop the skills and values necessary to fit into American society. Jefferson defended these alternatives as in the best interests of the Indians, because he believed that otherwise they faced extermination. But he also recognized that by becoming farmers they would need less land. "While they are learning to do better on less land," he noted, "our increasing numbers will be calling for more land."

The hard truth about white policies toward Indians was that however enlightened some individuals might be, the demographic pressure of high birthrates and aggressive expansion ensured conflict between the two cultures. Anglo-Americans never doubted the superiority of their ways. As William Henry Harrison, governor of the new Indiana Territory, confessed in 1801, "A great many of the Inhabitants of the Fronteers consider the murdering of the Indians in the highest degree meritorious." Even a disciple of the Enlightenment, such as Jefferson, could become cynical and encourage the policy of selling goods on credit in order to lure Indians into debt. "When these debts get beyond what the individuals can pay," the president observed, "they become willing to lop them off by a cession of lands." Between 1800 and 1810 whites pressed Indians into ceding more than 100 million acres in the Ohio River valley.

Destruction of Indian cultures

The loss of so much land to white settlement devastated traditional Indian cultures by reducing hunting grounds and making game and food scarce. "Stop your people from killing our game," the Shawnees complained in 1802 to federal Indian agents. "They would be angry if we were to kill a cow or hog of theirs, the little game that remains is very dear to us." Tribes also became dependent on white trade to obtain blankets, guns, metal utensils, alcohol, and decorative beads. To pay for these goods with furs, Indians often overtrapped, which forced them to invade the lands of neighboring tribes, provoking wars. The destructive effects of alcohol, which Indians turned to as a means of coping with cultural stress, were especially marked during these years, and increased production in white backcountry settlements during the 1790s and early 1800s made whiskey readily available. Indeed, white consumption of alcohol was also rising during these years, a symptom of the adjustment of white society to cultural stress.

Among the Shawnees in the Ohio River valley, the strain produced by white expansion led to alcoholism, growing violence among tribe members, family disintegration, and the collapse of the clan system designed to regulate relations among different villages. These problems might have been lessened by separation from white culture, but the Shawnees had become dependent on trade for articles they could not produce themselves. The question of how to deal with white culture became a matter of anguished debate. Black Hoof, as we have seen, attempted to take up farming and accommodate to white ways. But for most Indians, the course of assimilation proved unappealing and fraught with risk.

The Prophet, Tecumseh, and the Pan-Indian Movement

Other Shawnees decided not to adopt white ways but to revitalize their culture by severing all ties with the white world. In such efforts Indian religion often played a central role. During the 1790s a revival of religious fervor led by Handsome Lake took hold among the Iroquois, following the loss of most of the Iroquois lands and the collapse of their military power in western New York. Subsequently, Lalawethika, also known as the Prophet, sparked a religious revival among the Shawnees. The Prophet's early life was undistinguished: he was a poor hunter and as a child accidentally blinded himself in the right eye with an arrow. His portly build and homely looks reinforced his unsightly appearance, and the ridicule of his fellow tribe members drove him to alcoholism. Then, suddenly, in April 1805 he lapsed into a trance so deep that he was given up for dead. When he revived, he spoke of having died and been reborn. In this vision and others he later received, he outlined a new creed for the Shawnees. Renouncing alcohol, he took a new name, Tenskwatawa (the Open Door), to express his mission to "reclaim the Indians from bad habits and to cause them to live in peace with all mankind."

Tenskwatawa urged the Shawnees to renounce whiskey and white goods and return to their old ways of hunting with bows and arrows, eating customary foods such as corn and beans, and wearing traditional garb. Seeking to revitalize Shawnee culture, the Prophet condemned intertribal violence, promoted monogamous marriage, and denounced the idea of private instead of communal property. Except for guns, which could be used in self-defense, his followers were to discard all items made by whites.

Prophet's message

Not only was trade forbidden with white settlers, but so was intermarriage. Indian wives of white men were to leave their husbands and return to the tribe, and children of mixed parentage were to be barred from the village. Setting up headquarters at the newly built village of Prophetstown in Indiana in 1808, Tenskwatawa led a religious revival among the tribes of the Northwest, who were increasingly concerned about the loss of their lands. Just as thousands of white settlers traveled to Methodist

Tenskwatawa (left), "the Open Door," shown in traditional dress, led a religious movement to revitalize Shawnee culture and attracted a large following among the northwestern tribes. After the Battle of Tippecanoe, he was supplanted as leader of the Indian revitalization movement by his brother Tecumseh (right), who advocated political unity to preserve Indian lands and cultures. Tecumseh was the dominant figure among the western tribes until he died fighting alongside the British in the War of 1812.

The Indian Response to White Encroachment With land cessions and white western migration placing increased pressure on Indian cultures after 1790, news of the Prophet's revival fell on eager ears. It spread especially quickly northward along the shores of Lake Michigan and westward along Lake Superior and the interior of Wisconsin. Following the Battle of Tippecanoe, Tecumseh eclipsed the Prophet as the major leader of Indian resistance, but his trips south to forge political alliances met with less success.

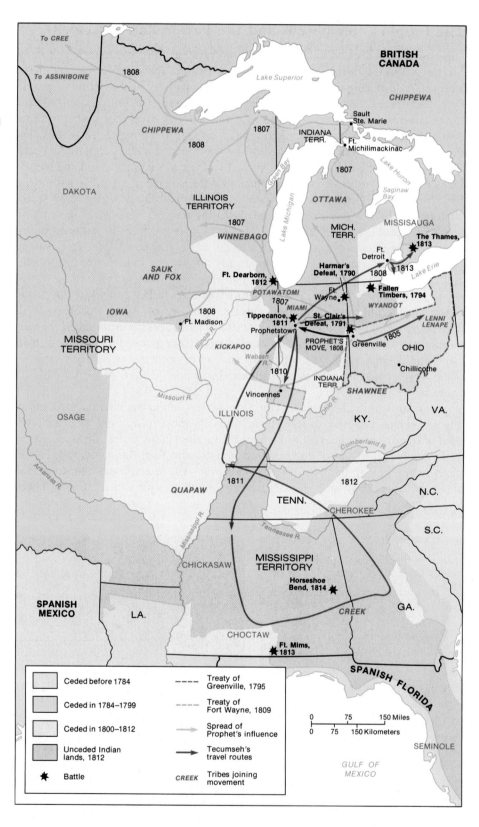

or Baptist camp meetings in the woods, where preachers denounced the evils of liquor and called for a return to a purer way of life, so thousands of Indians from northern tribes traveled to the Prophet's village for inspiration.

Whereas Tenskwatawa's strategy of revitalization was primarily religious, his older brother Tecumseh turned to political and military solutions. William Henry Harrison described Tecumseh as "one of those uncommon geniuses which spring up occasionally to produce revolutions and overturn the established order of things." Tall and athletic, an accomplished hunter and a renowned warrior, Tecumseh became active in 1809, after the Lenni Lenape and Miami tribes ceded yet another 3 million acres in Indiana and Illinois under the Treaty of Fort Wayne. Repudiating the treaty, he traveled throughout the Northwest, urging tribes to forget their ancient rivalries and unite under his leadership to protect their lands from white incursions. Tecumseh's confederacy brought together the Wyandot, Chippewa, Sauk and Fox, Winnebago, Potawatomi, and other tribes. As Tecumseh began to overshadow the Prophet, William Harrison aptly termed him "really the efficient man—the Moses of the family."

Tecumseh's movement

Tecumseh's message of Pan-Indian unity and centralized authority ran counter to many facets of traditional Indian cultures. He asked villages to pay less attention to their local leaders and join his larger movement; he also called on tribes to unite with their traditional enemies in a common cause. Although the amount of support he received was impressive, his following never matched that of the Prophet's earlier revivals. After recruiting allies among the northwestern tribes, Tecumseh in 1811 headed south, where he encountered greater resistance. In general, the southern tribes were more prosperous, were more acculturated, and felt less immediate pressure on their land from whites. In addition, the Choctaws and Chickasaws refused to forget long-standing feuds with northern tribes. So Tecumseh's southern mission ended largely in failure.

Tecumseh's failure in the South

To compound Tecumseh's problems, while he was away a force of Americans under Governor Harrison defeated the Prophet's forces at the Battle of Tippecanoe in November and then destroyed Prophetstown. As a result, Tecumseh became convinced that the best way to contain white expansion was to play off the Americans against the British in the Great Lakes region. Indeed, by 1811, the two nations were on the brink of war.

The Second War for American Independence

As Tecumseh worked to overcome obstacles to a Pan-Indian alliance, Jefferson encountered his own difficulties in trying to achieve American political unity. The president's goal was to woo all but the most extreme Federalists into the Republican camp. His reelection in 1804 showed how much progress he had made, as he defeated Federalist Charles Cotesworth Pinckney and carried 15 of 17 states. With the Republicans controlling three-quarters of the seats in Congress, Jefferson's goal of one-party rule seemed at hand.

But events across the Atlantic complicated the efforts to unite Americans. Only two weeks after Napoleon agreed to sell Louisiana to the United States, war broke out between France and Great Britain. As in the 1790s, the United States again found itself caught between the world's two greatest powers. Jefferson insisted that the nation should remain neutral in a European war that did not concern Americans. But the controversial policies he proposed to maintain American neutrality brought out the divisions in American society and momentarily revived the two-party system.

The Barbary Pirates and Cultural Identities

In seeking a common national identity, citizens of the United States often found it easier to define themselves in terms of what they were not. As conflict increased along the nation's western frontiers, most Americans believed they were not like the Indians, whom they perceived as nomadic and wild. As France and England harassed U.S. ships on the high seas, Americans insisted they should not be like the nations of Europe, where "Favoritism as well as Corruption prevails," as one American diplomat complained. And Americans drew another sharp cultural contrast during these decades: they protested they were not like the "Barbary pirates" of North Africa, who also preyed on American ships.

The Barbary states of North Africa—Algiers, Morocco, Tripoli, and Tunis—lay along the Mediterranean Sea's southern coast. During the seventeenth and eighteenth centuries their corsairs—light, maneuverable sailing vessels—plundered enemy ships, confiscating cargo and enslaving the captured crews. In doing so, the Barbary states behaved much like European nations along the Mediterranean, whose ships over the years had swept up North African cargo and crews. Indeed, the slavery imposed by the Barbary states was neither as harsh nor as extensive, in sheer numbers, as the slave trade engaged in by Europeans and Americans along the West African coast.

The United States and the Barbary States, 1801–1815 The young United States, like many European powers, found its trading vessels challenged by the Barbary states of Morocco, Algiers, Tunisia, and Tripoli. When the pasha of Tripoli declared war on the United States in 1801, Jefferson dispatched a force that blockaded Tripoli to bring the war to an end in 1805. Tribute paid to the other Barbary States continued until 1816, after a new naval force, led by Captain Stephen Decatur, forced the ruler of Algiers to end the practice.

Corsairs, light, maneuverable ships sailing out of Barbary ports like Tripoli (shown here), were well fitted for their purpose. As one historian noted, "Like stinging insects, their light, rapid vessels were designed to strike at unarmed or lightly armed merchantmen, while being able to flee very speedily at the mere approach of a warship."

But the Barbary states were Muslim; and to American (and European) eyes, that made the tyranny of their rulers particularly objectionable. A biography of Islam's prophet, Muhammad, published in the United States in 1802, was typical in its condemnation. Muhammad's whole life had been an "imposture" and his teachings a "system of blasphemy and iniquity" by which the followers of Islam had been "degraded to the rank of brutes." More powerful European nations, like Britain, France, and Holland, found it convenient to pay tributes to the Barbary states so their ships could sail unmolested. But both Jefferson and John Adams disliked that idea. The "policy of Christendom" of paying tribute, complained Adams, "has made Cowards of all their Sailors before the Standard of Mahomet." In Adams's eyes, the cultural and religious differences clearly added insult to the injuries inflicted by the Barbary corsairs.

For their part, the Barbary states bore no special hostility toward Americans; indeed, in 1778 Morocco was among the first states to recognize the fledgling United States and to request that it send an ambassador. Congress, however, was so weak and distracted with its own affairs that for many years it could spare neither the money for bribes nor even the diplomats to open negotiations with the Barbary states. By the time John Adams became president, he had subdued his outrage, and he agreed to tributes. But when Tripoli increased its demands in 1801, President Jefferson sent a small squadron of American ships to force a settlement. In 1803 Tripoli captured the *U.S.S. Philadelphia,* the second largest frigate in the navy, which caused Federalists to mock the president for having neglected the navy for so long. The following year, however, Lieutenant Stephen Decatur retrieved the situation by sneaking into Tripoli's harbor and burning the *Philadelphia.* The American blockade that followed forced Tripoli to sue for peace and give up any further demands for tribute. Even so, the United States continued paying tribute to the other Barbary states until 1816.

American perceptions of Islamic culture

Neutral Rights

Both France and Britain found that paying tribute to the Barbary states gave their ships a competitive advantage over those of less powerful nations, like the United States, who could not afford the demands. But Americans soon found their commerce in more danger from the warring nations of France and Britain.

At first the war benefited American trade because it disrupted European agriculture, increasing the demand for American foodstuffs and other raw materials. As the fighting drove most nonneutral ships from the seas, American foreign trade doubled between 1803 and 1805. But after 1805 the British navy began seizing American ships with increasing frequency, as it tightened its blockade of Europe.

Impressment

Adding to American anger, the British navy also resumed its impressment of sailors and even passengers from American ships. British authorities refused to recognize the right of its citizens to emigrate and become American citizens, insisting that even if naturalized by the United States they remained subjects of the Crown. Anywhere from 4000 to 10,000 sailors were impressed by British naval officers, who did not always bother to distinguish naturalized from native-born Americans.

Isaac Clark, for example, was a native of Randolph, Massachusetts, yet he was taken from the American ship *Jane* in June 1809 after it was stopped by the British. When he presented papers attesting to his American citizenship, the English captain tore them up and threw them overboard. Refusing to work, Clark was put in irons and given a daily allowance of a biscuit and a pint of water, and once a week he received two dozen lashes. Finally, half-starved and physically broken, Clark gave in. He served in the British navy for more than two and a half years until wounded in action against a French frigate. While in a hospital he was freed through the intervention of the American consul. Voicing American indignation, John Quincy Adams characterized impressment as an "authorized system of kidnapping upon the ocean."

American ships seized

By 1805, the war had demonstrated the British navy's clear superiority at sea, while Napoleon's army enjoyed a decisive edge on land. Adopting a strategy of attrition, each country began to raid America's ocean commerce with the other side. Between 1803 and 1807, Britain seized more than 500 American ships; France, more than 300. Britain issued new regulations in 1807, known as the Orders in Council,

Orders in Council

that required any ship trading with France or its satellites to put in first at a British port, pay a duty, and get a license. Napoleon retaliated with the Milan Decree of 1807, which announced that any ship that stopped in Britain in conformity with the Orders in Council would be treated as a British ship, subject to seizure. American merchants, caught in the middle, saw the number of seized ships again increase. An irate Jefferson complained of France and England, "The one is a den of robbers, the other of pirates." When in June 1807 a British frigate fired on the U.S. warship *Chesapeake* in American waters and seized four deserters from the Royal Navy, public opinion clamored for military retaliation.

The Embargo

Yet Jefferson shrank from declaring war. He announced instead a program of "peaceable coercion," designed to protect neutral rights without war. The plan not only prohibited American ships from trading with foreign ports but also stopped the export of all American goods. Jefferson was confident that American exports were so essential to the two belligerents that they would quickly agree to respect American neutral rights. In December 1807 Congress passed the Embargo Act.

The president had seriously miscalculated. France did not depend on American trade and so managed well enough, while British ships quickly took over the carrying trade as American vessels lay idle. Under the embargo, American exports plunged from $108 million in 1807 to a mere $22 million a year later. At the same time, imports fell from almost $145 million to about $58 million. As the center of American shipping, New England port cities were hurt the most and protested the loudest. And when their merchants were not protesting, they were smuggling behind American officials' backs. During his last months in office Jefferson simply gave up trying to enforce the act.

Madison and the Young Republicans

Following Washington's example, Jefferson did not seek a third term. A caucus of Republican members of Congress selected James Madison to run against Federalist Charles Cotesworth Pinckney. Although Madison triumphed easily, Pinckney swept all of New England, where feeling against the embargo was highest, and the Federalists picked up 24 seats in Congress. The party seemed on the verge of a revival.

Few men have assumed the presidency with more experience than James Madison. A leading nationalist in the 1780s, the father of the Constitution, a key floor leader in Congress, the founder of the Republican party, Jefferson's secretary of state and closest adviser, Madison had spent over a quarter of a century in public life. Yet his tenure as president proved disappointing, for despite his intellectual brilliance, he lacked the force of leadership and the inner strength to impose his will on less capable men. *Madison's character*

With a president reluctant to fight for what he wanted, leadership passed from the executive branch to Congress. The elections of 1810 swept in a new generation of Republicans, led by the adroit and magnetic 34-year-old Henry Clay of Kentucky, who gained the rare distinction of being elected Speaker in his first term. These younger Republicans were much more nationalistic than the generation led by Jefferson and Madison. They sought an ambitious program of economic development and were aggressive expansionists, especially those from frontier districts. Their feisty willingness to go to war earned them the name of War Hawks. Though they numbered fewer than 30 in Congress, they quickly became the driving force in the Republican party. *War Hawks*

The Decision for War

During Jefferson's final week in office in early 1809, Congress repealed the Embargo Act. To encourage the two great powers to respect neutral rights, a new act reopened trade with all nations except Britain and France and authorized the president to resume trade with either nation if it withdrew its restrictions. The following year Congress authorized trade with France and England but decreed that if one of the two belligerents agreed to stop interfering with American shipping, trade with the other would be prohibited.

In this situation, Napoleon cleverly outmaneuvered the British by announcing that he would set aside the French trade regulations. Madison eagerly took the French emperor at his word and reimposed a ban on trade with England. But as French raiders continued to seize American ships, it became clear that Napoleon's words were not matched by French deeds. Madison, who had boxed himself into a corner, refused to rescind his order unless the British revoked the Orders in Council. In the disputes that followed, American anger focused on the British, who seized many more ships than the French and continued to impress American sailors.

Declaration of war

The embargo produced hard times in Britain, and finally, on June 16, 1812, the British ministry suspended the Orders in Council. But it was too late. Two days earlier, unaware of the change in policy, Congress granted Madison's request for a declaration of war against Britain. The vote was 79 to 49 in the House and 19 to 13 in the Senate, mostly along party lines, with every Federalist voting against war. As the representatives of commercial interests, particularly in New England, Federalists were convinced that war would ruin American commerce. They also still identified with Britain as the champion of order and conservatism. The handful of Republicans who joined the Federalists represented coastal districts, which were most vulnerable to the Royal Navy.

Clearly, the vote for war could not be explained as a matter of outraged Americans protecting neutral rights. The coastal areas, which were most affected, preferred trade over high principle. On the other hand, members of Congress from the South and the West, regions that had a less direct interest in the issue, clamored most strongly for war. Their constituents were consumed with a desire to seize additional territory in Canada or in Florida (owned by Britain's ally Spain). In addition, they accused the British of stirring up hostility among the Indian tribes.

Perhaps most important, the War Hawks were convinced that Britain had never truly accepted the verdict of the American Revolution. To them, American independence—and with it republicanism—hung in the balance. For insecure Americans, hungering for acceptance in the community of nations, nothing rankled more than being treated by the British as colonials. John Quincy Adams expressed this point of view when he declared: "In this question something besides dollars and cents is concerned and no alternative [is] left but war or the abandonment of our rights as an independent nation."

National Unpreparedness

With Britain preoccupied by Napoleon, the War Hawks expected that the United States would win an easy victory. In truth, the United States was totally unprepared for war. Crippled by Jefferson's cutbacks, the navy was unable to lift the British blockade of the American coast, which bottled up the country's merchant marine and most of its navy. As for the U.S. army, it was small and poorly led. When Congress moved to increase its size to 75,000, even the most hawkish states failed to meet their quotas. Congress was also reluctant to levy taxes to finance the war.

Battle of Lake Erie

A three-pronged American invasion of Canada from Detroit, Niagara, and Lake Champlain failed dismally in 1812. Americans fared better the following year, as both sides raced to build a navy on the strategically located Lake Erie. Led by Commander Oliver Hazard Perry, American forces won a decisive victory at Put-In Bay in 1813. Perry's triumph gave the United States control of Lake Erie and greatly strengthened the American position in the Northwest.

"A Chance Such as Will Never Occur Again"

As the United States struggled to organize its forces, Tecumseh sensed that his long-awaited opportunity had come to drive Americans out of the western territories. "Here is a chance . . . such as will never occur again," he told a war council, "for us Indians of North America to form ourselves into one great combination." Joining

During the Battle of New Orleans, American troops under Jackson entrenched behind breastworks, while their artillery raked the advancing British forces with deadly fire. The ladders needed to scale the American works quickly became entangled in the disorganized British assault.

up with the British, Tecumseh traveled south in the fall to talk again with his Creek allies. To coordinate a concerted Indian offensive for the following summer, he left a bundle of red sticks with eager Creek soldiers. They were to remove one stick each day from the bundle and attack when the sticks had run out.

Defeat of the Creeks

A number of the older Creeks were more acculturated and preferred an American alliance. But about 2000 younger "Red Stick" Creeks launched a series of attacks, climaxed by the destruction of Fort Mims along the Alabama River in August 1813. Once again, the Indians' lack of unity was a serious handicap, as warriors from the Cherokee, Choctaw, and Chickasaw tribes, traditional Creek enemies, allied with the Americans. At the Battle of Horseshoe Bend in March 1814, General Andrew Jackson and his Tennessee militia soundly defeated the Red Stick Creeks. Jackson promptly dictated a peace treaty under which the Creeks ceded 22 million acres of land in the Mississippi Territory. They and the other southern tribes still retained significant landholdings, but Indian military power had been broken in the Southwest.

Tecumseh's death

Farther north, in October 1813 American forces under General William Henry Harrison defeated the British and their Indian allies at the Battle of the Thames. In the midst of heavy fighting Tecumseh was slain—and with him died any hope of a Pan-Indian movement.

The British Invasion

As long as the war against Napoleon continued, the British were unwilling to divert army units to North America. But in 1814 Napoleon was at last defeated. Free to concentrate on America, the British devised a coordinated strategy to invade the United States in the northern, central, and southern parts of the country. The main army headed south from Montreal but was checked when Captain Thomas Macdonough destroyed the British fleet on Lake Champlain.

Meanwhile, a smaller British force captured Washington and burned several public buildings, including the Capitol and the president's home. To cover the scars of this destruction, the executive mansion was painted with whitewash and became

The War of 1812 After the American victory on Lake Erie and the defeat of the western Indians at the Battle of the Thames, the British adopted a three-pronged strategy to invade the United States, climaxing with an attempt on New Orleans. But they met their match in Andrew Jackson, whose troops marched to New Orleans after fighting a series of battles against the Creeks and forcing them to cede a massive tract of land.

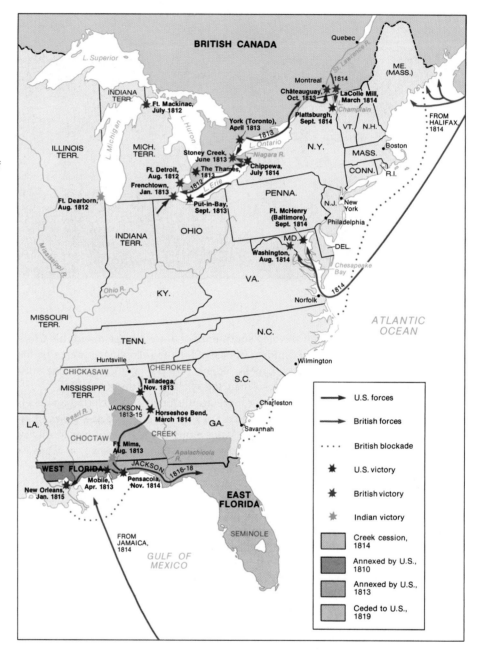

known as the White House. The burning of the capital was a humiliating event; President Madison and his wife, Dolley, were abruptly forced to flee, leaving their dinner to be eaten by the British. But the defeat had little military significance. The principal British objective was Baltimore, where for 25 hours their fleet bombarded Fort McHenry in the city's harbor. When he saw the American flag still flying above the fort at dawn, Francis Scott Key hurriedly penned the verses of "The Star Spangled Banner," which was eventually adopted as the national anthem.

The third British target was New Orleans, where a formidable army of 7500 British troops was opposed by a hastily assembled American force commanded by Major General Andrew Jackson. The Americans included regular soldiers; frontiersmen from Kentucky and Tennessee; citizens of New Orleans, including several companies of free African Americans; Choctaw Indians; and—for an added dash of color—a group of pirates. Jackson's outnumbered and ill-equipped forces won a stunning victory, which made the general an overnight hero. The Battle of New Orleans enabled Americans to forget the war's many failures and to boast that once again the United States had humbled the world's greatest military power.

Jackson's victory at New Orleans

The Hartford Convention

In December 1814, while Jackson was organizing the defense of New Orleans, New England Federalists met in Hartford to map strategy against the war. Yankee merchants, contemptuous of "Mr. Madison's War," had continued to trade with the enemy, while New England governors declined to make available the state militias. Finally the Massachusetts legislature called for a convention to discuss New England's grievances. Massachusetts, Connecticut, and Rhode Island sent delegates, but only three counties in New Hampshire and one in Vermont were represented.

Rejecting calls for secession, the delegates endorsed a series of proposed amendments to the Constitution that showed their displeasure with the government's economic policies and their resentment of the South's national political power. To their dismay, however, the committee sent to Washington to present the convention's demands arrived in the capital just as news of Andrew Jackson's victory was being trumpeted on the streets. The burst of national pride following Jackson's victory badly undercut the Hartford Convention's position, as did news from across the Atlantic that American negotiators in Ghent, Belgium, had signed a treaty ending the war. Hostilities had ceased, technically, on Christmas Eve 1814, two weeks before the Battle of New Orleans.

Like the war itself, the Treaty of Ghent accomplished little. All the major issues between the two countries, including impressment, neutral rights, trade, and the boundary between the United States and Canada, were either ignored or referred to future commissions for settlement. As John Quincy Adams commented, "Nothing was adjusted, nothing was settled—nothing in substance but an indefinite suspension of hostilities was agreed to." Both sides were simply relieved to end the conflict.

Treaty of Ghent

Adams was right in concluding that, in **America Turns Inward** terms of international relations, the war had settled nothing. Psychologically, however, the nation's mood had changed perceptibly. "Let any man look at the degraded condition of this country before the war," declaimed young Henry Clay, a leading War Hawk. "The scorn of the universe, the contempt of ourselves. . . . What is our present situation? Respectability and character abroad—security and confidence at home." Indeed, the return of peace hard on the heels of Jackson's victory sparked a new confidence in their country's destiny. "We have stood the contest, single-handed, against the conqueror of Europe," wrote Supreme Court justice Joseph Story to a friend, "and we are at peace, with all our blushing victories thick crowding on us."

National pride

The upsurge in national pride after the War of 1812 is reflected in the proud demeanor of these American soldiers, as portrayed by John Lewis Krimmel. Fourth of July parades routinely allowed soldiers to parade, drums beating and flags flying for the entertainment of civilians.

The upsurge in nationalism sounded the death knell of the Federalist party. The resistance of New England Federalists to the embargo and their disloyalty during the war had already weakened the party elsewhere, and the Hartford Convention tainted it with disunion and treason. Although the party had made its best showing in years in 1812, when Madison narrowly defeated his Federalist opponent, its support collapsed in the 1816 election. Madison's secretary of state, James Monroe, resoundingly defeated Federalist Rufus King of New York. Four years later Monroe ran for reelection unopposed.

The Missouri Crisis

The optimism of the era, however, was undercut by sectional rivalries that flared in 1819, when the Missouri Territory applied for admission as a slave state. Before the controversy over Missouri erupted, slavery had not been a major issue in American politics. Congress had debated the institution when it prohibited the African slave trade in 1808, the earliest year this step could be taken under the Constitution. In the absence of any specific federal legislation, however, slavery had crossed the Mississippi River into the Louisiana Purchase. Louisiana entered the Union in 1812 as a slave state, and in 1818 Missouri, which had about 10,000 slaves in its population, asked permission to come in too.

In 1818 the Union contained 11 free and 11 slave states. As the federal government became stronger and more active, both the North and the South became increasingly anxious about maintaining their political power. The North's greater population gave it a majority in the House of Representatives, 105 to 81. The Senate, of course, was evenly balanced, because each state had two senators regardless of population. But Maine, which previously had been part of Massachusetts, requested admission as a free state. That would upset the balance unless Missouri came in as a slave state.

Representative James Tallmadge of New York disturbed this delicate state of affairs when in 1819 he suddenly introduced an amendment designed to establish a program of gradual emancipation in Missouri. The debate that followed was bitter, as for the first time Congress directly debated the morality of slavery. The House approved the Tallmadge amendment, but the Senate refused to accept it, and the two houses deadlocked.

Missouri Compromise

When Congress reconvened in 1820, Henry Clay of Kentucky promoted what came to be known as the Missouri Compromise. Under its terms Missouri was admitted as a slave state and Maine as a free state. In addition, slavery was forever prohibited in the remainder of the Louisiana Purchase north of 36°30′ (the southern boundary of Missouri). Clay's proposal, the first of several sectional compromises he would engineer in his long career, won congressional approval and Monroe signed the measure, ending the crisis. But southern fears for the security of slavery and northern fears about its spread remained. As Thomas Jefferson had gloomily

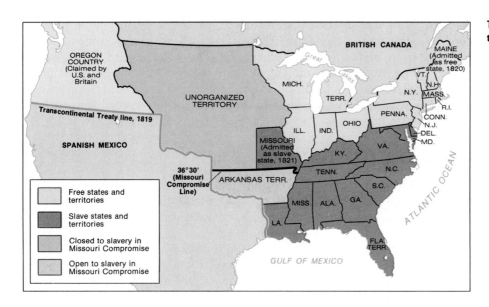

The Missouri Compromise and the Union's Boundaries in 1820

predicted, "A geographical line, coinciding with a marked principle, moral and political, once conceived and held up to angry passions of men, will never be obliterated; and every new irritation will mark it deeper and deeper."

Monroe's Presidency

The spirit of postwar harmony produced the so-called Era of Good Feelings, presided over by James Monroe, the last president of the Revolutionary generation. Monroe, like Jefferson before him, hoped to eliminate political parties, which he considered unnecessary in a free government. Like Washington, he thought of himself as the head of the nation rather than of a party.

Monroe's greatest achievements were diplomatic, accomplished largely by his talented secretary of state, John Quincy Adams, the son of President John Adams. An experienced diplomat, Adams thought of the Republic in continental terms and was intent on promoting expansion to the Pacific. Such a vision required dealing with Spain, which had never recognized the legality of the Louisiana Purchase. In addition, between 1810 and 1813 the United States had occupied and unilaterally annexed Spanish West Florida.

Spain, however, was preoccupied with events farther south in the Americas. In the first quarter of the nineteenth century, its colonies one after another had revolted and established themselves as independent nations. These revolutions increased the pressure on the Spanish minister to America, Luis de Onís, to come to terms with the United States. Furthermore, in 1818 Andrew Jackson marched into East Florida and captured several Spanish forts. Jackson had exceeded his instructions, but Adams understood well enough the additional pressure this aggression put on Onís and refused to disavow it.

Fearful that the United States might next invade Texas or other Spanish territory, Spain agreed to the Transcontinental, or Adams-Onís, Treaty in February 1819. Its terms set the boundary between American and Spanish territory all the way to the Pacific (map, above). Spain not only gave up its claims to the Pacific Northwest but also ceded Florida; in exchange, the U.S. government

Transcontinental Treaty

assumed $5 million in claims against Spain by American citizens. In order to obtain the line to the Pacific, the United States abandoned its contention that Texas was part of the Louisiana Purchase. Adams had wanted Texas, but he wanted the line to the Pacific even more. Understanding the strategic commitment to expanding across the continent, Adams wrote in his diary, "The acknowledgement of a definite line of boundary to the South Sea [the Pacific] forms a great epoch in our history."

The Monroe Doctrine

The United States came to terms not only with Spain but, even more important, with Great Britain as well. Following the War of 1812, the British abandoned their connections with the western Indian tribes and no longer attempted to block American expansion to the Rocky Mountains. In a growing spirit of cooperation, the Rush-Bagot Agreement in 1817 limited naval forces on the Great Lakes and on Lake Champlain. In 1818 the countries agreed to the 49th parallel as the northern boundary of the Louisiana Purchase and also to joint control of the Oregon Territory for 10 years, subject to renewal.

Improved relations with Britain

In this atmosphere of good will, George Canning, the British foreign secretary, proposed in August 1823 that the United States and Britain issue a joint statement disavowing any expansionist aims in Latin America and opposing the transfer of Spain's colonies to any foreign power. Monroe was inclined to accept the British offer, and both Jefferson and Madison urged him to do so. But John Quincy Adams forcefully argued that the United States should not make any pledge against acquiring territory in the future, particularly in Texas, Mexico, and the Caribbean. Adams also worried that in any joint statement the United States would appear to be merely a junior partner, coming along "as a cock-boat in the wake of a British man-of-war." Monroe finally agreed to make an independent statement.

Monroe Doctrine

He included it in his annual message to Congress, on December 2, 1823. Monroe reaffirmed that the United States would not intervene in European affairs, a principle of American foreign policy since Washington's Farewell Address. And he also announced that the United States would not interfere with already-established European colonies in the Western Hemisphere. But any intervention, he warned, in the new republics of Latin America would be considered a hostile act: "The American continents . . . are henceforth not to be considered as subjects for future colonization by any European powers." The essence of this policy, which was Adams's handiwork, was the concept of two worlds, one old and one new, each refraining from interfering in the other's affairs.

American public opinion hailed Monroe's statement and then promptly forgot it. Only years later would it be referred to as the Monroe Doctrine. Still, it represented the culmination of the American quest since 1776 for independence and sovereignty. The very fact that Britain had proposed a joint declaration demonstrated that, at last, the parent nation recognized its offspring as a legitimate and sovereign nation. Monroe's declaration underlined the United States' determination not to act in world affairs as a satellite of Britain. Ever since the adoption of the Constitution, the issue of independence had been at the center of American politics. It had surfaced during the 1790s, in Hamilton's quarrel with Jefferson over whether to favor Britain or France and in the differing responses of Americans to the French Revolution. It colored the debates over the embargo and finally once again came to a head in 1812 with the second war for American independence.

The End of an Era

The growing reconciliation with Great Britain ended the external threat to the Republic. Isolated from Europe and protected by the British fleet, the United States was free to turn its attention inward, to concentrate on expanding across the vast continent and on developing its resources. Yet how would the nation be developed? Jefferson had dreamed of an "empire of liberty," delighting in western expansion as the means to preserve a nation of small farmers like those Crèvecoeur had written about during the 1780s.

End of foreign threat

Younger, more nationalistic Republicans had a different vision. They spoke of internal improvements, protective tariffs to help foster American industries, better roads and canals to link farmers with towns, cities, and wider markets. The tone of these new Republicans was not aristocratic; they were not like the Federalists of old. Still, their dream of a national, commercial republic resembled Franklin's and Hamilton's more than Jefferson's. They looked to profit from speculation in land, from the increasing market for cotton, from the new methods of industrial manufacturing. If they represented the rising generation, what would be the fate of Crèvecoeur's semisubsistence farm communities? The answer was not yet clear.

In one of those remarkable coincidences that Americans hailed as a sign of Providence's favor, Thomas Jefferson and John Adams died within hours of each other on July 4, 1826, the fiftieth anniversary of the adoption of the Declaration of Independence. The lives of these two giants of the Revolution—Jefferson, the ever-hopeful, self-styled Revolutionary Virginia gentleman, and Adams, the prickly, independent Federalist of Braintree—intertwined with one another in the fabric of the nation's development. Partners in the struggle to secure American independence, these Revolutionary colleagues had become bitter foes in the heated party battles of the 1790s and resumed a warm friendship only after they had retired from public life. Their reconciliation was in tune with the surge of American nationalism, but their time was past. Leadership belonged now to a new generation of Americans, who confronted different problems and challenges. Revolutionary America had passed from the scene. The dawn of a new nation was at hand.

chapter summary

As president, Thomas Jefferson increasingly abandoned his earlier ideals in favor of nationalism, a trend that continued under his successors, James Madison and James Monroe.

- Before becoming president, Jefferson advocated the principles of agrarianism, limited government, and strict construction of the Constitution.

- Once in power, however, he failed to dismantle Hamilton's economic program and promoted western expansion by acquiring Louisiana from France despite his constitutional principles.

- The growth of nationalism was also reflected as the judiciary emerged as an equal branch of government.

  - Chief Justice John Marshall proclaimed that the courts were to interpret the meaning of the Constitution (judicial review).

- Many northern Indian tribes rallied to a religious movement led by the Shawnee prophet Tenskwatawa, which aimed to revive traditional Indian cultures.

  - The Prophet's brother Tecumseh advocated a political and military confederacy to protect Indians' lands, but a number of important tribes refused to support him.

  - Tecumseh's movement collapsed with his death during the War of 1812.

- France and Britain both interfered with neutral rights, and the United States went to war against Britain in 1812.

- In the years after 1815 there was a surge in American nationalism.

  - The Transcontinental Treaty with Spain (1819) foreshadowed American expansion by drawing a boundary line to the Pacific.

  - The Monroe Doctrine (1823) barred European intervention in the Western Hemisphere.

  - Britain's recognition of American sovereignty after 1815 ended the threat of foreign interference in America's internal affairs.

  - But the Missouri crisis was an early indication of growing sectional rivalries.

interactive learning

The Primary Source Investigator CD-ROM offers the following materials related to this chapter:

- Interactive maps: **Indian Expulsion, 1800–1890** (M8); **Exploration of America's Far West, 1803–1807** (M9); and **The War of 1812** (M10)

- A collection of primary sources investigating the early national period: paintings depicting the War of 1812, "Mad Tom" (Jefferson) in a rage, and the resolutions of the secessionist Hartford Convention. Other sources include the Barbary treaties, paintings of women quilting and a country wedding, and an Iroquois Nation creation story.

additional reading

A good survey of the presidencies of Jefferson and Madison is Marshall Smelser, *The Democratic Republic* (1968). Drew R. McCoy, *The Elusive Republic* (1980), skillfully analyzes the dilemmas Jefferson and Madison confronted in power. An important study of the Federalist party is David Hackett Fischer, *The Revolution of American Conservatism* (1965). For the origins of the War of 1812, see Roger H. Brown, *The Republic in Peril* (1964). The biographies of Jefferson and Madison, listed in the Bibliography, examine political developments in this period in detail.

Malcolm J. Rohrbough, *The Trans-Appalachian Frontier* (1978), traces the process of western settlement, while other aspects of western society are treated in John Boles, *The Great Revival in the South* (1972); and R. David Edmunds, *The Shawnee Prophet* (1983). Donald Jackson, *Thomas Jefferson and the Stony Mountains: Exploring the West from Monticello* (1979), is a fascinating analysis of western exploration in this period. The journals of the Lewis and Clark expedition, which have been published in several editions, are invaluable; a recent history is Stephen E. Ambrose, *Undaunted Courage* (1996).

The first part of George Dangerfield, *The Awakening of American Nationalism* (1965), capably covers Monroe's administration. Samuel F. Bemis traces American foreign policy during and after the war in *John Quincy Adams and the Foundations of American Foreign Policy* (1949). Ernest R. May, *The Making of the Monroe Doctrine* (1976), is the best study of the subject. For a fuller list of readings, see the Bibliography at www.mhhe.com/davidsonnation5.

significant events

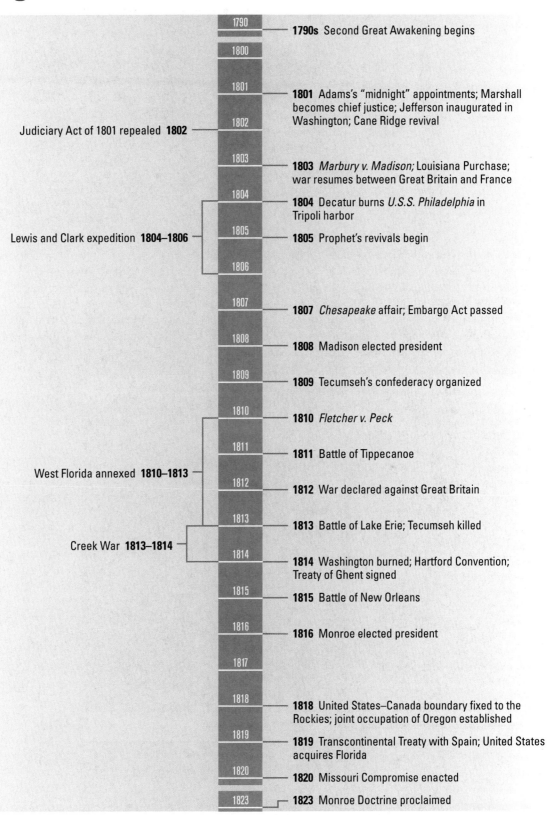

Year	Event
1790	**1790s** Second Great Awakening begins
1800	
1801	**1801** Adams's "midnight" appointments; Marshall becomes chief justice; Jefferson inaugurated in Washington; Cane Ridge revival
1802	Judiciary Act of 1801 repealed **1802**
1803	**1803** *Marbury v. Madison;* Louisiana Purchase; war resumes between Great Britain and France
1804	**1804** Decatur burns *U.S.S. Philadelphia* in Tripoli harbor
1805	Lewis and Clark expedition **1804–1806** · **1805** Prophet's revivals begin
1806	
1807	**1807** *Chesapeake* affair; Embargo Act passed
1808	**1808** Madison elected president
1809	**1809** Tecumseh's confederacy organized
1810	**1810** *Fletcher v. Peck*
1811	West Florida annexed **1810–1813** · **1811** Battle of Tippecanoe
1812	**1812** War declared against Great Britain
1813	**1813** Battle of Lake Erie; Tecumseh killed
1814	Creek War **1813–1814** · **1814** Washington burned; Hartford Convention; Treaty of Ghent signed
1815	**1815** Battle of New Orleans
1816	**1816** Monroe elected president
1817	
1818	**1818** United States–Canada boundary fixed to the Rockies; joint occupation of Oregon established
1819	**1819** Transcontinental Treaty with Spain; United States acquires Florida
1820	**1820** Missouri Compromise enacted
1823	**1823** Monroe Doctrine proclaimed

287

AFTER THE FACT
Historians Reconstruct the Past

Sally Hemings and Thomas Jefferson

The rumors began in Albemarle County, Virginia, more than two hundred years ago; they came to the notice of a journalist by the name of James Callender. A writer for hire, Callender had once lent his pen to the Republicans, but turned from friend into foe when the party failed to reward him with a political appointment. When his story splashed onto the pages of the *Recorder*, a Richmond newspaper, the trickle of rumor turned into a torrent of scandal. Callender alleged that Thomas Jefferson, during his years in Paris as the American minister, had contracted a liaison with one of his own slaves. The woman was the president's mistress even now, he insisted, in 1802. She was kept at

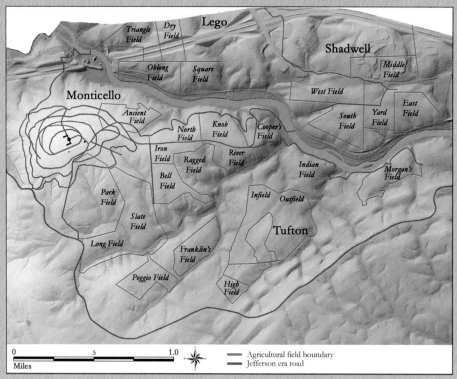

Jefferson owned 5000 acres of land in Albemarle County, Virginia, his "home farm" of Monticello and three "quarter farms"—Lego, Tufton, and Shadwell. Sally Hemings and her children lived at the Monticello plantation.

Monticello, and Jefferson had fathered children with her. Her name was Sally Hemings.

Solid information about Sally Hemings is scarce. She was one of six children, we know, born to Betty Hemings and her white master, John Wayles, a Virginia planter whose white daughter, Martha Wayles Skelton, married Jefferson in 1772. We know that Betty Hemings was the child of an African woman and an English sailor, which means Betty's children with Wayles, Sally among them, were quadroons—light-skinned men and women whose ancestry was one-quarter African. We know that Sally accompanied one of Jefferson's daughters to Paris as her maid in 1787 and that, upon returning to Virginia a few years later, she performed domestic work at Monticello. We know that she had six children and that the four who survived to adulthood escaped from slavery into freedom: Jefferson assisted her two eldest children, Beverly and Harriet, in leaving Monticello in 1822, and her two younger children, Madison and Eston, were freed by Jefferson's will in 1827. We know that shortly after Jefferson's death, his daughter, Martha Jefferson Randolph, freed Sally Hemings and that she lived with her two younger sons in Charlottesville until her own death in 1835.

We know, too, that Jefferson's white descendants stoutly denied (and, to this day, some still deny) any familial connection with the descendants of Sally Hemings. Even though Callender's scandal

This view of Monticello was painted shortly after Jefferson's death. It portrays his white descendants surrounded by a serene landscape.

quickly subsided, doing Jefferson no lasting political damage, his white grandchildren were still explaining away the accusations half a century later. In the 1850s, Jefferson's granddaughter, Ellen Coolidge Randolph, claimed that her brother, Thomas Jefferson Randolph, had told her that one of Jefferson's nephews, Samuel Carr, fathered Hemings's children. In the 1860s, Henry Randall, an early biographer of Jefferson, recalled a conversation with Thomas Jefferson Randolph in the 1850s in which he attributed paternity to another nephew, Samuel's brother Peter Carr.

Until the end of the twentieth century, most scholars resolved the discrepancy of this dual claim by suggesting that one of the Carr nephews had fathered Sally Hemings's children. And all of Jefferson's most eminent twentieth-century biographers—Douglass Adair, Dumas Malone, John Chester Miller, and Joseph J. Ellis—contended that a man of Jefferson's character and convictions could not have engaged in a liaison with a slave woman. After all, Jefferson was a Virginia gentleman and an American philosophe who believed that reason should rule over passion; he was also an eloquent apostle of equality and democracy and an outspoken critic of the tyrannical power of masters over slaves. And despite his opposition to slavery, Jefferson argued in his *Notes on the State of Virginia* (1785) for the likelihood that peoples of African descent were inferior intellectually and artistically to those of European descent. Because of that conviction, he warned of the dire consequences that would attend the mixing of the races.

The official version of events did not go unchallenged. Madison Hemings, a skilled carpenter who, a year after his mother's death, moved from Virginia to southern Ohio, publicly related an oral tradition repeated among his family. When interviewed by a Pike County, Ohio, newspaper in 1873, Madison reported that his mother had been Thomas Jefferson's "concubine" and that Jefferson had fathered all of her children. Even so, nearly a century passed before Madison Hemings's claims won wider attention. In 1968, the historian Winthrop Jordan noted that Sally Hemings's pregnancies coincided with Jefferson's stays at Monticello. In 1975, Fawn Brodie's best-selling "intimate history" of Jefferson portrayed his relationship with Sally Hemings as an enduring love affair; four years later, the African American novelist Barbara Chase-Rimboud set Brodie's findings to fiction.

An even more powerful case for Jefferson's paternity of all of Hemings's children was made in 1997 by Annette Gordon-Reed, an African American scholar. Gordon-Reed drew on her legal training to subject the handling of the evidence by Jefferson's biographers to a close and telling cross-examination. While they had dismissed Madison Hemings's recollections as mere family lore and wishful thinking, Gordon-Reed argued that such oral testimony was, in fact, no more or less reliable than the oral testimony of Jefferson's white Randolph descendants.

One year later, Gordon-Reed's arguments crested on a tidal wave of new revelations: A team of DNA research scientists headed by Eugene A. Foster discovered an exact match on the Y-chromosome markers between Thomas Jefferson's line and the descendants of Eston Hemings. (Eston was Sally's youngest child and the only one who left male-line descendants whose DNA could be tested.) Since the chance of such a match occurring randomly was less than one in a thousand, the DNA evidence made it highly probable that Thomas Jefferson fathered at least one of Sally Hemings's children. In addition, Foster's team found no DNA match between the Hemings line and the Carr family, thus discrediting the assertions of Jefferson's white descendants. Intrigued by these findings, the historian Fraser D. Neiman undertook a sophisticated statistical analysis of Hemings's conceptions and Jefferson's returns to Monticello (where he spent about half his time), which established a 99 percent probability that he had fathered all of Hemings's children.

Taken together, this new evidence has persuaded most historians that Thomas Jefferson conducted a monogamous liaison with Sally Hemings over thirty-eight years and that their union produced at least one and most likely all six of her children. Even scholars who still question whether Jefferson fathered all of Hemings's children now agree that the burden of proof has decisively shifted to those who doubt his paternity. As a result, the debate among historians has moved on to explore questions left unresolved by the new scientific findings.

One such question bears on how historians should assess the credibility of their sources. Specifically, how reliable are the oral traditions passed down through families? Both the DNA and statistical evidence bear out Madison Hemings's recollections. Surely that outcome, as Annette Gordon-Reed has urged, should prompt future historians to scrutinize the oral testimony of white masters like the Jeffersons and the Randolphs as closely as they do the narratives of slaves and the oral traditions of their descendants. But does it follow that historians should regard the recollections of nonliterate peoples as possessing a superior claim to being accurate recoveries of the past? Gordon-Reed and a host of other historians warn against that conclusion, arguing that all oral testimony must be tested against the findings yielded by the documentary record and scientific research. Their caution is warranted by the fact that the DNA findings to date have failed to show a match between the Jefferson line and that of Thomas Woodson, another Monticello slave whose African American descendants have long cited their own family's oral tradition as evidence of a biological connection to Jefferson.

An equally intriguing question concerns the character of the relationship between Sally Hemings and Thomas Jefferson. Was it forced and exploitative or

The names of Sally Hemings and her sons appear on this list of Thomas Jefferson's slaves.

This bell once belonged to Martha Wayles Jefferson, the wife of Thomas Jefferson. According to Hemings family tradition, she gave the bell to Sally Hemings, who was her half-sister.

consensual and even affectionate? On the one hand, the long duration of their liaison suggests that it may have been based on a shared emotional intimacy. (If Jefferson fathered all of Hemings's children, their involvement began in Paris during the late 1780s and endured at least until the birth of Eston Hemings in 1808.) As Annette Gordon-Reed points out, even stronger support for this interpretation is that Sally Hemings and all of her children were the only nuclear slave family at Monticello who finally attained their freedom. Furthermore, biographers have never doubted Jefferson's affection for his first wife, Martha Wayles Skelton, before she died in 1782. Is it not likely that Jefferson felt similarly toward Sally, who was in fact Martha's unacknowledged half-sister?

On the other hand, the sexual exploitation of black women was common among white masters in the Chesapeake, the Carolinas, and the Caribbean. Like them, Jefferson may have availed himself of the privileges of ownership to compel sexual favors over many years from a slave whom he fancied. Or perhaps Sally Hemings submitted to Jefferson's sexual demands because she hoped to win better treatment—and, in the end, freedom—for herself and her children. Many bondswomen (among them, perhaps, Sally's mother, Betty Hemings, and her grandmother) used that strategy to protect their children from the ravages of slavery. What lends added support to either of those interpretations is the testimony of Madison Hemings, who recalled that while Jefferson was affectionate with his white Randolph grandchildren, he was "not in the habit of showing partiality or fatherly affection" to his children with Sally Hemings.

In the last analysis, the significance of Sally Hemings's relationship with Thomas Jefferson may reside in its power to reveal the complexity of southern plantation societies between the American Revolution and the Civil War. In that place and time, the American South was not starkly divided into whites and blacks; instead it was a culture in which the races had been mingling for generations, yielding

This painting was discovered on the reverse side of a portrait of a Virginia gentleman. Experts believe that it dates from the early national period and the artist, still unknown, evidently shared Jefferson's criticisms of slavery.

many people of mixed ancestry like Sally Hemings. Israel Jefferson, who passed part of his life in slavery at Monticello, remembered her as being "mighty near white," with "long straight hair down her back." Because of their shared bonds of blood, such light-skinned slaves sometimes enjoyed greater privileges and freedoms from their masters, but they also had to negotiate more complicated relationships with them and with less favored members of the slave community.

BIBLIOGRAPHY The best study of the Jefferson-Hemings controversy that predates the DNA discoveries in 1998 is Scot A. French and Edward L. Ayers, "The Strange Career of Thomas Jefferson," in *Jeffersonian Legacies*, ed. Peter S. Onuf (1993). Among those published after the DNA findings, the most informed and comprehensive are a "Forum" piece in the *William and Mary Quarterly*, 57 (2000), entitled "Thomas Jefferson and Sally Hemings Redux" (which includes Fraser D. Neiman's important statistical study); and an anthology of essays edited by Jan Lewis and Peter S. Onuf, *Sally Hemings and Thomas Jefferson* (1999). Readers who wish to pursue the subject in more depth should consult Fawn Brodie's provocative biography, *Thomas Jefferson: An Intimate History* (1974); Annette Gordon-Reed's pathbreaking challenge to the existing scholarship, *Thomas Jefferson and Sally Hemings* (1997); and the November 5, 1998, issue of *Nature*, the British scientific journal in which Eugene A. Foster and his research team first published their DNA findings. Equally intriguing are the ways in which fiction writers and filmmakers have depicted the liaison between Jefferson and Hemings: the best place to begin is with Barbara Chase-Rimboud's novel, *Sally Hemings* (1979), and the Merchant-Ivory film of 1995, *Jefferson in Paris*—the cinematography is gorgeous, the dialogue is sensitive and intelligent, and the actress Thandie Newton shines as Sally Hemings.

THE REPUBLIC TRANSFORMED AND TESTED

Two remarkable transformations began sweeping the world in the late eighteenth century. So wrenching and far-reaching were these changes that both have been called revolutions. The first was a cascade of political revolts that led to increased democratic participation in the governing of many nation-states. The other was the application of machine labor and technological innovation to agricultural and commercial economies, known as the industrial revolution.

Proclaiming the values of liberty and equality, Americans in 1776 led the way with their own democratic revolution. As we have seen, the act of revolution itself did not solve the question of how regional and economic antagonisms could be adjusted peacefully in the new nation-state. Not until the Republicans succeeded the Federalists was a tradition of peaceful political change established within the framework of the Constitution. And not until a new generation of leaders arrived on the scene during the second war for independence did a national consciousness fully bloom.

These were notable milestones, but internationally, the center of revolutionary attention had shifted in 1789 to France. There, as in America, the ideals of the Enlightenment played a part in justifying the rejection of rule by monarchy. French liberals like the marquis de Lafayette were inspired by the example of the United States. Still, the crowds

marching through the streets of Paris adopted a more radical and violent stance, reflecting the burdens on peasants and workers of the harsh feudal system as well as other social pressures. The worldwide rise in population of the previous half century had left the French capital overcrowded, underfed, and thoroughly unruly.

The French citizenry proved that much more willing to arm themselves and march on the Bastille, on the palace at Versailles, against any perceived enemies of the Revolution. The countryside, too, suffering from a series of bad harvests, rose up in protest, sometimes brutally. Paradoxically, the population pressure that had pushed matters to a crisis was relieved as the Revolution gave way to the emperor Napoleon, whose wars of conquest killed almost as many French soldiers as the natural increase of the nation's population. When Napoleon was at last defeated at the Battle of Waterloo in 1815, Louis XVIII reestablished the French monarchy.

In Latin America, however, movements of democracy and nationalism spread. Just as Great Britain had attempted to pay for its colonial defenses with additional revenue from its colonies, so the Spanish Crown raised taxes in the Americas, with predictable results. The Creole class—Spanish who had been born in America—resented the preferential treatment and administrative positions given the *peninsulares*—colonial residents born in Spain. Although the Spanish colonies lacked the tradition of representative assemblies found in North America, the writings of Jefferson and Thomas Paine circulated, as did translations of the French *Declaration of the Rights of Man*. From 1808 to

GLOBAL EVENTS

Spinning jenny invented
1765

Steam engine invented
1769

French Revolution begins
1789

France abolishes slavery
1794

| 1765 | 1769 | 1775 | 1789 | 1797 | 1801 |
| | | | WASHINGTON | ADAMS | JEFFERSON |

1765
Stamp Act Congress

1775
American Revolution begins

1794
Slave revolt in Haiti

1793
Whitney invents cotton gin

1790
First American textile mill

AMERICAN EVENTS

1821 Spain's American provinces declared their independence one by one. Democracy did not always root itself in the aftermath of these revolutions, but democratic ideology remained a powerful social catalyst.

The industrial revolution was less violent but no less dramatic in its effects. It began in Great Britain, where canals built toward the end of the eighteenth century improved the transportation network, just as they would in the United States during the 1820s and 1830s. In Britain, too, James Watt in 1769 invented an engine that harnessed the power of steam, while innovations in textile production led to the use of water and later steam power to drive mechanical looms. At about the same time, steam power, along with other innovations, made it possible for coal mining and the manufacture of iron to be accomplished on a larger scale. (The British miner shown here was drawn in 1814.)

As steam power was applied to ships and rail locomotives, the reach of commercial markets widened. Regular shipping made it possible to bring Egyptian cotton from Alexandria to factories in British Manchester and American cotton from the Arkansas Red River country to New England. Just as skilled workers such as Samuel Slater smuggled the new technology out of England to the United States, others such as William Cockerill set up factories in Europe as the capabilities of steam and industrial manufacturing spread to the continent.

In many ways the narrative of the young American republic is the story of how one nation worked out the implications of these twin revolutions, industrial and democratic. It was only after the War of 1812 that a market economy began rapidly to transform the agricultural practices of Crèvecoeur's semisubsistence America. Urban areas of the North became more diversified and industrial as young

GLOBAL EVENTS

Revolutionary movements in Europe
1830

Slavery abolished within British empire
1833

First rail line in England
1825

| 1804 | 1809 | 1817 | 1825 | 1829 | 1837 | 1841 |
| | MADISON | MONROE | ADAMS | JACKSON | VAN BUREN | HARRISON/TYLER |

1825
Erie Canal completed

1829
Mexico abolishes slavery

1834
McCormick patents
mechanical reaper

1830
Total U.S. rail mileage, 13 miles

1815–1839
Cotton trade is the major
expansive force in the
American economy

1830–1838
Indians removed from Southwest

1840
Total U.S. rail and canal
mileage, 3300 miles each

1804–1824
Wars for independence in Latin America

1833
American Anti-Slavery Society founded

AMERICAN EVENTS

women took jobs in textile mills and young men labored in flour mills processing grain to be shipped east. The impact of industry on the North is probably clear enough in the popular imagination.

What is sometimes less appreciated is how the industrial revolution transformed the rural South. Cotton would never have become king there without the demand for it created by textile factories or without the ability to "gin" the seeds out of cotton by Eli Whitney's invention. (The "gin" in *cotton gin* is a clipped southern pronunciation of the word "engine.") Nor could cotton production have flourished without industrial advances in transportation, which allowed raw materials and factory goods to be shipped worldwide.

As the industrial and democratic revolutions developed side by side, the United States had to resolve the conflicts that the two presented each other. On the one hand, the advances in industry and commerce made it possible for resourceful entrepreneurs to reap profits on a scale that Americans of Crèvecoeur's day could never have imagined. They also created a labor force more impoverished than most Americans had been. In the North, factory workers found the conditions of labor increasingly harsh as the century progressed. In the South, the institution of slavery became even more economically entrenched because of the profits to be made using slave labor to raise cotton. The industrial revolution, in other words, made possible a society in which Americans could

become both richer and poorer than they had ever been before—a society more stratified and more unequal. On the other hand, the democratic revolution spreading across America was calling for greater equality among all citizens. This potential contradiction was one Americans wrestled with throughout the era.

The industrial revolution thus transformed both the North and the South—but in conflicting ways. Although the economies of the two regions depended on one another, slavery came increasingly to be the focus of disputes between them. The industrial revolution's demand for cotton increased both southern profits and the demand for slave labor. Yet the spread of democratic ideology worldwide was creating increased pressure to abolish

PART THREE

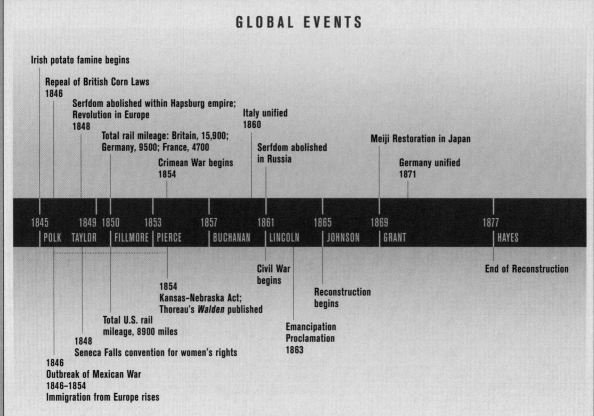

GLOBAL EVENTS

Irish potato famine begins

Repeal of British Corn Laws
1846

Serfdom abolished within Hapsburg empire;
Revolution in Europe
1848

Total rail mileage: Britain, 15,900;
Germany, 9500; France, 4700

Crimean War begins
1854

Italy unified
1860

Serfdom abolished
in Russia

Meiji Restoration in Japan

Germany unified
1871

| 1845 | 1849 | 1850 | 1853 | 1857 | 1861 | 1865 | 1869 | 1877 |
| POLK | TAYLOR | FILLMORE | PIERCE | BUCHANAN | LINCOLN | JOHNSON | GRANT | HAYES |

Civil War
begins

End of Reconstruction

Reconstruction
begins

1854
Kansas–Nebraska Act;
Thoreau's *Walden* published

Total U.S. rail
mileage, 8900 miles

Emancipation
Proclamation
1863

1848
Seneca Falls convention for women's rights

1846
Outbreak of Mexican War
1846–1854
Immigration from Europe rises

AMERICAN EVENTS

slavery everywhere. In France the revolutionary government struck it down in 1794. The British empire outlawed it in 1833, about the time that American abolitionists, influenced by their British friends, became more active in opposing it. In eastern Europe the near slavery of feudal serfdom was being eliminated as well: in 1848 within the Hapsburg em-pire; in 1861 in Russia; in 1864 in Romania.

If the purpose of a democratic republic is to resolve conflicts among its members in a nonviolent manner, then in 1861 the American republic failed. It took four years of bitter fighting to reconcile the twin paths of democracy and industrial development. Given the massive size of the territory involved and the depth of sectional divisions, it is perhaps not surprising that a union so diverse did not hold without the force of arms. That the separation was not final—that, in the end, reunion emerged out of conflict—is perhaps one reason why the tale is so gripping.

Chapter 10

I n the years before the Civil War, the name of Chauncey Jerome could be found traced in neat, sharp letters in a thousand different places across the globe: everywhere from the fireplace mantels of southern planters to the log cabins of Illinois prairie farmers and even in Chinese trading houses in Canton. Chauncey Jerome was a New England clockmaker whose clever, inexpensive, and addictive machines had conquered the markets of the world.

Jerome, the son of a Connecticut blacksmith, had apprenticed himself to a carpenter during his boyhood, but after serving in the War of 1812 he decided to try his luck as a clockmaker. For several years he eked out a living peddling his products from farmhouse to farmhouse. Then in 1824 his career took off thanks to a "very showy" bronze looking-glass clock. The new model he had designed sold as fast as the clocks could be manufactured. Between 1827 and 1837 Jerome's factory produced more clocks than any other in the country. But when the Panic of 1837 struck, Jerome had to scramble to avoid financial ruin.

The Opening of America

1815–1850

preview • In the quarter century after 1815 a market revolution transformed the United States into a boom-and-bust, geographically mobile society defined above all by materialism and wealth. New transportation networks encouraged entrepreneurs to sell to wider markets. Factories appeared, first in the textile industry, employing young women from rural families. As factory discipline structured time in more precise and demanding ways, workers protested by forming labor unions.

Looking for a new opportunity, he set out to produce an inexpensive brass "one-day" clock—so called because its winding mechanism kept it running that long. Traditionally, the works of these clocks were made of wood, and the wheels and teeth had to be painstakingly cut by hand. Furthermore, wooden clocks could not be exported overseas because the humidity on board ship swelled the wood and ruined them. Jerome's brass version proved more accurate than earlier types and cheaper to boot. Costs came down further when he began to use interchangeable parts and combined his operations for making cases and movements within a single factory in New Haven, Connecticut. By systematically organizing the production process, Jerome brought the price of a good clock within the reach of ordinary people. So popular were the new models that desperate competitors began attaching Jerome labels to their own inferior imitations.

Disaster struck again in 1855, when Jerome went into partnership with several unreliable associates. Within a few years his business faltered, then failed. At the age of 62, the once-prominent business leader found himself working again in a clock factory as an ordinary mechanic. He lived his last years in poverty.

Jerome rose higher than most Americans of his generation, and he fell further. Yet his fellow citizens shared his dreams of success, just as they were haunted by the fear of losing everything. For Jerome, it wasn't only material comforts that vanished; so did respect. "One of the most trying things to me now," he confessed in his autobiography, "is to see how I am looked upon by the community since I lost my property. I never was any better when I owned it than I am now, and never behaved any better. But how different is the feeling towards you, when your neighbors can make nothing more out of you. . . . You are passed by without notice."

Chauncey Jerome's life spanned the transition from the master-apprentice system of production to the beginnings of mechanization and the rise of the factory system. Crèvecoeur's vision of independent American farmers living mainly on what they themselves produced had, by 1850, become a dream of the past. In its place stood a commercial republic in which a full-blown national market drew together most settled areas of the country.

The concept of the market is crucial here. Americans tied themselves to one another eagerly, even aggressively, through the mechanism of the free market. They sold cotton or wheat and bought manufactured cloth or brass one-day clocks. They borrowed money not merely to buy a house or farm but also to speculate and profit. They relied, even in many rural villages, on cash and paper money instead of bartering for goods and services. American life moved from less to more specialized forms of labor. It moved from face-to-face local dealings to impersonal, distant transactions. It shifted from the mechanically sim-

Chauncey Jerome's brass clock revolutionized clock-making and made him wealthy. The label displaying Jerome's name, the equivalent of a modern trademark, is visible inside the case.

ple to the technologically complex and from less dense patterns of settlement on farms to more complex arrangements in cities and towns. Such were the changes Chauncey Jerome witnessed—indeed, changes he helped to bring about himself, with his clocks that divided the working days of Americans into more disciplined, orderly segments.

As these changes occurred about him, Jerome sensed that society had taken on a different tone—that the marketplace and its ethos had become dominant. "It is all money and business, business and money which make the man now-a-days," he complained. "Success is every thing, and it makes very little difference how, or what means he uses to obtain it." The United States, according to one foreign traveler, had become "one gigantic workshop, over the entrance of which there is the blazing inscription 'No admission here except on business.'"

The Market Revolution

In 1844 John Burrows heard that potatoes were selling for $2.00 a bushel in New Orleans. Potatoes fetched less than 50 cents a bushel in Davenport in the Iowa Territory where Burrows was a small merchant, so he loaded 2500 bushels on a flatboat and started down the Mississippi River. Along the way, he learned that other merchants, acting on the same information, had done the same and that the market in New Orleans was now glutted with potatoes. When he reached his destination 6 weeks later, he could not sell his load at all. Desperate, he finally swapped his potatoes at 8 cents a bushel, taking a load of coffee in return. He made nothing on the transaction, since it had cost him that much to ship the load to New Orleans.

Burrows's experience demonstrated that a national market economy required not just the efficient movement of goods but also rapid communications. Looking back many years later on the amazing transformation that had occurred in his lifetime, Burrows commented, "No one can realize the difficulties of doing a produce business in those days."

A truly national system of markets began to grow following the War of 1812, when the United States entered a period of unprecedented economic expansion. As it grew, the economy became varied enough to sustain and even accelerate its growth. Before the war it had been tied largely to international trade. The United States exported staples like cotton, wheat, tobacco, and timber; if the nations that bought these commodities suddenly stopped doing so, the domestic economy suffered. That happened during the European wars of the 1790s and again after 1803. Because so many Americans remained rural and primarily self-sufficient, they could not absorb any increase in goods produced by American manufacturers.

Growth of a domestic market

But the War of 1812 marked the turning point in the creation and expansion of a domestic market. First the embargo and then the war itself stimulated the growth of manufacturing, particularly in textiles. In 1808 the United States had 8000 spindles spinning cotton thread; by the end of the war the number had jumped to around 130,000. In addition, war had also bottled up capital in Europe. When peace was restored, this capital flowed into the United States, seeking investments. Finally, the war experience led the federal government to adopt policies designed to spur economic expansion.

The New Nationalism

After the war with Britain, leadership passed to a new generation of the Republic—younger men like Henry Clay, John C. Calhoun, and John Quincy Adams. All were ardent nationalists eager to use federal power to promote rapid development of the nation. Increasingly dominant within the Republican party, they advocated the "New Nationalism," a set of economic policies designed to foster the prosperity of all regions of the country and bind the nation more tightly together.

National bank

Even James Madison saw the need for increased federal activity, given the problems the government experienced during the war. The national bank had closed its doors in 1811 when its charter expired. Without it the country had fallen into financial chaos. Madison had opposed Hamilton's national bank in 1791, but now with his approval, Congress in 1816 chartered the Second Bank of the United States for a period of 20 years. Madison also agreed to a mildly protective tariff to aid budding American industries by raising the price of competing foreign goods.

Protective tariff

Passed in 1816, it set an average duty of 20 percent on imported woolen and cotton cloth, iron, and sugar. The measure enjoyed wide support in the North and West, but a number of southern representatives voted against it because most of its benefits went to northern manufacturers.

Madison also recommended that the government promote internal improvements such as roads, canals, and bridges. The war had demonstrated how cumbersome it was to move troops or supplies overland. Although Madison did not believe that federal funds could be used for merely local projects, he was willing to support projects broader in scope. His successor, James Monroe, approved additional ones.

The Cotton Trade

Cotton proved to be the key to American economic development after 1815. By the end of the eighteenth century, southern planters had discovered that short-fiber cotton would grow in the lower part of the South. But the cotton contained sticky green seeds that could not be easily separated from the lint by hand. The needed breakthrough came in 1793 when Eli Whitney invented the cotton gin, a mechanical device that removed the seeds from the lint. The gin allowed a laborer to clean 50 pounds of cotton a day, compared with only 1 pound by hand. With prices high on the world market, cotton production in the Lower South soared. By 1840 the South produced more than 60 percent of the world supply, which accounted for almost two-thirds of all American exports.

Whitney's cotton gin

The cotton trade was the major expansive force in the economy until the depression of 1839. Northern factories increasingly made money by turning raw cotton into cloth, while northern merchants reaped profits from shipping the cotton and then reshipping the textiles. Planters used the income they earned to purchase foodstuffs from the West and goods and services from the Northeast.

The Transportation Revolution

To become truly national, a market economy needed an efficient transportation network linking various regions of the nation. The economy had not become self-sustaining earlier partly because the only means of transporting goods cheaply was by water. Thus trade was limited largely to coastal and international markets, for even on rivers, bulky goods moved easily in only one direction—downstream.

All that changed, however, after 1815. From 1825 to 1855—the span of a single generation—the cost of transportation on land fell 95 percent while its speed increased fivefold. As a result, new regions were drawn quickly into the market.

The Canal Age

Canals attracted considerable investment capital, especially after the success of the wondrous Erie Canal. Built between 1818 and 1825, the canal stretched 364 miles from Albany on the Hudson River to Buffalo on Lake Erie. Its construction by the state was an act of faith, for in 1816 the United States had only 100 miles of canals, none longer than 28 miles. Then, too, the proposed route ran through forests, disease-ridden swamps, and unsettled wilderness. The canal's engineers lacked experience, but they made up for that by sheer ingenuity. Improving on European tools, they devised a cable and screw that allowed one man to pull down even the largest trees and a stump-puller that removed up to 40 stumps a day.

Erie Canal

The project paid for itself within a few years. The Erie Canal reduced the cost of shipping a ton of goods from Buffalo to New York City from more than 19 cents a mile to less than 3 cents a mile. By 1860 the cost had fallen to less than a penny a mile. Where its busy traffic passed, settlers flocked, and towns like Rochester and Lockport sprang up and thrived by moving goods and serving markets. "Everything in this bustling place appears to be in motion," wrote one English traveler about Rochester in 1827. The steady flow of goods eastward gave New York City the dominant position in the scramble for control of western trade.

New York's commercial rivals, like Philadelphia and Baltimore, were soon frantically trying to build their own canals to the West. Western states like Ohio and Indiana, convinced that prosperity depended on cheap transportation, constructed canals to link interior regions with the Great Lakes. By 1840 the nation had completed more than 3300 miles of canals—a length greater than the distance from New York City to Seattle—at a cost of about $125 million. Almost half of that amount came from state governments.

The Erie Canal promoted urban growth, economic development, and feverish activity along its route. Here boaters guiding their craft past busy laborers on the shore provide an indication of the commerce that quickly flourished on the waterway.

End of canal era

By 1850 the canal era was over. The depression of 1839 caused several states to halt or slow their construction, especially since many poorly planned canals lost money. Still, whether profitable or not, canals sharply reduced transportation costs and stimulated economic development in a broad belt along their routes.

Steamboats and Railroads

Because of its vast expanse, the United States was particularly dependent on river transportation. But shipping goods downstream from Pittsburgh to New Orleans took 6 weeks, and the return journey required 17 weeks or more. Steamboats reduced the time of a trip from New Orleans to Louisville from 90 to 8 days while cutting upstream costs by 90 percent.

Western steamboats

Robert Fulton demonstrated the commercial possibilities of propelling a boat with steam when his ship, the *Clermont,* traveled in 1807 from New York City to Albany on the Hudson River. But steamboats had the greatest effect on transportation on western rivers, where the flat-bottomed boats could haul heavy loads even when the water level was low. The number of steamboats operating in those waters jumped from 17 in 1817 to 727 in 1855. Since steamboats could make many more voyages annually, the carrying capacity on the western rivers increased 100-fold between 1820 and 1860.

Governments did not invest heavily in steamboats as they had in canals; instead their main assistance was removing fallen trees and other obstacles to navigation. Although railroads would end the steamboat's dominance by 1860, it was the major form of western transportation during the years in which the national market economy grew up, and it proved the most important factor in the rise of manufacturing in the Ohio and upper Mississippi valleys.

Railroads' later influence

In 1830 the nation had only 13 miles of railroad track, and most of the lines constructed in the following decade served as feeder lines to canals. But soon enough, cities and towns saw that their economic future depended on having good rail links, so that by 1840 railroad and canal mileage were almost exactly equal (3325 miles). By 1850, the nation had a total of 8879 miles of track. Railroad rates were usually higher than canal or steamboat charges, but the new iron roads operated year-round, offered more direct routes, and moved goods about twice as fast. Even so, not until the 1850s did they come to dominate the transportation system.

Agriculture in the Market Economy

The new forms of transportation had a remarkable effect on Crèvecoeur's yeoman farm families: they became linked ever more tightly to a national market system. Before the canal era, wheat could be shipped at a profit no farther than 50 miles. But given cheap transportation, farmers eagerly grew more grain and sold the surplus in distant markets.

In this shift toward commercial agriculture, farmers began cultivating more acres, working longer hours, and adopting scientific farming methods, including crop rotation and the use of manures as fertilizer. Instead of bartering goods with friends and neighbors, they more often paid cash or depended on banks to extend them credit. Instead of taking the crops to market themselves, they began to rely on regional merchants, intermediaries in a far-flung distribution system. Like southern planters, western wheat farmers increasingly sold in a world market. Banks and distributors advanced credit to farmers, who more and more competed in a market controlled by impersonal forces centered in distant locations.

As transportation and market networks connected more areas of the nation, they encouraged regional specialization. The South increasingly concentrated on staple crops for export, and the West grew foodstuffs, particularly grain. By 1850, Wisconsin and Illinois were major wheat-producing states. Eastern farmers,

Commercial agriculture

1800 TRAVEL TIMES

1830 TRAVEL TIMES

Travel Times, 1800 and 1830

unable to compete with wheat yields from fertile western farms, shifted to grazing sheep or producing fruits, vegetables, and dairy products for rapidly growing urban areas.

Although foreign commerce expanded too, it was overshadowed by the dramatic growth in domestic markets, which absorbed more and more of the goods and services being produced. The cities of the East no longer looked primarily to the sea for their trade; they looked to southern and western markets. That, indeed, was a revolution in markets.

John Marshall and the Promotion of Enterprise

For a national market system to flourish, a climate favorable to investment had to exist. Under the leadership of Chief Justice John Marshall the Supreme Court became the branch of the federal government most aggressive in protecting the new forms of business central to the growing market economy.

Marshall, who presided over the Court from 1801 to 1835, at first glance seemed an unlikely leader. Informal in manners and almost sloppy in dress, he was nonetheless a commanding figure: tall and slender, with twinkling eyes and a contagious, hearty laugh. His forceful intellect was reinforced by his genial ability to persuade. Time after time he convinced his colleagues to uphold the sanctity of private property and the power of the federal government to promote economic growth.

Constitutionality of the national bank

In the case of *McCulloch v. Maryland* (1819) the Court upheld the constitutionality of the Second Bank of the United States. Maryland had levied a tax on the Baltimore branch of the national bank, which the bank refused to pay, and the case went to the Supreme Court. The Court struck down the tax. Just as Alexander Hamilton had argued in the debate over the first national bank, Marshall emphasized that the Constitution gave Congress the power to make all "necessary and proper" laws to carry out its delegated powers. If Congress believed that a bank would help it meet its responsibilities, such as maintaining the public credit and regulating the currency, then it was constitutional. The bank only had to be useful, not essential. "Let the end be legitimate," Marshall wrote, "let it be within the scope of the Constitution, and all means which are appropriate, which are plainly adapted to that end, which are not prohibited . . . are constitutional." By upholding Hamilton's doctrine of implied powers, Marshall enlarged federal power to an extraordinary degree.

Interstate commerce

He also encouraged a more freewheeling commerce in *Gibbons v. Ogden* (1824). Under a New York law Aaron Ogden held a monopoly on steamboat traffic on the Hudson River between New Jersey and New York City. Thomas Gibbons, who had a federal license to operate a steamboat, set up a competing line and Ogden sued. The case gave Marshall a chance to define the greatest power of the federal government in peacetime, the right to regulate interstate commerce. In striking down a steamboat monopoly granted by the state of New York, the chief justice gave the term *commerce* the broadest possible definition, declaring that it covered all commercial dealings and that Congress's power over interstate commerce could be "exercised to its utmost extent." The result was increased business competition throughout society.

Protection of contracts

At the heart of most commercial agreements were private contracts, made between individuals or companies. Marshall took an active role in defining contract law, which was then in its infancy. The case of *Fletcher v. Peck* (1810) showed

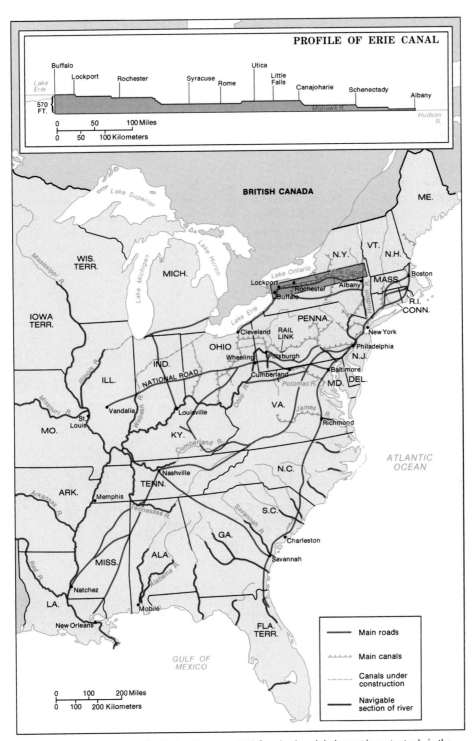

PROFILE OF ERIE CANAL

Buffalo
Lockport
Rochester
Syracuse
Rome
Utica
Little Falls
Canajoharie
Schenectady
Albany

Lake Erie
570 FT.
Mohawk R.
Hudson R.

0 50 100 Miles
0 50 100 Kilometers

BRITISH CANADA

ME.

Lake Superior
Lake Michigan
Lake Huron
Lake Ontario
Lake Erie

WIS. TERR.
MICH.
N.Y.
VT.
N.H.
MASS.
Boston
R.I.
CONN.

Mississippi R.

IOWA TERR.

Erie Canal
Lockport
Rochester
Albany
Buffalo

PENNA.
Cleveland
RAIL LINK
New York
Philadelphia
N.J.

OHIO
Wheeling
Pittsburgh

IND.
NATIONAL ROAD
Cumberland
Baltimore
MD.
DEL.

ILL.

Illinois R.
Wabash R.
Ohio R.
Potomac R.
VA.
James R.
Richmond

Missouri R.

St. Louis
Vandalia
Louisville

MO.
KY.
Cumberland R.

ATLANTIC OCEAN

N.C.

ARK.
Nashville
TENN.
Memphis
Tennessee R.
Savannah R.
S.C.

GA.
Charleston
Savannah

MISS.
ALA.
Alabama R.

Arkansas R.
Red R.
Natchez

LA.
Mobile

New Orleans
FLA. TERR.

GULF OF MEXICO

0 100 200 Miles
0 100 200 Kilometers

Main roads
Main canals
Canals under construction
Navigable section of river

The Transportation Network of a Market Economy, 1840 Canals played their most important role in the Northeast, where they linked eastern cities to western rivers and the Great Lakes. On the Erie Canal, a system of locks raised and lowered boats in a series of steps along the route. Steamboats were most crucial in the extensive river systems of the South and the West.

Daily Lives

TIME AND TRAVEL
Floating Palaces of the West

Plying the Mississippi River and its tributaries, the steamboat carried both freight and passengers, but it won its greatest fame as a mode of travel. The most luxurious boats, dubbed floating palaces, offered accommodations far beyond the experience of the average American. Steamboats also provided the cheapest form of inland transportation up to the Civil War. By midcentury, cabin passage for the 1400-mile trip from Louisville to New Orleans was only $12 to $15.

On the earliest steamboats passengers were housed on the main deck along with the cargo, but as the boats became larger, designers added a second, or boiler, deck (which, despite its name, was not where the boilers were located). Eventually a third level was added, the hurricane or texas, with additional accommodations. The boiler deck's saloon was the center of society, with the ladies' parlor at one end and the barroom at the other. Besides serving as a dining room and lounge, the saloon sometimes provided the sleeping quarters for men. Berths were arranged in two tiers on both sides and, at least on the better boats, contained bedding and a mattress. Women entered the saloon only for meals.

Steamboats also offered passage on the main deck for about one-fifth the price of a regular ticket. These passengers received no living quarters or toilet facilities and had to provide their own food. Then, too, boiler explosions, collisions, and sinkings from a snag took a much higher loss of life among lower-deck passengers, who were primarily the poor, immigrants, and African Americans. Between 1811 and 1851, 44 steamboats collided, 166 burned, 209 exploded, and 576 hit obstructions and sank, costing thousands of lives.

The steamboat was, as many travelers remarked, a "world in miniature," conveying slaves and planters, farmers and manufacturers, merchants and frontier families, soldiers and Indians, ministers and professional gamblers. As fares steadily dropped, people of widely different wealth and position were thrown together in the main cabin and mingled with democratic familiarity. Women spent

The luxurious saloon furnishings of a Mississippi steamboat, the *Princess*

how far he was willing to go to protect private property. The justices unanimously struck down a Georgia law taking back a land grant that a group of speculators had obtained by bribing members of the legislature. A grant was a contract, Marshall declared, and because the Constitution forbade states to impair "the obligation of contracts," the legislature could not interfere with the grant once it had been made. Although the framers of the Constitution probably meant *contracts* to refer only to agreements between private parties, Marshall made no distinction between public and private agreements, thereby greatly expanding the meaning of the contract clause.

their time talking, sewing, caring for children, and strolling the deck. Men passed the time in conversation about politics, the weather, business, and crops. The bar was the center of their social world, and gambling was rife.

The most famous vessels on the rivers boasted intricately carved gingerbread facings, painted a glistening white and trimmed in gold leaf—an architectural style known as "Steamboat Gothic." For all their luxurious veneer, however, steamboats lacked many amenities. Most six-by-six staterooms had two narrow shelves to sleep on and no lighting or heat. The washrooms in the main cabin contained tin basins and pitchers of cold water, a comb and brush, and a communal toothbrush. One traveler complained that there were only two towels for 70 men on one boat. Water, for both drinking and washing, came directly from the river and was laden with silt. Steamboat food was ample but often poorly prepared and saturated with grease. Furthermore, the average riverboat hardly lived up to the standards of the most famous packets. In 1843 John James Audubon journeyed from Louisville to St. Louis on what he described as "the very filthiest of all filthy old rattraps I ever traveled in." He grumbled particularly about a leaky roof, threadbare sheets, and pillows filled with corn husks.

In maintaining law and order, the captain was aided by the passengers, who in the tradition of the frontier sometimes formed their own courts to deal with those charged with minor offenses. Travelers accused of theft, illicit sexual relations, or cheating at gambling might find themselves flogged or put ashore at some desolate spot. In one case, when a young man and woman traveling together as "cousins" aroused suspicion, the passengers insisted on an investigation by the boat's officers, who discovered the pair sharing a berth. At the next stop, while the boat waited, indignant passengers marched the couple ashore, rounded up a minister, and compelled them to get married.

Despite the discomforts of swarming mosquitoes, heat from the boilers, and noisy engines at all hours of the night, observers agreed that journeying by steamboat was far more pleasant than taking a stagecoach, the principal alternative in the West before 1850. With their churning paddlewheels, gingerbread decks, and belching smokestacks, these gaudy vessels became the grandest showpieces of life along the commercial waterways of the Mississippi.

The most celebrated decision Marshall wrote on the contract clause was in *Dartmouth College v. Woodward*, decided in 1819. This case arose out of the attempt by New Hampshire to alter the college's charter granted by George III in 1769. The Court overturned the state law on the grounds that state charters were also contracts and could not be altered by later legislatures. By this ruling Marshall intended to protect corporations, which conducted business under charters granted by individual states.

Thus the Marshall Court encouraged economic risk taking. Its decisions protected property and contracts, limited state interference in business affairs, and created a climate of business confidence.

General Incorporation Laws

Importance of corporations

Corporations were not new in American business, but as the economy expanded, they grew in numbers. Corporations had the advantage of continuing beyond the lives of the individuals who created them. By pooling investors' resources, they also provided a way to raise capital for large-scale undertakings. Then, too, corporations offered the advantage of limited liability: that is, an investor was liable only for the amount he or she had invested, which limited a person's financial risk. Small and medium-sized businesses continued to be run as partnerships and individual ventures, but ventures such as banks, insurance companies, railroads, and manufacturing firms—which all required a large amount of capital—increasingly were incorporated.

Originally, state legislatures were required to approve a special charter for each new corporation. Beginning in the 1830s, states adopted general incorporation laws that automatically granted a corporation charter to any applicant who met certain minimum qualifications. This reform made it much easier and faster to secure a charter and stimulated organization of the national market.

A Restless Temper

"Eating on the first of May," commented one New York City resident, "is entirely out of the question." That day was "moving day," when all the leases in the city expired. On that date nearly everyone, it seemed, moved to a new residence or place of business. Bedlam prevailed as furniture and personal belongings cluttered the sidewalks and people, movers, and horses crowded the streets. To Frances Trollope, it looked as if the whole population was "flying from the plague." Whereas in Europe millions of ordinary folk had never ventured beyond their local village, a Boston paper commented in 1828, "here, the whole population is in motion."

A People in Motion

Between 1815 and 1850, the nation reverberated with almost explosive energy. "An American . . . wants to perform within a year what others do within a much longer period," observed Francis Lieber, a noted political scientist who emigrated from Germany. The famous French commentator Alexis de Tocqueville was astonished, like most Europeans, at the restless mobility of the average American. "Born often under another sky, placed in the middle of an always moving scene, . . . the American . . . grows accustomed only to change, and ends by regarding it as the natural state of man."

A high-speed society

This emphasis on speed affected nearly every aspect of American life. Americans ate so quickly that one disgruntled European insisted food was "pitchforked down." Steamboat captains risked boiler explosions for the honor of having the fastest boat on the river, prompting the visiting English novelist Charles Dickens to comment that traveling under these conditions was like taking up "lodgings on the first floor of a powder mill." American technology emphasized speed over longevity on the assumption that the present design would soon be obsolete. Unlike European railroads, American railroads were lightweight, were hastily constructed, and paid little heed to the safety or comfort of passengers. Even so, Americans quickly embraced this new mode of transportation because of its speed. Eighteen-year-old Caroline Fitch of Boston likened her first ride on a railroad to a

Europeans were shocked that Americans bolted their food or gorged themselves on anything within reach, as this English drawing indicates. Such habits reflected both the indifferent preparation of food and the frenetic tempo of American life.

"lightning flash": "It was 'whew!' and we were there, and 'whew!' and we were back again."

Even within railroad cars Americans were too fidgety to adapt to the European system of individual passenger compartments. Instead, American cars had a center aisle, allowing ever-restless passengers to wander the length of the train. Riding the rails in Texas, an English visitor was astounded that the passengers were "constantly jumping on and off whilst the train is in motion, and larking from one car to the other."

Horatio Greenough, a sculptor who returned to the United States in 1836 after an extended stay abroad, was amazed and a bit frightened by the pace he witnessed. "Go ahead! is the order of the day," he observed. "The whole continent presents a scene of scrambling and roars with greedy hurry." In the economic arena, the growth of a national market increased the sense of motion and restlessness. But social factors also contributed to this high-speed society.

Population Growth

The American population continued to double about every 22 years—more than twice the birthrate of Great Britain. The census, which counted fewer than 4 million Americans in 1790, surpassed 23 million in 1850. Although the birthrate peaked in 1800, it declined only slowly before 1840. During the 1840s, as urban areas grew rapidly, it dropped about 10 percent, the first significant decrease in American history. In cities, families were smaller, in part because the labor of children was not as critical to the family's economic welfare.

At the same time, many basic population characteristics changed little throughout the first half of the nineteenth century. Life expectancy did not improve significantly, the population remained quite young, and early marriage remained the norm, especially in rural areas.

From 1790 to 1820 natural increase accounted for virtually all the country's population growth. But immigration, which had been disrupted by the Napoleonic Wars in Europe, revived after 1815. In the 1830s some 600,000 immigrants arrived, more than double the number in the quarter century after 1790. And

Immigration rises after 1830

these newcomers proved to be merely a foretaste of the flood of immigrants that reached America beginning in the late 1840s.

The Federal Land Rush

The vast areas of land available for settlement absorbed much of the growing population. By 1850 almost half of all Americans lived outside the original 13 states. Well over 2 million lived beyond the Mississippi River. As settlers streamed west, speculation in western lands reached frenzied proportions. In the single year of 1818, at the peak of land-buying fever, the United States sold 3.5 million acres of its public domain. (In contrast, only 68,000 acres were sold in 1800.)

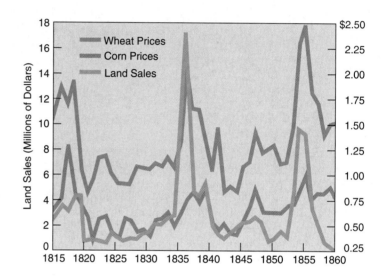

Purchase of Public Land

Year	Price per Acre	Minimum Acreage	Terms of Sale
1785	$1.00	640	Cash
1796	2.00	640	One-half cash; 1 year to pay balance
1800	2.00	320	Payment over 4 years
1804	2.00	160	Payment over 4 years
1820	1.25	80	Cash
1832	1.25	40	Cash
1841	Preemption (squatter could buy up to 160 acres at minimum price of $1.25 per acre)		
1854	Graduation (price of unsold lands reduced over time to a minimum of 12.5 cents per acre)		

Western Land Sales and the Price of Corn and Wheat Western farmers' expectations of future income were tied to the price of corn and wheat. As commodity prices rose, farmers eagerly bought land on credit, anticipating that future profits would enable them to pay off their mortgages. As the graph illustrates, when wheat and corn prices fell sharply in the Panic of 1819, land sales plummeted, and many farmers who had purchased on credit found themselves unable to pay their debts; a similar pattern is apparent in the 1830s. In the South there was a comparable relationship between land sales and the price of cotton. In order to encourage settlement, the terms to purchase public land (table, bottom) were made increasingly favorable, so that eventually a squatter could acquire the traditional 80-acre family farm on good land for only $100. Nevertheless, speculators continued to hold vast tracts of the public domain.

The Panic of 1819 sent sales and prices crashing, and in the depression that followed many farmers lost their farms. Congress reacted by abolishing credit sales and demanding payment in cash, but it tempered this policy by lowering the price of the cheapest lands to $1.25 an acre. (The best lands, sold at auction, fetched considerably higher prices, however.) The government also reduced the minimum tract to 80 acres, which meant that an ordinary farm could be purchased for $100.

Even so, speculators purchased most of the public lands sold, since the law put no limit on how many acres an individual or a land company could buy. These land speculators played a leading role in settlement of the West. To hasten sales, they usually sold land partially on credit—a vital aid to poorer farmers. They also provided loans to purchase needed tools and supplies, since the cost of establishing a farm was beyond the means of many young men. Many farmers became speculators themselves, buying up property in the neighborhood and selling it to latecomers at a tidy profit. "Speculation in real estate has been the ruling idea and occupation of the Western mind," one Englishman reported in the 1840s. "Clerks, labourers, farmers, storekeepers merely followed their callings for a living while they were speculating for their fortunes."

Speculators help settle western lands

Geographic Mobility

Given such rapid settlement, geographic mobility became one of the most striking characteristics of the American people. The 1850 census revealed that nearly half of all native-born free Americans lived outside the state where they had been born. In Boston from 1830 to 1860 perhaps one-third of the inhabitants changed their place of residence each year. Some owners, dissatisfied with their location, moved their houses instead. An astonished Charles Dickens recounted he once met a house "coming downhill at a good round trot, drawn by some twenty oxen!" The typical American "has no root in the soil," visiting Frenchman Michel Chevalier observed, but "is always in the mood to move on, always ready to start in the first steamer that comes along from the place where he had just now landed." Indeed, Americans were so mobile that Chevalier thought the national emblem should be a steamboat or locomotive.

On the road again

It was the search for opportunity, more than anything else, that accounted for such restlessness. An American moved, noted one British observer, "if by so doing he can make $10 where before he made $8." Often, the influence of the market uprooted Americans too. In 1851, a new railroad line bypassed the village of Auburn, Illinois, on the way to Springfield. "It seemed a pity," wrote one resident, "that so pretty a site as that of the old town should be abandoned for so unpromising a one . . . much of it mere swamp—but railroad corporations possess no bowels of compassion, the practical more than the beautiful being their object." After residents quickly moved to the new town that sprang up around the depot, a neighboring farmer purchased the site and plowed up the streets, and Auburn reverted to a cornfield.

Urbanization

Even with the growth of a national market, the United States remained a rural nation. Nevertheless, the four decades after 1820 witnessed the fastest rate of urbanization in American history. In 1820 there were only 12 cities with a population of more than 5000; by 1850 there were nearly 150. The 1820 census classified only about 9 percent of the American people as urban (living in towns with a population of 2500 or more). Forty years later the number had risen to 20 percent.

St. Louis, a major urban center that developed in the West, depended on the steamboat to sustain its commerce, as this 1859 illustration makes clear.

As a result, the ratio of farmers to city dwellers steadily dropped from 15 to 1 in 1800 to 5.5 to 1 in 1850. Improved transportation, the declining productivity of many eastern farms, the beginnings of industrialization, and the arrival of immigrants all stimulated the growth of cities.

Urban centers, old and new

The most heavily urbanized area of the country was the Northeast, where in 1860 more than a third of the population lived in cities.* The nation's largest city was New York, with more than half a million people, and older cities like Philadelphia, Boston, Baltimore, and New Orleans continued to be major urban centers. Equally significant, important urban centers such as St. Louis and Cincinnati arose in the West. Remarkably, by the century's midpoint, 40 percent of the nation's total urban population resided in interior cities. The South, with only 10 percent of its people living in cities, was the least urbanized region.

All these changes—the amazing growth of the population, the quickening movement westward, and the rising migration to the cities—pointed to a fundamental reorientation of American development. Expansion was the keynote of the new America, and the prospects it offered both excited and unsettled Americans.

The Rise of Factories

It was an isolated life, growing up in rural, hilly Vermont. But stories of the textile factories that had sprung up in Lowell and other towns in Massachusetts reached even small villages like Barnard. Fifteen-year-old Mary Paul was working there as a domestic servant when she asked her father for permission to move to Lowell. "I am in need of clothes which I cannot get about here," she explained. In

---

*The Northeast included New England and the mid-Atlantic states (New York, Pennsylvania, and New Jersey). The South comprised the slave states plus the District of Columbia.

1845 two friends from Barnard helped her find a job at the Lowell mills, from which she earned $128 in 11 months. After four years she returned home but now found "countryfied" life too confining. This time she left her rural hometown for good. She moved about and supported herself at several occupations before finally marrying and settling down in nearby Lynn.

Mary Paul was one of thousands of rural Americans whose lives were fundamentally altered by the economic transformation of the young republic. The changes in her lifestyle and her working habits demonstrated that the new factories and industries needed more than technological innovation to run smoothly. Equally crucial, the labor used to manufacture these goods needed to be reorganized.

Technological Advances

Before 1815 manufacturing had been done in homes or shops by skilled artisans who turned out a small number of finished goods, often made to order for local customers. As master craftworkers, they taught their trades to apprentices and journeymen. In addition, women often worked in their homes part-time under the putting-out system, making finished articles from raw material supplied by merchant capitalists. During the winter months many farm families manufactured items such as brooms and fans to supplement their income.

Small-scale manufacturing

After 1815 this older form of manufacturing began to give way to factories with machinery tended by unskilled or semiskilled laborers. Cheap transportation networks, the rise of cities, and the availability of capital and credit all stimulated the shift to factory production.

From England came many of the earliest technological innovations. But Americans often improved on the British machines or adapted them to more extensive uses. In contrast to the more traditional societies of Europe, "everything new is quickly introduced here," one visitor commented in 1820. "There is no clinging to old ways; the moment an American hears the word 'invention' he pricks up his ears." From 1790 to 1860 the United States Patent Office granted more patents than England and France combined.

Acceptance of technology

To protect their economic advantage, the British forbade the export of any textile machinery or emigration of any craftworker trained in their construction. But in 1790 a mill worker named Samuel Slater slipped past English authorities and built the first textile mill in America. Two decades later, the Boston merchant Francis Cabot Lowell imitated British designs for a power loom and then improved on them.

The first machines required highly skilled workers to both build and repair them. Eli Whitney had a better idea. Having won a contract to produce 10,000 muskets for the government, he developed machinery that would mass-produce parts that were interchangeable from one gun to another. Such parts had to be manufactured to rigid specifications that Whitney had difficulty attaining, but once the process was perfected after his death, a worker could assemble a musket quickly with only a few tools. Simeon North applied the same principle to the production of clocks, and Chauncey Jerome followed North's example and soon surpassed him.

Interchangeable parts

What rail and steam engines did for transportation, Samuel F. B. Morse's telegraph did for communications. Morse patented a device that sent electrical pulses over a wire in 1837, and before long, telegraph lines fanned out in all directions, linking various parts of the country instantaneously. By 1860 there were more than

Communication

50,000 miles of telegraph lines laid. The new telegraph sped business information, helped link the transportation network, and allowed newspapers to provide readers with up-to-date news.

Indeed, the invention of the telegraph and the perfection of a power press (1847) by Robert Hoe and his son Richard revolutionized journalism. The mechanical press sharply increased the speed with which sheets could be printed over the old hand method. Mass-produced newspapers, often selling for only a penny, gained huge circulations since ordinary families could afford them. Hoe's press had a similar impact on book publishing, as thousands of copies could be printed at affordable prices.

 ## The Postal System

The development of a national market economy depended on mass communications that transmitted commercial information and brought into contact producers and sellers separated by great distances. While postage was relatively expensive, the American postal system subsidized the distribution of newspapers and disseminated other forms of information widely. Indeed, in the years before the Civil War, the postal system had more employees than any other enterprise in the country. While the postal system's primary purpose was to promote commerce, it had a profound social impact by accustoming people to long-range and even impersonal communication. By 1840, the post office handled almost 41 million letters and 39 million newspapers.

When traveling in the United States in 1831, Tocqueville was amazed at the scope of the postal system. "There is an astonishing circulation of letters and newspapers among these savage woods," he reported from the Michigan frontier. There was hardly a village or town in the country, no matter how remote, that was not connected with the rest of the country through the postal system. Nothing in Europe, he noted, could match it. While the British and French post offices handled a greater volume of mail, the United States throughout these years had a much more extensive postal system. In 1828, there were almost twice as many post offices in the United States as in Great Britain, and over five times as many as in France.

In the Americas, the Canadian postal system was so limited that merchants and even government officials routinely used the United States postal system to get mail to other provinces, while by midcentury Mexico had only 49 post offices and no regularized service for the whole country. In China, the government maintained a very efficient military-courier system for official communications, but foreigners developed the first private postal system, mainly for business correspondence; it was not until the twentieth century that a mass-based postal system was established. Most countries had no true postal system in these years, since literacy was so limited.

Textile Factories

The factory system originated in the Northeast, where capital, water power, and transportation facilities were available. In New England, as in England, the production of cloth was the first manufacturing process to make significant use of the new technology on a large scale. Eventually all the processes of manufacturing cloth were brought together in a single location, from opening the cotton bales to weaving the cloth, and machines did virtually all the work.

In 1813 a group of wealthy Boston merchants chartered the Boston Manufacturing Company and established the first fully integrated textile factory at Waltham, Massachusetts. Expanding their highly profitable operations, these investors, known as the Boston Associates, set up operations in 1820 at Chelmsford, Massachusetts, which they renamed Lowell. Intended as a model community, Lowell soon became the nation's most famous center of textile manufacturing.

Lowell

Its founders sought to avoid the wretched misery that characterized the factory system in England by combining paternalism with high profits. Instead of relying primarily on child labor or a permanent working class, the Lowell mills employed daughters of New England farm families. Thus women were the first factory workers in the United States. They lived in company boardinghouses under the watchful eye of a matron. To its many visitors, Lowell presented an impressive sight: huge factories, well-kept houses, bustling shops. Female employees were encouraged to attend lectures and use the library. They even published their own magazine, the *Lowell Offering*.

In reality, however, factory life involved strict rules and long hours of tedious, repetitive work. At Lowell, for example, workers could be fined for lateness or misconduct, including talking on the job. Alcohol, cards, and gambling were forbidden in the shop or mill yard. The women's morals in the boardinghouses were strictly guarded; male visitors were supervised, and there was a 10 P.M. curfew. Work typically began at 7 A.M. (earlier in the summer) and continued until 7 at night, six days a week. With only 30 minutes for the noon meal, many workers had to run to the boardinghouse and back to avoid being late. Winter was the "lighting up" season, when work began before daylight and ended after dark. The only light after sunset came from whale oil lamps that filled the long rooms with smoke. Even in summer the factories were poorly lit and badly ventilated.

Hard work in the mills

Although the labor was hard, the female operators earned from $2.40 to $3.20 a week, wages that were considered good at the time. (Domestic servants and seamstresses, two of the most common jobs women held, were paid less than a dollar a week.) The average "mill girl," as they were called, was between 16 and 30 years old. Most were not working to support their families back home on the farm; instead they wanted to save some money for perhaps the first time in their lives and sample some of life's pleasures. "I must . . . have something of my own before many more years have passed," Sally Rice wrote in rejecting her parents' request that she return home to Somerset, Vermont. "And where is that something coming from if I go home and earn nothing?"

Mill workers, Lowell

The sense of sisterhood that united women in the boardinghouses made it easier for farm daughters to adjust to the stress and regimen the factory imposed on them. So did their view of the situation as temporary rather than permanent, for most women worked in the mills no more than five years before getting married.

As competition in the textile industry intensified, factory managers sought ways to raise productivity. In the mid-1830s the mills began to increase the workloads and speed up the machinery. Even these changes failed to maintain previous profits, and on several occasions factories cut wages. The ever-quickening pace of work finally provoked resistance among the mill workers. Several times in the 1830s wage cuts sparked strikes in which a minority of workers walked out. Management retaliated by firing strike leaders, hiring new workers, and blacklisting women who refused to return. In the 1840s workers' protests focused on the demand for a 10-hour day.

Transformation of Lowell

The quest for profits also undercut the owners' paternalism. As the mills expanded, a smaller proportion of the workers lived in company boardinghouses and moral regulations were relaxed. But the greatest change was a shift in the workforce from native-born women to Irish immigrants. In 1845 the Irish made up only 8 percent of the Lowell workforce. By 1860 they amounted to almost half, many of them men and children. Because these new workers were poor and desperate for work, wages declined further. And because they did not view their situation as temporary, a permanent working class began to take shape.

Lowell and the Environment

Lowell was a city built on water power. Early settlers had used the power of the Merrimack River to run mills, but never on the scale used by the new textile factories. As the market spread, Americans came to link progress with the fullest use of the natural resources of the environment. Just as they had done in Lowell itself, the Boston Associates sought to impose a sense of order and regularity on the surrounding physical environment in order to efficiently use its natural resources. In the process, they fundamentally reshaped the area's waterscape.

Reshaping the area's waterscape

As more and more mills were built, the Boston Associates sought to harness water for energy. By 1836, Lowell had seven canals, with a supporting network of locks and dams, to govern the Merrimack's flow and distribute water to the city's twenty-six mills. The Associates also built dams at several points along the river to store water and divert it into power canals for factories. At Lawrence, they constructed the largest dam in the world at the time, a 32-foot-high granite structure that spanned 1600 feet across the river. But even dammed, the Merrimack's waters proved insufficient. So the Associates gained control of a series of lakes in New Hampshire covering more than 100 square miles that fed into the river system. By damming these lakes, they could provide a regular flow of water down the river, especially in the drier summer months. In the course of establishing this elaborate water-control system, they came to see water as a form of property, divorced from the ownership of land along the river. Water became a commodity that was measured in terms of its power to operate a certain number of spindles and looms.

Damaging effects

By regulating the river's waters, the Boston Associates made the Merrimack Valley the greatest industrial center in the country in the first half of the nineteenth century. But not all who lived in the valley benefited. By raising water levels, the dams flooded farm lands, blocked the transportation of logs downstream, and damaged mills upstream by reducing the current and creating backwater that impeded waterwheels. The dams also devastated the fish population by preventing upstream spawning, while factories routinely dumped their wastes into the river to be carried downstream. These wastes, combined with sewage from the growing population, eventually contaminated water supplies. Epidemics of typhoid, cholera, and dysentery occurred with increasing frequency, so that by midcentury Lowell had a reputation as a particularly unhealthy community.

In the end, the factory system fundamentally transformed the environment. Far from existing in harmony with its rural surroundings, Lowell, with its clattering

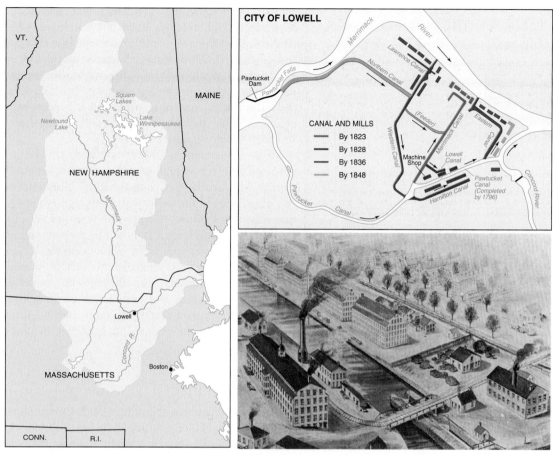

Development of the Lowell Mills As more mills were built at Lowell, the demand increased for water to power them. By 1859 the mills drew water from lakes 80 to 100 miles upstream, including Winnipesaukee, Squam, and Newfound. The map at left shows the watersheds affected. In the city of Lowell (right), a system of canals was enlarged over several decades. In the painting (done in 1845), the machine shop can be seen at left, with a row of mills alongside a canal. Rail links tied Lowell and Boston together.

machines and dammed rivers, presented a glaring contrast to rural life. The founding vision of Lowell had disappeared.

Industrial Work

For most workers, adaptation to the disciplined work routine of the factory did not happen easily. Traditionally, artisans had worked within the home. Apprentices were considered part of the family, and masters were responsible not only for teaching their apprentices a trade but also for providing them some education and for supervising their moral behavior. Journeymen took pride in their work, knowing that if they perfected their skill, they could become respected master artisans with their own shops. Skilled artisans worked not by the clock, at a steady pace, but rather in bursts of intense labor alternating with more leisurely time.

Artisan system

The factory changed that. Factory-produced goods were not as finished or elegant as those done by hand, and pride in craftsmanship gave way to rates of productivity. At the same time, workers were required to discard old habits, for

Transformation of work

TIME TABLE OF THE LOWELL MILLS,

To take effect on and after Oct. 21st, 1851.

The Standard time being that of the meridian of Lowell, as shown by the regulator clock of JOSEPH RAYNES, 43 Central Street.

	From 1st to 10th inclusive.				From 11th to 20th inclusive.				From 21st to last day of month.			
	1st Bell	2d Bell	3d Bell	Eve. Bell	1st Bell	2d Bell	3d Bell	Eve. Bell	1st Bell	2d Bell	3d Bell	Eve. Bell
January,	5.00	6.00	6.50	*7.30	5.00	6 00	6.50	*7.30	5.00	6.00	6.50	*7.30
February,	4.30	5.30	6.40	*7.30	4.30	5.30	6.25	*7.30	4.30	5.30	6.15	*7.30
March,	5.40	6.00		*7.30	5.20	5.40		*7.30	5.05	5.25		6.35
April,	4.45	5.05		6.45	4.30	4.50		6.55	4.30	4.50		7.00
May,	4.30	4.50		7.00	4.30	4.50		7.00	4.30	4.50		7 00
June,	"	"		"	"	"		"	"	"		"
July,	"	"		"	"	"		"	"	"		"
August,	"	"		"	"	"		"	"	"		"
September,	4.40	5.00		6.45	4.50	5.10		6.30	5.00	5.20		*7.30
October,	5.10	5.30		*7.30	5.20	5.40		*7.30	5.35	5.55		*7.30
November,	4.30	5.30	6.10	*7.30	4.30	5.30	6.20	*7.30	5.00	6.00	6.35	*7.30
December,	5.00	6.00	6.45	*7.30	5.00	6.00	6.50	*7.30	5.00	6.00	6.50	*7.30

* Excepting on Saturdays from Sept. 21st to March 20th inclusive, when it is rung at 20 minutes after sunset.

YARD GATES,

Will be opened at ringing of last morning bell, of meal bells, and of evening bells; and kept open Ten minutes.

MILL GATES.

Commence hoisting Mill Gates, Two minutes before commencing work.

WORK COMMENCES,

At Ten minutes after last morning bell, and at Ten minutes after bell which "rings in" from Meals.

BREAKFAST BELLS.

During March "Ring out"........at....7.30 a. m........."Ring in" at 8.05 a. m.
April 1st to Sept. 20th inclusive.....at....7 00 " " .... " " at 7.35 " "
Sept. 21st to Oct. 31st inclusive.....at....7.30 " " .... " " at 8.05 " "
Remainder of year work commences after Breakfast.

DINNER BELLS.

"Ring out"...................................12.30 p. m........."Ring in"....1.05 p. m.

In all cases, the *first* stroke of the bell is considered as marking the time.

Long hours and punctuality: that is the message of this Lowell timetable. Often accustomed to a less regimented life on a farm, machine operators complained of the pace of the machines and the tyranny of the factory bell that summoned and dismissed them each day. A song, "The Lowell Factory Girl," described factory life:

"The factory bell begins to
  ring,
and we must all obey,
And to our old employment go,
or else be turned away."

Lynn as the center of shoemaking

industrialism demanded a worker who was sober, dependable, and self-disciplined. The machines, whirring and clacking away, set a strict schedule that had to be followed. Absenteeism, lateness, and drunkenness hurt productivity and, since work was specialized, disrupted the regular factory routine. Thus industrialization not only produced a fundamental change in the way work was organized but transformed the very nature of work.

For newcomers to industrial ways, the factory clock became the symbol of the new order. One mill worker who finally quit complained of "obedience to the ding-dong of the bell—just as though we are so many living machines." Along with the loss of personal freedom came the loss of standing in the community. Whereas the master-apprentice relationship was a close bond, factories sharply separated workers from management. Few workers rose through the ranks to supervisory positions, and even fewer could achieve the artisan's dream of setting up one's own business. Even well-paid workers sensed their decline in status.

The Shoe Industry

Shoemaking illustrated the industrial process at work. Traditionally, a skilled cobbler knew how to judge the quality of leather, cut out the various parts of a shoe, and stitch and glue the parts together. He then sold the shoes in the same shop where he and his apprentices made them. Unlike the textile industry, shoemaking was not rapidly transformed in this period by a shift to heavy machinery. Even so, expanding national markets fundamentally altered the business.

Following in his father's footsteps, Micajah Pratt, a cobbler from Lynn, Massachusetts, began selling shoes in 1812 to customers in New England. He found, however, that there were ready markets in the South and West for cheaply made shoes. So he hired workers to produce shoes in larger and larger central shops. Pratt cut costs further by using new production techniques, such as standardized patterns and sole-cutting machines. He eventually employed as many as 500 men and women and produced about a quarter million pairs of shoes annually. Other shoe manufacturers adopted similar strategies, and Lynn soon became the nation's shoe-manufacturing center.

With the shoe industry booming, Lynn's population doubled every 20 years. Yet so great was the national market that manufacturers could not keep pace with demand. Increasingly they hired nearby farmers, fishermen, and their families to do part-time work at home. Women and girls sewed the upper parts of a shoe, men and boys attached the bottoms. While slow, this mode of production allowed wages to be reduced still further. A few highly paid workers performed critical tasks like cutting the leather, but most work was done either in large central shops or in homes. With workers no longer able to make an entire shoe, in little more than a generation shoemaking ceased to be a craft. Though not organized in a factory setting, it had become essentially an assembly-line process.

The Labor Movement

In this newly emerging economic order, workers sometimes organized to protect their rights and traditional ways of life. Craftworkers like carpenters, printers, and tailors formed unions, and in 1834 individual unions came together in the National Trades' Union.

The leaders of these groups argued that labor was degraded in America: workers endured long hours, low pay, and low status. Workers were not being rewarded according to the value of their labor, they argued; instead, the idle rich lived off the industrious poor. Unlike most American social thinkers of the day, a number of labor leaders accepted the idea of conflict between different classes. They did not believe that the interests of workers and employers could be reconciled, and they blamed the plight of labor on monopolies, especially banking and paper money, and on machines and the factory system.

If the unions' rhetoric sounded radical, the solutions they proposed were moderate. Reformers agitated for public education and abolition of imprisonment for debt to provide better opportunities for workers. Leaders saw effective unions and political action as the means to restore labor to its former honored position. Proclaiming the republican virtues of freedom and equality, they attacked special privilege and decried workers' loss of independence.

The labor movement gathered some momentum in the decade before the Panic of 1837, but in the depression that followed, its strength collapsed. During hard times, few workers were willing to strike or engage in collective action. Nor did skilled craftworkers, who spearheaded the union movement, feel a particularly strong bond with semiskilled factory workers and unskilled laborers. More than a decade of agitation did finally gain the 10-hour day for some workers by the 1850s, and the courts also recognized workers' right to strike, but these gains had little immediate impact.

Workers were united in resenting the industrial system and their loss of status. But they found themselves divided by a host of other factors: ethnic and racial antagonisms, gender, conflicting religious perspectives, occupational differences, party loyalties, and disagreements over tactics. For most workers, the factory and industrialism were not agents of opportunity but reminders of their loss of independence and a measure of control over their lives.

Farmers, workers, and merchants—all these Americans were affected, as individuals, by the revolution in markets.

Social Structures of the Market Society

Equally critical, the market revolution restructured American society as a whole. It created greater extremes between the rich and the poor, contributed to the rise of a growing middle class, placed greater emphasis on material goods, and even changed the way Americans thought about time.

Economic Specialization

To begin with, the spread of the market produced greater specialization. As we have seen, transportation networks made it possible for farmers to concentrate on producing certain crops, while factories could focus on making a single item such as cloth or shoes. Within factories, the division of labor broke down the manufacture of an item into smaller, more specialized (and less skilled) tasks. As we have seen, no longer did one cobbler produce a pair of shoes from start to finish.

This process evolved at different rates. Textiles and milling were completely mechanized. Other sectors of the economy, like shoes and men's clothing, depended little on machinery. Indeed, large factories were the exception rather than the rule. Much manufacturing was still done in smaller shops with few employees. Even so, the tendency was toward more technology, greater efficiency, and increasing specialization.

Decline of women's traditional work

Specialization had consequences at home as well. The average eighteenth-century American woman produced thread, cloth, clothing, and candles in the home for family use. With the growth of factories, however, household manufacturing all but disappeared. As a result, women lost many of the economic functions they had once performed at home. Again, textiles are a striking example. Between 1815 and 1860, the price of cotton cloth fell from 18 to 2 cents a yard. Because manufactured cloth was also smoother and more brightly colored than homespun, most women purchased cloth rather than make it themselves. Similarly, the new ready-made men's clothing reduced the amount of sewing women did, especially in cities, where more men purchased clothing from retail stores. As Chapter 12 will make clearer, the growth of industry led to an economic reorganization of the family and a new definition of women's role in society.

Materialism

Europeans who visited the United States during these years were struck by how hard Americans worked and how preoccupied they were with material goods and achievements. The new generation did not invent materialism, but the spread of the market after 1815 made it much more evident. "I know of no country, indeed," Tocqueville commented, "where the love of money has taken stronger hold on the affections of men." And in 1836 the American writer Washington Irving coined the classic phrase that captured the spirit of the age when he spoke, in one of his stories, of "the almighty dollar, that great object of universal devotion throughout the land."

Wealth and status

In a nation that had no legally recognized aristocracy, no established church, and class lines that were only informally drawn, wealth became the most obvious symbol of status. Dismissing birth as "a mere idea," one magazine explained, "Wealth is something substantial. Everybody knows that and feels it." Materialism reflected more than a desire for goods and physical comfort. It represented a quest for respect and recognition. "Americans boast of their skill in money making," one contemporary observed, "and as it is the only standard of dignity and nobility and worth, they endeavor to obtain it by every possible means."

The emphasis on money and material goods left its mark on the American character. Often enough, it encouraged sharp business practices and promoted a greater tolerance of wealth acquired by questionable means. Families were rated by the size, not the source, of their fortunes. Americans also emphasized practicality over theory. The esteem of the founding generation for intellectual achievement was mostly lost in the scramble for wealth that seemed to consume the new generation.

The Emerging Middle Class

In the years after 1815, a new middle class took shape in American society. A small class of shopkeepers, professionals, and master artisans had existed earlier, but the creation of a national market economy greatly expanded its size and influence. As specialization increased, manual and nonmanual labor were more often physically separated. Office work and selling became removed from the production and handling of merchandise. More frequently, businesspeople, professionals, storekeepers, clerks, office workers, and supervisors began to think of themselves as a distinct social group. "In America it is customary to denominate as 'clerk' all young men engaged in commercial pursuits," wrote one observer at midcentury. "Of course, the term is not applied to those engaged in mechanical trades." Members of the growing middle class had access to more education and enjoyed greater social mobility. They were paid not only more but differently. A manual worker might earn $300 a year, paid as wages computed on an hourly basis. White-collar employees received a yearly salary and might make $1000 a year or more.

Middle-class neighborhoods, segregated along income and occupational lines, also began to develop in towns and cities. Moreover, in large urban areas the separation of work from place of residence combined with improvements in transportation made it possible for many middle-class residents to live in surrounding suburbs and commute to work. Leisure also became segregated as separate working-class and middle-class social organizations and institutions emerged.

During these years, a distinct middle-class way of life evolved based in part on levels of consumption. Greater wealth meant the ability to consume more.

Separation of middle class from manual laborers

Material goods as emblems of success

This traffic jam in New York City conveys the rapid pace and impatient quality of American life in the first half of the nineteenth century. "In the streets all is hurry and bustle," one European visitor to the city reported. "Carts, instead of being drawn by horses at a walking pace, are often met at a gallop, and always in a brisk trot. . . . The whole population seen in the streets seem to enjoy this bustle and add to it by their own rapid pace, as if they were all going to some place of appointment, and were hurrying on under the apprehension of being too late."

Someone like Joseph Engles, a Philadelphia publishing agent, might boast a house furnished with not one but two sofas, a looking glass, thirteen chairs, five yards of ingrain carpet on the floors, and even a piano and stool. Material goods became emblems of success and status—as clockmaker Chauncey Jerome sadly discovered when his business failed and his wealth vanished. Indeed, this materialistic ethos was most apparent in the middle class, as they strove to set themselves apart from other groups in society.

The rise of a middle class would soon launch far-reaching changes in American society, as we will see in Chapter 12. The middle class came to embrace a new concept of marriage, the family, and the home. Along with occupation and income, moral outlook also marked class boundaries during this period.

The Distribution of Wealth

As American society became more specialized and differentiated, greater extremes of wealth appeared. After 1815, local tax records reveal a growing concentration of wealth at the top of the social pyramid. The concentration was greatest in large eastern cities and in the cotton kingdom of the South, but everywhere the tendency was for the rich to get richer and own a larger share of the community's total wealth. In New York, Brooklyn, Boston, and Philadelphia, the top 1 percent of the wealth holders owned a quarter of the total wealth in 1825; by 1850 they owned half. Similar trends appeared in western cities, such as Cincinnati and St. Louis. By 1860, 5 percent of American families owned more than 50 percent of the nation's wealth.

In contrast, those at the base of the social pyramid held a smaller percentage of a community's wealth. In Connecticut towns between 1831 and 1851 the number of inhabitants listed as having no property increased by 33 percent. In Cincinnati the lower half of the city's taxpayers held 10 percent of the wealth in 1817; in 1860 their share had dropped to less than 3 percent.

In a market society, the rich were able to build up their assets because those with capital were in a position to increase it dramatically by taking advantage of new investment opportunities. Although a few men, such as Cornelius Vanderbilt and John Jacob Astor, vaulted from the bottom ranks of society to the top, most of the nation's richest individuals came from wealthy families.

Social Mobility

The existence of great fortunes is not necessarily inconsistent with the idea of social mobility or property accumulation. Although the gap between the rich and the poor widened after 1820, even the incomes of most poor Americans rose, because the total amount of wealth produced in America had become much larger. From about 1825 to 1860 the average per capita income almost doubled to $300. Voicing the popular belief, a New York judge proclaimed, "In this favored land of liberty, the road to advancement is open to all."

Limits of social mobility

Social mobility existed in these years, but not as much as contemporaries boasted. Most laborers—or more often their sons—did manage to move up the social ladder, but only a rung or two. Few unskilled workers rose higher than to a semiskilled occupation. Even the children of skilled workers normally did not escape the laboring classes and enter the middle-class ranks of clerks, managers, or lawyers. For most workers, improved status came in the form of a savings account or home ownership, which gave them some security during economic downswings and in old age.

A New Sensitivity to Time

It was no accident that Chauncey Jerome's clocks spread throughout the nation along with the market economy. The new methods of doing business involved a new and stricter sense of time. Factory life required a more regimented schedule in which work began at the sound of a bell, workers kept machines going at a constant pace, and the day was divided into hours and even minutes.

Clocks began to invade private as well as public space. Before Jerome and his competitors began using standardized parts, only the wealthy owned clocks, but with mass production ordinary families could afford them. Even farmers became more sensitive to time as they became integrated into the marketplace. As one frontier traveler reported in 1844, "In Kentucky, in Indiana, in Illinois, in Missouri, and here in every dale in Arkansas, and in cabins where there was not a chair to sit on, there was sure to be a Connecticut clock."

The Market at Work: Three Examples

To sense how much America was leaving behind Crèvecoeur's vision of a land of subsistence farmers, consider three examples of the new market economy, from a small city on the East Coast to the distant frontier of the Rocky Mountains.

In 1820 Kingston, New York, was a small, rural-oriented community of 1000 people, located along the Hudson River halfway between New York City and Albany. But in 1828 the Delaware and Hudson Canal linked Kingston with the Pennsylvania coal fields, jolting the town out of its economic lethargy. The rise of the coal trade stimulated local commerce and greatly increased the number of banks and the variety of businesses. The rhythm of life in Kingston now focused on the docks, stores, and canal boats rather than on planting and harvest. By 1850 Kingston had a population of 10,000, ten times that in 1820. *The market transforms Kingston, New York*

Its landscape changed too. In 1820 most storekeepers and craftworkers had conducted business from their homes. By 1850 a commercial district boasted specialized stores, some handling china and glassware, others dry goods, clothing, or jewelry and watches. In addition, most manufacturing facilities were confined to two sections on the city's outskirts. Residential areas were separate from the commercial center and had become segregated along class lines, with different neighborhoods for the elite of the community, for skilled workers, and for unskilled laborers. By midcentury, street signs and gas lamps were going up, and numbers were being assigned to buildings. Kingston had become an urban center.

A thousand miles west lay the small prairie settlement of Sugar Creek, Illinois. The first white settlers had moved to Sugar Creek in 1817, as the market revolution was getting under way. The village's pioneers were primarily concerned about simply surviving. The land they plowed was on the edge of the forest, where girdled trees often remained standing among the crops until they could be cleared. The roads to larger towns like Springfield were mere cart paths, winding hither and yon among the trees. *Sugar Creek, Illinois*

By the 1840s and 1850s the market economy had made inroads at Sugar Creek. True, a farmer like Eddin Lewis might still keep an account book noting that James Wilson came by for "six days work planting corn [$]3.00." That was the traditional barter system in action, for no cash actually changed hands. Lewis was simply keeping tabs, noting also when he helped Wilson, so that eventually the account could be balanced. But Lewis had also begun to drive hogs to St. Louis, where he received cash in return. By 1848 he was shipping south 6000 pounds of barreled pork, as well as lard and 350 bushels of corn. Wealth had become more concentrated in Sugar Creek, too. The richest farmers concentrated on a few money-making crops and rented their surplus land to poorer tenants; their wives no longer had to produce large amounts of butter for market to make ends meet. Sugar Creek, in other words, was becoming more specialized, more stratified in its wealth, and more tied into regional and national markets.

Another thousand miles west a different sort of American roamed, who might at first seem unconnected to the bustle of urban markets. These were the legendary mountain men. Traveling across the Great Plains, along upland streams, and over the passes of the Rockies, hard-bitten outdoorsmen like Jim Bridger, Jedediah Smith, and James Walker wore buckskin hunting shirts, let their unkempt hair grow to their shoulders, and stuck pistols and tomahawks in their belts. In good times they feasted on raw buffalo liver and roasted hump; when game was scarce, some were not above holding their hands "in an anthill until they were covered with ants, then greedily [licking] them off," as one trapper recalled. Wild and exotic, the mountain men quickly became romantic symbols of the American quest for individual freedom.

Yet these wanderers too were tied to the market. During their heyday, from the mid-1820s to the early 1840s, they trapped beaver, whose pelts were shipped east and turned into fancy hats for gentlemen. The fur trade was not a sporting event but a business, dominated by organizations like John Jacob Astor's American Fur Company, and the trapper was part of a vast economic structure that stretched from the mountains to the eastern cities and on to Europe. The majority of these men went into the wilderness not to flee civilization but to make money. Their ultimate goal was to accumulate capital in order to set themselves up in society. Of those

Mountain men and the fur trade

Thomas Hicks's painting, *Calculating,* captures the spirit of the United States as the market revolution unfolded. Americans, one foreign visitor reported, were a "guessing, reckoning, expecting and calculating people." During this period the phrase "I calculate" came to mean "I think." The man carefully going over his figures wears a beaver hat, the end product of the fur trade. Indeed, business attitudes shaped and controlled the fur trade, and many mountain men ended up as calculating businessmen.

who survived the fur trade, almost none remained permanently outside the bounds of civilization; most returned and took up new careers. Far from repudiating society's values, the mountain men sought respectability and success as defined by the society they had temporarily left. They, like farmers, were expectant capitalists for whom the West was a land of opportunity.

Prosperity and Anxiety

The mountain men, the farmers of Sugar Creek, and the workers of Kingston were all alert to the possibilities of the market. As Americans saw their nation's frontiers expand and its economy grow, many began to view history in terms of an inevitable and continuous improvement. The path of commerce, however, was not steadily upward. Rather it advanced in a series of wrenching boom-bust cycles: accelerating growth and overheated expansion, followed by a crash and then depression.

The country remained extraordinarily prosperous from 1815 until 1819, only to sink into a depression that lasted from 1819 to 1823. During the next cycle, slow economic expansion in the 1820s gave way to almost frenzied speculation and investment in the 1830s. Then came the inevitable contraction in 1837, and the country suffered an even more severe depression from 1839 to 1843. The third cycle again followed the familiar pattern: gradual economic growth during the 1840s, frantic expansion in the 1850s, and a third depression that began in 1857 and lasted until the Civil War. In each of these depressions, thousands of workers were thrown out of work, overextended farmers lost their farms, and many businesses closed their doors.

Boom-bust cycle

The impact of the boom-bust cycle can be seen in the contrasting fates of two Americans who moved west in search of opportunity. In 1820, 17-year-old Benjamin Remington left Hancock, Massachusetts, for western New York, which was just being opened to white settlement. Possessing little money and no property, he tried his hand at several jobs before purchasing on credit a 150-acre farm near the growing city of Rochester. Remington's timing was ideal. In 1823, two years after his arrival, the new Erie Canal was completed as far as Rochester. Wheat prices rose, flour shipments from the region shot up, and Remington prospered supplying food for eastern markets. Over the years, he added to his acreage, built a comfortable house for his family, and was elected town supervisor. For Remington, the West was indeed a land of opportunity.

Somewhat younger, Addison Ward moved west when he came of age in 1831, leaving Virginia for Indiana. Unfortunately, by the time Ward arrived in Greene County, the best land had already been claimed. All he could afford was 80 acres of rough government land, which he bought in 1837 largely on credit. The region lacked adequate transportation to outside markets, but the economy was booming, land values were soaring, and the state had begun an ambitious internal improvements program. Ward's timing, however, could not have been worse. Almost immediately the country entered a depression, driving farm prices and land values downward. Overwhelmed by debts, Ward sold his farm and fell into the ranks of tenant farmers. He eventually moved on but never recovered financially. Catching the wrong end of the boom-bust cycle, Ward never achieved economic success and social respectability. As his experience demonstrated, the market revolution wore a double face, and the bright side did not shine on everyone.

In such an environment, prosperity, like personal success, seemed all too fleeting. Because Americans believed that the good times would not last—that the bubble would burst and another "panic" would set in—their optimism was often

Popular anxiety

tinged by insecurity and anxiety. They knew too many individuals like Chauncey Jerome, who had been rich and then lost all their wealth in a downturn.

The Panic of 1819

The initial shock of this boom-and-bust psychology came with the Panic of 1819, the first major depression in the nation's history. From 1815 to 1818 cotton had commanded truly fabulous prices on the Liverpool market, reaching 32.5 cents a pound in 1818. In this heady prosperity, the federal government extended liberal credit for land purchases, and the new national bank encouraged merchants and farmers to expand their operations by borrowing in order to catch the rising tide.

National depression

But in 1819 the price of cotton collapsed and took the rest of the economy with it. Once the inflationary bubble burst, land values, which had been driven to new heights by the speculative fever, plummeted 50 to 75 percent almost overnight. As the economy went slack, so did the demand for western foodstuffs and eastern manufactured goods and services, pushing the nation into a severe depression.

Because the market economy had spread to new areas, the downturn affected not only city folk but rural Americans as well. Many farmers, especially in newly settled regions, had bought their land on credit, and farmers in established areas had expanded their operations, looking to future profits. When prices fell, both groups were hard-pressed to pay their debts. New cotton planters in the Southwest, who were most vulnerable to the ups and downs of the world market, were especially hard hit.

The panic's economic stresses stirred sectional tensions, but the downturn affected the political life of the nation in even more direct ways. As the depression deepened and hardship spread, Americans viewed government policies as at least partly to blame. The postwar nationalism, after all, had been based on the belief that government should stimulate economic development through a national bank and protective tariff, by improving transportation, and by opening up new lands. As Americans struggled to make sense of their new economic order, they looked to take more direct control of the government that was so actively shaping their lives. During the 1820s, the popular response to the market and the Panic of 1819 produced a strikingly new kind of politics in the Republic.

chapter summary

By uniting the country in a single market, the market revolution transformed the United States during the quarter century after 1815.

- The federal government promoted the creation of a market through a protective tariff, a national bank, and internal improvements.

- The development of new forms of transportation, including canals, steamboats, and eventually

railroads, allowed goods to be transported cheaply on land.

- The Supreme Court adopted a pro-business stance that encouraged investment and risk taking.

- Economic expansion generated greater national wealth, but it also brought social and intellectual change.

  - Americans pursued opportunity, embraced a new concept of progress, viewed change as normal, developed a strong materialist ethic, and considered wealth the primary means to determine status.

  - Entrepreneurs reorganized their operations to increase production and sell in a wider market.

- The earliest factories were built to serve the textile industry, and the first laborers in them were young women from rural families.
  - Factory work imposed on workers a new discipline based on time and strict routine.
  - Workers' declining status led them to form unions and resort to strikes, but the depression that began in 1837 destroyed these organizations.
- The market revolution distributed wealth much more unevenly and left Americans feeling alternately buoyant and anxious about their social and economic status.
  - Social mobility still existed, but it was more limited than popular belief claimed.
  - The economy lurched up and down in a boom-bust cycle.
  - In hard times, such as the Panic of 1819, Americans looked to the government to relieve economic distress.

interactive learning

The Primary Source Investigator CD-ROM offers the following materials related to this chapter:

- Interactive maps: **Slavery and the Cotton Kingdom** (M11) and **The Transportation Revolution, 1830–1890** (M12)

- A collection of primary sources, including many exploring the massive economic expansion that occurred in this period. Other documents demonstrate social changes connected to the rise of the Cotton Kingdom, including an illustration of domestic slaves and servants, patent diagrams of the cotton gin, and advertisements selling western land investment opportunities. Also read about the building of the National Road.

additional reading

Charles Sellers, *The Market Revolution* (1991), is the most ambitious synthesis of social, economic, and political developments in this period, but it is marred by an overly romantic view of preindustrial society and a pronounced ideological bias. For a critique of Sellers's interpretation, see William E. Gienapp, "The Myth of Class in Jacksonian America," *Journal of Policy History*, 6 (1994), 232–281, with comments and a rejoinder. Additional assessments are offered in Melvin Stokes and Stephen Conway, eds., *The Market Revolution in America* (1996). Insightful discussions of a number of relevant topics can be found in Mary Kupiec Cayton et al., eds., *Encyclopedia of American Social History* (3 vols., 1993), a superb and wide-ranging collection based on the latest scholarship.

A very important overview of economic change is Douglass C. North, *The Economic Growth of the United States, 1790–1860* (1961). George Rogers Taylor, *The Transportation Revolution, 1815–1860* (1951), is the classic survey, while John Larson, *Internal Improvements* (2001), is an excellent recent study. Many of the social consequences of the new market economy are described in Jack Larkin, *The Reshaping of Everyday Life, 1790–1840* (1988), and more analytically in Christopher Clark, *The Roots of Rural Capitalism* (1990). Significant community studies include Stuart M. Blumin, *The Urban Threshold* (1976) and John Mack Faragher, *Sugar Creek* (1986). Workers' experiences are sympathetically examined in Thomas Dublin, *Women at Work* (1979); Paul G. Faler, *Mechanics and Manufacturers in the Early Industrial Revolution* (1981); and Sean Wilentz, *Chants Democratic: New York City and the Rise of the American Working Class, 1788–1850* (1984). Stuart Blumin's *The Emergence of the Middle Class* (1989) is an excellent treatment of a critical subject. For a fuller list of readings, see the Bibliography at www.mhhe.com/davidsonnation5.

significant events

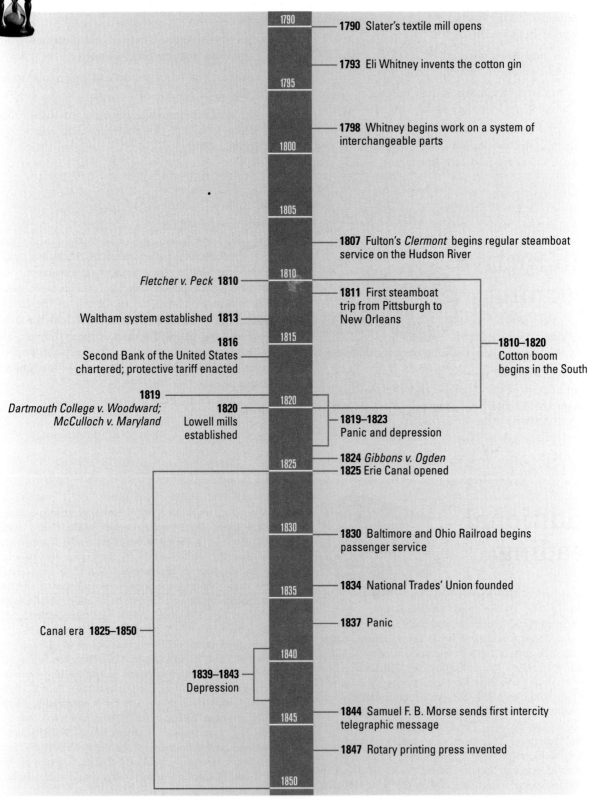

1790 Slater's textile mill opens

1793 Eli Whitney invents the cotton gin

1798 Whitney begins work on a system of interchangeable parts

1807 Fulton's *Clermont* begins regular steamboat service on the Hudson River

Fletcher v. Peck **1810**

Waltham system established **1813**

1811 First steamboat trip from Pittsburgh to New Orleans

1816
Second Bank of the United States chartered; protective tariff enacted

1810–1820
Cotton boom begins in the South

1819
Dartmouth College v. Woodward; McCulloch v. Maryland

1820
Lowell mills established

1819–1823
Panic and depression

1824 *Gibbons v. Ogden*
1825 Erie Canal opened

1830 Baltimore and Ohio Railroad begins passenger service

1834 National Trades' Union founded

Canal era **1825–1850**

1837 Panic

1839–1843
Depression

1844 Samuel F. B. Morse sends first intercity telegraphic message

1847 Rotary printing press invented

Chapter 11

The notice, printed in a local newspaper, made the rounds in the rural Pearl River district of Mississippi. A traveler, the advertisement announced, had lost a suitcase while fording the Tallahala River. The contents included "6 ruffled shirts, 6 cambric handkerchiefs, 1 hairbrush, 1 tooth-brush, 1 nail-brush, . . ."

As the list went on, the popular reaction would inevitably shift from amusement to disdain: "1 pair curling tongs, 2 sticks pomatum . . . 1 box pearl powder, 1 bottle Cologne, 1 [bottle] rose-water, 4 pairs silk stockings, and 2 pairs kid gloves." The howls of derision that filled the air could only have increased upon learning that anyone finding said trunk was requested to contact the owner—Mr. Powhatan Ellis of Natchez.

Powhatan Ellis was no ordinary backcountry traveler. Born into a genteel Virginia family, Ellis had moved in 1816 to the raw Southwest to increase his fortune. With his cultivated tastes, careful dress, and stately dignity, he upheld the tradition of the gentleman politician. In Virginia he would have commanded respect: indeed, in Mississippi he had been appointed district judge and U.S. senator. But for the voters along the Pearl River, the advertisement for his trunk of ruffled shirts, hair oils, and fancy "skunkwater" proved to be the political kiss of death. His opponents branded him an aristocrat and a dandy, and his support among the piney woods farmers evaporated faster than a morning mist along Old Muddy on a sweltering summer's day.

The Rise of DEMOCRACY

1824–1840

preview • In the 1820s and 1830s a new democratic political culture championed the wisdom of the people and the need for political parties. Andrew Jackson personified the new spirit, expanding the power of the presidency by rejecting South Carolina's doctrine of states' rights and by humbling the national bank. Paradoxically, democratic politics intensified racism, as Indians east of the Mississippi were forced from their lands and free African Americans met increased discrimination.

No one was more satisfied with this outcome than the resourceful Franklin E. Plummer, one of Ellis's political enemies. In truth, while the unfortunate Powhatan Ellis had lost a trunk fording a stream, he had never placed the advertisement trying to locate it. That was the handiwork of Plummer, who well understood the new playing field of American politics in the 1820s. If Powhatan Ellis typified the passing political world of the Revolutionary era, Plummer was a product of the raucous democratic system emerging in its place. Leaving his home in New England, Plummer had made his way as a young man to the new state of Mississippi, where he set himself up as an attorney, complete with a law library of three books. Plummer's shrewdness and oratorical talent made up for his lack of legal training, however, and he was quickly elected to the legislature.

Champion of the people   In 1830 Plummer's ambition led him to announce a run for Congress. At first few observers took his candidacy seriously. But Plummer boldly portrayed himself as the champion of the people battling against the aristocrats of Natchez. Contrasting his humble background with that of his wealthy opponent, Plummer proclaimed: "We are taught that the highway to office, distinction and honor, is as free to the *meritorious poor* man, as to the *rich;* to the man who has risen from obscurity by his own individual exertions, as to him who has inherited a high and elevated standing in society. . . ." Taking as his slogan "Plummer for the People, and the People for Plummer," he was easily elected.

By 1840 the new style of democratic politics was in full swing. This rally in Knoxville, Tennessee, uses a camp meeting–style platform in the woods to rally supporters. The makeup of this audience underscores another feature of Jacksonian democracy: the vote went only to adult white males.

On the campaign trail Plummer knew how to affect the common touch. Once, while canvassing the district with his opponent, the pair stopped at a farmhouse. When his opponent, seeking the farmer's vote, kissed the daughter, Plummer lifted up a toddling boy and began picking red bugs off him, telling the enchanted mother, "They are powerful bad, and mighty hard on babies." On another occasion, while his opponent slept, Plummer rose at dawn to help milk the family's cow—and won another vote.

As long as Plummer maintained his image as one of the people, fighting their battles against aristocrats, he remained invincible. But in 1835 when he became a candidate for the U.S. Senate, his touch deserted him. Borrowing money from a Natchez bank, he purchased a stylish coach, put his servant in a uniform, and campaigned across the state. Aghast at such pretensions, his followers promptly abandoned him, and he was soundly defeated. He died in 1852 in obscurity and poverty. Ah, Plummer! Even the staunchest of nature's noblemen may stumble, prey to the temptations of power and commerce!

Franklin Plummer was being pulled two ways by the forces transforming American society. As the previous chapter explained, the growth of commerce and new markets opened up opportunities for more and more Americans during these years. *Opportunity* was one of the bywords of the age. Through his connections with bankers and the well-to-do, Plummer saw the opportunity to accumulate wealth and to gain status and respect.

Yet at the same time that new markets were producing a more stratified, unequal society, the nation's politics were becoming more democratic. The new political system that developed after 1820 differed strikingly from that of the early Republic. Just as national markets linked the regions of America economically, the new system of national politics with its mass electioneering techniques involved more voters than ever before and created a new class of politicians. Plummer's world reflected that new political culture. And its central feature—another byword

Daily Lives

CLOTHING AND FASHION

The Plain Dark Democracy of Broadcloth

The emergence of democracy in American life was accompanied by a dramatic change in men's clothing. In the eighteenth century clothing was a prime indicator of social rank and set members of the upper class apart from ordinary citizens. A gentleman's finely tailored apparel—ruffled shirts, lace cuffs, silk stockings, decorative garters, and buckled shoes—was a mark of status because only elites could afford these expensive items. Because of the cost and extensive labor involved, most Americans owned only a few clothes, and these usually were made out of homespun—cloth woven from thread spun in the household. With a quick glance an observer could tell a person's social rank.

In the Jacksonian era, however, fashionable clothing became cheaper and much more widely available, and as a result dress no longer revealed social standing. By significantly lowering the cost, tex-

tile mills made good-quality cloth accessible to ordinary families. "All sorts of cotton fabrics are now so cheap that there is no excuse of any person's not being well provided," commented *The Young Lady's Friend* in 1836. Poor families and slaves did not share in this abundance, but most Americans' basic wardrobe expanded: now women usually owned more than a couple of dresses, and men ordinarily had more than a single jacket and one or two pairs of pants.

The colorful shirts, rude trousers, leather aprons, frocks, and heavy boots and shoes worn by farmers and mechanics while working were readily distinguishable from the coats and trousers of middle-class merchants, professionals, managers, and clerks. Outside the workplace, however, differences in clothing style, if not tailoring quality, largely disappeared. British traveler John Fowler in 1831 was amazed to see American workers, decked out in their Sunday best, walking the streets wearing "sleek coats, glossy hats, watchguards, and deerskin gloves!" Unlike men in the eighteenth century, these Americans dressed in somber colors. By the 1830s "black was the prevailing

color," one New Yorker recalled. "It was worn for promenade, parlor, church, ball, business," and "in such uniformity of style, as effectively to destroy all individuality."

As this nattily dressed butcher suggests, clothes were not much help in sorting out social status in America. Although the clothing of the upper class was often made of finer material and was more skillfully tailored, by the 1820s less-prosperous Americans wore similar styles. "The washerwoman's Sunday attire is now as nearly like that of the merchant's wife as it can be," commented one astonished observer.

---

on everyone's lips—was equality. In truth, the relationship between the new equalities of politics and the new opportunities of the market was an uneasy one.

Equality and Opportunity

Middle- and upper-class Europeans who visited the United States during these decades were especially sensitive to the egalitarian quality of American life. Coming from the more stratified society of Europe, they were immediately struck by the "democratic spirit" that had become "infused into all the national habits and all the customs of society." Europeans spent only a few days traveling American roads before the blunt contours of Franklin Plummer's world were brought home to them.

The emergence after 1840 of the ready-made clothing industry also had a decisive impact on men's fashions. A growing number of men in middle-class positions were anxious to create a proper image but could not afford the expert tailoring required to make a business suit. In response to this demand, tailors developed standardized patterns and a proportional sizing system and began mass-producing affordable ready-made clothing. Decently made, fashionable suits could be purchased off the rack, and thus clerks began wearing clothing identical in style to that worn by their employer. By eliminating the distinction between homemade apparel and that sewed by a tailor, ready-made clothing further democratized men's attire.

New ways of dressing began with the urban middle class and gradually spread throughout most of society. Ill-fitting clothes were increasingly a sign not of poverty but of isolation from the main avenues of transportation, commerce, and information.

Rather than distinguishing one class from another, democratic fashions increasingly set men apart from women. Fashion came to be considered a female concern, and ornamentation and bright colors now were associated with women's clothing. Ready-made clothing was not available for women, because female apparel required a close fit in the bodice. Nevertheless, the style of women's clothing also became standardized. American women sought to keep abreast of the latest Paris fashions, and if they could not afford a dressmaker's fitting, they sewed their own clothing. Illustrated magazines such as *Godey's Lady's Book* publicized the latest fashions, and even young women working in the mills at Lowell joined together to buy a subscription.

An English visitor reported that in the United States "men dress after the same type, differing only in finer or coarser material; every man would wear, if he could, a black satin waistcoat and a large diamond pin stick in the front of his shirt, as he certainly has a watch or a gild or gold chain of some sort or other. The mean white affects the style of the large proprietor of . . . capital as closely as he can. . . ." As one newspaper commented, Americans in the Jacksonian era were citizens of the "plain dark democracy of broadcloth."

To begin with, they discovered that only one class of seats was available on stagecoaches and rail cars. These were filled according to the rough-and-ready rule of first come, first served. In steamboat dining rooms or at country taverns, everyone ate at a common table, sharing food from the same serving plates. As one upper-class gentleman complained, "The rich and the poor, the educated and the ignorant, the polite and the vulgar, all herd on the cabin floor, feed at the same table, sit in each others laps, as it were."

Indeed, the democratic "manners" of Americans seemed positively shocking. In Europe social inferiors would speak only if spoken to. But Americans felt free to strike up a conversation with anyone, including total strangers. Frances Trollope was offended by the "coarse familiarity of address" between classes, while another visitor complained that in a nation where every citizen felt free to shake the hand of another, it was impossible to know anyone's social station. This informality—a forward, even *rude* attitude—could also be seen in the American custom of chewing tobacco and spitting everywhere: in taverns, courts, and hospitals, even in private homes. Fanny Kemble, an English actress, reported that on an American steamboat "it was a perfect shower of saliva all the time."

Americans were self-consciously proud of such democratic behavior, which they viewed as a valued heritage of the Revolution. The keelboaters who carried the future King Louis-Philippe of France on a trip down the Mississippi made their republican feelings plain when the keelboat ran aground. "You kings down there!" bellowed the captain. "Show yourselves and do a man's work, and help us three-spots pull off this bar!" The ideology of the Revolution made it clear that, in the American deck of cards at least, "three-spots" counted as much as jacks, kings, and queens. Kings were not allowed to forget that—and neither was Franklin Plummer.

The Tension between Equality and Opportunity

Opportunity and inequality of wealth

Although Americans praised both opportunity and equality, a fundamental tension existed between the two values. Inevitably, widespread opportunity would produce inequality of wealth. In Crèvecoeur's America, a rough equality of wealth and status had prevailed because of the lack of access to the market. In 1800 shoemakers in Lynn, with no way to ship large quantities of shoes across the country, could not become wealthy. Without steamboats or canals, farmers in Jefferson's day could not market surplus grain for profit. But by the 1820s and 1830s, as the opportunities of the market expanded, wealth became much more unevenly distributed. Thus the new generation had to confront contradictions in the American creed that their parents had been able to conveniently ignore.

Meaning of equality

By equality, Americans did not mean equality of wealth or property. "I know of no country where profounder contempt is expressed for the theory of permanent equality of property," Alexis de Tocqueville wrote. Nor did equality mean that all citizens had equal talent or capacity. Americans realized that individuals possessed widely differing abilities, which inevitably produced differences in wealth. "Distinctions in society will always exist under every just government," Andrew Jackson declared. "Equality of talents, or education, or of wealth cannot be produced by human institutions."

In the end, what Americans upheld was the equality of opportunity, not equality of condition. "True republicanism requires that every man shall have an equal chance—that every man shall be free to become as unequal as he can," one American commented. In an economy that could go bust as well as boom, Americans agreed that one primary objective of government was to safeguard opportunity. Thus the new politics of democracy walked hand in hand with the new opportunities of the market.

The New Political Culture of Democracy

The stately James Monroe, with his powdered hair and buckled shoes and breeches, was not part of the new politics. In 1824 as he neared the end of his second term, a host of new leaders in the Republican party looked to succeed him. Traditionally, a congressional caucus selected the party's presidential nominee, and the Republican caucus finally settled on Secretary of Treasury William H. Crawford of Georgia. Condemning "King Caucus" as undemocratic, three other Republicans, all ardent nationalists, refused to withdraw

Death of the caucus system

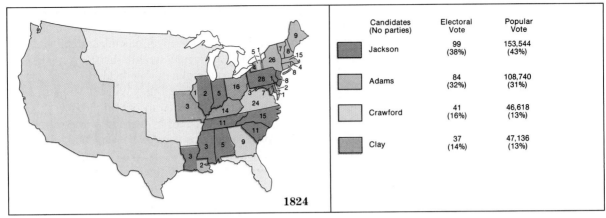

Candidates (No parties)	Electoral Vote	Popular Vote
Jackson	99 (38%)	153,544 (43%)
Adams	84 (32%)	108,740 (31%)
Crawford	41 (16%)	46,618 (13%)
Clay	37 (14%)	47,136 (13%)

Election of 1824

from the race: Secretary of State John Quincy Adams; John C. Calhoun, Monroe's secretary of war; and Henry Clay, the Speaker of the House.

None of these men bargained on the sudden emergence of another Republican candidate, Andrew Jackson, the hero of the Battle of New Orleans. Because of his limited political experience, no one took Jackson's candidacy seriously at first, including Jackson himself. But soon the general's supporters and rivals began receiving reports of his unusual popularity. From Cincinnati an observer wrote, "Strange! Wild! Infatuated! All for Jackson!" Savvy politicians soon flocked to his standard, but it was the people who first made Jackson a serious candidate.

The Election of 1824

Calhoun eventually dropped out of the race, but that still left four candidates, none of whom received a majority of the popular vote. Jackson led the field, however, and finished first in the Electoral College with 99 votes. Adams had 84, Crawford 41, and Clay 37. Under the Twelfth Amendment, the House was to select a president from the top three candidates. Clay, though himself eliminated, held enough influence as Speaker of the House to name the winner. After he met privately with Adams, he rallied the votes in the House needed to put Adams over the top.

Two days later, Adams announced that Clay would be his new secretary of state, the usual steppingstone to the presidency. Jackson and his supporters promptly charged that there had been a "corrupt bargain" between Adams and Clay. Before Adams had even assumed office, the 1828 race was under way.

Corrupt bargain

Even more significant, the election of 1824 shattered the old party system. Henry Clay and John Quincy Adams began to organize a new party, known as the National Republicans, to distinguish it from Jefferson's old party. Jackson's disappointed supporters eventually called themselves Democrats. To muddy the political waters even further, a third party arose out of a controversy that erupted in 1826 over a secret organization known as the Freemasons.

Anti-Masonry and the Defense of Equality

The Freemasons (or simply Masons) were a secret fraternal group whose chapters had spread through Europe and America during the eighteenth century. Members like George Washington and Benjamin Franklin shared the Enlightenment's belief in the power of reason and the idea of progress while also embracing the Masons' moral commitment to temperance, charity, and hard work. By 1826 the 150,000 American Masons were predominantly business leaders, manufacturers, and professionals. While Masons were often above average in wealth, their power and prestige stemmed more from the number of public offices they held.

Origins of the Anti-Masonic movement

It was in western New York along the Erie Canal that William Morgan, a disgruntled Mason, announced in 1826 that he intended to publish a book exposing the secrets of the order. Not long after, he was seized by a group of Masons, forced into a closed carriage, and spirited off. Morgan was never seen again, and little doubt exists that he was murdered, allegedly near Niagara Falls. When prominent Masons used their power to thwart any investigation, the Anti-Masonic movement began. Anti-Masons demanded that the Masonic order be rooted out and eliminated. By 1830, they had organized in 10 states as a political party. Two years later they ran a presidential ticket.

Appeal of Anti-Masonry

In national terms Morgan's disappearance was a relatively minor incident, but it touched raw nerves in an egalitarian society. The shadowy Masons seemed a sinister threat to equality and opportunity, since the members swore an oath to advance a "brother's" interests over those of nonmembers. Confronted with the power of such an "aristocratic" order, how could ordinary citizens compete? "The direct object of freemasonry," one Anti-Masonic writer charged, "is to benefit the few at the expense of the many, by creating a privileged class, in the midst of a community entitled to enjoy equal rights and privileges." The Anti-Masons undertook to reform society by arousing public opinion and involving more citizens in politics.

As a rule, Anti-Masonry was strongest in populous, rapidly developing, market-oriented towns. Poor farmers who lacked access to markets and desired new roads or canal lines were often suspicious of Masonic officeholders. So were farmers in newly opened areas who had become dependent on city banks and merchants for credit. By attacking Masonry as an infidel society that exalted reason over traditional religion, the Anti-Masonic movement also represented a fervent desire to Christianize society. As such it represented a protest against the increasingly secular aspects of American life, which the spread of the market had strengthened.

Second party system

The new parties were one indication of how much the political system was in flux. By the mid-1830s, the National Republicans gave way to the Whigs, a new party that absorbed many members of the fading Anti-Masons. The Democrats, the other major party, came together under the leadership of Andrew Jackson. Once established, this second American party system dominated the nation's politics until the 1850s.

Social Sources of the New Politics

New attitudes toward government

Why was it that a new style and new system of politics emerged in the 1820s? We have already seen that a revolution in markets, stimulated by new transportation networks, was under way. We have seen, too, that the scramble to bring western lands into the market generated a speculative land boom that collapsed in the Panic of 1819. The rise of the new political culture was rooted in these social conditions. During the sharp depression that followed, many Americans became convinced that government policy had aggravated, if not actually produced, hard times. As a result, they decided that the government had a responsibility to relieve distress and promote prosperity.

For the first time, large numbers of Americans saw politics as relevant to their daily lives. Agitation mounted, especially at the state level, for government to enact relief for those in debt and provide other forms of assistance. Elections soon became the means through which the majority expressed its policy preferences by voting for candidates pledged to specific programs. The older idea that representatives should be independent and vote according to their best judgment gave way to the notion that representatives were to carry out the will of the people, as expressed in the outcomes of elections.

With more citizens championing the "will of the people," pressure mounted to open up the political process. Most states eliminated property qualifications for voting in favor of white manhood suffrage, under which all adult white males were allowed to vote. Similarly, property requirements for officeholders were reduced or dropped.

Democratic reforms

Presidential elections became more democratic as well. By 1832 South Carolina was the only state in which the legislature rather than the voters still chose presidential electors. The Anti-Masons pioneered a convention as a more democratic method of nominating party candidates and approving a platform, and the other parties soon followed suit. And because a presidential candidate had to carry a number of states in different sections of the country, the backing of a national party, with effective state and local organizations, became essential.

These democratic winds of change affected European societies and eventually other areas of the world as well. In no other major country, however, were such reforms achieved as early, and with as little resistance, as in the United States. Suffrage provides a good example. In Britain, in response to growing demonstrations and the cautionary example of the French monarchy's overthrow in 1830, Parliament approved the Reform Bill of 1832, which enfranchised a number of property holders and gave Britain the broadest electorate in Europe. Yet in fact, only about 15 percent of the adult males in Britain enjoyed the right of suffrage after the bill's passage. In France the figure was less than one percent.

Male suffrage in Europe and Latin America

The democratic revolutions of 1848 championed universal male suffrage in France and Prussia. Yet this ideal soon suffered setbacks. By 1852 the French republic had been replaced by a monarchy under the emperor Louis Napoleon. And in Prussia, the new constitution essentially negated universal male suffrage by dividing the electorate into three classes according to wealth, a formula that enabled 5 percent of the voters to elect one-third of parliament. Belgium, which had the most liberal constitution in Europe, did not approximate manhood suffrage until 1848. Even the second Reform Act (1867) in Britain enfranchised only about one-third of the adult males.

Likewise, the Latin American republics established in the 1820s and 1830s imposed property requirements on voting or, like Uruguay, excluded certain occupational groups such as servants and peasants from the suffrage. One exception was Mexico, where a number of states adopted an extremely broad suffrage. A new constitution in 1836, however, established a much more centralized state and sharply limited voting rights. The most restricted suffrage existed in the republic of Haiti, where only army officers and a few other privileged individuals enjoyed the franchise. When the revolution of 1843 brought a new constitution with mass-based suffrage, it met widespread resistance among elites, and the government quickly failed.

As the new reforms went into effect, voter turnout soared. Whereas in the 1824 presidential election only 27 percent of eligible voters bothered to go to the

Voter turnout

polls, four years later the proportion had more than doubled to 56 percent. In 1840, 78 percent of eligible voters cast ballots, probably the highest turnout in American history.

The Acceptance of Parties

Rise of the professional politician

All these developments worked to favor the rise of a new type of politician: one whose life was devoted to party service and who often depended for his living on public office. As the number of state-sponsored internal improvement projects increased during the 1820s, so did the number of government jobs that could support party workers. No longer was politics primarily the province of the wealthy, who spent only part of their time on public affairs. Instead, political leaders were more likely to come from the middle ranks of society, especially outside the South. Many became economically established after entering politics, but as Franklin Plummer demonstrated, large sums of money were not required to conduct a campaign. Indeed, a successful politician now had to mingle with the masses and voice their feelings—requirements that put the wealthy elite at a disadvantage.

Van Buren champions the party system

In many ways, Martin Van Buren epitomized the new breed of politician. The son of a New York tavern keeper, Van Buren lacked great oratorical skills or a magnetic personality. But he was a master organizer and tactician, highly skilled at using the new party system. His abilities eventually carried him to the Senate and even the White House. Unlike the older Revolutionary generation, who regarded political parties as dangerous and destructive, Van Buren argued that they were not only "inseparable from free governments" but "in many and material respects . . . highly useful to the country." While conceding that political parties were subject to abuse, he stressed that competing parties would watch each other and check abuses at the same time that they kept the masses informed.

The Politics of the Common Man

New style of politics

Andrew Jackson was one of the first political leaders to grasp the new politics in which the ordinary citizen was celebrated as never before. "Never for a moment believe that the great body of the citizens . . . can deliberately intend to do wrong," he proclaimed. Party leaders everywhere avoided aristocratic airs when on the stump. "I have always dressed chiefly in *Home spun* when among the people," one North Carolina member of Congress explained. "If a Candidate be dressed Farmerlike he is well received and kindly remembered by the inmates of the Log Cabin, and there is no sensation among the children or the *chickens*."

Politics became mass entertainment, in which campaign hoopla often overshadowed the issues. Parades, glee clubs, massive rallies, and barbecues were used to rouse voters, and treating to drinks became an almost universal campaign tactic. ("The way to men's hearts is down their throats," quipped one Kentucky vote-getter.) Although politicians often talked about principles, political parties were pragmatic organizations, intent on gaining and holding power.

Limitations of the democratic political system

The Jacksonian era has been called the Age of the Common Man, but such democratic tendencies had distinct limits. Women and slaves were not allowed to vote, nor could free African Americans (except in a few states) and Indians. Nor did the parties always deal effectively with (or even address) basic problems in society. Still, Van Buren's insight was perceptive. Popular political parties provided an essential mechanism for peacefully resolving differences among competing interest groups, regions, and social classes.

"The Will of the People the Supreme Law" reads the banner at this county election. One of the few occasions when most of the men would assemble at the village, Election Day remained an all-male event as well as a time of excitement, heated debate, and boisterous celebration. As citizens give their oath to an election judge, diligent party workers dispense free drinks, solicit support, offer party tickets, and keep a careful tally of who has voted. Liquor and drinking are prominently featured: one elector enjoys another round, a prospective voter who is too drunk to stand is held up by a faithful party member, and on the right a groggy partisan sports a bandage as a result of a political brawl.

The new democratic style of politics **Jackson's Rise to Power**
first appeared on the state and local
levels: Van Buren deftly working behind the scenes in New York; Amos Kendall of Kentucky campaigning in favor of debtor relief; Davy Crockett of Tennessee carefully dressed in frontier garb and offering voters a drink from a jug of whiskey and a chew from a large plug of tobacco. The national implications of these changes, however, were not immediately clear.

John Quincy Adams's Presidency

When he assumed the presidency in 1825, John Quincy Adams might have worked to create a mass-based party. But Adams, a talented diplomat and a great secretary of state, possessed hardly a political bone in his body. Cold and tactless, he could build no popular support for the ambitious and often farsighted programs he proposed. His plans for the federal government to promote not only manufacturing and agriculture but also the arts, literature, and science left his opponents aghast.

Nor would Adams take any steps to gain reelection, though he earnestly desired it. Despite urgent pleas from Henry Clay and other advisers, he declined to remove from federal office men who actively opposed him. Since Adams refused to be a party leader, Clay undertook to organize the National Republicans. But with a reluctant candidate at the top of the ticket, Clay labored under serious handicaps. The new style of politics came into its own nationally only when Andrew Jackson swept to power at the head of a new party, the Democrats.

Jackson's election

Building a new party was a tricky business. Because Jackson's coalition was made up of conflicting interests, "Old Hickory" remained vague about his own position on many issues. Thus the campaign of 1828 soon degenerated into a series of personal attacks, splattering mud on all involved. Aided by enormous majorities in the South, Jackson won handily.

In one sense, the significance of the election was clear. It marked the beginning of politics as Americans have practiced it ever since, with two disciplined national parties actively competing for votes, an emphasis on personalities over issues, and the resort to mass electioneering techniques. Yet in terms of public policy, the meaning of the election was anything but clear. The people had voted for Jackson as a national hero without any real sense of what he would do with his newly won power.

President of the People

Certainly the people looked for change. "I never saw such a crowd here before," Daniel Webster wrote as inauguration day approached. "Persons have come 500

Jackson's stubborn determination shines through clearly in this portrait by Asher Durand, painted in 1835. "His passions are terrible," Jefferson noted. "When I was President of the Senate, he was Senator, and he could never speak on account of the rashness of his feelings. I have seen him attempt it repeatedly, and as often choke with rage. His passions are, no doubt, cooler now; he has been much tried since I knew him, but he is a dangerous man."

miles to see General Jackson, and they really seem to think that the country is rescued from some dreadful danger!" Some 15,000 supporters cheered wildly after Jackson was sworn in.

At the White House reception pandemonium reigned. Elbowing aside the invited dignitaries, thousands of ordinary citizens pushed inside to catch a glimpse of their idol. The new president had to flee after being nearly crushed to death by well-wishers. The crowd trampled on the furniture, broke glass, smashed mirrors, and ruined carpets and draperies. "It was a proud day for the people," boasted Amos Kendall, one of the new president's advisers. "General Jackson is their own president." Supreme Court Justice Joseph Story was less enraptured: "I never saw such a mixture. The reign of King Mob seemed triumphant."

Jackson's character

Whether loved as a man of the people or hated as a demagogue leading the mob, Jackson was the representative of the new democracy. The first president from west of the Appalachians, he moved as a young lawyer to the Tennessee frontier.

He had a quick mind but limited schooling and little use for learning; after his death a family friend acknowledged that the general had never believed that the Earth was round. A man of action, his decisiveness served him well as a soldier and also in the booming economy around Nashville, where he established himself as a large landowner and slaveholder. Tall and wiry, with flowing white hair, Jackson carried himself with a soldier's bearing. His troops had nicknamed him Old Hickory out of respect for his toughness, but that strength sometimes became arrogance, and he could be vindictive and a bully. He was not a man to provoke, as his reputation for dueling demonstrated.

For all these flaws, Jackson was a shrewd politician. He knew how to manipulate men and could be affable or abusive as the occasion demanded. He would sometimes burst into a rage to get his way with a hostile delegation, only to chuckle afterward, "They thought I was mad." He also displayed a keen sense of public opinion, skillfully reading the shifting national mood.

As the nation's chief executive, Jackson defended the spoils system, under which   **Spoils system**
public offices were awarded to political supporters, as a democratic reform. Rotation in office, he declared, would guard against insensitive bureaucrats who presumed that they held their positions by right. The cabinet, he believed, existed more to carry out his will than to offer counsel, and throughout his term he remained a strong executive who insisted on his way—and usually got it.

The Political Agenda in the Market Economy

Jackson took office at a time when the market economy was spreading through America and the nation's borders were expanding geographically. The three major problems his administration faced were directly caused by the resulting growing pains.

First, the demand for new lands put continuing pressure on Indians, whose valuable cornfields and hunting grounds could produce marketable commodities like cotton and wheat. Second, as the economies of the North, South, and West became more specialized, their rival interests forced a confrontation over the tariff. And finally, the booming economy focused attention on the role of credit and banking in society and on the new commercial attitudes that were a central part of the developing market economy. The president attacked all three issues in his characteristically combative style.

As a planter, Jackson benefited from the   **Democracy and Race**
international demand for cotton that
was drawing new lands into the market. He had gone off to the Tennessee frontier in 1788, a rowdy, ambitious young man who could afford to purchase only one slave. Caught up in the get-rich-quick mania of the frontier, he became a prominent land speculator, established himself as a planter, and by the time he became president owned nearly 100 slaves. His popularity derived not only from defeating the British but also from opening extensive tracts of valuable Indian lands to white settlement. Through military fighting and treaty negotiating, he was personally responsible for obtaining about a third of Tennessee for the United States, three-quarters of Florida and Alabama, a fifth of Georgia and Mississippi, and a tenth of Kentucky and North Carolina.

Even so, in 1820 an estimated 125,000 Indians remained east of the Mississippi River. In the Southwest the Choctaws, Creeks, Cherokees, Chickasaws, and

Seminoles retained millions of acres of prime agricultural land in the heart of the cotton kingdom. Led by Georgia, southern states demanded that the federal government clear these titles. In response, Monroe in 1824 proposed to Congress that the remaining eastern tribes be relocated west of the Mississippi River.

New attitudes toward race

As white pressure for removal intensified, a shift in the attitude toward Indians and race increasingly occurred. Previously whites had generally attributed cultural differences among whites, blacks, and Indians to the environment. After 1815 the dominant white culture stressed "innate" racial differences that could never be erased. A growing number of Americans began to argue that the Indian was a permanently inferior savage who blocked progress.

Accommodate or Resist?

The new, more aggressive attitudes among white Americans placed Indians and other minorities in the Old Southwest in a difficult position. During the seventeenth and eighteenth centuries the region reflected a multiracial character because Indians, Spanish, French, and Africans had all settled there. The intermixture of cultures could be seen in the garb of the Creek Indian chief William McIntosh (below), who adopted a style of dress that reflected both his Indian and white heritage. McIntosh's father was a Scot, his mother a Creek, his wife a Cherokee—and McIntosh himself had allied his people with Andrew Jackson's forces during the War of 1812. But not long after he signed a treaty for the cession of Creek lands in 1825, he was murdered by a rival faction of the tribe, who regarded the cession as an act of betrayal.

William McIntosh's attire reflects the multicultural nature of the Old Southwest. He wears the ruffled shirt and cravat of a white gentleman, but his robe, sash, leggings, and moccasins display with pride his Creek heritage.

As southern whites increased their clamor for Indian removal, similar tensions among various tribal factions increased.

Among the Seminoles, mixed-bloods (those with white as well as Indian ancestry) took the lead in urging military resistance to any attempt to expel them. In the Cherokee nation, on the other hand, mixed-bloods led by John Ross advocated a program of accommodation by adopting white ways to prevent removal. After a bitter struggle Ross prevailed, and in 1827 the Cherokees adopted a written constitution modeled after that of the United States. They also enacted the death penalty for any member who sold tribal lands to whites without consent of the governing general council. Developing their own alphabet, they published a bilingual newspaper, the *Cherokee Phoenix.* Similarly, the neighboring Creeks moved to centralize authority by strengthening the power of the governing council at the expense of local towns. They too made it illegal for individual chiefs to sell any more land to whites.

The division between traditionalists and those favoring accommodation reflected the fact that Indians too had been drawn into a web of market relationships. As more Cherokee families began to sell their surplus crops, they ceased to share property communally as in the past. Cherokee society became more stratified and unequal, just as white society had, and economic elites dominated the tribal government. Women's traditional economic role was transformed as well, as men now took over farming operations, previously a female responsibility. Nor were the Cherokees untouched by the cotton boom. Some of the tribe's leaders, particularly half-bloods who could deal easily with white culture, became substantial planters who owned large numbers of black slaves and thousands of acres of cotton land. Largely of mixed ancestry, slaveholders were wealthier, had investments in other enterprises such as gristmills and ferries, raised crops for market, were more likely to read English, and were the driving force behind acculturation.

As cotton cultivation expanded among the Cherokees, slavery became harsher and a primary means of determining status, just as in southern white society. The general council passed several laws forbidding intermarriage with African Americans and excluding African Americans and mulattoes from voting or holding office. Ironically, at the same time that white racial attitudes toward Indians were deteriorating, the Cherokees' racial attitudes toward blacks were also hardening, paralleling the increased racism among white Americans.

Changing nature of Cherokee society

Trail of Tears

As western land fever increased and racial attitudes sharpened, Jackson prodded Congress to provide funds for Indian removal. He watched sympathetically as the Georgia legislature overturned the Cherokee constitution, declared Cherokee laws null and void, and decreed that tribal members would be tried in state courts. In 1830 Congress finally passed a removal bill.

Pressure for Indian removal

But the Cherokees brought suit in federal court against Georgia's actions. In 1832 in the case of *Worcester v. Georgia,* the Supreme Court sided with the Cherokees. Indian tribes had full authority over their lands, wrote Chief Justice John Marshall in the opinion. Thus Georgia had no right to extend its laws over Cherokee territory. Pronouncing Marshall's decision "stillborn," Jackson ignored the Court's edict and went ahead with plans for removal.

Although Jackson assured Indians that they could be removed only voluntarily, he paid no heed when state governments harassed tribes into surrendering lands. Under the threat of coercion, the Choctaws, Chickasaws, and Creeks reluctantly agreed to move to tracts in present-day Oklahoma. In the process, Indians unaccustomed to white law and notions of property fell victim to shameful frauds, as land-hungry schemers cheated countless tribal members out of their lands. As much as 90 percent of the land allotments may have fallen into the hands of speculators.

Indian removal along the Trail of Tears

The Cherokees held out longest, but to no avail. In order to deal with more pliant leaders of the tribe, Georgia authorities kidnapped Chief John Ross, who led the resistance to relocation, and threw him into jail. Ross was finally released but not allowed to negotiate the treaty, which stipulated that the Cherokees leave their lands no later than 1838. When that time came, most refused to go. In response, President Martin Van Buren had the U.S. Army round up resistant members and force them, at bayonet point, to join the westward march. Of the 15,000 who traveled this Trail of Tears, approximately one-quarter died along the way of exposure, disease, and exhaustion, including Ross's wife. As for the western tracts awaiting the survivors, they were smaller and generally inferior to the rich lands that had been taken from the Cherokees.

Removal of the Cherokees

Indian Removal During Jackson's presidency, the federal government concluded nearly 70 treaties with Indian tribes, in the Old Northwest as well as in the South. Under their terms, the United States acquired approximately 100 million acres of Indian land.

▨ Northern Indian lands ceded during relocation	← Converging routes of major southern tribes
▨ New reservations of northern Indians	Note: Lands of major southern tribes are same color as their new reservations.

Military resistance

Some Indians chose resistance. In the Old Northwest a group of the Sauk and Fox led by Black Hawk recrossed the Mississippi into Illinois in 1832 and were crushed by federal troops and the militia. More successful was the military resistance of a minority of Seminoles under the leadership of Osceola. Despite his death, they held out until 1842 in the Everglades of Florida before being subdued and removed. In the end, only a small number of southern tribe members were able to escape removal. Most were shunted off onto worthless lands that whites did not want.

Except for a few missionaries and eastern reformers, Americans expressed little regret over the treatment of the eastern tribes. In his Farewell Address in 1837, Jackson defended his policy by piously asserting that the eastern tribes had been finally "placed beyond the reach of injury or oppression, and that [the] paternal care of the General Government will hereafter watch over them and protect them."

Indians, however, knew the bitter truth of the matter. Without effective political power, they found themselves at the mercy of the pressures of the marketplace and the hardening racial attitudes of white Americans.

Free Blacks in the North

Unlike Indian removal, the rising discrimination against free African Americans during this period did not depend directly on presidential action. Still, it was Jackson's Democratic party, which was in the vanguard of promoting white equality, that was also the most strongly proslavery and the most hostile to black rights. The intensifying racism that accompanied the emergence of democracy in American life bore down with particular force on free African Americans. "The policy and power of the national and state governments are against them," commented one northerner. "The popular feeling is against them—the interests of our citizens are against them. Their prospects . . . are dreary, and comfortless."

In the years before the Civil War, the free black population remained small: only about 171,000 in the North in 1840, about a quarter of whom were mulattoes. Although those numbers amounted to less than 2 percent of the North's population, most states enacted laws to keep African Americans in an inferior position. (For a discussion of free African Americans in the South, see Chapter 13.)

Most black northerners lacked meaningful political rights. Black men could vote on equal terms with whites in only five New England states. New York imposed a property requirement only on black voters, which disfranchised the vast majority. Moreover, in New Jersey, Pennsylvania, and Connecticut, African American men lost the right to vote after having previously enjoyed that privilege.

Discrimination against free blacks

Black northerners were also denied basic civil rights that whites enjoyed. Five states prohibited them from testifying against whites, and either law or custom excluded African Americans from juries everywhere except Massachusetts. In addition, several western states passed black exclusion laws prohibiting free African Americans from immigrating into the state. These laws were seldom enforced, but they were available to harass the African American population in times of social stress.

Segregation, or the physical separation of the races, was widely practiced in the free states. African Americans were assigned to separate sections on public transportation. Throughout the North they could not go into most hotels and restaurants, and if permitted to enter theaters and lecture halls, they sat in the corners and balconies. In white churches, they were put in separate pews and took communion after white members. In virtually every community, black children were excluded from the public schools or forced to attend overcrowded and poorly funded separate schools. Commented one English visitor: "We see, in effect, two nations—one white and another black—growing up together . . . but never mingling on a principle of equality."

Discrimination pushed African American males into the lowest-paying and most unskilled jobs in society: servants, sailors, waiters, and common laborers. In Philadelphia in 1838, 80 percent of employed black males were unskilled laborers, and three of five black families had less than $60 total wealth. African American women normally continued working after marriage, mostly as servants, cooks, laundresses, and seamstresses, because their wages were critical to the family's economic survival. Blacks were willing strikebreakers, because white workers, fearing economic competition and loss of status, were overtly hostile and excluded them from trade unions. A number of antiblack riots erupted in northern cities during these years. "Whenever the interests of the white man and the black come into collision,"

Black poverty

The Spread of White Manhood Suffrage White manhood suffrage became the norm during the Jacksonian era, but in a number of states free black males who had been voting by law or by custom lost the right to vote. After 1821 a $250 property requirement disfranchised about 90 percent of adult black males in New York.

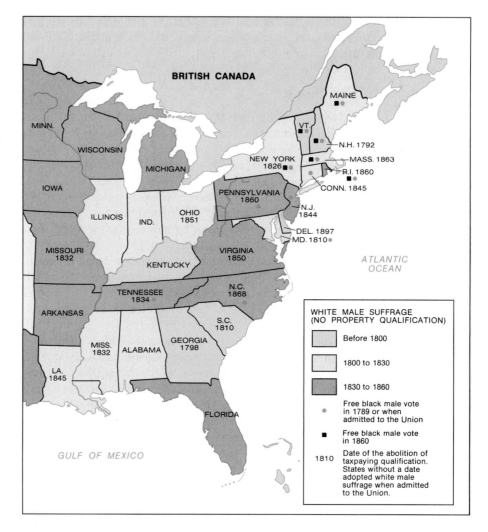

one foreign observer noted, "the black man goes to the wall. It is certain that, wherever labor is scarce, there he is readily employed; when it becomes plentiful, he is the first to be discharged." Driven into abject poverty, free blacks in the North suffered from an inadequate diet, were more susceptible to disease, and in 1850 had a life expectancy 8 to 10 years less than that of whites.

"None but those who experience it can know what it is—this constant, galling sense of cruel injustice and wrong," grieved Charlotte Forten, a free African American from Philadelphia.

The African American Community

African Americans responded to this oppression by founding self-help societies, and the black community centered on institutions such as black churches, schools, and mutual aid societies. They also agitated against slavery in the South and for equal rights in the North. After 1840 black frustration generated a nationalist movement that emphasized racial unity, self-help, and, for some, renewal of ties with Africa.

Because of limited economic opportunity, the African American community was not as diversified as white society in terms of occupation and wealth. There were distinctions, nevertheless, that rested on wealth and skin color. In general, mulattoes (lighter-skinned blacks) had greater opportunities to become more literate and skilled, were better off economically, and were more likely to be community leaders. Mulattoes' feelings of superiority were reflected in marriage choices, as they usually shunned darker-skinned blacks. "They have as much caste among themselves as we have," lamented the abolitionist Sarah Grimké, "and despise the poor as much I fear as their pale brethren."

The Minstrel Show

The racist attitudes of the day were very much reflected in popular culture, nowhere more than in minstrel shows, the most popular form of entertainment in Jacksonian America. Originating in the 1830s and 1840s and playing to packed houses in cities and towns throughout the nation, minstrel shows featured white actors performing in blackface. They dealt in the broadest of racial stereotypes, ridiculing blacks as physically different and portraying them as buffoons.

Appeal of minstrelsy

Although popular throughout the country, minstrelsy's primary audience was in northern cities. Its basic message was that African Americans could not cope with freedom and therefore did not belong in the North. Enslaved African Americans were portrayed as happy and contented, whereas free black Americans were caricatured either as strutting dandies or as helpless ignoramuses. Drawing its patrons from workers, Irish immigrants, and the poorer elements in society, minstrelsy assured these white champions of democracy that they remained superior.

The unsettling economic, social, and political changes of the Jacksonian era heightened white Americans' fear of failure, which stimulated racism. The popular yet unrealistic expectation was that any white man might become rich. Yet in fact, 20 percent or more of white adult males of this era never accumulated any property. Their lack of success encouraged them to relieve personal tensions through increased hostility to their black neighbors. Subjecting black Americans to legal

Deepening racism

Minstrel sheet music (left) illustrates the racist attitudes that pervaded Jacksonian democracy. Blacks, played by whites, were made to appear ridiculous through grotesque physical features, exaggerated poses, and pretentious airs. In contrast, the confident expression of this African American (right), who had this daguerreotype taken around 1856, evidences the dignity free blacks maintained in the face of unrelenting hostility and discrimination.

disabilities ensured that even the poorest whites would enjoy an advantage in the race for wealth and status. "The prejudice of race appears to be stronger in the states that have abolished slavery than in those where it still exists," Tocqueville noted, "and nowhere is it so intolerant as in those states where servitude has never been known." The power of racism in Jacksonian America stemmed, at least in part, from the fact that equality remained part of the nation's creed while it steadily receded as a social reality.

The Nullification Crisis

Indian removal and antiblack discrimination provided one answer to the question of who would be given equality of opportunity in America's new democratic society. Indians and African Americans would not. The issue of nullification raised a different, equally pressing question. As the market revolution propelled the economies of the North, South, and West toward increased specialization, how would various regions or interest groups accommodate their differences?

The Growing Crisis in South Carolina

South Carolina had been particularly hard hit by the depression of 1819. When prosperity returned to the rest of the nation, many of the state's cotton planters remained economically depressed. With lands exhausted from years of cultivation, they could not compete with the fabulous yields of frontier planters in Alabama and Mississippi.

Increasingly, South Carolinians viewed federal tariffs as the cause of their miseries. When Congress raised the duty rates in 1824, they assailed the tariff as an unfair tax that raised the prices of goods they imported while benefiting other regions of the nation. Other southern states opposed the 1824 tariff as well, though none so vehemently as South Carolina.

The one southern state in which black inhabitants outnumbered whites, South Carolina had also been growing more sensitive about the institution of slavery. In 1822 a slave conspiracy led by Denmark Vesey, a free black carpenter in Charleston, had been thwarted only at the last moment. A brilliant leader, literate, and well traveled, Vesey argued that slavery violated the principles of both republicanism and Christianity. He devised a well-coordinated plan to seize control of the city and raise the standard of black liberty, but several slaves betrayed the conspiracy at the last moment. Charleston authorities hurried to arrest Vesey and his lieutenants, who were tried, convicted, and either executed or banished. Even so, white South Carolinians were convinced that other undetected conspirators lurked in their midst.

Denmark Vesey's conspiracy

As an additional measure of security, the state's leaders pushed for stronger constitutional protection of slavery. After all, supporters of high tariffs had already claimed that the "implied powers" of the Constitution gave them the right to promote manufacturing. What was to stop this same broad interpretation from being used to end slavery? "In contending against the tariff, I have always felt that we were combatting against the symptom instead of the disease," argued Chancellor William Harper of South Carolina. "Tomorrow may witness [an attempt] to relieve . . . your slaves."

When Congress raised the duty rates still higher in 1828 with the so-called Tariff of Abominations, South Carolina's legislature published the *South Carolina*

Exposition and Protest, which outlined for the first time the theory of nullification. Only later was it revealed that its author was Jackson's own vice president, John C. Calhoun.

Calhoun's Theory of Nullification

Educated at Yale and at the most distinguished law school in the country, Calhoun was the most impressive intellect of his political generation. During the 1820s the South Carolina leader made a slow but steady journey away from nationalism toward an extreme states' rights position. When he was elected Jackson's vice president, South Carolinians assumed that tariff reform would soon be enacted. But Jackson and Calhoun quarreled, and Calhoun lost all influence in the administration.

In his theory of nullification, Calhoun addressed the problem of how to protect the rights of a minority in a political system based on the rule of the majority. The Union, he argued, was a compact between sovereign states. Thus the people of each state, acting in special popular conventions, had the right to nullify any federal law that exceeded the powers granted to Congress under the Constitution. The law would then become null and void in that state. In response, Congress could either repeal the law or propose a constitutional amendment expressly giving it the power in question. If the amendment was ratified, the nullifying state could either accept the decision or exercise its ultimate right as a sovereign state and secede from the Union.

Minority rights versus majority rule

As Daniel Webster outlines his nationalist theory of the Constitution and the Union, Senator Robert Hayne of South Carolina sits (front, left) with his hands together. The Senate gallery is filled, with most of the seats occupied by women, evidence of the widespread interest in politics.

Nationalists' theory of
the Union

When Senator Robert Hayne of South Carolina outlined Calhoun's theory in the Senate in 1830, Senator Daniel Webster of Massachusetts replied sharply that the Union was not a compact of sovereign states. The people and not the states, he argued, had created the Constitution. "It is the people's constitution, the people's government, made for the people, made by the people, and answerable to the people." Webster also insisted that the federal government did not merely act as the agent of the states but had sovereign powers in those areas in which it had been delegated responsibility. Finally, Webster endorsed the doctrine of judicial review, which gave the Supreme Court authority to determine the meaning of the Constitution.

The Nullifiers Nullified

When Congress passed another tariff in 1832 that failed to give the state any relief, South Carolina's legislature called for the election of delegates to a popular convention, which overwhelmingly adopted an ordinance in November that declared the tariffs of 1828 and 1832 "null, void, and no law, nor binding upon this state, its officers or citizens" after February 1, 1833.

Idea of a perpetual
Union

Jackson, who had spent much of his life defending the nation, was not about to tolerate any defiance of his authority or the federal government's. In his Proclamation on Nullification, issued in December 1832, he insisted that the Union was perpetual. Under the Constitution, there was no right of secession. Surprisingly, it had taken 40 years since the adoption of the Constitution to develop this point. To reinforce Jackson's announced determination to enforce the tariff laws, Congress passed the Force Bill, reaffirming the president's military powers.

Compromise of 1833

Yet Jackson was also a skillful politician. At the same time that he threatened South Carolina, he urged Congress to reduce the tariff rates. By holding out the hope of tariff reform, he managed to isolate South Carolina from the rest of the southern states. With no other state willing to follow South Carolina's lead, Calhoun reluctantly agreed to a compromise tariff, which Jackson signed on March 1, 1833, the same day he signed the Force Bill. South Carolina's convention repealed the nullifying ordinance, and the crisis passed.

Calhoun's doctrine had proved too radical for the rest of the South. Yet at the same time the controversy convinced many southerners that they were becoming a permanent minority. "It is useless and impracticable to disguise the fact," concluded nullifier William Harper, "that we are divided into slave-holding and non-slaveholding states, and this is the broad and marked distinction that must separate us at last." As that feeling of isolation grew, it was not nullification but the threat of secession that ultimately became the South's primary weapon.

The Bank War

Jackson understood well the political ties that bound the nation. He grasped much less firmly the economic and financial connections that linked different regions of the country through banks and national markets. In particular, the president was suspicious of the national bank and the power it possessed. His clash with the Second Bank of the United States brought on the greatest crisis of his presidency.

The National Bank and the Panic of 1819

Chartered by Congress in 1816 for a 20-year period, the Second Bank of the United States suffered initially from woeful mismanagement. At first it helped fuel the speculative pressures in the economy. Then it turned about-face and sharply contracted credit by calling in loans when the depression hit in 1819. The Bank regained a sound financial footing, but William Gouge, a Philadelphia journalist and economist, charged, "The Bank was saved and the people were ruined." Critics viewed the Bank's policies not as a consequence but as the cause of the financial downswing. To many Americans, the Bank had already become a monster.

Monster bank

The psychological effects of the Panic of 1819 were almost as momentous as the economic. In the midst of dizzying prosperity and unbounded optimism, Americans were suddenly plunged into privation, despair, and economic depression. That shock convinced many uneasy farmers and workers that the hard times were punishment for having lost sight of the old virtues of simplicity, frugality, and hard work. For them banks became a symbol of the commercialization of American society and the rapid passing of a simpler way of life.

Biddle's Bank

In 1823 Nicholas Biddle, a rich 37-year-old Philadelphia businessman, became president of the national bank. Biddle was intelligent and thoroughly familiar with the banking system, but he was also impossibly arrogant and had an inflated view of his importance. Seeking boldly to restore the Bank's damaged reputation, he set out to use the Bank to regulate the amount of credit available in the economy and thereby provide the nation with a sound currency.

Function as a central bank

Government revenues were paid largely in banknotes (paper money) issued by state-chartered banks. Because the Treasury Department regularly deposited U.S. funds in the national bank, the notes of state banks from all across the Union came into its possession. If Biddle believed that a state bank was overextended and had issued more notes than was safe, he presented them to that bank and demanded they be redeemed in specie (gold or silver). Because banks did not have enough specie reserves to back all the paper money they issued, the only way a state bank could continue to redeem its notes was to call in its loans and reduce the amount of its notes in circulation. This action had the effect of lessening the amount of credit in the economy.

On the other hand, if Biddle felt that a bank's credit policies were reasonable, he simply returned the state banknotes to circulation without presenting them for redemption. Being the government's official depository gave Biddle's bank enormous power over state banks and over the economy. As Biddle tactlessly admitted, "There are very few [state banks] which might not have been destroyed by an exertion of the powers of the bank." Under Biddle's direction the Bank became a financial colossus: it had 29 branches and made 20 percent of the country's loans, issued one-fifth of the total banknotes, and held fully a third of all deposits and specie. Yet for the most part, Biddle used the Bank's enormous power responsibly to provide the United States a sound paper currency, which the expanding economy needed.

Although the Bank had strong support in the business community, workers complained that they were often paid in depreciated state banknotes. Such notes could be redeemed for only a portion of their face value, a practice that in effect cheated

Opposition to paper money

workers out of part of their wages. They called for a "hard money" currency of only gold and silver. Hard money advocates viewed bankers and financiers as profiteers who manipulated the paper money system to enrich themselves at the expense of honest, hardworking farmers and laborers.

The Clash between Jackson and Biddle

Jackson's own experiences left him with a deep distrust of banks and paper money. In 1804 his Tennessee land speculations had brought him to the brink of bankruptcy, from which it took years of painful struggle to free himself. Reflecting on his personal situation, he became convinced that banks and paper threatened to corrupt the Republic.

As president, Jackson called for reform of the banking system from time to time, but Biddle refused even to consider curbing the Bank's powers. Already distracted by the nullification controversy, Jackson warned Biddle not to inject the bank issue into the 1832 campaign. When Biddle went ahead and applied for a renewal of the Bank's charter in 1832, four years early, Jackson was furious. "The Bank is trying to kill me," he stormed to Van Buren, "*but I will kill it.*"

Jackson's veto

Despite the president's opposition, Congress passed a recharter bill in the summer of 1832. Immediately Jackson vetoed it as unconstitutional (rejecting Chief Justice Marshall's ruling in favor of the Bank in *McCulloch v. Maryland*). The president went on to condemn the Bank as an agent of special privilege and as inconsistent with the republican principle of equality, because it made "the rich richer and the potent more powerful." Holding up the national bank as a symbol of aristocracy, the president pledged to protect "the humble members of society—the farmer, mechanics, and laborers"—against "the advancement of the few at the expense of the many." The message completely ignored the Bank's vital services in the economy.

As Jackson's veto message revealed, the struggle over the national bank tended to pit traditional farmers and workers against the world of commerce and national markets. Jackson's strongest supporters were workers and farmers outside the commercial economy and those who were disturbed by the changes that the market produced in their lives. Individuals who were more comfortable with the new commercial ethos rallied to the Bank's defense. In the end, most of them would wind up as members of the opposing Whig party.

The Bank Destroyed

When Congress failed to override Jackson's veto, the recharter of the Bank became a central issue of the 1832 campaign. Jackson's opponent was Henry Clay, a National Republican who eagerly accepted the financial support of Biddle and the national bank. Clay went down to defeat, and once reelected, Jackson was determined to destroy the Bank. He believed that as a private corporation the Bank wielded a dangerous influence over government policy and the economy, and he was justly incensed over its heavy-handed attempt to influence the election.

Removal of the deposits

To cripple the Bank, the president simply ordered all the government's federal deposits withdrawn. Because such an act clearly violated federal law, Jackson was forced to transfer one secretary of the treasury and fire another before he finally found in Roger Taney someone willing to take the job and carry

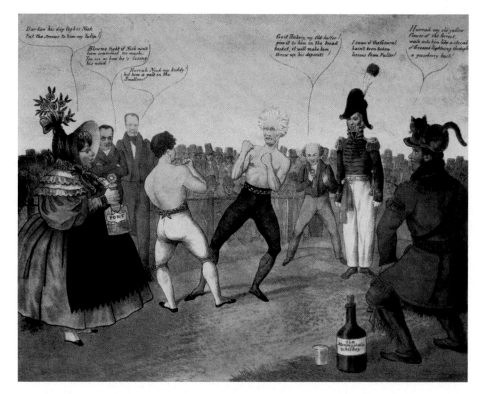

In this Bank War cartoon, Jackson boxes Biddle as Webster and Clay urge Biddle on and Van Buren shouts instructions from Old Hickory's corner. The heavyset woman holding a bottle of port (an upper-class beverage) represents the national bank, bloated with privilege and wealth, while a plain American in frontier garb keeps watch over Jackson's bottle of whiskey, the drink of the masses.

out the edict. Taney (pronounced "Taw-ney") began drawing against the government's funds to pay its debts while depositing new revenues in selected state banks.

Biddle fought back by deliberately precipitating a brief financial panic in 1833. "Go to Biddle," Jackson snapped to businesspeople seeking relief. "I never will restore the deposits. I never will recharter the United States Bank, or sign a charter for any other bank." Eventually Biddle had to relent, and Jackson's victory was complete. When the Bank's charter expired in 1836, no national banking system replaced it. Instead, Jackson continued depositing federal revenues in selected state banks. A large majority of these "pet banks" were controlled by Democrats.

Jackson's Impact on the Presidency

Jackson approached the end of his administration in triumph. Indian removal was well on its way to completion, the nullifiers had been confounded, and the "Monster Bank" had been destroyed. In the process, Jackson immeasurably enlarged the power of the presidency. "The President is the direct representative of the American people," he lectured the Senate when it opposed him. "He was elected by the people, and is responsible to them." With this declaration, Jackson redefined the character of the presidential office and its relationship to the people.

Jackson also converted the veto into an effective presidential power. During his two terms in office, he vetoed 12 bills, compared with only 9 for all previous presidents combined. Moreover, where his predecessors had vetoed bills only on strict constitutional grounds, Jackson felt free to block laws simply because he thought them bad policy. The threat of such action became an effective way to

Strengthening of presidential powers

shape pending legislation to his liking, which fundamentally strengthened the power of the president over Congress. The development of the modern presidency began with Andrew Jackson.

Van Buren and Depression

With the controls of the national bank removed, state banks rapidly expanded the amount of paper money in circulation. The total value of banknotes jumped from $82 million in January 1835 to $120 million in December 1836. As the currency expanded, so did the number of banks: from 329 in 1829 to 788 in 1837. A spiraling inflation set in as prices rose 50 percent after 1830 and interest rates by half as much.

As prices rose sharply, so did speculative fever. By 1836 land sales, which had been only $2.6 million four years earlier, approached $25 million. Almost all of these lands were bought entirely on credit with banknotes, many of which had little value. Settlers seeking land poured into the Southwest, and as one observer wryly commented, "under this stimulating process prices rose like smoke." In an attempt to slow the economy, Jackson issued the Specie Circular in July 1836, which decreed that the government would accept only specie for the purchase of public land. Land sales drastically declined, but the speculative pressures in the economy were already too great.

Specie Circular

This Whig cartoon blames the Democratic party for the depression that began during Van Buren's administration. Barefoot workers go unemployed, and women and children beg and sleep in the streets. Depositors clamor for their money from a bank that has suspended specie payments, while the pawnbroker and liquor store do a thriving business and the sheriff rounds up debtors.

"Van Ruin's" Depression

During Jackson's second term, his opponents had gradually come together in a new party, the Whigs. Led by Henry Clay, they charged that "King Andrew I" had dangerously concentrated power in the presidency. The Whigs also embraced Clay's "American System," designed to spur national economic development and particularly manufacturing. To do this the Whigs advocated a protective tariff, a national bank, and federal aid for internal improvements. In 1836 the Democrats nominated Martin Van Buren, who triumphed over three Whig sectional candidates.

Whig party

Van Buren had less than two months in office to savor his triumph before the speculative mania collapsed, and with it the economy. After a brief recovery, the bottom fell out of the international cotton market in 1839 and the country entered a serious depression. Arising from causes that were worldwide, the depression demonstrated how deeply the market economy had penetrated American society. It was not until 1843 that the economy revived.

Depression

Public opinion identified hard times with the policies of the Democratic party. Because he strongly opposed a new national bank, Van Buren instead persuaded Congress in 1840 to create an Independent Treasury to keep the government's funds. Its offices were forbidden to accept paper currency, issue any banknotes, or make any loans. The government's money would be safe, but it would also remain unavailable to banks to make loans and stimulate the economy.

Independent Treasury

As the depression deepened, thousands of workers were unemployed and countless businesses failed. Urban workers and their families were among the hardest hit. Nationally wages fell 30 to 50 percent. "Business of all kinds is completely at a stand," wrote one business leader in 1840, "and the whole body politic sick and infirm, and calling aloud for a remedy."

The Whigs' Triumph

The Whigs had done much to strengthen their party's national organization, and with the nation stuck in the worst depression of the century, they approached the election of 1840 in high spirits. To oppose Van Buren, they turned to William Henry Harrison, the military leader who had won fame defeating the Shawnee Indians at Tippecanoe. Using the democratic electioneering techniques that Jackson's supporters had first perfected, they portrayed Harrison as a man of the people while painting Van Buren as an aristocrat who wore a corset, ate off gold plates with silver spoons, and used cologne. Shades of Franklin Plummer!

First modern presidential campaign

This Illinois marching club benefited from the support of women.

Whig rallies featured hard cider and log cabins to reinforce Harrison's image as a man of the people. Ironically, Harrison had been born into one of Virginia's most aristocratic families and was living in a 16-room mansion in Ohio. But the Whig campaign, by portraying the election as a contest between aristocracy and democracy, was perfectly attuned to the prevailing national spirit.

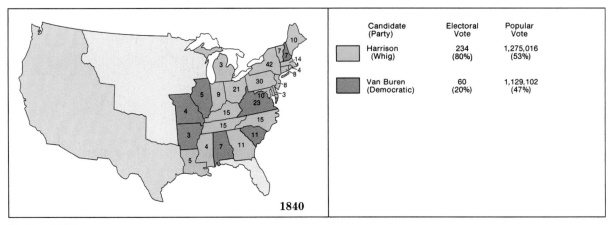

Candidate (Party)	Electoral Vote	Popular Vote
Harrison (Whig)	234 (80%)	1,275,016 (53%)
Van Buren (Democratic)	60 (20%)	1,129,102 (47%)

1840

Election of 1840

Both parties used parades, barbecues, liberty pole raisings, party songs, and mass meetings to stir up enthusiasm. But the Whigs pioneered a new aspect of mass political campaigning: they prominently involved women. Deeming themselves the party of morality, Whigs appealed directly to women for support, urging them to become politically informed in order to morally instruct their husbands. Women attended Whig rallies, conducted meetings, made speeches, and wrote campaign pamphlets, activities that before had been solely the duties of men. "I never took so much interest in politics in my life," Mary Steger of Richmond confessed to a friend. Uncertain what to make of this new Whig tactic, one Democrat observed, "This way of making politicians of their women is something new under the sun." Democrats had no choice but to eventually follow suit. Women's role in national politics began in 1840, and within a few years their presence at party rallies was commonplace.

Women take a new political role

Just as the Panic of 1819 had roused the voters to action, the depression and the two parties' response to it sparked mass interest. The result was a record turnout, as some 900,000 new voters were mobilized between 1836 and 1840 and nearly four-fifths of the eligible voters went to the polls. Although the popular vote was fairly close (Harrison led by about 150,000 votes out of 2.4 million cast), in the Electoral College Harrison won an easy victory, 234 to 60.

The "log cabin" campaign marked the final transition from the deferential politics of the Federalist era to the egalitarian politics that had emerged in the wake of the Panic of 1819. "We have been sung down, lied down, drunk down!" protested one indignant Democratic journal. As the *Democratic Review* conceded after the Whigs' victory in 1840, "We have taught them how to conquer us."

The Jacksonian Party System

It is easy, given the hoopla of democratic campaigning, to be distracted from the central fact that the new political system was directly shaped by the social and economic strains of an expanding nation. Whigs and Democrats held different attitudes toward the changes brought about by the market, banks, and commerce.

Democrats, Whigs, and the Market

Democratic ideology

The Democrats tended to view society as a continuing conflict between "the people"—farmers, planters, and workers—and a set of greedy aristocrats. The latter were not Europe's landed aristocrats, of course, but a "paper money aristocracy" of bankers, stock jobbers, and investors. This new class manipulated the banking system for its own profit, Democrats claimed, and sapped the nation's virtue by encouraging speculation and the desire for quickly gained, unearned wealth. For Democrats, the Bank War became a battle to restore the old Jeffersonian Republic with its values of simplicity, frugality, hard work, and independence. This attempt to retain those values is what Jackson was referring to when he said that removal of the deposits from Biddle's Bank would "preserve the morals of the people."

Jackson understood the dangers that private banks posed to a democratic society. Yet Democrats, in effect, wanted the rewards of the market without sacrificing the features of a simple agrarian republic. They wanted the wealth and goods that the market offered without the competitive, changing society, the complex dealings, the dominance of urban centers, and the loss of independence that came with it.

Whigs, on the other hand, were more comfortable with the market. For them, commerce and economic development were agents of civilization. Nor did the Whigs envision any conflict in society between farmers and mechanics on the one hand and businesspeople and bankers on the other. Economic growth would benefit everyone by creating jobs, stimulating demand for agricultural products, raising national income, and expanding opportunity. The government's responsibility was to provide a well-regulated economy that guaranteed opportunity for citizens of ability. In such an economy, banks and corporations were not only useful but necessary. A North Carolina Whig well expressed the party's vision of society: "All should be mutual friends and helpers to each other, and who ever aids and assists his fellow men from good motives, by lending money, by affording employment by precept or example, is a benefactor to his fellow men." **Whig ideology**

Whigs and Democrats differed not only in their attitudes toward the market but also in their view of how active government should be. Despite Andrew Jackson's inclination to be a strong president, Democrats as a rule believed in limited government. Government's role in the economy was to promote competition by destroying monopolies and special privileges. As one New Jersey Democratic newspaper declared, "All Bank charters, all laws conferring special privileges, with all acts of incorporation, for purposes of private gain, are monopolies, in as much as they are calculated to enhance the power of wealth, produce inequalities among the people and to subvert liberty." **Democrats' belief in limited government**

In *Charles River Bridge v. Warren Bridge* (1837) the Supreme Court strengthened the vision of an expanding capitalistic society undergirded by free competition. The opinion was written by Chief Justice Roger Taney, whom Jackson had appointed in 1835 to succeed John Marshall. At issue was whether in authorizing construction of a free bridge Massachusetts violated the rights of the owners of an adjacent toll bridge. Declaring that the public interest was the overriding concern, Taney's opinion struck down the idea of implied monopolies. In this decision, the Court sought to promote equality of opportunity and economic progress. **Opposition to monopolies**

In keeping with this philosophy of limited government, Democrats also rejected the idea that moral beliefs were the proper sphere of government action. Religion and politics, they believed, should be kept clearly separate, and they generally opposed humanitarian legislation as an interference with personal freedom. On the other hand, they supported debtor relief, which in their view curbed the wealthy aristocrats who tyrannized the common worker.

The Whigs, in contrast, viewed government power positively. They believed that it should be used to protect individual rights and public liberty and that it **Whigs' belief in active government** had a special role where individual effort was ineffective. By regulating the economy and competition, the government could ensure equal opportunity. Indeed, for Whigs the concept of government promoting the general welfare went beyond the economy. Northern Whigs in particular also believed that government power should be used to foster the moral welfare of the country. They were much more likely to favor temperance or antislavery legislation and aid to education. Whigs portrayed themselves not only as the party of prosperity but also as the party of respectability and proper behavior.

The Social Bases of the Two Parties

In some ways the social makeup of the two parties was similar. To be competitive, Whigs and Democrats both had to have significant support among farmers, the largest group in society, and workers. Neither party could carry an election by appealing exclusively to the rich or the poor.

Attitudes toward the market economy

The Whigs, however, enjoyed disproportionate strength among the business and commercial classes, especially following the Bank War. Whigs appealed to planters who needed credit to finance their cotton and rice trade in the world market, to farmers who were eager to sell their surpluses, and to workers who wished to improve their social position. Democrats attracted farmers isolated from the market or uncomfortable with it, workers alienated from the emerging industrial system, and rising entrepreneurs who wanted to break monopolies and open the economy to newcomers like themselves. The Whigs were strongest in the towns, cities, and rural areas that were fully integrated into the market economy, whereas Democrats dominated areas of semisubsistence farming that were more isolated and languishing economically. Attitude toward the market, rather than economic position, was more important in determining party affiliation.

Religious and ethnic factors

Religion and ethnic identities also shaped partisanship. As the self-proclaimed "party of respectability," Whigs attracted the support of high-status native-born church groups, including the Congregationalists and Unitarians in New England and Presbyterians and Episcopalians elsewhere. The party also attracted immigrant groups that most easily merged into the dominant Anglo-Protestant culture, such as the English, Welsh, and Scots. Democrats, on the other hand, recruited more Germans and Irish, whose more lenient observance of the Sabbath and (among Catholics) use of parochial schools generated native-born hostility. Democrats appealed to the lower-status Baptists and Methodists, particularly in states where they earlier had been subjected to disabilities. Both parties also attracted freethinkers and the unchurched, but the Democrats had the advantage because they resisted demands for temperance and sabbatarian laws, such as the prohibition of Sunday travel. In states where they could vote, African Americans were solidly Whig in reaction to the Democratic party's strong racism and hostility to black rights.

The Triumph of the Market

Clearly, Jacksonian politics evolved out of the social and economic dislocation produced by rapidly expanding economic opportunity. Yet efforts to avoid the costs of the market while preserving its benefits were doomed to failure. In states where the Democrats eliminated all banks, so much hardship and financial chaos ensued that some system of banking was soon restored. The expansion of the economy after 1815 had caught farmers as well as urban residents in an international network of trade and finance, tying them with a tightening grip to the price of cotton in Liverpool or the interest rates of the Bank of England. There was no rolling back the market in a return to the ideals of Crèvecoeur.

Still, Americans had evolved a system of democratic politics to deal with the conflicts that the new order produced. The new national parties—like the new markets spreading across the nation—had become essential structures uniting the American nation. They advanced an ideology of equality and opportunity, which stood as a goal for the nation even though women, African Americans, and Indians were excluded. The new politics developed a system of truly national parties, competing with one another, involving large numbers of ordinary Americans resolving differences through compromise and negotiation. Along with the market, democracy had become an integral part of American life.

chapter summary

Beginning in the 1820s, the United States experienced a democratic revolution that was identified with Andrew Jackson.

- The rise of democracy was stimulated by the Panic of 1819, which caused Americans to look toward both politicians and the government to address their needs.

- The new political culture of democracy included the use of conventions to make nominations, the celebration of the wisdom of the people, the adoption of white manhood suffrage, and the acceptance of political parties as essential for the working of the constitutional system.

- The new politics had distinct limits, however. Women were not given the vote, and racism intensified.

  - The eastern Indian tribes were forced to move to new lands west of the Mississippi River.

  - Free African Americans found themselves subject to increasingly harsh discrimination and exclusion.

- In politics, Andrew Jackson came to personify the new democratic culture. Through his forceful leadership, he significantly expanded the powers of the presidency.

  - Jackson threatened to use force against South Carolina when it tried to nullify the federal tariff using John C. Calhoun's theory of nullification, that is, that a state convention could nullify a federal law.

  - In response, nationalists advanced the idea of the perpetual Union. A compromise, which gradually lowered the tariff, ended the crisis (Compromise of 1833).

  - Jackson vetoed a bill to recharter the Second Bank of the United States and destroyed the Bank by removing its federal deposits.

- Under President Martin Van Buren, the nation entered a severe depression.

- Capitalizing on hard times and employing the democratic techniques pioneered by the Democrats, the Whigs gained national power in 1840.

- By 1840 the two parties had developed different ideologies.

  - The Whigs were more comfortable with the mechanisms of the market and linked commerce with progress.

  - The Democrats were uneasy about the market and favored limited government.

interactive learning

The Primary Source Investigator CD-ROM offers the following materials related to this chapter:

- Interactive maps: **Election of 1824** (M7), **Election of 1840** (M7), and **Indian Expulsion, 1800–1890** (M8)

- A short documentary movie on Indian removal along the Trail of Tears (D6)

- A collection of primary sources including Andrew Jackson's response to the Nullification issue, a cartoon satirizing the Jackson administration, and a caricature of Martin Van Buren. Several sources illustrate the Indian expulsion: audio clips of slave songs and field hollers, the orders to remove the Cherokees, the Treaty at Echota, a memorial from the ladies of Steubenville protesting the Indian removal, and a physician's report of emigrating Cherokees at Fort Payne, Alabama.

additional reading

Arthur M. Schlesinger Jr., *The Age of Jackson* (1945), marks the beginning of modern historiography on the Jacksonian era. Locating the main sources of Jacksonianism among eastern workers, Schlesinger emphasized the banking and currency issue as the defining issue of Jacksonian politics. Lightly researched, overwritten, and partisan in its analysis, Schlesinger's book provoked a flurry of works challenging its interpretation. Among the most important is the chapter on Jackson in Richard Hofstadter, *The American Political Tradition* (1948). Despite this withering criticism, Schlesinger is not without defenders. Charles Sellers, *The Market Revolution* (1991), offers an updated—and equally flawed—version of Schlesinger's argument.

A good recent interpretation of Jacksonian politics is Harry Watson, *Liberty and Power* (1990). Robert Remini places the features of the new democratic political system in bold relief in *The Election of Andrew Jackson* (1963). Important discussions of party ideologies include Marvin Meyers, *The Jacksonian Persuasion* (1957); Daniel Walker Howe, *The Political Culture of the American Whigs* (1979); and Lawrence Frederick Kohl, *The Politics of Individualism* (1988). For the Whig party, see Michael F. Holt's *The Rise and Fall of the American Whig Party* (1999), which provides a full and detailed account of the party's history. The best account of the nullification crisis is William W. Freehling, *Prelude to Civil War* (1966), and Robert Remini offers a succinct analysis of the banking issue in *Andrew Jackson and the Bank War* (1967). Paul Goodman, *Towards a Christian Republic* (1988), is the most valuable study of Anti-Masonry. For differing views on Indian removal, see Michael D. Green, *The Politics of Indian Removal* (1982), which deals with Creek society, and Robert Remini, *The Legacy of Andrew Jackson* (1988). For a fuller list of readings, see the Bibliography at www.mhhe.com/davidsonnation5.

significant events

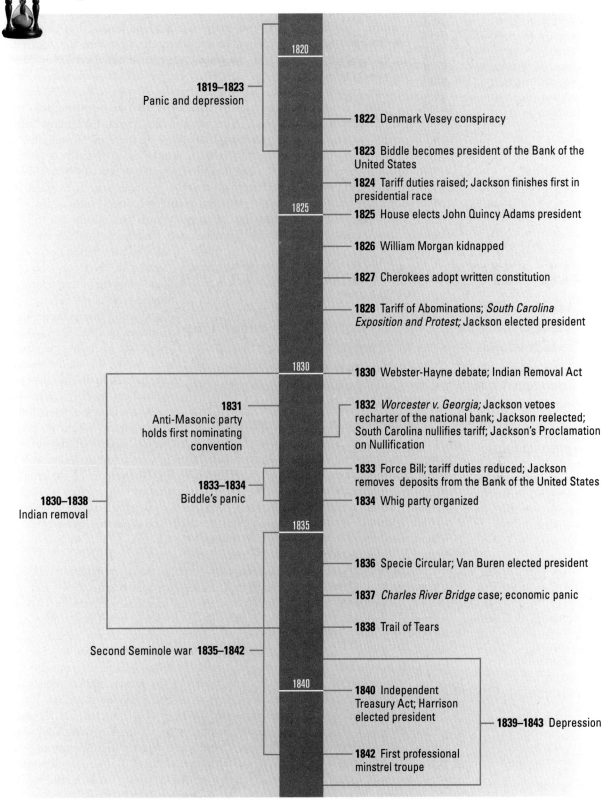

1819–1823
Panic and depression

1822 Denmark Vesey conspiracy

1823 Biddle becomes president of the Bank of the United States

1824 Tariff duties raised; Jackson finishes first in presidential race

1825 House elects John Quincy Adams president

1826 William Morgan kidnapped

1827 Cherokees adopt written constitution

1828 Tariff of Abominations; *South Carolina Exposition and Protest*; Jackson elected president

1830 Webster-Hayne debate; Indian Removal Act

1831
Anti-Masonic party holds first nominating convention

1832 *Worcester v. Georgia*; Jackson vetoes recharter of the national bank; Jackson reelected; South Carolina nullifies tariff; Jackson's Proclamation on Nullification

1833 Force Bill; tariff duties reduced; Jackson removes deposits from the Bank of the United States

1833–1834
Biddle's panic

1834 Whig party organized

1830–1838
Indian removal

1836 Specie Circular; Van Buren elected president

1837 *Charles River Bridge* case; economic panic

1838 Trail of Tears

Second Seminole war **1835–1842**

1840 Independent Treasury Act; Harrison elected president

1839–1843 Depression

1842 First professional minstrel troupe

361

Chapter 12

I n 1826 the Reverend Lyman Beecher was probably the most celebrated minister of the Republic, and the pulpit of Hanover Street Church was his to command. Beecher looked and spoke like a pious farmer, but every Sunday he was transformed when he mounted the pulpit of Boston's most imposing church. From there, he would blaze forth denunciations of dancing, drinking, dueling, or "infidelity," all the while punctuating his sermon with pump-handle strokes of the right hand.

Prophecies of the millennium

Nor were Beecher's ambitions small. His goal was nothing less than to bring the kingdom of Christ to the nation and the world. Like many ministers, Beecher had studied the intriguing final book of the New Testament, the Revelation to John. The Revelation foretold in Latter days of Earth a glorious millennium—a thousand years of peace and triumph—when the saints would rule and evil would be banished from the world. Beecher was convinced that the long-awaited millennium might well begin in the United States.

Personal experience reinforced this optimism. Born to a sturdy line of New England blacksmiths in 1775, Beecher entered Yale College during the high tide of postwar nationalism—and, some said, the lowest ebb of religion among young people. In the revivals of the Second Great Awakening that came to many colleges in 1802, Beecher had been one of those converted.

THE FIRES OF PERFECTION

1820–1850

preview • The Second Great Awakening unleashed a cascade of reform during the 1820s and 1830s. Middle-class women were prominent in these campaigns, reflecting the profound changes in their social roles wrought by the market economy. Some reformers withdrew from everyday life to create utopian communities; others sought humanitarian reforms such as temperance, educational improvement, women's rights, and—most disruptive to the political system—the abolition of slavery.

But he was hardly a stodgy Puritan. Much of Beecher's boundless energy went into raising a family of 11 children, every one of whom he prayed would take leading roles in bringing the kingdom of God to America. He loved to wrestle on the floor with his sons, climb the highest trees, or go "berrying" with his daughters. Still, the religious dimension of their lives was constant. The family attended two services on Sunday, a weekly prayer meeting, and a monthly "concert of prayer," where the devout met to pray for the conversion of the world. Beecher's son Thomas remembered his father commanding: "Overturn and overturn till He whose right it is shall come and reign, King of nations and King of saints."

To usher in the kingdom of God entire communities and even nations would have to be swept with a divine fire. Toward that end Beecher joined other Protestant ministers in supporting a host of religious reforms and missionary efforts. In 1810 the American Board of Commissioners for Foreign Missions was established, followed by the American Bible Society (1816) and the American Tract Society (1825), whose Bibles and religious pamphlets blanketed every sleepy hamlet in the country. Societies sprang up to promote Sunday schools and minister to sailors and the poor. By 1830 the most important of these organizations made up the loosely united "Benevolent Empire." To Beecher these organizations were signs of the coming kingdom.

Benevolent associations

As the new pastor at Hanover Street, Beecher also directed his righteous artillery on a host of evils that seemed to be obstructing God's kingdom. With scorn he attacked Unitarians, whose liberal, rational creed rejected the divinity of Jesus. In Boston, Unitarians were mainly upper class and cultured. But he also denounced what he viewed as sinful pastimes of the lower class: playing cards, gambling, and

Lyman Beecher (center) with his family in 1855. Five of his six sons, all of whom were ministers, stand in back. In front, daughters Catharine (holding his arm to steady it for the long exposure) and Isabella are on the left; Harriet, the author of *Uncle Tom's Cabin*, is at the far right.

drinking. And he denounced Roman Catholic priests and nuns as superstitious, devious agents of "Antichrist."

Beecher's efforts at "moral reform" antagonized many immigrants and other working people who enjoyed liquor or lotteries. Thus when a blaze broke out in the basement of his church in 1830, unsympathetic local firefighters stood by while the splendid structure burned to the ground. The fires of spiritual reform had been halted, temporarily, by a blaze of a literal sort.

Any fire, real or spiritual, is unpredictable as it spreads from one scrap of tinder to the next. That proved to be the case with reform movements of the 1820s and 1830s, as they moved in diverging, sometimes contradictory, ways. What did it mean, after all, to bring in Christ's kingdom? The goals of the early reform societies were moral rather than social. Leaders like Beecher sought to convert individuals and to church the unchurched, with the help of religious revivals and benevolent associations. Their conservative aim, as he expressed it, was to restore America to "the moral government of God."

Other Christians, however, began to focus on social issues like slavery, the inequality of women, and the operation of prisons. To these problems they demanded more radical solutions. Ironically, many of Beecher's children went well beyond his more conservative strategies for hastening the millennium. They spoke out for abolition, women's rights, and education in ways that left their father distinctly uncomfortable. In their activities the Beechers reflected the diversity of the reform impulse itself.

Revivalism and the Social Order

Society during the Jacksonian era was undergoing deep and rapid changes. The revolution in markets brought both economic expansion and periodic depressions, as its citizens competed—often anxiously—for status and wealth. In a nation where fortunes could be won and lost almost overnight, some reformers sought stability and moral order in religious community. The bonds of unity created by a revival brought a sense of peace in the midst of a society in change. Revivals could reinforce strength and discipline, too, in an emerging industrial culture that demanded sobriety and regular working habits.

Other reformers, however, sought to check the excesses of Jacksonian America by radically remaking institutions or devising utopian, experimental ways of living and working together. The drive for renewal, in other words, led reformers sometimes to preserve social institutions, other times to overturn them. It led them sometimes to liberate, other times to control. And the conflicting ways in which these dynamics operated could be seen in the electric career of Charles Grandison Finney.

Finney's New Measures

In 1821, as a young man, Finney experienced a soul-shattering conversion that led him to give up his law practice to become an itinerant minister. Eventually he was ordained in the Presbyterian church, although he lacked any formal theological training. He first attracted national attention when in the mid-1820s and early 1830s he conducted a series of spectacular revivals in the booming port cities along the new Erie Canal.

Charles Finney, about 1834

Like George Whitefield before him, Finney had an entrancing voice that carried great distances. His power over an audience was such that when he described the descent of a sinner into hell, those in the back of the hall rose to witness the final plunge. His success, however, resulted also from his use of special techniques—"the new measures"—and his casual attitude toward religious doctrine.

These new measures had been developed during the frontier revivals of the Second Great Awakening (page 266). Finney's contribution was to popularize the techniques and use them systematically. He held "protracted meetings" night after night to build up excitement. Speaking boldly and bluntly, he prayed for sinners by name, encouraged women to testify in public gatherings, and placed those struggling with conversion on the "anxious bench" at the front of the church. "A revival is not a miracle," he coolly declared, "it is a purely scientific result of the right use of constituted means."

Conversion experience

Finney and other evangelical* revivalists stressed the need for individuals to undergo an emotionally wrenching conversion experience and be reborn. Not all conversion experiences, however, occurred during revivals, prayer meetings, and religious gatherings. The slave Mortimer, for example, first heard a voice calling his name while he was in the field plowing. As he started to run, the cry "I am blessed but you are damned!" reverberated around him. Begging for mercy, Morte began to pray when a soft voice reassured him, "You are this day made alive and freed from hell." Deeply impressed by Morte's experience, his master told him henceforth he could preach on the plantation, and Morte thus commenced his life-long career as a preacher. Like Mortimer, born-again Christians could describe in detail their feelings and experiences when they were reborn. And, as in his case, religion could bring both peace and a sense of purpose in one's life.

---

*The word *evangelical* derives from a Greek word meaning the bringing of good news—in this case the Gospel. Protestant evangelicals stressed the need for individual conversion and rebirth stemming from an awareness of sinful guilt and Christ's act of atoning, through his death, for their sins.

The Philosophy of the New Revivals

Finney also rejected many religious doctrines of Calvinism, including predestination, which maintained that God had already determined which individuals were destined to be saved or damned and that no human effort could change this decision. But by the 1820s such a proposition seemed unreasonable to a generation that condemned hereditary distinctions, celebrated personal dignity, and praised human ability and activity. Leaving the Lord little role in the drama of human deliverance, Finney embraced the doctrine of free will. All men and women who wanted to could be saved. To those anxious about their salvation, he thundered, "Do it!" Finney's approach also made emotion paramount. His revivals were not as tumultuous as those on the southern frontier, but agonized prayers, groans, and uncontrolled crying often resounded through the hall.

Free will and perfectionism

With salvation within reach of every individual, what might be in store for society at large? "If the church would do her duty," Finney confidently predicted, "the millennium may come in this country in three years." By the 1830s Finney had taken to preaching not merely faith in human progress but something more—human perfectibility. Embracing this new theology of "perfectionism," he boldly asserted that all Christians should "aim at being holy and not rest satisfied until they are as perfect as God." And a true Christian would not rest until society was made perfect as well.

By preaching an optimistic message of free will and salvation to all, Finney and his eager imitators transformed Protestantism. But not all clergy applauded. For Lyman Beecher, as well as for many supporters of the Second Great Awakening, Finney's new measures went too far in generating excessive emotionalism, while his theology of perfectionism verged on heresy. Undaunted by such criticism, Finney continued his revivals. As for Lyman Beecher, he decided in 1832 to outflank his adversaries by moving west to become the president of Lane Seminary in Cincinnati. There he planned to train the right sort of revivalists to save the frontier for true religion and to bring about the kingdom of God in America.

In The Way of Good and Evil devout Christians are all helped on the path (right) to millennial perfection by the virtues of family, religion, education, and hard work. Sinners on the left, however, take the path of disobedience, intemperance, and lying—straight to hell.

Religion and the Market Economy

Revival audiences responded to the call for reform partly because they were unsettled by the era's rapid social changes. In the North, evangelical religion proved strongest not in isolated backwaters but in frontier areas just entering the market economy. Rochester, New York, a booming flour-milling center on the Erie Canal, epitomized that social environment.

Finney's Rochester revival

When Charles Finney came to town in the winter of 1830–1831, Rochester was a community in crisis. It had grown in a decade and a half from a village of 300 souls to a commercial city of more than 20,000. That wrenching expansion produced sharp divisions among the town's leaders, a large working class that increasingly lived apart from employers and beyond their moral control, and a rowdy saloon culture catering to canal boatmen and other transients.

Finney preached almost daily in Rochester for six months. He was assisted by local ministers with his revivals, which brought thousands to accept his message of voluntary salvation and doubled church membership. Religion helped bring order to what had been a chaotic and fragmented city.

Revivalism's appeal to the middle class

Although revivals like Finney's Rochester triumph drew converts from all segments of American society, they appealed especially to the middle class. Lawyers, merchants, retailers, and manufacturers all played central roles in the larger market economy and invested in factories and railroads. The market put intense pressure on these upwardly mobile citizens. They viewed success as a reflection of moral character, yet they also feared that with the ups and downs of the economy—boom, then bust—they would lose their wealth. Religion provided a way in which to cope with the tensions and uncertainties of their own lives.

Workers and church membership

Workers, too, were among the converted. Conversions among workers dramatically increased during the depression that began in 1839, as revivalists preached from street corners and held meetings in the workplace and homes. The Methodist church, which lacked the social respectability of some of the other evangelical churches, was particularly important in instilling the values of sobriety, frugality, and hard work in the urban working class.

Among other things, joining a church reflected a desire to get ahead in the new economy by accepting moral self-discipline. To a striking degree, social mobility and church membership were linked. In Rochester two-thirds of the male workers who were church members improved their occupational status in a decade. In contrast, workers who did not join a church rarely stayed in town more than a few years, and those who stayed were likely to decline in status.

Revivalists like Finney were interested in saving souls, not money, and their converts were most concerned with their spiritual state. Even so, evangelical Protestantism reinforced values needed to succeed in the new competitive economy. Churchgoers embraced the values of hard work, punctuality, and sobriety; they internalized the demand for self-control. In that sense, religion was one means of social control in a disordered society. And many employers put pressure on workers to give up their drinking habits, on and off the job, and to embrace religion.

The Rise of African American Churches

Independent black churches grew in size and importance as well because African Americans in urban areas increasingly resented being treated as second-class worshipers. In 1787, only a month after the close of the Constitutional Convention in Philadelphia, Richard Allen was praying at St. George's Church. Allen was not only a devout churchgoer but also a popular black preacher. But this Sunday morning his prayers were interrupted. "You must get up—you must not kneel here," a white usher whispered to Allen, who was not in the area reserved for black parishioners. Several white ushers roughly pulled him to his feet. Allen and other black members of the congregation walked out. In 1794 he organized the Bethel Church, where African Americans would be free to worship without discrimination.

In the early nineteenth century, similar tensions led to the formation of black Methodist and Baptist churches in a number of northern and southern cities. The most important was the African Methodist Episcopal (AME) Church. Growing fears for the security of slavery caused southern white communities, especially in the Deep South, to suppress independent black churches after 1820. But these churches, which were strongly evangelical, continued to grow in the North. In 1836 the AME Church, first organized in 1816, had 7,500 members. Twenty years later its membership was about 20,000. As with the black Baptist church, however, its major growth lay in the future and in the South following emancipation.

The Significance of the Second Great Awakening

As a result of the Second Great Awakening, the dominant form of Christianity in America became evangelical Protestantism. Membership in the major Protestant churches—Congregational, Presbyterian, Baptist, and Methodist—soared during the first half of the nineteenth century. By 1840 an estimated half of the adult population was nominally connected to some church, with the Methodists emerging as the largest Protestant denomination in both the North and the South.

Evangelicalism was in harmony with the basic values of early-nineteenth-century Americans. Its emphasis on the ability of everyone to bring about his or her salvation upheld the American belief in individualism. By catering to a mass audience without social distinctions, the revivals reinforced the American belief in democracy and equality. And Finney's invincibly optimistic doctrine of perfectionism was exactly attuned to the spirit of the age.

Evangelicalism bolsters individualism and equality

But not all—or even a majority—of Americans who flocked to revivals or # Women's Sphere

joined reform societies were men. On the contrary, female converts outnumbered males by about three to two. Usually the initial convert in a family was a woman, and many men who converted were related to women who had come forward earlier.

Women and Revivalism

Women's changing lives

Women played such an important role in the Awakening partly because of changes in their own social universe. Instead of parents arranging the marriages of their children, couples were beginning to wed more often on the basis of affection. Under such conditions, a woman's prospects for marriage became less certain, and in older areas like New England, the migration of so many young men to the West compounded this uncertainty. Yet marriage was deemed important for a woman's happiness, and it remained essential for her economic security.

The unpredictability of these social circumstances drew young women toward religion. Women between the ages of 12 and 25 were especially susceptible to conversion. Joining a church heightened a young woman's feeling of initiative and gave her a sense of purpose. By establishing respectability and widening her social circle of friends, church membership also enhanced her chances of marriage.

The Ideal of Domesticity

The era's changing economic order brought other pressures to bear on wives and mothers. Most men now worked outside the home, while the rise of factories led

As business affairs grew increasingly separate from the family in the nineteenth century, the middle-class home became a female domain. A woman's role as a wife and mother was to dispense love and moral guidance to her husband and her children. As this domestic scene makes clear, she was at the very center of the world of the family.

to a decline in part-time work such as spinning, which women had once performed to supplement family income. Moreover, except on the frontier, home manufacturing was no longer essential, for the family purchased articles that women previously had made, such as cloth, soap, and candles. "The transition from mother-and-daughter power to water-and-steam power," one New England minister noted, produced "a complete revolution of domestic life."

This growing separation of the household from the workplace meant that the home took on a new social identity. It was idealized as a place of "domesticity," a haven away from the competitive, workaday world, with the mother firmly at its center. This new view of women's role was elaborated largely by clergy and female authors in sermons, advice manuals, and pieces of sentimental fiction for an urban middle-class audience. But the ideal's significance and acceptance had far-reaching consequences. The idea of domesticity was based on the notion of separate sexual spheres. If men's sphere was the world of factories, offices, and fields, women's sphere was the home, where they were to dispense love and comfort and teach moral values to husbands and children. "Love is our life our reality, business yours," Mollie Clark told one suitor.

Women, who were considered morally stronger, were also held to a higher standard of sexual purity. A man's sexual infidelity, while hardly condoned, brought no lasting shame. But a woman who engaged in sexual relations before marriage or was unfaithful afterward was threatened with everlasting disgrace. Under this double standard, women were to be passive and submerge their identities in those of their husbands.

Most women of the era did not see this ideology as a rationale for male dominance. On the contrary, women played an important role in creating the ideal of domesticity, none more than Lyman Beecher's daughter Catharine. Like the earlier advocates of "republican motherhood," Catharine Beecher argued that women exercised power as moral guardians of the nation's future. The proper care of a middle-class household was also a crucial responsibility, and Beecher wrote several books on efficient home management. "There is no one thing more necessary to a housekeeper in performing her varied duties, than a habit of system and order," she told readers. "For all the time afforded us, we must give account to God."

Catharine Beecher was also a leading advocate of giving women greater educational opportunities so that they could become schoolteachers. Conceiving of the school as an extension of the home, she maintained that teachers, like mothers, should instill sound moral values in children. She argued that women's naturally pious character and their affection for children made them ideally suited to be teachers.

"Sisterhood" and social networks

Women also exerted their moral authority through the growing number of benevolent organizations, which fostered close friendships among women. Women gave emotionally much more to other family members than they received in exchange, and they turned to other women for comfort and support. This "sisterhood"—the common sense of identity and shared experiences— helped sustain reform movements launched by women to aid females of the lower classes.

The ideal of domesticity was not unique to the United States. The middle class became increasingly important in Europe, so that after 1850 it was culturally dominant and formulated society's values. Employment opportunities expanded for women as industrialization accelerated, yet the social expectation among the middle class was that women would not be employed outside the home. This redefinition of women's roles was more sweeping in Europe because previously, middle-class women had left the task of child-raising largely to hired nurses and governesses. By midcentury, these mothers devoted much more time to domestic duties, including rearing the children. Family size also declined, both in France and in England. The middle class was most numerous in England; indeed, the importance of the middle class in Britain during Queen Victoria's reign gave these ideals the label *Victorianism.*

Domesticity in Europe

The majority of white women hardly had time to make the ideal of domesticity the center of their lives. Farmers' wives had to work constantly, whereas lower-class families could not get by without the wages of female members. Still, most middle-class women tried to live up to the ideal, though many found the effort confining. "The great trial is that I have nothing to do," one complained. "Here I am with abundant leisure and capable, I believe, of accomplishing some good, and yet with no object on which to expend my energies."

Women's socially defined role as guardians of morality helps explain their prominence among revival converts. Religious activity was one way that women could exert influence over society and one area where wives need not be subordinate to their husbands. For some male critics, Finney's policy of giving women a prominent role in revivals threatened to bring about a dangerous equality between the sexes. One unhappy man in Rochester complained about the effect of Finney's visit to his home: "He *stuffed* my wife with tracts, and alarmed her fears, and nothing short of meetings, night and day, could atone for the many fold sins my poor, simple spouse had committed." Then, getting to the heart of the matter, he added, "She made the miraculous discovery, that she had been 'unevenly yoked.' From this unhappy period, peace, quiet, and happiness have fled from my dwelling, never, I fear, to return."

The Middle-Class Family in Transition

As the middle-class family adapted to the pressures of competitive society by becoming a haven of moral virtue, it developed a new structure and new set of attitudes closer in spirit to those of the modern family. One basic change was the rise of privacy. The family was increasingly seen as a sheltered retreat from the outside world. (See Daily Lives, "Privacy Begins at Home," pages 370–371.) In addition, the pressures to achieve success led middle-class young adults to delay marriage, since a husband was expected to have the financial means to support his wife.

Smaller family size was a result of the delay in marriage as well, since wives began bearing children later. But especially among the urban middle class, women began to use birth control to space children further apart and minimize the risks of pregnancy. In addition, it has been estimated that before 1860 one abortion was performed for every five or six live births. These practices contributed to a decline in the birthrate, from slightly more than 7 children per family in 1800 to 5.4 in 1850—a 25 percent drop. And over that 50-year period the decline became more abrupt beginning in the 1830s. Family size was directly related to the success ethic. On the farm, children working in the fields and around the house were an economic asset. In the new, market-oriented urban society, in contrast, children needed an extended education and special training in order to succeed. Thus they were a greater financial burden on their parents.

Decline in the birthrate

Daily Lives

PUBLIC SPACE/ PRIVATE SPACE
Privacy Begins at Home

In 1831 Olive Walkley made a significant decision: she moved the bed in which she and her husband, Stephen, slept out of the parlor and replaced it with a carpet. She also had the unfinished upstairs plastered and partitioned into bedrooms for their children. The Walkleys were farmers in Southington, Connecticut, but like middle-class urban families they were influenced by the new movement to separate public and private space in the home.

When the Walkleys were married in 1811, Americans were accustomed to living in close quarters, for most houses had few rooms. Further, the limited light and heat forced members to congregate together. Parents and sometimes the entire family slept in the parlor, where visitors were also entertained and where the family's most valuable possessions, including its best bed, were proudly displayed. Even in the wealthiest households, usually only the parents enjoyed separate sleeping quarters, and in most homes beds could be found in virtually every room.

In the years after 1820, however, the American home was reshaped to create specialized regions of privacy, service, and socializing. While houses increasingly faced the road, new designs provided greater privacy by creating an entry hall that served as a transition space from the outside world to the various parts of the house and by separating living and cooking quarters from areas for entertainment.

A sitting room was for the family's everyday use, whereas the parlor was reserved for public activity, including receiving company, giving recitals, and performing ceremonies such as weddings and funerals. As Americans developed a new sense of privacy, the parents' bed and the intimate activities associated with it were placed out of sight. In more prosperous homes an upholstered mahogany sofa replaced the bed in the parlor, and the floor was covered with a carpet, as much a symbol of the family's refine-ment as the mantel clock was of its modern outlook.

Food preparation and domestic work were done in a separate kitchen and adjoining back rooms. While rural families often continued to eat in the sitting room, houses more frequently contained a separate dining room. Stoves, which enlarged usable space by radiating heat, became common in more affluent homes, while the hearth and its fire—once the main source of food, heat, and light—ceased to be the center of

An architect confers with builders about the plans as a new house goes up in the background

With smaller families, however, parents could tend more carefully to their children's success. Increasingly middle-class families took on the expense of additional education to prepare their sons for a career in business. They also frequently equalized inheritances rather than favoring the eldest son or favoring sons over daughters.

American Romanticism

The rational-minded Unitarians in Boston had become accustomed to being attacked by evangelical ministers like Lyman Beecher. They were less prepared to be criticized by one of their own—and on their own home ground, no less. Yet that was what happened when a Unitarian minister named Ralph Waldo Emerson addressed the students of Harvard Divinity School on a warm summer evening in July 1838.

the family's life together. In addition, sleeping space became increasingly private and individual. Larger homes now contained bedrooms, normally on the second floor, and if space permitted, adolescent and grown unmarried children were given separate bedrooms, where they could withdraw from the rest of the family. Smaller family size as well as higher income enabled middle-class families to create new private space within the home.

The newer homes projected a sense of order as well, in sharp contrast to the run-down appearance of older houses, especially in the countryside. These were rarely painted, doors often did not fit, broken windows were patched with rags, and front yards remained unenclosed. Often enough, trash and garbage were simply tossed out the nearest window or door. However, as middle-class families (especially in the North) became increasingly sensitive to the home's exterior public face, they began to paint their houses and keep them in good repair. They also erected whitewashed fences around their front yards, planted ornamental trees and shrubs, trimmed the grass, and put their refuse in pits.

The new standards of domestic life also emphasized cleanliness and decoration. Lydia Maria Child's popular *The American Frugal Housewife* offered families of modest means numerous tips on cleaning and scouring as well as decorating. The market for brooms soared as wives sought to keep their homes clean. In 1798 only a few hundred broomcorn brooms were manufactured; in 1840 almost 2 million were sold. At the same time, women increasingly decorated their homes with mass-produced carpets, wallpaper, mirrors, lithographs, and curtains (which enhanced privacy from passersby).

A home's floor plan and furnishings not only determined comfort but also defined a family's status and aspirations. These signs of refinement were most often found in homes of professionals, prosperous farmers, and upwardly mobile skilled workers. The new domestic ideal of the home, which required additional floor space and the ownership of consumer goods, widened the gap between the middle and poorer ranks of society.

Emerson warned his listeners that the true church seemed "to totter to its fall, almost all life extinct." Outside, nature's world was alive and vibrant: "The grass grows, the buds burst, the meadow is spotted with fire and gold in the tint of flowers." But from the pulpits of too many congregations came lifeless preaching. "In how many churches, by how many prophets, tell me," Emerson demanded, "is man made sensible that he is an infinite Soul?" Leaving the shocked audience to ponder his message, Emerson and his wife drove home beneath a night sky illuminated by the northern lights.

Emerson's Divinity School Address glowed much like that July aurora. The address lacked the searing fire of Finney's revivals, yet it was bold in its own way because it reflected a second major current of thought that shaped the reform movements of the era. That current was the intellectual movement known as Romanticism.

Romantic movement

Romanticism began in Europe as a reaction against the Enlightenment. The Enlightenment had placed reason at the center of human achievement; Romanticism instead emphasized the importance of emotion and intuition as sources of truth. It gloried in the unlimited potential of the individual, who might soar if freed from the restraints of institutions. Romanticism extolled humanitarianism and sympathized with the oppressed.

In elevating inner feelings and heartfelt convictions, Romanticism reinforced the emotionalism of religious revivals. Philosophically, its influence was strongest among intellectuals who took part in the Transcendental movement and in the dramatic flowering of American literature. And like revivalism, Romanticism offered its own paths toward perfectionism.

Emerson and Transcendentalism

Above all, Romanticism produced individualists. Thus Transcendentalism is difficult to define, for its members resisted being lumped together. It blossomed in the mid-1830s, when a number of Unitarian clergy like George Ripley and Ralph Waldo Emerson resigned their pulpits, loudly protesting the church's smug, lifeless teachings. The new "Transcendentalist Club" attracted a small following among other discontented Boston intellectuals, including Margaret Fuller, Bronson Alcott, and Orestes Brownson.

Transcendentalist ideas

Like European Romantics, American Transcendentalists emphasized feeling over reason, seeking a spiritual communion with nature. By *transcend* they meant to go beyond or to rise above—specifically above reason and beyond the material world. As part of creation, every human being contained a spark of divinity, Emerson avowed. Transcendentalists also shared in Romanticism's glorification of the individual. "Trust thyself. Every heart vibrates to that iron string," Emerson advised. "The root and seed of democracy is the doctrine, judge for yourself." If freed from the constraints of traditional authority, the individual had infinite potential. So optimistic

In the summer of 1858 members of the cultural Saturday Club of Boston made an excursion to the Adirondacks to observe nature. In *Philosopher's Camp*, painted by William J. Stillman, who organized the expedition, a group on the left dissects a fish under the supervision of the famous scientist Louis Agassiz, while on the right others practice firing rifles. Symbolically, Ralph Waldo Emerson stands alone in the center contemplating the world in solitude.

was Transcendentalism in its view of human nature that it essentially denied the existence of evil.

Transcendentalism had much in common with Jacksonian America—optimism, individualism, and an egalitarian spirit. Like the devout at Finney's revivals, who sought to perfect themselves and society, listeners who flocked to Emerson's lectures were infused with the spirit of optimistic reform.

As the currents of Romanticism percolated through American society, the country's literature came of age. In 1820 educated Americans still tended to ape the fashions of Europe and read English books. But as the population grew, education increased, and the country's literary market expanded, American writers looked with greater interest at the customs and character of their own society. Improved printing presses made possible cheaper, mass-produced American books, and better transportation led to a wider distribution of printed material. By 1850 for every British book, two American books were sold in the United States.

Emergence of American literature

Emerson's address "The American Scholar" (1837) constituted a declaration of literary independence. "Our long dependence, our long apprenticeship to the learning of other lands draws to a close," he proclaimed. "Events, actions arise, that must be sung, that will sing themselves."

The Clash between Nature and Civilization

At the time Emerson spoke, James Fenimore Cooper was already making his mark as the first distinctive American novelist. In the Leatherstocking Tales, a series of five novels written between 1823 and 1841, he focused on the clash between nature and civilization. Cooper clearly admired his hero, Natty Bumppo, a self-reliant frontiersman who represented the nobility and innocence of the wilderness. At the same time, the novels portrayed the culture of the frontier as a threat to the civilization Cooper prized so highly.

Cooper and wilderness

In one scene in *The Pioneers* (1823), as frontier villagers slaughter thousands of pigeons, Leatherstocking laments the wanton destruction, only to hear a townsman express surprise that anyone would "grumble at the loss of a few pigeons. . . . If you had to sow your wheat twice, and three times, as I have done," he continues, "you wouldn't be so massyfully feeling'd toward the devils." As Americans began to exploit the resources of the hinterlands, many of the country's new Romantic writers betrayed a concern that the advance of civilization, with its market economy and crowded urban centers, might destroy the natural simplicity of the land. Natty Bumppo stood halfway between the savage and civilized worlds, not comfortable embracing either.

Henry David Thoreau, too, used nature as a backdrop to explore the conflict between the unfettered individual and the constraints of society. Thoreau grew up in Concord, Massachusetts, where he became part of Emerson's circle. In 1845 he built a cabin on the edge of Walden Pond, living in relative solitude for 16 months to demonstrate the advantages of self-reliance. His experiences became the basis for one of the classics in American literature, *Walden* (1854).

Thoreau and individualism

Thoreau argued that only in nature could one find true independence. By living simply, it was possible to master oneself and the world. Thoreau's own isolation, however, was less than total. When lonely or hungry, he walked to Emerson's home nearby for conversation and a slice of Lidia Emerson's apple pie, and most of the materials he used to build his "wilderness" cabin were store-bought. Still, *Walden* eloquently denounced Americans' frantic competition for material goods and wealth. "Money is not required to buy one necessity of the soul," Thoreau maintained.

"I see my townsmen, whose misfortune it is to have inherited farms, houses, barns, cattle, and farming tools. . . . Who made them serfs of the soil?" It seemed only too clear that "the mass of men lead lives of quiet desperation."

Thoreau's individualism was so extreme that he rejected any institution that contradicted his personal sense of right. "The only obligation which I have a right to assume, is to do at any time what I think right," he wrote in his essay "On Civil Disobedience." Voicing the anti-institutional impulse of Romanticism, he took individualism to its antisocial extreme.

Songs of the Self-Reliant and Darker Loomings

Walt Whitman, poet of democracy

In contrast to Thoreau's exclusiveness, Walt Whitman was all-inclusive, embracing American society in its infinite variety. A journalist and laborer in the New York City area, Whitman was inspired by the common people, whose "manners, speech, dress, friendships . . . are unrhymed poetry." In taking their measure in *Leaves of Grass* (1855), he pioneered a new, modern form of poetry, unconcerned with meter and rhyme and filled with frank imagery and sexual references.

Conceiving himself the representative of all Americans, Whitman exuberantly titled his first major poem "Song of Myself."

> I am your voice—It was tied in you—In me it began to talk.
> I celebrate myself to celebrate every man and woman alive.

Emerson and other critics were put off by his rough-hewn methods, but Whitman, like the Transcendentalists, exalted the emotions, nature, and the individual. At the same time, he endowed these ideas with a more joyous, democratic spirit.

More brooding in temperament was Nathaniel Hawthorne, who lived for a time in Concord. Unable to partake of Emerson's sunny optimism and repelled by the self-centered outlook of Thoreau, Hawthorne wrote of the power of the past to shape future generations and the consequences of pride, selfishness, envy, and secret guilt. In *The Scarlet Letter* (1850), set in New England's Puritan era, Hawthorne spun the tale of Hester Prynne, who bore an illegitimate child, and of the Puritan neighbors who harshly condemned her. Like the Puritans, Hawthorne had no illusions about creating a world without evil, and he rejected the American belief that a person or nation could free itself from the past.

Melville and nature's destructive power

Hawthorne found a soul mate in Herman Melville, whose dark masterpiece, *Moby-Dick* (1851), drew on his youthful experiences aboard a whaling ship. The novel's Captain Ahab relentlessly drives his ship in pursuit of the great white whale Moby-Dick. In Melville's telling, Ahab becomes a powerful symbol of American character: the prototype of the ruthless businessman despoiling nature's resources in his pursuit of success. "Swerve me?" he asks at one point. "The path to my fixed purpose is laid with iron rails, whereon my soul is grooved to run. Over unsound gorges, through the rifled hearts of mountains, under torrents' beds, unerringly I rush!" Ahab is Emerson's self-reliant man, but in him, self-reliance is transformed into a monomania that eventually destroys his ship, its crew, and himself.

Herman Melville

More clearly than any other writer, Melville recognized the dilemma created by Romanticism's emphasis on the individual. Liberated from institutional restraints, human possibilities seemed unlimited to Romantic philosophers. Yet as older traditions and institutions dropped away, the new individualism also led to a competitive materialism devoid of the older sense of community. How, Melville asked, could American society be made perfect, if it was based on self-interested materialism and individualism?

But awash in the many opportunities opening before them, most Americans were not attuned to such searching criticism. They preferred to celebrate, with Emerson, the glories of democracy and the individual's quest for perfection.

The Age of Reform

In the glowing fires of a fervent camp meeting, the quest for perfection often proved hard to control. At the Cane Ridge revival of 1801, the Methodist Peter Cartwright had his hands full trying to stop less orthodox preachers from gathering converts. Quite a few worshipers had joined a group known as the Shakers. Cartwright had to ride around the neighborhood "from cabin to cabin" trying to cure people of the Shaker "delusion."

The Shakers were only one group that demonstrated more radical possibilities for democratic change. While the mainline benevolent societies aimed at a more conservative reformation of individual sinners, the more radical offshoots of Romanticism and perfectionism sought to remake society at large.

Some schemers and dreamers for a better world harbored decidedly eccentric notions. Sylvester Graham, who argued that diet determined character, won lasting fame by inventing the cracker named after him. While he gained a small following, most Americans ignored him—except commercial bakers, who, knowing a threat when they saw one, mobbed this champion of homemade bread. Other reformers, however, decided that the best way to test untried ideas was to withdraw from the everyday world in order to demonstrate the possibilities of perfection.

Utopian Communities

Utopian communities aimed at reforming the world through example. They looked to replace the competitive individualism of American society with a purer spiritual unity and group cooperation. Some were directly linked to religion, but even the secular communities shared the optimism of perfectionism and millennialism.

Dancing was an integral part of the Shakers' religion, as this picture of a service at Lebanon, New York, indicates. In worshiping, men and women formed separate lines with their hands held out and moved back and forth in rhythm while singing religious songs. One Shaker hymn proclaimed, "With ev'ry gift I will unite, / And join in sweet devotion / To worship God is my delight, / With hands and feet in motion." Note the presence of African Americans in the community.

The Shakers

The Shakers proved to be one of the most long-lived utopian experiments. Ann Lee, the illiterate daughter of an English blacksmith, believed that God had a dual nature, part male and part female. Through a series of religious visions Lee became convinced that her own life would reveal the female side of the divinity, just as Christ had come to earth exemplifying the male side. In 1774 she led a small band of followers to America.

The Shaker movement's greatest growth, however, came after Lee's death, when her followers recruited converts at revivals like Cane Ridge. The new disciples founded about 20 communal settlements based on the teachings of Mother Ann, as she was known. Her followers sometimes shook in the fervent public demonstration of their faith—hence the name Shakers. Convinced that the end of the world was at hand and that there was no need to perpetuate the human race, Shakers practiced celibacy, separating the sexes as far as practical. Men and women normally worked apart, ate at separate tables in silence, entered separate doorways, and had separate living quarters.

Shaker communities accorded women unusual authority and equality. Community tasks were generally assigned along sexual lines, with women performing household chores and men laboring in the fields. Leadership of the church, however, was split equally between men and women. By the mid–nineteenth century, a majority of members were female.

Property in Shaker settlements was owned communally and controlled by the church hierarchy. The sect's members worked hard, lived simply, and impressed outsiders with their cleanliness and order. Lacking any natural increase, however, membership began to decline after 1850, from a peak of about 6000 members.

The Oneida Community and complex marriage

The Oneida Community, founded by John Humphrey Noyes, also set out to alter the relationship between the sexes, though in a markedly different way. Noyes, a convert of Charles Finney, took the doctrine of perfection to extremes. Whereas Finney argued that men and women should strive to achieve perfection, Noyes announced that he had actually reached this blessed state. Settling in Putney, Vermont, and, after 1848, in Oneida, New York, Noyes set out to create a community organized on his religious ideals.

In pursuit of greater freedom, Noyes relieved women of what he termed "kitchen slavery." Female members cooked only at breakfast and thereafter were free from household duties until the next morning. Noyes's ideas of liberation, however, went beyond the kitchen. Under his doctrine of "complex marriage," commune members were permitted to have sexual relations with one another, but only with the approval of the community and after a searching examination of the couple's motives. Noyes eventually undertook experiments in planned reproduction by selecting "scientific" combinations of parents to produce morally perfect children.

Under his charismatic leadership the Oneida Community grew to more than 200 members in 1851. But in 1879 an internal dispute drove him from power, and without his guiding hand the community soon fell apart. In 1881 its members reorganized as a business enterprise.

The Mormon Experience

The Church of Jesus Christ of Latter-day Saints, whose members are generally known as Mormons, was founded by a young man named Joseph Smith in Palmyra, in western New York, where the religious fires of revivalism flared up regularly. The son of a poor farmer, Smith was robust, charming, almost hypnotic in his appeal. In 1827, at the age of only 22, he announced that he had discovered a set of golden tablets on which was written the *Book of Mormon*. The tablets, which

Smith claimed to have translated, told the story of a band of Hebrews who in biblical times journeyed to America, splitting into two groups, the Nephites and Lamanites. The Nephites established a Christian civilization, only to be exterminated by the Lamanites, whose descendants are said to be the Indians of the Americas. Proclaiming that he had a commission from God to reestablish the true church, Smith gathered about him a group of devoted followers.

Like Charles Finney's more liberal theology, Mormonism placed little emphasis on predestination and proclaimed that salvation was available to all. Moreover, Mormon culture upheld the middle-class values of hard work, thrift, and self-control. It partook of the optimistic, materialist attitudes of American society. And by teaching that Christ would return to rule the earth, it shared in the hope of a coming millennial kingdom.

Mormonism was less an outgrowth of evangelicalism, however, than of the primitive gospel movement, which sought to reestablish the ancient church. Indeed, having seen the consequences of excessive emotion in the revivals of his youth, Smith soon curbed enthusiasm among his followers and downplayed the experience of conversion. In restoring what Smith called "the ancient order of things," he drew on both the Old and New Testaments. Thus Mormons created a theocracy uniting church and state, reestablished biblical priesthoods and titles, and adopted temple rituals. With its claims of continuing divine revelation, Mormonism attracted weary seekers of spiritual certainty and the true church.

Movement to restore the ancient church

After a revelation told Smith to gather the saints in the city of Zion in preparation for Christ's return to earth, he undertook to create a spiritual community first in Ohio and then in Missouri. But his unorthodox teachings provoked bitter persecution wherever he went, and mob violence finally hounded him and his followers out of Missouri in 1839. In response, Smith established a new holy city, which he named Nauvoo, located on the Mississippi River in Illinois.

Reinforced by a steady stream of converts from Britain, Nauvoo became the largest and fastest-growing city in Illinois, with a population of 10,000 by the mid-1840s. There, Smith introduced the most distinctive features of Mormon theology, including baptism for the dead, eternal marriage, and polygamy, or plural marriage. He also established the secret ceremonies of the Mormon temple, which rituals bore some resemblance to those of the Masonic order. As a result, Mormonism increasingly diverged from traditional Christianity and became a distinct new religion. Nauvoo's political organization was unorthodox too. To bolster his authority as a prophet, Smith established a theocratic government, under which church leaders controlled political offices and governed the community, with Smith as mayor.

City of Zion: Nauvoo

Discarding his earlier ideas of community property, Smith embraced private enterprise at Nauvoo. But speculation in land soon overran the city, rival neighborhoods vied to become the main commercial district, and dissident groups in the city challenged Smith's power. Neighboring residents, alarmed by the Mormons' growing political power and reports that church leaders were practicing polygamy, demanded that Nauvoo's charter be revoked and the church suppressed. In 1844, while in jail for destroying his opponents' press in Nauvoo, Smith was murdered by an anti-Mormon mob. In 1846 the Mormons abandoned Nauvoo, and the following year Brigham Young, Smith's successor, led them westward to Utah.

Socialist Communities

Not all utopian experiments were based on religious teachings. The hardship and poverty that accompanied the growth of industrial factories also inspired utopian communities based on science and reason. Robert Owen, a Scottish industrialist, came to the United States in 1824 committed to creating a society that balanced agriculture and manufacturing. Owen believed that the character of individuals was shaped by their surroundings and that by changing those surroundings, one could change human character.

Robert Owen and New Harmony

Unfortunately, most of the 900 or so volunteers who flocked to Owen's community in New Harmony, Indiana, lacked the skills and commitment needed to make it a success. Bitter factions soon split the settlement. Having lost most of his own fortune, Owen dissolved the community in 1827. More than 20 other American communities were founded on Owen's theories, but none were particularly successful.

Brook Farm

In 1841 Emerson's friend George Ripley organized Brook Farm, a Transcendentalist community and socialist experiment near Boston where members could live "a more wholesome and simple life than can be led amidst the pressure of our competitive institutions." Brook Farm attracted a number of prominent New England intellectuals, who remained for varying lengths of time. Its most important achievements were a magazine, *The Dial,* edited by Margaret Fuller, and its innovative school, whose curriculum included modern subjects such as history, art, and literature. The school's success, however, was overshadowed by the economic failure of the farm, and in 1847 the community disbanded.

The experiences of Brook Farm, New Harmony, and similar communities demonstrated that the United States was poor soil for socialistic experiments. Wages were too high and land too cheap to interest most Americans. And individualism was too strong to create a commitment to cooperative action.

The Temperance Movement

The most significant reform movements of the period sought not to withdraw from society but to change it directly. One of the most determined of these was the temperance movement.

Attack on drinking

The origins of the campaign against alcohol lay in the era's heavy drinking. Alcohol consumption soared after the Revolution, so that by 1830 the average American consumed four gallons of absolute alcohol a year, the highest level in American history and nearly triple present-day levels. Anne Royale, whose travels took her cross-country by stage, reported, "When I was in Virginia, it was too much whiskey—in Ohio, too much whiskey—in Tennessee, it is too, too much whiskey!" The social costs for such habits were high: broken families, abused and neglected wives and children, sickness and disability, poverty, and crime. The temperance movement undertook to eliminate these problems by curbing drinking.

Led largely by clergy, the movement at first focused on drunkenness and did not oppose moderate drinking. But in 1826 the American Temperance Society was founded, taking voluntary abstinence as its goal. During the next decade approximately 5000 local temperance societies were founded.

Annual Consumption of Distilled Spirits, per Capita, 1710–1920
Beginning in 1790, per capita levels of drinking steadily rose, until 1830, when the temperance movement produced a sharp decline over the next two decades.

As the movement gained momentum, annual per capita consumption of alcohol dropped sharply. By 1845 it had fallen below two gallons a year.

The temperance movement lasted longer and attracted many more supporters than other reforms did. It appealed to young and old, to urban and rural residents, to workers and businesspeople. Moreover, it was one of the few reform movements with significant support in the South. Its success came partly for social reasons. Democracy necessitated sober voters; factories required sober workers. In addition, temperance attracted the upwardly mobile—professionals, small businesspeople, and skilled artisans anxious to improve their social standing. Finally, temperance advocates stressed the suffering that men inflicted on women and children, and thus the movement appealed to women as a means to defend the home and carry out their domestic mission.

Educational Reform

In 1800 Massachusetts was the only state that required free public schools supported by community funds. The call for tax-supported education arose first among workers, as a way to restore their deteriorating position in society. But middle-class reformers quickly took control of the movement, looking to uplift the masses, make them responsible citizens, and preserve equal opportunity. Horace Mann, the leading proponent of common schools, hailed education as "the great equalizer of the conditions of men" and contended that it would eliminate poverty. Reformers appealed to business leaders by arguing that the new economic order needed educated workers.

Common school movement

Mann convinced Massachusetts to create a state board of education, which he oversaw from 1837 to 1848. Under his leadership, the state adopted a minimum-length school year, provided for training of teachers, and expanded the curriculum to include subjects such as history, geography, and various applied skills. Massachusetts also took the lead in requiring every town with a population of 500 or more to establish a high school. This innovation was slow to catch on elsewhere; by 1860 the nation could count only about 300 high schools, fully a third of them in Massachusetts. Moreover, compulsory attendance was rarely instated. Many poor parents out of necessity sent their children to work instead of school. Still, by the 1850s the number of schools, attendance figures, and school budgets had all increased sharply. School reformers enjoyed their greatest success in the Northeast and the least in the South, where planters opposed paying taxes to educate poorer white children.

Educational opportunities for women also expanded. Teachers like Catharine Beecher and Emma Hunt Willard established a number of private girls' schools, putting to rest the objection of many male educators that fragile female minds could not absorb large doses of mathematics, physics, or geography. In 1833 Oberlin became the nation's first coeducational college. Four years later Mary Lyon founded Mount Holyoke, the first American college for women.

Female education

The Asylum Movement

After 1820 there was also a dramatic increase in the number of asylums of every sort—orphanages, jails, and hospitals. Advocates of asylums called for isolating and separating the criminal, the insane, the ill, and the dependent from outside society. The goal of care in asylums, which had earlier focused on confinement, shifted to the reform of personal character.

American efforts to rehabilitate prisoners attracted international attention. Pennsylvania and New York developed systems to isolate prisoners, introducing the measures of solitary confinement and absolute silence to give inmates time to reflect on their past errors. The reformers assumed that environment produced criminal behavior and that the new prison routines would rehabilitate criminals. The new measures were not very effective, however, and under the strain of isolation some inmates went insane or committed suicide.

Prison reformers believed that rigid discipline, extensive rules, and (in some programs) solitary confinement were necessary to rehabilitate criminals. Prisoners often had to march lockstep under strict supervision and wear uniforms such as those seen in this photograph from the 1870s.

Dorothea Dix and the insane

Dorothea Dix, a Boston schoolteacher, took the lead in advocating state-supported asylums for the mentally ill. She attracted much attention to the movement by her report detailing the horrors to which the mentally ill were subjected, including being chained, kept in cages and closets, and beaten with rods. In response to her efforts, 28 states maintained mental institutions by 1860.

Like other reform movements, the push for new asylums and better educational facilities reflected overtones of both liberation and control. Asylums freed prisoners and the mentally ill from the harsh punishments and abuses of the past, but the new techniques of "rehabilitation" forced prisoners to march in lockstep. Education brought with it the freedom to question and to acquire knowledge, but some enthusiastic reformers hoped that schools would become as orderly as prisons. Louis Dwight, who advocated solitary confinement for prisoners at night and total silence by day, suggested eagerly that such methods "would greatly promote order, seriousness, and purity in large families, male and female boarding schools, and colleges."

Abolitionism

Late in the fall of 1834, Lyman Beecher was in the midst of his continuing efforts to "overturn and overturn" on behalf of the kingdom of God. As planned, he had gone to Cincinnati to assume leadership of Lane Seminary. The school had everything that an institution for training ministers to convert the West needed— everything, that is, except students. In October 1834 all but 8 of Lane's 100 scholars had departed after months of bitter fighting with Beecher and the trustees over the issue of abolition.

Beecher knew the source of his troubles: a scruffy yet magnetic student named Theodore Dwight Weld. Weld had been firing up his classmates over the need to immediately free the slaves. Beecher was not surprised, for Weld had been

William Lloyd Garrison (shown, left, at age 30) and Theodore Dwight Weld (right) represented different wings of the abolitionist movement. Garrison's growing radicalism led him to repudiate organized religion in the struggle against slavery. Weld, on the other hand, preferred to work through the evangelical churches and cooperate with the clergy.

converted by that firebrand Finney. He knew, too, that Weld had been influenced by the arguments of William Lloyd Garrison, whose abolitionist writings had sent shock waves across the entire nation. Indeed, Beecher's troubles at Lane Seminary provided only one example of how the flames of reform, when fanned, could spread along paths not anticipated by those who first kindled them.

The Beginnings of the Abolitionist Movement

William Lloyd Garrison symbolized the transition from a moderate antislavery movement to the more militant abolitionism of the 1830s. A sober, religious youngster deeply influenced by his Baptist mother, Garrison in the 1820s edited a newspaper sympathetic to many of the new reforms. In 1829 he was enlisted in the antislavery cause by Benjamin Lundy, a Quaker who edited a Baltimore antislavery newspaper, *The Genius of Universal Emancipation*. Calling for a gradual end to slavery, Lundy supported colonization, a strategy for overcoming southern fears of emancipation by transporting free black Americans to Africa.

Embracing colonization, Garrison went to Baltimore to help edit Lundy's paper. It was there that Garrison first encountered the opinions of free African Americans, who played a major role in the genesis of the abolitionist movement. To his surprise, Garrison discovered that most of them strongly opposed the colonization movement as proslavery and antiblack. "This is our home, and this is our country," a free black convention proclaimed in 1831. "Beneath its sod lie the bones of our fathers; for it some of them fought, bled, and died. Here we were born, and here we will die." Under their influence, Garrison soon developed views far more radical than Lundy's, and within a year of moving to Baltimore, the young firebrand was convicted of libel and imprisoned. Upon his release Garrison hurried back to Boston, determined to publish a new kind of antislavery journal.

Free blacks oppose colonization

On January 1, 1831, the first issue of *The Liberator* appeared, and abolitionism was born. In appearance, the bespectacled Garrison seemed frail, almost mousy. In print, however, he was abrasive, withering, and uncompromising. "On this subject,

I do not wish to think, or speak, or write with moderation," he proclaimed. "I am in earnest—I will not equivocate—I will not excuse—I will not retreat a single inch—AND I WILL BE HEARD." Repudiating gradual emancipation and embracing "immediatism," Garrison insisted that slavery end at once. He denounced colonization as a racist, antiblack movement and upheld the principle of racial equality. To those who suggested that slaveowners should be compensated for freeing their slaves, Garrison was firm. Southerners ought to be convinced by "moral suasion" to renounce slavery as a sin. Virtue was its own reward.

Garrison's immediatism

Garrison attracted the most attention, but other abolitionists spoke with equal conviction. Wendell Phillips, from a socially prominent Boston family, held listeners spellbound with his speeches. Lewis Tappan and his brother Arthur, two New York City silk merchants, boldly placed their wealth behind a number of humanitarian causes, including abolitionism. James G. Birney, an Alabama slaveholder, converted to abolitionism after wrestling with his conscience, and Angelina and Sarah Grimké, the daughters of a South Carolina planter, left their native state to speak against the institution. And there was Angelina's future husband, Theodore Weld, the restless student at Lane Seminary who had fallen so dramatically under Garrison's influence.

To abolitionists, slavery was a moral, not an economic, question. The institution seemed a contradiction of the principle of the American Revolution that all human beings had been created with natural rights. Then, too, it went against the Romantic spirit of the age, which celebrated the individual's freedom and self-reliance. Abolitionists condemned slavery because of the breakup of marriages and families by sale, the harsh punishment of the lash, slaves' lack of access to education, and the sexual abuse of black women. Most of all, they denounced slavery as outrageously contrary to Christian teaching. As one Ohio antislavery paper declared, "We believe slavery to be a sin, always, everywhere, and only, sin—sin, in itself." So persistent were abolitionists in their religious objections that they forced the churches to face the question of slavery head-on. In the 1840s the Methodist and Baptist churches each split into northern and southern organizations over the issue.

The Spread of Abolitionism

After helping organize the New England Anti-Slavery Society in 1832, Garrison joined with Lewis Tappan and Theodore Weld the following year to establish a national organization, the American Anti-Slavery Society. It coordinated a loosely affiliated network of state and local societies. During the years before the Civil War, perhaps 200,000 northerners belonged to an abolitionist society.

Geography of abolitionism

Abolitionists were concentrated in the East, especially New England, and in areas that had been settled by New Englanders, such as western New York and northern Ohio. The movement was not strong in cities or among businesspeople and workers. Most abolitionists were young, being generally in their twenties and thirties when the movement began, and had grown up in rural areas and small towns in middle-class families. Intensely religious, many had been profoundly affected by the revivals of the Second Great Awakening. Whatever their background, they shared a deep alienation from American society—its crass materialism, its shallow politics, and its lack of religion. More and more they came to feel that slavery was the fundamental cause of the Republic's degraded condition.

Certainly Theodore Weld was cut from this mold. After enrolling in Lane Seminary in 1833, he promoted immediate abolitionism among his fellow students.

When Lyman Beecher assumed the Lane presidency a year later, he confronted a student body dominated by committed abolitionists, impatient of any position that stopped short of Garrison's immediatism.

The radicalism of Lane students was also made clear in their commitment to racial equality. Unlike some abolitionists, who opposed slavery but disdained blacks as inferior, Lane students mingled freely with Cincinnati's free black community. Alarmed by rumors in the summer of 1834 that the town's residents intended to demolish the school, Beecher and Lane's trustees forbade any discussion of slavery on campus, restricted contact with the black community, and ordered students to return to their studies. "Who that has an opinion and a soul will enter L. Sem now?" one rebel asked. "Who can do it without degrading himself?" All except a few left the school and enrolled at Oberlin College. That debt-ridden institution agreed to their demands for guaranteeing freedom of speech, admitting black students, and hiring Charles Finney as professor of theology.

Lane Seminary rebellion

But Finney fared no better than Beecher with the Lane rebels. In the end, he too concluded that reform generated discord, distracting Christians from the greater good of promoting revivals. Both men conceived of sin in terms of individual immorality, not unjust social institutions. To the abolitionists, however, America could never become a godly nation until slavery was abolished. "Revivals, moral Reform, etc. will remain stationary until the temple is cleansed," Weld bluntly concluded.

Free African Americans, who made up the majority of subscribers to Garrison's *Liberator*, provided important support and leadership for the movement. Frederick Douglass assumed the greatest prominence. Having escaped from slavery in Maryland, he became an eloquent critic of its evils. Initially a follower of Garrison, Douglass eventually broke with him and started his own newspaper in Rochester. Other important black abolitionists included Martin Delany, William Wells Brown, William Still, and Sojourner Truth. Most black Americans endorsed peaceful means to end slavery, but David Walker in his *Appeal to the Colored Citizens of the World* (1829) urged slaves

Black abolitionists

Black abolitionist Frederick Douglass (second from left at the podium) was only one of nearly 50 runaway slaves who appeared at an abolitionist convention held in August 1850 in Cazenovia, New York. Other runaways included Emily and Mary Edmonson (both in plaid dresses). When the Edmonsons' attempt at escape failed, Henry Ward Beecher (Lyman Beecher's son) rallied his congregation in Brooklyn to raise the money to purchase the girls' freedom.

to use violence to end bondage. Aided by many other African Americans, these men and women battled against racial discrimination in the North as well as slavery in the South.

A network of antislavery sympathizers also developed in the North to convey runaway slaves to Canada and freedom. While not as extensive or as tightly organized as contemporaries claimed, the Underground Railroad hid fugitives and transported them northward from one station to the next. Free African Americans, who were more readily trusted by wary slaves, played a leading role in the Underground Railroad. One of its most famous conductors was Harriet Tubman, an escaped slave who repeatedly returned to the South and eventually escorted to freedom more than 200 slaves.

Opponents and Divisions

The drive for immediate abolition faced massive obstacles within American society. With slavery increasingly important to the South's economy, Southerners forced opponents of slavery to flee the region. In the North, where racism was equally entrenched, abolitionism provoked bitter resistance. Even abolitionists such as Garrison treated blacks paternalistically, contending that they should occupy a subordinate place in the antislavery movement.

On occasion, northern resistance turned violent. A hostile Boston mob seized Garrison in 1835 and paraded him with a rope around his body before he was finally rescued. Another anti-abolitionist mob burned down the headquarters of the American Anti-Slavery Society in Philadelphia. And in 1837 in Alton, Illinois, Elijah Lovejoy was murdered when he tried to protect his printing press from an angry crowd. The leaders of these mobs were not from the bottom of society but, as one of their victims noted, were "gentlemen of property and standing." Prominent leaders in the community, they reacted vigorously to the threat that abolitionists posed to their power and prosperity and to the established order.

Divisions among abolitionists

But abolitionists were also hindered by divisions among reformers. At Oberlin College Charles Finney preferred revivalism over Theodore Weld's abolitionism. Even more conservative than Finney, Lyman Beecher was shocked to hear that his son Edward had stood guard over Elijah Lovejoy's printing press the evening before the editor was murdered. Within another decade, Beecher would see his daughter Harriet Beecher Stowe write the most successful piece of antislavery literature in the nation's history, *Uncle Tom's Cabin*. Even the abolitionists themselves splintered, shaken by the opposition they encountered and unable to agree on the most effective response. More conservative reformers wanted to work within established institutions, using the churches and political action to end slavery. But for Garrison and his followers, the mob violence demonstrated that slavery was only part of a deeper national disease, whose cure required the overthrow of American institutions and values.

By the end of the decade, Garrison had worked out a program for the total reform of society. He embraced perfectionism and pacifism, denounced the clergy, urged members to leave the churches, and called for an end to all government. Condemning the Constitution as proslavery—"a covenant with death and an agreement with hell"—he publicly burned a copy one July 4th. No person of conscience, he argued, could vote or otherwise participate in the corrupt political system. This platform was radical enough on all counts, but the final straw for Garrison's opponents was his endorsement of women's rights as an inseparable part of abolitionism.

The Women's Rights Movement

Women faced many disadvantages in American society. They were kept out of most jobs, denied political rights, and given only limited access to education beyond the elementary grades. When a woman married, her husband became the legal representative of the marriage and gained complete control of her property. If a marriage ended in divorce, the husband was awarded custody of the children. Any unmarried woman was made the ward of a male relative.

When abolitionists divided over the issue of female participation, women found it easy to identify with the situation of slaves, since both were victims of male tyranny. Sarah and Angelina Grimké took up the cause of women's rights after they were criticized for speaking to audiences that included men as well as women. Sarah responded with *Letters on the Condition of Women and the Equality of the Sexes* (1838), arguing that women deserved the same rights as men. Abby Kelly, another abolitionist, remarked that women "have good cause to be grateful to the slave," for in "striving to strike his irons off, we found most surely, that we were manacled *ourselves.*"

Two abolitionists, Elizabeth Cady Stanton and Lucretia Mott, launched the women's rights movement after they were forced to sit behind a curtain at a world antislavery convention in London. In 1848 Stanton and Mott organized a conference in Seneca Falls, New York, that attracted about a hundred supporters. The meeting issued a Declaration of Sentiments, modeled after the Declaration of Independence, that began, "All men and women are created equal."

Seneca Falls convention

The Seneca Falls convention approved resolutions calling for educational and professional opportunities for women, laws giving them control of their property, recognition of legal equality, and repeal of laws awarding the father custody of the children in divorce. The most controversial proposal, and the only resolution that did not pass unanimously, was one demanding the right to vote. The Seneca Falls convention established the arguments and the program for the women's rights movement for the remainder of the century.

The women's rights movement won few victories before 1860. Several states gave women greater control over their property, and a few made divorce easier or granted women the right to sue in courts. But disappointments and defeats outweighed these early victories. Still, many of the important leaders in the crusade for women's rights that emerged after the Civil War had already taken their places at the forefront of the movement. They included Stanton, Susan B. Anthony, Lucy Stone, and—as Lyman Beecher by now must have expected, one of his daughters—Isabella Beecher Hooker.

The Schism of 1840

It was Garrison's position on women's rights that finally split antislavery ranks already divided over other aspects of his growing radicalism. The showdown came in 1840 at the national meeting of the American Anti-Slavery Society, when delegates debated whether women could hold office in the organization. Some of Garrison's opponents favored women's rights but opposed

Elizabeth Cady Stanton, one of the instigators and guiding spirits at the Seneca Falls convention, photographed with two of her children about that time.

linking the question to the slavery issue, insisting that it would drive off potential supporters. By packing the convention, Garrison carried the day. His opponents, led by Lewis Tappan, resigned to found the rival American and Foreign Anti-Slavery Society.

The schism of 1840 lessened the influence of abolitionism as a benevolent reform movement in American society. Although abolitionism heightened moral concern about slavery, it failed to convert the North to its program, and its supporters remained a tiny minority. For all the considerable courage they showed, their movement suffered from the lack of a realistic, long-range plan for eliminating so deeply entrenched an institution. Garrison even boasted that "the genius of the abolitionist movement is to have *no* plan." Abolitionism demonstrated the severe limits of moral suasion and individual conversions as a solution to deeply rooted social problems.

Reform Shakes the Party System

"What a fog-bank we are in politically! Do you see any head-land or light—or can you get an observation—or soundings?" The words came from a puzzled Whig politician writing a friend after the Massachusetts state elections of 1853. He was in such a confused state because reformers were increasingly entering the political arena to achieve results.

Reform enters politics

The crusading idealism of revivalists and reformers inevitably collided with the hard reality that society could not be perfected by converting individuals. In America's democratic society, politics and government coercion promised a more effective means to impose a new moral vision on the nation. Several movements, including those to establish public schools and erect asylums, had operated within the political system from the beginning. A growing number of other frustrated reformers abandoned the principle of voluntary persuasion and looked to governmental coercion to achieve their goals.

Politicians did not particularly welcome the new interest. Because the Whig and Democratic parties both drew on evangelical and nonevangelical voters, heated moral debates over the harmful effects of drink or the evils of slavery threatened to detach regular party members from their old loyalties and disrupt each party's unity. The strong opposition of German and Irish immigrants to temperance stimulated antiforeign sentiment among reformers and further divided both party coalitions, particularly the Democrats. "The temperance question is playing havock in the old party lines," commented one Indiana politician. The issue of abolition seemed even more disruptive.

Women and the Right to Vote

As the reform impulse shifted toward the political arena, women in particular lost influence. As major participants in the benevolent organizations of the 1820s and 1830s, they had used their efforts on behalf of "moral suasion." But because women could not vote, they felt excluded when the temperance and abolitionist movements turned to electoral action to accomplish their goals. By the 1840s female reformers increasingly demanded the right to vote as the means to change society. Nor were men blind to what was at stake: one reason they so strongly resisted female suffrage was because it would give women real power.

Previously, many female reformers had accepted the right of petition as their most appropriate political activity. But *The Lily,* a women's rights paper, soon changed its tack. "Why shall [women] be left only the poor resource of petition?" it asked. "For even petitions, when they are from women, without the elective franchise to give them backbone, are of but little consequence."

The Maine Law

The political parties could resist the women's suffrage movement because most of its advocates lacked the right to vote. Less easily put off were temperance reformers. Although drinking had significantly declined in American society by 1840, it had hardly been eliminated. After 1845 the arrival of large numbers of German and Irish immigrants, who were accustomed to consuming alcohol, made voluntary prohibition even more remote. In response, temperance advocates proposed state laws that would outlaw the manufacture and sale of alcoholic beverages. If liquor was unavailable, reformers reasoned, drinkers would be forced to reform whether they wanted to or not.

Struggle over prohibition

Party leaders tried to dodge the question of prohibition, since large numbers of Whigs and Democrats were found on both sides of the question. Temperance advocates countered with a strategy of endorsing the legislative candidates who pledged to support a prohibitory law. To win additional recruits, temperance leaders adopted techniques used in political campaigns, including house-to-house canvasses, parades and processions, bands and singing, banners, picnics, and mass rallies.

The movement's first major triumph came in 1851 in Maine. The Maine Law, as it was known, authorized search and seizure of private property and provided stiff penalties for selling liquor. In the next few years a number of states enacted similar laws, although most were struck down by the courts or later repealed. Prohibition remained a controversial political issue throughout the century.

Although prohibition was temporarily defeated, the issue badly disrupted the Whig and Democratic parties. It detached a number of voters from both coalitions, greatly increased the extent of party switching, and brought to the polls a large number of new voters, including many "wets" who wanted to preserve their right to drink. By dissolving the ties between so many voters and their parties, the temperance issue played a major role in the eventual collapse of the Jacksonian party system in the 1850s.

Abolitionism and the Party System

Abolition was the most divisive issue to come out of the benevolent reform movement. In 1835 abolitionists distributed more than a million pamphlets, mostly in the South, through the post office. A wave of excitement swept the South when the first batches arrived addressed to white southerners. Former senator Robert Hayne led a Charleston mob that burned sacks of U.S. mail containing abolitionist literature, and postmasters in other southern cities refused to deliver the material. The Jackson administration allowed southern states to censor the mail, leading abolitionists to protest that their civil rights had been violated. In reaction, the number of antislavery societies in the North nearly tripled.

Censorship of the mails

With access to the mails impaired, abolitionists began flooding Congress with petitions against slavery. Asserting that Congress had no power over the institution, angry southern representatives demanded action, and the House in response adopted the so-called gag rule in 1836. It automatically tabled without consideration any petition dealing with slavery. But southern leaders had made a tactical blunder. The gag rule allowed abolitionists not only to attack slavery but also to

Gag rule

speak out as defenders of white civil liberties. The appeal of the antislavery movement was broadened, and in 1844 the House finally repealed the controversial rule.

Many abolitionists outside Garrison's extreme circle began to feel that an antislavery third party offered a more effective means of attacking slavery. In 1840 these political abolitionists founded the Liberty party and nominated for president James Birney, a former slaveholder who had converted to abolitionism. Birney received only 7000 votes, but the Liberty party was the seed from which a stronger antislavery political movement would grow. From 1840 onward, abolitionism's importance would be in the political arena rather than as a voluntary reform organization.

After two decades of fiery revivals, benevolent crusades, utopian experiments, and Transcendental philosophizing, the ferment of reform had spread through urban streets, canal town churches, frontier clearings, and the halls of Congress. Abolition, potentially the most dangerous issue, seemed still under control in 1840. Birney's small vote, coupled with the disputes between the two national antislavery societies, encouraged political leaders to believe that the party system had turned back this latest threat of sectionalism. But the growing northern concern about slavery highlighted differences between the two sections. Despite the strength of evangelicalism in the South, the reform impulse spawned by the revivals found little support there, since reform movements were discredited by their association with abolitionism. The party system confronted the difficult challenge of holding together sections that, although sharing much, were also diverging in important ways. To the residents of both sections, the South increasingly appeared to be a unique society with its own distinctive way of life.

chapter summary

The Jacksonian era produced the greatest number of significant reform movements in American history.

- The movements grew out of the revivals of the Second Great Awakening, which emphasized emotion and preached the doctrines of good works and salvation available to all.

  - Evangelical Protestantism also endorsed the ideals of perfectionism and millennialism.

  - The revival theologies helped people adjust to the pressures in their daily lives created by the new market economy.

- Romanticism, which emphasized the unlimited potential of each individual, also strengthened reform.

- Women's role in society was now defined by the ideal of domesticity—that women's lives should center on the home and the family.

- Middle-class women turned to religion and reform as ways to shape society.

- Utopian communities sought to establish a model society for the rest of the world to follow.

- Humanitarian movements combated a variety of social evils.

  - Crusades for temperance, educational reform, and the establishment of asylums all gained significant support.

  - Abolitionism precipitated both strong support and violent opposition, and the movement itself split in 1840.

- Temperance, abolitionism, and women's rights movements each turned to political action to accomplish their goals.

- Although it survived, the party system was seriously weakened by these reform movements.

interactive learning

The Primary Source Investigator CD-ROM offers the following materials related to this chapter:

• A collection of primary sources exploring the growing fever for reform in the United States, including Abraham Lincoln's discussion of the Declaration of Independence and the Constitution in regards to slavery and the Declaration of Sentiments, an appeal to Americans for equal treatment of women. Other sources include a certificate of freedom for Harriet Bolling in Petersburg, Virginia; a newspaper produced for a nineteenth century factory; and an image of a homespun stocking.

additional reading

Considerable work has been done in recent years on the relationship between evangelical religion and society. Nathan O. Hatch, *The Democratization of American Christianity* (1989), is a good starting point. Whitney Cross, *The Burned Over District* (1950), explores the revivals of western New York, where evangelicalism was particularly strong. Paul Johnson, *A Shopkeeper's Millennium* (1978), is an interesting, well-written community study, but it strains the evidence somewhat to push its thesis that revivalism was a form of class domination. George H. Thomas, *Revivalism and Cultural Change* (1989), also examines the relationship between religion and the new market economy.

Ronald G. Walters, *American Reformers, 1815–1860* (1978), presents a general history of the reform impulse. A fuller treatment, with more emphasis on evangelical religion, is Alice Felt Tyler, *Freedom's Ferment* (1944), which captures the era's heady optimism. Good discussions of the concept of domesticity and women's lives can be found in Carl Degler, *At Odds* (1977), and Nancy Cott, *The Bonds of Womanhood* (1977). Mary P. Ryan, *The Cradle of the Middle Class* (1981), skillfully traces the connection between economic transformation and family structure. Specific reform movements are analyzed in Carl F. Kaestle, *Pillars of the Republic* (1983), which addresses the common school movement; Ellen C. DuBois, *Feminism and Suffrage* (1978); and James B. Stewart, *Holy Warriors* (1976), which is the best study of abolitionism. Lori D. Ginzberg, *Women and the Work of Benevolence* (1990), and Barbara Epstein, *The Politics of Domesticity* (1981), examine women's participation in reform. For a fuller list of readings, see the Bibliography at www.mhhe.com/davidsonnation5.

significant events

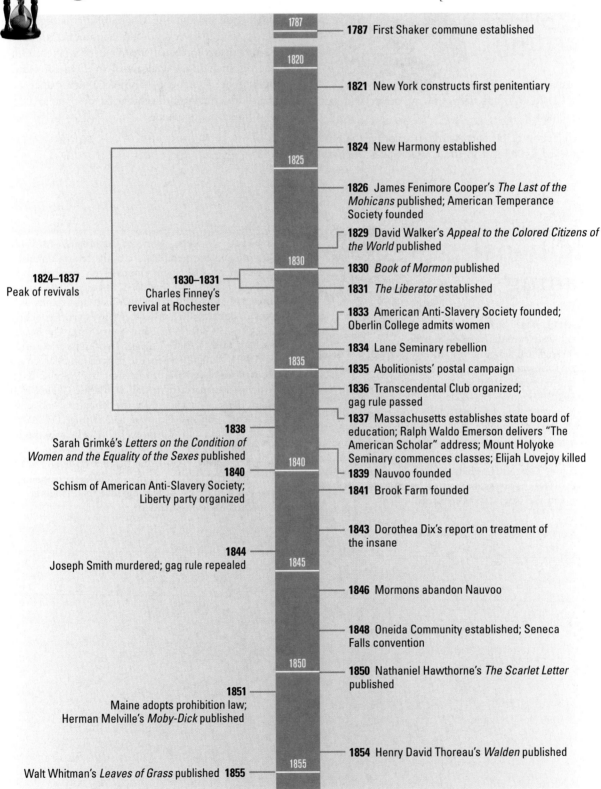

1787 First Shaker commune established

1821 New York constructs first penitentiary

1824 New Harmony established

1826 James Fenimore Cooper's *The Last of the Mohicans* published; American Temperance Society founded

1829 David Walker's *Appeal to the Colored Citizens of the World* published

1830 *Book of Mormon* published

1831 *The Liberator* established

1833 American Anti-Slavery Society founded; Oberlin College admits women

1834 Lane Seminary rebellion

1835 Abolitionists' postal campaign

1836 Transcendental Club organized; gag rule passed

1837 Massachusetts establishes state board of education; Ralph Waldo Emerson delivers "The American Scholar" address; Mount Holyoke Seminary commences classes; Elijah Lovejoy killed

1839 Nauvoo founded

1841 Brook Farm founded

1843 Dorothea Dix's report on treatment of the insane

1846 Mormons abandon Nauvoo

1848 Oneida Community established; Seneca Falls convention

1850 Nathaniel Hawthorne's *The Scarlet Letter* published

1854 Henry David Thoreau's *Walden* published

1824–1837
Peak of revivals

1830–1831
Charles Finney's revival at Rochester

1838
Sarah Grimké's *Letters on the Condition of Women and the Equality of the Sexes* published

1840
Schism of American Anti-Slavery Society; Liberty party organized

1844
Joseph Smith murdered; gag rule repealed

1851
Maine adopts prohibition law; Herman Melville's *Moby-Dick* published

Walt Whitman's *Leaves of Grass* published **1855**

Chapter 13

The impeccably dressed Colonel Daniel Jordan, master of 261 slaves at Laurel Hill, strolls down his oak-lined lawn to the dock along the Waccamaw River, a day's journey north of Charleston, to board the steamship *Nina*. On Fridays, it is Colonel Jordan's custom to visit the exclusive Hot and Hot Fish Club, founded by his fellow low-country planters, to play a game of lawn bowling or billiards and be waited on by black servants in livery as he sips a mint julep in the refined atmosphere that for him is the South.

Several hundred miles to the west another steamboat, the *Fashion*, makes its way along the Alabama River near the village of Claiborne. One of the passengers is upset by the boat's slow pace. He has been away from his plantation in the Red River country of Texas and is eager to get back. "Time's money, time's money!" he mutters to anyone who will listen. "Time's worth more'n money to me now; a hundred percent more, 'cause I left my niggers all alone; not a damn white man within four mile on 'em." When asked what they are doing, since the cotton crop has already been picked, he says, "I set 'em to clairin', but they ain't doin' a damn thing. . . . I know that as well as you do. . . . But I'll make it up, I'll make it up when I get thar, now you'd better believe." For this Red River planter, time is money and cotton is his world—indeed, cotton is what the South is all about. "I am a cotton man, I am, and I don't car who knows it," he proclaims. "I know cotton, I do. I'm dam' if I know anythin' but cotton."

At the other end of the South, the slave Sam Williams works in the intense heat of Buffalo Forge, an iron-making factory nine miles from Lexington, Virginia, in the Shenandoah Valley. As a refiner, Williams has the most important job at the forge, alternately heating pig iron in the white-hot coals, then slinging the ball of glowing metal on an anvil, where he pounds it with huge, water-powered hammers to remove the impurities. Ambitious and hard working, he earns extra money (at the same rate paid to whites) for any iron he produces beyond his weekly quota. In some years his extra income is more than $100. His wife, Nancy, who is in charge of the dairy, earns extra money as well, and their savings accounts at the local bank total more than $150. Additional income allows them to buy extra food and items for themselves and their four daughters, but more important, it helps keep their family intact in an unstable environment. They know that their owner is very unlikely to sell away slaves who work so hard. For Sam and Nancy Williams, family ties, worship at the local Baptist church, and socializing with their fellow slaves are what make life important.

In the bayous of the Deep South, only a few miles from where the Mississippi delta meets the Gulf, Octave Johnson hears the dogs coming. For over a year now Johnson has been a runaway slave. He fled from a Louisiana plantation in St. James

The Old South

1820–1860

preview • In the decades before the Civil War, the rural South depended on the export of staple crops like rice, tobacco, sugar, and cotton–and the slave labor used to produce them. Though most southern whites did not own slaves, those who did reaped prestige, political influence, and wealth. Excluded from white society, enslaved African Americans resisted bondage and developed their own culture, whose religion, songs, and shared experiences helped them survive a cruel and arbitrary regime.

Plantation Burial, painted about 1860 by John Antrobus, portrays the black slave community from a Louisiana plantation burying a loved one. Religion played a central role in the lives of slaves.

Parish when the work bell rang before daybreak and the overseer threatened to whip him for staying in bed. To survive, he hides in the swamps four miles behind the plantation—stealing turkeys, chickens, and pigs and trading with other slaves. As uncertain as this life is, nearly 30 other slaves have joined him over the past year.

The sound of the dogs warns Johnson and his companions that the hound master Eugene Jardeau is out again. This time when the pack bursts upon them, the slaves do not flee but kill as many dogs as possible. Then they plunge into the bayou, and as the hounds follow, alligators make short work of another six. For Octave Johnson the real South is a matter of weighing one's prospects between the uncertainties of alligators and the overseer's whip—and deciding when to say no.

Ferdinand Steel and his family are not forced, by the flick of the lash, to rise at five in the morning. They rise because the land demands it. Steel, in his twenties, owns 170 acres of land in Carroll County, Mississippi. Unmarried, he moved there from Tennessee with his widowed mother, sister, and brother in 1836, only a few years after the Choctaws had been forced to give up the region and march west. His life is one of continuous hard work, caring for the animals and tending the crops. His mother, Eliza, and sister, Julia, have plenty to keep them busy: making soap, fashioning dippers out of gourds, or sewing.

The Steel family grows cotton, too, but not with the single-minded devotion of the planter aboard the *Fashion.* Self-sufficiency and family security always come first, and Steel's total crop amounts to only five or six bales. His profit is never sufficient to consider buying even one slave. In fact, he would have preferred not to raise any cotton—"We are to[o] weak handed," he says—but the five bales mean cash, and cash means that when he goes to market in nearby Grenada, he can buy sugar and coffee, gunpowder and lead, a yard or two of calico, and quinine to treat the malaria that is so common in those parts. Though fiercely independent, Steel and his scattered neighbors help each other raise houses, clear fields, shuck corn, or quilt. They depend on one another and are bound together by blood, religion, obligation, and honor. For small farmers like Ferdinand Steel, these ties constitute the real South.

The portraits could go on: different people, different Souths, all of them real. Such contrasts underscore the difficulty of trying to define a regional identity. Encompassing in 1860 the 15 slave states plus the District of Columbia, the South was a land of great geographic diversity. It extended from the Tidewater coastal plain along the Atlantic seaboard to the prairies of Texas, from the Kentucky bluegrass region to the Gulf coast, from the mountains of western Virginia to the swamps of the Mississippi delta with its semitropical climate. The only geographic feature that separated the North and South was the Ohio River, and it was an avenue of trade rather than a source of division.

Yet despite its many differences of people and geography, the South was bonded by ties so strong, they eventually outpulled those of the nation itself. At the heart of this unity was an agricultural system that took advantage of the region's warm climate and long growing season. Cotton required 200 frost-free days, and rice and sugar even more, which meant that in the United

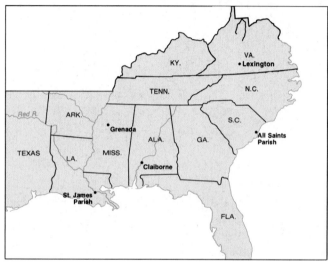

The Diverse South

States these staples could be grown only in the South. Most important, this rural agricultural economy was based on the institution of slavery, which had far-reaching effects on all aspects of southern society. It shaped not only the culture of the slaves themselves but also the lives of their masters and mistresses, and even of farm families and herders in the hills and backwoods who saw few slaves in their day-to-day existence. To understand the Old South, then, we must understand how the southern agricultural economy and the institution of slavery affected the social class structure of both white and black southerners.

The Social Structure of the Cotton Kingdom

We have already seen (in Chapter 10) that the spread of cotton stimulated the nation's remarkable economic growth after the War of 1812. Demand spurred by the textile industry sent the price of cotton soaring on the international market, and white southerners scrambled into the fresh lands of the Southwest to reap the profits to be made in the cotton sweepstakes.

The Boom Country Economy

Cotton pushes westward

Letters, newspapers, and word of mouth all brought tales of the black belt region of Alabama, where the dark soil was particularly suited to growing cotton, and of the tremendous yields from the soils along the Mississippi River's broad reaches. "The *Alabama Feaver* rages here with great violence and has *carried off* vast numbers of our Citizens," a North Carolinian wrote in 1817. "I am apprehensive if it continues to spread as it has done, it will almost depopulate the country." A generation later, as the removal of the southern Indian tribes opened vast tracts of land to white settlement, immigrants were still "pouring in with a ceaseless tide," one observer reported, "including 'Land Sharks' ready to swallow up the home of the redmen, or the white, as oportunity might offer."

By the 1840s planters even began to leave Mississippi and Alabama—virgin territory at the turn of the century—to head for the new cotton frontier along the Red River and up into Texas. A decade later the northern visitor Frederick Law Olmsted came across many abandoned southern homesteads, which he called "Gone to Texas" farms. Amazingly, by the eve of the Civil War nearly a third of the total cotton crop came from *west* of the Mississippi River.

As Senator James Henry Hammond of South Carolina boasted in 1858, cotton was king in the Old South. True, the region devoted more acreage to corn, but cotton was the primary export and the major source of southern wealth. Indeed, by 1860 the United States produced three-fourths of the world's supply of cotton. This boom fueled the southern economy so strongly that following the depression of 1839–1843, the southern economy grew faster than that in the North. Even so, per capita income in the South remained below that of the free states, and wealth was not as evenly distributed in the plantation South as in northern agricultural areas.

Southern prosperity

This prosperity, however, masked basic problems in the economy—problems that would become more apparent after the Civil War. Much of the South's new wealth resulted from migration of its population to more productive western lands. The amount of prime agricultural land was limited, and once it was settled, the South could not sustain forever its rate of expansion. Nor did the shift in population alter the structure of the southern economy, stimulate technological change, improve the way goods were produced and marketed, or generate internal markets.

The single-crop agriculture practiced by southern farmers rapidly wore out the soil. Tobacco was a particularly exhaustive crop, and corn also rapidly drained nutrients. To restore their soils, planters and farmers in the Upper South increasingly shifted to wheat production, but because they now plowed their fields rather than using a hoe, this shift intensified soil erosion. Destruction of the forests, particularly in the Piedmont, where commercial agriculture now took hold, had the same effect, and many streams quickly silted up and were no longer navigable. Row-crop agriculture made floods and droughts more common. In addition, reliance on a single crop increased toxins and parasites in the soil, making southern agriculture more vulnerable to destruction than varied agriculture was.

Environmental impact of single-crop agriculture

Only the South's low population density mitigated the impact on the environment. More remote areas remained heavily forested, wetlands were still common, and as late as 1860 eighty percent of the region was uncultivated (cattle and hogs, however, ranged over much of this acreage). Throughout much of the South, farmers fired the woods in the spring to destroy insects, burn off brush, and increase grass for their browsing stock.

Perhaps the most striking environmental consequence of the expansion of southern society was the increase in disease. The South, especially the Lower South, enjoyed a reputation for unhealthiness. Epidemic diseases such as malaria, yellow fever, and cholera were brought to the area by Europeans. The clearing of land—which increased runoff, precipitated floods, and produced pools of stagnant water—along with the growing white and black population, facilitated the spread of these diseases. In notoriously unhealthy areas, such as the coastal swamps of South Carolina's rice district, wealthy whites fled during the sickly summer months and were only part-time residents.

In this romanticized Currier and Ives print of a cotton plantation, field hands are waist-deep in cotton while other slaves haul the picked cotton to be ginned and then pressed into bales. Mounted on a horse, an overseer rides through the field supervising the work while the owner and his wife look on. Picking began as early as August and continued in some areas until late January. Because the bolls ripened at different times, a field had to be picked several times.

The Upper South's New Orientation

As cotton transformed the boom country of the Deep South, agriculture in the Upper South also adjusted.* Improved varieties and more scientific agricultural practices reversed the decline in tobacco that had begun in the 1790s. More important, however, farmers in the Upper South made wheat and corn their major crops. As early as 1840 the value of wheat grown in Virginia was twice that of tobacco.

Slave trade

Because the new crops required less labor, planters in the Upper South regularly sold their surplus slaves to cotton and sugar planters in the Deep South. Indeed, some planters in the Upper South maintained a profit margin only by these sales. The demand in the Deep South for field hands drove their price steadily up, so that by the late 1850s a prime field hand, who would have sold for $600 in the early 1840s, commanded $1500. Even with increased labor costs, southern agriculture flourished.

---

*The Upper South included the border states (Delaware, Maryland, Kentucky, and Missouri) and Virginia, North Carolina, Tennessee, and Arkansas. The states of the Deep South were South Carolina, Georgia, Florida, Alabama, Mississippi, Louisiana, and Texas.

The Rural South

The Old South, then, was dynamic, expanding, and booming economically. But the region remained overwhelmingly rural, with 84 percent of its labor force engaged in agriculture in 1860, compared with 40 percent in the North. Conversely, the South lagged in manufacturing, producing only 9 percent of the nation's manufactured goods. During the 1850s some southern propagandists urged greater investment in industry to diversify the South's economy. But as long as high profits from cotton continued, these advocates made little headway.

Lack of manufacturing

With so little industry, few cities developed in the South. New Orleans, with a population of 169,000 in 1860, was the only truly southern city of significant size. Only 1 in 10 southerners lived in cities and towns in 1860, compared with 1 out of 3 persons in the North. North Carolina, Alabama, Mississippi, Arkansas, and Texas did not contain a single city with a population of 10,000.

Absence of cities

As a rural society, the South evidenced far less interest in education. Southern colleges were inferior to those in the North, and public secondary schools were virtually nonexistent. Wealthy planters, who hired tutors or sent their children to private academies, generally opposed a state-supported school system. Thus free public schools were rare, especially in the rural districts that made up most of the South. Georgia in 1860 had only one county with a free school system, and Mississippi had

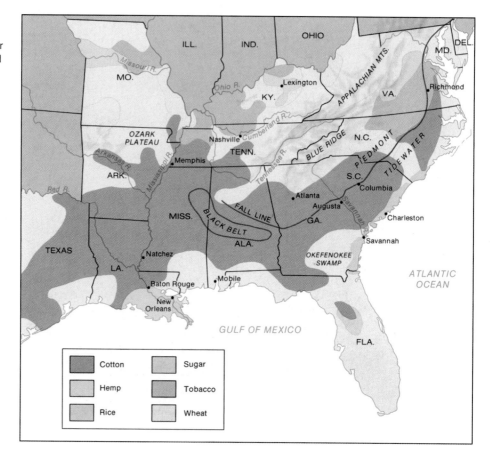

Cotton and Other Crops of the South By 1860, the cotton kingdom extended across the Lower South into the Texas prairie and up the Mississippi River valley. Tobacco and hemp were the staple crops of the Upper South, where they competed with corn and wheat. Rice production was concentrated in the swampy coastal region of South Carolina and Georgia as well as the lower tip of Louisiana. The sugar district was in southern Louisiana.

no public schools outside its few cities. On average southern white children spent only one-fifth as much time in school as did their northern counterparts.

The net result was that illiteracy rates were much higher in the South. Among native-born white citizens, the 1850 census showed that 20 percent were unable to read and write. The comparable figure was 3 percent in the middle states and 0.4 percent in New England. In some areas of the South, more than a third of all white residents were illiterate.

Distribution of Slavery

Even more than agrarian ways, slavery set the South apart. Whereas in 1776 slavery had been a national institution, by 1820 slavery was confined to the states south of Pennsylvania and the Ohio River. The South's "peculiar institution" bound white and black southerners together in a multitude of ways.

Slaves were not evenly distributed throughout the region. More than half lived in the Deep South, where African Americans outnumbered white southerners in both South Carolina and Mississippi by the 1850s. Elsewhere in the Deep South, the black population exceeded 40 percent in all states except Texas. In the Upper South, on the other hand, whites greatly outnumbered blacks. Only in Virginia and North Carolina did the slave population top 30 percent.

The distribution of slaves showed striking geographic variations within individual states as well. In areas of fertile soil, flat or rolling countryside, and good transportation, slavery and the plantation system dominated. In the pine barrens, areas isolated by lack of transportation, and hilly and mountainous regions, small family farms and few slaves were the rule.

Almost all enslaved African Americans, male and female, worked in agricultural pursuits, with only about 10 percent living in cities and towns. On large plantations, a few slaves were domestic servants and others were skilled artisans—blacksmiths, carpenters, or bricklayers—but most toiled in the fields. Only about 5 percent of the South's manufacturing employees in the 1850s were slaves like Sam Williams.

Slave occupations

Slavery as a Labor System

Slavery was, first and foremost, a system to manage and control labor. The plantation system, with its extensive estates and large labor forces, could never have developed without slavery, nor could it have met the world demand for cotton and other staples. Slaves represented an enormous capital investment, worth more than all the land in the Old South.

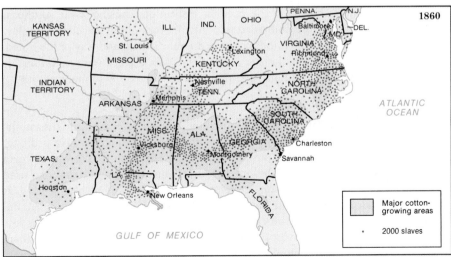

The Spread of Slavery, 1820–1860 Between 1820 and 1860, the slave population of the South shifted southward and westward, concentrating especially heavily in coastal South Carolina and Georgia, in the black belt of central Alabama and Mississippi (so named because of its rich soil), and in the Mississippi valley. Small farms with few slaves predominated in cotton-growing areas that lacked good transportation, such as northern Georgia, and in regions with poor soil, such as the piney woods of southern Mississippi.

Southern Population, 1860

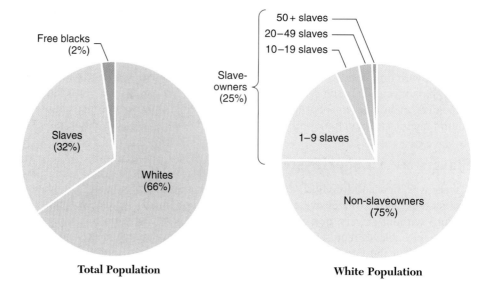

Total Population   White Population

Profitability of slavery

Furthermore, slavery remained a highly profitable investment. The average slaveowner spent perhaps $30 to $35 a year to support an adult slave; some expended as little as half that. Allowing for the cost of land, equipment, and other expenses, a planter could expect one of his slaves to produce more than $78 worth of cotton—which meant that even at the higher cost of support, a slaveowner took about 60 percent of the wealth produced by a slave's labor. For those who pinched pennies and drove slaves harder, the profits were even greater.

Slavery and aristocratic values

By concentrating wealth and power in the hands of the planter class, slavery shaped the tone of southern society. Planters were not aristocrats in the European sense of having special legal privileges or formal titles of rank. Still, the system encouraged southern planters to think of themselves as a landed gentry upholding the aristocratic values of pride, honor, family, and hospitality.

Whereas slavery had existed throughout most of the Americas at the beginning of the century, by the 1850s the United States, Cuba, and Brazil were the only slaveholding nations left in the region. Public opinion in Europe and in the North had grown more and more hostile to the peculiar institution, causing white southerners to feel increasingly like an embattled minority. Yet they clung tenaciously to slavery, for it was the base on which the South's economic growth and way of life rested. As one Georgian observed on the eve of the Civil War, slavery was "so intimately mingled with our social conditions that it would be impossible to eradicate it."

Class Structure of the White South

Once a year around Christmastime, James Henry Hammond gave a dinner for his neighbors at his South Carolina plantation, Silver Bluff. The richest man for miles around as well as an ambitious politician, the aristocratic Hammond used these dinners to put his neighbors under personal obligation to him as well as receive the honor and respect he believed his due. Indeed, Hammond's social and political ambitions caused him to carefully cultivate his neighbors, despite his low opinion of them, by hiring them to perform various tasks and by providing them a variety of services such as ginning their cotton and allowing them to use his grist mill. These services enhanced his ethic of paternalism, but his less affluent neighbors also displayed a strong personal pride. After he ungraciously complained about the inconvenience of these services, only three of his neighbors came to his Christmas dinner in 1837, a snub that enraged him. As Hammond's experience demonstrated, class relations among whites in the Old South were a complex blend of privilege, patronage, and equality.

The Slaveowners

In 1860 the region's 15 states had a population of 12 million, of which roughly two-thirds were white, one-third were black slaves, and about 2 percent were free African Americans. Because of the institution of slavery, the social structure of the antebellum South differed in important ways from that of the North. Even so, southern society was remarkably fluid, and as a result, class lines were not rigid.

Of the 8 million white southerners in 1860, only about 2 million (one-quarter) either owned slaves or were members of slaveowning families. Moreover, most slaveowners owned only a few slaves. If one uses the census definition of a planter as a person who owned 20 or more slaves, only about 1 out of every 30 white southerners belonged to families of the planter class.

A planter of consequence, however, needed to own at least 50 slaves, and there were only about 10,000 such families—less than 1 percent of the white population. This privileged group made up the aristocracy at the top of the southern class structure. Owners of large numbers of slaves were very rare; only about 2000 southerners such as Colonel Daniel Jordan owned 100 or more slaves. Although limited in size, the planter class nevertheless owned more than half of all slaves and controlled more than 90 percent of the region's total wealth.

The typical plantation had 20 to 50 slaves and 800 to 1000 acres of land. On an estate larger than that, slaves would have to walk more than an hour to reach the farthest fields, losing valuable work time. Thus larger slaveowners usually owned several plantations, with an overseer to manage the slaves on each while the owner attended to administrative and business matters. The slaves were divided into field hands, skilled workers, and house servants, with one or more slaves serving as "drivers" to assist the overseer. While planters pioneered the application of capitalistic methods, including specialization and division of labor, to agriculture, plantations remained labor-intensive operations. Only the production of sugar, among the southern staples, was heavily mechanized.

Plantation administration

Tidewater and Frontier

Southern planters shared a commitment to preserve slavery as the source of their wealth and stature. Yet in other ways they were a diverse group. On the one hand, the tobacco and rice planters of the Atlantic Tidewater were part of a settled region and a culture that reached back 150 to 200 years. States such as Mississippi and Arkansas, in contrast, were at or just emerging from the frontier stage, since most residents had arrived after 1815. Consequently, the society of the Southwest was rawer and more volatile.

It was along the Tidewater, especially the bays of the Chesapeake and the South Carolina coast, that the legendary "Old South" was born. Here, masters erected substantial homes, some of them—especially between Charleston and Columbia—the classic white-pillared mansions in the Greek revival style. Here, more than a few planters were urbane and polished.

Tidewater society

A Plantation Layout, Hopeton, Georgia Often covering a thousand acres or more, a plantation was laid out like a small village and contained several fields and usually extensive uncleared woods. Somewhere near the master's "big house" were the quarters—slave cabins clustered along one or more streets. Service buildings might include a smokehouse, stables, a gin house (for cotton) or a rice mill, and an overseer's dwelling. Like most large plantations, Hopeton produced a considerable amount of foodstuffs, but it grew both rice and cotton as staples. Most plantations concentrated on a single cash crop.

The ideal of the Tidewater South was the country gentleman of the English tradition. An Irish visitor observed that in Maryland and Virginia the great planters lived in "a style which approaches nearer to that of the English country gentleman than what is to be met with anywhere else on the continent." As in England, in the Tidewater South the local gentry often served as justices of the peace, and the Episcopal church remained the socially accepted road to heaven. Here, too, family names continued to be important in politics.

Society in the cotton kingdom

While the newer regions of the South boasted planters with cultivated manners, as a group the cotton lords were a different breed. They were basically entrepreneurs who had moved west for the same reason so many other Americans had: to make their fortunes. Some were planters, such as Thomas Dabney, fleeing the exhausted soils of the Tidewater; others were the sons of planters seeking to improve their lot. Not a few were northerners with an eye for opportunity, such as Henry Watson, who went south as a young tutor, settled in Greensboro, Alabama, and became a leading planter. Overseers sometimes rose into the ranks of slaveowners, as Ephraim Beanland of Mississippi did. Merchants and businessmen such as Maunsel White of New Orleans invested their profits in a plantation; land speculators rode the land grabs of the 1830s into the ranks of the elite. But by and large, the wealthy planters of the cotton gentry were self-made men, who through hard work, aggressive business tactics, and good luck had risen from ordinary backgrounds. For them, the cotton boom and the exploitation of enslaved men and women offered the opportunity to move up in a new society that lacked an entrenched elite.

"Time's money, time's money." For men like the impatient Texan, time was indeed money, slaves were capital, and cotton by the bale signified cash in hand. This business orientation was especially apparent in the cotton kingdom, where planters sought to maximize their profits and constantly reinvested their returns in land and slaves. As one visitor said of Mississippi slaveholders: "To sell cotton in order to buy negroes—to make more cotton to buy more negroes, 'ad infinitum,' is the aim and direct tendency of all the operations of the thorough-going cotton planter: his whole soul is wrapped up in the pursuit." One shocked Virginian who visited Vicksburg claimed that its citizens ran "mad with speculation" and did business "in a kind of phrenzy." And indeed there was money to be made. The combined annual income of the richest thousand families of the cotton kingdom approached $50 million, while the wealth of the remaining 666,000 families amounted to only about $60 million.

Slaveholders' values

This skillful portrait of John Stock, a wealthy South Carolina rice planter, depicts his aristocratic bearing and tastes.

Stately mansions could be found in a few areas of the cotton South. In general, though, most planters lived humbly. Although they ranked among the richest citizens in America, their homes were often simple one- or two-story unpainted wooden frame houses, and some were log cabins. A visitor to one Georgia plantation reported that the house did not have a pane of glass in the windows, a door between the rooms, or a ceiling other than the roof. "If you wish to see people worth millions living as [if] they were not worth hundreds," advised one southwestern planter in 1839, "come to the land of cotton and negroes."

Practical men, few of the new cotton lords had absorbed the culture and learning of the traditional country gentleman. During his extensive journeys in the South, the noted New Yorker Frederick Law Olmsted declared that he "did not see, except perhaps in one or two towns, a thermometer, nor a book of Shakespeare, nor a piano or sheet of music, nor a good reading lamp, nor an engraving or copy of any kind, or a work of art of the slightest merit. A large majority of all these houses were residences of slaveholders, a considerable proportion cotton planters."

The Master at Home

Whether supervising a Tidewater plantation or creating a cotton estate on the Texas frontier, the master had to coordinate a complex agricultural operation. He gave daily instructions concerning the work to be done, settled disputes between slaves and the overseer, and generally handed out rewards and penalties. In addition, the owner made the critical decisions concerning the planting, harvesting, and marketing of the crops. Planters also watched investments and expenditures, and they often sought to expand their production by clearing additional fields, buying more land or slaves, or investing in machinery such as cotton gins. As in any business, these decisions required a sound understanding of the domestic and international market as well as anticipation of future swings.

In performing his duties, the plantation owner was supposed to be the "master" of his crops, his family, and his slaves. Defenders of slavery held up this paternalistic ideal—the care and guidance of dependent "children"—maintaining that slavery promoted a genuine affection between caring master and loyal slaves.

Paternalism

In real life, however, market forces undermined this paternalistic ideal. Even in the Tidewater, planters were concerned with money and profits. Indeed, some of the most brutal forms of slavery existed on rice plantations, where the absenteeism of many owners combined with the sheer numbers of slaves made close personal ties impossible. Except for a few domestic servants, owners of large plantations had little contact with their slaves. Nor could paternalism mask the reality that slavery everywhere rested on violence, racism, and exploitation.

The Plantation Mistress

Upper-class southern white women, like those in the North, grew up with the ideal of domesticity, reinforced by the notion of a paternalistic master who was lord of the plantation. But the plantation mistress soon discovered that, given the demands placed on her, the ideal was hard to fulfill.

Mistress's duties

Growing up, a young genteel lady enjoyed a certain amount of leisure. But once she married and became a plantation mistress, a southern woman was often shocked by the magnitude of her responsibilities. Nursing the sick, making clothing, tending the garden, caring for the poultry, and overseeing every aspect of food preparation were all her domain. She also had to supervise and plan the work of the domestic servants and distribute clothing. After taking care of breakfast, one harried Carolina mistress recounted that she "had the [sewing] work cut out, gave orders about dinner, had the horse feed fixed in hot water, had the box filled with cork: went to see the carpenters working on the negro houses . . . now I have to cut out the flannel jackets." Sarah Williams, the New York bride of a North Carolina planter, admitted that her mother-in-law "works harder than any Northern farmer's wife I know."

Sarah Pierce Vick, the mistress of a plantation near Vicksburg, Mississippi, pauses to speak to one of her slaves, who may be holding feed for her horse. A plantation mistress had many duties and, while enjoying the comforts brought by wealth and status, often found her life more difficult than she had anticipated before marriage.

Unlike female reformers in the North, upper-class southern women did not openly challenge their role, but there is evidence that they found their sphere confining. The greatest unhappiness stemmed from the never-ending task of managing slaves. One southern mistress confessed, "I do not see how I can live my life amid these people! To be always among people whom I do not understand and whom I must guide, and teach and lead on like children. It frightens me." Yet without the labor of slaves, the lifestyle of these women was an impossibility.

Some women drew a parallel between their situation and that of the slaves. Both were subject to male dominance, and independent-minded women found the subordination of marriage difficult. Susan Dabney Smedes, in her recollection of growing up on an Alabama plantation, recalled that "it was a saying that the mistress of a plantation was the most complete slave on it." Some women particularly bristled at their lack of independence and at the necessity of obeying men. "How men can go blustering around, making everybody uncomfortable, simply to show that they are masters and we are only women and children at their mercy!" exclaimed Mary Chesnut, the wife of a South Carolina planter who termed her father-in-law "as absolute a tyrant as the Czar of Russia . . . or the Sultan of Turkey."

Miscegenation

Many women were deeply discontented, too, with the widespread double standard for sexual behavior and with the daily reminders of miscegenation some had to face. A man who fathered illegitimate children by slave women suffered no social or legal penalties, even in the case of rape (southern law did not recognize such a crime against slave women). On the other hand, a white woman guilty of adultery lost all social respectability.

Mary Chesnut, who knew the reality of miscegenation firsthand from her father-in-law's liaisons with slave women and discussed it more frankly than most, sneered in her diary at the assumptions of male superiority. "All the time they seem to think themselves patterns—models of husbands and fathers," she fumed, bitter at the enforced silence among wives. "Like the patriarchs of old, our men live all in one house with their wives and concubines; and the mulattoes one sees in every family partly resemble the white children. Any lady is ready to tell you who is the father of all the mulattoes one sees in everybody's household but her own. Those, she seems to think, drop from the clouds. My disgust sometimes is boiling over." One planter's wife spoke of "violations of the moral law that made mulattoes as common as blackberries," and another recalled, "I saw slavery in its bearing on my sex. I saw that it teemed with injustice and shame to all womankind and I hated it."

Still, only a small minority of women questioned either their place in southern society or the corrosive influence of slavery. Even fewer were willing to forgo the material comforts that slavery made possible. Moreover, racism was so pervasive within American society that the few white southern women who privately criticized the institution displayed little empathy for the plight of slaves themselves, including black women. Whatever the burdens of the plantation mistress, they were hardly akin to the bondage of slavery itself.

Yeoman Farmers

In terms of numbers, yeoman farm families were the backbone of southern society, accounting for more than half the southern white population. They owned no slaves and farmed the traditional 80 to 160 acres, like northern farmers. About 80 percent owned their own land, and the rest were tenant farmers who hoped one day to acquire a homestead. They settled almost everywhere in the South, except in the rice and sugar districts and valuable river bottomlands of the Deep South, which were monopolized by large slaveowners. Like Ferdinand Steel, most were semisubsistence farmers who raised primarily corn and hogs, along with perhaps a few bales of cotton or some tobacco, which they sold to obtain the cash needed to buy items like sugar, coffee, and salt. Some were not so much farmers as herdsmen, who set large herds of scrawny cattle or pigs to forage in the woods until it was time for the annual drive to market. Yeoman farmers lacked the wealth of planters, but they had a pride and dignity that earned them the respect of their richer neighbors.

Southern farmers led more isolated lives than their northern counterparts. Yet the social activities of these people were not much different from those of northern farmers. Religion played an important role at camp meetings held in late summer after the crops were laid by and before harvest time. As in the North, neighbors also met to exchange labor and tools, always managing to combine work with fun. The men rolled logs to clear fields of dead trees, turning the activity into a contest. Women met for quilting bees, and adults and children alike would gather to shuck corn. A Tennessee plain farmer recalled that his neighbors "seem to take delight in helping each other sutch as lay[ing] railings, cornshucking and house raising[.] they tried to help each other all they could and dancet all night." Court sessions, militia musters, political rallies—these too were occasions that brought rural folk together.

Because yeoman farmers lacked cheap slave labor, good transportation, and access to credit, they could not compete with planters in the production of staples. When it came to selling their corn and wheat, small farmers conducted only limited

Farmers and herders

Limits to economic opportunity

A majority of white southerners were members of nonslaveholding yeoman farm families. Ruggedly independent, these families depended on their own labor and lived under more primitive conditions than large plantation owners or small farmers in the North. Basil Hall, an Englishman traveling through the South in 1827 and 1828, sketched members of this Georgia family with the aid of a camera lucida, an optical device that projected an image from real life onto paper, where it could be traced with accuracy.

A FAMILY GROUP IN THE INTERIOR OF THE STATE OF GEORGIA.

business with planters, who usually grew as many of their own foodstuffs as possible. In the North urban centers became a market for small farmers, but in the South the lack of towns limited this internal market.

Thus while southern yeoman farmers were not poor, they suffered from a chronic lack of money and the absence of conveniences that northern farm families enjoyed, such as cast-iron stoves, sewing machines, specialized tools, and good furniture. A few chafed at the absence of public schools and greater opportunities. Josiah Hinds, who hacked a farm out of the isolated woods of northern Mississippi, worried that his children were growing up "wild." He complained that "education is but little prized by my neighbours," who were satisfied "if the corn and cotton grows to perfection . . . [and] brings a fare price, and hog meat is at hand to boil with the greens."

Absence of class conflict

In some ways, then, the worlds of yeoman farmers and upper-class planters were not only different but also in conflict. Still, a hostility between the two classes did not emerge. Yeoman farmers admired planters and hoped that one day they would join the gentry themselves. And even white southerners who owned no slaves accepted slavery as a means of controlling African Americans as members of an inferior social caste based on race. "Now suppose they was free," one poor farmer told Frederick Law Olmsted. "You see they'd all think themselves as good as we." Racism and fear of black people were sufficient to keep nonslaveholders loyal to southern institutions.

Poor Whites

The poorest white southerners were confined to land that no one else wanted: the wiregrass region of southeastern Georgia, the sand hills of central South Carolina, the pine barrens of the coastal plains from Virginia to southeastern Mississippi. In their backgrounds they were similar to other southerners, but they were the least efficient, the least enterprising, and the least lucky of the rural white population. Their numbers are difficult to estimate. A rough guess would be perhaps half a million, or a little more than 5 percent of the white population. Poverty-stricken, they lived in rough, unchinked, windowless log cabins located in the remotest areas and were often squatters without title to the land they were on. The men spent their time hunting and fishing, while women did the domestic work and what farming they could manage.

Circumstances made their poverty difficult to escape. Largely illiterate, they suffered from malnutrition stemming from a monotonous diet of corn, pork, and whiskey, and they were afflicted with malaria and hookworm, diseases that sapped their energy. Contemporaries repeatedly commented on their sickly cast, liberal use of whiskey and snuff, sexual immorality, and prematurely aged appearance. Encountering one woman of this class in a piney woods cabin, Olmsted described her as "apparently young" but with a face "dry and impassive as a dead man's. . . . Once in about a minute, [she] would suddenly throw up her chin, and spit with perfect precision into the hottest embers of the fire." Other white southerners scornfully referred to poor whites as crackers, white trash, sandhillers, and clay eaters.

Lives of poor whites

Because poor whites traded with slaves, exchanging whiskey for stolen goods, contemptuous planters often bought them out simply to rid the neighborhood of them. For their part, poor whites keenly resented planters, but their hostility toward African Americans was even stronger. Poor whites refused to work alongside slaves or perform any work commonly done by them and vehemently opposed ending slavery. Emancipation would remove one of the few symbols of their status—that they were, at least, free.

Relations with planters

The Peculiar Institution

Slaves were not free. That overwhelming fact must be understood before anything is said about the kindness or the cruelty that individual slaves experienced; before any consideration of healthy or unhealthy living conditions; before any discussion of how slave families coped with hardship, rejoiced in shared pleasures, or worshiped in prayer. The lives of slaves were affected day in and day out, in big ways and small, by the basic reality that slaves were not their own masters. If a slave's workload was reasonable, it remained so only at the master's discretion, not because the slave determined it to be. If slaves married or visited family or friends on a nearby plantation, they did so only with the master's permission. If they raised a family, they could remain together only as long as the master did not separate them by sale. Whatever slaves wanted to do, they had always to consider the response of their masters.

When power was distributed as unequally as it was between masters and slaves, every action on the part of the enslaved involved a certain calculation, conscious or unconscious. The consequences of every act, of every expression or gesture, had to be considered. In that sense, the line between freedom and slavery penetrated every corner of a slave's life, and it was an absolute and overwhelming distinction.

One other stark fact reinforced the sharp line between freedom and slavery: slaves were distinguished on the basis of color. While the peculiar institution was an economic system of labor, it was also a caste system based on race. The color line of slavery made it much easier to brand black people as somehow different. It made it easier to defend the institution and win the support of yeoman farmers and poor white southerners, even though in many ways the system held them back. Hence slavery must be understood on many levels: not only as an economic system but also as a racial and cultural one, not only in terms of its outward conditions of life and labor but also through the inner demands it made on the soul.

Slavery and race

Work and Discipline

The conditions slaves encountered varied widely, depending on the size of the farm or plantation, the crop being grown, the personality of the master, and whether he was an absentee owner. On small farms slaves worked in the fields with the own-ers and had much closer contact with whites. On plantations, in contrast, most slaves dealt primarily with the overseer, who was paid by the size of the harvest he brought in and was therefore often harsh in his approach. The largest planta-tions, which raised rice and sugar, also required the longest hours and the most grueling labor.

Organization of slave labor

House servants and the drivers, who supervised the field hands, were accorded the highest status, and skilled artisans such as carpenters and blacksmiths were also given special recognition. The hardest work was done by the field hands, both men and women, who sometimes were divided into plowhands and hoe gangs. In the summer of 1854 Olmsted watched a group of Mississippi slaves return to work in the fields after a thunderstorm. "First came, led by an old driver carrying a whip, forty of the largest and strongest women I ever saw together; . . . they carried them-selves loftily, each having a hoe over the shoulder, and walking with a free, power-ful swing like [soldiers] on the march." Behind them were the plowhands on the mules, "the cavalry, thirty strong, mostly men, but a few of them women." Bringing up the rear was "a lean and vigilant white overseer, on a brisk pony."

Some planters organized their slaves by the gang system, in which a white overseer or a black driver supervised gangs of 20 to 25 adults. Although this approach extracted long hours of reasonably hard labor, the slaves had to be con-stantly supervised and shirkers were difficult to detect. Other planters preferred the task system, under which each slave was given a specific daily assignment to complete, after which he or she was finished for the day. This system allowed slaves to work at their own pace, gave them an incentive to do careful work, and freed overseers from having to closely supervise the work. On the other hand, slaves resisted vigorously if masters tried to increase the workload. The task system was most common in the rice fields, whereas the gang system predominated in the cot-ton districts. Many planters used a combination of the two.

Slaves' workday

Toil began just before sunrise and continued until dusk. During cultivation and harvest, slaves were in the field 15 to 16 hours a day, eating a noonday meal there and resting before resuming labor. Work was uncommon on Sundays, and frequently only a half day was required on Saturdays. Even so, the routine was taxing. "We . . . have everybody at work before day dawns," an Arkansas cotton planter reported. "I am never caught in bed after day light nor is any body else on the place, and we continue in the cotton fields when we can have fair weather till it is so dark we can't see to work."

Black slave driver

Often masters gave money, additional food, gifts, and time off to slaves who worked diligently, but the threat of punishment was always present. Slaves could be denied passes; their food allowance could be reduced; and if all else failed, they could be sold. The most common instrument of punishment, how-ever, was the whip. The frequency of its use varied from plantation to planta-tion, but few slaves escaped the lash entirely. "We have to rely more and more on the power of fear," the planter James Henry Hammond acknowledged. "We are determined to continue masters, and to do so we have to draw the rein tighter and tighter day by day to be assured that we hold them in complete check."

Slave Maintenance

Clothing and housing

Planters generally bought rough, cheap cloth for slave clothing and each year gave adults at most only a couple of outfits and a pair of shoes that were worn out by the end of the year. Few had enough clothing or blankets to keep warm when the weather dipped below freezing. Some planters provided well-built housing, but more commonly slaves lived in cramped, poorly built cabins that were leaky in wet weather, drafty in cold, and furnished with only a few crude chairs, benches and a table, perhaps a mattress filled with corn husks or straw, and a few pots and dishes.

Sickness among the hands was a persistent problem. In order to keep medical expenses down, slaveowners treated sick slaves themselves and called in a doctor only for serious cases. Even conscientious masters often employed harmful treatments and dispensed quack patent medicines. Conditions varied widely, but on average, a slaveowner spent less than a dollar a year on medical care for each slave.

Even so, the United States was the only slave society in the Americas where the slave population increased naturally—indeed, at about the same rate as the white population. Nevertheless, a deficient diet, inadequate clothing and shelter, long hours of hard toil, and poor medical care resulted in a lower life expectancy among slaves. Infant mortality was more than double that of the free white population; for every 1000 live births among southern slaves, more than 200 died before the age of 5. As late as 1860, fewer than two-thirds of slave children lived to age 10. For those who survived infancy, enslaved African Americans had a life expectancy about 8 years less than that of white Americans.

Slaves' lower life expectancy

Resistance

Given the wide gulf between freedom and slavery, it was only natural that slaves resisted the bondage imposed on them. The most radical form of resistance was rebellion, which occurred repeatedly in slave societies in the Americas. In Latin America, slave revolts were frequent, involving hundreds and even thousands of slaves and pitched battles in which large numbers were killed. The most successful slave revolt occurred in France's sugar-rich colony Saint Domingue (the western part of the Caribbean island of Hispaniola). There, free blacks who had fought in the American Revolution because of France's alliance with the United States brought back the ideals of freedom and equality. Furthermore, the brutally overworked population of half a million slaves was ready to revolt and received further encouragement from the example of the French Revolution. Under the leadership of Toussaint L'Ouverture, rebellion led to the establishment of Haiti in 1804, the second independent republic in the Western Hemisphere.

Slave revolts in Latin America

Elsewhere, Jamaica averaged one significant slave revolt every year from 1731 to 1823, while in 1823 thousands rose in Guiana. Jamaica too witnessed an uprising, of some 20,000 slaves in 1831. These revolts, and ones in 1823 and 1824 in British-controlled Demarra, were savagely suppressed. And in Brazil, which had the largest number of slaves outside the United States, the government took 50 years to suppress with military force a colony of about 20,000 slaves who had sought refuge in the mountains.

In contrast, slave revolts were rare in the United States. Unlike in Latin America, in the Old South whites outnumbered blacks, the government was much more powerful, most slaves were native-born, and family life was much stronger. Slaves recognized the odds against them, and many potential leaders became fugitives instead. In a sense, what is remarkable is that American slaves revolted at all.

Infrequency of revolts in the United States

Early in the nineteenth century several well-organized uprisings in the United States were barely thwarted. In 1800 Gabriel Prosser, a slave blacksmith, recruited perhaps a couple hundred slaves in a plan to march on Richmond and capture the governor. But a heavy thunderstorm postponed the attack and a few slaves then betrayed the plot. Prosser and other leaders were eventually captured and executed. Denmark Vesey's conspiracy in Charleston in 1822 met a similar fate (page 348).

Nat Turner's rebellion

The most famous slave revolt, led by a literate slave preacher named Nat Turner, was smaller and more spontaneous. Turner, who lived on a farm in southeastern Virginia, enjoyed unusual privileges. His master, whom he described as a kind and trusting man, encouraged him to study the Bible and preach to other slaves on Sundays and gave him great personal freedom. Spurred on by an almost fanatic mysticism, Turner became convinced from visions of white and black angels fighting that God intended to punish white people and that he had been selected "to carry terror and devastation" throughout the countryside. One night in 1831 following an eclipse of the sun, he and six confederates stole out and murdered Turner's master and family. Gaining some 70 recruits as they went, Turner's band eventually killed 57 white men, women, and children. Along the way, the members voiced their grievances against slavery and announced that they intended to confiscate their masters' wealth.

The revolt lasted only 48 hours before being crushed. Turner himself eluded pursuers for more than two months but finally was captured, tried, and executed. While the uprising was quickly put down, it left white southerners throughout the region with a haunting uneasiness. Turner seemed a model slave, yet who could read a slave's true emotions behind the mask of obedience?

Day-to-day resistance

Few slaves followed Turner's violent example. But there were other, more subtle, ways of resisting a master's authority. Most dramatically, they could do as Octave Johnson did and run away. With the odds stacked heavily against them, few runaways escaped safely to freedom except from the border states. More frequently, slaves fled to nearby woods or swamps to avoid punishment or protest their treatment. Some runaways stayed out only a few days; others, like Johnson, held out for months.

Many slaves resisted by abusing their masters' property. They mishandled animals, broke tools and machinery, misplaced items, and worked carelessly in the fields. Olmsted observed one field gang that stopped hoeing every time the overseer turned his back. Slaves also sought to trick the master by feigning illness or injury and by hiding rocks in the cotton they picked. Slaves complained directly to the owner about an overseer's mistreatment, thereby attempting to drive a wedge between the two.

The most common form of resistance, and a persistent annoyance to slaveowners, was theft. Slaves took produce from the garden, raided the master's smokehouse, secretly slaughtered his stock, and killed his poultry. Slaves often distinguished between "stealing" from each other and merely "taking" from white masters. "Dey allus done tell us it am wrong to lie and steal," recalled Josephine Howard, a former slave in Texas, "but why did de white folks steal my mammy and her mammy? Dey lives . . . over in Africy. . . . Dat de sinfulles' stealin' dey is."

Slaves' hidden feelings

Slaves learned to outwit their masters by wearing an "impenetrable mask" around whites, one bondsman recalled. "How much of joy, of sorrow, of misery and anguish have they hidden from their tormentors." Frederick Douglass, the most famous fugitive slave, explained that "as the master studies to keep the slave ignorant, the slave is cunning enough to make the master think he succeeds."

Slave Culture

Trapped in bondage, faced with the futility of revolt, slaves could at least forge a culture of their own. By the nineteenth century, American slaves had been separated from much of their traditional African heritage, but that did not mean they had fully accepted the dominant white culture. Instead, slaves combined strands from their African past with customs that evolved from their life in America. This slave culture was most distinct on big plantations, where the slave population was large and slaves had more opportunity to live apart from white scrutiny.

The Slave Family

Maintaining a sense of family was one of the most remarkable achievements of African Americans in bondage, given the obstacles that faced them. Southern law did not recognize slave marriages as legally binding, nor did it allow slave parents complete authority over their children. Black women faced the possibility of rape by the master or overseer without legal recourse, and husbands, wives, and children had to live with the fear of being sold and separated. From 1820 to 1860 more than 2 million slaves were sold in the interstate slave trade. Perhaps 600,000 husbands and wives were separated by such sales. The chance that a slave family would be broken up—children taken from parents, brothers separated from sisters—was even greater. A slave mother whose three children had all been sold away grieved to Fredrika Bremer: "When they took from me the last little girl . . . I believed I never should have got over it! It almost broke my heart!"

Breakup of families

Despite their vulnerability, family ties remained strong, as slave culture demonstrated. The marriage ceremony among slaves varied from a formal religious service to jumping over a broomstick in front of the slave community to nothing more than the master giving verbal approval. Whatever the ceremony, slaves viewed the ritual as a public affirmation of the couple's commitment to their new duties and responsibilities. Rather than adopting white norms, slaves developed their own moral code concerning sexual relations and marriage. Although young slaves often

Family ties in slavery

An unknown artist (believed to be European) painted this slave auction in the 1850s, at which a young boy (left) is being examined by a prospective buyer as his mother clings to him. A planter and his wife (perhaps the owners?) look on. Once, while walking with a European visitor, Mary Chesnut, an upperclass South Carolinian, passed one such slave sale. "If you can stand that," she acidly remarked, "no other Southern thing need choke you."

engaged in premarital sex, they were expected to choose a partner and become part of a stable family. It has been estimated that at least one in five slave women had one or more children before marriage, but most of these mothers eventually married. "The negroes had their own ideas of morality, and they held them very strictly," the daughter of a Georgia planter recalled. "They did not consider it wrong for a girl to have a child before she married, but afterwards were very strict upon anything like infidelity on her part." Black churches played a leading role in condemning adultery.

Gender roles

The traditional nuclear family of father, mother, and children was the rule, not the exception, among slaves. Within the marriage the father was viewed as the traditional head of the family; wives were to be submissive and obey their husbands. Labor in the quarters was divided according to sex. Women did the indoor work, such as cooking, washing, and sewing, and men performed outdoor chores, such as gathering firewood, hauling water, and tending the animals and garden plots. The men also hunted and fished to supplement the spare weekly rations. "My old daddy . . . caught rabbits, coons an' possums," recalled Louisa Adams of North Carolina. "He would work all day and hunt at night." (See Daily Lives, "A Slave's Daily Bread," pages 414–415.)

Beyond the nuclear family, slaves developed strong kinship networks that promoted a sense of community. Aunts and uncles were expected to look after children who lost their parents through death or sale. When children were sold to a new plantation, a family in the slave quarters took them in. Thus all members of the slave society drew together in an extended network of mutual obligation.

Slave Songs and Stories

Protest and celebration

In the songs they sang, slaves expressed some of their deepest feelings about love and work and the joys and pain of life. "The songs of the slave represent the sorrows of his heart," commented Frederick Douglass. Surely there was bitterness as well as sorrow when slaves sang:

> We raise the wheat
> They give us the corn
> We bake the bread
> They give us the crust
> We sift the meal
> They give us the husk
> We peel the meat
> They give us the skin
> And that's the way
> They take us in

Yet songs were also central to the celebrations held in the slave quarters: for marriages, Christmas revels, and after harvest time. And a slave on the way to the fields might sing:

> Saturday night and Sunday too
> Young gals on my mind.
> Monday morning 'way 'fore day,
> Old master's got me gwine.
> Peggy does you love me now?

Lewis Miller of York, Pennsylvania, painted this picture of Virginia slaves dancing in 1853. Dancing and music were important components of slave culture and provided a welcome respite from work under slavery. Declared one runaway slave, "The sternest . . . master cannot frighten or whip the fun out of us."

Slaves expressed themselves through stories as well as song. Most often these folktales used animals as symbolic models for the predicaments in which slaves found themselves. In the best known of these, the cunning Brer Rabbit was a weak fellow who defeated larger animals like Brer Fox and Brer Bear by using his wits. Sometimes the identity of the trickster was no longer symbolic, but the slave. Because these latter stories contained more overt hostility to white people, slaves usually told them only among themselves. But the message, whether direct or symbolic, was much the same: to laugh at the master's shortcomings and teach the young how to survive in a hostile world.

Folktales

Steal Away to Jesus

At the center of slave culture was religion. The Second Great Awakening, which had begun on the southern frontier, converted many slaves, most of whom joined the Methodist and Baptist churches. Slaves constituted more than a quarter of the members of both of these southern churches.

Slaveowners encouraged a certain amount of religion among slaves as an effective means of social control. Masters provided slaves with a minister (often white), set the time and place of services, and usually insisted that a white person be present. "Church was what they called it," one former slave protested, "but all that preacher talked about was for us slaves to obey our masters and not to lie and steal. Nothing about Jesus was ever said and the overseer stood there to see that the preacher talked as he wanted him to talk." In response, some slaves rejected all religion, while others continued to believe in conjuring, voodoo, and various practices derived from African religion.

Most slaves, however, sought a Christianity firmly their own, beyond the control of the master. On many plantations they met secretly at night, in the

Slave religion

Daily Lives

FOOD/DRINK/DRUGS
A Slave's Daily Bread

Once a week on most plantations, slaves lined up to receive their rations from the master. Although quantities might vary, each adult could expect to receive about a peck of cornmeal, three or four pounds of bacon or salt pork, and some molasses for sweetener. Some masters added vegetables, fruits, or sweet potatoes in season, but only on rare occasions did slaves receive wheat flour, beef, lean meat, poultry, or eggs. Milk, when available at all, was reserved for children and was usually sour.

In terms of simple calories, this ration was ample enough to sustain life. A careful modern study of the slave diet has concluded that on the eve of the Civil War, adult slaves received almost 5400 calories, which exceeds today's recommended levels of consumption. More than 80 percent of the calories, however, came from corn and pork. This monotonous fare of hog-and-hominy lacked several essential nutrients as well as enough protein, afflicting many slaves with diet-related diseases like pellagra and beriberi. The malnutrition was due more to ignorance than miserliness or willful neglect on the part of masters. Although slaveowners and their families enjoyed more variety in their food and better cuts of meat, they too lacked a balanced diet.

On some plantations masters left all cooking to the slaves, who, before going to work in the morning, would eat breakfast and prepare their noon meal to take with them to eat in the fields. At night, they came home to fix a light supper. Other masters established a plantation kitchen where cooks prepared breakfast and dinner, though supper remained the responsibility of the individual slave or family. On these plantations a noon meal was brought to the fields. In general, the quality of food preparation was better under this system because slaves were often too exhausted after work to put much time or care into cooking. Naturally enough, slaves preferred to fix meals according to their own taste and eat as a family in some privacy. Fanny Kemble reported that on her husband's Georgia plantation the slaves sat "on the earth or doorsteps, and ate out of their little cedar tubs or an iron pot, some few with broken iron spoons, more with pieces of wood, and all the children with their fingers." The cooking itself was done in front of a large fireplace.

Wherever their masters permitted it, slaves tended their own vegetable gardens after work or

On one plantation, slaves working in the field who became thirsty during the heat of the day drank from this canteen. But so did the overseer or plantation owner, who was provided a separate spout. Which spout was for the slaves?

quarters or at "hush harbors" in the safety of the woods, where they broke into rhythmic singing and dancing, modeled on the ring shout of African religion. Even regular services were characterized by intense enthusiasm. "The way in which we worshiped is almost indescribable," one slave preacher recalled. "The singing was accompanied by a certain ecstasy of motion, clapping of hands, tossing of heads, which would continue without cessation about half an hour. The old house partook of the ecstasy; it rang with their jubilant shouts, and shook in all its joints." In an environment where slaves, for most of the day, were prevented from expressing their deepest feelings, such meetings served as a satisfying emotional release.

Religion also provided slaves with values to guide them through their daily experiences and give them a sense of self-worth. Slaves learned that God would redeem the poor and downtrodden and raise them one day to honor and glory. Rejecting the teaching of some white ministers that slavery was punishment, slave raised chickens and other animals. Not only did this practice provide eggs and other items not included in the weekly rations, but it also enabled slaves to sell their surplus to the master or in town and use their earnings to buy occasional luxuries such as coffee, sugar, and tobacco. Slaves also raided the master's smokehouse, secretly slaughtered his stock and killed his poultry, and stole from neighboring plantations. Richard Carruthers, a former slave, recalled, "If they didn't provision you 'nough, you just had to slip round and get a chicken."

Slaves who worked all day still had plenty of incentive to stir out at night to fish or to hunt raccoon or opossum. "The flesh of the coon is palatable," admitted Solomon Northup, a northern free black kidnapped into slavery, "but verily there is nothing in all butcherdom so delicious as a roasted 'possum." Possum was parboiled to soften it and then roasted with lard over the fire, along with sweet potatoes. Squirrel meat, though tougher, could be boiled long enough to soften it for squirrel pie served with dumplings. Rabbits, especially young ones, were tender enough to fry.

Along with such meat might come "hoecakes," a popular dish made by slapping cornmeal dough on the blade of a hoe and holding it over the coals. Vegetables were boiled in a pot with a bit of hog jowl, each new vegetable thrown in at the appropriate cooking time: beans first, then cabbage when the beans were half done, then squash, and finally okra. Whenever they could get them, slave cooks used spices to flavor their dishes. Some spices, such as sesame seeds, had come from Africa with the slaves. Red pepper, native to the Americas, added zing to innumerable dishes.

On holidays the master usually provided a banquet for all hands on the plantation. Slaves eagerly filled up on beef, mutton, roast pig, coffee, wheat bread, pies, and other dishes only rarely tasted. Although masters generally tried to keep whiskey away from their slaves, some slaveowners made an exception at Christmas. Feasting was one of the slaves' "princi[pal] sources of comfort," one former slave testified. "Only the slave who has lived all the year on his scanty allowance of meal and bacon, can appreciate such suppers."

preachers assured their congregations that they were the chosen people of God. Just as certainly, on the final Day of Judgment, masters would be punished for their sins. "This is one reason why I believe in hell," a former slave declared. "I don't believe a just God is going to take no such man as my former master into His Kingdom."

Again, song played a central role. Slaves sang religious "spirituals" at work and at play as well as in religious services. Seemingly meek and otherworldly, the songs often contained a hidden element of protest. Frederick Douglass disclosed that when slaves sang longingly of "Canaan, sweet Canaan," they were thinking not only of the Bible's Promised Land but also of the North and freedom. When slaves heard "Steal Away to Jesus" sung in the fields, they knew that a secret devotional meeting was scheduled that evening. Songs became one of the few ways that slaves could openly express, in the approved language of Christianity, their yearning for freedom. While

Slave spirituals

415

slaves sang lyrics that spoke of an otherworldly freedom from sin in heaven, their hearts were considering a this-worldly escape from physical bondage.

Religion, then, not only served to comfort slaves after days of toil and sorrow; it also strengthened their sense of togetherness and common purpose and held out the promise of eventual freedom in this world and the next. The faith that "some ob dese days my time will come" was one of the most important ways that slaves coped with bondage and resisted its pressure to rob them of their self-esteem.

The Slave Community

Hierarchy

Although slaves managed with remarkable success to preserve a sense of self-worth in a culture of their own, the hard reality of slavery made it impossible to escape fully from white control. Even the social hierarchy within the slave quarters never was entirely free from the white world. Slave preachers, conjurers, and herb doctors held status that no white conferred, but the prestige of a slave driver rested ultimately on the authority of the white master. Similarly, skilled slaves and house servants often felt superior to other slaves, an attitude masters consciously promoted. "We house slaves thought we was better'n the others what worked in the field," one personal servant confessed. Light-skinned slaves sometimes deemed their color a badge of superiority. Fanny Kemble recorded that one woman begged to be relieved of field labor, which she considered degrading, "on '*account of her color.*'"

Lucy Skipworth, who was the daughter of a driver and had been educated by her mistress, was a member of the slave elite on both counts. At Hopewell plantation in Alabama, she was in full charge of the main residence during her master's frequent absences. She ran a plantation school (despite white opposition) and, as a devout Baptist, supervised her fellow slaves' religious life. Eager for her master's approval, Skipworth on several occasions reported slave disobedience, which temporarily estranged her from the slave community. Yet in the end she was always welcomed back. While Skipworth never rebelled or apparently never considered running away, she was far from submissive. She defied white authority, protected her family, and used her influence to get rid of an overseer the slaves disliked. Like many house servants, she lived between two worlds—her master's and the slave quarters—and was never entirely comfortable in either.

But the realities of slavery and white racism inevitably drove black people closer together in a common bond and forced them to depend on one another to survive. New slaves on a plantation were immediately instructed in the mysteries of the quarters, including such vital matters as the best strategies for avoiding punishment. Walled in from the individualistic white society beyond, slaves out of necessity created a community of their own.

Free Black Southerners

Of the 4 million African Americans living in the South in 1860, only 260,000—about 7 percent—were free. More than 85 percent of them lived in the Upper South, with almost 200,000 in Maryland, Virginia, and North Carolina alone. Free black southerners were also much more urban than the southern white and slave populations. In 1860 almost a third of the free African Americans in the Upper South, and more than half in the Lower South, lived in towns and cities. As a rule, free African Americans were more literate than slaves, and they were disproportionately female and much more likely to be of mixed ancestry. Only 10 percent of all slaves were classified as mulattoes, compared to four times as many free African Americans.

Still, most free black southerners lived in rural areas, although usually not near plantations. A majority eked out a living farming or in low-paying unskilled jobs, but some did well enough to own slaves themselves. In 1830 about 3600 free blacks owned slaves, although commonly their "property" was their own wives or children, purchased because they could not be emancipated under state laws. A few free blacks, however, were full-fledged slaveowners.

Following Nat Turner's rebellion of 1831, southern legislatures increased the restrictions on free African Americans. Most states in the Deep South prohibited residents from freeing slaves in their wills, and some required any emancipated slaves to leave the state. All states forbade the entry of free African Americans, and those already living there were subject to ever greater restrictions. They had to carry their free papers, could not assemble when they wished, were subject to a curfew, often had to post a bond and be licensed to work, and could not vote, hold office, or testify in court against white people.

Lighter-skinned black southerners who were free, like their counterparts in the North, tended to set themselves apart from darker-skinned African Americans, free or slave. In such cities as Charleston and New Orleans, they established separate social and cultural organizations and maintained their own exclusive social network. Economically dependent on white customers, they developed close connections with white southerners yet were never accepted in the white world. Free African Americans occupied an uncertain position in southern society, well above black slaves but distinctly beneath even poorer white southerners. They were victims of a society that had no place for them.

This painting shows a free African American market woman in Baltimore. Urban blacks in the South, including slaves, enjoyed greater personal freedom and access to more social activities but had only limited economic opportunity.

Southern Society and the Defense of Slavery

From wealthy planters to yeoman farmers, from free black slaveholders to white mountaineers, from cotton field hands to urban craftworkers, the South was a remarkably diverse region. Yet it was united by its dependence on staple crops and above all by the institution of slavery. As the South's economy became more and more dependent on slave-produced staples, slavery became more central to the life of the South, to its culture and its identity.

The Virginia Debate of 1832

At the time of the Revolution, the leading critics of slavery had been southerners—Jefferson, Washington, Madison, and Patrick Henry among them. But beginning in the 1820s, in the wake of the controversy over admitting Missouri as a slave state (page 282), southern leaders became less apologetic about slavery and more aggressive in defending it. The turning point occurred in the early 1830s, when the South found itself increasingly under attack. It was in 1831 that William Lloyd Garrison began publishing his abolitionist newspaper, *The Liberator*. In that year too Nat Turner launched the revolt that frightened so many white southerners.

In response to the Turner insurrection, a number of Virginia's western counties, where there were few slaves, petitioned the legislature to adopt a program for gradual emancipation. Between January 16 and 25, 1832, the House of Delegates engaged in a remarkable debate over the merits of slavery. In the end, however, the legislature refused, by a vote of 73 to 58, to consider legislation to end slavery.

Significance of the Virginia debate

The Virginia debate represented the last significant attempt of white southerners to take action against the peculiar institution. In its aftermath, most felt that the subject was no longer open to debate. Instead, during the 1830s and 1840s, southern leaders defended slavery as a positive good, not just for white people but for black people as well. As John C. Calhoun proclaimed in 1837, "I hold that in the present state of civilization, where two races . . . distinguished by color and other physical differences, as well as intellectual, are brought together, the relation now existing in the slaveholding states between the two is, instead of an evil, a good— a positive good."

The Proslavery Argument

Politicians like Calhoun were not alone. White southern leaders justified slavery in a variety of ways. Ministers argued that under the law of Moses, Jews were authorized to enslave heathens and emphasized that none of the Biblical prophets or Christ himself had ever condemned slavery. They traced slavery's origins to the curse of Canaan, in which Canaan (the allegedly black grandson of Noah) was made a servant in punishment for his father's sin.

Religious arguments

Social and racial arguments

Defenders of the institution also pointed out that classical Greece and Rome depended on slavery. They even cited John Locke, that giant of the Enlightenment,

This 1841 proslavery cartoon contrasts the treatment of American slaves, who are allegedly well fed, well clothed, and well cared for, with the plight of English factory workers. Defenders of slavery made the same comparisons to northern laborers.

who had recognized slavery in the constitution he drafted for the colony of Carolina. African Americans belonged to an intellectually and emotionally inferior race, slavery's defenders argued, and therefore lacked the ability to care for themselves and required white guardianship. "Providence has placed [the black man] in our hands for his good, and has paid us from his labor for our guardianship," contended James Henry Hammond, the eminent planter and senator from South Carolina whose "guardianship" of several hundred slaves had netted him a tidy fortune.

Proslavery writers sometimes argued that slaves in the South lived better than factory workers in the North. Masters cared for slaves for life, whereas northern workers had no claim on their employer when they were unemployed, old, or no longer able to work. In advancing this argument, white southerners exaggerated the material comforts of slavery and minimized the average worker's standard of living—to say nothing, of course, about the incalculable psychological value of freedom. Still, to many white southerners, slavery seemed a more humane system of labor relations.

Defenders of slavery did not really expect to influence public opinion in the North. Their target was more often slaveowners themselves. As Duff Green, a southern editor and one of Calhoun's advisers, explained, "We must satisfy the consciences, we must allay the fears of our own people. We must satisfy them that slavery is of itself right—that it is not a sin against God—that it is not an evil, moral or political. In this way only," he went on, "can we prepare our own people to defend their institutions."

Closing Ranks

Not all white southerners could quell their doubts. To take only one example, Robert Scott, an antislavery advocate in the Virginia debate of 1832, was publicly calling slavery "an institution reprobated by the world" as late as 1849. Still, a striking change in southern opinion seems to have occurred in the three decades before the Civil War. Outside the border states, few white southerners after 1840 would admit even in private that slavery was wrong. Those who continued to oppose slavery found themselves harassed, assaulted, and driven into exile. Southern mobs destroyed the presses of antislavery papers and threatened the editors into either keeping silent or leaving the state. Southern mails were forcibly closed to abolitionist propaganda, and defenders of the South's institutions carefully scrutinized textbooks and faculty members in southern schools. Southerners like James Birney and Sarah and Angelina Grimké had to go to the free states to continue their fight against slavery.

Increasingly, too, the debate over slavery spread to the national political arena. Before 1836 Andrew Jackson's enormous popularity in the South blocked the formation of a competitive two-party system there. The rise of the abolitionist movement in the 1830s, however, left many southerners uneasy, and when the Democrats nominated the northerner Martin Van Buren in 1836, southern Whigs seized on the issue of the security of slavery and charged that Van Buren could not be counted on to meet the abolitionist threat. The Whigs made impressive gains in the South in 1836, carrying several states and significantly narrowing the margin between the two parties.

In later presidential elections, both parties in the South attacked the opposing party through its northern supporters as unreliable on slavery. This tactic was less successful in state elections, however, since both parties were led by

Economics and party
affiliation

slaveholders and were committed to protecting slavery. In addition, the depression that began in 1837 focused the attention of southern voters on economic matters. Southern Whigs appealed to the commercially oriented members of society: planters, business leaders and merchants, bankers, professionals, and residents of cities and the plantation black belts. Democrats won their share of slaveowners, but the party's greatest support came from small independent farmers in more isolated regions, where, as in the North, class and occupation were less important than one's economic and moral outlook. Southern voters most comfortable with the market and the changes it brought gravitated toward the Whig party. On the other hand, those farmers who feared the loss of personal independence that banks and commercial development brought with them tended to support the Democratic party.

During the Jacksonian era, most southern political battles did not revolve around slavery. Even so, southern politicians in both parties had to be careful to avoid the stigma of antislavery, since they were under mounting pressure from John Calhoun and his followers. Frustrated in his presidential hopes by the nullification crisis in 1832–1833 (page 348), Calhoun sought to unite the South behind his leadership by agitating the slavery issue, introducing inflammatory resolutions in Congress upholding slavery, seizing on the abolitionist mailing campaign to demand censorship of the mails, and leaping to his feet to insist on a gag rule to block antislavery petitions. During the 1830s and early 1840s, few southern politicians followed his lead, but they did become extremely careful about being in the least critical of slavery or southern institutions. They knew quite well that even if their constituents were not as fanatical as Calhoun, southern voters overwhelmingly supported slavery.

Sections and the Nation

Viewing the events of the 1830s and 1840s with the benefit of hindsight, one cannot help but concentrate on the Civil War looming in the distance and focus on the differences dividing the North and the South. Yet free white northerners and southerners had much in common as Americans.

Forces of national unity

The largest group in both sections was composed of independent farmers who cultivated their own land with their own labor and were devoted to the principles of personal independence and social egalitarianism. Although southern society was more aristocratic in tone, both sections were driven forcefully by the quest for material wealth. The Texas Red River planter for whom time was money did not take a backseat to the Yankee clockmaker Chauncey Jerome in the scramble for success and status. White Americans in both sections aspired to rise in society, and they looked to the expanding opportunities of the market to help them do so. Moreover, both northerners and southerners linked geographic mobility to opportunity, and both pushed westward in search of better land and a new start.

Many Americans, North and South, also adhered to the teachings of evangelical Protestantism. Southern churches were less open to social reform, primarily because of its association with abolitionism, and southern churches, unlike most in the North, defended slavery as a Christian institution. Eventually both the Methodist and the Baptist churches split into separate northern and southern organizations over this issue, but their attitudes on other matters often coincided.

Finally, white northerners and southerners shared a belief in democracy and white equality. To be sure, the existence of the planter class created greater tensions in southern society between democracy and aristocracy. But southern as well as northern states embraced the democratic reforms of the 1820s and 1830s, and the electorate in both sections favored giving all white males the vote and making public officeholders responsible to the people. Southerners insisted that the equality proclaimed in the Declaration of Independence applied only to white Americans (and really only to white males), but the vast majority of northerners in practice took no exception to this attitude. Both sections agreed on the necessity of safeguarding equality of opportunity rather than promoting equality of wealth.

With so much in common, it was not inevitable that the two sections would come to blows. Certainly, before 1840 few politicians believed that the differences between the two sections were decisive. It was only in the mid-1840s, when the United States embarked on a new program of westward expansion, that the slavery issue began to loom ominously in American life and Americans began to question whether the Union could permanently endure, half slave and half free.

chapter summary

The Old South was a complex, biracial society that increasingly diverged from the rest of the United States in the years before 1860.

- Southerners placed heavy emphasis on agriculture and upheld the superiority of the rural way of life. Few cities and towns developed.

  - Southern commercial agriculture produced staple crops for sale in northern and European markets: tobacco, sugar, rice, and, above all, cotton.

  - As southern agriculture expanded into the fresh lands of the Deep South, the slave population moved steadily westward and southward, and the Upper South became more diversified agriculturally.

- Slavery played a major role in shaping the class structure of the Old South.

  - Ownership of slaves brought privilege and status, and the largest slaveowners were extraordinarily wealthy.

  - Planters on the older eastern seaboard enjoyed a more refined lifestyle than those on the new cotton frontier.

- Most slaveowners, however, owned only a few slaves, and the majority of southern whites were nonslaveowning yeoman farmers.

  - At the bottom of the white class structure were the poor whites.

  - Slavery hurt nonslaveholding whites economically, but class tensions were muted in the Old South because of racial fears.

- The institution of slavery was both a labor system and a social system, regulating relations between the races.

  - Slaves resisted bondage in many ways, ranging from the subtle to the overt. Slave revolts, however, were rare.

  - Slaves developed their own culture in which the family, religion, and songs played key roles in helping slaves cope with the pressures of bondage.

  - Slaves' shared experiences created a community based on a common identity and mutual values.

- As slavery came under mounting attack, white southerners rallied to protect their peculiar institution.

  - They developed a set of arguments defending slavery as a positive good.

  - Both political parties in the South strongly defended the institution and southern rights.

- Many Americans, both North and South, shared the same values: personal independence, social egalitarianism, evangelical Protestantism. But beginning in the mid-1840s, with renewed westward expansion, the slavery issue increased sectional tensions.

interactive learning

The Primary Source Investigator CD-ROM offers the following materials related to this chapter:

- Interactive map: **Slavery and the Cotton Kingdom** (M11)

- A collection of primary sources exploring the meaning and effects of slavery in the United States. Sources include a Seaman's Protection certificate, which guaranteed freedom for a Black sailor; a sketch of Africans crowded on the slave ship *Wildfire;* and a variety of documents relating to John Brown.

additional reading

Few topics have received more historical attention than slavery and the Old South. The economics of slavery, the values of slaveowners, the nature of the region's social structure, and the content of slave culture are all matters of great controversy. The reports of Frederick Law Olmsted, conveniently available in Lawrence Powell, ed., *The Cotton Kingdom* (1984), provide a fascinating introduction to antebellum southern society. James Oakes, *Slavery and Freedom* (1990), is a good synthesis of the contradictions between slavery and freedom in southern life.

William W. Freehling, *The Road to Disunion* (1990), is a wide-ranging examination of the South to 1854 that emphasizes the diversity and divisions in southern society. James Oakes, *The Ruling Race* (1982), is a controversial study of slaveowners that emphasizes their capitalist orientation.

While old, Frank Owsley's *Plain Folk of the Old South* (1949) has not been superseded on southern yeoman farmers. The lives of upper-class southern white women and their servants are analyzed in Elizabeth Fox-Genovese, *Within the Plantation Household* (1988), while Victoria E. Bynum, *Unruly Women* (1992), deals with white and black women of lower status. The impact of geographic mobility on southern society can be studied in Joan E. Cashin, *A Family Venture* (1991). The best exploration of slavery as a labor system still remains Kenneth M. Stampp, *The Peculiar Institution* (1956), but the most perceptive treatment of slave culture is Eugene D. Genovese, *Roll, Jordan, Roll* (1974). Charles Joyner, *Down by the Riverside* (1984), is a very sensitive recreation of slave culture in the rice districts. Ira Berlin, *Slaves without Masters* (1974), is an excellent account of southern free blacks. Drew Faust, *A Sacred Circle* (1977), is a stimulating discussion of proslavery thought, while William J. Cooper Jr., *The Politics of Slavery* (1978), stresses the role of the slavery issue in southern politics. For a fuller list of readings, see the Bibliography at www.mhhe.com/davidsonnation5.

significant events

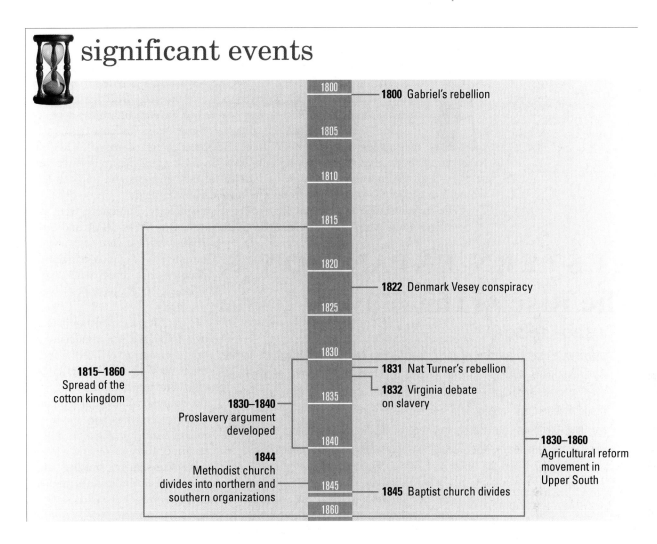

1800	**1800** Gabriel's rebellion
1805	
1810	
1815	
1820	
	1822 Denmark Vesey conspiracy
1825	
1830	
1815–1860 Spread of the cotton kingdom	**1831** Nat Turner's rebellion
1830–1840 Proslavery argument developed	**1832** Virginia debate on slavery
1835	
1840	**1830–1860** Agricultural reform movement in Upper South
1844 Methodist church divides into northern and southern organizations	
1845	**1845** Baptist church divides
1860	

Chapter 14

A t first the Crows, Arapahos, and other Indians of the Great Plains paid little attention to the new people moving out from the forests far to the east. After all, for as long as they could remember, nations like the Crow had called the plains their own. But the new arrivals were not to be taken lightly. Armed with superior weapons and bringing with them a great many women and children, they seemed to have an unlimited appetite for land. They attacked the villages of the Plains Indians, ruthlessly massacred women and children, and forced defeated tribes to live on reservations and serve their economic interests. In little more than a century and a half—from the first days when only a handful of their hunters and trappers had come into the land—they had become the masters of the plains.

The invaders who established this political and military dominance were *not* the strange "white men," who also came from the forest. During the 1830s and early 1840s, whites were still few in number. The more dangerous people—the ones who truly worried the Plains tribes—were the Sioux.

WESTERN EXPANSION & The Rise of the Slavery Issue

1820–1850

preview • The expansion of the United States to the Pacific was a process involving many overlapping and diverse frontiers–of cultures, peoples, and even animals and disease. From the east, the ideology of Manifest Destiny brought American settlers into conflict with Mexicans in Texas, New Mexico, and California, the British in Oregon, and Native Americans west of the Mississippi. Ominously, the acquisition of new lands also reopened the debate over slavery and the Union.

Westward expansion is usually told as a one-dimensional tale, centering on the wagon trains pressing on toward the Pacific. But frontiers, after all, are the boundary lines between contrasting cultures or environments, and during the nineteenth century, those in the West were constantly shifting and adapting. Frontier lines moved not only east to west, as with the white and Sioux migrations, but also south to north, as Spanish culture diffused, and west to east, as Asian immigrants came to California. Furthermore, frontiers marked not only human but also animal boundaries. Horses, cattle, and pigs, all of which had been imported from Europe, moved across the continent, usually in advance of European settlers. Often they transformed the way Indian peoples lived. Frontiers could also be technological, as in the case of trade goods and firearms. Moreover, as we have already seen, disease moved across the continent with disastrous consequences for natives who had not acquired immunity to European microorganisms.

Cultural interaction

Three frontiers altered the lives of the Sioux: those of the horse, the gun, and disease. The horse frontier spread ahead of white settlement from the southwest, where horses had first been imported by the Spanish. On the other hand, the Spanish, unlike English and French traders, refused to sell firearms to Indians, so the gun frontier moved in the opposite direction, from northeast to southwest. The two waves met and crossed along the upper Missouri during the first half of the eighteenth century. For the tribes that possessed them, horses provided greater mobility, both for hunting bison and for fighting. Guns, too, conferred obvious advantages, and the arrival of these new elements inaugurated an extremely unsettled era for Plains Indian cultures.

The Sioux were first lured from the forest onto the Minnesota prairie during the early 1700s to hunt beaver, whose pelts could be exchanged with white traders for manufactured goods. Having obtained guns in exchange for furs, the Sioux

The cultures of the Plains Indians depended on the large buffalo herds that roamed the plains. Here, two Plains Indians mounted on horses hunt buffalo with bows and arrows.

drove the Omahas, Otos, Cheyennes, and Missouris (who had not yet acquired guns) south and west. But by the 1770s their advantage in guns had disappeared, and any farther advance was blocked by powerful tribes like the Mandans and Arikaras. These peoples were primarily horticultural, raising corn, beans, and squash and living in well-fortified towns. They also owned more horses than the Sioux, which made it easier for them to resist attacks.

But the third frontier, disease, threw the balance of power toward the Sioux after 1779. European traders brought smallpox with them onto the prairie. The horticultural tribes were hit especially hard because they lived in densely populated villages, where the epidemic spread more easily. The Sioux embarked on a second wave of westward expansion in the late eighteenth century, so that by the time Lewis and Clark came through in 1804, they firmly controlled the upper Missouri as far as the Yellowstone River.

The Sioux's nomadic life, centered on the buffalo hunt, enabled them to avoid the worst ravages of disease, especially the smallpox epidemic of 1837, which reduced the plains population by as much as half. Indeed, the Sioux became the largest tribe on the plains and were the only one whose high birthrate approximated that of whites. From an estimated 5000 in 1804, they grew to 25,000 in the 1850s. Their numbers increased Sioux military power as well as the need for new hunting grounds, and during the first half of the nineteenth century, they pushed even farther up

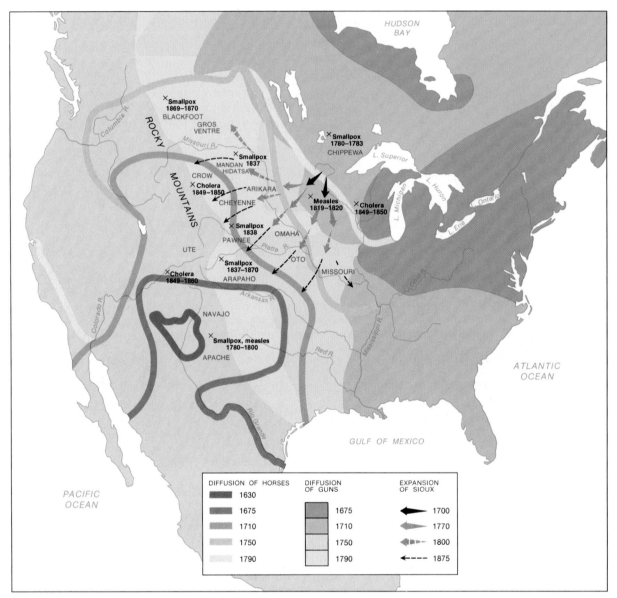

Sioux Expansion and the Horse and Gun Frontiers In 1710 the horse and gun frontiers had not yet crossed, but by 1750 the two waves began to overlap. The Sioux pushed west during the early eighteenth century thanks to firearms; they were checked from further expansion until the 1770s, when smallpox epidemics again turned the balance in their favor.

the Missouri, conquered the plains west of the Black Hills, and won control of the hunting grounds on the Platte River.

These shifting frontiers of animals, disease, firearms, and trade goods disrupted the political and cultural life of the Great Plains. And as white Americans moved westward, their own frontier lines produced similar disruptions, not only between white settlers and Indians but also between Anglo-American and Hispanic cultures.

Ironically, perhaps the greatest instability created by the moving frontiers occurred in established American society. As the political system of the United States struggled to incorporate territories, the North and South engaged in a fierce debate over whether the new lands should become slave or free. Just as the Sioux's cultural identity was brought into question by the moving frontier, so too was the identity of the American Republic.

Manifest (and Not So Manifest) Destiny

"Make way . . . for the young American Buffalo—he has not yet got land enough," roared one American politician in 1844. In the space of a few years, the United States acquired Texas, California, the lower half of the Oregon Territory, and the lands between the Rockies and California: nearly 1.5 million square miles in all. John L. O'Sullivan, a prominent Democratic editor in New York, struck a responsive chord when he declared that it had become the United States' "manifest destiny to overspread the continent allotted by Providence for the free development of our yearly multiplying millions." The cry of "Manifest Destiny" soon echoed in other editorial pages and in the halls of Congress.

Manifest Destiny

The Roots of the Doctrine

Many Americans had long believed that their country had a special, even divine, mission, which could be traced back to the Puritans' attempt to build a "city on a hill." Manifest Destiny also contained a political component, inherited from the ideology of the Revolution. In the mid–nineteenth century, Americans spoke of extending democracy, with widespread suffrage among white males, no king or aristocracy, and no established church, "over the whole North American continent."

Americans believed that their social and economic system, too, should spread around the globe. They pointed to its broad ownership of land, individualism, and free play of economic opportunity as superior features of American life. Of course,

With the Star of Empire blazing from her forehead, the Spirit of Progress dominates John Gast's painting *Manifest Destiny*. Indians and wild animals retreat in the face of advancing progress, illustrated by white settlers and farmers, railroads and other forms of transportation, telegraph lines, schools symbolized by a book, and, in the distance, cities. In reality, the movement of the frontier was hardly one-dimensional, as Hispanic, Indian, Asian, and white cultures clashed.

Manifest Destiny also had its self-interested side. American business interests recognized the value of the fine harbors along the Pacific Coast, which promised a lucrative trade with Asia, and they hoped to make those harbors American.

Finally, underlying the doctrine of Manifest Destiny was a widespread racism. The same belief in racial superiority that was used to justify Indian removal under Jackson, to uphold slavery in the South, and to excuse segregation in the North also proved handy to defend expansion westward. The United States had a duty to regenerate the backward peoples of America, declared politicians and propagandists. Their reference was not so much to Indians—who refused to assimilate into American society—but to Mexicans, whose Christian nation had its roots in European culture. The Mexican race "must amalgamate and be lost, in the superior vigor of the Anglo-Saxon race," proclaimed O'Sullivan's *Democratic Review,* "or they must utterly perish."

Before 1845 most Americans assumed that expansion would be achieved peacefully. American settlement would spread westward, and when the time was right, neighboring provinces, like ripe fruit, would fall naturally into American hands. Texas, New Mexico, Oregon, and California—areas that were sparsely populated and weakly defended—dominated the American expansionist imagination. With time, Americans became less willing to wait patiently for the fruit to fall.

The Mexican Borderlands

The heart of Spain's American empire was Mexico City, where spacious boulevards spread out through the center of the city and the University of Mexico, the oldest university in North America, had been accepting students since 1553, a full 85 years longer than Harvard. From the Mexican point of view, the frontier was 1000 miles to the north, a four-week journey to Texas, another two weeks to New Mexico, and three months by land and sea to the missions of California. Being so isolated, these provinces developed largely free from supervision.

California society

California's settlements were anchored by four coastal *presidios,* or forts, at San Diego, Santa Barbara, Monterey, and San Francisco. Between them lay 21 Catholic missions run by a handful of Franciscans (there were only 36 in 1821). The

Although Indians in California worked on both Spanish missions and *ranchos* in conditions of near slavery, Indians were encouraged to adopt Spanish religion and customs. Here an Indian woman, dressed in Spanish fashion, grinds corn for tortillas using a stone roller and a slab.

missions controlled enormous tracts of land on which grazed gigantic herds of cattle, sheep, and horses. The animals and irrigated fields were tended by about 20,000 Indians, who worked for all practical purposes as slaves.

When Mexico won its independence from Spain in 1821, California at first was little affected. But in 1833 the Mexican Congress freed the Indians of California and stripped the Catholic church of its lands. These lands were turned over to Mexican cattle ranchers, usually in massive grants of 50,000 acres or more. The new *rancheros* ruled their estates much like great planters of the Old South. Labor was provided by Indians, who once again were forced to work for little more than room and board. Indeed, the mortality rate of Indian workers was twice that of southern slaves and four times that of the Mexican Californians. At this time the Mexican population of California was approximately 4000. During the 1820s and 1830s Yankee traders set up shop in California in order to buy cattle hides for the growing shoe industry at Lynn and elsewhere. Still, in 1845 the American population in California amounted to only 700.

Spanish settlement of New Mexico was more dense: the province had about **New Mexico** 44,000 inhabitants in 1827. But like that of California, its society was dominated by *ranchero* families who grazed large herds of sheep along the upper Rio Grande valley between El Paso and Taos. A few individuals controlled most of the wealth, while their workers eked out a meager living. Mining of copper and gold was also important, and here too the profits enriched a small upper class. Spain had long outlawed any commerce with Americans, but after Mexico declared its independence in 1821, yearly caravans from the United States began making the long journey along the Santa Fe Trail. Although this trade flourished over the next two decades, developments in the third Mexican borderland, neighboring Texas, worsened relations between Mexico and the United States.

The Texas Revolution

At first, the new government in Mexico encouraged American immigration to Texas, **American immigration** where only about 3000 Mexicans, mostly ranchers, lived. In 1821 Moses Austin, an **to Texas** American, received a grant from the Spanish government to establish a colony. After his death, his son Stephen took over the project, laying out the little town of San Felipe de Austin along the Brazos River and offering large grants of land at almost no cost. By 1824 the colony's population exceeded 2000. Stephen Austin was only the first of a new wave of American land agents, or *empresarios,* who obtained permission from Mexican authorities to settle families in Texas. Ninety percent of the new arrivals came from the South. Some, intending to grow cotton, brought slaves.

Tensions between Mexicans and American immigrants grew with the Texas **Cultural conflict** economy. Most settlers from the States were Protestant. Although the Mexican government did not enforce its law that all citizens become Catholic, it barred Protestant churches. In 1829 Mexico abolished slavery, then looked the other way when Texas slaveholders evaded the law. In the 1830s the Mexican government began to have second thoughts about American settlement and passed laws prohibiting any new immigration. But Texans were most disturbed because they had little say in their government, whose legislature lay about 700 miles to the south.

For a time the Mexican authorities enforced these policies only erratically and in 1833 allowed American immigration to resume. But the flood of new settlers only made the situation worse. By mid-decade the American white population of 30,000 was nearly 10 times the number of Mexicans in the territory. Mexico also seemed determined to enforce the abolition of slavery. Even more disturbing to the

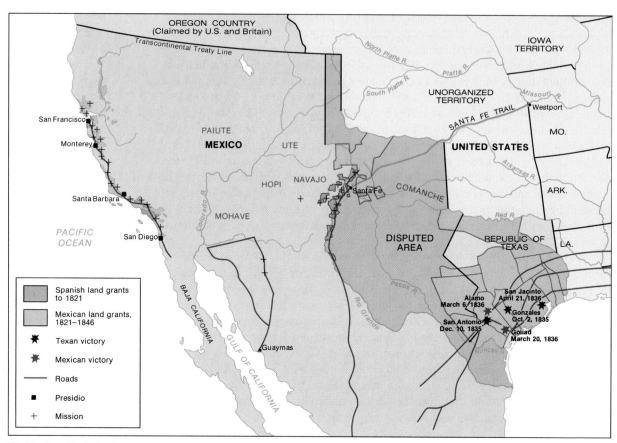

The Mexican Borderlands

American newcomers, in 1834 General Antonio Lopez de Santa Anna dissolved the Mexican Congress and proclaimed himself dictator. When Santa Anna led a military expedition north to enforce his new regime, a ragtag Texas army drove back the advance party and then captured Mexican troops in nearby San Antonio. A full-scale revolution was under way.

The Texas Republic

As Santa Anna massed his forces, a provisional government on March 2, 1836, proclaimed Texan independence. The constitution of the new Republic of Texas borrowed heavily from the U.S. Constitution, except that it explicitly prohibited the new Texas Congress from interfering with slavery. Meanwhile, Santa Anna's troops overran a Texan garrison at an old mission in San Antonio, known as the Alamo, and killed all of its 187 defenders. The Mexicans, however, paid dearly for the victory, losing more than 1500 men. The massacre of another force at Goliad after it surrendered further inflamed American resistance.

But anger was one thing; organized resistance was another. The commander of the Texas forces was Sam Houston, a former governor of Tennessee. Of striking physique and something of an eccentric, Houston had a flair for wearing colorful clothing to attract attention. His political career in Tennessee might have continued, except that the failure of his marriage led him to resign abruptly as governor and go live with the Indians. Eventually he made his way to Texas, where his intellectual ability and unexcelled talent as a stump speaker propelled him to the forefront of the independence movement. Steadily retreating eastward, Houston adeptly forged his ragged army into a disciplined fighting force.

Sam Houston, the first president of the Texas Republic, once set tongues wagging by appearing at a ball in a suit of black velvet lined with white satin and sporting a large hat trailing plumes of feathers. This daguerreotype, taken about 1850, shows the aging lion's firm determination.

By late April Houston was ready to fight. Reinforced by eager volunteers from the United States, Houston's army surprised the Mexican army camped along the San Jacinto River. With the first Mexican volley rattling overhead, the Texans charged, shouting "Remember the Alamo!" In only 15 minutes they overwhelmed the Mexicans (who had been enjoying an afternoon siesta) and captured Santa Anna.

Threatened with execution, the Mexican commander signed treaties recognizing Texan independence and establishing the Rio Grande as the southern boundary of the Texas Republic. The Mexican Congress (which had been reestablished in 1835) repudiated this agreement and launched several unsuccessful invasions into Texas. In the meantime, Houston assumed office in October 1836 as the first president of the new republic, determined to bring Texas into the Union as quickly as possible.

As an old Tennessee crony of Andrew Jackson's, Houston assumed that the United States would quickly annex such a rich and inviting territory. But Jackson worried that any such move would revive sectional tensions and hurt Martin Van Buren's chances in the 1836 presidential election. Only on his last day in office did he extend formal diplomatic recognition to the Texas Republic. Van Buren, distracted by the economic panic that broke out shortly after he entered office, took no action during his term.

Rebuffed, Texans decided to go their own way. In the 10 years following independence, the Lone Star Republic attracted more than 100,000 immigrants by offering free land to settlers. Mexico, however, refused to recognize Texan independence, and the vast majority of its citizens still wished to join the United States, where most of them, after all, had been born. There matters stood when the Whigs and William Henry Harrison won the presidency in 1840.

Texan independence

The Trek West

As thousands of Americans were moving into Texas, a much smaller trickle headed toward the Oregon country. Since 1818 the United States and Great Britain had occupied that territory jointly, as far north as latitude 54°40′. Although white settlement remained sparse, by 1836 American settlers outnumbered the British in the Willamette valley.

Pushed by the Panic of 1837 and six years of depression and pulled by tales of Oregon's lush, fertile valleys and the healthy, frost-free climate along California's Sacramento River, many American farmers struck out for the West Coast. Missouri was "cleaned" out of money, worried farmer Daniel Waldo, and his wife was even more adamant about heading west: "If you want to stay here another summer and shake your liver out with the fever and ague, you can do it," she announced to her husband, "but in the spring I am going to take the children and go to Oregon, Indians or no Indians." The wagon trains began rolling west.

The Overland Trail

Only a few hundred emigrants reached the West in 1841 and 1842, but in 1843 more than 800 followed the Overland Trail across the mountains to Oregon. From

Migration west

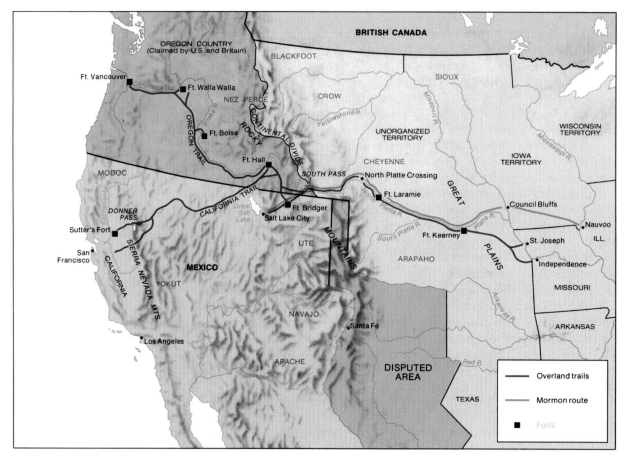

The Overland Trail Beginning at several different points, the Overland Trail followed the Platte and Sweetwater rivers across the plains to South Pass, where it crossed the Continental Divide. The trail split again near Fort Hall. Between 1840 and 1860 more than a quarter of a million emigrants made the trek. Following news of the gold strikes in 1848, the flow of westward emigrants increased and shifted toward California.

then on, they came by the thousands. Every spring brought a new rush of families to Independence or later to St. Joseph, Missouri, or to Council Bluffs, Iowa, where they waited for the spring rains to end and the trails to become passable. The migration was primarily a family enterprise, and many couples had only recently married. Most adults were between 20 and 50, since the hard journey discouraged the elderly. Furthermore, a family of four needed about $600 to outfit its journey, an amount that excluded the poor.

Caravans of 20 to 30 wagons were not uncommon the first few years, but after 1845 parties traveled in smaller trains of 8 to 10 wagons. Large companies used up the grass quickly, disagreements were more likely, and breakdowns (and hence halts) were more frequent. The trip itself lasted about 6 months, since the wagons normally covered only 15 miles a day, and the weather, repairs, deaths, and other eventualities necessitated occasional halts.

Women on the Overland Trail

The journey west placed a special strain on women, for the rugged life along the trail disrupted their traditional sense of the home. Few wives were as eager as Dan Waldo's to undertake the journey. "Poor Ma said only this morning, 'Oh I wish we never had started,'" one daughter reported, "and she looks so sorrowful and dejected." In one study of Oregon-bound parties, three-fourths of the women did not want to make the move.

At first, parties divided work by gender, as had been done back home. Women cooked, washed, sewed, and took care of the children, while men drove the wagons, cared for the stock, stood guard, and did the heavy labor. Necessity placed new demands on women, however, and eventually altered their roles. Within a few weeks, they found themselves helping to repair wagons and construct bridges. When men became exhausted, sick, or injured, women stood guard and drove the oxen. The change in work assignments proceeded only in one direction, however, for few men undertook "women's work."

Breakdown of women's traditional role

The extra labor did not bring women new authority or power within the family. Nor, by and large, did they seek it. Women resisted efforts to blur the division between male and female work and struggled to preserve their traditional role and image. Quarrels over work assignments often brought into the open long-simmering family tensions. One woman reported that there was "not a little fighting" in their company, which was "invariably the outcome of disputes over divisions of labor." The conflicting pressures a woman might feel were well illustrated by Mary Ellen Todd, a teenaged daughter who spent hours practicing how to crack the bull-whip. "How my heart bounded," she recalled, "when I chanced to hear father say to mother, 'Do you know that Mary Ellen is beginning to crack the whip.' Then how it fell again when mother replied, 'I am afraid it isn't a very lady-like thing for a girl to do.' After this, while I felt a secret joy in being able to have a power that set things going, there was also a sense of shame over this new accomplishment."

As women strove to maintain a semblance of home on the trail, they often experienced a profound sense of loss. Trains often worked or traveled on the Sabbath, which had been ladies' day back home and an emblem of women's moral authority. Women also felt the lack of close companions to whom they could turn for comfort. One woman, whose husband separated their wagon from the train after a dispute, sadly watched the other wagons pull away: "I felt that indeed I had left all my friends to journey over the dreaded plains without one female acquaintance even for a companion—of course I wept and grieved about it but to no purpose."

Women's sense of loss

Often fatigued, their sense of moral authority eroded, and their ultimate home uncertain, women complained, as one put it, that "we had left all civilization behind us." Civilization to women meant more than law, government, and schools; it also meant their homes and domestic mission. Once settled in the West, they strove to reestablish that order.

Indians and the Trail Experience

The nations whose lands were crossed by white wagon trains reacted in a number of ways to the westward tide. The Sioux, who had long been trading with whites, were among the tribes who regularly visited overlanders to trade for blankets, clothes, cows, rifles, and knives. On the other hand, white migrants took a heavy toll on the Plains Indians' way of life: the emigrant parties scared off game and reduced buffalo herds, overgrazed the grass, and depleted the supply of wood. Having petitioned unsuccessfully in 1846 for government compensation, the Sioux decided to demand payment from the wagon trains crossing their lands. Whether parties paid or not depended on the relative strength of the two groups, but whites complained bitterly of what seemed to them naked robbery.

Pressures on the Plains Indians

Daily Lives

TIME AND TRAVEL

Seeing the Elephant on the Overland Trail

In an era when traveling circuses proved a welcome though rare attraction, Americans used the expression "I have seen the elephant" to indicate they had gotten all—or considerably more than—they had bargained for. To the quarter of a million men and women who migrated overland to the Pacific coast, "seeing the elephant" meant ceasing to be a greenhorn by overcoming hardship and succeeding. The greeting "Have you seen the elephant?" became the unofficial password of the Overland Trail.

Some walked, rode horseback, or accompanied mule pack trains, but the overwhelming majority of emigrants traveled in wagons. Wagons could haul more pounds per animal, did not have to be packed each day, could carry the sick and injured, and could be arranged in a defensive circle at night. Most often, emigrants modified a common farm wagon, about 10 feet long. The wooden wagon bed, made of seasoned hardwood to withstand extreme heat, cold, and moisture, was arched over by cloth or waterproofed canvas that could be closed at each end. Many owners adorned their wagon covers with personal information and slogans or decorated them with paintings and pictures of animals (the elephant was a popular choice) so they would stand out in the crowd.

Pulled usually by four to six oxen, one wagon could carry provisions and gear for a family of four. Most farm families were larger, however, and took at least one additional wagon. Packed within was a supply of bacon, breadstuffs (mostly flour), and coffee. For sleeping, families brought blankets and frequently a tent; a well-equipped wagon might have

Joseph Goldsborough Bruff, who traveled the Overland Trail to California, drew this picture of a Platte River crossing.

Their fears aroused by sensational stories, overland parties were wary of Indians, but this menace was greatly exaggerated, especially on the plains. Few wagon trains were attacked by Indians, and less than 4 percent of deaths on the trail were caused by Indians. In truth, emigrants killed more Indians than Indians killed emigrants. For overlanders the most aggravating problem posed by Indians was theft of stock. Many companies received valuable assistance from Indians, who acted as guides, directed them to grass and water, and transported stock and wagons across rivers.

As trail congestion and conflict increased, the government constructed a string of protective forts and in 1851 summoned the Plains Indians to a conference at Fort Laramie. The U.S. government agreed to make an annual payment as compensation for the damages caused by the wagon trains but also required tribes to confine themselves to areas north or south of a corridor through which the Overland Trail ran. Some tribes were unwilling to surrender their freedom of movement and refused to agree. The Sioux, the most powerful tribe on the plains, signed and then ignored the terms.

a feather bed laid over the packed possessions in the wagon. Parents normally slept there for privacy while children used the tent.

Before starting, the adult male members of a company elected their leaders. In the first years, when trains often ran to 30 wagons or more, a complex set of rules and procedures was adopted. With experience these were simplified. Still, disputes inevitably arose, and leaders were sometimes deposed midjourney. Samuel Tetherow recalled that his father, the captain of an 1845 train, "was capable as well as popular." "But," he continued, if you think it's any snap to run a wagon train of 66 wagons with every man in the train having a different idea of what is the best thing to do, all I can say is that some day you ought to try it."

At first, overlanders were gripped by a spirit of adventure; this feeling soon passed, however, as the monotonous daily routine set in. Women rose before daybreak to cook breakfast and food for lunch; the men followed at around five to care for the animals; the train was off at seven with the call of a bugle. Men and older sons walked alongside the team or herded stock in the rear. Women and children could ride in the wagon as it jolted along, but before long they walked as much as possible to conserve the animals' strength. After a noonday stop for a cold lunch, the journey resumed; by midafternoon the men seemed almost asleep as they plodded under the baking sun beside their teams. At evening camp the men attended to the animals while the women and children collected buffalo dung for fuel and hauled water. Women cooked the evening meal and afterward washed the dishes, took care of the bedding, cleaned the wagons, aired provisions, and mended clothes. After a guard was posted, the exhausted emigrants turned in for the night.

Once the Great Plains were crossed and the Rockies loomed, mutual assistance was critical. The final third of the route lay across deserts, along twisting rivers with difficult crossings, on paths barely wide enough for a wagon. Wagons had to be double- and triple-teamed up steep grades and hoisted over canyon walls with ropes, chains, and winches. Because most wagons lacked brakes, drivers locked the wheels when going down steep slopes, dragged a weight behind, or lowered the wagon by a rope attached to a tree. At some desert crossings, a tradition developed: travelers used supplies left by earlier groups, then hauled water and grass back, after they had safely crossed, for the next party.

Improvements in the 1850s shortened the trip and reduced the hardships. Still, it required considerable courage to embark on the journey and great fortitude to complete it. "To enjoy such a trip," an anonymous overlander testified, "a man must be able to endure heat like a Salamander, . . . dust like a toad, and labor like a jackass. He must learn to eat with his unwashed fingers, drink out of the same vessel with his mules, sleep on the ground when it rains, and share his blanket with vermin. . . . It is a hardship without glory." When they reached their new homes, those who traveled the Overland Trail could boast that they had, indeed, seen the elephant.

The Political Origins of Expansion

President William Henry Harrison made the gravest mistake of his brief presidential career when he ventured out one raw spring day, bareheaded and without an overcoat, to buy groceries at the Washington markets. He caught pneumonia and died only one month after his inauguration.

For the first time in the nation's history, a vice president succeeded to the nation's highest office upon the death of the president. John Tyler of Virginia had been a Democrat who supported states' rights so strongly that, during the nullification crisis, he was the only senator to vote against the Force Bill (page 350). After that, Jackson and the Democrats would have nothing to do with him, so Tyler joined the Whigs despite his strict constructionist principles. In 1840 the Whigs put him on the ticket with Old Tip in order to balance the ticket sectionally. In the rollicking 1840 campaign, the Whigs sang all too accurately: "And we'll vote for Tyler, therefore, / Without a why or wherefore."

Tyler becomes president

435

Tyler's Texas Ploy

Tyler breaks with the Whigs

Tyler's courteous manner and personal warmth masked a rigid mind. Repeatedly, when Henry Clay and the Whigs in Congress passed a major bill, Tyler opposed it. After Tyler twice vetoed bills to charter a new national bank, disgusted congressional Whigs formally expelled their president from the party. Most Democrats, too, avoided him as an untrustworthy "renegade."

Tyler, in short, was a man without a party. Surrounded by a group of flatterers, the president could claim almost no support except among federal officeholders, who could be fired if they did not endorse him. Still, Tyler's ambition led him to believe that he might win another four years in the White House if only he latched onto the right popular issue. Nursing their own personal and political dreams, his advisers began to whisper in his ear that that issue was the annexation of Texas.

The Texas movement

That advice came mostly from Democrats disgruntled with Martin Van Buren. Jackson's successor was, in their eyes, an ineffective leader who had stumbled through a depression and in 1840 gone down in ignominious defeat. "They mean to throw Van overboard," reported one delighted Whig, who caught wind of the plans. Meanwhile, Tyler's allies launched rumors designed to frighten southerners into pushing for annexation. Britain was ready to offer economic aid if Texas would abolish slavery, they claimed. (The rumor was false.) In April 1844 Tyler sent to the Senate for ratification a treaty he had secretly negotiated to bring Texas into the Union.

Van Overboard

The front runners for the Whig and Democratic presidential nominations were Clay and Van Buren. Although rivals, they were both moderates who feared the slavery issue. Apparently by prearrangement, both men issued letters opposing annexation on the grounds that it threatened the Union and would provoke war with Mexico.

As expected, the Whigs unanimously nominated Clay on a platform that ignored the expansion issue entirely. The Democrats, however, had a more difficult time. Those who opposed Van Buren persuaded the Democratic convention to adopt a rule requiring a two-thirds vote to nominate a candidate. That blocked Van Buren's nomination.

Polk's nomination

On the ninth ballot the delegates finally turned to James K. Polk of Tennessee, who was pro-Texas. The 1844 Democratic platform called for the "reannexation" of Texas (under the claim it had been part of the Louisiana Purchase) and the "reoccupation" of Oregon, all the way to its northernmost boundary at 54°40′.

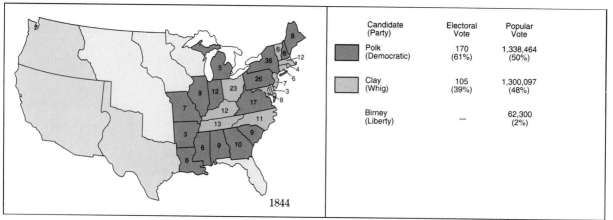

Candidate (Party)	Electoral Vote	Popular Vote
Polk (Democratic)	170 (61%)	1,338,464 (50%)
Clay (Whig)	105 (39%)	1,300,097 (48%)
Birney (Liberty)	—	62,300 (2%)

1844

Election of 1844

The status of slavery in the territories became more than an abstract question when the Senate in 1848 ratified the Treaty of Guadalupe Hidalgo. Under its terms the United States acquired Mexico's provinces of New Mexico and Upper California in return for approximately $18 million. That translated into a half million square miles of territory along with about 75,000 Spanish-speaking inhabitants. With the United States in control of the Pacific Coast from San Diego to Puget Sound, Polk's continental vision had become a reality.

Peace treaty with Mexico

As Hispanic, Indian, Asian, and Anglo-American cultures mixed, the patterns

New Societies in the West

of settlement along the frontier varied widely. Some settlers recreated the farm economies and small towns of the Anglo-American East; others continued the cattle-ranching life of the Hispanic West. In California the new settlements were overwhelmingly shaped by the rush for gold after 1848. And in the Great Basin around Salt Lake, the Mormons established a society whose sense of religious mission was as strong as that of the Puritans.

Farming in the West

The overlanders expected to replicate the societies they had left behind. When a wagon train arrived at its destination, members had usually exhausted their resources and thus quickly scattered in search of employment or a good farm site. "Friday, October 27.—Arrived at Oregon City at the falls of the Willamette," read one pioneer diary. "Saturday, October 28.—Went to work."

In a process repeated over and over, settlers in a new area set up the machinery of government. Although violence was common on the frontier, farming communities tended to resolve problems by traditional means. Churches took longer to establish, for ministers were hard to recruit and congregations were often not large enough to support a church. As the population grew, however, a more conventional society evolved. Towns and a middle class developed, the proportion of women increased, schools were established, and the residents became less mobile.

Evolution of western society

Although opportunity was greater on the frontier and early arrivals had a special advantage, more and more the agricultural frontier of the West resembled the older society of the East. With the development of markets and transportation, wealth became concentrated, some families fell to the lower rungs of society, and those who were less successful left, seeking yet another fresh start.

The Gold Rush

In January 1848, while constructing a sawmill along the American River, James Marshall noticed gold flecks in the millrace. More discoveries followed, and when the news reached the East, it spread like wildfire. The following spring the Overland Trail was jammed with eager "forty-niners." Some 80,000 emigrants journeyed to California that year, about 55,000 of whom took the overland route. In only two years, from 1848 to the end of 1849, California's population jumped from 14,000 to 100,000. By 1860 it stood at 380,000.

Among those who went to California was William Swain, a 27-year-old farmer in western New York. Deciding that he had had enough of the hard work of farming, he bid good-bye to his wife and daughter in 1849 and set off for the gold fields to make his fortune. Upon his arrival in November, he entered a partnership and staked a claim along the Feather River, but after several months of back-breaking work in icy waters, he and his partners discovered that their claim was "worth nothing." He sold out and joined another company, but early rains soon forced them to stop work. In October 1850, after less than a year in the diggings, Swain decided to return home. With only a few hundred dollars to show for his labor, he counted himself one of the vast majority of miners who had seen "their bright daydreams of golden wealth vanish like the dreams of night." He arrived home the following February and resumed farming.

Life in the mining camps

Those like Swain intent on making a fortune and returning home gave no thought to putting down roots. Most agreements were made by the month. Mining camps literally appeared and died overnight, as word of a new strike sent miners racing off to another canyon, valley, or streambed. Most settlements were hardly more than a single street, littered with debris and lined with stores, buildings, and miners' shacks—often no more than blankets or cloth tacked to a wooden frame. A saloon and gambling hall, which might double as a hotel and sometimes a brothel, was usually the most prominent building in town. More than 80 percent of the prospectors who poured into the gold country were Americans, including free blacks. Mexicans, Australians, Hawaiians, Chinese, French, English, and Irish also came. Whatever their nationality, the new arrivals were overwhelmingly unmarried men in their twenties and thirties.

The constant movement, the hard labor of mining, the ready cash, and the rootlessness all made camp society unstable. "There is an excitement connected with the pursuit of gold which renders one restless and uneasy—ever hoping to do something better," explained one forty-niner. Removed from the traditional forms of social control, miners engaged in gambling, swearing, drinking, and fighting. One startled minister reported from the California gold fields that unlike back home, immorality "is in the open, unmasked, makes no apologies and asks none." Indeed, he said, "It unfurls its flag in the most public and conspicuous places."

Women in the camps

Only about 5 percent of gold rush emigrants were women or children; given this relative scarcity, men were willing to pay top dollar for women's domestic skills.

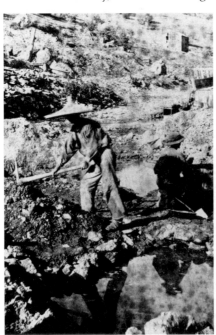

With their distinctive clothing and bamboo hats, Chinese miners could be seen throughout the diggings. Chinese immigration reached a peak in 1852, when 20,000 arrived in California. In the heyday of the mining camps, perhaps 20 percent of the miners were Chinese. Confronted with intense hostility from other miners, they worked abandoned claims and unpromising sites with primitive and less expensive equipment.

Women supported themselves by cooking, sewing, and washing, as well as by running hotels and boardinghouses. "A smart woman can do very well in this country," one woman informed a friend in the East. "It is the only country I ever was in where a woman received anything like a just compensation for work." Likewise, they suffered no shortage of suitors. "I had men come forty miles over the mountains, just to look at me," Eliza Wilson recalled, "and I never was called a handsome woman, in my best days, even by my most ardent admirers." Women went to the mining frontier to be with their husbands, to make money, or to find adventure. But the class most frequently seen in the diggings was prostitutes, who numbered perhaps 20 percent of female Californians in 1850.

Predictably, mining the miners offered one of the more reliable roads to prosperity.

Perhaps half the inhabitants of a mining town were shopkeepers, businesspeople, and professionals who provided services for prospectors. Also conspicuous were gamblers, card sharks, and other outcasts, all bent on separating the miner from his riches. In such an atmosphere, violence was prevalent, so when a new camp opened, miners adopted a set of rules and regulations. Justice was dispensed promptly, either by a vote of all the miners or by an elected jury. While effective when administered fairly, the system at times degenerated into lynch law.

Observers praised the diggings' democratic spirit. Yet such assertions overlooked strongly held nativist prejudices: when frustrated by a lack of success, American miners directed their hostility toward foreigners. The miners ruthlessly exterminated the Indians in the area, mob violence drove Mexicans out of nearly every camp, and the Chinese were confined to claims abandoned by Americans as unprofitable. The state eventually enacted a foreign miners' tax that fell largely on the Chinese. Free African Americans felt the sting of discrimination as well, both in the camps and in state law. White American miners proclaimed that "colored men were not privileged to work in a country intended only for American citizens."

Nativist and racial prejudices

Before long, the most easily worked claims had been played out, and competition steadily drove down the average earnings from $20 a day in 1848 to $6 in 1852. That was still higher than eastern wages, but goods and services cost significantly more too. As gold became increasingly difficult to extract, larger corporations using heavy equipment and employing miners working for wages came to dominate the industry. Men who had come to California filled with visions of wealth usually found only shovels of mud. As the era of the individual miner passed, so too did mining camps and the unique society they spawned.

The damage mining did to the land endured longer. Abandoned prospect holes and diggings pockmarked the gold fields and created piles of debris that heavy rains would wash down the valley, choking streams and ruining lands below. Excavation of hillsides, construction of dams to divert rivers, and the destruction of the forest cover to meet the heavy demand for lumber and firewood caused serious erosion of the soil and spring floods. The attitude of the individual miners differed little from that of the capitalists who succeeded them: both sought to exploit the environment as rapidly as possible with little thought to long-term consequences. Untempered by any sense of restraint, the quest for rapid wealth left long-lasting scars on the landscape of the gold country.

Environmental impact of mining

Instant City: San Francisco

When the United States assumed control of California, San Francisco had a population of perhaps 200. But thousands of emigrants took the water route west, passing through San Francisco's harbor on their way to the diggings. By 1856 the city's population had jumped to an astonishing 50,000. In a mere 8 years the city had attained the size New York had taken 190 years to reach.

The product of economic self-interest, San Francisco developed in helter-skelter fashion. Land prices soared, speculation was rampant, and commercial forces became paramount. Residents lived in tents or poorly constructed, half-finished buildings. To enlarge the commercial district, hills began to be leveled, with the dirt used to fill in the bay (thereby creating more usable land). Since the city government took virtually no role in directing development, almost no land was reserved for public use. Property owners defeated a proposal to widen the streets, prompting the city's leading newspaper to complain, "To sell a few more feet of lots, the streets were compressed like a cheese, into half their width."

San Francisco's chaotic growth

San Francisco in 1852

The Migration from China

The gold rush that swelled San Francisco's streets was a global phenomenon. Americans predominated in the mining population, but Latin Americans, Europeans, Australians, and Chinese swarmed into California. An amazing assortment of languages could be heard on the city's streets: indeed, in 1860 San Francisco was 50 percent foreign-born.

The most distinctive of the ethnic groups was the Chinese. They had come to Gum San, the land of the golden mountain. Those who arrived in California overwhelmingly hailed from the area of southern China around Canton—and not by accident. Although other provinces of China also suffered from economic distress, population pressures, social unrest, and political upheaval, Canton had a large European presence, since it was the only port open to outsiders. That situation changed after the first Opium War (1839–1842), when Britain forced China to open other ports to trade. For Cantonese, the sudden loss of their trade monopoly produced widespread economic hardship. At the same time, a series of religious and political revolts in the region led to severe fighting that devastated the countryside. A growing number of residents concluded that emigration was the only way to survive, and the presence of western ships in the harbors of Canton and nearby Hong Kong (a British possession since 1842) made it easier to migrate to California rather than southeast Asia.

Between 1849 and 1854, some 45,000 Chinese flocked to California. Among those who went was 16-year-old Lee Chew, who left for California after a man from his village returned with great wealth from the "country of the American wizards." Like the other gold seekers, these Chinese immigrants were overwhelmingly young and male, and they wanted only to accumulate savings and return home to their families. (Indeed, only 16 Chinese women arrived before 1854.) Generally poor, Chinese immigrants arrived already in debt, having borrowed the price of their steamship ticket; they fell further into debt to Chinese merchants in San Francisco, who loaned them money to purchase needed supplies.

When the Chinese were harassed in the mines, many opened laundries in San Francisco and elsewhere, since little capital was required—soap, scrub board, iron, and ironing board. The going rate at the time for washing, ironing, and starching shirts was an exorbitant $8 per dozen. Many early San Franciscans actually found it cheaper to send their dirty laundry to Canton or Honolulu, to be returned several months later. Other Chinese around San Francisco set up restaurants or worked in the fishing industry. In these early years they found Americans less hostile, as long as they stayed away from the gold fields. As immigration and the competition for jobs increased, however, anti-Chinese sentiment intensified.

Gradually, San Francisco took on the trappings of a more orderly community. The city government established a public school system, erected streetlights, created a municipal water system, and halted further filling in of the bay. Industry was confined to the area south of the city; several new working-class neighborhoods grew up near the downtown section. Fashionable neighborhoods sprouted on several hills, as high rents drove many residents from the developing commercial center, and churches and families became more common. By 1856, the city of the gold rush had been replaced by a new city whose stone and brick buildings gave it a new sense of permanence.

The Mormons in Utah

The makeshift, often chaotic society spawned by the gold rush was a product of largely uncontrolled economic forces. In contrast, the society evolving in the Great Basin of Utah exhibited an entirely different but equally remarkable growth. Salt Lake City became the center of a religious kingdom established by the Church of Jesus Christ of Latter-day Saints.

After Joseph Smith's death in 1844 (page 377), the Mormon church was led by Brigham Young, who lacked Smith's religious mysticism but was a brilliant organizer. Young decided to move his followers to the Great Basin, an isolated area a thousand miles from the settled parts of the United States. In 1847 the first thousand settlers arrived, the vanguard of thousands more who extended Mormon settlement throughout the valley of the Great Salt Lake and the West. Church officials also held the government positions, and Young had supreme power in legislative, executive, and judicial matters as well as religious affairs. In 1849 the state of Deseret was officially established, with Brigham Young as governor. It applied for admission to the Union.

State of Deseret

The most controversial church teaching was the doctrine of polygamy, or plural marriage, which Young finally sanctioned publicly in 1852. Visitors reported with surprise that few Mormon wives seemed to rebel against the practice. Some plural wives developed close friendships; indeed, in one sample almost a third of plural marriages included at least two sisters. If the wives lived together, the system allowed them to share domestic work. When the husband established separate households, wives enjoyed greater freedom, since the husband was not constantly present. Moreover, because polygamy distinguished Mormonism from other religions, plural wives saw it as an expression of their religious faith. "I want to be assured of *position in God's estimation*," one such wife explained. "If polygamy is the Lord's order, we must carry it out."

Polygamy

The Mormons connected control of water to their sense of mission and respect for hierarchy. The Salt Lake valley, where the Mormons established their holy community, lacked significant rivers or abundant sources of water. Thus success

Irrigation and community

depended on irrigating the region, something never before attempted. When the first Mormons arrived from the East, they had no experience with irrigation and little capital. But they made up for that lack with a strong sense of unity bolstered by a religious commission to exploit the environment and make it fruitful. By constructing a coordinated series of dams, aqueducts, and ditches, they brought life-giving water to the valleys of the region. Fanning out from their original settlement, they founded a series of colonies throughout the West, all tied to Salt Lake City and joined by ribbons of water. Mormon farmers grew corn, wheat, hay, and an assortment of fruits and vegetables. By 1850, there were more than 16,000 irrigated acres in what would eventually become the state of Utah. The Mormons were the first Anglos to extensively use irrigation in North America.

Manipulation of water reinforced the Mormons' sense of hierarchy and group discipline. Centralization of authority in the hands of church officials made possible an overall plan of development, allowed for maximum exploitation of resources, and freed communities from the disputes over water rights that plagued many settlements in the arid West. In a radical departure from American ideals, church leaders insisted that water belonged to the community, not individuals, and vested this authority in the hands of the local bishop. Control of water resources, which were vital for survival in the desert, reinforced the power of the church hierarchy over not just the faithful but dissidents as well. Community needs, as interpreted by church leaders, took precedence over individual rights. Thus irrigation did more than make the desert bloom. By checking the Jeffersonian ideal of an independent, self-sufficient farmer, it also made possible a centralized, well-regulated society under the firm control of the church.

Temple City: Salt Lake City

In laying out the Mormons' "temple city" of Salt Lake, Young was also determined to avoid the commercial worldliness and competitive individualism that had plagued the Mormons at Nauvoo. City lots, which were distributed by lottery, could not be subdivided for sale, and real estate speculation was forbidden.

Salt Lake City's orderly growth

The city itself was laid out in a checkerboard grid well suited to the level terrain. Streets were 132 feet wide (compared with 60 feet in San Francisco), and each square block contained eight home lots of 1.25 acres each. Unlike in early San

Francisco, the family was the basic social unit in Salt Lake City, and almost from the beginning the city had an equal balance of men and women. The planners also provided for four public squares in various parts of the city. The city lacked any traditional secular authority: it was divided into 18 wards, each under the supervision of a bishop, who held civil as well as religious power.

As the city expanded, the original plan had to be modified to accommodate the developing commercial district by dividing lots into sizes more suitable for stores. Experience and growth also eventually dictated smaller blocks and narrower streets, but the city still retained its spacious appearance and regular design. Through religious and economic discipline church leaders succeeded in preserving a sense of common purpose.

Shadows on the Moving Frontier

Transformations like Salt Lake City and San Francisco were truly remarkable. But it is important to remember that Americans were not coming into a trackless, unsettled wilderness. As frontier lines crossed, 75,000 Mexicans had to adapt to American rule.

The Treaty of Guadalupe Hidalgo guaranteed Mexicans in the ceded territory "the free enjoyment of their liberty and property." As long as Mexicans continued to be a sizable majority in a given area, their influence was strong. But wherever Anglos became more numerous, they demanded conformity to American customs. When Mexicans remained faithful to their heritage, language, and religion, these cultural differences worked to reinforce Hispanic powerlessness, social isolation, and economic exploitation.

New Mexico had the largest Hispanic population as well as the fewest Anglos in the Mexican cession. As a result, the upper-class Mexicans who owned the land and employed large numbers of mixed-blood workers on their ranches managed to maintain their position. This class had cultivated American allies during the Santa Fe trade, and their connections grew stronger as American businesspeople slowly entered the territory in the 1850s. Neither group had much interest in the lower-class Hispanics, whom both exploited.

The rush of American emigrants quickly overwhelmed Hispanic settlers in   Hispanic-Anglo conflict
California. Even in 1848, before the discovery of gold, Americans in California

Town plazas, such as this one in San Antonio, were commercial centers in the Mexican Southwest. Traders from outlying *ranchos* enjoy refreshments while their goods, loaded on oxcarts, await sale.

outnumbered Mexicans two to one, and by 1860 Hispanics amounted to only 2 percent of the population. At the time of the American conquest, the 200 or so *ranchero* families owned about 14 million acres, but changes in California land law required verification of their original land grants by a federal commission. Since the average claim took 17 years to complete and imposed complex procedures and hefty legal fees, many *rancheros* lost large tracts of land to Americans.

Lower-class Mexicans scratched out a bare existence on ranches and farms or in the growing cities and towns. Scorned by the dominant Anglo majority and without skills and resources, they were often reduced to extreme poverty. As the Hispanic population in California became primarily urban, women assumed a larger role in the family. Many men were seasonal workers who were absent part of the year, and thus women played a greater role in sustaining the family economically.

Mexicans in Texas were also greatly outnumbered: they totaled only 6 percent of the population in 1860. Stigmatized as inferior, they were the poorest group in free society. One response to this dislocation, an option commonly taken by persecuted minorities, was social banditry. An example was the folk hero Juan Cortina. A member of a displaced landed family in southern Texas, Cortina was driven into resistance in the 1850s by American harassment. He began stealing from wealthy Anglos to aid poor Mexicans, proclaiming, "To me is entrusted the breaking of the chains of your slavery." Cortina continued to raid Texas border settlements until finally imprisoned by Mexican authorities. While failing to produce any lasting change, Cortina demonstrated the depth of frustration and resentment among Hispanics over their abuse at the hands of the new Anglo majority.

Escape from Crisis

Issue of slavery's extension

With the return of peace, Congress confronted the problem of whether to allow slavery in the newly acquired territories. David Wilmot, in his controversial proviso, had already proposed to outlaw slavery throughout the Mexican cession. John C. Calhoun, representing the extreme southern position, countered that slavery was legal in all territories. The federal government had acted as the agent of all the states in acquiring the land, he argued, and southerners had a right to take their property there, including slaves. Only when the residents of a territory drafted a state constitution could they decide the question of slavery.

Between these extremes were two moderate positions. One proposed extending the Missouri Compromise line of 36°30′ to the Pacific, which would have continued the earlier policy of dividing the national domain between the North and the South. The other proposal, championed by Senator Lewis Cass of Michigan and Senator Stephen A. Douglas of Illinois, was to allow the people of the territory rather than Congress to decide the status of slavery. This solution, which became known as popular sovereignty, was deliberately ambiguous, since its supporters refused to specify whether the residents could make this decision at any time or only when drafting a state constitution, as Calhoun insisted.

When Congress organized the Oregon Territory in 1848, it prohibited slavery there, since even southerners admitted that the region was too far north to grow the South's staple crops. But this seemingly straightforward decision made it impossible to apply the Missouri Compromise line to the other territories. Without Oregon as a part of the package, the bulk of the remaining land would be open to slavery, something at which the North balked. Almost inadvertently, one of the two moderate solutions had been discarded by the summer of 1848.

A Two-Faced Campaign

In the election of 1848 both major parties tried to avoid the slavery issue. The Democrats nominated Lewis Cass, a supporter of popular sovereignty, while the Whigs bypassed all their prominent leaders and selected General Zachary Taylor, who had taken no position on any public issue and who remained silent throughout the campaign. The Whigs adopted no platform and planned instead to emphasize the general's war record.

But the slavery issue would not quietly go away. Instead, a new antislavery coalition, the Free Soil party, came together. Alienated by Polk's policies and still angry over the 1844 convention, northern Democrats loyal to Van Buren spearheaded its creation. They were joined by "Conscience Whigs," who disavowed Taylor's nomination because he was a slaveholder. Furthermore, political abolitionists like Salmon P. Chase left the Liberty party in favor of this broader coalition. To widen its appeal, the Free Soil platform focused on the dangers of extending slavery rather than on the evil of slavery itself. Ironically, the party's convention named as its candidate Martin Van Buren—the man who for years had struggled to keep the slavery issue out of politics.

Free Soil party

With the Free Soilers strongly supporting the Wilmot Proviso, the Whigs and Democrats could not ignore the slavery question. The two major parties responded by running different campaigns in the North and the South. To southern audiences, each party promised that it would protect slavery in the territories; to northern voters, each claimed that it would keep the territories free. In this two-faced, sectional campaign, the Whigs won their second national victory. Taylor held on to the core of Whig voters in both sections (Van Buren and Cass, after all, had long been Democrats). But in the South, where the contest pitted a southern slaveholder against two northerners, Taylor won many more votes than Clay had in 1844. As one southern Democrat complained, "We have lost hundreds of votes, solely on the ground that General Cass was a Northerner and General Taylor a Southern man." Furthermore, Van Buren polled five times as many votes as the Liberty party had four years earlier. It seemed that the national system of political parties was being gradually pulled apart.

The Compromise of 1850

Once he became president, Taylor could no longer remain silent. The territories gained from Mexico had to be organized; furthermore, by 1849 California had gained enough residents to be admitted as a state. In the Senate the balance of power between North and South stood at 15 states each. California's admission would break the sectional balance.

Taylor's plan

Called "Old Rough and Ready" by his troops, Taylor was a forthright man of action, but he was politically inexperienced and oversimplified complex problems. Since even Calhoun conceded that entering states had the right to ban slavery, Taylor proposed that the way to end the sectional crisis was to skip the territorial stage by combining all the Mexican cession into two very large states, New Mexico and California. So the president sent agents to California and New Mexico with instructions to set the machinery in motion for both territories to draft constitutions and apply for statehood directly. Even more shocking to southern Whigs, he proposed to apply the Wilmot Proviso to the entire area, since he was convinced that slavery would never flourish there. By the time Congress convened in December 1849, California had drafted a constitution and applied for admission as a free state. Taylor reported that New Mexico (which included most of Arizona, Utah, and Colorado) would soon do the same and recommended that both be admitted as free states. The president's plan touched off the most serious sectional crisis the Union had yet confronted.

Into this turmoil stepped Henry Clay, now 73 years old and nearing the end of his career. A savvy card player all his life, Clay loved politics: the bargaining, the wheeling and dealing, the late-night trade-offs eased along by a bottle of bourbon. Thirty years earlier he had engineered the Missouri Compromise, and in 1833 he had helped defuse the nullification crisis. Clay decided that a grand compromise was needed to save the Union. Already, Mississippi had summoned other southern states to meet in a convention at Nashville to discuss the crisis, and southern extremists were pushing for secession. The points of disagreement went beyond the question of the western territories. Many northerners considered it disgraceful that slaves were bought and sold in the nation's capital, where slavery was still permitted. Southerners complained bitterly that northern states ignored the 1793 fugitive slave law and prevented them from reclaiming runaway slaves.

Clay's compromise

Clay's compromise, submitted in January 1850, addressed all these concerns. California, he proposed, should be admitted as a free state, which represented the

The Great Triumvirate—Clay, Webster, and Calhoun—served together in public life for almost four decades. Clay (left) and Webster (center) supported the Compromise of 1850, whereas in his last speech in the Senate, the dying Calhoun (right) opposed it. By midcentury, power was passing to a new generation of politicians more accustomed to sectional conflict and less amenable to compromise.

clear wishes of most settlers there. The rest of the Mexican cession would be
organized as two territories, New Mexico and Utah, under the doctrine of popular
sovereignty. Thus slavery would not be prohibited from these regions. Clay also
proposed that Congress abolish the slave trade but not slavery itself in the District
of Columbia and that a new, more rigorous fugitive slave law be passed to enable
southerners to reclaim runaway slaves. To reinforce the idea that both North and
South were yielding ground, Clay combined those provisions that dealt with the
former Mexican territory and several others adjusting the Texas–New Mexico
boundary into a larger package known as the Omnibus Bill.

   With the stakes so high, the Senate debated the bill for six months. Daniel Webster of Massachusetts, always deep-voiced, seemed more somber than usual when he

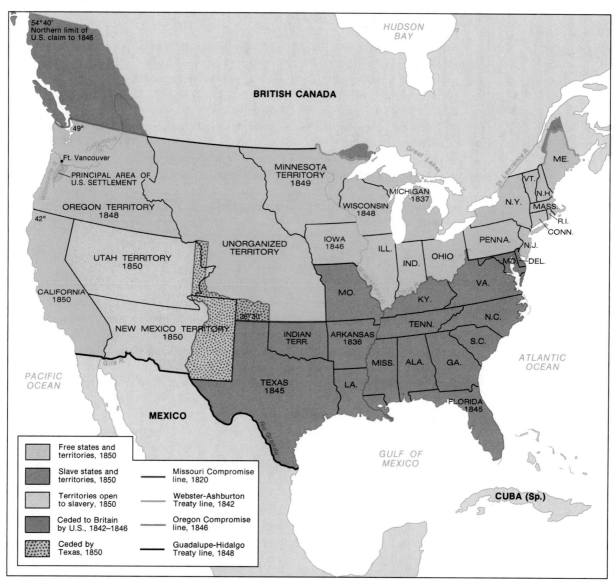

Territorial Growth and the Compromise of 1850 The Webster-Ashburton Treaty established Maine's
northern boundary as well as the American-Canadian boundary west of the Great Lakes.

delivered a pro-compromise speech on the seventh of March. "I wish to speak today not as a Massachusetts man, not as a Northern man, but as an American. . . . I speak today for the preservation of the Union. Hear me for my cause." Calhoun, whose aged, crevassed face mirrored the lines that had been drawn so deeply between the two sections, was near death and too ill to deliver his final speech to the Senate, which a colleague read for him as he listened silently. The "cords of Union," he warned—those ties of interest and affection that held the nation together—were snapping one by one. Only equal rights for the South and an end to the agitation against slavery could preserve the Union.

Clay, wracked by a hacking cough, spent long hours trying to line up the needed votes. But for once, the great whist enthusiast had misplayed his hand. The Omnibus Bill required that the components of the compromise be approved as a package. Extremists in Congress from both regions, however, combined against the moderates and rejected the bill.

Passage of the Compromise

With Clay exhausted and his strategy in shambles, Democrat Stephen A. Douglas assumed leadership of the pro-compromise forces. The sudden death in July of President Taylor, who had threatened to veto Clay's plan, aided the compromise movement. One by one, Douglas submitted the individual measures for a vote. Northern representatives provided the necessary votes to admit California and abolish the slave trade in the District of Columbia, while southern representatives supplied the edge needed to organize the Utah and New Mexico territories and pass the new fugitive slave law. On the face of it, everyone had compromised. But in truth, only 61 members of Congress, or 21 percent of the membership, had not voted against some part of the Compromise.

By September 17 all the separate parts of the Compromise of 1850 had passed and been signed into law by the new president, Millard Fillmore. The Union, it seemed, was safe.

Away from the Brink

The general public, both North and South, rallied to the Compromise. At the convention of southern states in Nashville, the fire-eaters—the radical proponents of states' rights and secession—found themselves voted down by more moderate voices.

Rejection of secession

Even in the Deep South, coalitions of pro-Compromise Whigs and Democrats soundly defeated secessionists in the state elections that followed. Still, most southerners felt that a firm line had been drawn. With California's admission, they were now outnumbered in the Senate, so it was critical that slaveholders be granted equal legal access to the territories. They announced that any breach of the Compromise of 1850 would justify secession.

Fugitive slave law

The North, for its part, found the new fugitive slave law the hardest measure of the Compromise of 1850 to swallow. The controversial law denied an accused runaway a trial by jury, and it required that all citizens assist federal marshals in its enforcement. Harriet Beecher Stowe's popular novel *Uncle Tom's Cabin* (1852) presented a powerful moral indictment of the law—and of slavery as an institution. (See Daily Lives, "Uncle Tom by Footlights," pages 478–479.) Despite sentimental characters, a contrived plot, and clumsy dialect, the book profoundly moved its readers. Emphasizing the duty of Christians toward the downtrodden, it reached a greater audience than any previous abolitionist work and heightened moral opposition to the institution.

In reality, however, fewer than 1000 slaves a year ran away to the North, many of whom did not succeed. Despite some cases of well-publicized resistance, the

1850 fugitive slave law was generally enforced in the free states. Many northerners did not like the law, but they were unwilling to tamper with the Compromise. Stephen Douglas spoke accurately enough when he boasted in 1851, "The whole country is acquiescing in the compromise measures—everywhere, North and South. Nobody proposes to repeal or disturb them."

And so calm returned. In the lackluster 1852 presidential campaign, both the Whigs and the Democrats endorsed the Compromise. Franklin Pierce, a little-known New Hampshire Democrat, soundly defeated the Whig candidate, Winfield Scott. Even more significant, the antislavery Free Soil candidate received only about half as many votes as Van Buren had four years before. With the slavery issue seemingly losing political force, it appeared that the Republic had weathered the storm unleashed by the Wilmot Proviso.

But the moving frontier still had changes to work. It had leaped from the Mississippi valley to the Pacific, but in between remained territory still unorganized. And as the North became increasingly industrialized and the South more firmly committed to an economy based on cotton and slavery, the growing conflict between the two sections would shatter the Jacksonian party system, reignite the slavery issue, and shake the Union to its foundation.

chapter summary

In the 1840s the United States expanded to the Pacific, a development that involved the cultural interaction of Americans with other groups and led to the rise of the slavery issue in national politics.

- In the 1840s Americans proclaimed that it was the United States' Manifest Destiny to expand across the North American continent.

- Americans in Texas increasingly clashed with Mexican authorities, and in 1836 Texans revolted and established an independent republic.

- Americans headed for Oregon and California on the Overland Trail.

  - The journey put special pressures on women as the traditional division of labor by gender broke down.

  - White migration also put pressure on Plains Indians' grazing lands, wood supplies, and freedom of movement.

  - The gold rush spawned a unique society that was overwhelmingly male, highly mobile, and strongly nativist and racist.

  - Led by Brigham Young, the Mormons established a tightly organized, centrally controlled society in the Great Salt Lake basin.

  - Throughout the Southwest the Hispanic population suffered at the hands of the new Anglo majority.

- President James K. Polk entered office with a vision of the United States as a continental nation.

  - He upheld President John Tyler's annexation of Texas and agreed to divide the Oregon country with Britain.

  - The United States eventually went to war with Mexico and acquired California and the Southwest.

- The Mexican War reinjected into national politics the issue of slavery's expansion.

  - The Wilmot Proviso sought to prohibit slavery from any territory acquired from Mexico.

  - The struggle over the Proviso eventually disrupted both major parties.

  - Congress momentarily stilled the sectional crisis with the Compromise of 1850.

interactive learning

The Primary Source Investigator CD-ROM offers the following materials related to this chapter:

* Interactive map: **The Mexican War, 1846–1848** (M13)

* A collection of primary sources demonstrating the dramatic impact of slavery on the Union as it expanded westward. Also discover the dynamic and socially disruptive slave trade that emerged to feed the plantations to the west through images of slave pens where humans were held until their sale. Explore the westward expansion with the journal of Maximillian Alexander Philipp. As the nation expanded, conflict with Mexico erupted: view a portrait of Stephen F. Austin, one of the founders of the Republic of Texas, to go along with the interactive map illustrating the Mexican War.

additional reading

In recent years the field of western American history has dramatically expanded to include cultural diversity, environmental problems, racial interaction, and the role of gender, themes that were largely ignored in earlier accounts of western expansion. Good introductions to the "new western history" are Richard White's inelegantly titled *It's Your Misfortune and None of My Own* (1991) and William Cronon et al., *Under an Open Sky* (1992).

David J. Weber, *The Mexican Frontier, 1821–1846* (1982), is a superb study of the Southwest prior to American control. Two excellent accounts from different perspectives of the Overland Trail experience are John D. Unruh Jr., *The Plains Across* (1979), and John Mack Faragher, *Women and Men on the Overland Trail* (1979). Thomas R. Hietala offers a stimulating analysis of the social roots of expansionism in *Manifest Design* (1985). Leonard J. Arrington and Davis Bitton, *The Mormon Experience,* 2nd ed. (1992), is a good survey. Women's experiences in the West are analyzed in Julie R. Jeffrey, *Frontier Women* (1979), while Donald D. Jackson, *Gold Dust* (1980), examines the gold rush. The fullest treatment of politics in this decade is William R. Brock, *Parties and Political Conscience* (1970). The drive to annex Texas is carefully untangled in William W. Freehling, *The Road to Disunion* (1990), and its impact on the Democratic party is the focus of James C. N. Paul's *Rift in the Democracy* (1961). The best discussion of Polk's handling of the Oregon and Texas issues is Charles G. Sellers Jr., *James K. Polk, Continentalist, 1843–1846* (1966). Michael F. Holt presents a magisterial analysis of the Whig party's difficulties in this decade in *The Rise and Fall of the American Whig Party* (1999). Holman Hamilton, *Prologue to Conflict* (1964), is an excellent study of the Compromise of 1850. For a fuller list of readings, see the Bibliography at www.mhhe.com/davidsonnation5.

significant events

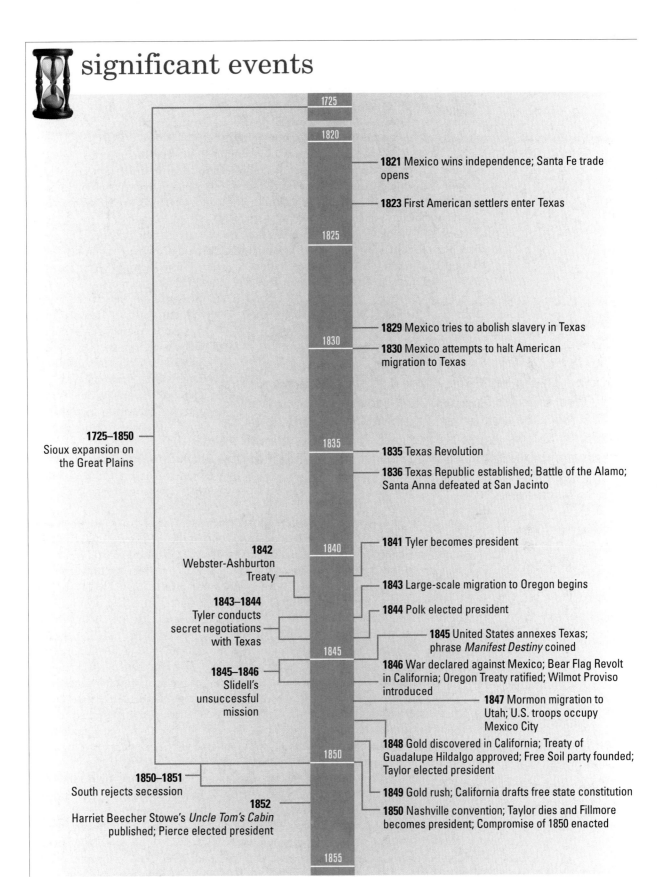

1725–1850
Sioux expansion on
the Great Plains

1842
Webster-Ashburton
Treaty

1843–1844
Tyler conducts
secret negotiations
with Texas

1845–1846
Slidell's
unsuccessful
mission

1850–1851
South rejects secession

1852
Harriet Beecher Stowe's *Uncle Tom's Cabin*
published; Pierce elected president

1725

1820

1821 Mexico wins independence; Santa Fe trade opens

1823 First American settlers enter Texas

1825

1829 Mexico tries to abolish slavery in Texas

1830

1830 Mexico attempts to halt American migration to Texas

1835

1835 Texas Revolution

1836 Texas Republic established; Battle of the Alamo; Santa Anna defeated at San Jacinto

1840

1841 Tyler becomes president

1843 Large-scale migration to Oregon begins

1844 Polk elected president

1845 United States annexes Texas; phrase *Manifest Destiny* coined

1845

1846 War declared against Mexico; Bear Flag Revolt in California; Oregon Treaty ratified; Wilmot Proviso introduced

1847 Mormon migration to Utah; U.S. troops occupy Mexico City

1848 Gold discovered in California; Treaty of Guadalupe Hildalgo approved; Free Soil party founded; Taylor elected president

1850

1849 Gold rush; California drafts free state constitution

1850 Nashville convention; Taylor dies and Fillmore becomes president; Compromise of 1850 enacted

1855

Chapter 15

I
nto town they rode, several hundred strong, their faces flushed with excitement. They were unshaven, rough-talking men, "armed . . . to the teeth with rifles and revolvers, cutlasses and bowie-knives." At the head of the procession an American flag flapped softly in the warm May breeze. Alongside it was another with a crouching tiger emblazoned on black and white stripes, followed by banners proclaiming "Southern Rights" and "The Superiority of the White Race." At the rear rolled five artillery pieces, which were quickly dragged into range of the town's main street. Watching intently from a window in his office, Josiah Miller, the editor of the Lawrence *Kansas Free State,* predicted, "Well, boys, we're in for it."

For the residents of Lawrence, Kansas, the worst seemed at hand. The town had been founded by the New England Emigrant Aid Company, a Yankee association that recruited settlers in an effort to keep Kansas Territory from becoming a slave state. Accepting Stephen Douglas's idea that the people should decide the status of slavery, the town's residents intended to see to it that under popular sovereignty Kansas entered the Union as a free state. Emigrants from the neighboring slave state of Missouri were equally determined that no "abolition tyrants" or "negro thieves" would control the territory. There had been conflict in Kansas almost immediately: land disputes, horse thievery, shootings on both sides.

THE UNION BROKEN

1850–1861

preview • During the 1850s the building of a vast railroad network and a rising tide of immigration benefited the North in terms of both economic and political power. As a result, sectional tensions grew. But it was the debate over slavery in the newly acquired territories–especially in Kansas–that brought the crisis to a head. By 1861 the old party system had collapsed, Republican Abraham Lincoln had been elected entirely on the strength of northern votes, and secession was imminent.

In the ensuing turmoil, the federal government seemed to back the proslavery forces. In the spring of 1856, a U.S. district court indicted several of Lawrence's leading citizens for treason, and federal marshal Israel Donaldson called for a posse to help make the arrests. Donaldson's posse, swelled by eager volunteers from across the Missouri border, arrived outside Lawrence on the night of May 20.

Meanwhile, Lawrence's "committee of safety" had agreed on a policy of nonresistance. Most of those indicted had fled, but Donaldson arrested two men without incident. Then he dismissed his posse.

The posse, however, was not ready to go home. Already thoroughly liquored up, it marched into town cheering. Ignoring the pleas of some leaders, its members smashed the presses of two newspapers, the *Herald of Freedom* and the *Kansas Free State.* Then the horde unleashed its wrath on the now-deserted Free State Hotel, which more closely resembled a fort. The invaders unsuccessfully attempted to batter it down with cannon fire and blow it up with gunpowder; finally they put a torch to the building. When the mob finally rode off, it left the residents of Lawrence unharmed but thoroughly terrified.

Retaliation by free state partisans was not long in coming. Hurrying north along a different road to Lawrence, an older man with a grim face and steely eyes heard the news the next morning that the town had been attacked. "Old Man Brown," as everyone called him, was on his way with several of his sons to provide reinforcements. A severe, God-fearing Calvinist, John Brown was also a staunch abolitionist who had once remarked to a friend that he believed "God had raised him up on purpose to break the jaws of the wicked." Brooding over the failure of the free-staters to resist

A torchlight parade staged by the Republican Wide-Awakes, New York City, 1860. In remarkably few years, the new sectional party sensed victory within its reach in the presidential election.

The Free State Hotel was destroyed and burned by the proslavery band that attacked Lawrence, Kansas, on May 21, 1856. News of the so-called Sack of Lawrence greatly agitated northern public opinion and strengthened the struggling Republican party.

Pottawatomie massacre

the "slave hounds" from Missouri, Brown ordered his followers to sharpen their heavy cutlasses. "Caution," he announced, "is nothing but the word of Cowardice."

On the night of May 24, 1856, Brown headed toward Pottawatomie Creek with a half dozen others, including four of his sons. Announcing that they were "the Northern Army" come to serve justice, they burst into the cabin of James Doyle, a proslavery man from Tennessee, with cutlasses drawn. As Brown marched off Doyle and his three sons, Doyle's terrified wife, Mahala, begged him to spare her youngest, and the old man relented. The others were led no more than 100 yards down the road before Owen and Salmon Brown hacked them to death with broadswords. Old Man Brown then walked up to James Doyle's body and put a bullet through his forehead. Before the night was done, two more cabins had been visited and two more proslavery settlers brutally executed. Not one of the five murdered men owned a single slave or had any connection with the raid on Lawrence.

Brown's action precipitated a new wave of fighting in Kansas, and the news of the tumult further angered residents in both sections of the nation. "Everybody here feels as if we are upon a volcano," remarked one congressman in Washington.

The country was indeed atop a smoldering volcano that would finally erupt in the spring of 1861, showering death and destruction across the land. Popular sovereignty, the last remaining moderate solution to the controversy over the expansion of slavery, had failed dismally in Kansas. The violence and disorder in the territory provided a stark reply to Stephen Douglas's proposition: What could be more peaceable, more fair than the notion of popular sovereignty?

Sectional Changes in American Society

The road to war was not a straight or short one. Six years elapsed between the Compromise of 1850 and the crisis in "Bleeding Kansas." Another four would pass before the first shot was fired. And the process of separation involved more than ineffective politicians and an unwillingness to compromise. As we have seen, Americans were bound together by a growing transportation network, by national markets, and by a national political system. These social and political ties—the "cords of Union," Calhoun called them—could not be severed all at once. Increasingly, however, the changes occurring in American society heightened sectional tensions. As the North continued to industrialize, its society came into conflict with that of the South. The Old Northwest, which had long been a political ally of the South, became more closely linked to the East. The coming of civil war, in other words, involved social and economic changes as well as political ones.

The Growth of a Railroad Economy

By the time the Compromise of 1850 produced a lull in the tensions between North and South, the American economy had left behind the depression of the early 1840s and was roaring again. Its basic structure, however, was changing. Cotton remained the nation's major export, but it was no longer the driving force for American economic growth. After 1839 this role was taken over by the construction of a vast railroad network covering the eastern half of the continent. By 1850 the United States possessed more than 9000 miles of track; 10 years later it had over 30,000 miles, more than the rest of the world combined. Much of the new construction during the 1850s occurred west of the Appalachian Mountains—more than 2000 miles in Ohio and Illinois alone.

Because western railroads ran through less settled areas, they were especially dependent on public aid. State and local governments made loans to rail companies, invested in their stocks and bonds, backed them with government credit, and sometimes exempted them temporarily from taxes. About a quarter of the cost of railroad construction came from state and local governments, but federal land grants were crucial, too. By mortgaging or selling the land to farmers, the railroad raised construction capital and also stimulated settlement, which increased its business and profits. By 1860 Congress had allotted about 28 million acres of federal land to 40 different companies.

On a national map, the rail network in place by 1860 looked impressive, but these lines were not fully integrated. A few trunk-line roads such as the New York Central had combined a number of smaller lines to facilitate the shipment of freight. But roadbeds had not yet been standardized, so that no fewer than 12 different gauges, or track widths, were in use. Moreover, cities at the end of rail lines jealously strove to maintain their commercial advantages, not wanting to connect with competing port cities for fear freight would pass through to the next city down the line.

The effect of the new lines rippled outward through the economy. Farmers along the tracks began to specialize in cash crops and market them in distant locations. With their profits they purchased manufactured goods that earlier they might have made at home. Before the railroad reached Athens, Tennessee, the surrounding counties produced about 25,000 bushels of wheat, which sold for less than

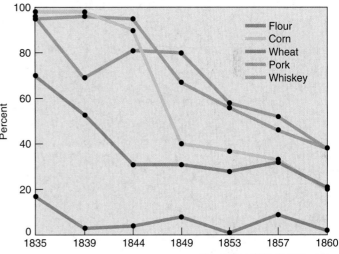

Proportion of Western Exports Shipped via New Orleans, 1835–1860 In 1835 nearly 100 percent of western exports of corn, pork, and whiskey were being shipped via New Orleans. By 1860 only about 40 percent of pork and whiskey and 20 percent of flour and corn were. The change in shipping patterns weakened the political ties between the South and the Old Northwest.

Railroads' impact on the economy

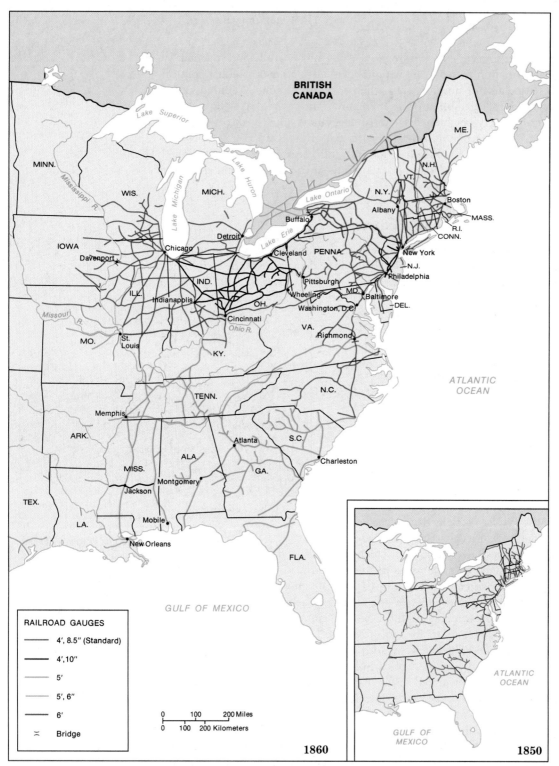

BRITISH CANADA

MINN.

WIS.

MICH.

Lake Superior

Lake Huron

Lake Michigan

Lake Erie

Lake Ontario

ME.

N.H.

VT.

N.Y.

Boston

Albany

MASS.

R.I.

CONN.

Buffalo

Detroit

Cleveland

PENNA.

New York

N.J.

Philadelphia

IOWA

Davenport

Chicago

IND.

Pittsburgh

Wheeling

MD.

Baltimore

DEL.

ILL.

Indianapolis

OH.

Washington, D.C.

Missouri R.

Mississippi R.

MO.

St. Louis

Cincinnati

Ohio R.

VA.

Richmond

KY.

N.C.

ATLANTIC OCEAN

TENN.

ARK.

Memphis

ALA.

Atlanta

S.C.

Charleston

MISS.

Montgomery

GA.

TEX.

Jackson

LA.

Mobile

New Orleans

FLA.

GULF OF MEXICO

RAILROAD GAUGES

— 4', 8.5" (Standard)

— 4', 10"

— 5'

— 5', 6"

— 6'

⋈ Bridge

0   100   200 Miles

0   100   200 Kilometers

1860

ATLANTIC OCEAN

GULF OF MEXICO

1850

Railroads, 1850 and 1860, with Track Gauges During the 1850s a significant amount of railroad track was laid, but total track mileage is misleading, because the United States lacked a fully integrated rail network in 1860. A few trunk-line roads had combined a number of smaller lines into a single system to facilitate shipment. The Pennsylvania Railroad, for example, connected Philadelphia and Pittsburgh. But the existence of five major track gauges as well as minor ones meant that passengers and freight often had to be transferred from one line to the next. And north-south traffic was further disrupted by the lack of bridges over the Ohio River.

50 cents a bushel. Once the railroad came, farmers in these same counties grew 400,000 bushels and sold their crop at a dollar a bushel. Railroads also stimulated other areas of the economy, notably the mining and iron industries.

The new rail networks shifted the direction of western trade. In 1840 most northwestern grain was shipped down the Mississippi River to the bustling port of New Orleans. But low water made steamboat travel risky in summer, and ice shut down traffic in winter. Products such as lard, tallow, and cheese quickly spoiled if stored in New Orleans' sweltering warehouses. Increasingly, traffic from the Midwest flowed west to east, over the new rail lines. Chicago became the region's hub, linking the farms of the upper Midwest to New York and other eastern cities by more than 2000 miles of track in 1855. Thus while the value of goods shipped by river to New Orleans continued to increase, the South's overall share of western trade dropped dramatically. *Reorientation of western trade*

A sharp rise in demand for grain abroad also encouraged farmers in the Northeast and Midwest to become more commercially oriented. Wheat, which in 1845 commanded $1.08 a bushel in New York City, fetched $2.46 in 1855; in similar fashion the price of corn nearly doubled. Farmers responded by specializing in cash crops, borrowing to purchase more land, and investing in equipment to increase productivity. These new patterns of commerce and agriculture weakened the traditional political alliance between the South and the West, which had been based on shared economic interests. "The power of cotton over the financial affairs of the Union has in the last few years rapidly diminished," the *Democratic Review* remarked in 1849, "and bread stuffs will now become the governing power." *The new commercial agriculture*

Railroads and the Prairie Environment

As railroad lines fanned out from Chicago, farmers began to acquire open prairie land in Illinois and then Iowa, putting its deep black soil into production. Commercial agriculture transformed this remarkable treeless environment.

To settlers accustomed to woodlands, the thousands of square miles of tall grass were an awesome sight. Indian grass, Canadian wild rye, and native big bluestem all grew higher than a person. In 1838 Edmund Flagg gazed upon "the tall grasstops waving in . . . billowy beauty in the breeze; the narrow pathway winding off like a serpent over the rolling surface, disappearing and reappearing till lost in the luxuriant herbage." Long-grass prairies had their perils too: summer or winter storms sent travelers searching for the shelter of trees along river valleys. Dewitt Smith recalled the fierce green-headed flies awaiting the unsuspecting. "A journey across the big praries was, in the summer time, undertaken only at night," he recalled, "because on a hot summer day horses would be literally stung and worried to death."

Because eastern plows could not penetrate the densely tangled roots of prairie grass, the earliest settlers erected farms along the boundary separating the forest from the prairie. In 1837, however, John Deere patented a sharp-cutting steel plow that sliced through the sod without soil sticking to the blade. In addition, Cyrus McCormick refined a mechanical reaper that harvested 14 times more wheat with the same amount of labor. By the 1850s McCormick was selling 1000 reapers a year and could not keep up with demand, while Deere turned out 10,000 plows annually. *Impact of technology*

The new commercial farming fundamentally altered the landscape and the environment. Indians had grown corn in the region for years, but never in such large fields as did white farmers, whose surpluses were shipped east. Prairie farmers also introduced new crops that were not part of the earlier ecological system, notably wheat, along with fruits and vegetables. Native grasses were replaced by a small number of plants cultivated as commodities. Corn had the best yields, but *Changes in the landscape* it was primarily used to feed livestock or make whiskey. Because bread played a key role in the American and European diet, wheat became the major cash crop. Tame grasses replaced native grasses in pastures for making hay.

Western farmers altered the landscape by reducing the annual fires, often set by Indians, that had kept the prairie free from trees. In the fires' absence, trees reappeared on land not in cultivation and, if undisturbed, eventually formed woodlots. The earlier unbroken landscape gave way to independent farms, each fenced in the precise checkerboard pattern established by the Northwest Ordinance. It was an artificial ecosystem of animals, woodlots, and crops whose large, uniform layout made western farms more efficient than the irregular farms in the East.

Railroads and the Urban Environment

Railroads transformed the urban environment as well. Communities soon recognized that their economic survival depended on creating adequate rail links to the countryside and to major urban markets. Large cities feared they would be left behind in the struggle to be the dominant city in the region. Smaller communities saw their very survival at stake in the battle for rail connections. When the new railroad line bypassed the prairie village of Auburn, Illinois, its fate was sealed, and residents quickly abandoned it for more promising locations.

Influence on location of towns

Even communities that obtained rail links found the presence of this new technology difficult to adjust to. When a railroad began serving nearby Jacksonville, Illinois, merchants complained about the noise, dirt, and billowing smoke when locomotives hissed through the business district. "The public square was filled with teams [of horses]," one resident recalled, "and whenever the engine steamed into the square making all the noise possible, there was such a stampede. . . . Many of the people were as much scared as the horses at the steaming monster. . . ." After a few years, the tracks were relocated on the outskirts of town. Jacksonville's experience became the norm: increasingly communities kept railroads away from fashionable neighborhoods and shopping areas. As the tracks became a physical manifestation of social and economic divisions, the notion of living "on the wrong side of the tracks" became crucial to defining the urban landscape.

Rising Industrialization

On the eve of the Civil War, 60 percent of American laborers worked on farms. In 1860, for the first time, that figure dropped below 50 percent in the North. The expansion of commercial agriculture spurred the growth of industry. Out of the 10 leading American industries, 8 processed raw materials produced by agriculture, including flour milling and the manufacture of textiles, shoes, and woolens. (The only exceptions were iron and machinery.) Industrial growth also spurted during the 1850s as water power was increasingly replaced by steam, since there were only a fixed number of water-power sites.

Most important, the factory system of organizing labor and the technology of interchangeable parts spread to other areas of the economy. Many industries during the 1850s adopted interchangeable parts. Isaac Singer began using them in 1851 to mass-produce sewing machines, which made possible the ready-made clothing industry, while workers who assembled farm implements performed a single step in the process over and over again. By 1860 the United States had nearly a billion dollars invested in manufacturing, almost twice as much as in 1849.

Immigration

The surge of industry required a large factory labor force. Natural increase helped swell the population to more than 30 million by 1860, but only in part, since the birthrate had begun to decline. On the eve of the Civil War the average white mother bore five children, compared to seven at the turn of the century. It was the beginning of mass immigration to America during the mid-1840s that kept population growth soaring.

In the 20 years from 1820 to 1840, about 700,000 newcomers had entered the United States. That figure jumped to 1.7 million in the 1840s, then to 2.6 million in the 1850s. Though even greater numbers arrived after the Civil War, as a percentage of the nation's total population, the wave from 1845 to 1854 was the largest influx of immigrants in American history. Most newcomers were young people in the prime of life: out of 224,000 arrivals in 1856, only 31,000 were under 10 and only 20,000 were over 40.

Influx of immigrants

Certainly the booming economy and the lure of freedom drew immigrants, but they were also pushed by deteriorating conditions in Europe. In Ireland, a potato blight in 1846 produced widespread famine. Out of a population of 9 million, as many as a million perished, while a million and a half more emigrated, two-thirds to the United States.

The Irish tended to be poorer than other immigrant groups of the day. Although the Protestant Scots-Irish continued as before to emigrate, the decided majority of the Irish who came after 1845 were Catholic. The newcomers were generally mostly

New sources of immigration

Conditions of famine across Ireland led many to buy passage on ships like this one, departing for the United States. New York was the major port of entry for immigrants who surged into the United States during the 1840s and 1850s.

unmarried younger sons and daughters of hard-pressed rural families. Because they were poor and unskilled, the Irish congregated in the cities, where the women performed domestic service and took factory jobs and the men did manual labor.

Germans and Scandinavians also had economic reasons for leaving Europe. They included small farmers whose lands had become marginal or who had been displaced by landlords, and skilled workers thrown out of work by industrialization. Others fled religious persecution. Some, particularly among the Germans, left after the liberal revolutions of 1848 failed, in order to live under the free institutions of the United States. Since coming to America, wrote a Swede who settled in Iowa in 1850, "I have not been compelled to pay a penny for the privilege of living. Neither is my cap worn out from lifting it in the presence of gentlemen."

The revolutions of 1848

Unprecedented unrest and upheaval prevailed in Europe in 1848, the so-called year of revolutions. The famine that had driven so many Irish out of their country was part of a larger food shortage caused by a series of poor harvests. Mounting unemployment and overburdened relief programs increased suffering. In this situation middle-class reformers, who wanted civil liberty and a more representative government, joined forces with lower-class workers to overthrow several regimes, sometimes by also appealing to nationalist feelings. France, Austria, Hungary, Italy, and Prussia all witnessed major popular uprisings. Yet though these revolts gained temporary success, they were all quashed by the forces of the old order. Liberal hopes for a more open, democratic society suffered a severe setback.

In the aftermath of this failure, a number of hard-pressed German workers and farmers, as well as disillusioned radicals and reformers, emigrated to the United States, the symbol of democratic liberalism in the world. They were joined by the first significant migration from Asia, as thousands of Chinese headed to the gold rush in California and other strikes (page 444). This migration was simply part of a century-long phenomenon, as approximately 50 million Europeans, largely from rural areas, would migrate to the Western Hemisphere.

Although many Germans and Scandinavians arrived in modest straits, few were truly impoverished, and many could afford to buy a farm or start a business. Unlike the Irish, Germans tended to emigrate as families, and wherever they settled, they formed social, religious, and cultural organizations to maintain their language and customs. Whereas the Scandinavians, Dutch, and English immigrants were Protestant, half or more of the Germans were Catholics.

Immigrants and industrialization

Factories came more and more to depend on immigrant labor, including children, since newcomers would work for lower wages and were less prone to protest harsh working conditions. The shift to an immigrant workforce could be seen most clearly in the textile industry, where by 1860 more than half the workers in New England mills were foreign-born. Tensions between native- and foreign-born workers, as well as among immigrants of various nationalities, made it difficult for workers to unite.

Urban resources strained

The sizable foreign-born population in many American cities severely strained urban resources. Immigrants who could barely make ends meet were forced to live in overcrowded, unheated tenement houses, damp cellars, and even shacks—"the hall was dark and reeking with the worst filth," reported one New York journalist; the house was "filled with little narrow rooms, each one having five or six occupants; all very filthy." Urban slums became notorious for crime and drinking, which took a heavy toll on families and the poor. In the eyes of many native-born Americans, immigrants were to blame for driving down factory wages and pushing American workers out of jobs. Overshadowing these complaints was a fear that America might not be able to assimilate the new groups, with their unfamiliar social customs, strange languages, and national pride. These fears sparked an outburst of political nativism in the mid-1850s.

Southern Complaints

With British and northern factories buying cotton in unprecedented quantities, southern planters prospered in the 1850s. Their operations, like those of northern commercial farmers, became more highly capitalized to keep up with the demand. But instead of machinery, white southerners invested in slaves. During the 1850s, the price of prime field hands reached record levels.

Nonetheless, a number of southern nationalists, who advocated that the South should become a separate nation, pressed for greater industrialization to make the region more independent. "At present, the North fattens and grows rich upon the South," one Alabama newspaper complained in 1851, noting that "we purchase all our luxuries and necessities from the North," including clothing, shoes, implements and machinery, saddles and carriages, and even books. But most southerners ignored such pleas. As long as investments in cotton and slaves absorbed most of the South's capital, efforts to promote southern industry made little headway.

Despite southern prosperity, the section's leaders complained that the North used its power over banking and commerce to convert the South into a colony. In the absence of any significant southern shipping, northern intermediaries controlled the South's commodities through a complex series of transfers from planter to manufacturer. Storage and shipping charges, insurance, port fees, and commissions together added an estimated 20 percent to the cost of cotton and other commodities. These revenues went into the pockets of northern merchants, shippers, and bankers. The idea that the South was a colony of the North was inaccurate, but southern whites found it a convincing explanation of the North's growing wealth. More important, it reinforced their resistance to federal aid for economic development, which they were convinced would inevitably enrich the North at southern expense. This attitude further weakened the South's political alliance with the West, which needed federal aid for transportation.

Southern economic dependence

White southerners also feared that the new tide of immigration would shift the sectional balance of power. Some immigrants did settle in the South's few cities,

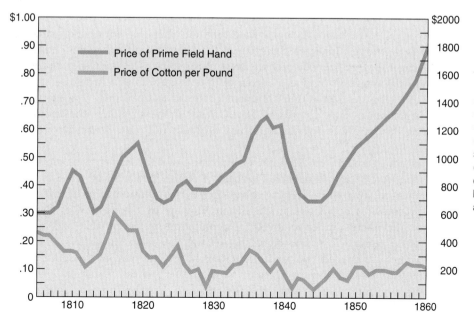

Prices of Cotton and Slaves
From 1815 to 1850, cotton and slave prices generally moved together, as southerners plowed their profits from growing cotton into buying more land and slaves. During the 1850s, however, the booming southern economy and bumper cotton crops drove the price of slaves steeply upward compared to cotton prices, squeezing slave-owners' profit margins and heightening southern anxieties about the future.

but most shunned the South because they did not want to compete with cheap slave labor. The lack of industry and the limited demand for skilled labor also shunted immigrants northward. As a result, the North surged even further ahead of the South in population, thereby strengthening its control of the House of Representatives and heightening southern concern that the North would rapidly settle the western territories.

The Political Realignment of the 1850s

When Franklin Pierce (he pronounced it "Purse") assumed the presidency in 1853, he was only 48 years old, the youngest man yet to be elected president. He was also a supporter of the "Young America" movement of the Democratic party, which eagerly looked to spread democracy across the globe by annexing additional territory to the United States.

The believers in Young America felt it idle to argue about slavery when the nation could be developing new resources. But they failed to appreciate how each new plan for expansion would stir up the slavery issue. In 1853 Pierce did manage to conclude the Gadsden Purchase, thereby gaining control of about 45,000 square miles of Mexican desert that contained the most practical southern route for a transcontinental railroad (see map, page 467).

Gadsden Purchase

Pierce had no success, however, with his major goal, the acquisition of Cuba, a rich sugar-producing region in which slavery had once been strong and still existed. For years many Americans had assumed the United States would eventually acquire Cuba, but Spain rebuffed all efforts to purchase it. Then, in 1854, three American ministers meeting at Ostend in Belgium confidentially recommended that if Spain would not sell Cuba, the island should be seized. The contents of this "Ostend Manifesto" soon leaked, and Pierce was forced to repudiate the notion of acquiring Cuba through naked aggression. In any case, he soon had his hands full with the proposals of another Democrat of the Young America stamp, Senator Stephen A. Douglas of Illinois.

Ostend Manifesto

The Kansas-Nebraska Act

Known as the Little Giant, Douglas was ambitious, bursting with energy, and impatient to get things done. As chairman of the Senate's Committee on Territories, he was eager to organize federal lands west of Missouri as part of his program for economic development. And as a citizen of Illinois, he wanted Chicago selected as the eastern terminus of the transcontinental railroad to California. Chicago would never be chosen over St. Louis and New Orleans, however, unless the rest of the Louisiana Purchase was organized, for any northern rail route would have to run through that region.

Repeal of the Missouri Compromise

Under the terms of the Missouri Compromise of 1820, slavery was prohibited in this portion of the Louisiana Purchase. Douglas had already tried in 1853 to organize the area while keeping a ban on slavery—only to have his bill voted down by southern opposition in the Senate. Bowing to a good deal of southern pressure, the Illinois leader removed the prohibition on slavery that had been in effect for 34 years. The Kansas-Nebraska Act was passed in May 1854.

Popular sovereignty

The new act created two territories: Kansas, directly west of Missouri, and a much larger Nebraska Territory, located west of Iowa and the Minnesota Territory. The Missouri Compromise was explicitly repealed. Instead, popular sovereignty was to determine the status of slavery in both territories, though it was left unclear

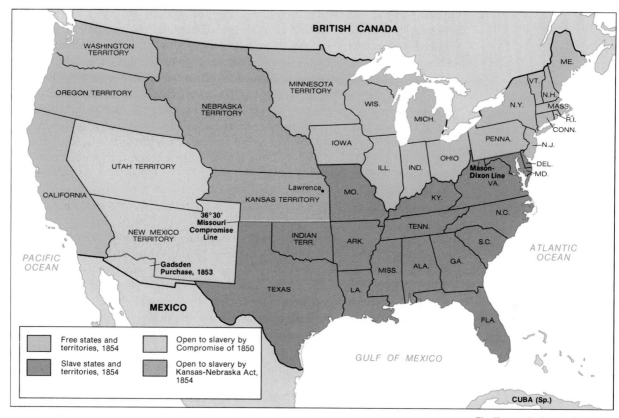

The Kansas-Nebraska Act
When the Kansas-Nebraska Act of 1854 opened the remaining portion of the Louisiana Purchase to slavery under the doctrine of popular sovereignty, conflict between the two sections focused on control of Kansas, directly west of the slave state of Missouri.

whether residents of Kansas and Nebraska could prohibit slavery at any time or only at the time of statehood, as southerners insisted. Still, most members of Congress assumed that Douglas had split the region into two territories so that each section could claim another state: Kansas would be slave and Nebraska free.

The Kansas-Nebraska Act outraged northern Democrats, Whigs, and Free Soilers alike. Critics rejected Douglas's contention that popular sovereignty would keep the territories free. As always, most northerners spoke little of the moral evils of slavery; it was the chance that the Slave Power might gain new territory that concerned them. So great was the northern outcry that Douglas joked he could "travel from Boston to Chicago by the light of my own [burning] effigy."

The Collapse of the Second American Party System

The furor over the Kansas-Nebraska Act laid bare the underlying social and economic tensions that had developed between the North and the South. These tensions put mounting pressure on the political parties, and in the 1850s the Jacksonian party system collapsed. Voters who had been loyal to one party for years, even decades, began switching allegiances, while new voters were mobilized. By the time the process of realignment was completed, a new party system had emerged, divided this time along clearly sectional lines.

Political realignment

In part, the old party system decayed because new problems had replaced the traditional economic issues of both Whigs and Democrats. The Whigs alienated many of their traditional Protestant supporters by openly seeking the support of

Disillusionment with the parties

Catholics and recent immigrants. Then, too, the growing agitation by Protestant reformers for the prohibition of alcohol divided both parties, especially the Whigs. Finally, both the Whigs and the Democrats were targets of popular disillusionment, with the existing parties perceived as little more than corrupt engines of plunder designed "to keep a lot of [Old Fogies] in office." Observed one Ohio Whig in 1853, "There is prevailing generally a sort of 'don't care a damn' spirit."

Thus the party system was already weakened when the Kansas-Nebraska Act divided the two major parties along sectional lines. Northern congressional Whigs, who unanimously opposed the bill, found themselves deserted by virtually all their southern colleagues. And fully half the northern Democratic representatives in the House voted against Douglas's bill.

The Know-Nothings

In such an unstable atmosphere, with party loyalties declining, independent parties flourished. The most dramatic challenge to the Whigs and Democrats came first from a movement worried about the recent flood of immigrants.

New York City was the primary gateway for immigrants, and it was here that the American party, a secret nativist society, first organized. Its members were sworn to secrecy and instructed to answer inquiries by replying "I know nothing." In 1853 the Know-Nothings, as they were quickly dubbed, began organizing in several other states; after only a year they had become the fastest-growing party in the nation. Not coincidentally, 1854 also marked the peak of the new wave of immigration.

Nativist impulse

Taking as its slogan "Americans should rule America," the American party advocated that immigrants be forced to wait not 5 but 21 years before becoming naturalized citizens. It also called on voters to oust from office corrupt politicians who openly bid for foreign and Catholic votes. Know-Nothings denounced illegal voting by immigrants, the rising crime and disorder in urban areas, and immigrants' heavy drinking. They were also strongly anti-Catholic, convinced that the "undemocratic" hierarchy of priests, bishops, and archbishops controlled by the pope in Rome was conspiring to undermine American democracy.

To young native-born American workers, the Know-Nothing message was particularly appealing. It was they who bore the brunt of the economic dislocations caused by industrialization and who had to compete with immigrants for jobs. In the 1854 elections, the Know-Nothings won a series of remarkable victories.

Their showing spelled doom for the Whigs, already weakened by the Kansas-Nebraska Act, as the rank and file deserted in droves to the Know-Nothings. Fueled by its success, the American party turned its attention south, and in a few months it had organized in every state of the Union. With perhaps a million voters enrolled in its lodges in 1855, Know-Nothing leaders confidently predicted that they would elect the next president.

Know-Nothings' decline

Yet only a year later—by the end of 1856—the party had collapsed as quickly as it had risen. Many Know-Nothing officeholders proved woefully incompetent. Voters deserted them when the party failed to enact its program. But the death knell of the party was rising sectional tensions. In 1856 a majority of northern delegates walked out of the American party's national convention when it adopted a proslavery platform. Significantly, they deserted to the other new party, the Republicans. This party, unlike the Know-Nothings, had no base in the South. It intended to elect a president by sweeping the free states, which controlled a majority of the electoral votes.

In this nativist print, an eagle guards a schoolhouse while a group of Catholic laborers try to undermine its foundation. Directing the work is a priest, who receives instructions from the pope sitting on a throne. Nativist propaganda extolled the importance of public schools in safeguarding democracy and portrayed Catholics as hostile to American institutions.

The Republicans and Bleeding Kansas

Initially, the Republican party made little headway in the North. Although it attracted in 1854 a variety of Whigs, anti-Nebraska Democrats, and Free Soilers, many moderate Whigs and Democrats viewed the party as too radical. Again in 1855 Republican candidates met defeat almost everywhere they ran. A Democratic newspaper expressed the prevailing view when it declared, "Nobody believes that this Republican movement can prove the basis of a permanent party."

Such predictions, however, did not take into account the emotions stirred up by developments in Kansas. Most early settlers migrated to Kansas for the same reasons other white Americans headed west—the chance to prosper in a new land. But Douglas's idea of popular sovereignty transformed the process of settlement into a referendum on slavery in the territories. A race soon developed between northerners and southerners to settle Kansas first. To the proslavery residents of neighboring Missouri, free-state communities like Lawrence seemed ominous threats. "We are playing for a mighty stake," former senator David Rice Atchison insisted. "If we win, we carry slavery to the Pacific Ocean; if we fail we lose Missouri, Arkansas and Texas and all the territories; the game must be played boldly."

When the first Kansas elections were held in 1854 and 1855, Missourians poured over the border, seized the polls, and stuffed the ballot boxes. A later congressional investigation concluded that more than 60 percent of the votes were cast illegally. This massive fraud tarnished popular sovereignty at the outset and greatly aroused public opinion in the North. It also provided proslavery forces with a commanding majority in the Kansas legislature, where they promptly expelled the legally elected free-state members and enacted a strict legal code designed to intimidate antislavery settlers. This Kansas Code limited such time-honored rights as freedom of speech, impartial juries, and fair elections. Mobilized into action, the free-staters in the fall of 1855 organized a separate government, drafted a state constitution prohibiting slavery, and asked Congress to admit Kansas as a free state. In such a polarized situation, violence quickly broke out between the two factions.

Turmoil in Kansas

Proslavery and antislavery settlers clash in 1856 at the town
of Hickory Point in the Kansas
Territory. Full-scale battles with
artillery were rare in Kansas,
but a number of skirmishes took
place between the two factions
in the territory, which gave cre-
dence to the image of "Bleeding
Kansas."

The Caning of Charles Sumner

In May 1856, only a few days before the proslavery attack on Lawrence, Republican
senator Charles Sumner of Massachusetts delivered a scathing speech, "The Crime
against Kansas." Sumner was passionate in his condemnation of slavery, and his
speech included remarks that deliberately insulted the state of South Carolina and
one of its senators, Andrew Butler. Preston S. Brooks, a South Carolina congressman who was related to Butler, was outraged that Sumner had insulted his relative
and mocked his state.

Several days later, on May 22, Brooks strode into the Senate after it had
adjourned, went up to Sumner, who was seated at his desk, and proceeded to beat
the Massachusetts leader over the head with his cane. The cane shattered into three
pieces from the violence of the attack, but Brooks, swept up in the emotion of the
moment, furiously continued hitting Sumner until the senator collapsed to the
floor, drenched in blood.

Significance of the
caning

Northerners were electrified to learn that a senator of the United States had
been beaten unconscious in the Senate chamber. But what caused them even greater
consternation was southern reaction to Sumner's caning—for in his own region,
Preston Brooks was promptly lionized as a hero. Instantly, the Sumner caning
breathed life into the fledgling Republican party. Its claims about "Bleeding Kansas"
and the Slave Power now seemed credible. Sumner, reelected in 1857 by the Massachusetts legislature, was unable to return to the Senate until 1860, his chair left
vacant as a symbol of southern brutality.

The Election of 1856

Given the storm that had arisen over Kansas, Democrats concluded that no candidate associated with the repeal of the Missouri Compromise had a chance to win.
So the Democrats turned to James Buchanan of Pennsylvania as their presidential
nominee. Buchanan's supreme qualification was having the good fortune to have
been out of the country when the Kansas-Nebraska Act was passed. The American
party, split badly by the Kansas issue, nominated former president Millard Fillmore.

SOUTHERN CHIVALRY — ARGUMENT versus CLUB'S.

The caning of Senator Charles Sumner of Massachusetts by Representative Preston S. Brooks of South Carolina inflamed public opinion. In this northern drawing, the fallen Sumner, a martyr to free speech, raises his pen against Brooks's club. In the background, several prominent Democrats look on in amusement. Printmakers, rushing to capitalize on the furor, did not know what the obscure Brooks looked like and thus had to devise ingenious ways of portraying the incident. In this print, Brooks's face is hidden by his raised arm.

The Republicans chose John C. Frémont, a western explorer who had helped liberate California during the Mexican War. The party's platform denounced slavery as a "relic of barbarism" and demanded that Kansas be admitted as a free state. Throughout the summer the party hammered away on Bleeding Sumner and Bleeding Kansas. "A constantly increasing excitement is kept up by the intelligence coming every day from Kansas," wrote one observer. "I have never known political excitement—I ought rather to say exasperation—approach that which now rages."

Ideology of the Republican party

A number of basic principles guided the Republican party, including the ideal of free labor. Slavery degraded labor, Republicans argued, and would inevitably drive free labor out of the territories. Condemning the South as a stagnant, hierarchical, and economically backward region, Republicans praised the North as a fluid society of widespread opportunity where enterprising individuals could improve their lot through hard work and self-discipline. Stopping the expansion of slavery, in Republican eyes, would preserve this heritage of opportunity and economic independence for white Americans. Republicans by and large remained blind to ways in which industrialization was closing off avenues of social mobility for poor workers.

Also important was the moral opposition to slavery, which works like Harriet Beecher Stowe's *Uncle Tom's Cabin* had strengthened. Republican speakers and editors stressed that slavery was a moral wrong, that it was incompatible with the ideals of the Republic and Christianity. "Never forget," Republican leader Abraham Lincoln declared on one occasion, "that we have before us this whole matter of the right and wrong of slavery in this Union, though the immediate question is as to its spreading out into new Territories and States."

Concept of the Slave Power

More negatively, Republicans gained support by shifting their attacks from slavery itself to the Slave Power, or the political influence of the planter class. Pointing to the Sumner assault and the incidents in Kansas, Republicans contended that the Slave Power had set out to destroy the liberties of northern whites. "The question has passed on from that of slavery for negro servants, to that of tyranny over free white men," one Republican insisted in the 1856 campaign.

Heritage of republicanism

All these fears played on a strong northern attachment to the heritage of the American Revolution. Just as the nation's founders had battled against slavery, tyranny, aristocracy, and minority rule, so the North faced the unrepublican Slave Power. "The liberties of our country are in tenfold the danger that they were at the commencement of the American Revolution," warned one Republican paper. "We then had a distant foe to contend with. Now the enemy is within our borders."

In the election, Buchanan all but swept the South (losing only Maryland to Fillmore) and won enough free states to push him over the top, with 174 electoral votes to Frémont's 114 and Fillmore's 8. Still, the violence in Kansas and Sumner's caning nearly carried Frémont into the presidency. He ran ahead of both Buchanan and Fillmore in the North and won 11 free states out of 16. Had he carried Pennsylvania plus one more, he would have been elected. For the first time in American history, an antislavery party based entirely in the North threatened to elect a president and snap the bonds of union.

The Worsening Crisis

Buchanan's character

James Buchanan had spent much of his life in public service: more than 20 years in the House and the Senate, secretary of state under Polk, and minister to Russia and to Great Britain. A tall, heavyset man with flowing white hair, Buchanan struck White House visitors as exceptionally courteous: an eye defect caused him to tilt his head slightly forward and to one side, which reinforced the impression of deference and attentiveness. A dutiful party member, he had over the years carefully cultivated wide personal support, yet he was a cautious and uninspiring leader who had a strong stubborn streak, deeply resented opposition, and overrated his ability to enforce party discipline on those who disagreed with his policies.

Moderates in both sections hoped that the new president would thwart Republican radicals and secessionists of the Deep South, popularly known as "fire-eaters." Throughout his career, however, Buchanan had taken the southern position on sectional matters, and he proved remarkably insensitive to the concerns of northern Democrats. Moreover, on March 6, 1857, only two days after Buchanan's inauguration, the Supreme Court gave the new administration an unintended jolt with one of the most controversial decisions in its history.

The *Dred Scott* Decision

Dred Scott

Protection of slavery

The owner of a Missouri slave named Dred Scott had taken him to live for several years in Illinois, a free state, and in the Wisconsin Territory, in what is now Minnesota, where slavery had been banned by the Missouri Compromise. Scott had returned to Missouri with his owner, only to sue eventually for his freedom on the grounds that his residence in a free state and a free territory had made him free. His case ultimately went to the Supreme Court. Two northern justices joined all five southern members of the Court in ruling 7 to 2 that Scott remained a slave. The majority opinion was written by Chief Justice Roger Taney of Maryland, who argued that under Missouri law, which took precedence, Scott was still a slave.

Had the Court stopped there, the public outcry would have been minimal. But the Court majority believed that they had a responsibility to deal with the larger controversy between the two sections. In particular, Chief Justice Taney wanted to strengthen the judicial protection of slavery. Taney, a former Maryland slaveowner who had freed his slaves, ruled that African Americans could not be and never had been citizens of the United States. Instead, he insisted that at the time the Constitution was adopted, they were "regarded as beings of an inferior order, so far inferior that they had no rights which the white man was bound to respect." In addition, the Court ruled that the Missouri Compromise was unconstitutional. Congress, it declared, had no power to ban slavery from *any* territory of the United States.

While southerners rejoiced at this outcome, Republicans denounced the Court. Their platform declared, after all, that Congress ought to prohibit slavery in all territories. "We know the court . . . has often over-ruled its own decisions," Abraham Lincoln observed, "and we shall do what we can to have it over-rule this." But the decision was sobering. If all territories were now open to slavery, how long would it be before a move was made to reintroduce slavery in the free states? For Republicans, the Court's decision foreshadowed the spread of slavery throughout the West and even throughout the nation.

But the decision also was a blow to Douglas's more moderate solution of popular sovereignty. If Congress had no power to prohibit slavery in a territory, how could it authorize a territorial legislature to do so? Although the Court did not rule on this point, the clear implication of the *Dred Scott* decision was that popular sovereignty was also unconstitutional. The Court, in effect, had endorsed John C. Calhoun's radical view that slavery was legal in all the territories. In so doing, the Court, which had intended to settle the question of slavery in the territories once and for all, instead succeeded only in strengthening the forces of extremism in American politics.

Reaction to the decision

Chief Justice Roger Taney

The Panic of 1857

As the nation grappled with the *Dred Scott* decision, an economic depression aggravated sectional conflict. Once again, boom gave way to bust as falling wheat prices and contracted credit hurt commercial farmers and overextended railroad investors. The Panic of 1857 was nowhere near as severe as the depression of 1837–1843. But the psychological results were far-reaching, for the South remained relatively untouched. With the price of cotton and other southern commodities still high, southern secessionists hailed the panic as proof that an independent southern nation was economically workable. Insisting that cotton sustained the international economy, James Henry Hammond, a senator from South Carolina, boasted: "What would happen if no cotton was furnished for three years? England would topple headlong and carry the whole civilized world with her save the South. No, you dare not make war on cotton. No power on earth dares to make war on it. Cotton is king."

Economic issues increase sectional tensions

For their part, northerners urged federal action to spur the economy. Southerners defeated an attempt to increase the tariff duties, at their lowest level since 1815, and Buchanan, under southern pressure, vetoed bills to improve navigation on the Great Lakes and to give free farms to western settlers. Many businesspeople and conservative ex-Whigs condemned these southern actions and now endorsed the Republican party.

The Lecompton Constitution

Although the *Dred Scott* decision and economic depression weakened the bonds of the Union, Kansas remained at the center of the political stage. In June 1857, when the territory elected delegates to draft a state constitution, free-state voters

Attempt to make Kansas a slave state

boycotted the election, thereby giving proslavery forces control of the convention that met in Lecompton. The delegates drafted a constitution that made slavery legal. Even more boldly, they scheduled a referendum in which voters could choose only whether to admit additional slaves into the territory. They could not vote against the constitution, and they could not vote to get rid of slavery entirely. Once again, free-staters boycotted the election, and the Lecompton constitution was approved.

As a supporter of popular sovereignty, President Buchanan had pledged a free and fair vote on the Lecompton constitution. But the outcome offered him the unexpected opportunity to satisfy his southern supporters by pushing the Lecompton constitution through Congress. This action was too much for Douglas, who broke party ranks and denounced the Lecompton constitution as a fraud. Nevertheless, the administration prevailed in the Senate. Buchanan now pulled out all the stops to gain the necessary votes in the House to admit Kansas as a slave state. But the House, where northern representation was much stronger, rejected the constitution. In a compromise, Congress, using indirect language, returned the constitution to Kansas for another vote.

Defeat of the Lecompton constitution

This time it was decisively defeated, 11,300 to 1788. No doubt remained that as soon as Kansas had sufficient population, it would come into the Union as a free state.

The attempt to force slavery on the people of Kansas drove many conservative northerners into the Republican party. And Douglas, once the Democrats' strongest potential candidate in 1860, now found himself assailed by the southern wing of his party. On top of that, in the summer of 1858, Douglas faced a desperate fight in his race for reelection to the Senate against Republican Abraham Lincoln.

The Lincoln-Douglas Debates

"He is the strong man of his party . . . and the best stump speaker, with his droll ways and dry jokes, in the West," Douglas commented when he learned of Lincoln's nomination to oppose him. "He is as honest as he is shrewd, and if I beat him my victory will be hardly won." Tall (6 feet, 4 inches) and gangly, Lincoln had a gaunt face, high cheekbones, deep-socketed gray eyes, and a shock of unruly hair. He appeared awkward as he spoke, never knowing quite what to do with his large, muscular hands. Yet his finely honed logic, his simple, eloquent language, and his sincerity carried the audience with him. His sentences, as spare as the man himself, had none of the oratorical flourishes common in that day. "If we could first know *where* we are, and *whither* we are tending, we could then better judge *what* to do, and *how* to do it," Lincoln began, in accepting his party's nomination for senator from Illinois in 1858. He quoted a proverb from the Bible:

Lincoln's view of the crisis

> A house divided against itself cannot stand.
>
> I believe this government cannot endure, permanently half *slave* and half *free*.
>
> I do not expect the Union to be *dissolved*—I do not expect the house to *fall*—but I *do* expect it will cease to be divided.
>
> It will become *all* one thing, or *all* the other.
>
> Either the *opponents* of slavery, will arrest the further spread of it, and place it where the public mind shall rest in the belief that it is in course of ultimate extinction; or its *advocates* will push it forward, till it shall become alike lawful in all the States, *old* as well as new—*North* as well as *South*.

The message echoed through the hall and across the pages of the national press.

Lincoln's character

Born in the slave state of Kentucky, Lincoln had grown up mostly in southern Indiana and central Illinois. He could split rails with the best frontier farmer, loved

Superb debaters, Douglas and Lincoln nevertheless had very different speaking styles. The deep-voiced Douglas was constantly on the attack, drawing on his remarkable memory and showering points like buckshot in all directions. Employing sarcasm and ridicule rather than humor, he never tried to crack a joke. Lincoln, who had a high-pitched voice and a rather awkward platform manner, developed his arguments more carefully and methodically, and he relied on his sense of humor and unmatched ability as a storyteller to drive his points home to the audience.

telling stories, and was at home mixing with ordinary folk. Yet his intense ambition had lifted him above the backwoods from which he came. He compensated for a lack of formal schooling through disciplined self-education, and he became a shrewd courtroom lawyer of respectable social standing. Known for his sense of humor, he was nonetheless subject to fits of acute depression, and his eyes often mirrored a deep melancholy.

Lincoln's first love was always politics. A fervent admirer of Henry Clay and his economic program, Lincoln entered the state legislature when he was only 25 and soon became an important Whig manager. After the party's decline, he joined the Republicans and became one of their key leaders in Illinois. In a series of seven joint debates, Lincoln challenged Douglas to discuss the issues of slavery and the sectional controversy.

In the campaign, Douglas sought to portray Lincoln as a radical whose "House Divided" speech preached sectional warfare. The nation *could* endure half slave and half free, Douglas declared, as long as states and territories were left alone to regulate their own affairs. Accusing Lincoln of believing that blacks were his equal, Douglas countered that the American government had been "made by the white man, for the white man, to be administered by the white man."

Lincoln responded by denying any intention to interfere with slavery in the South, but he insisted that the spread of slavery to the territories was a blight on the Republic. Douglas could not be counted on to oppose slavery's expansion, Lincoln warned, for he had already admitted that he didn't care whether slavery

Douglas and Lincoln on the slavery issue

was voted "down or up." For his part, Lincoln denied any "perfect equality between the negroes and white people" and opposed allowing blacks to vote, hold office, or intermarry with whites. But, he concluded,

> notwithstanding all this, there is no reason in the world why the negro is not entitled to all the natural rights enumerated in the Declaration of Independence, the right to life, liberty and the pursuit of happiness. . . . I agree with Judge Douglas [that the negro] is not my equal in many respects—certainly not in color, perhaps not in moral or intellectual endowment. But in the right to eat the bread, without leave of anybody else, which his own hand earns, *he is my equal and the equal of Judge Douglas, and the equal of every living man.*

Freeport Doctrine

At the debate held at Freeport, Illinois, Lincoln asked Douglas how under the *Dred Scott* decision the people of a territory could lawfully exclude slavery before statehood. Douglas answered, with what became known as the Freeport Doctrine, that slavery could exist only with the protection of law and that slaveowners would never bring their slaves into an area that did not have a slave code. Therefore, Douglas explained, if the people of a territory refused to pass a slave code, slavery would never be established there.

In a close race, the legislature elected Douglas to another term in the Senate.* But on the national scene, southern Democrats angrily repudiated him and condemned the Freeport Doctrine. And although Lincoln lost, Republicans thought his impressive performance marked him as a possible presidential contender for 1860.

The Beleaguered South

While northerners increasingly feared that the Slave Power was conspiring to extend slavery into the free states, southerners worried that the "Black Republicans" would hem them in and undermine their political power.

South's internal crisis

The very factors that brought prosperity during the 1850s stimulated the South's sense of crisis. As the price of slaves rose sharply, the proportion of southerners who owned slaves had dropped almost a third since 1830. Land also was being consolidated into larger holdings, evidence of declining opportunity for ordinary white southerners. Between 1850 and 1860 the average farm size rose in the South by 20 percent. Furthermore, California and Kansas had been closed to southern slaveholders—unfairly, in their eyes. Finally, Douglas's clever claim that a territory could effectively outlaw slavery using the Freeport Doctrine seemed to negate the *Dred Scott* decision that slavery was legal in all the territories.

Several possible solutions to the South's internal crisis had failed. Agricultural reform to restore worn-out lands had made significant headway in Virginia and Maryland, but elsewhere the rewards of a single-crop economy were just too great. Like most Americans, southerners preferred to exploit the soil and then move west. Another alternative—industrialization—had also failed. Indeed, the gap between the North and the South steadily widened in the 1850s. A few militant southerners launched their own private military expeditions during the 1850s, hoping to add Cuba, Mexico, or Nicaragua to the United States as slave territories. But all these "filibustering" expeditions came to naught.

---

*State legislatures elected senators until 1913, when the Seventeenth Amendment was adopted. While Lincoln and Douglas both campaigned for the office, Illinois voters actually voted for candidates for the legislature who were pledged to one of the senatorial candidates.

The South's growing sense of moral and political isolation made this crisis more acute. By the 1850s slavery had been abolished throughout most of the Americas, and in the United States the South's political power was steadily shrinking. Only the expansion of slavery held out any promise of new slave states needed to preserve the South's political power and protect its way of life. "The truth is," fumed one Alabama politician, ". . . the South is excluded from the common territories of the Union. The right of expansion claimed to be a necessity of her continued existence, is practically and effectively denied the South."

Failed solutions

The Road to War

In 1857 John Brown—the abolitionist firebrand—had returned to the East from Kansas, consumed with the idea of attacking slavery in the South itself. With financing from a number of prominent northern reformers, Brown gathered 21 followers, including 5 free blacks, in hope of fomenting a slave insurrection. On the night of October 16, 1859, the group seized the unguarded federal armory at Harpers Ferry in Virginia. But no slaves rallied to Brown's standard: few even lived in the area to begin with. Before long the raiders found themselves holed up in the armory's engine house with hostile townspeople taking potshots at them. Charging with bayonets fixed, federal troops commanded by Colonel Robert E. Lee soon captured Brown and his band.

John Brown's raid

John Brown

Reaction to the raid

Brown's raid at Harpers Ferry was yet another blow weakening the forces of compromise and moderation at the nation's political center. The invasion itself was a dismal failure, as were most of the enterprises Brown undertook in his troubled life. But the old man knew well how to bear himself with a martyr's dignity. "Had I so interfered in behalf of the rich, the powerful, the intelligent, the so-called great," he declared at his trial, ". . . it would have been all right. Every man in this court would have deemed it an act worthy of reward rather than punishment. . . . I believe that to have interfered as I have done in behalf of [God's] despised poor, is no wrong, but a right." On December 2, 1859, the state of Virginia hanged Brown for treason.

John Brown's enduring legacy sprang not from his ill-fated raid but from the popular reaction to his cause. Republicans made haste to denounce Brown's raid, lest they be tarred as radicals, but other northerners were less cautious. Ralph Waldo Emerson described Brown as a "saint, whose martyrdom will make the gallows as glorious as the cross," and on the day of his execution, church bells tolled in many northern cities. Only a minority of northerners endorsed Brown, but southerners were shocked by such public displays of sympathy. And they were firmly convinced that the Republican party was secretly connected to the raid. "I have always been a fervid Union man," one North Carolina resident wrote, "but I confess the endorsement of the Harpers Ferry outrage has shaken my fidelity and I am willing to take the chances of every probable evil that may arise from disunion, sooner than submit any longer to Northern insolence and Northern outrage."

A Sectional Election

When Congress convened in December, there were ominous signs everywhere of the growing sectional rift. Intent on destroying Douglas's Freeport Doctrine, southern radicals demanded a congressional slave code to protect slavery in the territories. To northern Democrats, such a platform spelled political death. As one Indiana Democrat put it, "We cannot carry a single congressional district on that doctrine in the state."

Daily Lives

POPULAR ENTERTAINMENT
Uncle Tom by Footlights

In 1850 theaters remained a controversial if popular form of public entertainment. The Puritans had roundly condemned plays of any sort, and many religious critics still frowned on theatergoing as sinful. Nevertheless, with the rise of cities the stage became a medium for mass entertainment and increasingly attracted the urban middle class.

In 1852 George C. Howard, the head of the Museum Theater in Troy, New York, was looking for new material. He was attracted to the issue of slavery by a controversial new novel, *Uncle Tom's Cabin.* Written by Harriet Beecher Stowe, one of the Reverend Lyman Beecher's energetic daughters, the book was a runaway bestseller, with more than 300,000 copies printed in the first year.

The book's plot followed a host of characters to a multitude of locales. George and Eliza Harris, a mulatto slave couple, learn that their young son is to be sold. Eliza flees with her child across the ice-choked Ohio River to freedom, while George escapes separately. At the same time, Tom, an older slave and a devout Christian, is sold and taken to Louisiana. He is bought by the father of Evangeline St. Clare, an innocent, golden-haired child who treats Tom kindly, but after both Evangeline and her father die, Tom is sold to Simon Legree, a hard-drinking, blasphemous Yankee. When Tom refuses to whip other slaves on the plantation, Legree beats him to death; Tom is a martyr to his faith in God and his love for his fellow man.

In this playbill advertising a dramatic production of *Uncle Tom's Cabin,* vicious bloodhounds pursue the light-skinned Eliza, who clutches her child as she frantically leaps to safety across the ice-choked Ohio River.

Disruption of the Democratic party

At the Democratic convention in April in Charleston, South Carolina, southern radicals boldly pressed their demand for a federal slave code. After a heated debate, however, the convention adopted the Douglas platform upholding popular sovereignty, whereupon the delegations from eight southern states walked out. Unable to agree on a candidate, the convention finally reassembled two months later in Baltimore and nominated Douglas. At this point most of the remaining southern Democrats left in disgust. Joining with the Charleston seceders, they nominated their own candidate, Vice President John C. Breckinridge of Kentucky, on a platform supporting a federal slave code. The last major national party had shattered.

In May the Republicans met in Chicago, where they turned to Abraham Lincoln, a moderate on the slavery issue who was strong in Illinois and the other northern states the party had lost in 1856. Republicans also sought to broaden their appeal by supporting economic proposals for a moderately protective tariff, a homestead bill, and a northern transcontinental railroad.

The election that followed was really two contests in one. In the North, which had a majority of the electoral votes, only Lincoln and Douglas had any chance of carrying a state. In the South, the race pitted Breckinridge against John Bell of

Compressing this complex story was not easy. Then, too, no American play on the subject of slavery had been produced before, and many theater managers believed that the public would not accept a black hero. But Howard wanted to cast his four-year-old daughter, Cordelia (already an experienced trouper), as young Eva, and so George Aiken, a member of the repertory company, wrote an adaptation that focused on Tom's experiences in the St. Clare household.

The play's success prompted Aiken to write a sequel based on the Legree section of the novel; finally he combined the two plays into a 6-act, 30-scene epic that took an entire evening to perform. To make the plot coherent would have required almost twice as many scenes, but Aiken's adaptation became the classic stage version. From Troy the production moved to New York City, where it ran for an unprecedented 325 performances and then achieved similar triumphs in other northern cities. No play had ever attracted such large audiences.

Aiken had a good eye for the dramatic: a slave auction, Eva's death after a long illness, and Tom's defiance of Legree when threatened with a whipping. ("My soul a'nt yours, mas'r; you haven't bought it—ye can't buy it.") Eliza's flight across the icy Ohio River—described in two paragraphs in the book—became one of the major scenes, with a pack of bloodhounds added for good measure. As in minstrel shows, blacks were played by whites wearing lampblack.

Aiken added more humor to the plot, but the play remained faithful to the book's antislavery message. Howard worked hard to attract a new middle-class audience. He banned the prostitutes who frequented theaters and in the lobby displayed the endorsements of prominent religious leaders and reformers on posters. A further innovation, matinee performances, attracted women and children. As one reporter for the New York *Atlas* commented, instead of newsboys and apprentices, he saw "many people who have been taught to look on the

stage with horror and contempt." Blacks, who normally were barred from New York theaters, were seated in a segregated section.

The play moved audiences of all backgrounds. After wrestling with his religious scruples, John Kirk, a salesman, finally went to see a Chicago production. "The appeals of the dying little Eva to her father, for Uncle Tom's freedom, were overwhelmingly affecting," he testified. "I never saw so many white pocket handkerchiefs in use at the same time, and, for the same purpose before. I was not the only one in that large audience to shed tears I assure you." Equally striking, the play affected the workers and apprentices who made up the theater's normal clientele. Traditionally hostile to abolitionism, these groups cheered wildly over Eliza's escape and shouted approval of her antislavery speeches. By providing vivid images of the cruelty of slavery, theatrical presentations of *Uncle Tom's Cabin*, even more than the book, heightened the sectional tensions that divided the nation in the 1850s.

Tennessee, the candidate of the new conservative Constitutional Union party. Although Lincoln received less than 40 percent of the popular vote and had virtually no support in the South, he won 180 electoral votes, 27 more than needed for election. For the first time, the nation had elected a president who headed a completely sectional party and who was committed to stopping the expansion of slavery.

Secession

Although the Republicans had not won control of either house of Congress, Lincoln's election struck many southerners as a blow of terrible finality. Lincoln had been lifted into office on the strength of the free states alone. With Republicans opposed to slavery's expansion, the South's power base could only diminish. It was not unrealistic, many fire-eaters argued, to believe that Lincoln would use federal aid to induce the border states to voluntarily free their slaves. Once slavery disappeared there, and new states were added, the necessary three-fourths majority would exist to approve a constitutional amendment abolishing slavery. Or perhaps Lincoln might send other John

Southern fears

479

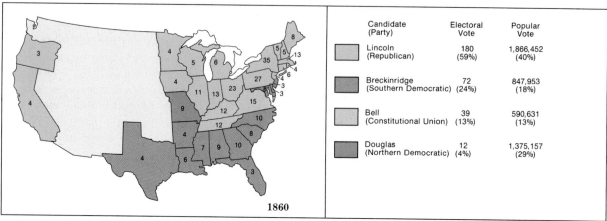

Candidate (Party)	Electoral Vote	Popular Vote
Lincoln (Republican)	180 (59%)	1,866,452 (40%)
Breckinridge (Southern Democratic)	72 (24%)	847,953 (18%)
Bell (Constitutional Union)	39 (13%)	590,631 (13%)
Douglas (Northern Democratic)	12 (4%)	1,375,157 (29%)

1860

Election of 1860 Although Lincoln did not win a majority of the popular vote, he still would have been elected even if the votes for all three of his opponents had been combined, because he won a clear majority in every state he carried except California, Oregon, and New Jersey (whose electoral votes he split with Douglas).

Confederate States of America

Crittenden Compromise fails

Lincoln's approach to the crisis

Browns into the South to stir up more slave insurrections. The Montgomery (Alabama) *Mail* accused Republicans of intending "to free the negroes and force amalgamation between them and the children of the poor men of the South."

Secession seemed the only alternative left to protect southern equality and liberty. South Carolina, which had challenged federal authority in the nullification crisis, was determined to force the other southern states to act. On December 20, 1860, a popular convention unanimously passed a resolution seceding from the Union. The rest of the Deep South followed, and on February 7, 1861, the states stretching from South Carolina to Texas organized the Confederate States of America and elected Jefferson Davis president.

But the Upper South and the border states declined to secede, hoping that once again Congress could patch together a settlement. Senator John Crittenden of Kentucky proposed a constitutional amendment extending to California the old Missouri Compromise line of 36°30′. Slavery would be prohibited north of this line and given federal protection south of it in all territories, including any acquired in the future. Furthermore, Crittenden proposed an "unamendable amendment" to the Constitution, forever preserving slavery in states where it already existed.

But the Crittenden Compromise was doomed for the simple reason that the two groups who were required to make concessions—Republicans and secessionists—had no interest in doing so. "The argument is exhausted," representatives from the Deep South announced, even before Crittenden had introduced his package. "We have just carried an election on principles fairly stated to the people," Lincoln wrote in opposing compromise. "Now we are told in advance, the government shall be broken up, unless we surrender to those we have beaten, before we take the offices. If we surrender, it is the end of us, and of the government." Only the unamendable amendment passed, but war ended any possibility that it would be ratified.

The Outbreak of War

As he prepared to take office, Lincoln pondered what to do about secession. In his inaugural address on March 4, he sought to reassure southerners that he had no intention, "directly or indirectly, to interfere with the institution of slavery in the States where it exists." But he maintained that "the Union of these states is perpetual," echoing Andrew Jackson's Proclamation on Nullification, and that no state could leave the Union by its own action. He also announced that he intended to "hold, occupy and possess" federal property and collect customs duties under the

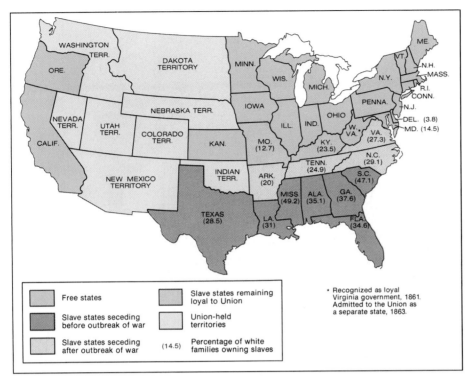

The Pattern of Secession Led by South Carolina, the Deep South seceded between Lincoln's election in November and his inauguration in March. The Upper South did not secede until after the firing on Fort Sumter. The four border slave states never seceded and remained in the Union throughout the war. As the map indicates, secession sentiment was strongest in states where the highest percentage of white families owned slaves.

tariff. He closed by calling for a restoration of the "bonds of affection" that united all Americans.

The new president hoped for time to work out a solution, but on his first day in office he was handed a dispatch from Major Robert Anderson, commander of the federal garrison at Fort Sumter in Charleston harbor. Sumter was one of the few remaining federal outposts in the South. Anderson informed the government that he was almost out of food and that, unless resupplied, he would have to surrender in six weeks. For a month Lincoln looked for a way out, but he finally sent a relief expedition. As a conciliatory gesture, he notified the governor of South Carolina that supplies were being sent and that if the fleet were allowed to pass, only food, and not men, arms, or ammunition, would be landed.

Fort Sumter

The burden of decision now shifted to Jefferson Davis. From his point of view, secession was a constitutional right and the Confederacy was not a bogus but a legitimate government. To allow the United States to hold property and maintain military forces within the Confederacy would destroy its claim of independence. Davis therefore instructed the Confederate commander at Charleston to demand the immediate surrender of Fort Sumter and, if refused, to open fire. When Anderson declined the ultimatum, Confederate batteries began shelling the fort on April 12 at 4:30 A.M. Some 33 hours later Anderson surrendered. When in response Lincoln called for 75,000 volunteers to put down the rebellion, four states in the Upper South, led by Virginia, also seceded. Matters had passed beyond compromise.

Upper South secedes

The Roots of a Divided Society

And so the Union was broken. After 70 years, the forces of sectionalism and separatism had finally outpulled the ties binding "these United States." Why did affairs come to such a pass?

AN EMINENT SOUTHERN CLERGYMAN,

During an eloquent discourse, is wonderfully assisted in finding scriptural authority for Secession and Treason, and the divine ordination of Slavery.

When news of secession spread, many southern white women wore decorative cockades made of woven palmetto leaves and silk (right). "In every direction could be seen Palmetto cockades, fastened with a blue ribbon; there were hundreds of them," reported one observer. Northerners reacted differently. Envelopes like the one shown here (left) portrayed a secessionist southern preacher inspired by the devil to give "an eloquent discourse" on "Treason" and God's approval of slavery.

Diverging economies

In some ways, as we have seen, the revolution in markets that transformed the nation during these years served to link together northerners and southerners. The cotton planter who rode the steamship *Fashion* along the Alabama River ("Time's money! Time's money!") was wearing ready-made clothes manufactured in New York from southern cotton. Chauncey Jerome's clocks from Connecticut were keeping time not only for commercial planters but also for Lowell mill workers like Mary Paul, who learned to measure her lunch break in minutes. Farmers in both Tennessee and Iowa were interested in the price of wheat in New York, for it affected the profits that could be made shipping their grain by the new railroad lines. American society had become far more specialized, and therefore far more interdependent, since the days of Crèvecoeur's self-sufficient farmer of the 1780s.

But a specialized economy had not brought unity. For the North, specialization meant more factories, a higher percentage of urban workers, and a greater number of cities and towns. Industry affected midwestern farmers as well, for their steel plows and McCormick reapers allowed them to farm larger holdings and required greater capital investment in the new machinery. For its part, the South was transformed by the industrial revolution too, as textile factories made cotton the booming mainstay of its economy. But for all its growth, the region remained largely a rural society. Its prosperity stemmed from expansion westward into new areas of cotton production, not new forms of production or technology. The dominant planter class reinforced its traditional concepts of honor, hierarchy, and deference.

Above all, the intensive labor required to produce cotton, rice, and sugar made slavery an inseparable part of the southern way of life—"so intimately mingled with our social conditions," as one Georgian admitted, "that it would be impossible to eradicate it." An increasing number of northerners viewed slavery as evil, not so much out of high-minded sympathy toward slaves but as a labor system that threatened the republican ideals of white American society.

If the United States had not grown so dynamically—if its frontier had not swept so quickly toward the Pacific—the nation might have been able to postpone the day of reckoning on slavery until some form of gradual emancipation could be adopted. But the luxury of time was not available. The new territories became the battlegrounds for two contrasting ways of life, with slavery at the center of the debate. Nor did those Americans, North and South, black and white, who saw the issue in moral terms think the question should be postponed.

It fell to the political system to try to resolve sectional conflict through a system of national parties that represented various interest groups and promoted democratic debate. But the political system had critical weaknesses. The American process of electing a president gave the winning candidate a state's entire electoral vote, regardless of the margin of victory. That procedure made a northern sectional party possible, since the Republicans could never have carried an election on the basis of a popular vote alone. In addition, the four-year fixed presidential term allowed Presidents Pierce and Buchanan to remain in office, pursuing disruptive policies on Kansas even after the voters had rejected those policies in the midterm congressional elections in 1854 and 1858. Finally, since 1844 the Democratic party had required a two-thirds vote to nominate its presidential candidate. Unintentionally, this requirement made it difficult to pick any truly forceful leader and gave the South a veto over the party's candidate. Yet the South, by itself, could not elect a president.

Weaknesses of the political system

The nation's republican heritage also contributed to the political system's vulnerability. Ever since the Revolution, when Americans accused the king and Parliament of deliberately plotting to deprive them of their liberties, Americans were on the watch for political conspiracies. Such an outlook often stimulated exaggerated fears, unreasonable conclusions, and excessive reactions. For their part, Republicans emphasized the existence of the Slave Power bent on eradicating northern rights. Southerners, on the other hand, accused the Black Republicans of conspiring to destroy southern equality. Each side viewed itself as defending the country's republican tradition from an internal threat.

Belief in conspiracies against liberty

In 1850 southerners might have been satisfied if their section had been left alone and the agitation against slavery had ended. But a decade later, many Americans both North and South had come to accept the idea of an irrepressible conflict between two societies, one based on freedom, the other on slavery, in which only one side could ultimately prevail. At stake, it seemed, was control of the nation's future. Four years later, as a weary Abraham Lincoln looked back to the beginning of the conflict, he noted, "Both parties deprecated war, but one of them would *make* war rather than let the nation survive, and the other would *accept* war rather than let it perish, and the war came."

chapter summary

In the 1850s, the slavery issue reemerged in national politics and increasingly disrupted the party system, leading to the outbreak of war in 1861.

• Fundamental economic changes heightened sectional tensions in the 1850s.

— The construction of a vast railroad network reoriented western trade from the South to the East.

— A tide of new immigrants swelled the North's population (and hence its political power) at the expense of the South, thereby stimulating southern fears.

• The old Jacksonian party system was shattered by the nativist movement and by a renewed controversy of the expansion of slavery.

— In the Kansas-Nebraska Act, Senator Stephen A. Douglas tried to defuse the slavery debate by incorporating popular sovereignty (the idea that the people of a territory should decide the status of slavery there). This act effectively repealed the Missouri Compromise.

- Popular sovereignty failed in the Kansas Territory, where fighting broke out between proslavery and antislavery partisans.

- Sectional violence reached a climax in May 1856 with the attack on Lawrence, Kansas, and the caning of Senator Charles Sumner of Massachusetts by Representative Preston S. Brooks of South Carolina.

- Sectional tensions sparked the formation of a new antislavery Republican party, and the party system realigned along sectional lines.

  - The Supreme Court's *Dred Scott* decision, the Panic of 1857, the congressional struggle over the proslavery Lecompton constitution, and John Brown's attack on Harpers Ferry in 1859 strengthened the two sectional extremes.

- In 1860 Abraham Lincoln became the first Republican to be elected president.

  - Following Lincoln's triumph, the seven states of the Deep South seceded.

  - When Lincoln sent supplies to the Union garrison in Fort Sumter in Charleston harbor, Confederate batteries bombarded the fort into submission.

  - The North rallied to Lincoln's decision to use force to restore the Union, and in response the four states of the Upper South seceded.

interactive learning

The Primary Source Investigator CD-ROM offers the following materials related to this chapter:

- Interactive maps: **Election of 1860** (M7) and **The Transportation Revolution, 1830–1890** (M12)

- A collection of primary sources illuminating the political and social strife of the 1850s, including "Free At Last!", a document about the role of African Americans in their emancipation, and the First and Second Confiscation Acts. Other sources capture the anxiety of the age, such as a letter written by John Boston proclaiming his freedom and a letter regarding how to handle contraband slaves.

additional reading

The problem of the coming of the Civil War has attracted considerable historical attention over the years. David M. Potter, *The Impending Crisis, 1848–1861* (1976), is a superior political treatment of the period, shrewd in its judgments and penetrating in its analysis. Fuller in its coverage but more melodramatic is Allan Nevins, *Ordeal of the Union* (2 vols., 1947) and *The Emergence of Lincoln* (2 vols., 1950). A stimulating work that, unlike these, focuses on the problem and complexities of the antebellum political realignment is Michael F. Holt, *The Political Crisis of the 1850s* (1978).

The heavy immigration during these years is described in Philip D. Taylor, *The Distant Magnet* (1971). Holt's book, noted in the previous paragraph, presents the most astute discussion of the Know-Nothing party. John McCardell's *The Idea of a Southern Nation* (1979) is a solid, well-written treatment of southern nationalism in this period. The most thorough examination of the blend of factors that produced the Republican party is William E. Gienapp, *The Origins of the Republican Party, 1852–1856* (1987). Eric Foner, in *Free Soil, Free Labor, Free Men* (1970), focuses on the ideas of Republican party leaders. For the turbulent history of Kansas in this period, see James A. Rawley, *Race and Politics* (1969). The critical events of 1857 are the focal point of Kenneth M. Stampp's *America in 1857* (1990). The secession movement has largely been investigated in specific southern states. A particularly good example of this approach is Stephen A. Channing's account of secession in South Carolina, *Crisis of Fear* (1974). Kenneth M. Stampp, *And the War Came* (1950), is the best study of northern public opinion during the secession crisis. An excellent examination of the war's origins, sophisticated in its analysis and up-to-date in its scholarship, is Gabor S. Boritt, ed., *Why the War Came* (1996). For a fuller list of readings, see the Bibliography at www.mhhe.com/davidsonnation5.

significant events

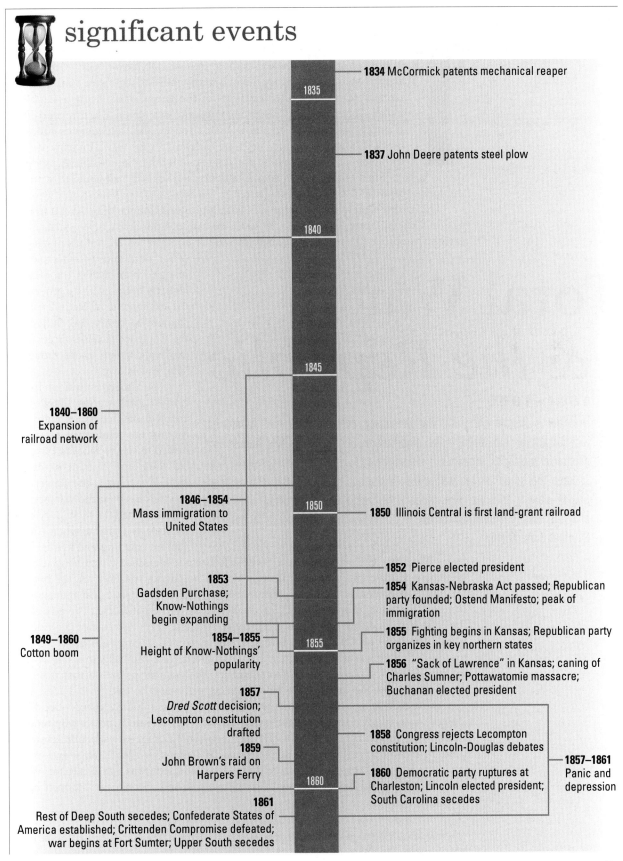

1834 McCormick patents mechanical reaper

1835

1837 John Deere patents steel plow

1840

1845

1840–1860
Expansion of
railroad network

1846–1854
Mass immigration to
United States

1850

1850 Illinois Central is first land-grant railroad

1852 Pierce elected president

1853
Gadsden Purchase;
Know-Nothings
begin expanding

1854 Kansas-Nebraska Act passed; Republican
party founded; Ostend Manifesto; peak of
immigration

1849–1860
Cotton boom

1854–1855
Height of Know-Nothings'
popularity

1855

1855 Fighting begins in Kansas; Republican party
organizes in key northern states

1856 "Sack of Lawrence" in Kansas; caning of
Charles Sumner; Pottawatomie massacre;
Buchanan elected president

1857
Dred Scott decision;
Lecompton constitution
drafted

1858 Congress rejects Lecompton
constitution; Lincoln-Douglas debates

1859
John Brown's raid on
Harpers Ferry

1860

1857–1861
Panic and
depression

1860 Democratic party ruptures at
Charleston; Lincoln elected president;
South Carolina secedes

1861
Rest of Deep South secedes; Confederate States of
America established; Crittenden Compromise defeated;
war begins at Fort Sumter; Upper South secedes

Chapter 16

Total War & the Republic

1861–1865

preview • As the first total war in history, the Civil War was fought not just by armies but through the mobilization of each society's human and economic resources. Lincoln's leadership was key. He moved slowly at first, to keep the border states within the Union, but later accepted the destruction of slavery as a war aim. Indeed, the freeing of four million slaves was only the most monumental of the war's many transformations, in both the South and the North.

The war won't last sixty days!" Of that Jim Tinkham was confident. With dreams of a hero's return, Tinkham quit his job as a grocery store clerk and enlisted for three months in a Massachusetts regiment. Soon he was transferred to Washington as part of the Union army being assembled under General Irvin McDowell. Tinkham was elated when in mid-July the army was finally ordered to march toward the Confederates concentrated at Manassas Junction, 25 miles away. On the way, Tinkham passed carriages carrying members of Congress and other jaunty sightseers, their picnic baskets filled with provisions and fine wines. They too had come to witness the battle that would crush the rebellion.*

The battle began at dawn on July 21, with McDowell commanding 30,000 troops against General Pierre Beauregard's 22,000. Tinkham did not arrive on the field until early afternoon. As his regiment pushed toward the front, he felt faint at his first sight of the dead and wounded, some mangled horribly. But the Massachusetts troops were caught up in the excitement of battle as they charged up Henry Hill. Suddenly the Confederate ranks broke and exuberant Union troops shouted, "The war is over!"

The timely arrival of fresh Confederate troops, however, enabled the rebels to regroup. Among the reinforcements who rushed to Henry Hill was 19-year-old Randolph McKim of Baltimore. A student at the University of Virginia when the war began, McKim joined the First Maryland Infantry as a private when Abraham Lincoln imposed martial law in his home state. "The cause of the South had become identified with liberty itself," he explained. After only a week of drill, McKim boarded a train on July 21 bound for Manassas. When he and his comrades disembarked, they could hear the cannon firing in the distance, so they marched double-quick to the battlefield. The arrival of the First Maryland and other reinforcements in the late afternoon turned the tide of battle. The faltering Confederate line held, then charged, giving full throat for the first time to the famous "rebel yell." "There is nothing like [the yell] this side of the infernal region," explained one Union soldier. "The peculiar sensation that it sends down your backbone under these circumstances can never be told."

The Union troops gave way slowly at first, but discipline dissolved once Mc-Dowell ordered a retreat, and the army quickly degenerated into a frightened, stampeding mob. Troops threw away their equipment, shoved aside officers who tried to stop them, and raced frantically past the wagons, artillery pieces, and civilian carriages that clogged the road. Joining the stampede was Jim Tinkham, who confessed he would have continued on to Boston if he had not been stopped by a

---

*The Union and Confederacy often gave different names to a battle. The Confederates called the first battle Manassas; the Union, Bull Run.

Reveille rouses drowsy Union soldiers on a wintry morning as a drummer boy warms his hands. Instead of the glory they expected, reveille, roll call, and drill constituted Civil War soldiers' usual camp routine. A hired black laborer is already at work as the troops awaken.

guard after crossing the Long Bridge into Washington. All the next day in a drizzling rain, mud-spattered troops straggled into the capital in complete disorder. One dispirited officer, conceding that they were "pretty well whipped," declared that he'd had "enough of fighting to last my lifetime" and announced that he was going home.

The rout at Bull Run sobered the North. Gone were dreams of ending the war with one glorious battle. Gone was the illusion that 75,000 volunteers serving three months could crush the rebellion. As one perceptive observer noted, "We have undertaken to make war without in the least knowing how." Having cast off his earlier illusions, a newly determined Jim Tinkham reenlisted for a three-year hitch.

Still, it was not surprising that both sides underestimated the magnitude of the conflict. Previous warfare as it had evolved in Europe consisted largely of maneuverings that took relatively few lives, respected private property, and left civilians largely unharmed. The Civil War, on the other hand, was the first war whose major battles routinely involved more than 100,000 troops. So many combatants could be equipped only through the use of factory-produced weaponry, they could be

Meaning of total war

moved and supplied only with the help of railroads, and they could be sustained only through the concerted efforts of civilian society as a whole. The morale of the population, the quality of political leadership, and the utilization of industrial and economic might were all critical to the outcome. Quite simply, the Civil War was the first total war in history.

The Demands of Total War

When the war began, the North had an enormous advantage in manpower and industrial capacity. The Union's population was 2.5 times larger, and its advantage in white men of military age even greater. The North had a much larger merchant marine; produced more iron, firearms, and textiles; contained more railroad track and rolling stock; and possessed more than ten times the industrial capacity.

From a modern perspective, the South's attempt to defend its independence against such odds seems a hopeless cause. Yet this view indicates how much the conception of war has changed. European observers, who knew the strength and resources of the two sides, believed that the Confederacy, with its large area, poor roads, and rugged terrain, could never be conquered. Indeed, the South enjoyed definite strategic advantages. To be victorious, it did not need to invade the North—only to defend its own land and prevent the North from destroying its armies. Southern soldiers knew the topography of their home country better, and a friendly population regularly supplied them with intelligence about Union troop movements.

Southern advantages

Resources of the Union and the Confederacy, 1861

	Union	Confederacy	Union Advantage
Total population	23,300,000	9,100,000*	2.5 to 1
White male population (18–45 years)	4,600,000	1,100,000	4.2 to 1
Bank deposits	$207,000,000	$47,000,000	4.4 to 1
Value of manufactured goods	$1,730,000,000	$156,000,000	11 to 1
Railroad mileage	22,000	9,000	2.4 to 1
Shipping tonnage	4,600,000	290,000	16 to 1
Value of textiles produced	$181,000,000	$10,000,000	18 to 1
Value of firearms produced	$2,290,000	$73,000	31 to 1
Pig iron production (tons)	951,000	37,000	26 to 1
Coal production (tons)	13,680,000	650,000	21 to 1
Corn and wheat production (bushels)	698,000,000	314,000,000	2.2 to 1
Draft animals	5,800,000	2,900,000	2 to 1
Cotton production (bales)	43,000	5,344,000	1 to 124

*Slaves accounted for 3,500,000, or 40 percent.

Sources: U.S. Census 1860; E. B. Long, *The Civil War Day by Day* (New York: Doubleday, 1971), p. 723.

The North, in contrast, had to invade and conquer the Confederacy and destroy the southern will to resist. To do so, it would have to deploy thousands of soldiers to defend long supply lines in enemy territory, a situation that significantly reduced the northern advantage in manpower. Yet in the end, the Confederacy was not only invaded and conquered but also utterly destroyed. By 1865 the Union forces had penetrated virtually every part of the 500,000 square miles of the Confederacy and were able to move almost at will. The Civil War demonstrated the capacity of a modern society to overcome the problems of distance and terrain with technology.

Political Leadership

To sustain a commitment to total war required effective political leadership. This task fell on Abraham Lincoln and Jefferson Davis, presidents of the rival governments.

Jefferson Davis grew up in Mississippi accustomed to life's advantages. Educated at West Point, he fought in the Mexican War, served as Franklin Pierce's secretary of war, and became one of the South's leading advocates in the Senate. Although he was hardworking and committed to the cause he led, his temperament was not well suited to his new post. He quarreled tactlessly with generals and politicians and refused to work with those he disliked. "He cannot brook opposition or criticism," one member of the Confederate Congress testified, "and those who do not bow down before him have no chance of success with him." His narrow, legalistic approach to problems hampered his efforts to rouse the southern people.

Jefferson Davis

Yet for all Davis's personal handicaps, he faced an institutional one even more daunting. The Confederacy had been founded on the ideology of states' rights. Yet to meet the demands of total war, Davis would need to increase the authority of the central government beyond anything the South had ever experienced.

When Lincoln took the oath of office, his national experience consisted of one term in the House of Representatives. But Lincoln was a shrewd judge of character and a superb politician. To achieve a common goal, he willingly overlooked withering criticism and personal slights. (The commander of the Union army, General George McClellan, for one, continually snubbed the president and referred to him as "the original Gorilla.") He was not easily humbugged, overawed, or flattered and never allowed personal feelings to blind him to his larger objectives.

Lincoln's leadership

"This is essentially a People's contest," Lincoln asserted at the start of the war, and few presidents have been better able to communicate with the average citizen. He regularly visited Union troops in camp, in the field, and in army hospitals. "The boys liked him," wrote Joseph Twichell, from a Connecticut regiment. "[I]n fact his popularity with the army is and has been universal." Always Lincoln reminded the public that the war was being fought for the ideals of the Revolution and the Republic. It was a test, he remarked in his famous address at Gettysburg, of whether a nation "conceived in Liberty, and dedicated to the proposition that all men are created equal" could "long endure."

Lincoln also proved the more effective military leader. Jefferson Davis took his title of commander in chief literally, interfering with his generals even on the

Lincoln at the time of the Gettysburg Address

smallest matters. But he failed to formulate an effective overarching strategy. In contrast, Lincoln had a clear grasp of the challenge confronting the Union. He accepted General Winfield Scott's proposal to blockade and surround the Confederacy, cut off its supplies, and slowly strangle it into submission, just as the anaconda snake squeezes its prey. But unlike Scott, he realized that an "anaconda plan" was not enough. The South would also have to be invaded and defeated, not only on an eastern front in Virginia but also in the West, where Union control of the Mississippi would divide the Confederacy fatally. Lincoln understood that the Union's superior manpower and matériel would become decisive only when the Confederacy was simultaneously threatened along a broad front. The Union forces could then break through at the weak points. It took time before the president found generals able to execute this novel strategy.

The Border States

When the war began, only Delaware of the border slave states was certain to remain in the Union. Lincoln's immediate political challenge was to retain the loyalty of Maryland, Kentucky, and Missouri. Maryland especially was crucial, for if it was lost, Washington itself would have to be abandoned.

Suppression in Maryland

The danger became immediately apparent when pro-Confederate forces destroyed the railroad bridges near Baltimore and isolated Washington. Only with difficulty was the administration able to move troops to the city. Once the capital was safe, Lincoln moved vigorously—even ruthlessly—to secure Maryland. He suspended the writ of habeas corpus, the right under the Constitution of an arrested person either to be charged with a specific crime or to be released. That done, he held without trial prominent Confederate sympathizers and suppressed pro-Confederate newspapers. Intervention by the army ensured that Unionists won a complete victory in the fall state election. The election ended any possibility that Maryland would join the Confederacy.

Kentucky's neutrality

At the beginning of the conflict, Kentucky officially declared its neutrality. "I think to lose Kentucky is nearly to lose the whole game," Lincoln wrote with obvious concern. "Kentucky gone, we can not hold Missouri, nor, as I think, Maryland. These all against us, and the job on our hands is too large for us." Union generals requested permission to occupy the state, but the president refused, preferring to act cautiously and wait for Unionist sentiment to assert itself. After Unionists won control of the legislature in the summer election, a Confederate army entered the state, giving Lincoln the opening he needed. He quickly sent in troops, and Kentucky stayed in the Union.

In Missouri, skirmishing broke out between Union and Confederate sympathizers. Only after the Union victory at the Battle of Pea Ridge in March 1862 was Missouri secure from any Confederate threat. Even so, guerrilla warfare continued in the state throughout the remainder of the war.

In Virginia, internal divisions led to the creation of a new border state, as the hilly western counties, where slavery was not strong, refused to support the Confederacy. After adopting a congressionally mandated program of gradual emancipation, West Virginia was formally admitted to the Union in June 1863.

Importance of the border states

The Union scored an important triumph in holding the border states. The population of all five equaled that of the four states of the Upper South that had joined the Confederacy, and their production of military supplies—food, animals, and minerals—was greater. Furthermore, Maryland and West Virginia contained key railroad lines and were critical to the defense of Washington, while

Kentucky and Missouri gave the Union army access to the major river systems of the western theater, down which it launched the first successful invasions of the Confederacy.

As with so many Civil War battles, **Opening Moves**
the Confederate victory at Bull Run
achieved no decisive military results. But a sobered Congress authorized the enlistment of half a million volunteers to serve for three years. Lincoln named 34-year-old George McClellan, a West Point graduate, to be the new commander of the Union army. Energetic and ambitious, McClellan had been working as a railroad executive when the war began. For the next eight months he appeared the very model of businesslike efficiency as he settled into the much-needed task of organizing and drilling the Army of the Potomac.

Blockade and Isolate

The U.S. Navy began the war with only 42 ships available to blockade 3550 miles of Confederate coastline. By the spring of 1862, it had secured several key bases for the blockading squadrons, and the navy also began building powerful gunboats to operate on the rivers. In April 1862 Flag Officer David G. Farragut ran a gauntlet of Confederate shore batteries to capture New Orleans, the Confederacy's largest city and most important port. Memphis, another important river city, fell to Union forces in June.

The blockade was hardly leakproof, and Confederates slipped through it using small, fast ships. Still, southern trade suffered badly. In hopes of lifting the blockade, the Confederacy converted the wooden U.S.S. *Merrimack,* which was rechristened the *Virginia,* into an ironclad gunboat. In March 1862 a Union ironclad, the *Monitor,* battled it to a standoff, and the Confederates were forced to scuttle the *Virginia* when they evacuated Norfolk in May. After that, the Union's naval supremacy was secure.

Ironclads

The South looked to diplomacy as another means to lift the blockade. With cotton so vital to European economies, especially Great Britain's, southerners believed that Europe would formally recognize the Confederacy and come to its aid. The North, for its part, claimed that it was merely putting down a domestic insurrection, and Secretary of State William Seward warned European nations against intervening in America's internal affairs. Nevertheless, European countries extended belligerent status to the government at Richmond, which allowed the Confederacy to purchase supplies abroad.

King Cotton diplomacy

By 1862 cotton supplies were dwindling, and France was ready to recognize the Confederacy, but only if Britain would follow suit. The British government favored the South, but it hesitated to act until Confederate armies demonstrated that they could win the war. Meanwhile, new supplies of cotton from Egypt and India enabled the British textile industry to recover. In the end, Britain and the rest of Europe refused to recognize the Confederacy, and the South was left to stand or fall on its own resources.

Grant in the West

In the western war theater, the first decisive Union victory was won by a short, shabbily dressed, cigar-chomping general named Ulysses S. Grant. An undistinguished student at West Point, Grant eventually resigned his commission. He failed

The War in the West, 1861–1862
Grant's push southward stalled after his costly victory at Shiloh; nevertheless, by the end of 1862 the Union had secured Kentucky and Missouri, as well as most of Confederate Tennessee and the upper and lower stretches of the Mississippi River.

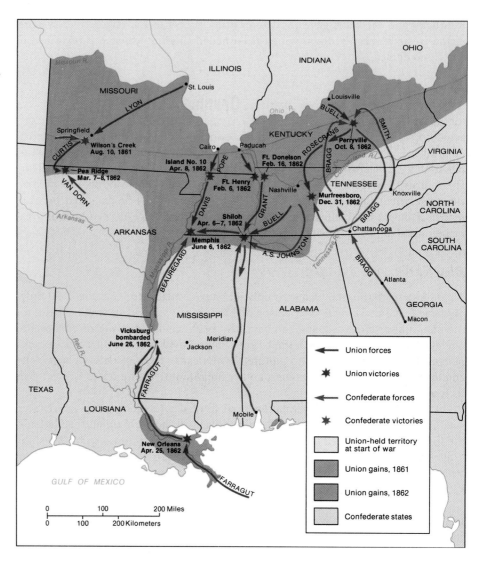

Grant's character

at everything he tried in civilian life, and when the war broke out he was a store clerk in Galena, Illinois. Almost 39, he promptly volunteered, and two months later became a brigadier general.

Grant's quiet, self-effacing manner gave little indication of his military ability or iron determination. Alert to seize any opening, he remained extraordinarily calm and clear-headed in battle. He absorbed details on a map almost photographically, and in battles that spread out over miles, he was superb at coordinating an attack. He would "try all sorts of cross-cuts," recalled one staff officer, "ford streams and jump any number of fences to reach another road rather than go back and take a fresh start." Grant also took full advantage of the telegraph to track troop movements, stringing new lines as he advanced. (Some of his Union telegraphers were so adept that they could receive messages before a station was set up by touching the end of the wire to their tongues to pick up Morse code.) Most important, Grant grasped that hard fighting, not fancy maneuvering, would bring victory. "The art of war is simple," he once explained. "Find out where your enemy is, get at him as soon as you can and strike him as hard as you can, and keep moving on."

Grant realized that rivers were avenues into the interior of the Confederacy. In February 1862, supported by Union gunboats, he captured Fort Henry on the Tennessee River and Fort Donelson on the Cumberland. These victories forced the Confederates to withdraw from Kentucky and middle Tennessee. Grant continued south with 40,000 men, but he was surprised on April 6 by General Albert Sidney Johnston at Shiloh, just north of the Tennessee-Mississippi border. Johnston was killed in the day's fierce fighting, but by nightfall his army had driven the Union troops back to the Tennessee River, where they huddled numbly as a cold rain fell. William Tecumseh Sherman, one of Grant's subordinates, found the general standing under a dripping tree, his coat collar drawn up against the damp, puffing on a cigar. Sherman was about to suggest retreat, but something in Grant's eyes, lighted by the glow of his stogie, made him hesitate. So he said only, "Well, Grant, we've had the devil's own day, haven't we?" "Yes," the Union commander quietly replied. "Lick 'em tomorrow, though." And he did. With the aid of reinforcements, which he methodically ferried across the river all night, Grant counterattacked the next morning and drove the Confederates from the field.

> Shiloh

But victory came at a high price, for Shiloh inflicted more than 23,000 casualties. "The scenes on this field would have cured anyone of war," Sherman testified. Grant, who before had doubted the commitment of Confederate troops, came away deeply impressed by their determination. "At Shiloh," he wrote afterward, "I gave up all idea of saving the Union except by complete conquest."

Eastern Stalemate

Grant's victories did not silence his critics, who charged he drank too much. But Lincoln was unmoved. "I can't spare this man. He fights." That was a quality in short supply in the East, where General McClellan directed operations.

The short, handsome McClellan looked like a general, but beneath his arrogance and bravado lay a self-doubt that rendered him excessively cautious. As the months dragged on and McClellan did nothing but train and plan, Lincoln's frustration grew. "If General McClellan does not want to use the army I would like to *borrow* it," he remarked sarcastically. In the spring of 1862 the general finally transported his 130,000 troops to the Virginia coast and began inching toward Richmond, the Confederate capital. In May, when McClellan was within five miles of Richmond, General Joseph Johnston suddenly attacked him near Fair Oaks, from which he barely escaped.* Worse for McClellan, when Johnston was badly wounded the formidable Robert E. Lee took command of the Army of Northern Virginia.

> Lincoln fears "McClellan has the slows"

Where McClellan was cautious and defensive, the aristocratic Lee was daring and ever alert to assume the offensive. His first name, one of his colleagues commented, should have been Audacity: "He will take more chances, and take them quicker than any other general in this country." Joining Lee was Thomas "Stonewall" Jackson, a deeply religious Calvinist whose rigorous discipline honed his troops to a hard edge. In the Seven Days' battles, McClellan maneuvered brilliantly to parry the attacks of Lee and Jackson; still, he always stayed on the defensive,

> Lee's generalship

---

*Not to be confused with Albert Sidney Johnston, the Confederate general in the western theater killed at Shiloh.

With almost 23,000 casualties, Antietam was the bloodiest single day of the war. A group of Confederate soldiers are shown where they fell along the Hagerstown Pike, the scene of some of the heaviest fighting. Said one Union officer of the fighting there: "Men, I cannot say fell; they were knocked out of the ranks by dozens."

finally retreating until he was under the protection of the Union gunboats. Frustrated, Lincoln ordered the Peninsula campaign abandoned and formed a new army under John Pope. After Lee badly mauled Pope at the second Battle of Bull Run, Lincoln restored McClellan to command.

Lee's invasion fails

Realizing that the Confederacy needed a decisive victory, Lee convinced Davis to allow him to invade the North, hoping to detach Maryland and isolate Washington. But as the army crossed into Maryland, Union soldiers discovered a copy of Lee's orders, accidentally left behind at a campsite by a Confederate officer. From this document McClellan learned that his forces vastly outnumbered Lee's—yet still he hesitated before launching a series of badly coordinated assaults near Antietam Creek on September 17 that Lee barely repulsed. The bloody exchanges horrified both sides for their sheer carnage. Within the space of seven hours, nearly 5000 soldiers were killed and another 18,000 wounded, making it the bloodiest single day in American history. When McClellan allowed the Confederate army to escape back into Virginia, the president permanently relieved him of command in November.

The winter of 1862 was the North's Valley Forge, as morale sank to an all-time low. It took General Ambrose Burnside, who assumed McClellan's place, little more than a month to demonstrate his utter incompetence. In December, at the Battle of Fredericksburg, he suffered a disastrous defeat, which prompted Lincoln to put "Fighting Joe" Hooker in charge. In the West, Grant had emerged as the dominant

The War in the East, 1861–1862
McClellan's campaign against Richmond failed when Joseph Johnston surprised him at Fair Oaks. Taking command of the Army of Northern Virginia, Lee drove back McClellan in the Seven Days' battles and then won a resounding victory in the second Battle of Bull Run. He followed this up by invading Maryland, dividing his forces to take advantage of McClellan's caution, and capturing Harpers Ferry. McClellan checked his advance at Antietam. The Army of the Potomac's devastating defeat at Fredericksburg ended a year of frustration and failure for the Union in the eastern theater.

figure, but the Army of the Potomac still lacked a capable commander, the deaths kept mounting, and no end to the war was in sight.

Emancipation

In 1858 Lincoln had proclaimed that an American "house divided" could not stand and that the United States would eventually become either all slave or all free. When the house divided, however, Lincoln hesitated to strike at slavery. He perceived, accurately, that most white northerners were not deeply committed to emancipation. He feared the social upheaval that such a revolutionary step would cause, and he did not want to alarm the wavering border states. Thus when Congress met in special session in July 1861, Lincoln fully supported a resolution offered by John J. Crittenden of Kentucky, which declared that the war was being fought solely "to defend and maintain the supremacy of the Constitution and to preserve the Union." The Crittenden Resolution passed the House by 117 to 2 and the Senate by 30 to 5.

Crittenden Resolution

Lincoln gives priority to the Union

Still, Republican radicals like Senator Charles Sumner and Horace Greeley pressed Lincoln to adopt a policy of emancipation. Slavery had caused the war, they argued; its destruction would hasten the war's end. Lincoln, however, placed first priority on saving the Union. "My paramount object in this struggle *is* to save the Union, and is *not* either to save or to destroy slavery," he told Greeley in 1862. "If I could save the Union without freeing *any* slave I would do it, and if I could save it by freeing *all* the slaves I would do it, and if I could save it by freeing some and leaving others alone, I would also do that." This statement summarized Lincoln's policy during the first year of the war.

The Logic of Events

Congressional attack on slavery

As the Union army began to occupy Confederate territory, slaves flocked to the Union camps. Octave Johnson, the runaway who hid in the Louisiana bayous for more than a year (page 392), was only one of many slaves who presented themselves to occupying forces. In May 1861 the army adopted the policy of declaring runaway slaves "contraband" of war and refused to return them to their rebel owners. In the Confiscation Act of August 1861, Congress provided that slaves used for military purposes by the Confederacy would become free if they fell into Union hands. For a year Lincoln accepted that position but would go no further. When two of his generals, acting on their own authority, abolished slavery in their districts, he countermanded their orders.

By the time Congress reconvened in December 1861, opinion was beginning to shift. When reintroduced, the Crittenden Resolution was soundly defeated. Congress also prohibited federal troops from capturing or returning fugitive slaves and freed the 2000 slaves living in the District of Columbia with compensation to their owners. In July 1862 it passed the Second Confiscation Act, which declared that the slaves of anyone who supported the rebellion would be freed if they came into federal custody. Unlike with the first act, it did not matter whether the slaves had been used for military purposes.

Process of emancipation during the Civil War

Lincoln's decision for emancipation

Lincoln signed this bill and then proceeded to ignore it. Instead, he emphasized state action, since slavery was a domestic institution. In his first annual message to Congress, he proposed that the federal government provide grants to compensate slaveowners in any state-sponsored program of gradual emancipation. Twice the president summoned white representatives from the border states and prodded them to act before the war destroyed slavery of its own momentum. Both times they rejected his plea.

Following the failure of his second meeting with the border state leaders, Lincoln on July 22, 1862, presented to his cabinet a proposed proclamation freeing the slaves in the Confederacy. He was increasingly confident that the border states would remain in the Union, and he wanted to strike a blow that would weaken the Confederacy militarily. By making the struggle one of freedom versus slavery, such a proclamation would also undermine Confederate efforts to obtain diplomatic recognition. But Lincoln decided to wait for a Union military victory so that the act would not appear one of desperation.

The Emancipation Proclamation

Terms of the Proclamation

On September 22, following the victory at Antietam, Lincoln announced that all slaves within rebel lines would be freed unless the seceded states returned to their allegiance by January 1, 1863. When that day came, the Emancipation Proclamation went formally into effect. Excluded from its terms were the Union slave states, all of Tennessee, and the other areas of the Confederacy that were under Union control. In all, about 830,000 of the nation's 4 million slaves were not covered by its provisions. Because Lincoln justified his actions on strictly military grounds, he believed that there was no legal right to apply the Proclamation to areas not in rebellion.

Following initial criticism of the Proclamation, European public opinion swung toward the Union. In the North, Republicans generally favored Lincoln's decision, while the Democrats made it a major issue in the 1862 elections. "Every white man in the North, who does not want to be swapped off for a free Nigger, should vote the Democratic ticket," urged one party orator. Although the Democrats improved their showing in the elections that fall, the results offered no clear verdict on the Proclamation.

Despite the mixed reaction, the Emancipation Proclamation had immense symbolic importance, for it redefined the nature of the war. The North was fighting not to save the old Union but to create a new nation. The war had become, in Lincoln's words, "remorseless revolution."

Reaction to the Proclamation

African Americans' Civil War

Contrary to white southerners' fears that a race war would erupt behind the lines, the institution of slavery did not explode: it simply disintegrated. Well before federal troops entered an area, slaves took the lead in undermining the institution by openly challenging white authority and claiming greater personal freedom. One experienced overseer reported in frustration that now the "slaves will do only what pleases them, go out in the morning when it suits them, come in when they please, etc." The wife of a Texas planter away at war wrote that she had discontinued whipping, for it only made matters worse. Throughout the Confederacy the vital psychological relationship between master and slave was strained, and sometimes it snapped.

Early in the conflict slaves concluded that emancipation would be one consequence of a Union victory. Perhaps as many as half a million—one-seventh of the total slave population of the Confederacy—fled to Union lines, where they faced an uncertain reception since northern troops manifested a deep-seated racism and were often hostile. The ex-slaves, called freedmen, ended up living in refugee or contraband camps that were overcrowded and disease-ridden and provided only rudimentary shelter and food. "The poor Negroes die as fast as ever," one northern missionary reported. "The children are all emaciated to the last degree and have such violent coughs and dysenteries that few survive."

Convinced that freed slaves would not work on their own initiative, the U.S. government put some contrabands to work assisting the army as cooks, teamsters, woodchoppers, and other unskilled laborers. Their wages were well below those

Black men, including runaway slaves, joined the Union army and navy beginning in 1863. These photographs show Hubbard Pryor before (left) and after (right) enlistment. As soldiers, former slaves developed a new sense of pride and confidence. "I felt like a man with a uniform on and a gun in my hand," declared one ex-slave, and Elijah Marrs recalled that at his first roll call, "I felt freedom in my bones."

Slaves within Union lines

paid white citizens for the same work. In the Mississippi valley, where two-thirds of the freedpeople under Union control were located, most were forced to work on plantations leased or owned by loyal planters. This policy was officially adopted in the summer of 1863 as a way to free the army from the cost of supporting former slaves and strengthen Unionism in the South. Freedpeople had no say in the contracts negotiated between military authorities and planters, found themselves strictly disciplined, and had so many deductions taken from their wages that in the end most received only room and board. In short, the conditions often approximated slavery.

Black Soldiers

Blacks in combat

In adopting the policy of emancipation, Lincoln also announced that African Americans would be accepted in the navy and, more controversially, the army. (Throughout its history, the navy had been hard-pressed to get enough recruits, and as a result that service had always included some black sailors.) Resistance to accepting black volunteers in the army remained especially strong in the Midwest. Black northerners themselves were divided over whether to enlist, but Frederick Douglass spoke for the vast majority when he argued that once a black man had served in the army, there was "no power on earth which can deny that he has earned the right of citizenship in the United States."

In the end, nearly 200,000 African Americans served in the Union forces, constituting about 10 percent of the Union's total military manpower. Some, including two of Douglass's sons, were free, but most were former slaves who enlisted after escaping to the Union lines. As a concession to the racism of white troops, blacks served in segregated units under white officers. They were paid only $10 a month, with $3 deducted for clothing. White soldiers, in contrast, received $13 a month plus a $3.50 clothing allowance. Not until June 1864 did Congress finally grant equal pay to black soldiers.

At first given undesirable duties such as heavy labor and burial details, black soldiers successfully lobbied for the chance to fight. They impressed white troops with their courage under fire. "I have been one of those men, who never had much confidence in colored troops fighting," one Union officer admitted, "but these doubts are now all removed, for they fought as bravely as any troops in the Fort." In the end 37,000 African American servicemen gave their lives, a rate of loss about 40 percent higher than among white soldiers. Black recruits had good reason to fight fiercely. They knew that the freedom of their race hung in the balance, they hoped to win civil rights at home by their performance on the battlefield, they resented racist sneers about their loyalty and ability, and they knew that capture might mean death. The effect on African American pride was also apparent. Slaves admired the confidence of the black troops as they marched through the South. One soldier, who discovered his former master among the prisoners he was guarding, summed up the situation succinctly. "Hello, massa," he called cheerfully, "bottom rail on top dis time!"

The Confederate Home Front

"How shall we subsist this winter?" John Jones wondered in the fall of 1862. A clerk in the War Department in Richmond, Jones found it increasingly difficult to make ends meet on his salary. Prices kept going up, essential items were in short supply, and the signs of hardship were everywhere: in the darned and patched clothing, the absence of meat from the market, the desperation on people's faces. Some of the residents of Richmond "look like vagabonds," Jones noted in his diary. "We see men and women and children in the streets in dingy and dilapidated clothes; and some seem gaunt and pale with hunger. . . ." Coffee was a luxury Jones could no longer afford, he sold his watch to buy fuel, and he worried incessantly about being able to feed his family. "I cannot afford to have more than an ounce of meat daily for each member of my family of six," he recorded in 1864. "The old cat goes staggering about from debility, though Fannie [a daughter] often gives him her share. We see neither rats nor mice about the premises now." By the end of the year a month's supply of food and fuel was costing him $762, a sum sufficient to have supported his family for a year in peacetime. "This is war, terrible war!"

Nowhere were the profound effects of war more complete than within the Confederacy. These changes were especially ironic because the southern states had seceded in order to preserve their traditional ways. Not only did the war send hundreds of thousands of "Johnny Rebs" off to the front; it also put extreme burdens on the women and families at home. It fundamentally transformed the southern economy and forced the Confederate government to become more centralized. And, of course, it ended by destroying the institution of slavery, which the South had gone to war to preserve.

The New Economy

With the Union blockade tightening, the production of foodstuffs became crucial to the South's economy. Many men who normally worked in the fields had gone into the army, and with the lessening of discipline, slaves became increasingly assertive and independent. More and more plantations switched from growing cotton to raising grain and livestock. As a result, cotton production dropped from 4.5 million bales in 1861 to 300,000 in 1864. Even so, food production declined. By the last two years of the war, the shortage was serious.

The Union blockade also made it impossible to rely on European manufactured goods. So the Confederate War Department built and ran factories, took over the region's mines, and regulated private manufacturers so as to increase the production of war goods. Although the Confederacy never became industrially self-sufficient, its accomplishments were impressive. As Josiah Gorgas, head of the Confederate Ordnance Department, noted:

Attempts to industrialize

> We began in April, 1861, without an arsenal, laboratory or powder mill of any capacity, and with no foundry or rolling mill except at Richmond, and before the close of 1863, . . . we had built up foundries and rolling mills, smelting works, chemical works, a powder mill far superior to any in the United States, and a chain of arsenals, armories and laboratories equal in their capacity and their improved appointments to the best of those in the United States.

In fact, the Confederacy sustained itself far better in industrial goods than it did in agricultural produce. It was symbolic that when Lee surrendered, his troops had sufficient guns and ammunition to continue, but they had not eaten in two days.

New Opportunities for Southern Women

Southern white women took an active role in the war. Some gained notoriety as spies; others smuggled military supplies into the South. Women also spent a good deal of time knitting and sewing clothes for soldiers. "We never went out to pay a

New responsibilities and opportunities

"Nannie" McKenzie Semple was one of many southern white women who worked for the Confederate government. Semple's salary, from working as a "Treasury Girl," netted her more than what the average soldier received.

visit without taking our knitting along," recalled a South Carolina woman. Perhaps most important, with so many men fighting, women took charge of agricultural production. On plantations the mistress often supervised the slaves as well as the wrenching shift from cotton to foodstuffs. "All this attention to farming is uphill work with me," one South Carolina woman confessed to her army husband.

One such woman was 33-year-old Emily Lyles Harris, the wife of a small slaveowner and farmer in upcountry South Carolina. When her husband joined the army in 1862, she was left to care for her seven children as well as supervise the slaves and manage the farm. Despite the disruptions of wartime, she succeeded remarkably, one year producing the largest crop of oats in the neighborhood and always making enough money for her family to live decently. She took little pride, however, in her achievements. "I shall never get used to being left as the head of affairs at home," she wrote on one occasion. "The burden is very heavy, and there is no one to smile on me as I trudge wearily along in the dark with it. . . . I am not an independent woman nor ever shall be." And on another occasion, realizing that the work was behind schedule, she complained, "I'm tired to death with urging children and negroes to work." Self-doubt, lack of privacy, and the burdens of responsibility left her depressed, and while she persevered, by 1865 she openly hoped for defeat.

The war also opened up new jobs for women off the farm. Given the manpower shortage, "government girls" became essential to fill the growing Confederate bureaucracy; and with economic conditions so desperate, the secretary of the treasury found he had 100 applications for every vacancy. At first women were paid half the wages of male coworkers, but by the end of the war they had won equal pay. White women also staffed the new factories springing up in southern cities and towns, undertaking even dangerous work that normally would have been considered off-limits. A majority of the workers in the South's munitions factories were women, some of whom lost their lives in accidental explosions. "Of all the principles developed by the late war," wrote one Alabama planter, "I think the capability of our Southern women to take care of themselves was by no means the least important."

Confederate Finance and Government

The most serious domestic problem the Confederate government faced was finance, for which officials at Richmond never developed a satisfactory program. The South had few banks and only $27 million in specie when the war began. European governments refused to float major loans, which left taxation as the unappealing alternative. Only in 1863 did the government begin levying a graduated income tax (from 1 to 15 percent) and a series of excise taxes. Most controversial, the government resorted to a tax-in-kind on farmers that, after exempting a certain portion, took one-tenth of their agricultural crops. Even more unpopular was the policy of impressment, which allowed the army to seize private property for its own use, often with little or no compensation.

Above all, the Confederacy financed the war effort simply by printing paper money not backed by specie, some $1.5 billion, which amounted to three times more than the federal government issued. The result was runaway inflation, so that by 1865 a Confederate dollar was worth only 1.7 cents in gold and prices had soared to 92 times their prewar base. Prices were highest in Richmond, where flour sold for $275 a barrel by early 1864 and coats for $350. By the end of the war, flour had reached an astronomical $1000 a barrel. Inflation that ate away at their standard of living was one of the great wartime hardships borne by the southern people.

Soaring inflation

In politics even more than in finance, the Confederacy exercised far greater powers than those of the federal government before 1861. Indeed, Jefferson Davis strove to meet the demands of total war by transforming the South into a centralized, national state. He sought to limit state authority over military units, and in April 1862 the Confederacy passed the first national conscription law in American history, drafting all white males between 18 and 35 unless exempted. As conditions worsened, those age limits widened to 17 and 50, mobilizing virtually the entire military-age white population. Civilians, too, felt the effects of government control, for in 1862 the Congress authorized Davis to invoke martial law and suspend the writ of habeas corpus.

Centralization of power

Critics protested that Davis was destroying states' rights, the cardinal principle of the Confederacy. Concerned foremost about their states' safety, governors wanted to be able to recall troops if their own territory was threatened. When President Davis suspended the writ of habeas corpus, his own vice president, Alexander H. Stephens, accused him of aiming at a dictatorship. Davis, however, used those powers for a limited time and only with the permission of Congress, yet in practice it made little difference whether the writ was suspended or not. With disloyalty a greater problem than in the Union, Confederate authorities more stringently regulated civil liberties, and the army arrested thousands of civilians.

Opposition to Davis

But the Confederate draft, more than any other measure, produced an outcry. The law allowed the rich to provide substitutes, at a cost that eventually rose, on the open market, to as much as $6000. The Confederacy eventually abolished this privilege, but as one Georgia leader complained, "It's a notorious fact if a man has influential friends—or a little money to spare he will never be enrolled." Most controversially, the draft exempted from service one white man on every plantation with 20 or more slaves (later reduced to 15). This law was designed to preserve control of the slave population, but more and more nonslaveholders complained that it was a rich man's war and a poor man's fight. Denouncing the war as a slaveholders' plot, one Alabama yeoman claimed that "all they want is to git you pumped up and go to fight for their infernal negroes and after you do their fighting you may kiss their hind parts for all they care." In some counties where the draft was unenforceable, conscription officers ventured only at risk to their own safety.

Hostility to conscription

Hardship and Suffering

By the last year of the conflict, food shortages had become so severe that ingenious southerners concocted various substitutes: parched corn in place of coffee, strained blackberries in place of vinegar. One scarce item for which there was no substitute was salt, which was essential for curing meat. Scarcity bred speculation, hoarding, and spiraling prices. The high prices and food shortages led to riots in several cities, most seriously in Richmond early in April 1863. There, about 300 women and children chanting "Bread!" wrecked a number of stores and helped themselves to bread, food, and other items. Nor were rural areas immune from these outbreaks. Country women attacked wagon trains carrying supplies and on several occasions even invaded towns and looted stores.

As always, war corroded the discipline and order of society. With the value of paper money dropping and the future uncertain, many southerners spent money in frenzied haste. Gambling halls were crowded with revelers seeking relief, while soldiers on furlough drank heavily, aware of their increasingly poor chances of survival at the front. Even in the army, theft became common, and in Richmond, the House of Representatives was robbed and Jefferson Davis's favorite horse stolen.

The search for escape from the grim reality of the war led to a forced gaiety for those who could afford it. "The cities are gayer than before the war," one refugee reported, "—parties every night in Richmond, suppers costing ten and twenty thousand dollars." Walking home at night after spending several hours at the bedside of a dying soldier, Judith McGuire passed a house gay with laughter, music, and dancing. "The revulsion . . . was sickening," she wrote afterward in her diary. "I thought of the gayety of Paris during the French Revolution, . . . the ball at Brussels the night before the battle of Waterloo, and felt shocked that our own Virginians, at such a time, should remind me of scenes which we were wont to think only belonged to . . . foreign society." The war was a cancer that ate away not only at southern society but at the southern soul itself.

The Union Home Front

Because the war was fought mostly on southern soil, northern civilians rarely felt its effects directly. Yet to be effective, the North's economic resources had to be organized and mobilized.

Government Finances and the Economy

Measures to raise money

To begin with, the North required a comprehensive system to finance its massive campaign. Taxing the populace was an obvious means, and taxes paid for 21 percent of Union war expenses, compared with only 1 percent of the Confederacy's. In August 1861 Congress passed the first federal income tax, 3 percent on all incomes over $800 a year. When that, along with increased tariff duties, proved insufficient, Congress enacted a comprehensive tax law in 1862 that for the first time brought the tax collector into every northern household. Excise fees taxed virtually every occupation, commodity, or service; income and inheritances were taxed, as were corporations and consumers. A new bureaucracy, the Internal Revenue Bureau, oversaw the collection process.

The government also borrowed heavily, through the sale of some $2.2 billion in bonds, and financed the rest of the war's cost by issuing paper money. In all, the Union printed $431 million in greenbacks (so named because of their color on one side). Although legal for the payment of debts, they could not be redeemed in specie, and therefore their value fluctuated. Congress also instituted a national banking system, allowing nationally chartered banks to issue notes backed by U.S. bonds. By taxing state banknotes out of circulation, Congress for the first time created a uniform national currency.

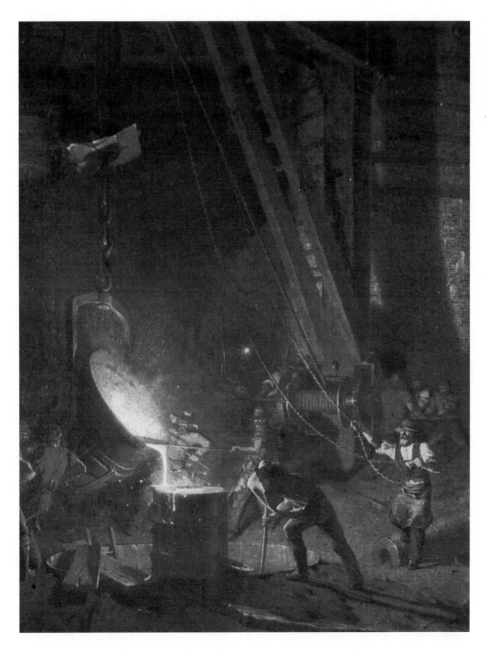

The superiority of northern industry was an important factor in the war's eventual outcome. Here molten ore is cast into cannons at a foundry in West Point, New York. This factory produced 3000 cannons during the war.

During the war, the Republican-controlled Congress encouraged economic development. Tariffs to protect industry from foreign competition rose to an average rate of 47 percent, compared to 19 percent in 1860. To encourage development of the West, the Homestead Act of 1862 granted 160 acres of public land—the size of the traditional American family farm—to anyone (including women) who settled and improved the land for five years. Over a million acres were distributed during the war years alone. In addition, the Land Grant College Act of 1862 donated the proceeds from certain land sales to finance public colleges and universities. Eventually 69 institutions of higher learning were created under its provisions, many in the West.

Western development

A Rich Man's War

Over the course of the war the government purchased more than $1 billion worth of goods and services. In response to this heavy demand, the economy boomed and business and agriculture prospered. Wages increased 42 percent between 1860 and 1864, but because prices rose faster than wages, workers' real income dropped almost 30 percent, from $363 in 1860 to $261 in 1865. That meant the working class paid a disproportionate share of the war's costs.

Corruption and fraud

The Republican belief that government should play a major role in the economy also fostered a cozy relationship between business and politics. In the rush to profit from government contracts, some suppliers sold inferior goods at inflated prices. Uniforms made of "shoddy"—bits of unused thread and recycled cloth— were fobbed off in such numbers that the word became an adjective describing inferior quality. Unscrupulous dealers sold clothing that dissolved in the rain, shoes that fell apart, spoiled meat, broken-down horses, and guns that would not fire. A War Department investigation later revealed that at least 20 percent of government expenditures involved fraud.

Stocks and dividends rose with the economy as investors scrambled after profitable new opportunities. An illegal cotton trade flourished in the Mississippi valley, where northern agents bribed military authorities for passes to go through the lines in order to purchase cotton bales from southern planters. The Confederate government quietly traded cotton for contraband such as food, medicine, and enough arms and equipment to maintain an army of 50,000 men. One War Department investigator asserted in 1863, "Every colonel, captain or quartermaster is in secret partnership with some operator in cotton."

Moral decline

Speculation during the last two years of the war became particularly feverish, and the fortunes made went toward the purchase of ostentatious luxuries. The Chicago *Tribune* admitted: "We are clothed in purple and fine linen, wear the richest laces and jewels and fare sumptuously every day." Like Richmond, Washington became the symbol of this moral decay. Prostitution, drinking, and corruption reached epidemic proportions in the capital, and social festivities became the means to shut out the numbing horror of the casualty lists.

Women and the Workforce

Even more than in the South, the war opened new opportunities for northern women. Countless wives ran farms while their husbands were away at war. One traveler in Iowa reported, "I met more women driving teams on the road and saw more at work in the fields than men." The war also stimulated the shift to mechanization, which made the northern labor shortage less severe. By 1865 three times as many reapers and harvesters were in use as in 1861.

Beyond the farm, women increasingly found work in industry, filling approximately 100,000 new jobs during the war. Like women in the South, they worked as clerks in the expanding government bureaucracy. The work was tedious and the workload heavy, but the new jobs offered good wages, a sense of economic independence, and a pride in having aided the war effort.

Women and medicine

The war also allowed women to enter and eventually dominate the profession of nursing. "Our women appear to have become almost wild on the subject of hospital nursing," protested one army physician, who like many others opposed the presence of women in military hospitals. Led by Drs. Emily and Elizabeth Blackwell, Dorothea Dix, and Mary Ann Bickerdyke, women fought the bureaucratic

A nurse tends a wounded Union soldier in a military hospital in Nashville, Tennessee. Despite the opposition of army doctors, hundreds of female volunteers worked in army hospitals for each side. Nursing became a female profession after the war.

inefficiency of the army medical corps. Their service in the wards of the maimed and dying reduced the hostility to women in medicine.

Clara Barton, like so many other nurses, often found herself in battlefield hospitals, amidst massive death and suffering. During the battle of Fredericksburg, she wiped the brows of the wounded and dying, bandaged wounds, and applied tourniquets to stop the flow of blood. She later recalled that as she rose from the side of one soldier, "I wrung the blood from the bottom of my clothing, before I could step, for the weight about my feet." She steeled herself at the sight of amputated arms and legs casually tossed in piles outside the front door as the surgeons cut away, yet she found the extent of suffering overwhelming. She was jolted by the occasional familiar face among the tangled mass of bodies: the sexton of the church in her hometown, his face caked in blood; a wayward boy she had befriended years ago; an officer who had kindly assisted her on the way to the front, already dead when she discovered him. Sleeping in a tent nearby, she drove herself to the brink of exhaustion until the last patients were transferred to permanent hospitals. She then returned to her home in Washington, where she broke down and wept.

Before 1861 teaching, too, had been dominated by males, but the shortage of men forced school boards in both sections to turn to women, who were paid half to two-thirds of what men received. After the war teaching increasingly became a female profession, as many women came to see teaching as a career and not just a temporary occupation. Women also contributed to the war effort through volunteer work. The United States Sanitary Commission was established in 1861 to provide

Women and teaching

medical supplies and care. Much of its work was performed by women, who raised funds, collected supplies, and worked in hospitals alongside paid nurses.

Civil Liberties and Dissent

Suspension of the writ
of habeas corpus

In order to mobilize northern society, Lincoln did not hesitate to curb dissenters. Shortly after the firing on Fort Sumter, he suspended the writ of habeas corpus in specified areas, which allowed the indefinite detention of anyone suspected of disloyalty or activity against the war. Although the Constitution permitted such suspension in time of rebellion or invasion, Lincoln did so without consulting Congress (unlike President Davis), and he used his power far more broadly, expanding it in 1862 to cover the entire North for cases involving antiwar activities. The president also decreed that those arrested under its provisions could be tried under the stricter rules of martial law by a military court. Eventually more than 20,000 individuals were arrested, most of whom were never charged with a specific crime or brought to trial.

Democrats attacked Lincoln as a tyrant bent on destroying the Constitution. Among those arrested was Clement Vallandigham, an Ohio Democratic congressman who in a speech delivered in May 1863 called for an armistice. He was convicted by a military commission and banished to the Confederacy (in 1864 he returned to the North). The Supreme Court refused to review the case, but once the war was over, in *Ex parte Milligan* (1866) it struck down the military conviction of another civilian, accused of plotting to free Confederate prisoners of war. The Court ruled that as long as the regular courts were open, civilians could not be tried by military tribunals.

The Copperheads

Republicans labeled those who opposed the war Copperheads, conjuring up the image of a venomous snake waiting to strike the Union. Copperheads constituted the extreme peace wing of the Democratic party. Often they had been hurt by the economic changes of the war, but more crucial was their bitter opposition

In this 1862 painting, Lincoln battles the Copperhead dragon to preserve the Union. He is held back by an Irish Democrat from Tammany Hall, who invokes the Constitution and democracy to oppose the war effort. The heavy-handed caricature of the Irish was common in Republican propaganda during the war.

to emancipation and also the draft, which they reviled as a violation of individual freedom and an instrument of special privilege. According to the provisions enacted in 1863, a person would be exempt from the present (but not any future) draft by paying a commutation fee of $300, about a year's wages for a worker or an ordinary farmer. Or those drafted could hire a substitute, the cost of which was beyond the reach of all but the wealthy. Despite this criticism, in reality poor men also bought their way out of the draft, often by pooling their resources; in addition, the government of some communities paid the commutation fee for any resident who was drafted. In all, approximately 118,000 men provided substitutes, and another 87,000 paid the commutation fee. Perhaps another 160,000 northerners illegally evaded the draft. Only 46,000 men were actually drafted into the Union army, out of more than 2 million who served.

New York City draft riot

In July 1863, when the first draftees' names were drawn in New York, workers in the Irish quarter rose in anger. Rampaging through the streets, the mob attacked draft officials and prominent Republicans, ransacked African American neighborhoods, and lynched black residents who fell into its hands. By the time order was restored four days later, at least 105 people had been killed, the worst loss of life from any riot in American history. (See pages 525–528.)

Gone to Be a Soldier

Marcus Spiegel came to the United States after the revolution of 1848 failed in Germany. The son of a rabbi, Spiegel married an American woman, became a naturalized citizen, and was trying to make it in the warehouse business in Ohio when the war began. As an immigrant, he considered it his duty to preserve the Union for his children, and the regular pay of an officer was also enticing, so he enlisted in November 1861 as a lieutenant and eventually became one the few Jewish colonels in the army. A loyal Democrat, Spiegel did not go to war to end slavery and flatly proclaimed that black people were not "worth fighting for." By early 1864, however, his views had changed as a result of his service. He had "learned and seen more of what the horrors of Slavery was than I ever knew before," and though he still doubted African Americans' capabilities, he now was "in favor of doing away with the institution of Slavery." He assured his wife that "this is no hasty conclusion but a deep conviction." A few weeks later, Marcus Spiegel died of wounds he received while fighting in Louisiana.

Fervently committed or not, by war's end about 2 million men had served the Union cause and another million, the Confederate. They were mostly young; almost 40 percent of entering soldiers were age 21 or younger. They were not drawn disproportionately from the poor, and in both the North and the South, farmers and farm laborers accounted for the largest group of soldiers. Unskilled workers, who were poorer than other groups, were actually underrepresented in the ranks. It is also a myth that the North hired an army of foreign-born mercenaries. The overwhelming majority of those who wore the blue and the gray were native-born, and the proportion of immigrants in both armies was roughly the same as in the eligible military population.

Most soldiers, like Marcus Spiegel, took patriotism seriously, and although officers tended to be more ideological, enlisted men were not ignorant of the issues of the war. Chiefly volunteers, they usually expressed their motivation for fighting in general terms, either to defend the Union or protect the South. Only with time did the majority of Union soldiers, like Spiegel, come to endorse the destruction of slavery as a war aim.

Daily Lives

FOOD/DRINK/ DRUGS

Hardtack, Salt Horse, and Coffee

"**If a person** wants to know how to appreciate the value of good vi[c]tuals he had better enlist," a Vermont soldier declared. "I have seen the time when I would have been glad to [have] picked the crusts of bread that mother gives to the hogs." Whether in the field or in quarters, food was generally Johnny Reb's and Billy Yank's first concern.

At the beginning of the war, the prescribed daily allowance for each soldier included 12 ounces of pork or 20 ounces of beef, a pound or more of bread or flour, and ample quantities of rice, beans, sugar, and coffee. Although both armies experienced shortages from time to time, in general northern soldiers had more food and in greater variety than their opponents. As the war ground on, the Confederacy was forced to reduce sharply the daily ration because of shortages, bureaucratic inefficiency, and the lack of adequate transportation.

Meat, bread, and coffee: these were the soldier's mainstays. The meat was either pork or beef and was usually salted to preserve it. Soldiers, who called salt pork "sowbelly" and pickled beef "salt horse," preferred the former, since the beef was so briny that it was inedible unless thoroughly soaked in water. Many soldiers left salted beef in a creek overnight before they tried to eat it.

Union soldiers normally were given wheat bread or flour, but for Confederates cornbread was the standby. This monotonous fare prompted a Louisiana soldier near the end of the war to grumble, "If any person offers me cornbread after this war comes to a close I shall *probably* tell him to—go to hell." Both armies often replaced bread with hardtack, crackers half an inch thick that were so hard, soldiers dubbed them "teeth-dullers." Cynics claimed that they were more suitable for building breastworks, and some Yanks insisted that the "B.C." (for Brigade Commissary) stamped on the boxes they came in referred to their date of manufacture. The crackers became moldy and worm-infested with age, and hence veterans preferred to eat them in the dark.

Coffee was the other main staple, eagerly consumed. Because of the Union blockade, the Confederacy could not get enough, and Rebel troops resorted to various unappealing substitutes. Despite official opposition, troops often fraternized during lulls in the fighting, swapping tobacco, which was in short supply on the Union side, for coffee and sugar, which Confederates desired most. When the two armies spent the winter of 1862 camped on opposite sides of the Rappahannock River, enlisted

An infantry private from New York eats a meal in camp.

Discipline

The near-holiday atmosphere of the war's early months soon gave way to dull routine. Men from rural areas, accustomed to the freedom of the farm, complained about the endless recurrence of reveille, roll call, and drill. "When this war is over," one Rebel promised, "I will whip the man that says 'fall in' to me." Troops in neither army cared for the spit and polish of regular army men. "They keep us very strict here," noted one Illinois soldier. "It is the most like a prison of any place I ever saw."

By modern standards training was minimal and discipline lax in both armies. Troops from rural families found it harder to adjust to army routine than did urban men ferried cargoes of sugar and coffee to one bank and tobacco to the other, using makeshift toy boats.

In an effort to create portable rations, the Union War Department produced an experimental "essence of coffee," a forerunner of the modern instant variety. But the beverage was so vile that men would not drink it, and it was eventually abandoned. More long-lasting was the use of dehydrated potatoes, which few men ever developed a taste for, and desiccated mixed vegetables, which were issued in hard, dry cakes that troops dubbed "baled hay."

Members of both armies supplemented their diet by foraging (the army's polite term for stealing), although Union soldiers, being most often in enemy territory, relied more heavily on this tactic. Hungry troops regularly raided pigpens, poultry houses, orchards, gardens, cornfields, and smokehouses. "When we started the colonel tried to prevent our foraging," one Massachusetts soldier reported, "but . . . [soon] we were as expert at it as any of the old hands."

During training and in winter quarters, cooks normally prepared food for an entire company. Neither army, however, established a cooks' or bakers' school, and troops contended that officers regularly selected the poorest soldiers to be cooks. "A company cook is a most peculiar being," one soldier recalled after the war. "He generally knows less about cooking than any other man in the company. Not being able to learn the drill, and too dirty to appear on inspection, he is sent to the cook house to get him out of the ranks." Once the army went on the march, men usually cooked for themselves or formed a mess of four to eight soldiers, taking turns cooking. Either way, food was rarely prepared with any skill.

By war's end, soldiers on both sides had developed a new appreciation for food. One hungry Texan promised that when he got home he was going "to take a hundred biscuit and two large hams, call it three days rations, then . . . eat it all at *one* meal." A poetic Yankee summed up the situation succinctly:

The soldiers' fare is very rough,
The bread is hard, the beef is
  tough;
If they can stand it, it will be,
Through love of God, a mystery.

soldiers, especially factory workers, who were more familiar with impersonal organizations and used to greater social control. Many southerners were "not used to control of any sort," one Rebel noted, "and were not disposed to obey anyone except for good and sufficient reason given." Manifesting strong feelings of equality that clashed with military hierarchy, Yanks and Rebs alike complained about officers' privileges and had no special respect for rank. "We had enlisted to put down the rebellion," an Indiana private explained, "and had no patience with the red-tape tomfoolery" of the regular army. "The boys recognized no superiors, except in the line of legitimate duty." The Union discontinued the election of lower officers, but this tradition was retained in the Confederate army, which further undermined discipline, since those known as strict disciplinarians were eventually defeated.

Camp Life

Disease and medical care

On average, soldiers spent 50 days in camp for every day in battle. Camp life was often unhealthy as well as unpleasant. Poor sanitation, miserable food, exposure to the elements, and primitive medical care contributed to widespread sickness and disease. Officers and men alike regarded army doctors as nothing more than quacks and tried to avoid them. It was a common belief that if a fellow went to the hospital, "you might as well say good bye." Conditions were even worse in the Confederate hospitals, for the Union blockade produced a shortage of medical supplies. Twice as many soldiers died from dysentery, typhoid, and other diseases as from wounds.

Treatment at field hospitals was a chilling experience. More than anything else, ignorance was responsible for the existing conditions and practices, because nothing was known about germs or how wounds became infected. Years later an appalled federal surgeon recounted:

> We operated in old blood-stained and often pus-stained coats. . . . We used undisinfected instruments . . . and still worse, used marine sponges which had been used in prior pus cases and had been only washed in tap water. . . . Our silk to tie blood vessels was undisinfected. . . . We dressed the wounds with clean but undisinfected sheets, shirts, tablecloths, or other old soft linen rescued from the family ragbag. . . . We knew nothing about antiseptics and therefore used none.

Decline of morality

The boredom of camp life, the horrors of battle, and the influence of an all-male society all corrupted morals. Swearing and heavy drinking were common, and one Mississippian reported that after payday games of chance were "running night and day, with eager and excited crowds standing around with their hands full of money." Prostitutes flooded the camps of both armies, and an Illinois private stationed in Pulaski, Tennessee, wrote home that the price schedule in each of the brothels in town was quite reasonable. "You may think I am a hard case," he conceded, "but I am as pious as you can find in the army." As in the gold fields of

Soldiers leaving for war often had their pictures taken with their loved ones. The Confederate soldier on the left posed with his two sisters. On the right, a member of the Union forces sits with his family for a farewell portrait. Such photographs are reminders of how much the war and its mounting death toll touched civilians as well as soldiers on both sides.

California, the absence of women stimulated behavior that would have been checked back home by the frowns of family and society.

With death so near, some soldiers sought solace in religion. Religious fervor was greater in the Confederate camps, and a wave of revivals swept the ranks during the last two winters of the war, producing between 100,000 and 200,000 conversions. Significantly, the first major revivals occurred after the South's twin defeats at Vicksburg and Gettysburg. Then, too, as battle after battle thinned Confederate ranks, the prospect of death became increasingly large.

The Changing Face of Battle

As in all modern wars, technology revolutionized the conditions under which Civil War soldiers fought. Smoothbore muskets, which at first served as the basic infantry weapon, gave way to the rifle, so named because of the grooves etched into the barrel to give a bullet spin. A new bullet, the minié ball, allowed the rifle to be easily loaded, and the invention of the percussion cap rendered it serviceable in wet weather. More important, the new weapon had an effective range of 400 yards—five times greater than that of the old musket. As a result, soldiers fought each other from greater distances, and battles took much longer to fight and produced many more casualties.

Impact of technology

Under such conditions, the defense became a good deal stronger than the offense. The larger artillery pieces also adopted rifled barrels, but they lacked good fuses and accurate sighting devices and could not effectively support attacking troops. They were a deadly defensive weapon, however, that decimated advancing infantry at close range. Confederate general D. H. Hill described the devastating barrage as his men charged the Union line at Malvern Hill: "As each brigade emerged from the woods, from 50 to 100 guns opened upon it, tearing great gaps in its ranks. Most of them had an open field half a mile wide to cross, under the fire of field artillery and heavy ordnance. It was not war—it was murder." More than 100 regiments on both sides suffered in excess of 50 percent casualties in a single battle.

Strength of the defense

As the haze of gunfire covered the land and the constant spray of bullets mimicked rain pattering through the treetops, soldiers discovered that their romantic notions about war had no place on the battlefield. Men witnessed horrors they had never envisioned as civilians and choked from the stench of decaying flesh and mortal slaughter. They realized that their efforts to convey to those back home the gruesome truth of combat were inadequate. "No tongue can tell, no mind can conceive, no pen portray the horrible sights I witnessed this morning," a Union soldier wrote after Antietam. And still they tried.

Soldiers' hardening outlook

An Indiana soldier at Perryville (7600 casualties): "It was an awful sight to see there men torn all to pieces with cannon balls and bom shells[.] the dead and wounded lay thick in all directions." An Ohio soldier at Antietam (23,000 casualties), two days after the fighting: "The smell was offul . . . there was about 5 or 6,000 dead bodes decaying over the field . . . I could have walked on the boddees all most from one end too the other." A Georgian, the day after Chancellorsville (30,000 casualties): "It looked more like a slaughter pen than anything else. . . . The shrieks and groans of the wounded . . . was heart rending beyond all description." A Maine soldier who fought at Gettysburg (50,000 casualties): "I have Seen . . . men rolling in their own blood, Some Shot in one place, Some another . . . our dead lay in the road and the Rebels in their hast to leave dragged both their baggage wagons and artillery over them and they lay mangled and torn to pieces so that Even friends could not tell them. You can form no idea of a battle field."

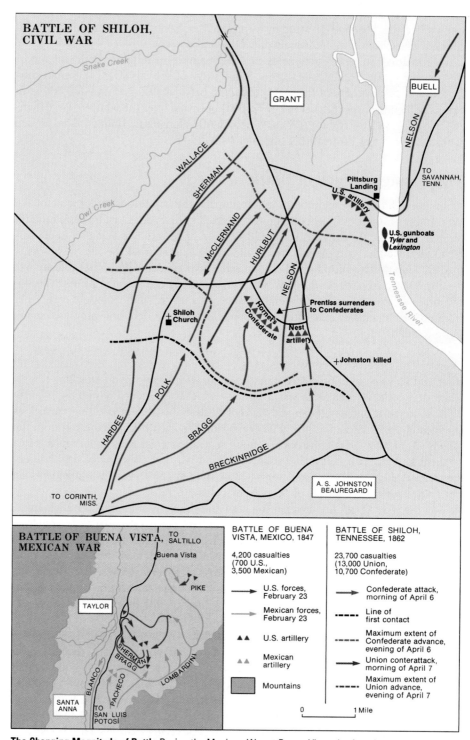

BATTLE OF SHILOH, CIVIL WAR

Snake Creek

Owl Creek

WALLACE

SHERMAN

McCLERNAND

HURLBUT

NELSON

GRANT

BUELL

NELSON

TO SAVANNAH, TENN.

Pittsburg Landing

U.S. artillery

U.S. gunboats *Tyler* and *Lexington*

Tennessee River

+ Shiloh Church

Hornet's Confederate

Nest artillery

Prentiss surrenders to Confederates

+ Johnston killed

HARDEE

POLK

BRAGG

BRECKINRIDGE

TO CORINTH, MISS.

A. S. JOHNSTON BEAUREGARD

BATTLE OF BUENA VISTA, MEXICAN WAR

TO SALTILLO

Buena Vista

PIKE

TAYLOR

SHERMAN

BRAGG

LOMBARDINI

BLANCO

PACHECO

SANTA ANNA

TO SAN LUIS POTOSÍ

BATTLE OF BUENA VISTA, MEXICO, 1847

4,200 casualties
(700 U.S.,
3,500 Mexican)

→ U.S. forces, February 23

→ Mexican forces, February 23

▲▲ U.S. artillery

▲▲ Mexican artillery

Mountains

BATTLE OF SHILOH, TENNESSEE, 1862

23,700 casualties
(13,000 Union,
10,700 Confederate)

→ Confederate attack, morning of April 6

---- Line of first contact

---- Maximum extent of Confederate advance, evening of April 6

→ Union conterattack, morning of April 7

---- Maximum extent of Union advance, evening of April 7

0   1 Mile

The Changing Magnitude of Battle During the Mexican War at Buena Vista, the American army of 4800 men was overextended trying to defend a two-mile line against 15,000 Mexicans. At Shiloh, in contrast, battle lines stretched almost six miles. (The maps are drawn to the same scale.) Against 40,000 Confederates, Grant galloped back and forth, rallying some 35,000 troops organized under five subordinates and coordinating the overnight reinforcement of 25,000 troops. The size of the armies, the complexity of their organization, the length of battle lines, and the number of casualties all demonstrate the extent to which the magnitude of battle had changed.

Hardening Attitudes

Throughout the Civil War, soldiers continued to speak in terms of the traditional ideals of duty, honor, and patriotism. Nevertheless, military service profoundly changed them. For the volunteers of 1861, the war was a test of courage and manhood, and thus they believed the winning side would display superior valor. Expecting a restrained war that would uphold this moral code, they admired the courage of the foe and considered it pointless to kill an isolated soldier.

But the reality of combat did not fit such expectations, and by 1864 the nature of war had been transformed. Soldiers discovered the futility of mass frontal assaults, and under the rain of fire on the battlefield sought cover wherever they could find it. As the fighting intensified, they sought to kill enemy soldiers any way they could in order to hasten the war's end. At the same time, they became indifferent to death and suffering. "The daily sight of blood and mangled bodies," observed a Rhode Island soldier, "so blunted their finer sensibilities as almost to blot out all love, all sympathy from the heart." This hardening of attitudes produced a steady erosion of moral standards. Combatants began taking personal property from the dead and wounded and even prisoners after a battle.

Eroding moral values

As they repudiated their earlier moral assumptions, the soldiers in both armies felt increasingly alienated from civilians back home. In reaction, they developed a stronger sense of comradeship with enemy soldiers, based on their belief that only other soldiers could understand what they had gone through and why they acted the way they did. They felt less an actor in the war than an impersonal object caught in a relentless process of destruction.

In the face of what Charles Francis Adams Jr. termed "the carnival of death," soldiers braced themselves with a grim determination to see the war through to the end. Not glorious exploits but endurance became the true measure of heroism. Exclaimed one chastened Georgia soldier, "What a scourge is war."

The Union's Triumph

While talking to a neighbor, Dolly Lunt suddenly saw the bluecoats coming down the road. Thinking to herself, "Oh God, the time of trial has come!" she ran home as fast as she could. Lunt had left Maine as a young woman and gone to teach school in Covington, Georgia, where she married a local planter. After his death, she took charge of the plantation and its slaves and was still managing it when the Civil War began. Now William Tecumseh Sherman's dreaded army had arrived at her gate. As the Union troops swarmed over the yard, they cleaned out the smokehouse and dairy, stripped the kitchen and cellar of their contents, and killed her fowl and hogs. They broke open locks, smashed down doors, seized items of no military value such as kitchen utensils and even a doll, wantonly destroyed furnishings and personal items, and marched off some of the male slaves. Not content with plundering the main house, the troops entered the slave cabins and rifled them of every valuable, even the money some of the slaves had made by doing extra work. Overcome with anxiety, Lunt spent a supperless night huddled in the house with her remaining slaves, who were clutching their meager possessions. As darkness descended, she reported, "the heavens from every point were lit up with flames from burning buildings." Total war had come to Dolly Lunt's doorstep.

Confederate High Tide

In the spring of 1863 matters still looked promising for Lee. At the battle of Chancellorsville, he brilliantly defeated Lincoln's latest commander, Joseph Hooker. But during the fighting Stonewall Jackson was accidentally shot by his own men, and he died a few days later—a grievous setback for the Confederacy. Determined to take the offensive, Lee invaded Pennsylvania in June with an army of 75,000. Lincoln's newest general, George Gordon Meade, warily shadowed the Confederates. On the first of July, advance parties from the two armies accidentally collided at the town of Gettysburg, and the war's greatest battle ensued.

Gettysburg

For once it was Lee who had the extended supply lines and was forced to fight on ground chosen by his opponent. After two days of assaults failed to break the Union left or right, Lee made the greatest mistake of his career, sending 14,000 men under General George Pickett in a charge at the center of the Union line on Cemetery Ridge. "Pickett's division just seemed to melt away in the blue musketry smoke which now covered the hill," one Confederate officer wrote. "Nothing but stragglers came back." The Union casualties of more than 23,000 represented a quarter of Meade's effective strength, but Lee lost between 25,000 and 28,000—more than a third of his troops. Never again was he able to assume the offensive.

Lincoln Finds His General

Capture of Vicksburg

To the west, Grant had been trying for months to capture Vicksburg, a Rebel stronghold on the Mississippi. In a daring maneuver, he left behind his supply lines and marched inland, calculating that he could feed his army from the produce of Confederate farms, weakening southern resistance in the process. These actions were the tactics of total war, and seldom had they been tried before Grant used them. His troops drove the defenders of Vicksburg back into the city and starved them into submission. On July 4, the city surrendered. With the fall of Port Hudson, Louisiana, four days later, the Mississippi was completely in Union hands. Grant had divided the Confederacy and isolated Arkansas, Texas, and part of Louisiana from the rest of the South.

He followed up this victory by rescuing Union forces holed up in Chattanooga. His performance confirmed Lincoln's earlier judgment that "Grant is my man, and I am his the rest of the war." Congress now revived the rank of lieutenant general, held before only by George Washington, which Lincoln bestowed on Grant. In March 1864 Lincoln brought him east and put him in command of all the Union armies.

Grant in command

Grant recognized that the Union possessed the resources to wear down the Confederacy but that its larger armies had "acted independently and without concert, like a balky team, no two ever pulling together." He intended to change that. While he launched a major offensive against Lee in Virginia, William Tecumseh Sherman, who replaced Grant as commander of the western army, would drive a diagonal wedge through the Confederacy from Tennessee across Georgia. Grant's orders to Sherman were as blunt as his response had been that rainy night when the two had conferred at Shiloh: "Get into the interior of the enemy's country so far as you can, inflicting all the damage you can against their war resources."

Union's summer offensive

In May and June 1864 Grant tried to maneuver Lee out of the trenches and into an open battle. But Lee was too weak to win head-on, so he opted for a strategy of attrition, hoping to inflict such heavy losses that the northern will to continue would break. It was a strategy that nearly worked, for Union casualties were staggering. In a month of fierce fighting, the Army of the Potomac lost 60,000 men—the size of Lee's entire army at the beginning of the campaign. Yet at the

The War in the East, 1863–1865 Lee won his most brilliant victory at Chancellorsville, then launched a second invasion of the North, hoping to score a decisive victory. When the two armies accidentally collided at Gettysburg on July 1, 1863, the Union's Army of the Potomac was driven back through the town until it took up a strong defensive position, shaped like a fishhook and anchored by a hill at each end. On July 2 the Confederate attack drove back the Union's left flank but failed to dislodge the right. Lee's assault on the center of the Union line on July 3 ended in a shattering defeat, and the Army of Northern Virginia retreated back to Virginia. In 1864 Grant delivered a series of heavy blows against Lee's outnumbered forces in Virginia. Despite staggering losses, Grant relentlessly pressed on in a ruthless demonstration of total war. (Note the casualties listed for the spring and summer of 1864; from mid-May to mid-June Grant lost nearly 60,000 men, equal to Lee's strength.) Sheridan's devastating raids against the civilian farms of the Shenandoah Valley helped deprive Lee of desperately needed supplies. In April 1865, too weak to defend Richmond any longer, Lee surrendered at Appomattox Courthouse.

end of the campaign Grant's reinforced army was larger than when it started, whereas Lee's was significantly weaker.

After especially bloody losses at the battle of Cold Harbor, Grant changed tactics. He marched his army around Richmond and settled into a siege of Petersburg, which guarded Richmond's last remaining rail link to the south. A siege would be agonizingly slow, but he counted on his numerical superiority to eventually stretch Lee's line to the breaking point. In the west, meanwhile, the gaunt and grizzled Sherman fought his way by July to the outskirts of Atlanta, which was heavily defended and gave no sign of capitulating. "Our all depends on that army at Atlanta," wrote Mary Chesnut in August, based on her conversations with Confederate leaders in Richmond. "If that fails us, the game is up."

War in the Balance

The game was nearly up for Lincoln as the 1864 election approached. In 1863 the victories at Gettysburg and Vicksburg sparked Republican victories, indicating that public opinion seemed to be swinging toward emancipation. But as the Union war machine swept more and more northerners south to their deaths and as Grant and Sherman bogged down on the Virginia and Georgia fronts, even leaders in Lincoln's own party began to mutter out loud that he was not equal to the task.

1864 election

Perhaps the most remarkable thing about the 1864 election is that it was held at all. Indeed, before World War II, the United States was the only democratic government in history to carry out a general election in wartime. But Lincoln firmly believed that to postpone it would be to lose the priceless heritage of republicanism itself: "We cannot have free government without elections, and if the rebellion could force us to forego or postpone a national election, it might fairly claim to have already conquered and ruined us." Exploiting his control of the party machinery, Lincoln easily won the Republican nomination, and he made certain that the Republican platform called for the adoption of a constitutional amendment abolishing slavery. To balance the ticket, the convention selected Andrew Johnson, the military governor of Tennessee and a prowar Democrat, as his running mate. The two men ran under the label of the "Union" party.

The Democrats nominated George McClellan, the former Union commander. Their platform pronounced the war a failure and called for an armistice and a peace conference. Warned that a cessation of fighting would lead to disunion, McClellan partially repudiated this position, insisting that "the Union is the one condition of peace—we ask no more." In private he made it clear that if elected he intended to restore slavery. Late in August, Lincoln was still gloomy about his prospects as well as those of the Union itself. But Admiral David Farragut won a dramatic victory at Mobile Bay, and a few weeks later, in early September, Sherman finally captured Atlanta. As Secretary of State Seward gleefully noted, "Sherman and Farragut have knocked the bottom out of the Chicago [Democratic] nominations."

Significance of Lincoln's reelection

Polling an impressive 55 percent of the popular vote, Lincoln won 212 electoral votes to McClellan's 21. Eighteen states allowed soldiers to vote in the field, and Lincoln received nearly 80 percent of their ballots. One lifelong Democrat described the sentiment in the army: "We all want peace, but none any but an honorable one. I had rather stay out here a lifetime (much as I dislike it) than consent to a division of our country." Jefferson Davis remained defiant, but the last hope of a Confederate victory was gone.

Equally important, the election of 1864 ended any doubt that slavery would be abolished in the reconstructed Union. The Emancipation Proclamation had not put an end to the question, for its legal status remained unclear. Lincoln argued that as a war measure, it would have no standing once peace returned; and in any case, it had not freed slaves in the border states or those parts of the Confederacy already under Union control. Thus Lincoln and the Republicans believed that a constitutional amendment was necessary to secure emancipation.

In 1864 the Senate had approved an amendment that freed all slaves without compensating their owners, but the measure did not receive the necessary two-thirds vote in the House. After the election, Lincoln threw all his influence behind the drive to round up the necessary votes, and it passed the House on January 31, 1865. By December, enough states had ratified the Thirteenth Amendment to make it part of the Constitution.

Thirteenth Amendment

The abolition of slavery in the United States was part of a worldwide drive against slavery. The antislavery movement was spearheaded in Britain, where Parliament abolished slavery in the empire in 1833. The other colonial powers were much slower to act. Portugal did not end slavery in its New World colonies until 1836, Sweden in 1847, Denmark and France in 1848, Holland in 1863, and Spain not until 1886. Most of the Latin American republics had ended slavery when they threw off Spanish or Portuguese control, but the institution remained important in Cuba and Brazil; Spain abolished slavery in Cuba in 1886, and Brazil ended the institution in 1888. European reformers also crusaded against slavery in Africa and Asia, and indeed the antislavery movement increased European presence in Africa. At the same time, European nations ended the medieval institution of serfdom. In Russia, where serfdom had most closely approximated slavery, Czar Alexander II emancipated the serfs in 1861, an act that led him to strongly favor the Union in the American Civil War.

Abolition as a global movement

The Twilight of the Confederacy

For the Confederacy, the outcome of the 1864 election had a terrible finality. At the beginning of the war, Vice President Stephens had proclaimed slavery the cornerstone of the Confederacy, but now both Lee and Davis endorsed enlisting slaves in the army. In March 1865 the Confederate Congress authorized recruiting 300,000 slaves for military service. When signing the bill, Davis announced that freedom would be given to those who volunteered and to their families. That same month he offered through a special envoy to abolish slavery in exchange for British diplomatic recognition. A Mississippi paper denounced this proposal as "a total abandonment of the chief object of this war" and added that "if the institution [of slavery] is already irretrievably undermined the rights of the States are buried with it." The British rejected the offer, and the war ended before any slaves were mustered into the Confederate army, but the abandonment of slavery surely completed the Confederacy's internal revolution. The demands of total war had forced Confederate leaders to forsake the Old South's most important values and institutions.

Confederacy's abandonment of slavery

In the wake of Lincoln's reelection, the Confederate will to resist rapidly disintegrated. White southerners had never fully united behind the war effort, but the large majority had endured great suffering to uphold it. As Sherman pushed deeper into the Confederacy and General Philip Sheridan mounted his devastating raid on the Shenandoah Valley, the war came home to southern civilians as never before. "We haven't got nothing in the house to eat but a little bit o meal," wrote the wife of one Alabama soldier in December 1864. "Try to get off and come home and fix us all up some and then you can go back. . . . If you put off a-coming, 'twont be no use to come, for we'll all . . . [be] in the grave yard." He deserted. In the last months of the fighting, more than half the Confederacy's soldiers were absent without leave.

U.S. Gunboat *Cimerone*   Steamer landing troops from Harrison

U.S. TROOPS BURNING The COLE HOUSE and PLANTATION. OPPOSITE HARRISON'S
LANDING JAMES RIVER on the night of 1st August 1862

General William Sherman demonstrated the tactics of total war in the autumn of 1864. "Destroyed all we could not eat . . . burned their cotton and gins . . . burned and twisted their railroads . . . ," wrote one of Sherman's soldiers. This drawing, done by a Union private, depicts a similar destructive raid on a plantation along Virginia's James River in 1862, but by the spring of 1865, Confederate armies were increasingly unable to resist the Union might.

March to the sea

After the fall of Atlanta, Sherman gave a frightening demonstration of the meaning of total war. Detaching a portion of his forces to engage General John Hood's army, which moved back into Tennessee, Sherman imitated Grant's strategy by abandoning his supply lines for an audacious 300-mile march to the sea. He intended to deprive Lee's army of the supplies it desperately needed to continue and to break the southern will to resist. Or as he bluntly put it, "to whip the Rebels, to humble their pride, to follow them to their recesses, and make them fear and dread us."

Moving in four columns, Sherman's army covered about 10 miles a day, cutting a path of destruction 50 miles wide. "We had a gay old campaign," one of his soldiers wrote. "Destroyed all we could not eat, stole their niggers, burned their cotton and gins, spilled their sorghum, burned and twisted their railroads and raised Hell generally." Sherman estimated that his men did $100 million in damage, of which $20 million was necessary to supply his army and the rest was wanton destruction. After he captured Savannah in late December, he turned north and wreaked even greater havoc in South Carolina, which Union troops considered the seedbed of the rebellion.

Meanwhile, General George H. Thomas defeated Hood's forces in December at Nashville, leaving the interior of the Confederacy essentially conquered. Only Lee's army remained, entrenched around Petersburg, Virginia, as Grant relentlessly extended his lines, stretching the Confederates thinner and thinner. On April 2 Confederate forces evacuated Richmond.

Grant doggedly pursued the Army of Northern Virginia westward for another hundred miles. After Union forces captured supplies waiting for Lee at Appomattox

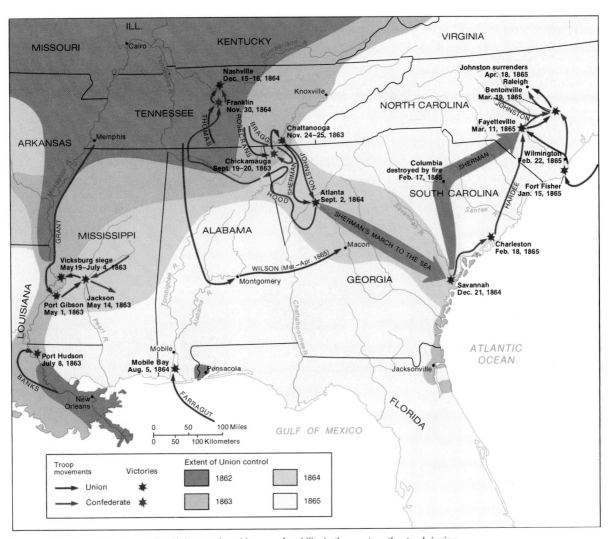

The War in the West, 1863–1865 The Union continued its war of mobility in the western theater, bringing more Confederate territory under its control. After Grant captured Vicksburg, the entire Mississippi lay in Union hands. His victories at Lookout Mountain and Missionary Ridge, near Chattanooga, ended the Confederate threat to Tennessee. In 1864 Sherman divided the Confederacy by seizing Atlanta and marching across Georgia; then he turned north. When Joseph Johnston surrendered several weeks after Lee's capitulation at Appomattox, the war was effectively over.

Courthouse, the weary gentleman from Virginia asked to see Grant. Lee surrendered on April 9, 1865. As the vanquished foe mounted his horse, Grant saluted by raising his hat; Lee raised his respectfully and rode off at a slow trot. "On our part," one federal officer wrote, there was "not a sound of trumpet . . . nor roll of drum; not a cheer . . . but an awed stillness rather." The guns were quiet.

Lee's surrender

With Lee's army gone, remaining resistance throughout the Confederacy collapsed within a matter of weeks. Visiting the captured city of Richmond on April 4, Lincoln was enthusiastically greeted by the black population. He looked "pale, haggard, utterly worn out," noted one observer. The lines in his face showed how much the war had aged him in only four years. Often his friends had counseled rest, but Lincoln had observed that "the tired part of me is *inside* and out of reach." Day after day, the grim telegrams had arrived at the War Department, or

The war's greatest generals, Ulysses S. Grant (left) and Robert E. Lee (right), confronted each other in the eastern theater during the last year of the war. A member of a distinguished Virginia family, the tall, impeccably dressed Lee was every inch the aristocratic gentleman. Grant, a short, slouched figure with a stubby beard, dressed indifferently, often wearing a private's uniform with only the stars on his shoulders to indicate his rank. But his determination is readily apparent in this picture, taken at his field headquarters in 1864.

mothers had come to see him, begging him to spare their youngest son because the other two had died in battle. The burden, he confessed, was almost too much to bear.

Back in Washington the president received news of Lee's surrender with relief. The evening of April 14, Lincoln, seeking a welcome escape, went to see a comedy at Ford's Theater. In the midst of the performance John Wilkes Booth, an unstable actor and Confederate sympathizer, slipped into the presidential box and shot him. Lincoln died the next morning. As he had called upon his fellow Americans to do in his Gettysburg Address, the sixteenth president had given his "last full measure of devotion" to the Republic.

Lincoln's assassination

The Impact of War

Cost of war

The assassination, which capped four years of bloody war, left a tiredness in the nation's bones—a tiredness "inside" and not easily within reach. In every way the conflict had produced fundamental, often devastating changes. There was, of course, the carnage. Approximately 620,000 men on both sides lost their lives, almost as many as in all the other wars the nation has fought from the Revolution through Vietnam combined. In material terms, the conflict cost an estimated $20 billion, or about 10 times the value of all slaves in the country in 1860 and more

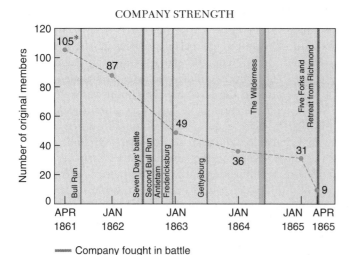

COMPANY STRENGTH

Original members	122
Killed in battle and died of wounds*	17
Died of disease	14
Discharged for various causes	29
Transferred to other commands	6
Prisoners of war at war's end	27
On leave, hospitalized, or at home	8
Deserted	12
Surrendered at Appomattox	9

*Fifty-three members were wounded
one or more times and survived.

▬▬ Company fought in battle
▬▬ Company absent from battle

*Note: 17 members left the company at an
unknown time and are excluded from the graph.

The Attrition of War: Company D, 7th Virginia Infantry, Army of Northern Virginia Organized on April 25, 1861, Company D declined dramatically from its original strength over the course of the war. Combat, disease, and desertion took their toll, but the most important causes of the drop were discharges (often because of wounds) and being captured. As the graph shows, the sharpest declines occurred in 1862 and in 1865, when the company saw heavier military action. The losses also illustrate the relative impact of offensive versus defensive warfare. The sustained, largely offensive campaigning in 1862 reduced the company to half its initial members. In contrast, it missed the brunt of the fighting during Grant's 1864 offensive. The company experienced another sharp falloff in 1865, when most of the remaining original members were captured on the hasty retreat from Richmond. Of those who had volunteered at the beginning of the war, only nine were still in the ranks when the Army of Northern Virginia surrendered at Appomattox Courthouse.

than 11 times the total amount spent by the federal government from 1789 to 1861. Even without adding the market value of freed slaves, southern wealth declined 43 percent, transforming what had been the richest section in the nation (on a white per capita basis) into the poorest.

The effects of total war, however, went well beyond upheaval and destruction. The Civil War rearranged and reordered not only the national economy but also economic relations worldwide. In the nation, demand for the machines of war stimulated industrialization, especially in the heavy industries of iron and coal, machinery, and agricultural implements. Manufacturers were forced to supply the army on an unprecedented scale over great distances. One consequence was the creation of truly national industries in flour milling, meat packing, clothing and shoe manufacture, and machinery making.

People across the globe felt the effects of the war, particularly due to changes in the cotton trade. By 1860 the South was supplying more than three-quarters of all cotton imported by Britain, France, Germany, and Russia. When the war cut off that supply, manufacturers scrambled to find new sources. India, Egypt, and Brazil all improved their railroad facilities and ports in order to encourage planters to open new cotton fields. The Indian city of Bombay experienced explosive growth handling the flood of new cotton. The effect of the trade on Egypt was so great, historians of that nation rank the American Civil War along with the construction of the Suez Canal as the most crucial events in its nineteenth-century history. In the end, the efforts of cotton merchants, textile operators, and European governments

The war's effects on the cotton trade worldwide

marked the first steps by European powers toward a more aggressive imperialism that flourished in the late nineteenth century.

Politically, the war dramatically changed the balance of power. The South lost its substantial influence, as did the Democratic party, while the Republicans emerged in a dominant position. The Union's military victory also signaled the triumph of nationalism. The war destroyed the idea that the Union was a voluntary confederacy of sovereign states, which theorists like John C. Calhoun had argued, and that the states had the right to secede. It was perpetual, as Andrew Jackson had first suggested—truly an indivisible nation. In an important symbolic change, Americans now spoke of the United States in the singular rather than the plural.

Spiritual toll of war

In the short run, the price was disillusionment and bitterness. The South had to live with the humiliation of military defeat and occupation, while former slaves anxiously waited to see what their situation would be in freedom. The war's corrosive effect on morals corrupted American life and politics, destroyed idealism, and severely crippled humanitarian reform. Millennialism and perfectionism were victims of the war's appalling slaughter, forsaken for a new emphasis on practicality, order, materialism, and science. As the war unfolded, the New York *Herald* recognized the deep changes: "All sorts of old fogy ideas, manners, and customs have gone under, and all sorts of new ideas, modes, and practices have risen to the surface and become popular."

George Ticknor, a prominent author and critic who was sensitive to shifting intellectual and social currents, reflected on the changes that had shaken the nation in only a few short years. The war, it seemed to him, had left "a great gulf between what happened before it in our century and what has happened since. . . . It does not seem to me as if I were living in the country in which I was born."

chapter summary

For the first total war in history, the Civil War's outcome depended not just on armies but also on the mobilization of each society's human, economic, and intellectual resources.

- Confederate president Jefferson Davis's policy of concentrating power in the government at Richmond, along with the resort to a draft and impressment of private property, provoked strong protests from many southerners.

- Abraham Lincoln's policies, especially his suspension of the writ of habeas corpus and his interference with civil liberties, were equally controversial.

- But Lincoln skillfully handled the delicate situation of the border states in the first year of the war, keeping them in the Union.

- Lincoln at first resisted pressure to make emancipation a Union war aim, but he eventually issued the Emancipation Proclamation, which transformed the meaning of the war.

- African Americans helped undermine slavery in the Confederacy and made a vital contribution to the Union's military victory.

- The war had a powerful impact on the home front.

  - Women confronted new responsibilities and enjoyed new occupational opportunities.

  - In the Confederacy, hardship and suffering became a fact of life.

  - The Confederate government's financial and tax policies and the tightening Union blockade increased this suffering.

- Both societies also experienced the ravages of moral decay.

- The Civil War changed the nature of warfare.

  - Technology, particularly the use of rifles and rifled artillery, revolutionized tactics and strategy.

- The Union eventually adopted the strategy of attacking the civilian population of the South.
- Soldiers in both armies suffered from disease and inadequate medical care, poor food, moral corruption, and the mounting death toll.

- Union soldiers were more accustomed to order and control and adjusted more effectively to the war's demands.
- The war altered the nation's political institutions, its economy, and its values.

interactive learning

The Primary Source Investigator CD-ROM offers the following materials related to this chapter:

- Interactive maps: **Slavery and the Cotton Kingdom** (M11) and **Civil War, 1861–1864** (M15)
- A short documentary movie on the process of emancipation during the Civil War (D9)

- A collection of primary sources exploring the course of America's first "total war." Several documents reveal African Americans' role in the war: a photograph of contrabands crossing a river, a map of the distribution of slaves, and an image of the 6th Colored Regiment's flag. Other documents explore how the international community reacted to America's Civil War: a political cartoon illustrating England's concerns over its cotton supply, an English cartoon depicting Lincoln asking slaves for help in the war, and a cartoon showing Britannia sympathizing with the Union over Lincoln's assassination.

additional reading

Histories of the Civil War tend to concentrate on either the home front or the military, and on either the Confederacy or the Union. A good single-volume history of the war, up-to-date in its scholarship and balanced in its judgments, covering all these topics is James M. McPherson, *Battle Cry of Freedom* (1988). In recent years military historians have devoted more attention to the relationship between society and the military. An interesting example that traces the evolution of the Union's strategy toward southern civilians is Mark Grimsley, *The Hard Hand of War* (1995).

The best biography of Lincoln, based on extensive research, is David Donald, *Lincoln* (1995). William E. Gienapp, *Abraham Lincoln and Civil War America* (2002), is a concise biography that focuses on the presidential years. Mark E. Neely has written two innovative studies of civil liberties in wartime: *The Fate of Liberty* (1991) examines the Union and *Southern Rights* (1999) deals with the Confederacy. For the South's bid for

independence, Emory M. Thomas, *The Confederate Nation, 1861–1865* (1979), is the standard account. The fullest discussion of southern politics is George C. Rable, *The Confederate Republic* (1994). After years of relative neglect, historians have turned their attention to the vital home front. Drew Faust, *Mothers of Invention* (1996), is an imaginative study of slaveholding women in the Confederacy; Daniel Sutherland, *Seasons of War* (1995), and William Blair, *Virginia's Private War* (1998), analyze the experiences of several Virginian counties in the war; and Stephen V. Ash, *When the Yankees Came* (1995), examines southerners under Union occupation. For the northern home front, see J. Matthew Gallman, *The North Fights the Civil War* (1994). Leon Litwack, *Been in the Storm So Long* (1979), is a gracefully written account of African Americans' experiences during the war, and James L. Roark's *Masters without Slaves* (1977) discusses the collapse of the southern slaveholders' world. Gerald F. Linderman, *Embattled Courage* (1987), presents an interesting assessment of soldiers in both armies. Two excellent collections of essays that evaluate the war's outcome from various angles are David H. Donald, ed., *Why the North Won the Civil War* (1961), and Gabor S. Boritt, ed., *Why the Confederacy Lost* (1992). For a fuller list of readings, see the Bibliography at www.mhhe.com/davidsonnation5.

significant events

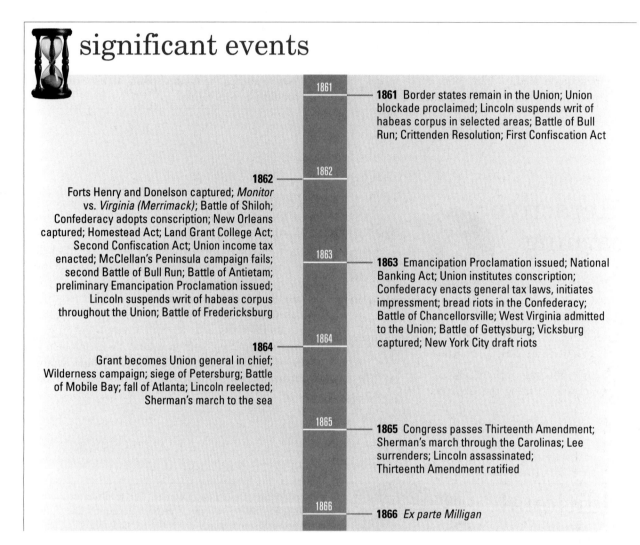

1861 Border states remain in the Union; Union blockade proclaimed; Lincoln suspends writ of habeas corpus in selected areas; Battle of Bull Run; Crittenden Resolution; First Confiscation Act

1862
Forts Henry and Donelson captured; *Monitor* vs. *Virginia (Merrimack)*; Battle of Shiloh; Confederacy adopts conscription; New Orleans captured; Homestead Act; Land Grant College Act; Second Confiscation Act; Union income tax enacted; McClellan's Peninsula campaign fails; second Battle of Bull Run; Battle of Antietam; preliminary Emancipation Proclamation issued; Lincoln suspends writ of habeas corpus throughout the Union; Battle of Fredericksburg

1863 Emancipation Proclamation issued; National Banking Act; Union institutes conscription; Confederacy enacts general tax laws, initiates impressment; bread riots in the Confederacy; Battle of Chancellorsville; West Virginia admitted to the Union; Battle of Gettysburg; Vicksburg captured; New York City draft riots

1864
Grant becomes Union general in chief; Wilderness campaign; siege of Petersburg; Battle of Mobile Bay; fall of Atlanta; Lincoln reelected; Sherman's march to the sea

1865 Congress passes Thirteenth Amendment; Sherman's march through the Carolinas; Lee surrenders; Lincoln assassinated; Thirteenth Amendment ratified

1866 *Ex parte Milligan*

AFTER THE FACT
Historians Reconstruct the Past

What Caused the New York Draft Riots?

Atop a platform, with a small crowd looking on, a blindfolded man stood beside a cylinder as an attendant cranked it around. When the cylinder stopped, the blindfolded man reached in and pulled out a rolled-up slip of paper with a name on it. The day was Saturday, July 11, 1863, and in New York City the Union draft had begun. The day's selections were completed without incident.

Monday, however, was another story. Bright and early, hundreds of laborers streamed up Eighth and Ninth avenues. Waving "No Draft" placards, they rousted other workers from the stores and factories that they passed, stopping at last outside the draft office. Someone fired a pistol. Then members of the mob burst in, destroyed the selection cylinder, and set the building afire. Firefighters tried to stop the blaze from spreading, but another angry mob arrived in time to prevent them. All over the city the chaos spread. "Men left their various pursuits," wrote one reporter; store owners "put up their shutters; factories were emptied, conductors or drivers left their cars" until a "concourse of over twelve thousand" men, women, and children were roaming the streets.

CHARGE OF THE POLICE ON THE RIOTERS AT THE "TRIBUNE" OFFICE.

Over the next several days, the riots became even more violent. Fires burned out of control, telegraph wires were cut, railroad tracks were torn up, and crowds staged pitched battles with police and troops. Targets of the mob's wrath included both high officials and lowly citizens. Homes of the wealthy were looted and set afire, but so was the Colored Orphan Asylum. Policemen caught by the rioters were stripped of their clothes, and their faces were beaten to bloody pulps. Abraham Franklin, a crippled black coachman, was dragged from his rooms and hung while onlookers cheered for Jefferson Davis. By Friday order was at last restored by troops that had been rushed back from their recent victory at Gettysburg. At least 105 people, mostly rioters, lost their lives, and more than a million dollars in property had been destroyed. It was the highest loss of life in any civil disturbance in American history. A month later, the draft resumed in New York City.

What was the cause of such an immense tumult? "Absolute disloyalty," huffed the Republican New York *Tribune*. "It is absurd . . . to attribute this ruffianism to anything else than sympathy with the Rebels." The Democratic New York *World*, which had condemned the draft beforehand, offered an equally straightforward answer. The riot was a spontaneous protest against Lincoln's "wanton exercise of arbitrary powers." Having perverted the war into a struggle to destroy slavery, the paper complained, the administration was now determined to enforce an unconstitutional conscription law that allowed the rich to escape while sweeping the poor into the army's ranks.

At first glance, the *World's* emphasis on the draft seems sufficient. Rioters, after all, carried "No Draft" placards. They attacked draft officials and, by direct intimidation, forced the government to suspend the draft. Eyewitnesses agreed, moreover, that the rioters were overwhelmingly workers and mostly immigrants. These men certainly could not afford to pay the $300 commutation fee to avoid the draft. For them, $300 represented a year's wages or more.

Still, a closer look at the evidence suggests that there was more to these riots than a simple protest of the Union draft. For one thing, the draft did not apply to immigrants unless they were naturalized citizens or had declared their intention to be naturalized. Thus many foreign-born rioters were not even eligible. In addition, observers noted that rioters, including some of the most violent, were remarkably young. Dismissing talk of an oppressive conscription law, the New York *Times* asserted that "three-fourths of those who have been actively engaged in violence have been boys and young men under twenty years of age and not at all subject to Conscription." And if the $300 clause was what most angered the mobs, why did they attack free blacks, who were also subject to the draft and almost all of whom were too poor to pay the fee?

Historians who have examined Union conscription records cast further doubt on this explanation. Despite complaints by Democrats that the $300 fee was an instrument of class privilege, in reality poor men as well as wealthy ones bought their way out of the draft. In New York City, the rate of commutation was as high in poorer wards as in wealthy ones. In fact, over the course of the war 98 percent of the men drafted in the Irish districts of the city either paid the fee or provided substitutes. For as little as $10, workers could buy the equivalent of draft insurance by joining commutation clubs, in which members pooled their money to pay the fee for any contributor who was drafted.

SACKING A DRUG STORE IN SECOND AVENUE.
Observers noted that many rioters were boys.

If the draft was not the sole cause of the riots, what else was behind the mob's anger? For historians, evidence is not easy to come by. Members of rioting crowds rarely leave written records. More often, descriptions are the work of unsympathetic observers. Still, for historians actions can speak as loudly as words. Look closely at what the mobs did. Whom did they choose as the targets of their violence? Did different mobs express their anger in different ways? By examining the riots as they evolved over several days, it is possible to discover vital evidence concerning motivation. In the New York City disturbances, the makeup of the crowds changed dramatically from one day to the next, and the targets the rioters attacked also varied.

On Monday morning, industrial laborers and skilled workers, especially from the building trades, took a leading role. They were joined by some of the city's fire companies. Although some native-born workers participated, the protesters were largely immigrants, Germans as well as Irish. As they marched to the draft office, they announced a one-day strike in protest against the draft. By noon this throng of workers had halted the selection process.

Other rioters, however, began to attack the police and free blacks. As the mayhem escalated, some members of the morning demonstration, including those from several fire companies, now aided the authorities in trying to restore order. For those who switched sides, opposition to the draft had been paramount, and they were unwilling to sanction looting or murder.

When the riots continued on Tuesday and Wednesday, the crowds became much more heavily Irish. German Americans, some of whom were Republicans, no longer joined in. In fact, on several occasions they stepped in to protect free blacks. Skilled workers such as bricklayers, painters, and stonecutters for the most part also held back. Instead, rioters were largely industrial workers and common laborers and included many women and children. Their anger was directed no longer against the draft but against the Republican government and all its policies, including emancipation. Thus they vandalized homes of prominent Republicans, chanted pro-Confederate slogans, and fought pitched battles with the police and soldiers. The offices of Horace Greeley's pro-Republican New York

Common laborers in particular vented their anger on African Americans. As with colonial mob actions, such protests exhibited ritualistic overtones. The victim here not only is being hanged and burned but is being shot as well.

527

Tribune were attacked several times, and Greeley was forced to hide in a nearby restaurant to escape a beating.

For common laborers—longshoremen, street pavers, cartmen—African Americans increasingly became the target of vengeance. Mobs assaulted blacks and lynched at least twelve, ransacked businesses that catered to black customers, and destroyed tenements in which African Americans lived. These attacks were designed to purge neighborhoods of any black presence, especially in areas where black workers had been used to break strikes. These common laborers sought to restore the traditional racial order threatened by Republican policies, most notably emancipation.

In contrast, attacks on blacks and black residences were not common in wards where large numbers of industrial workers lived. While heavily Irish, industrial laborers in iron foundries and railroad shops did not work alongside African Americans. Although hostile to blacks, they aimed their anger more directly at the Republican party. Rather than roaming throughout the city as many common laborers did, industrial workers concentrated on their own neighborhoods, from which they tried to remove all reminders of Republican authority, particularly draft officials, policemen, and soldiers.

Although many policemen were not Republicans, the Metropolitan Police had been created by the Republican party in 1857, and its members had been particularly zealous in arresting individuals suspected of disloyalty.

In the end, no single grievance can explain New York's draft riots. Hostility to Republican employers, Protestant reformers, and authorities merged with antiblack racism, fears of job competition, and economic marginality. By itself, opposition to the draft did not produce the escalating violence and extraordinary destruction. But when that inflammatory issue sparked an avalanche of protest, it provided an outlet for more deeply rooted grievances. The result was the most serious civil disturbance of the war.

BIBLIOGRAPHY Iver Bernstein, *The New York City Draft Riots* (1990), does an admirable job of placing the riots within the context of changing class relations and work patterns. Adrian Cook, *The Armies of the Streets* (1974), presents a fuller, more straightforward narrative. For the Union draft, including a discussion of the impact of commutation, see James W. Geary, *We Need Men: The Union Draft in the Civil War* (1991). James M. McPherson, *The Negro's Civil War* (1965), contains primary sources detailing black New Yorkers' experiences during the riots.

Chapter 17

J oseph Davis had had enough. Well on in years and financially ruined by the war, he decided to quit farming. In November 1866, he sold his Mississippi plantations Hurricane and Brierfield to Benjamin Montgomery and his sons. The sale of southern plantations was common enough after the war, but this transaction was bound to attract attention, since Joseph Davis was the elder brother of Jefferson Davis. Indeed, before the war the Confederate president had operated Brierfield as his own plantation, although his brother retained legal title to it. In truth, the sale was so unusual that the parties involved agreed to keep it secret, since the Montgomerys were black, and Mississippi law prohibited African Americans from owning land.

Though a slave, Montgomery had been the business manager of the two Davis plantations before the war. He had also operated a store on Hurricane Plantation for white as well as black customers with his own line of credit in New Orleans.

Reconstructing the

UNION

1865–1877

preview • Reconstruction became the battleground of attempts to define the new shape of the Union. Congress rejected Andrew Johnson's lenient terms for the South's reentry and enacted a program that included the principle of black suffrage. African Americans asserted their freedom by uniting divided families, establishing churches, and seeking education and land. But when northern whites became disillusioned with reform, the ideology of white supremacy brought Reconstruction to an end.

In 1863 Montgomery fled to the North, but when the war was over, he returned to Davis Bend, where the federal government was leasing plots of the land on confiscated plantations, including Hurricane and Brierfield, to black farmers. Montgomery quickly emerged as the leader of the African American community at the Bend.

Then, in 1866, President Andrew Johnson pardoned Joseph Davis and restored his lands. By then Davis was over 80 years old and lacked the will and stamina to rebuild, yet unlike many ex-slaveholders, he still felt bound by obligations to his former slaves. Convinced that with proper encouragement African Americans could succeed economically in freedom, he sold his land secretly to Benjamin Montgomery. Only when the law prohibiting African Americans from owning land was overturned in 1867 did Davis publicly confirm the sale to his former slave.

For his part, Montgomery undertook to create a model society at Davis Bend based on mutual cooperation. He rented land to black farmers, hired others to work his own fields, sold supplies on credit, and ginned and marketed the crops. To the growing African American community, he preached the gospel of hard work, self-reliance, and education.

Various difficulties dogged these black farmers, including the destruction caused by the war, several disastrous floods, insects, droughts, and declining cotton prices. Yet before long, cotton production exceeded that of the prewar years, and in 1870 the black families at Davis Bend produced 2500 bales. The Montgomerys eventually acquired another plantation and owned 5500 acres, which made them reputedly the third largest planters in the state. They won national and international awards for the quality of their cotton. Their success demonstrated what African Americans, given a fair chance, might accomplish.

The experiences of Benjamin Montgomery during the years after 1865 were not those of most black southerners, who did not own land or have a powerful white

A Visit from the Old Mistress, by Winslow Homer, captures the conflicting, often awkward, emotions felt by both races after the war.

benefactor. Yet Montgomery's dream of economic independence was shared by all African Americans. As one black veteran noted, "Every colored man will be a slave, and feel himself a slave until he can raise him own bale of cotton and put him own mark upon it and say dis is mine!" Blacks could not gain effective freedom simply through a proclamation of emancipation. They needed economic power, including their own land that no one could unfairly take away.

For nearly two centuries the laws had prevented slaves from possessing such economic power. If those conditions were to be overturned, black Americans needed political power too. Thus the Republic would have to be reconstructed to give African Americans political power that they had been previously denied.

War, in its blunt way, had roughed out the contours of a solution, but only in broad terms. Clearly, African Americans would no longer be enslaved. The North, with its industrial might, would be the driving force in the nation's economy and retain the dominant political voice. But beyond that, the outlines of a reconstructed Republic remained vague. Would African Americans receive effective power? How would the North and the South readjust their economic and political relations? These questions lay at the heart of the problem of Reconstruction.

Presidential Reconstruction

Throughout the war Abraham Lincoln had considered Reconstruction his responsibility. Elected with less than 40 percent of the popular vote in 1860, he was acutely aware that once the states of the Confederacy were restored to the Union, the Republicans would be weakened unless they ceased to be a sectional party.

By a generous peace, Lincoln hoped to attract former Whigs in the South, who supported many of the Republicans' economic policies, and build up a southern wing of the party.

Lincoln's 10 Percent Plan

Lincoln outlined his program in a Proclamation of Amnesty and Reconstruction issued in December 1863. When a minimum of 10 percent of the qualified voters from 1860 took a loyalty oath to the Union, they could organize a state government. The new state constitution had to be republican in form, abolish slavery, and provide for black education, but Lincoln did not insist that high-ranking Confederate leaders be barred from public life. Once these requirements had been met, the president would recognize the new civilian state government.

Disavowing any thought of trying prominent Confederate leaders, Lincoln indicated that he would be generous in granting pardons and did not rule out compensation for slave property. Moreover, while he privately suggested permitting some black men to vote in the disloyal states, "as for instance, the very intelligent and especially those who have fought gallantly in our ranks," he did not demand social or political equality for black Americans, and he recognized pro-Union governments in Louisiana, Arkansas, and Tennessee that allowed only white men to vote.

Radical Republicans

The Radical Republicans found Lincoln's approach much too lenient. Strongly antislavery, Radical members of Congress had led the struggle to make emancipation a war aim. Now they were in the forefront in advocating rights for the freedpeople. They were also disturbed that Lincoln had not enlisted Congress in devising Reconstruction policy. Lincoln argued that the executive branch should bear the responsibility for restoring proper relations with the former Confederate states. The Radicals, on the other hand, believed that it was the duty of Congress to set the terms under which states would regain their rights in the Union. Though the Radicals often disagreed on other matters, they were united in a determination to readmit southern states only after slavery had been ended, black rights protected, and the power of the planter class destroyed.

Wade-Davis bill

Under the direction of Senator Benjamin Wade of Ohio and Representative Henry Winter Davis of Maryland, Congress formulated a much stricter plan of Reconstruction. It proposed that Confederate states be ruled temporarily by a military governor, required half the white adult males to take an oath of allegiance before drafting a new state constitution, and restricted political power to the hard-core Unionists in each state. When the Wade-Davis bill passed on the final day of the 1864 congressional session, Lincoln exercised his right of a pocket veto.* Still, his own program could not succeed without the assistance of Congress, which refused to seat Unionist representatives who had been elected from Louisiana or Arkansas. As the war drew to a close, Lincoln appeared ready to make concessions to the Radicals. He suggested that he might favor different—and conceivably more rigorous—Reconstruction plans for different states. At his final cabinet meeting, he approved placing the defeated

---

*If a president does not sign a bill after Congress has adjourned, it has the same effect as a veto.

South temporarily under military rule. But only a few days later Booth's bullet found its mark, and Lincoln's final approach to Reconstruction would never be known.

The Mood of the South

Northerners worried about the attitude of ex-Confederates at war's end. In the wake of defeat, the immediate reaction among white southerners was one of shock, despair, and hopelessness. Some former Confederates, of course, were openly antagonistic. A North Carolina innkeeper remarked bitterly that Yankees had stolen his slaves, burned his house, and killed all his sons, leaving him only one privilege: "To hate 'em. I git up at half-past four in the morning, and sit up till twelve at night, to hate 'em." Most Confederate soldiers were less defiant, having had their fill of war. Even among hostile civilians the feeling was widespread that the South must accept northern terms. And some, like Captain Samuel Foster, a Confederate soldier from Texas, marveled that "mens minds can change so sudden, from opinions of life long, to new ones a week old." Men "who actually owned and held slaves up to this time,—have now changed in their opinions regarding slavery . . . to see that for a man to have property in man was wrong, and that the 'Declaration of Independence' meant more than they had ever been able to see before."

The mood of white southerners at the end of the war was mixed. Many, like the veteran caricatured here by northern cartoonist Thomas Nast, remained hostile. Others, like Texas captain Samuel Foster, came to believe that the institution of slavery "had been abused, and perhaps for that abuse this terrible war . . . was brought upon us as a punishment."

This psychological moment was critical. To prevent a resurgence of resistance, the president needed to lay out in unmistakable terms what white southerners had to do to regain their old status in the Union. Any confusion in policy, or wavering on the peace terms, could only increase the likelihood of resistance. Perhaps even a clear and firm policy would not have been enough. But with Lincoln's death, the executive power came to rest in far less capable hands.

Johnson's Program of Reconstruction

Andrew Johnson, the new president, had been born in North Carolina and eventually moved to Tennessee, where he worked as a tailor. Barely able to read and write when he married, he rose to political power by portraying himself as the champion of the people against the wealthy planter class. "Some day I will show the stuck-up aristocrats who is running the country," he vowed as he began his political career. He had not opposed slavery before the war—in fact, he hoped to disperse slave ownership more widely in southern society. Although he accepted emancipation as one consequence of the war, Johnson remained a confirmed racist. "Damn the negroes," he said during the war, "I am fighting these traitorous aristocrats, their masters."

Johnson's character and values

Because Johnson disliked the planter class so strongly, Republican Radicals in Congress expected him to uphold their views on Reconstruction. In fact, the

Andrew Johnson's contentious personality masked a deep-seated insecurity.

new president did speak of trying Confederate leaders and breaking up planters' estates. Unlike most Republicans, however, Johnson strongly supported states' rights and opposed government aid to business. Given such differences, conflict between the president and the majority in Congress was inevitable, but Johnson's personality and political shortcomings made the situation worse. Scarred by his humble origins, he remained throughout his life an outsider. When challenged or criticized, he became tactless and inflexible, alienating even those who sought to work with him.

Johnson's program

At first, Johnson seemed to be following Lincoln's policy of quickly restoring the southern states to their rightful place in the Union. He prescribed a loyalty oath ordinary white southerners would have to take to have their property, except for slaves, restored and to regain their civil and political rights. Like Lincoln, Johnson excluded high Confederate officials from this group, but he added those with property worth over $20,000, which included his old foes in the planter class. These groups had to apply to the president for individual pardons.

Loyal state governments could be formed after a provisional governor, appointed by the president, called a convention to draft a new state constitution. Voters and delegates had to qualify under the 1860 state election laws and take the new loyalty oath. Once elections were held to choose a governor, legislature, and members of Congress, Johnson announced, he would recognize the new state government, revoke martial law, and withdraw Union troops. Again, the plan was similar to Lincoln's, though more lenient. Unlike the formula Lincoln adopted, Johnson spoke only informally of requiring southern states to repeal their ordinances of secession, repudiate the Confederate debt, and ratify the proposed Thirteenth Amendment abolishing slavery.

The Failure of Johnson's Program

Southern defiance

The southern delegates who met to construct new governments soon demonstrated that they were in no frame of mind to follow Johnson's recommendations. Several states merely repealed instead of repudiating their ordinances of secession, rejected the Thirteenth Amendment, or refused to repudiate the Confederate debt.

Black codes

Nor did any of the new governments allow African Americans any political rights or make any effective provisions for black education. In addition, each state passed a series of laws, often modeled on its old slave code, that applied only to African Americans. These "black codes" did grant African Americans some rights that had not been enjoyed by slaves. They legalized marriages performed under slavery and allowed black southerners to hold and sell property and to sue and be sued in state courts. Yet their primary purpose was to keep African Americans as propertyless agricultural laborers with inferior legal rights. The new freedpeople could not serve on juries, testify against whites, or work as they pleased. South Carolina forbade blacks to engage in anything other than agricultural labor without a special license; Mississippi prohibited them from buying or renting farmland. Most states ominously provided that black people who were vagrants could be arrested and hired out to landowners. Many northerners were incensed by the restrictive black codes, which violated their conception of freedom.

Southern voters under Johnson's plan also defiantly elected prominent Confederate military and political leaders to office, headed by Alexander Stephens, the vice president of the Confederacy, who was elected senator from Georgia. At this point, Johnson could have called for new elections or admitted that a different program of Reconstruction was needed. Instead he caved in. For all his harsh rhetoric, he shrank from the prospect of social upheaval, and he found it enormously gratifying when upper-class planters praised his conduct and requested pardons. As the lines of ex-Confederates waiting to see him lengthened, he began issuing special pardons almost as fast as they could be printed. In the next two years he pardoned some 13,500 former rebels.

Elections in the South

In private, Johnson warned southerners against a reckless course. Publicly he put on a bold face, announcing that Reconstruction had been successfully completed. But many members of Congress were deeply alarmed, and the stage was set for a serious confrontation.

Johnson's Break with Congress

The new Congress was by no means of one mind. A small number of Democrats and a few conservative Republicans backed the president's program of immediate and unconditional restoration. At the other end of the spectrum, a larger group of Radical Republicans, led by Thaddeus Stevens, Charles Sumner, Benjamin Wade, and others, was bent on remaking southern society in the image of the North. Reconstruction must "revolutionize Southern institutions, habits, and manners," thundered Representative Stevens, ". . . or all our blood and treasure have been spent in vain."

Thaddeus Stevens, Radical leader in the House

As a minority, the Radicals could accomplish nothing without the aid of the moderate Republicans, the largest bloc in Congress. Led by William Pitt Fessenden and Lyman Trumbull, the moderates hoped to avoid a clash with the president, and they had no desire to foster social revolution or promote racial equality in the South. But they wanted to keep Confederate leaders from reassuming power, and they were convinced that the former slaves needed federal protection. Otherwise, Trumbull declared, the freedpeople would "be tyrannized over, abused, and virtually reenslaved."

The central issue dividing Johnson and the Radicals was the place of African Americans in American society. Johnson accused his opponents of seeking "to Africanize the southern half of our country," while the Radicals championed civil and political rights for African Americans. Convinced that southern white Unionists were too small a nucleus to build a party around, Radicals believed that the only way to maintain loyal governments and develop a Republican party in the South was to give black men the ballot. Moderates agreed that the new southern governments were too harsh toward African Americans, but they feared that too great an emphasis on black civil rights would alienate northern voters.

Issue of black rights

In December 1865, when southern representatives to Congress appeared in Washington, a majority in Congress voted to exclude them. Congress also appointed a joint committee, chaired by Senator Fessenden, to look into Reconstruction.

The growing split with the president became clearer when Congress passed a bill extending the life of the Freedmen's Bureau. Created in March 1865, the

Johnson's vetoes

bureau provided emergency food, clothing, and medical care to war refugees (including white southerners) and took charge of settling freedpeople on abandoned lands. The new bill gave the bureau the added responsibilities of supervising special courts to resolve disputes involving freedpeople and establishing schools for black southerners. Although this bill passed with virtually unanimous Republican support, Johnson nevertheless vetoed it, and Congress failed to override his veto.

Johnson also vetoed a civil rights bill designed to overturn the more flagrant provisions of the black codes. The law made African Americans citizens of the United States and granted them the right to own property, make contracts, and have access to courts as parties and witnesses. For most Republicans Johnson's action was the last straw, and in April 1866 Congress overrode his veto, the first major legislation in American history to be enacted over a presidential veto. Congress then approved a slightly revised Freedmen's Bureau bill in July and promptly overrode the president's veto. Johnson's refusal to compromise drove the moderates into the arms of the Radicals.

The Fourteenth Amendment

To prevent unrepentant Confederates from taking over the reconstructed state governments and denying African Americans basic freedoms, the Joint Committee on Reconstruction proposed an amendment to the Constitution, which passed both houses of Congress with the necessary two-thirds vote in June 1866. The amendment, coupled with the Freedmen's Bureau and civil rights bills, represented the moderates' terms for Reconstruction.

Provisions of the amendment

The Fourteenth Amendment put a number of matters beyond the control of the president. The amendment guaranteed repayment of the national war debt and prohibited repayment of the Confederate debt. To counteract the president's wholesale pardons, it disqualified prominent Confederates from holding office and provided that only Congress by a two-thirds vote could remove this penalty. Because moderates, fearful of the reaction of white northerners, balked at giving the vote to African Americans, the amendment merely gave Congress the right to reduce the representation of any state that did not have impartial male suffrage. The practical effect of this provision, which Radicals labeled a "swindle," was to allow northern states to restrict suffrage to whites if they wished, since unlike southern states they had few African Americans and thus would not be penalized.

The amendment's most important provision, Section 1, defined an American citizen as anyone born in the United States or naturalized, thereby automatically making African Americans citizens. Section 1 also prohibited states from abridging "the privileges or immunities" of citizens, depriving "any person of life, liberty, or property, without due process of law," or denying "any person . . . equal protection of the laws." The framers of the amendment probably intended to prohibit laws that applied to one race only, such as the black codes, or that made certain acts felonies when committed by black but not white people, or that decreed different penalties for the same crime when committed by white and black lawbreakers. The framers probably did not intend to prevent African Americans from being excluded from juries or to forbid segregation (the legal separation of the races) in schools and public places.

Nevertheless, Johnson denounced the proposed amendment and urged southern states not to ratify it. Ironically, of the seceded states only the president's own state ratified the amendment, and Congress readmitted Tennessee with no further restrictions. The telegram sent to Congress by a longtime foe of Johnson announcing Tennessee's approval ended, "Give my respects to the dead dog in the White House." The amendment was ratified in 1868.

The Elections of 1866

When Congress blocked his policies, Johnson undertook a speaking tour of the East and Midwest in the fall of 1866 to drum up popular support. But the president found it difficult to convince northern audiences that white southerners were fully repentant. News that summer of major race riots in Memphis and New Orleans heightened northern concern. Forty-six African Americans died when white mobs invaded the black section of Memphis, burning homes, churches, and schoolhouses. About the same number were killed in New Orleans when whites attacked both black and white delegates to a convention supporting black suffrage. "The negroes now know, to their sorrow, that it is best not to arouse the fury of the white man," boasted one Memphis newspaper. When the president encountered hostile audiences during his northern campaign, he only made matters worse by trading insults and ranting that the Radicals were traitors. Even supporters found his performance humiliating.

Antiblack riots

Not to be outdone, the Radicals vilified Johnson as a traitor aiming to turn the country over to rebels and Copperheads. Resorting to the tactic of "waving the bloody shirt," they appealed to voters by reviving bitter memories of the war. In a classic example of such rhetoric, Governor Oliver Morton of Indiana proclaimed that "every bounty jumper, every deserter, every sneak who ran away from the draft" was a Democrat; everyone "who murdered Union prisoners," every "New York rioter in 1863 who burned up little children in colored asylums called himself a Democrat. In short, the Democratic party may be described as a common sewer."

Voters soundly repudiated Johnson, as the Republicans won more than a two-thirds majority in both houses of Congress, every northern gubernatorial contest, and control of every northern legislature. The Radicals had reached the height of their power, propelled by genuine alarm among northerners that Johnson's policies would lose the fruits of the Union's victory. Johnson was a president virtually without a party.

Repudiation of Johnson

With a clear mandate in hand, congressional Republicans passed their own program of Reconstruction, beginning with the first Reconstruction Act in March 1867. Like all later pieces of Reconstruction legislation, it was repassed over Johnson's veto.

Congressional Reconstruction

Placing the 10 unreconstructed states under military commanders, the act provided that in enrolling voters, officials were to include black adult males but not former Confederates who were barred from holding office under the Fourteenth Amendment. Delegates to the state conventions would frame constitutions that provided for black suffrage and that disqualified prominent ex-Confederates from office. The first state legislatures to meet under the new constitution were required to ratify the Fourteenth Amendment. Once these steps were completed and Congress approved the new state constitution, a state could send representatives to Congress.

Resistance of southern whites

White southerners found these requirements so obnoxious that officials took no steps to register voters. Congress then enacted a second Reconstruction Act, also in March, ordering the local military commanders to put the machinery of Reconstruction into motion. Johnson's efforts to limit the power of military commanders produced a third act, passed in July, that upheld their superiority in all matters. When elections were held to ratify the new state constitutions, white southerners boycotted them in large numbers. Undaunted, Congress passed the fourth Reconstruction Act (March 1868), which required ratification of the constitution by only a majority of those voting rather than those who were registered.

By June 1868 Congress had readmitted the representatives of seven states. Georgia's state legislature expelled its black members once it had been readmitted, granting seats to those barred by Congress from holding office. Congress ordered the military commander to reverse these actions, and Georgia was then admitted a second time in July 1870. Texas, Virginia, and Mississippi did not complete the process until 1869.

Post-Emancipation Societies in the Americas

With the exception of Haiti's revolution (1791–1804), the United States was the only society in the Americas in which the destruction of slavery was accomplished by violence. But the United States, uniquely among these societies, enfranchised former slaves almost immediately after the emancipation. Thus in the United States former masters and slaves battled for control of the state in ways that did not occur in other post-emancipation societies. In most of the Caribbean, property requirements for voting left the planters in political control. Jamaica, for example, with a population of 500,000 in the 1860s, had only 3,000 voters.

Moreover, in reaction to political efforts to mobilize disfranchised black peasants, Jamaican planters dissolved the assembly and reverted to being a Crown colony governed from London. Of the sugar islands, all but Barbados adopted the same policy, thereby blocking the potential for any future black peasant democracy. Nor did any of these societies have the counterparts of the Radical Republicans, a group of outsiders with political power that promoted the fundamental transformation of the post-emancipation South. These comparisons highlight the radicalism of Reconstruction in the United States, which alone saw an effort to forge an interracial democracy.

The Land Issue

Blacks' desire for land

While the political process of Reconstruction proceeded, Congress confronted the question of whether land should be given to former slaves to foster economic independence. At a meeting with Secretary of War Edwin Stanton near the end of the war, African American leaders declared, "The way we can best take care of ourselves is to have land, and till it by our own labor." During the war, the Second Confiscation Act of 1862 had authorized the government to seize and sell the property, including land, of supporters of the rebellion. In June 1866, however, President Johnson ruled that confiscation laws applied only to wartime.

Congress debated land confiscation off and on from December 1865 until early 1867. Thaddeus Stevens, a leading Radical in the House, advocated confiscating

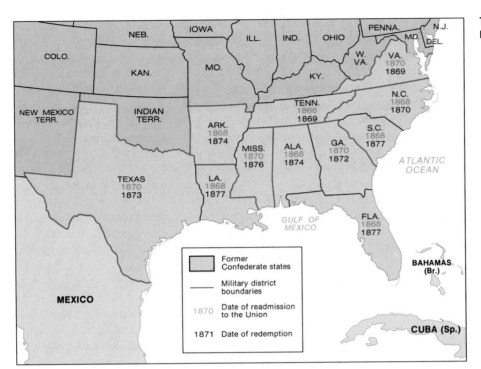

The Southern States during Reconstruction

394 million acres of land from about 70,000 of what he termed the "chief rebels" in the South, who made up less than 5 percent of the South's white families. He proposed to give 40 acres to every adult male freedperson and then sell the remaining land, which would amount to nine-tenths of the total, to pay off the public debt, compensate loyal southerners for losses they suffered during the war, and fund Union veterans' pensions. Land, he insisted, would be far more valuable to African Americans than the right to vote.

But in the end Congress rejected all proposals. Even some Radicals were opposed to land redistribution. Given Americans' strong belief in self-reliance, little sympathy existed for the idea that government should support any group. In addition, land redistribution represented an attack on property rights, another cherished American value. "A division of rich men's lands amongst the landless," argued the *Nation*, a Radical journal, "would give a shock to our whole social and political system from which it would hardly recover without the loss of liberty." By 1867 land reform was dead.

Failure of land redistribution

Few freedpeople acquired land after the war, a development that severely limited African Americans' economic independence and left them vulnerable to white coercion. It is doubtful, however, that this decision was the basic cause of the failure of Reconstruction. In the face of white hostility and institutionalized racism, African Americans probably would have been no more successful in protecting their property than they were in maintaining the right to vote.

Impeachment

Throughout 1867 Congress routinely overrode Johnson's vetoes. Still, the president had other ways of undercutting congressional Reconstruction. He interpreted the

Tenure of Office Act

new laws as narrowly as possible and removed military commanders who vigorously enforced them. Congress responded by restricting Johnson's power to issue orders to military commanders in the South. It also passed the Tenure of Office Act, which forbade Johnson to remove any member of the cabinet without the Senate's consent. The intention of this law was to prevent him from firing Secretary of War Edwin Stanton, the only Radical in the cabinet.

When Johnson tried to dismiss Stanton in February 1868, the determined secretary of war barricaded himself in his office (where he remained night and day for about two months). Angrily, the House of Representatives approved articles of impeachment. The articles focused on the violation of the Tenure of Office Act, but the charge with the most substance was that Johnson had conspired to systematically obstruct Reconstruction legislation. In the trial before the Senate, his lawyers argued that a president could be impeached only for an indictable crime, which Johnson clearly had not committed. The Radicals countered that impeachment applied to political offenses and not merely criminal acts.

Johnson acquitted

In May 1868 the Senate voted 36 to 19 to convict, one vote short of the two-thirds majority needed. The seven Republicans who joined the Democrats in voting for acquittal were uneasy about using impeachment as a political weapon. Their vote against conviction established the precedent that a president could be removed from office only for indictable offenses, which greatly lessened the effectiveness of the threat of impeachment.

Reconstruction in the South

The refusal of Congress to convict Johnson sent a clear signal: the power of the Radicals in Congress was waning. Increasingly the success or failure of Reconstruction hinged on developments not in Congress but in the southern states themselves. Power there rested with the new Republican parties, representing a coalition of black and white southerners and transplanted northerners.

Black Office Holding

Almost from the beginning of Reconstruction, African Americans had lobbied for the right to vote. After they received the franchise, black men constituted as much as 80 percent of the Republican voters in the South. They steadfastly opposed the Democratic party with its appeal to white supremacy. As one Tennessee Republican explained, "The blacks know that many conservatives [Democrats] hope to reduce them again to some form of peonage. Under the impulse of this fear they will roll up their whole strength and will go entirely for the Republican candidate whoever he may be."

Throughout Reconstruction, African Americans never held office in proportion to their voting strength. No African American was ever elected governor, and only in South Carolina, where more than 60 percent of the population was black, did they control even one house of the legislature. During Reconstruction between 15 and 20 percent of the state officers and 6 percent of members of Congress (2 senators and 15 representatives) were black. Only in South Carolina did black officeholders approach their proportion of the population.

Blacks who held office generally came from the top levels of African American society. Among state and federal officeholders, perhaps four-fifths were literate, and more than a quarter had been free before the war, both marks of distinction in the black community. Their occupations also set them apart: two-fifths were professionals (mostly clergy), and of the third who were farmers, nearly all owned land. Among black members of Congress, all but three had a secondary school education, and four had gone to college. In their political and social values, African American leaders were more conservative than the rural black population was, and they showed little interest in land reform.

Hiram Revels, a minister and educator, became the first African American to serve in the U.S. Senate, representing Mississippi. Later he served as president of Alcorn University.

Background of black political leaders

White Republicans in the South

Black citizens were a majority of the voters only in South Carolina, Mississippi, and Louisiana. Thus in most of the South the Republican party had to secure white votes to stay in power. Opponents scornfully labeled white southerners who allied with the Republican party scalawags, yet an estimated quarter of white southerners at one time voted Republican. Although the party appealed to some wealthy planters, they were outnumbered by Unionists from the upland counties and hill areas who were largely yeoman farmers. Such voters were attracted by Republican promises to rebuild the South, restore prosperity, create public schools, and open isolated areas to the market with railroads.

The other group of white Republicans in the South was known as carpetbaggers. Originally from the North, they allegedly had arrived with all their worldly possessions stuffed in a carpetbag, ready to loot and plunder the defeated South. Some did, certainly, but northerners moved south for a variety of reasons. Those in political office were especially well educated. Though carpetbaggers made up only a small percentage of Republican voters, they controlled almost a third of the offices. More than half of all southern Republican governors and nearly half of Republican members of Congress were originally northerners.

The Republican party in the South had difficulty agreeing on a program or maintaining unity. Scalawags were especially susceptible to the race issue and social pressure. "Even my own kinspeople have turned the cold shoulder to me because I hold office under a Republican administration," testified a Mississippi white Republican. As black southerners pressed for greater recognition and a greater share of the offices, white southerners increasingly defected to the Democrats. Carpetbaggers, in contrast, were less sensitive to race, although most felt that their black allies needed guidance and should be content with minor offices. The friction between scalawags and carpetbaggers, which grew out of their rivalry for party honors, was particularly intense.

Divisions among southern Republicans

From the beginning of Reconstruction, African Americans demanded the right to vote as free citizens. The Fifteenth Amendment, ratified in 1870, secured that right for black males. In New York, black citizens paraded in support of Ulysses Grant for president. Parades played a central role in campaigning: this parade exhibits the usual banners, flags, costumes, and a band. Blacks in both the North and the South voted solidly for the Republican party as the party of Lincoln and emancipation, although white violence in the South increasingly reduced black turnout.

The New State Governments

New state constitutions

The new southern state constitutions enacted several significant reforms. They put in place fairer systems of legislative representation, allowed voters to elect many officials who before had been appointed, and abolished property requirements for officeholding. In South Carolina, for the first time, voters were allowed to vote for the president, governor, and other state officers.* The Radical state governments also assumed some responsibility for social welfare and established the first statewide systems of public schools in the South. Although the Fourteenth Amendment prevented high Confederate officials from holding office, only Alabama and Arkansas temporarily forbade some ex-Confederates to vote.

Race and social equality

All the new constitutions proclaimed the principle of equality and granted black adult males the right to vote. On social relations they were much more cautious. No state outlawed segregation, and South Carolina and Louisiana were the only states that required integration in public schools (a mandate that was almost universally ignored). Sensitive to status, mulattoes pushed for prohibition of social discrimination, but white Republicans refused to adopt such a radical policy.

Economic Issues and Corruption

The war left the southern economy in ruins, and problems of economic reconstruction were as difficult as those of politics. The new Republican governments encouraged industrial development by providing subsidies, loans, and even

*Previously, presidential electors as well as the governor had been chosen by the South Carolina legislature.

temporary exemptions from taxes. These governments also largely rebuilt the southern railroad system, often offering lavish aid to railroad corporations. These investments in the South's industrial base helped: in the two decades after 1860, the region doubled its manufacturing establishments. Yet the harsh reality was that the South steadily slipped further behind the booming industrial economy of the North. Between 1854 and 1879, 7000 miles of railroad track were laid in the South, but in the same period 45,000 miles were constructed in the rest of the nation.

The expansion of government services offered temptations for corruption. In many southern states, officials regularly received bribes and kickbacks for their award of railroad charters, franchises, and other contracts. By 1872 the debts of the 11 states of the Confederacy had increased by $132 million, largely because of railroad grants and new social services such as schools. The tax rate grew as expenditures went up, so that by the 1870s it was four times the rate of 1860.

Corruption, however, was not only a southern problem: the decline in morality affected the entire nation. During these years in New York City alone, the Democratic Tweed Ring stole more money than all the Radical Republican governments in the South combined. Moreover, corruption in the South was hardly limited to Republicans. Many Democrats and white business leaders participated in these corrupt practices both before and after the Radical governments were in power. Louisiana governor Henry Warmoth, a carpetbagger, told a congressional committee that the legislature was as good as the people it represented. "Everybody is demoralizing down here. Corruption is the fashion."

Corruption in Radical governments undeniably existed, but southern whites exaggerated its extent for partisan purposes. Conservatives just as bitterly opposed honest Radical regimes as they did notoriously corrupt ones. In the eyes of most white southerners, the real crime of the Radical governments was that they allowed black citizens to hold some offices and tried to protect the civil rights of African Americans. Race was the conservatives' greatest weapon. And it would prove the most effective means to undermine Republican power in the South.

Corruption

Emancipation came to slaves in different ways and at different times. For some it

Black Aspirations

arrived during the war when Union soldiers entered an area; for others it came some time after the Confederacy's collapse, when Union troops or officials announced that they were free. Whatever the timing, freedom meant a host of precious blessings to people who had been in bondage all their lives.

Experiencing Freedom

The first impulse was to think of freedom as a contrast to slavery. Emancipation immediately released slaves from the most oppressive aspects of bondage—the whippings, the breakup of families, the sexual exploitation. Freedom also meant movement, the right to travel without a pass or white permission. Above all, freedom meant that African Americans' labor would be for their own benefit. One Arkansas freedman, who earned his first dollar working on a railroad, recalled that when he was paid, "I felt like the richest man in the world."

Freedom included finding a new place to work. Changing jobs was one concrete way to break the psychological ties of slavery. Even planters with

Changing employment

Daily Lives

PUBLIC SPACE/ PRIVATE SPACE

The Black Sharecropper's Cabin

On the plantations of the Old South, slaves had lived in cabins along a central path in the shadow of the white master's "big house." These quarters were the center of their community, where marriages and other festivals were celebrated and family life went on. But with the coming of emancipation, freedpeople looked to leave the old quarters, which stood as a symbol of bondage and of close white supervision. African Americans either built new housing or dismantled their old cabins and hauled them to the plots of land they rented as tenants or sharecroppers. Moving enabled them to live on the land they farmed, just as white farmers and tenants did.

In selecting a cabin site, freedpeople tried to locate within a convenient distance of their fields but close to the woods as well, since cutting wood was a year-round task for boys. To improve drainage, cabins were often built on a knoll or had a floor raised above the ground. A nearby stream, spring, or well provided not only water but also a place to cool butter and other perishable dairy products.

Like slave cabins, most sharecroppers' dwellings were one story high, about 16 feet square, and usually built of logs chinked with mud. The few windows had shutters to protect against the weather; glass was rare. Though the inside walls normally lacked plaster or sheeting, they were given a coat of whitewash annually to brighten the dark interior. To provide a bit of cheer, women often covered the walls with pictures from seed catalogues and magazines. The floor, packed dirt that was as smooth and hard as concrete, was covered with braided rugs made from scraps of cloth and worn-out clothing.

The main room served as kitchen and dining room, parlor, bathing area, and the parents' bedroom. To one side might be a homemade drop-leaf table (essential because of cramped space), which served as a kitchen work counter and a dining table. The other side of the room had a few plain beds, their slats or rope bottoms supporting corn shuck or straw mattresses. (Featherbeds were considered a remarkable luxury.) The social center of the

Chimneys on sharecroppers' cabins were often tilted deliberately so that they could be pushed away from the house quickly if they caught fire.

reputations for kindness sometimes found that most of their former hands had departed. The cook who left a South Carolina family even though they offered her higher wages than her new job explained, "I must go. If I stays here I'll never know I'm free."

Importance of names

Symbolically, freedom meant having a full name, and African Americans now adopted last names. More than a few took the last name of some prominent individual; more common was to take the name of the first master in the family's oral history as far back as it could be recalled. Most, on the other hand, retained their first name, especially if the name had been given to them by their parents (as most room was the fireplace, the only source of heat and the main source of light after dark. Pots and pans were hung on the wall near the fireplace, and the mother and daughters did the cooking stooped over an open fire. Clothing was hung on pegs in the wall.

The cabin's chimney was made of small logs notched together and covered with several layers of clay to protect it from the heat. It often narrowed toward the top, and sometimes its height was extended by empty flour barrels. A taller chimney drew better, which kept smoke from blowing back down into the house and kept sparks away from the roof. After the evening meal the family gathered around the fireplace, the children to play with homemade dolls and toys, the mother to sew, and the father perhaps to play the fiddle. At bedtime a trapdoor in the ceiling offered access up a ladder to the loft beneath the gabled roof, where older children slept, usually on pallets on the floor, as had been the case in slavery.

In the summer, cooking was done outdoors over an open fire. Women generally preferred to cook under a tree, which offered some protection from rain as well as relief from the sun and the high humidity. Sharecropper families rarely had separate cooking rooms attached to or next to the cabin. Separate kitchens, which were a sign of prosperity, were more common among black landowners and white tenant farmers.

Gradually, as black sharecroppers scraped together some savings, they improved their homes. By the end of the century, frame dwellings were more common, and many older log cabins had been covered with wood siding. The newer homes were generally larger, with wood floors, and often had attached rooms such as a porch or kitchen. In addition, windows had glass panes, roofs were covered with shingles instead of planking, and stone and brick chimneys were less unusual. Ceramic dishes were more frequently seen, and wood-burning stoves made cooking easier for women and provided a more efficient source of heat.

Without question, the cabins of black sharecroppers provided more space than the slave quarters had, and certainly more freedom and privacy. Still, they lacked many of the comforts that most white Americans took for granted. Such housing reflected the continuing status of black sharecroppers as poverty-stricken laborers in a caste system based on race.

often had been the case among slaves). It had been their form of identity in bondage, and for those separated from their family it was the only link with their parents. Whatever name they took, it was important to black Americans that they make the decision themselves without white interference.

The Black Family

African Americans also sought to strengthen the family in freedom. Because slave marriages had not been recognized as legal, thousands of former slaves insisted on

Upholding the family

being married again by proper authorities, even though a ceremony was not required by law. Blacks who had been forcibly separated in slavery and later remarried confronted the dilemma of which spouse to take. Laura Spicer, whose husband had been sold away in slavery, received a series of wrenching letters from him after the war. He had thought her dead, had remarried, and had a new family. "You know it never was our wishes to be separated from each other, and it never was our fault. I had rather anything to had happened to me most than ever have been parted from you and the children," he wrote. "As I am, I do not know which I love best, you or Anna." Declining to return, he closed, "Laura, truly, I have got another wife, and I am very sorry. . . ."

Like white husbands, black husbands deemed themselves the head of the family and acted legally for their wives. They often insisted that their wives would not work in the fields as they had in slavery, a decision that had major economic repercussions for agricultural labor. "The [black] women say they never mean to do any more outdoor work," one planter reported, "that white men support their wives and they mean that their husbands shall support them." In negotiating contracts, a father also demanded the right to control his children and their labor. All these changes were designed to insulate the black family from white control.

The Schoolhouse and the Church

Black education

In freedom, the schoolhouse and the black church became essential institutions in the black community. Next to ownership of land, African Americans saw education as the best hope for advancement. At first, northern churches and missionaries, working with the Freedmen's Bureau, set up black schools in the South. Tuition represented 10 percent or more of a laborer's monthly wages. Yet these schools were full. Many parents sent their children by day and attended classes themselves at night. Eventually, the Bureau schools were replaced by the new public school systems, which by 1876 enrolled 40 percent of African American children.

Black adults had good reasons for seeking literacy. They wanted to be able to read the Bible, to defend their newly gained civil and political rights, and to protect themselves from being cheated. One elderly Louisiana freedman explained that giving children an education was better than giving them a fortune, "because if you left them even $500, some man having more education than they had would come along and cheat them out of it all." Both races saw that education would undermine the old servility that slavery had fostered.

Teachers in black schools

Teachers in the Freedmen's Bureau schools were primarily northern middle-class white women sent south by northern missionary societies. "I feel that it is a precious privilege," Esther Douglass wrote, "to be allowed to do something for these poor people." Many saw themselves as peacetime soldiers, struggling to make emancipation a reality. Indeed, on more than one occasion, hostile white southerners destroyed black schools and threatened and even murdered white teachers. Teachers in urban schools often lived together in comfortable housing, which provided a social network, created a sense of sisterhood, and helped sustain morale. In rural areas, however, teachers often had to live alone or with black families because of white hostility. Then there were the everyday challenges: low pay, dilapidated buildings, lack of sufficient books, classes of 100 or more children, and irregular attendance. Meanwhile, the Freedmen's Bureau undertook to quickly train

After living for years in a society where teaching slaves to read and write was usually illegal, freedpeople viewed literacy as a key to securing their newfound freedom. Blacks were not merely "*anxious* to learn," a school official in Virginia reported, they were "*crazy* to learn."

black teachers, and by 1869 a majority of the approximately 3000 teachers in freedmen's schools were black.

Before the war, most slaves had attended white churches or services supervised by whites. Once free, African Americans quickly established their own congregations led by black preachers. In the first year of freedom, the Methodist Church South lost fully half of its black members. By 1870 the Negro Baptist Church had increased its membership threefold when compared to the membership in 1850, and the African Methodist Episcopal Church expanded at an even greater rate.

Independent black churches

Black churches were so important because they were the only major organizations in the African American community controlled by blacks. A white missionary reported that "the Ebony preacher who promises perfect independence from White control and direction carried the colored heart at once." Black ministers were respected leaders, and many of the black men elected to office during Reconstruction were preachers. As it had in slavery, religion offered African Americans a place of refuge in a hostile white world and provided them with hope, comfort, and a means of self-identification.

New Working Conditions

As a largely propertyless class, blacks in the postwar South had no choice but to work for white landowners. Except for paying wages, whites wanted to retain the old system of labor, including close supervision, gang labor, and physical punishment. Determined to remove all emblems of servitude, African Americans refused to work under these conditions, and they demanded time off to devote to their own interests. Convinced that working at one's own pace was part of freedom, they simply would not work as long or as hard as they had in slavery. Because of shorter

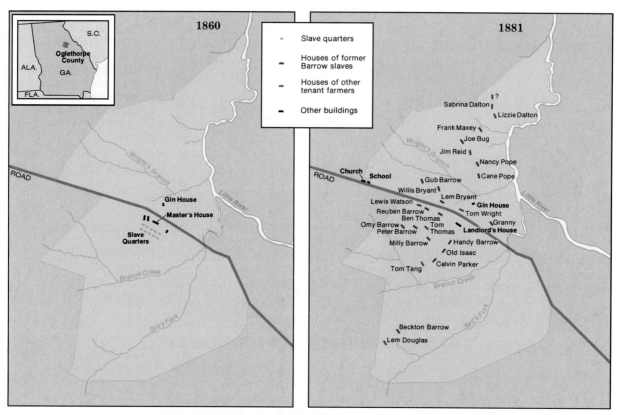

A Georgia Plantation after the War After emancipation, sharecropping became the dominant form of agricultural labor in the South. Black families no longer lived in the old slave quarters but dispersed to separate plots of land that they farmed themselves. At the end of the year each sharecropper turned over part of the crop to the white landowner.

hours and the withdrawal of children and women from the fields, work output declined by an estimated 35 percent in freedom. Blacks also refused to live in the old slave quarters located near the master's house. Instead, they erected cabins on distant parts of the plantation. Wages at first were $5 or $6 a month plus provisions and a cabin; by 1867, they had risen to an average of $10 a month.

Sharecropping

These changes eventually led to the rise of sharecropping. Under this arrangement African American families farmed separate plots of land and then at the end of the year divided the crop, normally on an equal basis, with the white landowner. Sharecropping had higher status and offered greater personal freedom than being a wage laborer. "I am not working for wages," one black farmer declared in defending his right to leave the plantation at will, "but am part owner of the crop and as [such,] I have all the rights that you or any other man has." Although black per capita agricultural income increased 40 percent in freedom, sharecropping was a harshly exploitative system in which black families often sank into perpetual debt.

The Freedmen's Bureau

The task of supervising the transition from slavery to freedom on southern plantations fell to the Freedmen's Bureau, a unique experiment in social policy supported by the federal government. Assigned the task of protecting freedpeople's economic rights, approximately 550 local agents supervised and regulated working conditions in southern agriculture after the war. The racial attitudes of Bureau agents varied widely, as did their commitment and competence. Then, too, they had to depend on the army to enforce their decisions.

Most agents encouraged or required written contracts between white planters and black laborers, specifying not only wages but also the conditions of employment. Although agents sometimes intervened to protect freedpeople from unfair treatment, they also provided important help to planters. They insisted that black laborers not desert at harvest time; they arrested those who violated their contracts or refused to sign new ones at the beginning of the year; and they preached the gospel of work and the need to be orderly and respectful. Given such attitudes, freedpeople increasingly complained that Bureau agents were mere tools of the planter class. "They are, in fact, the planters' guards, and nothing else," claimed the New Orleans *Tribune,* a black newspaper. One observer reported, "Doing justice seems to mean seeing that the blacks don't break contracts and compelling them to submit cheerfully."

The primary means of enforcing working conditions were the Freedmen's Courts, which Congress created in 1866 in order to avoid the discrimination African Americans received in state courts. These new courts functioned as military tribunals, and often the agent was the entire court. The sympathy black laborers received varied from state to state. In 1867 one agent summarized the Bureau's experience with the labor contract system: "It has succeeded in making the freedman work and in rendering labor secure and stable—but it has failed to secure to the Freedman his just dues or compensation."

In 1869, with the Bureau's work scarcely under way, Congress decided to shut it down, and by 1872 it had gone out of business. Despite its mixed record, it was the most effective agency in protecting blacks' civil and political rights. Its disbanding signaled the beginning of the northern retreat from Reconstruction.

Bureau's mixed record

End of the Bureau

Planters and a New Way of Life

Planters and other white southerners faced emancipation with dread. "All the traditions and habits of both races had been suddenly overthrown," a Tennessee planter recalled, "and neither knew just what to do, or how to accommodate themselves to the new situation."

The old ideal of a paternalistic planter, which required a facade of black subservience and affection, gave way to an emphasis on strictly economic relationships. Mary Jones, a Georgia slaveholder before the war who did more for her workers than the law required, lost all patience when two workers accused her of trickery and hauled her before a Freedmen's Bureau agent, with whom she won her case. Upon returning home, she announced to the assembled freedpeople that "I have considered them friends and treated them as such but now they were only laborers under contract, and only the law would rule between us." Only with time did planters develop new norms and standards to judge black behavior. What in 1865 had seemed insolence was viewed by the 1870s as the normal attitude of freedom.

Planters' new values

Slavery had been a complex institution that welded black and white southerners together in intimate relationships. After the war, however, planters increasingly embraced the ideology of segregation. Because emancipation significantly reduced the social distance between the races, white southerners sought psychological separation and kept dealings with African Americans to a minimum. By the time Reconstruction ended, white planters had developed a new way of life based on the institutions of sharecropping and segregation and undergirded by a militant white supremacy.

Although most planters kept their land, they did not regain the economic prosperity of the prewar years. Rice plantations, which were not suitable to tenant farming, largely disappeared after the war. In addition, southern cotton growers faced increased competition from new areas such as India, Egypt, and Brazil. Cotton prices began a long decline, and southern per capita income suffered as a result. By 1880 the value of southern farms had slid 33 percent below the level of 1860.

The Abandonment of Reconstruction

On Christmas Day 1875, a white acquaintance approached Charles Caldwell on the streets of Clinton, Mississippi, and invited him into Chilton's store to have a drink to celebrate the holiday. A former slave, Caldwell was a state senator and the leader of the Republican party in Hinds County, Mississippi. But the black leader's fearlessness made him a marked man. Only two months earlier, he had been forced to flee the county to escape an armed white mob angry about a Republican barbecue he and his fellow Republicans had organized. For four days the mob hunted down and killed nearly 40 Republican leaders for presuming to hold a political meeting. Despite that hostility, Caldwell had returned to vote in the November state election. Even more boldly, he had led a black militia company through the streets to help quell the disturbances. Now, as Caldwell and his "friend" raised their glasses in a holiday toast, a gunshot exploded through the window. Caldwell collapsed, mortally wounded from a bullet to the back of his head. He was taken outside, where his assassins riddled his body with bullets. He died in the street.

Charles Caldwell shared the fate of more than a few black Republican leaders in the South during Reconstruction. Southern whites used violence, terror, and political assassination to challenge the federal government's commitment to sustaining Reconstruction. If northerners had boldly countered such terrorism, Reconstruction might have ended differently. But in the years following President Johnson's impeachment trial in 1868, the influence of Radical Republicans steadily waned. The Republican party was being drained of the crusading idealism that had stamped its early years.

The Election of Grant

Immensely popular after the war, Ulysses S. Grant was the natural choice of Republicans to run for president in 1868. Although Grant was elected, Republicans were shocked that despite his great military stature, his popular margin was only 300,000 votes. An estimated 450,000 black Republican votes had been cast in the South, which meant that a majority of whites casting ballots had voted Democratic. The 1868 election helped convince Republican leaders that an amendment securing black suffrage throughout the nation was necessary.

Fifteenth Amendment

In February 1869 Congress sent the Fifteenth Amendment to the states for ratification. It forbade any state to deny the right to vote on grounds of race, color, or previous condition of servitude. Some Radicals had hoped to forbid literacy or property requirements to protect blacks further. Others wanted a simple declaration that all adult male citizens had the right to vote. But the moderates in the party were aware that many northerners were increasingly worried about the number of immigrants who were again entering the country and wanted to be able to restrict their voting. As a result, the final amendment left loopholes that eventually allowed southern states to disfranchise African Americans. The amendment was ratified in March 1870, aided by the votes of the four southern states that had not completed the process of Reconstruction and thus were also required to endorse this amendment before being readmitted to Congress.

Lucy Stone, a major figure in the women's rights movement.

Proponents of women's suffrage were gravely disappointed when Congress refused to prohibit voting discrimination on the basis of sex as well as race. The Women's Loyal League, led by Elizabeth Cady Stanton and Susan B. Anthony, had pressed for first the Fourteenth and then the Fifteenth Amendment to recognize women's public role. But even most Radicals, contending that black rights had to be ensured first, were unwilling to back women's suffrage. The Fifteenth Amendment ruptured the feminist movement. Although disappointed that women were not included in its provisions, Lucy Stone and the American Woman Suffrage Association urged ratification. Anthony and Stanton, on the other hand, broke with their former allies among the Radicals, denounced the amendment, and organized the National Woman Suffrage Association to work for passage of a new amendment giving women the ballot. The division hampered the women's rights movement for decades to come.

Women's suffrage rejected

The Grant Administration

Ulysses Grant was ill at ease with the political process. His simple, quiet manner, while superb for commanding armies, did not serve him as well in public life, and his well-known resolution withered when he was uncertain of his goal. Also, he lacked the moral commitment to make Reconstruction succeed.

A series of scandals wracked Grant's presidency. Although Grant did not profit personally, he remained loyal to his friends and displayed little zeal to root out wrongdoing. His relatives were implicated in a scheme to corner the gold market, and his private secretary escaped conviction for stealing federal whiskey revenues only because Grant interceded on his behalf. His secretary of war resigned to avoid impeachment. James W. Grimes, one of the party's founders, denounced the Republican party under Grant as "the most corrupt and debauched political party that has ever existed."

Corruption under Grant

Nor was Congress immune from the lowered tone of public life. In such a climate ruthless state machines, led by men who favored the status quo, came to dominate the party. Office and power became ends in themselves, and party leaders worked in close cooperation with northern industrial interests. The few Radicals still active in public life increasingly repudiated Grant and the Republican governments in the South. Congress in 1872 passed an amnesty act, removing the restrictions of the Fourteenth Amendment on officeholding except for about 200 to 300 ex-Confederate leaders.

Grant swings from a trapeze while supporting a number of associates accused of corruption. Among those holding on are Secretary of the Navy George M. Robeson (top center), who was accused of accepting bribes in the awarding of navy contracts; Secretary of War William W. Belknap (top right), who was forced to resign for selling Indian post traderships; and the president's private secretary, Orville Babcock (bottom right), who was implicated in the Whiskey Ring scandal. Although not personally involved in the scandals during his administration, Grant was reluctant to dismiss from office supporters accused of wrongdoing.

As corruption in both the North and the South worsened, reformers became more interested in cleaning up government than in protecting blacks' rights. These liberal Republicans opposed the continued presence of the army in the South, denounced the corruption of southern governments as well as the national government, and advocated free trade and civil service reform. In 1872 they broke with the Republican party and nominated for president Horace Greeley, the editor of the New York *Tribune*. A onetime Radical, Greeley had become disillusioned with Reconstruction and urged a restoration of home rule in the South as well as adoption of civil service reform. Democrats decided to back the Liberal Republican ticket. The Republicans renominated Grant, who, despite the defection of a number of prominent Radicals, won an easy victory with 56 percent of the popular vote.

Growing Northern Disillusionment

During Grant's second term, Congress passed the Civil Rights Act of 1875, the last major piece of Reconstruction legislation. This law prohibited racial discrimination in all public accommodations, transportation, places of amusement, and juries. At the same time, Congress rejected a ban on segregation in public schools, which was almost universally practiced in the North as well as the South. Although some railroads, streetcars, and public accommodations in both sections were desegregated after the bill passed, the federal government made little attempt to enforce the law, and it was ignored throughout most of the South. In 1883 the Supreme Court struck down its provisions except the one relating to juries.

Civil Rights Act of 1875

Despite passage of the Civil Rights Act, many northerners were growing disillusioned with Reconstruction. They were repelled by the corruption of the southern governments, they were tired of the violence and disorder in the South, and they had little faith in black Americans. William Dodge, a wealthy New York capitalist and an influential Republican, wrote in 1875 that the South could never develop its resources "till confidence in her state governments can be restored, and this will never be done by federal bayonets." It had been a mistake, he went on, to make black southerners feel "that the United States government was their special friend, rather than those . . . among whom they must live and for whom they must work." He concluded, "We have tried this long enough. Now let the South alone."

Waning northern concern

As the agony of the war became more distant, the Panic of 1873 diverted public attention from Reconstruction to economic issues. In the severe depression that followed over the next four years, some 3 million people found themselves out of work. Congress became caught up in the question of whether printing greenbacks would help the economy prosper. Battered by the panic and the corruption issue, the Republicans lost a shocking 77 seats in Congress in the 1874 elections, and along with them control of the House of Representatives for the first time since 1861. "The truth is our people are tired out with the worn out cry of 'Southern outrages'!!" one Republican concluded. "Hard times and heavy taxes make them wish the 'ever lasting nigger' were in hell or Africa." Republicans spoke more and more about cutting loose the unpopular southern governments.

Depression and Democratic resurgence

The Triumph of White Supremacy

As northern commitment to Reconstruction waned, southern Democrats set out to overthrow the remaining Radical governments. Already white Republicans in the South felt heavy pressure to desert their party. In Mississippi one party member justified his decision to leave on the grounds that otherwise he would have "to live a life of social oblivion" and his children would have no future.

Racism

This campaign badge from 1868 made the sentiments of white Democrats clear.

OUR TICKET.

for President   Vice President.

SEYMOUR.   BLAIR.

OUR MOTTO:

THIS IS A WHITE MAN'S COUNTRY: LET WHITE MEN RULE.

Entered according to Act of Congress, A. D. 1868, by
B. W. Hitchcock, in the Clerk's office of the U. S.
District Court for the Southern Dist. of New York.

To poor white southerners who lacked social standing, the Democratic appeal to racial solidarity offered great comfort. As one explained, "I may be poor and my manners may be crude, but . . . because I am a white man, I have a right to be treated with respect by Negroes. . . . That I am poor is not as important as that I am a white man; and no Negro is ever going to forget that he is not a white man." The large landowners and other wealthy groups that led southern Democrats objected less to black southerners voting. These well-to-do leaders did not face social and economic competition from African Americans, and in any case, they were confident that if outside influences were removed, they could control the black vote.

Democrats also resorted to economic pressure to undermine Republican power. In heavily black counties, white observers at the polls took down the names of black residents who cast Republican ballots and published them in local newspapers. Planters were urged to discharge black tenants who persisted in voting Republican. But terror and violence provided the most effective means to overthrow the Radical regimes. A number of paramilitary organizations broke up Republican meetings, terrorized white and black Republicans, assassinated Republican leaders, and prevented black citizens from voting. The most famous was the Ku Klux Klan, founded in 1866 in Tennessee. It and similar groups functioned as unofficial arms of the Democratic party.

Congress finally moved to break the power of the Klan with the Force Act of 1870 and the Ku Klux Klan Act of 1871. These laws made it a felony to interfere with the right to vote; they also authorized use of the army and suspension of the writ of habeas corpus. The Grant administration eventually suspended the writ of habeas corpus in nine South Carolina counties and arrested hundreds of suspected Klan members throughout the South. Although these actions weakened the Klan, terrorist organizations continued to operate underground.

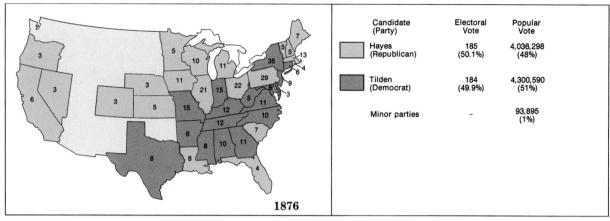

Election of 1876

Then in 1875 Democrats inaugurated what became known as the Mississippi Plan, the decision to use as much violence as necessary to carry the state election. Several local papers trumpeted, "Carry the election peaceably if we can, forcibly if we must." When Republican governor Adelbert Ames requested federal troops to stop the violence, Grant's advisers warned that sending troops to Mississippi would cost the party the Ohio election. In the end the administration told Ames to depend on his own forces. Bolstered by terrorism, the Democrats swept the election in Mississippi. Violence and intimidation prevented as many as 60,000 black and white Republicans from voting, converting the normal Republican majority into a Democratic majority of 30,000. Mississippi had been "redeemed."

Mississippi Plan

The Disputed Election of 1876

With Republicans on the defensive across the nation, the 1876 presidential election was crucial to the final overthrow of Reconstruction. The Republicans nominated Ohio governor Rutherford B. Hayes to oppose Samuel Tilden of New York. Once again, violence prevented many Republican votes, this time an estimated quarter of a million, from being cast in the South. Tilden had a clear majority of 250,000 in the popular vote, but the outcome in the Electoral College was in doubt because both parties claimed South Carolina, Florida, and Louisiana, the only reconstructed states still in Republican hands. Hayes needed all three states to be elected, for even without them, Tilden had amassed 184 electoral votes, one short of a majority. Republican canvassing boards in power disqualified enough Democratic votes to give each state to Hayes.

To arbitrate the disputed returns, Congress established a 15-member electoral commission: 5 members each from the Senate, the House, and the Supreme Court. By a straight party vote of 8–7, the commission awarded the disputed electoral votes—and the presidency—to Hayes.

When angry Democrats threatened a filibuster to prevent the electoral votes from being counted, key Republicans met with southern Democrats on February 26 at the Wormley Hotel in Washington. There they reached an informal understanding, later known as the Compromise of 1877. Hayes's supporters agreed to withdraw federal troops from the South and not oppose the new Democratic state

Compromise of 1877

governments. For their part, southern Democrats dropped their opposition to Hayes's election and pledged to respect African American rights.

Without federal support, the Republican governments in South Carolina and Louisiana promptly collapsed, and Democrats took control of the remaining states of the Confederacy. By 1877, the entire South was in the hands of the Redeemers, as they called themselves. Reconstruction and Republican rule had come to an end.

Redeemers take control

Racism and the Failure of Reconstruction

Reconstruction failed for a multitude of reasons. The reforming impulse that had created the Republican party in the 1850s had been battered and worn down by the war. The new materialism of industrial America inspired in many Americans a jaded cynicism about the corruption of the age and a desire to forget uncomfortable issues. In the South, African American voters and leaders inevitably lacked a certain amount of education and experience; elsewhere, Republicans were divided over policies and options.

Yet beyond these obstacles, the sad fact remains that the ideals of Reconstruction were most clearly defeated by the deep-seated racism that permeated American life. Racism was why the white South so unrelentingly resisted Reconstruction. Racism was why most white northerners had little interest in black rights except as a means to preserve the Union or to safeguard the Republic. Racism was why northerners were willing to write off Reconstruction and with it the welfare of African Americans. While Congress might pass a constitutional amendment abolishing slavery, it could not overturn at a stroke the social habits of two centuries.

Certainly the political equations of power, in the long term, had been changed. The North had fought fiercely during the war to preserve the Union. In doing so, it

Benjamin Montgomery, together with his sons, purchased Jefferson Davis's plantation along the Mississippi River after the war. A former slave, Montgomery pursued the dream of black economic independence by renting land to black farmers at Davis Bend.

had secured the power to dominate the economic and political destiny of the nation. With the overthrow of Reconstruction, the white South had won back some of the power it had lost in 1865. But even with white supremacy triumphant, African Americans did not return to the social position they had occupied before the war. They were no longer slaves, and black southerners who walked dusty roads in search of family members, sent their children to school, or worshiped in churches they controlled knew what a momentous change emancipation was. Even under the exploitative sharecropping system, black income rose significantly in freedom. Then, too, the principles of "equal protection" and "due process of law" had been written into the Constitution. These guarantees would be available for later generations to use in championing once again the Radicals' goal of racial equality.

End of the Davis Bend experiment

But this was a struggle left to future reformers. For the time being, the clear trend was away from change or hope—especially for former slaves like Benjamin Montgomery and his sons, the owners of the old Davis plantations in Mississippi. In the 1870s bad crops, lower cotton prices, and falling land values undermined the Montgomerys' financial position, and in 1875 Jefferson Davis sued to have the sale of Brierfield invalidated.

A lower court ruled against Davis, since he had never received legal title to the plantation. Davis appealed to the state supreme court, which, following the overthrow of Mississippi's Radical government, had a white conservative majority. In a politically motivated decision, the court awarded Brierfield to Davis in 1878, and the Montgomerys lost Hurricane as well. The final outcome was not without bitter irony. In applying for restoration of his property after the war, Joseph Davis had convinced skeptical federal officials that he—and not his younger brother—held legal title to Brierfield. Had they decided instead that the plantation belonged to Jefferson Davis, it would have been confiscated.

But the waning days of Reconstruction were times filled with such ironies: of governments "redeemed" by violence, of Fourteenth Amendment rights designed to protect black people being used by conservative courts to protect giant corporations, of reformers taking up other causes. Disowned by its northern supporters and unmourned by public opinion, Reconstruction was over.

chapter summary

Presidents Abraham Lincoln and Andrew Johnson and the Republican-dominated Congress each developed a program of Reconstruction to quickly restore the Confederate states to the Union.

- Lincoln's 10 percent plan required that 10 percent of qualified voters from 1860 swear an oath of loyalty to begin organizing state government.

- Following Lincoln's assassination, Andrew Johnson changed Lincoln's terms and lessened Reconstruction's requirements.

- The more radical Congress repudiated Johnson's state governments and eventually enacted its own program of Reconstruction, which included the principle of black suffrage.

  – Congress passed the Fourteenth and Fifteenth Amendments and also extended the life of the Freedmen's Bureau, a unique experiment in social welfare.

  – Congress rejected land reform, however, which would have provided the freedpeople with a greater economic stake.

  – The effort to remove Johnson from office through impeachment failed.

- The Radical governments in the South, led by black and white southerners and transplanted northerners, compiled a mixed record on matters such as racial equality, education, economic issues, and corruption.

- Reconstruction was a time of both joy and frustration for former slaves.

  – Former slaves took steps to reunite their families and establish black-controlled churches.

  – They evidenced a widespread desire for land and education.

  – Black resistance to the old system of labor led to the adoption of sharecropping.

  – The Freedmen's Bureau fostered these new working arrangements and also the beginnings of black education in the South.

- Northern public opinion became disillusioned with Reconstruction during the presidency of Ulysses S. Grant.

- Southern whites used violence, economic coercion, and racism to overthrow the Republican state governments.

- In 1877 Republican leaders agreed to end Reconstruction in exchange for Rutherford B. Hayes's election as president.

- Racism played a key role in the eventual failure of Reconstruction.

interactive learning

The Primary Source Investigator CD-ROM offers the following materials related to this chapter:

- Interactive maps: **Election of 1876** (M7) and **Barrow Plantation** (M18)

- A collection of primary sources concerning the United States at the close of the Civil War, including an interview with an ex-slave and an engraving of people celebrating the anniversary of the Emancipation Proclamation. Other sources demonstrate the extent to which African Americans' lives changed after the war and during Reconstruction, such as a picture of a black schoolhouse and a number of firsthand accounts of life after slavery. Several documents reveal increased attempts to restrict and punish newly emancipated slaves during Reconstruction, including examples of the black codes passed by many southern states.

additional reading

Historians' views of Reconstruction have dramatically changed in recent decades. Modern studies offer a more sympathetic assessment of Reconstruction and the experience of African Americans. Indicative of this trend is Eric Foner, *Reconstruction* (1988), the fullest modern treatment. Foner devotes considerable attention to black southerners' experiences but seriously neglects the North. The book is also available in an abridged edition.

Eric L. McKitrick, *Andrew Johnson and Reconstruction* (1966), while very critical of Johnson and his policies, argues that impeachment was unjustified. A different conclusion is reached by Michael Les Benedict in *The Impeachment and Trial of Andrew Johnson* (1973), which is the most thorough treatment of Congress's effort to remove Johnson from office. Political affairs in the South during Reconstruction are examined in Dan T. Carter, *When the War Was Over* (1985), and Thomas Holt, *Black over White* (1977), an imaginative study of black political leadership in South Carolina. Leon Litwack, *Been in the Storm So Long* (1979), and Willie Lee Rose, *Rehearsal for Reconstruction* (1964), sensitively analyze former slaves' transition to freedom, and James L. Roark, *Masters without Slaves* (1977), discusses former slaveholders' adjustment to the end of slavery. Two excellent studies of changing labor relations in southern agriculture are Julie Saville, *The Work of Reconstruction* (1995), and John Rodrique, *Reconstruction in the Cane Fields* (2001). George R. Bentley, *A History of the Freedmen's Bureau* (1955), is a sympathetic treatment of that unique institution; Donald Nieman, *To Set the Law in Motion: The Freedmen's Bureau and the Legal Rights of Blacks, 1865–1868* (1979), is more critical. Different perspectives on the overthrow of Reconstruction appear in William Gillette, *Retreat from Reconstruction, 1869–1879* (1980), which focuses on national politics and the federal government, and in Michael Perman, *The Road to Redemption* (1984), which looks at developments in the South. For a fuller list of readings, see the Bibliography at www.mhhe.com/davidsonnation5.

significant events

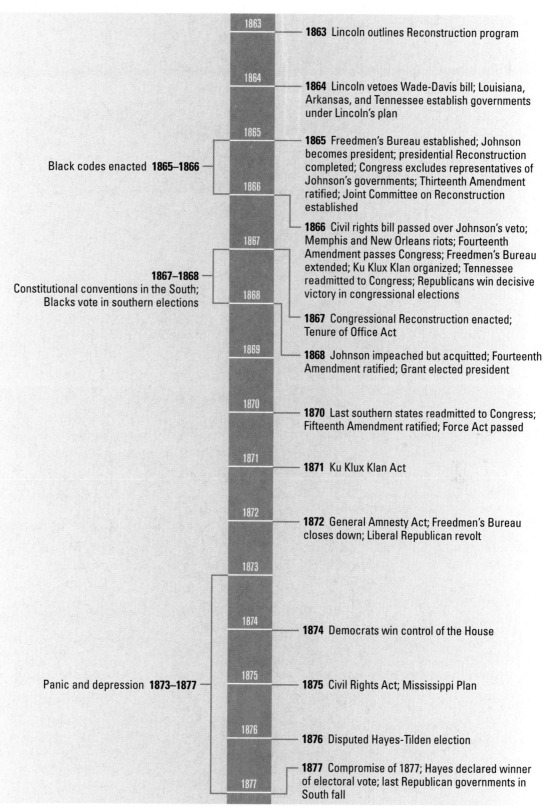

1863	**1863** Lincoln outlines Reconstruction program
1864	**1864** Lincoln vetoes Wade-Davis bill; Louisiana, Arkansas, and Tennessee establish governments under Lincoln's plan
1865	**1865** Freedmen's Bureau established; Johnson becomes president; presidential Reconstruction completed; Congress excludes representatives of Johnson's governments; Thirteenth Amendment ratified; Joint Committee on Reconstruction established
1866	
	1866 Civil rights bill passed over Johnson's veto; Memphis and New Orleans riots; Fourteenth Amendment passes Congress; Freedmen's Bureau extended; Ku Klux Klan organized; Tennessee readmitted to Congress; Republicans win decisive victory in congressional elections
1867	
1868	**1867** Congressional Reconstruction enacted; Tenure of Office Act
1869	**1868** Johnson impeached but acquitted; Fourteenth Amendment ratified; Grant elected president
1870	**1870** Last southern states readmitted to Congress; Fifteenth Amendment ratified; Force Act passed
1871	**1871** Ku Klux Klan Act
1872	**1872** General Amnesty Act; Freedmen's Bureau closes down; Liberal Republican revolt
1873	
1874	**1874** Democrats win control of the House
1875	**1875** Civil Rights Act; Mississippi Plan
1876	**1876** Disputed Hayes-Tilden election
1877	**1877** Compromise of 1877; Hayes declared winner of electoral vote; last Republican governments in South fall

Black codes enacted **1865–1866**

1867–1868
Constitutional conventions in the South;
Blacks vote in southern elections

Panic and depression **1873–1877**

THE UNITED STATES IN AN INDUSTRIAL AGE

The Statue of Liberty has now stood watch over New York harbor for more than a hundred years. Looking back today, most Americans view the tired, huddled masses who passed beneath Liberty's torch as part of the continuing stream of immigrants stretching back to the English Pilgrims, the French fur traders of Canada, and the Spanish friars of Old California. But the tide of immigration that swelled during the mid–nineteenth century was strikingly different from the great majority of those who traveled to America in an earlier age. Innovations in transportation, communications, and industry created an international network that for the first time made possible voluntary migration on a massive scale.

In the 300 years before 1820 most new arrivals in North and South America did not come voluntarily. Nearly 8 million Africans were brought to the Americas during those years, virtually all as slaves. That number was four to five times the number of Europeans who came during the same period. In contrast, between 1820 and 1920 nearly 30 million free immigrants arrived from Europe.

Nor was this new flood directed only toward America. At least as many Europeans settled in other regions of Europe or the world. From eastern Europe millions followed the Trans-Siberian Railway (completed in 1905) into Asiatic Russia. The Canadian prairie provinces of Manitoba and Saskatchewan competed for homesteaders with Montana and the Dakotas. And as cowboys began driving American steers to railheads for shipment east, gauchos in western Argentina were rounding up cattle to be shipped to Buenos Aires. Before 1900 two out of three emigrating Italians booked passage not for the United States but for Brazil or Argentina.

This broad movement could not have taken place without a global network of communication, markets, and transportation. By midcentury, urbanization and industrialization were well under way in both America and Europe. The British, who led in revolutionizing industry, also discovered its harsh side effects. Without efficient transportation, British urban workers were forced to live within walking distance of factories. The resulting overcrowding and filth were almost stupefying. Families jammed into dark, dingy row houses built with few windows. In the streets and alleys beyond, open sewers flowed with garbage. In London one construction engineer reported that the overflow from privies had collected to the depth of three feet in the cellars of nearby houses.

Spurred by a deadly cholera epidemic in 1848, social reformer Edwin Chadwick led a campaign to install a system of cheap iron pipes and tile drains to provide running water and sewers throughout major cities. In addition, French and German research during the 1860s and 1870s established the germ theory of disease, confirming the need for better sanitation.

Other urban planners admired the radical renovation of Paris begun in the 1850s by Baron Georges Haussmann. Haussmann's

GLOBAL EVENTS

Darwin's *On the Origin of Species* published
1859

Suez Canal completed
1869

Franco–Prussian War;
Britain produces half the world's pig iron
1870

Refrigerated ships permit
export of beef from Argentina
1876

Pogroms against
Russian Jews
spur emigration
1880s

1850   1860   1870   1880

GRANT   HAYES   GARFIELD   ARTHUR

1869
Transcontinental railroad completed

1876
Bell invents telephone

Rockefeller founds Standard Oil

1877
Reconstruction
ends

1853
Commodore Perry visits Japan

1881
American Federation of Labor founded

AMERICAN EVENTS

workers tore down the city's medieval fortress walls, widened major streets into boulevards, and set aside land for pleasant green parks. American cities had no ancient walls and fewer narrow roads, and Americans were often more willing to rebuild and enlarge. Their innovations led Europeans to adopt horse-drawn streetcars and, later, electric trolleys. With an intracity transportation network in place, the old "walking cities" were able to add suburbs, partially easing the crush of earlier industrial crowding.

As hubs of the new industrial networks, cities needed efficient links to raw materials as well as markets for their finished products. Much of the late nineteenth century can be seen as a scramble of Western nations for those natural resources and markets.

Miners combed the hills of California for gold in 1849, as they did two years later in Victoria, Australia. In South Africa, the rush was for diamonds discovered along the Vaal and Orange rivers and gold near present-day Johannesburg. In Canada, Argentina, Australia, and New Zealand, farmers and cattle ranchers moved steadily toward larger commercial operations. All these enterprises extracted value from previously untapped natural resources.

The end result of the scramble was the age of imperialism, as the European powers sought to dominate newly acquired colonies in Africa and Asia. The United States joined the rush somewhat late, in part because it was still extracting raw materials from its own "colonial" regions, the

booming West and the defeated South.

European imperialists sometimes justified their rule over nonwhite races in Darwinian fashion, as the survival of the fittest. "The path of progress is strewn with the wreck . . . of inferior races," one English professor proclaimed in 1900. British poet Rudyard Kipling even suggested that Europeans were making a noble sacrifice on behalf of their subject peoples. "Take up the White Man's Burden," he exhorted them. "Send forth the best ye breed—/ Go bind your sons to exile / To serve your captives' need."

But the burdens were far greater for the coolie laborers of Kipling's India, who died by the thousands clearing jungles for tea plantations. Imperialism's costs were also

GLOBAL EVENTS

Berlin Conference concluded;
European powers partition Africa;
Indian National Congress

Slavery abolished
in Brazil
1888

Germany enacts a social security system;
Japan establishes the Meiji Constitution
1889

Boxer Rebellion in China;
Freud's *Interpretation of Dreams* published

Outbreak of
Russo–Japanese War;
Social welfare legislation
in France
1904

Spanish–American War
1898

| 1885 | 1890 | 1895 | 1900 |
| CLEVELAND | HARRISON | CLEVELAND | McKINLEY | ROOSEVELT |

Sherman Antitrust Act

1897
First U.S. subway opens
(Boston)

1901
J. P. Morgan creates
U.S. Steel

1896
Plessy v. Ferguson
upholds segregation

Carnegie Steel produces
more steel than all Great
Britain

Twain's *Huckleberry Finn* published

1893
Three-year depression begins

AMERICAN EVENTS

harsh for black miners laboring in South Africa and for Chinese workers in Australia and the United States who found themselves excluded and segregated after both gold rushes. A similar racialism—the widely accepted practice of categorizing and ranking people according to race—thwarted southern black sharecroppers in the United States and made it easier for successive waves of prospectors, cowhands, and sodbusters to drive American Indians off their lands.

The racial undercurrent of both European imperialism and American expansion was something most white Americans of the era ignored. But farmers in both the South and the West did lash out at industrial "robber barons" and railroad "monopolists." These business leaders seemed to epitomize the abuses of the new industrial order. As we shall see, the underlying causes of the era's social strain could not be so conveniently placed at the door of a few greedy villains.

PART FOUR

GLOBAL EVENTS

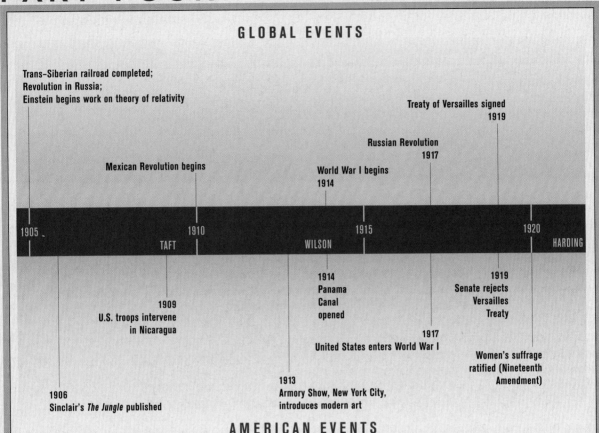

Trans–Siberian railroad completed;
Revolution in Russia;
Einstein begins work on theory of relativity

Treaty of Versailles signed
1919

Russian Revolution
1917

Mexican Revolution begins

World War I begins
1914

| 1905 | 1910 | 1915 | 1920 |
| TAFT | | WILSON | HARDING |

1914
Panama
Canal
opened

1919
Senate rejects
Versailles
Treaty

1909
U.S. troops intervene
in Nicaragua

1917
United States enters World War I

Women's suffrage
ratified (Nineteenth
Amendment)

1906
Sinclair's *The Jungle* published

1913
Armory Show, New York City,
introduces modern art

AMERICAN EVENTS

Industrialization created a whole new order of complex, interlocking systems that fostered an increasingly stratified society.

Just as cotton farmers in the American South found themselves in debt to merchants who charged exorbitant interest rates, small cotton growers in India, Egypt, and Brazil faced similar pressures. A global industrial system determined prices and wages in ways that frustrated and baffled ordinary workers. One official, traveling into the "more distant parts of the cotton-growing tracts of [India's] Provinces," reported that growers there found "some difficulty in realizing the present state of the trade, and the fact that, by means of the Electric Telegraph, the throbbings of the pulse of the Home markets communicate themselves instantly to Hingunghat and other trade centres throughout the country." They attributed sudden rises and falls in the price of cotton to "war" or "luck" or perhaps a demand for cotton because "the Queen had given every one in England new clothes" on the occasion of a royal wedding.

The social strains arising out of such wrenching changes forced political systems to adjust as well. In the United States both Populist and Progressive reformers called on the government to play a more active part in managing the excesses of the new industrial order. In Europe, both radical reformers like Karl Marx and more moderate socialists pushed for change. As strikes became more common and labor unions more powerful, industrializing nations passed social legislation that included the first social security systems and health insurance. In the end, however, the political system was unable to manage the new global order of commerce and imperialism. With the coming of World War I, it was shaken to its roots.

Chapter 18

T
he news spread across the South during the late 1870s. Perhaps a man came around with a handbill telling of cheap land, or a letter might arrive from friends or relatives and be read aloud at church. The news spread in different ways, but in the end, it always spelled Kansas.

Few black farmers had been that far west themselves. More than a few knew that the abolitionist Old John Brown had made his home in Kansas before coming east to raid Harpers Ferry. Black folks, it seemed, might be able to live more freely in Kansas. "You can buy land at from a dollar and a half to two dollars an acre," wrote one settler to his friend in Louisiana. There was another distinct advantage: "They do not kill Negroes here for voting."

In 1878 such prospects excited hundreds of black families already stretched to their limits by hardship and violence. With Rutherford Hayes president, Reconstruction was at an end. Southern state governments had been "redeemed" by conservative whites, and the future seemed uncertain. "COME WEST," concluded *The Colored Citizen,* a newspaper in Topeka. "COME TO KANSAS."

The New South & The Trans-Mississippi West

1870–1896

preview • In the decades following Reconstruction, the South and the West became more tightly linked to the economy of the Northeast. Both regions supplied the agricultural goods and raw materials that fueled urban and industrial growth in the northeastern and north central states. Tragically, both were also racially divided societies in which whites often used violence to assert their dominance.

St. Louis learned of these rumblings in the first raw days of March 1879, as steamers from downriver began unloading freedpeople in large numbers. Some came with belongings and money; others, with only the clothes on their backs. While the weather was still cold, they sought shelter beneath tarpaulins along the river levee, built fires by the shore, and got out frying pans to cook meals while their children jumped rope nearby. By the end of 1879, more than 20,000 had arrived.

When the crowds overwhelmed the wharves and temporary shelters, the city's black churches banded together to house the "refugees," feed them, and help them continue toward Kansas. Repeated rumors that rail passage would not be free failed to shake their hopes. "We's like de chilun ob Israel when dey was led from out o' bondage by Moses," one explained, referring to the Bible's tale of exodus from Egypt. So the "Exodusters," as they became known, pressed westward.

The Exodusters

In the end, more black emigrants settled in growing towns like Topeka, Lincoln, and Kansas City. Men worked as hired hands; women took in laundry. With luck, couples made $350 a year, saved a bit for a home, and put down roots. Bill Sims, an emigrant who settled in Ottawa, Kansas, put down roots literally—working at tree husbandry for a living. By the 1930s, when he was in his nineties, he could boast that his oldest daughter had been the "first colored girl to ever graduate" from Ottawa University. On the courthouse grounds at the center of town, the trees he had planted years before were still standing, a silent monument to his place in the community.

Sims and the host of Exodusters who poured into Kansas were part of a human flood westward. It had many sources—played-out farms of New England and the South, crowded cities, all of Europe. In 1879, as African Americans traveled up the

Benjamin Singleton and S. A. McClure pose in front of a riverboat as they prepare to leave Nashville, Tennessee, for Kansas on April 15, 1876. The crush of people on and around the boat offers graphic evidence of the lure of the West for African Americans and others in search of a fresh start.

Mississippi to St. Louis, 1000 white emigrants arrived in Kansas every week. Special trains brought settlers to the plains, all eager to start anew. During the 1880s the number of Kansans jumped from a million to a million and a half. Other western states experienced similar booms.

The optimism of boomers black and white could not mask the serious strains in the rapidly expanding nation, especially in the South and the trans-Mississippi West. As largely agricultural regions, they struggled to find their place in the new age of industry emerging from Reconstruction. In the South, despite a strong push to industrialize, the continuing dominance of white supremacy undercut economic growth, encouraging the scourge of sharecropping and farm tenancy and spawning a system of racial violence and caste to replace slavery. For its part, the booming West began to realize at least some of the dreams of antebellum reformers: for free homesteads in Kansas and beyond, for a railroad that spanned the continent, for land-grant colleges to educate its people. Yet the West, too, built a society based on racial violence and caste.

Much as the national markets emerging after the War of 1812 drew the lands beyond the Appalachian Mountains into their economic orbit, the industrial economy emerging after the Civil War incorporated the South and the trans-Mississippi region as well. By the end of the nineteenth century, both the South and West had assumed their place as suppliers of raw materials, providers of foodstuffs, and consumers of finished goods. A nation of "regional nations" was thus knit together in

Relations between the South, West, and Northeast

the last third of the nineteenth century. Not all southerners and westerners were happy with the result. As we shall see in Chapter 21, their frustrations mounted as the Northeast enriched itself at their expense and the powers in Washington ignored their plight.

The Southern Burden

Inequities between the agricultural South and the industrial North infuriated Henry Grady, the editor of the *Atlanta Constitution.* Grady often liked to tell the story of the poor cotton farmer buried in a pine coffin in the pine woods of Georgia. Except the coffin hadn't been made in Georgia but in Cincinnati. The nails in the coffin had been forged in Pittsburgh, though an iron mine lay near the Georgia cemetery. Even the farmer's cotton coat was made in New York and his trousers in Chicago. The "South didn't furnish a thing on earth for that funeral but the corpse and the hole in the ground!" fumed Grady. The irony of the story was the tragedy of the South. The region had human and natural resources aplenty but, alas, few factories to manufacture the goods it needed.

The gospel of a "New South"

In the 1880s Grady campaigned to bring about a "New South" of bustling industry, cities, and commerce. The business class and its values would displace the old planter class as southerners raced "to out-Yankee the Yankee." Grady and other publicists recognized the South's potential. Extending from Delaware south to Florida and west to Texas, the region took in a third of the nation's total area. It held a third of its arable farmlands, vast tracts of lumber, and rich deposits of coal, iron, oil, and fertilizers. To overcome the destruction of the Civil War and the loss of slaveholding wealth, apostles of the New South campaigned to catch up with the industrial North.

Yet no amount of hopeful talk could change the economic structure of southern society that had emerged from the Civil War—decentralized, rural, and agricultural. As late as 1890 the census counted less than 10 percent of all southerners as urban dwellers, compared with more than 50 percent in the North Atlantic states. Well into the twentieth century, Grady's New South remained the poorest section of the country. And the South suffered as well the burden of an unwieldy labor system that was often unskilled, usually underpaid, and always divided along lines of race.

Agriculture in the New South

A cotton-dominated economy

For all the talk of industry, the economy of the postwar South remained agricultural, tied to crops like tobacco, rice, sugar, and especially cotton. By using fertilizers, planters were able to introduce cotton into areas once considered marginal. The number of acres planted in cotton more than doubled between 1870 and 1900. Some southern farmers sought prosperity in crops other than cotton. George Washington Carver, of Alabama's Tuskegee Institute (page 683), persuaded many poor black farmers to plant peanuts. But most southern soils were too acidic and the spring rains too heavy for other legumes and grains to flourish. Parasites and diseases plagued cattle herds. Work animals like mules were raised more cheaply in other regions. Try as southerners might to diversify, cotton still dominated their economy. "When southern cotton prices drop, every man feels the blow," noted one observer. "When southern cotton prices advance, every industry thrives with vigor."

From 1880 to 1900 world demand for cotton grew slowly, and prices fell. As farms in other parts of the country were becoming larger and more efficient and were tended by fewer workers per acre, southern farms decreased in size. This decrease reflected the breakup of large plantations, but it also resulted from a high birthrate. Across the country, the number of children born per mother was dropping, but in the South, large families remained common because more children meant more farmhands. Each year, fewer acres of land were available for each person to cultivate. Even though the southern economy kept pace with national growth, per capita income fell behind.

Tenancy and Sharecropping

To freedpeople across the South, the end of slavery brought hopes of economic independence. Surely John Solomon Lewis was one such hopeful soul. After the war Lewis rented land to grow cotton in Tensas Parish, Louisiana. A depression in the 1870s dashed his dreams. "I was in debt," Lewis explained, "and the man I rented land from said every year I must rent again to pay the other year, and so I rents and rents and each year I gets deeper and deeper in debt."

After the Civil War, African Americans marked their freedom by ending field labor for most women and children. The women instead played a vital role in the domestic economy. Home garden plots supplemented the family food supply.

The dream of economic independence was rooted in a theory of landholding called the "agricultural ladder," in vogue after the Civil War. According to this theory, any poor man could work his way up, rung by rung, until he finally owned his own land. Each rung in the agricultural ladder brought greater autonomy and—with it—the chance to achieve self-sufficiency and independence. At the bottom was the hired hand, who worked for wages on someone else's farm. On the next rung, the sharecropper was paid no wages but instead received a share of the proceeds when the owner sold the harvest, about half minus whatever debts had been incurred. The tenant, higher still, rented a parcel of land, had his own tools and work animals, and owned the crop itself. As rent, the tenant turned over part of the harvest, usually a quarter of the cotton crop and a third of any grains, to the landowner. Through ruthless penny-pinching, the tenant eventually could purchase land and rise finally to the status of independent farmer.

Agricultural ladder

In practice, harsh realities overwhelmed theory, as John Solomon Lewis and other poor farmers—black and white—learned. Most of the best land in the South remained in the hands of large plantation owners. Few freedpeople or poor whites ever had enough money to acquire property. The problem lay in a ruinous system of credit. The harvest, whether produced by croppers or tenants or even small, independent farmers, was rarely enough for the worker to make ends meet, let alone to pay off debts and move up the agricultural ladder. Most farmers had to borrow money in the spring just to buy seeds, tools, or necessities such as food and clothing. Usually the only source of supplies and credit was the country store.

Crop-lien system

When John Solomon Lewis and other tenants entered the store, they saw two prices, one for cash and one for credit. The credit price might be as much as 60 percent higher. (Creditors justified the difference on the grounds that high interest rates protected them against the high numbers of unpaid loans.) As security for

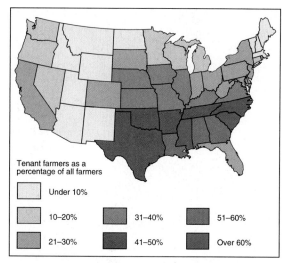

Tenant Farmers, 1900 Tenant farming dominated southern agriculture after the Civil War. But notice that by 1900 it also accounted for much of the farm labor in the trans-Mississippi West, where low crop prices, high costs, and severe environmental conditions forced independent farmers into tenancy.

Debt peonage in India, Egypt, and Brazil

Boom in textiles

the loan, independent farmers mortgaged their land and soon slipped into tenancy as debts mounted and creditors foreclosed on their farms. The only asset tenants had was the crop they owned or the share they received. So they put up a mortgage or "lien" on the crop. The lien gave the shop-keeper first claim on the crop until the debt was paid.

Across the South, sharecropping and crop liens reduced many farmers to virtual slavery by shackling them to perpetual debt. Year after year, they rented or worked the land and borrowed against their future returns until they found themselves so deeply in debt that they could never escape. This economic dependence, known as debt peonage, turned the agricultural ladder into an agricultural slide, robbing small farmers of their land and sending them to the bottom rungs of tenancy, sharecropping, and migrant farm work. By the 1880s three of every four African American farmers in the black belt states of Mississippi, Alabama, and Georgia were croppers. Twenty years later, a majority of southern white farmers had fallen into sharecropping. Few had the freedom to move up. The landlord or shopkeeper (often the same person) could insist that tenants grow only cash crops such as cotton rather than produce they could eat. Most landlords also required that cotton be ginned, baled, and marketed through their mills—at rates they controlled. Sharecropping, crop liens, and monopolies on ginning and marketing added up to inequality and crushing poverty for the small farmers of the South, black or white.

The slide of sharecroppers and tenants into debt peonage occurred elsewhere in the cotton-growing world. In India, Egypt, and Brazil agricultural laborers gave up subsistence farming to raise cotton as a cash crop during the American Civil War, when the North prevented southern cotton from being exported to textile manufacturers in Europe. New railroad and telegraph lines built in these new growing regions helped make the export of cotton more efficient. But when prices fell, growers borrowed to make ends meet, as in the American South. In India money-lenders charged interest as high as 24 percent annually on such debts; in Egypt the rates soared sometimes to 60 percent. The pressures on cotton growers led them to revolt in the mid-1870s. In India growers attacked prominent money-lenders, while Brazilian protesters destroyed land records and refused to pay taxes. As we shall see in Chapter 21, American farmers rose up too, in the 1890s.

Southern Industry

The crusade for a New South did bring change. From 1869 to 1909, industrial production grew faster than the national rate. So did productivity for southern workers. A boom in railroad building after 1879 furnished the region with good transportation. In two areas, cotton textiles and tobacco, southern advances were striking. With cotton fiber and cheap labor close at hand, 400 cotton mills were humming by 1900, when they employed almost 100,000 workers.

Most new textile workers were poor white southerners escaping competition from black farm laborers or fleeing the hardscrabble life of the mountains. Entire families worked in the mills. Older men had the most trouble adjusting. They lacked the experience, temperament, and dexterity to tend spindles and looms in cramped mills. Only over time, as farm folk adapted to the tedious rhythm of

This girl had been working in a cotton mill in Whitnel, North Carolina, for about a year, sometimes on the night shift. She made 48 cents a day. When asked how old she was, she hesitated, then said, "I don't remember." But then she added, confidentially, "I'm not old enough to work, but do just the same."

factories, did southerners become competitive with workers from other regions of the United States and western Europe.

Tobacco and cigarettes

The tobacco industry also thrived in the New South. Before the Civil War, American tastes had run to cigars, snuff, and chewing tobacco. In 1876, James Bonsack, an 18-year-old Virginian, invented a machine to roll cigarettes. That was just the device Washington Duke and his son James needed to boost the fortunes of their growing tobacco business. Cigarettes suited the new urban market in the North. Unlike chewing tobacco and snuff, they were, according to one observer, "clean, quick, and potent."

Between 1860 and 1900, the annual rate of tobacco consumption nearly quadrupled. Americans spent more money on tobacco than on clothes or shoes. The sudden interest in smoking offered southerners a rare opportunity to control a national market. But the factories were so hot, the stench of tobacco so strong, and the work so exhausting that native-born white southerners generally refused the jobs. Duke solved the labor problem by hiring Jewish immigrants, experts in making cigars, to train black southerners in the techniques of tobacco work. Then he promoted cigarettes in a national advertising campaign, using gimmicks like collectible picture cards. By the 1890s his American Tobacco Company led the industry.

Limited growth

The growth of the textile and tobacco industries encouraged urbanization and investment in regional development. But investment and urbanization could not by themselves lift the region from poverty. Low wages reflected the pattern of southern agriculture rather than the higher wage patterns of industries in the Northeast and upper Midwest. As immigrants flooded into those regions, they created skilled workforces and expanded markets. Low wages discouraged them from settling in the South. Isolated from the international labor pool, the southern labor force grew almost exclusively from natural increase.

Timber and Steel

The realities of southern economic life were more accurately reflected in lumber and steel than in tobacco and textiles. After the Civil War, the South possessed more than 60 percent of the nation's timber resources. With soaring demand from towns and cities, lumber and turpentine became the South's chief industries and employers. If anything, however, aggressive lumbering left the South far poorer. Corruption of state officials and a relaxed federal timber policy allowed northerners and foreigners to acquire huge forest tracts at artificially low prices. The timber was then sold as raw lumber rather than as more profitable finished products such as cedar shingles or newsprint (or the coffins Henry Grady liked to mention). Only in North Carolina did the manufacture of furniture flourish.

Aggressive logging added little to local economies. Logging camps were isolated and temporary. Visitors described the lumberjacks as "single, homeless, and possessionless." Once loggers leveled the forests around their camps, they moved on to other sites. Most sawmills operated for only a few years before the owners followed the loggers to a new area. Thus loggers and millers had little time to put down roots and invest their cash in the community.

Environmental costs

The environmental costs were equally high. In the South, as elsewhere, overcutting and other logging practices stripped hillsides bare. As spring rains eroded soil and unleashed floods, forests lost their capacity for self-renewal. By 1901 a Georgian complained that "from most of the visible land the timber is entirely gone." With it went the golden eagles, the peregrine falcons, and other native species of wildlife.

Turpentine mills, logging, and lumber milling provided young black southerners with their greatest source of employment. Occasionally an African American rose to be a supervisor, though most supervisors were white. Because the work was dirty and dangerous and required few skills, turnover was high and morale low. Southerners often blamed the workers, not the operators, for the industry's low standards. As one critic complained, "The sawmill negro is rather shiftless and is not inclined to stay in any one location and consequently there is little incentive on the part of the owner or operator to carry on welfare work in any extensive manner." In fact, most black workers left the mills in search of higher wages or to sharecrop in order to marry and support families.

This railroad served a lumber mill. The lumber industry in the South exploited large stands of timber, but overcutting led to erosion and tended to impoverish the region.

The iron and steel industry most disappointed promoters of the New South. The availability of coke as a fuel made Chattanooga, Tennessee, and Birmingham, Alabama, major centers for foundries. By the 1890s the Tennessee Coal, Iron, and Railway Company (TCI) of Birmingham was turning out iron pipe for gas, water, and sewer lines vital to cities. Unfortunately Birmingham's iron deposits were ill-suited for the kinds of steel in demand. In 1907 the financially strapped TCI was sold to the giant U.S. Steel Corporation, controlled by northern interests.

Birmingham steel

The pattern of lost opportunity was repeated in other southern industries—mining, chemical fertilizers, cottonseed oil, and railroads. Under the campaign for a New South, all grew dramatically in employment and value, but not enough to end poverty or industrialize the region. The South remained largely rural, agricultural, and poor.

The Sources of Southern Poverty

Why did poverty persist in the New South? Many southerners claimed that the region was exploited by outside interests. In effect, they argued, the South became a colonial economy controlled by business interests in New York or Pittsburgh rather than Atlanta or New Orleans. Raw materials such as minerals, timber, and cotton were shipped to other regions, which earned larger profits by turning them into finished goods. Profits that might have been used to foster development in the South were thereby siphoned off to other regions.

Three other factors also contributed to the region's poverty. First, the South began to industrialize later than the Northeast. Northern workers produced more not because they were more energetic or disciplined but because they were more experienced. Once southern workers overcame their inexperience, they competed well.

Late start in industrializing

Second, the South commanded only a small technological community to guide its industrial development. Northern engineers and mechanics seldom followed northern capital into the region. Few people were available to adapt modern technology to southern conditions or to teach southerners how to do it themselves.

Education might have overcome the problem by upgrading the region's workforce. But no region in the nation spent less on schooling than did the South. Southern leaders, drawn from the ranks of the upper class, cared little about educating ordinary white residents and openly resisted educating black southerners. Education, they contended, "spoiled" workers by leading them to demand higher wages and better conditions. In fact, the region's low wages encouraged educated workers to leave the South for higher pay. Few southern states invested in technical colleges and engineering schools, and so none could match those of the North.

Undereducated labor

Lack of education aggravated a third source of southern poverty: the isolation of its labor force. In 1900 agriculture still dominated the southern economy. It required unskilled, low-paid sharecroppers and wage laborers. Southerners feared that outsiders, with their new ways, might spread discontent among workers. So southern states discouraged social services and opportunities that might have attracted human and financial resources. The South remained poor because it received too little, not too much, outside investment.

The isolated southern labor market

Many a southern man, noted a son of the region, loved "to toss down a pint of raw whiskey in a gulp, to fiddle and dance all night, to bite off the nose or gouge out the eye of a favorite enemy, to fight harder and love harder than the next man, to

Life in the New South

be known far and wide as a hell of a fellow." Life in the New South was a constant struggle to balance this love of the vigorous life with the equally powerful pull of Christian piety.

Divided in its soul, the South was also divided by race. Even after the Civil War ended slavery, some 90 percent of African Americans continued to live in the rural South. Without slavery, however, southerners lost the system of social control that had defined race relations. Over time they substituted a new system of racial separation that eased, but never eliminated, white fear of African Americans.

Rural Life

Pleasure, piety, race—all divided southern life, in town and country alike. And life separated along lines of gender as well, especially in the rural areas where most southerners lived.

Hunting

Southern males found one source of pleasure in hunting. Hunting offered men welcome relief from heavy farm work. For rural people a successful hunt could also add meat and fish to a scanty diet. And through hunting many boys found a path to manhood. Seeing his father and brothers return with wild turkeys, young Edward McIlhenny longed for "the time when I would be old enough to hunt this bird." The prospect of danger, perhaps a fall from a horse, only added to the excitement.

The thrill of illicit pleasure also drew many southern men to events of violence and chance, including cockfighting. They valued combative birds and were convinced that their champions fought more boldly than did northern bantams. Gambling doubtless heightened the thrills. Such sport offended churchgoing southerners by its cruelty and wantonness. They condemned as sinful "the beer garden, the base ball, the low theater, the dog fight and cock fight and the ring for the pugilist and brute."

Farm entertainments

Many southern customs involved no such disorderly behavior. Work-sharing festivals such as house raisings, log rollings, quiltings, and road work gave isolated farm folk the chance to break their daily routine, to socialize, and to work for a common good. These events, too, were generally segregated along gender lines. Men did the heavy chores and competed in contests of physical prowess. Women shared more domestic tasks. Community gatherings also offered young southerners a relaxed place for courtship. In one courting game, the young man who found a rare red ear of corn "could kiss the lady of his choice"—although in the school, church, or home under adult supervision, such behavior was discouraged.

Town

For rural folk, a trip to town brought special excitement, along with a bit of danger. Saturdays, court days, and holidays provided an occasion to mingle. Once again, there were male and female domains. For men the saloon, the blacksmith shop, or the storefront was a place to do business and to let off steam. Few men went to town without participating in social drinking, but when men turned to roam the streets, the threat of brawling and violence drove most women away.

Court week, when a district judge arrived to mete out justice, drew the biggest crowds. Some people came to settle disputes; most came to enjoy the spectacle or do some business like horse trading. Peddlers and entertainers worked the crowds with magic tricks, patent medicines, and other wares. Town also offered a chance to attend the theater or a traveling circus.

The Church

At the center of southern life stood the church as a great stabilizer and custodian of social order. "When one joined the Methodist church," a southern woman remembered, "he was expected to give up all such things as cards, dancing, theatres, in fact all so called worldly amusements." Many devout southerners pursued these ideals, although such restraint asked more of people than many were willing to show, except perhaps on Sunday.

Congregations were often so small and isolated that they could attract a preacher only once or twice a month. Evangelicals counted on the Sunday sermon to steer them from sin. In town, a sermon might last 30 to 45 minutes, but in the country, a preacher could go on for two hours or more, whipping up his congregation until "even the little children wept."

Rural religion

By 1870 southern churches were segregated by race. Indeed, the black church was the only institution controlled by African Americans after slavery and thus a principal source of leadership and identity in addition to comfort (page 547). Within churches both black and white, congregations were segregated by gender, too. As a boy entered manhood, he moved from the female to the male section. Yet churches were, at base, female domains. Considered guardians of virtue, more women were members, attended services, and ran church activities.

Church was a place to socialize as well as worship. Many of the young went simply to meet those of the opposite sex. Church picnics and all-day sings brought as many as 30 or 40 young people together for hours of eating, talk, services, and hymn singing. Still, these occasions could not match the fervor of a weeklong camp meeting. In the late summer or early fall, town and countryside alike emptied as folks set up tents in shady groves and listened to two or three ministers preach day and night in the largest event of the year. The camp meeting refired evangelical faith while celebrating traditional values of home and family.

For Baptists in the South, both white and black, the ceremony of adult baptism included total immersion, often in a nearby river. The ritual symbolized the waters of newfound faith washing away sins that had been forgiven by God's free grace. Here, a black congregation looks on, some holding umbrellas to protect against the sun.

Segregation

Nothing challenged tradition in the post–Civil War South more than race. With the abolition of slavery and the end of Reconstruction, white northerners and southerners achieved sectional harmony by sacrificing the rights of black citizens. During the 1880s, Redeemer governments (pages 535–536) moved to formalize a new system of segregation or racial separation. Redeemers were Democratic politicians who came to power in southern states to end the Republican rule established during Reconstruction. They were eager to reap the benefits of economic expansion and to attract the business classes—bankers, railroad promoters, industrial operators. As their part of the bargain, the Redeemers assured anxious northerners that Redeemer rule would not mean political disfranchisement of the freedpeople. That promise they would not keep.

Pressure to reach a new racial accommodation in the South increased as more African Americans moved into southern towns and cities, competing for jobs with poor whites. One way to preserve the social and economic superiority of white southerners, poor as well as rich, was to separate blacks as an inferior caste. But federal laws designed to enforce the Civil Rights Act of 1866 and the Fourteenth Amendment stood in the way. In effect, these laws established social equality for all races in public gathering places such as hotels, theaters, and railroads.

In 1883, however, the Supreme Court ruled (in the *Civil Rights Cases*) that hotels and railroads were not "public" institutions because private individuals owned them. The Fourteenth Amendment was thus limited to protecting citizens from violations of their civil rights by states, not by private individuals. The national policy of laissez faire in race relations could not have been made any clearer.

A long line of African American voters waits to cast ballots in Caddo Parish, Louisiana, in 1894. Clearly, interest in voting remained high among black citizens. Two years later Louisiana followed the lead of other Southern states in disfranchising most of its black voters (as well as many poor whites).

Within 20 years every southern state had enacted segregation as law. The earliest laws legalized segregation in trains and other such public conveyances where blacks and whites were likely to mingle. Soon a complex web of Jim Crow statutes had drawn an indelible color line separating the races in prisons, parks, hotels, restaurants, hospitals, and virtually all public gathering places except streets and stores. (The term *Jim Crow*, used to denote a policy of segregation, originated in a song of the same name sung in minstrel shows of the day.)

Jim Crow laws

In 1892, African American leaders in Louisiana decided to challenge the legality of segregation. Homer Adolph Plessy, an African American, agreed to test a state law requiring segregated railroad facilities by sitting in the all-white section of a local train. He was promptly arrested, and state judge John H. Ferguson ruled against him. Slowly the case of *Plessy v. Ferguson* worked its way up to the Supreme Court. In 1896, the Court ruled that segregation did not constitute discrimination as long as accommodations for both races were "separate but equal." Justice John Marshall Harlan (ironically from a former slaveholding family) issued the lone dissent: separate, whether equal or not, was always a "badge of servitude" and a violation of the "color-blind" Constitution. Harlan's dissent was in vain: the doctrine of separate but equal became part of the fabric of American law and governed race relations for more than half a century to come. When coupled with a growing campaign in the 1890s to disfranchise black voters across the South (see page 682), segregation provided a formidable barrier to African American progress.

Plessy v. Ferguson

By the turn of the century segregation was firmly in place, stifling economic competition between the races and reducing African Americans to second-class citizenship. Many kinds of employment, such as work in the textile mills, went largely to whites. Skilled and professional black workers generally served black clients. African Americans were barred from juries and usually received far stiffer penalties than whites for the same crimes.

Spending on Education in the South before and after Disfranchisement With disfranchisement and segregation, education was separate, but hardly equal, for blacks and whites. In these states, after blacks were disfranchised, spending on white students rose while spending on black students decreased.

[*Source:* Data from Robert A. Margo, *Disfranchisement, School Finance, and the Economics of Segregated Schools in the U.S. South, 1890–1910* (New York: Garland Press, 1985), table I-1.]

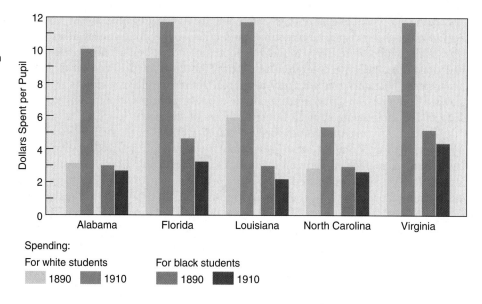

Spending:

For white students		For black students	
▨ 1890	▨ 1910	▨ 1890	▨ 1910

As Jim Crow laws became entrenched, so did social custom. Black southerners always addressed white southerners as Mister, Miss, and Ma'am—even those of lower status. But white southerners called black southerners by their first names or more simply Sister or Boy, no matter their age or profession. Any African American who crossed the color line risked violence. Some were tarred and feathered, others whipped and beaten, and many lynched. Of the 187 lynchings averaged each year of the 1890s, some 80 percent occurred in the South. The victims were almost always African Americans.

Western Frontiers

The black Exodusters flooding into Kansas in the 1870s and 1880s were only part of the vast migration west. Looking beyond the Mississippi in the 1840s and 1850s, white "overlanders" had set their sights on California and Oregon and the promise of land. They headed across the Mississippi River, pushing the frontier of Anglo settlement to the edge of the continent.

The overlanders went west in search of opportunity and "free" land. They found opportunity elusive to those without money or power. They also found Indians—perhaps as many as 360,000—and "Hispanos," settlers of Spanish descent, who hardly considered the land free for use by Anglos.

Moving frontiers

The overlanders discovered as well that the West was not one region but many, each governed by a different ecology. And its frontiers moved in many directions, not just from east to west. Before the Civil War, the frontier for easterners had moved beyond the Mississippi to the timberlands of Missouri but skipped over the Great Plains, as the overlanders settled in California and Oregon. But another frontier then pushed east from the Pacific coast, following miners into the Sierra Nevada. For Texans, the frontier moved from south to north as cattle ranchers sought new grazing land, as had the ancestors of the Spanish rancheros of the Southwest. And for American Indians, these constantly shifting frontiers shaped and reshaped their ways of life.

Western Landscapes

Whatever perspective one adopts, the West is above all a place of varied landscapes. Early travelers from the United States labeled the vast region beyond the Mississippi the "Great American Desert." Most of the land between the 98th meridian and the lush lowlands of the West Coast receives less than 20 inches of rain a year, making the Great Plains a treeless expanse of prairie grass and dunes. Infrequent stands of timber cluster along river bottoms, and wood for housing and fences is scarce. Overlanders of the 1840s and 1850s compared its vast windy spaces to the oceans: a "sea of grass" stretching to the horizon and crossed by "prairie schooners."

Dry territory west of the 98th meridian

But the plains are only part of the trans-Mississippi West. And even they can be divided. The Great Plains west of the 98th meridian are semiarid, but the eastern Prairie Plains are favored with good soil and abundant rain. Beyond the plains the jagged peaks of the Rocky Mountains stretch from Alaska to New Mexico. And west of the mountains lies the Great Basin of Utah, Nevada, and eastern California. There temperatures climb above 100 degrees and the ground cracks. Near the coast rise the Sierra Nevada and Cascades, rich in minerals and lumber and sloping to the temperate shores and fertile valleys of the Pacific.

Easterners who watched the wagons roll west liked to conjure up the image of a "trackless wilderness." In truth, even in the 1840s, the Great Plains and mountain frontier comprised a complex web of cultures and environments in which Spanish, Anglo-American, and Indian cultures interacted and often produced swift change. One example is the horse, introduced into North America by the colonial Spanish. By the eighteenth century horses were grazing on prairie grass across the Great Plains. By the nineteenth century the Comanche, Cheyenne, Apache, and other tribes had become master riders and hunters who could shoot their arrows with deadly accuracy at a full gallop. The new mobility of the Plains Indians far extended the area in which they could hunt buffalo, which soon became a staple of their existence. Their lives shifted from settled, village-centered agriculture to nomadic hunting.

Indian Peoples and the Western Environment

Some whites embraced the myth of the Indian as "noble savage" who lived in perfect harmony with the natural world. To be sure, Plains Indians were inventive in using scarce resources. Cottonwood bark fed horses in winter, and the buffalo supplied not only meat but also bones for tools, fat for cosmetics, sinews for thread, even dung for fuel. Yet Indians could not help but shape their ecosystems. Plains Indians hunted buffalo by stampeding herds over cliffs, which often led to waste. They irrigated crops and set fires to improve vegetation and game. By the mid–nineteenth century some tribes had become so enmeshed in trade with whites that they overtrapped their own hunting grounds.

Ecosystems, in turn, helped to shape Indian cultures. Although big-game hunting was common among many western tribes, the nomadic buffalo culture of the Great Plains Indians was hardly representative. In the lush forests and mountain ranges of the Pacific Northwest, Yuroks, Chinook, and other tribes hunted bear, moose, elk, and deer. Along the rocky coast they took whales, seals, and a variety of fish from the ocean. The Yakamas and Walla Wallas moved into the river valleys for the great salmon runs. The early Hohokams and later the Pima and other

Variety of Indian cultures

The cultures of western Indians were remarkably varied, ranging from the nomadic Plains tribes to the more settled peoples of the northwest coast who lived off the sea. This Sioux woman gathers firewood; the photograph was taken by Edward Curtis, who spent many years recording the faces and lives of native peoples of the West.

tribes in New Mexico and Arizona developed irrigation to allow farming of beans, squash, and corn in the arid climate.

Despite their diversity, Indian peoples shared certain values. Most tribes were small extended kinship groups of 300 to 500 people in which the well-being of all outweighed the needs of each member. Although some tribes were better off than others, the gap between rich and poor within tribes was seldom large. Such small material differences often promoted communal decision making. The Cheyenne, for example, employed a council of 44 to advise the chief.

Indians also shared a reverence for nature, whatever their actual impact on the natural world. They believed human beings were part of an interconnected world of animals, plants, and other natural elements. All had souls of their own but were bound together, as if by contract, to live in balance through the ceremonial life of the tribe and the customs related to plants and animals. The Taos of New Mexico thought that each spring the pregnant earth issued new life. To avoid disturbing "mother" earth, they removed the hard shoes from their horses, while they themselves walked in bare feet or soft moccasins. Whites were mystified by the explanation of one chief for why his people refused to farm: "You ask me to plow the ground! Shall I take a knife and tear my mother's bosom? . . . You ask me to cut grass and make hay and sell it, and be rich like white men! But how dare I cut off my mother's hair?"

Regard for the land thus endowed special places with religious meaning often indecipherable to whites. Where the Sioux saw in the Black Hills the sacred home of Wakan Tanka—the burial place of the dead and the site of their vision quests—whites saw grass for grazing and gold for the taking. From such contrasting views came conflict.

Whites and the Western Environment: Competing Visions

As discoveries of gold and silver lured whites into Indian territory, many adopted the decidedly un-Indian outlook of Missouri politician William Gilpin. Only a lack of vision prevented the opening of the West for exploitation, Gilpin told an Independence, Missouri, audience in 1849. What were most needed were cheap lands and a railroad linking the two coasts "like ears on a human head." Distance, climate, topography, and even the Indians were mere obstacles.

By 1868 a generous Congress had granted western settlers their two greatest wishes: free land under the Homestead Act of 1862 and a transcontinental railroad. As the new governor of Colorado, Gilpin crowed about the region's limitless resources. One day, he believed, the West would support more than a billion people. Scarce rainfall and water did not daunt him, for in his eyes the West was an Eden-like garden, not "the great American Desert." Once the land had been planted, Gilpin assured listeners, the rains would develop naturally. He subscribed to the popular notion that "rain follows the plow," a myth sustained by an unusually wet cycle from 1878 to 1886. When the dry weather returned in the late 1880s, not rain but hardship followed farmers who moved west.

Unlike the visionary Gilpin, John Wesley Powell knew something about water and farming. After losing an arm in the Civil War, geologist Powell went west. In 1869 and 1871 he led scientific expeditions down the Green and

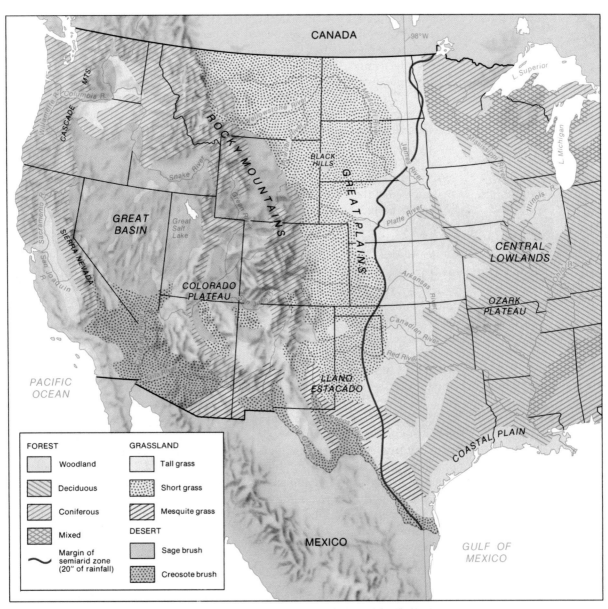

Natural Environment of the West With the exception of Oregon and Washington in the Pacific Northwest, few areas west of the 20-inch rainfall line receive enough annual precipitation to support agriculture without irrigation. Consequently, water has been the key to growth and development in the area west of the 98th meridian, which encompasses more than half the land area of the continental United States. The dominance of short grasses and coniferous (evergreen) trees reflects the rainfall patterns.

Colorado rivers through the Grand Canyon. Navigating the swirling rapids that blocked his way, he returned to warn Congress that developing the West required more scientific planning. Much of the region had not even been mapped or its resources identified.

In 1880 Powell became director of the recently formed U.S. Geological Survey. He, too, had a vision of the West, but one based on the limits of its environment.

Water as a key resource

The key was water, not land. In the water-rich East, the English legal tradition of river rights prevailed. Whoever owned the banks of a river or stream controlled as much water as they might take, regardless of the consequence for those downstream. Such a practice in the water-starved West, Powell recognized, would enrich the small number with access while spelling ruin for the rest.

The alternative was to treat water as community property. The practice would benefit many rather than a privileged few. To that end Powell suggested that the federal government establish political boundaries defined by watersheds and regulate the distribution of the scarce resource. But his scientific realism could not overcome the popular vision of the West as the American Eden. Powerful interests ensured that development occurred with the same helter-skelter, laissez-faire credo that captivated the East. The first to feel the effects of this unrestrained expansion would be the Indian and Latino residents of the region.

The War for the West

So marginal did federal officials consider the Great Plains that they left the lands to the Indians. By the end of the Civil War, some two-thirds of all Indian peoples lived on the Great Plains. Even before the war, a series of gold and silver discoveries beginning in 1848 signaled the first serious interest by white settlers in the arid and semiarid lands beyond the Mississippi. To open more land to white settlement and to protect the Indians from white settlers, federal officials introduced in 1851 a policy of "concentration." They pressed tribes to sign treaties limiting the boundaries of their hunting grounds to "reservations"—the Sioux to the Dakotas, the Crows to Montana, the Cheyenne to the foothills of Colorado—where they would be taught to farm.

Policy of concentration

Such treaties often claimed that their provisions would last "as long as waters run," but time after time, land-hungry pioneers broke the promises of their government by squatting on Indian lands and demanding federal protection. The government, in turn, forced more restrictive agreements on the western tribes. This cycle of promises made and broken continued, until a full-scale war for the West raged between whites and Indians.

Contact and Conflict

The policy of concentration began in the Pacific Northwest and produced some of the earliest clashes between whites and Indians. In an oft-repeated pattern, resistance led to war and war to Indian defeat. In the 1850s, as territorial governor Isaac Stevens was browbeating local tribes into giving up millions of acres in Washington Territory, a gold strike flooded the Indian homelands with miners. The tribes fought them off, only to be crushed and forced onto reservations.

In similar fashion, by 1862 the lands of the Santee Sioux had been whittled down to a strip 10 miles wide and 150 miles long along the Minnesota River. Lashing out in frustration, the tribe attacked several undefended white settlements along the Minnesota frontier. In response, General John Pope arrived in St. Paul declaring his intention to wipe out the Sioux. "They are to be treated as maniacs or wild beasts and by no means as people," he instructed his officers. When Pope's forces captured 1800 Sioux, white Minnesotans were outraged that President Lincoln ordered only 38 hanged.

The campaign under General Pope was the opening of a guerrilla war that continued on and off for some 30 years. The conflict gained momentum in 1864, when Governor John Evans of Colorado sought to end all land treaties with Indian peoples in eastern Colorado. In November, a force of 700 Colorado volunteers under Colonel John Chivington fell upon a band of friendly Cheyenne gathered at Sand Creek under army protection. Chief Black Kettle raised an American flag to signal friendship, but Chivington would have none of it. "Kill and scalp all, big and little," he told his men. The troops massacred at least 150, including children holding white flags of truce and mothers with babies in their arms. A joint congressional investigation later condemned Chivington. In 1865 virtually all Plains Indians joined in the First Sioux War to drive whites from their lands.

Chivington massacre

Among the soldiers who fought the Plains Indians were African American veterans of the Civil War. In 1866 two regiments of black soldiers were organized into the Ninth and Tenth Calvary under the command of white officers. Their Indian foes dubbed them "buffalo soldiers," reflecting the similarity they saw between the hair of African Americans and that of the buffalo. It was also a sign of hard-won respect. The buffalo soldiers fought Indians across the West for more than 20 years. They also subdued bandits, cattle thieves, and gunmen—from the rugged country of Big Bend to the badlands of South Dakota. And they helped to prepare the way for white settlement by laying the foundations for posts such as Fort Sill in Oklahoma and by locating water, wood, and grasslands for eager homesteaders.

Buffalo soldiers

War was only one of several ways in which white settlement undermined tribal cultures. Over the course of centuries only an estimated 4000 Indians (and about 7000 whites) were killed in direct warfare—a paltry few compared to the casualty lists of the Civil War. Far more devastating forces were at work. Disease, including smallpox, measles, and cholera, killed more Indians than combat did. Liquor furnished by white traders entrapped many a brave in a deadly cycle of alcoholism. Trading posts altered traditional ways of life with metal pots and pans, traps, coffee, and sugar but furnished no employment and thus few ways for their Indian customers to pay for these goods. Across the West mines, crops, grazing herds, and fences disturbed traditional hunting and farming lands of many tribes.

On the Great Plains the railroad disrupted the migratory patterns of the buffalo and thus the patterns of the hunt. When buffalo robes became popular in the East in the 1870s and hides became a source of leather for industrial belts, commercial companies hired hunters, who could kill more than 100 bison an hour. Military commanders promoted the butchery as a way of undermining Indian resistance. By 1883 bison had nearly disappeared from the plains (see After the Fact, "Where Have All the Bison Gone?" on pages 605–608). With them went a way of life that left the Plains Indians more vulnerable to white expansion.

Custer's Last Stand—and the Indians'

The Sioux War ended in 1868 with the signing of the Treaty of Fort Laramie. It established two large Indian reservations, one in Oklahoma and the other in the Dakota Badlands. Only six years later, however, in the summer of 1874, Colonel George Armstrong Custer led an expedition into *Paha Sapa*, the sacred Black Hills of the Sioux. In doing so, he flagrantly disregarded the treaty of 1868. Custer, a Civil War veteran, already had a reputation as a "squaw killer" for his

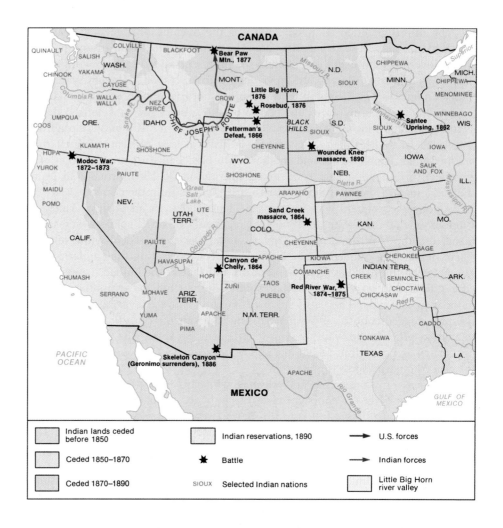

Legend

Indian lands ceded before 1850	Indian reservations, 1890	➡ U.S. forces
Ceded 1850–1870	✦ Battle	➡ Indian forces
Ceded 1870–1890	SIOUX Selected Indian nations	Little Big Horn river valley

The Indian Frontier As conflict erupted between Indian and white cultures in the West, the government sought increasingly to concentrate tribes on reservations. Resistance to the reservation concept helped unite the Sioux and Cheyenne, traditionally enemies, in the Dakotas during the 1870s. Along the Little Big Horn River, the impetuous Custer underestimated the strength of his Indian opponents and attacked before the supporting troops of Reno and Benteen were in a position to aid him.

cruel warfare against Indians in western Kansas. To open the Black Hills to whites, his expedition spread rumors of gold "from the grass roots down." Prospectors poured into Indian country. Once again, federal authorities tried to force a treaty to gain control of the Black Hills. When negotiations failed, President Grant ordered all "hostiles" in the area rounded up and driven onto the reservations.

In reaction the Cheyenne for the first time allied with the Sioux, led by a young war chief named Crazy Horse and medicine man Sitting Bull. Against them marched several army columns, including Custer's Seventh Cavalry, a force of about 600 troops. Custer, eager for glory, arrived at the Little Big Horn River a day earlier than the other columns. Hearing of a native village nearby, he attacked, only to discover that he had stumbled onto an encampment of more than 12,000 Sioux and Cheyenne extending for almost 3 miles. From a deep ravine Crazy Horse charged Custer, killing him and some 250 soldiers.

Battle of Little Big Horn

As he led the attack, Crazy Horse yelled "It is a good day to die!"—the traditional war cry. Even in the midst of victory he spoke truly. Although Custer had been conquered, railroads stood ready to extend their lines, prospectors to make fortunes, and soldiers to protect them. By late summer the Sioux were forced to split into small bands in order to evade the army. Sitting Bull barely escaped to Canada; Crazy Horse and 800 with him surrendered in 1876 after a winter of suffering and starvation.

The battles along the Platte and upper Missouri rivers did not end the war between whites and Indians, but never again would it reach such proportions. Even peaceful tribes like the Nez Percé of Idaho found no security once whites began to hunger for their land. The Nez Percé had become breeders of livestock, rich in horses and cattle that they grazed in the meadows west of the Snake River canyon. Their business enterprise did not prevent the government from trying to force them onto a small reservation in 1877.

Rather than see his people humiliated, Chief Joseph led almost 600 Nez Percé toward Canada, pursued by the U.S. Army. In just 75 days they traveled more than 1300 miles. Every time the army closed to attack, Chief Joseph and his warriors drove them off. But before the Nez Percé could reach the border, they were trapped and forced to surrender. Chief Joseph's words still ring with eloquence: "Hear me, my chiefs, I am tired; my heart is sick and sad. From where the sun now stands I will fight no more forever." The government then shipped the defeated tribe to the bleak Indian Country of Oklahoma. There disease and starvation finished the destruction begun by the army.

Chief Joseph

Killing with Kindness

Over these same years Indians saw their legal sovereignty being whittled away. Originally, federal authorities had treated various tribes as autonomous nations existing within the United States, with whom treaties could be made. That tribal status began shrinking in 1831, when the Supreme Court declared Indians "domestic dependent nations." Although the United States continued to negotiate treaties with the tribes, government officials began treating Indians as wards, with as little regard for them as for inept children. In 1869 President Grant created the Board of Indian Commissioners, whose members were chosen by Protestant churches to help settle conflicts with local tribes and to spread Christian values and white styles of living. Finally, in 1871, Congress abandoned the treaty system altogether and with it the legal core of Indian autonomy.

La Fleche and Jackson

Some whites and Indians spoke out against the tragedy taking place on the Great Plains. In the 1870s, Susette La Fleche, daughter of an Omaha chief, lectured eastern audiences about the mistreatment of Indian peoples and inspired reformers to action. Similarly moved, the poet Helen Hunt Jackson turned her energies to lobbying for Indian rights and attacking government policy. In 1881, she published *A Century of Dishonor*. The best-selling exposé detailed government fraud and corruption in dealing with Indians, as well as the many treaties broken by the United States.

Reformers began pressing for assimilation of Indians into white society, ironically as the only means of preserving Indians in a society that seemed bent on destroying them. The Women's National Indian Association, created in 1874, and the later Indian Rights Association, joined by Helen Hunt Jackson, sought to end the Indian way of life by suppressing communal activities, reeducating Indian children, and establishing individual homesteads.

Dawes Act

Reformers also recognized that the policy of concentrating Indians on reservations had failed. Deprived of their traditional lands and culture, reservation tribes became dependent on government aid. In any case, whites who coveted Indian lands were quick to violate treaty terms. With a mix of good intentions and unbridled greed, Congress adopted the Dawes Severalty Act in 1887. It ended reservation policy by permitting the president to distribute land to Indians who had severed their attachments to their tribes. The goals of the policy were simple: to draw Indians into white society as farmers and small property owners and (less high-mindedly) to bring Indian lands legally into the marketplace.

In practice, the Dawes Act was more destructive than any blow struck by the army. It undermined the communal structure on which Indian tribal life was based. Lands held by tribes would now be parceled out to individuals: 160 acres to the head of a family and 80 acres to single adults or orphans. But as John Wesley Powell had warned, small homestead farms in the West could not support a family—white or Indian—unless the farms were irrigated. Most Indians, moreover, had no experience with farming, managing money, or other white ways.

The sponsors of the Dawes Act, knowing that whites might swindle Indians out of their private holdings, arranged for the government to hold title to the land for 25 years. That arrangement did not stop unscrupulous speculators from "leasing" lands. Furthermore, all reservation lands not allocated to Indians were opened to non-Indian homesteaders. In 1881, Indians held more than 155 million acres of land. By 1890 the figure had dropped to 104 million and by 1900 to just under 78 million.

Against such a dismal future, some Indians sought solace in the past. In 1890 a religious revival swept the Indian nations when word came from the Nevada desert that a humble Paiute named Wovoka had received revelations from the Great Spirit. Wovoka preached that if his followers adopted his mystical rituals and lived together in love and harmony, the Indian dead would come back, whites would be driven from the land, and game would be thick again. As the rituals spread, alarmed settlers referred to the strange shuffling and chanting as the "Ghost Dance." The army moved to stop the proceedings among the Sioux for fear of

Wounded Knee

another uprising. At Wounded Knee in South Dakota the cavalry fell upon one band and with devastating machine-gun fire killed some 146 men, women, and children.

Wounded Knee was a final act of violence against an independent Indian way of life. After 1890 the battle was over assimilation, not extinction. The system of markets, rail networks, and extractive industries was linking the Far West with the rest of the nation. Free-roaming bison were being replaced by herded cattle and sheep, nomadic tribes by prairie sodbusters, and sacred hunting grounds with gold fields. Reformers relied on education, citizenship, and allotments to move Indians from their communal lives into white society. Most Indians were equally determined to preserve their tribal ways and separateness as a people.

Borderlands

The coming of the railroad in the 1880s and 1890s brought wrenching changes to the Southwest as well, especially to the states and territories along the old border with Mexico. But here there was a twist. As new markets and industries sprang up, new settlers poured in not only from the east but also from the south, across the Mexican border. Indians such as the Navajo and the Apache thus faced the hostility of newcomers—Anglos and Mexicans alike—as well as of Hispanos, those settlers of Spanish descent already in the region. Before the Mexican War of 1846, the governors of northern Mexico had offered bounties for Indian scalps.

Like Indians, Hispanos discovered that they had either to accommodate or to resist the flood of new Anglos. The elite, or Ricos, often aligned themselves with Anglos against their countryfolk to protect their status and property. Others, including Juan José Herrera, resisted the newcomers. When Anglo cattle ranchers began forcing Hispanos off their lands near Las Vegas, New Mexico, Herrera assembled a band of masked nightriders known as Las Gorras Blancas (the White Caps). In 1889 and 1890 as many as 700 White Caps burned Anglo fences, haystacks, and occasionally barns and houses. Herrera's followers also set thousands of railroad ties afire when the Atchison, Topeka and Santa Fe Railroad refused to raise the low wages it paid Hispano workers.

Juan José Herrera and the White Caps

New Anglos frequently fought Hispanos. But it was western lawyers and politicians, using legal tactics, who deprived Hispanos of most of their property. Thomas

Western cities attracted ethnically diverse populations. This chili stand in San Antonio served the city's large Latino population.

Catron, an ambitious New Mexico lawyer, squeezed out many Hispanos by contesting land titles so aggressively that his holdings grew to 3 million acres. In those areas of New Mexico and California where they remained a majority, Hispanos continued to play a role in public life. During the early 1890s Herrera and his allies formed a "People's Party," swept local elections, and managed to defeat a bid by Catron to represent the territory in Congress.

Mexican immigrants

With the railroads came more white settlers as well as Mexican laborers from south of the border. Just as the southern economy depended on African American labor, the Southwest grew on the labor of Mexicans. Mexican immigrants worked mostly as contract and seasonal laborers for railroads and large farms. Many of them settled in the growing cities along the rail lines: El Paso, Albuquerque, Tucson, Phoenix, and Los Angeles. They lived in segregated barrios, Spanish towns, where their cultural traditions persisted. But by the late nineteenth century, most Hispanics, whether in barrios or on farms and ranches, had been excluded from power.

Formation of regional communities

Yet to focus on cities alone would distort the experience of most southwesterners of Spanish descent, such as those who lived in the small villages of northern New Mexico and southern Colorado. In those areas emerged a pattern of adaptation and resistance to Anglo penetration. As the market economy advanced, Hispanic villagers turned to migratory labor to adapt. Women continued to work in the old villages, whereas men traveled from job to job in mining, in farming, and on the railroads. The resulting network of villages and migrant workers furnished a base from which Hispanics could seek employment and a haven to which they could return. This "regional community" allowed for both the preservation of the communal life of the old Hispanic village and an entry into the new world of market capitalism that was transforming the West.

Ethno-Racial Identity in the New West

The New West met the Old South in the diamond-shaped Blackland Prairie of central Texas. Before the Civil War, King Cotton had thrived in its rich soil. Afterward, Texas became the leading cotton-producing state in the country. Having embraced the slave system of the Old South, Texas also adopted the New South's system of segregation, with its racial separation, restrictions on black voting, and biracial labor force of African Americans and poor whites.

Yet Texas was also part of the borderlands of the American West, where the Anglo culture of European Americans met the Latino culture of Mexicans and Mexican Americans. Many Mexicanos had lived in Texas since before the 1840s, when it had been part of Mexico. In the late nineteenth and early twentieth centuries, more newcomers crossed the Rio Grande in search of work. Between 1890 and 1910, the Spanish-speaking population of the Southwest nearly doubled. In central Texas, the presence of this large and growing force of Mexicano laborers complicated racial matters. The black-and-white poles of European and African Americans that had defined identity in the Old South were now replaced by a new

A new racial triad

racial triad of black, white, and brown that negotiated identity and status among themselves.

Like African Americans, Mexican Americans and Mexican immigrants in Texas were separated from Anglos by a color line and were considered inferior by most whites. Unlike African Americans, however, Texans of Mexican descent sometimes found themselves swinging between the white world of privilege and the black world of disadvantage. In 1914, for example, Mexicans gained status by joining Anglos in the Land League, a radical organization of Texas renters dedicated to land reform. Its secretary, frustrated over the reluctance of whites to sign on, extolled the virtues of Mexican members: "Mexican tenants not only join the League but will starve before they will submit to a higher rent than the League and the law says is just." And whites could lose status, as had the many Texans who sank into landlessness and poverty on the eve of the First World War. White landowners disdained them as "white trash" and a "white scourge," found them to be more expensive tenants, and thus were more likely to rent to what they now regarded as "hard-working" Mexican Americans and Mexican immigrants.

Such complex bargaining over racial status and privilege occurred within a New West of corporate enterprise and wage labor. As small white operators lost their farms and ranches to large corporations, they saw the social distance shrink between themselves and black and brown laborers, sharecroppers, and tenants. By the 1920s, a multiracial labor force of landless wage earners worked on giant ranches and large farms across the Southwest. In Texas, the labor force was triracial, but in California it also included Asian Americans, and, elsewhere, American Indians as well. Thus racial identity in the New West would be more complicated and, for Mexicans and Mexican Americans, more fluid.

Opportunity in the West lay in land and resources, but wealth also accu-

Boom and Bust in the West

mulated in the towns and cities. Each time a speculative fever hit a region, new communities sprouted to serve those who rushed in. The western boom began in mining—with the California gold rush of 1849 and the rise of San Francisco (see page 443). In the decades that followed, new hordes threw up towns in Park City in Utah, Tombstone in Arizona, Deadwood in the Dakota Territories, and other promising sites. All too often, busts followed booms, transforming boom towns into ghost towns.

Mining Sets a Pattern

The gold and silver strikes of the 1840s and 1850s set a pattern that was followed by other booms. Stories of easy riches attracted single prospectors with their shovels and wash pans. Almost all were male, and nearly half were foreign born. Someone entering the local saloon could expect to hear English, the Irish brogue, German, French, Spanish, Chinese, Italian, Hawaiian, and various Indian dialects. Muddy mining camps sprang up in which a prospector could register a claim, get provisions, bathe, and buy a drink or a companion.

Prostitution flourished openly in mining towns (as it did in cattle towns). Such communities provided ideal conditions: large numbers of rootless men, few women, and money enough to buy sexual favors. In the booming towns of Gold Hill and Virginia City near the Comstock Lode of Nevada, men outnumbered women by a ratio of 2 to 1 in 1875. Almost 1 woman in 12 was a prostitute. Usually the prostitutes were young, in their teens and twenties. They walked the streets and plied their trade in one-room shacks called "cribs." If young and in demand, they worked in dance halls, saloons, and brothels. Pay varied by race, with Anglos at the top of the scale, followed by African Americans, Mexicans, and Indians. All told, as many as 50,000 women worked as prostitutes in the trans-Mississippi West before the turn of the century.

Prostitution was one source of revenue, but a far more profitable one came from outfitting these boom societies with the equipment they needed. Such sales siphoned

Prostitution

Blasting away with pressurized water jets, miners loosen gold-bearing gravel. Such techniques damaged the environment in the rush to exploit western resources. The artist, Mrs. Jonas Brown, lived in Idaho City during the height of its gold rush.

riches into the pockets of store owners and other suppliers. Once the quick profits were gone, a period of consolidation brought more order to towns. Police departments replaced vigilantes. Brothels, saloons, and gambling dens were limited to certain districts. And larger scale came to regional businesses. In the mine fields, that meant corporations with the capital for hydraulic water jets to blast ore loose and for other heavy equipment to crush rock and extract silver and gold from deeper veins.

Environmental costs of mining

In their quest for quick profits, such operations often led to environmental disaster. With each snow melt and rain, the gravel from hydraulic mining worked its way down into river systems. The resulting floods, mudslides, and dirty streams threatened the livelihood of farmers in the valleys below. Outside Sacramento, 39,000 acres of farmland lay under the debris by the 1890s, and another 14,000 acres were nearly ruined. In 1893 Congress created the Sacramento River Commission to eliminate flooding with series of dams and canals, effectively ending free-flowing rivers in California. Meanwhile, underground mining consumed so much timber that one observer called the Comstock Lode in Nevada "tomb of the forest of the Sierras." In Butte, Montana, the smoke from sulfur-belching smelters turned the air so black that by the 1880s townsfolk had trouble seeing even in daylight.

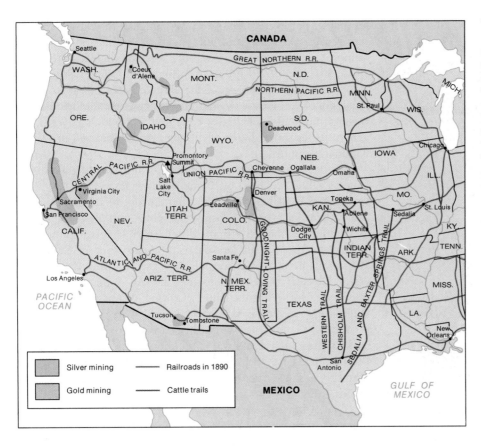

The Mining and Cattle Frontiers
In the vast spaces of the West, railroads, cattle trails, and gold mining usually preceded the arrival of enough settlers to establish towns and cities. The railroads forged a crucial link between the region's natural resources and urban markets in the East and in Europe, but by transecting the plains they also disrupted the migratory patterns of the buffalo herds, undermining Plains Indian cultures while opening the land to cattle grazing and farming.

In corporate mining operations, paid laborers replaced the independent prospectors of earlier days. As miners sought better wages and working conditions, shorter hours, and the right to unionize, management fought back. In Coeur d'Alene, Idaho, troops crushed a strike in 1892, killing seven miners. The miners then created the Western Federation of Miners. In the decade after 1893 the union attracted some 50,000 members and gained a reputation for militancy. In a common cycle, the rowdy mining frontier of small-scale prospectors was integrated into the industrial system of wage labor, large-scale resource extraction, and high-finance capital.

The Transcontinental Railroad

As William Gilpin predicted in 1849, the development of the West awaited the railroads. Before the Central and Union Pacific railroads were joined to span the continent in 1869, travel across the West was slow and dusty. Vast distances and sparse population gave entrepreneurs little chance to follow the eastern practice of building local railroads from city to city.

In 1862 Congress granted the Central Pacific Railroad the right to build the western link of the transcontinental railroad eastward from Sacramento. To the Union Pacific Corporation fell responsibility for the section from Omaha westward. Generous loans and gifts of federal and state lands made the venture wildly

Railroad land grants

profitable. For every mile of track completed, the rail companies received between 200 and 400 square miles of land—some 45 million acres by the time the route was completed. Fraudulent stock practices, corrupt accounting, and wholesale bribery (involving a vice president of the United States and at least two members of Congress) swelled profits even more. More than 75 western railroads eventually benefited from such government generosity, as did millions of ordinary Americans and the entire national economy.

General Grenville Dodge, an army engineer on leave to the Union Pacific, recruited his immense labor force from Civil War veterans as well as Irish and other European immigrants. He drove them with ruthless army discipline, completing as much as 10 miles of track in a single day. Charles Crocker of the Central Pacific had no similar source of cheap labor in California. Worse yet, he faced the formidable task of cutting through the Sierra Nevada. When his partner Leland Stanford suggested importing workers from China, Crocker dismissed him with a laugh—at first. But it was some 10,000 Chinese laborers who accomplished the feat. With wheelbarrows, picks, shovels, and baskets they inched eastward, building trestles like the one at Secrettown (left) and chipping away at the Sierras' looming granite walls. On the worst stretches they averaged only eight inches a day.

Once Chinese crews broke into the flat country of the desert basin, the two railroads raced to claim as much federal land as possible. In the resulting scramble, the two sides passed each other, laying more than 200 miles of parallel track before the government ordered them to join. On May 10, 1869, at Promontory Summit, Utah, a silver hammer pounded a gold spike into the last tie. East and West were finally linked by rail. Travel time across the continent was slashed from months to little more than a week.

As the railroads pushed west in the 1860s, they helped spawn cities like Denver and later awakened sleepy communities such as Los Angeles. Railroads opened the Great Plains to cattle drives that in the 1870s brought great herds to "cow towns" like Sedalia, Missouri, and Cheyenne, Wyoming, where cattle could be shipped to market. Fast behind the cattle boom came the "sodbusters" in the late 1870s to till the hard prairie soils left open by the destruction of the buffalo. By the 1890s the once barren Great Plains were crisscrossed by rails, dotted with towns, and divided into farms, ranches, and Indian reservations.

The rail companies recognized early the strategic value of their enterprise. If a key to profiting from the gold rush was supplying miners, one way to prosper from the West was to control transportation. Just by threatening to bypass a town, a railroad could extract concessions on rights-of-way, taxes, and loans. That coercion was one reason why westerners developed such mixed feelings—gratitude for the transportation, rage at the bullying—toward the railroads.

Cattle Kingdom

Westerners realized that railroads were crucial components of the cattle industry. Cow towns like Abilene, Denver, and Cheyenne flourished from the business of the growing cattle kingdom. By 1860, some 5 million head of longhorn cattle were wandering the grassy plains of Texas. Ranchers allowed their herds to roam the unbroken or "open" range freely, identified only by a distinctive mark on their hides. Each spring cowboys rounded up the herds, branded the calves, and selected the steers to send to market.

Cattle ranching in the United States had begun in Texas and California, largely by Tejanos and Californios of Spanish descent. Anglo Americans who came to Texas readily adopted the equipment of Tejanos: the tough mustangs and broncos (horses suited to managing mean-spirited longhorns), the branding iron for marking the herds, the corral for holding cattle, and the riata, or lariat, for roping. The cowboys also wore Mexican chaps, spurs, and broad-brimmed sombreros, or "hats that provide shade." In Texas, at least a third of all cowboys were Mexicans and black freedmen after the Civil War, the rest largely Confederate veterans. And sometimes rivalries developed among them. One Mexican *corrido,* or ballad, boasted of a herd of 500 steers that could not be corralled by 30 Anglo cowboys, when suddenly five Mexican *vaqueros* arrived: *"Esos cinco mexicanos al momento los echaron / y los trienta americanos se quedaron azorados."* ("Those five Mexicans in a moment put in the steers / and the thirty Americans were left astonished.")

In 1866, as rail lines swept west, Texas ranchers began driving their herds north to railheads for shipment to market. These "long drives" lasted two to three months and sometimes covered more than 1000 miles. When early routes to Sedalia, Missouri, proved unfriendly, ranchers scouted alternative paths. The Chisholm Trail led from San Antonio to Abilene and Ellsworth in Kansas. More westerly routes soon ran to Dodge City and even Denver and Cheyenne.

Clara Williamson painted this herd on the long drive north from Texas. Cowboys normally worked in pairs, opposite each other, as shown here; the chuck wagon can be seen at the rear of the train. So strenuous was the work that each cowboy brought with him about eight horses so that fresh mounts would always be available.

Home on the range

Because cattle grazed on the open range, early ranches were primitive. Most had a house for the family, a bunkhouse for the hired hands, and about 30 to 40 acres of grazing land per animal. Women were scarce in the masculine world of the cattle kingdom. Most were ranchers' wives, strong and resourceful women who cooked, nursed the sick, and helped run the ranch. Some women ranched themselves. When Helen Wiser Stewart of Nevada learned in July 1884 that her husband had been murdered, she took over the ranch, buying and selling cattle, managing the hands, and tending to family and crops.

Farmers looking for their own homesteads soon became rivals to the cattle ranchers. The "nesters," as ranchers disdainfully called them, fenced off their lands, thus shrinking the open range. Vast grants to the railroads also limited the area of free land, and ranchers intent on breeding heavier cattle with more tender beef began to fence in their stock to prevent them from mixing with inferior strays. Before long, farmers and ranchers found themselves locked in deadly "range wars" over grazing and water rights. Farmers usually won.

Conflicts also arose between cattle ranchers and herders of another animal introduced by the Mexicans—sheep. Cattle ranchers had particular contempt for the sheep raiser and the "woolies." Sheep cropped grasses so short that they ruined land for cattle grazing. To protect the range they saw as their own from the "hooved locust," cattle ranchers attacked shepherds and their flocks. On one occasion enraged cattle ranchers clubbed 8000 sheep to death along the Green River in Wyoming. The feuds often burst into range wars, some more violent than those between farmers and ranchers.

Western boom and bust

The cattle boom that began with the first long drive of 1866 reached its peak from 1880 to 1885. Ranchers came to expect profits of 25 to 40 percent a year. Millions of dollars poured into the West from eastern and foreign interests eager to cash in on soaring cattle prices. Ranching corporations extended the open range from Texas into Wyoming and Montana.

As in all booms, forces were at work bringing the inevitable bust. High profits soon swelled the size of the herds and led to overproduction. Increased competition from cattle producers in Canada and Argentina caused beef prices to fall. And nature imposed its own limits. On the plains, nutritious buffalo and gamma grasses were eaten to the nub, only to be replaced by unpalatable species. In the Great Basin, overgrazing destroyed the delicate balance between sagebrush and an understory of perennial bunch grasses. In their place came Russian thistle and cheatgrass that could support only small herds. When overgrazing combined with drought, as in New Mexico in the 1880s and 1890s, the results could be disastrous. In all these regions, as vegetation changed, erosion increased, further weakening the ecosystem. In 1870, 5 acres of plains land were needed to feed a steer. By the mid-1880s, 50 acres were required.

There was, moreover, simply not enough grass along the trails to support the millions of head on their way to market. Diseases like "Texas fever" sometimes wiped out entire herds. Then in 1886 and 1887 came two of the coldest winters in recorded history. The winds brought blizzards that drove wandering herds up against fences, where they froze or starved to death. Summer brought no relief. Heat and drought scorched the grasslands and dried up waterholes. In the Dakotas, Montana, Colorado, and Wyoming, losses ran as high as 90 percent.

By the 1890s the open range and the long drives had largely vanished. What prevailed were the larger cattle corporations such as the King Ranch of Texas. Only the large corporations had enough capital to acquire and fence vast grazing lands, hire ranchers to manage herds, and pay for feed during winter months. As for the cowboys, most became wage laborers employed by the ranching corporations. Like the mining industry, the cattle industry in the West was succumbing to the eastern pattern of economic concentration and labor specialization.

In the 1860s they had come in a trickle; in the 1870s they came in a torrent. # The Final Frontier

They were farmers from the East and Midwest, black freedpeople from the rural South, and peasant-born immigrants from Europe. What bound them together was a craving for land. They had read railroad and steamship advertisements and heard stories from friends about millions of free acres in the plains west of the 98th meridian. Hardier strands of wheat like the "Turkey Red" from Russia, improved machinery, and new farming methods made it possible to raise crops in what once had been the "Great American Desert." The number of farms in the United States jumped from around 2 million on the eve of the Civil War to almost 6 million in 1900.

A Rush for Land

The desire for land was so intense that in the spring of 1889 nearly 100,000 people made their way by wagon, horseback, carriage, buckboard, mule, and on foot to a line near present-day Oklahoma City, in the center of land once reserved for the Indians. These people were "Boomers," gathered for the last great land rush in the trans-Mississippi West. At noon on April 22, 1889, the Boomers raced across the line to claim some 2 million acres of Indian territory just opened for settlement. Beyond the line lay the "Sooners"—those who had jumped the gun and hidden in gullies and thickets, ready to leap out an instant after noon to claim a stake in prosperity.

Boomers and Sooners

Even as the hopefuls lined up in Oklahoma, thousands of other settlers were abandoning their farms to escape mounting debts. The dream of the West as a garden paradise was already being shaken by harsh weather, overproduction, and competition from abroad. Wheat sold for $1.60 a bushel during the Civil War. It fell to 49 cents in the 1890s. Holding on as best they could, plains farmers braved a harsh climate in isolation.

Farming on the Plains

Farmers looking to plow the plains faced a daunting task. Under the Homestead Act (1862), government land could be bought for $1.25 an acre or claimed free if a homesteader worked it for 5 years. But the best parcels—near a railroad line,

Homestead Act

Sod houses could often make living difficult. It might be dry in a downpour, but afterward, the soaked roof would begin to drip and rain for hours. This Kansas sod house, built in 1899, looks simple enough from the outside, but the four windows hint that it was better furnished than most. For its interior, see the next page.

with access to eastern markets—were owned by the railroads themselves or by speculators and sold for around $25 an acre.

Once land was acquired, expenses only mounted because farming in the arid Great Plains required special equipment. Sturdy steel-tipped plows and spring-toothed harrows, which turned over sun-baked prairie soil and left a blanket of dust to reduce evaporation, were needed for "dry farming" in parched climates. Newly developed threshers, combines, and harvesters brought in the crop, and powerful steam tractors pulled the heavy equipment. For such machinery, along with horses, seed, and other farm tools, the average farmer spent $1200, a small fortune in 1880. (Bigger operators invested 10 or 20 times that total.) If their land abutted a ranch, farmers also had to erect fences to keep cattle from trampling fields. Lacking wood, they found the answer in barbed wire, first marketed by Illinois farmer Joseph Glidden in 1874. Crop yields of wheat increased tenfold as a result of these innovations.

Tracts of 160 acres granted under the Homestead Act might be enough for eastern farms, but in the drier West more land was needed to produce the same harvest. Farms of more than 1000 acres, known as "bonanza farms," were most common in the wheat lands of the northern plains. A steam tractor working a bonanza farm could plow, harrow, and seed up to 50 acres a day—20 times more than a single person could do without machinery. Against such competition, small-scale farmers could scarcely survive. Like the southerners, many westerners became tenants on land owned by someone else. Bonanza farmers hired as many as 250 laborers to work each 10,000 acres in return for room, board, and 50 cents a day in wages.

Bonanza farms

A Plains Existence

For poor farm families, life on the plains meant sod houses or dugouts carved from hillsides for protection against the wind. Tough, root-bound sod was cut into bricks a foot wide and three feet long and laid edgewise to create walls. Sod bricks covered rafters for a roof. The average house was seldom more than 18 by 24 feet, and in severe weather it had to accommodate animals as well as people. One door

The interior of the sod house shown on the previous page. Mr. and Mrs. Bartholomew sit proudly amid their possessions, including two ample bookcases, a pedal organ (note the fancy swiveled seat), wallpapered walls, pictures, and rugs on the floor.

and often a single window provided light and air. The thick walls kept the house warm in winter and cool in summer, but a heavy, soaking rain or snow could bring the roof down or drip mud and water into the living area. As soon as a home was established, armies of flies, gnats, mosquitoes, and fleas moved in. Katherine Gibson of the Dakota territories went to light her stove one cold morning only to be attacked by a rattlesnake and its offspring.

The heaviest burdens fell to women. With stores and supplies scarce, they spent long days over hot tubs preparing tallow wax for candles or soaking ashes and boiling lye with grease and pork rinds to make soap. In the early years of settlement wool was in such short supply that resourceful women used hair from wolves and other wild animals to make cloth. Buttons had to be fashioned from old wooden spoons.

Nature added its hardships. In summer, searing winds blasted the plains for weeks. Grasses grew so dry that a single spark could ignite thousands of acres. Farmers in the Southwest lived in dread of stinging centipedes and scorpions that inhabited wall cracks. From Missouri to Oregon, nothing spelled disaster like locusts. They descended without warning in swarms 100 miles long. Beating against houses like hailstones, they stripped all vegetation, including the bark of trees. Winter held special horrors. Blizzards swept the plains, piling snow to the rooftops and halting all travel. Settlers might awaken to find their food frozen and snow on their beds. Weeks would pass before farm families saw an outsider.

In the face of such hardships many westerners found comfort in religion. Indians turned to traditional spiritualism and Hispanics to the Catholic church as a means of coping with nature and change. Though Catholics and Jews came west, evangelical Protestants dominated the Anglo frontier in the mining towns and in other western communities. Worship offered an emotional outlet and some intellectual stimulation as well as a means of preserving old values and sustaining hope. In the West, as in the rural South, circuit riders compensated for the shortage of preachers, while camp meetings offered the chance to socialize. Both brought contact with a world beyond the prairie. In many communities it was the churches that first instilled order on public life, addressing problems such as the need for schools or charity for the poor.

Religion

The Urban Frontier

Not all westerners lived in isolation. By 1890 the percentage of those in cities of 10,000 or more was greater than in any other section of the country except the Northeast. Usually unruly, often chaotic and unplanned, western cities were mostly the products of history, geography, technology, and commerce.

Some western cities—San Antonio, El Paso, and Los Angeles—were old Spanish towns whose growth had been sparked by the westward march of Anglo migrants, the northward push of Mexican immigrants, and the spread of railroad lines. Other cities profited from their location near commercial routes, such as Portland near the Columbia River in Oregon. Still others, such as Wichita, Kansas, arose to serve the cattle and mining booms of the West. And as technology freed people from the need to produce their own food and clothing, westerners turned to the business of supplying goods and services, enterprises that required the labor of more densely populated cities.

Most newer cities had wide streets and large blocks. Whereas the streets of eastern cities measured 30 to 60 feet across, street widths of 80 feet or more were typical in the West. Streets had to be broad enough to allow ox-drawn wagons to turn, but they also bespoke the big plans of town promoters. "Every town in the

Daily Lives

FOOD/DRINK/ DRUGS

The Frontier Kitchen of the Plains

Out on the treeless plains the Indians had adjusted to scarcity of food, water, and other necessities by adopting a nomadic way of life. Their small kinship groups moved each season to wherever nature supplied the food they needed. Such mobility discouraged families from acquiring extensive material possessions. Tools and housing had to be light and portable. Even tribes that raised crops as part of their subsistence cycle often moved with the seasons.

White settlement was different. Farmers, ranchers, and townspeople rooted themselves to a single place. What the surrounding countryside could not supply had to be brought from afar, generally at great effort and expense. In areas distant from the railroad or other transportation links, families generally had to learn either to do without or to improvise from materials at hand. Keeping food on the table was nearly impossible some seasons of the year. Coffee and sugar were staples in such short supply that resourceful women invented a variety of substitutes. "Take a gallon of bran, two tablespoonsful of molasses, scald and parch in an oven until it is somewhat browned and charred," one woman suggested. Something as simple as finding water suitable for drinking or cooking became a problem in many western areas, where the choice might be between "the strong alkaline water of the Rio Grande or the purchase of melted manufactured ice (shipped by rail) at its great cost."

Gardening, generally a woman's responsibility, brought variety to the diet and color to the yard. The legume family of peas and beans, in particular, provided needed protein. Flowers were much prized but seldom survived the winds, heat, and dry periods. Dishwater and laundry water helped keep flowers alive. One woman was so excited by the discovery of a hardy dandelion that she cultivated it with care and planted its seeds each spring. To prepare for the lean winter months, women stocked their cellars and made wild fruits into leathery cakes eaten to ward off the scurvy that resulted from vitamin deficiency.

Until rail lines made the shipment of goods cheap and until Sears, Roebuck "wishbooks" brought mail order to the frontier, a woman's kitchen was fairly modest. A cast iron stove that sold for $25 in the East was in such demand and so expensive to ship that it fetched $200 in some areas of the West. One miner's wife in

Like southern women, women in the West played an essential role in the family economy. There was time for fun, too: this woman has found a rather remarkable way to feed her cat.

West," marveled one European, "is laid out on a plan as vast as though it were destined, at no distant future, to contain a million of inhabitants."

Denver

Denver, Colorado, was typical. Founded in 1859, Denver's growth was boosted by the discovery of gold at the mouth of Cherry Creek. It catered largely to miners with a mix of supply stores, saloons, gambling parlors, and brothels. As it grew, so did its reputation for violence. "A city of demons," said one disgusted visitor, where "a man's life is of no more worth than a dog's." Until the early 1860s, when the city hired its first police force, vigilante committees kept the peace with "the rope and the revolver."

In the 1870s Denver embarked on a new phase of growth. The completion of the Denver Pacific and Kansas Pacific railroads made it the leading city on the eastern slope of the Rocky Mountains. Its economy diversified, and its population soared from about 5000 in 1870 to more than 100,000 by 1890. It soon ranked behind only Los Angeles and Omaha among western cities.

Like much of the urban West, Denver grew outward rather than upward, spreading across the open landscape. Such sprawling patterns of growth produced a city

Montana during the 1870s considered her kitchen "well-furnished" with two kettles, a cast iron skillet, and a coffeepot. A kitchen cupboard might be little more than a box nailed to a log. One "soddie" recalled that her kitchen remained snug and dry during a rainstorm, but after the sun came out, the water trapped in the thick sod roof seeped slowly down. She ended up frying pancakes on her stove under the protection of an umbrella while the sun shone brightly outside.

Without doctors, women learned how to care for the hurt and the sick. Most folk remedies did little more than ease pain. Whiskey and patent medicines were often more dangerous than the disease, but they were used to treat a range of ills from frostbite to snakebite and from sore throats to burns and rheumatism. Settlers believed that onions and gunpowder had valuable medicinal properties. Cobwebs could bandage small wounds; turpentine served as a disinfectant. Mosquitoes were repelled with a paste of vinegar and salt. Most parents thought the laxative castor oil could cure any childhood malady. And if a family member had a fever, one treatment was to bind the head with a cold rag, wrap the feet in cabbage leaves, and then force down large doses of sage tea, rhubarb, and soda. Some women adapted remedies used on their farm animals. Sarah Olds, a Nevada homesteader whose family was plagued by fleas and lice, recalled that "we all took baths with plenty of sheep dip in the water. . . . I had no disinfectant . . . so I boiled all our clothing in sheep dip and kerosene."

Gradually, as the market system penetrated the West, families had less need to improvise in matters of diet and medicine. Through catalogs one might order spices like white pepper or poultry seasoning and appliances like grinders for real coffee. If a local stagecoach passed by the house, a woman might send her eggs and butter to town to be exchanged for needed store-bought goods like thread and needles. It took a complex commercial network to bring all that the good life required to a land that produced few foods and necessities in abundance.

with sharply divided districts for business, government, and industry. Workers lived in one section of town; managers, owners, and other wealthier citizens lived in another.

Development was so rapid that Denver struggled to keep up with itself. Within a decade of plotting its initial tracts, the city began construction of the first of several horse-drawn railways. In 1891 the electrified trolley made its first appearance. By 1900, the city contained 800 miles of streets, but only 24 of them were paved. A British observer marveled at "how [Denver's] future vast proportions seem to exist already in the minds of its projectors. Instead of its new streets and buildings being huddled as with us in our urban beginnings, they are placed here and there at suitable points, with confidence that the connecting links will soon be established." So, too, with the rest of the urban West.

The West and the World Economy

In its cities or on its open ranges, deep in its mine shafts or on the sun-soaked fields of its bonanza farms, the West was being linked to the world economy. Longhorn cattle that grazed on Texas prairies fed city dwellers in the eastern United States and in Europe as well. Wood from the forests of the Pacific Northwest found its way into the hulls of British schooners and the furniture that adorned the parlors of Paris. Wheat grown on the Great Plains competed with grain from South America and Australia. Gold and silver mined in the Rockies were minted into coins around the world.

The ceaseless search for western resources depended ultimately on money. As raw materials flowed out of the region, capital flowed in, most of it from the East and from Europe. With it, westerners built great railroads, sank mine shafts, cut towering forests, and raised cattle and crops that found their way to national and international markets. Foreign investments varied from industry to industry but generally came in two forms: direct stock purchases and loans to western corporations and individuals. The great open-range cattle boom of the 1870s and 1880s, for example, brought an estimated $45 million into the western livestock industry from Great Britain alone. The Scottish-owned Prairie Cattle Company owned nearly 8000 square miles of western cattle land in three huge tracts. By 1887, Congress had become so alarmed at foreign ownership that it enacted the Alien Land Law, which prohibited the purchase of any land in western territories by foreign corporations or by individuals who did not intend to become citizens. Capital-hungry westerners paid little attention. A decade later, there had been virtually no forfeitures of land under the law.

Like southerners, westerners rarely consumed what they took from the ground. In most instances, they located the resources, extracted them, and sent them outside the region to be turned into finished products. Only when manufactured goods returned to the West did westerners finally consume them. But westerners were more than consumers. They were part of a worldwide network of production and trade. Between 1865 and 1915, world population increased by more than 50 percent, and demand mushroomed. Better and cheaper transportation, fed by a new industrial order, allowed westerners to supply raw materials and agricultural goods to places they knew only as exotic names on a map. Still, global reach came at a cost. Decisions made elsewhere—in London and Paris, in Tokyo and Buenos Aires—now determined what westerners charged and how much they made. A bumper crop in Europe could drive down grain prices so sharply that debt-ridden farmers lost their land. And the effect in Europe was just as devastating, squeezing peasant farmers out and sending many of them to the Great Plains, where they increased the rivalry for land and profits.

Packaging and Exporting the "Wild West"

No one linked the West to the wider world and shaped perceptions of the region more than William F. ("Buffalo Bill") Cody. Already a well-known scout for the frontier army and a buffalo hunter for hungry railroad crews, Cody garnered added fame when Edward Judson, writing under the pen name "Ned Buntline," published a series of novels in the 1870s based loosely on Cody's life. In them, the dashing Buffalo Bill fought desperadoes and Indians, saved distressed damsels, and brought order to the wild frontier. He became an icon of a mythic West: where opportunity was there for the taking, where good always triumphed over evil, where all Indians hunted bison and lived in tepees, and where romance and adventure obscured the realities of Anglo conquest, unchecked exploitation, and growing corporate control.

Buffalo Bill Cody's Wild West show

Trading on his fame and a flair for showmanship, Cody packaged the West in 1883, when he created the "Wild West, Rocky Mountain, and Prairie Exhibition" and took it on tour. Rope-twirling, gun-slinging cowboys, savage-looking Indians, and Annie Oakley, as celebrated for her beauty as for her pinpoint aim, entertained audiences as large as 40,000 or more in giant, open-air theaters. They reenacted famous frontier events, including Custer's Last Stand, and performed daring feats of marksmanship, horseback riding, and calf-roping. Cody even hired Sitting Bull, the most famous Indian in America, to stare glumly at gawking ticket holders.

Marginalized as a people, Indians were now typecast and commercialized as a commodity and packaged along with other stereotypes of the American West, including, of course, the sturdy, brave cowboy of legend. Yet the show also broke stereotypes that spoke to Cody's own reformist impulses—for women's rights in the graceful, gun-toting Annie Oakley and for the preservation of Indian life in its remnant representatives whooping and galloping across the arena.

The popularity of Buffalo Bill's Wild West show soon extended overseas. Cody's troupe, animals and all, circled the globe by steamship, train, and wagon. The photograph here shows them embarking for London from New York in 1887, but they played to audiences as far away as Outer Mongolia. Queen Victoria saw them twice, and Prince Albert I of Monaco traveled to Cody, Wyoming, to meet the man who embodied the West, and to "kill a grizzly or two" with the legendary hunter. Indeed, for many Europeans the "Wild West" of Buffalo Bill Cody was America itself.

Examining the census records of 1890, the superintendent of the census noted that landed settlements stretched so far that "there can hardly be said to be a

This photograph of Buffalo Bill Cody (standing in front with his hand resting on a rope) and the cast of his Wild West was taken on a cross-Atlantic voyage to England in 1887. By the 1880s, when Cody created the show, Americans were already longing for the "vanishing frontier." Buffalo Bill provided it for them, complete with mythical stereotypes that reinforced the image of the West as a savage land in need of taming but also an Eden of boundless opportunity and adventure. The reach of such fantasies was truly global, and cultural exchange flowed in both directions, as the poster for the grand opening of the Wild West's new amphitheater suggests. Note the Arabs and cowboys on horseback and exotic camels. Note, too, the use of new technology—electric spotlighting—which allowed for a second, evening show by making "night as light as day."

frontier line." One after another, territories became states: Nebraska in 1867; Colorado in 1876; North Dakota, South Dakota, Montana, and Washington in 1889; Wyoming in 1890; Utah in 1896; Oklahoma in 1907; and New Mexico and Arizona in 1912. A new West was emerging as a mosaic of ethnicities, races, cultures, and climates but with the shared identity of a single region.

That sense of a regional identity was heightened for both westerners and southerners because so many of them felt isolated from the mainstream of industrial America. Ironically, it was not their isolation from northern industry but their links to it that marginalized them. The campaign for a New South to out-Yankee the industrial Yankee could not overcome the low wages and high fertility rates of an older South. The promoters of the West had greater success in adapting large-scale industry and investment to mining, cattle ranching, and farming. Still, they too confronted the limits of their region, whose resources were not endless and whose rainfall did not follow the plow. Like easterners, citizens of the West found that large corporations with near-monopoly control over markets and transportation bred inequality, corrupt politics, and resentment.

What beggared the South and conquered the West was a vast new industrial order that was reshaping the entire Western world. It first took hold in Great Britain at the end of the eighteenth century, then spread to Europe and abroad. In the United States, the new machine age engulfed the North and the East after the Civil War, nourished industrial cities from Pittsburgh to Chicago, and pulled millions of immigrants from Europe, Latin America, and Asia to work in its factories. By the turn of the twentieth century, the new industrial order would enrich the United States beyond imagining. The country would stand as the mightiest industrial power on earth. But the attending conflicts of race, class, region, and ethnicity would bedevil Americans for the next hundred years and beyond.

chapter summary

In the years after the Civil War, both the South and the West became more closely linked to the industrial Northeast.

- Despite differences in geography and history, the South and the West shared many features.

  - Both became sources of agricultural goods and raw materials that fed urban and industrial growth in the northeastern and north central states.

  - Both were racially divided societies in which whites often used violence to assert their dominance.

  - Both looked beyond their regions for the human and financial resources needed to boost their economies.

  - Southerners embraced the philosophy of the "New South" that industrialization would bring prosperity.

- The South nonetheless remained wedded to agriculture, especially cotton, and to a system of labor that exploited poor whites and blacks.

  - Important in the South were the *crop-lien system,* which shackled poor southerners to the land through debt, and *Jim Crow segregation,* which kept blacks and whites apart.

- White westerners too exploited people of other races and ethnicities through settlement, conquest, and capture.

  - By 1890, the emergence of the Ghost Dance and the closing of the frontier signaled that Indians must adapt to life within the boundaries set by white culture despite their efforts at resistance.

  - Latinos were increasingly subjected to similar exploitation but resisted and adapted more effectively to the intrusions of white culture and market economy.

- In a pattern that became typical for western mining, ranching, and agriculture, small operators first grabbed quick profits and then were followed by large corporations that increased both the scale and the wealth of these industries.

interactive learning

The Primary Source Investigator CD-ROM offers the following materials related to this chapter:

- Interactive maps: **Indian Expulsion, 1800–1890** (M8); **Mining Towns, 1848–1883** (M14); and **African Americans and Crop Lien** (M19)

- A collection of primary sources exploring the United States in an industrial age. A number of documents capture changes in rural life, including a photograph of a sharecropper's shack and a series of photographs documenting the disappearing Indian culture. Other documents reveal the social pressures that accompanied the rise of industry in the United States: the Chinese Exclusion Act; a photograph of a Native American school in Pine Ridge, South Dakota; and a selection on social Darwinism.

additional reading

The themes of change and continuity have characterized interpretations of southern history after Reconstruction. For years C. Vann Woodward's classic *The Origins of the New South* (1951) dominated thinking about the region with its powerful argument for a changing South. Edward Ayers, *The Promise of the New South* (1992), offers a fresh, comprehensive synthesis that sees both change and continuity. Gavin Wright, *Old South, New South* (1986), destroys the myth of the southern colonial economy. Ted Ownby, *Subduing Satan* (1990), provides a valuable discussion of southern social life, especially the role of religion. On the issue of race relations see Joel Williamson, *The Crucible of Race: Black-White Relations in the South since Emancipation* (1984).

The contours of western history were first mapped by Fredrick Jackson Turner in his famous address "The Significance of the Frontier in American History" (1893) but have been substantially reshaped by Richard White, *"It's Your Own Misfortune and None of My Own": A New History of the American West* (1992); Patricia Limerick, *A Legacy of Conquest: The Unbroken Past of the American West* (1987);

Gregory Nobles, *American Frontier: Cultural Encounter and Continental Conquest* (1997); and Donald Worster, *Rivers of Empire* (1985). Each describes the history of the West less as a traditional saga of frontier triumphs than as an analysis of how the region and its resources have been exploited by various peoples and cultures. On John Wesley Powell and his seminal role in the West, see Donald Worster, *A River Running West: The Life of John Wesley Powell* (2001). Sarah Deutsch, *No Separate Refuge: Culture, Class, and Gender on an Anglo-Hispanic Frontier in the American Southwest, 1880–1940* (1987), develops the concept of regional community to depict the interpenetration of cultures and their impact on gender in New Mexico and Colorado, and Robert M. Utley offers an excellent survey of American Indians in *The Indian Frontier of the American West 1846–1890* (1984). On the growing literature of ethnoracial identity in the West, see Neil Foley, *White Scourge: Mexicans, Blacks, and Poor Whites in Texas Cotton Culture* (1997), and David Gutiérrez, *Walls and Mirrors: Mexican Americans, Mexican Immigrants, and the Politics of Ethnicity* (1995). For an excellent account of the African American experience in shaping the West, see Quintard Taylor, *In Search of the Racial Frontier: African Americans in the American West, 1528–1990* (1998). For a fuller list of readings, see the Bibliography at www.mhhe.com/davidsonnation5.

significant events

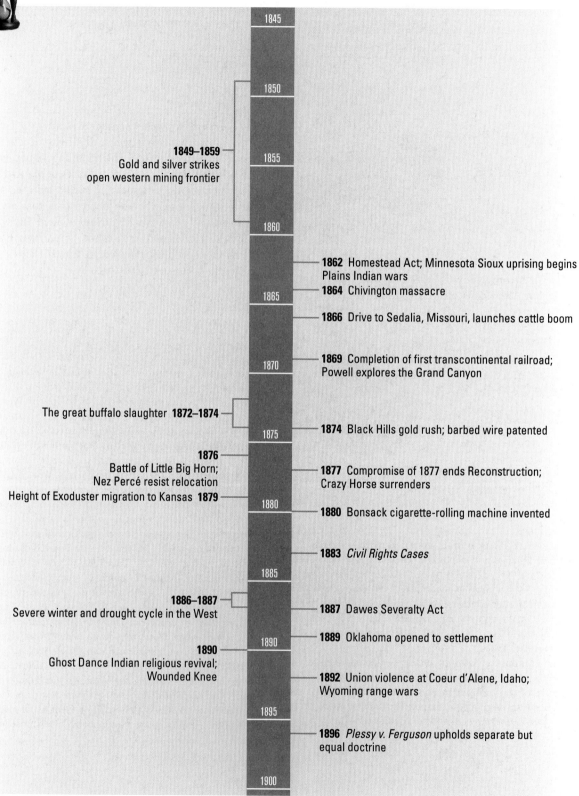

1845

1850

1849–1859
Gold and silver strikes
open western mining frontier

1855

1860

1862 Homestead Act; Minnesota Sioux uprising begins
Plains Indian wars
1864 Chivington massacre

1865

1866 Drive to Sedalia, Missouri, launches cattle boom

1869 Completion of first transcontinental railroad;
Powell explores the Grand Canyon

1870

The great buffalo slaughter **1872–1874**

1874 Black Hills gold rush; barbed wire patented

1875

1876
Battle of Little Big Horn;
Nez Percé resist relocation

1877 Compromise of 1877 ends Reconstruction;
Crazy Horse surrenders

Height of Exoduster migration to Kansas **1879**

1880

1880 Bonsack cigarette-rolling machine invented

1883 *Civil Rights Cases*

1885

1886–1887
Severe winter and drought cycle in the West

1887 Dawes Severalty Act

1889 Oklahoma opened to settlement

1890

1890
Ghost Dance Indian religious revival;
Wounded Knee

1892 Union violence at Coeur d'Alene, Idaho;
Wyoming range wars

1895

1896 *Plessy v. Ferguson* upholds separate but
equal doctrine

1900

AFTER THE FACT
Historians Reconstruct the Past

Where Have All the Bison Gone?

In late summer of 1875 a herd of great American bison—the largest animals in North America—grazed lazily along a shallow creek bed. Summering on the highlands of the southern plains, they fed on the mid and tall grasses of early spring and the late-sprouting short grasses of summer. They groomed, played, and mated before beginning their slow trek down to the river bottoms, where naturally cured short grasses and cottonwood bark nourished them during the winter months.

So the cycle had spun for thousands of years. But on this day in 1875 the bison of this herd began mysteriously to die. One by one, they dropped to the ground as if swatted by a huge, invisible hand. Those at the herd's edges went first. Occasionally the animals gathered about a carcass and sniffed at the warm blood. Or they raised their heads to scent the wind for

trouble. With the poorest eyesight on the plains, the bison could see little—certainly not the puff of smoke that appeared downwind as each new bison staggered and fell.

The hunter lay perfectly still. No need to move—his powerful .50-caliber Sharps rifle could drop a "shaggy" at 600 feet. No need for horses—they would only spook the herd. The man lay quietly downwind, ideally firing one, maybe two rounds a minute, keeping the pace of killing slow and steady. With care, a good hunter might bag as many as a hundred bison a day. And Tom Nixon was a good hunter, a professional in it for profit.

On this day in 1875, legend has it, Nixon killed 120 bison in 40 minutes. The barrel of his Sharps grew so hot that his bullets wobbled in flight. He forgot about the slow and steady kill, forgot even

The buffalo robe of a Hidatsa warrior. Kiowa Indians kept calendars on buffalo skin robes, which historians have used to help estimate bison populations.

about his rifle, which was ruined in the hunt. That day he was out for a record, and he got it. The season was as profitable as the day. From September 15 to October 20, Nixon killed 2127 bison.

Other hunters fared well too. A buffalo robe fetched as much as $5 in the East. Operating in bands of three or four—a shooter, two skinners, and a cook—professional hunters wreaked havoc with the southern herd of the Great Plains in the 1870s. And within a decade, the northern herd had nearly vanished. By some counts, the 30 million bison that roamed the plains in the early nineteenth century shrank to 5000 by the mid-1880s.

Where had all the bison gone? Popular historical accounts have focused almost entirely on the gun-toting white hunters of legend and the smoke-belching railroad: symbols of a market economy penetrating the West. Without doubt, the market economy played a role in eliminating the vast herds. As far back as the 1830s and 1840s, fur trappers and traders were eating buffalo meat; so too were the

railroad crews who extended tracks west. More to the point, the new rail lines provided easy transport of bulky robes and skins to the East. Railroad companies also brought whole trainloads of tourists to shoot at the herd from open windows or atop the cars. In all, the great hunts brought about 10 million bison hides to market.

Ten million is an immense number. But even conservative estimates have suggested that 30 million buffalo had been roaming the plains. What other factors can account for the precipitous drop?

Understanding the fate of the bison herds has required historians to analyze the entire ecology of the plains, of which the bison were an integral part. In many ways, the decades of the 1870s and 1880s represent the end of a process begun much earlier. In reconstructing that process, historians have assembled evidence ranging from traditional accounts of traders and trappers to Indian oral traditions, agricultural census data for livestock, and meteorology reports. They have even found ingenious ways to evaluate the rings of trees and pollen sediment.

One piece of the bison puzzle appears in the 1850s, nearly 20 years before the great white hunts. Starving Indians began to appear across the central and southern plains. Traders reported that the Cheyenne were eating their treasured horses, and other tribes were raiding Mexico for stock. Historians are also able to catch a glimpse of these hard times in the painted robe calendars of the Kiowa. The calendars show the sign for "few or no bison" for four successive years beginning in 1849.

Contemporaries blamed white emigrants headed overland to the Pacific coast. But the pressures of overland migration alone were not enough to bring the Indians to starvation. From accounts in their diaries and letters, overlanders themselves admitted to being poor hunters of bison. Few recorded ever killing more than a handful at a time. More puzzling, many overlanders reported seeing the "blanched skulls and bones" of bison in the early 1840s, *before* the height of the overland migration. Most puzzling, bison were disappearing first from the western portion of the central plains, where whites were most scarce.

Here, in the western plains, was precisely where Indians were plentiful. Since the seventeenth century, Indian peoples had been lured to the bison-rich plains. The bison became a staple of Indian life, providing a "grocery store on the hoof," hides for clothing and shelter, and a source of powerful religious

This Blackfoot robe records the history of one warrior's exploits. It also shows the importance in plains culture of the horse, which competed with the bison for food, especially during the winter. Dozens of horseshoes record animals stolen from enemies.

created buffer zones between them. These contested spaces served as refuges for bison, because hunting could be conducted only sporadically for fear of enemy attack. But after 1840 Indian diplomacy brought peace among many rival tribes. The bison began to disappear as Indians stepped up the hunt across the former buffer zones of the western range. They especially favored two- to five-year-old bison cows for their tender meat and their thinner, more easily processed hides. The death of these cows, the most fertile members of the herd, sharply reduced the number of new births.

Yet more was at work on the plains than the on-slaught of hunters, white or Indian. A broader biotic invasion was under way. Incoming whites and Indi-ans carried animals with them. Indians brought tens of thousands of horses, while the Pacific-bound overlanders brought oxen, cattle, mules, and sheep. These ungulates carried diseases new to the plains—brucellosis, tuberculosis, and a variety of parasites. Later in the century, bison in refuges were found to be riddled with these deadly ailments. The new species also competed for grazing land. So over-landers and Indians were weakening the herds less through slaughter than by occupying the *habitats* of the bison and consuming their food.

Then, beginning in the late 1840s, two decades of unusually heavy rainfall were followed by years of drought. Scientists can deduce these conditions us-ing the science of dendrochronology, which focuses on reading tree rings to provide clues about the weather of a particular era. Around 1850 tree rings began to shrink, indicating the onset of a cycle with more frequent droughts. As highland springs and creeks dried up and summer short grasses grew poorly, more bison began to disappear.

symbols. Most Plains Indians followed the herds for their subsistence, but as the commercial trade in buf-falo robes grew in the 1870s, tribes such as the Black-feet were being drawn into the hunt for profit. In the first half of the nineteenth century, moreover, new In-dian peoples had come to the plains, pushed by the westward advance of European Americans and by hostile tribes from the Great Lakes region. The Indian population in the central plains grew from perhaps 8000 in 1820 to as many as 20,000 in the 1850s.

For a time, the competition between tribes actu-ally helped protect the bison. Warring groups

By comparing the rings from this pine tree taken from the Grand Canyon, historians can date the years of its growth. The widest ring, indicating the wettest year, was 1767.

In contrast, 1754 was extremely dry.

Earlier cycles of drought had led to the virtual disappearance of bison from the plains. No bison bones appear, for example, at archaeological levels that match pollen data indicating droughts between 5000 and 2500 B.C.E. and 500 to 1300 C.E. Thereafter a cycle of above-average rainfall and cooler weather created a more hospitable climate for bison. Unusually abundant rains in the early nineteenth century allowed the herds to grow much larger than normal, as Indian calendars also noted. When drought set in, the herds started to shrink.

In the end, the bison were brought low not by one factor but by many. Drought, Indian population increases, and Indian market hunting weakened the great herds. The disturbances created by overlanders and their animals, the appearance of new bovine diseases, and the increased competition for grazing land only made matters worse. By the time the great white hunts began, the bison, though still numerous, were already in crisis.

BIBLIOGRAPHY Mari Sandoz, *The Buffalo Hunters: The Story of the Hide Men* (1954), provides a vivid description of white hunters in the 1870s and 1880s. Dan Flores sets that traditional tale in a broader context in his pathbreaking article "Bison Ecology and Bison Diplomacy: The Southern Plains from 1800 to 1840," *Journal of American History* (September 1991): 465–485. Flores focuses on the southern plains, but more recently, Elliott West has come to similar conclusions about the central plains in *The Way to the West: Essays on the Central Plains* (1995). His essays move beyond the bison and include broader discussions of the interplay of climate, animals, plants, and people in the region.

Chapter 19

I t was so dark, Robert Ferguson could not see his own feet. Inching along the railroad tracks, he suddenly pitched forward and felt his breath taken away as the ground vanished beneath him. To his dismay, he found himself wedged between two railroad ties, his legs dangling in the air. Scrambling back to solid ground, he retreated along the tracks to the railroad car, where he sat meekly until dawn.

Ferguson, a Scot visiting America in 1866, had been in Memphis, Tennessee, only two days earlier, ready to take the "Great Southern Mail Route" east some 850 miles to Washington. Things had gone badly from the start. About 50 miles outside of town, a broken river bridge forced him to take a ferry. He spent the next 10 miles bumping along in a mule-drawn truck before learning that the rail line did not resume for another 40 miles. Disheartened, he decided to return to Memphis to try again.

The train to Memphis arrived six hours late, dawdled its way home, and then, barely three miles from the city, derailed in the middle of the night. When a few passengers decided to hike the remaining distance into town, Ferguson tagged along. It was then that he had fallen between the tracks and retreated to the railcar. At dawn he discovered to his horror that the tracks led onto a flimsy, high river bridge. Ferguson had trouble managing the trestle even in daylight.

The New Industrial Order

1870–1900

preview • At the heart of the new order reshaping American society was not just industry but *systems* of industry–systems of transportation and communication, systems for managing large corporations and raising the money to finance them. Workers fought to create systems of labor as well, by forming unions. Industrialization came at a price that was often steep, but by 1890 the United States had transformed itself into the most industrialized nation in the world.

Before he finally reached Washington, Robert Ferguson faced six more days of difficult travel. One line ended, and passengers and freight would be forced onto another because rail gauges—the width of the track—differed from line to line. Or a bridge was out, or there was no bridge at all. Trains had no meals "on board" or any sleeping cars. "It was certainly what the Americans would call 'hard travelling,'" Ferguson huffed; "—they do not make use of the word 'rough,' because roughness may be expected as a natural condition in a new country."

Cross-country travel proved so rough that it inspired even an American to fantasy. In 1859, the *Southern Literary Messenger* carried the first of several installments describing Miss Jane Delaware Peyton's trip to Washington, D.C., from Rasselas, Oregon, in 2029, 170 years in the future. Elegant trains whisked her from one end of the country to the other in only 8 days at speeds of 60 miles an hour. While this "immense velocity" presented no physical problems, Miss Peyton had to guard against "Tourbilliere," an all-too-common mental disorder of the twenty-first century. After 10 or more hours on a speeding train, quick-witted passengers found perception accelerating but memory lapsing. "The mind loses an idea almost as soon as it has been formed," Miss Peyton reported. The only cure was to stop and let the mind catch up to its changing surroundings. So every few days Miss Peyton and her fellow travelers disembarked from their train to sit quietly at a depot until their symptoms subsided. Such persons were said to be "waiting for their brains."

By the 1880s, some of our writer's fantasies had come true, as T. S. Hudson discovered in 1882 when he launched a self-proclaimed "Scamper through America." Hudson, another British tourist, did not cross the continent in quite

Giant egg-shaped Bessemer converters remove carbon from molten iron ore to make steel at Andrew Carnegie's steelworks in Pittsburgh. Factory temperatures soared to over 100 degrees, and Carnegie ran his mills 24 hours a day, every day a year except for July 4th.

8 days, but it took him just 60 days to go from England to San Francisco and back. And he booked his rail ticket from a single agent in Boston. Such centralization would have been unthinkable in 1859, when a transcontinental railroad was still a decade from completion.

Hudson's trains had Pullman Palace cars with luxury sleeping quarters and a full breakfast of coffee, iced milk, eggs, "game in their season," and fresh fruits. Newly installed air brakes made trains safer and their stops smoother. Bridges appeared where none had been before, including a "magnificent" span over the Mississippi at St. Louis. Hudson also found himself in the midst of a communications revolution. Traveling across the plains, he was struck by the number of telephone poles along the route.

An industrial transformation

What made America in the 1880s so different from just a few decades earlier was not the speed and comfort of travel or the wonders of the new technology. The true marvel was the emerging industrial order that underlay those technologies and made them possible. Because this order was essentially in place by the beginning of the twentieth century, we tend to take its existence for granted. Yet its growth in scale and complexity was at first slow and required innovations in many different areas of society to achieve its effects.

The process of industrialization began in the United States at least three decades before the Civil War, with small factories producing light consumer goods such as clothing, shoes, and furniture. Despite these early national markets, much of the economy remained local. Only after the 1850s did the industrial economy develop a set of interlocking systems that allowed larger factories, using more and bigger machines, to produce goods with greater efficiency and market them on a national and international scale.

The transformation, remarkable as it was, brought pain along with progress. The demand for natural resources led to virgin forests being cut down and open-pit mines spewing hazardous runoffs. Factory-lined rivers of the Northeast were left toxic with industrial wastes. In 1882, the year Hudson scampered by rail across America, an average of 675 people were killed on the job every week. Like most people, workers scrambled—sometimes literally—to adjust. Few Americans anywhere had time to "wait for their brains" to catch up to the dizzying pace of change.

Change came nonetheless as industrialization transformed the nation from an agrarian republic of merchants and small farmers into the mightiest industrial empire the world had ever known. As we saw in the last chapter, this new industrial order quickly incorporated the South and the West as suppliers of raw materials and as markets for manufactured goods. As we shall see in the next chapter, industrialization also spawned a new urban order whose products and culture spread outward across the country, reshaping virtually every aspect of American life. By the 1890s, the strains of such rapid change ignited an era of violent protest and progressive reform.

The Development of Industrial Systems

The new industrial order can best be understood as a web of complex industrial systems woven together in the second half of the nineteenth century. By "industrial system," we mean a set of orderly arrangements or processes—whether of extraction, production, transportation, distribution, or finance—organized to make the whole industrial order function smoothly. Look, for example, at the industrial systems required to build the bridge across the Mississippi that T. S. Hudson so admired. When James B. Eads constructed its soaring arches in 1874, he needed steel, most likely made

The magnificent steel arches of the Eads Bridge, the engineering marvel that awed T. S. Hudson, spanning the Mississippi River at St. Louis. The steel came from the mills of Andrew Carnegie.

from iron ore mined in northern Michigan. Giant steam shovels scooped up the ore and loaded whole freight cars in a few strokes. A transportation system—railroads, boats, and other carriers—probably moved the ore to Pittsburgh, where the factory system furnished the labor and machinery to finish the steel. The capital to create such factories came itself from a system of finance that linked investment banks and stock markets to entrepreneurs in need of money. Only with a national network of industrial systems could the Eads bridge be built and a new age of industry arise.

Natural Resources and Industrial Technology

The earliest European settlers had marveled at the "merchantable commodities" of America, from the glittering silver mines of the Spanish empire to the continent's hardwood forests. What set the new industrial economy apart from that older America were the scale and efficiency of using such natural resources. New technologies made it possible to exploit them in ways undreamed of only decades earlier.

Steel, for example, had been made from iron and carbon alloyed with other metals and forged into swords as far back as the Middle Ages. In the 1850s, inventors in England and America discovered a cheaper way—called the Bessemer process after its British developer—to convert large quantities of iron into steel. By the late 1870s, the price of steel had dropped by more than half. Steel was lighter than iron, could support 20 times as much weight, and lasted 20 years instead of 3. Steel tracks soon carried most rail traffic; steel girders replaced the old cast iron frames; steel cables supported new suspension bridges.

Bessemer process

Industrial technology made some natural resources more valuable. New distilling methods transformed a thick, smelly liquid called petroleum into kerosene for lighting lamps, oil for lubricating machinery, and paraffin for making candles. Beginning in 1859, new drilling techniques began to tap vast pools of petroleum below the surface. About the same time, Frenchman Etienne Lenoir constructed the first practical internal combustion engine. After 1900, new vehicles like the gasoline-powered carriage turned the oil business into a major industry.

Petroleum industry

Steel Production, 1880 and 1914
While steel production jumped in western industrial nations from 1880 to 1914, it skyrocketed in the United States because of rich resources, cheap labor, and aggressive management.

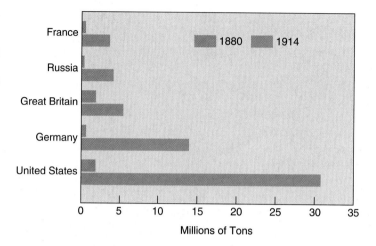

Millions of Tons

Environmental costs

The vast scale of these operations used equally vast amounts of resources and produced huge quantities of waste. Coal mining, logging, and the industrial toxins of factories led to only the most obvious forms of environmental degradation—scarred land, vanishing forests, contaminated waters. As giant water cannons blasted away hillsides in search of gold in California, rock and gravel washed into rivers, raising their beds and threatening populations downstream with floods. Some industrialists did succeed in limiting pollution, often to turn a profit as much as to protect the environment. Chicago meat packers stretched their imaginations to use every conceivable part of the animals that came into their plants. Straight-length bones were turned into cutlery, hoofs and feet into glue and oil, fat into oleomargarine.

Systematic Invention

Industrial technology rested on invention. For sheer inventiveness, the 40 years following the Civil War have rarely been matched in American history. Between 1790 and 1860, 36,000 patents were registered with the government. Over the next three decades, the U.S. Patent Office granted more than half a million. The process of invention became systematized as small-scale inventors were replaced by orderly "invention factories"—forerunners of expensive research labs.

Edison's contributions

No one did more to bring system, order, and profitability to invention than Thomas Alva Edison. In 1868, at the age of 21, Edison went to work for a New York brokerage house and promptly improved the design of the company's stock tickers. Granted a $40,000 bonus (worth perhaps $400,000 in current dollars), he set himself up as an independent inventor. For the next five years, Edison patented a new invention almost every five months.

Edison was determined to bring system and order to the process of invention. Only then could breakthroughs come in a steady and profitable stream. He moved 15 of his workers to Menlo Park, New Jersey, where in 1876 he created an "invention factory." Like a manufacturer, Edison subdivided the work among gifted inventors, engineers, toolmakers, and others.

The spread of an electrical power system

This orderly bureaucracy soon evolved into the Edison Electric Light Company. Its ambitious owner aimed at more than perfecting his new electric light bulb. Edison wanted to create a unified electrical power system—central stations to generate electric current, wired to users, all powering millions of small bulbs in homes and businesses. To launch his enterprise, Edison won the backing of several large banking houses by lighting up the Wall Street district in 1882. It was like "writing by daylight," recorded one reporter. Soon Edison power plants sprang up in major cities across the country.

Electricity was more flexible than earlier sources of energy. Factories no longer had to be built near rivers and falls to make use of water power. Before the end of the century, electricity was running automatic looms, trolley cars, subways, and factory machinery. Electricity not only revolutionized industry; it also worked in the homes of ordinary citizens. The electric motor, developed commercially by George Westinghouse and Nikola Tesla in 1886, powered everything from sewing machines to Edison's "gramophone," later known as the record player.

George Eastman revolutionized photography by making the consumer a part of his inventive system. In the process, he democratized picture taking, once the province of the skilled professional, by inventing a camera that anyone could use at a price ($25) many could afford. In 1888 Eastman marketed the "Kodak" camera. The small black box weighed just over two pounds and contained a strip of celluloid film that replaced hundreds of pounds of photography equipment. After 100 snaps of the shutter, the owner simply sent the camera back to Eastman's Rochester factory, along with a $10 fee, then waited for the developed photos and a reloaded camera to return by mail. "You press the button—we do the rest" was Eastman Kodak's apt slogan. So successful was he that Eastman had to fight off competitors for legal control of his patents. In a pattern that has held ever since, other inventors faced similar court battles.

What united these innovations was the notion of rationalizing inventions—of making a systematic process out of them. By 1913, Westinghouse Electric, General Electric, U.S. Rubber Company, and other firms had set up research laboratories. And by the middle of the century research laboratories had spread beyond business to the federal government, to universities, to trade associations, and to labor unions.

Thomas Edison, unkempt and wrinkled, in his research lab

Transportation and Communication

Abundant resources and new inventions remained worthless to industry until they could be moved to processing plants, factories, and offices. With more than 3.5 million square miles of land in the United States, distance alone was daunting. Where 100 miles of railroad track would do for shipping goods in Germany and England, 1000 miles was necessary in America.

The problem of scale

An efficient transportation system created an integrated national market and tied the United States into an emerging international economy. By the 1870s railroads crisscrossed the country, and steam-powered ships (introduced before the Civil War) were pushing barges down rivers and carrying passengers and freight across the oceans. The time of transatlantic travel was cut in half, to about 10 days. Between 1870 and 1900, the value of American exports tripled. Eventually the rail and water transportation systems fused. By 1900 railroad companies owned nearly all the country's domestic steamship lines.

A thriving industrial nation also required effective communication. Information was a precious commodity, as essential to industry as were resources or technology. In the early 1840s, it took newspapers as long as 10 days to reach Indiana from New York and 3 months to arrive by ship in San Francisco. In 1844 Samuel Morse succeeded in sending the first message over an electrical wire between cities. By

Telegraph

Daily Lives

TIME AND TRAVEL
The Rise of Information Systems

In 1877, a year after its invention, advertisements were already touting Alexander Graham Bell's "speaking telegraph": "Conversation can easily be carried on after slight practice and occasional repetition of a word or sentence. . . . [A]fter a few trials the ear becomes accustomed to the peculiar sound."

It was not so for everyone. Some people had great difficulty understanding the strange sounds. Others reported terrifying "stage fright" that left them speechless. Still others had no idea how to greet callers. Bell answered with a chipper "Ahoy!" Operators at the first public telephone exchange used the old-fashioned "What is wanted?" But it was Thomas Edison's melodious "Hello" (derived from "Halloo," the traditional call to bring hounds to the chase) that won out by 1880.

At first Bell's electrical toys could be rented only in pairs by individuals who wanted to connect two places. In 1877 the advantages of such direct communication led to the first intercity hookup, between New York and Boston. Before the turn of the century, the Bell-organized American Telephone and Telegraph Company had combined more than 100 local telephone companies to furnish business and government with long-distance service. When rates dropped after 1900, telephones found their way into ordinary American homes.

The telephone revolutionized communications, cutting time and obliterating distances. It also liberated social relations by freeing people from the nineteenth-century convention of addressing only those to whom they had been properly introduced. And it acted as a great social leveler. Almost overnight, telephone operators (called "hello girls") began connecting people of different locales and classes who might never have spoken to each other at all, let alone as peers.

The telephone and other innovations were the basis of the information system required of any thriving industrial nation. The increased specialization at all stages of production required information about markets, prices, and supply sources—and required it quickly.

During the first half of the nineteenth century, information had traveled mostly through the

Systems of finance and communications intersected at Wall Street, New York, where the nation's most important investment banks and markets were located. The Great Blizzard of 1888 buried the district with snow and also shadowed in white the crisscrossing "blizzard" of wires needed for the communications networks.

1861 the Western Union Company had strung 76,000 miles of telegraph lines across the country. If a bank collapsed in Chicago, bankers in Dallas knew of it that day. Railroads could keep traffic unsnarled through the dots and dashes of Morse's code. So useful to railroads was the telegraph that they allowed poles and wires to be set along their rights-of-way in exchange for free telegraphic service. By the turn of the century a million miles of telegraph wire handled some 63 million messages a year, not to mention those flashing across underwater cables to China, Japan, Africa, and South America.

A second innovation in communication, the telephone, vastly improved on the telegraph. Alexander Graham Bell, a Scottish immigrant, was teaching the deaf when he began experimenting with ways to transmit speech electrically. In 1876, he transmitted his famous first words to a young assistant: "Mr. Watson, come here! I want

Telephone

mails. In 1844 Samuel F. B. Morse sent the first intercity message across electrical wires, thereby achieving instantaneous communication. But the telegraph had drawbacks. Instantaneous communication was hardly direct. Messages had to be taken to a telegraph office, where trained clerks could translate them into Morse code, an unwieldy system of dots and dashes. Only then could they be transmitted by electrical impulse. When they arrived at the receiving station, messages were recast into understandable language, then carried by hand to their precise destination. This system was a far cry from the telephone, which was both instantaneous and direct.

Another device that increased business efficiency was the typewriter. C. Latham Sholes, a Milwaukee printer and editor, had been tinkering with an automatic numbering machine when a friend suggested he develop a mechanical letter-writing device. In 1868 he patented the "Type-Writer." In the 1870s the Remington Arms Company began mass-producing them. By the early twentieth century the typewriter had taken its modern shape—a keyboard with upper- and lowercase letters and a carriage that allowed typists to see the output.

At first typewriters were used mainly by writers, editors, ministers, and others from the world of letters. (Legend has it that Mark Twain's *The Adventures of Tom Sawyer* was the first book manuscript to be typed.) Early critics charged that "machine-made" letters were too impersonal. When farmers complained about receiving them, Sears, Roebuck hired secretaries to write their business letters by hand. Nevertheless, machine writing soon became standard business practice.

The need for speed and efficiency in the office led to other breakthroughs. Carbon paper, designed for making a typewritten copy along with the original, was patented in 1872. In 1890 Alfred Dick invented the mimeograph to reproduce many copies of a single document cheaply, a communications boon not only to businesses but also to churches, reform organizations, and political groups. Communications, like the rest of the new industrial order, were steadily becoming more orderly and efficient, permitting the rapid distribution of information to those people who desired it.

you." No longer did messages require a telegraph office, the unwieldy Morse code, and couriers to deliver them.

President Rutherford B. Hayes installed the first telephone in the White House in 1878, when the instrument was still a curiosity. The same year, the city of New Haven, Connecticut, opened the first telephone exchange in America. By 1895 there were 310,000 of Bell's machines in America. Five years later there were 1.5 million. The telephone patent proved to be the most valuable ever granted. In the scramble for profits, the Bell Telephone Company battled challenges from competitors and suits from rivals who claimed that their contributions were worth a share of the rights.

Along with other innovations in communication (see Daily Lives, "The Rise of Information Systems," above), telephones modernized offices and eased business transactions. In 1915 the American Telephone and Telegraph Company opened the first transcontinental line. A business executive in New York now could speak personally to an associate in San Francisco. When commercial rates dropped after the turn of the century, the telephone became part of a social revolution. Like the railroad and the telegraph, it compressed distances and reduced differences across the country. In time, remote farms and isolated villages would be connected to distant neighbors and vital hospitals and fire departments.

Finance Capital

As industry grew, so did the demand for investment capital—the money spent on land, buildings, and machinery. The scale of industry required more funds than ever. Between 1870 and 1900, the number of workers in an average iron and steel firm grew from 100 to 400, and the capital invested jumped to nearly $1 million, about seven times what it had been in 1870.

The need for capital was great especially because so many new industrial systems were being put into place at once. A railroad, for example, had enormous start-up costs. Miles of track had to be laid, workers hired, engines and cars bought, depots constructed. Industrial processes involving so many expensive systems could not take shape until someone raised the necessary funds.

Sources of capital   Where did the money come from? For the first three-quarters of the nineteenth century, investment capital came mostly from the savings of firms. In the last half of the century "capital deepening"—a process essential for industrialization—took place. Simply put, as national wealth increased, people began to save and invest more of their money, which meant that more funds could be loaned to companies seeking to start up or expand.

Savings and investment grew more attractive with the development of a complex network of financial institutions. Commercial and savings banks, investment houses, and insurance companies gave savers new opportunities to channel money to industry. The New York Stock Exchange, in existence since 1792, linked eager investors with money-hungry firms. By the end of the nineteenth century, the stock market had established itself as the basic means of making capital available to industry.

The Corporation

For those business leaders with the skill to knit the industrial pieces together, large profits awaited. This was the era of the "robber barons," entrepreneurs who bulled their way to success at the expense of competitors and employees. To be sure, sheer ruthlessness went a long way in the fortune-building game. "Law? Who cares about law!" railroad magnate Cornelius Vanderbilt once boasted. "Hain't I got the power?"

To survive in the long term, business leaders could not depend on ruthlessness alone. They had to have ingenuity, an eye for detail, and the gift of foresight. The growing scale of enterprise and need for capital led them to adapt an old device, the corporation, to new needs. Corporations had existed since colonial times, when governments granted charters of incorporation to organizations that ran public facilities such as turnpikes, canals, and banks. After the Civil War the modern corporation came into use for raising money and protecting business holdings.

Advantages of the corporation   The corporation had several advantages over more traditional forms of ownership: the single owner and the partnership. A corporation could raise large sums quickly by selling "stock certificates," or shares in its business. It could also outlive its owners (or stockholders) because it required no legal reorganization if one of the owners died. It limited liability because owners were no longer personally responsible for corporate debts. And it separated owners from day-to-day management of the company. Professional managers could now operate complex businesses. So clear were these advantages that before the turn of the century, corporations were making two-thirds of all manufactured products in the United States.

An International Pool of Labor

Last, but hardly least important for the new industrial order, was a pool of labor. In the United States the demand for workers was so great that the native-born could not fill it. In 1860 it took about 4.3 million workers to run all the factories, mills, and shops in the United States. By 1900 there were approximately 20 million workers in industrial and associated enterprises.

In part, the United States relied on a vast global network to fill its need for workers. In Europe as well as Latin America, Asia, Africa, and the Middle East, seasonal migrations provided a rich source of workers for many nations, including the United States. Beginning in the 1870s, for example, rural laborers and tenant farmers from the Mezzogiorno in Italy traveled throughout Europe seeking wage work in construction during the building season, which stretched from spring through early fall. Poor Irish workers migrated to Great Britain, where they constituted a reserve source of industrial labor during the nineteenth century. Mechanization, poverty, oppression, and ambition pushed many of these rural laborers from farms into industrial cities and soon to other continents once steamships made transoceanic travel easier.

To draw these workers to the United States, industrialists advertised in newspapers, distributed pamphlets, and sent agents fanning out across the globe. Between 1870 and 1890, more than 8 million immigrants arrived in the United States, another 14 million by 1914. Some came from Asia and Latin America, but most came from Europe and settled in industrial cities. Like migratory laborers elsewhere, they hoped to find work, fatten their purses, and go home. According to one estimate, between 25 and 60 percent of all immigrants returned to their homelands from the United States during these years.

Global labor network

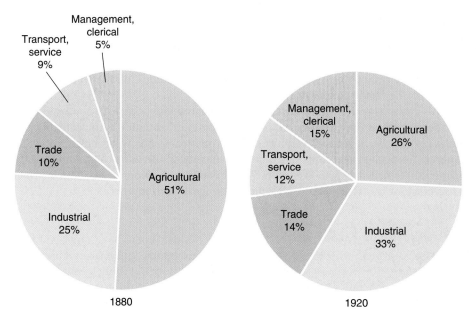

1880

1920

Occupational Distribution, 1880 and 1920 Between 1880 and 1920, management and industrial work—employing white- and blue-collar workers—grew at the expense of farm work.

Migration chains

In the United States as in other countries, immigrants relied on well-defined migration chains of family and friends to get jobs. A brother might find work with other Slavs in the mines of Pennsylvania; or the daughter of Greek parents, in a New England textile mill filled with relatives. Labor contractors also served as a funnel to industry. Tough and savvy immigrants themselves, they met newcomers at the docks and train stations with contracts to work in local factories, mines, and other industries. For their trouble they took a fee or a slice of the new workers' wages. Among Italians they were known as *padrones;* among Mexicans, as *enganchistas.* By the end of the nineteenth century such contractors controlled two-thirds of the labor in New York.

Mexicans, too, formed part of this transnational labor pool, streaming across the border especially after the Mexican Revolution in 1910. But even before, seasonal migration of Mexican laborers to plant and pick crops from Texas to California was common enough to spawn cross-border family networks. One man was responsible for bringing 27 families from Mexico to California. "Come! Come! Come over," a Mexican migrant remembered being told by friends. Mexican laborers also helped build the transcontinental railroad and, after the turn of the century, moved farther north for jobs in the tanneries, meatpacking plants, foundries, and rail yards of Chicago, St. Louis, and other centers of industry.

Domestic sources

Rural Americans—some 11 million between 1865 and 1920—provided a home-grown source of labor, similar in the roots and patterns of their movements to migrants from abroad. Driven from the farm by machines and bad times or just following dreams of a new life, they moved first to small, then to larger, cities in search of work. Most lacked the skills for high-paying jobs. But unlike their foreign counterparts, they spoke English, many could read and write, and few were certain of returning home. In iron and steel cities as well as in coal-mining towns, the better industrial jobs and supervisory positions often went to them. Other rural migrants found work in retail stores or offices and slowly entered the new urban middle class of white-collar workers.

Chicago laborer

Most African Americans continued to work the fields of the South. About 300,000 moved to northern cities between 1870 and 1910, perhaps more to southern cities. Between 1880 and 1910, the black urban population across the South jumped, more than doubling in industrial cities such as Birmingham. In some instances, black migrants were escaping domineering fathers; in others, seeking the excitement of the city; and in still others, following a husband or fleeing the prejudices of the Old South. These migrants too relied on family migration chains in their journey, sometimes traveling in groups, sometimes alone. On occasion, they brought siblings or spouses and children, often one by one, after they had found work.

All came in search of opportunity, and all faced the burden of continued discrimination when they arrived. Newer industries such as textile manufacturing and railroad shop work refused to hire African Americans, but some businesses, like Andrew Carnegie's steel mills in Pittsburgh, employed blacks as janitors and wage laborers. Women found jobs as domestic servants and laundresses. Still, by 1890 an average of less than one black man in ten worked in industry.

Railroads: America's First Big Business

The system was a mess: any good railroad executive knew as much. Along the tracks that spanned the country, each town—each rail station—set its clocks separately by the sun. In 1882, the year T. S. Hudson scampered across America, New York and Boston were 11 minutes and 45 seconds apart. Stations often had several clocks showing the time on different rail lines, along with one displaying "local mean time." In 1883, without consulting anyone, the railroad companies solved the problem by dividing the country into four zones, each an hour apart. One Chicago newspaper compared the feat to Joshua's making the sun stand still. Cities and towns soon adjusted, but Congress did not get around to making the division official until 1918.

Railroad time

At the center of the new industrial systems lay the railroads, moving people and freight, spreading communications, reinventing time, ultimately tying the nation together. Railroads also stimulated economic growth, simply because the sheer building of them required so many resources—coal, wood, glass, rubber, brass, and by the 1880s 75 percent of all U.S. steel. By lowering transportation costs, railroads allowed manufacturers to reduce prices, attract more buyers, and increase business. Perhaps most important, as America's first big business they devised new techniques of management, soon adopted by other companies.

A Managerial Revolution

To the men who ran them, railroads provided a challenge in organization and finance. In the 1850s the Pepperell textile mills of Maine, one of the largest industrial enterprises in America, employed about 800 workers. By the early 1880s the Pennsylvania Railroad had nearly 50,000 people on its payroll. From setting schedules and rates to determining costs and profits, everything required a level of coordination unknown in earlier businesses.

The so-called trunk lines pioneered in devising new systems of management. Scores of early companies had serviced local networks of cities and communities, often with less than 50 miles of track. During the 1850s longer trunk lines emerged east of the Mississippi to connect the shorter branches, or "feeder" lines. By the outbreak of the Civil War, four great trunk lines linked the eastern seaboard with the Great Lakes and western rivers. After the war, trunk lines grew in the South and West.

Pioneering trunk lines

The operations of large lines spawned a new managerial elite, beneath owners but with wide authority over operations. Cautious by nature, they preferred to negotiate and administer rather than compete. In the 1850s, Daniel McCallum, superintendent of the New York and Erie Railroad, laid the foundation for this system by drawing up the first table of organization for an American company. A tree trunk with roots represented the president and board of directors; five branches constituted the main operating divisions; leaves stood for the local agents, train crews, and other workers. Information moved up and down the trunk so that managers could get daily reports to and from the separate parts.

The new managers

By the turn of the century, these managerial techniques had spread to other industries. Local superintendents were responsible for daily activities. Central offices served as corporate nerve centers, housing divisions for purchases, production, transportation, sales, and accounting. A new class of middle managers ran them and imposed new order on business operations. Executives, managers, and workers were being taught to operate in increasingly precise and coordinated ways.

Competition and Consolidation

Although managers made operations more systematic, the struggle among railroad companies to dominate the industry was anything but precise and rational. In the 1870s and 1880s the pain of railroad progress began to tell.

An 1886 office furniture catalog underlines the need for efficiency that was a hallmark of the rising middle-level office manager. Filing cabinets and one of Edison's mimeograph machines are near at hand. Workers dress in a more dignified style reserved for professionals, while framed pictures on the wall lend a homey air.

Erie Wars

Pooling

By their nature, railroads were saddled with enormous fixed costs—land, equipment, debts. These remained constant regardless of the volume of traffic. To generate added revenue, railroads constructed more lines in hopes of increasing their traffic. Soon the railroads had overbuilt. With so much extra capacity, railroad owners schemed to win new accounts. They gave free passes to favored shippers, promised them free sidings at their plants, offered free land to lure businesses to their territory.

The most savage and costly competition came over the rates charged for shipping goods. Managers lowered rates for freight that was shipped in bulk, on long hauls, or on return routes (since the cars were empty anyway). They used "rebates"—secret discounts to preferred customers— to drop prices below the posted rates of competitors (and then recouped the losses by overcharging small shippers like farmers). When the economy plunged or a weak line sought to improve its position, rate wars broke out. By 1880, 65 lines had declared bankruptcy.

One way to prevent the ravages of competition was to buy up competing lines. It was often expensive and could ignite even fiercer warfare. From 1866 to 1868 Cornelius Vanderbilt of the New York Central waged a futile battle to gain control of the Erie Railroad. The Erie was headed by a trio of railroad sharks: the corporate buccaneer Daniel Drew, the flamboyant speculator James Fisk Jr., and the unscrupulous Jay Gould. Vanderbilt fought the trio in the courts, where each side bought its own judges. He fought them in the legislature, where both sides bribed legislators (for $15,000 apiece, some said). He fought them on the streets with gangs of hired toughs and on the seas, where Fisk himself served as admiral of a Hudson River fleet armed with riflemen.

The "Erie Wars" ended in a standoff. The Erie paid Vanderbilt a huge ransom to end his attack. Gould and Drew retained control of the company, until they turned against each other. By 1877, the Erie was bankrupt, mismanaged and drowned in a sea of "watered stock." (Such stock, issued in excess of the company's assets, derived its name from the rancher's trick of having cattle drink water before weighing in for sale.) Gould emerged unscathed from the fight. When he died of tuberculosis at the age of 56 in 1892, his estate totaled $74 million.

Cooperation worked better than competition. During the 1870s railroad managers created regional federations to pool traffic, set prices, and divide profits among members. Pooling—informal agreements among competing companies to act together—was designed to remove the competition that led to rate wars. Without the force of law, however, pools failed. Members broke ranks by cutting prices in hopes of quick gain. In the end, rate wars died down only when weaker lines failed or stronger ones bought up competitors.

The Challenge of Finance

Earlier in the nineteenth century, many railroads relied on state governments for financial help. Backers also looked to counties, cities, and towns for bonds and other forms of aid. People living near the ends of rail lines, who stood to gain from

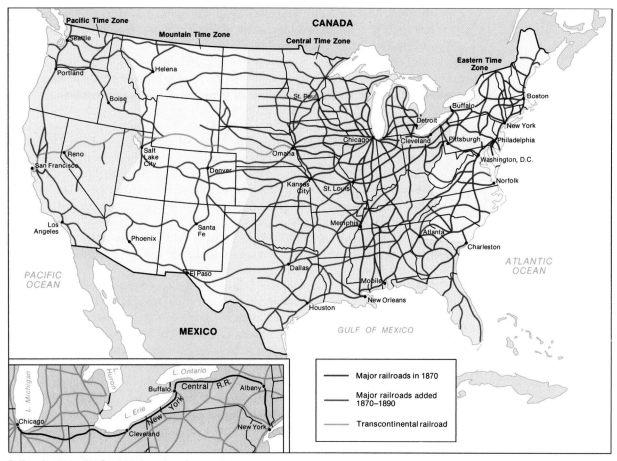

Railroads, 1870–1890 By 1890, the railroad network stretched from one end of the country to the other, with more miles of track than in all of Europe combined. New York and Chicago, linked by the New York Central trunk line, became the new commercial axes.

construction, were persuaded to take railroad stock in exchange for land or labor. In the 1850s and 1860s western promoters went to Washington for help and returned with $65 million in loans to six western railroads and some 131 million acres of land.

Federal aid helped to build only part of the nation's railroads. Most of the money came from private investors. The New York Stock Exchange expanded rapidly as railroad corporations began to trade their stocks and bonds. Large investment banks developed financial networks to track down money at home and abroad. By 1898 a third of the assets of American life insurance companies had gone into railroads, while Europeans owned nearly a third of all American railroad stocks.

New ways of raising money

Because investment bankers played such large roles in funding railroads, they found themselves advising companies about their business affairs. If a company fell into bankruptcy, bankers sometimes served as the "receivers" who oversaw the property until financial health returned. By absorbing smaller lines into larger ones, eliminating rebates, and stabilizing rates, the bankers helped reduce competition and impose order and centralization. In the process, they often came to control the companies they counseled.

By 1900, the new industrial systems had transformed American railroads. Some 200,000 miles of track were in operation, 80 percent of it owned by only six groups of railroads. Time zones coordinated schedules; standardized track made cross-country freighting easier. Soon passengers were traveling 16 billion miles a year. To that traffic could be added farm goods, raw materials, and factory-finished products. Everything moved with a new regularity that allowed businesses to plan and prosper.

The Growth of Big Business

In 1865, 26-year-old John D. Rockefeller sat stone-faced in the office of his Cleveland oil refinery, about to conclude the biggest deal of his life. Rockefeller's business was flourishing, but not his partnership with Maurice Clark. The two had fallen out over how quickly to expand. Rockefeller was eager to grow fast; the cautious Clark was not. They dissolved their partnership and agreed to bid for the company. Bidding opened at $500, rocketed to $72,500, and abruptly stopped. "The business is yours," said Clark. The men shook hands and a thin smile crept across Rockefeller's face.

Twenty years later, Rockefeller's Standard Oil Company controlled 90 percent of the nation's refining capacity and an empire that stretched well beyond Cleveland. Around the clock, trains sped Standard executives to New York, Philadelphia, and other eastern cities. The railroads were a fitting form of transportation for Rockefeller's company; in many ways they were the key to his oil empire. They carried his oil products and discounted his rates, giving him the edge to squeeze out rivals. And they pioneered the business systems on which Rockefeller was building. As we shall see with other American firms, Standard Oil was improving on the practices of the railroads to do bigger and bigger business.

Strategies of Growth

But first a great riddle had to be solved: How to grow and still control the ravages of competition? In Michigan in the 1860s, salt producers found themselves fighting for their existence. The presence of too many salt makers had begun an endless round of price-cutting that was driving them all out of business. Seeing salvation in combination, they drew together in the nation's first pool. In 1869 they formed the Michigan Salt Association. They voluntarily agreed to divide production, assign markets, and set prices—at double the previous rate.

The pool

Competition often plagued salt processing and other manufacturers of consumer goods because their start-up costs were low.* Horizontal combination—joining loosely together with rivals that produced the same goods or services—had saved Michigan salt producers. The railroads were among the first big businesses to employ pools. By the 1880s there was a whiskey pool, a cordage pool, and countless others. Such informal arrangements ultimately proved unenforceable and therefore unsatisfactory. (After 1890 they were also considered illegal restraints on trade.) But other forms of horizontal growth, such as formal mergers, spread in the wake of an economic panic in the 1890s.

Horizontal growth

Some makers of consumer products worried less about direct competition and concentrated on boosting efficiency and sales. They adopted a growth strategy called "vertical integration," in which one company gained control of two or more

Vertical integration

Consumer goods such as food and clothing are products that fill the needs and wants of individuals, while *producer* or *capital goods* such as factory equipment are used to turn out other goods or services.

stages of a business operation. A fully integrated manufacturing company, for example, possessed its own raw materials, transportation facilities, factories, and marketing outlets.

Gustavus Swift, a New England butcher, saw the advantages of such integration when he arrived in Chicago in the mid-1870s. Aware of the demand for fresh beef in the East, he acquired new refrigerated railcars to ship meat from western slaughter-houses and a network of ice-cooled warehouses in eastern cities to store it. By 1885 he had created the first national meatpacking enterprise, Swift and Company. Swift moved upward, closer to consumers, by putting together a fleet of wagons to distrib-ute his beef to retailers. He moved down toward raw materials, extending and coor-dinating the purchase of cattle at the Chicago stockyards. By the 1890s Swift and Company was a fully integrated, vertically organized corporation operating on a nationwide scale. Soon Swift, Armour and Company, and three other giants—together called the "Big Five"—controlled 90 percent of the beef shipped across state lines.

Vertical growth generally brought producers of consumer goods closer to the marketplace. For them, profit came from high-volume sales. The Singer Sewing Machine Company and the McCormick Harvester Company created their own retail sales arms. Manufacturers began furnishing ordinary consumers with tech-nical information, credit, and repair services in an effort to expand sales. Adver-tising expenditures grew, to some $90 million by 1900, to identify markets, shape buying habits, and drum up business.

Carnegie Integrates Steel

Industrialization encouraged vertical integration in heavy industry but more often downward, toward reliable sources of raw materials. These firms made heavy machinery and materials for big users like railroads and factory builders. Their markets were easily identified and changed little. For them, profits lay in securing limited raw materials and in holding down costs.

Andrew Carnegie led the way in steel. A Scottish immigrant, he worked his way up from bobbin boy in a textile factory to expert telegrapher to superinten-dent of the western division of the Pennsylvania Railroad at the age of 24. A string of wise investments paid off handsomely. He owned a share of the first sleeping car, the first iron railroad bridge, a locomotive factory, and finally an iron factory that became the nucleus of his steel empire.

In 1872, on a trip to England, Carnegie chanced to see the new Bessemer process for making steel. Awestruck by its fiery display, he rushed home to build the biggest steel mill in the world. The J. Edgar Thomson Mills (shrewdly named in honor of the president of the Pennsylvania Railroad) opened in 1875, in the midst of a severe depression. Over the next 25 years, Carnegie added mills at Homestead and elsewhere in Pennsylvania and moved from railroad building to city building. He supplied steel for the Brooklyn Bridge, New York City's elevated railway, and the Washington Monument.

Bessemer process

Carnegie succeeded, in part, by taking advantage of the boom-and-bust business cycle. He jumped in during hard times, building and buying when equipment and businesses were cheap. But he also found skilled managers who employed the admin-istrative techniques of the railroads. And Carnegie knew how to compete. He scrapped machinery, workers, even a new mill to keep costs down and undersell competitors.

Keys to Carnegie's success

The final key to Carnegie's success was expansion. His empire spread horizon-tally by purchasing rival steel mills and constructing new ones. It spread vertically, buying up sources of supply, transportation, and eventually sales. Controlling such

Carnegie Furnaces, Braddock, Pennsylvania

an integrated system, Carnegie could ensure a steady flow of materials from mine to mill and market as well as a steady stream of profits. In 1900 his company turned out more steel than Great Britain and netted him $40 million.

Integration of the kind Carnegie employed expressed the logic of the new industrial age. More and more, the industrial activities of society were being linked together in one giant, interconnected process.

Rockefeller and the Great Standard Oil Trust

John D. Rockefeller began his career as a refiner of petroleum and soon accomplished in oil what Carnegie achieved in steel. And he went further, developing an innovative business structure—the trust—that promised greater control than even Carnegie's integrated system. At first Rockefeller grew horizontally by buying out or joining competing oil refiners. To cut costs, he expanded vertically, with oil pipelines, warehouses, and barrel factories. By 1870, when he and five partners formed the Standard Oil Company of Ohio, his high-caliber, low-cost products could compete with any other.

Rockefeller's methods of expansion

Because the oil refining business was a jungle of competitive firms, Rockefeller proceeded to twist arms. He bribed rivals, spied on them, created phony companies, and slashed prices. His decisive edge came from the railroads. Desperate for business, they granted Standard Oil not only rebates on shipping rates but also "drawbacks," a fee railroaders paid Standard for any product shipped by a rival. Within a decade Standard dominated the oil business with a vertically integrated empire that stretched from drilling to selling.

Throughout the 1870s Rockefeller kept his empire stitched together through informal pools and other business combinations. But they were weak and afforded him too little control. He could try to expand further, except that corporations were restricted by state law. In Rockefeller's home state of Ohio, for example, corporations could not own plants in other states or own stock in out-of-state companies.

In 1879 Samuel C. T. Dodd, chief counsel of Standard Oil, came up with a solution, the "trust." Under the trust, the stockholders of corporations surrendered their shares "in trust" to a central board of directors with the power to control all property. In exchange, stockholders received certificates of trust that paid hefty dividends. Because it did not literally own other companies, the trust violated no state law.

The trust

In 1882 the Standard Oil Company of Ohio formed the country's first great trust. It brought Rockefeller what he sought so fiercely—centralized management of the oil industry. Other businesses soon created trusts of their own—in meatpacking, wiremaking, and farm machinery, for example. Just as quickly, trusts became notorious for crushing rivals and fixing prices.

The Mergers of J. Pierpont Morgan

The trust was only a stepping-stone to an even more effective means of avoiding competition, managing people, and controlling business: the corporate merger. The idea of two corporations merging—one buying out another—remained impossible until 1889, when New Jersey began to permit corporations to own other corporations.

In 1890, the need to find a substitute for the trust grew urgent. Congress outlawed trusts under the Sherman Antitrust Act (page 630). The Sherman Act specifically banned business from "restraining trade" by setting prices, dividing markets, or engaging in other unfair practices. The ever-inventive Samuel Dodd came up with a new idea, the "holding company," a corporation of corporations that had the power to hold shares of other companies. Many industries converted their trusts into holding companies, including Standard Oil, which moved to New Jersey in 1899.

The holding company

Two years later came the biggest corporate merger of the era, created by a financial wizard named J. Pierpont Morgan. His orderly mind detested the chaotic competition that threatened his profits. "I like a little competition," Morgan used to say, "but I like combination more." After the Civil War he had taken over his father's powerful investment bank. For the next 50 years, the House of Morgan played a part in consolidating almost every major industry in the country.

Morgan's greatest triumph was in steel, where for years Carnegie had refused to combine with rivals. In January 1901, with the threat of a colossal steel war looming, Morgan convinced Carnegie to put a price tag on his company. When a messenger brought back the scrawled reply—more than $400 million—Morgan merely nodded and said, "I accept this price." He then bought Carnegie's eight largest competitors and announced the formation of the United States Steel Corporation.

U.S. Steel gobbled up more than 200 manufacturing and transportation companies, 1000 miles of railways, and the whole Mesabi iron range of Minnesota. The mammoth holding company produced nearly two-thirds of all American steel. Its value of $1.4 billion exceeded the national debt and made it the country's first billion-dollar corporation.

The merger movement

What Morgan helped to create in steel was rapidly coming to pass in other industries. A wave of mergers swept through American business after the depression of 1893. As the economy plunged, cutthroat competition bled businesses until they were eager to sell out. Giants sprouted almost overnight. By 1904, in each of 50 industries one firm came to account for 60 percent or more of the total output.

Corporate Defenders

The gospel of wealth

As Andrew Carnegie's empire grew, his conscience turned troubled. Preaching a "gospel of wealth," he urged the rich to act as stewards for the poor, "doing for them better than they would or could do for themselves." He devoted his time to philanthropy by creating foundations and endowing libraries and universities with some $350 million in contributions.

Defenders of the new corporate order were less troubled than Carnegie was about the rough-and-tumble world of big business. They justified the system by stressing the opportunity created for individuals by economic growth. Through frugality, acquisitiveness, and discipline—the sources of cherished American individualism—anyone could rise like Andrew Carnegie.

Social Darwinism

When most ordinary citizens failed to follow in Carnegie's footsteps, defenders blamed the individual. Failures were lazy, ignorant, or morally depraved, they said. British philosopher Herbert Spencer added the weight of science by applying Charles Darwin's theories of evolution where naturalist Darwin had never intended—to society. Spencer maintained that in society, as in biology, only the "fittest" survived. The competitive social jungle doomed the unfit to poverty and rewarded the most fit with property and privilege.

Spencer's American apostle, William Graham Sumner, argued that competition was natural and had to proceed without any interference, including government regulation. Millionaires were simply the "product of natural selection." Such "social Darwinism" found strong support among turn-of-the-century business leaders. The philosophy of ruthless competition certified their success even as they worked to destroy the very competition it celebrated.

Corporate Critics

Andrew Carnegie invoked the gospel of wealth to justify his millions, but a group of radical critics looked on his libraries and foundations as desperate attempts to buy peace of mind. For all the contemporary celebrations of wealth and big business, they saw the new industrial order as exploitative, divisive, and immoral. It was built on the backs of ordinary "toilers," whose labors profited the few Carnegies of the world.

Henry George, a journalist and self-taught economist, began his critique with a simple question. How could poverty exist when industrial progress had created such wealth? George pointed to greedy landowners who bought property when it was cheap and then held it until the forces of society—labor, technology, and speculation on nearby sites—had increased its value. They reaped most of the rewards, despite the hard work of others. In his best-selling book *Progress and Poverty* (1879), George proposed a single tax on these "unearned" profits to end monopoly landholding. With all other taxes abolished, income would be slowly redistributed. "Single-tax" clubs sprang up throughout the country, and George nearly won the race for mayor of New York in 1886.

The journalist Edward Bellamy tapped the same popular resentment against the inequalities of industrial capitalism. In his best-selling novel *Looking Backward* (1888) Julian West, a fictional Bostonian, falls asleep in 1887 and awakens Rip Van Winkle–like in the year 2000. In place of the competitive, class-ridden society of the nineteenth century is an orderly utopia managed by a benevolent government trust. "Fraternal cooperation," shared abundance, and "nationalism," which puts the interests of the community above those of the individual, are the guiding principles. By 1892, Bellamy's philosophy had spawned over 160 clubs in 27 states with followers demanding redistribution of wealth, civil service reform, and nationalization of railroads and utilities.

Less popular but equally hostile to capitalism was the Socialist Labor party, formed in 1877. Under Daniel De Leon, a West Indian immigrant, it stressed class conflict and called for a revolution to give workers control over production. De Leon refused to compromise his radical beliefs, and the socialists ended up attracting more intellectuals than workers. Some immigrants found its class consciousness appealing, but most rejected its radicalism and rigidity. A few party members, bent on gaining greater support, revolted and in 1901 founded the more successful Socialist Party of America. Workers were beginning to organize their own responses to industrialism.

By the mid-1880s, in response to the growing criticism of big business, several states in the South and West enacted laws limiting the size of corporations. But these laws proved all too easy to evade when states such as New Jersey and Delaware eased their rules to allow corporations to grow nationwide.

DESIGN FOR A TABLET IN ANTIQUE BRASS TO BE PLACED IN THE CHICAGO UNIVERSITY

This drawing is from a 1905 edition of *Collier's* magazine, famous for exposing corporate abuses. Here it mocks John D. Rockefeller, head of the Standard Oil Company, as the new God of the industrial age by parodying the Protestant doxology of thanks: "Praise God from whom all blessings flow, Praise him all creatures here below!"

Socialist Labor party

Sherman Antitrust Act

In 1890, the public clamor against trusts finally forced Congress to act. The Sherman Antitrust Act relied on the only constitutional authority the federal government had over business: its right to regulate interstate commerce. The act outlawed "every contract, combination in the form of trust or otherwise, or conspiracy, in restraint of trade or commerce." The United States stood practically alone among industrialized nations in regulating such business combinations.

Its language was purposefully vague, but the Sherman Antitrust Act did give the government the power to break up trusts and other big businesses. So high was the regard for the rights of private property, however, that few in Congress expected the government to exercise that power or the courts to uphold it. They were right. Before 1901, the Justice Department filed only 14 antitrust suits against big businesses, virtually none of them successful. And in 1895, the Supreme Court dealt the law a major blow by severely limiting its scope when the government brought suit against the E. C. Knight Company, which controlled over 90 percent of sugar refining in the country. *United States v. E. C. Knight Co.* held that businesses involved in manufacturing (as opposed to "trade or commerce") lay outside the authority of the Sherman Act. The ruling thus excluded most firms other than transportation companies that carried goods across state lines. Not until after the turn of the century would the law be used to bust a trust.

United States v. E. C. Knight Co.

The Costs of Doing Business

The heated debates between the critics and defenders of industrial capitalism made clear that the changes in American society were two-edged. Big businesses certainly helped to order or rationalize production, increase national wealth, and tie the country together. Yet they also concentrated power, corrupted politics, and made the gap between rich and poor more apparent than ever. In 1890, the richest 9 percent of Americans held nearly three-quarters of all wealth in the United States. But by 1900, one American in eight (nearly 10 million people) lived below the poverty line.

The boom-and-bust cycle

More to the point, the practices of big business subjected the economy to enormous disruptions. The banking system could not always keep pace with the demand for capital, and businesses failed to distribute enough profits to sustain the purchasing power of workers. The supply of goods regularly outstripped the demand for them, and then the wrenching cycle of boom and bust set in. Three

Boom and Bust Business Cycle, 1865–1900 Between 1865 and 1900, industrialization produced great economic growth but also wild swings of prosperity and depression. During booms, productivity soared and near-full employment existed. But the rising number of industrial workers meant high unemployment during deep busts.

severe depressions—1873–1879, 1882–1885, and 1893–1897—rocked the economy in the last third of the nineteenth century. With hard times came fierce competition as managers searched frantically for ways to cut costs, and the industrial barons earned their reputations for ruthlessness.

At seven in the morning, Sadie Frowne sat at her sewing machine in a Brooklyn garment factory. ## The Workers' World

The boss, a man she barely knew, dropped a pile of unfinished skirts next to her. She pushed one under the needle and began to rock her foot quickly on the pedal that powered her machine. Sometimes Sadie pushed the fabric too hastily, and the needle pierced her finger. "The machines go like mad all day because the faster you work the more money you get," Sadie explained of the world of industrial work in 1902.

The cramped sweatshops, the vast steel mills, the dank tunnels of the coal fields—all demanded workers and required them to work in new ways. Farmers or peasants who had once timed themselves by the movement of the sun now lived by the clock and labored in the twilight of gaslit factories. Instead of being self-employed, they had to deal with supervisors and were paid by the piece or hour. Not the seasons but the relentless cycle of machines set their pace. Increasingly, workers bore the brunt of depressions, faced periodic unemployment, and toiled under dangerous conditions as they struggled to bring the new industrial processes under their control.

Industrial Work

In 1881, the Pittsburgh Bessemer Steel Company opened its new mill in Homestead, Pennsylvania. Nearly 400 men and boys went to work in its 60 acres of sheds. They kept the mill going around the clock by working in two shifts: 12 hours a day the first week, 12 hours a night the next. In the furnace room, some men fainted from the heat, while the vibration and screeching of machinery deafened others. There were no breaks, even for lunch. "Home is just the place where I eat and sleep," said a steelworker. "I live in the mills."

Few industrial workers labored under conditions quite so harsh, but the Homestead mill reflected the common characteristics of industrial work: the use of machines for mass production; the division of labor into intricately organized, menial tasks; and the dictatorship of the clock. At the turn of the century, two-thirds of all industrial work came from large-scale mills.

Under such conditions labor paid dearly for industrial progress. By 1900, most of those earning wages in industry worked 6 days a week, 10 hours a day. They held jobs that required more machines and fewer skills. Repetition of small chores replaced fine craftwork. In the 1880s, for example, almost all the 40 different steps that had gone into making a pair of shoes by hand could be performed by a novice, or "green hand," with a few days of instruction at a simple machine.

With machines also came danger. Tending furnaces in a steel mill or plucking tobacco from cigarette-rolling machines was tedious. If a worker became bored or tired, disaster could strike. Each year from 1880 to 1900 industrial mishaps killed an average of 35,000 wage earners and injured over 500,000. Workers could expect no payment from employers or the government for death or injury. Accidents were assumed to be workers' own fault.

Industrial workers rarely saw an owner. The foreman or supervisor exercised complete authority over the unskilled in his section, hiring and firing them, even

Pattern of industrial work

Industrial accidents

The laborers in Thomas Anschutz's painting *Steel-workers—Noontime* were luckier than those at Homestead. They could escape the factory's stifling heat for a brief break. Workers fortunate enough to bring food used a "lunch pail" like the one at left.

setting their wages. Skilled workers had greater freedom, yet they too felt the pinch of technology and organization. By the 1880s, carpenters were finding that machine-made doors were replacing the ones they once constructed at the site. Painters no longer mixed their own paints. "I regard my people," said one manager, "as I regard my machinery. So long as they can do my work for what I choose to pay them, I keep getting out of them all I can."

Taylorism

Higher productivity and profits were the aims, and for Frederick W. Taylor, efficiency was the way to achieve them. During the 1870s and 1880s, Taylor undertook careful time-and-motion studies of workers' movements in the steel industry. He set up standard procedures and offered pay incentives for beating his production quotas. On one occasion, he designed 15 ore shovels, each for a separate task. One hundred forty men were soon doing the work of 600. By the early twentieth century "Taylorism" was a full-blown philosophy, complete with its own professional society. "Management engineers" prescribed routines from which workers could not vary.

For all the high ideals of Taylorism, ordinary laborers refused to perform as cogs in a vast industrial machine. In a variety of ways, they worked to maintain control. Many European immigrants continued to observe the numerous saints' days and other religious holidays of their homelands, regardless of factory rules. When the pressure of six-day weeks became too stifling, workers took an unauthorized "blue Monday" off. Or they slowed down to reduce the grueling pace. Or they simply walked off the job. Come spring and warm weather, factories reported turnover rates of 200 to 300 percent.

Worker citizens

For some laborers, seizing control of work was more than a matter of survival or self-respect. Many workers regarded themselves as citizens of a democratic republic. They expected to earn a "competence"—enough money to support and educate their families and enough time to stay abreast of current affairs. Few but highly skilled workers could realize such democratic dreams. More and more, labor was being managed as another part of an integrated system of industry.

Children, Women, and African Americans

In the mines of Pennsylvania, nimble-fingered eight- and nine-year-olds snatched bits of slate from amid the chunks of coal. In Illinois glass factories, quick-footed "dog boys" dashed with trays of red-hot bottles to the cooling ovens. By 1900, the industrial labor force included some 1.7 million children, more than double the number 30 years earlier. Parents often had no choice. As one union leader observed, "Absolute necessity compels the father . . . to take the child into the mine to assist him in winning bread for the family." On average, children worked 60 hours a week and carried home paychecks a third the size of those of adult males.

Women had always labored on family farms, but by 1870 one out of every four nonagricultural workers was female. In general they earned one-half of what men did. Nearly all were single and young, anywhere from their mid-teens to their mid-twenties. Most lived in boardinghouses or at home with their parents. Usually they contributed their wages to the family kitty. Once married, they took on a life of full-time housework and child rearing.

Injured boy from the mills

Only 5 percent of married women held jobs outside the home in 1900. Married black women (in need of income because of the low wages paid to their husbands) were four times more likely than married whites to work away from home. Domestic service was by far the most common occupation for these women. But industrialization inevitably pushed women into new jobs. Mainly they worked in industries considered extensions of housework: food processing, textiles and clothing, and cigar making. And many women actually preferred factory labor, with its long hours and dirty conditions, to being a live-in servant, where they were at work over six days a week and on call 24 hours a day.

New methods of management and marketing opened positions for white-collar women as "typewriters," "telephone girls," bookkeepers, and secretaries. On rare occasions women entered the professions, though law and medical schools still regarded them as unwelcome invaders. Such discrimination drove ambitious, educated women into nursing, teaching, and library work. Their growing presence soon "feminized" these professions, pushing men upward into managerial slots or out entirely.

Even more than women, African American men faced discrimination in the workplace. They were paid less than whites and given menial jobs. Their greatest opportunities in industry often came as strikebreakers to replace white workers. Once a strike ended, however, black workers were replaced themselves and hated by the white regulars whom they had replaced. The service trades furnished the largest single source of jobs. Waiting on whites in restaurants or on railroads lay within the boundaries set by the prevailing color line. Craftworkers and a sprinkling of black professionals could usually be found in cities. After the turn of the century, black-owned businesses thrived in the growing black neighborhoods of the North and South.

The American Dream of Success

Whatever their separate experiences, working-class Americans did improve their overall lot. Though the gap between the very rich and the poor widened, most wage earners made some gains. Between 1860 and 1890 real daily wages—pay in terms of buying power—climbed some 50 percent, more the result of gradually falling prices than of increases in pay. And after 1890, the number of hours on the job began a slow decline.

Rising real wages

Yet most unskilled and semiskilled workers in factories continued to receive low pay. In 1890, an unskilled laborer could expect about $1.50 for a 10-hour day;

Clerks' jobs, traditionally held by men, came to be filled by women as growing industrial networks created more managerial jobs for men. In this typical office, male managers literally oversee female clerks.

Social mobility

a skilled one, perhaps twice that amount. It took about $600 to make ends meet, but most manufacturing workers made under $500 a year. Native-born white Americans tended to earn more than immigrants, those who spoke English more than those who did not, men more than women, and all others more than African Americans, Latinos, and Asians.

Few workers repeated the rags-to-riches rise of Andrew Carnegie. But some did rise despite periodic unemployment and ruthless wage cuts. About one-quarter of the manual laborers in one study entered the lower middle class in their own lifetimes. More often such unskilled workers climbed in financial status within their own class. Most workers, seeing some improvement, believed in the American dream of success, even if they did not fully share in it.

The Systems of Labor

Putting in more hours to save a few pennies, walking out in exhaustion or disgust, slowing down on the job—in these ways individual workers coped with industrial America. Sporadic and unorganized, such actions stood little chance of bringing the new industrial order under the control of labor. For ordinary workers to begin to shape industrialization they had to combine, as businesses did. They needed to combine horizontally—organizing not just locally but on a national scale. And they needed to integrate vertically by coordinating action across a wide range of jobs and skills, as Andrew Carnegie coordinated the production of steel.

Unions were the workers' systematic response to industrialization. The most radical unions echoed the moral critics of capitalism by pointing to the oppressiveness of the new industrial order and worked to overturn it. Others embraced the new industrial order but wanted to improve the position of workers within it. Yet whatever their views, unionists believed that power had swung out of balance and only an organized response could correct it.

Early Unions

In the United States unions began forming before the Civil War. Skilled craft-workers—carpenters, iron molders, cigar makers—joined together to protect themselves against the growing power of management. Railroad "brotherhoods" also furnished insurance for those hurt or killed on the accident-plagued lines. Largely local and exclusively male, these early craft unions remained weak and unconnected to each other as well as to the growing mass of unskilled workers.

After the Civil War, a group of craft unions, brotherhoods, and reformers united skilled and unskilled workers in a nationwide organization. The National Labor Union (NLU) hailed the virtues of a simpler America, when workers controlled their workday, earned a decent living, and had time to be good citizens. NLU leaders attacked the wage system as unfair and enslaving and urged workers to manage their own factories. By the early 1870s, NLU ranks had swelled to more than 600,000.

National Labor Union

The NLU pressed energetically for the eight-hour workday, the most popular labor demand of the era. Workers saw it as a way not merely of limiting their time on the job but of limiting the power of employers over their lives. "Eight hours for work; eight hours for rest; eight hours for what we will!" proclaimed a banner at one labor rally. Despite the popularity of the issue, the NLU wilted during the depression of 1873.

The Knights of Labor

More successful was a national union born in secrecy. In 1869 Uriah Stephens and nine Philadelphia garment cutters founded the Noble and Holy Order of the Knights of Labor. They draped themselves in ritual and regalia to deepen their sense of solidarity and met in secret to evade hostile owners. The Knights remained small and fraternal for a decade. Their strongly Protestant tone repelled Catholics, who made up almost half the workforce in many industries.

In 1879 the Knights elected Terence V. Powderly as their Grand Master Workman. Handsome, dynamic, Irish, and Catholic, Powderly threw off the Knights' secrecy, dropped their rituals, and opened their ranks. He called for "one big union" to embrace the "toiling millions"—skilled and unskilled, men and women, natives and immigrants, all religions, all races. By 1886, membership had leaped to over 700,000, including nearly 30,000 African Americans and 3000 women.

Terence Powderly

Like the NLU, the radical Knights of Labor looked to abolish the wage system. In its place they wanted to construct a cooperative economy of worker-owned mines, factories, and railroads. The Knights set up more than 140 cooperative workshops, where workers shared decisions and profits, and sponsored some 200 political candidates, who enjoyed only sporadic success. To tame the new industrial order, they supported the eight-hour workday and the regulation of trusts. Underlying this program was a moral vision of society. If only people renounced greed, laziness, and dishonesty, Powderly argued, corruption and class division would disappear, and democracy would flourish. To reform citizens, the Knights promoted the prohibition of child and convict labor and the abolition of liquor.

It was one thing to proclaim a national union, quite another to coordinate the activities of so many members. Powderly soon found locals resorting to strikes and violence, actions he condemned. In the mid-1880s, such stoppages wrung concessions from the western railroads, but the organization soon became associated with unsuccessful strikes and violent extremists. Even the gains against the railroads were wiped out when the Texas and Pacific Railroad broke a strike by local Knights.

By 1890 the Knights of Labor, symbol of organized labor's resistance to industrial capitalism, teetered near extinction.

The American Federation of Labor

Samuel Gompers

The Knights' position as the premier union in the nation was taken by the rival American Federation of Labor (AFL). The AFL reflected the practicality of its leader, Samuel Gompers. Born in a London tenement, the son of a Jewish cigar maker, Gompers had immigrated in 1863 with his family to New York's Lower East Side. Unlike the visionary Powderly, Gompers preached accommodation, not resistance. He urged his followers to accept capitalism and the wage system. What he wanted was "pure and simple unionism"—a worker organization that bargained for higher wages, fewer hours, improved safety, more benefits.

Gompers chose to organize highly skilled craftworkers because they were difficult to replace. He bargained with employers and used strikes and boycotts only as last resorts. With the Cigar Makers' Union as his base, Gompers helped create the first national federation of craft unions in 1881. In 1886, it was reorganized as the American Federation of Labor. Twenty-five labor groups joined, representing nearly 140,000 skilled workers.

Here was labor's answer to the corporation and the trust: a horizontal organization trying to minimize competition among skilled workers. Gompers fought off radicals and allied himself with whatever candidate supported labor. Stressing gradual, concrete gains, he made the AFL the most powerful union in the country. By 1901 it had more than a million members, almost a third of all skilled workers in America.

Failure of organized labor

Despite the success of the AFL, the laboring classes did not organize themselves as systematically as did the barons of industrial America. For one thing, Gompers and the AFL were less interested in vertical integration that combined skilled and unskilled workers and had little inclination to include women and African Americans. For another, workers themselves were separated by language and culture, divided along lines of race and gender, and fearful of retaliation by management. A strong strain of individualism made many workers regard any collective action as un-American. And so they often resisted unionization. In 1900, union membership comprised less than 10 percent of industrial workers.

The Limits of Industrial Systems

It was the vagaries of the marketplace and stubbornness of owners that in the end broke the labor movement and set the limits of industrial systems for workers. As managers increased their control over the workplace, workers often found themselves at the mercy of the new industrial order. Even in boom times, one in three workers was out of a job at least three or four months a year. The word *unemployment* dates from the late nineteenth century.

Spontaneous protests

When a worker's pay dropped and frustration mounted, when a mother worked all night and fell asleep during the day while caring for her children, when food prices suddenly jumped—anger might boil over into protest. "A mob of 1,000 people, with women in the lead, marched through the Jewish quarter of Williamsburg last evening and wrecked half a dozen butcher shops," reported the *New York Times* in 1902. In the late nineteenth century a wave of labor activism swept the nation. More often than mobs, it was strikes and boycotts that challenged the authority of employers and gave evidence of working-class identity and discontent.

Most strikes broke out spontaneously, organized by informal leaders in a factory. "Malvina Fourtune and her brother Henry Fourtune it was them who started

In this painting by Robert Koehler, entitled *The Strike* (1886), labor confronts management in a strike that may soon turn bloody. One worker reaches for a stone as an anxious mother and her children look on.

the strike," declared a company informer in Chicopee, Massachusetts. "They go from house to house and tells the people to keep up the strike." Thousands of rallies and organized strikes were staged as well, often on behalf of the eight-hour workday, in good times and bad, by union and nonunion workers alike.

Molly Maguires

Some workers resorted to terrorism to resist the new industrial order. In the coalfields of Pennsylvania, Irish miners organized a secret society called the Molly Maguires, after an earlier group of protesters in Ireland who had disguised themselves as women and roamed the Irish countryside beating and sometimes killing tyrannical landlords. The American Mollys founded their society in 1866, and for the next decade the small but dedicated band resorted to intimidation, arson, and murder to combat the horrid working conditions of coal miners. In 1876, twenty Mollys were brought to trial and a year later executed for sixteen murders. For most Americans, justice was served, despite the questionable legality of the trial—and in its wake, the secret society vanished. But for those who had joined the Mollys, violence was a long-established tradition, imported from Ireland and employed as both a form of protest and a means of achieving "retributive justice" against oppressors.

Great Railroad Strike

In 1877, in the midst of a deep depression, the country's first nationwide strike opened an era of confrontation between labor and management. When the Baltimore and Ohio Railroad cut wages by 20 percent, a crew in Martinsburg, West Virginia, seized the local depot and blocked the line. President Hayes sent federal troops to enforce a court order ending the strike, but instead two-thirds of the nation's tracks were shut down in sympathy. The novel tactic suggested a growing sense of solidarity among workers. The country ground to a halt.

When owners brought in strikebreakers, workers torched rail yards, smashed engines and cars, and tore up track. Local police, state militia, and federal troops finally quashed the strike after 12 bloody days. The "Great Railroad Strike" of 1877 left 100 people dead and more than $10 million worth of railroad property in rubble. It signaled the rising power and unity of labor and sparked fears, as one newspaper warned, that "this may be the beginning of a great civil war in this country, between labor and capital."

Laundresses strike

The Civil War between North and South was still fresh in the minds of Atlantans when 3000 laundresses struck for higher wages in 1881. Over 98 percent of the city's domestic workers were black women, just a decade and a half out of slavery. Pitiful wages already had led many of them to employ informal strategies to protest. They took unauthorized breaks, pretended to be sick, or "pantoted" (stole) leftovers from the kitchens of their white employers. Washerwomen were among the most privileged domestics because they neither worked nor lived with their employers. Instead they labored together in common spaces in their neighborhoods, where they built social and political networks. In 1881 they formed the Washing Society and threatened to leave much of the city without clean clothes unless their demands for higher wages were met. Though little resulted from the strike, it nonetheless showed the growing appeal of organized protest against economic inequality and laid the groundwork for later civil rights protests.

Haymarket Square riot

In 1886, tension between labor and capital exploded in the "Great Upheaval"—a series of strikes, boycotts, and rallies. One of the most violent episodes occurred at Haymarket Square in Chicago. A group of anarchists was protesting the recent killing of workers by police at the McCormick Harvester Company. As rain drenched the small crowd, police ordered everyone out of the square. Suddenly a bomb exploded. One officer was killed; 6 others were mortally wounded. When police opened fire, the crowd fired back. Nearly 70 policemen were injured, and at least 4 civilians died.

Conservatives charged that radicals were responsible for the "Haymarket Massacre." Though the bomb thrower was never identified and though no evidence connecting the accused to the bombing was ever presented, a jury found eight anarchists guilty of conspiracy to commit murder. Four were hanged, one killed himself, and three remained in jail until they were pardoned by Governor John Peter Altgeld in 1893. He considered their conviction a miscarriage of justice, but ordinary citizens who had supported labor grew fearful of what newspapers called its "Samson-like power." Cities enlarged their police forces, and states built more National Guard armories on the borders of working-class neighborhoods.

Management Strikes

The strikes, rallies, and boycotts of 1886 were followed by a second surge of labor activism in 1892. In the remote silver mines of Coeur d'Alene, Idaho, at the Carnegie steel mill in Homestead, Pennsylvania, in the coal mines near Tracy City, Tennessee, strikes flared, only to be crushed by management. Often state and federal troops joined company guards and private detectives from the Pinkerton agency to fight workers.

Pullman strike

The broadest confrontation between labor and management took place two years later. A terrible depression had shaken the economy for almost a year when George Pullman, owner of the Palace Car factory and inventor of the plush railroad car, laid off workers, cut wages (but kept rents high on company-owned housing), and refused to discuss grievances. In 1894 workers struck and managed to convince the new American Railway Union to support them by boycotting all trains that used Pullman cars. Quickly the strike spread to 27 states and territories.

Anxious railroad owners appealed to President Grover Cleveland for federal help. On the slim pretext that the strike obstructed mail delivery (strikers had actually been willing to handle mail trains without Pullman cars), Cleveland secured a court order halting the strike. He then called several thousand special deputies into Chicago to enforce it. In the rioting that followed, 12 people died and scores were arrested. But the strike was crushed.

"GIVING THE BUTT"—THE WAY THE "REGULAR" INFANTRY TACKLES A MOB.

Government troops were often called in to help management quell strikes. In the Pullman Strike of 1894, U.S. Regulars "give the butt" to angry laborers in this drawing by Frederick Remington.

In all labor disputes the central issue was the power to shape the new industrial systems. Employers always enjoyed the advantage. They hired and fired workers, set the terms of employment, and ruled the workplace. They fought unions with "yellow dog" contracts that forced workers to refuse to join. Blacklists circulated the names of labor agitators. Lockouts kept protesting workers from plants, and company spies infiltrated their organizations. With a growing pool of labor, employers could replace strikers and break strikes.

Management could also count on local, state, and federal authorities for troops to break strikes. In addition, businesses used a powerful new legal weapon, the injunction. These court orders prohibited certain actions, including strikes, by barring workers from interfering with their employer's business. It was just such an order that had brought federal deputies into the Pullman strike and put Eugene Debs, head of the American Railway Union, behind bars. The Indiana-born Debs, a former locomotive fireman and early labor organizer, received a six-month jail sentence for violating the court injunction. After his release, he abandoned the Democratic party to become the foremost Socialist leader in America. Yet despite the protests of workers such as Debs, employers had become masters of the mightiest industrial economy on earth.

In a matter of only 30 or 40 years, the new industrial order transformed the landscape of America. Whether rich or poor, worker, entrepreneur, or industrial baron, Americans were being drawn closer by the new industrial systems. Ore scooped from Mesabi might end up in a steel girder on James Eads's Mississippi bridge, in a steel needle for Sadie Frowne's sewing machine in Brooklyn, or in a McCormick reaper slicing across the Nebraska plains. When a textile worker in Massachusetts struck, a family in Alabama might well pay more for clothes. A man in Cleveland now set his watch to agree with the time of a man in New York, regardless of the position of the sun. Such changes might seem effortless to someone like T. S. Hudson, scampering across the rails of America in 1882. But as the nineteenth century drew to a close, material progress went hand in hand with social pain and upheaval.

Management weapons

chapter summary

In the last third of the nineteenth century, a new industrial order reshaped the United States.

- New systems—of resource development, technology, invention, transportation, communications, finance, corporate management, and labor—boosted industrial growth and productivity.

- Businesses grew big, expanding vertically and horizontally to curb costs and competition and to increase control and efficiency.

- Industrialization came at a price.

  - Workers found their power, job satisfaction, and free time reduced as their numbers in factories mushroomed.

  - The environment was degraded.

  - A vicious cycle of boom and bust afflicted the economy.

- Workers both resisted and accommodated the new industrial order.

  - Some resisted through informal mechanisms such as slowdowns, absenteeism, and quitting and through spontaneous and more formal ones, including radical unions like the Knights of Labor.

  - Other workers were more accommodating, accepting low-paying jobs and layoffs and creating "pure-and-simple" unions, such as the American Federation of Labor, that accepted the prevailing system of private ownership and wage labor while bargaining for better wages and working conditions.

- The benefits of industrialization were equally undeniable.

  - Life improved materially for many Americans.

  - The real wages of even industrial workers climbed.

- The United States rocketed from fourth place among industrial nations in 1860 to first by 1890.

interactive learning

The Primary Source Investigator CD-ROM offers the following materials related to this chapter:

- Interactive map: **The Transportation Revolution, 1830–1890** (M12)

- A collection of primary sources capturing the effects of the rise of capitalism in the United States, including the Gold Standard Act and a number of photos by Jacob Riis. Several documents also illustrate rapid improvements in technology: see a van used to carry photographic equipment and learn about Thomas Edison's invention of the light bulb.

additional reading

For a useful introduction to the period, see Edward C. Kirland, *Industry Comes of Age: Business, Labor, and Public Policy, 1860–1897* (1967). Mechanization and its impact are the focus of Siegfried Giedion's classic *Mechanization Takes Command* (1948). The best overview of American labor is American So-

cial History Project, *Who Built America? Working People and the Nation's Economy, Politics, Culture, & Society,* Volume Two: *From the Gilded Age to the Present* (1992). Herbert Gutman, *Work, Culture, and Society in Industrializing America: Essays in American Working-Class History* (1976), explores the development of working-class communities in the nineteenth century, especially the role of ethnicity in creating a working-class culture. David Montgomery offers a broad look at the impact of industrialization on American labor in *The Fall of the House of Labor: The Workplace, the State, and American Labor Activism, 1865–1925* (1987), and Leon Fink, *Workingmen's Democracy:*

The Knights of Labor and American Politics (1983), examines early efforts of the Knights of Labor to challenge corporate capitalism by organizing workers and socializing them into a labor culture. Alice Kessler-Harris, *Out to Work: A History of Wage-Earning Women in the United States* (1982), surveys female wage earners and their effect on American culture, family life, and values. Kevin Kenny, *Making Sense of the Molly Maguires* (1998), is a superb study not only of the mysterious Mollys and their tragic end but of immigration, working-class violence, and the history of the Irish in America.

No book did more to set the idea of big business as ruthless robber barons than Matthew Josephson, *The Robber Barons: The Great American Capitalists, 1861–1901* (1934).

An early revision of this bleak image can be found in Allan Nevins's biography of John D. Rockefeller, *A Study in Power: John D. Rockefeller, Industrialist and Philanthropist*, 2 vols. (1953). Business historian Alfred D. Chandler Jr.'s *Strategy and Structure: Chapters in the History of American Industrial Enterprise* (1962) and *The Visible Hand: The Managerial Revolution in American Business* (1977) are seminal accounts of business organization and management that stress the adaptations of business structures and the emergence of a new class of managers. For a comparative view of the rise of big business in the United States, Great Britain, and Germany, see his *Scale and Scope* (1988). For a fuller list of readings, see the Bibliography at www.mhhe.com/davidsonnation5.

significant events

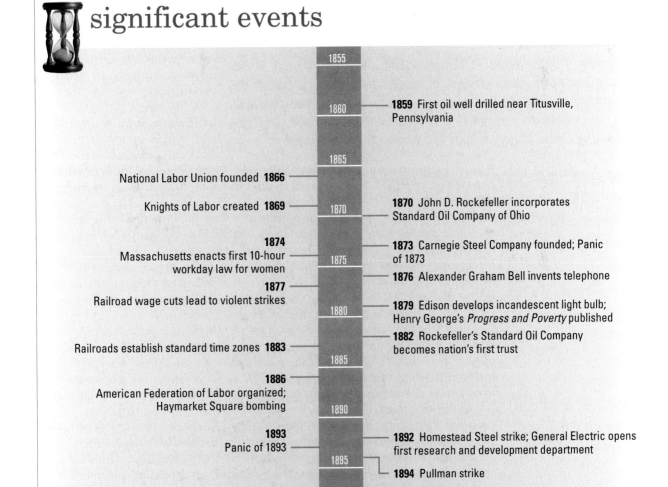

1855

1859 First oil well drilled near Titusville, Pennsylvania

1860

1865

National Labor Union founded **1866**

Knights of Labor created **1869**

1870

1870 John D. Rockefeller incorporates Standard Oil Company of Ohio

1874
Massachusetts enacts first 10-hour workday law for women

1875

1873 Carnegie Steel Company founded; Panic of 1873

1876 Alexander Graham Bell invents telephone

1877
Railroad wage cuts lead to violent strikes

1880

1879 Edison develops incandescent light bulb; Henry George's *Progress and Poverty* published

Railroads establish standard time zones **1883**

1885

1882 Rockefeller's Standard Oil Company becomes nation's first trust

1886
American Federation of Labor organized; Haymarket Square bombing

1890

1893
Panic of 1893

1895

1892 Homestead Steel strike; General Electric opens first research and development department

1894 Pullman strike

1900

1901 U.S. Steel Corporation becomes nation's first billion-dollar company

1905

Chapter 20

Graziano's bootblack stand was jammed with people milling about, looking for help. Above the crowd, enthroned like an Irish king, sat George Washington Plunkitt, ward boss of Manhattan's Fifteenth Assembly District. There to help, Plunkitt asked little in return, only votes on election day. Plunkitt understood the close relationship between help and votes. "There's got to be in every ward," another boss explained, "somebody that any bloke can come to—no matter what he's done—and get help. *Help, you understand; none of your law and justice, but help.*" Plunkitt knew the reverse to be true as well: to maintain power, political bosses had to be able to count on the support of those they helped.

For years Plunkitt had been a leader of Tammany Hall, the Democratic party organization that ruled New York City politics from 1850 to 1930. Much of Plunkitt's daily routine was taken up with helping. One typical day began when a bartender roused him at two in the morning to get a friend out of jail. Plunkitt succeeded but didn't return to bed until after three. Howling fire sirens woke him at six. Before dawn he was assisting burned-out tenants with food, clothing, and shelter. Home by eleven, he found four out-of-work men waiting for help. Within hours each had a job. A quick bite of lunch and he was off again, this time to a pair of funerals. Plunkitt brought flowers for the bereaved and offered condolences, all in full view of the assembled. From there he rushed to attend a "Hebrew confirmation." Early evening found him at district headquarters, helping his election captains plot ways of "turning out the vote."

The Rise of an Urban Order

1870–1900

preview • At the center of the new industrial order was the city. But to accommodate the global migration of laborers and families, to support the sprawling factories and the masses who kept them going, urban centers of the late nineteenth century had to reinvent themselves. Transportation systems, residential housing, political and social cultures all changed.

After a quick stop at a church fair, it was back to the party clubhouse. He helped some local teams by buying tickets for their next game. Before leaving, he pledged to help two dozen pushcart peddlers by trying to stop the police from harassing them. He arrived at a wedding reception at half past ten (already having helped the bride and groom with "a handsome wedding present"). Finally, at midnight, he crawled into bed, after a day of helping all he could.

Such relentless effort helped Plunkitt as well. Born poor to Irish immigrants, he died a millionaire in 1924. His pluck and practicality would have made him the envy of any industrialist. As with the Carnegies and Rockefellers, fierce ambition fueled his rise from butcher boy to political boss. City politics was his way out of the slums in a world that favored the rich, the educated, and the well-established.

In the late nineteenth century the needs of rapidly growing cities gave political bosses like George Washington Plunkitt their chance. "I seen my opportunities and I took 'em," Plunkitt used to say. Every city contract and bond issue, every tax assessment, every charter for a new business offered Plunkitt and his cronies an opportunity to line their pockets. Money made from defrauding the public was known as "boodle," or honest graft. ("Black" graft came from vice and extortion.) How much boodle bosses collected depended on how well their organization managed to elect sympathetic officials. That explained why Plunkitt spent so much time helping his constituents.

Plunkitt's New York was the first great city in history to be ruled by ordinary people in an organized and continuing way. Bosses and their cronies came from

Boodle

Realist painters like George Bellows, who were scorned by critics as the "Ashcan School," captured the grittiness and vibrancy of teeming urban life. *Cliff Dwellers* makes dramatic use of light and dark, relying on line, mass, and color to achieve its naturalism.

the streets and saloons, the slums and tenements, the firehouses and funeral homes. Many of their families had only recently arrived in America. While the Irish of Tammany Hall ran New York, Germans governed St. Louis, Scandinavians Minneapolis, and Jews San Francisco.

In an earlier age political leadership had been drawn from the ranks of the wealthy and native-born. America had been an agrarian republic where personal relationships were grounded in small communities. By the late nineteenth century, the country was in the midst of an urban explosion. Industrial cities of unparalleled size and diversity were transforming American life. They lured people from all over the globe, created tensions between natives and newcomers, reshaped the social order. For Plunkitt, as for so many Americans, a new urban age was dawning. The golden door of opportunity opened onto the city.

A New Urban Age

The modern city was the product of industrialization. Cities contained the great investment banks, the smoky mills and dingy sweatshops, the spreading railroad yards, the grimy tenements and sparkling mansions, the new department stores and skyscrapers. People came from places as near as the countryside and as far as Italy, Russia, and Armenia. By the end of the nineteenth century America had entered a new urban age, with tens of millions of "urbanites," an urban landscape, and a growing urban culture.

The Urban Explosion

During the 50 years after the Civil War, the population of the United States quadrupled—from 23 million to 92 million. Yet the number of people living in American cities increased nearly sevenfold. In 1860, only one American in six lived in a city with a population of 8000 or more; in 1900, one in three did. By 1910 nearly half the nation lived in cities large and small.

Cities grew in every region of the country, some faster than others. In the Northeast and upper Midwest early industrialization created more cities than in the West and the South, although those regions contained big cities as well. Atlanta, Nashville, and later Dallas and Houston boomed under the influence of railroads. Los Angeles had barely 6000 people in 1870. By 1900 it trailed only San Francisco among large cities on the Pacific coast, with a population of 100,000.

Large urban centers dominated whole regions and tied the country together in a complex urban network. New York, the nation's banker, printer, and chief marketplace, ruled the East. Smaller cities operated within narrower spheres of influence and often specialized. Milwaukee was famous for its beer, Tulsa for oil, and Hershey, Pennsylvania, for chocolate.

Cities' relations to regions around them

Cities even shaped the natural environment hundreds of miles beyond their limits. Chicago became not only the gateway to the West but also a powerful agent of ecological change. As its lines of commerce and industry radiated outward, the city transformed the ecosystems of the West. Wheat to feed Chicago's millions replaced sheltering prairie grasses. Great stands of white pine in Wisconsin vanished, only to reappear in the furniture and frames of Chicago houses or as fence rails shipped to prairie farms.

The Great Global Migration

Between 1820 and 1920, some 60 million people left farms and villages for cities across the globe. They formed part of a migrating pool of labor, moving from country to country in search of work. Beginning in the 1870s, the use of ocean-going, steam-powered ships made it possible for migrating laborers to seek work across continents, and in Europe mushrooming populations, aided by scientific breakthroughs and advances in technology, gave the emigrants a powerful push out. The end of the Napoleonic Wars in 1815 launched a cycle of baby booms that continued at 20-year intervals for the rest of the century. Improved diet and sanitation, aided by Louis Pasteur's discovery that bacteria cause infection and disease, reduced deaths. Meanwhile machinery cut the need for farm workers. In 1896 one man in a wheat field could do what had taken 18 men just 60 years earlier.

Push and pull factors

Surplus farm workers formed a ragtag army of migrants both in America and in Europe. The prospect of factory work for better pay and fewer hours lured especially the young to cities. Labor agents combed Europe, pulling immigrants to the United States with often false promises of high-paying jobs and unimagined riches. "They told me that in America the streets were paved with gold," reported one immigrant. "When I got here, I found the streets were not paved with gold, they were not paved at all, and they expected me to pave them." In America, young farm women spearheaded the migration. Mechanization and the rise of commercial agriculture made them less valuable in the fields, while mass-produced goods from mail-order houses made them less useful at home.

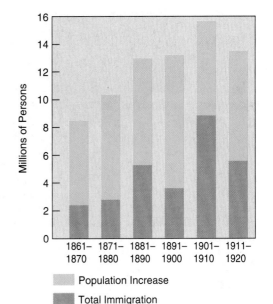

*Includes immigrants from Great Britain, Ireland, Germany, and the Scandinavian countries.

†Includes immigrants from Poland, Russia, Italy, and other Baltic and East European countries.

Immigration and Population, 1860–1920 Between 1860 and 1920, immigration increased dramatically as the sources of immigrants shifted from northern Europe to southeastern Europe. Despite fears to the contrary, the proportion of newcomers as a percentage of population increases did not show nearly the same jump.

Asia sent comparatively fewer newcomers to the United States, Canada, and other industrializing nations hungry for workers, but Asian immigrants followed migration patterns similar to those of the workers leaving Europe and for similar reasons. In China, for example, several factors combined to push some 370,000 people out of the country and into the United States and Hawaii between 1850 and 1882. Defeats in the Opium Wars (1839–1842) and the Anglo-Chinese War (1856–1860) forced the Chinese to pay large indemnities to Great Britain and to limit the duties charged on foreign imports. When the Chinese government raised taxes to make up the difference, small landowners unable to afford them lost their farms, tenants unable to pay higher rents lost their plots, and peasants who had turned their homes into centers of small industry lost income. They simply could not compete with the now-cheaper manufactured goods from the West.

Chinese immigrants

To that international context could be added domestic upheavals, interethnic rivalries, and local wars in central and southern China that devastated those regions. Many of the people displaced by taxation and turmoil moved within the country, but those from Guangdong Province in southeastern China, especially around the coastal city of Canton, often left the country entirely. Canton had long been a thriving port of trade at which foreigners called and from which the Cantonese ventured abroad. Agents from America and Europe could recruit workers more easily in Canton, and ships stood ready in the harbor to transport them across the Pacific and elsewhere. In Japan and other Asian nations, similar forces of push and pull sparked migration into the United States, including some 400,000 Japanese between 1885 and 1924.

Earlier in the century, European immigrants had come to the United States from northern and western Europe. In the 1880s, "new" immigrants from southern and eastern Europe began to arrive. Some, like Russian and Polish Jews, were fleeing religious and political persecution. Others left to evade famine or diseases

The "new" immigration

By the 1890s, European immigrants were arriving at the new receiving center on Ellis Island in New York harbor (left). Asian immigrants came through Angel Island in San Francisco Bay (right). On both coasts, physical examinations, like the eye inspections shown, became part of standard screening practices as immigration policies stiffened. The rapid rise in immigration ignited nativist fears that immigrants were taking over the country. In the 1870s cartoon, immigrants literally gobble up Uncle Sam.

such as cholera, which swept across southern Italy in 1887. But most came for the same reasons as migrants from the countryside—a job, more money, a fresh start.

Ambitious, hardy, and resourceful, immigrants found themselves tested every step of the way to America. They left behind the comfort of family, friends, and old ways. The price of one-way passage by steamship—about $50 in 1904—was far too expensive for most to bring relatives, at least at first. And the trip was dangerous even before immigrants stepped on board a ship. They traveled for weeks, stealing across heavily guarded borders, just to reach a port like Le Havre in France. At dockside, shipping lines vaccinated, disinfected, and examined them to ensure against their being returned at company expense.

It took one to two weeks to cross the Atlantic aboard steam-powered ships. Immigrants spent most of the time belowdecks in cramped, filthy compartments called "steerage." Most arrived at New York's Castle Garden or the newer facility on nearby Ellis Island, opened in 1892. If coming from Asia, they landed at Angel Island in San

Francisco Bay. Sometimes they were held in the facility for weeks. As one Chinese newcomer gazed out on San Francisco Bay, he scribbled a poem on the gray walls:

> Why do I have to languish in this jail?
> It is because my country is weak and my family poor.
> My parents wait in vain for news;
> My wife and child, wrapped in their quilt, sigh with loneliness.

Immigrants had to pass another medical examination, have their names recorded by customs officials, and pay an entry tax. At any point, they could be detained or shipped home.

Immigrants arrived in staggering numbers—over 6 million between 1877 and 1890, some 30 million by 1920. By 1900 they made up nearly 15 percent of the population. Most were young, between the ages of 15 and 40. Few spoke English or had skills or much education. Unlike earlier arrivals, who were mostly Protestant, these new immigrants worshiped in Catholic, Greek, or Russian Orthodox churches and Jewish synagogues. Almost two-thirds were men. A large number came to make money for buying land or starting businesses back home. Some changed their minds and sent for relatives, but those returning were common enough to be labeled "birds of passage."

Immigrant profile

Jews were an exception. Russian Jews escaped from Europe by the tens of thousands after the assassination of Czar Alexander II in 1881 rekindled anti-Semitic "pogroms," or riots. Between 1880 and 1914, a third of eastern Europe's Jews left. They made up 10 percent of all immigration to the United States during those years. Almost all stayed and brought their families, often one by one. They had few choices. As one Jewish immigrant wrote of his Russian homeland, "Am I not despised? Am I not urged to leave? . . . Do I not rise daily with the fear lest the hungry mob attack me?"

The Shape of the City

In colonial days, Benjamin Franklin could walk from one end of Boston to the other in an hour. Only Franklin's adopted home, Philadelphia, spilled into suburbs. Over the years these colonial "walking cities" developed ringed patterns of settlement. Merchants, professionals, and the upper classes lived near their shops and offices in the city center. As one walked outward, the income and status of the residents declined.

Cities of the late nineteenth century still exhibited this ringed pattern, except that industrialization had reversed the order of settlement and increased urban sprawl. As the middle and upper classes moved out of a growing industrial core, the poor, some immigrants, African Americans, and lower-class laborers filled the void. They took over old factories and brownstones, shanties and cellars. By sheer weight of numbers they transformed these areas into the slums of the central city.

Patterns of settlement

Curled around the slums was the "zone of emergence," an income-graded band of those on their way up. It contained second-generation city dwellers, factory workers, skilled laborers, and professional mechanics. They lived in progressively better tenements and neater row houses as the distance from center city increased. Poverty no longer imprisoned them, but they could still slip back in hard times.

Farther out was the suburban fringe, home to the new class of white-collar managers and executives. They lived in larger houses with individual lots on neat, tree-lined streets. The very wealthy still maintained mansions on fashionable city avenues, but by the 1870s and 1880s, they too began to keep suburban homes.

Growth of New Orleans to 1900
Streetcars helped cities spread beyond business districts while still functioning as organic wholes. By 1900, streetcar lines in New Orleans reached all the way to Audubon Park and Tulane University, bringing these once-distant points within the reach of city dwellers and creating "streetcar suburbs."

Urban Transport

For all their differences, the circles of settlement held together as a part of a massive and interdependent whole. One reason was an evolving system of urban transportation. Civic leaders came to understand that the modern city could not survive, much less grow, without improved transportation. San Francisco installed trolley cars pulled by steam-driven cables. It worked so well in San Francisco that Chicago, Seattle, and other hilly cities installed cable systems in the 1880s. Some cities experimented with elevated trestles to carry steam locomotives, others, with cable lines high above crowded streets. But none of the breakthroughs quite did the trick. Cables remained slow and unreliable; the elevated railways, or "els," were dirty, ugly, and noisy.

Role of electricity

Electricity rescued city travelers. In 1888 Frank Julian Sprague, a naval engineer who had once worked for Thomas Edison, installed the first electric trolley line in Richmond, Virginia. Electrified streetcars were soon speeding along at 12 miles an hour, twice as fast as horses. By 1902 electricity drove nearly all city railways. Sprague's innovations also meant that "subways" could be built without having to worry about tunnels filled with a steam engine's smoke and soot. Between 1895 and 1897 Boston built the first underground electric line. New York followed in 1904 with a subway that ran from City Hall on the southern tip of Manhattan north to Harlem. Once considered too far afield, Harlem soon became dotted with new apartment and tenement developments. When the white middle class of

New York refused to move so far uptown, Philip A. Peyton convinced landlords to allow his Afro-American Realty Company to handle the properties. Within a decade Harlem had become the black capital of America.

The rich had long been able to keep homes outside city limits, traveling to and fro in private carriages. New systems of mass transit freed the middle class and even the poor to live miles from work. For a nickel or two, anyone could ride from central shopping and business districts to the suburban fringes and back. A network of moving vehicles held the segmented and sprawling city together and widened its reach out to "streetcar suburbs."

Bridges and Skyscrapers

Because cities often grew along rivers and harbors, their separate parts sometimes had to be joined over water. The principles of building large river bridges had already been worked out by the railroads. It remained for a German immigrant and his son, John and Washington Roebling, to make the bridge a symbol of urban growth.

The Brooklyn Bridge, linking New York City with Brooklyn, took 13 years to complete. It cost $15 million and 20 lives, including that of designer John. When it opened in 1883, it stretched more than a mile across the East River, with passage broad enough for a footpath, two double carriage lanes, and two railroad lines. Its arches were cut like giant cathedral windows, and its supporting cables hung, said an awestruck observer, "like divine messages from above." Soon other suspension bridges were spanning the railroad yards in St. Louis and the bay at Galveston, Texas.

Even as late as 1880 church steeples dominated the urban landscape. They towered over squat factories and office buildings. But growing congestion and the increasing value of land pushed architects to search for ways to make buildings taller. In place of thick walls of brick that restricted factory floor space, builders used cast iron columns. The new "cloudscrapers" were strong, durable, and fire-resistant. Their open floors were ideal for warehouses and also for office buildings and department stores.

Steel, tougher in tension and compression, turned cloudscrapers into skyscrapers. William LeBaron Jenney first used steel in his 10-story Home Insurance Building (1885) in Chicago. By the end of the century steel frames and girders raised buildings to 30 stories or more. New York City's triangular Flatiron building (at right), named for its shape, used the new technology to project an angular yet remarkably delicate elegance. In Chicago, Daniel Burnham's Reliance Building (1890) relied so heavily on new plate glass windows that contemporaries called it "a glass tower fifteen stories high."

It was no accident that many of the new skyscrapers arose in Chicago, for the city had burned nearly to the ground in 1871. The "Chicago school" of architects helped rebuild it. The young maverick Louis H. Sullivan promised a new urban profile in which the skyscraper would be "every inch a proud and soaring thing." In the Wainwright Building (1890) in St. Louis and the Carson, Pirie, and Scott

Flatiron Building, New York City

department store (1889–1904) in Chicago, Sullivan produced towering structures that symbolized the modern industrial city.

Architects did not create the towering landscapes of modern industrial cities without help. Soaring skyscrapers were of little value without an efficient, safe means of transporting people aloft. In 1861, Elisha Graves Otis developed a trustworthy, fast elevator. By the 1890s, new electric elevators were whisking people to the tops of towering buildings in seconds. The elevator extended the city upward, just as the streetcar extended it outward, and in the process both transformed the physical and social space of urban America.

Slum and Tenement

Far below the skyscrapers lay the slums and tenements of the inner city. In cramped rooms and sunless hallways, along narrow alleys and in flooded basements lived the city poor. They often worked there, too, in "sweaters' shops" where as many as 18 people labored and slept in foul two-room flats.

Perils of the slum neighborhood

In New York, whose slums were the nation's worst, crime thrived in places called "Bandit's Roost" and "Hell's Kitchen." Bands of young toughs with names like the "Sewer Rats" and the "Rock Gang" stalked the streets in search of thrills and easy money. Gambling, prostitution, and alcoholism all claimed their victims most readily in the slums. The poor usually turned to such crime in despair. A 20-year-old prostitute supporting a sickly mother and four brothers and sisters made no apologies: "Let God Almighty judge who's to blame most, I that was driven, or them that drove me to the pass I'm in."

The poor diets of slum dwellers left them vulnerable to disease, but it was their close quarters and often filthy surroundings that raised their rates of infection to epidemic levels. Cholera, typhoid, and an outbreak of yellow fever in Memphis in the 1870s killed tens of thousands. Tuberculosis was deadlier still. As late as 1900, among infectious diseases it ranked behind only influenza and pneumonia *combined* as a killer. Slum children—all city children—were most vulnerable. Almost a quarter of children born in American cities in 1890 never lived to see their first birthday.

"Dumbbell" tenements were designed to use every inch of available space in the standard 25-by-200-foot city lot while providing ventilation and reducing the spread of disease.

The installation of new sewage and water purification systems helped. The modern flush toilet came into use only after the turn of the century. Until then people relied on water closets and communal privies. Some catered to as many as 800. All too often cities dumped waste into old private vaults or rivers used for drinking water. In 1881 an exasperated mayor of Cleveland called the Cuyahoga River "an open sewer through the center of the city."

Slum housing was often more dangerous than the water. The tubercle bacillus flourished in musty, windowless tenements. In 1879 New York enacted a new housing law requiring a window in all bedrooms of new tenements. Architect James E. Ware won a competition with a design that contained an indentation on both sides of the building. When two tenements abutted each other, the indentations formed a narrow shaft for air and light. From above, the buildings looked like giant dumbbells. Up to 16 families lived on a floor, with only two toilets in the hall.

Originally hailed as an innovation, Ware's dumbbell tenement spread over such cities as Cleveland, Cincinnati, and Boston "like a scab," said an unhappy reformer. Ordinary blocks contained 10 such tenements and housed as many as 4000 people. The airshafts became giant silos for trash. They blocked what little light had entered and, worse still, carried fires from one story to the next. When the

New York housing commission met in 1900, it concluded that conditions were worse than when reformers had started 33 years earlier.

Every new arrival to the city brought dreams and altogether too many needs.

Running and Reforming the City

Schools and houses had to be built, streets paved, garbage collected, sewers dug, fires fought, utility lines laid. Running the city became a full-time job, and a new breed of professional politician rose to the task. So, too, did a new breed of reformer, determined to help the needy cope with the ravages of urban life.

The need for change was clear. Many city charters dating from the eighteenth century included a cumbersome system of checks and balances. Mayors vetoed city councils; councils ignored mayors. Jealous state legislatures allowed cities only the most limited and unpopular taxes, such as those on property. But to the cities more than the states fell responsibility for providing services. Municipal government grew into a tangle of little governments—fragmented, scattered, at odds with one another. By 1890, Chicago had 11 branches of government, each with its own regulations and taxing authority. Just as such decentralization paralyzed city governments, the traditional sources of political leadership evaporated. The middle and upper classes were being drawn into business and moving to the suburbs. As immigrants and rural newcomers flocked to factories and tenements, the structures of urban government strained to adapt.

Boss Rule

"Why must there be a boss," journalist Lincoln Steffens asked Boss Richard Croker of New York, "when we've got a mayor—and a city council?" "That's why," Croker broke in. "It's because we've got a mayor and a council and judges—*and*—a hundred other men to deal with." The boss was right. He and his system furnished cities with the centralization, authority, and services they sorely needed.

Bosses ruled through the political machine. Often, like New York's Tammany Hall, machines dated back to the late eighteenth and early nineteenth centuries. They began as fraternal and charitable organizations. Over the years they became centers of political power. In New York the machine was Democratic; in Philadelphia, Republican. Some were less centralized, as in Chicago; some less ethnically mixed, like Detroit's. Machines could be found even in rural areas. In Duval County, Texas, for instance, the Spanish-speaking Anglo boss Archie Parr molded a powerful alliance with Mexican American landowners.

In an age of enterprise, the political machine operated similarly to a corporation. Like a corporate executive, the boss looked on politics as a business. His office might be a saloon, a funeral home, or, like George Washington Plunkitt's, a shoeshine stand. His managers were party activists, connected in a corporate-style chain of command. Local committeemen reported to district captains, captains to district leaders, district leaders to the boss or bosses who directed the machine.

The boss as entrepreneur

The stock in trade of the machine was simple: a Christmas turkey, a load of coal for the winter, jobs for the unemployed, English language classes for the recently arrived. Bosses sponsored fun, too—sports teams, glee clubs, balls and barbecues with bands playing and drink flowing. This system, rough and uneven as it was, served as a form of public welfare at a time when private charity could not cope with the crush of demands. To the unskilled, the boss doled out jobs in public construction. For bright, ambitious young men, he had places in city offices or in

A crude welfare system

This stereotyped depiction of the "party boss" as a larger-than-life thug has him handing out "special privilege" and "immunity from arrest," among other gifts. Cartoons such as this one could be powerful weapons. The political cartoons of Thomas Nast, which appeared in the *New York Times,* especially angered Boss William Tweed. His supporters might not have been able to read, but they surely could understand pictures. Tweed offered Nast $100,000 to "study art" in Europe. Nast refused the bribe.

the party. These positions represented the first steps into the middle class.

In return, citizens were expected to show their gratitude at the ballot box. Sometimes the grateful were not enough, so bosses turned elsewhere. "Little Bob" Davies of Jersey City mobilized the "graveyard vote." He drew names from tombstones to pad lists of registered voters and hired "repeaters" to vote under the phony names. When reformers introduced the Australian (secret) ballot in the 1880s to prevent fraud, bosses pulled the "Tasmanian dodge" by premarking election tickets. Failing that, they dumped whole ballot boxes into the river or drove unpersuaded voters from the polls with hired thugs.

Rewards, Costs, and Accomplishments

Why did bosses go to such lengths? Some simply loved the game of politics. More often bosses loved money. Their ability to get it was limited only by their ingenuity or the occasional success of reform. The record for brassiness must go to Boss William Tweed. During his reign in the 1860s and 1870s, Tweed swindled the city of New York out of a fortune. His masterpiece was a chunky three-story courthouse in lower Manhattan originally budgeted at $250,000. When Tweed was through, the city had spent more than $13 million, over 60 percent of which ended up in the pockets of Tweed and his cronies. They got kickbacks from favored contractors; they padded bills, inflated costs, and even hired nonexistent employees whose salaries they kept for themselves. Tweed died in prison, but with such profits to be made, it was small wonder that bosses rivaled the pharaohs of Egypt as builders.

In their fashion bosses played a vital role in the industrial city. Rising from the bottom ranks, they guided immigrants into American life and helped some of the underprivileged up from poverty. They changed the urban landscape with massive construction programs and modernized city government by uniting it and making it more effective. Choosing the aldermen, municipal judges, mayors, and administrative officials, bosses exerted new control to provide the contracts and franchises to run cities. Such accomplishments fostered the notion that government could be called on to help the needy. The welfare state, still decades away, had some of its roots here.

The toll was often outrageous. Inflated taxes, extorted revenue, and unpunished vice and crime were only the obvious costs. A woman whose family enjoyed Plunkitt's Christmas turkey might be widowed by an accident to her husband in a sweatshop kept open by timely bribes. Filthy buildings might claim her children, as corrupt inspectors ignored serious violations. Buying votes and selling favors, bosses turned democracy into a petty business—as much a "business," said Plunkitt, "as the grocery or dry-goods or the drug business." Yet they were the forerunners of the new breed of full-time, professional politicians who would soon govern the cities and the nation as well.

Nativism, Revivals, and the Social Gospel

Urban blight and the condition of the poor inspired social as well as political activism, especially within churches. Not all of it was positive. The popular Congregationalist minister Josiah Strong concluded that the city was "a menace to society." Along with anxious economists and social workers, he held immigrants responsible for everything from corruption to unemployment and urged restrictions on their entry into the country.

In the 1880s and 1890s, two depressions sharpened such anxieties. Nativism, a defensive and fearful nationalism, peaked as Americans blamed their economic woes on foreigners and foreign competition. New organizations like the Immigration Restriction League attacked Catholics and the foreign-born for subverting democracy, taking jobs, and polarizing society. Already the victims of racial prejudice, the Chinese were an easy target. In 1882 Congress enacted the Chinese Exclusion Act. It banned the entry of Chinese laborers and represented an important step in the drive to restrict immigration. In 1897 the first bill requiring literacy tests for immigrants passed Congress, but President Grover Cleveland vetoed it.

Some clergy took their missions to the slums to bridge the gap between the middle class and the poor. Beginning in 1870 Dwight Lyman Moody, a 300-pound former shoe salesman, won armies of lowly converts with revivals in Boston, Chicago, and other cities. Evangelists helped to found American branches of the British Young Men's Christian Association and the Salvation Army. By the end of the century the Salvation Army had grown to 700 corps staffed by some 3000 officers. They ministered to the needy with food, music, shelter, and simple good fellowship.

The Sawdust Trail, painted by George Bellows in 1916, depicts one of the revival meetings of William Ashley ("Billy") Sunday in Philadelphia. Sunday, a hard-drinking professional baseball player turned evangelist, began his religious revivals in the 1890s and drew thousands. Here, Sunday leans down from the platform to shake the hand of an admirer. In the foreground, a swooning woman, overcome with a sense of her sins, is carried away.

A small group of ministers rejected the old ethos that weak character explained sin and that society would be perfected only as individual sinners were converted. They spread a new "Social Gospel" that focused on improving the conditions of society in order to save individuals. In *Applied Christianity* (1886), the influential Washington Gladden preached that the church must be responsible for correcting social injustices, including dangerous working conditions and unfair labor practices. Houses of worship, such as William Rainford's St. George's Episcopal Church in New York, became centers of social activity, with boys' clubs, gymnasiums, libraries, glee clubs, and industrial training programs.

The Social Settlement Movement

The settlement house

Church-sponsored programs sometimes repelled the immigrant poor when they saw them as thinly disguised missionary efforts. Not all were. Many urban church programs, such as A. B. Simpson's in New York City, served body and soul successfully and without heavy-handed evangelizing. Immigrants and other slum dwellers were more receptive to a bold experiment called the settlement house. Often situated in the worst slums, these early community centers were run by middle-class women and men to help the poor and foreign-born. At the turn of the century there were more than 100 of them, the most famous being Jane Addams's Hull House in Chicago. When Hull House opened in 1889, it occupied a crumbling mansion on South Halstead Street. Slowly it grew to a dozen buildings over more than a city block. In 1898 the Catholic church sponsored its first settlement house in New York, and in 1900 Bronson House opened its doors to the Latino community in Los Angeles.

High purposes inspired settlement workers. They left comfortable middle-class homes to live in settlement houses and dedicated themselves (like the "early Christians," said one) to service and sacrifice. Teaching immigrants American ways and creating a community spirit would foster "right living through social relations." But immigrants were also urged to preserve their heritages through festivals, parades, and museums. Like political bosses, settlement reformers furnished help, from day nurseries to English language and cooking classes to playgrounds and libraries. Armed with statistics and personal experiences, they also lobbied for social legislation to improve housing, women's working conditions, and public schools.

City Life

Urban social stratification

City life reflected the stratified nature of American society in the late nineteenth century. Every city had its tenements and slums but also its fashionable avenues for the rich, who constituted barely 1 percent of the population but owned a fourth of all wealth. In between tenement and mansion lived the broad middle of urban society—educated professionals, white-collar clerks and salespeople, shopkeepers, corporate managers and executives, public employees, and their families. They composed nearly a third of the population and owned about half the nation's wealth. With more money and more leisure time, their power and influence were growing.

In the impersonal city of the late nineteenth century, class distinctions continued to be based on wealth and income. But no longer were dress and manners enough to distinguish one class from another. Such differences were more often reflected in where people lived, what they bought, which organizations they joined, and how they spent their time.

The Immigrant in the City

When the ship put into port, the first thing an immigrant was likely to see was a city. Perhaps it was Boston or New York or Galveston, Texas, where an overflow of Jewish immigrants was directed after the turn of the century. Enough of the newcomers traveled inland so that by 1900 three-quarters of the residents of Minnesota and Wisconsin and nearly two-thirds in Utah had at least one foreign-born parent.* But some 70 percent of all immigrants, exhausted physically and financially, settled in cities.

---

*Mormons serving as missionaries in Europe and Great Britain especially swelled Utah's population with converts.

Cities developed well-defined mosaics of ethnic communities, because immigrants usually clustered together on the basis of Old World villages or provinces. But these neighborhoods were constantly changing. As many as half the residents moved out every 10 years, often because they got better-paying jobs or had more family members working. Though one nationality usually dominated a neighborhood, there were always others. **Ethnic neighborhoods**

Ethnic communities served as havens from the strangeness of American society and as springboards to a new life. From the moment they stepped off the boat, newcomers felt pressed to learn English, don American clothes, and drop their "greenhorn" ways. Yet in their neighborhoods they also found comrades who spoke their language, theaters that performed their plays and music, restaurants that served their food. Houses of worship were always at the center of neighborhood life, often reflecting the practices of individual towns or provinces. Foreign-language newspapers reported events from both the Old World and the New in a tongue first-generation immigrants could understand. Meanwhile, immigrant aid societies furnished assistance with housing and jobs and sponsored baseball teams, insurance programs, and English classes. **Adapting to America**

Sometimes immigrants combined the old and new in creative adaptations. Italians developed a pidgin dialect called "Italglish." It permitted them to communicate quickly with Americans and to absorb American customs. So the Fourth of July became "Il Forte Gelato" (literally "The Great Freeze"), a play on the sound of the words. Other immigrant groups invented similar idioms, like Chuco, a dialect that developed among border Mexicans in El Paso.

The backgrounds and cultural values of immigrants often influenced the jobs they took. Because Chinese men did not scorn washing or ironing, more than 7500 of them could be found in San Francisco laundries by 1880. Sewing ladies' garments seemed unmanly to many native-born Americans but not to Russian and Italian tailors. Slavs tended to be physically robust and valued steady income over education. They worked in the mines for better pay than in factories and pulled their children from school to send them to work.

On the whole, immigrants married later and had more children than the native-born. Greeks and eastern European Jews prearranged marriages according to tradition. **Family life**

Entertainment in immigrant neighborhoods often resulted in a cross-fertilization of cultures. The New Cathay Boys Club Band, a marching band of Chinese Americans (shown here), was formed in San Francisco's Chinatown in 1911. It was inspired by the Columbia Park Boys Band of Italians from nearby North Beach and played American music only.

They imported "picture brides," betrothed by mail with a photograph. After marriage men ruled the household, but women managed it. Although child-rearing practices varied, immigrants resisted the relative permissiveness of American parents. Youngsters were expected to contribute like little adults to the welfare of the family.

In these "family economies" of working-class immigrants, key decisions—over whether and whom to marry, over work and education, over when to leave home—were made on the basis of collective rather than individual needs. Though boys were more likely to work outside the home than girls, daughters in immigrant families went to work at an early age so sons could continue their education. It was customary for one daughter to remain unmarried so she could care for younger siblings or aged parents.

Special situation of the Chinese

The Chinese were an exception to the pattern. The ban on the immigration of Chinese laborers in the 1880s (page 653) had frozen the sex ratio of Chinese communities into a curious imbalance. Like other immigrants, most Chinese newcomers had been single men. In the wake of the ban, those in the United States could not bring over their wives and families. Nor by law in 13 states could they marry whites. With few women, Chinese communities suffered from high rates of prostitution, large numbers of gangs and secret societies, and low birth totals. When the San Francisco earthquake and fire destroyed birth records in 1906, resourceful Chinese immigrants created "paper sons" (and less often "paper daughters") by forging American birth certificates and claiming their China-born children as American citizens.

Acculturation

Caught between past and present, immigrants from all countries clung to tradition and acculturated slowly. Their children adjusted more quickly. They soon spoke English like natives, married whomever they pleased, and worked their way out of old neighborhoods. Yet the process was not easy. Children faced heartrending clashes with parents and rejection from peers. Sara Smolinsky, the immigrant heroine of Anzia Yezierska's novel *Bread Givers* (1925), broke away from her tyrannical family, only to discover a terrible isolation: "I can't live in the old world and I'm yet too green for the new."

Bicycling became a popular middle-class recreation as cycle designs improved. These African American cyclists, photographed around 1900, had just crossed a bridge over the South Platte River in Denver.

Urban Middle-Class Life

Life and leisure for the urban middle class revolved around home and family. By the turn of the century just over a third of middle-class urbanites owned their homes. Often two or three stories, made of brick or brownstone, these houses were a measure of their owners' social standing. The plush furniture, heavy drapes, antiques, and curios all signaled status and refinement.

The home as haven and status symbol

Such homes, usually on their own lots, served as havens to protect and nourish the family. Seventeenth-century notions of children as inherently sinful had given way to more modern theories about the shaping influence of environment. Calm and orderly households with nurturing mothers would launch children on the right course. "A clean, fresh, and well-ordered house," stipulated a domestic adviser in 1883, "exercises over its inmates a moral, no less than physical influence, and has a direct tendency to make members of the family sober, peaceable, and considerate of the feelings and happiness of each other."

A woman was judged by the state of her home. The typical homemaker prepared elaborate meals, cleaned, laundered, and sewed. Each task took time. Baking bread alone required several hours, and in 1890, four of five loaves were still made at home. Perhaps 25 percent of urban households had live-in servants to help with the work. They were on call about 100 hours a week, were off just one evening and part of Sunday, and averaged $2 to $5 a week in salary.

By the 1890s a host of new consumer products eased the burdens of housework. Brand names trumpeted a new age of commercially prepared food—Campbell's soup, Quaker oats, Pillsbury flour, Jell-O, and Cracker Jacks, to name a few. New appliances such as "self-working" washers offered mechanical assistance, but shredded shirts and aching arms testified to how far short mechanization still fell.

Toward the end of the century, Saturday became less of a workday and more of a family day. Sunday mornings remained a time for church, still an important center of family life. Afternoons had a more secular flavor. There were shopping trips (city stores often stayed open) and visits to lakes, zoos, and amusement parks (usually built at the end of trolley lines to attract more riders). Outside institutions of all kinds—fraternal organizations, uplift groups, athletic teams, and church groups— were becoming part of middle-class urban family life.

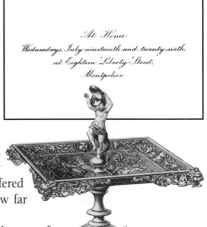

Newly developed "electroplating," which deposited a thin layer of silver or gold over less expensive material, allowed manufacturers to sell to middle-class consumers wares previously reserved for the wealthy. Pictured here are a silver- and gold-plated card receiver and a calling card, once part of the courtly culture of elites and by the 1880s found in more and more middle-class homes. This "downward mobility" of manners and material culture allowed the middle class to ape the conventions of their social superiors, in this case by using calling cards to reinforce social networks and to serve as social barriers should personal contact be unwanted.

Victorianism and the Pursuit of Virtue

Middle-class life reflected a code of behavior called Victorianism, named for Britain's long-reigning Queen Victoria (1837–1901). It emerged in the 1830s and 1840s as part of an effort to tame the turbulent urban-industrial society developing in Europe.

Victorianism dictated that personal conduct be based on orderly behavior and disciplined moralism. It stressed sobriety, industriousness, self-control, and sexual modesty. It taught that demeanor, particularly proper manners, was the backbone of society. And it strictly divided the gender roles of men and women, especially in the realm of sexuality. According to its rules, women were "pure vessels" devoid of sexual desire, men wild beasts unable to tame their lust. A woman's job was to control the "lower natures" of her husband by withholding sex except for procreation.

Women's fashion mirrored Victorian values. Strenuously laced corsets ("an instrument of torture," one woman called them) pushed breasts up, stomachs in, and rear ends out. Internal organs pressed unnaturally against one another; ribs occasionally cracked; uteruses sagged. Fainting spells and headaches were all too common. But the resulting wasplike figure accentuated the image of women as child bearers. Ankle-length skirts were draped over bustles, hoops, and petticoats to make hips look larger and suggest fertility. Such elegant dress symbolized wealth, status, and modesty. It also set off middle- and upper-class women from those below, whose plain clothes signaled lives of drudgery and want.

Woman's Christian Temperance Union

When working-class Americans failed to follow Victorian guidelines, reformers helped them pursue virtue. It seemed natural to Frances Willard that women, who cared for the moral and physical well-being of their families, should lead the charge. She resigned her position as dean of women at Northwestern University and in 1879 became the second president of the newly founded Woman's Christian Temperance Union (WCTU, organized in 1874). The very title of the organization, stressing the singular "woman," spoke for the unity of women. Under Willard's leadership, the organization grew by the 1890s to 150,000 members, all of them women and most of them middle-class and white. By the turn of the century it was the largest women's organization in the world.

Initially the WCTU focused on temperance—the movement, begun in the 1820s, to stamp out the sale of alcoholic beverages and to end drunkenness. For these women, the campaign seemed not merely a way to reform society but also a way to protect their homes and families from abuse at the hands of drunken husbands and fathers. And in attacking the saloon, Willard also sought to spread democracy by storming these all-male bastions, where political bosses conducted so much political business and where women were refused entry. Soon, under the slogan of "Do Everything," the WCTU was also promoting suffrage for women, prison reform, better working conditions, and an end to prostitution. Just as important, it offered talented, committed women an opportunity to move out of their homes and churches and into the public arena of lobbying and politics.

Comstock Law

Anthony Comstock crusaded with equal vigor against what he saw as moral pollution, ranging from pornography and gambling to the use of nude art models. In 1873 President Ulysses S. Grant signed the so-called Comstock Law, a statute banning from the mails all materials "designed to incite lust." Two days later Comstock went to work as a special agent for the Post Office. In his 41-year career, he claimed to have made more than 3000 arrests and destroyed 160 tons of vice-ridden books and photographs.

Victorian crusaders like Comstock were not simply missionaries of a stuffy morality. They were apostles of a middle-class creed of social control and discipline who responded to growing alcoholism, venereal disease, gambling debts, prostitution, and unwanted pregnancies. No doubt they overreacted in warning that the road to ruin lay behind the door of every saloon, pool hall, or bedroom. Yet the new urban environment did indeed reflect the disorder of a rapidly industrializing society.

The insistence with which moralists warned against "impropriety" suggests that many people did not heed their advice. Three-quarters of women surveyed toward the turn of the century reported that they enjoyed sex. The growing variety of contraceptives—including spermicidal douches, sheaths made of animal intestines, rubber condoms, and forerunners of the diaphragm—testified to the desire for pregnancy-free intercourse. Abortion, too, was prevalent. According to one estimate, a third of all pregnancies were aborted, usually with the aid of a midwife. (By the 1880s abortion had been made illegal in most states, following the lead of the first antiabortion statute in England in 1803.) Despite Victorian marriage manuals, middle-class Americans became more conscious of sexuality as an emotional dimension of a satisfying union.

Challenges to Convention

A few bold men and women openly challenged conventions of gender and propriety. Victoria Woodhull, publisher of *Woodhull & Claflin's Weekly,* divorced her husband, ran for president in 1872 on the Equal Rights party ticket, and pressed the case for sexual freedom. "I am a free lover!" she shouted to a riotous audience in New York. "I have the inalienable, constitutional, and natural right to love whom I may, to love as long or as short a period as I can, to change that love every day if I please!" Woodhull made a strong public case for sexual freedom. But in private she believed in strict monogamy and romantic love for herself.

Victoria Woodhull

The same cosmopolitan conditions that provided protection for Woodhull's unorthodox beliefs also made possible the growth of self-conscious communities of homosexual men and women. Earlier in the century, Americans had idealized romantic friendships among members of the same sex, without necessarily attributing sexual overtones to those friendships. But for friendships with an explicitly sexual dimension, the anonymity of large cities provided new meeting grounds. Single factory workers and clerks, living in furnished rooms rather than with their families in small towns and on farms, were freer to seek others who shared their sexual orientation. Homosexual men and women began forming social networks: on the streets where they regularly met or at specific restaurants and clubs, which, to avoid controversy, sometimes passed themselves off as athletic associations or chess clubs. Such places could be found in New York City's Bowery, around the Presidio military base in San Francisco, and at Lafayette Square in Washington, D.C.

Urban homosexual communities

Only toward the end of the century did physicians begin to notice homosexual behavior, usually to condemn it as a disease or an inherited infirmity. Indeed, not until the turn of the century did the term *homosexual* come into existence. Certainly homosexual love itself was not new. But for the first time in the United States, the conditions of urban life allowed gay men and lesbians to define themselves in terms of a larger, self-conscious community, even if they were stoutly condemned by Victorian morality.

City Culture

"We cannot all live in cities," reformer Horace Greeley lamented just after the Civil War, "yet nearly all seemed determined to do so." Economic opportunity drew people to the teeming industrial city. But so, too, did a vibrant urban culture, boasting temples of entertainment, electrified trolleys and lights, the best schools, stores and restaurants, the biggest newspapers, and virtually every museum, library, art gallery, bookshop, and orchestra in America. In the beckoning cities of the late nineteenth century, Americans sought to realize their dreams of success.

Public Education in an Urban Industrial World

Those at the bottom and in the middle ranks of city life found one path to success in public education. Although the campaign for public education began in the Jacksonian era, it did not make real headway until after the Civil War, when industrial cities began to mushroom. As late as 1870 half the children in the country received no formal education at all, and one American in five could not read.

Between 1870 and 1900, an educational awakening occurred. As more and more businesses required workers who could read, write, and figure sums, attendance in public schools more than doubled. The length of the school term rose from 132 to 144 days. Illiteracy fell by half. At the turn of the century, nearly all

Educational reformers in the 1870s pushed elementary schools to include drawing as a required subject. Their goal was not to turn out gifted artists but to train students in the practical skills needed in an industrial society. Winslow Homer's portrait of a teacher by her blackboard shows the geometric shapes behind practical design.

the states outside the South had enacted mandatory education laws. Almost three of every four school-age children were enrolled. Even so, the average American adult still attended school for only about five years, and less than 10 percent of those eligible ever went to high school.

The average school day started early, but by noon most girls were released under the assumption that they needed less formal education. Curricula stressed the fundamentals of reading, writing, and arithmetic. Courses in manual training, science, and physical education were added as the demand for technical knowledge grew and opportunities to exercise shrank. Students learned by memorization, sitting in silent study with hands clasped or standing erect while they repeated phrases and sums. Few schools encouraged creative thinking. "Don't stop to think," barked a Chicago teacher to a class of terrified youngsters in the 1890s, "tell me what you know!"

A rigid social philosophy underlay the harsh routine. In an age of industrialization, massive immigration, and rapid change, schools taught conformity and values as much as facts and figures. Teachers acted as drillmasters, shaping their charges for the sake of society. "Teachers and books are better security than handcuffs and policemen," wrote a New Jersey college professor in 1879. In *McGuffey's Reader,* a standard textbook used in grammar schools throughout the nineteenth century, students learned not only how to read but also how to behave. Hard work, Christian ethics, and obedience to authority would lead boys to heroic command, girls to blissful motherhood, and society to harmonious progress.

As Reconstruction faded, so did the impressive start made in black education. Most of the first generation of former slaves had been illiterate. So eager were they to learn that by the end of the century nearly half of all African Americans could read. But discrimination soon took its toll. For nearly 100 years after the Civil War, the doctrine of "separate but equal," upheld by the Supreme Court in *Plessy v. Ferguson* (1896), kept black and white students apart but scarcely equal (page 577). By 1882 public schools in a half dozen southern states were segregated by law, the rest by practice. Underfunded and ill-equipped, black schools served dirt-poor families whose every member had to work. In fact, only about a third of the South's black children attended and rarely for the entire school year.

Like African Americans, immigrants saw education as a way of getting ahead. Some educators saw it as a means of Americanizing newcomers. They assumed that immigrant and native-born children would learn the same lessons in the same language and turn out the same way. Only toward the end of the century, as immigration mounted, did eastern cities begin to offer night classes that taught English, along with civics lessons for foreigners. When public education proved inadequate, immigrants established their own schools. Catholics, for example, started an elaborate expansion of their parochial schools in 1884.

By the 1880s educational reforms were helping schools respond to the needs of an urban society. Opened first in St. Louis in 1873, American versions of innovative German "kindergartens" put four- to six-year-olds in orderly classrooms while parents went off to work. "Normal schools" multiplied to provide teachers with more professional training. By 1900 almost one teacher in five had a professional degree. In the new industrial age, science and manual training supplemented more conventional subjects in order to supply industry with better-educated workers. And vocational education reduced the influence of unions. Now less dependent on a system of apprenticeship controlled by labor, new workers were also less subject to being recruited into unions.

Higher Learning and the Rise of the Professional

As American society grew more organized, mechanized, and complex, the need for managerial, technical, and literary skills brought greater respect for college education. The Morrill Act of 1862 generated a dozen new state colleges and universities, eight mechanical and agricultural colleges, and six black colleges. Private charity added more. Railroad barons like Johns Hopkins and Leland Stanford used parts of their fortunes to found colleges named after them (Hopkins in 1873, Stanford in 1890). The number of colleges and universities nearly doubled between 1870 and 1910, though less than 5 percent of college-age Americans enrolled in them.

Higher education

A practical impulse inspired the founding of several black colleges. In the late nineteenth century, few institutions mixed races. Church groups and private foundations, such as the Peabody and Slater funds (supported by white donors from the North), underwrote black colleges after Reconstruction. By 1900, a total of 700 black students were enrolled. About 2000 had graduated. Through hard work and persistence, some even received degrees from institutions normally reserved for whites.

In keeping with the new emphasis on practical training, professional schools multiplied to provide training beyond a college degree. American universities adopted the German model requiring young scholars to perform research as part of their training. The number of law and medical schools more than doubled between 1870 and 1900; medical students almost tripled. Ten percent of them were women, though their numbers shrank as the medical profession became more organized and exclusive.

Professionals of all kinds—in law, medicine, engineering, business, academics—swelled the ranks of the middle class. Slowly they were becoming a new force in urban America, replacing the ministers and gentleman freeholders of an earlier day as community leaders.

Higher Education for Women

Before the Civil War women could attend only three private colleges. After the war they had new ones all their own, among them Smith (1871), Wellesley (1875), and Bryn Mawr (1885). Many land-grant colleges, chartered to serve all people, admitted women from the start. By 1910 some 40 percent of college students were women, almost double the 1870 figure. Only one college in five refused to accept them.

Potent myths continued to make college life hard for women. As Dr. Edward Clarke of the Harvard Medical School told thousands of students in *Sex in Education* (1873), the rigors of a college education could lead the "weaker sex" to physical or mental collapse, infertility, and early death. Women's colleges therefore included a strict program of physical activity to keep students healthy. Many also offered an array of courses in "domestic science"—cooking, sewing, and other such skills—to counter the claim that higher education would be of no value to women.

College students, together with office workers and female athletes, became role models for ambitious young women. These "new women," impatient with custom, cast off Victorian restrictions. Fewer of them married, and more were self-supporting. They shed their corsets and bustles and donned lighter, more comfortable clothing, including "shirtwaist" blouses (styled after men's shirts) and lower-heeled shoes. Robust and active, they could be found ice-skating in the winter, riding bicycles in the fall and spring, playing golf and tennis in the summer.

A Culture of Consumption

The city spawned a new material culture built around consumption. As standards of living rose, American industries began providing "ready-made" clothing to replace garments that had once been made at home. Similarly, food and furniture were mass-produced in greater quantities. The city became a giant marketplace for these goods, where new patterns of mass consumption took hold. Radiating outward to more rural areas, this urban consumer culture helped to level American society. Increasingly, city businesses sold the same goods to farmer and clerk, rich and poor, native-born and immigrant.

Department stores

Well-made, inexpensive merchandise in standard sizes and shapes found outlets in new palaces of consumption called "department stores" because they displayed their goods in separate sections or departments. The idea was imported from France, where shopping arcades had been built as early as the 1860s. Unlike the small exclusive shops of Europe, department stores were palatial, public, and filled with inviting displays of furniture, housewares, and clothing.

The French writer Emile Zola claimed that department stores "democratized luxury." Anyone could enter free of charge, handle the most elegant and expensive goods, and buy whatever was affordable. When consumers found goods too pricey, department stores pioneered layaway plans with deferred payments. Free delivery and free returns or exchanges were available to all, not just the favored customers of exclusive fashion makers. The department store also educated people by showing them what "proper" families owned and the correct names for things like women's wear and parlor furniture. This process of socialization was taking place not only in cities but in towns and villages across America. Mass consumption was giving rise to a mass culture.

Chain stores and mail-order houses

"Chain stores" (a term coined in America) spread the culture of consumption without frills. They catered to the working class, who could not afford department stores, and operated on a cash-and-carry basis. Owners kept their costs down by buying in volume to fill the small stores in growing neighborhood chains. Founded in 1859, the Great Atlantic and Pacific Tea Company was the first of the chain stores. By 1876 its 76 branch stores had added groceries to its original line of teas.

Far from department and chain stores, rural Americans joined the community of consumers by mail. In 1872, Aaron Montgomery Ward sent his first price sheet to farmers from a livery stable loft in Chicago. Ward eliminated the intermediary and promised savings of 40 percent on fans, needles, trunks, harnesses, and scores of other goods. By 1884, his catalog boasted 10,000 items, each illustrated by a woodcut. Similarly, Richard W. Sears and Alvah C. Roebuck built a $500 million mail-order business by 1907. Schoolrooms that had no encyclopedia used a Ward's or Sears' catalog instead. Children were drilled in reading and spelling from them. When asked the source of the Ten Commandments, one farm boy replied that they came from Sears, Roebuck.

Leisure

As mechanization slowly reduced the number of hours on the job, factory workers found themselves with more free time. So did the middle class, with free weekends, evenings, and vacations. A new, stricter division between work and leisure developed. City dwellers turned their free time into a consumer item that often reflected differences in class, gender, and ethnicity.

Sports, for example, had been a traditional form of recreation for the rich. They continued to play polo, golf, and the newly imported English game of tennis. Croquet had more middle-class appeal because it required less skill and special equipment. Perhaps as important, croquet could be enjoyed in mixed company, like the new craze of bicycling. Bicycles evolved from unstable contraptions with large front wheels into "safety" bikes with equal-sized wheels, a dropped middle bar, pneumatic tires, and coaster brakes. A good one cost about $100, far beyond the reach of a factory worker but within the grasp of a mechanic or a well-paid clerk. On Sunday afternoons city parks became crowded with cyclists. Women also rode the new safety bikes, although social convention forbade them to ride alone. But cycling broke down conventions too. It required looser garments, freeing women from corsets. Lady cyclists demonstrated that they were hardly too frail for physical exertion.

Sports and class distinctions

Organized spectator sports attracted crowds from every walk of life. Baseball overshadowed all others. For city dwellers with dull work, tight quarters, and isolated lives, baseball offered the chance to join thousands of others for an exciting outdoor spectacle. By the 1890s it was attracting crowds of 60,000. Baseball began to take its modern form in 1869, when the first professional team, the Cincinnati Red Stockings, appeared. Slowly the game evolved: umpires began to call balls and strikes, the overhand replaced the underhand pitch, and fielders put on gloves.

Spectator sports for the urban masses

Artist Edward Shinn's *Sixth Avenue Shoppers* shows a nighttime scene in the city's shopping district. In an era of more flexible gender roles, Shinn nonetheless captures a traditional division of gender with the women (at the left of the painting) crowded around shopping stalls and men (at the right) hunched over a cockfight.

Teams from eight cities formed the National League of Professional Baseball Clubs in 1876, followed by the American League in 1901. League players were distinctly working class. At first, teams featured a few black players. When African Americans were barred in the 1880s, black professionals formed their own team, the Cuban Giants of Long Island, New York, looking to play anyone they could. Their name was chosen with care. In an age of racial separation, the all-black team hoped to increase its chances of playing white teams by calling itself "Cuban."

Horse racing, bicycle tournaments, and other sports of speed and violence helped to break the monotony, frustration, and routine of the industrial city. In 1869, without pads or helmets, Rutgers beat Princeton in the first intercollegiate football match. By the 1890s the service academies and state universities fielded teams. Despite protests against rising death tolls (18 players died in 1905), football soon attracted crowds of 50,000 or more. Beginning in 1891 when Dr. James Naismith nailed a peach basket to the gymnasium wall at the YMCA Training School in Springfield, Massachusetts, "basketball" became the indoor interlude between the outdoor sports of spring and fall.

Bare-knuckled prizefighting, illegal in some states, took place secretly in saloons and commercial gyms. In the rough-and-tumble world of the industrial city, the ring gave young men from the streets the chance to stand out from the crowd and to prove their masculinity. "Sporting clubs" of German, Irish, and African American boxers sprouted up in cities along the East Coast. *The National Police Gazette* and other magazines followed the bouts with sensational stories chronicling matches in detail. When the sport adopted the Marquis of Queensbury rules in the 1880s, including the use of gloves, boxing gained new respectability and appeal. Soon boxing, like other sports, was being commercialized with professional bouts, large purses, and championship titles.

Boxing (margin note)

City Entertainment at Home and on the Road

City entertainment, like city life, divided along lines of class. For the wealthy and middle class there were symphonies, operas, and theater. Highbrow productions of Shakespearean plays catered to the aspirations of the American upper class for culture and European refinement. Popular melodramas gave their largely middle-class audiences the chance to ignore the ambiguities of modern life, if only for an evening. They booed villains and cheered heroes, all the while marveling at the tricky stage mechanics that made ice floes move and players float heavenward. By 1900, people were bringing their entertainment home, snapping up new phonograph recordings at the rate of 3 million a year.

Workingmen found a haven from the drudgery of factory, mill, and mine in the saloon. It was an all-male preserve—a workingmen's club—where one could drink and talk free from Victorian finger-wagging. Rougher saloons offered fulfillment of still more illicit desires in the form of prostitutes, gambling, and drugs. Young working women found escape alone or on dates at vaudeville shows (pages 666–667), dance halls, and the new amusement parks with their mechanical "thrill rides." In the all-black gaming houses and honky-tonks of St. Louis and New Orleans, the syncopated rhythms of African American composer Scott Joplin's "Maple Leaf Rag" (1899) and other ragtime tunes heralded the coming of jazz.

Traveling circuses (margin note)

As much as any form of entertainment, the traveling circus brought together all classes and races in a way that embodied the changes of the new urban, industrial world. The circus made use of the latest techniques of organization, transportation, and advertising. These new spectacles were much bigger than the small bands of wandering performers that constituted the first American circuses of a century earlier. They traveled by rail, not wagon, and over much greater distances. Most of all they reflected their day: the business culture, ethnoracial diversity, more fluid gender roles, and imperial ambitions of late-nineteenth-century America.

The new traveling circuses moved outward from their bases in large cities. By 1910, there were over 30 crisscrossing the country. Like good businesses, they planned and advertised tightly scheduled tours months in advance. The largest, the mammoth New York–based Barnum and Bailey Circus, carried dozens of gilded show wagons, hundreds of animals, tons of equipment, and sometimes thousands of performers, work hands, and animal tenders. Their reach stretched across the nation (after the first transcontinental circus tour in 1869) and later around the globe (when steamships transported them to Europe, Asia, and Australia).

With factory-like precision, circus workers erected and dismantled small tent cities in hours, moved them across vast spaces in days or weeks, and performed as many as three shows daily. They drew audiences from every class, ethnicity, and race, sometimes numbering in the tens of thousands under huge canvas "big tops." Not the small menageries of the eighteenth century but impressive collections of elephants, big cats, apes, and other exotic animals filled their shows. These modern circuses also contained a greater number of female performers—acrobats, bareback riders, flying trapeze artists, singing and dancing girls—and included women of color. And they had sideshows with dwarfs, giants (and "giantesses"), bearded and fat ladies, "dog-faced" boys, and other "human oddities" that inverted gender roles and blurred the distinction between animals and humans.

Circuses were popular entertainment and big businesses, but they also were disseminators of culture that both supported and subverted social conventions. When owners reassured customers that their scantily clad dancers came from

This lithograph is from an 1894 poster for the Barnum & Bailey Circus. It depicts a menagerie tent in which exotic animals are displayed side by side with "Strange and Savage Tribes," thus collapsing the boundaries between animals and human beings. Much smaller than the Big Top, menagerie tents allowed Euro-American patrons to examine animals and humans up close. The Barnum show presented its first "ethnological congress" of "native" peoples in 1886, as the United States began its drive for empire abroad. The human specimens were meant to give Americans a glimpse of foreign cultures and to be instructive. "Even the best informed and most intellectual had something to learn," boasted a circus route book.

Daily Lives

POPULAR ENTERTAINMENT
The Vaudeville Show

It looked like a palace or some high-toned concert hall. Patrons walked through a richly ornamented arched gateway to gold-domed, marble ticket booths. Ushers guided them through a stately lobby cushioned with velvet carpets. Large mirrors and brass ornaments hung on brocaded walls. There were "gentlemen's smoking and reading rooms" and suites with dressing cases and free toiletries for the ladies. The house seats were thick and comfortable and positioned well back from the stage. Thousands of electrical fixtures set the place aglow. When the lights dimmed, the audience sank into polite silence as the show began.

Benjamin Franklin Keith, who had worked in circuses, tent shows, and dime museums, opened the New Theatre in Boston in 1894.

Seeing housewives with children as a source of new profits, resourceful theater owners such as Keith had cleaned up the bawdy variety acts of saloons and music halls, borrowed the animal and acrobat acts from circuses and Wild West shows and the comedy acts of minstrel shows, and moved them to plusher surroundings. They called the new shows "vaudeville," after the French "pièces de vaudeville" developed at eighteenth-century street fairs. In 1881 Tony Pastor opened the first vaudeville theater, on Fourteenth Street, in New York City. Within a decade more elegant palaces like Keith's New Theatre were opening in cities across the country.

Balconies at vaudeville shows, like this one depicted by Charles Dana Gibson, attracted a wide variety of customers. Most seats cost $1, and theater owners scheduled performances from morning until night.

respectable Victorian families or their muscular lady acrobats prized the Victorian ideals of family, motherhood, and domesticity, they winked slyly because they knew that the very appearance of these women, let alone their talents, defied the Victorian ideal of dainty and demure femininity. The Adam Forepaugh Shows staged spectacles such as "Scenes & Battles from the American Revolution" that entertained but also gave audiences—foreign and native-born alike—a history lesson, however rosy. In 1886, Barnum & Bailey displayed exotic peoples and animals in the first "Ethnological Congress" ever to accompany a traveling circus. Patrons saw living embodiments of "strange and savage tribes" from Africa, the Middle East, and Asia. These displays opened American eyes to a wider world while reinforcing prevailing notions of white supremacy. At just this moment, when the United States was embarking on a quest for empire (see Chapter 21), circuses trumpeted national expansion with celebrations of American might and exceptionalism. To audiences at home, reenactments of famous battles abroad brought faraway places near and made abstract principles of foreign policy real. To foreign audiences, those same reenactments trumpeted the rise of a new world power.

As the nineteenth century drew to a close the city was reshaping the country, just as the industrial system was creating a more specialized, diversified, and interlocking

For anywhere from a dime to two dollars, a customer could see up to nine acts—singers, jugglers, acrobats, magicians, trained animals, and comics. The mix of performers reflected the urban tempo and new urban tastes. Skits often drew on the experience of immigrants, and early comedy teams had names like "The Sport and the Jew" and "Two Funny Sauerkrauts." Divided into acts that came in rapid-fire succession, "continuous shows" ran one after another, from early morning until late at night. "After breakfast go to Proctor's," trumpeted one advertisement for F. F. Proctor's vaudeville show, "after Proctor's go to bed."

Saloon music halls had catered to a rowdy all-male, working-class clientele, who smoke, drank, stomped, and jeered at the players. Vaudeville was aimed at middle-class and wealthier working-class families who could no longer afford "legitimate" theater and light opera. Keith worked diligently to make each of his theaters "as 'homelike' an amusement resort as it was possible to make it." Backstage he tacked signs warning performers not to say "slob" or "son-of-a-gun" or "'hully-gee' . . . unless you want to be canceled peremptorily." In the interest of good taste, all his chorus girls wore stockings. Within a few years Keith was producing the kind of show, as one comedian put it, "to which any child could bring his parents."

The audience, too, was instructed on proper behavior. No liquor was served. No cigars or cigarettes were permitted. Printed notices directed patrons to "kindly avoid the stamping of feet and pounding of canes on the floor. . . . Please don't talk during acts, as it annoys those about you, and prevents a perfect hearing of the entertainment."

Enjoying its heyday from 1890 to 1920, vaudeville became big business. Nearly one in five city dwellers went to a show once every seven days. Headliners earned $1,000 a week, theaters $20,000. Owners like Keith and Edward Albee merged their operations into gigantic circuits. By the time of Keith's death in 1914, the Keith-Albee circuit had built an empire of 29 theaters in more than seven cities.

Vaudeville became middle-class mass entertainment. Moderate and moral, it furnished cheap recreation that also reinforced genteel values. Skits encouraged audiences to pursue success through hard work. An emerging star system made American heroes out of performers like Will Rogers and George M. Cohan and American models out of Fanny Brice and Mae West. Ethnic comics defused tensions among immigrants with spoofs that exaggerated stereotypes and stressed the common foibles of all humanity. And theatergoers learned how to behave. Order and decorum replaced the boisterous atmosphere of saloons and music halls. Vaudeville audiences adopted the middle-class ideal of behavior—passive and polite. Americans were learning to defer to experts in the realms of public conduct and popular entertainment, as elsewhere in the new urban, industrial society.

national and even international economy. Most Americans were ambivalent about this process. Cities beckoned migrants from the countryside and immigrants from abroad with unparalleled opportunities for work and pleasure. The playwright Israel Zangwill celebrated the city's transforming power in his 1908 Broadway hit *The Melting Pot*. "The real American," one of his characters explained, "is only in the Crucible, I tell you—he will be the fusion of all the races, the coming superman."

The Melting Pot

Where Zangwill saw a melting pot with all its promise for a new superrace, champions of traditional American values, such as the widely read Protestant minister Josiah Strong, saw "a commingled mass of venomous filth and seething sin, of lust, of drunkenness, of pauperism, and crime of every sort." Both the champions and the critics of the late nineteenth century had a point. Corruption, crudeness, and disorder were no more or less a part of the cities than the vibrancy, energy, and opportunities that drew people to them. The gap between rich and poor yawned most widely in cities. As social critic Henry George observed, progress and poverty seemed to go hand in hand.

In the end moral judgments, whether pro or con, missed the point. Cities stood at the hubs of the new industrial order. All Americans, whatever they thought about the new urban world, had to search for ways to make that world work.

chapter summary

The modern city was the product of industrialization, lying at the center of the new integrated systems of transportation, communications, manufacturing, marketing, and finance.

- Fed by a great global migration of laborers, cities began to grow and to assume their modern shape of ringed residential patterns around central business districts and strict divisions among different classes, races, and ethnic groups.

- The challenge for the political system was to find within its democratic traditions a way to bring order out of the seeming chaos of unchecked urban growth.

- The urban boss and the urban political machine met the needs of cities for centralized authority but at a terrible cost in corruption, while social settlement houses, the Salvation Army, and the Social Gospel churches represented only start at coping with the problems of poverty and urban blight.

- As cities grew, the middle-class code of behavior—called Victorianism—spread, teaching the values of sobriety, hard work, self-control, and modesty that served the needs of new industrial society for efficiency and order and the middle-class need for protection against the turbulence of city life.

- Yet for all the emphasis on skills, discipline, and order, the vibrancy of city culture remained attractive, drawing millions in search of education, entertainment, and opportunity and radiating outward to almost every corner of the country.

interactive learning

The Primary Source Investigator CD-ROM offers the following materials related to this chapter:

- Interactive map: **Streetcar Suburbs in 19th-Century New Orleans** (M17)

- A collection of primary sources demonstrating the rise of urban order in the United States. Sources include a video clip of immigrants arriving at Ellis Island. An advertisement in Godey's Lady's Book illustrates some fashions among middle-class Victorian women.

additional reading

The best treatment of the rise of cities is Howard B. Chudacoff, *The Evolution of American Urban Society* (rev. ed., 1981). John Stilgoe, *Borderland: The Origins of the American Suburb, 1820–1929* (1988), chronicles the growth of suburban America. William Cronon, *Nature's Metropolis: Chicago and the Great West* (1991), looks at Chicago as part of the ecological landscape. In *Boss Cox's Cincinnati: Urban Politics in the Progressive Era* (1968), Zane Miller reassesses the urban political machine, and Paul Boyer explores efforts at controlling city life in *Urban Masses and Moral Order in America, 1820–1920* (1978). John F. Kasson, *Rudeness & Civility: Manners in Nineteenth-Century Urban America* (1990), and Lawrence Levine, *Highbrow/Lowbrow: The Emergence of Cultural Hierarchy in America* (1988), investigate the emerging urban culture. For a penetrating examination of traveling circuses as conduits for cultural exchanges, see Janet M. Davis's *The Circus Age: Culture and Society under the American Big Top* (2002).

Marcus Lee Hanson's classic *The Atlantic Migration, 1607–1860* (1940) began the shift in immigration history away from the national and toward a more global perspective. For richly detailed comparative examinations of the immigrant experience, see Roger Daniels, *Coming to America: A History of Immigration and Ethnicity in American Life* (1990), and Ronald Takaki, *A Different Mirror: A History of Multicultural America* (1993). Susan A. Glenn, *Daughters of the Shtetl: Life and Labor in the Immigrant Generation* (1990), throws light on the issue of gender by probing the lives and labor of immigrant women, with particular attention to the shaping effect of Old World Jewish culture. Virginia Yans-McLaughlin, ed., *Immigration Reconsidered: History, Sociology, and Politics* (1990), offers a collection of penetrating essays that places American immigration in its international context. For a fuller list of readings, see the Bibliography at www.mhhe.com/davidsonnation5.

significant events

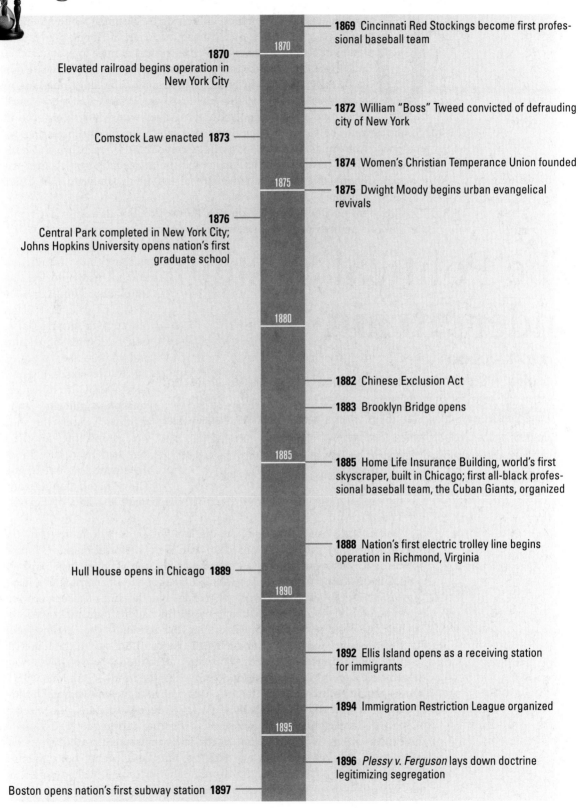

1869 Cincinnati Red Stockings become first professional baseball team

1870

1870
Elevated railroad begins operation in New York City

1872 William "Boss" Tweed convicted of defrauding city of New York

Comstock Law enacted **1873**

1874 Women's Christian Temperance Union founded

1875

1875 Dwight Moody begins urban evangelical revivals

1876
Central Park completed in New York City; Johns Hopkins University opens nation's first graduate school

1880

1882 Chinese Exclusion Act

1883 Brooklyn Bridge opens

1885

1885 Home Life Insurance Building, world's first skyscraper, built in Chicago; first all-black professional baseball team, the Cuban Giants, organized

1888 Nation's first electric trolley line begins operation in Richmond, Virginia

Hull House opens in Chicago **1889**

1890

1892 Ellis Island opens as a receiving station for immigrants

1894 Immigration Restriction League organized

1895

1896 *Plessy v. Ferguson* lays down doctrine legitimizing segregation

Boston opens nation's first subway station **1897**

Chapter 21

On May 1, 1893, an eager crowd of nearly half a million people jostled into a dramatic plaza fronted on either side by gleaming white buildings overlooking a sparkling lagoon. Named the Court of Honor, the plaza was the center of a strange ornamental city that was at once awesome and entirely imaginary. At one end stood a building whose magnificent white dome exceeded even the height of the capitol in Washington. Unlike the marble-built capitol, however, this building was all surface: a stucco shell plastered onto a steel frame and then sprayed with white oil paint to make it glisten. Beyond the Court of Honor stretched thoroughfares encompassing over 200 colonnaded buildings, piers, islands, and watercourses. Located five miles south of Chicago's central business district, this city of the imagination proclaimed itself the "World's Columbian Exposition" in honor of the 400th anniversary of Columbus's voyage to America.

World's Columbian Exposition

President Grover Cleveland opened the world's fair in a way that symbolized the nation's industrial transformation. He pressed a telegrapher's key. Instantly electric current set 7000 feet of shafting into motion—motion that in turn unfurled flags, set fountains pumping, and lit 10,000 electric bulbs. The lights played over an array of exhibition buildings soon known far and wide as the "White City."

The Political System under **Strain**

1877–1900

preview • Struggling to come to terms with the inequalities of the new urban and industrial order, the political system became locked in a near stalemate, broken only during the 1890s when a deep depression sparked labor protests and a revolt of farmers. The needs of industry for raw materials and markets also encouraged Americans to look abroad, in order to seek their "Manifest Destiny" in a commercial and even a territorial empire.

In Cleveland's judgment the neoclassical architecture was both "magnificent" and "stupendous." Surely the sheer size was astonishing, for the buildings had been laid out not by the square foot but by the acre. The Hall of Manufactures and Liberal Arts alone spread its roof over 30 acres, twice the area of Egypt's Great Pyramid.

One English visitor dismissed the displays within as little more than "the contents of a great dry goods store mixed up with the contents of museums." In a sense he was right. Visitors paraded by an unending collection of typewriters, pins, watches, agricultural machinery, cedar canoes, and refrigerators, to say nothing of a map of the United States fashioned entirely out of pickles. But this riot of mechanical marvels, gewgaws, and bric-a-brac was symbolic too of the nation's industrial transformation. The fair resembled nothing so much as a tangible version of the new mail-order catalogs whose pages were now introducing the goods of the city to the hinterlands.

The connections made by the fair were international as well. This event was the *World's* Columbian Exposition, with exhibits from 36 nations. Germany's famous manufacturer of armaments, Krupp, had its own separate building. It housed a 120-ton rifled gun. Easily within the range of its gunsights was a replica of the U.S. battleship *Illinois,* whose own bristling turrets stood just offshore of the exposition, on Lake Michigan. At the fair's amusement park, visitors encountered exotic cultures—and not just temples, huts, and totems, but exhibits in the living flesh. The Arabian village featured Saharan camels, veiled ladies, and elders in turbans. Nearby, Irish peasants boiled potatoes over turf fires while Samoan men threw axes.

In 1893 the World's Columbian Exposition set the night ablaze with a towering searchlight visible 60 miles away. Here the beam spotlights the fair's theme, "The World United," just as the giant exhibition halls highlighted the way the new industrial order was reshaping the globe.

Like all such fairs, the Columbian Exposition created a fantasy. Beyond its boundaries, the new industrial order was showing signs of strain. Early in 1893 the Philadelphia and Reading Railroad had gone bankrupt, setting off a financial panic. By the end of the year, nearly 500 banks and 15,000 businesses had failed. Although millions of tourists continued to marvel at the fair's wonders, crowds of worried and unemployed workers also gathered elsewhere in Chicago. On Labor Day, Governor John Altgeld of Illinois told a crowd that the government was powerless to soften the "suffering and distress" brought by this latest economic downturn.

In truth, the political system was ill equipped to cope with the economic and social revolutions reshaping America. The executive branch remained weak, while members of Congress and the courts found themselves easily swayed by the financial interests of the industrial class. The crises of the 1890s strained the political order and forced it to confront such inequities.

Strains on the political system

The political system also had to take into account developments abroad. Industrialization had sent American businesses around the world in search of raw materials and new markets. As that search intensified, many influential Americans argued that the United States needed to compete with European nations in acquiring territory overseas. By the end of the century, the nation's political system had taken its first steps toward modernization, including a major political realignment

International consequences

at home and a growing empire abroad. The changes launched the United States into the twentieth century and an era of prosperity and global power.

The Politics of Paralysis

During the 1880s and 1890s, as the American political system came under strain, Moisei Ostrogorski was traveling across the United States. Part of a flood of foreign observers, the Russian political scientist had come to see the new democratic experiment in action. His verdict was as blunt as it was widely shared: "the constituted authorities are unequal to their duty." It seemed that the glorious experiment had fallen victim to greed, indifference, and political mediocrity.

In fact, there were deeper problems: a great gulf between rich and poor; a wrenching cycle of boom and bust; the unmet needs of African Americans, Indians, and women. Politics was the traditional medium of resolution, but it was grinding into a dangerous stalemate.

Political Stalemate

From 1877 to 1897 American politics rested on a delicate balance of power that left neither Republicans nor Democrats in control. Republicans inhabited the White House for 12 years; Democrats, for 8. Margins of victory in presidential elections were paper thin. No president could count on having a majority of his party in both houses of Congress for his entire term. Usually Republicans controlled the Senate and Democrats the House of Representatives.

With elections so tight, both parties worked hard to turn out the vote. Brass bands, parades, cheering crowds of flag-wavers were "the order of the day and night from end to end of the country," reported a British visitor. In cities party workers

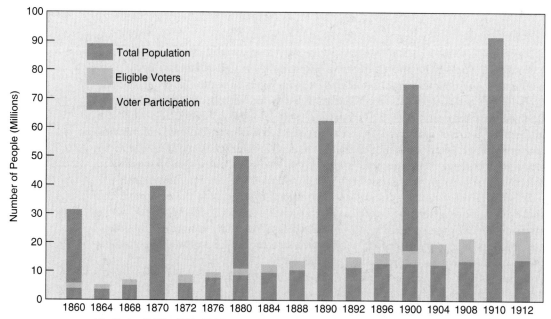

The Voting Public, 1860–1912 Between 1860 and 1910 the population and the number of eligible voters increased nearly threefold. As reforms of the early twentieth century reduced the power of political machines and parties, the percentage of voter participation actually declined.

handed out leaflets and pinned campaign buttons on anyone who passed. When Election Day arrived, stores and businesses shut down. At political clubs and corner saloons men lined up to get voting orders (along with free drinks) from ward bosses. In the countryside, fields went untended as farmers took their families to town, cast their ballots, and bet on the outcome.

An average of nearly 80 percent of eligible voters turned out for presidential elections between 1860 and 1900, a figure higher than at any time since. New party discipline and organization helped to turn out the vote, but it is also true that in this era the electorate made up a smaller percentage of the population. Strict voting qualifications limited participation. Only one American in four qualified to vote, and only one in five actually voted in presidential elections from 1876 to 1892. Most voters were white males. Women could vote in national elections only in a few western states, and beginning in the 1880s, the South erected barriers that eventually disfranchised many African American voters.

Party loyalty rarely wavered. In every election, 16 states could be counted on to vote Republican and 14 Democratic (the latter mainly in the South). In only six states—the most important being New York and Ohio—were the results in doubt. National victories often hung on their returns.

Voter turnout

The Parties

What inspired such loyalty? While Republicans and Democrats shared broad values, they also had differences. Both parties supported business and condemned radicalism, and neither offered embattled workers or farmers much help. Democrats believed in states' rights and limited government, while Republicans favored federal activism to foster economic growth. The stronghold of Democrats lay in the South, where they reminded voters that they had led the states of the Old Confederacy, "redeemed" them from Republican Reconstruction, and championed white supremacy. Republicans dominated the North with strong support from industry and business. They, too, invoked memories of the Civil War to secure votes, black as well as white. "Not every Democrat was a rebel," they chanted, "but every rebel was a Democrat."

Ethnicity and religion also cemented voter loyalty. Republicans relied on old-stock Protestants, who feared new immigrants and put their faith in promoting pious behavior throughout society. In the Republican party, they found support for immigration restriction, prohibition, and English-only schools. In the North, the Democratic party attracted urban political machines, their immigrant voters, and the working poor. Often Catholic, these voters saw salvation in following their own religious rituals, not in dictating the conduct of others.

"For three months processions, usually with brass bands, flags, badges, crowds of cheering spectators, are the order of the day and night from end to end of the country," commented a British observer. Here, Denver Republicans lead a nighttime parade to celebrate the election of Benjamin Harrison in the presidential contest of 1888.

Ethnic and religious factors

Region, religion, and ethnicity thus bound voters to each party, but outside the two-party system, reformers often fashioned political organizations of their own. Some formed groups that aligned themselves behind issues rather than parties. Opponents of alcohol created the Woman's Christian Temperance Union (1874) and the Anti-Saloon League (1893). Champions of women's rights joined the National Woman Suffrage Association (1890), a reunion of two branches of the women's suffrage movement that had split in 1869.

Like these political organizations, third political parties also crystallized around a single concern or a particular group. Advocates of temperance rallied to the Prohibition party (1869). Those who sought inflation of the currency formed the Greenback party (1874). Angry farmers in the West and South created the Populist, or People's, party (1892). All drew supporters from both conventional parties, but as largely single-interest groups they mobilized minorities, not majorities.

The Issues

In the halls of Congress, attention focused on well-worn issues: veterans' benefits, appointments, tariffs, and money. The presidency had been weakened by the impeachment of Andrew Johnson, the scandals of Ulysses S. Grant, and the contested victory of Rutherford B. Hayes in 1876. So Congress enjoyed the initiative in making policy. Time after time, legislators squandered it amid electioneering and party infighting or simply were swamped by the ever-increasing flood of proposed legislation.

Some divisive issues were the bitter legacy of the Civil War. Republicans and Democrats waved symbolic "bloody shirts," each tarring the other with responsibility for the war. The politics of the Civil War also surfaced in the lobbying efforts of veterans. The Grand Army of the Republic, an organization of more than 400,000 Union soldiers, petitioned Congress for pensions to make up for poor wartime pay and to support the widows and orphans of fallen comrades. By the turn of the century Union army veterans and their families were receiving $157 million annually. It was one of the largest public assistance programs in American history, which at its peak accounted for nearly half of the federal budget. It was also one of the first government programs to offer benefits to African Americans and laid the foundations of the modern welfare state.

More important than welfare was the campaign for a new method of staffing federal offices. From barely 53,000 employees at the end of the Civil War, the federal government had grown to 166,000 by the early 1890s. Far more of these new jobs required special skills. But dismantling the reigning "spoils system" proved difficult for politicians who had rewarded faithful supporters with government jobs regardless of their qualifications. Reacting to the scandals of the Grant administration, a group of independents formed the National Civil Service Reform League in 1881. The league promoted the British model of civil service based on examination and merit. But in Congress neither party was willing to take action when it held power (and thus controlled patronage).

Pendleton Act

One July morning in 1881, a frustrated office seeker named Charles Guiteau unwittingly broke the log jam. As President James Garfield hurried to catch a train, Guiteau jumped from the shadows and shot him twice. Garfield's death finally produced reform. In 1883 the Civil Service Act, or Pendleton Act, created a bipartisan civil service commission to administer competitive examinations for some federal jobs. By 1896 almost half of all federal workers came under civil service jurisdiction.

The protective tariff also stirred emotions in Congress. Since 1812, tariffs, or taxes on imported goods, had been used to shield "infant industries" in the United States from foreign competition. But by the 1880s many American industries had grown into strapping adults, no longer in need of such protection. Worse still, tariff revenues had created a budget surplus so large that it could undermine prosperity by depriving the economy of money for investment in employment and productivity.

As promoters of business, Republicans usually championed tariffs and were joined by industrialists, westerners who sold protected raw materials like wool and timber, and even many workers, who believed that the tariff safeguarded their jobs and their wages. Democrats, with their strength in the agricultural South, sought to reduce tariffs in order to lower the prices that farmers and other consumers paid for manufactured goods.

In 1890, when Republicans controlled the House, Congress enacted the McKinley Tariff, named for its sponsor, Ohio senator William McKinley. It raised tariff rates so high that they threatened to choke off all manufactured imports. It also contained a novel twist to appease reductionists. A "reciprocity" clause allowed the president to lower rates if other countries did the same. It was not enough to soothe opponents, who helped to drive McKinley and other Republicans from office in the elections of 1890. For the next two decades and more, a national tug-of-war would be waged over the tariff.

McKinley Tariff

Just as divisive was the issue of currency. For most of the nineteenth century, currency was backed by both gold and silver. The need for more money during the Civil War had led Congress to issue "greenbacks"—currency printed on paper with a green back and not convertible to gold or silver. For the next decade and a half Americans argued over whether to print more such paper money or take it

In this cartoon, Uncle Sam sits securely behind a locked door, protected by the soon-to-be-enacted Dingley Tariff bill (1897) from the riotous clamor of foreigners seeking entry into U.S. markets. Whenever reformers tried to reduce tariffs, political support for protection made the task nearly impossible. In 1882 Congress had created a commission to consider lowering tariffs, but it was quickly captured by the interests who stood to gain most from high tariffs. Complained one senator: "There was a representative of the wool growers on the commission; . . . of the iron interest . . . of the sugar interest. . . . And those interests were very carefully looked out for."

out of circulation. Farmers and other debtors favored printing greenbacks as a way of inflating prices and thus reducing their debts. For the opposite reasons, bankers and creditors stood for "sound money" backed by gold. Fear of inflation led Congress first to reduce the number of greenbacks and then in 1879 to make all remaining paper money convertible into gold.

A more heated battle was developing over silver-backed money. By the early 1870s so little silver was being used that Congress officially stopped coining it in 1873, touching off a steep economic slide as the supply of money contracted. With it came charges that a conspiracy of bankers had been responsible for "demonetizing" silver and wrecking the economy in what was widely referred to as the "Crime of '73." In truth, the money supply was inadequate. By the late nineteenth century, the supply of goods had expanded more rapidly than the amount of money in circulation. As the demand for money grew, pressure to raise interest rates, the charges for borrowing, grew as well. So, too, did deflation, or falling prices, as too little money chased too many goods. All added to economic instability and increased calls for enlarging the money supply.

In 1878 the Bland-Allison Act inaugurated a limited form of silver coinage. But pressure for unlimited coinage of silver—coining all silver presented at U.S. mints—mounted as silver production quadrupled between 1870 and 1890. In 1890 pressure for silver peaked in the Sherman Silver Purchase Act. It obligated the government to buy 4.5 million ounces of silver every month. Paper tender called "treasury notes," redeemable in either gold or silver, would pay for it. The compromise satisfied both sides only temporarily.

Crime of '73

Bland-Allison Act

The White House from Hayes to Harrison

From the 1870s through the 1890s a string of nearly anonymous presidents presided over the country. Not all were mere caretakers. Some tried to energize the office, but Congress continued to dominate Washington.

Republican Rutherford B. Hayes was the first of the "Ohio dynasty," which included three presidents from 1876 to 1900. He moved quickly to end Reconstruction and tried unsuccessfully to woo southern Democrats with promises of economic support. His pursuit of civil service reform ended only in splitting his party between "Stalwarts" (who favored the old spoils systems) and "Half-Breeds" (who opposed it and favored reform). Hayes left office after a single term, happy to be "out of a scrape."

In 1880, Republican James Garfield, another Ohioan, succeeded Hayes by a handful of votes. He spent his first hundred days in the White House besieged by office hunters and failing to placate the rival sections of his party. After Garfield's assassination only six months into his term, Chester A. Arthur, the "spoilsman's spoilsman," became president. To everyone's surprise, the dapper Arthur turned out to be an honest president. He broke with machine politicians, including his mentor and Stalwart leader Roscoe Conkling of New York. He worked to lower the tariff, warmly endorsed the new Civil Service Act, and reduced the federal surplus by beginning construction of a modern navy. Such evenhandedness left him little chance for renomination from divided party leaders.

The dirty election of 1884

The election of 1884 was one of the dirtiest ever recorded. Senator James G. Blaine, leader of the reform-minded Half-Breeds in the Republican party, fought off charges of corrupt dealings with the railroads, while Democrat Grover Cleveland, the former governor of New York, admitted to fathering an illegitimate child. In the last week of the race a New York minister labeled the Democrats the party of "Rum, Romanism, and Rebellion" (alcohol, Catholicism, and the Civil War). In reaction the Irish Catholic vote swung strongly to Cleveland and with it New York and the election.

Cleveland was the first Democrat elected to the White House since James Buchanan in 1856, and he was more active than many of his predecessors. He pleased reformers by expanding the civil service, and his devotion to gold-backed currency, economy, and efficiency earned him praise from business. He supported the growth of federal power by endorsing the Interstate Commerce Act (1887), new agricultural research, and federal arbitration of labor disputes.

Cleveland's presidential activism nonetheless remained limited. He vetoed two of every three bills brought to him, more than twice the number of all his predecessors. Toward the end of his term, embarrassed by the large federal surplus, Cleveland finally reasserted himself by attacking the tariff, but to no avail. The Republican-controlled Senate blocked his attempt to lower it.

A Chinese laborer, holding his queue of long hair in hand, proudly displays patches in support of the 1888 Democratic presidential candidate, Grover Cleveland, and his running mate, Allen B. Thurman. Cleveland and Thurman lost to Benjamin Harrison and Levi P. Morton, a wealthy New York banker. After his victory, Harrison, a pious Presbyterian, grabbed the hand of Senator Matthew Quay and crowed, "Providence has given us the victory." "Providence hadn't a damn thing to do with it," Quay said later, irked that Harrison seemed to have no idea how many Republicans "were compelled to approach the gates of the penitentiary to make him President."

In 1888 Republicans nominated a sturdy defender of tariffs, Benjamin Harrison, the grandson of President William Henry Harrison. President Cleveland won a plurality of the popular vote but lost in the Electoral College. The "human iceberg" (as Harrison's colleagues called him) worked hard, rarely delegated management, and turned the White House into a well-regulated office. He helped to shape the Sherman Silver Purchase Act (1890), kept up with the McKinley Tariff (1890), and accepted the Sherman Antitrust Act (1890) to limit the power and size of big businesses.

At the end of Harrison's term in 1893, Congress had completed its most productive session of the era, including the first billion-dollar peacetime budget. The growing federal surplus had become an embarrassment, and Republicans spent it, mostly on giveaway and pork-barrel projects that blatantly benefited their own states and districts. To Democratic jeers of a "Billion Dollar Congress," Republican House Speaker Thomas Reed shot back, "This is a billion-dollar country!"

Ferment in the States and Cities

Despite its growing expenditures and more legislation, most people expected little from the federal government. Few newspapers even bothered to send correspondents to Washington. Public pressure to curb the excesses of the new industrial order mounted closer to home, in state and city governments. Experimental and often effective, state programs began to grapple with the problems of corporate power, discriminatory shipping rates, political corruption, and urban decay.

State commissions

Starting in 1869 with Massachusetts, states established commissions to investigate and regulate industry, especially railroads, America's first big business. By the turn of the century, almost two-thirds of the states had them. These early commissions gathered and publicized information on shipping rates and business practices and furnished advice about public policy.

In the Midwest, on the Great Plains, and in the Far West, merchants and farmers pressed state governments to rein in high railroad rates and stop the rebates given to large shippers. In California, one newspaper published a schedule of freight rates to Nevada, showing that lower rates had been charged by wagon teams before the railroads were built. On the West Coast and in the Midwest, state legislatures empowered commissions to end rebates and monitor freight rates. In 1870 Illinois became the first of several states to define railroads as public highways subject to regulation, including setting maximum rates.

Concern over political corruption and urban blight led to state municipal conventions, the first in Iowa in 1877. Philadelphia sponsored a national conference on good city government in 1894. A year later reformers founded the National Municipal League. It soon had more than 200 branches. Its model city charter advanced such farsighted reforms as separate city and state elections, limited contracts for utilities, and more authority for mayors. Meanwhile cities and states in the Midwest enacted laws closing stores on Sundays, prohibiting the sale of alcohol, and making English the language of public schools—all in an effort to standardize social behavior and control the habits of new immigrants.

National Municipal League

The Revolt of the Farmers

In 1890, the politics of stalemate cracked as the patience of farmers across the South and the western plains reached an end. Beginning in the 1880s, a sharp depression drove down agricultural prices and forced thousands from their land. But farmers suffered from a great deal more, including heavy mortgages, widespread poverty, and railroad rates that sometimes discriminated against them. In 1890 their resentment boiled over. An agrarian revolt—called Populism—swept across the political landscape and helped break the political stalemate of the previous 20 years.

The Harvest of Discontent

The revolt of the farmers stirred first on the southern frontier, spread eastward from Texas through the rest of the Old Confederacy, then moved west across the plains. Farmers blamed their troubles on obvious inequalities: manufacturers protected by the tariff, railroads with sky-high shipping rates, wealthy bankers who held their mounting debts, expensive intermediaries who stored and processed their commodities—all seemed to profit at their expense.

The true picture was fuzzier. The tariff protected industrial goods but also supported some farm commodities such as wool and sugar. Railroad rates, however high, actually fell from 1865 to 1890. And while mortgages were heavy, most were short, no more than four years. Farmers often refinanced them and used the money to buy more land and machinery, thus increasing their debts. Millers and operators of grain elevators or storage silos earned handsome profits, yet every year more of them came under state regulation.

Targets of farm anger

In hard times, of course, none of this mattered. And in the South many poor farmers seemed condemned forever to hard times. Credit lay at the root of their problem, because most southern farmers had to borrow money to plant and harvest their crops. The inequities of sharecropping and the crop-lien system (pages 569–570) forced them into debt. When the prices for their crops fell, they borrowed still more, stretching the financial resources of the South beyond their meager limits. Within a few years after the Civil War, Massachusetts' banks had five times as much money as all the banks of the Old Confederacy.

Beginning in the 1870s, nearly 100,000 debt-ridden farmers a year picked up stakes across the Deep South and fled to Texas to escape this ruinous system of credit, only to find it waiting for them. Others stood and fought, as one pamphlet exhorted in 1889, "not with glittering musket, flaming sword and deadly cannon, but with the silent, potent and all-powerful ballot."

The Origins of the Farmers' Alliance

Before farmers could vote together, they had to get together. Life on the farm was harsh, drab, and isolated. Such conditions shocked Oliver Hudson Kelley as he traveled across the South after the Civil War. In 1867 the young government clerk founded the Patrons of Husbandry to brighten the lives of farmers and broaden their horizons. Local chapters, called "granges," brought farmers and their families together to pray, sing, and learn new farming techniques. The Grangers sponsored fairs, picnics, dances, lectures—anything to break the bleakness of farm life. By 1875 there were 800,000 members in 20,000 locals, most in the Midwest, South, and Southwest.

At first the Grangers swore off politics. But in a pattern often repeated, socializing led to economic and then political action. By pooling their money to buy supplies and equipment to store and market their crops, Grangers could avoid the high charges of intermediaries. By the early 1870s they also were lobbying midwestern legislatures to adopt "Granger laws" regulating rates charged by railroads, grain elevator operators, and other intermediaries.

Eight "Granger cases" came before the Supreme Court in the 1870s to test the new regulatory measures. *Munn v. Illinois* (1877) upheld the right of Illinois to regulate private property (in this case, the giant elevators for storing grain) as long as it was "devoted to a public use." Later decisions allowed state regulation of railroads, but only within state lines. Congress responded in 1887 by creating the Interstate Commerce Commission, a federal agency that could regulate commerce across state boundaries. In practice, it had little power, but it was a key step toward establishing the public right to oversee private corporations.

Slumping prices in the 1870s and 1880s bred new farm organizations. Slowly they blended into what the press called the "Alliance Movement." The Southern Alliance, formed in Texas in 1875, spread rapidly after Dr. Charles W. Macune took command in 1886. A doctor and lawyer as well as a farmer, Macune planned to expand the state's network of local chapters, or suballiances, into a national network of state Alliance Exchanges. Like the Grangers, the exchanges pooled their resources in cooperatively owned enterprises for buying and selling, milling and storing, banking and manufacturing.

Mary Shelley's novel of a man-made monster who turns against its creator strikes the theme for this 1874 cartoon titled "The American Frankenstein." Here, the railroad is a monstrous creation that crushes the common people in its path. It carries the symbols of wealth and might—a cloak of ermine and a club of capital. "Agriculture, commerce, and manufacture are all in my power," the monster bellows in the caption. Figures of authority, like the policeman at the lower right, can only snap to attention and salute.

Granger cases

Southern Alliance

Soon the Southern Alliance was publicizing its activities in local newspapers, publishing a journal, and sending lecturers across the country. For a brief period, between 1886 and 1892, the Alliance cooperatives grew to more than a million members throughout the South and challenged accepted ways of doing business. Macune claimed that his new Texas Exchange saved members 40 percent on plows and 30 percent on wagons. But most Alliance cooperatives were managed by farmers without the time or experience to succeed. Usually opposed by irate local merchants, the ventures eventually failed.

Colored Farmers' Alliance

Although the Southern Alliance admitted no African Americans, it encouraged them to organize. A small group of black and white Texans founded the Colored Farmers' National Alliance and Cooperative Union in 1886. By 1891 a quarter of a million farmers had joined. Its operations were largely secret, because public action often brought swift retaliation from white supremacists. When the Colored Farmers' Alliance organized a strike of black cotton pickers near Memphis in 1891, white mobs hunted down and lynched 15 strikers. The murders went unpunished, and the Colored Alliance began to founder.

The Alliance Peaks

Farmer cooperation reached northward to the states of the Midwest and Great Plains in the National Farmers' Alliance, created in 1880. In June 1890 Kansas organizers formed the first People's party to compete with Democrats and Republicans. Meanwhile the Southern Alliance changed its name to the National Farmers' Alliance and Industrial Union, incorporated the strong Northern Alliances in the Dakotas and Kansas, and made the movement truly national.

The key to Alliance success was not organization but leadership, both at the top and in the middle. Alliance lecturers fanned out across the South and the Great Plains, organizing suballiances and teaching new members about finance and cooperative businesses. At least one-quarter of Alliance members were women. The Alliance movement continued the old Grange practice of sponsoring family-oriented activities, such as songfests, parades, picnics, and even burial services. Although Alliance members remained sharply divided over woman suffrage, more than a few women became speakers and organizers. "Wimmin is everywhere," noted one observer of the Alliance. The comment seemed to apply literally to Alliance member Mary Elizabeth Lease, who in the summer of 1890 alone gave 160 speeches.

In 1890, members of the Alliance met in Ocala, Florida, and issued the "Ocala Demands." The manifesto reflected their deep distrust of "the money power"—large corporations and banks whose financial power gave them the ability to manipulate the "free" market. The Ocala Demands called on government to correct such abuses by reducing tariffs, abolishing national banks, regulating railroads, and coining silver money freely. The platform also demanded a federal income tax and the popular election of senators to make government more responsive to the public.

The most innovative feature of the platform came from Charles Macune. His "subtreasury system" would have required the federal government to furnish warehouses for harvested crops and low-interest loans to tide farmers over until prices rose. Under such a system farmers would no longer have had to sell in a glutted market, as they did under the crop-lien system. And they could have exerted control over the money supply, expanding it simply by borrowing at harvest time.

Mary Elizabeth Lease, the "Kansas Pythoness," was admitted to the bar as a young woman but soon turned to radical activism. A charismatic speaker, she campaigned for Populist candidates in the 1890s, on one occasion warning the industrial Northeast that "the people are at bay, let the bloodhounds of money beware."

In the elections of 1890 the old parties faced hostile farmers across the nation. In the South, the Alliance continued to work within the Democratic party and elected 4 governors, won 8 legislatures, and sent 44 members of Congress and 3 senators to Washington. In the Great Plains, Alliance candidates drew farmers from the Republican party. Newly created farmer parties elected 5 representatives and 2 senators in Kansas and South Dakota and took over both houses of the Nebraska legislature.

In the West especially, Alliance organizers began to dream of a national third party that would be free from the corporate influence, sectionalism, and racial tensions that split Republicans and Democrats. In their minds, it would be a party not just of farmers but also of the downtrodden and the "toilers," including industrial workers.

In February 1892, as the presidential election year opened, a convention of 900 labor, feminist, farm, and other reform delegates (100 of them black) met in St. Louis. They founded the People's, or Populist, party and called for another convention to nominate a presidential ticket. Initially southern Populists held back, clinging to their strategy of working within the Democratic party. But when newly elected Democrats failed to support Alliance programs, southern leaders such as Tom Watson of Georgia abandoned the Democrats and began recruiting black and white farmers for the Populists. Although he was a wealthy farmer, Watson sympathized with the poor of both races.

The People's Party

The national convention of Populists met in Omaha, Nebraska, on Independence Day, 1892. Their impassioned platform promised to return government "to the hands of 'the plain people.'" More conservative southern Populists succeeded in blocking a plank for woman suffrage, though western Populists joined the campaign that would win women the right to vote in Colorado in 1893. Planks advocated the subtreasury plan, unlimited coinage of silver and expansion of the money supply, direct election of senators, an income tax, and government ownership of railroads, telegraph, and telephone. To attract wage earners the party endorsed the eight-hour workday, restriction of immigration, and a ban on the use of Pinkerton detectives in labor disputes—for the Pinkertons had engaged in a savage gun battle with strikers that year at Andrew Carnegie's Homestead steel plant. Delegates rallied behind the old greenbacker and Union general James B. Weaver, carefully balancing their presidential nomination with a one-legged Confederate veteran as his running mate.

The Election of 1892

The Populists enlivened the otherwise dull campaign of 1892, as Democrat Grover Cleveland and Republican incumbent Benjamin Harrison refought the election of 1888. This time, however, Cleveland won, and for the first session since the Civil War, Democrats gained control of both houses of Congress. The Populists, too, enjoyed success. Weaver polled over a million votes, the first third-party candidate to do so. Populists elected 3 governors, 5 senators, 10 representatives, and nearly 1500 members of state legislatures.

Despite these victories, the election revealed dangerous weaknesses in the People's party. Across the nation thousands of voters did change political affiliations, but most often from the Republicans to the Democrats, not to the Populists. No doubt a Democratic party campaign of intimidation and repression hurt the People's party in the South, where white conservatives had been appalled by Tom Watson's open courtship of black southerners. ("You are kept apart that you may be separately

Longer-term weaknesses of the Populists

fleeced of your earnings," Watson had told his racially mixed audiences.) In the North, Populists failed to win over labor and most city dwellers. Both were more concerned with family budgets than with the problems of farmers and the downtrodden.

The darker side of Populism also put off many Americans. Its rhetoric was often violent; it spoke ominously of conspiracies and stridently in favor of immigration restriction. In fact, in 1892 the Alliance lost members, an omen of defeats to come. But for the present, the People's party had demonstrated two conflicting truths. It showed how far from the needs of many ordinary Americans the two parties had drifted and how difficult it would be to break their power.

The Rise of Jim Crow Politics

In 1892, despite the stumping of Populists like Tom Watson, African Americans had cast their ballots for Republicans, when they were permitted to vote freely. But increasingly, their voting rights were being curtailed across the South.

As the nineteenth century drew to a close, a long-standing racialism—categorizing people on the basis of race—deepened. The arrival of "new" immigrants from eastern and southern Europe and the acquisition of new overseas colonies highlighted differences among races and helped encourage prejudices that stridently justified segregation and other forms of racial control (see pages 576–577). In the South racialism was enlisted into a political purpose—preventing an alliance of poor blacks and whites that might topple white conservative Democrats. The white supremacy campaign, on the face of it directed at African Americans, also had a broader target in the world of politics: rebellion from below, whether black or white.

Disfranchisement

Mississippi, whose Democrats had led the move to "redeem" their state from Republican Reconstruction, in 1890 took the lead in disfranchising African Americans. A new state constitution required voters to pay a poll tax and pass a literacy test, requirements that eliminated the great majority of black voters. Conservative Democrats favored the plan because it also reduced voting among poor whites, who were most likely to join opposition parties. Before the new constitution went into effect, Mississippi contained more than 250,000 eligible voters, black and white. By 1892, after its adoption, there were fewer than 77,000. Soon an all-white combination of conservatives and "reformers"—those disgusted by frequent election-stealing with blocs of black votes—passed disfranchisement laws across the South. Between 1895 and 1908, campaigns to limit voting won out in every southern state.

The disfranchisement campaign succeeded in achieving its broad aim of splitting rebellious whites from blacks, as the tragic fate of Tom Watson demonstrated. Only a dozen years after his biracial campaign of 1892, Watson was promoting black disfranchisement and white supremacy in Georgia. Like other southern Populists, Watson returned to the Democratic party still hoping to help poor whites. But under the increased atmosphere of intolerance, only by playing a powerful race card could he hope to win election. "What does civilization owe the negro?" he asked bitterly. "Nothing! Nothing!! NOTHING!!!"

The African American Response

To mount a successful campaign for disfranchisement, white conservatives inflamed racial passions. They staged "White Supremacy Jubilees" and peppered newspaper editorials with complaints of "bumptious" and "impudent" African Americans. The lynchings of blacks peaked during the 1890s, averaging over a hundred a year for the decade. Most took place in the South. White mobs in cities such as Atlanta and New Orleans terrorized blacks for days in the newly heightened atmosphere of tension.

African Americans worked out their own responses to the climate of intolerance. Ida B. Wells, a black woman born into slavery, turned her talents into a nationwide campaign against lynching when a friend, Thomas Moss, and two of his partners in the People's Grocery were brutally murdered after a fight with a white competitor in 1892. Wells meticulously documented the murders of African Americans across the South, demonstrating an astounding 200 percent increase between 1882 and 1892. Wells turned antilynching into a personal crusade. She spent much of her time educating Americans about the use of lynching and other forms of mob violence as devices for terrorizing African Americans in the absence of slavery. Black men like Thomas Moss, who might want to start black-owned businesses or alter race relations in the South, were particular targets, for they threatened the prevailing racial and economic hierarchy in the South. Though her lobbying failed to produce a federal antilynching law, Wells did help organize black women, eventually into the National Association of Colored Women in 1896. It supported wide-ranging reforms, including in education, housing, and health care, and, of course, antilynching.

Wells's campaign had focused on mob violence, but another former slave, Booker T. Washington, stressed instead the need for accepting the framework for race relations and working within it. "I love the South," Washington reassured an audience of white and black southerners in Atlanta in 1895. He conceded that white prejudice against blacks existed throughout the region but nonetheless counseled African Americans to accept what was offered them and work for their economic betterment through manual labor. Every laborer who learned a trade, every farmer who tilled the land could increase his or her savings. And those earnings would amount to "a

Ida B. Wells

Booker T. Washington

In keeping with Booker T. Washington's emphasis on manual training, the Tuskegee Institute, opened in Alabama in 1881, was training 1400 students in 30 trades by 1900. Academic subjects received attention, too, as evidenced by this photograph of a history class (segregated by gender) learning about Captain John Smith and Pocahontas.

little green ballot" that "no one will throw out or refuse to count." Toward that end, Washington organized the Tuskegee Institute and created a curriculum stressing vocational skills for farming, manual trades, and industrial work.

Many white Americans hailed Washington's "Atlanta Compromise," for it struck the note of patient humility they were so eager to hear. For African Americans, it made the best of a bad situation. Washington, an astute politician, discovered that philanthropists across the nation hoped to make Tuskegee an example of their generosity. He was the honored guest of Andrew Carnegie at his imposing Skibo Castle. California railroad magnate Collis Huntington became his friend, as did other business executives eager to discuss "public and social questions."

Washington always preached accommodation to the racial caste system. He accepted segregation (as long as separate facilities were equal) and qualifications on voting (if they applied to white citizens as well). Above all Washington sought economic self-improvement for common black folk in fields and factories. In 1900 he organized the National Negro Business League to help establish African Americans in business as the leaders of their people. The rapid growth of local chapters (320 by 1907) extended his influence across the country.

In the "Solid South" (as well as an openly racist North) it was Washington's restrained approach that set the agenda for most African Americans. The ferment of the early 1890s, among black Populists and white, was replaced by a lily-white Democratic party that dominated the region but remained in the minority on the national level.

The New Realignment

On May 1, 1893, President Cleveland was in Chicago to throw the switch that set ablaze 10,000 electric bulbs and opened the World's Columbian Exposition (page 670). The gleaming White City with its grand displays stood as a monument to the nation's glorious progress. Four days later a wave of bankruptcies destroyed major firms across the country, and stock prices sank to all-time lows, setting off the depression of 1893. By the time the exposition closed in October, Chicago's mayor estimated the number of unemployed in the city to be near 200,000, a fraction of the millions who had already lost their jobs nationwide.

The sharp contrast between the exposition's White City and the nation's economic misery demonstrated the inability of the political system to smooth out the economy's cycle of boom and bust. In the slow recovery from the depression of 1873, the economy had overexpanded, and in 1893 the inevitable contraction began. By increasing production, opening markets, and tying Americans closer together, the new industrial order had brought soaring prosperity. But in 1893, the price of interdependence became obvious, as a downturn in one sector of the economy quickly affected others. With no way to control the swings in the business cycle, depression came on a scale as large as that of the booming prosperity. Out of it emerged a new realignment that left the Republican party in control of national politics for decades to come.

The Depression of 1893

Railroad baron and descendant of two presidents Charles Francis Adams Jr. called the depression a "convulsion," but the country experienced it as crushing idleness. In August 1893, unemployment stood at 1 million; by the middle of 1894, it was 3 million. At the end of the year nearly one worker in five was out of a job.

Working and middle-class families took in boarders, laundry, and sewing to make ends meet. With so many fathers and husbands unemployed, more and more wives and children left home to work. In the 1890s the number of laboring women actually increased, from 4 million to 5.3 million, but mainly in the exploitative fields of domestic and clerical work. In the South, where half the nation's working children were employed, child labor rose by 160 percent in textile mills during the decade. Concern for the young became so acute that middle-class women created the League for the Protection of the Family in 1896. Among other things it advocated compulsory education to keep children out of factories and mines.

The federal government had no program at all to combat the effects of the depression. "While the people should patriotically and cheerfully support their Government," President Cleveland had said at his inauguration, "its functions do not include the support of the people." The states offered little more. Relief, like poverty, was considered a private matter. The burden fell on local charities, benevolent societies, churches, labor unions, and ward bosses. In city after city, citizens organized relief committees to distribute bread and clothing until their meager resources gave out.

Others were less charitable. As the popular preacher Henry Ward Beecher told his congregation, "No man in this land suffers from poverty unless it be more than his fault—unless it be his sin." But the scale of hardship was so great, its targets so random, that anyone could be thrown out of work—an industrious neighbor, a factory foreman with 20 years on the job, a bank president. Older attitudes about personal guilt and responsibility for poverty began to give way to new ideas about its social origins and the obligation of public agencies to help.

Charles Dana Gibson, the Massachusetts-born illustrator famous for his portraits of well-bred young women in the 1890s, tackles a different subject in this ink drawing, a bread line of mixed classes during the depression of 1893.

The Rumblings of Unrest

Even before the depression, rumblings of unrest had begun to roll across the country. The Great Railroad Strike of 1877 had ignited nearly two decades of labor strife (pages 636–638). After 1893 discontent mounted as wages were cut, employees laid off, and factories closed. During the first year of the depression, 1400 strikes sent more than half a million workers from their jobs.

Uneasy business executives and politicians saw radicalism and the possibility of revolution in every strike. But the depression of 1893 had unleashed another force: simple discontent. In the spring of 1894, it focused on government inaction. On Easter Sunday, "General" Jacob Coxey, a 39-year-old Populist and factory owner, launched the "Tramps' March on Washington" from Massillon, Ohio. His "Commonweal Army of Christ"—some 500 men, women, and children—descended on Washington at the end of April to offer "a petition with boots on" for a federal program of public works. President Cleveland's staff tightened security around the White House as other "armies" of unemployed mobilized: an 800-person contingent left from Los Angeles; a San Francisco battalion of 600 swelled to 1500 by the time it reached Iowa.

On May 1, Coxey's troops, armed with "clubs of peace," massed at the foot of the Capitol. When Coxey entered the Capitol grounds, 100 mounted police routed

Coxey's Army

the demonstrators and arrested the general for trespassing on the grass. Nothing came of the protest, other than to signal a growing demand for federal action.

Federal help was not to be found. Grover Cleveland had barely moved into the White House when the depression struck. The country blamed him; he blamed silver. In his view the Sherman Silver Purchase Act of 1890 had shaken business confidence by forcing the government to use its shrinking reserves of gold to purchase (though not coin) silver. Repeal of the act, Cleveland believed, was the way to build gold reserves, restore confidence, and achieve recovery. After bitter debate, Congress complied. But this economic tinkering only strengthened the resolve of "silverites" in the Democratic party to overwhelm Cleveland's conservative "gold" wing.

Worse for the president, repeal of silver purchases brought no economic revival. In the short run abandoning silver hurt the economy by shrinking the money supply just when expansion might have stimulated it by providing needed credit. As panic and unemployment spread, Cleveland's popularity wilted. Democrats were buried in the congressional elections of 1894. Dropping moralistic reforms and stressing national activism, Republicans won control of both the House and the Senate. With the Democrats now confined to the South, the politics of stalemate was over. All that remained for the Republican party was to capture the White House in 1896.

The Battle of the Standards

The campaign of 1896 quickly became known as the "battle of the standards"—a reference to the burning question of whether gold alone or gold and silver should become the monetary standard. Most Republicans saw gold as the stable base for building business confidence and economic prosperity. They adopted a platform calling for "sound money" supported by gold alone. Their candidate, Governor William McKinley of Ohio, cautiously supported the gold plank and firmly believed in high tariffs to protect American industry.

William Jennings Bryan made the first of his three presidential bids in 1896, when he ran on both the Democratic and Populist tickets. Passionate in his convictions and devoted to the plain people, the "Great Commoner" is depicted in this hostile cartoon as a Populist snake devouring the Democratic party.

Silverites, on the other hand, campaigned for "free and independent" coinage of silver, in which the Treasury freely minted all the silver presented to it, independent of other nations. The supply of money would increase, prices would rise, and the economy would revive—or so their theory held. But the free silver movement was more than a monetary theory. It was a symbolic protest of region and class—of the agricultural South and West against the commercial Northeast, of debt-ridden farm folk against industrialists and financiers.

Free silver

Silverites controlled the Democratic national convention from the start. They paraded with silver banners, wore silver buttons, and wrote a plank into the anti-Cleveland platform calling for free and unlimited coinage of the metal. The high point came when William Jennings Bryan of Nebraska stepped to the lectern, threw back his head, and offered himself to "a cause as holy as the cause of liberty—the cause of humanity." The crowd was in a near frenzy as he reached the dramatic climax and spread his arms in mock crucifixion: "You shall not crucify mankind upon a cross of gold." The next day the convention nominated him for the presidency.

"Cross of Gold" speech

Populists were in a quandary. They expected the Democrats to stick with Cleveland and gold, sending unhappy silverites headlong into their camp. Instead, the Democrats stole their thunder. "If we fuse [with the Democrats] we are sunk," complained one Populist. "If we don't fuse, all the silver men we have will leave us for the more powerful Democrats." At a bitter convention, fusionists nominated Bryan for president. The best antifusionists could do was drop the Democrats' vice presidential candidate in favor of the fiery agrarian rebel from Georgia, Tom Watson.

Bryan knew he faced an uphill battle. Adopting a more active style that would be imitated in future campaigns, he traveled 18,000 miles by train, gave as many as 30 speeches a day, and reached perhaps 3 million people in 27 states. The nomination of the People's party actually did more harm than good by labeling Bryan a Populist (which he was not) and a radical (which he definitely was not). Devoted to the "plain people," the Great Commoner spoke for rural America and Jeffersonian values: small farmers, small towns, small government.

McKinley knew he could not compete with Bryan's barnstorming, so he contented himself with sedate speeches from his front porch in Canton, Ohio. The folksy appearance of the campaign belied its reality. From the beginning, it had

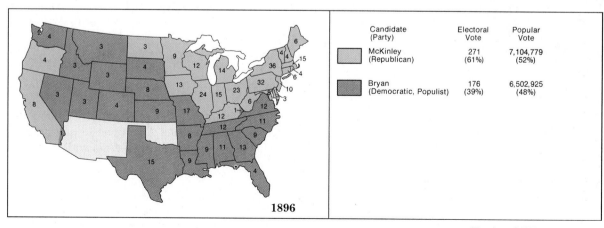

Candidate (Party)	Electoral Vote	Popular Vote
McKinley (Republican)	271 (61%)	7,104,779 (52%)
Bryan (Democratic, Populist)	176 (39%)	6,502,925 (48%)

1896

Election of 1896

been engineered by Marcus Alonzo Hanna, a talented Ohio industrialist. Hanna relied on modern techniques of organization and marketing. He advertised McKinley, said Theodore Roosevelt, "as if he were patent medicine." His well-oiled campaign brought to Canton tens of thousands, who cheered the candidate's promises of a "full dinner pail." Hanna also saturated the country with millions of leaflets, along with 1400 speakers attacking free trade and free silver. Frightened conservatives poured some $4 million into McKinley's war chest.

The election also proved to be one of the most critical in the Republic's history.* Over the previous three decades, political life had been characterized by vibrant campaigns, slim party margins, high voter turnout, and low-profile presidents. The election of 1896 signaled a new era of dwindling party loyalties and voter turnout, stronger presidents, and Republican rule. William McKinley's victory broke the political stalemate and forged a powerful coalition that dominated politics for the next 30 years. It rested on the industrial cities of the Northeast and Midwest and combined old support from business, farmers, and Union army veterans with broader backing from industrial wage earners. The Democrats controlled little but the South. And the Populists vanished, but not before leaving a compound legacy: as a catalyst for political realignment, a cry for federal action from the South and West, and a prelude to a new age of reform.

Republican coalition

McKinley in the White House

An 1896 Republican campaign poster features presidential hopeful William McKinley atop a giant gold coin engraved with the words "sound money" and supported by workers and businessmen alike. The poster promises domestic prosperity and respect overseas. The links between prosperity and empire as well as commerce and civilization were made not only in McKinley's campaign but also by later presidents.

In William McKinley, Republicans found a skillful chief with a national agenda and personal charm. He cultivated news reporters, openly walked the streets of Washington, and courted the public with handshakes and flowers from his own lapel. Firmly but delicately, he curbed the power of old-time state bosses. When need be, he prodded Congress to action. In all these ways, he foreshadowed "modern" presidents, who would act as party leaders rather than as executive caretakers.

Fortune at first smiled on McKinley. When he entered the White House, the economy had already begun its recovery, as the cycle of economic retrenchment hit bottom. Factory orders were slowly increasing, and unemployment dropped. Farm prices climbed. New discoveries of gold in Alaska and South Africa expanded the supply of money without causing "gold bugs" to panic that currency was being destabilized by silver.

Freed from the burdens of the economic crisis, McKinley called a special session of Congress to revise the tariff. In 1897 the Dingley Tariff raised protective rates still higher but allowed the tariffs to come down if other nations lowered theirs. McKinley also sought a solution for resolving railroad strikes, like the earlier Pullman conflict, before they turned violent. The Erdman Act of 1898 set up machinery for government mediation. McKinley even began laying plans for stronger regulation of trusts.

But affairs overseas competed for his attention. The same expansive forces that had transformed the United States were also causing Americans to look increasingly beyond their borders. McKinley found himself facing a crisis with Spain that

---

*Five elections, in addition to the contest of 1896, are often cited as critical shifts in voter allegiance and party alignments: the Federalist defeat of 1800, Andrew Jackson's rise in 1828, Lincoln's Republican triumph of 1860, Al Smith's Democratic loss in 1928, and—perhaps—Ronald Reagan's conservative tide of 1980.

would force the nation to decide whether a democratic, industrial republic should also become an imperial nation. Regulation—and a true age of reform—would await the next century.

Visions of Empire

The crisis with Spain was only the affair of the moment that turned American attention abroad. Underlying the conflict were larger forces linking the destiny of the United States with international events. By the 1890s, southern farmers were exporting half their cotton crop to factories worldwide, while western wheat farmers earned some 30 to 40 percent of their income from markets abroad. John D. Rockefeller's Standard Oil Company shipped about two-thirds of its refined products overseas, and Cyrus McCormick supplied Russian farmers with the reaper.

More than these growing commercial ties turned American heads overseas. Since the 1840s expansionists had spoken of a Manifest Destiny to overspread the North American continent from the Atlantic to the Pacific. It was perhaps only natural that as they brought the American West under control, visions of a new empire stretching from Latin America to Asia danced before their eyes, realized less by conquest than by opening the doors of trade to foreign markets and resources. It was perhaps natural too then that as Americans spun visions of empire in Asia and Latin America they would encounter other nations—old imperial powers Great Britain, France, Belgium, and Spain and newcomers Germany and Japan—who had imperial visions of their own.

European Expansion Worldwide

The scramble for empire was well under way by the time the Americans, Germans, and Japanese entered the fray in the late nineteenth century. Spain and Portugal still clung to the remnants of their colonial empires, dating from the fifteenth and sixteenth centuries. In the early nineteenth century, England, France, and Russia accelerated their drive to control foreign peoples and lands. But the late nineteenth century became the new age of imperialism because the technology of arms and the networks of communication, transportation, and commerce brought the prospect of effective, truly global empires within much closer reach.

From the very first years of settlement, the success of European expansion into colonial North America benefited from ecological factors. European diseases, animals, and plants often devastated and disrupted the new worlds they entered. The coming of smallpox and measles; of pigs, cattle, and horses; and of sugar and wheat played equally important roles in opening the Western Hemisphere and the Pacific basin to European domination. In areas like the Middle East, Asia, and Africa, where populations already possessed hardy domesticated animals and plants (as well as their

Ecological factors

Balance of U.S. Imports and Exports, 1870–1910 After the depression of 1893, both imports and exports rose sharply, suggesting one reason why the age of imperialism was so closely linked with the emerging global industrial economy.

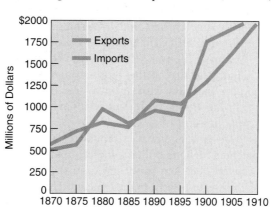

own devastating disease pools), European penetration was less complete and sometimes relied on naked force alone.

The speed and efficiency with which Europeans took over in the Niger and Congo basins of Africa in the 1880s prompted many Americans to argue for this European-style imperialism of conquest and possession. Germany, Japan, and Belgium were eagerly joining the hunt for colonies. But other Americans preferred a more indirect imperialism: one that exported products, ideas, and influence. To them, this American imperialism seemed somehow purer, for they could portray Americans as bearers of long-cherished values: democracy, free-enterprise capitalism, and Protestant Christianity.

Forces encouraging American imperialism

While Americans tried to justify imperial control in the name of such values, social, economic, and political forces were drawing them rapidly into the imperial race. The growth of industrial networks linked them to international markets as never before, whether they were Arkansas sharecroppers dependent on world cotton prices or Pittsburgh steelworkers whose jobs were made possible by orders for Singer sewing machines for Europe, China, and the Hawaiian Islands. As economic systems became more tightly knit and political systems more responsive to industrialists and financiers, a rush for markets and distant lands was perhaps unavoidable.

The Shapers of American Imperialism

Although the climate for expansion and imperialism was present at the end of the nineteenth century, the small farmer or steelworker was little concerned with how the United States advanced its goals abroad. An elite group—Christian missionaries, intellectuals, business leaders, and commercial farmers—joined navy careerists to shape a more active American imperialism. In doing so, they lobbied the White House and Congress, where foreign policy was made, and the State and War departments, where it was carried out.

By 1880 the once-proud Civil War fleet of more than 600 warships was rotting from neglect. The U.S. Navy ranked twelfth in the world, behind Denmark and Chile. The United States had a coastal fleet but no functional fleet to protect its interests overseas. Discontented navy officers combined with trade-hungry business leaders to lobby Congress for a modern navy.

Mahan calls for a strong navy

Alfred Thayer Mahan, a Navy captain and later admiral, formulated their ideas into a widely accepted theory of navalism. In *The Influence of Sea Power upon History* (1890), Mahan argued that great nations were seafaring powers that relied on foreign trade for wealth and might. In times of overproduction and depression, as had occurred repeatedly in the United States after the Civil War, overseas markets assumed even greater importance. The only way to protect foreign markets, Mahan reasoned, was with large cruisers and battleships. These ships, operating far from American shores, would need coaling stations and other resupply facilities throughout the world.

Mahan's logic was so persuasive and the profits to be reaped by American factories so great that in the 1880s Congress launched a program to rebuild the old wood-and-sail navy with steam vessels made of steel. By 1900, the U.S. Navy ranked third in the world. With a modern navy, the country had the means to become an imperial power.

Missionaries

Protestant missionaries provided a spiritual rationale for imperialism that complemented Mahan's military and economic arguments. As devout Americans sought to convert "heathen" unbelievers in the faraway lands of China, the Middle East, and the western Pacific, they encountered people whose cultural differences often made them unreceptive to the Christian message. Many missionaries believed that

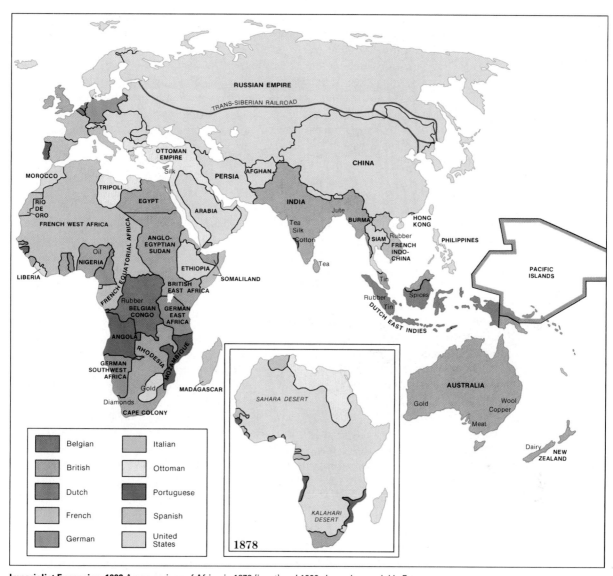

Imperialist Expansion, 1900 A comparison of Africa in 1878 (inset) and 1900 shows how quickly Europeans extended their colonial empires. Often resource-poor countries like Japan and England saw colonies as a way to acquire raw materials, such as South African diamonds and tin from Southeast Asia. Closer scrutiny shows that four of the most rapidly industrializing countries—Germany, Japan, Russia, and the United States—had few if any overseas possessions, even in 1900. And while China appears to be undivided, all the major powers were eagerly establishing spheres of influence there.

natives first had to become Western in culture before turning Christian in belief. They introduced Western goods, schools, and systems of government administration—any "civilizing medium," as one minister remarked when he invited the Singer Company to bring its famous sewing machines to China. Yet most missionaries were not territorial imperialists. They eagerly took up what they called "the White Man's Burden" of introducing Western civilization and religion to what they regarded as the inferior, "darker" races of the world. But they opposed outright military or political intervention.

Daily Lives

TIME AND TRAVEL
The New Navy

Early on February 3, 1874, a fleet of chunky monitors, steam frigates, and sloops lumbered out of Key West at a slow 4.5 knots. It was the largest assembly of American naval power since the Civil War. To the officers watching from shore, this fleet was an embarrassment. "Two modern vessels of war would have done us up in thirty minutes," a future admiral later observed.

In the era after the Civil War technology transformed the navies of Europe. Compound engines, improved armor plating, self-propelled torpedoes, and large rifled guns revolutionized naval warfare. The U.S. Navy, in contrast, sailed into the past. With 3000 miles of ocean as protection and no colonies to defend, a large blue-water fleet seemed unnecessary. Even steamships seemed impractical. The United States had no coaling stations in foreign wa-

ters to fuel them. By 1878 the navy had just 6000 sailors, the smallest force since the presidency of Andrew Jackson.

In 1873, as the U.S. Navy fell into disrepair, the British launched the *Devastation,* a single-masted, steam-driven vessel with heavy armor and powerful twin turrets.

A forerunner of the modern battleship, it could steam across the Atlantic and back without stopping for coal. Less than a decade later, a British fleet smashed Alexandria, Egypt, whose fortifications were sturdier than those of American ports. That battle convinced Congress that the American coast

Passengers on riverboats and yachts saluted the new steel-hulled, steam-powered American fleet as it steamed triumphantly up the Hudson River after naval victories in the Spanish-American War. Within a few years, these modern ships would be obsolete because an international arms race forced rapid innovation in naval design.

Social Darwinism

From scholars, academics, and scientists came racial theories to justify European and American expansion. Charles Darwin's *On the Origin of Species* (1859) had popularized the notion that among animal species, the fittest survived through a process of natural selection. Social Darwinists like Herbert Spencer in England and William Graham Sumner in the United States argued that the same laws of survival governed the social order. By natural as well as divine law, the fittest people (those descended from Anglo-Saxon and Teutonic stock, said Spencer and Sumner) would assert their dominion over "lesser peoples" of the world.

Commercial factors

Perhaps more compelling than either religious or racial motives for American expansion was the need for trade. The business cycle of boom and bust reminded Americans of the unpredictability of their economy. In hard times, people sought salvation wherever they could, and one obvious road to recovery lay in markets abroad. Entrepreneurs such as Minor Keith and his Tropical Fruit Company (later the mammoth United Fruit Company) had already constructed a railroad in Costa Rica and begun importing bananas from Central America. In Cuba and Hawaii, American planters were reaping harvests of sugarcane, pineapples, and other commercial crops to be processed and sold in domestic and foreign markets. By 1900, was no longer safe. In 1883 it appropriated $1.3 million for four modern, steel-hulled vessels—the cruisers *Atlanta, Boston,* and *Chicago,* each 3000 to 4500 tons, and the 1500-ton dispatch boat *Dolphin.* These early "protected" cruisers (so named for the armored deck built over boilers, engines, and other machinery) were an odd mix of old and new. All three had full sail rigs yet were completely electrified and contained watertight compartments and double bottoms. The *Chicago* had twin propellers but engines and boilers so antiquated that one observer compared them to a sawmill. The steel breech-loading guns were vast improvements over the iron muzzle loaders, yet gunners still aimed them the old-fashioned way, by looking down the barrels through open sights.

The naval program that began as a halfhearted effort had become a major commitment by the turn of the century. The fleet included additional protected cruisers, larger armored cruisers, and its first full-sized battleships—the *Indiana, Massachusetts,* and *Oregon,* each

displacing more than 10,000 tons. (Soon after 1900 giant battleships were displacing 20,000 tons; on the eve of World War I they reached more than 30,000 tons.) With five more first-class battleships commissioned by 1896, the U.S. Navy rose to fifth place in the world. The prestige of naval service had risen, too, and with it the number of sailors: nearly 10,000 in uniform.

The new navy, unlike the civilian world, was not a democratic culture. Privileges of rank were everywhere apparent. Commanders lived in wood-paneled luxury and dined on specially prepared cuisine, capped by coffee, brandy, and cigars. The crew ate salted meats, beans, and potatoes. Officers had private quarters, while enlisted men, so the saying went, lived under the place where they slept and slept under the place where they ate. At night the tables and benches used for dining in the common quarters were stowed between overhead beams from which hammocks were hung.

Battery drill was held twice a day, but under fire American marksmanship proved poor. Dur-

ing one battle in the Spanish-American War, Americans fired more than 8000 shells at fleeing Spanish cruisers. An examination of their hulls later revealed only 120 hits.

In 1907 President Theodore Roosevelt decided to put American naval power on display. He sent 16 battleships on a 46,000-mile, 14-month world tour. Ironically, the Great White Fleet (named for the gleaming white hulls of its ships) was already out of date. In 1906 Great Britain had commissioned the *Dreadnought,* a warship whose new guns rendered all its competitors obsolete. Unlike conventional battleships with guns of varying sizes, the Dreadnought carried guns so powerful that the ship had twice the firepower of anything else afloat. In a single stroke the new American navy, the proud product of a quarter century of effort, was outclassed—but not for long. The United States would match the British, for it had joined a naval arms race that would lead the world down the path to the carnage of the First World War.

the Singer Sewing Machine Company was sending some 60,000 sales agents to China and across the globe to hawk the virtues of their "iron tailor." It is no wonder, then, that as American companies extended their investments abroad and the depression of 1893 deepened at home, the National Association of Manufacturers insisted that the "expansion of our foreign trade is [the] only promise of relief."

Such arguments were often embraced even by anti-imperialists who favored expansion but believed it was a tactical mistake to acquire colonies. Yet their voices were drowned out by calls for an American-style empire. The growing chorus of imperialists in and out of government included social critics Henry and Brooks Adams, grandsons of former president and secretary of state John Quincy Adams, Massachusetts senator Henry Cabot Lodge, Secretary of State John Hay, and Theodore Roosevelt, who by the 1890s was serving as assistant secretary of the navy.

No one had done more to initiate the idea of a "new Empire" for the United States than William Henry Seward, secretary of state (1861–1869) under Lincoln and Andrew Johnson. Seward believed that "empire has . . . made its way constantly westward . . . until the tides of the renewed and decaying civilizations of the world meet on the shores of the Pacific Ocean." The United States must thus be prepared to win

William Henry Seward

Missionaries often viewed the Chinese as uncivilized "heathen" whose souls needed saving and whose culture needed civilizing. This cartoon, published around 1900, pokes fun at the common stereotype by suggesting what the Chinese must think of American "heathen." "Contributions Received Here to Save the Foreign Devils," reads the sign of the Chinese "preacher," who laments the uncivilized behavior of corrupt American city governments, feuding backwoodsmen, rioting laborers, and mobs tormenting Chinese and black Americans.

supremacy in the Far East—not by planting colonies or sending troops but by pursuing commerce. The idea that a commercial empire could be gained by demanding equal access to foreign markets was what made Seward's strategy truly revolutionary.

While he pursued ties to Japan, Korea, and China, Seward promoted a transcontinental railroad at home and a canal across the Central American isthmus. Link by link, he was trying to connect eastern factories to western ports in the United States and, from there, to markets in the Far East. In pursuit of these goals Seward made

Acquisition of Midway and Alaska

two acquisitions in 1867: Midway Island in the Pacific and Alaska. Unimportant by itself, the value of Midway lay as a way station to Asia not far from Hawaii, where missionary planters were already establishing an American presence. Critics called Alaska "Seward's Folly," but he paid only about 2 cents an acre for a mineral-rich territory twice the size of Texas.

Seward's conviction that the future of the United States lay in the Pacific and Asia produced little in his lifetime. But it flourished in the 1890s, when Mahan provided the naval theory necessary to make the leap and the vanishing American frontier supplied an economic rationale for extending Manifest Destiny beyond the nation's continental borders. But in the 1880s, Secretary of State James G. Blaine began to look for ways to expand American trade and influence southward into Central and South America, where Great Britain had interests of its own to protect.

Looking to Latin America

Blaine launched a campaign to cancel the Clayton-Bulwer Treaty (1850), which shared with Great Britain rights to any canal built in Central America. At the same time, he tried to shift Central American imports from British to U.S. goods by proposing that a "customs union" be created to reduce trade barriers in the Americas. His efforts resulted only in a weak Pan-American Union to foster peaceful understanding in the region, for Latin American nations balked at lowering their tariffs. In response, Blaine threatened to ban any export to the United States of the products of their generally single-crop economies. With Latin America dependent on such exports, only three nations—Colombia, Haiti, and Venezuela—had the will to resist.

Blaine's Pan-American Union

Gold, with its capacity to muddy the waters from which it was panned, stirred trouble in the jungles of Venezuela. In the 1880s, prospectors unearthed a 32-pound nugget along the border between Venezuela and British Guiana. Both Britain and Venezuela laid claim to the territory, which included the mouth of the Orinoco River, gateway to trade in the interior of South America's northern coast. In 1895, President Cleveland intervened, insisting on the right of the United States to mediate the dispute under the Monroe Doctrine. Great Britain and the United States rattled their sabers at each other but neither could afford war. The British finally accepted an American mediated settlement and in 1897 signed a treaty with Venezuela that left Venezuela with what it wanted most, control of access to the Orinoco, and the United States with what it wanted, the opportunity to assert its supremacy in the hemisphere.

The Venezuelan Boundary Dispute

Anglo-American tensions eased in the wake of the crisis and reached a new peak of friendship with a treaty concluded by Secretary of State John Hay and British ambassador Julian Pauncefote in 1901. The Hay-Pauncefote Treaty ceded British interest in building a canal across the Central American isthmus and required the United States to leave such a canal open to ships of all nations. The campaign begun years earlier by James Blaine to pave the way for a U.S.-owned canal had finally come to an end.

Reprise in the Pacific

In the Pacific, the United States confronted Great Britain and Germany as they vied for control of the strategically located islands of Samoa. In 1878 a treaty gave America the rights to the fine harbor at Pago Pago. When the Germans sent marines to secure their interests in 1889, the British and Americans sent gunboats. As tensions rose, a typhoon struck, sinking the rival fleets and staving off conflict. Ten years later the three powers finally carved up the islands, with the United States retaining Pago Pago.

Sugar was the key to Hawaii's English- and American-dominated plantations. Polynesians were culturally ill suited to the backbreaking labor that sugar cultivation demanded. Planters filled their labor needs by recruiting Japanese workers like this one.

If American expansionists wanted to extend trade across the Pacific to China, Hawaii was the crucial link. It afforded a fine naval base and a way station along the route to Asia. In 1893, American sugar planters overthrew the recently enthroned Queen Liliuokalani, a Hawaiian nationalist eager to rid the island of American influence. Their success was ensured when a contingent of U.S. marines arrived ashore on the pretext of protecting American lives. Eager to avoid the McKinley Tariff's new tax on sugar imported into the United States, planters lobbied for the annexation of Hawaii, but President Cleveland refused. He was no foe of expansion but was, as his secretary of state noted, "unalterably opposed to stealing territory, or of annexing people against their consent, and the people of Hawaii do not favor annexation." The idea of incorporating the nonwhite population also troubled Cleveland. For a time, matters stood at a stalemate.

The Imperial Moment

In 1895, after almost 15 years of planning from exile in the United States, José Martí returned to Cuba to renew the colony's struggle for independence from Spain. With cries of "Cuba libre," Martí and his rebels cut railroad lines, destroyed sugar mills, and set fire to the cane fields. Within a year, rebel forces controlled more than half the island. But even as they fought the Spanish, the rebels worried about the United States. Their island, just 90 miles off the coast of Florida, had long been a target of American expansionists and business interests. Martí had no illusions. "I have lived in the bowels of the monster," he explained of his exile in the United States, "and I know it."

Cuba in revolt

The Spanish overlords struck back at Martí and his followers with brutal force. Governor-General Valeriano Weyler herded half a million Cubans from their homes into fortified camps where filth, disease, and starvation killed perhaps 200,000. Outside these "reconcentration" camps, Weyler chased the rebels across the countryside, polluting drinking water, killing farm animals, burning crops.

The revolt in Cuba was only the first round in a struggle that would eventually end in a war between the United States and Spain. By the time it was over, the Spanish-American War would leave Spain defeated and banished from the Western Hemisphere, Cuba free of Spanish rule, the United States with new colonial possessions in the Pacific and the Caribbean, and the knotty problem of what to do with them the subject of a national debate. For better or worse, America's imperial moment had arrived.

Mounting Tensions

President Cleveland had little sympathy for the Cuban revolt, but in the Republican party, expansionists such as Theodore Roosevelt and Massachusetts senator Henry Cabot Lodge urged a forceful policy of recognizing Cuban independence—a step that if taken would likely provoke war with Spain. When William McKinley entered the White House in 1897, however, his Republican supporters discovered that they had elected only a moderate expansionist. Cautiously, privately, he lobbied Spain to stop cracking down on the rebels and destroying American-owned property. With over $50 million invested in Cuban sugar and an annual trade of over $100 million, American business interests had much to lose.

In October 1897 Spain promised to remove the much-despised Weyler, end the reconcentration policy, and offer Cuba greater autonomy. The shift encouraged McKinley to resist pressure at home for more hostile action. But leaders of the Spanish army in Cuba had no desire to compromise. Although Weyler was removed, the military renewed efforts to quash the rebellion and encouraged pro-army riots in the streets of Havana. Early in 1898, McKinley dispatched the

An investigation years later concluded that the sinking of the *Maine* resulted from a spontaneous explosion aboard ship, but at the time fervent patriots turned the event into a call for war and, as can be seen in the lower left corner, memorabilia, here in the form of a button carrying the famous rallying cry, "Remember the Maine." The peaceful arrival of the *Maine* in Havana harbor is depicted on the upper-left-hand corner of the painting, the grizzly aftermath of the explosion on the upper-right-hand corner.

battleship *Maine* to show that the United States meant to protect its interests and its citizens.

The de Lôme letter

Then in February 1898 the State Department received a stolen copy of a letter to Cuba sent by the Spanish minister in Washington, Enrique Dupuy de Lôme. So did William Randolph Hearst, a pioneer of sensationalist, or "yellow," journalism who was eager for war with Spain. "WORST INSULT TO THE UNITED STATES IN ITS HISTORY," screamed the headline of Hearst's *New York Journal*. What had de Lôme actually written? After referring to McKinley as a "would-be politician," the letter admitted that Spain had no intention of changing policy in Cuba. The Spanish planned to crush the rebels. Red-faced Spanish officials immediately recalled de Lôme, but most Americans now believed that Spain had deceived the United States.

Sinking of the *Maine*

On February 15, 1898, as the USS *Maine* lay peacefully at anchor in the Havana harbor, explosions ripped through its hull. Within minutes the ship sank to the bottom, killing some 260 American sailors. Much later, an official investigation concluded that the explosion was the result of spontaneous combustion in a coal bunker aboard ship. Most Americans at the time, however, inflamed by hysterical news accounts, concluded that Spanish agents had sabotaged the ship. McKinley sought a diplomatic solution but also a $50 million appropriation "to get ready for war."

Teller Amendment

Pressures for war proved too great, and on April 11, McKinley asked Congress to authorize "forceful intervention" in Cuba. Nine days later Congress recognized Cuban independence, insisted on the withdrawal of Spanish forces, and gave the president authority to use military force. In a flush of idealism, Congress also adopted the Teller Amendment, renouncing any aim to annex Cuba. Certainly both idealism and moral outrage led many Americans down the path to war. But in the end, the "splendid little war" (as Secretary of State Hay called it) resulted from less lofty ambitions—empire, trade, glory.

The Imperial War

For the 5462 men who died, there was little splendid about the Spanish-American War. Only 379 gave their lives in battle. The rest suffered from accidents, disease, and the mismanagement of an unprepared army. As war began, the American force totaled only 30,000, none of whom had been trained for fighting in tropical climates. The sudden expansion to 60,000 troops and 200,000 volunteers overtaxed the army's graft-ridden system of supply. Rather than tropical uniforms, some troops were issued winter woolens, and some fed on rations that were diseased, rotten, or even lethally spoiled. Others found themselves fighting with weapons from the Civil War.

Dewey at Manila

The navy fared better. Decisions in the 1880s to modernize the fleet now paid off handsomely. Naval battles largely determined the outcome of the war. As soon as war was declared, Admiral George Dewey ordered his Asiatic battle squadron from China to the Philippines. Just before dawn on May 1, he began shelling the Spanish ships in Manila Bay. Five hours later the entire Spanish squadron lay at the bottom of the bay. Three hundred eighty-one Spaniards were killed but only one American, a ship's engineer who died of a heart attack. Dewey had no plans to follow up his stunning victory with an invasion. His fleet carried no marines with which to take Manila. So ill-prepared was President McKinley for war, let alone victory, that only after learning of Dewey's success did he order 11,000 American troops to the Philippines.

Halfway around the globe, another Spanish fleet had slipped into Santiago harbor in Cuba just before the arrival of the U.S. Navy. The navy, under Admiral William Sampson, blockaded the island, expecting the Spanish to flee under the cover of darkness. Instead, on July 3, the Spanish fleet made a desperate dash for the open seas in broad daylight. So startled were the Americans that several of their ships nearly collided as they rushed to attack their exposed foes. All seven Spanish ships were sunk, with 474 casualties. Only one American was killed and one wounded. With Cuba now cut off from Spain, the war was virtually won.

War in Cuba

Few Americans had heard of the Philippine Islands; fewer still could locate them on a globe. McKinley himself followed news from the Pacific front on an old textbook map. But most Americans knew the location of Cuba and how close it lay to the Florida coast.

Racial tensions

Before the outbreak of hostilities, Tampa, Florida, was a sleepy coastal town with a single railroad line. But when it became the port of embarkation for the Cuban expeditionary force, some 17,000 troops arrived in the spring of 1898 alone. Tampa's overtaxed facilities soon broke down, spawning disease, tension, and racial violence. President McKinley had authorized the army to raise five volunteer regiments of black soldiers. By the time war was declared, over 8000 African Americans had signed up, half of them stationed around segregated Tampa. They found that although they could sail off to die freeing the peasants of Cuba, they were forbidden to buy a soda at the local drugstore. "Is America any better than Spain?" one dismayed black chaplain wondered. After drunken white troops shot at a black child, black troops in Tampa rioted. Three white and 27 black Americans were wounded in the melee.

Matters were scarcely less chaotic as 17,000 disorganized troops and hundreds of reporters finally scrambled aboard ship. There they sat for a week, until sailing on June 14 for Santiago and battle. By June 30, the Americans had landed to

Black veterans of the western Indian wars along with volunteers, segregated and commanded by white officers, made up almost a quarter of the American force that invaded Cuba. Members of the Tenth Cavalry, shown here, were clearly in no mood to be subjected to the harassment they and other black troops encountered around Tampa. Later the Tenth Cavalry supported a charge by Colonel Teddy Roosevelt's Rough Riders at the battle of San Juan Hill.

challenge some 24,000 Spanish, many equipped with modern rifles. The following day 7000 Americans—including the black soldiers of the Ninth and Tenth Cavalry regiments—stormed up heavily fortified San Juan and nearby Kettle hills. Their objective was the high ground north and east of Santiago.

Among them Lieutenant Colonel Theodore Roosevelt thrilled at the experience of battle. He had raised a cavalry troop of cowboys and college polo players, originally called "Teddy's Texas Tarantulas." By the time they arrived in Cuba, the volunteers were answering to the nickname "Rough Riders." As they charged toward the high ground, Roosevelt yelled: "Gentlemen, the Almighty God and the just cause are with you. Gentlemen, charge!" The withering fire drowned out his shrill, squeaky voice, so he repeated the call. Charge they did and conquer the enemy, though the battle cost more than 1500 American casualties. (See "After the Fact," pages 707–711.)

The Rough Riders

Without a fleet for cover or any way to escape, the Spanish garrison surrendered on July 17. In the Philippines, a similar brief battle preceded the American taking of Manila on August 13. The "splendid little war" had ended in less than four months.

Peace and the Debate over Empire

Conquering Cuba and the Philippines proved easier than deciding what to do with them. The Teller Amendment had renounced any American claim to Cuba. But clearly the United States had not freed the island to see chaos reign or American business

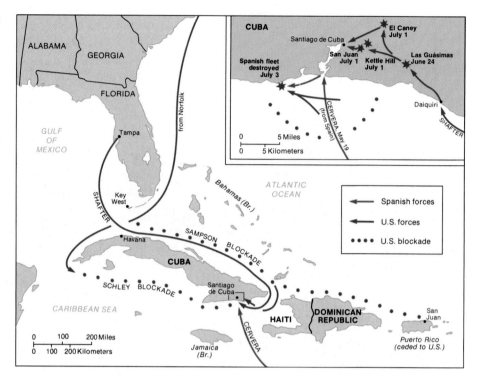

and military interests excluded. And what of the Philippines—and Spanish Puerto Rico, which American forces had taken without a struggle? Powerful public and congressional sentiment pushed McKinley to claim empire as the fruits of victory.

The president himself favored such a course. The battle in the Pacific highlighted the need for naval bases and coaling stations. "To maintain our flag in the Philippines, we must raise our flag in Hawaii," the New York *Sun* insisted. On July 7 McKinley signed a joint congressional resolution annexing Hawaii, as planters had wanted for nearly a decade.

Annexing Hawaii

The Philippines presented a more difficult problem. Filipinos had greeted the American forces as liberators, not new colonizers. The popular leader of the rebel forces fighting Spain, Emilio Aguinaldo, had returned to the islands on an American ship. But to the rebels' dismay, McKinley insisted that the islands were under American authority until the peace treaty settled matters.

Aguinaldo

Such a settlement, McKinley knew, would have to include American control of the Philippines. He had no intention of leaving Spain in charge or of seeing the islands fall to other European rivals. American military advisers warned that without control of the entire island of Luzon, its capital, Manila, would be indefensible as the naval base McKinley wanted. Nor, McKinley felt certain, were the Filipinos capable of self-government. Aguinaldo and his rebels thought otherwise, and in June Aguinaldo declared himself president of a new Philippine republic.

Anti-imperialists

Many influential Americans—former president Grover Cleveland, steel baron Andrew Carnegie, novelist Mark Twain—opposed annexation of the Philippines. Yet even these anti-imperialists favored expansion, if only in the form of trade. Business leaders especially believed that the country could enjoy the economic benefits of the Philippines without the costs of maintaining it as a colony. Annexation would mire the United States too deeply in the quicksands of Asian politics, they argued. More important, a large, costly fleet would be necessary to defend the

The United States in the Pacific In the late nineteenth century both Germany and the United States emerged as major naval powers and as contestants for influence and commerce in China. The island groups of the central and southwest Pacific, though of little economic value, had potential strategic significance as bases and coaling stations along the routes to Asia. Rivalry (as in the case of Samoa) sometimes threatened to erupt into open conflict. Control of Hawaii, Midway, Samoa, Guam, and the Philippines gave the United States a string of strategic stepping-stones to the Orient.

islands. To the imperialists that was precisely the point: a large fleet was crucial to the interests of a powerful commercial nation.

Racial ideas shaped both sides of the argument. Imperialists believed that the racial inferiority of nonwhites made occupation of the Philippines necessary, and they were ready to assume the "White Man's Burden" and govern. Filipinos, they argued, would gradually be taught the virtues of Western civilization, Christianity, democracy, and self-rule. (In fact, most Filipinos were already Catholic after many years under Spanish rule.) Anti-imperialists, on the other hand, feared racial inter-mixing and the possibility of Asian workers flooding the American labor market. They also maintained that dark-skinned people would never develop the capacity for self-government. An American government in the Philippines could be sustained only at the point of bayonets—yet the U.S. Constitution made no provision for governing people without representation or equal rights. Such a precedent abroad, the anti-imperialists warned, might one day threaten American liberties at home.

The role of race

Still, when the Senate debated the Treaty of Paris ending the Spanish-American War in 1898, the imperialists had the support of the president, most of Congress, and the majority of public opinion. Even an anti-imperialist like William Jennings Bryan, defeated by McKinley in 1896, endorsed the treaty. In it Spain surrendered title to Cuba, ceded Puerto Rico and Guam to the United States, and in return for $20 million turned over the Philippines as well.

Eager to see war ended, Bryan and other anti-imperialists believed that once the United States possessed the Philippines, it could free them. The imperialists had other notions. Having acquired an empire and a modern navy to protect it, the United States could now assert its new status as one of the world's great powers.

From Colonial War to Colonial Rule

Acquiring an empire was one thing, managing it quite another. As the Senate debated annexation of the Philippines in Washington, rebels fought with an American patrol outside of Manila. The few Americans who paid attention to the ensuing clash called it the "Filipino insurrection," but to those who fought, it was a brutal war. When it ended more than three years later, nearly 5000 Americans, 25,000 rebels, and perhaps as many as 200,000 civilians lay dead.

Racial antagonism spurred the savage fighting. American soldiers tended to dismiss Filipinos as nearly subhuman. Their armed resistance to American occupation often transformed the frustrations of ordinary troops into brutality and torture. To avenge a rebel attack, one American officer swore he would turn the surrounding countryside into a "howling wilderness." Before long the American force was resorting to a garrison strategy of herding Filipinos into concentration camps while destroying their villages and crops. The policy was embarrassingly reminiscent of the tactics of "Butcher" Weyler in Cuba. Only after the Americans captured Aguinaldo himself, in 1902, did the war end.

In contrast to the bitter guerrilla war, the United States ruled the Philippines with relative benevolence. Under William Howard Taft, the first civilian governor, the Americans built schools, roads, sewers, and factories and inaugurated new farming techniques. The aim, said Taft, was to prepare the island territory for independence, and in keeping with it, he granted great authority to local officials. These advances—social, economic, and political—benefited the Filipino elite and thus

The American decision to occupy the Philippines rather than give it independence forced Filipino nationalists to fight U.S. troops, as they had already been fighting the Spanish since 1896. Forces like the ones pictured at the right were tenacious enough to require more than 70,000 Americans (left) to put down the rebellion. Sporadic, bloody guerrilla fighting continued until 1902, and other incidents persisted until 1906.

earned their support. Decades later, on July 4, 1946, the Philippines were finally granted independence.

The United States played a similar role in Puerto Rico. As in the Philippines, executive authority resided in a governor appointed by the U.S. president. Under the Foraker Act of 1900 Puerto Ricans received a voice in their government as well as a nonvoting representative in the U.S. House of Representatives and certain tariff advantages. All the same, many Puerto Ricans chafed at the idea of such second-class citizenship. Some favored eventual admission to the United States as a state; others advocated independence—a division of opinion that persists even today.

Puerto Rico

An Open Door in China

Like a reciprocal equation, interest in Asia drove the United States to annex the Philippines, and annexation of the Philippines only whetted American interest in Asia. As ever, the possibility of markets in China—whether for Christian souls or consumer goods—proved an irresistible lure.

Both the British, who dominated China's export trade, and the Americans, who wanted to, worried that China might soon be carved up by other powers. Japan had defeated China in 1895, encouraging Russia, Germany, and France to join in demanding trade concessions. Each nation sought to establish an Asian "sphere of influence" in which its commercial and military interests reigned. Often such spheres resulted in restrictions against rival powers. Since Britain and the United States wanted the benefits of trade rather than actual colonies, they tried to limit foreign demands while leaving China open to all commerce.

In 1899, at the urging of the British, Secretary of State Hay circulated the first of two "open-door" notes among the imperial powers. He did not ask them to give up their spheres of influence in China, only to keep them open to free trade with other nations. The United States could hardly have enforced even so modest a proposal, for it lacked the military might to prevent the partitioning of China. Still, Japan and most of the European powers agreed in broad outline with Hay's policy out of fear that the Americans might tip the delicate balance by siding with a rival. Hay seized on the tepid response and brashly announced that the open door in China was international policy.

The open-door notes

Unrest soon threatened to close the door. Chinese nationalists, known to Westerners as Boxers for their clenched fist symbol, formed secret societies to drive out the *fon kwei*, or foreign devils. Encouraged by the Chinese empress, Boxers murdered hundreds of Christian missionaries and their followers and set siege to foreign diplomats and citizens at the British Embassy in Beijing. European nations quickly dispatched troops to quell the uprising and free the diplomats, while President McKinley sent 2500 Americans to join the march to the capital city. Along the way, the angry foreign armies plundered the countryside and killed civilians before reaching Beijing and breaking the siege.

Boxer Rebellion

Hay feared that once in control of Beijing the conquerors might never leave. So he sent a second open-door note in 1900, this time asking foreign powers to respect China's territorial and administrative integrity. They endorsed the proposal in principle only. In fact, the open-door notes together amounted to little more than an announcement of American desires to maintain stability and trade in Asia. Yet they reflected a fundamental purpose to which the United States dedicated itself across the globe: to open closed markets and to keep open those markets that other empires had yet to close. The new American empire would have its share of colonies, but in Asia as elsewhere it would be built primarily on trade.

Sense of mission

To expansionists like Alfred Thayer Mahan, Theodore Roosevelt, and John Hay, American interests would be secure only when they had been established worldwide, a course of action they believed to be blessed by divine providence. "We will not renounce our part in the mission of the race, trustee under God of the civilization of the world," declared Senator Albert Beveridge. But to one French diplomat, more accustomed to wheeling and dealing in the corridors of international power, it seemed that the Americans had tempted fate. With a whiff of Old World cynicism or perhaps a prophet's eye, he remarked, "The United States is seated at the table where the great game is played, and it cannot leave it."

On New Year's Eve at the State House in Boston a midnight ceremony ushered in the twentieth century. The crowd celebrated with psalms and hymns. There was a flourish of trumpets, and in the absence of a national anthem everyone sang "America."

Solemn and patriotic, the dawn of the new century brought an end to an era of political uncertainty and a decade of social upheaval. Prosperity returned at home; empire beckoned abroad. But deep divisions—between rich and poor, farmers and factory workers, men and women, native-born and immigrant, black and white—split the country. A younger generation of leaders stood in the wings, fearful of the schisms but confident it could bridge them. Theodore Roosevelt, who had looked eagerly toward war with Spain and the chance to expand American horizons, did not mince words with an older opponent. "You and your generation have had your chance. . . . Now let us of this generation have ours!"

chapter summary

The end of the nineteenth century witnessed a crisis arising out of years of political stalemate at home as well as the realization of dreams of empire abroad.

- Republicans and Democrats ground politics into near-gridlock over the well-worn issues of regional conflict, tariff, and monetary reform.

- Discontented Americans often fashioned political instruments of their own, whether for woman suffrage, temperance, monetary change, antilynching and civil rights, or farm issues.

- The political deadlock finally came to an end in the turbulent 1890s, when depression-spawned labor strife and a revolt of farmers produced the People's, or Populist, party and a political realignment that left the Republicans in control of national politics.

- By the 1890s, too, the tradition of Manifest Destiny combined powerfully with the needs of the new industrial order for raw materials and markets and the closing of the American frontier to produce a powerful drive toward empire, which rested on these two principles of American foreign policy:

  - The old Monroe Doctrine (1823), which warned European powers to stay out of the Americas.

  - The newer open-door notes of Secretary of State John Hay (1899–1900), which stressed the importance of equal commercial access to the markets of Asia.

- Most Americans favored an overseas empire for the United States but disagreed over whether it should be territorial or commercial.

- In the end America's overseas empire was both territorial and commercial. A victory in the Spanish-American War (1898) capped an era of territorial and commercial expansion by furnishing colonial possessions in the Caribbean and the Pacific and at the same time providing more stepping-stones to the markets of Asia.

interactive learning

The Primary Source Investigator CD-ROM offers the following materials related to this chapter:

- Interactive maps: **Election of 1896** (M7) and **The Spanish-American War in Cuba, 1898** (M20)

- A collection of primary sources exploring the American political system under strain in the industrial age, including a cartoon of Theodore Roosevelt and reforms passed by Congress, the Sherman Anti-Trust Act, and the Great Seal of the United States. Other documents illuminate U.S. territorial expansion: the joint resolution annexing Hawaii, for example.

additional reading

Sean Dennis Cashman, *America in the Gilded Age: From the Death of Lincoln to the Rise of Theodore Roosevelt* (1984), is a fine overview of the era. The importance of the presidential politics of the Gilded Age is stressed in H. Wayne Morgan, *From Hayes to McKinley: National Party Politics, 1877–1896* (1969), but for the importance of ethnicity and religion see Paul Kleppner, *The Cross of Culture: A Social Analysis of Midwestern Politics, 1850–1900* (1970). John Hicks's classic *The Populist Revolt* (1931) emphasizes poverty as the driving force behind Populism, while Lawrence Goodwyn points to the "movement culture" of the Alliance in reevaluating the Populists as crusaders for radical democratic change in *Democratic Promise: The Populist Movement in America* (1976). Charles Hoffman, *The Depression of the Nineties: An Economic History* (1970), furnishes a lucid account of the economy and the depression of 1893. On the spread of segregation in the post-Reconstruction South, see C. Vann Woodward's classic *The Strange Career of Jim Crow* (3rd rev. ed., 1974). Woodward focuses on changes in the law, while John Cell, *The Highest Stage of White Supremacy* (1982), points to the role of the city. For Booker T. Washington's approach to race relations, see Louis Harlan, *Booker T. Washington* (1972) and *Booker T. Washington: The Wizard of Tuskegee* (1983). David Levering Lewis, *W. E. B. DuBois: Biography of a Race* (1993), is the fullest account of the early life and career of the civil rights leader.

For a conventional view of the rise of the welfare state in the 1930s, see Harold Wilensky and Charles N. Lebeaux, *Industrial Society and Social Welfare* (1958). A revision of those views can be found in Theda Skocpol's *Protecting Soldiers and Mothers: The Political Origins of Social Policy in the United States* (1994), which stresses the nineteenth-century origins of the welfare state and the interplay between the state and nongovernmental political groups.

For broad interpretive views of American foreign policy, see Michael Hunt, *Ideology and American Foreign Policy* (1984); John Dobson, *America's Ascent: The United States Becomes a Great Power, 1880–1914* (1978); and Walter LaFeber, *The American Age* (1989). LaFeber contains a rich bibliography, and his *Inevitable Revolutions* (3rd ed., 1993) is good on Central America. Michael Hunt, *The Making of a Special Relationship: The United States and China to 1914* (1983), is excellent on Sino-American relations. On the role of missionaries, especially women, see Jane Hunter's *The Gospel of Gentility: American Women Missionaries in Turn-of-the-Century China* (1984). For the Philippines, see Stanley Karnow, *In Our Image* (1989). For a fuller list of readings, see the Bibliography at www.mhhe.com/davidsonnation5.

significant events

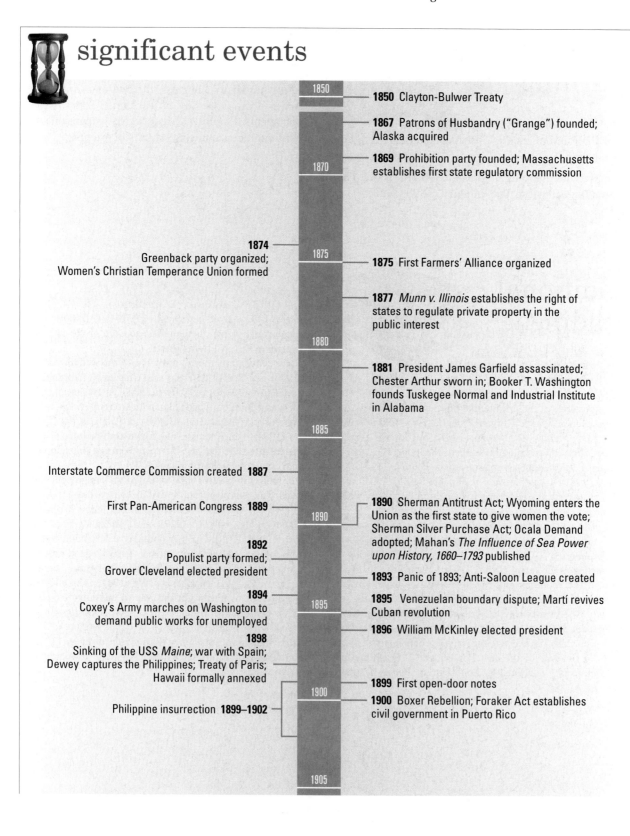

1850 Clayton-Bulwer Treaty

1867 Patrons of Husbandry ("Grange") founded; Alaska acquired

1869 Prohibition party founded; Massachusetts establishes first state regulatory commission

1874
Greenback party organized;
Women's Christian Temperance Union formed

1875 First Farmers' Alliance organized

1877 *Munn v. Illinois* establishes the right of states to regulate private property in the public interest

1881 President James Garfield assassinated; Chester Arthur sworn in; Booker T. Washington founds Tuskegee Normal and Industrial Institute in Alabama

Interstate Commerce Commission created **1887**

First Pan-American Congress **1889**

1890 Sherman Antitrust Act; Wyoming enters the Union as the first state to give women the vote; Sherman Silver Purchase Act; Ocala Demand adopted; Mahan's *The Influence of Sea Power upon History, 1660–1793* published

1892
Populist party formed;
Grover Cleveland elected president

1893 Panic of 1893; Anti-Saloon League created

1894
Coxey's Army marches on Washington to demand public works for unemployed

1895 Venezuelan boundary dispute; Martí revives Cuban revolution

1896 William McKinley elected president

1898
Sinking of the USS *Maine*; war with Spain; Dewey captures the Philippines; Treaty of Paris; Hawaii formally annexed

1899 First open-door notes

1900 Boxer Rebellion; Foraker Act establishes civil government in Puerto Rico

Philippine insurrection **1899–1902**

AFTER THE FACT
Historians Reconstruct the Past

Engendering the Spanish-American War

"WHAT, ARE YOU COWARDS?" The shrill voice could barely be heard above the gunfire, but for the man who possessed it, the only sounds that mattered would be the cries of Spanish troops surrendering on the San Juan Heights. For the second time Lieutenant Colonel Theodore Roosevelt was assaulting a hill during the soggy Cuban summer of 1898. The first attack had only just ended, with Roosevelt and his "Texas Tarantulas" (recently dubbed the "Rough Riders") helping to overrun what the Americans called Kettle Hill. The colonel had been easy to spot: he was the only man on horseback. But Roosevelt had his reasons for the daring display, as he explained later: "It is always hard to get men to start when they can not see whether their comrades are going." And perhaps there was another reason: it showed manly grit to defy death.

The second charge was aimed at nearby San Juan Hill, this time on foot. With a pistol recovered from the sunken battleship *Maine* and a pair of eyeglasses in each of his ten custom-made pockets, Roosevelt stormed the Spanish entrenchment—practically alone, as it turned out. Bubbling with excitement, he had neglected to give the order to attack. A hundred yards into the assault, he realized what had happened and returned to rally his men. Finally they charged and, of course, conquered.

Roosevelt's triumph during the Spanish-American War gave him a legendary, career-launching victory and the manly glory he had pursued since childhood. The sickly, bespectacled boy became a man, proving his courage, honor, and character in the

way he thought best, in war. "San Juan," he recalled years later, "was the great day of my life."

For many Americans, especially those born after the Civil War or too young to have fought in it, the Spanish-American War was the grand moment when their country became a great power and they a new generation of war heroes. Ever since, debates have raged over how they got that chance. Why did the United States go to war with Spain in 1898?

Historians have not wanted for explanations. Some see economic motives and stress the commercial rewards expected from newly acquired markets overseas. Others view the war as the global extension of the nation's "manifest destiny" to overspread the continent. Still others emphasize a geostrategic push for coaling stations in the Pacific to fuel a growing navy and for the islands in the Caribbean to block European imperialism. Humanitarian concern for the Cubans, a mission of Christian uplift for "lesser breeds," the glory of empire, political advantage at home and the spread of democracy abroad, revenge for the sinking of the *Maine*, frantic war cries from overheated journalists—all these factors, to a greater or lesser degree, enter into the historical calculus, depending on which historian is doing the math.

Yet the motives are so varied, the drums of war beating from so many quarters, historians have had difficulty tying the multiple causes into a coherent purpose. Is there a common thread among those who wanted war with Spain, apart from the conviction that war was necessary? Recent work has pointed to the broad-based political culture of shared values, institutions, and assumptions as the source of American belligerency. Within that political culture, some historians have highlighted gender as key.

Is it possible that constructions of gender somehow helped to breed war fever or to tie together the trumpeters of war? It may seem far-fetched to look for the sources of the Spanish-American War in the cultural roles assigned to men and women. Gender, after all, deals with the identity of individuals, whereas the study of international relations lies in the realm of sovereign nations. But the evidence pointing toward the role of gender in this war is intriguing, to say the least.

Political cartoons offer a graphic clue. William Randolph Hearst's *New York Journal* took the lead in howling for war on its front pages, in its editorials, and in its political cartoons. Even someone who couldn't read the cartoons' bold labels could hardly mistake the author's message. Over a hundred years later the fine-lined drawings still have bite. By 1898 other newspapers were imitating Hearst's swashbuckling style of sensational words and images.

A surprising number of cartoons relied on then-popular images of masculinity and femininity to make their case. In one drawing, a determined Uncle Sam spoils for a fight as he rips his jacket from his chest. "Off comes his coat—now look out!" reads the caption. In another, Sam looks down from behind a cannon at an aristocrat labeled "Spain." The Spaniard holds a bloody sword and a burning torch. At his feet lie a ravaged mother ("Cuba") and her child. "Peace—But Quit That!" says Sam. In yet another cartoon, President McKinley, who had his doubts about fighting the Spanish, is depicted as an "Old Woman" trying to "Sweep Back the Sea" of congressional and public support for war. A final cartoon has Secretary of State John Sherman wagging his finger in disapproval at a diminutive Alfonso XIII, the boy-king of Spain, who stands near a shackled prisoner, a beheaded statuette,

This detail from the popular painting by W. G. Read captured the Rough Riders' legendary charge up Kettle Hill—manly, courageous, romantic, and all wrong, as the much more accurate painting by Frederic Remington (inset) shows. Only Roosevelt rode his horse ("Little Texas"). The Rough Riders ran up the hill on foot—literally for their lives—to avoid being hit by rifle fire.

and a cage filled with Americans. Alfonso carries a label, "SPANISH CRUELTIES TO PRISONERS," lest the reader miss the point of Sherman's lecture.

In these and other political cartoons, we find notions of masculinity and femininity at the center of the message. Resolute males, whether mythic ones such as Uncle Sam or real ones such as Secretary of State Sherman, stand ready to fight or to rebuke those who break the codes of chivalry. Men opposing war or indecisive about it, such as McKinley, are dressed as women. The Spanish, on the other hand, are reduced to puny figures, like the petulant little Alfonso, or are made out to be bloodthirsty violators of helpless womanhood. True men, the cartoons seem to be saying, go to war to protect the principles of chivalry and the women who embody them; dishonorable, cowardly men ravage women or become them.

Words, too—in the halls of Congress, in boardrooms, on street corners, on the pages of newspapers—furnish more evidence. The country must take up arms, thundered Representative James R. Mann of Illinois, as Congress debated war—not because of some "fancied slight" or "commercial wrong" or lust for empire but "because it has become necessary to fight if we would uphold our manhood." When the *Maine* was sunk, Senator Richard R. Kenny of Delaware exploded over the insult: "American manhood and American chivalry give back the answer that innocent blood shall be avenged." Some urged arbitration to resolve the matter, but Senator George Perkins rejected it as unmanly: "Men do not arbitrate questions of honor," he insisted.

To others, Congress was too eager—and too male—to do anything but go to war. Alice Stone Blackwell, editor of the pro-suffrage *Woman's Journal,* put it bluntly: "Assuming for the sake of argument that this war is . . . utterly inexcusable . . . it is a Congress of men that has declared it." Other words—"courage," "virility," "glory," "character," "valor"—rang across the nation as Americans pondered war with Spain.

Such language, some historians have concluded, reflected a larger "crisis of manhood" imperiling American politics at the end of the nineteenth century. As they

"Off comes his coat—now look out!"

see it, the new industrial order spawned a "self-interested materialism" that was undermining the country's collective sense of civic virtue, dividing working classes from the middle class and splintering the republic. Just as bad, the creature comforts of the industrial age were making men sluggish and soft, particularly upper- and middle-class men who were the source of political leadership. Worse still, the hot pursuit of money and things was corroding the manly sense of honor, integrity, and valor that contemporaries believed to be essential for good government and the basis of leadership in politics.

As if these dangers were not enough, the rise of the "New Woman" threatened to emasculate men as women charged into the all-male preserve of politics. Woman activists laid claim to the right to vote and asserted the superiority of feminine virtue, which was needed to temper the corrupt "male" influence dominating the political system. Morality and intelligence rather than manliness, these women maintained, should be the touchstones of politics.

The depression of 1893 only aggravated the crisis. Men lost their jobs, their self-respect, and with them their independence and vitality. In a Darwinian

"Peace—But Quit That."

"Another Old Woman Tries to Sweep Back the Sea."

world of killing competition—in other words, the world as Americans of the late nineteenth century conceived it—the loss of male vigor could spell disaster at home and abroad.

Whatever else it did, the Spanish-American War offered a resolution to this crisis of manhood. The war furnished an opportunity for valorous action in the tradition of the legendary father figures who fought in the American Revolution and the Civil War and thereby set the mold for political leadership. The war would toughen American men for survival in the realm of domestic politics as well as in the rough-and-tumble world of great imperial powers. At the same time, rescuing the Cubans from Spanish oppression would restore the heroic sense of honor believed to be so vital to leadership. In the process, the "New Woman" would be defanged. Women would resume their "proper" roles as nurturers who respected their men and raised their children to be the next generation of brave, honorable males and gentle, domesticated females.

Undoubtedly, such gendered rhetoric is arresting. Whether it serves to tie together the various explanations for war and empire is another matter. Establishing the identity of a single individual is complicated enough, for character is shaped not only by gender but also by race, ethnicity, religion, class, education, and many other factors. National identity and the actions that derive from it are more complex still, and the actions of real people in the real world are perhaps thorniest of all. Even as staunch a booster of war and manly vigor as Theodore Roosevelt, to take one example, was ca-

pable as president of pursuing the "unmanly" path of arbitration to end the Russo-Japanese War in 1905.

Traditional diplomatic historians may never be satisfied with the notion that gender plays any role in international relations, which they see as the interaction of competing sovereign powers, commercial or territorial ambitions, and clear-cut concerns over national safety. It is also important to remember that bringing gender into the equation does not necessarily invest it with explanatory power. To say that gender shaped policy, after all, is different from saying that gender created policy. Still, constructions of gender did play a role in the Spanish-American War, if only in their widespread use by those who sold the country on war and by those who fought it.

BIBLIOGRAPHY Gender has become an increasingly important category of analysis for historians, even for those of American foreign policy. We draw heavily here on the innovative and provocative work of Kristin L. Hoganson, *Fighting for American Manhood: How Gender Politics Provoked the Spanish-American and Philippine-American Wars* (1998). For a broader view of the impact of gender on late-nineteenth-

"Secretary Sherman Talks to the Boy-King."

and early-twentieth-century America, see Gail Bederman's *Manliness and Civilization: A Cultural History of Gender and Race in the United States, 1880–1917* (1995). The myriad interpretations of the Spanish-American War are summarized in Luis Perez Jr.'s *The War of 1898: The United States and Cuba in History and Historiography* (1998). For his part, Perez stresses the largely ignored role of the Cuban *insurrectos,* who he feels were close to winning Cuban independence when the United States intervened to ensure that it controlled Cuba's future. Lewis L. Gould's *The Spanish-American War and President McKinley* (1982) tells the story from the presidential vantage point, while Theodore Roosevelt's *The Rough Riders* (1899) offers TR's own inflated recollections of his role in the Cuban campaign.

Chapter 22

Quitting time, March 25, 1911. The long day was about to end at the Triangle Shirtwaist Company near Washington Square at the lower end of Manhattan. The deafening whir of some 1500 sewing machines would soon be silenced as hundreds of workers—mostly young immigrant women—were set free. To some, quitting time seemed like an emancipation. Twelve-hour days in stifling, crowded workrooms, weekly paychecks of only $3 to $15, fines for the tiniest mistakes, deductions for needle and thread, even for electricity, made the young seamstresses angry. Two years earlier, their frustration had boiled over into an industrywide strike for better wages and working conditions. Despite a union victory, the only change visible at Triangle was that every morning the doors were locked to keep workers in and labor organizers out.

The fire broke out in the lofts as the workers were leaving their machines. In minutes the top stories were ablaze. Terrified seamstresses groped through the black smoke, only to find exits locked or clogged with bodies. All but one of the few working fire escapes collapsed. When the fire trucks arrived, horrified firefighters discovered that their ladders could not reach the top stories. "Spectators saw again and again pitiable companionships formed in the instant of death—girls who placed their arms around each other as they leaped," read one news story. Their bodies hit the sidewalk with a sickening thud or were spiked on the iron guard rails. One hundred forty-six people died, most of them young immigrant women. In far-off Russia and Poland, news of the disaster sent families into spasms of grief. "Most of these old parents had an idea of America as one big town," explained one immigrant. "Each of them was almost sure that their daughter was a victim of that terrible catastrophe."

A few days later 80,000 New Yorkers joined the silent funeral procession snaking slowly up Fifth Avenue in the rain. A quarter of a million watched. At the Metropolitan Opera House, union leader Rose Schneiderman told a rally, "This is not the first time that girls have been burned alive in the city. Every year thousands of us are maimed." A special state commission investigated the tragedy. Over the next four years its recommendations produced 56 state laws regulating fire safety, hours, machinery, and home work. They amounted to the most far-reaching labor code in the country.

The Triangle fire shocked the nation and underscored a widespread fear: modern industrial society had created profound strains, widespread misery, and deep class divisions. Corporations grew to unimagined size, bought and sold legislators, dictated the terms of their own profit. Men, women, and children worked around the clock in unsafe factories for wages that barely supported them. In cities across America, tenement-bred diseases took innocent lives. Criminals threatened people and property, while saloons tied the working poor to dishonest political bosses. Even among the middle class, inflation was shrinking wallets at

The Progressive Era
1890–1920

preview • The first truly broad-based, national reform movement, Progressivism addressed problems arising out of industrialization, urbanization, and immigration. Led by members of the urban middle class—many of them women—progressives were moderate modernizers who looked to bring order and efficiency as well as social justice to economic and political life. During the presidencies of Theodore Roosevelt and Woodrow Wilson, they established the modern, activist state.

By 1900 a wave of corporate mergers led muckraking reformers to use imagery like this grasping octopus, by George Luks, to dramatize the evils of monopoly. Progressives sought to counter the new powers of industrial society by invigorating government.

the rate of 3 percent a year. "It was a world of greed," concluded one garment worker; "the human being didn't mean anything."

But human beings did mean something to followers of an influential reform movement sweeping the country. Progressivism had emerged as a political force in the mid-1890s and would continue to shape politics through World War I. The movement sprang from many impulses, mixing a liberal concern for the poor and working class with conservative efforts to stabilize business and avoid social chaos. But liberal or conservative, most progressives shared a desire to soften the harsher aspects of industrialization, urbanization, and immigration.

Progressivism thus began in the cities, where the wellspring of misery was fullest, political corruption deepest, and social division clearest. It was organized by an angry, idealistic middle class and percolated up from neighborhoods to city halls, state capitals, and, finally, Washington. Though usually pursued through politics, the goals of progressives were broadly social—to create a "good society" where people could live decently, harmoniously, and prosperously, along middle-class lines.

Unlike past reformers, progressives saw government as a protector, not an oppressor. Only government possessed the resources for the broad-based reforms they sought. Progressivism spawned the modern activist state, with its capacity to regulate the economy and manage society. And because American society had

In 1911 the fiery deaths of 146 people at the Triangle Shirtwaist Company shocked the nation. Firefighters arrived within minutes, but their ladders could not reach the top stories. Trapped by locked doors, those who failed to escape perished within or leaped to their deaths on the streets below. Following the horrifying episode, New York enacted the most ambitious labor code in the country.

become so interdependent, progressivism became the first nationwide reform movement. No political party monopolized it; no single group controlled it. It flowered in the presidencies of Republican Theodore Roosevelt and Democrat Woodrow Wilson. In 1912 it even gave birth to its own party, the Progressive, or "Bull Moose," party. But by then progressivism had filtered well beyond politics into every realm of American life.

The Roots of Progressive Reform

Families turned from their homes; an army of unemployed on the roads; hunger, strikes, and bloody violence across the country—the wrenching depression of 1893 forced Americans to take a hard look at their new industrial order. They found common complaints that cut across lines of class, religion, and ethnicity. If streetcar companies raised fares while service deteriorated, if food processors doctored their canned goods with harmful additives, if politicians skimmed money from the public till, everyone suffered. And no one could stop it alone.

Aims of progressives

The result was not a coherent progressive movement but a set of loosely connected goals. Some progressives fought to make government itself efficient and honest. Others called for greater regulation of business and a more orderly economy. Some sought social justice for the poor and working classes; others, social welfare to protect children, women, and consumers. Still other progressives looked to purify society by outlawing alcohol and drugs, stamping out prostitution and slums, and restricting the flood of new immigrants. And all tried to make business and government more responsive to the democratic will of the people.

Paternalistic by nature, progressives often imposed their solutions, no matter what the less "enlightened" poor or oppressed saw as their own best interests. Then, too, reformers acted partly out of nostalgia. In a rapidly changing world, they wanted to redeem such traditional American values as democracy, opportunity for the individual, and the spirit of public service. Yet if the ends of progressives were traditional, their means were distinctly modern. They used the systems and methods of the new industrial order—the latest techniques of organization, management, and science—to fight its excesses.

The Progressive System of Beliefs

Progressives were moderate modernizers—reformers, not revolutionaries. They accepted the American system as sound, only in need of adjustment. Many drew on the increasingly popular Darwinian theories of evolution to buttress this gradual approach to change. With its notion of slowly changing species, evolution undermined the acceptance of fixed principles that had guided social thought in the Victorian era. Progressives saw an evolving landscape and ever-shifting values. They denied the old Calvinist doctrine of inborn sinfulness and instead saw people as having a greater potential for good than for evil.

Yet progressives had seen the mean side of industrialism and somehow had to explain the existence of evil and wrongdoing. Most agreed that they were "largely, if not wholly, products of society or environment." People went wrong, wrote one progressive, because of "what happens to them." By changing what happened, the human potential for good could be released. As reformer Jane Addams explained, "what has been called 'the extraordinary pliability of human nature'" made it "impossible to set any bounds to the moral capabilities which might unfold under ideal civic and educational conditions."

With an eye to results, progressives asked not "Is it true?" but "Does it work?" Philosopher Charles Peirce called this new way of thinking "pragmatism." William James, the Harvard psychologist, became its most famous popularizer. For James, pragmatism meant "looking towards last things, fruits, consequences, facts."

Pragmatism

The Pragmatic Approach

Pragmatism led educators, social scientists, and lawyers to adopt new approaches to reform. John Dewey, the master educator of the progressive era, believed that environment shaped the patterns of human thought. Instead of demanding mindless memorization of abstract and unconnected facts, Dewey tried to "make each one of our schools an embryonic community life." At his School of Pedagogy, founded in 1896 with his wife, Alice, he let students unbolt their desks from the floor, move about, and learn by doing so they could train for real life.

Psychologist John B. Watson believed that human behavior could be shaped at will. "Give me a dozen healthy infants," he wrote, ". . . and my own specified world to bring them up in, and I'll guarantee to take any one at random and train him to become any specialist I might select, doctor, lawyer, artist, merchant, chief, and yes, even beggarman and thief." "Behaviorism" swept the social sciences and later advertising, where Watson himself eventually landed.

Behaviorism

John Dewey, progressive philosopher and educator

Lawyers and legal theorists applied their own blend of pragmatism and behaviorism. Justice Oliver Wendell Holmes Jr., appointed to the Supreme Court in 1902, rejected the idea that the traditions of law were constant and universal. "Long ago I decided I was not God," said Holmes. Law was a living organism to be interpreted according to experience and the needs of a changing society.

This environmental view of the law, known as "sociological jurisprudence," found a skilled practitioner in Louis Brandeis. Shaken by the brutal suppression of the Homestead steel strike of 1892, Brandeis quit his corporate practice and proclaimed himself the "people's lawyer." The law must "guide by the light of reason," he wrote, by which he meant bringing everyday life to bear in any court case. Whereas older court

Sociological jurisprudence

opinions had been based largely on legal precedent, progressives asked courts to look at the world around them and realize that society had undergone changes so fundamental that many precedents of the past no longer applied. Past and present must stand on equal footing in interpreting the law, they said.

Brandeis Brief

Brandeis had a chance to test his practical principles when laundry owner Curt Muller challenged an Oregon law that limited his laundresses to working 10 hours a day. Brandeis defended the statute before the Supreme Court in 1908. His famous legal brief in *Muller v. Oregon* contained 102 pages describing the damaging effects of long hours on working women and only 15 pages of legal precedents. The Supreme Court upheld Oregon's right to limit the working hours of laborers and thus legitimized the "Brandeis Brief."

The Progressive Method

Seeing the nation riven by conflict, progressives tried to restore a sense of community through the ideal of a single public interest. Christian ethics were the guide, to be applied after using the latest scientific methods to gather and analyze data about a social problem. The modern corporation furnished an appealing model for organization. Like corporate executives, progressives relied on careful management, coordinated systems, and specialized bureaucracies to carry out reforms.

Between 1902 and 1912 a new breed of journalists investigated wrongdoers, named them in print, and described their misdeeds in vivid detail. Most exposés began as articles in mass-circulation magazines. *McClure's* magazine stirred controversy and boosted circulation when it sent reporter Lincoln Steffens to uncover the crooked ties between business and politics. Steffens's "Tweed Days in St. Louis" appeared in the October 1902 issue of *McClure's* and was followed in the November issue by Ida M. Tarbell's *History of the Standard Oil Company,* another stinging, well-researched indictment. Soon a full-blown literature of exposure was covering every ill from unsafe food to child labor.

Muckrakers

A disgusted Theodore Roosevelt thought the new reporters had gone too far and called them "muckrakers," after the man who raked up filth in the seventeenth-century classic *Pilgrim's Progress.* But by documenting dishonesty and blight, muckrakers not only aroused people but also educated them. No broad reform movement of American institutions would have taken place without them.

Voluntary organizations

To move beyond exposure to solutions, progressives stressed volunteerism, civic responsibility, and collective action. They drew on the organizational impulse that seemed everywhere to be bringing people together in new interest groups. Between 1890 and 1920 nearly 400 organizations were founded, many to combat the ills of industrial society. Some, like the National Consumers' League, grew out of efforts to promote general causes—in this case protecting consumers and workers from exploitation. Others, such as the National Tuberculosis Association, aimed at a specific problem.

When voluntary action failed, progressives looked to government to protect the public welfare. They mistrusted legislators, who might be controlled by corporate interests or political machines. So they strengthened the executive branch by increasing the power of individual mayors, governors, and presidents. Then they watched those executives carefully.

Professionals

Progressives also drew on the expertise of the newly professionalized middle class. Confident, cosmopolitan professionals—doctors, engineers, psychiatrists, city planners—mounted campaigns to stamp out venereal disease and dysentery, to reform prisons and asylums, and to beautify cities. At all levels—local, state, federal—new agencies and commissions staffed by impartial experts began to investigate and regulate lobbyists, insurance and railroad companies, public health, even government itself.

If progressivism ended in politics, it **The Search for the Good Society**
began with social reform: the need to
reach out, to do something to bring the "good society" a step closer. Ellen Richards had just such ends in mind in 1890 when she opened the New England Kitchen in downtown Boston. Richards, a chemist and home economist, designed the Kitchen to sell cheap, wholesome food to the working poor. For a few pennies, customers could choose from a nutritious menu, every dish of which had been tested in Richards's laboratory at the Massachusetts Institute of Technology.

The New England Kitchen promoted social as well as nutritional reform. Women freed from the drudgery of cooking could seek gainful employment. And as a "household experiment station" and center for dietary information, the Kitchen tried to educate the poor and Americanize immigrants by showing them how the middle class prepared meals. According to philanthropist Pauline Shaw, it was also a "rival to the saloon." A common belief was that poor diets fostered drinking, especially among the lower classes.

In the end, the New England Kitchen served more as an inexpensive eatery for middle-class working women and students than as a resource for the poor or an agency of Americanization. Still, Ellen Richards's experiment reflected a pattern typical of progressive social reform: the mix of professionalism with uplift of the poor and needy, socially conscious women entering the public arena, the hope of creating a better world along middle-class lines.

Pattern of reform

Poverty in a New Light

During the 1890s crime reporter and photographer Jacob Riis launched a campaign to introduce middle-class audiences to urban poverty. Writing in vivid detail in *How the Other Half Lives* (1890), Riis brought readers into the teeming tenement. Accompanying the text were shocking photos of poverty-stricken Americans—Riis's "other half." He also used slide shows to publicize their plight. His pictures of slum life appeared artless, merely recording the desperate poverty before the camera. But Riis used them to tell a moralistic story, much the way the earlier English novelist Charles Dickens had used his melodramatic tales to attack the abuses of industrialism in England. People began to see poverty in a new, more sympathetic light, the result less of flawed individuals than of environment.

A haunting naturalism in fiction and painting followed the tradition introduced by Riis's gritty photographic essays. In *McTeague* (1899) and *Sister Carrie* (1900), novelists Frank Norris and Theodore Dreiser spun dark tales of city dwellers struggling to keep body and soul intact. The "Ashcan school" painted urban life in all its grimy realism. Photographer Alfred Stieglitz and painters such as John Sloan and George Bellows chose slums, tenements, and dirty streets as subjects. Poverty began to look less ominous and more heartrending.

Naturalism

A new profession—social work—proceeded from this new view of poverty. Social work developed out of the old settlement house movement (page 654). Like the physicians from whom they drew inspiration, social workers studied hard data to diagnose the problems of their "clients." Unlike nineteenth-century philanthropists,

Social work

the new social workers refused to do things to or for people. Instead they worked with their clients, enlisting their help to solve their own problems. A social worker's "differential casework" attempted to treat individuals case by case, each according to the way the client had been shaped by environment.

In reality poverty was but a single symptom of many personal and social ills. Most progressives continued to see it as a by-product of political and corporate greed, slum neighborhoods, and "institutions of vice" such as the saloon. Less clear to them was how deeply rooted poverty had become. Simple middle-class good-will or even the era's most up-to-date scientific treatments were not enough to banish the alcoholism, drug addiction, and mental illness associated with poverty.

Expanding the "Woman's Sphere"

Progressive social reform attracted a great many women seeking what Jane Addams called "the larger life" of public affairs. In the late nineteenth century, women found that protecting their traditional sphere of home and family forced them to move beyond it. Bringing up children, making meals, keeping house, and caring for the sick now involved community decisions about schools, public health, and countless other matters.

Women's organizations

In the nineteenth century, many middle- and upper-middle-class women received their first taste of public life from women's organizations, including mothers' clubs, temperance societies, and church groups. By the turn of the century, some 500 women's clubs boasted over 160,000 members. Through the General Federation of Women's Clubs, they funded libraries and hospitals and supported schools, settlement houses, compulsory education, and child labor laws. Eventually they moved beyond the concerns of home and family to endorse such controversial causes as woman suffrage and unionization. To that list the National Association of Colored Women added the special concerns of African Americans, none more urgent than the fight against lynching.

By 1900 one-fourth of the non-farm labor force was female. On average, women industrial workers made $3 less a week than did unskilled men. Here, at a Labor Day parade in San Diego in 1910, women demand equal pay for equal work.

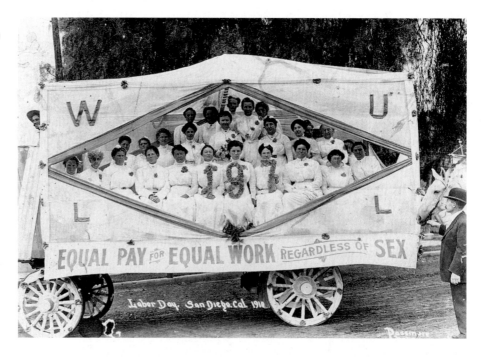

The dawn of the century saw the rise of a new generation of women. Longer lived, better educated, and less often married than their mothers, they were also willing to pursue careers for fulfillment. Usually they turned to professions that involved the traditional role of nurturer—nursing, library work, teaching, and settlement house work.

Custom and prejudice still restricted these new women. The faculty at the Massachusetts Institute of Technology, for example, refused to allow Ellen Richards to pursue a doctorate. Instead they hired her to run the gender-segregated "Woman's Laboratory" for training public school teachers. At the turn of the century, only about 1500 women lawyers practiced in the whole country, and in 1910 women made up barely 6 percent of licensed physicians. That figure rapidly declined as male-dominated medical associations grew in power and discouraged the entry of women.

Margaret Sanger sought to free women from the bonds of chronic pregnancy. Sanger, a visiting nurse on the Lower East Side of New York, had seen too many poor women overburdened with children, pregnant year after year, with no hope of escaping the cycle. The consequences were sometimes deadly but always crippling. "Women cannot be on equal footing with men until they have complete control over their reproductive functions," she argued.

The insight came as a revelation one summer evening in 1912 when Sanger was called to the home of a distraught immigrant family on Grand Street. Sadie Sachs, mother of three, had nearly died a year earlier from a self-induced abortion. In an effort to terminate another pregnancy, she had accidentally killed herself. Sanger vowed that night "to do something to change the destiny of mothers whose miseries were as vast as the sky." She became a crusader for what she called "birth control." By distributing information on contraception, she hoped to free women from unwanted pregnancies and the fate of Sadie Sachs.

Single or married, militant or moderate, professional or lay, white or black, more and more middle-class urban women thus became "social housekeepers." From their own homes they turned to the homes of their neighbors and from there to all of society.

Margin notes: New woman; Margaret Sanger

Social Welfare

In the "bigger family of the city," as one woman reformer called it, settlement house workers found that they could not care for the welfare of the poor alone. If industrial America, with its sooty factories and overcrowded slums, were to be transformed into the good society, individual acts of charity would have to be supplemented by government. Laws had to be passed and agencies created to promote social welfare, including improved housing, workplaces, parks, and playgrounds; the abolition of child labor; and the enactment of eight-hour-day laws for working women.

By 1910 the more than 400 settlement houses across the nation had organized into a loose affiliation, with settlement workers ready to help shape government policy. Often it was women who led the way. Julia Lathrop, a Vassar College graduate, spent 20 years at Jane Addams's Hull House before becoming the first head of the new federal Children's Bureau in 1912. By then two-thirds of the states had adopted some child labor legislation, although loopholes exempted countless youngsters from coverage. Under Lathrop's leadership, Congress was persuaded to pass the Keating-Owen Act (1916), forbidding goods manufactured by children to cross state lines.*

Margin note: Keating-Owen Act

---

*The Supreme Court struck down the law in 1918 as an improper regulation of local labor; nonetheless, the law focused greater attention on the abuses of child labor.

Florence Kelley, who had also worked at Hull House, spearheaded a similar campaign in Illinois to protect women workers by limiting their workday to eight hours. As general secretary of the National Consumers' League, she also organized boycotts of companies that treated employees inhumanely. Eventually most states enacted laws restricting the number of hours women could work.

Woman Suffrage

The movement for woman's suffrage

No one had ever seen pickets in front of the White House before, let alone picketing women. But there they were, starting on January 10, 1917. From ten in the morning until half past five in the evening, they stood stiff and silent at the front gates, six days a week, rain or shine. The "Silent Sentinels," as they called themselves, let their banners speak for them. One quoted the words of Inez Milholland. Only a year earlier, she had collapsed at a suffrage rally in Los Angeles as she rose to speak in favor of granting women the right to vote. "Mr. President," she had said with her dying breath, "how long must women wait for liberty?"

Ever since the conference for women's rights held at Seneca Falls in 1848, women reformers had pressed for the right to vote on the grounds of equal opportunity and simple justice. Progressives embraced woman suffrage by stressing what they saw as the practical results: reducing political corruption, protecting the home, and increasing the voting power of native-born whites. The "purer sensibilities" of women—an ideal held by Victorians and progressives alike—would help cleanse the political process of selfishness and corruption, while their sheer numbers would keep the political balance tilted away from immigrant newcomers.

The suffrage movement benefited, too, from new leadership. In 1900 Carrie Chapman Catt became president of the National American Woman Suffrage Association, founded by Susan B. Anthony in 1890. Politically astute and a skilled organizer, Catt mapped a grassroots strategy of education and persuasion from state to state. She called it "the winning plan." As the map on page 721 shows, victories came first in the West, where women and men had already forged a more equal partnership to overcome the hardships of frontier life. By 1914, 10 western states (and Kansas) had granted women the vote in state elections, as Illinois had in presidential elections.

"BEAN HIM!"*

*Note for ignorami—Hit him in the head

In this cartoon from a 1914 issue of *Life* magazine, a burly feminist catcher tells a suffragist pitcher to "bean" the male batter at the plate.

Militant suffragists

The slow pace of progress drove some suffragists to militancy. The shift in tactics had its origins abroad. In England, the campaign for woman suffrage had peaked after 1900, when Emmeline Pankhurst and her daughters Christabel and Sylvia turned militant to make their point. They and their followers chained themselves to the visitors' gallery in the House of Commons and slashed paintings in museums. When those tactics failed, they invaded the time-honored bastion of British manhood—the golf course—and scrawled "VOTES FOR WOMEN" in acid on the greens. They smashed the windows of department stores, broke up political meetings, even burned the houses of members of Parliament.

British authorities responded to the violence by arresting suffragists and throwing them in jail, Emmeline Pankhurst included. When the women went on hunger strikes in prison, wardens tied them down, held open their mouths with wooden clamps, and fed them by force. Rather than permit the protesters to die as mar-

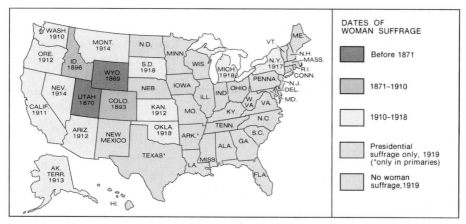

Woman Suffrage Western states were the first to grant women the right to vote. Sparsely populated and more egalitarian than the rest of the nation, the West was used to women participating fully in settlement and work. Other sections of the country, notably the Midwest, granted women partial suffrage that included voting for school boards and taxes. Suffragists encountered the most intractable resistance in the South, where rigid codes of social conduct elevated women symbolically but shackled them practically.

tyrs, Parliament passed the Cat and Mouse Act, a statute of doubtful constitutionality that allowed officials to release starving prisoners and then rearrest them once they returned to health.

Among the British suffragists was a small American with large, determined eyes. In 1907, barely out of her teens, Alice Paul had gone to England to join the suffrage crusade. When asked why she had enlisted, she recalled her Quaker upbringing. "One of their principles . . . is equality of the sexes," she explained. Paul marched arm-in-arm with British suffragists through the streets of London and more than once was imprisoned and refused to eat. In 1910, she returned to the United States and brought the aggressive tactics with her. Three years later, in 1913, Paul organized 5000 women to parade in protest at President Woodrow Wilson's inauguration. Wilson himself was skeptical of women voting and favored a state-by-state approach to the issue. Half a million people watched as a near riot ensued. Paul and other suffragists were hauled to jail, stripped naked, and thrown into cells with prostitutes.

In 1914, Paul broke with the more moderate National American Woman Suffrage Association and formed the Congressional Union, dedicated to enacting national woman suffrage at any cost through a constitutional amendment. She allied her organization with western women voters in the militant National Woman's party in 1917. It was also Paul who organized the Silent Sentinels at the White House the same year, when the president refused to see any more delegations of women urging a constitutional amendment. She was arrested at the gates of the White House and received a seven-month sentence. Guards dragged her off to a cell block in the Washington jail, where she and others refused to eat. Prison officials declared her insane, but a public outcry over her treatment soon led to her release.

Such repression only widened public support for woman suffrage in the United States and elsewhere. So did the contributions of women to the First World War at home and abroad (see Chapter 23). In the wake of the war, Great Britain granted women (over age thirty) the right to vote in 1918, Germany and Austria in 1919, and the United States in 1920 through the Nineteenth Amendment. Overnight the number of eligible voters in the country doubled.

Nineteenth Amendment

Daily Lives

PUBLIC SPACE/ PRIVATE SPACE

"Amusing the Million"

On a sunny May morning in 1903, 45,000 people poured through the gates of Luna Park at Coney Island, just south of Brooklyn. What they saw on opening day amazed them: "a storybook land of trellises, columns, domes, minarets, lagoons, and lofty aerial flights." Barkers beckoned them into a Venetian city, a Japanese garden, and a bustling Asian Indian celebration. They could hop aboard the "Switchback" Railroad, a forerunner of the roller coaster, or careen on flat-bottomed boats down a steep incline into the "Shoot-the-Chutes" lagoon. They could even witness a disaster. In "Fire and Flames," mock firefighters doused a four-story blaze as mock residents jumped from top floors to safety nets below—all on cue. Those who spent their days in crowded tenements rolling cigars or sleeping nights in stuffy apartments might well blink in awe as a quarter of a million electric lights, strung like glittering pearls across the buildings, turned night into enchanted day.

Coney Island was but one of a host of similar parks that popped up across the country at the turn of the century. Soaring urban populations, increases in leisure time, more spending money, and new trolley systems that made for cheap excursions from the city led to the opening of Boston's Paragon Park, Cleveland's Euclid Beach, Atlanta's Ponce de Leon Park, and Los Angeles's Venice Beach.

All traded in entertainment, but of a sort new to city dwellers. Earlier Victorian reformers had promoted two models of public entertainment: the spacious city park and the grand public exposition. Both were meant to instruct as well as amuse. Their planners hoped to

Gondolas in Venice Canal, Venice, California

The Venice Amusement Park in California was meant to conjure up Venice, Italy, complete with a network of canals. (Note the gondola in the foreground.) The founders dubbed Venice Park "the Coney Island of the Pacific."

Controlling the Masses

"Observe immigrants," wrote one American in 1912. "You are struck by the fact that from ten to twenty percent are hirsute, low-browed, big-faced persons of obviously low mentality. . . . They clearly belong in skins, in wattled huts at the close of the Ice Age." The writer was neither an uneducated fanatic nor a stern opponent of change. He was Professor Edward A. Ross, a progressive from Madison, Wisconsin, who prided himself on his scientific study of sociology.

Faced with the chaos and corruption of urban life, more than a few progressives feared they were losing control of their country. Saloons and dance halls lured youngsters and impoverished laborers; prostitutes walked the streets; vulgar amusements pandered to the uneducated. Strange Old World cultures clashed with "all-American" customs, and races jostled uneasily. The city challenged middle-class reformers to convert this riot of diversity into a more uniform society. To maintain reduce urban disorder by raising public taste and refining public conduct. When it opened in 1858, New York City's Central Park became a model pastoral retreat in the midst of the city. Its rustic paths, tranquil lakes, and woodsy views were designed as respites from the chaos of urban life. According to designer Frederick Law Olmsted, such vistas would have "a distinctly harmonizing and refining influence" on even the rudest fellow.

The World's Columbian Exposition of 1893 in Chicago also reflected an elevating vision of society. Its neoclassical buildings were designed to instruct citizens about their country's marvelous wealth and industry (see pages 670–671). At the center of the exposition stood an impressive 100-foot statue, "The Republic," a toga-draped figure holding an eagle perched on a globe. Some amusement parks, like Venice Beach's, mimicked the style of the exposition.

But it did not escape the amusement park operators that people wanted to have fun. At the Columbian Exposition, the amusements section, a mile-long strip of theaters, restaurants, sideshows, and rides, had lured more people than did the free public exhibits. As one owner put it, parks were in the business of "amusing the million." Coney Island's Luna Park drew 5 million paying customers in a single season.

Jostling with crowds, eating ice cream and hot dogs, riding Shoot-the-Chutes, young workingmen and working women, single, in couples, or married, and even the newest immigrant could feel gloriously free and independent, gloriously American. A sense of solidarity drew the mostly working-class crowds together, and the zaniness of the setting loosened social restraints. "I have heard some of the high people with whom I have been living say that Coney Island is not tony," reported one 20-year-old servant girl. "The trouble is that these high people don't know how to dance." In this girl's mind, the Victorian values of sober industry, thrift, and orderly conduct could hardly compete with the democratic abandon and gaiety of the new amusement parks. The parks heralded the rise of mass culture, invading public space with the private dreams of ordinary people.

control progressives sometimes moved beyond education and regulation and sought restrictive laws to control the masses.

Stemming the Immigrant Tide

A rising tide of immigrants from southern and eastern Europe especially troubled native-born Americans, including reformers anxious over the changing ethnic complexion of the country. In northern cities progressives often succeeded in reducing immigrant voting power by increasing residency requirements.

A new science called "eugenics" lent respectability to the idea that newcomers were biologically inferior. Eugenicists believed that heredity largely shaped all human behavior, and they therefore advocated selective breeding for human improvement. By 1914 more magazine articles discussed eugenics than slums, tenements,

Eugenics

and living standards combined. In *The Passing of the Great Race* (1916), upper-crust New Yorker and amateur zoologist Madison Grant helped popularize the notion that the "lesser breeds" threatened to "mongrelize" America. So powerful was the pull of eugenics that it captured the support of some progressives, including birth control advocate Margaret Sanger.

Americanization

Most progressives, however, believed in the shaping impact of environment and so favored either assimilating immigrants into American society or restricting their entry into the country. Jane Addams, for one, stressed the cultural "gifts" immigrants brought with them: folk rituals, dances, music, and handicrafts. With characteristic paternalism, she and other reformers hoped to "Americanize" the foreign-born (the term was newly coined) by teaching them middle-class ways. Education was one key. Progressive educator Peter Roberts, for example, developed a lesson plan for the Young Men's Christian Association that taught immigrants to dress, tip, buy groceries, and vote.

Literacy test

Less-tolerant citizens sought to restrict immigration as a way of reasserting control and achieving social harmony. Though white, Protestant, and American-born, these nativists were only occasionally progressives themselves, but they did employ progressive methods of organization, investigation, education, and legislation. The first solid victory for restrictionists came in 1882, when they succeeded in barring the entry of Chinese laborers into the country. After the turn of the century, restrictionists gained strength as the tidal wave of eastern and southern European immigrants crested. Active since the 1890s, the Immigration Restriction League pressed Congress in 1907 to require a literacy test for admission into the United States. Presidents Taft and Wilson vetoed it in 1913 and 1915, but Congress overrode Wilson's second veto in 1917, when war fever raised defensive nationalism to a new peak.

The Curse of Demon Rum

Tied closely to concern over immigrants was an attack on saloons. Part of a broader crusade to clean up cities, the antisaloon campaign drew strength from the century-old drive to lessen the consumption of alcohol. Women made up a disproportionate number of alcohol reformers. The temperance movement reflected their growing campaign to storm male domains—in this case the saloon—and to contain male violence, particularly the wife and child abuse associated with drinking.

By 1900 the dangers of an alcoholic republic seemed all too real. Alcohol consumption had risen to an annual rate of more than two gallons per person. Over half of Boston and Chicago visited a bar at least once a day. Often political bosses owned saloons or conducted their business there. To alcohol reformers, taverns and saloons thus seemed at the center of many social problems—gambling and prostitution, political corruption, drug trafficking, unemployment, and poverty. Few reformers recognized the complex cycle of social decay that produced such problems, fewer still the role of saloons as "workingmen's clubs." The saloon was often the only place to cash a check, find out about jobs, eat a cheap meal, or take a bath.

Anti-Saloon League

Reformers considered a national ban on drinking unrealistic and intrusive. Instead they concentrated on prohibiting the sale of alcohol at local and state levels and attacked businesses that profited from it. Led by the Anti-Saloon League (1893), a massive publicity campaign bombarded citizens with pamphlets and advertisements. Doctors cited scientific evidence linking alcohol to cirrhosis, heart disease, and insanity. Social workers connected drink to the deterioration of the family; employers, to accidents on the job and lost efficiency.

By 1917 three out of four Americans lived in "dry" counties. Nearly two-thirds of the states had adopted laws outlawing the manufacture and sale of alcohol. Not all progressives were prohibitionists, but the many who were sighed with relief at having taken the profit out of human pain and corruption.

Prostitution

No urban vice worried reformers more than prostitution. In their eyes it was a social evil that threatened young city women with a fate much worse than death. The Chicago Vice Commission of 1910 estimated that 5000 full-time and 10,000 occasional prostitutes plied their trade in the city. Other cities, small and large, reported similar numbers.

An unlikely group of reformers united to fight the vice: feminists who wanted husbands to be as chaste as their wives, public health officials worried about the spread of sexually transmitted disease, and immigration restrictionists who regarded the growth of prostitution as yet another sign of corrupt newcomers. Progressives condemned prostitution but saw the problem in economic and environmental terms. "Poverty causes prostitution," concluded the Illinois Vice Commission in 1916. On average, prostitutes earned five times the income of factory workers.

Some reformers saw more active agents at work. Rumors spread of a vast and profitable "white slave trade." Men armed with hypodermic needles were said to be lurking about streetcars, amusement parks, and dance halls in search of young women. Although the average female rider of the streetcar was hardly in danger of abduction, in every city there could be found cribs with locked doors where women were held captive and forced into prostitution. By conservative estimates they made up some 10 percent of all prostitutes.

As real abuses blended with sensationalism, Congress passed the Mann Act (1910), prohibiting the interstate transport of women for immoral purposes. By 1918 reformers succeeded in banning previously tolerated red-light districts in most cities. Once again, progressives went after those businesses that, like the liquor trade, made money from misery.

The "Inebriate's Express," loaded with drunken riders, is heading straight for hell. This detail from a chromolithograph, published around 1900, was typical of Victorian-era responses to the problems posed by alcohol. To the all-seeing eye of the omnipotent God, faith, hope, charity, and the Bible are sufficient to cure the problems of drinking.

"For Whites Only"

Most progressives paid little attention to the misery suffered by African Americans. The 1890s had been a low point for black citizens, most of whom still lived in the South. Across the region, the lynching of African Americans increased dramatically, as did restrictions on black voting and the use of segregated facilities to separate whites from blacks. Signs decreeing "For Whites Only" appeared on drinking fountains and restrooms and in other public places.

A few progressives, such as muckraker Ray Stannard Baker and settlement-house worker Lillian Wald, decried racial discrimination, but most ignored it—or used it to their political advantage. Throughout the South, white progressives and even old-guard politicians, including Senator Ben Tillman of South Carolina and Governor James K. Vardaman of Mississippi, used the rhetoric of reform to support white supremacy. Such "reformers" won office by promising to disfranchise African Americans in order to break the power of corrupt political machines that rested on the black vote, much as northern machines marshaled the immigrant vote.

In the face of such discrimination, African Americans fought back. After the turn of the century, black critics in the North rejected the accommodation of Booker T. Washington's "Atlanta Compromise," a cautious approach to race relations that counseled African Americans to accept segregation and work their way up the economic ladder by learning a vocational trade (pages 683–684). W. E. B. Du Bois, a professor at Atlanta University, leveled the most stinging attack in *The Souls of Black Folk* (1903). Du Bois saw no benefit for African Americans in sacrificing intellectual growth for narrow vocational training. Nor was he willing to abide the humiliating stigma that came from the South's discriminatory caste system. A better future would come only if black citizens struggled politically to achieve suffrage and equal rights.

W. E. B. Du Bois

Instead of exhorting African Americans to pull themselves up slowly from the bottom, Du Bois called on the "talented tenth," a cultured black vanguard, to blaze a trail of protest against segregation, disfranchisement, and discrimination. In 1905 he founded the Niagara Movement for political and economic equality, and in 1909 a coalition of blacks and white reformers transformed the Niagara Movement into the National Association for the Advancement of Colored People. As with other progressive organizations, its membership was largely limited to the middle class. It worked to extend the principles of tolerance and equal opportunity in a color-blind fashion by mounting legal challenges to the Jim Crow system of segregation and bigotry. By 1914, the NAACP had some 6,000 members in 50 branches throughout the country. Accommodation was giving way to new combative organizations and new forms of protest.

NAACP

The Politics of Municipal and State Reform

Reform the system. In the end, so many urban problems seemed to come back to the premise that government had to be overhauled. Jane Addams learned as much outside the doors of her beloved Hull House in Chicago. For months during the early 1890s, garbage had piled up in the streets. The filth and stench drove Addams and her fellow workers to city hall in protest—700 times in one summer—but to no avail. In Chicago, as elsewhere, corrupt city bosses had made garbage collection a plum to be awarded to the company that paid them the most for it.

In desperation, Addams herself submitted a bid for garbage removal in the ward. When it was thrown out on a technicality, she won an appointment as garbage inspector. For almost a year she dogged collection carts, but boss politics kept things dirty. So Addams ran candidates in 1896 and 1898 against local ward boss Johnny Powers. They lost, but Addams kept up the fight for honest government and social reform—at city hall, in the Illinois legislature, and finally in Washington. Politics turned out to be the only way to clean things up.

The Reformation of the Cities

For middle-class reformers, the urban battleground furnished the first test of political reform. And a series of colorful and independent mayors demonstrated that cities could be run humanely without changing the structure of government.

In Detroit, shoe magnate Hazen Pingree turned the mayor's office into an instrument of reform when elected in 1889. By the end of his fourth term, Detroit had new parks and public baths, fairer taxes, ownership of the local light plant, and a work-relief program for victims of the depression of 1893. In 1901, Cleveland mayor Tom Johnson launched a similar reform campaign. Before he was through, municipal franchises had been limited to a fraction of their previous 99-year terms and the city ran the utility company. By 1915 nearly two out of three cities in the nation had copied some form of this "gas and water socialism" to control the runaway prices of utility companies.

Tragedy dramatized the need to alter the very structure of government. On a hot summer night in 1900 a tidal wave from the Gulf of Mexico smashed the port city of Galveston, Texas. Floods killed one of every six residents. The municipal government sank into confusion and political wrangling. In reaction business leaders won approval of a new charter that replaced the mayor and city council with a powerful commission. Each of five commissioners controlled a municipal department, and together they ran the city. By 1920 nearly 400 cities had adopted the plan. Expert commissioners enhanced efficiency and helped to check party rule in municipal government.

In other cities, elected officials appointed an outside expert, or "city manager," to run things. The first was hired in Staunton, Virginia, in 1908. Within a decade, 45 cities had them. At lower levels experts took charge of services: engineers oversaw utilities; accountants, finances; doctors and nurses, public health; specially trained firefighters and police, the safety of citizens. Broad civic reforms attempted to break the corrupt alliance between companies doing business with the city and the bosses who controlled the wards. Citywide elections replaced the old ward system, and civil service laws helped create a nonpartisan bureaucracy. Political machines and ethnic voters lost power, while city government gained efficiency.

Jane Addams founded her settlement at Hull House in Chicago because she was convinced, like many progressives, that reform must be practical, arising out of the needs of individuals within a community. As Addams continued her campaigns, she also looked beyond the local neighborhood to reform political structures of municipal and state governments.

City-manager plan

Progressivism in the States

"Whenever we try to do anything, we run up against the charter," complained the reform mayor of Schenectady, New York. Charters granted by state governments defined the powers of cities. The rural interests that generally dominated state legislatures rarely gave cities adequate authority to levy taxes, set voting requirements, draw up budgets, or legislate reforms. State legislatures, too, found themselves under the influence of business interests, party machines, and county courthouse rings. Reformers therefore tried to place their candidates where they could do some good—in the governors' mansions.

Weaknesses of city government

La Follette

believes in the American people. He believes that YOU should know the TRUTH about the inside workings of YOUR government and the records of your representatives at Washington.

So with the help and approval of a score of other fighters for the common good, Senator La Follette established

La Follette's Magazine

devoted to fearless discussion of the most important public questions, and has departments for the home, special articles, stories, a Farm Department, fiction, humor, important news of the world.

Published monthly. Regular price $1.00 per year. To permit you to get acquainted with the magazine we will send it to you on trial

3 Months for 25c.

Simply send a quarter with your name and address to

LA FOLLETTE'S, Box 45, Madison, Wis.

On the state level, progressives made their greatest impact in Wisconsin, where Robert La Follette led the fight to regulate railroads, control corruption, and expand the civil service. In trying to do an end run around political party bosses, he used his publication, *La Follette's Magazine,* to reach ordinary Americans directly.

State progressivism enjoyed its greatest success in the Midwest, under the leadership of Robert La Follette of Wisconsin. La Follette first won election to Congress in 1885 by toeing the Republican line of high tariffs and the gold standard. When a Republican boss offered him a bribe in a railroad case, La Follette pledged to break "the power of this corrupt influence." In 1900 he won the governorship of Wisconsin as an uncommonly independent Republican.

Over the next six years "Battle Bob" La Follette made Wisconsin, in the words of Theodore Roosevelt, "the laboratory of democracy." La Follette's "Wisconsin idea" produced the most comprehensive set of state reforms in American history. There were new laws regulating railroads, controlling corruption, and expanding the civil service. His direct primary weakened the hold of party bosses by transferring nominations from the backrooms of party conventions and caucuses to the voters at large. Among La Follette's notable "firsts" were a state income tax, a state commission to oversee factory safety and sanitation, and a Legislative Reference Bureau at the University of Wisconsin. University-trained experts poured into state government.

Other states copied the Wisconsin idea or hatched their own. By 1916 all but three had direct primary laws. To cut the power of party organizations and make officeholders directly responsible to the public, progressives worked for three additional reforms: initiative (voter introduction of legislation), referendum (voter enactment or repeal of laws), and recall (voter-initiated removal of elected officials). By 1912 a dozen states had adopted initiative and referendum, and seven, recall. A year later the Seventeenth Amendment to the Constitution permitted the direct election of senators, previously selected by state legislatures.

Almost every state established regulatory commissions with the power to hold public hearings and to examine company books and question officials. Some could set maximum prices and rates. Yet it was not always easy to define, let alone serve, the "public good." All too often commissioners found themselves refereeing battles within industries—between carriers and shippers, for example—rather than between what progressives called "the interests" and "the people." Regulators had to rely on the advice of experts drawn from the business community itself. Many commissions thus became captured by the industries they regulated.

Social welfare received special attention from the states. The lack of workers' compensation for injury, illness, or death on the job had long drawn fire from reformers and labor leaders. American courts still operated on the common-law assumption that employees accepted the risks of work. Workers or their families could collect damages only if they proved employer negligence. Most accident victims received nothing. In 1902 Maryland finally adopted the first workers' compensation act. By 1916, most states required insurance for factory accidents and over half had employer liability laws. Thirteen states also provided pensions for widows with dependent children.

More and more it was machine politicians and women's organizations that pressed for working-class reforms. Despite the progressive attack on machine politics, political bosses survived, in part by adapting the climate of reform to the needs of their working-class constituents. After the Triangle fire of 1911, for example, it was Tammany Democrats Robert F. Wagner and Alfred E. Smith who led the fight for a new labor code.

This working-class "urban liberalism" also found advocates among women's associations, especially those concerned with mothers, children, and working women. The

Federation of Women's Clubs led the fight for mothers' pensions (a forerunner of aid to dependent children). When in 1912 the National Consumers' League and other women's groups succeeded in establishing the Children's Bureau, it was the first federal welfare agency and the only female-run national bureau in the world. At a time when women lacked the vote, they nonetheless sowed the seeds of the welfare state as they helped to make urban liberalism a powerful instrument of social reform.

Seeds of the welfare state

Progressivism Goes to Washington

On September 6, 1901, at the Pan-American Exposition in Buffalo, New York, Leon Czolgosz stood nervously in line. He was waiting among well-wishers to meet President William McKinley. Unemployed and bent on murder, Czolgosz shuffled toward McKinley. As the president reached out, Czolgosz fired two bullets into his chest. McKinley slumped into a chair. Eight days later the president was dead. The mantle of power passed to Theodore Roosevelt. At 42 he was the youngest president ever to hold office.

Roosevelt's entry into the White House was a political accident, as he himself acknowledged. Party leaders had seen the weak office of vice president as a way of removing him from power, but the tragedy in Buffalo foiled their plans. "It is a dreadful thing to come into the presidency this way," he remarked, "but it would be a far worse thing to be morbid about it." Surely progressivism would have come to Washington without Theodore Roosevelt, and while there he was never its most daring advocate. In many ways he was quite conservative. He saw reform as a way to avoid more radical change. Yet without Roosevelt, progressivism would have had neither the broad popular appeal nor the buoyancy he gave it.

TR

TR, as so many Americans called him, was the scion of seven generations of wealthy, aristocratic New Yorkers. A sickly boy, he built his body through rigorous exercise, sharpened his mind through constant study, and pursued a life so strenuous that few could keep up. He learned to ride and shoot, roped cattle in the Dakota Badlands, mastered judo, and later in life climbed the Matterhorn, hunted African game, and explored the Amazon.

In 1880, driven by an urge to lead and serve, Roosevelt won election to the New York State Assembly. In rapid succession he became a civil service commissioner in Washington, New York City police commissioner, assistant secretary of the navy, and the Rough Rider hero of the Spanish-American War. At the age of 40 he won election as reform governor of New York and two years later as vice president. Through it all, TR remained a solid Republican, personally flamboyant but committed to mild change only.

To the Executive Mansion (he renamed it the "White House"), Roosevelt brought a passion for order, a commitment to the public, and a sense of presidential possibilities. Most presidents believed the Constitution set specific limits on their power. Roosevelt thought that the president could do anything not expressly forbidden in the document. Recognizing the value of publicity, he gave reporters the first press room in the White House and favored them with all the stories they wanted. He was the first president to ride in an automobile, fly in an airplane, and dive in a submarine—and everyone knew it.

To dramatize racial injustice, Roosevelt invited black educator Booker T. Washington to lunch at the White House in 1901. White southern journalists

Bullnecked and barrel-chested, Theodore Roosevelt was "pure act," said Henry Adams. TR may have had the attention span of a golden retriever, as one critic charged, but he also embodied the great virtues of his day—honesty, hard work, constancy, courage, and, while in power, self-control.

called such mingling with African Americans treason, but for Roosevelt the gesture served both principle and politics. His lunch with Washington was part of a "black and tan" strategy to build a biracial coalition among southern Republicans. He denounced lynching and appointed black southerners to important federal offices in Mississippi and South Carolina.

Sensing the limits of political feasibility, Roosevelt went no further. Perhaps his own racial narrowness stopped him too. In 1906, when Atlanta exploded in a race riot that left 12 people dead, he said nothing. Later that year he discharged "without honor" three entire companies of African American troops because some of the soldiers were unjustly charged with having "shot up" Brownsville, Texas. All lost their pensions, including six winners of the Medal of Honor. The act stained Roosevelt's record. (Congress acknowledged the wrong in 1972 by granting the soldiers honorable discharges.)

Brownsville incident

A Square Deal

Philosophy of the Square Deal

By temperament, Roosevelt was not inclined to follow the cautious course McKinley had charted. He had more energetic plans in mind. He accepted growth—whether of business, labor, or government—as natural. In the pluralistic system he envisioned, big labor would counterbalance big capital, big farm organizations would offset big food processors, and so on. Standing astride them all, mediating when needed, was a big government that could ensure fair results for all. Later, as he campaigned for a second term in 1904, Roosevelt named this program the "Square Deal."

Anthracite coal strike

In a startling display of presidential initiative, Roosevelt in 1902 intervened in a strike that idled 140,000 miners and paralyzed the anthracite (hard) coal industry. As winter approached, public frustration with the mine owners mounted. They refused even to recognize the miners' union, let alone negotiate worker demands for higher wages and fewer hours. Roosevelt summoned both sides to the White House. John A. Mitchell, the young president of the United Mine Workers, agreed to arbitration, but management balked. Roosevelt leaked word to Wall Street that the army would take over the mines if the owners did not yield.

Seldom had a president acted so boldly, and never on behalf of strikers. In late October 1902 the owners settled by granting miners a 10 percent wage hike and a nine-hour day in return for increases in coal prices and no recognition of the union. Roosevelt was equally prepared to intervene on the side of management, as he did when he sent federal troops to end strikes in Arizona in 1903 and Colorado in 1904. His aim was to establish a vigorous presidency ready to deal squarely with all sides.

Roosevelt especially needed to face the issue of economic concentration. Financial power had become consolidated in giant trusts following a wave of mergers at the end of the century. As large firms swallowed smaller ones, Americans feared that monopoly would destroy individual enterprise and free competition. A series of government investigations revealed a rash of corporate abuses—rebates, collusion, "watered" stock, payoffs to government officials. The conservative courts showed little willingness to break up the giants or blunt their power. In *United States v. E. C. Knight* (1895), the Supreme Court had crippled the Sherman Antitrust Act by ruling that the law applied only to commerce and not to manufacturing. The decision left the American Sugar Refining Company in control of 98 percent of the nation's sugar factories.

U.S. v. E. C. Knight

In his first State of the Union message, Roosevelt told Congress that he did not oppose business concentration. As he saw it, large corporations were not only inevitable but more productive than smaller operations. He wanted to regulate, not destroy, them, to make them fairer and more efficient. Only then would the economic order be humanized, its victims protected, and class violence avoided. Like individuals, trusts had to be held to strict standards of morality. Conduct, not size, was the yardstick TR used to measure "good" and "bad" trusts.

With a progressive's faith in the power of publicity and a regulator's need for the facts, Roosevelt moved immediately to strengthen the federal power of investigation. He called for the creation of a Department of Commerce with a Bureau of Corporations that could force companies to hand over their records. Congressional conservatives shuddered at the prospect of putting corporate books on display. Finally, in 1903, after Roosevelt charged that John D. Rockefeller was orchestrating the opposition, Congress enacted the legislation and provided the Justice Department with additional staff to prosecute antitrust cases.

Northern Securities

In 1902, to demonstrate the power of government, Roosevelt had Attorney General Philander Knox file an antitrust suit against the Northern Securities Company. The mammoth holding company virtually monopolized railroads in the Northwest. Worse still, it had bloated its stock with worthless certificates. Here, clearly, was a symbol of the "bad trust."

J. P. Morgan, one of the company's founders, rushed to the White House. "Send your man [the attorney general] to my man [Morgan's lawyer] and they can fix it up," he told Roosevelt and Knox. "We don't want to fix it up," replied the attorney general. "We want to stop it." A trust-conscious nation cheered as the Supreme Court ordered the company to dissolve in 1904. Ultimately, the Roosevelt administration brought suit against 44 giants, including the Standard Oil Company, the American Tobacco Company, and the Du Pont Corporation.

Railroad regulation

Despite his reputation for trustbusting, Roosevelt always preferred regulation. The problems of the railroads, for example, were newly underscored by a recent round of consolidation that had contributed to higher freight rates. Roosevelt pressed Congress to strengthen the weak Interstate Commerce Commission (ICC) (page 679). In 1903 Congress enacted the Elkins Act, which gave the ICC power to end rebates. Even the railroads supported the act because it saved them from the costly practice of granting special reductions to large shippers.

By the election of 1904 the president's boldness had won him broad popular support. He trounced his two rivals, Democrat Alton B. Parker, a jurist from New York, and Eugene V. Debs of the Socialist party. No longer was he a "political accident," Roosevelt boasted.

Conservatives in his own party opposed Roosevelt's meddling in the private sector. But progressives, goaded by Robert La Follette, demanded still more regulation of the railroads, in particular a controversial proposal for making public the value of all rail property. In 1906, the president finally reached a compromise typical of his restrained approach to reform. The Hepburn Railway Act allowed the ICC to set ceilings on rates and to regulate sleeping car companies, ferries, bridges, and terminals. La Follette did not gain his provision to disclose company value, but the Hepburn Act drew Roosevelt nearer to his goal of continuous regulation of business.

Bad Food and Pristine Wilds

Extending the umbrella of federal protection to consumers, Roosevelt belatedly threw his weight behind two campaigns for healthy foods and drugs. In 1905 Samuel Hopkins Adams of *Collier's Weekly* wrote that in its patent medicines "Gullible America" would get "huge quantities of alcohol, an appalling amount of opiates and narcotics," and worse—axle grease, acid, glue. Adams sent the samples he had collected to Harvey Wiley, chief chemist at the Agriculture Department. Wiley's "Poison Squad" produced scientific evidence of Adams's charges.

Several pure food and drug bills had already died at the hands of lobbyists, despite a presidential endorsement. The appearance of Upton Sinclair's *The Jungle* in 1906 spurred Congress to act. Sinclair intended to recruit people to socialism by exposing the plight of workers in the meatpacking industry. His novel contained a brief but vivid description of the slaughter of cattle infected with tuberculosis, of meat covered with rat dung, and of men falling into cooking vats and being served to the public as "Durham's Pure Leaf Lard." Readers paid scant attention to the workers, but their stomachs turned at what they might be eating for breakfast. The Pure Food and Drug Act of 1906 sailed through Congress, and the Meat Inspection Act soon followed.

Roosevelt had come late to the consumer cause, but on conservation he led the nation. An outdoors enthusiast, he galvanized public concern over the reckless use of natural resources. His chief forester, Gifford Pinchot, persuaded him that planned management under federal guidance was needed to protect the natural domain. Cutting trees must be synchronized with tree plantings, oil needed to be pumped from the ground under controlled conditions, and so on.

Conservation through planned management

In the western states water was the problem, as U.S. Geological Survey director John Welsey Powell had noted years earlier (pages 580–582). Economic growth, even survival, depended on it. Two visions of what to do about Powell's water-starved West emerged. One emphasized the conservation of water (and other scarce resources) through planned use; the other, preservation of resources in a pristine state. Supporters of conservation pointed to the economic benefits flowing from planned water use: bringing marginal land into production, luring settlers into a region that was land-rich and people-poor, implanting agriculture and industry on an unimagined scale. Advocates of preservation pointed to the ecological costs of developing a region whose scarce water could be drained or contaminated and whose natural environment was thus ill-suited for agriculture and industry.

As fragmented local and state water policies sparked controversy, violence, and waste, many progressives campaigned for a federal program to replace the chaotic web of rules. Democratic senator Frederick Newlands of Nevada introduced the Reclamation Act of 1902 to set aside proceeds from the sale of public lands for irrigation projects. The Reclamation Act signaled a progressive step toward the conservationist goal of rational resource development.

Conservation often conflicted with the more radical vision of preservationists, led by naturalist and wilderness philosopher John Muir. Muir founded the Sierra Club in 1892 in hopes of maintaining such natural wonders as Yosemite and its neighboring Hetch-Hetchy valley in a state "forever wild" to benefit future generations. Many conservationists saw such valleys only as sites for dams and reservoirs to manage and control water. Controversy flared after 1900, when San Francisco announced plans to create a reservoir in the Hetch-Hetchy valley. For 13 years Muir waged a publicity campaign against the reservoir and its "devotees of ravaging commercialism." Pinchot enthusiastically backed San Francisco's claim. Roosevelt, torn by his friendship with Muir, did so less loudly. Not until 1913 did President Woodrow Wilson finally decide the issue in favor of San Francisco. Conservation had won over preservation.

John Muir and preservation

Roosevelt nonetheless advanced many of Muir's goals. Over the protests of cattle and timber interests, he added nearly 200 million acres to government forest reserves; placed coal and mineral lands, oil reserves, and water-power sites in the public domain; and enlarged the national park system. When Congress balked, he

Edward Curtis and documenting Native American culture

The Sierra Club, founded by naturalist John Muir, believed in the importance of preserving wilderness in its natural state. "In God's wildness," Muir wrote in 1890, "lies the hope of the world—the great fresh unblighted, unredeemed wilderness." Muir helped persuade President Theodore Roosevelt to double the number of national parks. Here, some Sierra Club members lounge at the base of a giant redwood in Big Basin in 1905.

appropriated another 17 million acres of forest before the legislators could pass a bill limiting him. Roosevelt also set in motion national congresses and commissions on conservation and mobilized governors across the country. Like a good progressive, he sent hundreds of experts to work applying science, education, and technology to environmental problems.

As Roosevelt acted more forcefully, conservatives lashed back. So far his record had been modest, but his chief accomplishment—invigorating the presidency—could lead to deeper reform. When another dip in the business cycle produced financial panic on Wall Street in 1907, business leaders and conservative politicians blamed the president. Roosevelt blamed the "speculative folly and the flagrant dishonesty of a few men of great wealth."

Clearly shaken, however, Roosevelt assured business leaders that he would do nothing to interfere with their efforts at recovery. That included a pledge not to file an antitrust suit if the giant U.S. Steel bought the Tennessee Coal and Iron Company. The economy recovered, and having declared he would not run in 1908, the 50-year-old Roosevelt prepared to give over his office to William Howard Taft.

The Troubled Taft

On March 4, 1909, as snow swirled outside the White House, William Howard Taft readied himself for his inauguration. Over breakfast with Roosevelt, he warmed in the glow of recent Republican victories. Taft had beaten Democrat William Jennings Bryan in the "Great Commoner's" third and last bid for the presidency. Republicans had retained control of Congress, as well as a host of northern legislatures. Reform was at high tide, and Taft was eager to continue the Roosevelt program.

"Will," as Roosevelt called Taft, was his handpicked successor. A distinguished jurist and public servant, the first American governor-general of the Philippines, and Roosevelt's secretary of war, Taft had great administrative skill and personal charm. But he disliked the political maneuvering of Washington and preferred conciliation to confrontation. Even Roosevelt had doubts. "He's all right," TR had told a reporter on inauguration day. "But he's weak. They'll get around him. They'll"—and here Roosevelt pushed the reporter with his shoulder—"lean against him."

Trouble began early when progressives in the House moved to curb the near-dictatorial power of the conservative Speaker, Joseph Cannon. Taft waffled, first supporting them and then abandoning them to preserve the tariff reductions he was seeking. When progressives later broke Cannon's power without Taft's help, they scorned the president. And Taft's compromise was wasted. Senate protectionists peppered the tariff bill with so many amendments that rates jumped nearly to their old levels.

William Howard Taft—big, good-natured, and modest—was reluctant to run for the presidency in 1908. At the outset of the campaign, President Roosevelt sent him pointed advice: "Photographs on horseback, yes, tennis, no, and golf is fatal." But Taft played anyway. He loved golf despite its reputation as a "dude's game."

Late in 1909, the rift between Taft and the progressives reached the breaking point in a dispute over conservation. Taft had appointed Richard Ballinger secretary of the interior over the objections of Roosevelt's old friend and mentor Chief Forester Pinchot. When Ballinger opened a million acres of public lands for sale, Pinchot rebelled openly. He charged that shady dealings had led Ballinger to transfer Alaskan public coal lands to a syndicate that included J. P. Morgan. Early in 1910, Taft fired Pinchot for insubordination. Angry progressives saw the Ballinger-Pinchot controversy as another betrayal by Taft. They began to look longingly across the Atlantic, where TR was stalking big game in Africa.

Despite his failures, Taft was no conservative pawn. He ended up protecting more land than Roosevelt, and he pushed Congress to enact a progressive program regulating safety standards for mines and railroads, creating a federal children's bureau, and setting an eight-hour workday for federal employees. Taft's support of a graduated income tax—sometimes fiery, sometimes mild—was finally decisive. Early in 1913 it became the Sixteenth Amendment. Historians view it as one of the most important reforms of the century, for it eventually generated the revenue for many new social programs.

Taft's accomplishments

Yet no matter what Taft did, he managed to alienate conservatives and progressives alike. That spelled trouble for the Republicans as the presidential election of 1912 approached.

Roosevelt Returns

In June 1910 Roosevelt had come home laden with hunting trophies and exuberant as ever. He found Taft unhappy and progressive Republicans threatening to defect. Party loyalty kept Roosevelt quiet through most of 1911, but in October Taft pricked him personally on the sensitive matter of busting trusts. Like TR, Taft accepted trusts as natural, but he failed to make Roosevelt's distinction between "good" and "bad" ones. He demanded, more impartially, that all trusts be prevented from restraining trade. In four years as president, Taft had brought nearly twice the antitrust suits Roosevelt had in seven years.

In October 1911 the Justice Department charged U.S. Steel with having violated the Sherman Antitrust Act by acquiring the Tennessee Coal and Iron

Company. Roosevelt regarded the action as a personal rebuke, because he himself had allowed U.S. Steel to proceed with the acquisition. Taft "was playing small, mean, and foolish politics," complained TR.

New Nationalism

Roosevelt decided to play big, high-minded, and presidential. Already, in a speech at Osawatomie, Kansas, in 1910, he had outlined a program of sweeping reform. His "New Nationalism" stressed the interests of the nation as a whole and the value of government as an agent of reform. It accepted consolidation in the economy—whether big business or big labor—but insisted on protecting the interests of individuals through big government. The New Nationalism promised government planning and efficiency under a powerful executive, "a steward of the public welfare." It promoted taxes on incomes and inheritances and greater regulation of industry. And it embraced social justice, specifically workers' compensation for accidents, minimum wages and maximum hours, child labor laws, and "equal suffrage"—a nod to women and loyal black Republicans. Roosevelt, a cautious reformer as president, grew daring as he set his sights again on the White House.

The Election of 1912

"My hat is in the ring!" Roosevelt announced in February 1912, to no one's surprise. Taft responded by claiming that the New Nationalism had won support only from "radicals," "emotionalists," and "neurotics." In fact, the enormously popular Roosevelt won most of the primaries, but by the time Republicans met in Chicago in June 1912, Taft had used presidential patronage and promises to secure the nomination. A frustrated Roosevelt bolted and took progressive Republicans with him. Two months later, amid choruses of "Onward Christian Soldiers," delegates to the newly formed

Progressive, or "Bull Moose," party

Progressive party nominated Roosevelt for the presidency. "I'm feeling like a bull moose!" he bellowed. Progressives suddenly had a symbol for their breakaway party.

The Democrats met in Baltimore, jubilant over the prospect of a divided Republican party. Delegates chose as their candidate Woodrow Wilson, the progressive governor of New Jersey. Wilson wisely concentrated his fire on Roosevelt. He coun-

Woodrow Wilson's New Freedom

tered the New Nationalism with his "New Freedom." It rejected the economic consolidation that Roosevelt embraced. Bigness itself was a sin, no matter how big corporations acted, because it crowded out competition, thereby promoting inefficiency and reducing economic opportunity. Only by strictly limiting the size of business

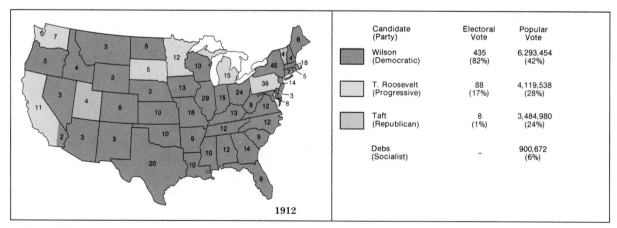

Candidate (Party)	Electoral Vote	Popular Vote
Wilson (Democratic)	435 (82%)	6,293,454 (42%)
T. Roosevelt (Progressive)	88 (17%)	4,119,538 (28%)
Taft (Republican)	8 (1%)	3,484,980 (24%)
Debs (Socialist)	–	900,672 (6%)

1912

Election of 1912

enterprises could the free market be preserved and Americans be released from the control of the wealthy and powerful. And only by keeping government small could individual liberty be protected. "Liberty," Wilson cautioned, "has never come from government," only from the "limitation of governmental power."

Increasingly voters found Taft beside the point. In an age of reform, even the Socialists looked good. Better led, financed, and organized than ever, the Socialist party had enlarged its membership to nearly 135,000 by 1912. Socialist mayors ran 32 cities. The party also had an appealing candidate in Eugene V. Debs, a home-grown Indiana radical. He had won 400,000 votes for president in 1904. Now, in 1912, he summoned voters to make "the working class the ruling class."

On Election Day voters gave progressive reform a resounding endorsement. Wilson won 6.3 million votes, Roosevelt 4.1 million, Taft just 3.6 million. Debs received almost a million votes. Together the two progressive candidates amassed a three to one margin. The Republican split, moreover, had broken the party's hold on national politics. For the first time since 1896, a Democrat would sit in the White House—and with his party in control of Congress.

Woodrow Wilson and the Politics of Morality

Woodrow Wilson was not shy about his good fortune. Soon after the election he confessed to William McCombs, chairman of the Democratic National Committee: "God ordained that I should be the next President of the United States." To the White House Wilson brought a passion for reform and the conviction that he was meant to accomplish great things. Under him, progressivism peaked.

Early Career

From the moment of his birth in 1856, Thomas Woodrow Wilson could not escape a sense of destiny. It was all around him. In the family's Presbyterian faith, in the sermons of his minister father, in dinnertime talk ran the unbending belief in a world predetermined by God and ruled by saved souls, the "elect." Wilson ached to be one of them and behaved as if he were.

To prepare to lead, young Tommy Wilson studied the fiery debates of the British Parliament and wandered the woods reciting them from memory. Like most southerners, he grew up loving the Democratic party, hating the tariff, and accepting racial separation. (Under his presidency, segregation would return to Washington for the first time since Reconstruction.)

An early career in law bored him, so he turned to political science and became a professor. His studies persuaded him that a modern president must act as a "prime minister," directing and uniting his party, shaping legislation and public opinion, exerting continuous leadership. In 1910, after a stormy tenure as head of Princeton University, Wilson was helped by Democratic party bosses to win the governorship of New Jersey. In 1912 they helped him again, this time to the presidency of the country.

The Reforms of the New Freedom

As governor, Wilson had led New Jersey on the path of progressive reform. As president, he was a model of executive leadership. More than Theodore Roosevelt, he shaped policy and legislation. He went to Congress to let members know he intended to work personally with them. He kept party discipline tight and mobilized public opinion when Congress refused to act.

Lowering the high tariff was Wilson's first order of business. Progressives had long attacked the tariff as another example of the power of trusts. By protecting American manufacturers, Wilson argued, such barriers weakened the competition he cherished. When the Senate threatened to raise rates, the new president appealed directly to the public. "Industrious" and "insidious" lobbyists were blocking reform, he cried to reporters. A "brick couldn't be thrown without hitting one of them."

Underwood-Simmons Tariff

The Underwood-Simmons Tariff of 1913 marked the first downward revision of the tariff in 19 years and the biggest since before the Civil War. To compensate for lost revenue, Congress enacted a graduated income tax under the newly adopted Sixteenth Amendment. It applied solely to corporations and the tiny fraction of Americans who earned more than $4000 a year. It nonetheless began a momentous shift in government revenue from its nineteenth-century base—public lands, alcohol taxes, and customs duties—to its twentieth-century base—personal and corporate incomes.

Wilson turned next to the perennial problems of money and banking. Early in 1913 a congressional committee under Arsene Pujo revealed that a few powerful banks controlled the nation's credit system. They could choke Wilson's free market by raising interest rates or tightening the supply of money. As a banking reform bill moved through Congress in 1913, Wall Street conservatives lobbied for a privately controlled, centralized banking system that could issue currency and set interest rates. Rural Democrats favored a decentralized system of regional banks run by local bankers. Populists and progressives—including William Jennings Bryan and Robert La Follette—wanted government control.

Federal Reserve Act

Wilson split their differences in the Federal Reserve Act of 1913. The new Federal Reserve System contained 12 regional banks scattered across the country. But it also created a central Federal Reserve Board in Washington, appointed by the president, to supervise the system. The board could regulate credit and the money

Woodrow Wilson came to the White House with promises to reform government. In this 1913 cartoon titled "A New Captain in the District," the newly elected president strides through corrupt Washington, ready to police such abuses as easy land grants and pork barreling, the much-criticized congressional practice of voting for projects that benefit home districts and constituents.

supply by setting the interest rate it charged member banks, by buying or selling government bonds, and by issuing paper currency called Federal Reserve notes. Thus the Federal Reserve System sought to stabilize the existing order by increasing federal control over credit and the money supply.

When Wilson finally took on the trusts, he moved closer to the New Nationalism of Theodore Roosevelt. The Federal Trade Commission Act of 1914 created a bipartisan executive agency to oversee business activity. The end—to enforce orderly competition—was distinctly Wilsonian, but the means—an executive commission to regulate commerce—were pure Roosevelt.

Federal Trade Commission

Roosevelt would have stopped there, but Wilson made good on his campaign pledge to attack trusts. The Clayton Antitrust Act (1914) barred some of the worst corporate practices—price discrimination, holding companies, and interlocking directorates (directors of one corporate board sitting on others). Yet despite Wilson's bias against size, the advantages of large-scale production and distribution were inescapable. In practice his administration chose to regulate rather than break up bigness. Under Wilson the Justice Department filed fewer antitrust suits than under the Taft administration and negotiated more "gentlemen's agreements" (voluntary agreements by companies to change practices) than under Roosevelt.

Clayton Antitrust Act

Labor and Social Reform

For all of Wilson's impressive accomplishments, voters turned lukewarm toward the New Freedom. In the elections of 1914 Republicans cut Democratic majorities in the House and won important industrial and farm states. To strengthen his hand in the presidential election of 1916, Wilson began edging toward the social reforms of the New Nationalism he had once criticized as paternalistic and unconstitutional. Early in 1916 he signaled the change when he nominated his close adviser Louis D. Brandeis to the Supreme Court. The progressive Brandeis had fought for the social reforms lacking on Wilson's agenda. His appointment also broke the tradition of anti-Semitism that had previously kept Jews off the Court.

In a host of other ways, Wilson revealed his willingness to intervene more actively in the economy. He helped pass laws improving the working conditions of merchant seamen and setting an eight-hour day for workers on interstate railroads. He endorsed the Keating-Owen Child Labor Act (page 719) and threw his support to legislation providing farmers with low-interest loans. And just before the election Wilson intervened to avert a nationwide strike of rail workers.

The Limits of Progressive Reform

Woodrow Wilson's administration capped a decade and a half of heady reform. Seeing chaos in the modern industrial city, progressive reformers had worked to reduce the damage of poverty and the hazards of industrial work, control the rising immigrant tide, and spread a middle-class ideal of morality. In city halls and state legislatures, they tried to break the power of corporate interests and entrenched political machines. In Washington, they enlarged government and broadened its mission from caretaker to promoter of public welfare.

Progressivism did not always succeed. Reformers sometimes betrayed their high ideals by denying equality to African Americans, Asians, and other minorities. They preferred to Americanize foreigners rather than accept the contributions of their cultures. Too often government commissions that were designed to be "watchdog" agencies found themselves captured by the interests they were supposed to oversee. Well-meaning but cumbersome regulation crippled industries like the railroads for decades. Although the direct primary, the popular election of senators, and other reforms weakened the power of political machines, boss rule survived.

For all its claims of sweeping change, progressivism left the system of market capitalism intact. Neither the New Nationalism of Theodore Roosevelt, with its emphasis on planning and regulation, nor Woodrow Wilson's New Freedom, which promoted competition through limits on corporate size, aimed to do more than improve the system. But the Gilded Age philosophy of laissez faire—of giving private enterprise a free hand—had clearly been rejected. Both state and federal governments established their right to regulate the actions of private corporations for the public good.

The reforms thus achieved, including the eight-hour workday, woman suffrage, direct election of senators, graduated income taxes, and public ownership of utilities, began to address the problems of an urban industrial society. Under progressive leadership, the modern state—active and interventionist—was born.

American confidence soared as the new century unfolded. A golden age of peace, prosperity, and human advancement seemed within reach, at least to progressives. But in 1914, as progressivism crested in America, the guns of a hot August shattered the uneasy calm in Europe and plunged the world into war. Few people anywhere were prepared for the bloodbath that followed.

chapter summary

Progressivism was a broad-based reform movement, the first truly national reform movement in American history, that attempted to address problems arising from industrialization, urbanization, and immigration.

- Progressive reform sprang from many impulses:

  - Desires to curb the advancing power of big business and to end political corruption.

  - Efforts to bring order and efficiency to economic and political life.

  - Attempts by new interest groups to make business and government more responsive to the needs of ordinary citizens.

  - Moralistic urges to rid society of industries such as the liquor trade that profited from human misery, to bridge the gap between immigrants and native-born Americans, and to soften the consequences of industrialization through social justice and social welfare.

- Led by members of the urban middle class, progressives were moderate modernizers, attempting to redeem such traditional American values as democracy, Judeo-Christian ethics, individualism, and the spirit of volunteerism and public service while employing the newest techniques of management and planning, coordinated systems, and specialized bureaucracies of experts.

- The twin drives for social justice and social welfare often relied on women, who extended their traditional sphere of home and family to become "social housekeepers" and crusaders for women's rights, especially the right to vote.

- Increasingly, progressivism animated politics, first at the local and state levels, then in the presidencies of Theodore Roosevelt and Woodrow Wilson.

- In the end, the weaknesses of progressivism—the fuzziness of its conception of the public interest, the exclusion of African Americans and other minorities, the ease with which its regulatory mechanisms were "captured" by those being regulated—were matched by its accomplishments in establishing the modern, activist state.

interactive learning

The Primary Source Investigator CD-ROM offers the following materials related to this chapter:

- Interactive maps: **Election of 1912** (M7) and **Woman Suffrage, 1871–1919** (M16)

- Short documentary movies on the movement for women's suffrage (D15); and Edward Curtis and documenting Native American culture (D11)

- A collection of primary sources examining America during the progressive era: the promotional poster for the movie *The Jungle,* the Keating-Owen Child Labor Act, an article on conditions in Chicago's meatpacking plants, and the Meat Inspection Act of 1906. Other sources reveal the prominent role of environmentalism in the progressive era, including the congressional act establishing Yellowstone National Park.

additional reading

The long interpretive debate over progressivism is best covered in Arthur Link and Richard L. McCormick, *Progressivism* (1985). Benchmarks in that debate include George Mowry, *The California Progressives* (1951), and Richard Hofstadter, *The Age of Reform: From Bryan to FDR* (1955), both of which see progressives as a small elite seeking to recapture its fading status and influence. Gabriel Kolko, *The Triumph of Conservatism: A Reinterpretation of American History 1900–1916* (1963), makes the controversial case of the New Left that business "captured" reform to control competition and stave off stricter federal regulation. Richard McCormick stresses the transformation of political culture accompanying the decline of political parties and the rise of interest groups in *From Realignment to Reform: Political Change in New York State, 1893–1910* (1981). The social history of progressivism is best covered in Steven J. Diner's *A Very Different Age: Americans of the Progressive Era* (1998).

John M. Blum, *The Republican Roosevelt* (1954), remains the most incisive rendering of TR, and Lewis L. Gould, *The Presidency of Theodore Roosevelt* (1991), is the best single-volume study of the White House years. Unsurpassed for its detail and depth is Arthur Link, *Woodrow Wilson,* 5 vols. (1947–1965). Robert Crunden, *Ministers of Reform: The Progressives' Achievements in American Civilization, 1889–1920* (1982), emphasizes the cultural origins and impact of progressivism, and Ellen Chesler, *Woman of Valor: Margaret Sanger and the Birth Control Movement in America* (1992), looks through a feminist lens at the life and times of social reformer Margaret Sanger. For a fuller list of readings, see the Bibliography at www.mhhe.com/davidsonnation5.

significant events

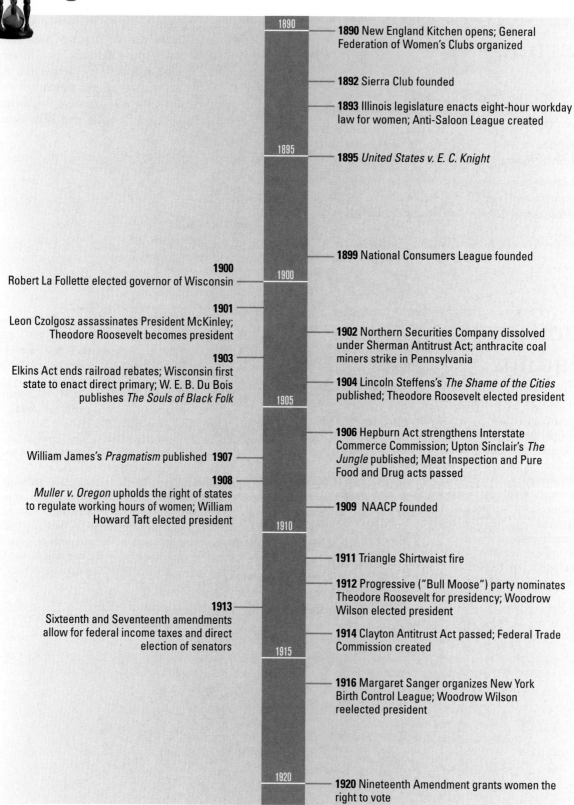

1890 New England Kitchen opens; General Federation of Women's Clubs organized

1892 Sierra Club founded

1893 Illinois legislature enacts eight-hour workday law for women; Anti-Saloon League created

1895 *United States v. E. C. Knight*

1899 National Consumers League founded

1900 Robert La Follette elected governor of Wisconsin

1901 Leon Czolgosz assassinates President McKinley; Theodore Roosevelt becomes president

1902 Northern Securities Company dissolved under Sherman Antitrust Act; anthracite coal miners strike in Pennsylvania

1903 Elkins Act ends railroad rebates; Wisconsin first state to enact direct primary; W. E. B. Du Bois publishes *The Souls of Black Folk*

1904 Lincoln Steffens's *The Shame of the Cities* published; Theodore Roosevelt elected president

1906 Hepburn Act strengthens Interstate Commerce Commission; Upton Sinclair's *The Jungle* published; Meat Inspection and Pure Food and Drug acts passed

William James's *Pragmatism* published **1907**

1908 *Muller v. Oregon* upholds the right of states to regulate working hours of women; William Howard Taft elected president

1909 NAACP founded

1911 Triangle Shirtwaist fire

1912 Progressive ("Bull Moose") party nominates Theodore Roosevelt for presidency; Woodrow Wilson elected president

1913 Sixteenth and Seventeenth amendments allow for federal income taxes and direct election of senators

1914 Clayton Antitrust Act passed; Federal Trade Commission created

1916 Margaret Sanger organizes New York Birth Control League; Woodrow Wilson reelected president

1920 Nineteenth Amendment grants women the right to vote

War! War! WAR!" The news had flashed across the country in the spring of 1898. As tens of thousands of eager young men signed up to fight the Spanish in Cuba, the USS *Oregon* left San Francisco Bay on a roundabout route toward its battle station in the Caribbean. It first headed south through the Pacific, passing Central America and leaving it thousands of miles behind. Then, in the narrow Strait of Magellan at South America's tip, the ship encountered a gale so ferocious, the shore could not be seen. All communication ceased, and Americans at home feared the worst. But the *Oregon* passed into the Atlantic and steamed north until finally, after 68 days and 13,000 miles at sea, it helped win the Battle of Santiago Bay.

The daring voyage electrified the nation but worried its leaders. Since the defeat of Mexico in 1848, the United States had stretched from the Atlantic to the Pacific without enough navy to go around. As an emerging power, the country needed a path between the seas—a canal across the narrow isthmus of Colombia's Panamanian province in Central America—to defend itself and to promote its growing trade.

The United States & *The Old World Order*

1901–1920

preview • With the outbreak of World War I, the old order of colonial imperialism and carefully balanced military alliances came crashing down. Wilson at first proclaimed Americans neutral, in hopes of brokering a peace settlement. But American economic and cultural ties to the Allies, along with German submarine warfare, brought Americans into the war. By its end, Woodrow Wilson's hopes for a progressive "peace without victory" and a new world order were dashed.

"I took the isthmus," Theodore Roosevelt later told a cheering crowd. In a way he did. As president, in 1903 he negotiated an agreement with Colombia to lease the needed strip of land. Holding out for more money and greater control over the canal, the Colombian senate refused to ratify the agreement.

Privately, TR talked of seizing Panama. But when he learned of a budding independence movement in Panama, he let it be known that he would welcome a revolt. On schedule and without bloodshed, the Panamanians rebelled late in 1903. The next day a U.S. cruiser dropped anchor offshore to prevent Colombia from landing troops. The United States quickly recognized the new Republic of Panama and signed a treaty for a renewable lease on a canal zone 10 miles wide. Panama received $10 million plus an annual rent of $250,000 (the same terms offered to Colombia). One of the few critics called it "a rough-riding assault upon another republic." Roosevelt never apologized, but in 1921, after oil had been discovered in the Canal Zone, Congress voted $25 million to Colombia.

In November 1906 Roosevelt pulled into port at Panama City aboard the USS *Louisiana,* newly launched and the biggest battleship in the fleet. He spent the next three days traveling the length of the canal site in the pouring rain. Soaked from head to toe, his huge panama hat and white suit sagging about his body, he splashed through labor camps and asked workers for their complaints. He toured the hospital at Ancon and met Dr. William Gorgas, the sanitation engineer in charge of eradicating the yellow fever–bearing mosquito. He walked railroad ties at the cuts and made speeches in the mud. "This is one of the great works of the world," he told an assembly of black diggers, some 30,000 of whom had been brought from the West Indies to accomplish the task. When completed, the canal

African American artist Horace Pippin lost the use of his right arm in the First World War. In 1930, after three years of work, he completed *The End of the War: Starting Home*. It shows black troops, bayonets at the ready, forcing a German surrender.

stretched some 50 miles across the Isthmus of Panama. At $352 million, its final cost was four times that of the Suez Canal.

The Panama Canal embodied Roosevelt's muscular foreign policy of respect through strength. He modernized the army and tripled its size, created a general staff for planning and mobilization, and established the Army War College. As a pivot point between the two hemispheres, his canal allowed the United States to flex its strength across the globe.

These expanding horizons came about largely as an outgrowth of American commercial and industrial expansion, just as the imperialist empires of England, France, Germany, Russia, and Japan reflected the spread of their own industrial and commercial might. The Americans, steeped in democratic ideals, frequently seemed uncomfortable with the naked ambitions of European empire-builders. Roosevelt's embrace of the canal, however, showed how far some progressives had come in being willing to shape the world.

Expansionist diplomats at home and abroad assured each other that global order could be maintained by balancing power through a set of carefully crafted

Panama Canal—Old and New Transoceanic Routes Tropical forests cover three-fourths of Panama, including the Canal Zone. Vegetation is denser at high elevations but tightly packed even below 1000 feet. The terrain is rugged, but the distance saved by the canal (nearly 8000 miles) made the ordeal of construction worthwhile.

alliances. But that system and the spheres of influence it spawned did not hold. In 1914, the year the Panama Canal opened, the old world order collapsed in a terrible war.

Progressive Diplomacy

Foundations of progressive diplomacy

As the Panama Canal was being built, progressive diplomacy was taking shape. Like progressive politics, it stressed moralism and order as it stretched presidential power to new limits in an effort to mold and remake the international environment. It rested on faith in the superiority of Anglo-American stock and institutions. "Of all our race, [God] has marked the American people as His chosen nation to finally lead in the redemption of the world," said one senator in 1900. Every Western leader assumed that northern Europeans were racially superior, too. The darker peoples of the tropical zones, observed a progressive educator, dwelled in "nature's asylum for degenerates." In this global vision of Manifest Destiny, few progressives questioned the need to uplift them.

Economic expansion underlay the commitment to a "civilizing" mission. The depression of 1893 had encouraged American manufacturers and farmers to look overseas for markets, and that expansion continued after 1900. By 1918, at the end of World War I, the United States had become the largest creditor in the world, with networks of commerce that reached as far away as the deserts of Arabia and river valleys of central China. Every administration committed itself to opening doors of trade and keeping them open.

Big Stick in the Caribbean

Theodore Roosevelt liked to invoke the old African proverb "Walk softly and carry a big stick." But in the Caribbean he moved both loudly and mightily. The Panama Canal gave the United States a commanding position in the Western Hemisphere. Its importance required the country to "police the surrounding premises," explained

Secretary of State Elihu Root. Before granting Cuba independence in 1902, the United States reorganized its finances and attached the Platt Amendment to the Cuban constitution. The amendment gave American authorities the right to intervene in Cuba if the independence or internal order of the country were threatened. Claiming that power, U.S. troops occupied the island twice between 1906 and 1923. **Platt Amendment**

In looking to enforce a favorable environment for trade in the Caribbean, Roosevelt also worried about European intentions. The Monroe Doctrine of 1823 had declared against further European colonization of the Western Hemisphere, but in the early twentieth century the rising debts of Latin Americans to Europeans invited intrusion. "If we intend to say hands off to the power of Europe, then sooner or later we must keep order ourselves," Roosevelt warned. In his balance-of-power system, it was the obligation of great powers to avoid the spheres of others while keeping order in their own. Across the globe, great powers would thus check each other, much as big government held big business in check at home.

Going well beyond Monroe's concept of resisting foreign intrusions into the Western Hemisphere, Roosevelt tightened his grip on the region. In 1904, when the Dominican Republic defaulted on its debts, he added the "Roosevelt Corollary" to the Monroe Doctrine by claiming the right to intervene directly if Latin Americans failed to keep their own financial households in order. Invoking its sweeping (and self-proclaimed) power, the United States assumed responsibility for several Caribbean states, including the Dominican Republic, Cuba, and Panama. **Roosevelt Corollary to the Monroe Doctrine**

A "Diplomatist of the Highest Rank"

In the Far East Roosevelt exercised ingenuity rather than force, because he realized that few Americans would support armed intervention half a world away. Like McKinley before him, TR committed himself only to maintaining an "open door" of equal access to trade in China and to protecting the Philippines, "our heel of Achilles."

The key to success lay in offsetting Russian and Japanese ambitions in the region. When Japan attacked Russian holdings in the Chinese province of Manchuria in 1904, Roosevelt offered to mediate. He worried that if unchecked, Japan might threaten American interests in China and the Philippines. At the U.S. Naval Base near Portsmouth, Maine, Roosevelt guided the Russians and the Japanese to the Treaty of Portsmouth in 1905. It recognized the Japanese victory (the first by an Asian power over a European country) and ceded to Japan Port Arthur, the southern half of Sakhalin Island, and, in effect, control of Korea. Japan promised to leave Manchuria as part of China and keep trade open to all foreign nations. The balance of power in Asia and the open door in China thus had been preserved. For his contributions, Roosevelt received the Nobel Peace Prize in 1906. **Treaty of Portsmouth**

Japanese nationalists resented the peace treaty for curbing Japan's ambitions in China. Their anger surfaced in a protest lodged, of all places, against the San Francisco school board. In 1906, rising Japanese immigration led San Francisco school authorities to place the city's 93 Asian students in a separate school. In Japan citizens talked of war over the insult. Roosevelt, furious at the "infernal fools in California," summoned the mayor of San Francisco and seven school board members to the White House. In exchange for an end to the segregation order Roosevelt offered to arrange a mutual restriction of immigration between Japan and the United States. In 1907 all sides accepted his "gentlemen's agreement." **Gentlemen's agreement**

The San Francisco school crisis sparked wild rumors that Japan was bent on taking Hawaii, or the Philippines, or the Panama Canal. In case Japan or any other nation

Great White Fleet

thought of upsetting the Pacific balance, Roosevelt sent 16 gleaming white battleships on a world tour. "By George, isn't it magnificent!" he crowed as the "Great White Fleet" steamed out of Hampton Roads, Virginia, in 1907 (see pages 692–693). The fleet made its most conspicuous stop in Japan. Some Europeans predicted disaster. Instead, cheering crowds turned out in Tokyo and Yokohama, where a group of Japanese children sang "The Star-Spangled Banner" in English. The show of force heralded a new age of American naval might but had an unintended consequence that haunted Americans for decades: it spurred Japanese admirals to expand their own navy.

Watching Roosevelt in his second term, an amazed London *Morning Post* honored him as a "diplomatist of the highest rank." Abroad as at home, his brand of progressivism was grounded in an enthusiastic nationalism that mixed force with finesse to achieve balance and order. Yet despite TR's efforts, imperial rivalries, an unchecked arms race, and unrest in Europe threatened to plunge the world into chaos.

Dollar Diplomacy

Instead of force or finesse, William Howard Taft stressed private investment to promote economic stability, keep peace, and tie debt-ridden nations to the United States. "Dollar diplomacy" simply amounted to "substituting dollars for bullets," Taft explained. He and Philander Knox, his prickly secretary of state, treated the restless nations of Latin America like ailing corporations, injecting capital and reorganizing management. By the time Taft left office in 1913, half of all American investments abroad were in Latin America.

Nicaraguan intrusion

In Nicaragua dollar diplomacy was not enough. In 1909, when the Nicaraguan legislature balked at American demands to take over its customshouse and national bank, a U.S. warship dropped anchor off the coast. The lawmakers hastily changed their minds, but in 1912 a revolution led Taft to dispatch 2000 marines to protect American lives and property. Sporadic American intrusions lasted more than a dozen years.

Failure dogged Taft overseas as it did at home. In the Caribbean his dollar diplomacy was linked so closely with unpopular regimes, corporations, and banks that Woodrow Wilson scrapped it as soon as he entered the White House. Taft's efforts to strengthen China with investments and trade only intensified rivalry with Japan and made China more suspicious of all foreigners, including Americans. In 1911 the southern Chinese provinces rebelled against foreign intrusion and overthrew the monarchy. Only persistent pressure from the White House kept dollar diplomacy in Asia alive at all.

Woodrow Wilson and Moral Diplomacy

The Lightfoot Club had been meeting in the Reverend Wilson's hayloft for months when the question of whether the pen was mightier than the sword came up. Young Tommy Wilson, who had organized the debating society, jumped at the chance to argue that written words were more powerful than armies. But when the boys drew lots, Tommy ended up on the other side. "I can't argue that side," he protested. "I can't argue for something I don't believe in." Thomas Woodrow Wilson eventually dropped his first name, but he never gave up his boyhood conviction that morality, at least as he defined it, should guide all conduct. To the diplomacy of order, force, and finance, Wilson added a missionary's commitment to spreading his system of beliefs—justice, democracy, and the Judeo-Christian values of harmony and cooperation.

Missionary Diplomacy

As president, Woodrow Wilson revived and enlarged Jefferson's notion of the United States as a beacon of freedom. "We are chosen, and prominently chosen," he noted, "to show the way to the nations of the world how they shall walk in the paths of liberty." Such paternalism only thinly masked Wilson's assumption of Anglo-American superiority and his willingness to force others to accept American-style democracy and Christian morality through force.

Wilson's missionary diplomacy had a practical side. In the twentieth century foreign markets would serve as America's new frontier. American industries "will burst their jackets if they cannot find free outlets in the markets of the world," Wilson cautioned in 1912. His special genius lay in reconciling this commercial self-interest with a global idealism. In his eyes, exporting American democracy and capitalism would promote peace, prosperity, and human advancement throughout the world.

Solitary and self-assured, Wilson conducted foreign policy on his own. Bypassing the State Department, he sent personal emissaries to foreign leaders and often typed his own dispatches. Sometimes Secretary of State William Jennings Bryan had no idea of what was happening. In rare moments of doubt, Wilson turned to his trusted friend, Edward M. House. The honorary "Colonel" House had hooked himself to Wilson in the early days of his political career and wielded power behind the scenes.

In Asia and the Pacific Wilson moved to put "moral and public considerations" ahead of the "material interests of individuals." He pulled American bankers out of a six-nation railroad project in China backed by President Taft. The scheme

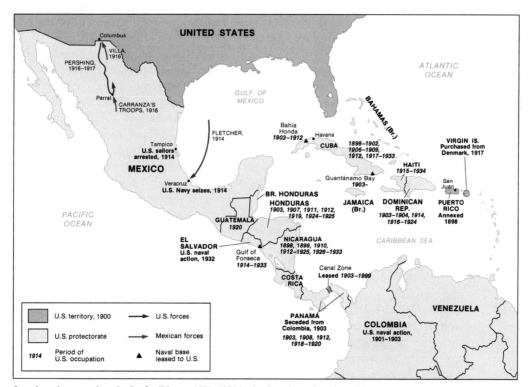

American Interventions in the Caribbean, 1898–1930 In the first three decades of the twentieth century, U.S. diplomacy transformed the Caribbean into an American lake as armed and unarmed intervention became part of the country's diplomatic arsenal.

Twenty-one Demands

encouraged foreign intervention and undermined Chinese sovereignty, said Wilson. The United States became the first major power to recognize the new Republic of China in 1911 when nationalists overthrew the last Manchu emperor. And in 1915 Wilson strongly opposed Japan's "Twenty-one Demands" for control of China. At the end of Wilson's first administration, the Philippines gained limited self-government, the first step toward the eventual independence finally granted in 1946.

In the Caribbean and Latin America, Wilson discovered that interests closer to home could not be pursued through high-minded words alone. In August 1914 he convinced Nicaragua, already occupied by American troops, to yield control of a naval base and grant the United States an alternate canal route. Upheavals in Haiti and the Dominican Republic brought in the U.S. Marines. By the end of his administration American troops were still stationed there and also in Cuba. All four nations were economically dependent on the United States and were virtual protectorates. Missionary diplomacy, it turned out, could spread its gospel with steel as well as cash.

Intervention in Mexico

Mexican Revolution

A lingering crisis in Mexico turned Wilson's "moral diplomacy" into a mockery. A common border, 400 years of shared history, and millions of dollars in investments made what happened in Mexico of urgent importance to the United States. In 1910 a revolution overthrowing the aged dictator Porfirio Díaz plunged the country into turmoil. Just as Wilson was entering the White House in 1913, the ruthless general Victoriano Huerta emerged as head of the government. Wealthy landowners and foreign investors endorsed Huerta, a conservative militarist who was likely to protect their holdings. Soon a bloody civil war was raging between Huerta and his rivals.

Most European nations recognized the Huerta regime immediately, but Wilson refused to accept the "government of butchers." (Huerta had murdered the popular leader Francisco Madera with the approval of the Taft administration.) When Huerta proclaimed himself dictator, Wilson banned arms shipments to Mexico. He threw his support to rebel leader Venustiano Carranza, on the condition that Carranza participate in American-sponsored elections. No Mexican was ready to tolerate such foreign interference. Carranza and his "constitutionalists" rejected the offer. With few options, Wilson armed the rebels anyway.

Wilson's distaste for Huerta was so great that he used a minor incident as a pretext for an invasion. In April 1914 the crew of the USS *Dolphin* landed without permission in the Mexican port city of Tampico. Local police arrested the sailors, only to release them with an apology. Unappeased, their squadron commander demanded a 21-gun salute to the American flag. Agreed, replied the Mexicans, but only if American guns returned the salute to Mexico. Learning of a German shipload of weapons about to land at Veracruz, Wilson broke the impasse by ordering American troops to take the city. Instead of the bloodless occupation they expected, U.S. marines encountered stiff resistance as they stormed ashore; 126 Mexicans and 19 Americans were killed before the city fell. The intervention accomplished little except the unlikely feat of uniting the rival Mexican factions against the United States.

Pancho Villa

Only the combined diplomacy of Argentina, Brazil, and Chile (the "ABC powers") staved off war between Mexico and the United States. When a bankrupt Huerta resigned in 1914, Carranza formed a new constitutionalist government but refused to follow Wilson's guidelines. Wilson turned to Francisco "Pancho" Villa, a wily, peasant-born general who had broken from Carranza. Together with Emiliano Zapata, another peasant leader, Villa kept a rebellion flickering.

General John J. "Black Jack" Pershing led U.S. forces into Mexico on a "punitive action" to catch rebel leader Pancho Villa "dead or alive." Villa (pictured here) eluded the Americans for several months before they abandoned the expedition. Audacious and ruthless, he was worshiped by Mexican peasants, who extolled his exploits in folktales and ballads after his assassination in 1923.

A year later, Wilson finally recognized the Carranza regime, which only turned Villa against the United States. In January 1916 Villa abducted 18 Americans from a train in Mexico and slaughtered them. In March, he galloped into Columbus, New Mexico, killed 19 people, and left the town in flames. Wilson ordered 6000 troops into Mexico to capture Villa "dead or alive." A reluctant Carranza agreed to yet another American invasion.

For nearly two years, General John "Black Jack" Pershing (nicknamed for the all-black unit he commanded in the Spanish-American War) chased Villa on horseback, by automobile, and in airplanes. There were bloody skirmishes with government troops but not a single one with Villa and his rebels. As the chase grew wilder and wilder, Carranza withdrew his consent for U.S. troops on Mexican soil. Early in 1917 Wilson pulled Pershing home. The "punitive expedition," as the president called it, poisoned Mexican-American relations for the next 30 years. But in 1917, Americans worried that an unstable Mexico might be fertile ground for Europeans to export to the New World the war then ravaging the Old World.

The Road to War

In early 1917, around the time Wilson recalled Pershing, the British liner *Laconia* was making a voyage across the Atlantic. As the ship steamed through the inky night, passengers belowdecks talked almost casually of the war raging in Europe since 1914. "What do you think are our chances of being torpedoed?" asked Floyd Gibbons, an American reporter who was aboard. Since Germany had stepped up its submarine attacks, the question was unavoidable. "I should put our chances at 250 to 1 that we don't meet a sub," replied a British diplomat.

"At that minute," recalled Gibbons later, "the torpedo hit us." Suddenly whistle blasts echoed through the corridors and the passengers were forced to abandon ship. They watched in horror from lifeboats as a second torpedo struck its target. The *Laconia*'s bow rose straight in the air as its stern sank; then the entire ship slid silently beneath icy waters. After a miserable night spent bobbing in the waves,

Fervent nationalism heightened the imperial rivalries that pulled European nations into World War I. Flags became important patriotic symbols, masses of morale-boosting color deployed above parades of marching troops and cheering citizens. The American artist Childe Hassam demonstrated that Americans shared this patriotic penchant. Here, flags of the Allies are featured.

Gibbons was rescued. But by 1917 other neutral Americans had already lost their lives at sea. And in April, despite Woodrow Wilson's best efforts at peace, the United States found itself dragged into war.

The Guns of August

Causes of World War I

For a century, profound strains had been pushing Europe toward war. Its population tripled, its middle and working classes swelled, discontent with industrial society grew. The United States had experienced many of the same strains, of course, yet in Europe these pressures played out on a field that was at once more stratified socially and more divided ethnically and culturally. As the continent's political systems adjusted to the new industrial order, both imperialism and nationalism flourished. Abroad, European nations competed for empire, acquiring colonies that could supply industrial raw materials and cheap labor. At home, nationalism proved an equally useful political card to play. It papered over internal division and dissent by directing ambitions and rivalries toward other nations. By 1914 empires jostled uneasily against one another across the globe.

Europe responded to the increased competition with an arms race. Great Britain became convinced that its mastery of the seas depended on maintaining a navy equal in power to the combined navies of its closest two rivals. France and Germany both doubled the size of their standing armies between 1870 and 1914. Led by Kaiser Wilhelm II, Germany aligned itself with Turkey and Austria-Hungary. The established imperial powers of England and France looked to contain Germany by supporting its foe, Russia. Soon Europe bristled with weapons, troops, and armor-plated navies. These war machines were linked to one another through a web of diplomatic alliances—all of them committed to war should someone or some nation set chaos in motion.

That moment came in 1914, in the Slavic province of Bosnia in southwestern Austria-Hungary. Since the 1870s the Ottoman, or Turkish, empire had been slowly disintegrating, allowing a host of smaller, ethnically based states to emerge. Serbia was one of them, and many Serbs dreamed of uniting other Slavic peoples in a "Pan-Slavic" nation. Their ambitions had been blocked in 1908, when Austria-Hungary annexed neighboring Bosnia. Tensions in the region were high when the Archduke Franz Ferdinand, heir to the Austro-Hungarian throne, visited Sarajevo, Bosnia's capital. On June 28, 1914, the Archduke and his wife were gunned down by a Serbian nationalist.

Assassination of Archduke Franz Ferdinand

Austria-Hungary mobilized to punish Serbia. In response, rival Russia called up its 6-million-soldier army to help the Serbs. Germany joined with Austria-Hungary, France with Russia. On July 28, after a month of insincere demands for apologies, Austria-Hungary declared war on Serbia. On August 1, Germany issued a similar declaration against Russia, and, two days later, against France. Following a battle plan drawn up well in advance, German generals pounded neutral Belgium with siege cannons the size of freight cars. Within days, five German columns were slicing west through the Belgian countryside, determined to overrun France before Russia could position its slow-moving army on the eastern front.

The guns of August heralded the first global war. Like so many dominoes, the industrialized nations fell into line: Britain, Japan, Romania, and later Italy to the side of "Allies" France and Russia; Bulgaria and Turkey to the "Central Powers" of Germany and Austria-Hungary. Armies fought from the deserts of North Africa to the plains of Flanders in Belgium. Fleets battled off the coasts of Chile and Sumatra. Soldiers came from as far away as Australia and India. Nearly 8 million never returned.

Neutral but Not Impartial

The outbreak of war in Europe shocked most Americans. Few knew Serbia as anything but a tiny splotch on the map of Europe. Fewer still were prepared to go to war in its defense. President Wilson issued an immediate declaration of neutrality and approved a plan for evacuating Americans stranded in Belgium. "The more I read about the conflict," he wrote a friend, "the more open it seems to me to utter condemnation."

The Course of War in Europe, 1914–1917 When World War I erupted between the Central and Allied Powers in 1914, few countries in Europe remained neutral. The armies of the Central Powers penetrated as far west as France and as far east as Russia, but by 1917, the European war had settled into a hideous standoff along the deadly line of trenches on the western front.

Wilson's neutral ideals

Wilson came to see the calamity as an opportunity. America could lead warring nations to a new world order. Selfish nationalism would give way to cooperative internationalism, power politics to collective security and Christian charity. Progressive faith in reason would triumph over irrational violence. Everything hinged on maintaining American neutrality. Only if the United States stood above the fray could it lead the way to a higher peace. Americans must remain "impartial in thought as well as action," Wilson insisted in 1914.

True impartiality was impossible. Americans of German and Austrian descent naturally sympathized with the Central Powers, as did Irish Americans, on the grounds of England's centuries-old domination of Ireland. The bonds of language, culture, and history tied most Americans to Great Britain. And gratitude for French aid during the American Revolution still lived. When the first American division marched through Paris years later, its commander stopped to salute Lafayette's tomb with the cry, "Nous voilà, Lafayette!"—Lafayette, we are here!

American economic ties to Britain and France also created a financial investment in Allied victory. After faltering briefly in 1914, the American economy boomed with the flood of war orders. The commanding British navy ensured that the Atlantic trade went mostly to the Allies. Between 1914 and 1916 trade with the Allies rocketed from $800 million to $3 billion. The Allies eventually borrowed more than $2 billion from American banks to finance their purchases. In contrast, a British naval blockade reduced American "contraband" commerce with the Central Powers to a trickle.

Few Americans cared. Although some progressives admired German social reforms, Americans generally saw Germany as an iron military power bent on conquest. Americans read British propaganda about spike-helmeted "Huns" raping Belgian women, bayoneting their children, pillaging their towns. Some of the stories were true, some embellished, some manufactured, but all worked against Germany in the United States.

The Diplomacy of Neutrality

Though Wilson insisted that all warring powers respect the right of neutrals to trade with any nation, he hesitated to retaliate against Great Britain's blockade of Germany. He recognized that the key to strangling Germany, a land power, was Britain's all-powerful navy and its iron blockade. Breaking it would cripple the Allied war effort. Meanwhile, Great Britain enforced its blockade with caution where the Americans were concerned. When Britain forbade the sale of cotton to the Central Powers in 1915, the British government bought American surpluses. It also agreed to compensate American firms for their losses when the war was over. By the end of 1915 the United States had all but accepted the British blockade of Germany, while American supplies continued to flow to England. True neutrality was dead. America became the quartermaster of the Allies.

Early in 1915, Germany turned to a dreadful new weapon to even the odds at sea. It mounted a counterblockade of Great Britain with two dozen submarines, or *Unterseebootes,* called U-boats. Before submarines, sea raiders usually gave crews and passengers the chance to escape. But if thin-skinned U-boats surfaced to obey these conventions, they risked being rammed or blown from the water. So submarines attacked without warning and spared no lives. Invoking international law and national honor, President Wilson threatened to hold Germany to "strict accountability" for any American losses. Germany promised not to sink any American ships, but soon a new issue grabbed the headlines: the safety of American passengers on belligerent vessels. *Submarine warfare*

On the morning of May 7, 1915, the British passenger liner *Lusitania* appeared out of a fog bank off the coast of Ireland on its way from New York to Southampton. The commander of the German U-20 could hardly believe his eyes: the giant ship filled the viewfinder of his periscope. He fired a single torpedo. A tremendous roar followed as one of the *Lusitania*'s main boilers exploded. The ship stopped dead in the water and listed so badly that lifeboats could barely be launched before the vessel sank. Nearly 1200 men, women, and children perished, including 128 Americans. *Lusitania*

Former president Theodore Roosevelt charged that such an "act of piracy" demanded war against Germany. Wilson, horrified at this "murder on the high seas," nevertheless urged restraint. "There is such a thing as a nation being so right that it does not need to convince others by force," he said a few days later. He sent notes of protest but did little more.

Secretary of State Bryan, an advocate of what he called "real neutrality," wanted equal protests lodged against both German submarines and British blockaders. He suspected that the *Lusitania* carried munitions as well as passengers and was thus a legitimate target. (Much later, evidence proved him right.) Relying on passengers for protection against attack, Bryan argued, was "like putting women and children in front of an army." Rather than endorse Wilson's policy, Bryan resigned.

Battling on two fronts in Europe, Germany wanted to keep the United States out of the war. But in February 1916 a desperate Germany declared submarine warfare on all *armed* vessels, belligerent or neutral. A month later a U-boat commander mistook the French steamer *Sussex* for a mine layer and torpedoed the unarmed vessel as it ferried passengers and freight across the English Channel. Several Americans were injured.

In mid-April, Wilson issued an ultimatum. If Germany refused to stop sinking nonmilitary vessels, the United States would break off diplomatic relations. War would surely follow. Without enough U-boats to control the seas, Germany agreed to Wilson's terms, all but abandoning its counterblockade. This *Sussex* pledge gave Wilson *Sussex pledge* a great victory but carried a grave risk. If German submarines resumed unrestricted attacks, the United States would have to go to war. "Any little German [U-boat] commander can put us into the war at any time," Wilson admitted to his cabinet.

Peace, Preparedness, and the Election of 1916

While hundreds of young Yanks slipped across the border to enlist in the Canadian army, most Americans agreed neutrality was the wisest course. Before the war a peace movement had taken seed in the United States, nourished in 1910 by a gift of $10 million from Andrew Carnegie. In 1914 social reformers Jane Addams, Charlotte Perkins Gilman, and Lillian Wald founded the Women's International League for Peace and Freedom and the American Union Against Militarism. Calling on Wilson to convene a peace conference, they lobbied for open diplomacy, disarmament, an end to colonial empires, and an international organization to settle disputes. In time these aims would become the core of Wilson's peace plan.

Pacifists might condemn the war, but Republicans and corporate leaders argued that the nation was woefully unprepared to keep peace. The army numbered only 80,000 men in 1914, the navy just 37 battleships and a handful of new "dreadnoughts," or supercruisers. Advocates of "preparedness" called for a navy larger than Great Britain's, an army of millions of reservists, and universal military training.

By the end of 1915, frustration with German submarines led Wilson to join the preparedness cause. He toured the country promoting preparedness and promised a "navy second to none." In Washington, he pressed Congress to double the army, increase the National Guard, and begin construction of the largest navy in the world. To foot the bill progressives pushed through new graduated taxes on higher incomes and on estates as well as additional levies on corporate profits.

Whoever paid for it, most Americans were thinking of preparedness for peace, not war, in 1916. The Democrats discovered the political power of peace early in the presidential campaign. As their convention opened in St. Louis in June, the keynote speaker began what he expected to be a dull description of Wilson's recent diplomatic maneuvers—only to have the crowd roar back in each case, "What did we do? What did we do?" The speaker knew the answer and shouted it back: "We didn't go to war! We didn't go to war!" The next day Wilson was renominated by acclamation. "He Kept Us Out of War" became his campaign slogan.

"He Kept Us Out of War"

The Republicans had already nominated Charles Evans Hughes, the former governor of New York. He endorsed "straight and honest" neutrality and peace. But despite his moderate stand, Democrats succeeded in painting Hughes as a warmonger, partly because Theodore Roosevelt had rattled his own sabers so loudly. As the election approached, Democrats took out full-page advertisements in newspapers across the country: "If You Want WAR, Vote for HUGHES! If You Want Peace with Honor VOTE FOR WILSON!"

As the polls closed on election day, Wilson squeaked out a paper-thin victory. He carried the South and key states in the Midwest and West on a tide of prosperity, progressive reform, and, most of all, promises of peace. As the British ambassador reported, "Americans desire nothing so much as to keep out of war."

Wilson's Final Peace Offensive

Twice since 1915 Wilson had sent his trusted adviser Edward House to Europe to negotiate a peace among the warring powers, and twice House had failed. With the

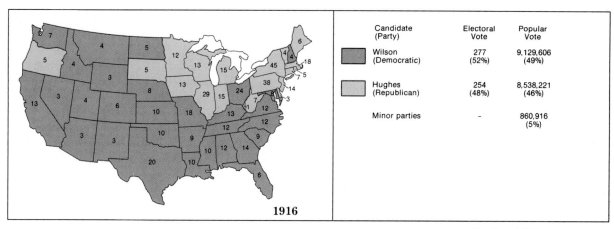

Candidate (Party)	Electoral Vote	Popular Vote
Wilson (Democratic)	277 (52%)	9,129,606 (49%)
Hughes (Republican)	254 (48%)	8,538,221 (46%)
Minor parties	–	860,916 (5%)

1916

Election of 1916

election over, Wilson opened his final peace offensive. But when he asked the belligerents to state their terms for a cease-fire, neither side responded. Frustrated, fearful, and genuinely agonized, Wilson called for "peace without victory": no victor, no vanquished, no embittering division of the spoils of war, only "a peace among equals," he said in January 1917.

As Wilson spoke, a fleet of U-boats was cruising toward the British Isles. Weeks earlier German military leaders had persuaded the Kaiser to take one last desperate gamble to starve the Allies into submission. On January 31, 1917, the German ambassador in Washington announced that unrestricted submarine warfare would resume the next day.

Wilson's dream of keeping the country from war collapsed. He asked Congress for authority to arm merchant ships and early in February severed relations with Germany. Then British authorities handed him a bombshell—an intercepted telegram from the German foreign secretary, Arthur Zimmermann, to the Kaiser's ambassador in Mexico. In the event of war with the United States, the ambassador was instructed to offer Mexico guns, money, and its "lost territory in Texas, New Mexico, and Arizona" to attack the United States. Already frustrated by Pancho Villa's raids across the U.S.-Mexican border, Wilson angrily released the Zimmermann telegram to the press. Soon after, he ordered gun crews aboard merchant ships and directed them to shoot U-boats on sight.

Zimmermann telegram

The momentum of events now propelled a reluctant United States toward war. On March 12 U-boats torpedoed the American merchant vessel *Algonquin*. On March 15, a revolution in Russia toppled Czar Nicholas II. A key ally was crumbling from within. By the end of the month U-boats had sunk nearly 600,000 tons of Allied and neutral shipping. For the first time reports came to Washington of cracking morale in the Allied ranks.

On April 2, 1917, accompanied by armed cavalry, Wilson rode down Pennsylvania Avenue and trudged up the steps of the Capitol. He delivered to Congress a stirring war message, full of idealistic purpose. "We shall fight for the things we have always carried nearest our hearts—for democracy, for the right of those who submit to authority to have a voice in their own governments, for the rights and liberties of small nations."

Pacifists held up the war resolution until it finally passed on April 6, Good Friday. Six senators and 50 House members opposed it, including the first woman in Congress, Jeannette Rankin of Montana. Cultural, economic, and historical ties

Jeannette Rankin

to the Allies, along with the German campaign of submarine warfare, had tipped the country toward war. Wilson had not wanted it, but now the battlefield seemed the only path to a higher peace.

War and Society

In 1915 the German zeppelin LZ-38, hovering at 8000 feet, dropped a load of bombs that killed seven Londoners. For the first time in history, civilians died in an air attack. Few aerial bombardments occurred during the First World War, but they signaled the growing importance of the home front in modern combat. Governments not only fielded armies but also mobilized industry, controlled labor, even rationed food. In the United States, traditions of cooperation and volunteerism helped government to organize the home front and the battle front, often in ways that were peculiarly progressive.

The Slaughter of Stalemate

Trench warfare

While the United States debated entry into the Great War, the Allies were coming perilously close to losing it. Following the German assault in 1914, the war had settled into a grisly stalemate. A continuous, immovable front stretched from Flanders in the north to the border of Switzerland in the south. Troops dug ditches, six to eight feet deep and four to five feet wide, to escape bullets, grenades, and artillery. Twenty-five thousand miles of these "trenches"—enough to circle the globe—slashed a muddy scar across Europe. Men lived in them for years, prey to disease, lice, and a plague of rats.

War in the machine age gave the advantage to the defense. When soldiers bravely charged "over the top" of the trenches, they were shredded by machine

The ideal of neat, sharply defined spaces for living and fighting is exemplified by these model trenches in northern France (left). Trench warfare, wrote one general, was "marked by uniform formations, the regulation of space and time by higher commands down to the smallest details . . . fixed distances between units and individuals." The reality (right) was something else again.

guns that fired 600 rounds a minute. Poison gas choked them in their tracks. Giant howitzers lobbed shells on them from positions too distant to see. In the Battle of the Somme River in 1916 a million men were killed in just four months of fighting, all to enable the British army to advance barely seven miles. Only late in the war did new armored "landships"—code-named "tanks"—return the advantage to the offense by surmounting the trench barriers with their caterpillar treads.

By then Vladimir Lenin was speeding home to Russia aboard a special train provided by the Germans. Lenin had been exiled to Switzerland during the early stages of the Russian Revolution but returned to lead his Bolshevik ("majority" in Russian) party to power in November 1917. Soon the Bolshevik-controlled government negotiated a separate peace with Germany, which promptly transferred a million of its soldiers to the western front for the coming spring offensive.

"You're in the Army Now"

The Allies' plight forced the U.S. Army into a crash program to send a million soldiers to Europe by the spring of 1918. The United States had barely 180,000 men in uniform. Volunteers rushed to recruitment offices, especially in ethnic communities, where Mexican Americans enlisted in numbers proportionally higher than any other group. But they were not enough.

To raise the necessary force, Congress passed the Selective Service Act in May 1917. Young men between the ages of 20 and 30 would be conscripted into the armed forces. Feelings over forced military service ran high. "There is precious little difference between a conscript [draftee] and a convict," protested the House Speaker in 1917. Progressives were more inclined to see military service as an opportunity to unite America and promote democracy: "Universal [military] training will jumble the boys of America all together, . . . smashing all the petty class distinctions that now divide, and prompting a brand of real democracy."

At ten in the morning on July 20, 1917, Secretary of War Newton Baker tied a blindfold over his eyes, reached into a huge glass bowl, and drew the first number in the new draft lottery. Some 24 million men were already registered. Almost 3 million were drafted; another 2 million volunteered. Most were white and young, between the ages of 21 and 31. Some 20,000 women served as clerks, telephone operators, and nurses. In a nation of immigrants, nearly one draftee in five was born in another country. Training often aimed at educating and Americanizing ethnic recruits. In special "development battalions" drill sergeants barked out orders while volunteers from the YMCA taught American history and English.

Like Mexican Americans, African Americans volunteered in disproportionately high numbers. They quickly filled the four all-black army and eight National Guard units already in existence. They were also granted fewer exemptions from the draft than white Americans were. Only 10 percent of the population, blacks made up 13 percent of all draftees. Abroad, where 200,000 black troops served in France, just one in five (compared with two of every three whites) was permitted in combat. Southern Democrats in Congress had opposed training African Americans to arms, fearful of the prospect of putting "arrogant, strutting representatives of black

With hostility remaining high between Mexico and the United States after President Wilson sent U.S. troops into Mexico, many Mexican laborers returned to Mexico rather than be drafted into a foreign army whose goals they did not share. On the other hand, Mexican Americans, especially those whose families had long lived in the United States, enlisted in the U.S. Army. Felix Sanchez of New Mexico was one such recruit.

soldiery in every community." But four regiments of the all-black 93rd Division, brigaded with the French army, were among the first Americans in the trenches and among the most decorated units in the U.S. Army.

Houston riot

Racial violence sometimes flared among the troops, notably in Houston in the summer of 1917. Harassed by white soldiers and by the city's Jim Crow laws, seasoned black regulars rioted and killed 17 white civilians. Their whole battalion was disarmed and sent under arrest to New Mexico. Thirteen troopers were condemned to death and hanged within days, too quickly for appeals even to be filed.

Progressive reformers did not miss the chance to put the social sciences to work in the army. Most recruits had fewer than seven years of education, yet they had to be classified and assigned quickly to units. Psychologists saw the chance to use new intelligence tests to help the army and prove their own theories about the value of "IQ" (intelligence quotient) in measuring the mind. In fact, these new "scientific" IQ tests often measured little more than class and cultural origins. Questions such as "Who wrote 'The Raven'?" exposed background rather than intelligence. More than half the Russian, Italian, and Polish draftees and almost 80 percent of blacks showed up as "inferior." The army stopped the testing program in January 1919, but schools across the country adopted it after the war, reinforcing many ethnic and racial prejudices.

On the home front, moral crusaders waged a war against sin, often pursuing old reforms with the help of mushrooming patriotism. Temperance leaders pressured the War Department to prohibit the sale of liquor to anyone in uniform in the vicinity of training camps. Alcohol would only impair a soldier's ability to fight. The army also declared war on venereal disease. "A Soldier who gets a dose is a Traitor!" warned one poster. The Commission on Training Camp Activities produced thousands of pamphlets, films, and lectures on the dangers of sexual misconduct. The drive constituted the first serious sex education many young Americans had ever received.

Mobilizing the Economy

To equip, feed, and transport an army of nearly 5 million demanded a national effort. The production of even a single ammunition shell brought components from every section of the country (plus vital nitrates from Chile) to assembly plants in New Jersey, Virginia, and Pennsylvania and from there to military installations or Atlantic ports.

At the Treasury Department, Secretary William Gibbs McAdoo fretted over how to finance the war, which cost, finally, $32 billion. The old revenue base of excise (luxury) taxes and customs duties gave way to a new one of taxes on incomes and profits. And with the reduction of the minimum level of taxable income to $1000, the number of Americans paying taxes jumped tenfold, from 437,000 in 1916 to 4,425,000 in 1918.

New taxes financed about a third of all war costs. The rest came from the sale of "Liberty" and "Victory" bonds and war savings certificates. At huge bond drives, movie stars Douglas Fairbanks and Mary Pickford, along with other celebrities, exhorted Americans to buy bonds. Boy Scouts sold them under the slogan "Every Scout to Save a Soldier." All five bond issues were oversubscribed, but more than money was at stake. The fund-raising campaign was also designed to raise patriotism. "Every person who refuses to subscribe," Treasury Secretary McAdoo warned a California audience, "is a friend of Germany." Meanwhile, the Federal Reserve

System expanded the money supply to make borrowing easier. The national debt, which had stood at $2 billion in 1917, soared to $20 billion only three years later.

With sweeping grants of authority provided by Congress, President Wilson constructed a massive bureaucracy to manage the home front. What emerged was a more managed economy, ironically similar to the New Nationalism envisioned by Theodore Roosevelt. Nearly 5000 new executive agencies employed business leaders from mammoth machinery makers John Deere and Evinrude as well as other corporate giants, the readiest source of expert managers. For a nominal "dollar a year," these executives served their country and built a partnership between big business and government. Industrial and trade associations as well as professional associations of engineers and scientists tied industry and science to a web of federal agencies. Antitrust suits, recalled one official, were simply put "to sleep until the war was over."

Under the leadership of Wall Street wizard Bernard Baruch, a War Industries Board (WIB) coordinated production through networks of industrial and trade associations. Though it had the authority to order firms to comply, the WIB relied instead on persuasion through publicity and "cost-plus" contracts that covered all costs, plus a guaranteed profit. When businesses balked—as when Henry Ford refused to accept government curbs on the manufacture of civilian automobiles— Baruch could twist arms. In this case, he threatened to have the army run Ford's factories. Ford quickly reversed himself. Overall, corporate profits tripled and production soared during the war years.

War Industries Board

The Food Administration encouraged farmers to grow more and citizens to eat less wastefully. Herbert Hoover, who had saved starving refugees as chairman of the Commission for Relief in Belgium in 1914, was appointed administrator. Like the WIB, the Food Administration mobilized what Hoover called "the spirit of self-sacrifice." Huge publicity campaigns promoted "wheatless" and "meatless" days each week and encouraged families to plant "victory" gardens. Stirred by high commodity prices, farmers brought more marginal lands into cultivation, and their real income increased 25 percent.

A Fuel Administration met the army's energy needs by increasing production and limiting domestic consumption. Transportation snarls required more drastic action. In December 1917 the U.S. Railroad Administration took over rail lines for the duration of the war. Government coordination, together with a new system of permits, got freight moving and kept workers happy. Federally imposed "daylight savings time" stretched the workday and saved fuel as well. Rail workers saw their wages grow by $300 million. Railroad unions won recognition, an eight-hour day, and a grievance procedure. For the first time in decades labor unrest subsided, and the trains ran on schedule.

The modern bureaucratic state received a powerful boost during the 18 months of American participation in the war. Accelerating trends that were already under way, hundreds of federal agencies centralized authority as they cooperated with business and labor to mount an unprecedented war effort. The number of federal employees more than doubled between 1916 and 1918, to over 850,000. The wartime bureaucracy was quickly dismantled at the end of the war, but it set an important precedent for the growth of government.

Bureaucratic state

War Work

The war benefited working men and women, though not as much as it benefited their employers. Government contracts guaranteed high wages, an eight-hour day, and equal pay for comparable work. To encourage people to stay on the job, federal contracting agencies set up special classes to teach employers the new science of personnel management in order to supervise workers more efficiently and humanely. American industry moved one step closer to the "welfare capitalism" of the 1920s, with its promises of profit sharing, company unions, and personnel departments to forestall worker discontent.

National War Labor Board

Personnel management was not always enough to guarantee industrial peace. In 1917 American workers called over 4000 strikes, the largest annual outbreak in American history. To keep factories running smoothly, President Wilson created the National War Labor Board (NWLB) early in 1918. The NWLB arbitrated more than 1000 labor disputes, helped to increase wages, established overtime pay, and supported the principle of equal pay for women. In return for pledges not to strike, the board guaranteed the rights of unions to organize and bargain collectively. Membership in the American Federation of Labor jumped from 2.7 million in 1914 to nearly 4 million by 1919.

Women in the workforce

As doughboys went abroad, the war brought nearly a million more women into the labor force. Most were young and single. Sometimes they took over jobs once held by men as railroad engineers, drill press operators, and electric lift truck drivers. Here, too, government tried to mediate between labor and management. In 1917 the Labor Department opened the Women in Industry Service (WIS) to recommend guidelines for using female labor. Among the most important were an eight-hour day, rest periods and breaks for meals, and equal pay for equal work. Most women never worked under such conditions, but for the first time, the federal government tried to upgrade their working conditions.

The prewar trend toward higher-paying jobs for women intensified. Most still earned less than the men they replaced as they moved into clerical and light industrial work. And some of the most spectacular gains in defense and government work evaporated after the war as male veterans returned and the country demobilized. Tens of thousands of army nurses, defense workers, and war administrators lost their jobs. Agencies such as the Women's Service Section of the Railroad Administration, which fought sexual harassment and discrimination, simply went out of business.

The constraints of war brought more women than ever into the job market. These women work on a production line manufacturing bullets. The novelty of the situation seems evident from the fashionable high-heeled high-button shoes that they wear—ill suited to the conditions in an armaments plant.

Women in war work nonetheless helped to energize a number of women's causes and organizations. Radical suffragist Alice Paul and others who had protested against the war now argued for women's rights, including the right to vote, on the basis of it. As women worked side by side with men in wartime factories and offices, in nursing stations at home or at the front, and in patriotic and other volunteer organizations, they could argue more convincingly for both economic and political equality. One step in that direction came after the war with the ratification of the Nineteenth Amendment in 1919 granting women the right to vote (page 721).

Great Migrations

War work sparked massive migrations of laborers. As the fighting abroad choked off immigration and the draft depleted the workforce, factory owners scoured the country and beyond for willing workers. Pressed by railroads and large-scale farmers, Congress waived immigration requirements in 1917 for agricultural workers from Mexico. A year later, the waiver was extended to workers on railroads, in mines, and on government construction projects.

Latino migrations

Industrial cities, no matter how small, soon swelled with newcomers, many of them Mexican and Mexican American. Between 1917 and 1920, some 50,000 Mexicans legally crossed the border into Texas, California, New Mexico, and Arizona. At least another 100,000 entered illegally. Some Mexican Americans left the segregated barrios and farmlands of the West, pushed out by this cheaper labor from Mexico, and migrated to Chicago, Omaha, and other midwestern cities. Mexican *colonias,* or communities, sprang up across the industrial heartland. But most Mexicans and Mexican Americans continued to work on the farms and ranches of the Southwest, where they were freed from military service by the deferment granted to all agricultural labor.

Northern labor agents fanned out across the rural South to recruit young African Americans, while black newspapers like the Chicago *Defender* summoned them up to the "Land of Hope." Over the war years more than 400,000 moved to the booming industrial centers of the North. Largely unskilled and semiskilled, they worked in the steel mills of Pennsylvania, the war plants of Massachusetts, the brickyards of New Jersey. Southern towns were decimated by the drain. Finally, under pressure from southern politicians, the U.S. Employment Service suspended its program to assist blacks moving north.

African Americans

These migrations—of African Americans into the army as well as into the city— aggravated racial tensions. Lynching parties murdered 38 black southerners in 1917 and 58 in 1918. In 1919, after the war ended, more than 70 African Americans were hung, some still in uniform. Housing shortages and job competition helped spark race riots across the North.

In almost every city black citizens, stirred by war rhetoric of freedom and democracy, showed new militancy by fighting back. In mid-1917 some 40 black and 9 white Americans died when East St. Louis erupted in racial violence. During the "red summer" of 1919, blood flowed in the streets of Washington, D.C., Omaha, Nebraska, New York City, and Chicago, where thousands of African Americans were burned out of their homes and hundreds injured. "The Washington riot gave me the *thrill that comes once in a life time,*" wrote a young black woman in 1919. "At last our men had stood like men, struck back, were no longer dumb driven cattle."

Propaganda and Civil Liberties

"Once lead this people into war," President Wilson warned before American entry into the First World War, "and they'll forget there ever was such a thing as tolerance." Americans succumbed to war hysteria, but they had help. Wilson knew how reluctant Americans had been to enter the war, and he created the Committee on Public Information (CPI) to boost American commitment to the war.

Committee on Public Information

Under George Creel, a California journalist, the CPI launched "a fight for the *minds* of men, for the conquest of their convictions." A zealous publicity campaign produced 75 million pamphlets, patriotic "war expositions" attended by 10 million people in two dozen cities, and colorful war posters, including James Flagg's famous

"I Want *You* for the U.S. Army." Seventy-five thousand fast-talking "Four-Minute Men" invaded movie theaters, lodge halls, schools, and churches to keep patriotism at "white heat" with four minutes of war tirades. The CPI organized "Loyalty Leagues" in ethnic communities and sponsored parades and rallies, among them a much-publicized immigrant "pilgrimage" to the birthplace of George Washington.

100 percent Americanism

The division between patriotism and intolerance proved impossible to maintain. As war fever rose, voluntary patriotism blossomed into an orgy of "100 percent Americanism" that distrusted all aliens, radicals, pacifists, and dissenters. German Americans became special targets. In Iowa the governor made it a crime to speak German in public. Hamburgers were renamed "Salisbury steak"; German measles, "liberty measles." When a mob outside St. Louis lynched a naturalized German American who had tried to enlist in the navy, a jury found the leaders not guilty.

Espionage and Sedition acts

Congress gave hysteria more legal bite by passing the Espionage and Sedition acts of 1917 and 1918. Both set out harsh penalties for any actions that hindered the war effort or that could be viewed as even remotely unpatriotic. Following their passage, 1500 citizens were arrested for offenses that included denouncing the draft, criticizing the Red Cross, and complaining about wartime taxes.

Radical groups received especially severe treatment. The Industrial Workers of the World (IWW), a militant labor union centered in western states, saw the war as a battle among capitalists and threatened to strike mining and lumber companies in protest. Federal agents raided the Chicago headquarters of the IWW—familiarly known as the "Wobblies"—and arrested 113 of its leaders in September 1917. The crusade destroyed the union.

Similarly, the Socialist party stridently opposed the "capitalist" war. In response, the postmaster general banned a dozen Socialist publications from the mail, though

The Final German Offensive and Allied Counterattack, 1918 On the morning of March 21, 1918, the Germans launched a spring offensive designed to cripple the Allies. Sixty-three German divisions sliced through Allied lines for the first time since 1914 and plunged to within 50 miles of Paris. The tide turned in July, when the Germans were stopped at the Marne. The Allied counterattack, with notable American successes at Château-Thierry, Belleau Wood, Saint-Mihiel, and Meuse-Argonne, broke the German war effort.

the party was a legal organization that had elected mayors, municipal officials, and members of Congress. In June 1918 government agents arrested Eugene V. Debs, the Socialist candidate in the presidential election of 1912, for attacking the draft. A jury found him guilty of sedition and sentenced him to 10 years in jail. Running for the presidency from his jail cell in 1920, Debs received nearly 1 million votes.

The Supreme Court condoned the wartime assault on civil liberties. In *Schenck v. United States* (1919), the Court unanimously affirmed the use of the Espionage Act to convict a Socialist party officer who had mailed pamphlets urging resistance to the draft. Free speech had limits, wrote Justice Oliver Wendell Holmes, and the pamphlets created "a clear and present danger" to a nation at war. In *Abrams v. United States* (1919) the Court upheld the verdict against Russian immigrant Jacob Abrams, whose pamphlets had denounced an American intervention in Russia to fight the Bolsheviks. Although Holmes saw no "clear and present danger," the majority ruled that the pamphlets tended to discourage the American war effort and thus violated the Sedition Act.

The horror of battle is graphically captured in this detail from a painting by Georges Leroux titled *L'Enfer*. The figures in the center, with helmets and gas masks, crouch in what looks like a muddy shell hole as they try to escape artillery fire and poison gas. "My impression," according to one report of a battle, "was that if the men at the heads of all the warring governments had to spend a few hours in the hell on earth that was going on there, the war would be over in short order."

Over There

The first American doughboys landed in France in June 1917, but they saw no battle. Not until November would the first Americans die in action. General John Pershing held back his raw troops until they could receive more training. He also separated them in a distinct American Expeditionary Force to preserve their identity and avoid Allied disagreements over strategy.

In the spring of 1918, as the Germans pushed within 50 miles of Paris, Pershing rushed 70,000 American troops to the front. American units helped block the Germans both at the town of Château-Thierry and a month later, in June, at Belleau Wood. At Belleau, it cost half their force to drive the enemy from the woods. Two more German attacks, one at Amiens, the other just east of the Marne River, ended in costly German retreats. On September 12, 1918, half a million American soldiers and a smaller number of French troops overran the German stronghold at Saint-Mihiel in four days.

With their army in retreat and civilian morale low, Germany's leaders sought an armistice. They hoped to negotiate terms along the lines laid out by Woodrow Wilson in a speech to Congress in January 1918. Wilson's bright vision of peace encompassed his "Fourteen Points." The key provisions called for open diplomacy, free seas and free trade, disarmament, democratic self-rule, and an "association of nations" to guarantee collective security. It was nothing less than a new world order to end selfish nationalism, imperialism, and war.

Wilson's Fourteen Points

Allied leaders were not impressed. "President Wilson and his Fourteen Points bore me," French premier Georges Clemenceau said. "Even God Almighty has only ten!" But Wilson's idealistic platform was also designed to save the Allies deeper embarrassment. Almost as soon as it came to power in 1917, the new Bolshevik government in Moscow began publishing secret treaties from the czar's archives. They revealed that the Allies had gone to war for territory and colonies, not the high principles they claimed. Wilson's Fourteen Points now gave their cause a nobler purpose.

Among Allied nations, Wilson's ideals stirred the hearts of ordinary citizens more than those of their leaders. But with public support, Wilson believed he could carry the peace, daring his European allies to accept his vision or risk defeat at the polls. On October 6, 1918, liberals in Germany gave him the chance when a telegram arrived from Berlin requesting an immediate truce on the basis of the Fourteen Points. Within a month Turkey and Austria surrendered. Early in November the Kaiser was overthrown and fled to neutral Holland. On November 11, 1918, just before dawn, German officers filed into Allied headquarters in a converted railroad car near Compiègne, France, and signed the armistice.

Of the 2 million Americans who served in France, some 116,500 died. Over 200,000 were wounded. By comparison, the war claimed 1.8 million Germans, 1.7 million Russians, 1.4 million French, 1.2 million Austro-Hungarians, and nearly a million Britons. The American contribution had nonetheless been crucial, providing vital convoys at sea and fresh, confident troops on land. The United States emerged from the war stronger than ever. Europe, on the other hand, looked forward—as one newspaper put it—to "Disaster . . . Exhaustion . . . Revolution."

The Influenza Pandemic of 1918–1919

In the months before the armistice, a scourge more lethal than war began to engulf the globe. It started innocently enough. At Fort Riley, Kansas, on the morning of March 11, 1918, company cook Albert Mitchell reported to the infirmary on sick call. His head and muscles ached, his throat was sore, and he had a low-grade fever.

It was the flu, dangerous for infants and the old but ordinarily no threat to a robust young man like Mitchell. By noon, 107 soldiers had reported symptoms. Within a week, the number had jumped to over 500. Cases of the flu were being reported in virtually every state in the Union, even on the isolated island of Alcatraz in San Francisco Bay. And robust young adults Mitchell's age were dying from it.

Cartoon by D. C. Boonzaier in *De Burger*, 16/10/1918

In October 1918 artist D. C. Boonzaier drew this grim cartoon of the Spanish flu— *Spaanse Griep*—when it came to South Africa. In his diary Boonzaier spoke of "the presence of some universal calamity, from which there was no escape. Death stalked by your side incessantly, you looked into its face wherever you turned."

The discovery that influenza was a virus was still years away. This eruption probably had its origin in birds, who passed it to pigs, who passed it to humans. It may have been spread initially by brush fires set on the Kansas plains, which scattered microbes from fecal matter and the earthworms that ingested it. Once it was airborne, there was virtually no stopping it.

The first wave of flu produced few deaths in the United States. But as the virus mutated over the next year, its victims experienced more distressing symptoms: vomiting, dizziness, labored breathing, incessant sweating. Eventually victims drowned in their own bodily fluids from the pneumonia that accompanied the infection.

Soldiers and others living in close quarters were especially vulnerable, and for reasons still unknown, so were young adults 20 to 34 years old, precisely the ages of most in the services. For every 50 people infected, 1 died. In the United States alone, the death toll rose to at least 600,000, more than the American battle deaths in World War I, World War II, the Korean War, and the war in Vietnam combined.

Ironically, the United States was the country least affected by this worldwide epidemic, called a "pandemic." American soldiers seem to have carried the disease to Europe, where it jumped from one country to another in the spring and summer of 1918. French troops and civilians soon were suffering from it, then British and Germans. General Eric von Ludendorf counted the flu as one of the causes of the failure of the final German offensive in July 1918, which almost won the war for Germany. In Spain, it infected as many as 8 million people.

With steamships and railroads carrying people all over the globe, virtually no place was safe. By the summer of 1918, the virus had leapt from North America and Europe to Asia and Japan; by fall, to Africa and South America. As far north as the Russian city of Archangel, officials were reporting 30 influenza deaths a day by October 1918. In densely packed India, one account claimed that at least 12 million perished from influenza. Six of every ten Inuit died from it in the villages north of Nome, Alaska, and on the Samoan islands in the Pacific, nearly 90 percent of the population caught the flu.

Global spread of the pandemic

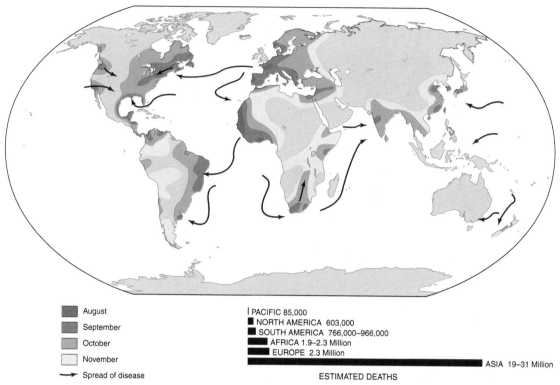

■ August	| PACIFIC 85,000
■ September	■ NORTH AMERICA 603,000
October	■ SOUTH AMERICA 766,000–966,000
November	AFRICA 1.9–2.3 Million
→ Spread of disease	EUROPE 2.3 Million
	ASIA 19–31 Million

ESTIMATED DEATHS

Spread of Influenza Pandemic: Second Stage, Autumn 1918 After the milder outbreak in the spring of 1918, a more deadly form of influenza spread outward from the coast of France at the beginning of August. The worldwide transportation system quickly dispersed the disease, sending it first to the western coast of Africa (beginning at Freetown, Liberia) and the eastern coast of North America (at Boston). The disease reached virtually all continents, although Australia's strict quarantine delayed entrance of the flu there until 1919. By far, the continent hardest hit was Asia, where anywhere from 12 to 20 million died in India alone. American mortality, though serious, totaled only about 550,000.

Sixteen months after Albert Mitchell had first reported to sick call, the flu vanished as quickly and mysteriously as it had appeared. Conservative estimates placed the number of dead worldwide at 25 million, making the influenza pandemic of 1918–1919 the most lethal outbreak of disease on an annual basis in human history. Global war had helped spread this particular disease, but improvements in transportation and two centuries of migrations had also spawned pandemics. As automobiles and airplanes continued to shrink the globe, similar pandemics, though less deadly, would be repeated in years to come.

The Lost Peace

As the USS *George Washington* approached the coast of France in mid-December 1918 the mist suddenly lifted in an omen of good hope. Woodrow Wilson had come to represent the United States at the Paris peace conference at Versailles, once the glittering palace of Louis XIV. A world of problems awaited him and the other Allied leaders. Europe had been shelled into ruin and scarred with the debris of war. Fifty million people lay dead or maimed from the fighting. Throughout the Balkans and the old Turkish empire, ethnic rivalries, social chaos, and revolution loomed.

With the old world order so evidently in shambles, Wilson felt the need to take vigorous action. Thus the president handpicked the peace commission of experts that accompanied him. It included economists, historians, geographers, and political scientists—but not a single member of the Republican-controlled Senate. What promised to make peace negotiations easier, however, created a crippling liability in Washington, where Republicans cast a hostile eye on the mirrored halls of Versailles.

The Treaty of Versailles

Everywhere he went, cheers greeted the president. In Paris 2 million people showered him with flowers. In Italy they hailed him as the "peacemaker from America." And Wilson believed them, unaware of how determined the victors were to punish the vanquished Germans. David Lloyd George of England, Georges Clemenceau of France, Vittorio Orlando of Italy, and Wilson made up the Big Four at the conference that included some 27 nations. War had united them; now peacemaking threatened to divide them.

Wilson's sweeping call for reform had taken Allied leaders by surprise. Hungry for new colonies, eager to see Germany crushed and disarmed, they had already drawn up secret treaties dividing the territories of the Central Powers. Germany had offered to surrender on the basis of Wilson's Fourteen Points, but the Allies refused to accept them. When Wilson threatened to negotiate peace on his own, Allied leaders finally agreed—but only for the moment.

Noticeably absent when the peace conference convened in January 1919 were the Russians. None of the Western democracies had recognized the Bolshevik regime in Moscow out of fear that the communist revolution might spread. Instead, France and Britain were helping to finance a civil war to overthrow the Bolsheviks. Even Wilson had been persuaded to send a small number of American troops to join the Allied occupation of Murmansk in northern Russia and Vladivostok on the Sea of Japan. The Soviets would neither forget nor forgive this invasion of their soil.

Grueling peace negotiations forced Wilson to yield several of his Fourteen Points. Britain, with its powerful navy, refused even to discuss the issues of free trade and freedom of the seas. Wilson's "open diplomacy" was conducted behind closed doors by the Big Four. The only mention of disarmament involved Germany, which was permanently barred from rearming. Wilson's call for "peace without victory" gave way to a "guilt clause" that saddled Germany with responsibility for the war. Worse still, the victors imposed on the vanquished an impoverishing debt of $33 billion in reparations.

Wilson did achieve some successes. His pleas for national self-determination led to the creation of a dozen new states in Europe, including Yugoslavia, Hungary, and Austria. (Newly created Poland and Czechoslovakia, however, contained

Allied leaders convened the peace conference in the palace of Louis XIV at Versailles. Woodrow Wilson faces the painter, as British prime minister David Lloyd George and French premier Georges Clemenceau confer. On June 28, 1919, representatives of the new German republic were herded into the famed Hall of Mirrors, where they glumly signed the peace treaty they had no hand in writing. The Germans, observed one reporter, suffered a "horrible humiliation."

Daily Lives

TIME AND TRAVEL
The Doughboys Abroad

When Secretary of War Newton Baker drew the first number in a new draft lottery on July 20, 1917, the United States had barely 180,000 men in the service. By the time World War I ended in November 1918, nearly 2 million men had donned uniforms, learned the manual of arms and close order drill, and gone off to fight in Europe. For the first time the New World was invading the Old, and for most of those who went, it was their first trip from home.

Armed against the enemy, scrubbed and clothed, drilled until they dropped, the "doughboys" marched out of their training camps and up the gangplanks of the "Atlantic Ferry"—the ships that conveyed them to Europe. (Infantrymen were called "doughboys" for the "dough" of clay that soldiers had used to clean their white belts in the 1850s.) Each man was outfitted with a pack, a weapon, a set of uniforms, and a "safety" razor, a new device that quickly altered American shaving habits.

Some soldiers were fortunate enough to ship out on refitted luxury liners, but most made the voyage belowdecks in converted freighters, "the blackest, foulest, most congested hole that I ever set foot into," reported one private. A few died from anthrax in the horsehair of their new shaving brushes. It was a poignant taste of things to come. Disease killed more Americans than enemy fire did. Some 62,000 troops died of influenza and other diseases.

The first American troops, a division of army regulars and a battalion of marines, had arrived in France at the end of June 1917. Two months later the first volunteers landed, wearing spring

After months of training stateside, the American Expeditionary Force sailed to Europe on the troop ships of the "Atlantic Ferry." Most soldiers departed from Hoboken, New Jersey, and almost half made the journey aboard British vessels.

---

millions of ethnic Germans.) Former colonies gained new status as "mandates" of the victors, who were obligated to prepare them for independence. The old German and Turkish empires in the Middle East and Africa became the responsibility of France and England, while Japan took over virtually all German possessions in the Pacific north of the equator.

League of Nations

Wilson never lost sight of his main goal—a League of Nations. He had given so much ground precisely because he believed this new world organization would correct any mistakes in the peace settlement. As constituted, the League was composed of a general Body of Delegates, a select Executive Council, and a Court of International Justice. Members promised to submit all war-provoking disagreements to arbitration and to isolate aggressors by cutting off commercial and military trade. Article X (Wilson called it "the heart of the covenant") bound members to respect one another's independence and territory and to join together against attack. "It is definitely a guarantee of peace," the president told the delegates in February 1919.

parade uniforms and carrying just 10 rounds of ammunition apiece. They were squeezed into "40-and-8's"—French freight cars designed to hold 40 men and 8 horses—and carried inland to training areas.

With the United States at war for such a short time, most American soldiers spent more time in training and on leave than in the trenches. To keep the men from becoming restless, company commanders marched their troops against imaginary enemies in never-ending exercises. "Every hill in this vicinity has been captured or lost at least ten times," wrote one weary infantryman who had to keep training even after the armistice. Soldiers complained about "cooties" (lice) and food (so bad that many reported a 10 percent weight loss within weeks of arriving). Used to freewheeling individualism and equality, they positively hated military discipline.

Enlisted men groused about army life, but the Old World awed them. Paris was titillating, with women who danced the "Can-Can" and cried "oo-la-la." The antiquity of Europe struck the doughboys even more: "The church here is very, very old, probably built sometime in the 12th or 13th century. Saint Louis the Crusader, King of France, attended a service there on three occasions and Jeanne d'Arc was there several times." The Europeans seemed old and old-fashioned, too. Elderly women in black shawls of mourning often were the only ones left in shattered villages. "They still harvest with cradles and sickles," noted one soldier. Everything endorsed the American myth of the Old World as hidebound and worn and the New as modern and vital.

It was as if they had become crusaders, off on what one doughboy called "a glorious adventure" to save beleaguered Europe. Disillusion and discontent overcame British and French troops after years in the trenches, but most doughboys never fought long enough to lose their sense of wonder and delight. A year after the war ended a veteran wrote: "I know how we all cried to get back to the States. But now that we are here, I must admit for myself at least that I am lost and somehow strangely lonesome. These our own United States are truly artificial and bare. There is no romance or color here, nothing to suffer for and laugh at."

The Battle for the Treaty

Wilson left immediately for home to address growing opposition in Congress. In the off-year elections of 1918, voters unhappy with wartime controls, new taxes, and attacks on civil liberties had given both houses to the Republicans. A slim Republican majority in the Senate put Wilson's archrival, Henry Cabot Lodge of Massachusetts, in the chairman's seat of the all-important Foreign Relations Committee. "I never expected to hate anyone in politics with the hatred I feel toward Wilson," Lodge confessed.

While most of the country favored the League, Lodge was against it. For decades he had fought to preserve American freedom of action in foreign affairs. Now he worried that the League would force Americans to subject themselves to "the will of other nations." And he certainly did not want Democrats to win votes by taking credit for the treaty. Securing the signatures of enough senators to block any treaty, Lodge rose in the Senate just before midnight on March 3, 1919, to read a "round robin" resolution against the League. "Woodrow Wilson's League of Nations died in the Senate tonight," concluded the New York *Sun*.

Wilson formally presented the treaty in July. "Dare we reject it and break the heart of the world?" he asked the senators. Fourteen Republicans and two Democrats were happy to do just that. "Irreconcilable" opponents of internationalism, they vowed to kill "the unholy thing with the holy name." Twenty-three "strong reservationists," led by Lodge, sought to amend the treaty with major changes requiring yet another round of Allied negotiations. Twelve "mild reservationists" wanted minimal alterations, mainly interpretive in nature.

Wilson's only hope of winning the necessary two-thirds majority for passage of the treaty lay in compromise, but temperamentally he could not abide it. Worn out by the concessions already wrung from him in Paris, afflicted increasingly by numbing headaches and a twitch in his left eye, he resisted any more changes. Despite his doctor's warnings, Wilson took his case to the people in a month-long stump across the nation.

Wilson's stroke

In Pueblo, Colorado, a crowd of 10,000 heard perhaps the greatest oration of Wilson's career. He spoke of American soldiers killed in France and American boys whom the League one day would spare from death. Listeners wept openly. That evening, utterly exhausted, Wilson collapsed in a spasm of pain. On October 2, four days after being rushed to the White House, he fell to the bathroom floor, knocked unconscious by a stroke.

For six weeks Wilson could do no work at all and for months after worked little more than an hour a day. His second wife, Edith Bolling Wilson, handled the routine business of government along with the president's secretary and his doctor. The country knew nothing of the seriousness of his condition. Wilson recovered slowly but never fully. More and more the battle for the treaty consumed his fading energies.

On November 19 Lodge finally reported the treaty out of committee with 14 amendments to match Wilson's Fourteen Points. The most important asserted that the United States assumed no obligation under Article X to come to the aid of League members unless Congress consented. Wilson believed Lodge had delivered a "knife thrust at the heart of the treaty" and refused to accept any changes. Whatever ill will Lodge bore Wilson, his objections did not destroy the treaty but only weakened it by protecting the congressional prerogative to declare war.

Under orders from the president, Democrats joined Republicans and "Irreconcilables" to defeat the treaty with Lodge's reservations. An attempt to pass the unamended treaty failed. Although four-fifths of the senators favored it in some form, Wilson and Lodge refused to compromise. When the amended treaty came before the Senate in March 1920, enough Democrats broke from the president to produce a majority but not the required two-thirds. The Treaty of Versailles was dead, and loyal Democrats had been forced to deliver the killing blow. Not until July 1921 did Congress enact a joint resolution ending the war. The United States, which had fought separately from the Allies, made a separate peace as well.

Red Scare

Peace abroad did not bring peace at home. On May Day 1919, six months after the war ended, mobs in a dozen cities broke up Socialist parades, injured hundreds, and killed three people. Later that month, when a spectator at a Victory Loan rally in Washington refused to stand for the national anthem, a sailor shot him in the back. The stadium crowd applauded. On the floor of the Senate Kenneth

McKellar of Tennessee advocated sending citizens with radical beliefs to a penal colony on Guam.

The spontaneous violence and extremism occurred because Americans believed they were under attack. Millions of soldiers had returned home, now unemployed and looking for jobs. With prices rising and war regulations lifted, laborers were demanding higher wages and striking when they failed to get them. In Boston even the police walked off their jobs. When a strike by conservative trade unionists paralyzed Seattle for five days in January, Mayor Ole Hanson draped his car in an American flag and led troops through the streets in a show of force. Hanson blamed radicals, while Congress ascribed the national ills to Bolshevik agents inspired by the revolution in Russia.

The menace of radical subversion was entirely overblown. With Socialist Eugene Debs in prison, his dwindling party numbered only about 30,000. Radicals at first hoped that the success of the Russian Revolution would help reverse their fortunes in the United States. But most Americans found the prospect of "Bolshevik" agitators threatening, especially after March 1919, when the new Russian government formed the Comintern to spread revolution abroad. Furthermore, the Left itself splintered. In 1919 dissidents deserted the Socialists to form the more radical Communist Labor party. About the same time, a group of mostly Slavic radicals created a separate Communist party. Both organizations counted no more than 40,000 members.

On April 28 Mayor Hanson received a small brown parcel at his office, evidently another present from an admirer of his tough patriotism. It was a homemade bomb. Within days, 20 such packages were discovered, including ones sent to John D. Rockefeller, Supreme Court Justice Oliver Wendell Holmes, and Postmaster General Albert Burleson. On June 2 bombs exploded simultaneously in eight different cities. One of them demolished the front porch of A. Mitchell Palmer, the attorney general of the United States. The bomb thrower was blown to bits, but enough remained to identify him as an Italian anarchist from Philadelphia. Already edgy over Bolshevism and labor militancy, many Americans assumed that an organized conspiracy was being mounted to overthrow the government.

Palmer, a Quaker and a staunch progressive, hardened in the wake of the bombings. In November 1919 and again in January 1920, he launched raids in cities across the United States. In a single night in January, government agents invaded private homes, meeting halls, and pool parlors in 33 cities. They took 4000 people into custody without warrants, sometimes beating those who resisted. Many were Russians, some were communists, but most were victims of suspicion run amok. In Detroit, 300 innocent people were arrested and confined for a week, one day without food. Prisoners were marched through streets in chains, crammed into dilapidated jails, and held incommunicado without hearings. Over 200 aliens, most of whom had no criminal records, were deported to the Soviet Union.

Arrests continued at the rate of 200 a week through March. State after state passed new statutes outlawing radical unions. Local vigilance committees even screened the loyalty of schoolteachers. In Centralia, Washington, vigilantes spirited radical labor organizer Wesley Everest from jail, castrated him, and hanged him from the Chehalis River bridge as they riddled his body with bullets. The county coroner ruled it a suicide.

Such abuses of civil liberties finally provoked a backlash. After the New York legislature expelled five duly elected Socialists in 1919, responsible politicians—from former presidential candidate Charles Evans Hughes to Ohio senator Warren Harding—began to denounce the action. Assistant Secretary of Labor Louis Post refused to issue more deportation orders, and the "deportation delirium" ended early in 1920.

In September 1919 some 350,000 steelworkers struck for higher wages, recognition of their union, and a reduction in their 70-hour workweeks. Mill owners countered by hiring black strike-breakers and armed guards and by launching a potent publicity campaign that depicted the strike as a plot of "Red agitators." Here, armed police ride down strikers in Philadelphia.

Palmer finally overreached himself by predicting a revolutionary uprising for May 1, 1920. Buildings were put under guard and state militia called to readiness. Nothing happened. Four months later, when a wagonload of bombs exploded on Wall Street, Palmer blamed a Bolshevik conspiracy. Despite 35 deaths and more than 200 injuries, Americans saw it as the work of a few fanatic anarchists (which it probably was) and went about business as usual.

In early August 1914 the Panama Canal opened without fanfare, but no one could miss its significance: the new American empire now spanned the globe, stretching from the Caribbean to the Pacific and linked by a path between the seas. There were plans for a tremendous celebration in which the battleship *Oregon*, whose 1898 "race around the Horn" had inspired the idea of an American-owned canal, would lead a flotilla of ships through the locks. But the plans had to be scrapped, for in that fateful month of August, the old world order of spheres of influence, balances of power, military alliances, and imperial colonies collapsed into a world war.

When they finally entered it, the war changed Americans. They experienced a managed economy for the first time. Propaganda shaped diverse ethnic, racial, class, and gender differences into a uniform set of national issues. Such single-mindedness would not quickly disappear. War work drew millions from country to city, from farm to factory. The army mixed millions more. They learned to fight but also to read, to sleep in a bed, to eat regular meals, and to take regular baths. After seeing Europe, they returned like tourists in uniform to tell of its wonders. Americans became at once more worldly and more wary of the world.

Not for another 20 years would the United States assume a leading position in international affairs. The nation turned from idealistic crusades to remake the world to the practical business of getting and spending. At home the spirit of reform dimmed as a dynamic new era of prosperity dawned. Abroad an uneasy peace reigned in Europe and Asia. Yet within a decade both prosperity and peace would vanish, victims of the failure to establish a new global order.

chapter summary

The First World War marked the beginning of the end of the old world order of colonial imperialism, military alliances, and balances of power; it also marked a failed effort to establish a new world order based on the progressive ideals of international cooperation and collective security.

- Progressive diplomacy—whether through Theodore Roosevelt's big stick diplomacy, William Taft's dollar diplomacy, or Woodrow Wilson's missionary diplomacy—stressed moralism and order, championed "uplifting" nonwhites, and stretched presidential authority to its limits.

- With the outbreak of the First World War in 1914, Woodrow Wilson saw an opportunity for the United States to lead the world to a higher peace of international cooperation and collective security by remaining neutral and brokering the peace settlement.

- However, American sympathy for the Allies, heavy American investments in the Allies, and the German campaign of unrestricted submarine warfare finally drew the country into the war in 1917.

- Progressive faith in government, planning, efficiency, and publicity produced a greatly expanded bureaucratic state that managed the war effort on the home front.
  - The darker side of progressivism also flourished as the war transformed progressive impulses for assimilation and social control into campaigns for superpatriotism and conformity that helped to produce a postwar Red scare in 1919 and 1920.
  - Meanwhile, changes already under way, including more women in the labor force and migrations of African Americans and Mexican Americans from rural to urban America, vastly accelerated with the expansion of opportunities for war work.

- When the war ended, Wilson's hopes for "peace without victory" and a new world order, embodied in his Fourteen Points, were dashed when his European allies imposed a harsh settlement on Germany and the U.S. Senate failed to ratify the Treaty of Versailles.

interactive learning

The Primary Source Investigator CD-ROM offers the following materials related to this chapter:

- Interactive maps: **The United States in Latin America, 1895–1941 (M21); America in World War I (M23);** and **Spread of Influenza Pandemic: Second Stage, Autumn 1918 (M24)**

- A collection of primary sources exploring the First World War, including Woodrow Wilson's "Fourteen Points" speech on international policy. Several other sources capture the sharp social and political conflicts at home during and immediately after the war, including a recording of a popular anti-immigrant song, an image of sailors destroying a socialist flag, and a cartoon on literacy and voting.

additional reading

The diverse vectors of progressive diplomacy, as practiced by Theodore Roosevelt and Woodrow Wilson, are the subject of Howard K. Beale, *Theodore Roosevelt and the Rise of America to World Power* (1956), and Arthur Link, *Woodrow Wilson: Revolution,* *War, and Peace* (1968). Ernest R. May examines American prewar diplomacy and the policies of the Great Powers, especially Germany's U-boat campaign, in *The World War and American Isolation, 1914–1917* (1957). David M. Kennedy, *Over Here: The First World War and American Society* (1980), is the definitive account of mobilization and the home front, but see also Maurine W. Greenwald, *Women, War, and Work* (1980), a detailed look at the status of women, and Joel William Trotter Jr., *The Great Migration in Historical Perspective* (1991), a fine collection of essays that stresses gender and class in the wartime experience of African Americans. Frank

Freidel re-creates the horrors of trench warfare in *Over There: The Story of America's First Great Overseas Crusade* (1964). For African Americans on the battle front, see Arthur E. Barbeau and Henri Florette, *The Unknown Soldiers: Black American Troops in World War I* (1974). Robert Ferrell, *Woodrow Wilson and World War I* (1985), analyzes Wilson's wartime diplomacy, the peace negotiations, and the fate of the Treaty of Versailles. The most informed account of the influenza pandemic can be found in Alfred W. Crosby, *America's Forgotten Pandemic: The Influenza of 1918* (1989).

The debate over American entry into World War I has a long history. Early revisionist accounts emphasizing a financial conspiracy to bring the nation to war include Charles Beard, *The Open Door to War* (1934), and Charles C. Tansill, *America Goes to War* (1938). A good account from the school of realists, which is critical of Wilson's moral motives, is found in George Kennan, *American Diplomacy, 1900–1950* (rev. ed., 1971). For a fuller list of readings, see the Bibliography at www.mhhe.com/davidsonnation5.

significant events

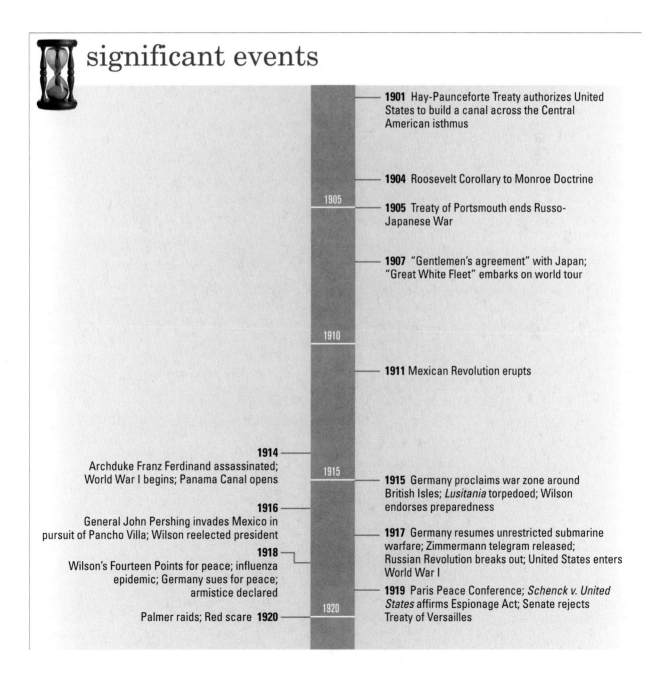

1901 Hay-Paunceforte Treaty authorizes United States to build a canal across the Central American isthmus

1904 Roosevelt Corollary to Monroe Doctrine

1905

1905 Treaty of Portsmouth ends Russo-Japanese War

1907 "Gentlemen's agreement" with Japan; "Great White Fleet" embarks on world tour

1910

1911 Mexican Revolution erupts

1914
Archduke Franz Ferdinand assassinated; World War I begins; Panama Canal opens

1915

1915 Germany proclaims war zone around British Isles; *Lusitania* torpedoed; Wilson endorses preparedness

1916
General John Pershing invades Mexico in pursuit of Pancho Villa; Wilson reelected president

1917 Germany resumes unrestricted submarine warfare; Zimmermann telegram released; Russian Revolution breaks out; United States enters World War I

1918
Wilson's Fourteen Points for peace; influenza epidemic; Germany sues for peace; armistice declared

1919 Paris Peace Conference; *Schenck v. United States* affirms Espionage Act; Senate rejects Treaty of Versailles

1920

Palmer raids; Red scare **1920**

GLOBAL ESSAY

THE PERILS OF DEMOCRACY

In the wake of World War I, the editors of the American progressive journal *The New Republic* despaired that "the war did no good to anybody. Those of its generation whom it did not kill, it crippled, wasted, or used up." With the specter of Russian Bolshevism looming, parliamentary governments across Europe struggled to establish what President Warren Harding in the United States called "normalcy": a mixture of material prosperity and political stability.

By the mid-1920s despair had given way to hope. The postwar recession had lifted in the United States, and Woodrow Wilson's vision of a world made safe for democracy no longer seemed a naive hope. In both political and material terms democracy seemed to be advancing almost everywhere. Great Britain eliminated restrictions on suffrage for men, and between 1920 and 1928 women gained the vote in both Britain and the United States. Hapsburg Germany transformed itself into the Weimar Republic, whose constitution provided universal suffrage and a bill of rights. Across central and eastern Europe, the new nations carved out of the old Russian and Austro-Hungarian empires attempted to create governments along similarly democratic lines. So did the previously independent Romania, Bulgaria, Greece, and Albania.

The winds of political reform blew from Europe across the Middle East through Asia. Some Asians, like Mao Zedong in China and Ho Chi Minh in Indochina (Vietnam), saw in communism the means to liberate their peoples from imperialist rule. But even Asian Marxists aligned themselves with the powerful force of nationalism. In India, the Congress party formed by Mohandas K. Gandhi united socialists and powerful industrial capitalists. Through tactics of nonviolence and boycotts of British goods, Indian nationalists pushed the British to grant them greater political representation, economic autonomy, and eventual self-government. In Turkey, Kemal Atatürk in 1923 abolished the sultanate and established the Turkish Republic, with all the trappings of a Western democratic state.

The spread of democracy had a material side as well. The credibility of parliamentary governments depended heavily on their ability to restore and maintain prosperity. In the second half of the 1920s the world economy expanded.

Some optimists suggested that innovations in manufacturing, like Henry Ford's moving assembly line, would usher in an era in which plenty would replace want. Increased earnings encouraged a democratic culture of consumption, whether it was buying radios in France or Western-style fashions in Tokyo (below). Products like the automobile, once available only to the rich, were increasingly accessible to people of all classes. Ford himself became an international hero, and German and Russian engineers used the term *Fordismus* to characterize modern industrial techniques.

Along with the automobile the mass media introduced a revolution in world culture. The impact of movies, radio, and mass circulation magazines, while greatest in

GLOBAL EVENTS

Inflation plagues defeated Germany
1920s

Washington Conference on naval armaments

Mussolini marches on Rome;
James Joyce's *Ulysses*

Atatürk establishes Turkish Republic

Kellogg-Briand Pact outlaws war

| 1920 | 1921 HARDING | 1922 | 1923 COOLIDGE | 1925 | 1928 |

Teapot Dome scandal exposed

Sinclair Lewis's *Babbitt*
published

F. Scott Fitzgerald's *The Great Gatsby* published;
Scopes trial debates evolution

Stock market
boom under way

KDKA, Pittsburgh, first commercial radio station on air;
Prohibition takes effect

AMERICAN EVENTS

the United States, was felt around the globe. Once-remote people and places became accessible and familiar. Stories, names, phrases, images, and ideas could become the common property of all. "In short, it seems to be the nature of radio to encourage people to think and feel alike," two prominent psychologists concluded. Consumption of culture as well as manufactured goods seemed to walk hand in hand with the democracy of the masses.

But the foundations upon which democracy rested were fragile. In the new Soviet Union, communists led by Lenin and the young Joseph Stalin demonstrated how readily talk of "the masses" and "democratic socialism" could mask an iron totalitarianism. In Japan, democracy was hampered by that nation's persistent feudal traditions and the rise of militarism. Although its parliamentary government was controlled for a time by liberal, westernized factions, nationalists from the old samurai class joined with the nation's economically powerful families in quest of a Japanese East Asian empire.

Fear of communist revolution led some nationalists in Europe to reject democracy. With Italy's parliamentary government seemingly paralyzed by postwar unrest, Benito Mussolini and his Fasci di Combattimento, or fascists, used terrorism, murder, and intimidation to create an "all-embracing" single-party state, outside which "no human or spiritual values can exist, let alone be desirable." They rejected both the liberals' belief in political parties and the Marxist concept of class solidarity. Instead, they glorified the nation-state dominated by the middle class, small business-people, modest property owners, and small farmers.

Fascism thus gave a sinister twist to the liberal ideal of national solidarity, but one that others embraced as a no-nonsense means of blunting Marxism. Adolf Hitler, like many Germans, resented the stinging defeat that war brought in 1919 and blamed communists, among others, for the sorry state of German life. Like Mussolini, Hitler used the politics of discontent to rise to power. Having achieved it in 1933, his Nazi party destroyed democracy. Under one-party rule, the Gestapo secret political police ensured that Germans expressed only those ideas that conformed

GLOBAL EVENTS

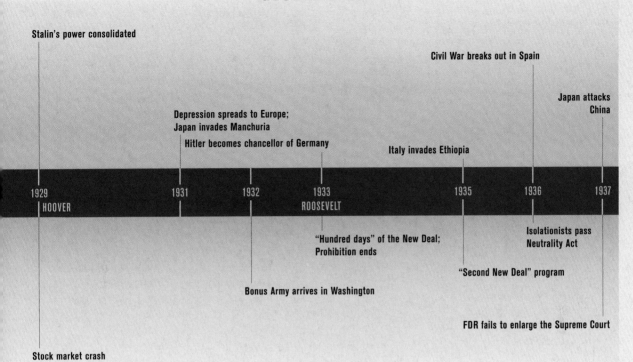

Stalin's power consolidated

Civil War breaks out in Spain

Japan attacks China

Depression spreads to Europe;
Japan invades Manchuria

Hitler becomes chancellor of Germany

Italy invades Ethiopia

| 1929 | | 1931 | 1932 | 1933 | | 1935 | 1936 | 1937 |

HOOVER

ROOSEVELT

"Hundred days" of the New Deal;
Prohibition ends

Isolationists pass
Neutrality Act

"Second New Deal" program

Bonus Army arrives in Washington

FDR fails to enlarge the Supreme Court

Stock market crash

AMERICAN EVENTS

to the views of their national leader, the Führer.

Hitler succeeded partly because the prosperity of the 1920s was shattered worldwide by the corro-sive hardships of the Great Depression. Farmers were particularly hard hit: during the 1920s the opening of new lands to cultivation had already led to overproduction. In Java, for example, the use of scientific agricultural techniques created a glut in the sugar market. By 1930 the price of wheat, measured in gold, reached its lowest point in 400 years. And those urban unemployed who walked the street in search of a job ("I seek work of any sort," reads the German's sign at left) were often ready to believe that only the forceful leadership of one could unite the many. Even in the United States, the business newspaper *Barron's* voiced the thoughts of more than a few when it mused that "a mild species of dictatorship" might "help us over the roughest spots in the road ahead."

Still, the rise of Hitler and Mussolini shook those people who had faith in the possibilities of mass politics. While Franklin Roosevelt used his radio "fireside chats" to bring government closer to the people, Hitler's fiery speeches and mass rallies seemed bent on encouraging racist fears and manipulating public opinion. While Hollywood produced films that affirmed popular faith in democratic government, a capitalist economy, and the success ethic, the German director Leni Riefenstahl used her cinematic gifts to combine myth, symbolism, and documentary into an evocation of the Führer as a pagan god of strength and a Christian savior. The "mass" aspects of the media were a two-edged sword. Perceptive critics recognized that even in democracies,

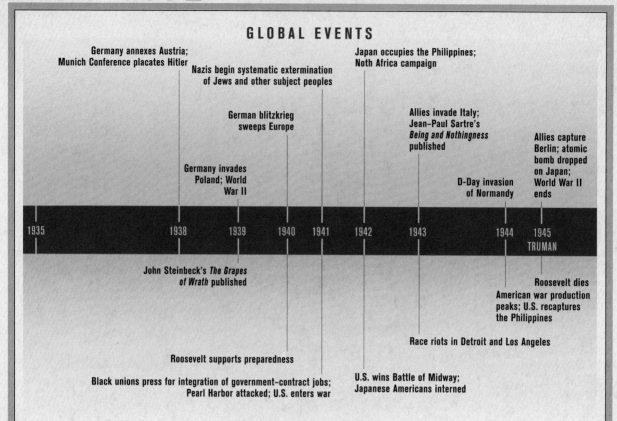

GLOBAL EVENTS

Germany annexes Austria;
Munich Conference placates Hitler

Nazis begin systematic extermination
of Jews and other subject peoples

Japan occupies the Philippines;
Noth Africa campaign

German blitzkrieg
sweeps Europe

Allies invade Italy;
Jean-Paul Sartre's
Being and Nothingness
published

Allies capture
Berlin; atomic
bomb dropped
on Japan;
World War II
ends

Germany invades
Poland; World
War II

D-Day invasion
of Normandy

| 1935 | 1938 | 1939 | 1940 | 1941 | 1942 | 1943 | 1944 | 1945 |
| | | | | | | | | TRUMAN |

John Steinbeck's *The Grapes
of Wrath* published

Roosevelt dies

American war production
peaks; U.S. recaptures
the Philippines

Race riots in Detroit and Los Angeles

Roosevelt supports preparedness

Black unions press for integration of government–contract jobs;
Pearl Harbor attacked; U.S. enters war

U.S. wins Battle of Midway;
Japanese Americans interned

AMERICAN EVENTS

mass culture was devoted primarily to the entertainment and escapism of light comedy and melodrama rather than serious social criticism.

Thus the Depression shook both the political and the material pillars of democratic culture. On the eve of World War II the number of European democracies had been reduced from 27 to 10. Latin America was ruled by a variety of dictators and military juntas that differed little from the dictatorships of Europe. China suffered not only from invasion by Japan's militarists and civil war but also from the corrupt and ineffectual one-party dictatorship of Chiang Kai-shek. Almost alone, the New Deal attempted to combat the Depression through the methods of parliamentary democracy. The totalitarian states that had promised stability, national glory, and an end to the communist menace instead led the world to chaos and war, from which both communism and democracy emerged triumphant.

Chapter 24

J ust before Christmas 1918 the "Gospel Car" pulled into Los Angeles. Bold letters on the side announced: "JESUS IS COMING—GET READY." Aimee Semple McPherson, the ravishing redheaded driver, had completed a cross-country drive to seek her destiny in the West. With only "ten dollars and a tambourine" to her name, Sister Aimee at first found destiny elusive. After three years of wandering the state, she landed in San Diego. With the highest rates of illness and suicide in California, it was the perfect place for Sister Aimee to preach the healing message of her "Foursquare Gospel." Her revival attracted 30,000 people, who witnessed her first proclaimed miracle: a paralytic walked.

Sister Aimee had a Pentecostal message for her flock: "Jesus is the healer. I am only the little office girl who opens the door and says, 'Come in.'" After the miracle in San Diego, her fame spread. She returned triumphantly to Los Angeles, where nearly three-quarters of a million people, many from the nation's heartland, had migrated in search of opportunity, sun, and perhaps salvation. In heading west, most had lost touch with the traditional Protestant denominations at home. Sister Aimee put her traveling gospel tent away. She would minister to the lost flock at her doorstep.

The New Era

1920–1929

preview • The 1920s ushered in a "New Era" in which key features of modern life took hold: mass society, mass culture, and mass consumption. Urban America led the way in rejecting social conventions that had limited Americans, especially women and children, while more traditional regions defended their ways of life through immigration restriction, Prohibition, Fundamentalism, and a reborn Ku Klux Klan. In the end the roaring economy crashed, undone by underlying weaknesses.

To the blare of trumpets on New Year's Day, 1923, she unveiled the $1.5 million Angelus Temple, graced by a 75-foot, rotating electrified cross. It was visible at night from 50 miles away. Inside was a 5000-seat auditorium, radio station KFSG (Kall Four Square Gospel), a "Cradle Roll Chapel" for babies, and a "Miracle Room" filled with crutches and canes discarded by the cured faithful. Services were not simply a matter of hymn, prayer, and sermon. Sister added pageants, Holy Land slide shows, circuses, and healing sessions.

Aimee Semple McPherson succeeded because she was able to blend old and new. Her lively sermons carried the spirit of what people were calling the "New Era" of productivity and consumerism. Where country preachers menaced their congregations with visions of eternal damnation, Sister Aimee, wrote a reporter, offered "flowers, music, golden trumpets, red robes, angels, incense, nonsense, and sex appeal." Her approach revealed a nose for publicity and a sophisticated understanding of the booming media industries of the 1920s. Here was one brand of evangelism suited to a new consumer age.

Modernizing the gospel was just one symptom of the New Era. Writing in 1931, journalist Frederick Lewis Allen found the changes of the preceding decade so breathtaking that he could not believe that 1919 was *Only Yesterday*, as he titled his book. To give a sense of the transformation, Allen followed an average American couple, the fictitious "Mr. and Mrs. Smith," through the 1920s. The same revolution in industry and technology that allowed the sweet-voiced Aimee McPherson to save souls by the thousands had also transformed the Smiths' home with the sounds of radio, the miracles of canned foods, and the savings in time and energy generated

Sister Aimee Semple McPherson, billed as "the world's most pulchritudinous evangelist," in her robe.

Blues, painted in 1929 by African American artist Archibald Motley Jr., evokes the improvised rhythms of the Jazz Age. New Orleans–born Motley was one of a group of black genre painters in the 1920s who became part of the Harlem Renaissance.

by a host of new electrical gadgets. But the most striking and visible changes involved the revolution in women's fashions and behavior. By the end of the decade, Mrs. Smith's corset vanished, and her hemline jumped from her ankle to her knee. Mimicking stylish young flappers, she bobbed, or cut, her long hair to the popular, near-boyish length and flattened her breasts for greater freedom of movement.

With Prohibition in full force, Mrs. Smith and other women of her day walked into illegal speakeasy saloons as readily as men. In the trendy hotels she and her husband danced to jazz. Modern couples like the Smiths sprinkled their conversations with references to "repressed sexual drives" and the best methods of contraception. But perhaps the most striking change about these "average" Americans was that they lived in the city. The census of 1920 showed that for the first time just over half the population were urbanites. Here, in urban America, the New Era worked its changes and sent them rippling outward.

Yet the city-dwelling Smiths of Frederick Allen's imagination were hardly average. Nearly as many Americans still lived on isolated farms, in villages, and in small towns as in cities. In fact, many "city" dwellers lived there, too. By defining cities as incorporated municipalities with 2500 people or more, the Census Bureau had created hundreds of statistical illusions. New York with its millions of inhabitants ranked in the census tables alongside Sac Prairie, Wisconsin, whose population

Urban role in the New Era

hovered barely above the mystical mark of 2500, and tiny Hyden, along the Cumberland plateau of eastern Kentucky.

Most citizens, the Smiths aside, dwelled in an earlier America and clung to its traditions. The technology of the New Era had yet to penetrate many urban American homes, let alone the hinterlands. As late as 1927, two-thirds of American households still had no washing machines or vacuum cleaners and half had no telephones. Nearly all American farms lacked electricity.

The poet August Derleth grew up under just such conditions in Sac Prairie. As a 10-year-old in 1919 he could hear the "howl of wolves" at night. The town observed changing seasons not with new fashions but by the appearance and disappearance of plants and animals. In Hyden, Kentucky, Main Street was still unpaved. By 1930 there were still only 10 automobiles in the county. God-fearing Baptists worshiped together as their parents had before them and still repaired to the Middle Fork of the Kentucky River for an open-air baptism when they declared their new birth in Christ. They would have nothing to do with flapper girls or the showy miracles of Aimee McPherson.

As much as some Americans resisted the transforming forces of modern life, the New Era could not be walled out. Industrial breakthroughs led to a host of new consumer goods, while large corporations developed more "modern" bureaucracies to make production more efficient and profitable. Whether Americans embraced the New Era or condemned it, change came nonetheless, in the form of a mass-produced consumer economy, a culture shaped by mass media, and a more materialistic society. A new ethic of getting and spending took hold, driving the economy to dizzying heights. Most Americans believed the New Era of peace and prosperity would last forever and ripple outward across the globe. Little did they realize that their roaring economy was honeycombed with weaknesses, and in 1929, to their astonishment, it crumbled.

The Roaring Economy

In the 1920s, the United States was in the midst of a revolution in production. Not only did the amount of goods manufactured increase sharply—by 64 percent over the decade—but workers became more efficient in manufacturing them. Output per worker—productivity—increased by 40 percent. The sale of electricity doubled; the consumption of fuel oil more than doubled. Between 1922 and 1927 the economy grew by 7 percent a year—the largest peacetime rate ever. If anything roared in the "Roaring Twenties," it was the economy.

Technology and Consumer Spending

Technology was partly responsible. Steam turbines and shovels, electric motors, belt and bucket conveyors, and countless other new machines became common at work sites. Machines replaced 200,000 workers each year, and a new phrase—"technological unemployment"—entered the vocabulary. Even so, rising demand, especially for new consumer goods, kept the labor force growing at a faster rate than the population. And pay improved. Between 1919 and 1927, average income climbed nearly $150 for each industrial worker.

As the industrial economy matured, more consumer goods appeared on store shelves—cigarette lighters, wristwatches, radios, panchromatic film. Under their impact, American customs changed, sometimes with unintended results. Electric washing machines and vacuum cleaners lightened the load of a "Blue Monday" spent washing clothes by hand and reduced the drudgery of cleaning house. At the same time these innovations boosted standards of household cleanliness and meant hours more of work for homemakers. Commercial laundries disappeared, and the long-term trend toward fewer domestic servants intensified.

As production of consumer goods grew, improvements in productivity helped keep prices down. The cost of a tire and an inner tube, for example, dropped by half between 1914 and 1929. Meanwhile, real wages (wages valued in purchasing power) jumped by 20 percent. Americans enjoyed the highest standard of living any people had ever known.

Yet for all the prosperity, a dangerous imbalance was developing in the economy. Most Americans saved little in the mistaken belief that prosperity was here to stay. Falling prices made many items seem like good buys, and the rapid expansion of credit (see page 792) allowed consumers to put off paying for what they purchased. As a result, personal debt was rising two and a half times faster than personal income, an unhealthy sign of consumers scrambling to spend.

The Booming Construction Industry

Along with technology and consumer spending, new "boom industries" promoted economic growth. In a rebound after the war years, construction boomed. Even cities the size of Beaumont, Texas; Memphis, Tennessee; and Syracuse, New York, were erecting buildings of 20 stories or more. New York got a new skyline of tall towers, topped in 1931 when the Empire State Building rose to the world-record height of 86 stories.

Residential construction doubled as people moved from cities to suburbs. Suburban Grosse Point, near Detroit, grew by 700 percent, and Beverly Hills, on the outskirts of Los Angeles, by 2500 percent. Road construction made suburban life possible and pumped millions of dollars into the economy. In 1919 Oregon, New Mexico, and Colorado hit on a novel idea for financing roads—a tax on gasoline. Within a decade every state had one.

Construction stimulated other businesses: steel, concrete, lumber, home mortgages, and insurance. It even helped change the nation's eating habits. The limited storage space of small "kitchenettes" in new apartments boosted supermarket chains and the canning industry. As shipments of fresh fruits and vegetables sped across new roads, interest in nutrition grew. Vitamins, publicized with new zeal, appeared on breakfast tables.

The Automobile

No industry boomed more than automobile manufacturing. Although cars had first appeared on streets at the turn of the century, for many years they remained little more than expensive toys. By 1920 there were 10 million in America, a sizable number. But by 1929 the total had jumped to 26 million, 1 for every 5 people (compared to 1 for every 43 in Britain and 1 for every 7000 in Russia). Automakers bought one-seventh of the nation's steel and more rubber, plate glass, nickel, and lead than any other industry. By the end of the decade, one American in four somehow earned a living from automobiles.

Henry Ford helped to make the boom possible by pushing standardization and mass production to such ruthless extremes that the automobile became affordable. Trading on his fame as a race-car manufacturer, he founded the Ford Motor Company in 1903 with the dream of building a "motor car for the multitude." "Everybody wants to be somewhere he ain't," Ford observed. The way to succeed was to drive down costs by making all the cars alike, "just like one pin is like another

Henry Ford

Henry Ford at the turn of the century

pin." In 1908 Ford perfected the Model T. It had a 20-horsepower engine and a body of steel. It was high enough to ride the worst roads, and it came in only one color: black.

Priced at $845, the Model T was cheap by industry standards but still too costly and too time-consuming to build. Two Ford engineers suggested copying a practice of Chicago meatpacking houses, where beef carcasses were carried on moving chains past meat dressers. In 1914 Ford introduced the moving assembly line. A conveyor belt, positioned waist high to eliminate bending or walking, propelled the chassis at six feet per minute as stationary workers put the cars together. The process cut assembly time in half. In 1925 new Model Ts were rolling off the line every 10 seconds. At $290, almost anybody could buy one. By 1927 Ford had sold 15 million of his "tin lizzies."

Doctrine of high wages

Ford was also a social prophet. Breaking with other manufacturers, he preached a "doctrine of high wages." According to it, workers with extra money in their pockets would buy enough to sustain a booming prosperity. In 1915 Ford's plants in Dearborn established the "Five-Dollar Day," twice the wage rate in Detroit. He reduced working hours from 48 to 40 a week and cut the workweek to five days. By 1926 he also employed 10,000 African Americans, many of whom had advanced far enough to hire and fire their white subordinates.

Yet Ford workers were not happy. Ford admitted that the repetitive operations on his assembly line made it scarcely possible "that any man would care to continue long at the same job." The Five-Dollar Day was designed, in part, to reduce the turnover rate of 300 percent a year at Ford plants. And Ford recouped his profits by speeding up the assembly line and enforcing ruthless efficiencies. Ford workers could not talk, whistle, smoke, or sit on the job. They wore frozen expressions called "Fordization of the face" and communicated in the "Ford whisper" without moving their lips. A Sociological Department spied on workers in their homes, and the Education Department taught plant procedures but also Americanization classes where immigrant workers learned English, proper dress, and even etiquette.

General Motors copied Ford's production techniques but not his business strategies. While Ford tried to sell everyone the same car, GM created "a car for every purse and purpose." There were Cadillacs for the wealthy, Chevrolets for the modest. GM cars were painted in a rainbow of colors, and every year the style changed. In a standardized society, such details made automobiles symbols of distinction as well as prestige.

A car culture

By making automobiles available to nearly everyone, the industry changed the face of America. The spreading web of paved roads fueled urban sprawl, real estate booms in California and Florida, and a new roadside culture of restaurants, service stations, and motels. Thousands of "auto camps" opened to provide tourists with tents and crude toilets. "Auto clubs" such as the Tin Can Tourists Association (named for the tin can tied to the radiator cap of a member's car) sprang up to aid travelers. Automobile travel broke down the isolation and provincialism of Americans and helped to standardize dialects and manners.

Across the country the automobile gave the young unprecedented freedom from parental authority. After hearing 30 cases of "sex crimes" (19 had occurred in cars), an exasperated juvenile court judge declared that the automobile was "a house of prostitution on wheels." It was, of course, much more. The automobile was to the 1920s what the railroad had been to the nineteenth century: the catalyst for economic growth, a transportation revolution, and a cultural symbol.

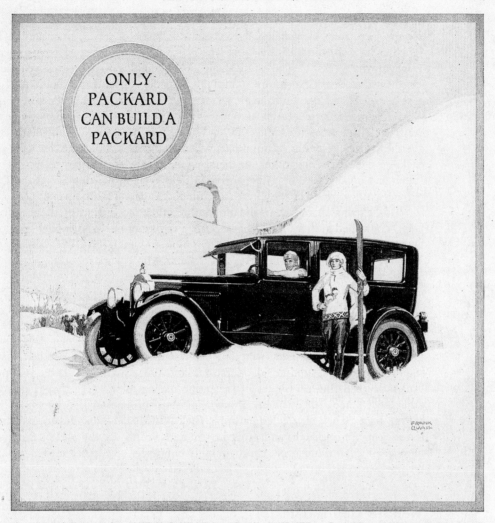

ONLY PACKARD CAN BUILD A PACKARD

FRANK QUAIL

A MAN IS KNOWN BY THE CAR HE KEEPS

In the old days men were rated by the homes in which they lived

and few but their friends saw them.

Today, men are rated by the cars they drive

and everybody sees them—

for the car is mobile and the home is not.

To own a Packard is an evidence of discriminating taste.

Woman, with her observing eye, has known this for twenty-five years.

And woman, proverbial for her greater thrift, will insist upon the family motor car being a Packard once she learns that the Packard Six costs less to own, operate and maintain than the ordinary car the family has been buying every year or two.

Packard Six and Packard Eight both furnished in ten body types, open and enclosed. Packard's extremely liberal monthly payment plan makes possible the immediate enjoyment of a Packard, purchasing out of income instead of capital.

A S K   T H E   M A N   W H O   O W N S   O N E

In the 1920s, automobile advertising shifted gears by broadening its audience and making the automobile a symbol of social success. Earlier advertisements had stressed the technical advantages of automobiles and were aimed strictly at men. Here an automobile advertisement from 1925 emphasizes the subliminal rewards of owning a luxury car. Prestige, power, wealth, and romantic love belong to a man who owns a Packard automobile. And women are not ignored. The advertisement points out to women that owning a Packard is not only "evidence of discriminating taste" but also a sign of cost-consciousness for family-minded females.

The Business of America

In business, said Henry Ford, the "fundamentals are all summed up in the single word, 'service.'" President Calvin Coolidge echoed the theme of service to society in 1925: "The business of America is business. The man who builds a factory builds a temple. The man who works there worships there." A generation earlier, progressives had criticized business for its social irresponsibility. But the wartime contributions of business managers and the return of prosperity in 1922 gained them a renewed respect.

Corporate consolidation

Encouraged by federal permissiveness, a wave of mergers swept the country. Between 1919 and 1930, some 8000 firms disappeared as large gobbled small. Oligopolies (where a few firms dominated whole industries) flourished in steel, meat-packing, cigarettes, and other businesses. National chains began to replace local "mom and pop" stores. By 1929, one bag of groceries in ten came from the 15,000 red-and-gold markets of the Great Atlantic and Pacific Tea Company.

Managerial elite

This expansion and consolidation meant that the capital of the nation was being controlled not by individuals but by corporations. The model of modern business was the large, bureaucratic corporation, in which those who actually managed the company had little to do with those who owned it—the shareholders. Stocks and bonds were becoming so widely dispersed that few individuals held more than 1 or 2 percent of any company.

A salaried bureaucracy of executives and plant managers formed a new elite, which no longer set their sights on becoming swashbuckling entrepreneurs like the Carnegies and Rockefellers of old. The new managers looked to work their way up a corporate ladder. They were less interested in risk than in productivity and stability. Managers subdivided operations and put experts in charge. Corporate leaders learned the techniques of "scientific management" taught at Harvard and other new schools of business through journals, professional societies, and consulting firms. They channeled earnings back into their companies to expand factories, carry on research, and grow in size and wealth. By the end of the decade, more than a thousand firms had research laboratories and half the total industrial income was concentrated in 100 corporations.

Welfare Capitalism

The new "scientific management" also stressed smooth relations between managers and employees. The rash of postwar strikes had left business leaders as suspicious as ever of labor unions and determined to find ways to limit their influence.

The American Plan

Some tactics were more strong-armed than scientific. In 1921 the National Association of Manufacturers, the Chamber of Commerce, and other employer groups launched the "American Plan," aimed at opening "closed shops," factories where only union members could work. Employers made workers sign agreements disavowing union membership. Labor organizers called them "yellow dog contracts." Companies infiltrated unions with spies, locked union members out of factories if they protested, and boycotted firms that hired union labor.

The gentler side of the American Plan involved a social innovation called "welfare capitalism." Companies such as General Electric and Bethlehem Steel pledged to care for their employees and give them incentives for working hard. They built clean, safe factories, installed cafeterias, hired trained dietitians, formed baseball teams and glee clubs. Several hundred firms encouraged perhaps a million workers to buy company stock. Millions more enrolled in company unions. Called "Kiss-Me Clubs" for their lack of power, they offered what few independent unions could match: health and safety insurance; a grievance procedure; and representation for African Americans, women, and immigrants.

But welfare capitalism embraced barely 5 percent of the workforce and often gave benefits only to skilled laborers, the hardest to replace. Most companies cared more for production than for contented employees. In the 1920s a family of four could live in "minimum health and decency" on $2000 a year. The average industrial wage was $1304, and almost one family in six was labeled as "chronically destitute." Thus working-class families often needed more than one wage earner just to get by. Over a million children ages 10 to 15 still worked full-time in 1920. Some received as little as 20 cents an hour.

In 1927, the most famous strike of the decade idled 2500 mill hands in Gastonia, North Carolina, where workers labored for 10- to 12-hour shifts in 90-degree heat and endured regular "stretch-outs," the textile equivalent of assembly-line speedups. Even strikebreakers walked out. Eventually, however, authorities broke the strike, presaging a national trend. A year later there were a record-low 629 strikes. Union membership sank from almost 5 million in 1921 to less than 3.5 million in 1929. "The AF of L [American Federation of Labor] machinery has practically collapsed," reported one union official.

The Consumer Culture

During the late nineteenth century the economy had boomed, too, but much of its growth had gone into producer goods: huge steel factories and rail, telephone, and electric networks. By World War I, these industrial networks had penetrated enough of the country to create mass markets for consumer goods such as refrigerators, bicycles, and other products for ordinary Americans. As an increasing percentage of the nation's industries turned out consumer goods, prosperity hinged more and more on consumption. If consumers purchased more goods, production would increase at the same time that costs would decrease. Lower production costs would allow for lower prices, which would lift sales, production, and employment still higher.

Everything in this cycle of prosperity depended on consumption. In the consumer economy, wives ceased to be homemakers and became purchasers of processed food and manufactured goods. Husbands were not merely workers but, equally important, consumers of mortgages and other forms of credit. Even vacationers became consumers—in this case, consumers of leisure time as more employees got two-week (unpaid) vacations. Consumption was the key to prosperity, and increased consumption rested on two innovations: advertising to help people buy, and credit to help them pay.

Around the turn of the century, advertisers began a critical shift from emphasizing *products* to stressing a consumer's *desires*: health, popularity, social status. During the First World War the Committee on Public Information, the federal propaganda agency, demonstrated the power of emotional appeals as an instrument of mass persuasion. Like the war propaganda, advertising copy aimed at emotions and cynically regarded the "average normal American," in the words of one executive, as having the "literate capacity of a 12- or 14-year-old." Behavioral psychologists like John B. Watson, who left Johns Hopkins University for an advertising agency in the 1920s, helped advertisers develop more sophisticated techniques for attracting customers.

Role of advertising

Earlier in the century Albert Lasker, the owner of Chicago's largest advertising firm, Lord and Thomas, had created modern advertising in America. His eye-catching ads were hard-hitting, positive, and often preposterous. To expand the sales of Lucky Strike cigarettes, Lord and Thomas advertisements claimed smoking made

This pen-and-ink drawing depicts a cavernous street in New York City awash in advertising. Its title, *Picturesque America,* is a play on the growing use of signs to sell products. Already by 1909, when the graphic artist Harry Grant Dart drew the piece, advertising and the consumer culture were overtaking the country, in this case transforming buildings into billboards for hawking everything from foreign language courses to cigars, furs, and automobiles. "Electric signs," promises one electrified sign, "make night beautiful." The artist did not agree.

people slimmer and more courageous. "Luckies" became one of the most popular brands in America. Bogus doctors and dentists endorsed all kinds of products, including toothpaste containing potassium chloride—eight grams of which was lethal. "Halitosis" was plucked from the pages of an obscure medical dictionary and used to sell Listerine mouthwash.

Installment buying as credit

Advertisers encouraged Americans to borrow against tomorrow to purchase what advertising convinced them they wanted today. Installment buying had once been confined to sewing machines and pianos. In the 1920s it grew into the tenth biggest business in the United States. In 1919 Alfred Sloan created millions of new customers by establishing the General Motors Acceptance Corporation, the nation's first consumer credit organization. By 1929 Americans were buying most of their cars, radios, and furniture on the installment plan. Consumer debt jumped to $7 billion, almost twice the federal budget.

A Mass Society

In the evening after a day's work in the fields—perhaps in front of an adobe house built by one of the western sugar-beet companies—Mexican American workers might gather to chat or sing a *corrido* or two. The *corrido*, or ballad, was an old Mexican folk tradition whose subjects matched the concerns of the day. One corrido during the 1920s told of a field laborer distressed that his family had rejected old Mexican customs in favor of new American fashions. His wife, he sang, now had "a bob-tailed dress of silk" and, wearing makeup, went about "painted like a *piñata.*" As for his children:

> My kids speak perfect English
> And have no use for our Spanish
> They call me "fader" and don't work
> And are crazy about the Charleston.

It was enough to make him long for Mexico.

For Americans from all backgrounds, the New Era was witness to "a vast dissolution of ancient habits," commented columnist Walter Lippmann. Mass marketing and mass distribution led not simply to a higher standard of living but also to a life less regional and diverse. In the place of moral standards set by local communities and churches came "modern" fashions and attitudes, spread by the new mass media of movies, radio, and magazines. In the place of "ancient habits" came the forces of mass society: independent women, freer love, standardized culture, urban energy and impersonality, and deep alienation.

A "New Woman"

In the tumultuous 1890s, a "New Woman" had appeared, one who was more assertive, athletic, and independent than her Victorian peers. By the 1920s, more modern versions of this New Woman were being charged with nothing less than leading what Frederick Lewis Allen called the "revolution in manners and morals" of the twenties. The most flamboyant of them wore close-fitting felt hats and makeup, long-waisted dresses and few undergarments, strings of beads, and unbuckled galoshes (which earned them the nickname "flappers"). Cocktail in hand, cigarette in mouth, footloose and economically free, the New Woman became a symbol of liberation and sexuality to some. To others she represented the decline of civilization.

World War I had served as a social catalyst, while the decade before it had stimulated changes for women workers. Single and married women poured into the workforce after the turn of the century. From a fifth of the labor force in 1900, women jumped to a quarter by 1930, with the greatest gains coming before the war. But most female workers remained in poor-paying jobs, and few found new freedom after quitting time. The war nonetheless prompted a change in attitudes. Before it, women were arrested for smoking cigarettes openly, using profanity, appearing on public beaches without stockings, and driving automobiles without men beside them. But with women bagging explosives, running locomotives, and drilling with rifles, the old taboos often seemed silly.

Disseminating birth control information by mail had also been a crime before the war. By the armistice there was a birth control clinic in Brooklyn, a National Birth Control League, and later an American Birth Control League led by Margaret Sanger. Sanger's crusade had begun as an attempt to save poor women from the burdens of unwanted

"Street selling was torture for me," Margaret Sanger recalled of her efforts to promote the *Birth Control Review.* Hecklers often taunted Sanger and her colleagues. "Have you never heard God's word to 'be fruitful and multiply and replenish the earth'?" one asked. The reply came back, "They've done that already."

Margaret Sanger

Daily Lives

CLOTHING AND FASHION
The Beauty Contest

Early in September 1921 eight young women stood nervously on the boardwalk at Atlantic City, New Jersey. For a week the seaside resort had presented a succession of swimming exhibitions, dance contests, and automobile races. A giant parade featured clowns, bands, and a float carrying King Neptune escorted by mermaids. All the marchers except the clowns wore bathing suits, even the mayor and members of the chamber of commerce. They had been instrumental in organizing the week's central event—a national beauty contest to select the first "Miss America."

The American beauty contest drew on an old heritage. In colonial times the traditional May Day celebration crowned a Queen of the May as a symbol of fertility. Queens embodied fruitfulness and community. Though physical beauty mattered in the selection, qualities such as civic leadership and popularity also counted. By the middle of the nineteenth century many cities began holding such festivals to publicize their virtues.

In 1854 showman P. T. Barnum conceived of a competition among women to judge their beauty. Because Victorian codes prohibited such displays, Barnum attracted only contestants of "questionable reputation." To lure middle-class women, he announced that "daguerreotypes," or photographs, could be submitted. Participants did not even have to send their names. The idea spread. When the promoters of the St. Louis Exposition advertised a beauty contest in 1905, some 40,000 women applied.

Promoters had conceived of the Miss America pageant as a way of extending the summer season past September 1. The contest measured physical beauty alone, with the high point being a bathing suit competition. (Only later did the pageant add a talent show.) After the turn of the century, bathing suits had grown alarmingly scant, exposing arms and discarding billowy bloomers in favor of revealing tights. Organizers worried that straitlaced visitors might balk at

Margaret Gorman of Washington, D.C., crowned in 1921 as the first Miss America.

pregnancies (page 719). In the 1920s her message found a receptive middle-class audience. Surveys showed that by the 1930s nearly 90 percent of college-educated couples practiced contraception.

Being able to a degree to control the matter of pregnancy, women felt less guilt about enjoying sex and less fear over the consequences. In 1909 Sigmund Freud had come to America to lecture on his theories of coping with the unconscious and overcoming harmful repressions. Some of Freud's ideas, specifically his emphasis on childhood sexuality, shocked Americans, while most of his complex theories sailed blissfully over their heads. As popularized in the 1920s, however, Freudian psychology stamped sexuality as a key to health.

Such changes in the social climate were real enough, but the life of a flapper girl hardly mirrored the lives and work routines of most American women. Over the decade, the female labor force grew by only 1 percent. As late as 1930 nearly 60 percent of all working women were African American or foreign-born and generally held low-paying jobs in domestic service or the garment industry.

The New Era did spawn new careers for women. The consumer culture capitalized on a preoccupation with appearance and led to the opening of some 40,000 beauty parlors staffed by hairdressers, manicurists, and cosmeticians. "Women's fields" the sight of middle-class women strutting seminude before a panel of judges.

Aware of such perils, pageant officials depicted entrants as wholesome, conventional, and unsophisticated. None of the contestants was permitted to wear short bobbed hair or makeup—both symbols of the racy modern woman. To underscore the lightheartedness of the pageant, local police dressed like Keystone Kops, the bumbling heroes of Mack Sennett's comedy films.

As the contestants waited anxiously, officials announced the winner—Margaret Gorman of Washington, D.C. She radiated wholesomeness and athletic vigor. "She represents the type of womanhood America needs," observed Samuel Gompers of the American Federation of Labor, "—strong, red-blooded, able to shoulder the responsibilities of home-making and motherhood."

The Miss America pageant was an immediate success. Newspapers across the country reported the results. In 1922 representatives of 58 cities competed, and a crowd of 200,000 watched the opening parade. The much-feared protests did materialize. In 1928 organizers were forced to cancel the pageant when hotel owners objected that their middle-class clientele found the display offensive. The pageant was revived again in 1935, and a Miss America has reigned ever since.

Miss America and other beauty contests evolved as commercialism and advertising took hold and Victorianism declined in the early twentieth century. But the lengths to which pageant organizers went to gain respect demonstrated the strength of the older social ideals. The Miss America pageant in particular came to symbolize the middle-class ideal of womanhood. Physical beauty remained the chief component, marriage and motherhood the chief ends. The message was graphic: men competed in sports gear, business attire, and professional garb; women, in bathing suits. That fashion would be slow to change.

carved out by progressive reformers expanded opportunities in education, libraries, and social welfare. Women earned a higher percentage of doctoral degrees (from 1 percent in 1910 to 15.4 percent in 1930) and held more college teaching posts than ever (32 percent). But in most areas, professional men resisted the "feminization" of the workforce. The number of female doctors dropped by half. Medical schools imposed restrictive quotas, and 90 percent of all hospitals rejected female interns.

In 1924 two women—Nellie Ross in Wyoming and Miriam ("Ma") Ferguson in Texas—were elected governors, the first female chief executives. But for the most part, women continued to be marginalized in party politics while remaining widely involved in educational and welfare programs. Operating outside male-dominated political parties, women activists succeeded in winning passage of the Sheppard-Towner Federal Maternity and Infancy Act in 1921 to fight infant mortality with rural prenatal and baby-care centers. It was the first federal welfare statute. Yet by the end of the decade the Sheppard-Towner Act had lapsed.

In the wake of their greatest success, the hard-won vote for women, feminists splintered. The National Woman Suffrage Association disbanded in 1920. In its place the new League of Women Voters encouraged informed voting with nonpartisan publicity. For the more militant Alice Paul and her allies, that was not enough. Their

**Equal Rights
Amendment**

National Woman's party pressed for a constitutional Equal Rights Amendment (ERA). Social workers and others familiar with the conditions under which women labored opposed it. Death and injury rates for women were nearly double those for men. To them the ERA meant losing the protection as well as the benefits women derived from mothers' pensions and maternity insurance. Joined by most men and a majority of Congress, they fought the amendment to a standstill.

Mass Media

In balmy California, where movies could be made year-round, Hollywood helped give the New Woman notoriety as a temptress and trendsetter. When sexy Theda Bara (the "vamp") appeared in *The Blue Flame* in 1920, crowds mobbed theaters. And just as Hollywood dictated standards of physical attraction, it became the judge of taste and fashion in countless other ways because motion pictures were a virtually universal medium. There was no need for literacy or fluency, no need even for sound, given the power of the pictures parading across the screen.

Motion pictures

Motion pictures, invented in 1889, had first been shown in tiny neighborhood theaters called "nickelodeons." For a nickel, patrons watched a silent screen flicker with moving images as an accompanist played music on a tinny piano. The audience was anything but silent. The theater reverberated with the cracking of Indian nuts, the day's equivalent of popcorn, while young cowboys shot off their Kilgore repeating cap pistols during dramatic scenes. Often children read the subtitles aloud to their immigrant parents, translating into Italian, Yiddish, or German.

After the first feature-length film, *The Great Train Robbery* (1903), productions became rich in spectacle, attracted middle-class audiences, and turned into America's favorite form of entertainment. By 1926 more than 20,000 movie houses offered customers lavish theaters with overstuffed seats, live music, and a celluloid dream world—all for 50 cents or less. At the end of the decade, they were drawing over 100 million people a week, roughly the equivalent of the national population.

In the spring of 1920 Frank Conrad of the Westinghouse Company in East Pittsburgh rigged up a research station in his barn and started transmitting phonograph music and baseball scores to local wireless operators. An ingenious Pittsburgh newspaper began advertising radio equipment to "be used by those who listen to Dr. Conrad's programs." Six months later Westinghouse officials opened the first licensed broadcasting station in history, KDKA, to stimulate sales of their supplies. By 1922 the number of licensed stations had jumped to 430. And by 1930 nearly one home in three had a radio ("furniture that talks," comedian Fred Allen called it).

At first radio was seen as a civilizing force. "The air is your theater, your college, your newspaper, your library," exalted one ad in 1924. But with the growing number of sets came commercial broadcasting, catering to more common tastes. By 1931 advertisers were paying $10,000 an hour for a national hookup, and the most popular show on radio was *Amos 'n' Andy,* a comedy about African Americans created by two white vaudevillians in 1926. It borrowed its style from black comedians Aubrey Lyles and Flournoy Miller, who occasionally wrote dialogue for the show. A slice of black culture, often stereotyped, sometimes mocked, nonetheless entered mainstream American life.

The vibrant energy of the New Woman is reflected in the geometric designs of this fashionable evening wrap (1928), whose jagged lines also suggest the era's newest vaulting skyscrapers. The beaded handbag (1925) conveys a similar excitement.

At night families gathered around the radio instead of the hearth, listening to a concert, perhaps, rather than going out to hear music. Ticket sales at vaudeville theaters collapsed. The aged, the sick, and the isolated, moreover, could be "at home but never alone," as one radio ad declared. Linked by nothing but airwaves, Americans were finding themselves part of a vast new community of listeners.

Print journalism also broadened its audience during the 1920s. In 1923 Yale classmates Henry R. Luce and Briton Hadden rewrote news stories in a snappy style, mixed them with photographs, and created the country's first national weekly, *Time* magazine. Fifty-five giant newspaper chains distributed 230 newspapers with a combined circulation of 13 million by 1927. Though they controlled less than 10 percent of all papers, the chains pioneered modern mass news techniques. Editors relied on central offices and syndicates to prepare editorials, sports, gossip, and Sunday features for a national readership.

Newspaper chains

In a world in which Americans were rapidly being reduced to anonymous parts of mass, industrialized society, media offered them a chance to identify with the achievements of individuals by creating a world of celebrities and heroes. Sports figures, business executives, and movie stars found their exploits splashed across the front pages of newspapers and magazines and followed on radio by millions hungry for excitement and eager to project their own dreams onto others.

No hero attracted more attention than a shy, reed-thin youth named Charles Lindbergh. Early on the morning of May 20, 1927, "Lucky Lindy" streaked into the skies above Long Island aboard a silver-winged monoplane called the *Spirit of St. Louis* and headed east. Thirty-three hours and thirty minutes later he landed just outside Paris, the first flier to cross the Atlantic alone. Eight others had died trying. An ecstatic mob swamped him and nearly tore his plane to pieces in search of souvenirs.

Charles Lindbergh

Lindbergh, dubbed by reporters the "Lone Eagle," returned with his plane aboard the warship USS *Memphis.* In New York City alone, he was greeted by nearly

The Roxy, the largest theater in the world when it opened in 1926, in all its palatial glory. Such lavish movie houses sought to attract more prosperous middle-class audiences with splendor reminiscent of European cathedrals. On the night the Roxy opened, pealing chimes marked the beginning of the show, whereupon a man dressed as a monk strode onto center stage, pointed to the balcony, and declared, "Let there be light!" Blazing spotlights then set the orchestra aglow. "Does God live here?" asked a little girl in a *New Yorker* cartoon.

4 million cheering fans, and when he sailed up the Potomac, he received a 21-gun salute, an honor previously reserved only for heads of state. Lindbergh had "fired the imagination of mankind," observed one newspaper. Never had one person mastered a machine so completely or conquered nature so courageously. To Americans ambivalent about mass society and worried about being overwhelmed by technology and bureaucracy, Lindbergh's accomplishment was a sign. Perhaps they could control the New Era without losing their cherished individualism. For a moment, Charles Lindbergh made it seem possible, and the media lionized him for it.

Youth Culture

By the 1920s, the drive for public education had placed a majority of teenagers in high school for the first time in American history. College enrollment reached 10 percent of the eligible population by 1928; in 1890 it had been less than 3 percent. A full-blown "peer culture" emerged, as children and adolescents spent more time outside the family among people their own age. Revolving around school and friends, its components were remarkably modern—athletics, clubs, sororities and fraternities, dating, proms, "bull sessions," and moviegoing.

Tolerance for premarital sex among young adults seems to have grown in the 1920s ("necking" and "petting" parties replaced sedate tea parties), but the new subculture of youth still tied sexual relations to love. Casual sex remained rare; what changed was the point at which sexual intimacy occurred. A growing minority of young women reported having premarital intercourse, for example, but only with their future husbands. Unsupervised dating and "going together" replaced chaperoned courting.

For all the frivolity and rebelliousness it promoted, the new youth culture tended to fuse the young to the larger society by promoting widely held values—competitiveness, merit through association, service, prestige. Even notorious young flappers usually ended their courting days with marriages that emphasized the conventional roles of wife and mother.

"Ain't We Got Fun?"

Spectator sports

"Ev'ry morning, ev'ry evening, ain't we got fun?" ran the 1921 hit song. As the average hours on the job each week decreased from 47.2 in 1920 to 42 by 1930, spending on amusement and recreation tripled. Spectator sports came of age. In 1921, some 60,000 fans paid $1.8 million to see Jack Dempsey, the "Manassas Mauler," knock out French champion Georges Carpentier. Millions more listened as radio took them ringside for the first time in sports history. Universities constructed huge stadiums for football—a 60,000-seater at Berkeley, a 64,000-seater at Ohio State. By the end of the decade college football games were outdrawing major league baseball.

Baseball remained the national pastime but became a bigger business. An ugly World Series scandal in 1919 led owners to appoint Judge Kenesaw Mountain Landis as "czar" of the sport early in the decade. His strict rule reformed the game. In 1920 the son of immigrants revolutionized it. George Herman "Babe" Ruth hit 54 home runs and made the New York Yankees the first club to attract a million fans in one season. A heroic producer in an era of consumption, Ruth was also baseball's bad boy. He smoked, drank, cursed, and chased every skirt in sight. Under the guidance of the first modern sports agent, Christy Walsh, Ruth became the highest-paid player in the game and made a fortune endorsing everything from clothing to candy bars.

At parties old diversions—charades, card tricks, recitations—faded in popularity as dancing took over. The ungainly camel walk, the sultry tango, and in 1924 the frantic Charleston were the urban standards. Country barns featured a revival of square dancing with music provided by Detroit's WBZ, courtesy of Henry Ford. And from the turn-of-the-century brothels and gaming houses of New Orleans, Memphis, and St. Louis came a rhythmic, compelling music that swept into nightclubs and over the airwaves: jazz.

Jazz was a remarkably complex blend of several older African American musical traditions, combining the soulfulness of the blues with the brighter syncopated rhythms of ragtime music. The distinctive style of jazz bands came from a marvelous improvising as the musicians embellished melodies and played off one another. The style spread when the "Original Dixieland Jazz Band" (hardly original but possessed of the advantage of being white) recorded a few numbers for the phonograph. The music became a sensation in New York in 1917 and spread across the country. Black New Orleans stalwarts like Joe "King" Oliver's Creole Jazz Band began touring, and in 1924 Paul Whiteman inaugurated respectable "white" jazz in a concert at Carnegie Hall. When self-appointed guardians of good taste denounced such music as "intellectual and spiritual debauchery," Whiteman disagreed: "Jazz is the folk music of the machine age." *Jazz*

The Art of Alienation

Before World War I a generation of young writers had begun to rebel against Victorian purity. The savagery of the war drove many of them even farther from any faith in reason or progress. Instead they embraced a "nihilism" that denied all meaning in life. When the war ended, they turned their resentment against American life, especially its small towns and big businesses, its conformity, technology, and materialism. Some led unconventional lives in New York City's Greenwich Village. Others, called expatriates, left the country altogether for the artistic freedom of London and Paris. *Expatriates* Their alienation helped produce a literary outpouring unmatched in American history.

On the eve of World War I the poet Ezra Pound had predicted an "American Risorgimento" that would "make the Italian Renaissance look like a tempest in a teapot." From Europe the expatriate Pound began to make it happen. Abandoning rhyme and meter in his poetry, he decried the "botched civilization" that had produced the war. Another voluntary exile, T. S. Eliot, bemoaned the emptiness of modern life in his epic poem *The Waste Land* (1922). Ernest Hemingway captured the disillusionment of the age in *The Sun Also Rises* (1926) and *A Farewell to Arms* (1929), novels where resolution came as it had in war—by death.

At home Minnesota-born Sinclair Lewis, the first American to win a Nobel Prize in literature, sketched a scathing vision of midwestern small-town life in *Main Street* (1920). The book described "savorless people . . . saying mechanical things about the excellence of Ford automobiles, and viewing themselves as the greatest race in the world." His next novel, *Babbitt* (1922), dissected small-town businessman George Follansbee Babbitt, a peppy realtor from the fictional city of Zenith. Faintly absurd and supremely dull, Babbitt was the epitome of the average.

The novels of another Minnesotan, F. Scott Fitzgerald, glorified youth and romantic individualism but found redemption nowhere. Fitzgerald's heroes, like Amory Blaine in *This Side of Paradise* (1920), spoke for a generation "grown up to find all Gods dead, all wars fought, all faiths in man shaken." Like most writers of the decade, Fitzgerald saw life largely as a personal affair—opulent, always self-absorbing, and ultimately tragic.

A "New Negro"

As World War I seared white intellectuals, so too did it galvanize black Americans. Wartime labor shortages had spurred a migration of over a million African Americans out of the rural South into northern industrial cities. But postwar unemployment and racial violence quickly dashed black hopes for equality. Common folk in these urban enclaves found an outlet for their alienation in a charismatic nationalist from Jamaica named Marcus Garvey.

Garvey brought his organization, the Universal Negro Improvement Association (UNIA), to America in 1916 in hopes of restoring black pride by returning African Americans to Africa and Africa to Africans. "Up you mighty race," he told his followers, "you can accomplish what you will." When Garvey spoke at the first national UNIA convention in 1920, over 25,000 supporters jammed Madison Square Garden in New York to listen. Even his harshest critics admitted there were least half a million members in more than 30 branches of his organization. It was the first mass movement of African Americans in history. But in 1925 Garvey was convicted of mail fraud and sentenced to prison for having oversold stock in his Black Star Line, the steamship company founded to return African Americans to Africa. His dream shattered.

As Garvey rose to prominence a renaissance of black literature, painting, and sculpture was brewing in Harlem. Since the completion of Manhattan's subway system in 1904, Harlem had grown black after eagerly expected white renters failed to appear. By the end of World War I, Harlem had become the cultural capital of black America.

The first inklings of a renaissance in Harlem came in 1922 when Claude McKay, another Jamaican immigrant, published a book of poems entitled *White Shadows*. In his most famous, "If We Must Die," McKay mixed defiance and dignity: "Like men we'll face the murderous, cowardly pack / Pressed to the wall, dying but fighting back!" Often supported by white patrons, or "angels," the young black writers and artists of Harlem found their subjects in the street life of cities, the folkways of the rural South, and the primitivism of preindustrial cultures. Poet Langston Hughes reminded his readers of the ancient heritage of African Americans in "The Negro Speaks of Rivers," while Zora Neale Hurston collected folktales, songs, and prayers of black southerners.

Born in Jamaica in 1887, Marcus Garvey founded his "Back to Africa" movement in 1914. He went to prison for mail fraud in 1925, but it was like "jailing a rainbow," said one observer. President Coolidge pardoned Garvey in 1927, then deported him to Jamaica.

Though generally not a racial protest, the Harlem Renaissance drew on the new assertiveness of African Americans as well as on the alienation of white intellectuals. In 1925 Alain Locke, a black professor from Howard University, collected a sampling of their works in *The New Negro*. The New Negro, Locke wrote, was "not a cultural foundling without his own inheritance" but "a conscious contributor . . . collaborator and participant in American civilization." The title of the book reflected not only an artistic movement but also a new racial consciousness.

Defenders of the Faith

As mass society pushed the country into a future of machines, organization, middle-class living, and cosmopolitan diversity, not everyone approved. Dr. and Mrs. Wilbur Crafts, the authors of *Intoxicating Drinks and Drugs in All Lands and Times,* set forth a litany of sins that tempted young people in this "age of cities." "Foul pictures, corrupt literature, leprous shows, gambling slot machines, saloons, and Sabbath breaking. . . . *We are trying to raise saints in hell.*"

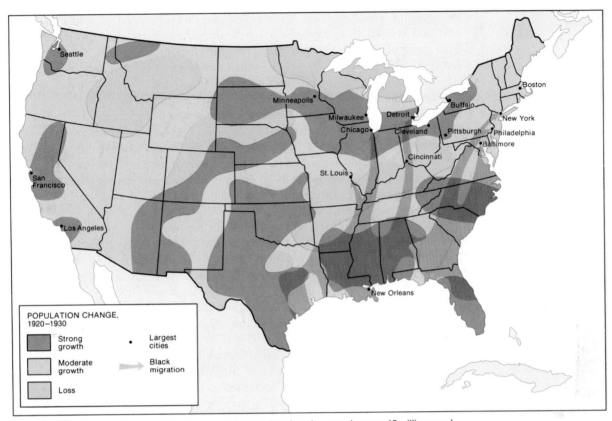

Areas of Population Growth In the 1920s the population of urban America grew by some 15 million people, at the time the greatest 10-year jump in American history. Spurred first by the industrial demands of World War I and then by declining farm income, cities grew largely by depopulating rural areas. The biggest gains were in the South and West, where farmers followed opportunity to cities in climates similar to their own. In the most dramatic manifestation of the overall trend, more than a million African Americans migrated from the rural South to the urban North in hopes of escaping poverty and discrimination.

The changing values of the New Era seemed especially threatening to traditionalists like the Crafts. Their deeply held beliefs reflected the rural roots of so many Americans: an ethic that valued neighborliness, small communities, and a sameness of race, religion, and ethnicity. Improvements in mass media—radio, movies, magazines—made it impossible for isolated communities to avoid national trends, even when they disapproved of them. Opponents of the new ways could be found among countryfolk and rural migrants to cities as well as an embattled Protestant elite. All were determined to defend the older faiths against the modern age.

Nativism and Immigration Restriction

In 1921, two Italian aliens, who freely admitted to being radical anarchists, presented a dramatic challenge to those older faiths. Nicola Sacco and Bartolomeo Vanzetti were sentenced to death—on the face of it, for a shoe company robbery and murder in South Braintree, Massachusetts, committed a year earlier. But the evidence against them was controversial, and critics charged that Sacco and Vanzetti were convicted primarily because they were foreign-born radicals. During

Sacco and Vanzetti

the trial, the presiding judge had scorned them in private as "anarchist bastards" and later refused all motions for a retrial, in spite of a confession to the robbery by a member of a well-known gang. For protesters around the world, Sacco and Vanzetti's execution in 1927 was a symbol of American bigotry and prejudice.

By then, nativism—a rabid hostility to foreigners—had produced the most restrictive immigration laws in American history. In the aftermath of World War I immigration was running close to 1 million a year, almost as high as prewar levels. Most immigrants came from eastern and southern Europe and from Mexico; most were Catholics and Jews. Alarmed white native-born Protestants warned that if the flood continued, Americans might become "a hybrid race of people as worthless and futile as the good-for-nothing mongrels of Central America and Southeastern Europe." Appreciating the wage benefits of a shrunken labor pool, the American Federation of Labor supported restriction.

Mexican Americans

In the Southwest, Mexicans and Mexican Americans became a target of concern. The Spanish had inhabited the region for nearly 400 years, producing a rich blend of European and Indian cultures. By 1900 about 300,000 Mexican Americans lived in the United States. In the following decade Mexicans fleeing poverty and a revolution in 1910 almost doubled the Latino population of Texas and New Mexico. In California it quadrupled. During World War I, labor shortages led authorities to relax immigration laws, and in the 1920s American farmers opened a campaign to attract Mexican farm workers.

Thousands of single young men, known as *solos,* also crossed the border to catch trains for northern industrial cities. By the end of the 1920s, thriving communities of Mexicans could be found in the "barrios"—Mexican neighborhoods—of Kansas City, Detroit, and elsewhere. Spanish-speaking newcomers settled into an immigrant life of family and festivals, churchgoing, hard work, and slow adaptation. As with other immigrants, some returned home, but some brought their families. The census of 1930 listed nearly 1.5 million Mexicans living in the United States, not including an untold number who had entered the country illegally.

National Origins acts

Mexicans were just one target of the first National Origins Act, passed in 1921. It capped all immigration at 350,000 and parceled out the slots by admitting up to 3 percent of each nationality living in the United States as of 1910. That system of quotas privileged "races" commonly believed to be superior—"Nordics"—over those considered inferior—"Alpines" and "Mediterraneans." Asian immigration was virtually banned. In 1924 a second National Origins Act cut the quota to 150,000, reduced the percentage to 2, and pushed the base year back to 1890, before the bulk of southern and eastern Europeans had arrived. To control the flow of illegal aliens, Congress also created the Border Patrol. Its 450 agents, stationed along the boundaries with Canada and Mexico, were scarcely enough to make anything other than a symbolic statement of restrictionist sentiment.

The National Origins Act fixed the pattern of immigration for the next four decades. Immigration from southern and eastern Europe was reduced to a trickle. The free movement of Europeans to America, a migration of classes and nationalities that had been unimpeded for 300 years, came to an end.

The "Noble Experiment"

Eighteenth Amendment

For nearly a hundred years reformers had tried—with sporadic success—to reduce the consumption of alcohol. Their most ambitious campaign climaxed in January 1920 when the Eighteenth Amendment, sanctioning the prohibition of liquor, went

Prohibition spawned a new industry—"bootlegging," or the illegal manufacture and sale of alcohol. The term derived from the practice of hiding an object, say a bottle of alcohol, in the leg of a high boot. This pen-and-ink illustration by Winsor McCay depicts the bootlegger, as its title, *A Giant of Evil*, indicates, as raining down bottles of whiskey.

into effect. Prohibition was not total: private citizens could still drink. They simply could not make, sell, transport, or import any "intoxicating beverage" containing 0.5 percent alcohol or more. The aim was to take the profit out of the liquor trade and reduce alcohol consumption without trampling too heavily on the rights of individuals. By some estimates, the consumption of liquor was cut in half.

From the start, however, enforcement was underfunded and understaffed. In large cities "speakeasies"—taverns operating under cover—were plentiful. Rural stills continued to turn out "moonshine." Even so, the consequences of so vast a social experiment were significant and often unexpected. Prohibition reversed the prewar trend toward beer and wine, because hard liquor brought greater profits to bootleggers. Prohibition also advanced women's rights. Whereas saloons had discriminated against "ladies," either barring them or having them enter by a separate door, speakeasies welcomed them. Prohibition helped to line the pockets and boost the fame of gangsters, including "Scarface" Al Capone. Like Capone, thousands of poor immigrants looked to illegal bootlegging to move them out of the slums. As rival gangs fought over territory, cities erupted in violence. To save lives and profits, gangsters organized crime as if they were nineteenth-century business moguls, dividing their operations and territory and imposing a hierarchical structure of management.

For all its unhappy consequences, Prohibition enjoyed wide backing. The best science of the day taught that alcohol was bad for health; the best social science, that it corroded family life and weakened society. Corporate executives and labor leaders supported Prohibition to promote an efficient and healthy workforce. So did many Catholics, who saw the road to pain and perdition lined with liquor bottles. And the liquor industry hurt itself with a terrible record of corrupting legislatures and, worse still, corrupting minors, who were one target of its aggressive campaign to recruit new drinkers in the competitive saloon business.

Consequences of Prohibition

Yet Prohibition can also be understood as cultural and class legislation. Support had always run deepest in Protestant churches, especially among the evangelical Baptists and Methodists. And there had always been a strong antiurban and anti-immigrant bias among reformers. As it turned out, the steepest decline in drinking occurred among working-class ethnics. Only the well-to-do had enough money to drink regularly without risking death or blindness, the common effects of cheap, tainted liquor. Traditionalists might celebrate the triumph of the "noble experiment," but modern urbanites either ignored or resented it.

Fundamentalism versus Darwinism

Although Aimee Semple McPherson embraced the fashions of the New Era, many Protestants, especially in rural areas, felt threatened by the secular aspects of modern life. Beginning in the late nineteenth century, scientists and intellectuals spoke openly about the relativity of moral values, questioned the possibility of miracles, and analyzed the Bible as if it were simply a historical document. They depicted Christianity as just another step in the development of the ancient Hebrew people and religiosity as the result of hidden psychological needs. Darwinism, pragmatism, and other philosophical and scientific theories left traditional religious teachings open to skepticism or even scorn. Pastors noted that despite an increase of nearly 13 million in church membership, church attendance was slipping. Some churches abandoned Sunday evening services altogether.

Among Protestants, conservatives of various sects worried that their liberal brethren had wandered too far from their faith. As early as the 1870s, liberal Protestants had sought to make Christianity more relevant to contemporary life. Their movement became known as "Modernism," defined by one leader as "the use of scientific, historical and social methods in understanding and applying evangelical Christianity to the needs of living persons."

The Fundamentals

Conservatives disagreed with this updating of orthodoxy, nowhere more publicly than in a series of pamphlets called *The Fundamentals* published between 1910 and 1915 and subsidized by two wealthy oilmen from Los Angeles, Lyman and Milton Stewart. The 3 million copies distributed nationwide called for a return to what they considered to be the fundamentals of belief, among them the virgin birth and resurrection of Jesus, a literal reading of the Creation account in Genesis, and the divinely inspired authorship of the Bible. Where liberal theologians saw the Bible as the product of human beings observing and interpreting godly action within their historical and cultural context, conservatives insisted the Bible was the timeless, revealed word of God. After 1920 a wide variety of conservative Protestants began calling themselves "Fundamentalists," those "willing to do battle royal for the Fundamentals."

The Fundamentalist movement grew dramatically in the first two decades of the twentieth century, fed by fears of Protestant Modernism but also of the Catholic and Jewish immigrants flooding into the country and by colorful evangelists such as former baseball player Billy Sunday. Fundamentalists maintained effective ministries nationwide but especially among Southern Baptists. Nothing disturbed them more than Darwinian theories of evolution that called into question the divine origins of humankind. In 1925 what began as an in-house fight among Protestants became a national brawl when the Tennessee legislature made it illegal to teach that "man has descended from a lower order of animals." Oklahoma, Florida, Mississippi, and Arkansas passed similar statutes.

Encouraged by the newly formed American Civil Liberties Union, a number of skeptics in the town of Dayton, Tennessee, decided to test the law. In the spring of 1925 a bespectacled biology teacher named John T. Scopes was arrested for teaching evolution. Behind the scenes, Scopes's sponsors were as much preoccupied with boosting their town's commercial fortunes as with the defense of academic freedom.

Scopes trial

When the Scopes trial opened in July, it took on the flavor of a championship boxing match. Millions listened over the radio to the first trial ever broadcast. Inside the courtroom Clarence Darrow, the renowned defense lawyer from Chicago and a professed agnostic, acted as co-counsel for Scopes. Serving as a co-prosecutor was William Jennings Bryan, the three-time presidential candidate who had recently joined the antievolution crusade. It was urban Darrow against rural Bryan in what Bryan described as a "duel to the death" between Christianity and evolution.

As Bryan saw it, nonbelievers as well as believers had a stake in the trial's outcome, at least if they lived in small-town America. The industrial revolution, he argued, had brought unprecedented organization to society and had concentrated power in big business and big government. The result was the erosion of community control and personal autonomy. Thus, for Bryan, the teaching of evolution became another battlefield in the struggle between localities and centralized authority, whether in business or government or even science, that was far removed from ordinary citizens. "It isn't proper to bring experts in here to try to defeat the purpose of the people," he said. "I have all the information I want to live by and die by." The presiding judge ruled that scientists could not be used to defend evolution. He considered their testimony "hearsay" because they had not been present at the Creation. The defense virtually collapsed until Darrow called Bryan to the stand as an "expert on the Bible." Under withering examination Bryan admitted, to the horror of his followers, that the Earth might not have been made "in six days of 24-hours." Even so, the Dayton jury took only eight minutes to find Scopes guilty of violating the law and fine him $100.

By then the excesses of the Scopes trial had transformed it into more of a national joke than a confrontation between darkness and light. Yet the debate over evolution raised a larger issue that continued to reverberate across the twentieth century. As scientific, religious, and cultural standards clashed, how much should religious beliefs influence public education?

In the wake of the Scopes trial, the question was resolved in favor of secular over religious instruction, at least in public schools. Before the trial, public education had always contained explicitly religious—indeed, Protestant—components. Now it became increasingly nonreligious. As for the Fundamentalists, they sought shelter. In the public mind, all of Fundamentalism had collapsed into the single image of the Bible-thumping southern redneck clinging to outmoded beliefs. The faith of these true believers never wavered, however. They spent the next two decades spreading their word over the radio and through Bible study and other parachurch groups, biding their time and growing in numbers.

KKK

On Thanksgiving Day 1915, just outside Atlanta, 16 men trudged up a rocky trail to the crest of Stone Mountain. There, as night fell, they set ablaze a large wooden cross and swore allegiance to the Invisible Empire, Knights of the Ku Klux Klan. The KKK was reborn.

As the Ku Klux Klan grew in influence after World War I, race riots erupted in over 25 cities beginning in 1919, including Chicago; Longview, Texas; Knoxville, Tennessee; and Omaha, Nebraska. More than 70 African Americans were lynched in the first year of peace, and 11 were burned alive. Many blacks fought back, their experience in World War I having made them determined to resist repression. In June 1921, rioting in Tulsa left 21 African Americans as well as 11 whites dead. As the billowing smoke in this photograph indicates, white mobs burned whole neighborhoods of the black community. Four companies of the National Guard were called out to reestablish order.

RUNING THE NEGRO OUT OF TULSA   JUNE TH 1. 1921

New Klan

The modern Klan, a throwback to the hooded order of Reconstruction days (page 554), reflected the insecurities of the New Era. Klansmen worried about the changes and conflicts in American society, which they attributed to the rising tide of new immigrants, "uppity women," and African Americans who refused to "recognize their place." Whereas any white man could join the old Klan, the new one admitted only "native born, white, gentile [Protestant] Americans." And the reborn Klan was not confined to the rural South, like the hooded nightriders of Reconstruction. In Texas, Klansmen fed off hatred of Mexicans; in California, of Japanese; in New York, of Jews and other immigrants. By the 1920s the capital of the Klan was Indianapolis, Indiana. More than half of its leadership and over a third of its members came from cities of more than 100,000 people.

The new Klan drew on the culture of small-town America and responded to some of its anxieties about lost personal independence and waning community control. The Klan, organized in local units called "klaverns," gave to local charities and drew on local hatreds. It was avowedly patriotic and bound members together in a special community of "true Americans." It boasted the kind of outfits and rituals familiar in any of the fraternal lodges that blanketed towns and villages across the country. Klan members wore white hooded sheets and satin robes, sang songs called "klodes," and even used a secret hand "klasp."

The "Women of the Ku Klux Klan" had chapters in 36 states, including Indiana, where almost a third of all native-born white women joined. Klanswomen were often God-fearing members of their communities who shunned the "revolution in manners and morals" and saw the Klan as the keeper of traditional values. A typical gathering brought the whole family to a barbecue with fireworks and hymn singing, the evening capped by the burning of a giant cross.

Members came mostly from the middle and working classes: small businesspeople, clerical workers, independent professionals, farmers, and laborers with few skills. Some lived on the edge of poverty. The Klan offered them status, security, and the promise of restoring an older America. It touted white supremacy, chastity, fidelity, and parental authority and fought for laissez-faire capitalism and fundamental Protestantism. When boycotts and whispering campaigns failed to cleanse communities of Jews, Mexicans, Japanese, or others who offended their social code, the Klan resorted to floggings, kidnappings, acid mutilations, and murder.

Using modern methods of promotion, the Klan enrolled perhaps 3 million dues-paying members by the early 1920s. Moving into politics, Klan candidates won control of legislatures in Indiana, Texas, Oklahoma, and Oregon. The organization was instrumental in electing six governors, three senators, and thousands of local officials. In the end, however, the Klan was undone by sex scandals and financial corruption. In November 1925 David Stephenson, grand dragon of the Indiana Klan and the most powerful leader in the Midwest, was sentenced to life imprisonment for rape and second-degree murder.

Republicans Ascendant

"The change is amazing," wrote a Washington reporter shortly after the inauguration of Warren G. Harding on March 4, 1921. Sentries disappeared from the gates of the White House, tourists again walked the halls, and reporters freely questioned the president. The reign of "normalcy," as Harding called it, had begun. "By 'normalcy,'" he explained, ". . . I mean normal procedure, the natural way, without excess."

The Politics of "Normalcy"

"Normalcy"—Harding's misreading of the word *normality*—turned out to be anything but normal. After eight years of Democratic rule, Republicans controlled the White House from 1921 to 1933 and both houses of Congress from 1918 to 1930. Fifteen years of bold reform gave way to eight years of cautious governing. A strengthened executive fell into weak hands. The cabinet and the Congress set the course of the nation.

Harding and his successor, Calvin Coolidge, were content with delegating power. Harding appointed to the cabinet some men of quality, as he promised: jurist Charles Evans Hughes as secretary of state, farm leader Henry C. Wallace as secretary of agriculture, and Herbert Hoover, savior of Belgian war refugees and former head of the Food Administration, as secretary of commerce. He also made, as one critic put it, some "unspeakably bad appointments": his old crony Harry Daugherty as attorney general and New Mexico senator Albert Fall as interior secretary. Daugherty sold influence for cash and resigned in 1923. Only a divided jury saved him from jail. In 1929 Albert Fall became the first cabinet member to be convicted of a felony. In 1922 he had accepted bribes of more than $400,000 for secretly leasing naval oil reserves at Elk Hill, California, and Teapot Dome, Wyoming, to private oil companies.

Harding died suddenly in August 1923, before most of the scandals came to light. Though he would be remembered as lackluster, his tolerance and moderation had a calming influence on the strife-ridden nation. Slowly he had even begun to lead. In 1921 he created a new Bureau of the Budget that brought modern accounting techniques to the management of federal revenues. Toward the end of his administration he cleared an early scandal from the Veterans' Bureau and set an agenda for Congress that included expanding the merchant marine.

To his credit Calvin Coolidge handled Harding's unfavorable legacy with skill and dispatch. He created a special investigatory commission, prosecuted the wrongdoers,

Warren G. Harding

Calvin Coolidge

and restored public confidence. Decisiveness, when he chose to exercise it, was one of Coolidge's hallmarks. He believed in small-town democracy and minimalist government. "One of the most important accomplishments of my administration has been minding my own business," he boasted. Above all Coolidge worshiped wealth. "Civilization and profits," he once said, "go hand in hand."

Coolidge had been in office barely a year when voters returned him to the White House by a margin of nearly two to one in the election in 1924. It was another sign that Americans had wearied of reform and delighted in surging prosperity. Whether the business-dominated policies served the economy or the nation well in the long term is open to question.

The Policies of Mellon and Hoover

Coolidge retained most of Harding's cabinet, including his powerful treasury secretary, Andrew Mellon. The former president of aluminum giant Alcoa, Mellon believed that prosperity "trickled down" from rich to poor through investment, which would raise production, employment, and wages. For more than a decade Mellon devoted himself to encouraging investment by reducing taxes on high incomes and corporations. By the time he was through, Congress had nearly halved taxes.

Unlike Mellon, Commerce Secretary Herbert Hoover (another Harding holdover) was not a traditional Republican. Hoover promoted a progressive brand of capitalism called "associationalism." It involved cooperation between business and government through trade associations, groups of private companies organized industry by industry. Approximately 2000 trade associations had come into being by 1929, many of them nurtured in the heyday of business-government cooperation during World War I. The role of government, as Hoover saw it, was to promote cooperation among businesses, to advise them on how best to act in the public

Associationalism

Andrew Mellon, secretary of the treasury and the millionaire head of an aluminum monopoly, is flanked by Grace and Calvin Coolidge on the lawn of the White House. A disciple of business, President Coolidge believed that what was of "real importance to wage-earners was not how they might conduct a quarrel with their employers but how the business of the country might be so organized as to insure steady employment at a fair rate of pay. If that were done there would be no occasion for a quarrel, and if it were not done a quarrel would do no good."

interest, and to ensure that everyone obeyed the rules. Through associationalism, Hoover married the individualism of the past with what progressives had seen as the efficiency, organization, and cooperation of the future. As such, he represented the best of the New Era.

Conferences sponsored by the Department of Commerce advised trade associations on how to standardize the products of member businesses, share information about pricing and costs, and develop new markets. The Bureau of Standards not only set standards for product design and manufacturing but also researched and published information about marketing and other business practices. The aim was to eliminate waste, cut costs, and end the boom-and-bust business cycle of ruthless competition. In that way, Hoover moved beyond old conservatives who had sought to fashion a healthy environment for business. Instead he aimed to aid business directly by supporting voluntary cooperation and by spreading the new gospel of efficiency and growth.

Both Hoover and Mellon ended up placing government in service of business. Mellon's tax policies helped concentrate wealth in the hands of fewer individuals and corporations, while Hoover's associationalism, for all its faith in the ability of businesses to act for public good, helped them consolidate their power at the expense of the public. By the end of the decade, 200 giant corporations controlled almost half the corporate wealth and nearly a fifth of national wealth. In keeping with this government-sponsored trend, the Anti-Trust Division of the Justice Department offered few objections, while the Supreme Court affirmed the constitutionality of trade associations. And for all the talk of limiting government, its role in the economy grew. So did its size, by more than 40,000 employees between 1921 and 1930. Building on their wartime partnership, government and business dropped all pretense of a laissez-faire economy. "Never before, here or elsewhere, has a government been so completely fused with business," noted the *Wall Street Journal*.

Distress Signals at Home and Abroad

Some economic groups remained outside the magic circle of Republican prosperity. Ironically, they included those people who made up the biggest business in America: farmers. In 1920 farming still had an investment value greater than manufacturing, all utilities, and all railroads combined. A third of the population relied on farming for a living.

Yet the farmers' portion of the national income shrank by almost half during the 1920s. The government withdrew wartime price supports for wheat and ended its practice of feeding refugees with American surpluses. As European farms began producing again, the demand for American exports dropped. New dietary habits meant that average Americans of 1920 ate 75 fewer pounds of food annually than they had 10 years earlier. New synthetic fibers drove down demand for natural wool and cotton fibers.

In 1921 a group of southern and western senators organized the "farm bloc" in Congress to coordinate relief for farmers. Over the next two years they succeeded in bringing stockyards, packers, and grain exchanges under federal supervision. Other legislation exempted farm cooperatives from antitrust actions and created a dozen banks for low-interest farm loans. But regulation and credit were not enough, and over the decade the purchasing power of farmers continued to slide.

For the five years that Coolidge ran a "businessman's government," workers reaped few gains in wages, purchasing power, and bargaining rights. Although welfare capitalism promised workers profit-sharing and other benefits, only a handful of companies put it into practice. Those that did often used it to weaken independent unions. As dangerous imbalances in the economy developed, Coolidge ignored them.

If most Americans paid little attention to the distress signals at home, they ignored economic unrest abroad. At the end of World War I, Europe's victors had forced Germany to take on $33 billion in war costs or reparations, partly to repay their own war debts to the United States. When Germany defaulted in 1923, French forces occupied the Ruhr valley, the center of German industry. Germany struck back by printing more money to cope with the crushing burden of debt. Runaway inflation soon wiped out the savings of the German middle class, shook confidence in the new democratic Weimar Republic, and eventually threatened the economic structure of all Europe.

The Dawes plan

In 1924 American business leader Charles G. Dawes persuaded the victorious Europeans to scale down reparations. In return the United States promised to help stabilize the German economy. Encouraged by the State Department, American bankers made large loans to Germany, with which the Germans paid their reparations. The European victors then used those funds to repay *their* war debts to the United States. It amounted to taking money out of one American vault and depositing it in another. In 1926 the United States also reduced European war debts. Canceling them altogether would have made more sense, but few Americans were that forgiving.

Two grand, if finally futile, gestures reflected the twin desires for peace and economy. In 1921, in a conference held in Washington, the sea powers of the world agreed to freeze battleship construction for 10 years and to set ratios on the tonnage of each navy. The Five-Power Agreement was the first disarmament treaty in modern history. A more extravagant gesture came in 1928, when the major nations of the world (except the Soviet Union) signed the Kellogg-Briand Pact outlawing war. "Peace is proclaimed," announced Secretary of State Frank Kellogg as he signed the document with a foot-long pen of gold.

Kellog-Briand Pact

But what seemed so bold on paper proved timid in practice. The French resented the lower limits set on their battleships under the Five-Power Agreement and touched off a new arms race by building smaller warships such as submarines, cruisers, and destroyers. And with no means of enforcement, the Kellogg-Briand Pact remained a hollow proclamation.

The Election of 1928

On August 2, 1927, in a small classroom in Rapid City, South Dakota, Calvin Coolidge handed a terse, typewritten message to reporters: "I do not choose to run for President in nineteen twenty-eight." Republicans honored the request and nominated Herbert Hoover. Hoover was not a politician but an administrator who had never once campaigned for public office. It did not matter. Republican prosperity made it difficult for any Democrat to win. Hoover, perhaps the most admired public official in America, made it impossible.

The Democratic party continued to fracture between its rural supporters in the South and West and ethnic laborers in the urban Northeast. The two factions had clashed during the 1924 convention, scuttling the presidential candidacy of New York governor Al Smith. By 1928 the shift in population toward cities had given an edge to the party's urban wing. Al Smith won the nomination on the first ballot, even though his handicaps were evident. When the New York City–bred Smith spoke "poysonally" on the "rha-dio," his accent made voters across America wince. Though he pledged to enforce Prohibition, he campaigned against it and

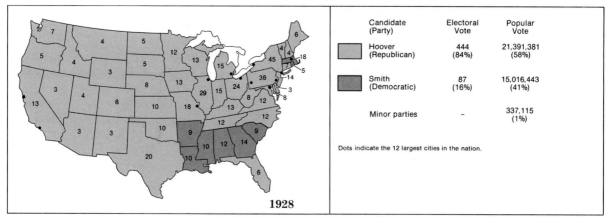

1928

Candidate (Party)	Electoral Vote	Popular Vote
Hoover (Republican)	444 (84%)	21,391,381 (58%)
Smith (Democratic)	87 (16%)	15,016,443 (41%)
Minor parties	–	337,115 (1%)

Dots indicate the 12 largest cities in the nation.

even took an occasional drink (which produced the false rumor that he was a hopeless alcoholic). Most damaging of all, Smith was Catholic at a time when anti-Catholicism remained strong in many areas of the country.

In the election of 1928, nearly 60 percent of the eligible voters turned out to give all but eight states to Hoover. The solidly Democratic South cracked for the first time. Still, the stirrings of a major political realignment lay buried in the returns. The 12 largest cities in the country had gone to the Republicans in 1924; in 1928 the Democrats won them. Western farmers, ignored by Republicans for a decade, also voted for Smith. The Democrats were becoming the party of the cities, of immigrants, and of the long-ignored. Around this core, they would build the most powerful vote-getting coalition of the twentieth century.

Just as important, a new kind of electorate was emerging. No longer were voters part of a vast partisan army whose loyalties were tied to the party year in and year out by barbecues, rallies, and torchlight parades. The reforms of the progressive era had restricted the power of machines and the discipline they could exert over voters. The culture of consumption that had shaped American life in the 1920s also worked to shape politics. Increasingly, parties courted voters with newspaper advertisements and radio "spots." In 1929 the Democrats created the first public relations department in American politics. Paradoxically, the twentieth century would witness a deterioration of party loyalty as the growing reliance on the media to communicate with "consumer/voters" weakened traditional party networks.

Election of 1928 Historians still debate whether the election of 1928 was a pivotal one that produced a significant political realignment. Hoover cracked the solidly Democratic South, which returned to the Democratic fold in 1932. On the other hand, Democrat Al Smith won the twelve largest cities in the country (the black dots on the map), all of which had voted Republican in 1924 but stayed in the Democratic fold in 1932.

Strolling across the felt-padded floor of **The Great Bull Market**
the New York Stock Exchange, Superintendent William Crawford greeted the New Year with swaggering confidence. Nineteen twenty-eight had been a record-setter, with more than 90,500,000 shares traded. The "bulls," or buyers of stock, had routed the bears, those who sell. It was the greatest bull market in history as eager purchasers drove prices to new highs. At the end of the last business day of 1928, Crawford surveyed the floor and declared flatly, "The millennium's arrived."

Veteran financial analyst Alexander Noyes had his doubts. Speculation—buying and selling on the expectation that rising prices will yield quick gains—had taken over the stock market. "Something has to give," said Noyes in September 1929. Less than a month later, the Great Bull Market fell in a heap.

The Rampaging Bull

New blood

No one knows exactly what caused the wave of speculation that boosted the stock market to dizzying heights. Driven alternately by greed and fear, the market succumbed to greed in a decade that considered it a virtue. A new breed of aggressive outsiders helped spread the speculative fever. William Durant of General Motors, the Fisher brothers from Detroit, and others like them bought millions of shares, crowded out more conservative investors from the East, and helped send prices soaring.

New money

Money and credit to fuel the market became plentiful. From 1922 to 1929, some $900 million worth of gold flowed into the country. The money supply expanded by $6 billion. Over the decade corporate profits grew by 80 percent. At interest rates as high as 25 percent, more could be made from lending money to brokers (who then made "brokers' loans" to clients for stock purchase) than from constructing new factories. By 1929 brokers' loans had almost tripled from two years earlier.

"Margin requirements," the cash actually put down to purchase stock, hovered around 50 percent for most of the decade. Thus buyers had to come up with only half the price of a share. The rest came from credit furnished by brokers' loans. As trading reached record heights in August 1929, the Federal Reserve Board tried to dampen speculation by raising the interest rates. Higher interest rates made borrowing more expensive and, authorities hoped, would rein in the galloping bull market. They were wrong. It was already too late.

The Great Crash

At the opening bell on Thursday, October 24, 1929, a torrent of sell orders flooded the Exchange, triggered by nervous speculators who had been selling for the past week. Prices plunged as panic set in. By the end of "Black Thursday" nearly 13 million shares had been traded—a record. Losses stood at $3 billion, another record. Thirty-five of the largest brokerage houses on Wall Street issued a joint statement of reassurance: "The worst has passed."

The worst had just begun. Prices rallied for the rest of the week, buoyed by a bankers' buying pool organized at the House of Morgan. The following Tuesday, October 29, 1929, the bubble burst. Stockholders lost $10 billion in a single day. Within a month industrial stocks lost half of what they had been worth in September. And the downward slide continued for almost four years. At their peak in 1929 stocks had been worth $87 billion. In 1933 they bottomed out at $18 billion.

ON THE FLOOR — N.Y. STOCK EXCHANGE   REGINALD MARSH

The Great Crash did not cause the Great Depression, but it did damage the economy and break the unbounded optimism on which the New Era rested. Although only about 500,000 people were actually trading stocks by the end of the decade, their investments had helped to sustain prosperity. Thousands of middle-class investors lost their savings and their futures. Commercial banks—some loaded with corporate stocks, others financing brokers' loans—reeled in the wake of the crash.

Role of the Crash

The Sickening Slide in Global Perspective

The Great Crash signaled the start of the greatest depression in the history of the modern world. In the United States, the gains of the 1920s were wiped out in a few years. In the first three years after the crash, national income fell by half, factory wages by almost half. By some estimates 85,000 businesses failed.

Although the Great Depression was less prolonged in other countries, the shock waves from the United States rippled across the globe, helping to topple already fragile economies in Europe. American loans, investments, and purchases had propped up Europe since the end of World War I. When those American resources dried up, European governments defaulted on war debts. More European banks failed; more businesses collapsed; unemployment surged to at least 30 million worldwide by 1932.

Europeans scrambled to protect themselves. Led by Great Britain in 1931, 41 nations abandoned the gold standard. Foreign governments hoped to devalue their currencies by expanding their supplies of money. Exports would be cheaper and foreign trade would increase. But several countries did so at once, while each country raised tariffs to protect itself from foreign competition. Devaluation failed, and the resulting trade barriers only deepened the crisis. Between 1929 and 1933 world exports declined by two-thirds, from a high of nearly $3 billion to less than $1 billion. (See the chart at right.)

In Latin America and other regions where countries depended on exporting raw materials, the slide varied. Shrinking sales of metallic minerals, timber, and hides crippled Chile, Bolivia, Peru, and Malaya, while exports of fuel oils still needed to warm homes and run factories shielded Venezuela. Only the Soviet Union escaped catastrophe, with its limited exports and a command economy that had launched a breakneck campaign of industrialization. Even in the Soviet Union, however, bumper crops of Russian wheat forced onto the world market at deflated prices led millions of peasants to starve to death in 1932–1933. Virtually everywhere else economies cracked under the weight of slackening demand and contracting world trade.

In the United States declining sales abroad sent crop prices to new lows. Farm income dropped by more than half—to a paltry $5 billion. The epidemic of rural bank failures spread to the cities. Nervous depositors rushed to withdraw their cash. Even healthy banks could not bear the strain. In August 1930 every bank in

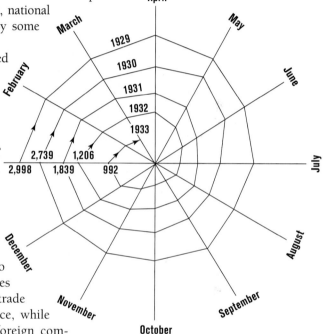

(in millions of dollars)

Declining World Trade, 1929–1933 As the Great Depression deepened, world trade spiraled downward. Here the imports of 75 countries are tracked from 1929 to 1933. (The amounts are measured in millions of U.S. gold dollars.) The greatest annual decline occurred between 1930 and 1931 as production plummeted and nation after nation began to erect high tariff barriers to protect their domestic markets from cheaper imports. Over the four-year period, world import trade fell by almost two-thirds, only underscoring the growing interdependence of the global economy.

Toledo but one closed its doors. Between 1929 and 1933 collapsing banks took more than $20 billion in assets with them. The economy was spiraling downward, and no one could stop it.

The Causes of the Great Depression

What, then, caused the Great Depression in the United States? In the months before the crash, with national attention riveted on the booming stock market, hardly anyone paid attention to existing defects in the American economy. But by 1928 the booming construction and automobile industries began to lose vitality as demand sagged. In fact, increases in consumer spending for all goods and services slowed to a lethargic 1.5 percent for 1928–1929. Warehouses began to fill as business inventories climbed, from $500 million in 1928 to $1.8 billion in 1929.

Overexpansion and relative decline in purchasing power

In one sense, businesses had done all too well. Corporations had boosted their profits by some 80 percent during the 1920s. They had done so by keeping the cost of labor and raw materials low as well as by increasing productivity. But the profits that business reaped were used to expand factories rather than to pay workers higher wages. Without strong labor unions or government support, real wages increased (due largely to falling prices) but never kept pace with productivity, which led to a paradox. As consumers, workers did not have enough money to buy the products they were making ever more efficiently and at lower cost.

Consumer debt and uneven distribution of wealth

People made up the difference between earnings and purchases by borrowing. Consumers bought "on time," paying for merchandise a little each month. During the decade, consumer debt rose by 250 percent. Few could afford to keep spending at that rate. Nor could the distribution of wealth sustain prosperity. By 1929, 1 percent of the population owned 36 percent of all personal wealth. The wealthy had more money than they could possibly spend and saved too much. The working and middle classes had not nearly enough to keep the economy growing, spend though they might.

Banking system

Another problem lay with the banking system. Mismanagement, greed, and the emergence of a new type of executive—half banker, half broker—led banks to divert more funds into speculative investments. The uniquely decentralized American banking system left no way to set things right if a bank failed. At the end of the decade, half of the 25,000 banks in America lay outside the Federal Reserve System. Its controls even over member banks were weak, and during the decade, 6000 banks failed.

Corporate structure and public policy

A shaky corporate structure only made matters worse. No government agency at all monitored the stock exchanges, while big business operated largely unchecked. Insider stock trading, shady stock deals, and outright stock fraud ran rampant. Meanwhile, public policy encouraged corporate consolidation and control because the government filed fewer antitrust suits. High profits and the Mellon tax program helped make many corporations wealthy enough to avoid borrowing. Thus changes in interest rates—over which the Federal Reserve exercised some control—had little influence on such corporations. Free from government regulation, fluctuating prices, and the need for loans, big businesses ruled the economy. And they ruled badly.

"Sick" industries

Unemployment began to increase as early as 1927, a sign of growing softness in the economy. By the fall of 1929 some 2 million people were out of work. Many of them were in textiles, coal mining, lumbering, and railroads. All were "sick" industries during the decade because they suffered from overexpansion, reduced demand, and weak management. Farmers were in trouble too. As European agriculture revived after World War I, farm prices tumbled. American farmers earned 16 percent of the national income in 1919 but only 9 percent in 1929. As more farmers went bust, so did many of the rural banks that had lent them money.

Finally, plain economic ignorance contributed to the calamity. High tariffs protected American industries but discouraged European business from selling to the world's most profitable market. Because Europeans weren't profiting, they lacked the money for American goods being shipped to Europe. Only American loans and investments supported demand abroad. When the American economy collapsed, those vanished and with them went American foreign trade. Furthermore, the Federal Reserve had been stimulating the economy both by expanding the money supply and by lowering interest rates. Those moves only fed the speculative fever by furnishing investors with more money at lower costs. A decision finally to raise interest rates in 1929 to stem speculation ended up speeding the slide.

Economic ignorance

"Everyone ought to be rich," proclaimed one enthusiastic investment adviser in *The Ladies Home Journal*—at a time when the economy was still bubbling and the stock market was setting new highs. Americans like him had nothing but faith in their New Era: in its capacity to produce abundance and spread wealth, in its promise of technological freedom from toil and want, in its ability to blend the vast differences among Americans into a mass culture in which individuals would nonetheless retain their identities. They put their money, some quite literally, on this modernism. Others objected to the price being paid in lost community and independence. They wanted to resurrect a world less organized, less bureaucratized, less complex and varied—a world less modern. In the 1920s, the tensions between these contrasting ideals sparked the first culture wars of the twentieth century.

As the economy began to collapse in upon itself, the heady optimism of the decade vanished as quickly as the culture wars. The first modern decade gave way to a depression more severe and prolonged than any in history, and no one—not the brokers of Wall Street nor the captains of industry, not the leaders of government nor the citizens on Main Street—had any clear notion of what to do about it.

chapter summary

The New Era of the 1920s brought a booming economy and modern times to America, vastly accelerating the forces of change—bureaucracy, productivity, technology, advertising and consumerism, mass media, peer culture, and suburbanization. Urban-rural tensions peaked with shifts in population that gave cities new power. But as the decade wore on, weaknesses in the economy and a new ethos of getting and spending, too much of it on credit, proved to be the New Era's undoing.

- Technology, advertising and consumer spending, and such boom industries as automobile manufac-

turing and construction fueled the largest peacetime economic growth in American history.

- Key features of modern life—mass society, mass culture, and mass consumption—took hold, fed by mass media in the form of radio, movies, and mass-circulation newspapers and magazines.

- Modern life unsettled old ways and eroded social conventions that had limited life especially for women and children, leading to the emergence of a New Woman and a youth culture.

- Great migrations of African Americans from the rural South to the urban North and of Latinos from Mexico to the United States reshaped the social landscape.

- Traditional culture, centered in rural America, hardened and defended itself against change through immigration restriction, Prohibition, Fundamentalism, and a reborn Ku Klux Klan.

- A galloping bull market in stocks reflected the commitment of government to big business and economic growth.

- When the stock market crashed in 1929, weaknesses in the economy—overexpansion, declining purchasing power, uneven distribution of wealth, weak banking and corporate structures, "sick" industries, and economic ignorance—finally brought the economy down, and with it the New Era came to a close.

interactive learning

The Primary Source Investigator CD-ROM offers the following materials related to this chapter:

- Interactive maps: **Election of 1928** (M7); **Breakdown of Rural Isolation: Expansion of Travel Horizons in Oregon, IL** (M22); and **Areas of Population Growth, 1920–1930** (M25)

- A collection of primary sources revealing the rapid changes experienced by Americans in the 1920s: a photo of a Model T Ford and a collection of beauty tips for women. Other documents recount the rise of racism and hate crimes in the United States: the constitution of the Ku Klux Klan, a political cartoon depicting Uncle Sam's resistance to illiterate voters, and a number of sources on the trial and execution of Sacco and Vanzetti.

additional reading

For years, Frederick Lewis Allen, *Only Yesterday: An Informal History of the 1920s* (1931), shaped the stereotyped view of the decade as a frivolous interlude between World War I and the Great Depression. William Leuchtenburg, *The Perils of Prosperity, 1914–1932* (1958), began an important reconsideration by stressing the serious conflict between urban and rural America and the emergence of modern mass society. Lynn Dumenil updates Leuchtenburg in her excellent *The Modern Temper: American Culture and Society in the 1920s* (1995). Ann Douglas, *Terrible Honesty: Mongrel Manhattan in the 1920s* (1995), puts Manhattan at the core of the cultural transformation in the 1920s, especially its success at bringing African American folk and popular art into the mainstream. On the Scopes trial, see Edward J. Larson, *Summer for the Gods: The Scopes Trial and America's Continuing Debate over Science and Religion* (1997), for a thorough and nuanced discussion of the religious roots of the controversy over Darwinism.

Roland Marchand, *Advertising the American Dream: Making Way for Modernity, 1920–1940* (1985), analyzes the role of advertising in shaping mass consumption, values, and culture, and Ellis Hawley, *The Great War and the Search for a Modern Order* (1979), emphasizes economic institutions. Three recent studies explore continuity and change for women in the 1920s: Kathleen M. Blee, *Women of the Klan: Racism and Gender in the 1920s* (1991); Virginia Scharff, *Taking the Wheel: Women and the Coming of the Motor Age* (1991); and Jacqueline Jones, *Labor of Love, Labor of Sorrow: Black Women, Work, and Family, from Slavery to the Present* (1985).

The most thorough and readable examination of the stock market and its relation to the economy and public policy in the 1920s is still Robert Sobel, *The Great Bull Market: Wall Street in the 1920s* (1968). The best books on the disintegration of the American economy remain Lester Chandler, *America's Greatest Depression, 1929–1941* (1970), and, from a global standpoint, Charles Kindleberger, *The World in Depression, 1929–1939* (1973). For an analysis of the Great Depression from the perspective of Keynesian economics that stresses declining purchasing power and investment, see John Kenneth Galbraith, *The Great Crash* (rev. ed., 1988). For the argument of monetarists, who see the roots of the depression in the shrinking money supply, see Milton Friedman and Anna Jacobson Schwartz, *Monetary History of the United States* (1963), and Peter Temin, *Did Monetary Forces Cause the Great Depression?* (1976). For a fuller list of readings, see the Bibliography at www.mhhe.com/davidsonnation5.

significant events

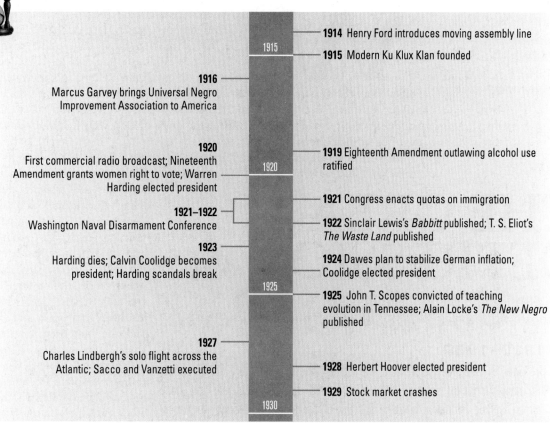

1914 Henry Ford introduces moving assembly line

1915

1915 Modern Ku Klux Klan founded

1916
Marcus Garvey brings Universal Negro
Improvement Association to America

1920
First commercial radio broadcast; Nineteenth
Amendment grants women right to vote; Warren
Harding elected president

1919 Eighteenth Amendment outlawing alcohol use
ratified

1920

1921 Congress enacts quotas on immigration

1921–1922
Washington Naval Disarmament Conference

1922 Sinclair Lewis's *Babbitt* published; T. S. Eliot's
The Waste Land published

1923
Harding dies; Calvin Coolidge becomes
president; Harding scandals break

1924 Dawes plan to stabilize German inflation;
Coolidge elected president

1925

1925 John T. Scopes convicted of teaching
evolution in Tennessee; Alain Locke's *The New Negro*
published

1927
Charles Lindbergh's solo flight across the
Atlantic; Sacco and Vanzetti executed

1928 Herbert Hoover elected president

1929 Stock market crashes

1930

Chapter 25

W inner, South Dakota, November 10, 1933. "Dammit, I don't WANT to write to you again tonight. It's been a long, long day, and I'm tired." All the days had been long since Lorena Hickok began her cross-country trek. Four months earlier Harry Hopkins, in charge of the federal relief program in President Franklin Roosevelt's new administration, had hired the journalist to report on government efforts to help Americans. Forget about statistics or the "social worker angle," he told her. "Talk with the unemployed, those who are on relief and those who aren't, and when you talk to them," he added, "don't ever forget that but for the grace of God you, I, any of our friends might be in their shoes."

As she toured the country in 1933 and 1934, Hickok found that Roosevelt's relief program was falling short. Its half-billion-dollar subsidy to states, localities, and charities was still leaving out too many Americans, such as the sharecropper Hickok discovered near Raleigh, North Carolina. He and his daughters had been living in a tobacco barn for two weeks on little more than weeds and table scraps. "Seems like we just keep goin' lower and lower," said the blue-eyed 16-year-old. To Hickok's surprise, hope still flickered in those eyes. She couldn't explain it until she noticed a pin on the girl's chest. It was a campaign button from the 1932 election—"a profile of the President." Hope sprang from the man in the White House.

THE GREAT DEPRESSION & *The New Deal*

1929–1939

preview • The Great Depression, the longest one in the history of the nation, left many Americans shaken. Rates of birth and marriage declined, and many women worked additional hours in and out of the home. Sufferings were most acute among agricultural migrants, African Americans, Latinos, and American Indians. Franklin Roosevelt's New Deal attacked the Depression along three broad fronts: recovery for the economy, relief for the needy, and reforms designed to ward off future depressions. It succeeded in all but the quest for recovery.

Before Franklin D. Roosevelt, the White House was far removed from ordinary citizens. His predecessor, President Herbert Hoover, had been distant and austere. The only federal agency with which Americans had any contact at all was the post office. And after 1929, it usually delivered bad news. The old order was widely perceived to have failed, and nothing, least of all government, seemed capable of reviving it.

As Lorena Hickok traveled the country in 1933, a year after Roosevelt's election, she detected a change. Perhaps people talked about long-awaited contributions to relief or maybe reforms in securities and banking or the new recovery programs for industry and agriculture. Just as likely it was Franklin Roosevelt they were talking about. Hickok seldom heard voters call themselves "Republicans" or "Democrats" anymore. Instead, she wrote, they were "for the president."

The mail carried other signs that plain people were looking to Washington, the federal government, and the president as at no time since the Civil War. The first weekend after Roosevelt's inauguration nearly half a million letters and telegrams poured into the White House. For years the average remained a record 5000 to 8000 a day. Over half the letters came from those at the bottom of the economic heap. Most sought help, offered praise, or just expressed their gratitude.

Migrants flocked to California during the Great Depression, often in jalopies like the one pictured behind these laborers in John Langley Howard's mural. By 1932 over a million homeless Americans wandered the nation. But a sign of the New Deal can be seen in the mural also: Shasta Dam along the Sacramento River, one of many dams built with federal funds that extended the power of the New Deal, quite literally in this case, all across the country.

Whatever the individual messages, their collective meaning was clear: Franklin D. Roosevelt and his "New Deal" for the American people had begun to restore hope. Though it never brought about a full recovery, the New Deal did improve economic conditions and did provide relief to thousands of Americans. It reformed the economic system and committed the federal government to managing its ups and downs. Finally, the New Deal extended the progressive drive to soften the impact of industrialization and translated decades of growing concern for the disadvantaged into a federal aid program. For the first time, Americans believed Washington would help them through a terrible crisis. The liberal state came of age: active, interventionist, and committed to social welfare.

The Human Impact of the Great Depression

Long breadlines snaked around corners. Vacant-eyed apple-sellers stood shivering in the wind. A man with his hat in his hand came to the back door asking for food in exchange for work. Fewer automobiles rode the streets; more hoboes rode the rails. Between 1929 and 1932

Shantytowns (called "Hoover-villes" after President Herbert Hoover) sprang up around most cities as the Depression deepened. Sometimes the down-and-out turned to desperate action. In 1931 a hunger riot broke out when the unemployed stormed a grocery store in Oklahoma City. Meanwhile, thousands occupied the Seattle County-City Building to protest conditions there. Two years later in Chicago, 55 citizens were arrested when they were found tearing down a four-story building and taking it away brick by brick.

an average of 100,000 people lost their jobs every week until some 13 million Americans were jobless. At least one worker in four could find no work at all.

The Great Depression was a great leveler that reduced differences in the face of common want. The New York seamstress without enough piecework to pay her rent felt the same pinch of frustration and anger as the Berkeley student whose college education was cut short when the bank let her father go. Not everyone was devastated. Most husbands had some job. Most wives continued as homemakers. Most Americans got by as best they could, often cooperating with one another, practicing a ruthless underconsumption to make ends meet. "We lived lean," recalled one Depression victim. So did most of the American people—northern and southern, urban and rural, black, white, brown, yellow, and red.

Hard Times

Subsistence incomes

Hard times lasted for a decade. Even before the Great Crash many Americans were having trouble making a living. Economists calculated that for the barest necessities a family of four in the golden year of 1929 required $2000 a year—more money than 60 percent of American families earned.

As soup kitchens opened and breadlines formed in cities across the nation, survival often became the goal. Millions stayed alive by foraging like animals, and city hospitals began receiving new patients ill from starvation. Pellagra and other diseases associated with malnutrition increased. Despite official claims that "no one has starved," the New York City Welfare Council reported 29 victims of starvation and 110 dead of malnutrition in 1932. Most were children.

Unable to pay mortgages or rent, many families lived off the generosity of forgiving landlords. Some traded down to smaller quarters or simply lost their homes. By 1932 between 1 million and 2 million Americans were homeless wanderers, among them an estimated 25,000 nomadic families. For the first time, emigration out of the United States exceeded immigration into it because Americans could find no work in their own country.

Marriages and births, symbols of faith in the future, decreased. For the first time in three centuries the curve of population growth began to level, as many young couples postponed having children. Experts worried about an impending "baby crop shortage." Strong families hung together and grew closer; weak ones languished or fell apart. Although divorce declined, desertion—the "poor man's divorce"—mushroomed. Under the strain, rates of mental illness and suicide rose as well. **Marriage and family**

Many fathers, whose lives had been defined by work, suddenly had nothing to do. They grew listless and depressed. Most mothers stayed home and found their traditional roles as nurturer and household manager less disrupted than the roles of their husbands as breadwinners. Between 1929 and 1933 living costs dropped 25 percent, but family incomes tumbled by 40 percent. Homemakers watched household budgets with a closer eye than ever. They canned more food and substituted less expensive fish for meat. When they earned extra money, they often did so within the confines of the "woman's sphere" by taking in boarders, laundry, and sewing; opening beauty parlors in their kitchens; and selling baked goods. **Fathers and mothers**

Family life took on new importance, and the home emerged as the center of recreation. Surveys showed that while Americans dreamed of the outdoors—swimming, boating, or playing tennis—they spent most of their free time at home. Board games such as Monopoly and card games like contract bridge enjoyed great popularity. Between 1934 and 1937, phonograph record sales jumped a hundredfold, and reading became the number one form of entertainment.

For those women who worked outside the home, prejudice still relegated them to so-called women's work. Over half the female labor force continued to work in domestic service or the garment trades, while others found traditional employment as schoolteachers, social workers, and secretaries. Only slowly did the female proportion of the workforce reach pre-Depression levels, until it rose finally to 25 percent by 1940, largely because women were willing to take almost any job.

Whether in the renewed importance of homemaking and family life or the reemergence of home industries, the Great Depression sent ordinary Americans scurrying for the reassuring shelter of past practices and left many of them badly shaken. Shame, self-doubt, and pessimism became epidemic as people blamed themselves for their circumstances and turned their anger inward. "Shame? You tellin' me?" recalled one man. "I would go stand on the relief line [and] bend my head low so nobody would recognize me." The lasting legacy of humiliation and fear—that you had caused your own downfall; that the bottom would drop out again; that life would be leveled once more; that the next depression might not end—was what one writer called an "invisible scar." **Psychological impact**

The Golden Age of Radio and Film

By the end of the decade almost 9 out 10 families owned radios. People depended on radios for nearly everything—news, sports, and weather; music and entertainment; advice on how to bake a cake or find God. Some programming helped change national habits. When *The Sporting News* conducted a baseball poll in 1932, editors were surprised to discover that a "new crop of fans has been created by radio . . . the women." Many women were at home during the day when most games were played, and broadcasters went out of their way to educate these new listeners. Night games soon outran day games in attendance, in part because husbands began taking wives and daughters, whose interest was sparked by radio. **Programming**

Radio entered a golden age of commercialism. Advertisers hawked their products on variety programs like *Major Bowes' Amateur Hour* and comedy shows with

George Burns and Gracie Allen. Daytime melodramas (called "soap operas" because they were sponsored by soap companies) aimed at women with stories of the personal struggles of ordinary folk.

Radio continued to bind the country together. A teenager in Splendora, Texas, could listen to the same wisecracks from Jack Benny, the same music from Guy Lombardo, as kids in New York and Los Angeles. In 1938 Orson Welles broadcast H. G. Wells's classic science fiction tale *The War of the Worlds.* Americans everywhere listened to breathless reports of an "invasion from Mars," and many believed it. In Newark, New Jersey, cars jammed roads as families rushed to evacuate the city. The nation, bombarded with reports of impending war in Europe and used to responding to radio advertising, was prepared to believe almost anything, even reports of invaders from Mars.

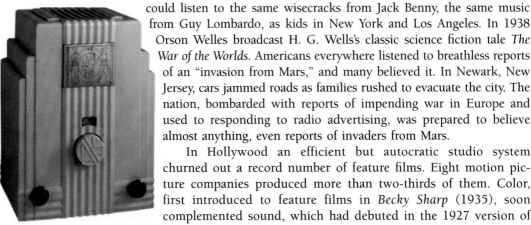

Art Deco radio, 1930. Art Deco, popularized in the 1920s, relied on the geometrical patterns of machines arranged in decorative designs.

In Hollywood an efficient but autocratic studio system churned out a record number of feature films. Eight motion picture companies produced more than two-thirds of them. Color, first introduced to feature films in *Becky Sharp* (1935), soon complemented sound, which had debuted in the 1927 version of *The Jazz Singer.* Neither alone could keep movie theaters full. As attendance dropped early in the Depression, big studios such as Metro-Goldwyn-Mayer and Universal lured audiences back with films that shocked, titillated, and just plain entertained.

By the mid-1930s more than 60 percent of Americans were going to the movies at least once a week. They saw tamer films as the industry began regulating movie content in the face of growing criticism. In 1933 the Catholic Church created the Legion of Decency to monitor features. To avoid censorship and boycotts, studios stiffened their own regulations. Producers could not depict homosexuality, abortion, drug use, or sex. (Even the word *sex* was banned, as was all profanity.) If couples were shown in bed, they had to be clothed and one foot of each partner had to touch the floor. Middle-class morality reigned on the screen, and most Depression movies, like most of popular culture, preserved traditional values.

"Dirty Thirties": An Ecological Disaster

Dust Bowl

Each year between 1932 and 1939 an average of nearly 50 dust storms, or "black blizzards," turned 1500 square miles between the Oklahoma panhandle and western Kansas into a gigantic "Dust Bowl." The baleful effects were felt as far north as the Dakotas and as far south as Texas. It was one of the worst ecological disasters in modern history. Nature played its part, scorching the earth and whipping the winds. But the "dirty thirties" were mostly human-made. The semiarid lands west of the 98th meridian were not suitable for agriculture or livestock. Sixty years of intensive farming and grazing had stripped the prairie of its natural vegetation and rendered it defenseless against the elements. When the dry winds came, one-third of the Great Plains just blew away.

The dust storms lasted anywhere from hours to days. Walking into one was like walking into "a wall of dirt." "This is the ultimate darkness," despaired a Kansan in the midst of one storm. "So must come the end of the world." Winds carried the dust aloft so high that yellow grit from Nebraska collected on the windowsills of the White House, and ships 300 miles off the East Coast found bits of Montana and Wyoming on their decks. Even the fish died—from lack of oxygen in dust-coated rivers.

"Black blizzards" dwarfed all fabricated structures. The drought that gave rise to the huge dust storms lasted from 1932 until 1936, and few who lived through a black blizzard ever forgot it. "Noon was like night," reported a conductor on the Santa Fe railroad. "There was no sun, and, at times, it was impossible to see a yard. The engineer could not see the signal lights." In a single day in 1934, 12 million tons of western dirt fell on Chicago.

Some 3.5 million plains people abandoned their farms. Landowners or corporations forced off about half of them as large-scale commercial farming slowly spread into the heartland of America. Commercial farms were more common in California, where 10 percent of the farms grew more than 50 percent of the crops. As in industrial America, the strategy in agricultural America was to consolidate and mechanize. As farms grew in size, so did the number of tenants. In most Dust Bowl counties people owned less than half the land they farmed. American agriculture was turning from a way of life into an industry. And as the economy contracted, owners cut costs by cutting workers.

Relief offices around the country reported a change in migrant families. Rather than black or brown, more and more were white and native-born, typically a young married couple with one child. Most did not travel far, perhaps to the next county. Long-distance migrants from Oklahoma, Arizona, and Texas usually set their sights on California. Handbills and advertisements promised jobs picking fruit and harvesting vegetables. If they were like the Joad family in John Steinbeck's classic novel *The Grapes of Wrath* (1939), they drove west along Route 66 through Arizona and New Mexico, their belongings piled high atop rickety jalopies, heading for the West Coast.

More than 350,000 Oklahomans migrated to California—so many that "Okie" came to mean any Dust Bowler, even though most of Oklahoma lay outside the Dust Bowl. The poor were only a small minority of new arrivals, but enough came to make Californians edgy. By the middle of the decade Los Angeles police had formed "bum blockades" to keep migrants out. "Negroes and Okies upstairs," read one sign in a San Joaquin Valley theater. Native-born whites had never encountered such discrimination before.

Only one in two or three migrants actually found work. The labor surplus allowed growers to set their own terms. A migrant family earned about $450 a year, less than a third the subsistence level. Families that did not work formed wretched enclaves called "little Oklahomas." The worst were located in the fertile Imperial Valley. There, at the end of the decade, relief officials discovered a family of 10 living in a 1921 Ford. When told to go, the mother responded vacantly, "I wonder where?"

Impact of commercial farming

Mexican Americans and Repatriation

Cesar Chavez

The Chavez family lost their farm in the North Gila River valley of Arizona in 1934. They had owned a small homestead near Yuma for two generations, but the Depression pushed them out. Cesar, barely six years old at the time, remembered only images of the departure: a "giant tractor" leveling the corral; the loss of his room and bed; a beat-up Chevy hauling the family west; his father promising to buy another farm someday.

The elder Chavez could never keep his promise. Instead he and his family lived on the road, "following the crops" in California. In eight years Cesar went to 37 schools. The family was forced to sell their labor to unscrupulous *enganchistas*, or contractors, for less than $10 a week. The father joined strikers in the Imperial Valley in the mid-1930s, but they were crushed. "Some people put this out of their minds and forget it," said Cesar Chavez years later. "I don't." Thirty years later he founded the United Farm Workers of America, the first union of migratory workers in the country.

Repatriation

A deep ambivalence had always characterized American attitudes toward Mexicans, but the Great Depression turned most Anglo communities against them. Cities such as Los Angeles, fearing the burden of relief, found it cheaper to ship Mexicans home. Some migrants left voluntarily. Others were driven out by frustrated officials or angry neighbors. Beginning in 1931 the federal government launched a series of deportations, or "repatriations," of Mexicans back to Mexico. These deportations often included the Mexicans' American-born children, who by law were citizens of the United States. During the decade the Latino population of the Southwest dropped by 500,000. In Chicago, the Mexican community shrank almost by half. Staying in the United States often turned out to be as difficult as leaving. The average income of Mexican American families in the Rio Grande valley of Texas was $506 a year. The sum represented the combined income of parents and children. Following the harvest made schooling particularly difficult: fewer than 2 Mexican American children in 10 completed five years of school.

LULAC and ethnic identity

For Americans of Mexican descent, the Great Depression only deepened anxiety over identity. Were they Mexicans, as many Anglos regarded them, or were they Americans, as they regarded themselves? In the 1920s, such questions had produced several organizations founded to assert the American identity of native-born and naturalized Mexican Americans and to pursue their civil rights. In 1929, on the eve of the Depression, many of these organizations were consolidated into the League of United Latin American Citizens (LULAC). By the early 1940s, "Flying Squadrons" of LULAC organizers had founded some 80 chapters nationwide, making it the largest Mexican American civil rights association in the country.

LULAC permitted only those Latinos who were American citizens to join, thus excluding hundreds of thousands of ethnic Mexicans who nonetheless regarded the United States as their home. It pointedly conducted meetings in English, relied heavily on the assimilated middle class for leadership, and stressed desegregation of public schools, voter registration, and an end to discrimination in public facilities and on juries.

Perhaps LULAC's clearest statement of intent in the 1930s came in its support for immigration restriction from Mexico as a means of both establishing the "Americanness" of its members and creating more jobs for Mexican Americans already here. Still, LULAC counted small farmers, ranchers, and wage laborers among its rank and file, many of whom identified strongly with Mexico. And despite

LULAC's efforts to distance itself from Mexican immigrants, women members raised funds for milk, eyeglasses, Christmas toys, and clothes for the new arrivals.

African Americans in the Depression

Hard times were nothing new to African Americans. "The Negro was born in depression," opined one black man. "It only became official when it hit the white man." Still, when the Depression struck, black unemployment surged. By 1932 it reached 50 percent, twice the national level. By 1933 several cities reported between 25 and 40 percent of their black residents with no support except relief payments. Even skilled black workers who retained their jobs saw their wages cut in half, according to one study of Harlem in 1935.

During the 1930s, with crop failures common, the annual income for black sharecroppers in the South averaged little more than $200. This poignant drawing in charcoal, titled *There Were No Crops*, won a first-place prize at the American Negro Exposition in Chicago in 1940 for the African American artist Charles White.

Migration out of the rural South, up by 800,000 during the 1920s, dropped by 50 percent in the 1930s. As late as 1940 three of four African Americans still lived in rural areas, yet conditions there were just as bad as in cities. In 1934 one study estimated the average income for black cotton farmers at under $200 a year. Millions of African Americans made do by stretching meager incomes, as they had for years.

Father Divine and Elijah Muhammad

Like many African Americans, George Baker refused to be victimized by the Depression. Baker had moved from Georgia to Harlem in 1915. He changed his name to M. J. Divine and founded a religious cult that promised followers an afterlife of full equality. In the 1930s Father Divine preached economic cooperation and opened shelters, or "heavens," for regenerate "angels," black and white. In Detroit, Elijah Poole changed his name to Elijah Muhammad and in 1931 established the Black Muslims, a blend of Islamic faith and black nationalism. He exhorted African Americans to celebrate their African heritage, to live a life of self-discipline and self-help, and to strive for a separate all-black nation.

The Depression inflamed racial prejudice. "Dust has been blown from the shotgun, the whip, and the noose," reported *The New Republic* in 1931, "and Ku Klux Klan practices were being resumed in the certainty that dead men not only tell no tales but create vacancies." Lynchings tripled between 1932 and 1933. In 1932 the Supreme Court ordered a retrial in the most celebrated racial case of the decade. A year earlier nine black teenagers had been accused of raping two white women on a train bound for Scottsboro, Alabama. Within weeks all-white juries had sentenced eight of them to death. The convictions rested on the testimony of the women, one of whom later admitted that the boys had been framed. Appeals kept the case alive for almost a decade. In the end charges against four of the "Scottsboro boys" were dropped. The other five received substantial prison sentences.

Scottsboro boys

The Tragedy of Herbert Hoover

The presidency of Herbert Hoover began with great promise but soon became the worst ordeal of his life. "I have no fears for the future of our country," he had announced at his inauguration in March 1929. "It is bright with hope." Within seven months a "depression" had struck. (Hoover himself coined the term to minimize the crisis.) Try as he might, he could not beat it and the nation turned against him. "People were starving because of Herbert Hoover," sputtered an angry mother in 1932. "Men were killing themselves because of Herbert Hoover, and their fatherless children were being packed away to orphanages . . . because of Herbert Hoover." The charge was unfair, but it stuck. For all of Hoover's promise and innovative intelligence, his was to be a transitional presidency, important as a break from the do-nothing presidents of past depressions and as a herald of the new, more active presidents to come.

The Failure of Relief

Private charity

By the winter of 1931–1932 the story was the same everywhere: relief organizations with too little money and too few resources to make much headway against the Depression. Once-mighty private charity had dwindled to 6 percent of all relief funds. Ethnic charities tried to stave off disaster for their own. Mexican Americans and Puerto Ricans turned to *mutualistas*, traditional societies that provided members with social support, life insurance, and sickness benefits. In San Francisco, the Chinese Six Companies offered food and clothing to needy Chinese Americans. But as the head of the Federation of Jewish Charities warned, private efforts were failing. The government would be "compelled, by the cruel events ahead of us, to step into the situation and bring relief on a large scale."

City services

An estimated 30 million needy people nationwide quickly depleted city treasuries, already pressed because nearly 30 percent of city taxpayers had fallen behind in paying the taxes they owed. In Philadelphia relief payments to a family of four totaled $5.50 a week, the highest in the country. Some cities gave nothing to unmarried people or childless couples, no matter how impoverished they were. New Orleans refused all new applications for aid in 1931. By the end of 1931, Detroit, Boston, and scores of other cities were bankrupt.

Louis Ribak's *Home Relief Station* grimly portrays the failing relief efforts of private charities and the humiliation of applying for relief. A crowd of broken men and women sits anxiously as a burly administrator interrogates a frail relief applicant. To go on relief, said one man, was to endure a "crucifixion."

Cities clamored for help from state capitals, but after a decade of extravagant spending and sloppy bookkeeping, many states were already running in the red. As businesses and property values collapsed, tax bases shrank and with them state revenues. Michigan, one of the few states to provide any relief, reduced funds by more than half between 1931 and 1932. Until New York established its Temporary Emergency Relief Administration (TERA) in 1931, no state had any agency at all to handle the problem of unemployment.

TERA

Some people refused to accept help even when they qualified. Before applications could even be considered, all property had to be sold, all credit exhausted, all relatives declared flat broke. After a half-hour grilling about his family, home, and friends, one applicant left, "feeling I didn't have any business living any more." Hostile officials attached every possible stigma to aid. Ten states enacted property requirements for voting. The destitute were being disfranchised.

The Hoover Depression Program

From the fall of 1930 onward, President Herbert Hoover took responsibility for ending the crisis, and as humanely as possible. It was a mark of his character. Orphaned at nine, he became one of Stanford University's first graduates and, before the age of 40, the millionaire head of one of the most successful mine engineering firms in the world. As a good Quaker, he balanced private gain with public service, saving starving Belgian refugees in 1915 after war broke out in Europe. He worked 14 hours a day, paid his own salary, and convinced private organizations and businesses to donate food, clothing, and other necessities. In his honor, Finns coined a new word: to "hoover" meant to help.

As secretary of commerce under Harding and Coolidge, Hoover perfected his associational philosophy (see page 808). It rested on the notion that government should foster private solutions to public problems by promoting voluntary cooperation among businesses and between businesses and government. Even so, when the Depression struck, his was no do-nothing presidency. Past presidents had feared that any intervention at all by government would upset the natural workings of the economy and that their sole responsibility was to keep the budget balanced. But Hoover understood the vicious cycle in which rising unemployment drove down consumer demand, and he appreciated the need for stimulating investment. He set in motion an unprecedented program of government activism.

Despite the president's best efforts, his program failed. As a good associationalist, Hoover rallied business leaders, who pledged to maintain employment, wages, and prices—only to see those leaders back down as the economy sputtered. He pushed a tax cut through Congress in 1930 in order to increase the purchasing power of consumers. But when the cuts produced an unbalanced federal budget, Hoover reversed course. At bottom he firmly believed that capitalism would generate its own recovery and that a balanced federal budget was required in order to restore the confidence of business. Too much government action, he worried, might destroy the very economic system he was seeking to save. So he agreed to tax increases in 1932, further undermining investment and consumption.

Herbert Hoover

Equally disastrous, the president endorsed the Smoot-Hawley Tariff (1930) to protect the United States from cheap foreign goods. That bill brought a wave of retaliation from countries abroad, which choked world trade and reduced American sales overseas. Even the $1 billion that Hoover spent on public works—more than the total spent by all his predecessors combined—did not approach the $10 billion needed to employ only half the jobless. Spending such huge sums seemed unthinkable, for the entire federal budget at the time was only $3.2 billion.

Reconstruction Finance Corporation

Under pressure from Congress, Hoover took his boldest action to save the banks. Between 1930 and 1932 some 5100 failed as panicky depositors withdrew their funds. Hoover agreed to permit the creation of the Reconstruction Finance Corporation (RFC) in 1932, an agency that could lend money to banks and their chief corporate debtors—insurance companies and railroads. Modeled on a similar agency created during World War I, the RFC had a capital stock of $500 million and the power to borrow four times that amount. Within three months bank failures dropped from 70 a week to 1 every two weeks. The Glass-Steagall Banking Act (1932) made it easier for banks to loan money by adding $2 billion of new currency to the money supply, backed by Federal Reserve government bonds.

Yet in spite of this success, Hoover drew criticism for rescuing banks and not people. From the start he rejected the idea of federal relief for the unemployed. It was not that the president was insensitive—far from it. He never visited a breadline or a relief shelter because he could not bear the sight of human suffering. He feared that a "dole," or giveaway program (of the kind being used in Britain), would damage the freedom and initiative of recipients, perhaps even produce a permanent underclass. The bureaucracy that would be needed to police recipients would inevitably meddle in the private lives of citizens and bring a "train of corruption and waste." Hoover assumed that neighborliness and cooperation would be enough.

Unemployment relief

As unemployment continued to worsen, Hoover slowly softened his stand on federal relief. In 1932 he allowed Congress to pass the Emergency Relief and Construction Act. It authorized the RFC to lend up to $1.5 billion for "reproductive" public works that paid for themselves—like toll bridges and slum clearance. Another $300 million went to states as loans for the direct relief of the unemployed. Yet in this Depression, $300 million was a pittance. When the governor of Pennsylvania requested loans to furnish the destitute with 13 cents a day for a year, the RFC sent only enough for 3 cents a day.

Stirrings of Discontent

Unprecedented though they were, Hoover's efforts were too little, too late. "The word revolution is heard at every hand," one writer warned in 1932. Some wondered if capitalism itself had gone bankrupt.

Farm Holiday Association

Here and there the desperate took matters into their own hands in 1932. In Wisconsin the Farm Holiday Association dumped thousands of gallons of milk on highways in a vain attempt to raise prices. Ten thousand striking miners formed a 48-mile motorcar "Coal Caravan" that worked its way in protest across southern Illinois. In March a demonstration turned ugly when communist sympathizers led a hunger march on Henry Ford's Rouge Assembly Plant in Dearborn, Michigan. As 3000 protesters surged toward the gates, Ford police drenched them with hoses, then opened fire at point-blank range. Four marchers were killed and more than 20 wounded.

Communist party

For all the stirrings of discontent, revolution was never a danger. In 1932 the Communist party of the United States had 20,000 members—up from 6500 only three years earlier but hardly large enough to constitute a political force. Deeply suspicious of Marxist doctrine, most Americans were unsympathetic to their cries for collectivism and an end to capitalism. Fewer than 1000 African Americans joined the party in the early 1930s. At first hostile to established politics, the Communists

In the early years of the Depression, demonstrations of the unemployed, some organized by Communists and other radicals, broke out all over the country. On March 6, 1930, a Communist-led protest at Union Square in New York turned into an ugly riot. In 1935 Communist parties, under orders from Moscow, adopted the more cooperative strategy of allying with democratic and socialist groups against fascism, proclaiming in the United States that "Communism is twentieth-century Americanism."

adopted a more cooperative strategy to contain Adolf Hitler when his Nazi party won control of Germany in 1933. The Soviet Union ordered Communist parties in Europe and the United States to join with liberal politicians in a "popular front" against Nazism. Thereafter party membership peaked in the mid-1930s at about 80,000.

The Bonus Army

Hoover sympathized with the discontented, but only to a point. In the summer of 1932, the "Bonus Army" learned the limits of his compassion. The army, a ragtag collection of World War I veterans, was hungry and looking to cash in the bonus certificates they had received from Congress in 1924 as a reward for wartime service. By the time they reached Washington, D.C., in June 1932, their numbers had swelled to nearly 20,000, the largest protest in the city's history. Hoover dismissed them as a special-interest lobby and refused to see their leaders, but the House voted to pay them immediately. When the Senate blocked the bonus bill, most veterans left.

About 2000 stayed to dramatize their plight, camping with their families and parading peaceably. Despite the efforts of the Washington police to evict them, the protesters refused to leave. By the end of July, the president had had enough. He called in the U.S. Army under the command of Chief of Staff General Douglas MacArthur. MacArthur arrived with four troops of saber-brandishing cavalry, six tanks, and a column of infantry with bayonets ready for action. By the time the smoke cleared the next morning, the Bonus marchers had vanished except for 300 wounded veterans.

Though he had intended that the army only assist the police, Hoover accepted responsibility for the action. And the sight of unarmed and unemployed veterans under attack by American troops soured most Americans. In Albany, New York,

Governor Franklin D. Roosevelt exploded at the president's failure: "There is nothing inside the man but jelly." Like the hero of a classical tragedy, Herbert Hoover, symbol of the New Era and the greatest humanitarian of his generation, came tumbling down.

The Election of 1932

At their convention in Chicago, Republicans still stuck with Hoover and endorsed his Depression program to the last detail. Democrats countered with Franklin D. Roosevelt, the charismatic New York governor. As a sign of things to come, Roosevelt broke all precedent by flying to Chicago and addressing the delegates in person. "I pledge you, I pledge myself to a new deal for the American people," he told them.

Without a national following, Roosevelt zigged and zagged in an effort to appeal to the broadest possible bloc of voters. One minute he attacked Hoover as a "profligate spender" and vowed to balance the budget; the next he called for costly public works and aid to the unemployed. He promised to help business, then spoke vaguely of remembering the "forgotten man" and "distributing wealth and products more equitably." For his part, Hoover denounced Roosevelt's New Deal as a "dangerous departure" from time-honored traditions, one that would destroy American values and institutions and "build a bureaucracy such as we have never seen in our history." None of it mattered. The deepening Depression ensured that virtually any Democratic candidate would defeat Hoover.

On Election Day, Roosevelt captured a decisive 57 percent of the popular vote and carried with him large Democratic majorities in the Congress. Just as telling as the margin of victory were its sources. Industrial workers in the North, poor farmers in the South and West, immigrants and big-city dwellers everywhere were being galvanized into a broad new coalition. These people had experienced firsthand the savage effects of the boom-and-bust business cycle and wanted change. But they were not radicals and found no appeal in the presidential campaigns of Socialist Norman Thomas or Communist William Z. Foster, both of whom had called for worker ownership of businesses. The Socialists polled less than a million votes, the Communists barely over 100,000. Instead Depression-era voters turned

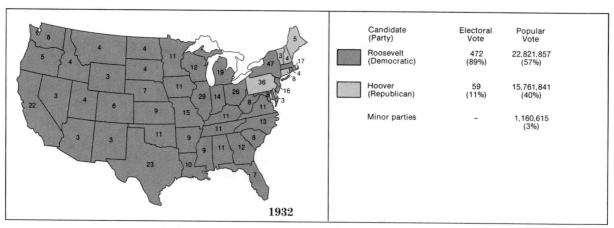

Election of 1932

to Roosevelt and the Democrats, who recognized that in a modern industrial state it was not enough to rally round business and hope that capitalism would right itself. Over 30 years of nearly unbroken Republican rule had come to an end.

The Early New Deal (1933–1935)

On March 4, 1933, as the clocks struck noon, Eleanor Roosevelt wondered if it were possible to "do anything to save America now." One-fourth of the workforce was unemployed. Thirty million families had no means of support. There wasn't enough money in the Treasury to meet the federal payroll.

Eleanor looked at her husband, who had just been sworn in as thirty-second president of the United States. Franklin faced the crowd of over 100,000 as millions more huddled around their radios: "Let me assert my firm belief that the only thing we have to fear is fear itself." Heeding the nation's call for "action, and action now," he promised to exercise "broad Executive power to wage a war against the emergency." The crowd cheered. Eleanor was terrified: "One has the feeling of going it blindly because we're in a tremendous stream, and none of us know where we're going to land."

The early New Deal unfolded in the spring of 1933 with a chaotic, three-month *Recovery, relief, reform* burst of legislation known as "the Hundred Days." It stressed recovery through planning and cooperation with business. It also furnished relief for the unemployed and began a reform of the economic system. Above all, the early New Deal revived national confidence. With Roosevelt in the White House, most Americans believed that they were in good hands, wherever they landed.

The Democratic Roosevelts

From the moment they entered it in 1933, Franklin and Eleanor—the Democratic Roosevelts—transformed the White House. No more footmen bowing and buglers playing, as they had when Hoover arrived in the dining room to partake of his customary seven-course meal. Instead visitors got fare fit for a boardinghouse. Roosevelt's lunches of hash and a poached egg cost 19 cents. With millions of Americans tightening their belts, the president joined them with a symbolic gesture that made his point of ending business as usual.

Such belt-tightening was new to Franklin Roosevelt. Born in 1882 of an old *Franklin Roosevelt* Dutch New York family, he grew up rich and pampered. He idolized his Republican cousin Theodore Roosevelt and mimicked his career, except as a Democrat. Like Theodore, Franklin was graduated from Harvard University (in 1904), won a seat in the New York State legislature (in 1910), secured an appointment as assistant secretary of the navy (in 1913), and ran for the vice presidency (in 1920). Then a disaster all his own struck. On vacation in the summer of 1921, Roosevelt fell ill with poliomyelitis. The disease paralyzed him from the waist down. For the rest of his life, he walked only with the aid of crutches and heavy steel braces.

Roosevelt seems to have emerged from the ordeal with greater patience, deeper conviction, and more empathy for the unfortunates of the world. He won the governorship of New York in 1928. When the Depression struck, he created the first state relief agency in 1931, the Temporary Emergency Relief Administration. Aid to the jobless "must be extended by Government, not as a matter of charity, but as a matter of social duty," he explained. He considered himself a progressive but moved well beyond the cautious use of federal power advocated by most progressives. A conventional budget balancer, he could abandon convention and be bold with sometimes costly social programs. He cared little about economic principles.

Franklin Roosevelt contracted polio in 1921 and remained paralyzed from the waist down for the rest of his life. Out of respect for his politically motivated wishes, photographers rarely showed him wearing heavy leg braces or sitting in a wheelchair. This photograph, snapped outside his New York City brownstone in September 1933 during his first year as president, is one of the few in which Roosevelt's braces are visible (just below the cuffs of his trousers). Note the wooden ramp constructed especially to help hold him up. To foster the illusion that he could walk, Roosevelt developed a technique for shifting his weight from one leg to the other as he leaned forward and supported himself on guard rails (as pictured here) or on the sturdy shoulder of an aide. Eleanor smiles approvingly from the doorway.

The Brains Trust

What he wanted were results. "Take a method and try it," he instructed his staff. "If it fails, try another. But above all try something." Experimentation became a hallmark of the New Deal.

Having followed a political path to the presidency, Roosevelt understood the value of public relations. As president, he held an unequaled number of press conferences (998) and hired the first press secretary. His famous "fireside chats" on radio brought him into American homes. When Roosevelt's reassuring voice came over the airwaves ("My friends, I want to tell you what has been done in the last few days, why it was done, and what the next steps are going to be"), people felt as if he had each of them in mind.

Eleanor Roosevelt redefined what it meant to be First Lady. Never had a president's wife been so visible, so much of a crusader, so cool under fire. She was the first First Lady to hold weekly press conferences. Her column, "My Day," appeared in 135 newspapers, and her twice-weekly broadcasts made her a radio personality rivaling her husband. She became his eyes, ears, and legs, traveling 40,000 miles a year. Secret Service men code-named her "Rover."

Eleanor believed that she was only a spur to her husband. But she was an activist in her own right, as a teacher and social reformer before Franklin became president and afterward as a tireless advocate of the underdog. In the White House, she pressed him to hire more women and minorities. She supported antilynching and anti–poll tax measures when he would not and experimental towns for the homeless. By 1939 more Americans approved of her than of her husband.

Before the election Roosevelt had gathered a group of lawyers and university professors called the "Brains Trust" to advise him on economic policy. Out of their recommendations came the early, or "first," New Deal of government planning, intervention, and experimentation. Brain Trusters disagreed over the means of achieving their goals but shared the broad aims of economic recovery, relief for the unemployed, and sweeping reform to soften the impact of the industrial order and to guard against the return of depression.

Saving the Banks

Roosevelt launched the New Deal with a record-breaking barrage of legislation in his first hundred days in office. Congress helped to shape the laws, but with an urgency and speed that left even the president feeling "a bit shell-shocked." Government began to dominate economic life so much that conservatives feared the end of capitalism had come, not from the Depression but from the White House. They need not have worried. Roosevelt meant to save capitalism by regulating and reforming it. The banks came first. Without a sound credit structure, there could be no borrowing; without borrowing, no investment; without investment, no recovery.

By the eve of the inauguration, governors in 38 states had temporarily closed their banks to stem the withdrawals of nervous depositors and to stop the failure of so many banks. On March 5, the day after his inauguration, Roosevelt ordered every bank in the country closed for four days (later extended to eight). He called it a "bank holiday." Instead of panicking, Americans acted as if it were a holiday, using home-made currencies called "scrip" and bartering their services. On March 9, the president introduced emergency banking legislation. The House passed the measure, sight unseen, and the Senate endorsed it later in the day. Roosevelt signed it that night.

Rather than nationalizing the banks as radicals wanted, the Emergency Banking Act followed the modest course of extending federal assistance to them. Sound banks would reopen immediately with government support. Troubled banks would be handed over to federal "conservators," who would guide them to solvency. On Sunday, March 12, Roosevelt explained what was happening in the first of his fireside chats. When banks reopened the next day, deposits exceeded withdrawals, even though legislation to insure those deposits had yet to be enacted.

To restore confidence in government, Roosevelt pushed through the Economy Act in March 1933, slashing $400 million in veterans' payments and $100 million in salaries from the federal budget. To guard against future stock crashes, financial reforms gave government greater authority to manage the currency and regulate stock transactions. In April 1933, Roosevelt dropped the gold standard and began experimenting with the value of the dollar to boost prices. Later that spring the Glass-Steagall Banking Act restricted speculation by banks and, more important, created federal insurance for bank deposits of up to $2500. Under the Federal Deposit Insurance Corporation, fewer banks failed for the rest of the decade than in the best year of the 1920s. The Securities Exchange Act (1934) established a new federal agency, the Securities and Exchange Commission, to oversee the stock market.

Emergency Banking Act

Federal Deposit Insurance

Relief for the Unemployed

Saving the banks and financial markets meant little if human suffering could not be relieved. Mortgage relief for the millions who had lost their homes came eventually in 1934 in the Home Owners' Loan Act. But to meet the need to alleviate starvation, Congress created the Federal Emergency Relief Administration (FERA) in May 1933. Sitting amid unpacked boxes, gulping coffee and chain-smoking, former social worker Harry Hopkins spent $5 million of a $500 million appropriation in his first two hours on the job. In its two-year existence, FERA furnished more than $1 billion in grants to states, local areas, and private charities.

Hopkins persuaded the president to expand relief with an innovative shift from government giveaways to a work program to see workers through the winter of 1933–1934. Paying someone "to do something socially useful preserves a man's morale," Hopkins argued. The Civil Works Administration (CWA) employed 4 million Americans on projects such as repairing schools, laying sewer pipes, and building roads. Alarmed at the high cost of the program, Roosevelt disbanded the CWA in the spring of 1934. It nonetheless furnished a new weapon against unemployment and an important precedent for future relief programs.

Work relief

Another work relief program established during Roosevelt's first hundred days proved even more creative. The Civilian Conservation Corps (CCC) was Roosevelt's pet project. It combined his concern for conservation with compassion for youth. The CCC took unmarried 18- to 25-year-olds from relief rolls and sent them into the woods and fields to plant trees, build parks, and fight soil erosion. During its 10 years, the CCC provided 2.5 million young men with jobs (which prompted critics who felt women were being neglected to chant, "Where's the she, she, she?").

New Dealers intended relief programs to last only through the crisis. The Tennessee Valley Authority (TVA)—a massive public works project created in 1933—helped to relieve unemployment but also made a continuing contribution

Tennessee Valley Authority

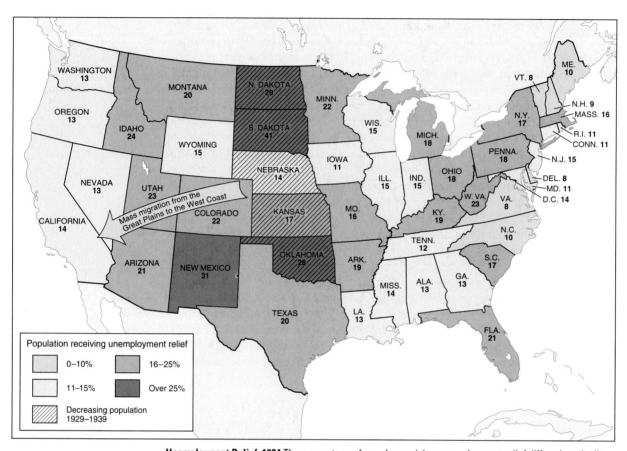

Unemployment Relief, 1934 The percentage of people receiving unemployment relief differed markedly throughout the nation. The farm belt of the plains was hit especially hard, with 41 percent of South Dakota's citizens receiving federal benefits. In the East, the percentage dropped as low as 8 percent in some states.

to regional planning. For a decade, planners had dreamed of transforming the flood-ridden basin of the Tennessee River, one of the poorest areas of the country, with a program of regional development and social engineering. The TVA constructed a series of dams along the seven-state basin to control flooding, improve navigation, and generate cheap electric power. In cooperation with state and local officials, it also launched social programs to stamp out malaria, provide library bookmobiles, and create recreational lakes.

Like many New Deal programs, the TVA left a mixed legacy. It saved three million acres from erosion, multiplied the average income in the valley tenfold, and repaid its original investment in federal taxes. Its cheap electricity helped bring down the rates of private utility companies and increase usage. But the experiment in regional planning also pushed thousands of families from their land, failed to end poverty, and created an agency that became one of the worst polluters in the country.

Planning for Industrial Recovery

Planning, not just for regions but for the whole economy, seemed to many New Dealers the key to recovery. Some held that if businesses were allowed to plan and cooperate, the ruthless competition that was driving down the economy might be

The Tennessee Valley Authority The Tennessee River basin encompassed parts of seven states. Rivers honeycombed the area, which received some of the heaviest rainfall in the nation. A longtime dream of Senator George Norris, the Tennessee Valley Authority, created in 1933, constructed some 20 dams and improved 5 others over the next 20 years to control chronic flooding and erosion and to produce cheap hydroelectric power and fertilizers.

controlled and the riddle of industrial recovery solved. Business leaders had been urging such a course since 1931. In June 1933, under the National Industrial Recovery Act (NIRA), Roosevelt put planning to work for industry.

Public Works Administration

The legislation created two new agencies. The Public Works Administration (PWA) was designed to boost consumer purchasing power and industrial activity with a $3.3 billion public works program. The workers it hired would spend their paychecks and stimulate production, while its orders for factory and other goods would send waves of capital rippling through the economy. Harold Ickes, the prickly interior secretary who headed PWA, built the Triborough Bridge and Lincoln Tunnel in New York, the port city of Brownsville, Texas, and two aircraft carriers. But he was so fearful of waste and corruption that he never spent funds quickly enough to jump-start the economy.

National Recovery Administration

A second federal agency, the National Recovery Administration (NRA), aimed directly at controlling competition. Under NRA chief Hugh Johnson, representatives from government and business (and also from labor and consumer groups) drew up "codes of fair practices." Industry by industry, the codes established minimum prices and wages and maximum hours. No company could seek a competitive edge by cutting prices or wages below certain levels or by working a few employees mercilessly and firing the rest. It also required business to accept key demands of labor, including union rights to organize and bargain with management (thus ensuring that if prices jumped, so too might wages). And each code promised improvements in working conditions and outlawed such practices as child labor and sweatshops.

No business was forced to comply, for fear that government coercion might be ruled unconstitutional. The NRA relied instead on voluntary participation. A publicity campaign of parades, posters, and massive public pledges exhorted businesses to join the NRA and consumers to buy only NRA-sanctioned products. More than two million employers eventually signed up. In store windows and on merchandise, shiny decals with blue-eagle crests alerted customers that "We Do Our Part."

For all the hoopla, the NRA failed to bring recovery. Big businesses shaped the codes to their advantage. Often they limited production and raised prices, sometimes beyond what they normally might have been. Not all businesses joined, and those that did often found the codes too complicated or costly to follow. The relatively few NRA inspectors had trouble keeping up with all the complaints. Even NRA support for labor faltered, because the agency had no way to enforce the rules granting unions the right to bargain. Business survived under the NRA, but by and large it did not grow. And without increased production and sales, there was no incentive for expansion, employment, and investment. Under such conditions hard times could last indefinitely. Despite an enthusiastic start, the NRA spawned little but evasion from businesses and criticism from consumers about "NRA prices and Hoover wages."

Schecter decision

On May 27, 1935, the Supreme Court struck down the floundering NRA in *Schecter Poultry Corp. v. United States.* The justices unanimously ruled that when the NRA regulated the Schecter brothers' poultry business within the state of New York, it exceeded the power granted the federal government to regulate commerce among the states. Privately Roosevelt was relieved to be rid of the NRA. But he and other New Dealers were plainly shaken by the Court's reasoning. They were relying on federal power to regulate commerce as a means of fighting the Depression. Their distress only grew when Justice Benjamin Cardozo added a chilling afterthought: the NRA's code-making represented "an unconstitutional delegation of legislative power" to the executive branch. Without the ability to make rules and regulations, *all* the executive agencies of the New Deal might flounder.

Planning for Agriculture

Agricultural Adjustment Administration

Like planning for industry, New Deal planning for agriculture relied on private interests—the farmers—to act as the principal planners. Under the Agricultural Adjustment Act of 1933, producers of basic commodities agreed to limit their own production. The government, in turn, paid farmers for not producing, while a tax on millers, cotton ginners, and other processors financed the payments. In theory, production quotas would reduce surpluses, and demand for farm commodities would rise, as would prices. Agriculture would recover.

In practice, the Agricultural Adjustment Administration (AAA) did help increase prices. Unlike the code-ridden NRA, the AAA wisely confined coverage to seven major commodities. As a way to push prices even higher, the new Commodity Credit Corporation gave loans to farmers who stored their crops rather than sell them—a revival of the Populists' old subtreasury plan (see page 680). Farm income rose from $5.5 billion in 1932 to $8.7 billion in 1935.

Not all the gains in farm income were due to government actions or were free of problems. The dust storms, droughts, and floods of the mid-1930s helped reduce harvests and push up prices. The AAA, moreover, failed to distribute its benefits equally. Large landowners were in a position to decide which of the fields would be left fallow. In the South this decision frequently meant that big farmers would cut the acreage of tenants and sharecroppers or force them out. Even when big farmers reduced the acreage that they themselves plowed, they could increase yields, because they had the money and equipment to cultivate more intensively.

In 1936 the Supreme Court voided the AAA. In *Butler v. U.S.*, the six-justice majority concluded that the government had no right to regulate agriculture, either by limiting production or by taxing processors. Congress hastily passed a replacement bill, the Soil Conservation and Domestic Allotment Act (1936), which addressed the Court's complaints. Farmers were now subsidized for practicing "conservation"—taking soil-depleting crops off the land—and paid from general revenues instead of a special tax. A second Agricultural Adjustment Act in 1938 returned production quotas.

Other agencies tried to help impoverished farmers. The Farm Credit Administration refinanced about a fifth of all farm mortgages. In 1935 the Resettlement Administration gave marginal farmers a fresh start by moving them to better land. Beginning in 1937 the Farm Security Administration furnished low-interest loans to help tenants buy family farms. In neither case did the rural poor have enough political leverage to obtain sufficient funds from Congress. Fewer than 5000 families (of a projected 500,000) were resettled, and less than 2 percent of tenant farmers received loans. Here, as elsewhere, the net effect was mixed. New Deal programs did help to stabilize the farm economy and provided an important precedent for future aid to farmers. At the same time, the favoritism shown large farmers promoted large-scale agribusiness or corporate-run farming.

After years of Hoover paralysis, Roosevelt's first hundred days finally broke national despair. The economic depression proved more resistant. Though Roosevelt regarded recovery as his primary goal, the New Deal never achieved it. Conditions improved, but the economy only limped along. Perhaps no one could have solved the riddle of recovery, but Roosevelt tried, and in 1935 he began to address a second riddle: how to reform the system so that the Great Depression did not return.

Despite the popularity of Roosevelt and the New Deal, there were critics. New federal agencies, designated by their initials, became easy targets of satirists and cartoonists. In this 1934 cartoon, a wincing Uncle Sam receives an unwelcome set of tattoos, each signifying a New Deal agency.

Recovery in Global Perspective

The Great Depression spread across the globe like a plague (see pages 813–814). In Europe and Asia, the economies of most industrial nations collapsed. But several countries did recover, and more quickly than the United States. By aggressively applying some of the same techniques of government planning and spending as did the United States, they were able to solve the riddle of recovery.

In Germany, where the Depression helped to install Adolf Hitler and his Nazi dictatorship in 1933, a bold program of public works—including a system of highways, or *Autobahns,* as well as housing, navigation, and railroad projects—far outspent the New Deal on a per capita basis. The Germans also stimulated economic growth through rearmament, subsidies to farmers and exporters, tax rebates to businesses, and government-sponsored cartels that regulated industrial output and prices. By 1936, the German economy had largely recovered and was approaching full employment.

Other industrial powerhouses had different experiences. Some recovered quickly, others barely, and still others almost immediately. Often recovery depended on how fast and how much they spent. In Britain, where unemployment was high during the 1920s and the economy listless, a similar program of government subsidies to industry and agriculture and government-sponsored cartels and public works (in this case, to clear slums and to construct low-income housing) helped to jump-start the economy. Unlike Germany, Britain already had unemployment insurance and relief services available, but it greatly expanded them in 1934. By 1937 limited British recovery, aided by booms in private residential construction and consumer goods, was under way. Although the Depression struck France later than either Britain or Germany, by 1935 conditions there were as bad as anywhere. Despite a wave of protests and strikes and a burst of reforms in 1936, no French government had the will, imagination, or staying power to do much. Industrial production remained below 1929 levels throughout the 1930s. Japan, on the other hand, dampened the effects of the Depression by arming itself to the teeth in preparation for expanding into Asia. The Japanese economy actually *grew* each year between 1929 and 1938 at an annual rate of 5 percent, the highest in the world.

A Second New Deal (1935–1936)

"Boys—this is our hour," concluded Harry Hopkins in the spring of 1935. A year earlier voters had broken precedent by returning the party in power to office, giving the Democrats their largest majorities in decades. With the presidential election of 1936 only a year away, Hopkins figured that time was short: "We've got to get everything we want—a works program, social security, wages and hours, everything—now or never."

Hopkins calculated correctly. Swept along by a torrent of protest, Roosevelt and the Congress produced a "second hundred days" of lawmaking and a "Second New Deal." The emphasis shifted from planning and cooperation with business to greater regulation of business, broader relief, and bolder reform. A limited welfare state emerged, in which government was finally committed—at least symbolically—to guaranteeing the well-being of needy Americans.

Voices of Protest

In 1934, a mob of 6000 stormed the Minneapolis city hall with demands for more relief and higher-paying jobs. Longshoremen shut down the docks in San Francisco, setting off a citywide strike. Before the end of the year, 1.5 million workers had joined in 1800 strikes. Conditions were improving but not quickly enough, and across the country, voices of protest gathered strength.

From the right came the charges of some wealthy business executives and conservatives that Roosevelt was an enemy of private property and a dictator in the making. In August 1934 they founded the American Liberty League. Despite spending $1 million in anti–New Deal advertising, the league won little support and only helped to convince the president that cooperation with business was failing.

Liberty League

In California discontented voters took over the Democratic party and nominated novelist Upton Sinclair, a Socialist, for governor. Running under the slogan "End Poverty in California," Sinclair proposed to confiscate idle factories and land and permit the unemployed to produce for their own use. Republicans mounted a no-holds-barred counterattack, including fake newsreels depicting Sinclair as a Bolshevik, atheist, and advocate of free love. Sinclair lost the election but won nearly one million votes.

"End Poverty in California"

Huey P. Long, the flamboyant senator from Louisiana, had ridden to power on a wave of rural discontent against banks, corporations, and machine politics as usual. As governor of Louisiana, he pushed through reforms regulating utilities, building roads and schools, even distributing free schoolbooks. By turns comical and ruthless, Long used his power to feather his own financial nest, and his private

Huey Long

police force was not above kidnapping political opponents. Detractors called him "dictator"; most Louisianans affectionately called him the "Kingfish" after a conniving character in the popular *Amos 'n' Andy* radio show.

Breaking with Roosevelt in 1933, Long pledged to bring about recovery by making "every man a king." His "Share Our Wealth" proposal was a drastic but simple plan: the government would limit the size of all fortunes and confiscate the rest. Every family would then be guaranteed an annual income of $2500 and an estate of $5000, enough to buy a house, an automobile, and a radio. (Long had already built a national following over the airwaves.)

Louisiana governor and U.S. senator Huey Long promised to make "every man a king," but critics predicted that only Long would wear the crown. Power-hungry and charismatic, the Kingfish made no secret of his presidential aspirations.

Despite his wild underestimates of the cost of subsidies for the have-nots, Long was addressing a real problem, the uneven distribution of wealth. By 1935, one year after his Share Our Wealth organization was begun, it boasted 27,000 clubs. Democratic National Committee members shuddered at polls showing that Long might capture up to 4 million votes in 1936, enough to put a Republican in the White House. But late in 1935, in the corridors of the Louisiana capitol, Long was shot to death by a disgruntled constituent whose family had been wronged by the Long political machine.

Father Charles Coughlin was Long's urban counterpart. Whereas Long explained the Depression as the result of bloated fortunes, Coughlin blamed the banks. In weekly broadcasts from the Shrine of the Little Flower in suburban Detroit, the Radio Priest told his working-class, largely Catholic audience that international bankers (many of them Jewish, Coughlin also charged) had toppled the world economy by manipulating gold-backed currencies.

Charles Coughlin

Across the urban North, 30 to 40 million Americans—the largest audience in the world—sat by their radios to listen. Like Long, Coughlin promised to cure the Depression with simple strokes: nationalizing banks, inflating the currency with silver, spreading work. When Roosevelt refused to adopt Coughlin's schemes, the priest broke with the president. In 1934 Coughlin organized the National Union for Social Justice to pressure both parties. As the election of 1936 approached, the union loomed ominously as a third-party threat.

A less ominous challenge came from Dr. Francis Townsend, a recently retired California physician. Moved by the plight of elderly Americans without pension plans or medical insurance, Townsend set up Old Age Revolving Pensions, Limited, in 1934. He proposed to have the government pay $200 a month to Americans aged 60 years or older who quit their jobs and spent the money within 30 days. For funding, the government would levy a 2 percent tax on commercial transactions. Thus Townsendites expected to spend more than half the national income to compensate less than one-tenth of the population. By 1936 Townsend clubs counted 3.5 million members, most of them small businesspeople and farmers at or beyond retirement age.

Francis Townsend

For all their differences, Sinclair, Long, Coughlin, and Townsend struck similar chords. Each proposed simplistic solutions for serious problems: a maldistribution of goods and wealth, inadequacies in the money supply, the plight of the elderly. Each attacked the growing control of corporations, banks, and government over individuals and communities. And they created mass political movements based on social as well as economic dissatisfaction. When Sinclair supporters pledged to produce for their own use and Long's followers swore to "share our wealth," when Coughlinites damned the "monied interests" and Townsendites thumped their Bibles at foul-ups in Washington, they were all also trying to protect their freedom and their communities from what they saw as the ills and intrusions of big business and big government.

The Second Hundred Days

By the spring of 1935, the forces of discontent were pushing Roosevelt to bolder action. So was Congress. With Democrats accounting for more than two-thirds of both houses, they were prepared to outspend even the president. The 100 days from April through mid-July, the "second hundred days," produced a legislative barrage that moved the New Deal toward Roosevelt's ultimate destination—"a little to the left of center," where government would permanently seek to soften the impact of industrial excesses, protect the needy, and compensate for the boom-and-bust business cycle.

Works Progress Administration

To help the many Americans who were still jobless, Roosevelt proposed the Emergency Relief Appropriation Act of 1935, with a record of $4.8 billion for relief and employment. Some of the money went to the new National Youth Administration for more than 4.5 million jobs for young people. But the lion's share went to the new Works Progress Administration (WPA), where Harry Hopkins mounted the largest work-relief program in history. Because his agency was not permitted to compete with private industry and stressed spending its money on wages, Hopkins showed remarkable ingenuity. WPA workers taught art classes in a Cincinnati mental hospital, drafted a Braille map for the blind in Massachusetts, and pulled a library by packhorse through the hills of Kentucky. Before its end in 1943, the WPA employed at least 8.5 million people and built or improved over 100,000 schools, post offices, and other public buildings.

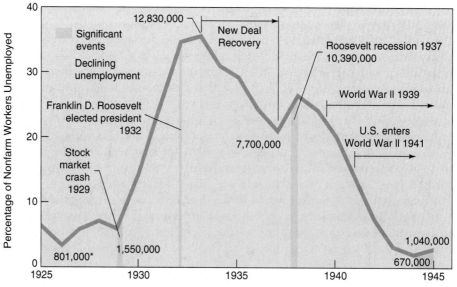

Unemployment, 1925–1945 Unemployment mushroomed in the wake of the stock market crash of 1929. It did not drop to 1929 levels until American entry into the Second World War in 1941. The purple bands indicate periods of declining unemployment.

The ambitious Social Security Act, passed in 1935, sought to help those people who could not help themselves—the aged poor, the infirm, dependent children. But Social Security went further, extending the umbrella of protection in the form of pensions for retirees and insurance for those suddenly laid off from their jobs. Equally important, the financial assistance Social Security provided would also act as an economic stabilizer to sustain consumer purchasing power in good times and bad. A payroll tax on both employers and employees underwrote pensions given to retirees over age 65, while an employer-financed system of insurance made possible government payments to unemployed workers.

Social Security marked a historic reversal in American political values. A new social contract between the government and the people replaced the gospel of self-help and the older policies of laissez faire. Government acknowledged a broad responsibility to protect the social rights of citizens. The welfare state, foreshadowed in the aid given veterans and their families after the Civil War, was institutionalized, though its coverage was limited. To win the votes of southern congressmen hostile to African Americans, the legislation excluded farm workers and domestic servants, doubtless among the neediest Americans but often black and disproportionately southern.

Congress had whittled down Roosevelt's plan for Social Security, but its labor legislation pushed well beyond the president's paternalistic goals. Roosevelt would have been happy providing moderate aid for workers in the form of pension plans, unemployment insurance, and, later, federal minimum wage standards. But New York senator Robert Wagner, the son of a janitor, wanted to give workers the power to fight their own battles. In 1933 Wagner had included union recognition in the NRA. When the Supreme Court killed the agency in 1935, Wagner introduced what became the National Labor Relations Act. (So important had labor support become to Roosevelt that he gave the bill his belated blessing.) The "Wagner Act" created a National Labor Relations Board (NLRB) to supervise the election of unions and ensure union rights to bargain. Most vital, the NLRB had the power to enforce these policies. By 1941, union membership had doubled.

Roosevelt responded to the growing hostility of business by turning against the wealthy and powerful in 1935. The popularity of Long's tirades against the rich and Coughlin's against banks sharpened Roosevelt's points of attack. The Revenue Act of 1935 (called the "Wealth Tax Act") threatened to "soak the rich," although Congress's final version of the law levied only moderate taxes on high incomes and inheritances. To control the powerful banking industry, the Banking Act of 1935 centralized the money market in the Federal Reserve Board. By controlling interest rates and the money supply, government increased its ability to compensate for swings in the economy. Finally, the Public Utilities Holding Company Act (1935) limited the size of widely unpopular utility empires. Long the target of progressive reformers, the giant holding companies produced high profits for speculators and higher prices for consumers. Although Congress diluted the act, as it had the wealth tax, New Dealers could still claim a political victory. "I am now on your bandwagon again," a Philadelphia voter told the president as the election of 1936 approached.

Social Security

National Labor Relations Act

The Election of 1936

In June 1936 Roosevelt traveled to Philadelphia, not to thank the loyal voter who had hopped aboard his bandwagon but to accept the Democratic nomination for a second term as president. "This generation of Americans has a rendezvous with destiny," he told a crowd of 100,000 packed into Franklin Field. Whatever destiny had in store for his generation, Roosevelt knew that the coming election would turn on a single issue: "It's myself, and people must be either for me or against me."

Roosevelt ignored his Republican opponent, Governor Alfred Landon of Kansas. Despite a bulging war chest of $14 million, Landon lacked luster as well as issues, because he favored the regulation of business and much of the New Deal. For his part Roosevelt turned the election into a contest between haves and have-nots. The forces of "organized money are unanimous in their hate for me," he told a roaring crowd at New York's Madison Square Garden, "and I welcome their hatred." The election returns shocked even experienced observers. Roosevelt won the largest electoral victory ever—523 to 8—and a whopping 60.8 percent of the popular vote. The margin of victory came from those at the bottom of the economic ladder, grateful for help furnished by the New Deal.

Roosevelt coalition

A dramatic political realignment was now clearly in place, one as important as the Republican rise to power in 1896. No longer did the Democratic Party depend for its strength primarily on the regional support of the "Solid South." Class replaced region as the dominant element in American politics. For the next 30 years, the Democrats would reign as the new majority party. The "Roosevelt coalition" rested on three pillars: traditional Democratic support in the South; citizens in the industrial cities, particularly ethnics and African Americans; and labor, both organized and unorganized. The minority Republicans became the party of big business and small towns.

The American People under the New Deal

Before 1939, farmers in the hill country of Texas spent their evenings in the light of 25-watt kerosene lamps. Their wives washed eight loads of laundry a week, all by hand. Every day the women hauled home 200 gallons of water—about 1500 pounds—from nearby wells. Farms had no milking machines, no washers, no water heaters, no refrigerators, and no radios. "Living—just living—was a problem," recalled one woman.

Rural Electrification Administration

The reason for this limited life was simple: the hill country had no electricity. Thus no agency of the Roosevelt administration changed the way people lived more dramatically than did the Rural Electrification Administration (REA), created in 1935. At the time, less than 10 percent of American farms had electricity. Six years later, 40 percent did, and by 1950, 90 percent did. The New Deal did not always make such a dramatic impact, and its overall record was mixed. But time and again it changed the lives of ordinary people as government never had before.

The New Deal and Western Water

In September 1936, President Roosevelt pushed a button in Washington, D.C., and sent electricity pulsing westward from the towering Boulder Dam on the Colorado River to cities as far away as Los Angeles. Its generators and turbines were the largest ever installed and could produce four times the electricity of Niagara Falls. The diverted waters irrigated 2.5 million acres, while the dam's floodgates protected millions in southern California, Nevada, and Arizona from the ravages of the Colorado River, the wildest in the West. In its water management programs, the New Deal further extended federal power, literally, across the country.

The Boulder Dam (begun under the Hoover administration) was one of several multipurpose dams completed under the New Deal in the arid West. The aim was simple: to control whole river systems for regional use. The task, of course, was more complicated, involving strings of dams, channels, and other projects costing billions. The Buchanan Dam on the lower Colorado River, the Bonneville and Grand Coulee dams on the Columbia, and many smaller versions curbed floods, generated cheap electric power, and developed river basins from Texas to Washington State. Beginning in 1938, the All-American Canal diverted the Colorado River to the Imperial Valley in California, 80 miles away, with a 130-mile extension to the Coachella Valley.

Such projects made the Bureau of Reclamation a powerful force in Washington and the West. It oversaw most water development and so provided not only employment for tens of thousands of westerners but also some of the cheapest electricity in the United States. Inexpensive power also helped to attract industry and to free regions, particularly the Pacific Northwest, from their dependence on extractive industries such as logging and mining. It was no wonder, then, that Franklin Roosevelt carried the West in every one of his four presidential elections.

The environmental price for such rewards soon became evident, as it did with the New Deal's experiment in eastern water use, the Tennessee Valley Authority. The once-mighty Columbia River, its surging waters checked by dams, flowed tamely from human-made lake to human-made lake, but without the salmon whose spawning runs were also checked. Blocked by the All-American Canal of its path to the sea, the Colorado River slowly turned salty. By 1950 its water was unfit for drinking or irrigation.

Bureau of Reclamation

The Limited Reach of the New Deal

In the spring of 1939, the Daughters of the American Revolution (DAR) refused to permit the black contralto Marian Anderson to sing at Constitution Hall. Eleanor Roosevelt quit the DAR in protest, and Secretary of the Interior Harold Ickes began looking for another site. On a nippy Easter Sunday, in the shadow of the Lincoln Memorial, Anderson finally stepped to the microphone and sang to a crowd of 7500. Lincoln himself would not have missed the irony.

In 1932 most African Americans cast their ballots as they had since Reconstruction—for Republicans, the party of Abraham Lincoln and emancipation. But disenchantment with decades of broken Republican promises was spreading, and by 1934 African Americans were voting for Democrats. "Let Jesus lead you and Roosevelt feed you," a black preacher told his congregation on the eve of the 1936 election. When the returns were counted, three of four black voters had cast their ballots for Roosevelt.

African Americans

The New Deal accounted for this voting revolution. Sympathetic but never a champion, Roosevelt regarded African Americans as one of many groups whose interests he brokered. Even that attitude was an improvement. Federal offices had been segregated since Woodrow Wilson's day, and in the 1920s black leaders called Hoover "the man in the lily-White House." Under Roosevelt, racial integration slowly returned to government, whose doors opened a bit wider to African Americans. Supporters of civil rights, such as Eleanor Roosevelt and Secretary of the Interior Ickes, brought political scientist Clark Foreman, economist Robert C. Weaver, and other black advisers into the administration. Mary McLeod Bethune, a sharecropper's daughter and founder of Bethune-Cookman College, ran a division of the National Youth Administration. Important as both symbols and activists, African American administrators created a "Black Cabinet" to help design federal policy.

Outside of government the Urban League continued to lobby for economic advancement, and the National Association for the Advancement of Colored People pressed to make lynching a federal crime. (Though publicly against lynching

California's multiethnic workforce

and privately in favor of an antilynching bill, Roosevelt refused to make it "must" legislation for fear of losing the powerful white southern members of Congress whom he needed "to save America.") In New York's Harlem, the Reverend John H. Johnson organized the Citizens' League for Fair Play in 1933 to persuade white merchants to hire black clerks. After picketers blocked storefronts, hundreds of African Americans got jobs with Harlem retailers and utility companies. Racial tension over employment and housing continued to run high, and in 1935 Harlem exploded in the only race riot of the decade.

Racial discrimination persisted under the New Deal. Black newspapers reported hundreds of cases in which businesses, under the guise of following NRA codes, replaced black workers with white ones or paid black workers lower wages than those paid to whites. Disgusted editors renamed the agency "Negroes Ruined Again." Federal efforts to promote grassroots democracy often gave control of New Deal programs to local governments, where discrimination went unchallenged. New Deal showplaces like the TVA's model town of Norris, Tennessee, and the subsistence homestead village of Arthurdale, West Virginia, were closed to African Americans.

African Americans reaped a few benefits from the New Deal. The WPA hired black workers for almost 20 percent of its jobs, even though African Americans made up less than 10 percent of the population. When it was discovered that the WPA was paying black workers less than whites, Roosevelt issued an executive order to halt the practice. Public Works Administrator Ickes established the first quota system for hiring black Americans. By 1941 the number of African Americans working for the government exceeded their percentage of the population.

Mexican Americans

Civil rights never became a goal of the New Deal, but for the nearly one million Mexican Americans in the United States, Latino culture sometimes frustrated meager federal efforts to help. Mexican folk traditions of self-help inhibited some from seeking aid; others remained unfamiliar with claim procedures. Still others failed to meet residency requirements, and some feared that applying for aid might lead to deportation, even when they were legal residents. Low voter turnout hampered the political influence of Latinos, and discrimination limited economic advancement. More important, from the Rio Grande Valley in Texas to the Imperial Valley in California, the majority of Mexicans and Mexican Americans served as farm workers, picking and planting for others. As such, they lay beyond most New Deal programs.

On Capitol Hill, Dennis Chavez of New Mexico, the only Mexican American in the Senate, channeled what funds he could into Spanish-speaking communities of the Southwest, but the results of his and other federal efforts were often mixed. The CCC and the WPA furnished some jobs for Mexican Americans in the Southwest and California, though fewer of them and for less pay than Anglos received. In southern Colorado, New Deal relief measures alleviated unemployment among Latinos, but the policy of emptying relief rolls just before the beet harvest to avoid competing with the wages offered by local growers only drove wages down. Crafts programs meant to generate income and preserve village life ended up preserving a marginalized, underpaid workforce as well. Federal training programs for midwives helped to bring down high rates of infant mortality but also raised the cost to patients and threatened village control of custom and culture. Like African Americans, most Mexican Americans remained mired in poverty.

Tribal Rights

The New Deal renewed federal interest in the 320,000 Indians living on reservations in Oklahoma, New Mexico, and other western states. Among the most disadvantaged Americans, Indian families rarely earned more than $100 a year. Their infant mortality was the highest in the country; their life expectancy was the shortest; their education level—usually no more than five years—was the lowest. Their rate of unemployment was three times the national average.

Part of the reason for new attention from Washington was John Collier. In the 1930s, Indians had no stronger friend. For years he had fought to restore tribal lands and culture, first as a social worker among the Pueblos and later as executive secretary of the American Indian Defense Association. Appointed as the new commissioner of the Bureau of Indian Affairs in 1933, Collier hired over 4000

In 1937 artist Amy Jones painted life on an Iroquois Indian reservation in the Adirondack Mountains. Indian rates for tuberculosis were high, and a doctor and nurse examine an Indian child for the disease (left side of the painting). On the right, Iroquois women and children weave baskets from wooden splints while Indian workers split logs to be made into splints for baskets. These themes of public health, manual labor, and Indian crafts formed powerful points of emphasis in the New Deal.

Indians. By the end of the decade they made up a fourth of all BIA employees. He cleaned out corruption and incompetence from the bureau, placed 77,000 young Indians in the CCC, and built Indian day schools with funds from the Public Works Administration.

John Collier's Indian Reorganization Act

The centerpiece of Collier's new program was the Indian Reorganization Act of 1934. It reversed the decades-old policy of assimilation and promoted tribal life. The 200 tribes on reservations, explained Collier, would be "surrounded by the protective guardianship of the federal government and clothed with the authority of the federal government." A special Court of Indian Affairs removed Indians from state jurisdiction. Tribal governments ruled reservations. Elders were urged to celebrate festivals, artists to work in native styles, children to learn the old languages. Perhaps most important, tribes regained control over Indian land. Since the Dawes Act of 1887, land had been allotted to individual Indians, who were often forced by poverty to sell to whites. By the end of the 1930s, Indian landholding had increased.

Indians split over Collier's policies. The Pueblos, with a strong communal spirit and already functioning communal societies, favored them. The tribes of Oklahoma and the Great Plains tended to oppose them. Individualism, the profit motive, and an unwillingness to share property with other tribe members fed their resistance. So did age-old suspicion of all government programs. And some Indians genuinely desired assimilation. The Navajos, under the leadership of J. C. Morgan, rejected the Indian Reorganization Act in 1935. Morgan saw tribal government as a step backward.

A New Deal for Women

As the tides of change washed across the country, a new deal for women was unfolding in Washington. The New Deal's welfare agencies offered unprecedented opportunity for social workers, teachers, and other women who had spent their lives helping the downtrodden. They were already experts on social welfare. Several were also friends with professional ties, and together they formed a network of activists in the New Deal promoting women's interests and social reform. Led by Eleanor Roosevelt and labor secretary Frances Perkins, women served on the consumers' advisory board of the NRA, helped to administer the relief program, and won appointments to the Social Security Board.

During the wave of agricultural strikes in California in 1933, Mexican laborers who had been evicted from their homes settled in camps such as this one in Corcoran. The camp held well over 3000 people, each family providing an old tent or burlap bags for habitation. Makeshift streets were named in honor of Mexican towns and heroes. By chance the field had been occupied previously by a Mexican circus, the Circo Azteca, which provided nightly entertainment.

In growing numbers women became part of the Democratic party machinery. At the 1936 Democratic National Convention 219 women served as delegates while more than 300 stood by as alternates. Social worker Mary W. "Molly" Dewson led the new Women's Division of the Democratic National Committee. It played a critical role in the election. Thousands of women mounted a "mouth-to-mouth" campaign, literally traveling from door to door to drum up support for Roosevelt and other Democrats. When the ballots were finally tallied, women formed an important part of the new Roosevelt coalition.

Federal appointments and party politics broke new ground for women, but in general the New Deal abided by existing social standards. Gender equality, like racial equality, was never high on its agenda. One quarter of all NRA codes permitted women to be paid less than men, and WPA wages averaged $2 a day more for men. The New Deal gave relatively few jobs to women, and when it did, the jobs were often in gender-segregated trades such as sewing. The percentage of women hired by the government fell below even that of the private sector.

Reflecting old conceptions of reform, New Dealers placed greater emphasis on aiding and protecting women than on employing them. The FERA built 17 camps for homeless women in 11 states. Social Security furnished subsidies to mothers with dependent children, and the WPA established emergency nursery schools (which became the government's first foray into early childhood education). But evenhanded protection for women was lacking. Social Security, for example, did not cover domestic servants, most of whom were women.

The Rise of Organized Labor

Although women and minorities discovered that the New Deal had limits to the changes it promoted, a powerful union movement arose in the 1930s by taking full advantage of the new climate. Workers themselves took the lead and ended up pushing Roosevelt well beyond his limits.

At the outset of the Great Depression, most workers were demoralized and languishing. Barely 6 percent belonged to a union. Though the New Deal left farm workers officially outside its coverage, its promise of support encouraged these workers, traditionally among the most unorganized laborers, to act on their own.

In California, where large agribusinesses employed migrant laborers to pick vegetables, fruit, and cotton, some 37 strikes involving over 50,000 workers swept the state after Roosevelt took office.

CAWIU farm strike

The most famous strike broke out in the cotton fields of the San Joaquin Valley under the auspices of the Cannery and Agricultural Workers Industrial Union (CAWIU). Most of the strikers were Mexican, supported more by a complex network of families, friends, and coworkers than by the weak CAWIU. Before the strike was over, local farmers killed three people, and local officials threatened to cut off all relief aid to strikers and to send them back to Mexico. The government finally stepped in to arbitrate a wage settlement, which resulted in an end to the strike but at a fraction of the pay the workers sought.

Such government support was not enough to embolden the cautious American Federation of Labor, the nation's premier union. Historically bound to skilled labor and organized on the basis of craft, it ignored the unskilled workers who by the 1930s made up most of the industrial labor force, and it almost never organized women or black workers. Thus the AFL avoided major industries such as rubber, automobiles, and steel. Because the NRA's regulations gave unions the right to organize and bargain, the AFL increased its membership, but its president, William Green, sought cooperation with management and made no changes in its policies toward the unskilled.

The thundering, barrel-chested John L. Lewis fought to unionize unskilled laborers. Tough, charismatic, practical, and dedicated to organizing all workers, Lewis headed the United Mine Workers (UMW), an affiliate of the AFL. He had supported Herbert Hoover in the 1932 presidential election, but when Roosevelt won, Lewis promptly paid a call on the new president to shore up his ties to the White House. He received little more than consolation from Roosevelt for his shrinking union. Yet the shrewd Lewis returned to the coalfields with a message he had never been given: "The president wants you to join a union." Within a year the UMW had 400,000 members. Raising his sights, Lewis called for the creation of a Steel Workers' Organizing Committee and for the admission of the United Auto Workers into the AFL.

At the annual AFL convention in Atlantic City in 1935, Lewis demanded a commitment to the "industrial organization of mass production workers." The delegates, mostly from craft unions, voted down the proposal. Near the end of the convention, as he passed "Big Bill" Hutcheson of the carpenters union, angry words passed between the two. Lewis spun and with a single punch sent Hutcheson sprawling in a bloody heap.

Congress of Industrial Organizations

The blow signaled the determination of industrial unions to break the AFL's domination of organized labor. A few weeks later, Lewis and the heads of seven other AFL unions announced the formation of the Committee for Industrial Organization (CIO). The AFL suspended the rogue unions in 1936. The CIO, later rechristened the Congress of Industrial Organizations, turned to the unskilled and embarked on a series of organizing drives in large-scale, mass-production industries.

Campaigns of the CIO

Sit-down strikes

CIO representatives concentrated on the mighty steel industry, which had clung to the open, or nonunion, shop since 1919. In other industries, militant members of the rank and file did not wait. Emboldened by the recent passage of the Wagner Act, a group of rubber workers in Akron, Ohio, simply sat down on the job in early 1936. Because the strikers occupied the plants, managers could not replace

Men looking through the broken windows of an automobile plant during the wave of sit-down strikes in 1937. The windows were smashed not by the men in this photograph but by women of the newly established "Emergency Brigade" when they heard that the men inside were being gassed. Women played a vital role in supporting the strikes, collecting and distributing food to strikers and their families, setting up a first-aid station, and furnishing day care. Women of the Emergency Brigade wore red tams, armbands with the initials "EB" ("Emergency Brigade"), and political buttons.

them with strikebreakers. Nor could the rubber companies call in the military or police without risk to their property. The leaders of the United Rubber Workers Union opposed the "sit-downs," but when the Goodyear Tire and Rubber Company laid off 70 workers, 1400 rubber workers struck on their own. An 11-mile picket line sprang up outside. Eventually Goodyear settled by recognizing the union and accepting its demands on wages and hours.

The biggest strikes erupted in the automobile industry. A series of spontaneous strikes at General Motors plants in Atlanta, Kansas City, and Cleveland spread to Fisher Body No. 2 in Flint, Michigan, late in December 1936. Singing the unionists' anthem, "Solidarity Forever," workers took over the plant while wives, friends, and fellow union members handed food and clothing through the windows. Local police tried to break up supply lines but were driven off by a hail of nuts, bolts, coffee mugs, and bottles.

In the wake of this "Battle of Running Bulls" (a reference to the retreating police), Governor Frank Murphy finally called out the National Guard, not to arrest but to protect strikers. General Motors surrendered in February 1937. Less than a month later U.S. Steel capitulated to the Steel Workers Organizing Committee without a strike. By the end of the year every automobile manufacturer except Henry Ford had negotiated with the UAW. Not until 1941 with the pressure of an impending war did Ford finally recognize the union.

Bloody violence accompanied some drives. On Memorial Day 1937, 10 strikers lost their lives when Chicago police fired on them as they marched peacefully toward the Republic Steel plant. Sit-down strikes often alienated an otherwise sympathetic middle class. (In 1939 the Supreme Court outlawed the tactic.) Yet a momentous transfer of power had nonetheless taken place. By 1940 nearly one worker in three belonged to a union. The unskilled had a powerful voice in the CIO.

Union gains

And membership in the craft unions of the AFL outnumbered CIO membership by more than a million. Women's membership in unions tripled between 1930 and 1940, and African Americans also made gains. Independent unions had become a permanent part of industrial America.

Government played an important but secondary role in the industrial union movement. Roosevelt courted workers, both organized and unorganized, but stood aside in the toughest labor battles. When the CIO tried to unionize the steel industry, the president declared "a plague o' both your houses." Yet doing nothing in favor of strikers was a vast improvement over the active hostility shown by earlier presidents. The Wagner Act afforded laborers an opportunity to organize and protection if they chose to request it. Leaders such as John L. Lewis, Walter Reuther of the United Auto Workers, and Philip Murray of the Steel Workers' Organizing Committee galvanized workers, who won their own victories.

"Art for the Millions"

No agency of the New Deal touched more Americans than Federal One, the bureaucratic umbrella of the WPA's arts program. For the first time, thousands of unemployed writers, musicians, painters, actors, and photographers went on the federal payroll, and millions of ordinary Americans saw their work. Public projects—from massive murals to tiny guidebooks—would make, as one New Dealer put it, "art for the millions."

A Federal Writers Project (FWP) produced about a thousand publications. Its 81 state, territorial, and city guides were so popular that commercial publishers happily printed them. A Depression-bred interest in American history prompted the FWP to collect folklore, study ethnic groups, and record the reminiscences of former slaves. Meanwhile, the Federal Music Project (FMP) employed some 15,000 out-of-work musicians. For a token charge, Americans could hear the music of Bach and Beethoven or the commissioned compositions of American composers such as Aaron Copland. In the Federal Art Project (FAP), watercolorists and drafters painstakingly prepared the Index of American Design, which offered elaborate illustrations of American material culture, from skillets to cigar-store Indians. At night, artists taught sculpture, painting, clay modeling, and carving in country churches, settlement houses, and schools.

Rivera and Orozco

The most notable contribution of the FAP came in the form of murals. Under the influence of Mexican muralists Diego Rivera and José Clemente Orozco, American artists adorned the walls of thousands of airports, post offices, and other government buildings with murals glorifying local life and work. The rare treatment of class conflict later opened the FAP to charges of communist infiltration, but most of the murals stressed the enduring qualities of American life—family, work, community.

The Federal Theater Project (FTP) reached the greatest number of people— some 30 million—and aroused the most controversy. As its head, Hallie Flanagan made government-supported theater vital, daring, and relevant. Living Newspapers dramatized headlines of the day in play-like form. Under the direction of Orson Welles and John Houseman, an all-black company (one of 16 "Negro Units") set Shakespeare's *Macbeth* in Haiti with voodoo priestesses and African drummers. Occasionally frank depictions of class conflict riled congressional conservatives, and beginning in 1938, the House Un-American Activities Committee investigated the FTP as "a branch of the Communistic organization." A year later Congress

Documentary realism

slashed its budget and brought government-sponsored theater to an end.

The documentary impulse to record life permeated the arts in the 1930s. Novels such as Erskine Caldwell's *Tobacco Road,* feature films such as John Ford's *The Grapes of Wrath,* and such federally funded documentaries as Pare Lorentz's *The River* stirred the social conscience of the country. New Dealers had practical motives for promoting such documentary realism. They wanted to blunt criticism of New Deal relief measures. In 1937 Rexford Tugwell established an Information Division in his Resettlement Administration. He put Roy Stryker, his former Columbia University teaching assistant, in charge of its Historical Section. Stryker hired talented photographers to produce an unvarnished record of the Great Depression. Their raw and haunting photographs turned history into both propaganda and art.

The New Deal government's pathbreaking documentary film *The River*

The End of the New Deal (1937–1940)

"I see one-third of a nation ill-housed, ill-clad, ill-nourished," the president lamented in his second inaugural address on January 20, 1937 (the first January inauguration under a new constitutional amendment). Industrial output had doubled since 1932; farm income had almost quadrupled. But full recovery remained elusive. Over 7 million Americans were still out of work. At the height of his popularity, with bulging majorities in Congress, Roosevelt planned to expand the New Deal. Within a year, however, the New Deal was largely over—drowned in a sea of economic and political troubles, some of them Roosevelt's own doing.

Packing the Courts

As Roosevelt's second term began, only the Supreme Court clouded the political horizon. In its first 76 years the Court had invalidated only two acts of Congress. Between 1920 and 1933 it struck down portions of 22 laws. This new judicial activism, spearheaded by a conservative majority, rested on a narrow view of the constitutional powers of Congress and the president. As the New Deal broadened those powers, the Supreme Court let loose a torrent of nullifications.

In 1935 the Court wiped out the NRA on the grounds that manufacturing was not involved in interstate commerce and thus lay beyond federal regulation. In 1936 it canceled the AAA, reducing federal authority that had been formerly justified under the taxing power and the general welfare clause of the Constitution. In *Moorehead v. Tipaldo* (1936) the Court ruled that a New York minimum-wage law was invalid because it interfered with the right of workers to negotiate a contract. A frustrated Roosevelt complained that the Court had thereby created a "'no-man's land,' where no government—State or Federal" could act.

Roosevelt was the first president since James Monroe to serve four years without having the opportunity to make a Supreme Court appointment. Among federal judges, Republicans outnumbered Democrats by more than two to one in 1933. Roosevelt intended to redress the balance by adding new judges to the federal bench, including the Supreme Court. Too many judges were "aged or infirm," Roosevelt declared early in February 1937. In the interest of efficiency he proposed to "vitalize" the judiciary with new members. When a 70-year-old judge who had served at least 10 years failed to retire, the president would add another, up to six to the Supreme Court and 44 to the lower federal courts.

Roosevelt badly miscalculated. He unveiled his plan without warning, expecting widespread support. He regarded courts as political, not sacred, institutions and had ample precedent for altering even the Supreme Court. (As recently as 1869 Congress had increased its size to nine.) But most Americans clung to the courts

Roosevelt's plan

Daily Lives

PUBLIC SPACE/ PRIVATE SPACE
Post Office Murals

"**How can a** finished citizen be made in an artless town?" asked the postmaster of Pleasant Hill, Missouri, in 1939. Such weighty matters as citizenship and art might have seemed beyond an ordinary postmaster, but he did not think so. Neither did the New Dealers in Washington. They had just made his post office the recipient of a new painting, titled *Back Home: April 1865*. His town, like so many others across America, had been "wholly without objects of art." Now it had one that showed common people at an epic moment in American history, the end of the Civil War. Townsfolk saw it every day, and every day it made them a bit more comfortable with art, more appreciative of the heritage of democracy, more secure in the knowledge that the Republic had endured other crises.

The Fine Arts Section (FAS) of the Treasury Department spon-sored the artwork for Pleasant Hill. It was only one of the New Deal programs for artists. The largest and most famous, the Works Progress Administration's Federal Art Project (1935–1943), produced 18,000 easel paintings, 17,000 sculptures, and 2500 murals. It employed thousands of needy artists and placed their work in state and municipal institutions.

The Treasury Department had a similar mission but focused on federal buildings. During its nine-year existence, the FAS hired 850 artists and authorized nearly 1400 works. Most were for the 1100 new post offices built during the New Deal.

Post offices were an ideal medium for democratizing art because they were often at the center of town and almost everyone used them. The rectangular brick buildings reflected the solidity, permanence, and service for which government stood.

Back Home: April 1865, presented to the Pleasant Hill, Missouri, post office in 1939, was commissioned by the Fine Arts Section of the Treasury Department as part of its program to democratize American art by adorning public buildings with it.

as symbols of stability. Few accepted Roosevelt's efficiency argument, and no one on Capitol Hill, with its share of 70-year-olds, believed that seven decades of life made a person incompetent. Worse still, the proposal ignited conservative-liberal antagonisms within the Democratic party.

In the midst of the controversy, the Court suddenly began to reverse direction. In April 1937, *N.L.R.B. v. Jones and Laughlin Steel Corporation* upheld the Wagner Act by one vote. A month later the justices sustained the Social Security Act as a legitimate exercise of the commerce power. And when Justice Willis Van Devanter, the oldest and most conservative justice, retired later that year, Roosevelt at last made an appointment to the Supreme Court.

With Democrats deserting him, the president abandoned his proposal in favor of a substitute measure that modestly reformed the lower federal courts. Roosevelt claimed victory nonetheless. After all, the Court had finally shifted course (and eventually he appointed nine Supreme Court justices). But victory came at a high

Rather than emphasizing government might with portraits of national heroes or friezes of eagles and flags, the new post office murals depicted the daily routines of common citizens from the community or region. Local committees helped select the artists and the subjects. Whenever possible, local artists did the work. Such regard for community participation was meant to temper the sense that people were surrendering control to an intrusive central government.

From the artists' point of view, post offices were hardly ideal settings. Muralists required space and light. Most post offices were small and dark. Available wall space was often no more than 6 by 12 feet, usually above the postmaster's door at the end of a long, cramped lobby.

Unlike the giant muralist Diego Rivera, whose controversial work had glorified the Mexican Revolution, post office muralists were encouraged to avoid controversy. Artists were rarely permitted to deal with inflammatory subjects such as war, radicalism, or poverty.

In a decade of fear and insecurity, the murals stressed the continuity of past and present. Grand themes were distilled to simple, timeless symbols embodied in everyday experiences: a family enjoying a Sunday picnic, friends picking fruit, skaters gliding across a frozen pond. Family, work, community—these lasting values bound Americans together in good times and saw them through bad.

Regionalism often influenced subject matter. Colonial and urban scenes predominated in New England and the mid-Atlantic states; agriculture and country life in the South; the frontier and Indian and Spanish culture in the West.

The caliber of the murals varied greatly, but in the end they achieved their aim. They reached millions of common folk by combining the ordinary and the aesthetic. And almost always they communicated a harmonious vision of America, inspiring viewers with faith in progress and in themselves.

price. The momentum of the 1936 election was squandered, the unity of the Democratic party was destroyed, and opponents learned that Roosevelt could be beaten. A conservative coalition of Republicans and rural Democrats had joined forces in the first of several anti–New Deal causes.

The New Deal at Bay

As early as 1936 Secretary of the Treasury Henry Morgenthau began to plead for fiscal restraint. With productivity rising and unemployment falling, Morgenthau felt that it was time to reduce spending, balance the budget, and let business lead the recovery. "Strip off the bandages, throw away the crutches," he said, and let the economy "stand on its own feet."

Morgenthau was preaching to the converted. Although the president had been willing to run budget deficits in a time of crisis, he was never comfortable with

John Maynard Keynes

them. To be sure, the British economist John Maynard Keynes had actually recommended the kind of deficit spending that Roosevelt was using. Keynes's startling theory called on government not to balance the budget but to spend its way out of depression. When prosperity returned, Keynes argued, government could pay off its debts through taxes. This deliberate policy of "countercyclical" action (spending in bad times, taxing in good) was designed to compensate for swings in the economy.

Recovery abroad

Keynes's theory was precisely the path chosen by several industrial nations in which recovery came more quickly than it did to the United States. Germany, in particular, built its rapid recuperation on spending. When Adolf Hitler and his National Socialist (Nazi) Party came to power in 1933, they went on a spending spree, constructing huge highways called *Autobahns,* enormous government buildings, and other public works. Later they ran up deficits for rearmament as they prepared for war. Between 1933 and 1939 the German national debt almost quadrupled, while in the United States it rose by barely 50 percent. For Germans, the price in lost freedoms was incalculable, but by 1936, their depression was over.

Similarly, fascist dictator Benito Mussolini created a corporate state in partnership with business that helped lift Italy from economic ruin, in part through government financing of public works and military expansion. In Japan militarists launched a spending campaign that led to full employment by the end of 1936. When the minister of finance attempted to curb it, he was assassinated.

Not all nations relied on military spending. And many of them, such as Great Britain and France, had not shared in the economic expansion of the 1920s, which meant their economies had a shorter distance to rise in order to reach pre-Depression levels. Yet spending of one kind or another helped solve the riddle of recovery in country after country. In Great Britain, for example, low interest rates plus government assistance to the needy ignited a housing boom, while government subsidies to the automobile industry and to companies willing to build factories in depressed areas slowed the

Federal Budget and Surplus/Deficit, 1920–1940 During the 1920s the federal government ran a modest surplus as spending dropped back sharply after World War I. Hoover's cautious Depression spending programs led to a small deficit in the early 1930s, which grew steadily as Franklin Roosevelt's New Deal spent boldly and as revenues from taxes and tariffs continued to sink. In 1937 federal spending cuts to balance the budget reduced the deficit but brought on a recession that was quickly followed by renewed federal spending and increasing deficits.

slide. In the 1930s, Britons still endured what they called the "Great Slump," but their economy was the first to surpass its performance in 1929, and by 1937 British unemployment had been cut nearly by half.

In the United States, Roosevelt ordered cuts in federal spending early in 1937. He slashed relief rolls by half and virtually halted spending on public works. Within six months, the economy collapsed. Industrial activity plummeted to 1935 levels. At the end of the year unemployment stood at 10.5 million. The president, sounding strangely like Hoover, told his cabinet to "sit tight and keep quiet." The "Roosevelt recession" only deepened. Finally spenders convinced him to propose a $3.75 billion omnibus measure in April 1938. Facing an election, Congress happily reversed relief cuts, quadrupled farm subsidies, and embarked on a new shipbuilding program. The economy revived but never recovered. Keynesian economics was vindicated, though decades would pass before it became widely accepted.

With Roosevelt vulnerable, conservatives in Congress struck. They cut back on public housing programs and minimum wage guarantees in the South. The president, wrote Harold Ickes in August 1938, "is punch drunk from the punishment." Vainly Roosevelt fought back. In the off-year elections of 1938, he tried to purge Democrats who had deserted him. The five senators he targeted for defeat all won. Republicans posted gains in the House and Senate and won 13 governorships. Democrats still held majorities in both houses but conservatives had the votes to block new programs. With the economy limping toward recovery, the New Deal passed into history, and the nation turned to a new crisis—a looming war abroad.

The Legacy of the New Deal

The New Deal lasted only five years, from 1933 to 1938, and it never spent enough to end the Depression. Though it pledged itself to the "forgotten" Americans, it failed the neediest among them—sharecroppers, tenant farmers, migrant workers. In many ways, it was quite conservative. It left capitalism intact, even strengthened, and it overturned few cultural conventions. Even its reforms followed the old progressive formula of softening industrialism by strengthening the state.

Yet for all its conservatism and continuities, the New Deal left a legacy of change. Under it, government assumed a broader role in the economy than progressives had ever undertaken. To the progressive goal of regulation was now added the more complicated task of maintaining economic stability—compensating for swings in the business cycle. In its securities and banking regulations, unemployment insurance, and requirements for wages and hours the New Deal created stabilizers to avoid future breakdowns. Bolstering the Federal Reserve system and enhancing control over credit strengthened the means by which government could shape the economy.

Franklin Roosevelt modernized the presidency. He turned the White House into the heart of government, the place where decisions were made. Americans looked to the president to set the public agenda, spread new ideas, initiate legislation, and assume responsibility for the nation. The power of Congress diminished but the scope of government grew. In 1932 there were 605,000 federal employees; by 1939 there were nearly a million (and by 1945, after World War II, some 3.5 million). The many programs of the New Deal—home loans, farm subsidies, bank deposit insurance, relief payments and jobs, pension programs, unemployment insurance, aid to mothers with dependent children, rural electrification, western water management—touched the lives of ordinary Americans, made them more secure, and formed the outlines of the new welfare state.

The welfare state had limits. Most of its relief measures were designed to last no longer than the crisis. Millions fell through even its more nearly permanent safety nets. Yet the commitment to furnishing minimum standards of life, not the failure to do so, marked a change so dramatic that the poor and working class threw their support to Roosevelt. He was, after all, the first president to try.

At a time when dictators and militarists took hold in Germany, Italy, Japan, and Russia, the New Deal strengthened democracy in America. Roosevelt acted as a democratic broker, responding first to one group, then another. And his "broker state" embraced groups previously spurned—unions, farm organizations, ethnic minorities, women. In short, during the 1930s the United States found a middle way between the extremes of communism and fascism. Still, the broker state had limits. The unorganized, whether in city slums or in sharecroppers' shacks, too often found themselves ignored.

Under the New Deal, the Democratic party became a mighty force in politics. In a quiet revolution, African Americans came into the party's fold, as did workers

What the New Deal Did . . .			
	RELIEF	RECOVERY	REFORM
FOR THE FARMER:	Rural Electrification Administration (1936) Farm Security Administration (1937)	Agriculture Adjustment Act (1933)	
FOR THE WORKER:		National Industrial Recovery Act (1933)	National Labor Relations Act (1935) Fair Labor Standards Act (1938)
FOR THE MIDDLE CLASS:	Home Owner's Loan Act (1934)		Revenue ("Wealth Tax") Act (1935) Public Utilities Holding Company Act (1935)
FOR THE NEEDY:	Federal Emergency Relief Act (1933) Civilian Conservation Corp (1933) Civil Works Administration (1933) National Public Housing Act (1937) Emergency Relief Appropriation Act (1935)		
FOR PROTECTION AGAINST FUTURE DEPRESSIONS:			Federal Deposit Insurance Corporation (1933) Securities Exchange Act (1934) Social Security Act (1935)

and farmers. Political attention shifted to bread-and-butter issues. In 1932 people had argued about Prohibition and European war debts. By 1935 they were debating Social Security, labor relations, tax reform, public housing, and the TVA. With remarkable speed, the New Deal had become a vital part of American life.

In February 1939 Eleanor Roosevelt addressed the National Youth Congress. Only six years earlier she had stood at her husband's inauguration, chilled with worry over the future of her country. As the decade drew to a close, she could take justifiable pride in the accomplishments of Franklin and the other New Dealers, including those in Congress. Blending public and private controls, the New Deal humanized industrial society and attempted to generate prosperity without sacrificing capitalism or democracy. And through it all, government—embodied in her husband—had taken the lead.

Yet New Dealers from the president down recognized that they could not do everything. "I never believed that the Federal government could solve the whole problem," Eleanor told the members of the Youth Congress. A measure of doubt crept into her voice: "It bought us time to think. . . . Is it going to be worthwhile?" Only future generations could say.

chapter summary

The Great Depression of the 1930s was the longest in the history of the nation; it forced virtually all Americans to live leaner lives and it spawned Franklin Roosevelt's New Deal.

- The Great Depression acted as a great leveler that reduced differences in income and status and left many Americans with an "invisible scar" of shame, self-doubt, and lost confidence.

  - Unemployment and suffering were especially acute among agricultural migrants, African Americans, Latinos, and American Indians.

  - Rates of marriage and birth declined, and many women found themselves working additional hours inside and outside the home to supplement family incomes.

  - Popular culture rallied to reinforce basic tenets of American life: middle-class morality, family, capitalism, and democracy.

- President Herbert Hoover represented a transition from the old, do-nothing policies of the past to the interventionist policies of the future. In the end, his program of voluntary cooperation and limited government activism failed, and in 1932 he lost the presidency to Franklin Roosevelt.

- Roosevelt's New Deal attacked the Great Depression along three broad fronts: recovery for the economy, relief for the needy, and reforms to ward off future depressions.

- The New Deal failed to achieve full recovery but did result in lasting changes:

  - The creation of economic stabilizers such as federal insurance for bank deposits, unemployment assistance, and greater control over money and banking that were designed to compensate for swings in the economy.

  - The establishment of a limited welfare state to provide minimum standards of well-being for all Americans.

  - The revitalization of the Democratic Party and the formation of a powerful new political coalition of labor, urban ethnics, women, African Americans, and the South.

  - The modernization of the presidency.

interactive learning

The Primary Source Investigator CD-ROM offers the following materials related to this chapter:

- Interactive maps: **Election of 1932** (M7) and **Unemployment Relief, 1934** (M26)

- A short documentary movie on the New Deal government's pathbreaking documentary film *The River* (D17)

- A collection of primary sources demonstrating how the Great Depression fundamentally altered American society and politics, such as with the Tennessee Valley Authority Act and the Social Security Act. Several sources document the effects of the Great Depression on the social fabric of the United States, including photographs of a dust storm, migrant mothers, and other images from the Farmer's Security Administration photographer Dorothea Lange.

additional reading

The best overall examination of the period encompassing the Great Depression and the Second World War is David M. Kennedy's *Freedom from Fear: The American People in Depression and War, 1929–1945* (1999). For a comparative look at responses to the Great Depression, see John A. Garraty, *The Great Depression* (1987). Robert Sobel, *The Great Bull Market: Wall Street in the 1920s* (1968), is a brief, evenhanded study of the stock market and Republican fiscal policies in the 1920s. Caroline Bird, *The Invisible Scar* (1966), remains the most sensitive treatment of the human impact of the Great Depression, but it should not be read without Studs Terkel, *Hard Times: An Oral History of the Great Depression* (1970), and Robert McElvaine, *The Great Depression: America, 1929–1941* (1984), which are especially good on Depression culture and values. Joan Hoff Wilson, *Herbert Hoover: Forgotten Progressive* (1975), traces Hoover's progressive impulses before and during his presidency.

Frank Freide, *Franklin D. Roosevelt: A Rendezvous with Destiny* (1990), is the best single-volume biography of Roosevelt, and William Leuchtenburg, *Franklin D. Roosevelt and the New Deal, 1932–1940* (1963), is the best single-volume study of the New Deal. Both fall within the liberal tradition of New Deal scholarship and are admiringly critical of Roosevelt's use of power. They emphasize the limits of political feasibility faced by New Dealers. For sharp criticism of New Left historians, see Paul Conkin, *The New Deal* (1967). For the bureaucratic constraints faced by the New Deal and the absence of "state capacity," see Theda Skocpol and Kenneth Finegold, "State Capacity and Economic Intervention in the Early New Deal," *Political Science Quarterly* (1982), 255–278.

Eleanor Roosevelt is analyzed in rich detail and from a frankly feminist viewpoint in Blanche Wiesen Cook, *Eleanor Roosevelt, Volume One, 1884–1993* (1992), and *Eleanor Roosevelt: Volume Two, 1933–1938* (1999). Susan Ware, *Beyond Suffrage: Women and the New Deal* (1981), locates a women's political network within the New Deal, and Harvard Sitkoff, *A New Deal for Blacks* (1978), studies a similar network of blacks and whites and surveys the mixed record of the New Deal for African Americans. The culture and politics of working men and women during the Great Depression are the subject of Lisabeth Cohen, *Making a New Deal: Industrial Workers in Chicago, 1919–1939* (1990), which depicts the erosion of ethnic communities and the acceptance among workers of federal activism and welfare capitalism during the Great Depression. Steve Fraser and Gary Gerstle, eds., *The Rise and Fall of the New Deal Order, 1930–1980* (1989), is an excellent collection of interpretive essays examining the origins, impact, and legacy of the New Deal. For a probing analysis of New Deal liberalism and its retreat from reform, see Alan Brinkley, *The End of Reform: New Deal Liberalism in Recession and War* (1995). For a fuller list of readings, see the Bibliography at www.mhhe.com/davidsonnation5.

significant events

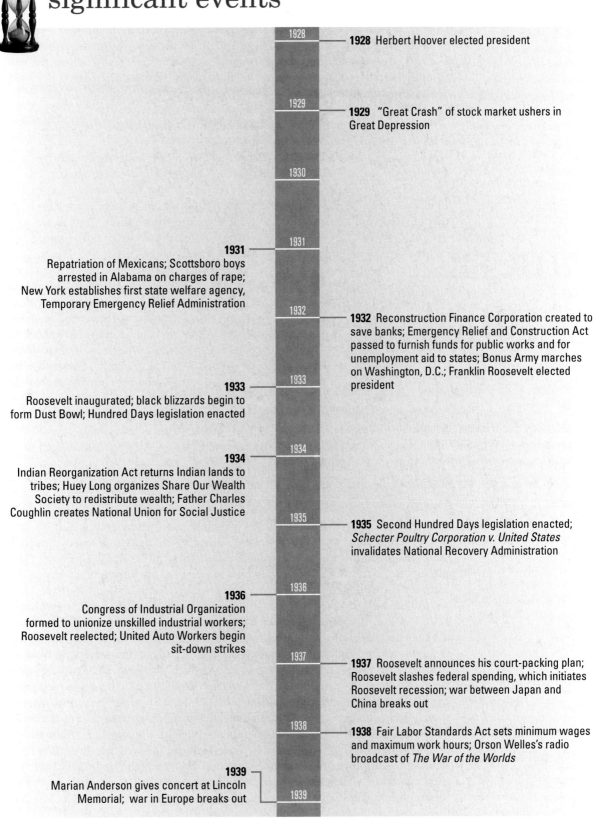

1928   1928 Herbert Hoover elected president

1929

1929   "Great Crash" of stock market ushers in Great Depression

1930

1931
1931
Repatriation of Mexicans; Scottsboro boys arrested in Alabama on charges of rape; New York establishes first state welfare agency, Temporary Emergency Relief Administration

1932
1932   Reconstruction Finance Corporation created to save banks; Emergency Relief and Construction Act passed to furnish funds for public works and for unemployment aid to states; Bonus Army marches on Washington, D.C.; Franklin Roosevelt elected president

1933
1933
Roosevelt inaugurated; black blizzards begin to form Dust Bowl; Hundred Days legislation enacted

1934
1934
Indian Reorganization Act returns Indian lands to tribes; Huey Long organizes Share Our Wealth Society to redistribute wealth; Father Charles Coughlin creates National Union for Social Justice

1935
1935   Second Hundred Days legislation enacted; *Schecter Poultry Corporation v. United States* invalidates National Recovery Administration

1936
1936
Congress of Industrial Organization formed to unionize unskilled industrial workers; Roosevelt reelected; United Auto Workers begin sit-down strikes

1937
1937   Roosevelt announces his court-packing plan; Roosevelt slashes federal spending, which initiates Roosevelt recession; war between Japan and China breaks out

1938
1938   Fair Labor Standards Act sets minimum wages and maximum work hours; Orson Welles's radio broadcast of *The War of the Worlds*

1939
Marian Anderson gives concert at Lincoln Memorial; war in Europe breaks out

1939

Chapter 26

John Garcia, a native Hawaiian, worked as a pipe fitter's apprentice at the Pearl Harbor Navy Yard in Honolulu. On Sunday, December 7, 1941, Garcia planned to enjoy a lazy day off. By the time his grandmother rushed in to wake him that morning at eight, he had already missed the worst of it. "The Japanese were bombing Pearl Harbor," he recalled her yelling at him. John listened in disbelief. "I said, 'They're just practicing.'" "No," his grandmother replied. It was real. He catapulted his huge frame from the bed, ran to the front porch, and caught sight of the antiaircraft fire in the sky. "Oh boy" were his only words.

Hopping on his motorcycle, Garcia sped the four miles to the harbor in 10 minutes. "It was a mess," he remembered. The USS *Shaw* was in flames. The battleship *Pennsylvania*, a bomb nesting one deck above the powder and ammunition, was about to blow. When ordered to put out its fires, he refused. "There ain't no way I'm gonna go down there," he told the navy officer. Instead, he spent the rest of the day pulling bodies from the water. There were so many, he lost count. He couldn't tell "how many were alive and how many were dead." Surveying the wreckage the following morning, he noted that the battleship *Arizona* "was a total washout." So was the *West Virginia*. The *Oklahoma* had "turned turtle, totally upside down." It took two weeks to get all the fires out.

America's Rise to Globalism

1927–1945

preview • As the Depression accelerated the rise of militarism in Europe and Asia, most Americans hoped to remain isolated from war. Only Japan's attack on Pearl Harbor brought the United States into the conflict. Eventually American industrial might supplied the Allies in both Europe and the Pacific, bringing renewed prosperity at home. And the dropping of two atomic bombs to end the war underscored America's new role as the preeminent power in a globally interdependent world.

The world had been at war since 1937, but Americans had largely been spared. The surprise attack at Pearl Harbor suddenly transformed the Pacific into an avenue of potential assault. Dennis Keegan, a young college student at the University of San Francisco, could not believe war had come, even though his younger brother Bill was training in Canada to fly with the Royal Air Force. "These places were so far away from us," Dennis said after hearing the radio reports on Pearl Harbor. "It just didn't seem possible that we were at war."

All along the West Coast panic spread. That night Keegan drove into downtown San Francisco. Market Street was "bedlam." "The United Artists Theater had a huge marquee with those dancing lights, going on and off," he recalled. "People were throwing everything they could to put those lights out, screaming Blackout! Blackout!" The next day a false army report of 30 Japanese planes flying toward the coast triggered air-raid sirens throughout the city. Los Angeles turned trigger happy. A young police officer named Tom Bradley (who later served as mayor of the city) heard "sirens going off, aircraft guns firing." "Here we are in the middle of the night," he said; "there was no enemy in sight, but somebody thought they saw the enemy." In January 1942 worried officials moved the Rose Bowl from Pasadena, California, to Durham, North Carolina. Though overheated, their fears were not entirely imaginary. Japanese submarines shelled Santa Barbara and Fort Stearns in Oregon. Balloons carrying incendiary devices caused several deaths in Oregon.

Images of its battleships in flames sent the United States into global war. Despite the apparent devastation, the losses at Pearl Harbor were more shocking than disabling. The *West Virginia*, shown here, settled to the bottom with guns firing and was later repaired.

Although the Japanese would never invade the mainland, in a world with long-range bombers and submarines no place seemed safe. This war was a global war, the first of its kind. Arrayed against the Axis powers of Germany, Italy, and Japan were the Allies—Great Britain, the Soviet Union, the United States, China, and the Free French. Their armies fought from the Arctic to the southwestern Pacific, in the great cities of Europe and Asia and the small villages of North Africa and Indochina, in malarial jungles and scorching deserts, on six continents and across four oceans. Perhaps as many as 100 million people took up arms; some 40 to 50 million lost their lives.

Tragedy on such a scale taught the generation of Americans who fought the war that they could no longer isolate themselves from any part of the world, no matter how remote it might seem. Manchuria, Ethiopia, and Poland had once seemed far away, yet the road to war had led from those distant places to the United States. Retreat into isolation had not cured the worldwide depression or preserved the peace. To avoid other such disasters, the United States would eventually assume a far wider role in managing the world's geopolitical and economic systems.

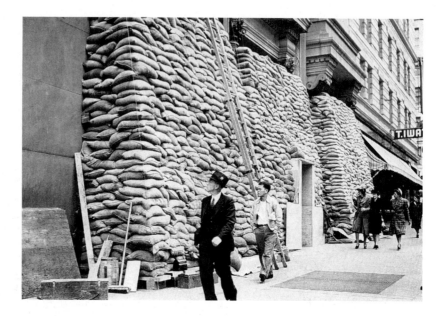

The Japanese attack on Pearl Harbor created a panic along the West Coast of the United States. Hasty defenses such as these sandbags stacked in front of the telephone company in San Francisco were thrown up to ward off an attack that never came.

The United States in a Troubled World

The outbreak of World War II had its roots in World War I. So vast was the devastation of the Great War that the victors suffered almost as much as the vanquished. Many of the victorious as well as the defeated nations were deeply dissatisfied with the peace terms adopted at Versailles. Over the next two decades Germany, the Soviet Union, Italy, Poland, and Japan all sought to achieve unilaterally what Allied leaders had denied them at Versailles. In central and eastern Europe rivalry among fascists, communists, and other political factions led to frequent violence and instability. Reparations imposed at Versailles shackled Germany's economy. As Germany struggled to recover, so did all of Europe. Although the United States possessed the resources to ease international tensions, it declined to lead in world affairs. It even rejected membership in the League of Nations.

Pacific Interests

A preference for isolation did not mean the United States could simply ignore events abroad. In assuming colonial control over the Philippines, Americans acquired a major interest in the western Pacific that created a potentially dangerous rivalry with Japan. The United States had also committed itself to an open-door policy (page 703) to prevent China from being divided up by foreign powers. That temptation seemed especially great during the 1920s, because China was wracked by civil war. In 1927 the Nationalist party, led by Chiang Kai-shek, consolidated power by attacking their former Communist party allies.

The Japanese had long dominated Korea, and during the 1920s they expanded their influence on the Chinese mainland. In 1931 Japanese agents staged an explosion on a rail line in Manchuria (meant to appear as if carried out by Chinese nationalists) that provided Japan with an excuse to occupy the whole province. A year later Japan converted Manchuria into a puppet state called Manchukuo.

Here was a direct threat to the Versailles system and the open door. But neither the major powers in Europe nor the United States was willing to risk a war with Japan over China. President Hoover would allow Secretary of State Henry Stimson only to protest that the United States would refuse to recognize Japan's takeover of Manchuria. The policy of "nonrecognition" became known as the Stimson Doctrine, even though Stimson himself doubted its worth. He was right to be skeptical. Three weeks later Japan's imperial navy shelled the Chinese port city of Shanghai. When the League of Nations condemned Japan in 1933, the Japanese withdrew from the League. The seeds of war in Asia had been sown.

Stimson Doctrine

Becoming a Good Neighbor

Trouble abroad encouraged the United States to improve relations with nations closer to home. By the late 1920s the United States had intervened in Latin America so often that the Roosevelt Corollary (page 747) had become an embarrassment. Slowly, Washington began to abandon some of its highhanded policies. In 1927, when Mexico confiscated American-owned properties, President Coolidge sent an ambassador, instead of the marines, to settle the dispute. In 1933, when critics compared the American position in Nicaragua to Japan's in Manchuria, Secretary Stimson ordered U.S. troops to withdraw. In those gestures and in President Hoover's efforts to cultivate goodwill south of the border lay the roots of a "Good Neighbor" policy.

Good Neighbor policy

Franklin Roosevelt pushed the good neighbor idea. To Roosevelt that meant correcting the political inequities between the United States and Latin America. At the seventh Pan-American Conference in 1933, his administration accepted a resolution denying any country "the right to intervene in the internal or external affairs of another." The following year he negotiated a treaty with Cuba that renounced the American right to intervene under the Platt Amendment (page 747). Henceforth the United States would replace direct military presence with indirect (but still substantial) economic influence.

The greatest test of the Good Neighbor policy came in 1937 and 1938, when Bolivia and Mexico expropriated the property of American oil companies. Roosevelt worried that intervention would push Mexico toward closer ties with potential enemies. When an arbitration committee decided that U.S. oil companies were entitled to only $24 million (not the $450 million they demanded), Roosevelt accepted the decision.

The Good Neighbor policy made Franklin Roosevelt unusually popular in Latin America, as this sheet music suggests. Roosevelt was the first American president to visit South America, and his diplomacy paid dividends when a largely united Western Hemisphere faced the world crisis.

As the threat of war increased during the 1930s, the United States found a new Latin willingness to cooperate in matters of common defense. In the first visit of an American president to the capital of Argentina, Roosevelt opened the Pan-American Conference in 1936. In a speech he declared that outside aggressors "will find a Hemisphere wholly prepared to consult together for our mutual safety and our mutual good." By the end of 1940 the administration had worked out defense agreements with every Latin American country but one. The United States faced the threat of war with the American hemisphere largely secured.

The Diplomacy of Isolationism

During the 1920s Benito Mussolini had appealed to Italian nationalism and fear of communism to gain power in Italy. Spinning dreams of a new Roman empire, Mussolini embodied the rising force of fascism. Then on March 5, 1933, one day after the inauguration of Franklin Roosevelt, the German legislature gave Adolf

The rise of fascism

Hitler control of Germany. Riding a wave of anticommunism and anti-Semitism, Hitler's Nazi party promised to unite all Germans in a Greater Third Reich that would last a thousand years. Just over a week earlier, Yosuke Matsuoka had led the Japanese out of the League of Nations. Governed by militarists, Japan began to carve out its own empire, which it called the Greater East Asia Co-Prosperity Sphere. The rise of fascism and militarism in Europe and Asia brought the world to war.

As much as Roosevelt wanted the United States to play a leading role in world affairs, the nation proved unwilling to follow. "It's a terrible thing to look over your shoulder when you are trying to lead—and to find no one there," he commented during the mid-1930s. Only when a potential economic interest was involved could the president command wide support for foreign initiatives. For example, in 1933 Roosevelt recognized the Communist regime in Russia, hoping that the Soviet Union would help contain Japanese expansion in Asia and fascism in Europe. Business leaders saw recognition largely as an opportunity to increase Russian-American trade. For every step Roosevelt took toward internationalism, the Great Depression forced him home again. Programs to revive the economy gained broad support; efforts to resolve crises abroad provoked controversy.

In 1935 Senator Gerald P. Nye of North Dakota headed investigations that revealed that bankers and munitions makers, so-called merchants of death, had made enormous profits during World War I. The Nye Committee report implied, but could not prove, that business interests had even steered the United States into war. "When Americans went into the fray," declared Senator Nye, "they little thought that they were there and fighting to save the skins of American bankers who had bet too boldly on the outcome of the war and had two billions of dollars of loans to the Allies in jeopardy."

Such charges provoked debate over how the United States should respond to the growing threats to peace. Internationalists like the League of Women Voters and former secretary of state Henry Stimson favored a policy of collective security—working actively with other nations. "The only certain way to keep out of a great war is to prevent war," Stimson declared. "The only hope of preventing war . . . is by the earnest, intelligent, and unselfish cooperation of the nations of the world towards that end."

On the other side stood the isolationists, united by their firm opposition to war and the conviction that the United States should avoid alliances with other nations. Yet many strange bedfellows made up the isolationist movement. It included liberal reformers like George W. Norris and conservatives like Robert A. Taft of Ohio, a concentration of midwesterners as well as major leaders from both coasts, and a number of Democrats as well as leading Republicans. Pacifists added yet another element to the debate. Powerful groups like the Women's International League for Peace and Freedom insisted that disarmament was the only road to peace.

Neutrality Legislation

Roused by the Nye Committee hearings, Congress debated a proposal to prohibit the sale of arms to belligerents in time of war. Internationalists opposed the idea. The embargo, they argued, should apply only to aggressor nations. Otherwise, aggressors could strike when they were ready and their victims would be ill prepared. The president, they believed, should have the authority to use the embargo selectively. The Neutrality Act of 1935 denied Roosevelt that power. At the isolationists' insistence, it required an impartial embargo of arms to all belligerents. The president had authority only to determine when a state of war existed. A troubled Roosevelt argued that the Neutrality Act might "drag us into war rather than keeping us out."

Recognition of the Soviet Union

Nye Committee

Internationalists versus isolationists

The limitations of formal neutrality became immediately apparent. In October 1935 Benito Mussolini ordered Italian forces into the North African country of Ethiopia. Against tanks and planes, the troops of Emperor Haile Selassie fought with spears and flintlock rifles. Roosevelt immediately invoked the Neutrality Act in hopes of depriving Italy of war goods. Unfortunately for Roosevelt, Italy needed not arms but oil, steel, and copper—materials not included under the Neutrality Act. When Secretary of State Cordell Hull called for a "moral embargo" on such goods, hard-pressed American businesses shipped them anyway. With no effective opposition from the League of Nations or the United States, Mussolini quickly completed his conquest. In a second Neutrality Act Congress added a ban on loans or credits to belligerents.

Neutrality legislation also benefited Nazi dictator Adolf Hitler. In March 1936, two weeks after Congress renewed the Neutrality Act, German troops thrust into the demilitarized area west of the Rhine River. This flagrant act violated the Treaty of Versailles. As Hitler shrewdly calculated, Britain and France did nothing, while the League of Nations sputtered out a worthless condemnation. Roosevelt remained aloof. The Soviet Union's lonely call for collective action fell on deaf ears.

Then came a rebellion against Spain's fledgling democracy. In July 1936 Generalissimo Francisco Franco, made bold by Hitler's success, revolted against the newly elected Popular Front government. The civil war that followed became a staging ground for World War II. Hitler and Mussolini sent supplies, weapons, and troops to Franco's Fascists, while the Soviet Union and Mexico aided the left-leaning government. The war divided opinion in Europe and America. Catholics supported the anti-communist Franco forces. Leftists embraced the Loyalists, who backed the democratic government. In the face of domestic political divisions Roosevelt refused to become involved in the conflict. By 1939 the Spanish republic had fallen to Franco.

Spanish Civil War

A flag company of Hitler youth parades past its *Führer,* Adolf Hitler (centered in the balcony doorway). Hitler's shrewd use of patriotic and party symbols, mass rallies, and marches exploited the possibilities for mass politics and propaganda.

Cash-and-carry

For its part, Congress searched for a way to allow American trade to continue (and thus to promote economic recovery at home) without drawing the nation into war itself. Under new "cash-and-carry" provisions in the Neutrality Act of 1937, belligerents could buy supplies other than munitions. But they would have to pay beforehand and carry the supplies on their own ships. If war spread, these terms favored the British, whose navy would ensure that supplies reached England.

Aggression in China

But the policy of cash-and-carry hurt China. In 1937 Japanese forces pushed into its southern regions. In order to give China continued access to American goods, Roosevelt refused to invoke the Neutrality Act, which would have cut off trade with both nations. But Japan had by far a greater volume of trade with the United States. Because the president lacked the freedom to impose a selective embargo, Japan could use American resources to support the invasion.

Inching toward War

With Italy, Germany, and Japan turning into armed camps, war seemed inevitable in both Europe and Asia. The three militant nations signed the Anti-Comintern Pact in 1937. On the face of it, the pact was merely a pledge of mutual support against the Soviet Union. But the Rome-Berlin-Tokyo axis freed those nations for further expansion. Roosevelt groped for some way to contain the Axis powers—these "bandit nations." In his first foreign policy speech in 14 months, he called for an international "quarantine" of aggressor nations. Most newspaper editorials applauded his remarks, yet Roosevelt quickly retreated. When Japanese planes sank the American gunboat *Panay* on China's Yangtze River in December, only two months later, he meekly accepted an apology for the unprovoked attack.

Quarantine speech

In truth, domestic pressures kept the president from risking a confrontation with powerful isolationists. His ill-fated plan to pack the Supreme Court in 1937 had emboldened opposition among both conservative Democrats and Republicans. In 1939, his request to Congress for flexibility in applying the arms embargo went down to defeat. "Well, Captain," Vice President John Nance Garner told him, "we may as well face the facts. You haven't got the votes, and that's all there is to it."

What made Roosevelt's impotence so frustrating was the growing Nazi menace. In 1938 German troops marched into Austria in yet another violation of the Treaty of Versailles. Hitler then insisted that the 3.5 million ethnic Germans in the Sudetenland of Czechoslovakia be brought into the Reich. With Germany threatening to invade Czechoslovakia, the leaders of France and Britain flew to Munich in September 1938, where they struck a deal to appease Hitler. Czechoslovakia would give up the Sudetenland in return for German pledges to seek no more territory in Europe. When British prime minister Neville Chamberlain returned to England, he told cheering crowds that the Munich Pact would bring "peace in our time." Six months later, in open contempt for the European democracies, Hitler took over the remainder of Czechoslovakia. "Appeasement" became synonymous with betrayal, weakness, and surrender.

Appeasement

Hitler's Invasion

By 1939 Hitler made little secret that he intended to recapture territory lost to Poland after World War I. Russia was the key to his success. If Soviet leader Joseph Stalin joined the Western powers, Hitler might be blocked. But Stalin suspected that the West hoped to turn Hitler against the Soviet Union. On August 24, 1939, the foreign ministers of Russia and Germany signed a nonaggression pact, shocking the rest of the world. The secret protocols of the agreement freed Hitler to invade Poland without having to fight a war with enemies attacking on two fronts. Stalin could extend his western borders by bringing eastern Poland, the Baltic states (Latvia, Estonia, and Lithuania), and parts of Romania and Finland into the Soviet sphere.

On the hot Saturday of September 1, 1939, German tanks and troops surged into Poland. "It's come at last," Roosevelt sighed. "God help us all." Within days France and England declared war on Germany. Stalin quickly moved into eastern Poland, where German and Russian armor took just three weeks to crush the Polish cavalry. As Hitler consolidated his hold on eastern Europe, Stalin invaded Finland.

Germany begins World War II

Once spring arrived in 1940, Hitler moved to protect his sea lanes by capturing Denmark and Norway. The French retreated behind their Maginot Line, a steel and concrete fortification at the German border. Undeterred, German panzer divisions supported by air power knifed through Belgium and Holland in a blitzkrieg—a "lightning war." The Low Countries fell in 23 days, giving the Germans a route into France. By May a third of a million British and French troops had been driven back onto the Atlantic beaches of Dunkirk. Only a strenuous rescue effort, staged by the Royal Navy and a flotilla of English pleasure craft, saved them. The way was clear for the Germans to march to Paris.

On June 22, less than six weeks after the German invasion, France capitulated. Hitler insisted that the surrender come in the very railway car in which Germany had submitted in 1918. William Shirer, an American war correspondent standing 50 yards away, watched the dictator through binoculars: "He swiftly snaps his hands on his hips, arches his shoulders, plants his feet wide apart. It is a magnificent gesture of defiance, of burning contempt for this place and all that it has stood for in the twenty-two years since it witnessed the humbling of the German Empire."

Retreat from Isolationism

Now, only Britain stood between Hitler and the United States. If the Nazis defeated the British fleet, the Atlantic Ocean could easily become a gateway to the Americas. Isolationism suddenly seemed dangerous. By the spring of 1940 Roosevelt had abandoned impartiality in favor of outright aid to the Allies. In May he requested funds to motorize the army (it had only 350 tanks) and build 50,000 airplanes a year (fewer than 3000 existed, most outmoded). Over isolationist protests he soon persuaded Congress to adopt a bill for the first peacetime draft in history.

That summer thousands of German fighter planes and heavy bombers struck targets in England. In the Battle of Britain Hitler and his air chief, Hermann Goering, sought to soften up England for a German invasion from occupied France. Radio reporters relayed graphic descriptions of London in flames and Royal Air Force pilots putting up a heroic defense. Such tales convinced a majority of Americans that the United States should help Britain win the war, though few favored military involvement. So Roosevelt adopted policies designed to help the British help themselves. In September 1940 he agreed to give Britain 50 old destroyers in return for leases on British bases in the Western Hemisphere. The destroyers-for-bases deal, Roosevelt told the nation, was the most important "reinforcement of our national defenses that has been taken since the Louisiana Purchase."

Battle of Britain

In the 1940 election campaign both Roosevelt and his Republican opponent, Wendell Willkie, favored an internationalist course short of war. In defeating Willkie, Roosevelt promised voters that "your boys are not going to be sent into any foreign wars." He portrayed the United States, instead, as "the great arsenal of democracy." Because the British no longer could pay for arms under the provisions

Lend-Lease aid

of cash-and-carry, Roosevelt proposed a scheme to "lease, lend, or otherwise dispose of" arms and supplies to countries whose defense was vital to the United States. That meant sending supplies to England on the dubious premise that they would be returned when the war ended. Roosevelt likened "lend-lease" to lending a garden hose to a neighbor whose house was on fire. Isolationist senator Robert Taft thought a comparison to "chewing gum" more apt. After a neighbor used it, "you don't want it back." In March 1941 Congress rejected isolationism, passing the Lend-Lease Act by a large majority.

By the summer of 1941 the United States and Germany were on the verge of war. American destroyers had begun to escort British ships as far as Iceland (though Roosevelt insisted it was a "patrol," not a convoy). The United States extended its defensive sphere to include Greenland and Iceland. Then Hitler, as audacious as ever, broke his alliance with the Soviet Union by launching a surprise invasion in June 1941. The Allies expected a swift Russian collapse. Soviet armies had fought poorly in the Finnish War, and Stalin in a series of purges three years earlier had executed much of his officer corps. But when the Russians threw up a heroic resistance, Roosevelt extended lend-lease to the Soviet Union.

Atlantic Charter

In August 1941 Roosevelt took a secret voyage to Argentia Bay off the coast of Newfoundland. There he met Britain's new war prime minister, Winston Churchill. Almost every day since England and Germany had gone to war, the two leaders had exchanged phone calls, letters, or cables. The Argentia meetings cemented this friendship—one key to Allied victory. Roosevelt and Churchill also drew up the Atlantic Charter, a statement of principles that the two nations held in common. The charter condemned "Nazi tyranny" and embraced the "Four Freedoms"—freedom of speech and expression, freedom of worship, freedom from want, and freedom from fear. In effect, the Atlantic Charter was an unofficial statement of war aims. It put humanitarian values ahead of narrow interests.

During World War II, Franklin Roosevelt and British prime minister Winston Churchill developed the closest relationship ever between an American president and the head of another government. The two distant cousins shared a sense of the continuities of Anglo-American culture and of the global strategy of the war.

By the time of the Argentia meetings, American destroyers in the North Atlantic were stalking German U-boats and reporting their whereabouts to British commanders. Given the harsh weather and aggressive American policy, incidents were inevitable. In October a U-boat sank the destroyer *Reuben James* with the loss of more than 100 American sailors. That attack increased public support for the Allied cause. Yet when interventionists criticized Roosevelt for being too cautious, isolationists charged him with being too provocative. As late as September 1941 eight of ten Americans opposed entering the hostilities. Few in the United States suspected that an attack by Japan, not Germany, would bring a unified America into the war.

Disaster in the Pacific

Worried most by the prospect of a German victory in Europe, Roosevelt avoided a showdown with Japan. The navy, the president told his cabinet, had "not got enough ships to go round, and every little episode in the Pacific means fewer ships in the Atlantic." But precisely because American and European attention lay elsewhere, Japan was emboldened to expand militarily into Southeast Asia.

Japanese leaders were able to justify their expansion easily enough. They viewed their Greater East Asia Co-Prosperity Sphere as simply an Asian version of the Monroe Doctrine. Japan, the preeminent power in the region, would replace the Europeans as a promoter of economic development. To American leaders, however, Japan's actions threatened the principles of the open-door policy and the survival of Chinese independence. By the summer of 1941 Japanese forces controlled the China coast and all major cities. When its army marched into French Indochina (present-day Vietnam) in July, Japan stood ready to conquer all of the Southeast Asian peninsula and the oil-rich Dutch East Indies.

Japan's thrust into Indochina forced Roosevelt to act. He embargoed trade, froze Japanese assets in American banks, and barred shipments of vital scrap iron and petroleum. When the Dutch slapped a similar embargo on their oil from the East Indies, Japan faced a turning point. If the United States would not supply needed petroleum, Japan would be forced to attack the Dutch East Indies. Prime Minister Fumimaro Konoye, still hoping to negotiate a settlement, proposed a summit meeting with Roosevelt. In fact, the two nations' goals were so at odds that no diplomatic resolution was possible. The Japanese ambassador pressed the United States to recognize recent conquests and Japanese dominance in Asia. Secretary of State Hull replied that Japan must renounce the Tripartite Pact with Italy and Germany and withdraw from China. Only then could summit talks begin.

In October the militant General Hideki Tojo replaced the more moderate Prime Minister Konoye. With the war party firmly in control, the military began preparing surprise attacks on American positions in Guam, the Philippines, and Hawaii. One final round of diplomacy, then war.

For their part, American military leaders urged Roosevelt to avoid conflict. The United States needed time to build up its national defenses. Massive Japanese troop movements southward indicated an assault on British and Dutch holdings. If the Japanese attacked American possessions, most expected the blow to fall on Guam or the Philippines. In late November American intelligence located, and then lost, a Japanese armada in Hitokappu Bay in Japan. Observing strict radio silence, the six carriers and their escorts steamed across the North Pacific toward the American base at Pearl Harbor in Hawaii. On Sunday morning, December 7, 1941, the first wave of Japanese planes roared down on the Pacific Fleet lying at anchor. For more than an hour the Japanese pounded the harbor and nearby airfields. Altogether

Japanese expansion

Pearl Harbor

19 ships—the heart of the Pacific Fleet—were sunk or battered. Practically all of the 200 American aircraft were damaged or destroyed. Only the aircraft carriers, by chance on maneuvers, escaped the worst naval defeat in American history.

In Washington, Secretary of War Henry Stimson could not believe the news. "My God! This can't be true, this must mean the Philippines." Later that day the Japanese did attack the Philippines, along with Guam, Midway, and British forces in Hong Kong and on the Malay peninsula. On December 8, Franklin Roosevelt told a stunned nation that "yesterday, December 7, 1941," was "a date which will live in infamy." America, the "reluctant belligerent," was in the war at last. Three days later Hitler declared war on the "half Judaized and the other half Negrified" people of the United States. Italy quickly followed suit.

Did Roosevelt deliberately invite war?

Had Roosevelt known the attack on Pearl Harbor was coming? Some critics have charged that the president deliberately contrived to bring about war. For months, American intelligence had been cracking some of Japan's secret codes. Much information indicated that Pearl Harbor was at risk. Yet Roosevelt left the fleet exposed, seeming almost to provoke an attack to bring the United States into the war. Was it mere coincidence that the vital aircraft carriers were at sea? That only the obsolete battleships were left at Pearl Harbor? This argument, however, is based on circumstantial, not documentary, evidence. Roosevelt's defenders (and they include most historians) have countered that he wanted to fight Germany more than Japan. If he really had wished to provoke an incident leading to war, one in Atlantic waters would have served him far better. More important, the intelligence signals intercepted by American code-breakers were confusing. Analysts lost track of the Japanese fleet as it moved toward Hawaii. Secretary of War Stimson had good reason to be astonished when the fleet attacked Pearl Harbor.

In the end, it seems equally plausible to argue that cultural misperceptions explained the coming of war better than any conspiracy theory. American leaders were surprised by the attack on Pearl Harbor because they could not quite believe that the Japanese were daring or resourceful enough to attack an American stronghold some 4000 miles from Japan. Japanese militarists counted on a surprise attack to give them time to build a line of defense strong enough to discourage weak-willed Westerners from continuing the war. As it turned out, both calculations were wrong.

A Global War

Prime Minister Churchill greeted the news of Pearl Harbor with shock but, even more, relief. Great Britain would no longer stand alone in the North Atlantic and the Pacific wars. "We have won the war," he thought, and that night he slept "the sleep of the saved and thankful."

Japan's shocking triumph over U.S. forces united Americans in a way Roosevelt had not. And as Churchill recognized, only with the Americans fully committed to war could the Allies make full use of the enormous material and human resources of the United States. Still, the Allies needed to secure an alliance between the Anglo-American democracies and the Soviet Communist dictatorship. And they needed to find a strategy to win both the war and the peace to follow.

Strategies for War

Within two weeks, Churchill was in Washington, meeting with Roosevelt to coordinate production schedules for ships, planes, and armaments. The numbers they announced were so large that some critics openly laughed—at first. A year later

World War II in Europe and North Africa Coordination of Allied strategy was crucial to victory. Until 1944 Soviet forces engaged the bulk of the Axis armies across a huge front. The battle of Stalingrad prevented Hitler from reinforcing Rommel against the British in North Africa. After winning North Africa, the Allies turned north to knock Italy out of the war. The final key to defeating the Nazis was the invasion of western Europe at Normandy. D-Day would not have been possible had the Allies been unable to use England as a base to gather their forces. Stalin supported D-Day with a spring offensive in eastern Europe.

combined British, Canadian, and American production boards not only met but exceeded the schedules.

Roosevelt and Churchill also planned grand strategy. Outraged by the attack on Pearl Harbor, many Americans thought Japan should be the war's primary target. But the two leaders had always agreed that Germany posed the greater threat. The Pacific war, they decided, would be fought as a holding action while the Allies concentrated on Europe. In a global war, in which arms and resources had to be allocated carefully, these long-range decisions would prove important. But in the short term, the Allies faced a daunting future indeed.

Defeat Germany first

Gloomy Prospects

By summer's end in 1942 the Allies faced defeat. The Nazis were massed outside the Soviet Union's three major cities—Leningrad, Moscow, and Stalingrad. In North Africa General Erwin Rommel, the famed "Desert Fox," swept into Egypt with his Afrika Korps and stood within striking distance of the Suez Canal—a crucial link to the resources of the British empire. German U-boats in the North Atlantic threatened to break the ocean link between the United States and Britain. U-boat sailors called the first six months of 1942 "the American hunting season" as they sank 400 Allied ships in U.S. territorial waters. So deadly were these "Wolfpacks" that merchant sailors developed a grim humor about sleeping. Those on freighters carrying iron ore slept above decks because the heavily laden ships could sink in less than a minute. On flammable oil tankers, however, sailors closed their doors, undressed, and slept soundly. If a torpedo hit, no one would survive.

In the Far East the Allies fared no better. Japanese forces had invaded the Philippines, British Malaya, and the Dutch East Indies. The supposedly impregnable British bastion of Singapore fell in just one week, and at the Battle of Java Sea, the Japanese navy destroyed almost the entire remaining Allied naval force in the western Pacific. In April 1942 General Douglas MacArthur, commander of American forces in the Philippines, fled to Australia. In what appeared to be an empty pledge, he vowed, "I shall return." Left behind with scant arms and food, American and Philippine

U-boat war

Fall of the Philippines

The U-Boat War In the world's first truly global war, the need to coordinate and supply troops and matériel became paramount. But as German U-boats took a heavy toll on Allied shipping, it became difficult to deliver American supplies to Europe. Avoiding the North Atlantic route forced an arduous 12,000-mile journey around Africa to the Persian Gulf and then across Iran by land. The elimination of German submarines greatly eased the shipping problem and, as much as any single battle, ensured victory.

troops on Bataan and Corregidor put up a heroic but doomed struggle. By summer no significant Allied forces stood between the Japanese and India or Australia.

The chain of spectacular victories disguised fatal weaknesses within the Axis alliance. Japan and Germany were fighting separate wars, each on two fronts. They never coordinated strategies. Vast armies in China and Russia drained them of both personnel and supplies. Brutal occupation policies made enemies of conquered populations. Axis armies had to use valuable forces to maintain control and move supplies. The Nazis were especially harsh. They launched a major campaign to exterminate Europe's Jews, Slavs, and Gypsies. Resistance movements grew as the victims of Axis aggression fought back. At the war's height 50 countries joined the Allies, who referred to themselves as the United Nations.

A Grand Alliance

Defeat at first obscured the Allies' strengths. Chief among these were the human resources of the Soviet Union and the industrial capacity of the United States. During World War II Americans would develop a global economy. Safe from the fighting, American farms and factories could produce enough food and munitions to supply two separate wars at once. By the end of the war American factories had turned out 300,000 airplanes, 87,000 ships, 400,000 artillery pieces, 102,000 tanks and self-propelled guns, and 47 million tons of ammunition.

The Allies benefited too from exceptional leadership. The "Big Three"—Joseph Stalin, Winston Churchill, and Franklin Roosevelt—all had shortcomings but were able to maintain a unity of purpose that eluded Axis leaders. All three understood the global nature of the war. To a remarkable degree they managed to set aside their differences in pursuit of a common goal—the defeat of Nazi Germany. The arch-anti-Communist Churchill pledged Britain's resources to assist the defense of the world's largest Communist state. The anti-imperialist Roosevelt poured American resources into the war effort of two of Europe's major imperial powers.

The Big Three

To be sure, each nation had its own needs. Russian forces faced 3.5 million Axis troops along a 1600-mile front in eastern Europe. To ease the pressure on those troops, Stalin repeatedly called on the Allies to open a second front in western Europe. So urgent were his demands that one Allied diplomat remarked that Stalin's foreign minister knew only four words in English: *yes, no,* and *second front.* But Churchill and Roosevelt felt compelled to turn Stalin down. In August 1942 the western Allies lacked the massive, well-trained force needed for a successful invasion of Europe. Churchill himself flew to Moscow to give Stalin the bad news: no second front in Europe until 1943. Postponed again until mid-1944, the second front became a source of festering Russian discontent.

Yet after his initial anger over the postponement, Stalin accepted Churchill's rationale for a substitute action. British and American forces would invade North Africa by the end of 1942. Code-named Operation Torch, the North African campaign could be mounted quickly. Equally important, it could bring British and American troops into direct combat with the Germans and stood an excellent chance of succeeding. Here was an example of how personal contact among the Big Three ensured Allied cooperation. The alliance sometimes bent but never broke.

Operation Torch

The Naval War in the Pacific

Despite the decision to concentrate on defeating Germany first, the Allies' earliest successes came in the Pacific. At the Battle of Coral Sea in May 1942 planes from

The Battle of Midway proved the importance of naval air power. The Japanese suffered major losses of aircraft carriers and pilots. Never again after Midway would the Japanese navy pose a major threat.

the aircraft carriers *Yorktown* and *Lexington* stopped a large Japanese invading force headed for Port Moresby in New Guinea (see the map, page 891). For the first time in history two fleets fought without seeing each other. The age of naval aviation had arrived. The Japanese fleet actually inflicted greater damage but decided to turn back to nurse its wounds. Had they captured Port Moresby, the Japanese could have severed Allied shipping routes to Australia.

Midway

To extend Japan's defenses, Admiral Isoruku Yamamoto ordered the capture of Midway, a small island guarding the approach west of Hawaii. The Americans, in possession of decoded messages, knew the Japanese were coming. On June 3, as the Japanese main fleet bore down on Midway, a patrol plane from the American carrier task force spotted smoke from the ships. Aircraft from the carriers *Hornet, Enterprise,* and *Yorktown* sank four enemy carriers, a cruiser, and three destroyers. The Japanese sank only the *Yorktown*. More important, the Japanese lost many of their best carrier pilots, who were more difficult to replace than planes. The Battle of Midway broke Japanese naval supremacy in the Pacific and stalled Japan's offensive. In August 1942 American forces launched their first offensive—on the Solomon Islands, east of New Guinea. With the landing of American marines on the key island of Guadalcanal, the Allies started on the bloody road to Japan and victory.

Turning Points in Europe

By the fall of 1942 the Allies had their first successes in the European war. At El Alamein, 75 miles from the Suez Canal, British forces under General Bernard Montgomery broke through Rommel's lines. Weeks later, the Allies launched Operation Torch, the invasion of North Africa. Under the command of General Dwight D. Eisenhower, Allied forces swept eastward through Morocco and Algeria. They were halted in February 1943 at the Kasserine Pass in Tunisia, but General George S. Patton regrouped them and masterminded an impressive string of victories. By May 1943 Rommel had fled from North Africa, leaving behind 300,000 German troops.

Stalingrad

Success in North Africa provided a stirring complement to the Russian stand at Stalingrad. From August 1942 until February 1943 Axis and Soviet armies pounded each other with more than a million troops. In one of the bloodiest engagements in history, each side suffered more casualties than the Americans did during the entire war. When it was over, the Germans had lost an army and their momentum. Stalin's forces went on the offensive, moving south and west through the Ukraine toward Poland and Romania. By the fall of 1942 the Allies had also gained the edge in the war for the Atlantic. Supplies moved easily after antisubmarine forces sank 785 out of the nearly 1200 U-boats the Germans built.

Those Who Fought

Mobilizing for war brought together Americans from all regions, social classes, and ethnic backgrounds. "The first time I ever heard a New England accent," recalled a midwesterner, "was at Fort Benning. The southerner was an exotic creature to me. The people from the farms. The New York street smarts." More than any other social institution the army acted as a melting pot. It also offered educational opportunities and job skills or suggested the need for them. "I could be a technical sergeant only I haven't had enough school," reported one Navajo soldier in a letter home to New Mexico. "Make my little brother go to school even if you have to lasso him."

In waging the world's first global war, the U.S. armed forces swept millions of Americans into new worlds and new experiences. When Pearl Harbor came, the army had 1.6 million men in uniform. By 1945 it had more than 7 million; the navy, 3.9 million; the army air corps, 2.3 million; and the marines, 600,000. Nineteen-year-olds who had never left home found themselves swept off to Europe or to the South Pacific. At basic training new recruits were subjected to forms of regimentation—the army haircut, foul-mouthed drill sergeants, and barracks life—they had seldom experienced in other areas of America's democratic culture.

In this war, as in most wars, the infantry bore the brunt of the fighting and dying. They suffered 90 percent of the battlefield casualties. In all, almost 400,000 Americans died and more than 600,000 were wounded. But service in the military did not mean constant combat. Most battles were reasonably short, followed by long periods of waiting and preparation. The army used almost 2 million soldiers just to move supplies. Yet even during the lull in battle, the soldiers' biggest enemy, disease, stalked them: malaria, dysentery, typhus, and even plague. In the Pacific theater, the thermometer sometimes rose to over 110 degrees Fahrenheit.

Wherever they fought, American soldiers usually lived in foxholes dug by hand with small shovels. Whenever possible they turned a hole in the ground into a home. "The American soldier is a born housewife," observed war correspondent Ernie Pyle. Between battles, movies were about the only entertainment many troops had. Each film was a tenuous link to a more comfortable world at home, a place American soldiers yearned for with special intensity. It was not a country or an idea for which they fought so much as a set of memories—a house, a car, Mom and Pop.

Many young GIs at first looked forward to going into battle. "I was going to gain my manhood," recalled one soldier. But combat soon hardened such troops. Donald Dickson's portrait of one such war-weary GI is titled *Too Many, Too Close, Too Long.*

Minorities at War

Minorities enlisted in unusually large numbers because the services offered training and opportunities unavailable in civilian life. Still, prejudice against African Americans and other minorities remained high. The army was strictly segregated and generally assigned black soldiers to noncombatant roles. The navy accepted them only as cooks and servants. At first the air corps and marines would not take them at all. The American Red Cross even kept "black" and "white" blood plasma separated, as

African Americans

In *Shipping Out,* black artist Jacob Lawrence commemorated black troops heading overseas in the crowded confines of a troop ship. African Americans in segregated units served more often in service roles than in combat. It was ironic that, in a war against Nazi racism, race remained a central issue among Americans. Lawrence was certainly aware of such ironies; the portrayal of soldiers crowded onto their bunks recalls eerily the packing of slave transport ships from earlier centuries.

if there were a difference. (Ironically, a black physician, Charles Drew, had invented the process allowing plasma to be stored.)

Despite the persistence of prejudice, more than a million black men and women served. As the war progressed, leaders of the black community pressured the military to ease segregation and allow black soldiers a more active role. The army did form some black combat units, usually led by white officers, as well as a black air corps unit. By mid-1942 black officers were being trained and graduated from integrated officer candidate schools at the rate of 200 a month. More than 80 black pilots won the Distinguished Flying Cross.

For both Mexican Americans and Asian Americans the war offered an opportunity to enter the American mainstream. Putting on a uniform was an essential act of citizenship. Mexican Americans had a higher enlistment rate than the population in general. A California congressional representative observed that "as I read the casualty list from my state, I find that anywhere from one-fourth to one-third of these names are names such as Gonzales and Sanchez." Chinese Americans served at the highest rate of all groups. As Harold Liu of New York's Chinatown recalled, "for the first time Chinese were accepted as being friends. . . . All of a sudden we became part of an American dream." Korean Americans were especially valuable in the Pacific theater because many could translate Japanese.

Like other Asian Americans, Filipinos had a powerful reason to enlist. Service offered an opportunity to fight for the liberation of their homeland from Japanese invaders. And like other minorities, Filipino Americans realized that in fighting for freedom abroad they were fighting for freedom at home. A Filipino soldier commented that he was doing something he had never before been allowed to do: serve "as an equal with American boys." Such loyalty had its rewards. Filipinos who volunteered became citizens. The California attorney general reinterpreted laws that had once prevented Filipinos from owning land. Now they could buy their own farms. Jobs opened in war factories. The status of other Asian Americans and Mexican Americans improved in similar ways. Minorities who served gained useful experience in dealing with the Anglo world. After the war, minority veterans would provide new leadership in their communities.

Choices for homosexuals

Homosexuals who wished to join the military faced a dilemma. Few Americans of the day had any knowledge of the gays in their midst, and fewer had much tolerance for homosexuality. Still, many gays risked exposure. Charles Rowland, from Arizona, recalled that he and other gay friends "were not about to be deprived the privilege of serving our country in a time of great national emergency by virtue of some stupid regulation about being gay." Homosexuals who did pass the screening test found themselves in gender-segregated bases, where life in an overwhelmingly male or female environment allowed many, for the first time in their lives, to meet like-minded gay men and women. Like other servicemen and -women, they served in a host of roles, fighting and dying on the battlefield or doing the unglamorous jobs that kept the army going.

Women at War

World War II brought an end to the military as an exclusive male enclave that women entered only as nurses. During the prewar mobilization, Eleanor Roosevelt and other female leaders had campaigned for a regular military organization for women. The War Department came up with a compromise that allowed women to join the Women's Army Auxiliary Corps (WAAC), but only with inferior status and lower pay. By 1943 the "Auxiliary" had dropped out of the title: WAACs became WACs, with full army status, equal ranks, and equal pay. (The navy had a similar force called the WAVEs.)   **WACs**

Women could look with a mixture of pride and resentment on their wartime military service. Thousands served close to the battlefields, working as technicians, mechanics, radio operators, postal clerks, and secretaries. Although filling a vital need, these jobs were largely traditional female ones that implied a separate and inferior status. Until 1944 women were prevented by law from serving in war zones, even as noncombatants. There were female pilots, but they were restricted to shuttling planes behind the lines. At many posts WAVEs and WACs lived behind barbed wire and could move about only in groups under armed escort.

When Pearl Harbor brought the United States into the war, Thomas Chinn sold **War Production** his publishing business and devoted himself full-time to war work. Like many other Chinese Americans, he was working for the first time outside Chinatown. He served as a supervisor in the Army Quartermaster Market Center, which was responsible for supplying the armed forces with fresh food as it was harvested across California. Chinn found himself coordinating a host of cold storage warehouses all the way from the Oregon border as far south as Fresno. "At times," he recalled, "in order to catch seasonal goods such as fresh vegetables, as many as 200 or 300 railroad cars would be shuttling in and out" of the warehouses.

Food production and distribution was only one of many areas that demanded attention from the government. After Pearl Harbor, steel, aluminum, and electric power were all in short supply, creating bottlenecks in production lines. Roosevelt recognized the need for more direct government control of the economy.

Although the conversion from peace to war came slowly at first, the president used a mix of compulsory and voluntary programs to control inflation and guarantee an ever-increasing supply of food, munitions, and equipment. In the end the United States worked a miracle of production that proved every bit as important to victory as any battle fought overseas. From 1939 to 1945 the gross national product grew from $91 billion to $166 billion. (In World War I it had not changed significantly.) So successful was war production that civilians suffered little deprivation.

Finding an Industrial Czar

Roosevelt's first attempt at coordinating the production effort was to set up a War Production Board (WPB) under the direction of former Sears, Roebuck president Donald M. Nelson. On paper, Nelson's powers were impressive. The WPB had authority to allocate resources and organize factories in whatever way promoted national defense. In one of its first acts, the WPB ordered an end to all civilian car and truck production. The American people would have no new cars until the war ended.

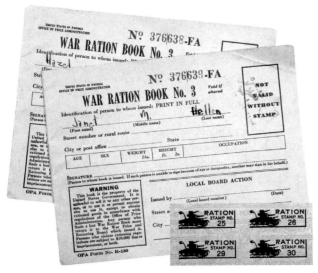

To fight inflation, the Office of Price Administration (OPA) imposed rationing on products in short supply. Consumers received coupons to trade for goods such as meat, shoes, and gasoline. The program was one of the most unpopular of the war.

In practice, Nelson was scarcely the dictator the economy needed. Other federal agencies with their own czars controlled petroleum, rubber, and labor resources, while military agencies continued their own procurement. To end the bottlenecks once and for all, the president in 1943 installed Supreme Court Justice James F. Byrnes as director of the new Office of War Mobilization (OWM). A canny political facilitator, Byrnes became the dictator the economy needed. His authority was so great and his access to Roosevelt so direct that he became known as the "assistant president." By assuming control over vital materials such as steel, aluminum, and copper, the OWM was able to allocate them more systematically. The bottlenecks disappeared. Such centralized planning helped ease the conversion to war production of industries both large and small. While the "Big Three" automakers—Ford, General Motors, and Chrysler—generated some 20 percent of all war goods, small business also played a vital role. A manufacturer of model trains, for example, made bomb fuses.

The career of Henry J. Kaiser, a California industrialist, illustrates how the war inspired creative financing and management. Kaiser sent his lobbyists to Washington, where they rustled up generous government loans for building factories. And because Kaiser needed steel to build new factories, they found ways around wartime restrictions. To attract workers to his new West Coast shipyards, Kaiser offered high wages and benefits, including day care for the children of working mothers. His innovative application of assembly line techniques reduced the time required to build cargo vessels, known as Liberty ships, from almost a year to only 56 days. His yards finished one in a record 14 days. Speed had its price: one Liberty ship actually split in half at its launching. Despite such occasional missteps, Kaiser built ships in the quantity the war effort demanded.

West Coast war industries

The aircraft industry also transformed the industrial landscape of the West Coast. When production of aircraft factories peaked in 1944, the industry had 2.1 million workers. Most of the new factories were located around Los Angeles, San Diego, and Seattle, where large labor pools, temperate climates, and available land made the locations attractive. The demand for workers opened opportunities for many Asian workers who had been limited to jobs within their own ethnic communities. In Los Angeles about 300 laundry workers closed their shops so that they could work on the construction of the ship *China Victory*. By 1943, 15 percent of all shipyard workers around San Francisco Bay were Chinese.

The military relied on large, established firms in part because they had more experience producing in large volume. At the same time lucrative war contracts helped big corporations increase their dominance over the economy. Workers in companies with more than 10,000 employees amounted to just 13 percent of the workforce in 1939; by 1944 they made up more than 30 percent. In agriculture a similar move toward bigness occurred. The number of people working on farms dropped by a fifth, yet productivity increased 30 percent as small farms were consolidated into larger ones. Large commercial farming by corporations rather than individuals (later called "agribusiness") came to dominate agriculture.

Productivity increased for a less tangible but equally important reason: pride in work done for a common cause. Civilians volunteered for civil defense, hospitals, and countless scrap drives. Children became "Uncle Sam's Scrappers" and "Tin-Can Colonels" as they scoured vacant lots for valuable trash. One teenager in Maywood, Illinois, collected more than 100 tons of paper between Pearl Harbor and D-Day. Backyard "victory" gardens added 8 million tons of food to the harvest in 1943; car pooling conserved millions of tires. As citizens put off buying new consumer goods, they helped limit inflation. Morale ran high because people believed that every contribution, no matter how small, helped defeat the Axis.

Science Goes to War

The striking success of aircraft against ships at Coral Sea and Midway demonstrated how science and technology changed the way war was fought. The air war in Europe spurred the development of a new generation of fighter planes and long-range bombers. To combat enemy bombers and submarines, English and American scientists rushed to perfect electronic detection devices such as radar and sonar.

Without sonar the Allies might never have won the submarine war in the North Atlantic. At the same time, improved American submarines crippled Japanese shipping in the western Pacific. By 1944 the home islands faced serious shortages of vital raw materials. Above the water, the newly developed techniques of radar-controlled naval and antiaircraft gunnery gave American ships a decided edge in crucial sea battles. It became possible to hit targets obscured by darkness, fog, or smoke. One of the most critical technical advances was also one of the best kept secrets of the war, the

The Manhattan Project required complex facilities to produce small amounts of nuclear materials for the first atom bombs. This plant at Oak Ridge, Tennessee, took advantage of abundant electricity from the Tennessee Valley Authority as well as the expertise of scientists from universities and private industry.

proximity fuse. By placing a small radio device in a warhead, scientists created a shell that did not need to hit a target to destroy it. Proximity fuses accounted for the success of American antiaircraft guns against Japanese planes and German V-1 bombs.

Scientific advances saved lives as well as destroying them. Insecticides, pesticides, and drugs limited the spread of infectious diseases like malaria and syphilis. Penicillin had its first widespread use in World War II. The health of the nation actually improved during the war. Life expectancy rose by three years overall and by five years for African Americans. Infant mortality was cut by more than a third, and in 1942 the nation recorded its lowest death rate in history. Still, such discoveries sometimes had unforeseen consequences. Although the pesticide DDT helped control malaria and other insect-borne diseases, its harmful effects on the environment became clear only years later.

Science made its most dramatic advances in atomic research. In 1938 German scientists discovered the process of fission, in which atoms of uranium-235 were split, releasing an enormous amount of energy. Leading European physicists who had come to America to escape the Nazis understood all too well the military potential of the German discovery. In 1939 Enrico Fermi, Albert Einstein, and Leo Szilard warned President Roosevelt "that extremely powerful bombs of a new type may thus be constructed."

The Manhattan Project

Roosevelt initiated what soon became the largest research and development effort in history, code-named the Manhattan Project. More than 100,000 scientists, engineers, technicians, and support workers from the United States, Canada, and England worked at 37 installations across the country to build an atomic bomb. The key to success was not so much secret discoveries but money (the project cost $2 billion) and industrial, scientific, and technical resources to produce nuclear fuels and a bomb design. Yet even with increased funding, scientists feared they might not win the race to produce an atomic bomb.

War Work and Prosperity

War production revived prosperity, but not without stress. As late as 1940 unemployment stood at almost 7 million. By 1944, it had virtually disappeared. Jeff Davies, president of Hoboes of America, reported in 1942 that 2 million of his members were "off the road." In retirement communities like San Diego nearly 4 retirees in 10 returned to work. Employers, eager to overcome the labor shortage, welcomed disabled workers. The hearing-impaired found jobs in deafening factories; dwarfs became aircraft inspectors because they could crawl inside wings and other cramped spaces. By the summer of 1943 nearly 3 million children aged 12 to 17 were working.

Tax reform

Roosevelt had to find some means to pay the war's enormous cost without undermining prosperity. His approach attempted to mix conservative and liberal elements. The Treasury Department tried to raise money voluntarily, by selling war bonds through advertising campaigns. To raise more funds, Secretary of the Treasury Henry Morgenthau also proposed a tax structure that was highly progressive— that is, it taxed higher income at a higher rate. Conservatives in Congress balked at sweeping tax reforms. After six months of wrangling, Congress passed a compromise, the Revenue Act of 1942, which levied a flat 5 percent tax on all annual incomes over $624. That provision struck hardest at low-income workers: in 1942 almost 50 million citizens paid taxes compared with 13 million the year before. The most innovative feature of the bill was a payroll deduction system. No longer would taxpayers have to set aside money to pay their total tax bill to the Internal Revenue Service at the end of the year.

Organized Labor

Wartime prosperity did not end the tug-of-war between business and labor. In 1941 alone more than 2 million workers walked off their jobs in protest. To end labor strife Roosevelt established the War Labor Board (WLB) in 1942. Like the agency Woodrow Wilson had created during World War I, the new WLB had authority to impose arbitration in any labor dispute. Its most far-reaching decision established a compromise between employers and unions that gave workers 15 days to leave the union after a contract was signed. Any worker who remained a member had to pay union dues for the life of the contract. That policy led to an almost 40 percent growth in union membership between 1941 and 1945, when a record 14.75 million workers held union cards.

War Labor Board

Despite the efforts of the WLB, strikes did occur. Dissatisfied railroad workers tied up rail lines in a wildcat strike in 1943. General George C. Marshall cursed it as the "damnedest crime ever committed against America." To break the impasse, the government seized the railroads and then granted wage increases. That same year the pugnacious John L. Lewis allowed his United Mine Workers to go on strike. "The coal miners of America are hungry," he charged. "They are ill-fed and undernourished." Roosevelt seized the mines and ran them for a time; he even considered arresting union leaders and drafting striking miners. But as Secretary of the Interior Harold Ickes noted, a "jailed miner produces no more coal than a striking miner." In the end the government negotiated a settlement that gave miners substantial new benefits.

Lewis leads a coal strike

John L. Lewis

Most Americans were unwilling to forgive Lewis or his miners. A huge coal shortage along the East Coast had left homes dark and cold. "John L. Lewis— Damn your coal black soul," wrote the military newspaper *Stars and Stripes*. In reaction, Congress easily passed the Smith-Connolly Act of 1943. It gave the president more authority to seize vital war plants shut by strikes and required union leaders to observe a 30-day "cooling-off" period before striking. Roosevelt vetoed the bill, only to be overridden in both houses.

Despite these incidents, workers remained dedicated to the war effort. Stoppages actually accounted for only about one-tenth of one percent of total work time during the war. When workers did strike, it was usually in defiance of their union leadership, and they left their jobs for just a few days.

Women Workers

The demands of war placed a double demand for labor: not only soldiers to fight but also workers to increase production. With as many as 12 million men in uniform, women (especially married women) became the nation's largest untapped source of labor. During the high-unemployment years of the Depression, both government and business had discouraged women from competing with men for jobs. With the onset of war, magazines and government bulletins suddenly began trumpeting "the vast resource of womanpower." The percentage of female workers grew from around a quarter in 1940 to more than a third by 1945. These women were no longer mostly young and single, as female workers of the past had been. A majority were either married or between 55 and 64 years old. Patriotism alone could not explain their willingness to leave families and homes for the factories.

"Womanpower" fills the labor shortage

Many women preferred the relative freedom of work and wages to the confines of home. With husbands off at war, millions of women needed additional income and had more free time. Black women in particular realized dramatic gains. Once concentrated in low-paying domestic and farm jobs with erratic hours and tedious labor, some 300,000 rushed into factories that offered higher pay and more regular hours. Given the chance to learn skills like welding, aircraft assembly, and electronics, women shattered many stereotypes about their capabilities. The diary of a ship welder in Oregon recorded both amazement and pride at what she accomplished:

> I, who hates heights, climbed stair after stair after stair till I thought I must be close to the sun. I stopped on the [tanker's] top deck. I, who hate confined spaces, went through narrow corridors, stumbling my way over rubber-coated leads. . . . I welded in the poop deck lying on the floor while another welder spattered sparks from the ceiling and chippers like giant woodpeckers shattered our eardrums. . . . I did overhead welding, horizontal, flat, vertical. . . . I made some good welds and some frightful ones. But now a door in the poop deck of an oil tanker is hanging, four feet by six of solid steel, by my welds. Pretty exciting!

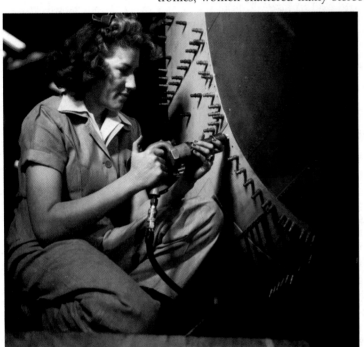

Between 1940 and 1945 the female labor force increased more than 50 percent. Many women performed jobs once restricted exclusively to males. Lionized with nicknames such as "Rosie the Riveter," women such as this airplane factory worker dispelled stereotypes about the work women were able to do.

Although the demand for labor improved the economic status of women, it did not alter conventional views about gender roles. Most Americans assumed that when the war ended, veterans would pick up their old jobs and women would return to the home. Surveys showed that the vast majority of Americans, whether male or female, continued to believe that child rearing was a woman's primary responsibility. The birthrate, which had fallen during the Depression, began to rise in 1943 as prosperity returned. And other traditional barriers continued to limit women's opportunities, even in wartime. Most professions admitted few women into graduate programs or other career paths. As women flooded into government bureaucracies, factory production lines, and corporate offices, few became managers. Supervision remained men's work.

The social stresses of wartime placed additional pressures on women. Alcohol abuse, teenage prostitution, divorce, and juvenile delinquency all were on the rise. Some observers blamed such trends on working mothers, who were said to neglect their families. In fact, studies showed that the families of mothers who stayed home fared no better than did those where mothers held outside jobs. The real problem lay with the extraordinary mobility created by the war. Crowded into new communities with inadequate schools and recreational facilities, young people had few outlets for their energies. Rather than build new recreational facilities, concerned public agencies were just as likely to recommend rules restricting mothers from work. Only labor shortages prevented the acceptance of such rules. The war inspired a change in economic roles for women without fomenting a revolution in attitudes about gender. That would come later.

Global Labor Migrations

A global war displaced people on a global scale. In Europe and Asia much of this movement was driven by the tide of battle. After the Japanese conquered the Chinese capital at Beijing and the new capital at Nanking, Chinese leader Chiang Kai-shek moved his government a thousand miles inland to Chungking. The combination of war with the Japanese and civil war with Communist forces uprooted Chinese people on a vast scale. One historian estimated a refugee population as high as 50 million. Facing a German invasion, the Soviet Union moved much of its heavy industry from western Russia and the Ukraine east behind the Ural Mountains. There it was safe from the German army and the Luftwaffe's bombers.

War economies had voracious appetites for labor. By using conquered people as workers, Germany and Japan freed their own people for military service. Both countries violated international law by exploiting military prisoners and captured civilians as slave labor. By war's end the Nazis had forced as many as 10 million foreign workers into German industries. They also used forced labor as part of their plan to eliminate whole populations such as Slavs and Jews. Japan had no such racial policy. Indeed, Japan made an effort to co-opt conquered people into voluntary service. In the Dutch East Indies, the Japanese so skillfully exploited anti-Dutch sentiment that most Javanese willingly supported their war effort. Facing labor shortages at home, the Japanese forced hundreds of thousands of Koreans to migrate to Japan. Of these, almost 100,000 were so-called comfort women who were impressed into sexual service.

In the United States the war changed the composition of the workforce and where people worked. The Census Bureau determined that between Pearl Harbor in 1941 and March 1945 at least 15.3 million people besides those in the military had changed addresses. Women were not the only new factory workers. "The war dispersed the reservation people as nothing ever had," recalled Vine DeLoria, an Indian activist. "Every day, it seemed, we would be bidding farewell to families as they headed west to work in defense plants on the coast." So many African Americans left the South that cotton growers began to buy mechanical harvesters to replace their labor. So many Appalachian hill people traveled back and forth from Kentucky to Detroit that the bus company added an express service. During the Depression, western states had forced almost half a million Mexican workers to return to Mexico. The Department of Agriculture set up the bracero, or contract labor, program with Mexico to bring workers back. Several hundred thousand Mexicans entered the Southwest legally and even more came in illegally. Their labor was vital to the war effort.

A Question of Rights

Franklin Roosevelt had been a government official during World War I. Now, presiding over a bigger world war, he was determined to avoid many of the patriotic excesses he had witnessed then: mobs menacing immigrants, the patriotic appeals to spy on neighbors, the raids on pacifist radicals. Even so, the conflicts arising over race, ethnic background, and class differences could not simply be ignored. In a society in which immigration laws discriminated against Asians by race, the war with Japan made life difficult for loyal Asian Americans of all backgrounds. Black and Latino workers faced as much discrimination in shipyards and airplane factories as they had in peacetime industries.

Little Italy

Aliens from enemy countries fared far better in World War II than in World War I. When the war began, about 600,000 Italian aliens and 5 million Italian Americans lived in the United States. Most still resided in Italian neighborhoods centered around churches, fraternal organizations, and clubs. Some had been proud of Mussolini and supported *fascismo*. "Mussolini was a hero," recalled one Italian American. "A superhero. He made us feel special." Those attitudes changed abruptly after Pearl Harbor. During the war, Italian Americans pledged their loyalties to the United States.

At first the government treated Italians without citizenship (along with Japanese and Germans) as "aliens of enemy nationality." They could not travel without permission, enter strategic areas, or possess shortwave radios, guns, or maps. By 1942 few Americans believed that German Americans or Italian Americans posed any kind of danger. Eager to keep the support of Italian voters in the 1942 congressional elections, Roosevelt chose Columbus Day 1942 to lift restrictions on Italian aliens. The segregation of Italian Americans ended. Henceforth they would maintain their ethnic unity as a matter of choice, not necessity.

Concentration Camps

Americans showed no such tolerance to the 127,000 Japanese living in the United States, whether they were aliens or citizens. Ironically, tensions were least high in Hawaii, where the war with Japan had begun. Local newspapers there expressed confidence in the loyalty of Japanese Americans, who in any case were crucial to Hawaii's economy. General Delos Emmons, the military governor of the islands, rebuffed pressures from Washington to evacuate as many as 20,000 "dangerous" Japanese. He branded a Justice Department report warning of widespread sabotage as being "so fantastic it hardly needs refuting."

On the mainland, Japanese Americans remained largely separated from the mainstream of American life. State laws and local custom threw up complex barriers to integration. In the western states, where they were concentrated around urban areas, most Japanese could not vote, own land, or live in decent neighborhoods. Approximately 47,000 Japanese aliens, known as "Issei," were ineligible for citizenship under American law. Only their children could become citizens. Despite such restrictions, some Japanese achieved success in small businesses like landscaping, while many others worked on or owned farms that supplied fruits and vegetables to growing cities.

West Coast politicians pressed the Roosevelt administration to evacuate the Japanese from their communities. It did not seem to matter that about 80,000 were American citizens, called "Nisei," and that no evidence indicated that they posed any threat. "A Jap's a Jap," commented General John De Witt, commander of West Coast defenses. "It makes no difference whether he is an American citizen or not." In response, the War Department in February 1942 drew up Executive Order 9066, which allowed the exclusion of any person from designated military areas. Under De Witt's authority, the order was applied only on the West Coast against Japanese Americans. By late February Roosevelt had agreed that both Issei and Nisei would be evacuated. But where would they go?

The army began to ship the entire Japanese community to "assembly centers." Most Nisei incurred heavy financial losses as they sold property at far below market value. Their distress became a windfall for people who had long resented their economic competition. "We've been charged with wanting to get rid of the Japs for selfish reasons," admitted the Grower-Shipper Vegetable Association. "We might as well be honest. We do. It's a question of whether the white man lives on the Pacific Coast or the brown man." At the assembly centers—racetracks, fairgrounds, and similar temporary locations—the army had not prepared basic sanitation, comfort, or privacy. "We lived in a horse stable," remembered one young girl. "We filled our

Issei

Nisei

The bleak landscape of the internment camp at Manzanar, California, was typical of the sites to which the government sent Japanese Americans. In such a harsh environment the Japanese had no real opportunity to create productive farm communities, as government officials had promised.

cheesecloth with straw—for our mattress." The authorities at least had the decency to keep families together.

Most Japanese were interned in 10 camps in remote areas of seven western states. Notions that the camps might become self-sufficient communities proved wishful thinking. Even resourceful farmers could not raise food in arid desert soil. No claim of humane intent could change the reality—these were concentration camps. Internees were held in wire-enclosed compounds by armed guards. Temporary tar-papered barracks housed families or small groups in single rooms. Each room had a few cots, some blankets, and a single light bulb. That was home.

Internment camps

Some Japanese within the camps protested. Especially offensive was a government loyalty questionnaire that asked Nisei citizens if they would be willing to serve in the armed forces. "What do they take us for? Saps?" asked Dunks Oshima, a camp prisoner. "First, they change my army status to 4-C [enemy alien] because of my ancestry, run me out of town, and now they want me to volunteer for a suicide squad so I could get killed for this damn democracy. That's going some, for sheer brass!" Yet thousands of Nisei did enlist, and many distinguished themselves in combat.

Other Japanese Americans challenged the government through the courts. Fred Korematsu in California and Gordon Hirabayashi in Washington State were arrested when they refused to report for relocation. "As an American citizen, I wanted to uphold the principles of the Constitution," recalled Hirabayashi. But the Supreme Court let stand military policies aimed specifically at Japanese Americans. The majority opinion stated that "residents having ethnic affiliations with an invading enemy may be a greater source of danger than those of different ancestry," even though the army had never demonstrated that any danger existed. And in *Korematsu v. United States* (1944), the Court upheld the government's relocation program as a wartime necessity. Three justices dissented, criticizing relocation as the "legalization of racism."

Korematsu and Hirabayashi

Concentration camps in America did not perpetuate the horror of Nazi death camps, but they were built on racism and fear. Worse, they violated the traditions of civil rights and liberties for which Americans believed they were fighting.

Minorities on the Job

Minority leaders saw the irony of fighting a war for freedom in a country in which civil rights were still limited. "A jim crow army cannot fight for a free world," the NAACP declared. Such ideas of racial justice had been the driving force in the life of A. Philip Randolph, long an advocate of greater militancy. Randolph had demonstrated his gifts as an organizer and leader of the Brotherhood of Sleeping Car Porters, the most powerful black labor organization. He was determined to break down the wall of discrimination that kept minority workers out of jobs in defense industries and segregated in government agencies, unions, and the armed forces. "The Administration leaders in Washington will never give the Negro justice," Randolph argued, "until they see masses—ten, twenty, fifty thousand Negroes on the White House lawn." In 1941 he began to organize a march on Washington.

A. Philip Randolph

President Roosevelt had the power to issue executive orders ending segregation in the government, defense industries, unions, and the armed forces, as Randolph demanded. It took the threat of the march to make him act. He issued Executive Order 8802 in June, which forbade discrimination by race in hiring either government or defense industry workers. To carry out the policy, the order established the Fair Employment Practices Commission (FEPC). In some ways creating the FEPC was the boldest step toward racial justice taken since Reconstruction. Even so, the new agency had only limited success in breaking down barriers against black and Hispanic Americans. It was one thing to ban discrimination, quite another to enforce that ban in a society still deeply divided by racial prejudice.

Fair Employment Practices Commission

Still, efforts by the FEPC did open industrial jobs in California's shipyards and aircraft factories, which had previously refused to hire Hispanic Americans. Thousands migrated from Texas, where job discrimination was most severe, to California, where war work created new opportunities. Labor shortages led the southwestern states to join with the Mexican government under the bracero program to recruit Mexican labor under specially arranged contracts. In Texas, in contrast, antagonism to braceros ran so deep that the Mexican government tried to prevent workers from going there. With support from labor unions, officials in the oil and mining industries routinely blocked Hispanics from training programs and job advancement. Not until late 1943 did the FEPC investigate the situation.

Bracero program

Black Americans experienced similar frustrations. More than half of all defense jobs were closed to minorities. In the aircraft industry, for example, which offered 100,000 skilled and high-paying jobs, blacks held about 200 janitorial positions. The federal agency charged with placing workers honored local "whites only" employment practices. Unions segregated black workers or excluded them entirely. One person wrote to the president with a telling complaint: "Hitler has not done anything to the colored people—it's people right here in the United States who are keeping us out of work and keeping us down."

Eventually the combination of labor shortages, pressure from black leaders, and initiatives from government agencies opened the door to more skilled jobs and higher pay. Beginning in 1943, the U.S. Employment Service rejected requests with racial stipulations. Faced with a dwindling labor pool, many employers finally opened their doors. By 1944 African Americans, who accounted for almost 10 percent of the population, held 8 percent of the jobs.

At War with Jim Crow

At the beginning of World War II three-quarters of the 12 million black Americans lived in the South. Hispanic Americans, whose population exceeded a million, were concentrated in a belt along the United States–Mexico border. When jobs for minorities opened in war centers, blacks and Hispanics became increasingly urban. In cities, too, they encountered deeply entrenched systems of segregation that denied them basic rights to decent housing, jobs, and political participation. Competition with whites for housing and the use of public facilities like parks, beaches, and transportation produced explosive racial tensions.

To ease crowding the government funded new housing. In Detroit, federal authorities had picked a site for minority housing along the edge of a Polish neighborhood. One such project, named in honor of the black abolitionist Sojourner Truth, included 200 units for black families. When the first of them tried to move in, they faced an angry mob of whites. Local officials had to send several hundred National Guardsmen to protect the newcomers from menacing Ku Klux Klan members. Tensions increased with the approaching hot summer, and riots broke out in June 1943, as white mobs beat up African Americans riding public trolleys or patronizing movie theaters, and black protesters looted white stores. Six thousand soldiers from nearby bases finally imposed a troubled calm, but not before the riot had claimed the lives of 24 black and 9 white residents. Although wartime labor shortages gradually improved the situation for African Americans in Detroit, local officials refused to accept responsibility. Instead, they blamed the NAACP and the "militant" Negro press for stirring up trouble.

Hispanics in southern California suffered similar indignities. By 1943 overt Anglo hostility had come to focus on the pachucos, or "zoot suiters." These young Hispanic men and boys had adopted the stylish fashions of Harlem hipsters: greased hair swept back into a ducktail; broad-shouldered, long-waisted suit coats; baggy pants, pegged at the ankles, polished off with a swashbuckling keychain. The Los Angeles city council passed an ordinance making it a crime even to wear a zoot suit. For most "zooters" this style was a modest form of rebellion; for a few it was a badge of criminal behavior; for some white servicemen it was a target for racism.

In June 1943 sailors from the local navy base invaded Hispanic neighborhoods in search of zooters who had allegedly attacked servicemen. The self-appointed vigilantes grabbed innocent victims, tore their clothes, cut their hair, and beat them. When Hispanics retaliated, the police arrested them, ignoring the actions of white sailors. Irresponsible newspaper coverage made matters worse. "ZOOTERS THREATEN L.A. POLICE" charged one Hearst paper. A citizens committee created at the urging of California governor Earl Warren rejected Hearst's inflammatory accusations. Underlying Hispanic anger were the grim realities of filthy housing, unemployment, disease, and white racism, which all added up to a level of poverty that wartime prosperity eased but did not end.

Minority leaders acted on the legal as well as the political front. The Congress of Racial Equality (CORE), a nonviolent civil rights group inspired by the Indian leader Mohandas K. Gandhi, used sit-ins and other peaceful tactics to desegregate some restaurants and movie theaters. In 1944 the Supreme Court outlawed the "all-white primary," an infamous device used by southerners to exclude blacks from voting in primary elections within the Democratic party. Because Democratic candidates in the South often ran unopposed in the general elections, the primary elections were usually the only true political contests. In *Smith v. Allwright* the Court ruled that since political parties were integral parts of public elections, they could

Detroit riots

Zoot suit riots

not deny minorities the right to vote in primaries. Thus the war sowed the seeds of future protest and reform. Asian, Hispanic, black, and Indian veterans would play leading roles in the postwar struggle for equality.

The New Deal in Retreat

After Pearl Harbor Roosevelt told reporters that "Dr. New Deal" had retired so that "Dr. Win-the-War" could get down to business. Political opposition, however, could not be eliminated even during a global conflict. The increasingly powerful anti–New Deal coalition of Republicans and rural Democrats saw in the war an opportunity to attack programs they had long resented. The president, for his part, never lost sight of the election returns. When war came, New Deal foes moved quickly. They ended the Civilian Conservation Corps, the National Youth Administration, and the largely ineffective National Resources Planning Board. They reduced the powers of the Farm Security Administration and blocked moves to extend Social Security and unemployment benefits. Seeming to approve such measures, voters in the 1942 elections sent an additional 44 Republicans to the House and another 9 to the Senate. The GOP began eyeing the White House.

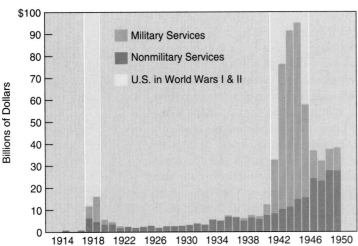

The Impact of World War II on Government Spending This chart shows that World War II more than the New Deal spurred government spending, even on nonmilitary sectors. Note that after both world wars, nonmilitary spending was higher than in the prewar years.

By the spring of 1944 no one knew whether Franklin Roosevelt would seek an unprecedented fourth term. The president's health had declined noticeably. Pallid skin, sagging shoulders, and shaking hands seemed open signs that he had aged too much to run. In July, one week before the Democratic convention, Roosevelt announced his decision: "All that is within me cries out to go back to my home on the Hudson River. . . . But as a good soldier . . . I will accept and serve." Conservative Democrats, however, made sure that Roosevelt's liberal vice president, Henry Wallace, would not remain on the ticket. In his place they settled on Harry S. Truman of Missouri, a loyal New Dealer and party stalwart. The Republicans chose the moderate governor of New York, Thomas E. Dewey, to run against Roosevelt, but Dewey never had much of a chance. Reports of victory in Europe and the Pacific undermined his charges that Roosevelt had mismanaged the war. Always pragmatic, Roosevelt made his domestic policies more conservative as well.

Roosevelt wins a fourth term

At the polls, voters gave Roosevelt 25.6 million popular votes to Dewey's 22 million, a clear victory, although the election was tighter than any since 1916. Like its aging leader, the New Deal coalition was showing signs of strain.

Winning the War and the Peace

To impress upon newly arrived officers the vastness of the war theater in the Pacific, General Douglas MacArthur laid out a map of the region. Over it, he placed an outline map of the United States. Running the war from headquarters in Australia, MacArthur pointed out, the distances were about the same as if, in the Western Hemisphere, the center was located in South America. On the same scale,

Tokyo would lie far up in northern Canada, Iwo Jima somewhere in Hudson Bay, Singapore in Utah, Manila in North Dakota, and Hawaii off the coast of Scotland.

In a war that stretched from one end of the globe to the other, the Allies had to coordinate their strategies on a grand scale. Which war theaters would receive equipment in short supply? Who would administer conquered territories? Inevitably, the questions of fighting a war slid into discussions of the peace that would follow. What would happen to occupied territories? How would the Axis powers be punished? If a more stable world order could not be created, the cycle of violence might never end. So as Allied armies struggled mile by mile to defeat the Axis, Allied diplomacy concentrated just as much on winning the peace.

The Fall of the Third Reich

After pushing the Germans out of North Africa in May 1943, Allied forces looked to drive Italy from the war. Late in July, two weeks after a quarter of a million British and American troops had landed on Sicily, Mussolini fled to German-held northern Italy. Although Italy surrendered early in September, Germany continued to pour in reinforcements. It took the Allies almost a year of bloody fighting to reach Rome, and at the end of the campaign they had yet to break German lines. Along the eastern front, Soviet armies steadily pushed the Germans out of Russia and back toward Berlin.

D-Day

General Dwight D. Eisenhower, fresh from battle in North Africa and the Mediterranean, took command of Allied preparations for Operation Overlord, a massive invasion of Europe striking from across the English Channel. By June 1944 all attention focused on the coast of France, for Hitler, of course, knew the Allies were preparing.

The Normandy landing involved complex problems of moving troops and matériel. The Rhino ferry allowed the landing forces to improvise docking facilities soon after the invasion forces landed. Sailors described these awkward craft as "ugly as hell, cranky as hell—but efficient as hell."

He suspected they would hit Calais, the French port city closest to the British Isles. Allied planners did their best to encourage this belief, even deploying fake armaments across the Channel. On the morning of June 6, 1944, the invasion began—not at Calais but on the less fortified beaches of Normandy (see the map, page 871). Almost 3 million men, 11,000 aircraft, and more than 2000 vessels took part in D-Day.

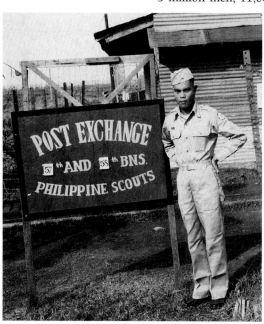

In the face of Japanese occupation, many Filipinos actively supported the American war effort. Valentine Untalan survived capture by the Japanese and went on to serve in the American army's elite Philippine Scouts. Like a growing number of Filipinos, he moved to the United States once the war was over.

As Allied forces hit the beaches, luck and Eisenhower's meticulous planning favored their cause. Persuaded that the Allies still wanted Calais, Hitler delayed sending in two reserve divisions. His indecision allowed the Allied forces to secure a foothold. Over the next few days more than 1.5 million soldiers landed on the beaches—but they still had to move inland. Slowed by difficult conditions, the Allied advance from Normandy took almost two months, not several weeks as expected. Once Allied tanks broke through German lines their progress was spectacular. In August Paris was liberated, and by mid-September the Allies had driven the Germans from France and Belgium.

All went well until December 1944, when Hitler threw his reserves into a last, desperate gamble. The unexpected German onslaught drove the Allied lines back along a 50-mile bulge. There the Germans trapped the 101st Airborne Division. When asked to surrender, General Tony MacAuliffe sent back a one-word reply: "Nuts!" His troops held, General George Patton raced to the rescue, and the last German offensive collapsed. Little stood between the Allies and Berlin.

Two Roads to Tokyo

In the bleak days of 1942 General Douglas MacArthur—flamboyant and jaunty with his dark sunglasses and corncob pipe—had emerged as America's only military hero. MacArthur believed that the future of America lay in the Far East. The Pacific theater, not the European, should have top priority, he argued. In March 1943 the Combined Chiefs of Staff agreed to his plan for a westward advance along the northern coast of New Guinea toward the Philippines and Tokyo. Naval forces directed by Admiral Chester Nimitz used amphibious warfare to move up the island chains of the Central Pacific (see the map on facing page).

By July 1944 the navy's leapfrogging campaign had reached the Marianas, east of the Philippines. From there B-29 bombers could reach the Japanese home islands. As a result, Admiral Nimitz proposed bypassing the Philippines in favor of a direct attack on Formosa (present-day Taiwan). MacArthur insisted instead on keeping his personal promise "to eighteen million Christian Filipinos that the Americans would return." President Roosevelt himself came to Hawaii to resolve the impasse, giving MacArthur the green light. Backed by more than 100 ships of the Pacific Fleet, the general splashed ashore on the island of Leyte in October 1944 to announce his return.

Battle of Leyte Gulf

The decision to invade the Philippines led to savage fighting until the war ended. As retreating Japanese armies left Manila, they tortured and slaughtered tens of thousands of Filipino civilians. The United States suffered 62,000 casualties redeeming MacArthur's pledge to return. A spectacular U.S. Navy victory at the Battle of Leyte Gulf spelled the end of the Japanese Imperial Navy as a fighting force. MacArthur and Nimitz prepared to tighten the noose around Japan's home islands.

The Pacific Campaigns of World War II The extraordinary distances of the Pacific spurred the United States to devise a two-front strategy to defeat Japan. MacArthur's army forces used Australia as a base of operations, aiming for the Philippines and the southeast coast of China. Once those areas were secured, forces could then launch air attacks on Japan. The navy, under command of Admiral Nimitz, set out to destroy the Japanese fleet and to conduct a series of amphibious landings on island chains in the Central Pacific. Meanwhile, British forces launched separate operations in Burma, forces under Chiang Kai-shek occasionally engaged Japanese forces on China's mainland, and in August 1945 Soviet troops attacked northern China.

Big Three Diplomacy

While the Allies cooperated to gain military victories in both Europe and the Pacific, negotiations over the postwar peace proved knottier. Churchill believed that only a stable European balance of power, not an international agency, could preserve peace. In his view the Soviet Union was the greatest threat to upsetting that balance of power. Premier Joseph Stalin left no doubt that an expansive notion of Russian security defined his war aims. For future protection Stalin expected to annex the Baltic states, once Russian provinces, along with bits of Finland and

Daily Lives

TIME AND TRAVEL
Air Power Shrinks the Globe

During World War I, the popular imagination thrilled to the stories of aerial dogfights and "flying aces." In reality, airplanes played only a secondary role in that war's military strategy. Short flying ranges and an inability to carry heavy loads limited what planes could do. Between the two wars, however, airframes grew stronger, engines more powerful, and payloads greater. Air-power strategists began to suggest that concerted waves of planes could attack industrial and military targets deep in enemy territory. Hitler grasped the strategic possibilities and insisted that Germany's air force as well as its army rearm and modernize.

During the blitzkriegs against Poland and France in the opening campaigns of the war, Hitler's air attacks terrorized civilian populations and disrupted enemy forces. Air Marshal Hermann Goering predicted that bombers from the German Luftwaffe would soon bring England to its knees. The Battle of Britain, fought during the winter of 1940–1941, signaled the start of the age of modern air warfare. For the first time in history, one nation tried to conquer another from the skies. Goering's boast failed as England continued doggedly to resist.

Despite the Luftwaffe's failure, Allied air-power strategists believed heavy bombers could cripple Germany and Japan. The first test of such "strategic bombing" came in 1942, when more than 1100 planes of the British Royal Air Force (RAF) destroyed some 20,000 homes, 1500 stores and offices, and about 60 factories around Cologne, Germany. Horrific as that sounds, the attack did not level the city, as RAF planners had predicted. Indeed, later studies indicated that for all the damage done, Axis productivity actually increased until the last months of the war. Still, strategic bombing disrupted Japanese and German industry, brought the war home to the civilian population, and diverted enemy forces from the front to home defense.

Raids on Dresden and on Tokyo dramatized the horrors of the new technology. Dresden, a charming German city almost untouched by the twentieth century, had largely been ignored until February 1945. The RAF hit it first; then, with fires still raging, the American bombing wave struck. A huge inferno drew all the oxygen out of the center of the city, so that victims who did not burn suffocated. The city and its 60,000 people died. In March 340 American bombers hit Tokyo with incendiary bombs. The resulting firestorms, whipped by strong winds, leveled 16 square miles, destroyed 267,000 homes, left 83,000 dead, and injured 41,000. The heat was so

The B-29 bombers gave the American air force much greater range, speed, and bomb loads. The *Enola Gay* (above), named after the pilot's mother, was modified to carry the first atom bomb, dropped on Hiroshima.

Romania and about half of prewar Poland. In eastern Europe and other border areas such as Iran, Korea, and Turkey, he wanted "friendly" neighbors. It soon became apparent that "friendly" meant regimes dependent on Moscow.

Early on, Franklin Roosevelt had promoted his own version of an international balance of power, which he called the "Four Policemen." Under its framework, the Soviet Union, Great Britain, the United States, and China would guarantee peace through military cooperation. But by 1944 Roosevelt was seeking an alternative both to this scheme and to Churchill's wish to return to a balance of power that safely hemmed in the Russians. He preferred to bring the Soviet Union into a peacekeeping system based on an international organization similar to the League of Nations. This time, Roosevelt intended that the United States, as well as all the great powers, would participate. Whether Churchill and Stalin—or the American people as a whole—would accept the idea was not yet clear.

intense that the water in canals boiled.

To ensure the success of aerial warfare, aircraft designers on both sides raced to make their planes bigger and faster. The first English raids used the Wellington bomber, a plane 65 feet long with a wing span of 86 feet and a bomb load of 1500 pounds. In contrast, the American B-29s that bombed Hiroshima and Nagasaki carried up to 10 tons on a plane that was about 50 percent larger. The Wellington flew 255 miles an hour and cruised as high as 12,000 feet, with a range of 2200 miles, whereas the new B-29s could travel more than 350 miles an hour, at altitudes up to 30,000 feet, with a range of up to 5000 miles—more than double the Wellington's. German scientists took an even more radical step. To increase the speed and range of their weaponry they produced a new V-1 pilotless "buzz bomb" (named for the sound of its jet engine) and the V-2 rocket, the first true missile used as a weapon. Launched from bases in Europe, V-1s and V-2s easily reached targets in England. For all the terror they inspired, however, they were inaccurate and the Germans could not launch them in sufficient quantities to mount a decisive threat.

With the development of long-range air power, the "front line" of traditional war vanished. Every civilian became a potential combatant, every village a potential target in a total war. Although air power was not decisive in the war, the creation of longer-range aircraft with heavier payloads forced Americans to rethink their ties to the world. After World War I, Americans had rejected the League of Nations and involvement in the political affairs of Europe. Arthur Vandenberg, a Republican senator from Michigan, became one of the nation's most outspoken isolationists. That was before Pearl Harbor and before Vandenberg visited London during the war. As German V-1 and V-2 missiles brought terror from the skies, the senator came to believe that an isolationist policy no longer made sense. Physical distance would never again be a safeguard from attack, because air power had reshaped the strategic map of the world. The United States was now a matter of hours, not days, away from both friends and potential enemies.

The Road to Yalta

The outlines—and the problems—of a postwar settlement became clearer during several summit conferences among the Allied leaders. In November 1943, with Italy's surrender in hand and the war against Germany going well, Churchill and Roosevelt agreed to make a hazardous trip to Teheran, Iran. There, the Big Three leaders met together for the first time and had a chance to take a personal measure of each other. ("Seems very confident," Roosevelt said of Stalin, "very sure of himself, moves slowly—altogether quite impressive.") The president tried to charm the Soviet premier, teasing Churchill for Stalin's benefit, keeping it up "until Stalin was laughing with me, and it was then that I called him 'Uncle Joe.'"

Teheran proved to be the high point of cooperation among the Big Three. It was there that Roosevelt and Churchill committed to the D-Day invasion Stalin

Teheran Conference

893

had so long sought. In return he promised to launch a spring offensive to keep German troops occupied on the eastern front. He also reaffirmed his earlier pledge to declare war against Japan once Germany was beaten.

Yalta Conference

But thorny disagreements over the postwar peace had not been resolved. That was clear in February 1945, when the Big Three met one last time, at the Russian resort city of Yalta, on the Black Sea. By then, Russian, British, and American troops were closing in on Germany. Roosevelt arrived tired, ashen. At 62, limited by his paralysis, he had visibly aged. He came to Yalta mindful that although Germany was all but beaten, Japan still held out in the Pacific. Under no circumstances did he want Stalin to withdraw his promises to enter the fight against Japan and to join a postwar international organization. Churchill remained profoundly mistrustful of Soviet intentions. As Germany and Japan disintegrated, he saw power vacuums opening up in both Europe and Asia. These the Russians appeared only too eager to fill. Most diplomats in the American State Department and a growing number of military officers and politicians shared Churchill's fears.

Dispute over Poland

Allied differences were most clearly reflected in the disagreements over Poland. For Britain, Hitler's invasion of Poland had been the flashpoint for war. It was fighting, in part, to ensure that Poland survived as an independent nation. For Stalin, Poland was the historic corridor of invasion used by Russia's enemies. After Soviet troops reentered Poland, he insisted that he would recognize only the Communist-controlled government at Lublin. Stalin also demanded that Russia receive territory in eastern Poland, for which the Poles would be compensated with German lands. That was hardly the "self-determination" called for in the Atlantic Charter. Roosevelt proposed a compromise. For the time being, Poland would have a coalition government; after the war, free elections would settle the question of who should rule. The Soviets would also receive the territory they demanded in eastern Poland, and the western boundary would be established later.

Similarly, the Allies remained at odds about Germany's postwar future. Stalin was determined that the Germans would never invade Russia again. Many Americans shared his desire to have Germany punished and its war-making capacity eliminated. At the Teheran Conference, Roosevelt and Stalin had proposed that the Third Reich be drastically dismembered, split into five powerless parts. Churchill was much less eager to bring low the nation that was the most natural barrier to Russian expansion. The era after World War I, he believed, demonstrated that a healthy European economy required an industrialized Germany.

Dividing Germany

Again, the Big Three put off making a firm decision. For the time being, they agreed to divide Germany into separate occupation zones (France would receive a zone carved from British and American territory). These four powers would jointly occupy Berlin, while an Allied Control Council supervised the national government.

When the Big Three turned their attention to the Far East, Stalin held a trump card. Roosevelt believed that only a bloody invasion of Japan itself could force a surrender. He thus secured from Stalin a pledge to enter the Pacific war within three months of Germany's defeat. His price was high. Stalin wanted to reclaim territories that Russia had lost in the Russo-Japanese War of 1904–1906, including islands north of Japan as well as control over the Chinese Eastern and South Manchurian railroads.

The agreements reached at Yalta depended on Stalin's willingness to cooperate. In public Roosevelt put the best face on matters. He argued that the new world organization (which Stalin had agreed to support) would "provide the greatest opportunity in all history" to secure a lasting peace. As if to lay to rest the isolationist sentiments that had destroyed Woodrow Wilson's dream, Roosevelt told Congress, "We shall take responsibility for world collaboration, or we shall have to bear the responsibility for another world conflict." Privately the president was less optimistic. He confessed to one friend that he doubted that, "when the chips were down, Stalin would be able to carry out and deliver what he had agreed to."

The Fallen Leader

The Yalta Conference marked one of the last and most controversial chapters of Franklin Roosevelt's presidency. Critics charged that the concessions to Stalin had been too generous and a threat to American national interests. Poland had been betrayed; China sold out; the United Nations crippled at birth. Yet Roosevelt gave to Stalin little that Stalin had not liberated with Russian blood and could have taken anyway. Even Churchill, an outspoken critic of Soviet ambitions, concluded that although "our hopeful assumptions were soon to be falsified . . . they were the only ones possible at the time."

What peace Roosevelt might have achieved can never be known. He returned from Yalta visibly ill. On April 12, 1945, while sitting for his portrait at his vacation home in Warm Springs, Georgia, he complained of a "terrific headache," then suddenly fell unconscious. Two hours later Roosevelt was dead, the victim of a cerebral hemorrhage. Not since the assassination of Lincoln had the nation so grieved. Under Roosevelt's leadership government had become a protector, the president a father and friend, and the United States the leader in the struggle against Axis tyranny. Eleanor recalled how many Americans later told her that "they missed the way the President used to talk to them. . . . There was a real dialogue between Franklin and the people."

Harry S. Truman faced the awesome task of replacing Roosevelt. "Who the hell is Harry Truman?" the chief of staff had asked when Truman was nominated for the vice presidency in 1944. In the brief period he served as vice president, Truman had met with Roosevelt fewer than 10 times. He knew almost nothing about the president's postwar plans and promises. When a reporter now addressed him as "Mr. President," he winced. "I wish you didn't have to call me that," he said. Sensing his own inadequacies, Truman adopted a tough pose and made his mind up quickly. People welcomed the new president's decisiveness as a relief from Roosevelt's evasive style. Too often, though, Truman acted before the issues were clear. He at least knew victory in Europe was near as Allied troops swept into Germany.

Truman becomes president

The Holocaust

The horror of war in no way prepared the invading armies for the liberation of the concentration camps. Hitler, they discovered, had ordered the systematic extermination of all European Jews, as well as Gypsies, homosexuals, and others considered deviant. The SS, Hitler's security force, had constructed six extermination centers in Poland. By rail from all over Europe the SS shipped Jews to die in the gas chambers.

No issue of World War II more starkly raised questions of human good and evil than what came to be known as the Holocaust. Tragically, the United States could have done more to save at least some of the 6 million Jews killed. Until the autumn of 1941 the Nazis permitted Jews to leave Europe, but few countries would accept them—including the United States. Americans haunted by unemployment feared that a tide of new immigrants would make competition for jobs even worse. Tales of persecution from war refugees had little effect on most citizens: opinion polls showed that more than 70 percent of Americans opposed

In April 1945, at the concentration camp in Buchenwald, Germany, Senator Alben Barkley of Kentucky viewed a grisly reminder of the horrors of the Nazis' "final solution." As vice president under Harry Truman, Barkley urged the administration to support an independent homeland in Israel for Jews.

easing quotas. After 1938 the restrictive provisions of the 1924 Immigration Act were made even tighter.

American Jews wanted to help, especially after 1942, when they learned of the death camps. But they worried that highly visible protests might only aggravate American anti-Semitism. They were also split over support for Zionists working to establish a Jewish homeland in Palestine. The British had blocked Jewish emigration to Palestine and, to avoid alienating the Arabs, opposed Zionism. Roosevelt and his advisers ultimately decided that the best way to save Jews was to win the war quickly, but that strategy still does not explain why the Allies did not do more. They could have bombed the rail lines to the camps, sent commando forces, or tried to destroy the death factories.

Influence of anti-Semitism

Anti-Semitism offers a partial answer. Assistant Secretary of State Breckinridge Long, the man responsible for immigration policy, personified a tradition of gentlemanly anti-Semitism. Polite on the surface but deeply bigoted, Long used his authority over visas to place obstacles in the way of desperate Jewish refugees. But Long went too far when he blocked a plan that both Treasury Secretary Henry Morgenthau and the president had approved to ransom Jews in Romania and 6000 Jewish children in France. Morgenthau, the only Jewish member of Roosevelt's cabinet, had at first shown little interest in the debate over Palestine and the refugees. Long's actions so disturbed him, however, that he sent Roosevelt a report titled "The Acquiescence of This Government in the Murder of the Jews." The president immediately stripped Long of his authority. He appointed a War Refugee Board charged with saving as many Jews as possible and promised to seek the establishment of a Jewish commonwealth in Palestine. But some 18 precious "long and heartbreaking" months had been lost and with them an untold number of lives.

A Lasting Peace

After 15 years of first depression and then war, the Allies sought a new international framework for cooperation among nations. That system, many believed, needed to be economic as well as political. At a 1944 meeting at Bretton Woods, a resort in New Hampshire, Americans led the way in creating two new economic organizations: the International Monetary Fund (IMF) and the International Bank for Reconstruction and Development, later known as the World Bank. The IMF hoped to promote trade by stabilizing national currencies, and the World Bank was designed to stimulate economic growth by investing in projects worldwide. Later that summer the Allies met at Dumbarton Oaks, a Washington estate, to lay out the structure for the proposed United Nations Organization (UNO, later known simply as the UN). An 11-member Security Council would oversee a General Assembly composed of delegates from all member nations. By the end of the first organizational meeting, held in San Francisco in April 1945, it had become clear that the United Nations would favor the Western powers in most postwar disputes.

Bretton Woods economic strategies

Dumbarton Oaks and the UNO

While the United Nations was organizing itself in San Francisco, the Axis powers were collapsing in Europe. As Mussolini attempted to escape to Germany, antifascist mobs in Italy captured and slaughtered him like a pig. Adolf Hitler committed suicide in his Berlin bunker on April 30. Two weeks later General Eisenhower accepted the German surrender.

In one final summit meeting, held in July 1945 at Potsdam (just outside Berlin), President Truman met Churchill and Stalin for the first time. Two issues dominated the meeting: Germany's political fate and how much the defeated nation would pay in reparations. The three leaders agreed that Germany should be occupied and demilitarized. The British and Americans, however, did not want to burden a defeated Germany once again with excessive reparations. Stalin insisted that Russia receive a minimum of $10 billion, regardless of how much it might hurt postwar Germany or the European economy. A complicated compromise allowed Britain and the United States to restrict reparations from their zones. But in large part Stalin had his way. For the foreseeable future, Germany would remain divided into occupation zones and without a central government of its own.

Potsdam summit

Atom Diplomacy

The most crucial factor affecting postwar relations never even reached the bargaining table in Potsdam. On July 16, 1945, the first atomic fireball rose from the desert in Alamogordo, New Mexico. Scientists at the Manhattan Project had successfully detonated their first explosive device. Upon receiving the news, Truman seemed a changed man—firmer, more confident. He "told the Russians just where they got on and off and generally bossed the whole meeting," observed Churchill. Several questions loomed. Should the United States now use the bomb? Should it warn Japan before dropping it? And perhaps equally vital, should Truman inform Stalin?

A few scientists had recommended not using the bomb or at least attempting to convince Japan to surrender by offering a demonstration of the new weapon's power. A high-level committee of administrators, scientists, and political and military leaders dismissed that idea, though some later regretted they did so. Nor did

Should the bomb be dropped?

Truman choose to tell Stalin about the bomb. He only mentioned obliquely that the United States possessed a weapon of "awesome destructiveness." Stalin, whose spies had already informed him of the bomb, showed no surprise. He only remarked casually that he hoped the Americans would use their new weapon to good effect against Japan. Atomic diplomacy had failed its first test. Stalin immediately stepped up the Russian program to build an atom bomb. After Potsdam the nuclear arms race was on.

Finally, Truman and Churchill decided to drop the first bomb with only an implied warning to the Japanese. In an ultimatum issued at Potsdam, they demanded unconditional surrender and threatened Japan with "inevitable and complete destruction" using the "full application of our military power" if it did not comply. Unaware of the warning's full meaning, officials in Tokyo made no formal reply.

Truman and Churchill knew Japan was on the verge of defeat. Japan's leaders had even sent peace feelers to the Russians. Why, then, did the Allies insist on unconditional surrender? Some historians have charged that Secretary of State James Byrnes, a staunch anticommunist, wanted a dramatic combat demonstration of the bomb that would serve to persuade Stalin to behave less aggressively in negotiations with the British and Americans. However much Byrnes had Soviet diplomacy on his mind, most evidence indicates that Truman decided to drop the bomb in order to end the war quickly.

Before leaving Potsdam, Truman ordered crews on Tinian Island in the South Pacific to proceed to their first target as soon as weather permitted. On August 6 the *Enola Gay*, a B-29 bomber, dropped a uranium bomb (given the name of "Little Boy") that leveled four square miles of Hiroshima, an industrial and military center. The blast immediately killed nearly 80,000 people (including 20 American prisoners of war). A German priest came upon soldiers who had looked up as the bomb exploded. Their eyeballs had melted from their sockets. Another eyewitness spoke of survivors "so broken and confused that they moved and behaved like automatons." Two days later the Soviet Union declared war on Japan, and on August 9 a second atom bomb (a plutonium weapon nicknamed "Fat Man") exploded over the port of Nagasaki. Another 60,000 people were killed instantly. In both cities many who lived through the horror began to sicken and die as radiation poisoning claimed tens of thousands of additional lives.

The bomb as a threat to the Soviets

The use of atomic bombs in World War II

This aerial view of Hiroshima gives stark testimony to the destructive force of the atomic blast. In one of the many bitter ironies, only the shells of the western-style buildings survived.

The two explosions left the Japanese stunned. Breaking all precedents, the emperor intervened and declared openly for peace. On September 3 a humiliated Japanese delegation boarded the battleship *Missouri* in Tokyo Bay and signed the document of surrender. World War II had ended.

"World War II changed everything," observed one admiral long after the war. The defeatism of the Depression gave way to the exhilaration of victory. Before the war Americans seldom exerted leadership in international affairs. After, the world looked to the United States to rebuild the economies of Europe and Asia and to maintain peace. World War II had not only shown the global interdependence of economic and political systems; it had also increased that interdependence. Out of the war developed a truly international economy. At home the trends toward bigness and centralization vastly accelerated. Advances in electronics, communications, and aviation brought the world closer to every home. Government grew, too. The size of the national debt alone guaranteed that Washington would continue to dominate the economy. Americans had come to believe in a strong defense, even if that meant a large federal bureaucracy and a generous military budget.

Still, a number of fears loomed, even as victory parades snaked down the nation's main streets. Would the inevitable cutbacks in spending bring on another depression? Would Soviet ambitions undo the new global peace, much as fascism and economic instability had undone the peace of Versailles? And then there was the shadow of the atom bomb looming over the victorious as well as the defeated. The United States might control atomic technology for the present, but what if the weapon fell into unfriendly hands? With the advent of the atomic age, no one in the world, not even in the United States, was safe anymore.

chapter summary

World War II deepened the global interdependence of nations and left the United States as the greatest economic and military power in the world.

- As fascism spread in Europe and as militarism spread in Asia, Franklin Roosevelt struggled to help America's allies by overcoming domestic political isolation and the fervor for neutrality.

- Despite German aggression against Poland in 1939, France and the Low Countries in 1940, and the Soviet Union in 1941, the United States did not enter the war until the Japanese surprise attack on Pearl Harbor in December 1941.

- The alliance forged among British prime minister Winston Churchill, Soviet premier Joseph Stalin, and President Franklin Roosevelt did not swerve from its decision to subdue Germany first, even though early defeats and America's lack of preparation slowed the war effort until 1943.

- At home America's factories produced enough goods to supply the domestic economy and America's allies.

  - Demands for labor created opportunities for women and minorities.

  - War hysteria aggravated old prejudices and led to the internment of Japanese Americans.

  - New Deal reform ended as "Dr. Win-the-War" replaced "Dr. New Deal."

- Although the successful landings in France on D-Day and the island-hopping campaign in the Pacific made it clear that the Allies would win the war, issues over Poland, Germany, and postwar boundaries raised doubts about the peace.

- The war ended with the atomic bombings of Hiroshima and Nagasaki, but not soon enough to limit the horrors of the Holocaust.

interactive learning

The Primary Source Investigator CD-ROM offers the following materials related to this chapter:

- Interactive map: **World War II** (M27)

- A short documentary movie on the use of atomic bombs in World War II (D18)

- A collection of primary sources illuminating the Second World War: Congress' declaration of war against Japan, the Lend-Lease Act with Britain, and numerous images from the battlefronts. Several documents highlight changes to society during the war: a number of war propaganda posters, photos of women working, and Norman Rockwell's Rosie the Riveter. Other sources illustrate the debate over the development of the nuclear bomb: read Einstein's letter to President Roosevelt and the president's letter to the lead scientist on the atomic project, Robert Oppenheimer.

additional reading

David Kennedy, *Freedom from Fear: The American People in Depression and War* (1999), covers the prewar and war years, especially political and social trends. For a good study of prewar diplomacy and isolationism see Robert Divine, *The Reluctant Belligerent* (2nd ed., 1979). John Keegan concentrates on military strategy in *The Second World War* (1989). Studs Turkel, *The Good War: An Oral History of World War II* (1984), offers the wartime recollections of Americans from varied walks of life. David Brinkley, *Washington Goes to War* (1988), offers a most readable look at the transformation wrought on our nation's capital. For broader treatments of the home front see John Blum, *"V" Was for Victory* (1976), and Richard Polenberg, *War and Society: The United States, 1941–1945* (1972). The internment of Japanese Americans is covered in Roger Daniels, *Concentration Camp USA* (1981), and Peter Irons, *Justice at War* (1983).

The decision to drop two atom bombs on Japan remains one of the most controversial legacies of the war. To better understand the racial dimension, see John Dower, *War without Mercy: Race and Power in the Pacific War* (1986). Richard Rhodes, *The Making of the Atomic Bomb* (1987), re-creates the history of the Manhattan Project. Gar Alperowitz, *The Decision to Use the Atomic Bomb* (1995), extends an interpretation he first advanced in *Atomic Diplomacy* (1965) that the Soviet Union was the planners' real target. Martin Sherwin, *A World Destroyed* (rev. ed., 1985), and J. Samuel Walker, *Prompt and Utter Destruction: Truman and the Use of the Atomic Bomb against Japan* (1997), view the decision more as a way to end the war quickly. David Holloway, *Stalin and the Bomb: The Soviet Union and Atomic Energy 1939–1956* (1994), uses Russian sources to trace the origins of atomic diplomacy. Students who wish to work with some of the original documents should see Michael Stoff et al., *The Manhattan Project: A Documentary Introduction to the Atomic Age* (1991). For a fuller list of readings, see the Bibliography at www.mhhe.com/davidsonnation5.

significant events

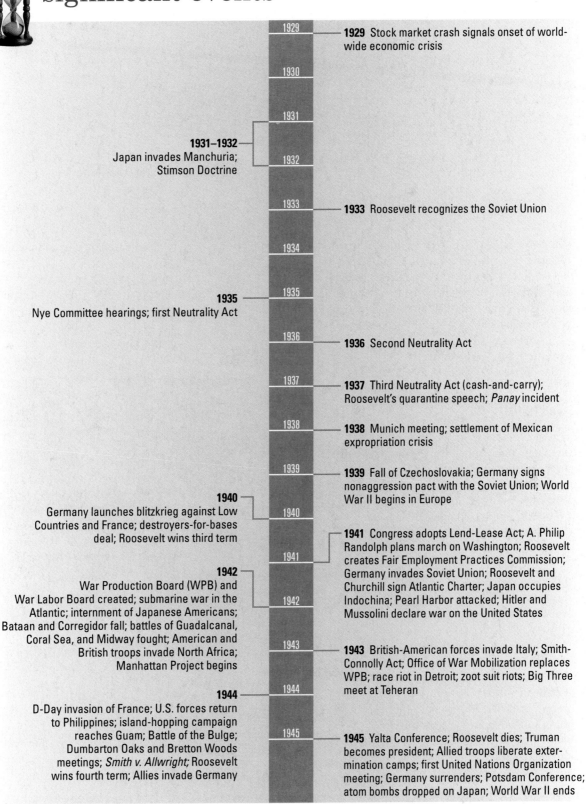

1929 Stock market crash signals onset of world-wide economic crisis

1931–1932
Japan invades Manchuria;
Stimson Doctrine

1933 Roosevelt recognizes the Soviet Union

1935
Nye Committee hearings; first Neutrality Act

1936 Second Neutrality Act

1937 Third Neutrality Act (cash-and-carry); Roosevelt's quarantine speech; *Panay* incident

1938 Munich meeting; settlement of Mexican expropriation crisis

1939 Fall of Czechoslovakia; Germany signs nonaggression pact with the Soviet Union; World War II begins in Europe

1940
Germany launches blitzkrieg against Low Countries and France; destroyers-for-bases deal; Roosevelt wins third term

1941 Congress adopts Lend-Lease Act; A. Philip Randolph plans march on Washington; Roosevelt creates Fair Employment Practices Commission; Germany invades Soviet Union; Roosevelt and Churchill sign Atlantic Charter; Japan occupies Indochina; Pearl Harbor attacked; Hitler and Mussolini declare war on the United States

1942
War Production Board (WPB) and War Labor Board created; submarine war in the Atlantic; internment of Japanese Americans; Bataan and Corregidor fall; battles of Guadalcanal, Coral Sea, and Midway fought; American and British troops invade North Africa; Manhattan Project begins

1943 British-American forces invade Italy; Smith-Connolly Act; Office of War Mobilization replaces WPB; race riot in Detroit; zoot suit riots; Big Three meet at Teheran

1944
D-Day invasion of France; U.S. forces return to Philippines; island-hopping campaign reaches Guam; Battle of the Bulge; Dumbarton Oaks and Bretton Woods meetings; *Smith v. Allwright;* Roosevelt wins fourth term; Allies invade Germany

1945 Yalta Conference; Roosevelt dies; Truman becomes president; Allied troops liberate extermination camps; first United Nations Organization meeting; Germany surrenders; Potsdam Conference; atom bombs dropped on Japan; World War II ends

AFTER THE FACT
Historians Reconstruct the Past

Did the Atomic Bomb Save Lives?

When news came that the United States had exploded a powerful new atomic device over Japan, it was hard for American troops in the Pacific to contain their joy. "We whooped and yelled like mad," recalled one veteran. "We downed all the beer we'd been stashing away. We shot bullets into the air and danced between the tent rows, because this meant maybe we were going to live."

Maybe we were going to live. The GIs in the field saw immediately that if the bomb ended the war, there would be no need for a massive invasion of Japan, similar to the D-Day invasion of Europe that had cost so many lives. As the lyrics of one popular song put it, "I believe the bomb that struck Hiroshima / was the answer to a fighting boy's prayers." After the war, Winston Churchill made the same point by calling the bomb "a miracle of deliverance." To conquer Japan "yard by yard might well require the loss of a million American lives," he told Congress. President Truman's memoirs put the totals somewhat lower: he referred to military estimates of over a million *casualties*, including half a million American deaths.

To most Americans, such large numbers made sense. Japanese resistance during the Pacific campaigns had been fierce. On the island of Okinawa alone, hand-to-hand fighting claimed over 12,000 American soldiers, sailors, and marines. American troops used flamethrowers to burn Japanese out of caves and holes. Rather than surrender, several thousand Japanese soldiers threw themselves off cliffs. In the half century following World War II, most historians assumed that dropping the bomb saved the

United States from mounting a bloody invasion of the Japanese home islands.

But how did Truman, Churchill, and other participants arrive at such casualty figures? The conclusion that the United States dropped the bomb to end the war quickly and to avoid 500,000 American deaths became one of the most controversial of World War II. The debate arose, in part, because of

the horror of nuclear weaponry. Critics have suggested that Japan might well have been persuaded to surrender without an atomic attack.

That debate—which began in earnest during the 1960s—has analyzed a host of factors affecting Truman's decision (see pages 897–898). Many navy and air corps officers believed that a naval blockade and conventional bombing were enough to force Japan's surrender without an invasion. The country,

> made use of this newly gained power. If the test should fail, then it would be even more important to us to bring about a surrender before we had to make a physical conquest of Japan. General Marshall told me that it might cost half a million American lives to force the enemy's surrender on his home grounds.

Harry S. Truman Memoirs, page 804 of typescript: an estimate of half a million deaths

Harry S. Truman, *Memoirs,* typescript, page 804: an estimate of half a million deaths. Reprinted by permission of Margaret Truman Daniel.

after all, was virtually without defense against bombing raids. Later critics have suggested that the Allies should have modified their demand for "unconditional surrender," instead allowing the Japanese to keep their revered institution of the emperor. (As events turned out, Japan surrendered only after such a guarantee was issued.) Others argue that the United States should have arranged for a demonstration of the bomb's power without actually detonating one over Japan.

Yet as the debates over these alternatives swirled during the 1960s and 1970s, no one challenged the estimates of a million-casualty invasion. That number had been put forward in 1947 by Henry Stimson, the highly respected former secretary of war. In an article for *Harper's* magazine Stimson wrote, "We estimated the major fighting would not end until the latter part of 1946 at the earliest. I was informed that such operations might be expected to cost over a million casualties, to American forces alone."

Stimson's account cast a long shadow. A few years later Harry Truman provided an air force historian with a significantly lower number. Truman recalled that General George Marshall, the army chief of staff, had told him in July 1945 that in an invasion of Japan one-quarter of a million casualties would be the cost as well as an equal number of Japanese. But when a White House aide checked Truman's memory against Stimson's account, he discovered the discrepancy—one million versus only a quarter million. "The President's casualty figure [should] be changed to conform with that of Secretary Stimson," the aide advised, "because presumably Stimson got his from Gen. Marshall; the size of the casualty figures is very important."

The last phrase is significant. Why were the numbers so important? Obviously, the higher the number of potential casualties, the stronger the case that using the bomb saved lives. So it is worth looking a bit more closely at Stimson's article.

In fact, the idea to write an article was not actually Stimson's. It came from another atomic policy maker, James Conant. Conant, the president of Harvard University, had become increasingly concerned

Hiroshima, August 6, 1945

about "the spreading accusation that it was unnecessary to use the atomic bomb at all." He complained privately in 1946 that "This type of sentimentalism . . . is bound to have a great deal of influence on the next generation. The type of person who goes into teaching, particularly school teaching, will be influenced a great deal by this type of argument." Conant believed that Stimson had the prestige to counter such criticisms. One of the nation's most distinguished public servants, he had been twice a secretary of war, an ambassador, and secretary of state.

Remains of a wristwatch from the atomic blast site at Hiroshima. The bomb exploded at 8:16 a.m.

So Stimson agreed to write an article. But where did he get his casualty estimates? During the war a memo from former president Herbert Hoover had been circulated, warning that an invasion could claim anywhere from half a million to a million American lives. At the time, in June 1945, a successful test of an atomic bomb was still a month away and the possibility of an invasion loomed larger. Stimson was convinced that the war might be ended without an invasion if the Allies would only assure the Japanese that the position of emperor would be protected. Hoover's dire warning about the costs of an invasion reinforced Stimson's argument against invading.

But unlike to the aide who later helped Truman with his memoirs, Stimson did not get similarly high casualty estimates from General Marshall. Marshall's staff thought Hoover's estimates were way too high. They estimated that the first-stage invasion (of Kyushu Island) might produce American casualties of perhaps 31,000, including about 7000 to 8000 deaths. If the invasion of Japan's main island, Honshu, took place, those numbers would rise to 120,000 casualties and 25,000 deaths. Estimates by General MacArthur were slightly higher, but within the same range. For reasons that remain unclear, however, when Stimson wrote his article after the war, he chose to use the higher estimates.

Thus, intentionally or not, Stimson's article greatly overestimated the number of invasion casualties predicted by the American military. And Conant's private worries show that those who dropped the bomb were more sensitive about their decision than they wished to admit. One of the most telling illustrations of the pressure to keep the estimates high can be seen in the successive drafts of Harry Truman's own memoirs, which were finally published in 1955. The assistants who helped Truman kept revising the figure upward. Truman's recollection, in 1952, mentioned only 250,000 casualties (not deaths); that figure jumped to 500,000 casualties in the first draft; then, in the published version, to a "half-million" *lives* saved.

Do the lower figures mean that historians should condemn Truman, Stimson, and others for preferring to use the bomb rather than invade Japan? Not

Japanese fighting on Okinawa and other Pacific islands produced high casualty and death rates for American forces, reinforcing the notion that an invasion of Japan would claim many American lives.

THE WHITE HOUSE
WASHINGTON Dec. 31, 1952

My dear Professor Cate:–
Your letter of Dec. 6th 1952 has
...been delivered to...

...I asked Gen. Marshall what it
would cost in lives to land on
the Tokio plane and other places
in Japan. It was his opinion that
1/4 million casualities would be
the minimum cost as well
as an equal number of the enemy.

Earlier letter
from Truman
to an Air Force
Historian

"1/4 million casualties"

Earlier letter from Truman to an air force historian. Here, Truman's and Marshall's estimate is a quarter of a million casualties, not deaths.

necessarily. After Japan's surprise attack on Pearl Harbor and its fierce resistance in the Pacific islands, American sentiments against the Japanese ran high. The atomic bomb had cost $2 billion to develop, and officials always assumed that if the bomb were successful, it would be used. Why else develop it? Truman (and most Americans) probably believed that even an invasion costing 25,000 lives would have justified using the bomb.

Even so, historians must constantly remind themselves that seemingly "impartial" accounts are influenced by the conditions under which they were created. Stimson set out not simply to tell the facts about the decision to drop the bomb. He wished to justify a decision he believed was necessary and proper. Like Conant, he understood that the record of the past is always shaped by those who do the telling. "History," he wrote in 1948, "is often not what actually happened but what is recorded as such."

BIBLIOGRAPHY Stimson's "The Decision to Use the Bomb" appears in the February 1947 issue of *Harper's* magazine. The debate over his casualty estimates and those of Truman and Churchill was launched by Barton J. Bernstein, "A Postwar Myth: 500,000 Lives Saved," *Bulletin of the Atomic Scientists* 42 (June/July 1986), and by Rufus Miles, "Hiroshima: The Strange Myth of Half a Million Lives Saved," *International Security* 10 (Fall 1985). Bernstein provides valuable background on Stimson's 1947 article in "Seizing the Contested Terrain of Nuclear History," *Diplomatic History* 19 (Winter 1993). Also useful is John Ray Skates, *The Invasion of Japan: Alternative to the Bomb* (1994). The debate over the projected invasion, of course, is only one aspect of the larger question of whether atom bombs should have been dropped on Japan. For readings on that topic, see the Bibliography.

GLOBAL ESSAY

THE UNITED STATES IN A NUCLEAR AGE

At Los Alamos in July 1945, during the final feverish days of work on the first atom bomb, a few scientists calculated the possible unexpected effects of an atomic blast. The strategic bombings at Dresden and Tokyo showed how a firestorm, once started, sucked oxygen from the surrounding atmosphere, feeding upon itself and enlarging the inferno. No one had ever set off an atomic explosion, and some scientists worried that an even greater chain reaction might follow, one that would not only ignite the atmosphere around it but envelop the earth's atmosphere, leaving the planet in ashes. Members of the team checked and rechecked the calculations before deciding that those fears were unwarranted.

In the half century after Hiroshima, the atomic nightmare returned repeatedly to haunt the world. The threat appeared to be not from the detonation of a single bomb but from an all-too-human chain reaction in which escalating violence leads to atomic strike and counterstrike, followed by a decades-long radioactive "nuclear winter," from which intelligent life could never fully recover.

During the heady victory celebrations of 1945, the threat of nuclear annihilation seemed distant. Although President Truman and other American leaders had become increasingly distrustful of Stalin, the United States preserved a clear atomic monopoly. The dangers from radioactive fallout impressed only a handful of officials and even fewer members of the public, who were treated to cheery fantasies of the

peacetime use of atomics. One such whimsy, featured in the May 1947 *Collier's* magazine, showed a recovered paraplegic emerging from the mushroom cloud of his atomic treatment, his wheelchair almost miraculously left behind.

By 1949, when fallout from Russian explosions indicated that the Soviet Union had gained the power of atomic weapons, the grim global realignment was already well established. Two superpowers, the Soviet Union and the United States, had replaced the players in the old balance of power that had defined European politics for two centuries.

The polarization of the globe into two camps, each dominated by a superpower, would have seemed strange even 20 years earlier. But in the long view, the result was not surprising. Since the sixteenth century, the expansion of European culture and power has been most significant along the continent's peripheries, both west and east. Along the west-facing rim, the Portuguese, Spanish, Dutch, French, and English reached beyond themselves for commercial and colonial empires. By the late nineteenth century England's colonial offshoot, the United States, was coming into its own even farther west. Over these same centuries of expansion, Europe's eastern flank saw Russian settlers pushing across the steppes of Eurasia, turning grasslands into cultivated fields. Farther north, Russian fur traders were bringing the forest and tundra of Siberia into the Russian orbit, just as French and English fur traders were mastering the forests of the Canadian shield.

GLOBAL EVENTS

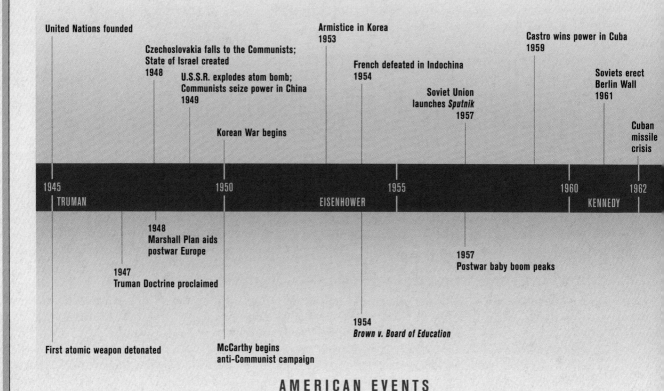

United Nations founded

Czechoslovakia falls to the Communists;
State of Israel created
1948

U.S.S.R. explodes atom bomb;
Communists seize power in China
1949

Korean War begins

Armistice in Korea
1953

French defeated in Indochina
1954

Soviet Union
launches *Sputnik*
1957

Castro wins power in Cuba
1959

Soviets erect
Berlin Wall
1961

Cuban
missile
crisis

| 1945 | 1950 | 1955 | 1960 | 1962 |

TRUMAN   EISENHOWER   KENNEDY

1948
Marshall Plan aids
postwar Europe

1947
Truman Doctrine proclaimed

1957
Postwar baby boom peaks

1954
Brown v. Board of Education

First atomic weapon detonated

McCarthy begins
anti-Communist campaign

AMERICAN EVENTS

In area and vastness of resources, the Soviet Union surpassed even the United States, its boundaries encompassing 12 time zones. Given the centuries-long tradition of authoritarian rule (*czar* is the Russian derivative of "caesar"), the Russian Revolution of 1917 took a firmly centralized approach to modernization. At sometimes frightful cost Stalin brought the Soviet Union to its position as superpower by the end of World War II. The peripheral powers of Europe—the United States and Russia—had become dominant. By the 1960s both relied on stockpiles of nuclear weapons to guarantee their security and power.

Deterrence—the knowledge of "mutual assured destruction"—would prevent either side from be-

ing the first to launch a missile attack. So, at least, nuclear strategists suggested. Yet that strategy was frightening precisely because the globe could not be cut neatly into communist and noncommu-

nist halves, each with clearly unified interests. The world was riven by ethnic, religious, and economic rivalries. When the prestige of either superpower became critically involved, such regional conflicts threatened to escalate into a full-scale nuclear war.

Both the Soviets and the Americans discovered the limits of projecting their power in regional conflicts. For more than a decade, the United States sought unsuccessfully to win a war against North Vietnam by conventional means before withdrawing in defeat. For another decade, the Soviet Union waged a similarly unsuccessful war in Afghanistan. In both cases, regional rivalries played a dominant role. In the Vietnam conflict, the Communist Ho Chi Minh was

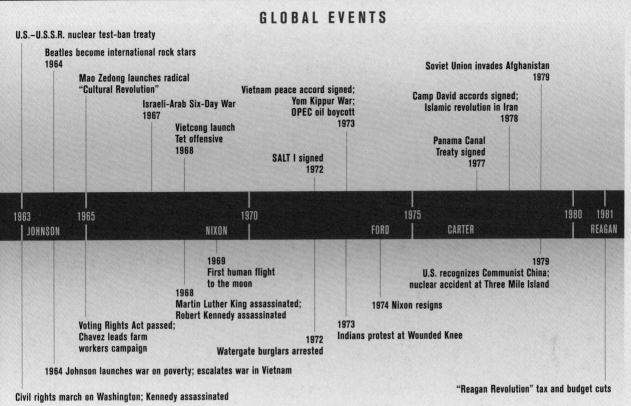

GLOBAL EVENTS

U.S.–U.S.S.R. nuclear test-ban treaty

Beatles become international rock stars
1964

Mao Zedong launches radical
"Cultural Revolution"

Israeli-Arab Six-Day War
1967

Vietcong launch
Tet offensive
1968

Vietnam peace accord signed;
Yom Kippur War;
OPEC oil boycott
1973

SALT I signed
1972

Soviet Union invades Afghanistan
1979

Camp David accords signed;
Islamic revolution in Iran
1978

Panama Canal
Treaty signed
1977

| 1963 | 1965 | | 1970 | | 1975 | | | 1980 | 1981 |
| JOHNSON | | | NIXON | | FORD | | CARTER | | REAGAN |

1969
First human flight
to the moon

1968
Martin Luther King assassinated;
Robert Kennedy assassinated

1974 Nixon resigns

1979
U.S. recognizes Communist China;
nuclear accident at Three Mile Island

1973
Indians protest at Wounded Knee

Voting Rights Act passed;
Chavez leads farm
workers campaign

1972
Watergate burglars arrested

1964 Johnson launches war on poverty; escalates war in Vietnam

"Reagan Revolution" tax and budget cuts

Civil rights march on Washington; Kennedy assassinated

AMERICAN EVENTS

enough of a nationalist to prefer nearly any form of government, including French colonial rule, to domination by Vietnam's traditional enemy, China. It did not matter that China was led by a Communist "comrade," Mao Zedong. During the war in Afghanistan, the Soviets discovered that their rebel opponents were inspired by their Islamic faith. The 1979 revolution in Iran brought the Ayatollah Khomeini to power and further demonstrated that Islamic fundamentalism would play a crucial role in the Middle East and the Saharan subcontinent. Those same religious divisions led increasingly to disputes within the Soviet Union, weakening that empire.

In the midst of the ongoing cold war, Europe recovered from the devastation of World War II, thanks in part to aid from the United States. Over the next few decades, the peacetime economic expansion that benefited the Americans also allowed both West Germany and Japan, their former enemies, to grow into modern industrial states with robust consumer economies. That prosperity, in part, helped nurture a new generation of "baby boomers," in Europe as well as America, who became politically active during the 1960s. In Africa and Asia, old colonial regimes gave way to newly independent nations.

But the global industrial economy did not expand indefinitely. In America, the boom and development mentality of the 1950s and 1960s was tempered in the 1970s as the environmental costs of air and water pollutants, strip mining, pesticides, and a host of other abuses became obvious. Similarly, by the mid-1970s major Soviet rivers like the Ural, Volga, and Dnieper had been polluted by industrial wastes. China, possessing coal reserves as great as those of the United States and the Soviet Union combined, had built so many coal-fired electrical plants that its northern cities were heavily polluted and damage from acid rain could be charted in neighboring regions. Satellite photos recorded such pollution, whether from factories, coal-fired electric plants, or even fires burning, as in the photo on page 910, in the islands of Indonesia.

By the end of the 1980s the natural limits of global growth and the strains of a nuclear standoff

GLOBAL EVENTS

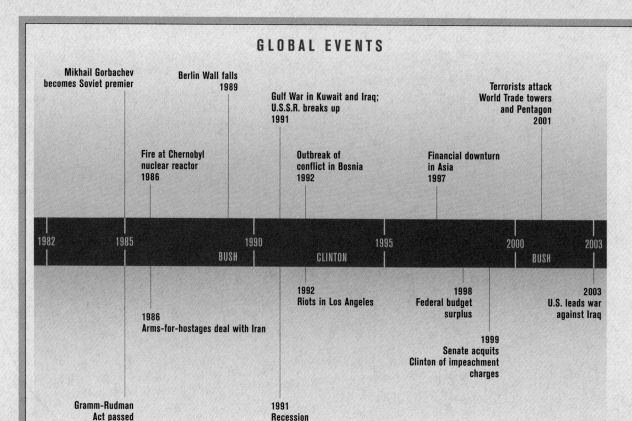

Mikhail Gorbachev becomes Soviet premier

Berlin Wall falls
1989

Gulf War in Kuwait and Iraq; U.S.S.R. breaks up
1991

Terrorists attack World Trade towers and Pentagon
2001

Fire at Chernobyl nuclear reactor
1986

Outbreak of conflict in Bosnia
1992

Financial downturn in Asia
1997

| 1982 | 1985 | 1990 | 1995 | 2000 | 2003 |

BUSH   CLINTON   BUSH

1992
Riots in Los Angeles

1998
Federal budget surplus

2003
U.S. leads war against Iraq

1986
Arms-for-hostages deal with Iran

1999
Senate acquits Clinton of impeachment charges

Gramm-Rudman Act passed

1991
Recession

AMERICAN EVENTS

were becoming clear. The Soviet empire, perhaps the last of the old colonial powers, saw its Eastern European satellite na-

tions break away. The Union of Soviet Socialist Republics itself split into a host of nations. Although some Americans cheered

at having "won" the cold war, the U.S. economy was suffering from an immense budget deficit run up in large part by military budgets aimed at checking Soviet power.

In the emerging multipolar world of the 1990s, the process of industrialization had created a truly global theater of markets, cultures, and politics. It also created such threats as a hole in the ozone layer and the possibility of a global warming trend. The United States, no longer such a dominant economic power, looked to rebuild its decayed public infrastructure, retrain displaced workers, and restore growth without further degrading the global environment.

Yet as the world's economies became more closely interconnected, instability in one part of the world affected other regions more directly. And where political systems stifled aspirations, terrorist tactics were taken up as a means for the relatively powerless to strike back. Terror had been a weapon used increasingly during the last half of the twentieth century, for a variety of religious or political reasons. The Vietcong had used it to challenge the United States and its allies, as had the Afghan rebels confronting the Soviet Union. Terror had been a weapon in smaller regional conflicts too, as in Northern Ireland and Israel. But the use of terror reached a new height on September 11, 2001, when Islamic extremists hijacked several airliners and turned them into potent weapons, flying into the Pentagon in Washington and destroying the massive World Trade towers of lower Manhattan.

Half a millennium after the civilizations of two hemispheres achieved sustained contact, their ultimate fates have been indivisibly and sometimes perilously intertwined. To grow and prosper, this nation of nations faced the task not only of empowering its own diverse peoples but also of working with nations worldwide to manage conflicts beyond the capability of a single superpower to control.

he war had been over for almost five months and still troop-ships steamed into New York and other ports. Timuel Black was packing his duffel belowdecks when he heard some of the white soldiers shout, "There she is! The Statue of Liberty!" Black felt a little bitter about the war. He'd been drafted in Chicago in 1943, just after race riots ripped the city. His father, a strong supporter of civil rights, was angry. "What the hell are you goin' to fight in Europe for? The fight is here." He wanted his son to go with him to demonstrate in Detroit, except the roads were blocked and the buses and trains screened to prevent more African Americans from coming in.

Instead, Black went off to fight the Nazis, serving in a segregated army. He'd gone ashore during the D-Day invasion, survived the Battle of the Bulge, and marched through one of the German concentration camps. "The first thing you get is the stench," he recalled. "Everybody knows that's human stench. You begin to realize something terrible had happened. There's quietness. You get closer and you begin to see what's happened to these creatures. And you get—I got more passionately angry than I guess I'd ever been." He thought: if it could happen here, to the Germans, it could happen anywhere. It could happen to black folk in America. So when the white soldiers called to come up and see the Statue of Liberty, Black's reaction was, "Hell, I'm not goin' up there. Damn that." But after all, he went up. "All of a sudden, I found myself with tears, cryin' and saying the same thing [the white soldiers] were saying. Glad to be home, proud of my country, as irregular as it is. Determined that it could be better."

At the same time Betty Basye was working across the continent as a nurse in a burn-and-blind center at Menlo Park, California. Her hospital treated soldiers shipped back from the Pacific: "Blind young men. Eyes gone, legs gone. Parts of the face. Burns—you'd land with a firebomb and be up in flames." She'd joke with the men, trying to keep their spirits up, talking about times to come. She liked to take Bill, one of her favorites, for walks downtown. Half of Bill's face was gone, and civilians would stare. It happened to other patients, too. "Nicely dressed women, absolutely staring, just standing there staring." Some people wrote the local paper, wondering why disfigured vets couldn't be kept on their own grounds and off the streets. Such callousness made Basye indignant. The war was over—"and we're still here." After a time, she started dating a soldier back from the South Pacific. "I got busy after the war," she recalled, "getting married and having my four children. That's what you were supposed to do. And getting your house in suburbia."

Yet as Basye and Black soon discovered, the return to "normal" life was filled with uncertainties. The first truly global war had left a large part of Europe in ruins and the old balance of power shattered. The dramatic events occurring month after month during 1945 and 1946 made it clear that whatever new world order emerged, the United States would have a central role in building it. Isolation

Cold War America

1945–1954

preview • The roots of the cold war lay both in Stalin's aggressive posture toward Eastern Europe and in the mutual suspicions of the Americans and the Soviets toward each other's newfound power. President Truman evolved a policy of containment designed to hedge in the U.S.S.R., but even so, the cold war turned hot in Korea. At home an anticommunist crusade against suspected subversives subsided only after its reckless leader, Senator Joseph McCarthy, was censured.

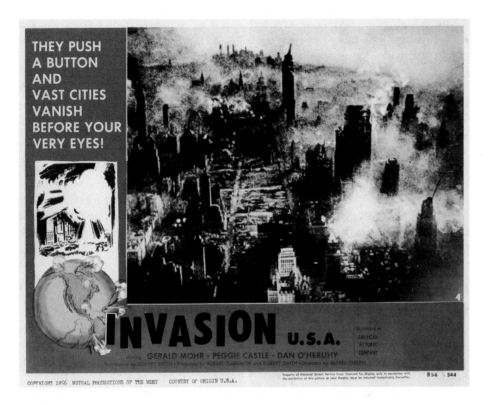

THEY PUSH
A BUTTON
AND
VAST CITIES
VANISH
BEFORE YOUR
VERY EYES!

INVASION U.S.A.

GERALD MOHR · PEGGIE CASTLE · DAN O'HERLIHY

With the rise of a cold war between the United States and the Soviet Union, the fears of an atomic war that might leave the world in ashes became a part of everyday life—and of popular culture. This poster advertising *Invasion U.S.A.*, a film first released in 1953, conjured up a New York City in ruins. Hollywood studios made a number of such low-budget movies that reflected American fears of the Communist menace.

seemed neither practical nor desirable in an era in which the power of the Soviet Union and communism seemed on the rise. To blunt that threat the United States converted not so much to peace as to a "cold war" against its former Soviet ally.

This undeclared war came to affect almost every aspect of American life. Abroad, it justified a far wider military and economic role for the United States in areas like the Middle East and the Pacific Rim nations of Asia, from Korea to Indochina. At home it sent politicians scurrying across the land in a search for Communist spies and "subversives." The Red hunt led from the State Department to the movie studios of Hollywood and even into college classrooms. Preparing for war in times of peace dramatically increased the role of the military-industrial-university complex formed during World War II.

Effects of the cold war

Like the return to "normalcy" after the First World War, the new postwar era was notable for what was *not* normal about it. In a time of peace, a cold war produced unprecedented military budgets, awesomely destructive weapons systems, and continued international tension. A nation that had traditionally followed an isolationist foreign policy now possessed military forces deployed across the globe. A people who had once kept government intrusion into the economy at a minimum now voted to maintain programs that ensured an active federal role. That economy produced prosperity beyond anything Americans had known before.

World War II devastated lands and people almost everywhere outside the

The Rise of the Cold War

Western Hemisphere. Once the war ended the world struggled to rebuild. Power that had once been centered in Europe shifted to nations on its periphery. In place of Germany, France, and England, the United States and the Soviet Union emerged

as the world's two reigning superpowers—and as enemies. Their rivalry was not altogether an equal one. The United States ended the war with a booming economy, a massive military establishment, and the atomic bomb. In contrast, much of the Soviet Union lay in ruins.

Americans fear Soviet intentions

But the defeat of Germany and Japan left no power in Europe or Asia to block the still formidable Soviet army. And many Americans feared that desperate, war-weary peoples would find the appeal of communism irresistible. If Stalin intended to extend the Soviet Union's dominion, only the United States had the economic and military might to block him. Events in the critical years of 1945 and 1946 persuaded most Americans that Stalin did have such a plan. The Truman administration concluded that "the USSR has engaged the United States in a struggle for power, or 'cold war,' in which our national security is at stake and from which we cannot withdraw short of national suicide." What had happened that led Western leaders to such a dire view of their former Soviet allies? How did the breach between the two nations become irreparable?

Cracks in the Alliance

When Truman entered the White House, he lacked Roosevelt's easy confidence that he could manage "Uncle Joe" Stalin. The new president approached the Soviets with a good deal more suspicion. "Stalin is an SOB, but of course he thinks I'm one, too," Truman commented after their meeting at Potsdam in July 1945. Roosevelt had hoped to strike a balance between the idealism of Wilsonian internationalism and the more practical reality that the major powers would continue to guarantee their own security. Spheres of influence would inevitably continue to exist. What was not clear was just how far each sphere would extend. That uncertainty contained the seeds of conflict. Behind all the diplomatic bowing and bluffing, what were the Soviets' real intentions? Their demand that Poland's borders be adjusted was easy to understand. The new boundaries there would strengthen Soviet national security.

What were Soviet ambitions?

Stalin had also asked that Russia join Turkey in assuming joint control of the Dardanelles, the narrow straits linking Soviet ports on the Black Sea with the Mediterranean (see the map, page 919). During the war, both Roosevelt and Churchill had been willing to consider such a change, especially because Turkey had leaned toward the Axis. In the uncertain postwar atmosphere, Stalin's intentions seemed less acceptable. The Russian dictator had also suggested that the Soviet Union become trustee of Libya, Italy's former African colony. As one British diplomat at Potsdam aptly put it, the great debate was "whether Russia [is] peaceful and wants to join the Western Club but is suspicious of us, or whether she is out to dominate the world and is hoodwinking us." Truman and his advisers, like the diplomat, tended to opt for the same answer: "It always seems safer to go on the worse assumption."

American suspicions were not eased when they looked to Greece, where local Communists led the fighting to overturn the traditional monarchy. And in November 1945 Soviet forces occupying northern Iran lent support to rebels seeking to break away from the Iranian government. Asia, too, seemed a target for Communist ambitions. Russian occupation forces in Manchuria were turning over captured Japanese arms to the Chinese Communist forces of Mao Zedong. Russian troops controlled the northern half of Korea. In Vietnam leftist nationalists were fighting against the return of colonial rule. To deal with this combination of menace and disorder Harry Truman and his advisers sought to frame a policy.

The View from West and East

Roots of the cold war

While postwar events heightened American suspicions of the Soviets, that mistrust had deeper roots. An ideological gulf had long separated the two nations. After the October Revolution of 1917, most Americans viewed Lenin's Bolshevik revolutionaries with a mixture of fear, suspicion, and loathing. In their grasp for power the Communists had often used violence, terror, and crime to achieve their ends. As Marxists they rejected both religion and the notion of private property, two institutions central to the American dream. Stalin's brutal purges during the late 1930s created a horrifying image of the Soviet Union as a totalitarian state ruled by terror. Then in 1939 Stalin had signed a cynical nonaggression pact with Germany, freeing him to divide Poland with Germany and make war on his Finnish neighbors. Would the defeat of Germany and Japan free the Soviet dictator to renew his expansion? If it did, how would the Western powers react?

Joseph Stalin

The events leading to World War II provided one lesson in what a policy of "appeasement" could mean. When Neville Chamberlain attempted to satisfy Hitler's demands in 1938, it only emboldened the Nazis to expand further. After the war, Secretary of the Navy James Forrestal applied the Munich analogy to the new situation in Europe. Giving in to Russian claims would only seem like an attempt "to buy their understanding and sympathy." As Forrestal saw it, "We tried that once with Hitler. . . . There are no returns on appeasement." To many of Truman's advisers, the Soviet dictator seemed to be every bit as much bent on conquest as Hitler had been.

Munich analogy

Toward Containment

The disagreements arising out of the conflicting Soviet and American points of view came to a head in the first months of 1946. For his part, Stalin announced in February that the Soviet Union would take unilateral steps to preserve its national security. In a world dominated by capitalism, he warned, future wars were inevitable. The Russian people had to ensure against "any eventuality" by undertaking a new five-year plan for economic development.

Some Americans thought Stalin was merely rallying Russian support for his domestic programs. Others saw their worst fears confirmed. *Time* magazine, an early voice for a "get tough" policy, called Stalin's speech "the most warlike pronouncement uttered by any top-rank statesman since V-J day." "I'm tired of babying the Soviets," remarked the president, who in any case seldom wore kid gloves. Even Truman's mother passed along a message: "Tell Harry to be good, be honest, and behave himself, but I think it is now time for him to get tough with someone." In March Winston Churchill warned that the Soviets had dropped an "Iron Curtain" between their satellite nations and the free world.

Iron Curtain

As policy makers groped for an effective way to deal with these developments, the State Department received a diplomatic cable, extraordinary for both its length (8000 words) and its impact in Washington. The author was George Kennan, chargé d'affaires in Moscow and long a student of Soviet conduct. Kennan argued that Russian leaders, including Stalin, were so paranoid that it was impossible to reach any useful accommodations with them. This temperament could best be explained by "the traditional and instinctive Russian sense of insecurity." That insecurity, when combined with Marxist ideology that viewed capitalism as evil, created a potent force for expansion. Soviet power, Kennan explained, "moves inexorably along a prescribed path, like a toy automobile wound up and headed in a given direction, stopping only when it meets some unanswerable force."

George Kennan defines containment

The response Kennan recommended was "containment." The United States must apply "unalterable counterforce at every point where [the Soviets] show signs of encroaching upon the interests of a peaceful and stable world." The idea of containment was not particularly novel, but Kennan's historical analysis provided leaders in Washington with a framework for analyzing Soviet behavior. It also laid out a plan for responding to that behavior. By applying firm diplomatic, economic, and military counterpressure, the United States could block Russian aggression. Eventually, that firmness might even persuade the Soviets to reform their domestic institutions. Only with free speech, a free press, and democratic elections in the Soviet Union would a reasonable accommodation between East and West be possible. Navy Secretary Forrestal was so impressed with Kennan's "long telegram," as it came to be known, that he sent copies to high officials in Washington as well as to American diplomats abroad. Truman wholeheartedly adopted the doctrine of containment.

The Truman Doctrine

At first it appeared that Iran, lying along the Soviet Union's southern border, would provide the first test for containment. An independent Iran seemed crucial in protecting rich fields of petroleum in the Persian Gulf region. In 1943 an oil mission sent to the area had reported that vast Middle Eastern oil fields would soon displace those in the United States as the center of world production. American oil companies had already taken a major position in the region alongside British fields established earlier in the century. During World War II the United States had adopted a far more active role in the affairs of Iran, Turkey, Saudi Arabia, and other Middle Eastern states.

The Iranian crisis

At war's end, Stalin failed to respect his treaty obligation to withdraw Russian troops from Iran. The presence of those troops might force Iran to grant economic and political concessions. In March 1946 Secretary of State James Byrnes went to the United Nations, determined to force a showdown over continued Soviet occupation of northern Iran. But before he could extract his pound of Russian flesh, the Soviets reached an agreement with Iran to withdraw.

Aid to Greece and Turkey

The face-off in Iran only intensified American suspicions. In Europe severe winter storms and a depressed postwar economy threatened to encourage domestic Communist movements. A turning point in the cold war came in early 1947, when Great Britain announced that it could no longer support the governments of Greece and Turkey. Without British aid, the Communists seemed destined to win critical victories. Truman decided that the United States should provide $400 million in military and economic aid. He went before Congress in March, determined to "scare hell out of the country." The world was now divided into two hostile camps, the president warned. To preserve the American way of life, the United States must now step forward and help "free people" threatened by "totalitarian regimes." This rationale for aid to Greece and Turkey soon became known as the Truman Doctrine.

Critics pointed out that the president had placed no limits on the American commitment. His was a proposal not simply to contain Communists in Greece and Turkey but to resist Soviet expansion everywhere. Robert Taft, once a leader of congressional isolationists, thought it was a mistake to talk about a bipolar world divided between Communist and anti-Communist camps. Congress, however, supported the new cold war crusade. It voted overwhelmingly to grant aid to Greece and Turkey.

As American fears of Soviet intentions increased, journalists often described communism as though it were a disease, an inhuman force, or a savage predator. In April 1946, *Time* magazine, a particularly outspoken source of anti-Communist rhetoric, portrayed the spread of "infection" throughout Europe and Asia as the "Red Menace."

The Truman Doctrine marked a new level of American commitment to a cold war. Just what responsibility the Soviets had for unrest in Greece and Turkey remained unclear. But Truman had linked communism with rebel movements all around the globe. That committed Americans to a relatively open-ended struggle. In the battle between communism and freedom, the president gained expanded powers to act when unrest threatened. Occasionally Congress would regret giving the executive branch so much power, but by 1947 anticommunism had become the dominant theme in American policy, both foreign and domestic.

The Marshall Plan

For all its importance, the Truman Doctrine did not address the area of primary concern to Washington, Western Europe. Across Europe desperate people scrounged for food and coal to heat their homes. Streets stood dark at night. National treasuries had neither capital nor credit needed to reopen darkened factories. American diplomats warned that without aid to revive the European economy, Communists would seize power in Germany, Italy, and France.

In June 1947 Secretary of State George C. Marshall stepped before a Harvard commencement audience to announce a recovery plan for Europe. He invited all European nations, East or West, to request assistance to rebuild their economies. Unlike Truman, Marshall did not emphasize the Communist menace. All the same, his massive aid plan was designed to eliminate conditions that produced the discontent Communists often exploited. Humanitarian aid also had its practical benefits. As Europe recovered, so would its ability to buy American goods. The secretary did not rule out Soviet participation, but he gambled that fears of American economic domination would lead the Soviets and their allies to reject his offer.

At first neo-isolationists in Congress argued that the United States could not afford such generosity. But when Communists expelled the non-Communists from Czechoslovakia's government, the cold war seemed to spread. Congress then approved the Marshall Plan, as it became known. And as the secretary anticipated, the Soviets blocked the efforts of Czechoslovakia and Poland to participate. The blame for dividing Europe fell, as Marshall guessed it would, on the Soviet Union, not the United States.

Communism in Czechoslovakia

The Fall of Eastern Europe

The intensive American efforts to stabilize Europe and the eastern Mediterranean provoked Stalin to take countermeasures. Most shocking to the Western nations were his steps to consolidate Soviet political and military domination over Eastern Europe. In 1947 he moved against Hungary, run since 1945 by a moderate government chosen under relatively free elections. Soviet forces imposed a Communist regime dependent on Moscow. In February 1948 Communists toppled the duly elected government of Czechoslovakia. Shortly after, news came that the popular Czech foreign minister, Jan Masaryk, had fallen to his death from a small bathroom window. Suicide was the official explanation, but many suspected murder. In response to the Marshall Plan, the Soviet foreign ministry initiated a series of trade agreements tightly linking the Soviet and Eastern European economies. It also established the Cominform, or Communist Information Bureau, to assert greater political control over foreign Communist parties.

Berlin airlift

The spring of 1948 brought another clash between the Soviets and their former allies, this time over Germany. There, the United States, Great Britain, and France decided to transform their occupation zones into an independent West German state. The Western-controlled sectors of Berlin, however, lay over 100 miles to the east, well within the Soviet zone. On June 24 the Soviets reacted by blockading land access to Berlin. Truman did not hesitate to respond. "We are going to stay, period." But he did say no when General Lucius Clay proposed to shoot his way through the blockade. Instead, the United States began a massive airlift of supplies that lasted almost a year. In May 1949 Stalin lifted the blockade, conceding that he could not prevent the creation of West Germany.

NATO formed

Stalin's aggressive actions accelerated the American effort to use military means to contain Soviet ambitions. By 1949 the United States and Canada had joined with Britain, France, Belgium, the Netherlands, and Luxembourg to establish the North Atlantic Treaty Organization (NATO) as a mutual defense pact. For the first time since George Washington had warned against the practice in his Farewell Address of 1793, the United States during peacetime entered into entangling alliances with European nations.

Israel recognized

Truman's firm handling of the Berlin crisis won him applause from both Democrats and Republicans. They were equally enthusiastic about another bold presidential action. Minutes after the Israelis announced their independence in May 1948, Truman recognized the new state of Israel. He had previously supported the immigration of Jews into Palestine despite the opposition of oil-rich Arab states and diplomats in the State Department. The president sympathized with Jewish aspirations for a homeland. He also faced a tough campaign in 1948 in which Jewish votes would be critical. As British prime minister Clement Attlee observed, "There's no Arab vote in America, but there's a heavy Jewish vote and the Americans are always having elections."

The Atomic Shield versus the Iron Curtain

The Berlin crisis forced Truman to consider the possibility of war. If it came, would atomic weapons again be used? That dilemma raised two other difficult questions. Should the decision to use atomic weapons rest in civilian or military hands? And was it possible to find a way to ease the atomic threat by creating an international system to control nuclear power?

The Atomic Energy Commission

On the question of civilian or military control of the bomb, Truman's response was firm. He was not going to have "some dashing lieutenant colonel decide when would be the proper time to drop one." In 1946 Congress seemed to have decided the issue in Truman's favor when it passed the McMahon Act. This bill established the Atomic Energy Commission (AEC), with control of all

Cold War Europe By 1956 the postwar occupation of Europe had hardened into rigid cold war boundaries. The United States reacted to the presence of Soviet conventional forces in Eastern Europe by rearming West Germany and creating the NATO alliance (1949) for the defense of nations from the North Atlantic through the Mediterranean basin. The U.S.S.R. formed a counteralliance under the Warsaw Pact (1955). Although Bonn became the de facto capital of West Germany, Berlin remained the official capital and into the 1960s the focus of the most severe cold war tensions.

fissionable materials for both peacetime and military applications. The AEC was a civilian, not a military, agency.

But civilian control was not as complete as Truman had demanded. The wartime head of the Manhattan Project, General Leslie Groves, had been working behind the scenes to give the military a decisive voice in atomic policy. During debate over the bill, Groves had leaked information about a Canadian atomic spy ring delivering secrets to the Soviet Union. That news spread doubts that scientists and civilians could be trusted with key secrets. Thus Groves persuaded Congress to allow the military to review many civilian decisions and even severely limit their actions.

Baruch plan

The idea of international control of atomic energy also fell victim to cold war fears. Originally, a high-level government committee proposed to Truman that the mining and use of the world's atomic raw materials be supervised by an agency of the United Nations. The committee argued that in the long run the United States would be more secure under a system of international control than relying on its temporary nuclear monopoly. But Truman chose Bernard Baruch, a staunch cold warrior, to draw up the recommendations to the United Nations in June 1946. Baruch's proposals ensured that the United States would dominate any international atomic agency. The Soviets countered with a plan calling for destruction of all nuclear bombs and a ban on their use. But Baruch had no intention of bargaining. It was either his plan or nothing, he announced. And so it was nothing. The Truman administration never seriously considered giving up the American nuclear monopoly. Stalin, for his part, gave top priority to the Soviet atomic bomb program. Failure at the United Nations thus promoted an arms race, not nuclear supremacy.

Atomic Deterrence

Ironically, because so much secrecy surrounded the bomb, many military planners knew little about it. Even Truman had no idea in 1946 how many bombs the United States actually possessed. (For the two years after Hiroshima, it was never more than two.) Military planners, however, soon found themselves relying more and more on atomic weapons. The Soviet army had at its command over 260 divisions. In contrast, the United States had reduced its forces by 1947 to little more than a single division. As the cold war heated up, American military planners were forced to adopt a nuclear strategy in face of the overwhelming superiority of Soviet forces. They would deter any Soviet attack by setting in place a devastating atomic counterattack.

At first, this strategy of nuclear deterrence was little more than a doomsday scenario to incinerate vast areas of the Soviet Union. A 1946 war plan, "Pincher," proposed obliterating 20 Soviet cities if the Soviets attacked Western Europe. By 1948 the war plan "Fleetwood" had raised the tally of cities to 77, with eight bombs aimed for Moscow, seven for Leningrad. Not until "Dropshot," the following year, did planners correct a major flaw in their strategy. If Moscow and Leningrad disappeared, who would be left to surrender? Dropshot recommended sparing those two cities until the second week.

By 1949, then, the cold war framed American foreign policy. The Joint Chiefs of Staff had committed themselves to a policy of nuclear deterrence. Western Europe was on its way to economic recovery, thanks to the Marshall Plan. Soviet pressure on Iran, Greece, and Turkey had abated. Many Americans had hopes that the United States might soon defeat communism.

Yet success brought little comfort. The Soviet Union was not simply a major power seeking to protect its interests and expand where opportunity permitted. In

The explosion of atomic bombs was not the only source of destruction. Scientists began to understand that radioactive fallout was a grave danger as well.

the eyes of many Americans, the Soviets were determined, if they could, to overthrow the United States from either without or within. This war was being fought not only around the globe but right in America, by unseen agents using subversive means. In this way, the cold war mentality soon came to shape the lives of Americans at home much as it did American policy abroad.

Postwar Prosperity

At war's end, many business leaders feared that a sudden drop in government purchases would bring back the hard times of the 1930s. Once war production ended, wartime boom towns might become ghost towns. Hard times would offer fertile ground for subversives, like the Communists, who fed on discontent. But the hard times never came. Instead, Americans entered into the longest period of prosperity in the nation's history, lasting until the 1970s. Even the fear of communism could not dampen the simple joys of getting and spending.

Two forces drove the postwar economic boom. One was unbridled consumer and business spending that followed 16 years of depression and war. High war wages had piled up in savings accounts and war bonds. Eager consumers set off to find the new cars, appliances, and foods unavailable during the war. Despite a sharp drop in government spending (from $83 billion in 1945 to only $31 billion in 1946), the gross national product fell less than 1 percent and employment actually increased. Consumers had taken up the slack.

Government expenditures at the local, state, and federal levels provided another boost to prosperity. The three major growth industries in the decades after World War II were health care, education, and government programs. Each of these was spurred by public spending. Equally important, the federal government poured millions of dollars into the military-industrial sector. The defense budget, which fell to $9 billion in 1947, reached $50 billion by the time Truman left office. Over the longer term, these factors promoting economic growth became clearer. In 1946, though, the road from war to peace seemed much more uncertain, especially for Americans at the margins of the economy.

Sources of prosperity

Postwar Adjustments

With millions of veterans looking for peacetime jobs, workers on the home front, especially women and minorities, found themselves out of work. Cultural attitudes added to the pressure on these groups to resume more traditional roles. War employment had given many women their first taste of economic independence. As peace came, almost 75 percent of the working women in one survey indicated that they hoped to continue their jobs. But as the troops came home, male social scientists stressed how important it was for women to accept "more than the wife's usual responsibility for her marriage" and offer "lavish—and undemanding—affection" on returning GIs. One marriage counselor urged women to let their husbands know "you are tired of living alone, that you want him now to take charge."

For minorities, the end of the war brought the return of an old labor practice, "last hired, first fired." At the height of the war over 200,000 African Americans and Hispanics had found jobs in shipbuilding. By 1946 that number had dwindled to fewer than 10,000. The influx of Mexican laborers under the bracero program temporarily halted. In the South, where the large majority of black Americans lived, wartime labor shortages had become surpluses, leaving few jobs available.

Minority workers

Having lived through twelve years of depression, Americans placed jobs at the top of their postwar domestic agenda. The Employment Act of 1946 shifted responsibility for a full-employment economy from the private sector to the federal government.

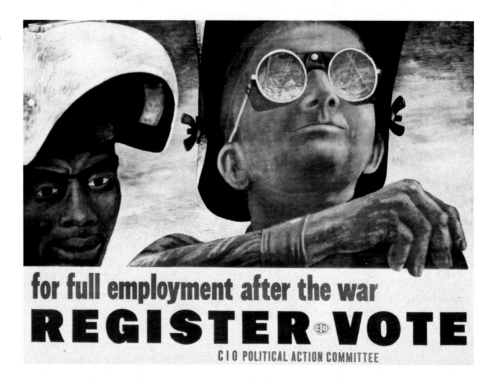

for full employment after the war
REGISTER·VOTE
CIO POLITICAL ACTION COMMITTEE

At the same time, many Hispanic and black veterans who had fought for their country during the war resented returning to a deeply segregated society. Such GIs "have acquired a new courage, have become more vocal in protesting the restrictions and inequalities with which they are confronted," noted one white Texan. When a funeral director in Three Rivers, Texas, refused to open its segregated cemetery for the burial of Felix Longoria, a Mexican American soldier killed in battle, his supporters organized. Led by Dr. Hector Garcia, a former army medical officer, the American G.I. Forum was founded in 1948 to campaign for civil rights. Longoria was finally buried in Arlington National Cemetery after the G.I. Forum convinced Congressman Lyndon Baines Johnson to intervene.

American G.I. Forum

Black veterans had a similar impact on the civil rights movement. Angered by violence, frustrated by the slow pace of desegregation, they breathed new energy into civil rights organizations like the NAACP and CORE (the Congress of Racial Equality). Voting rights was one of the issues they pushed. Registration drives in the South had the greatest success in urban centers like Atlanta. Other black leaders pressed for improved education. In rural Virginia, for example, a young Howard University lawyer, Spottswood Robinson, litigated cases for the NAACP to force improvement in segregated all-black schools. In one county Robinson and the NAACP even won equal pay for black and white teachers.

Black veterans and civil rights

Out in the countryside, however, segregationists used economic intimidation, violence, and even murder to preserve the Jim Crow system. White citizens in rural Georgia lynched several black veterans who had shown the determination to vote. Such instances disturbed President Truman, who saw civil rights as a key ingredient in his reform agenda. The president was especially disturbed when he learned that police in South Carolina had gouged out the eyes of a recently discharged black veteran. Truman responded in December 1946 by appointing a Committee on Civil Rights. A year later it published its report, *To Secure These Rights*.

To Secure These Rights

In San Antonio, Texas, Mexican American veterans helped form the Liga Pro Defensa Escolar, or School Improvement League. The huge crowd at this 1948 meeting demonstrated the interest among Hispanic Americans in tearing down the Jim Crow system of school segregation.

Discovering inequities for minorities, the committee exposed a racial caste system that denied African Americans employment opportunities, equal education, voting rights, and decent housing. But every time Truman appealed to Congress to implement the committee's recommendations, southern senators threatened to filibuster. That opposition forced the president to resort to executive authority to achieve even modest results. In his most direct attack on segregation, he issued an executive order in July 1948 banning discrimination in the armed forces. Segregationists predicted disaster, but experience soon demonstrated that integrated units fought well and exhibited minimal racial tension.

Several Supreme Court decisions gave added weight to Truman's civil rights initiatives. In cases that indicated a growing willingness to reconsider the doctrine that black facilities could be "separate but equal" (*Plessy v. Ferguson,* 1896), the Court struck down several state education laws clearly designed to create separate but inferior facilities.

For organized labor, reconversion brought an abrupt drop in hours worked and overtime paid. As wages declined and inflation ate into paychecks, strikes spread. Autoworkers walked off the job in the fall of 1945; steelworkers, in January 1946; miners, in April. In 1946 some 5 million workers struck, a rate triple that of any previous year. Antiunion sentiment soared. The crisis peaked in May 1946 with a national rail strike, which temporarily paralyzed the nation's transportation network. An angry President Truman asked, "What decent American would pull a rail strike at a time like this?"

Organized labor

At first, Truman threatened to seize the railroads and then requested from Congress the power to draft striking workers into the military. The strike was settled before the threat was carried out, but few people, whether conservative or liberal,

Daily Lives

POPULAR ENTERTAINMENT

*Jackie Robinson
Integrates Baseball*

After World War II, Branch Rickey of the Brooklyn Dodgers was determined to break the color line in baseball. For years he had wanted to give black players the opportunity to play in the majors. Equally to the point, he was convinced that this action would improve his team. "The greatest untapped reservoir of raw material in the history of the game is the black race," he explained, adding, "The Negroes will make us winners for years to come."

In the early years of professional baseball, African Americans had played on several major league teams. In 1887, however, as Jim Crow laws spread across the South, the threat of a boycott by some white players caused team owners to adopt an unwritten rule barring black players. That ban stood for 60 years. Even the most talented black ballplayers could only barnstorm at unofficial exhibitions or play in the Negro League.

World War II created a new climate. The hypocrisy of fighting racism abroad while promoting it at home was becoming harder for team owners to ignore. "If a black boy can make it on Okinawa and Guadalcanal," Commissioner Albert "Happy" Chandler told reporters in April 1945, "hell, he can make it in baseball." Economic factors played a role as well. The African American migration to northern cities during World War II created a new, untapped audience for major league baseball. Growing cold war tensions added another factor. Even a Mississippi newspaper saw blacks in the major leagues as "a good answer to our communist adversaries who say the Negro has no chance in America."

It is not difficult to identify Jackie Robinson in this photo of the Brooklyn Dodgers celebrating a key win in the 1948 pennant race. Though Robinson had made the Dodgers a much better team, full integration of major league sports took many more years.

approved the idea of using the draft to punish political foes. Labor leaders, for their part, became convinced they no longer had a friend at the White House.

Truman under Attack

In September 1945 Harry Truman had boldly claimed his intention to extend the New Deal into the postwar era. He called for legislation to guarantee full employment, subsidized public housing, national health insurance, and a peacetime version of the Fair Employment Practices Commission to fight job discrimination. Instead of promoting his liberal agenda, he found himself fighting a conservative

Rickey recognized the enormous hostility that the first black player would face. He found the ideal prospect in Jackie Robinson, a World War II veteran and a remarkable athlete who had lettered in four sports at UCLA. Rickey asked Robinson to a meeting in 1945, where he laid out his proposition. "I need a man that will take abuse, insults," he warned. Robinson would be carrying "the flag for [his] race."

Robinson was intensely proud of his people and his heritage. He had risked court-martial during the war to fight segregation. "Nobody's going to separate bullets and label them 'for white troops' and 'for colored troops,'" Robinson told a superior officer. But he let Rickey know that he would turn the other cheek. "If you want to take this gamble, I will promise you there will be no incident." Rickey assigned him to Montreal, where he led the Dodgers' farm team to a championship.

When the Dodgers invited Robinson to spring training, several southern-born players circulated a petition stating their opposition to playing with a black man. But manager Leo Durocher bluntly warned them they would be traded if they refused to cooperate. Robinson would make them all rich, Durocher insisted.

On April 15, 1947, Robinson made his debut with the Dodgers at Ebbets Field. A black newspaper, the Boston *Chronicle,* proclaimed, "TRIUMPH OF WHOLE RACE SEEN IN JACKIE'S DEBUT IN MAJOR LEAGUE BALL." Half the fans in the stands that day were African Americans. They cheered wildly at everything Robinson did. Indeed, blacks everywhere instantly adopted the Dodgers as their team, showing up in large numbers when Brooklyn was on the road.

If anything, the abuse heaped on Robinson was worse than Rickey had anticipated. Opposing players shouted vicious racial epithets. Robinson received death threats, his family was harassed, and some hotels barred him from staying with the team. He secretly wore a protective lining inside his hat in case he was beaned (he was hit a record 9 times during the season, 65 times in seven years), and on several occasions he was spiked by opposing players. Through it all, Robinson kept his temper, though not without difficulty. Once when a Cubs player kicked him, Robinson started to swing, then stopped. "I knew I was kind of an experiment," he recalled; ". . . the whole thing was bigger than me."

Robinson spoke with his glove, his bat, and his feet, not his fists. His daring base running, which he learned in the old Negro League, brought a new excitement to the game (he stole home 19 times in his career). In his first year, the Dodgers won the pennant and he was named Rookie of the Year. Two years later he was named the Most Valuable Player in the National League. After he retired in 1957, the skill and dignity he brought to the game earned him a place in baseball's Hall of Fame.

In the wake of his success, other teams added African Americans. Professional basketball and football followed baseball's lead. Still, the pace of integration was slow, and it was not until 1959 that all major league teams had at least one black member. Nevertheless, for once baseball had led the nation rather than following it: the armed services were not integrated until 1948, and the Supreme Court would not strike down segregation until seven years after Robinson first played for the Dodgers. Thanks to the vision of Branch Rickey and the courage of Jackie Robinson, America's pastime had become truly a national game.

backlash. Labor unrest was just one source of his troubles. The increased demand for consumer goods temporarily in short supply triggered a sharp inflation. For two years prices rose as much as 15 percent annually. Consumers blamed the White House for not doing more to manage the economy.

With Truman's political stock falling, conservative Republicans and Democrats blocked the president's attempts to revive and extend the New Deal. All he achieved was a watered-down full-employment bill, which created the Council of Economic Advisers to guide the president's policies. The bill did establish the principle that the government rather than the private sector was responsible for maintaining full employment. As the congressional elections of 1946 neared, Republicans pointed

"What next?" asked cartoonist Jack Lambert. Many Americans agreed that Harry Truman seemed overwhelmed by the burdens of the presidency.

Taft-Hartley Act

The GI Bill

to production shortages, the procession of strikes, the mismanagement of the economy. "To err is Truman," proclaimed the campaign buttons—or, more simply, "Had Enough?" Evidently many voters had. The Republicans gained control of both houses of Congress. Not since 1928 had the Democrats fared so poorly.

Leading the rightward swing was Senator Robert A. Taft of Ohio, son of former president William Howard Taft. Bob Taft not only wanted to halt the spread of the New Deal—he wanted to dismantle it. "We have to get over the corrupting idea we can legislate prosperity, legislate equality, legislate opportunity," he said in dismissing the liberal agenda. Taft especially wished to limit the power of the unions. In 1947 he pushed the Taft-Hartley Act through Congress, over Truman's veto. In the event of a strike, the bill allowed the president to order workers back on the job during a 90-day cooling-off period while collective bargaining continued. It also permitted states to adopt right-to-work laws, which banned the closed shop by eliminating union membership as a prerequisite for many jobs. Union leaders criticized the new law as a slave-labor act but discovered they could live with it, though it did hurt union efforts to organize, especially in the South.

A Welfare Program for GIs

Despite Republican gains, most Americans did not repudiate the New Deal's major accomplishments: Social Security, minimum wages, a more active role for government in reducing unemployment. The administration maintained its commitment to setting a minimum wage, raising it again in 1950, from 45 to 75 cents. Social Security coverage was broadened to cover an additional 10 million workers. Furthermore, a growing list of welfare programs benefited not only the poor but veterans, middle-income families, the elderly, and students. The most striking of these was the GI Bill of 1944, designed to reward soldiers for their service during the war.

For veterans, the "GI Bill of Rights" created unparalleled opportunity. Those with more than two years of service received all tuition and fees plus living expenses for three years of college education. By 1948 the government was paying the college costs of almost 50 percent of all male students as more than 2 million veterans took advantage of the GI Bill. Increased educational levels encouraged a shift from blue- to white-collar work and self-employment. Although the number of jobs in areas such as mining and manufacturing increased little, if at all, work in areas such as financial services, teaching, state and local governments, construction, and retailing all grew rapidly. Veterans also received low-interest loans to start businesses or farms of their own and to buy homes. By the 1950s the Veterans Administration, in charge of the program, was funding the purchase of some 20 percent of all new houses.

The GI Bill accelerated trends that would transform American society into a prosperous, heavily middle-class suburban nation. It also contributed to the economic advantages that white males held over minorities and females. Few women received benefits under the bill. Many lost their jobs or seniority to returning veterans. African Americans and Hispanics, even those eligible for veterans' benefits, were hampered by Jim Crow restrictions in segregated universities and in jobs in both the public and private sectors. The Federal Housing Administration even helped draw up "model" restrictive housing covenants. In order to "retain stability," neighborhoods were allowed to use the covenants to segregate according to "social and racial classes."

The Election of 1948

With his domestic program blocked, Harry Truman faced almost certain defeat in the election of 1948. The New Deal coalition that Franklin Roosevelt had held together for so long seemed to be coming apart. On the left Truman was challenged by Henry Wallace, who had been a capable secretary of agriculture and vice president under Roosevelt, then secretary of commerce under Truman. Wallace wanted to pursue New Deal reforms even more vigorously than Truman did, and he continually voiced his sympathy for the Soviet Union. Disaffected liberals bolted the Democratic party to support Wallace on a third-party Progressive ticket.

Henry Wallace and the progressives

Within the southern conservative wing of the party, archsegregationists resented Truman's moderate civil rights proposals for a voting rights bill and an antilynching law. When the liberal wing of the party passed a civil rights plank as part of the Democratic platform, delegates from several Deep South states stalked out of the convention. They banded together to create the States' Rights or "Dixiecrat" party, with J. Strom Thurmond, the segregationist governor of South Carolina, as their candidate.

Dixiecrats

With the Democrats divided, Republicans smelled victory. They sought to control the political center by rejecting the conservative Taft in favor of the more moderate former New York governor Thomas Dewey. Dewey proved so aloof that he inspired scant enthusiasm. "You have to know Dewey well to really dislike him," quipped one Taft supporter. Such shortcomings aside, it seemed clear to most observers that Dewey would walk away with the race. Pollster Elmo Roper stopped canvassing the voters two months before the election.

Truman, however, did not roll over and play dead. He launched a stinging attack against the "reactionaries" in Congress: that "bunch of old mossbacks . . . gluttons of privilege . . . all set to do a hatchet job on the New Deal." From the rear platform of his campaign train, he made almost 400 speeches in eight weeks. Over and over he hammered away at the "do-nothing" 80th Congress, which, he told farmers, "had stuck a pitchfork" in their backs. Still, on election day oddsmakers favored Dewey by as much as 20 to 1. Hours before the polls closed, the archconservative Chicago *Tribune* happily headlined "Dewey Defeats Truman." But the experts were wrong. Not only did the voters return Truman by over 2 million popular votes, but they also gave the Democrats commanding majorities in the House and Senate.

Truman fights back

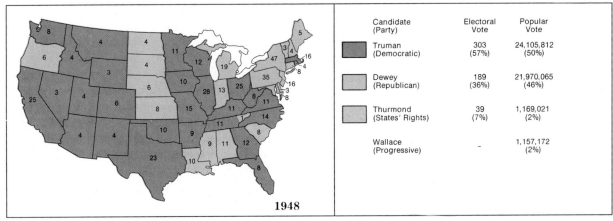

Candidate (Party)	Electoral Vote	Popular Vote
Truman (Democratic)	303 (57%)	24,105,812 (50%)
Dewey (Republican)	189 (36%)	21,970,065 (46%)
Thurmond (States' Rights)	39 (7%)	1,169,021 (2%)
Wallace (Progressive)	–	1,157,172 (2%)

1948

Election of 1948

The defection of the liberal and conservative extremes had allowed Truman to hold the New Deal coalition together after all. Jews grateful for his stand on Israel, Catholics loyal to the Democratic party, and ethnics all supported him. He had been the first major presidential candidate to campaign in Harlem. Farmers hurt by falling prices deserted the Republicans. An easing of inflation had reminded middle-income Americans that they had benefited significantly under Democratic leadership. "I have a new car and am much better off than my parents were. Why change?" one suburban voter remarked.

The Fair Deal

As he began his new term, Harry Truman expressed his conviction that all Americans were entitled to a "Fair Deal" from their government. His agenda called for a vigorous revival of New Deal programs such as national health insurance and regional TVA-style projects. Echoing an old Populist idea, Truman hoped to keep his working coalition together by forging stronger links between farmers and labor.

As before, a conservative coalition of Democrats and Republicans in Congress blocked any significant new initiatives. They voted down plans for a St. Lawrence Seaway in the Northeast, rejected national health insurance, and refused to approve federal aid to education. Furthermore, Truman could not forge a working coalition between farmers and labor. The farm bloc would not support labor in its attempts to repeal the Taft-Hartley Act, nor would labor vote to help pass farm price supports designed to encourage family farms at the expense of larger agribusinesses. On the domestic front Truman remained largely the conservator of Franklin Roosevelt's legacy.

The Cold War at Home

Bob Raymondi, a mobster serving a prison term in the late 1940s, was no stranger to extortion, racketeering, or gangland killings. In fact, he was so feared that he dominated the inmate population at Dannemora Prison. Raymondi began to make the acquaintance of a group of Communists who had been jailed for advocating the overthrow of the government. He enjoyed talking with people who had some education. When Raymondi's sister learned about his new friends, she was frantic. "My God, Bob," she told him. "You'll get into trouble."

Was something amiss? Most Americans judged it riskier to associate with Communists than with hardened criminals. Out of a population of 150 million, the Communist party in 1950 could claim a membership of only 43,000. (More than a few of those were FBI undercover agents.) But worry about Communists Americans did. In part, conscientious citizens were appalled by party members who excused Stalin's violent crimes against his own people. Millions of Russians had been executed or sent to Siberian labor camps; under those circumstances, most Americans found it outrageous to hear American Communists dismiss civil liberties as "bourgeois."

Conservative anti-Communism

Conservatives were especially outspoken about the Communist menace. Some honestly feared the New Deal as "creeping socialism." The president's advisers, it seemed to them, were either Communist agents or their unwitting dupes. Leftists, they believed, controlled labor unions, Hollywood, and other interest groups sympathetic to the New Deal. Their outrage grew as Stalin extended Soviet control in Eastern Europe and Asia. Many conservatives charged that a conspiracy within

Roosevelt's administration had sold out America to its enemies. More cynical conservatives used Red baiting simply to discredit people and ideas they disliked.

The Shocks of 1949

Truman won in 1948 in large part because of his strong leadership in foreign affairs. In 1949 a series of foreign policy shocks allowed Republicans to seize the anti-Communist issue. In August American scientists reported that rains monitored in the Pacific contained traces of hot nuclear waste. Only one conclusion seemed possible: the Soviet Union possessed its own atom bomb. When Truman announced the news, Congress was debating whether to spend $1.5 billion for military aid to the newly formed NATO alliance. The House stopped debating and voted the bill through, while Truman directed that research into a newer, more powerful fusion, or hydrogen, bomb continue. Senator Arthur Vandenberg, a Republican with wide experience in international affairs, summed up the reaction of many to the end of the American nuclear monopoly: "This is now a different world."

The H-bomb

Then in December came more bad news. The long-embattled Nationalist government of

China falls to Communists

The fall of China to the Communist forces of Mao Zedong was one of two great cold war shocks of 1949. Anti-Communists joined members of the China Lobby in blaming Truman for "losing China."

Chiang Kai-shek had fled mainland China to the offshore island of Formosa (present-day Taiwan). By January Communist troops under Mao Zedong were swarming into Beijing, China's capital city. Chiang's defeat came as no surprise to State Department officials, who had long regarded the Nationalists as hopelessly corrupt and inefficient. Despite major American efforts to save Chiang's regime and stabilize China, poverty and civil unrest spread in the postwar years. In 1947 full-scale civil war broke out, so Mao's triumph was hardly unexpected.

But Republicans, who had up until 1949 supported the president's foreign policy, now broke ranks. For some time, a group of wealthy conservatives and Republican senators had resented the administration's preoccupation with Europe. Time-Life publisher Henry Luce used his magazines to campaign for a greater concern for Asian affairs and especially more aid to defeat Mao Zedong. Luce and his associates, known as the "China Lobby," were supported in part with funds from the Chinese embassy. When Chiang at last collapsed, his American backers charged Democrats with letting the Communists win.

The Hiss case

Worries that subversives had sold out the country were heightened when former State Department official Alger Hiss was brought to trial in 1949 for perjury. Hiss, an adviser to Roosevelt at the Yalta Conference, had been accused by former Communist Whittaker Chambers of passing secrets to the Soviet Union during the 1930s. Though the evidence in the case was far from conclusive, the jury convicted Hiss for lying about his association with Chambers. And in February 1950 the nation was further shocked to learn that a high-ranking British physicist, Klaus Fuchs, had spied for the Russians while working on the Manhattan Project. Here was clear evidence of conspiracy at work.

The Loyalty Crusade

President Truman sought to blunt Republican accusations that he was "soft" on communism. Ten days after proposing the Truman Doctrine in March 1947, the president signed an executive order establishing a Federal Employee Loyalty Program designed to guard against the possible disloyalty of "Reds, phonies, and 'parlor pinks.'" Since the FBI could hardly find time to examine all of the 2 million government employees, the order required supervisors to review and certify the loyalties of those who worked below them, reporting to a system of federal loyalty review boards.

Loyalty Review Board

The system quickly got out of hand. Seth Richardson, the conservative who headed the Loyalty Review Board, brushed the Bill of Rights aside. In his opinion, the government could "discharge any employee for reasons which seem sufficient to the Government, and without extending to such employee any hearing whatsoever." After several years the difficulty of proving that employees were actually disloyal became clear, and Truman allowed the boards to fire those who were "potentially" disloyal or "bad security risks," such as alcoholics, homosexuals, and debtors. Suspect employees, in other words, were assumed guilty until proven innocent. After some 5 million investigations, the program identified a few hundred employees who, though not Communists, had at one time been associated with suspect groups. Rather than calm public fears, the loyalty program gave credibility to the growing Red scare.

HUAC, Hollywood, and Unions

About the same time Truman established the Loyalty Review Board, the House Committee on Un-American Activities (HUAC) began to investigate Communist influence in the film industry. Hollywood, with its wealth, glamour, and highly visible Jewish and foreign celebrities, had long aroused a mixture of attraction and suspicion among traditional Americans. "Large numbers of moving pictures that come out of Hollywood carry the Communist line," charged committee member John Rankin of Mississippi. Indeed, during the Depression some Hollywood figures had developed ties to the Communist party or had become sympathetic to party causes. To generate support for the Allies during the war, Hollywood (with Roosevelt's blessing) produced films with a positive view of the Soviet Union such as *Mission to Moscow* and *Song of Russia*.

HUAC called a parade of movie stars, screenwriters, and producers to sit in the glare of its public hearings. Some witnesses, such as Gary Cooper, Robert Montgomery, and Ronald Reagan, were considered "friendly" because they answered committee questions or supplied names of suspected leftists. Others refused to inform on their colleagues or to answer questions about earlier ties to the Communist party. Eventually 10 uncooperative witnesses, known as the "Hollywood Ten," refused on First Amendment grounds to say whether they were or ever had been Communists. They served prison terms for contempt of Congress.

Hollywood Ten

For all its probing, HUAC never offered convincing evidence that filmmakers were in any way subversive. About the most damning evidence presented was that one eager left-leaning extra, when asked to "whistle something" during his walk-on part, hummed a few bars of the Communist anthem the "Internationale." The investigations did, however, inspire nervous Hollywood producers to turn out films such as *The Iron Curtain* (1948), in which a Russian spy ring in the United States is exposed, and *I Was a Communist for the FBI* (1950). The studios also purged anyone suspected of disloyalty, adopting a blacklist that prevented admitted or accused Communists from finding work. Because no judicial proceedings were involved, victims of false charges, rumors, or spiteful accusations found it nearly impossible to clear their names.

Blacklisting

Suspicion of aliens and immigrants led finally to the passage, over Truman's veto, of the McCarran Act (1950). It required all Communists to register with the attorney general, forbade the entry of anyone who had belonged to a totalitarian organization, and allowed the Justice Department to detain suspect aliens indefinitely during deportation hearings. It was supported overwhelmingly in Congress. That same year a Senate committee began an inquiry designed to root out homosexuals holding government jobs. Even one "sex pervert in a Government agency tends to have a corrosive influence upon his fellow employees," warned the committee. The campaign had effects beyond government offices: the armed forces stepped up their rates of dismissal for sexual orientation, while city police more frequently raided gay bars and social clubs.

McCarran Act

The Ambitions of Senator McCarthy

By 1950 anticommunism had created a climate of fear in which legitimate concerns mixed with irrational hysteria. Joseph R. McCarthy, a Senate nonentity from Wisconsin, saw in that fear an issue with which to rebuild his political fortunes. To an audience in Wheeling, West Virginia, in February 1950 he waved a sheaf of papers in the air and announced that he had a list of 205—or perhaps 81, 57, or "a lot of"—Communists in the State Department. (No one, including the senator, could remember the number, which he continually changed.) In the following months McCarthy leveled charge after charge. He had penetrated the "iron curtain" of the State Department to discover "card-carrying Communists," the "top

The energetic and opportunistic Roy Cohn (left) served as a key strategist in the inquisition that made Senator Joseph McCarthy a figure to fear. He and fellow staffer David Schine (right) helped McCarthy turn a minor Senate subcommittee into a major power center.

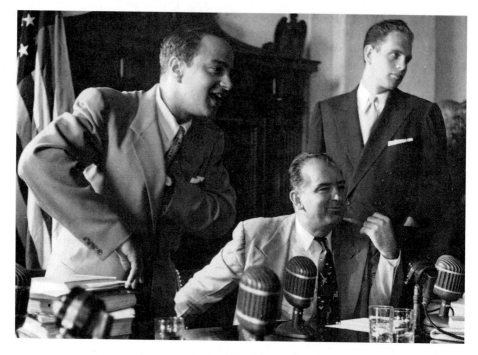

Russian espionage agent" in the United States, "egg-sucking phony liberals," and "Communists and queers" who wrote "perfumed notes."

It seemed not to matter that McCarthy never substantiated his charges. When examined, his lists contained names of people who had left the State Department long before or who had been cleared by the FBI. When forced into a corner, McCarthy simply lied and went on to another accusation. No one seemed beyond reach. In the summer of 1950 a Senate committee headed by Millard F. Tydings of Maryland concluded that McCarthy's charges were "a fraud and a hoax." Such candor among those in government did not last long, as "Jolting Joe" (one of McCarthy's favorite macho nicknames) in 1952 helped defeat Tydings and several other Senate critics.

McCarthy served as a blunt instrument that some conservative Republicans used to damage the Democrats. Without the support of these Republicans, McCarthy would have had little credibility. Many of his accusations came from information secretly (and illegally) funneled to him by FBI director J. Edgar Hoover. But McCarthyism was also the bitter fruit Truman and the Democrats reaped from their own attempts to exploit the anti-Communist mood. McCarthy, more than Truman, had tapped the fears and hatreds of a broad coalition of Catholic leaders, conservatives, and neo-isolationists who harbored suspicion of things foreign, liberal, internationalist, European, or a touch too intellectual. They saw McCarthy and his fellow witch-hunters as the protectors of a vaguely defined but deeply felt spirit of Americanism.

By the time Truman stepped down as president, 32 states had laws requiring teachers to take loyalty oaths, government loyalty boards were asking employees what newspapers they subscribed to or phonograph records they collected, and a library in Indiana had banned *Robin Hood* because the idea of stealing from the rich to give to the poor seemed rather too leftish. As one historian commented, "Opening the valve of anticommunist hysteria was a good deal simpler than closing it."

As the cold war heated up in 1949, the ## From Cold War to Hot War and Back
Truman administration searched for a
more assertive foreign policy—one that went beyond George Kennan's notion of "containment." The new policy was developed by the National Security Council (NSC), an agency created by Congress in 1947 as part of a plan to help the executive branch respond more effectively to cold war crises. The army, navy, and air force were united under a single Department of Defense. All overseas intelligence gathering and espionage activities became the responsibility of the Central Intelligence Agency. To the National Security Council fell the job of advising the president about foreign and military policy. From the beginning, the NSC had lobbied for an active policy not just to contain the Soviets but also to win the cold war. In April 1950 it sent Truman a document, NSC-68, which came to serve as the framework for American policy over the next 20 years.

NSC-68 argued that rather than merely hold the Soviets at bay, the United **NSC-68** States should "strive for victory." To that end NSC-68 called for an immediate increase in defense spending from $13 billion to $50 billion a year, to be paid for with a large tax increase. Most of the funds would go to rebuild conventional forces, but the NSC urged that the hydrogen bomb be developed to offset the Soviet nuclear capacity. At the same time the American people had to be mobilized to make the necessary sacrifices while the United States worked (NSC-68 never explained how) to make "the Russian people our Allies" in undermining their totalitarian government.

Efforts to carry out NSC-68 at first aroused widespread opposition. George Kennan argued that the Soviets had no immediate plans for domination outside the Communist bloc. Thus, NSC-68 was too simplistic and militaristic. Fiscal conservatives, both Democrat and Republican, resisted any proposal for higher taxes. Truman's own secretary of defense, Louis Johnson, warned that the new military budget would bankrupt the country. All such reservations were swept away on June 25, 1950. "Korea came along and saved us," Secretary of State Dean Acheson later remarked.

Police Action

In 1950 Korea was about the last place in the world Americans might have imagined themselves fighting a war. Since World War II the country had been divided along the 38th parallel, the north controlled by the Communist government of Kim Il Sung, the south by the dictatorship of Syngman Rhee. Preoccupied with China and the rebuilding of Japan, the Truman administration's interest had dwindled steadily after the war. When Secretary of State Acheson discussed American policy in Asia before the National Press Club in January 1950, he did not even mention Korea.

On June 24 Harry Truman was enjoying a leisurely break from politics at the **The North Korean** family home in Independence, Missouri. In Korea it was already Sunday morning **invasion** when Acheson called the president. North Korean troops had crossed the 38th parallel, Acheson reported, possibly to fulfill Kim Il Sung's proclaimed intention to "liberate" the South. Soon Acheson confirmed that a full-scale invasion was in progress. The United Nations, meeting in emergency session, had ordered a cease-fire, which the North Koreans were ignoring. With that, Truman flew back to

The Korean War In their opening offensive, North Korean troops almost pushed South Korean and American forces into the sea at Pusan. After MacArthur rallied UN forces, he commanded a successful landing at Inchon behind North Korean lines and then crossed the 38th parallel into North Korea. Red Chinese troops counterattacked, inflicting on U.S. troops one of the most humiliating defeats in American military history. Fighting continued for another two years.

Washington, convinced that Stalin and his Chinese Communist allies had ordered the invasion. Kim, Truman reasoned, would hardly have acted on his own. The threat of a third world war, this one atomic, seemed agonizingly real. Truman and his advisers wanted to respond firmly enough to deter aggression but without provoking a larger war with the Soviet Union or China.

Truman did not hesitate; American troops would fight the North Koreans, though the United States would not declare war. The fighting in Korea would be a "police action" supervised by the United Nations. On June 27 the Security Council passed a U.S. resolution to send United Nations forces to Korea. That move succeeded only because the Soviet delegate, who had veto power, was absent. Six months earlier he had walked out in protest over the council's refusal to seat mainland China. (Indeed, the Soviet absence from the Security Council vote undermines the idea that Stalin, rather than Kim Il Sung, had masterminded the North Korean attack.)

Truman's forceful response won immediate approval across America. Congress quickly voted the huge increase in defense funds needed to carry out the recommendations of NSC-68. American allies were less committed to the action. Though 16 nations contributed to the war effort, the United States provided half of the ground troops, 86 percent of the naval units, and 93 percent of the air force. By the time the UN forces could be marshaled, North Korean forces had pinned the South Koreans within a small defensive perimeter centered on Pusan. Then Douglas MacArthur, commander of the UN forces, launched a daring amphibious attack behind North Korean lines at Inchon, near the western end of the 38th parallel. Fighting eastward, MacArthur's troops threatened to trap the invaders, who fled back to the North.

The Chinese Intervene

MacArthur's success led Truman to a fateful decision. With the South liberated, he gave MacArthur permission to cross the 38th parallel, drive the Communists from the North, and reunite the country under Syngman Rhee. With Senator Joe McCarthy on the attack at home, the 1950 elections nearing, and the McCarran Act just passed, Truman was glad enough for the chance to vanquish the North Koreans. By Thanksgiving American troops had roundly defeated northern forces and were advancing on several fronts toward the frozen Yalu River, the boundary between Korea and China. MacArthur, emboldened by success, promised that the boys would be home by Christmas.

Marines in North Korea wait at a roadblock on December 1, 1950. American forces retreated after the Chinese crossed the Yalu. The harsh weather added to the casualties those forces suffered.

China, however, grew increasingly restive. Throughout the fall offensive, Premier Zhou Enlai warned that his country would not tolerate an American presence on its border. Washington officials did not take the warning seriously. Mao Zedong, they assumed, was a Soviet puppet, and Stalin had declared the Korean conflict to be merely a "civil war" and off-limits. Ignoring the Chinese warnings, MacArthur launched his end-the-war offensive. Not long after, American troops captured a Chinese prisoner—as Secretary of State Acheson recalled, "you began to know at that point something was happening." On November 26 some 400,000 Chinese troops poured across the Yalu, smashing through lightly defended UN lines. At Chosan they trapped 20,000 American and South Korean troops, inflicting one of the worst defeats in American military history. Within three weeks they had driven UN forces back behind the 38th parallel. So total was the rout that Truman wondered publicly about using the atom bomb. That remark sent a frightened British prime minister Clement Attlee flying to Washington to dissuade the president. He readily agreed that the war must remain limited and withdrew his nuclear threat.

Truman versus MacArthur

The military stalemate in Korea brought into the open a simmering feud between MacArthur and Truman. The general had made no secret of his political ambitions or of his differences with Truman over American policy in Asia. He was eager to bomb Chinese and Russian supply bases across the Korean border, to blockade China's coast, and to "unleash" Chiang Kai-shek on mainland China. On March 23 he issued a personal ultimatum to Chinese military commanders demanding total surrender. To his Republican congressional supporters he sent a letter declaring, "We must win. There is no substitute for victory."

To Truman, MacArthur's insubordination threatened the tradition that military policy remained under clear civilian control. Equally alarming, MacArthur's strategy appeared to be an open invitation to another world war. Despite the general's enormous popularity, Truman made plans to discipline him. When General Omar Bradley reported that MacArthur threatened to resign before Truman could act, the irate Truman replied, "The son of a bitch isn't going to resign on me. I want him fired!" Military leaders agreed that MacArthur had to go. On April 11 a stunned nation learned that the celebrated military commander had been relieved of his duties. On his return to the States, cheering crowds gave MacArthur one of the largest ticker-tape parades in New York City's history. Truman's move seemed one of the great political mistakes of his career. Congress gave MacArthur the unprecedented opportunity to address a joint session before a national television audience and the general's most fervent supporters tried to impeach Truman and Acheson.

The Global Implications of the Cold War

Behind the scenes Truman was winning this personal clash. At stake was not simply the issue of whether he or MacArthur would prevail. Rather, the outcome would determine the future direction of American foreign policy. The cold war crisis forced American leaders to think globally. Where in the world did the nation's interests lie? What region was most critical to the future? MacArthur believed that the Pacific basin would "determine the course of history in the next ten thousand years." To avoid being swept aside, the United States should make an all-out effort, not just to contain the Communist onslaught in Korea, but to play a major role throughout Asia. "What I advocate is that we defend every place, and I say that we have the capacity to do it," insisted MacArthur. Many conservative Republicans and groups like the China Lobby shared MacArthur's view. As Senator Robert Taft put it, the United States should pursue "the same policy in the Far East as in Europe."

Truman and his advisers continued to see Europe as the key to American foreign policy. Western Europe in particular, they believed, remained the center of the world's economic and military power. Political scientist Hans Morgenthau argued that "he who controls Europe is well on his way toward controlling the whole world." Further, Eurocentric Americans felt that the cultural differences between the United States and Asia were so great that the battle for Asia could not be won by military might. As theologian Reinhold Niebuhr put it, using American cold war weapons against the ideology of communism would be "like the spears of the knights when gunpowder challenged their reign."

Europe, not Asia, first

Secretary of State Acheson agreed with the Eurocentrists. Korea was to Acheson but a small link in a global "collective security system." The wider war in Asia that MacArthur favored would threaten American interests in Europe because American resources would be stretched too thinly. Or, as General Bradley told Congress, a war in Asia would lead to "the wrong war, at the wrong place, at the wrong time, and with the wrong enemy." In this debate the Eurocentric faction prevailed. Congressional leaders agreed with Truman that the war in Korea should remain limited and that American resources should go to rebuilding Europe's defenses.

Meanwhile, the war in Korea bogged down in stalemate. As peace negotiators argued over how to reunify Korea, the United States suffered another 32,000 casualties in an ugly war of attrition. By March 1952 Truman's popularity had sunk so low that he lost the New Hampshire presidential primary to Senator Estes Kefauver of Tennessee. With that defeat, he announced he would not run for reelection in 1952.

The Election of 1952

The Republican formula for victory in 1952 played on the Truman administration's obvious weaknesses. Republicans could capitalize on the stalemate over Korea, and several of Truman's advisers had been forced to resign for accepting mink coats and large freezers in return for political favors. The economy, however, remained remarkably healthy. Wage and price controls put in place by the administration prevented the sharp inflation that was expected to follow increased wartime spending.

The bigger problem for Republicans lay in choosing a candidate. Once General Dwight Eisenhower formally joined the Republican party, he became the choice of moderates and the northeastern establishment. Party regulars and the conservative wing were heavily committed to Robert Taft, who ran surprisingly well in the party primaries. But Ike was more popular with voters. His backers maneuvered their candidate to a first-ballot nomination. To heal the breach with the Taft delegates, the convention chose staunch anti-Communist senator Richard Nixon as Eisenhower's running mate.

Moderates like "Ike"

With no candidate as popular as Eisenhower, the Democrats drafted Illinois governor Adlai E. Stevenson. Few candidates could match Stevenson's eloquence, but, like Dewey before him, Stevenson lacked the common touch. Republican strategists turned his intelligence into a liability by dismissing him and his intellectual supporters as "eggheads." The GOP's campaign against communism and corruption, led by Nixon, put Stevenson on the defensive. Eisenhower, meanwhile, took the high road above the mudslinging. He promised voters that if elected, he would go to Korea to seek an end to the war.

Nixon's Checkers
speech

Righteous indignation over corruption mired the Republicans in a scandal of their own. Newspapers reported that a group of wealthy Californians had provided Richard Nixon with an $18,000 "slush fund" to help cover personal expenses. With his place on the ticket in peril, Nixon made an impassioned television appeal, portraying himself and his wife, Pat, as ordinary folks. Like other young couples, they had monthly payments to make on a mortgage and a car. Pat had only a sensible "Republican cloth coat," not furs. And yes, his daughter Tricia had received a cocker spaniel puppy named Checkers, but no matter what his enemies might say, his family was going to keep the dog. As soon as Nixon finished, sympathetic viewers deluged GOP headquarters with messages of support. Nixon's survival demonstrated the power of television to influence public opinion.

The election outcome was never much in doubt. Eisenhower's broad smile and confident manner won him more than 55 percent of the vote. "The great problem of America today," Eisenhower had said during the campaign, "is to take that straight road down the middle." Most Americans who voted for him were comforted to think that was just where they were headed.

Eisenhower and Korea

Even before taking office, Eisenhower's first priority was to end the stalemated Korean War. As president-elect, he fulfilled his campaign promise "to go to Korea" and appraise the situation firsthand. Once in office, he renewed negotiations with North Korea but warned that unless the talks made speedy progress, the United States might retaliate "under circumstances of our choosing." The carrot-and-stick approach worked. On July 27, 1953, the Communists and the UN forces signed an armistice ending a "police action" in which 54,000 Americans had died. Korea remained divided, almost as it had been in 1950. Communism had been "contained," but at a high price in human lives.

The Fall of McCarthy

It was less clear, however, whether domestic anticommunism could be contained. Eisenhower boasted that he was a "modern" Republican, distinguishing himself from what he called the more "hidebound" members of the GOP. Their continuing anti-Communist campaigns caused him increasing embarrassment. Senator McCarthy's reckless antics, at first directed at Democrats, began to hit Republican targets as well.

By the summer of 1953 the senator was on a rampage. He dispatched two young staff members, Roy Cohn and David Schine, to investigate the State Department's overseas information agency and the Voice of America radio stations. Behaving more like college pranksters, the two conducted a whirlwind 18-day witch-hunt through Western Europe, condemning government libraries for possessing "subversive" books, including volumes by John Dewey and Foster Rhea Dulles, a conservative historian and cousin of Eisenhower's secretary of state. Some librarians, fearing for their careers, burned a number of books. That action drove President Eisenhower to denounce "book burners," though soon after he reassured McCarthy's supporters that he did not advocate free speech for Communists.

The administration's own behavior contributed to the hysteria on which McCarthy thrived. The president launched a loyalty campaign, which he claimed resulted in 3000 firings and 5000 resignations of government employees. It was a godsend to McCarthyites: What further proof was needed that subversives were lurking in the federal bureaucracy? Furthermore, a well-publicized spy trial had led to the conviction of Ethel and Julius Rosenberg, a couple accused of passing atomic secrets to the Soviets. Although the evidence was not conclusive, the judge sentenced both Rosenbergs to the electric chair, an unusually harsh punishment even in cases of espionage. When asked to commute the death sentence to life imprisonment, Eisenhower refused, and the Rosenbergs were executed in June 1953.

A year later the Atomic Energy Commission turned its investigative eyes on physicist J. Robert Oppenheimer. During World War II it was Oppenheimer's administrative and scientific genius that had led to the development of the atom bomb. Widely respected by his colleagues, he had raised the hackles of many politicians in 1949 when he opposed the construction of a hydrogen bomb. Despite left-wing associations from the 1930s (which army officials had known about), no one had ever accused him of passing on national security information. Nonetheless, the Atomic Energy Commission in effect suggested Oppenheimer was a traitor by barring him from sensitive research.

The case of J. Robert Oppenheimer

Once the Soviet Union developed its own nuclear capability, Americans felt vulnerable to a surprise atomic attack. This advertisement from the *New York Times* in 1954 promised consumers that their valuables could be stored deep in a mountain vault.

In such a climate—where Democrats remained silent for fear of being called leftists and Eisenhower cautiously refused to "get in the gutter with *that* guy"—McCarthy lost all sense of proportion. When the army denied his aide David Schine a commission, McCarthy decided to investigate communism in the army. The new American Broadcasting Company network, eager to fill its afternoon program slots, televised the hearings. For three weeks, the public had an opportunity to see McCarthy badger witnesses and make a mockery of Senate procedures. Soon after, his popularity began to slide and the anti-Communist hysteria ebbed as well. In 1954 the Senate finally moved to censure him. He died three years later, destroyed by alcohol and the habit of throwing so many reckless punches.

McCarthy versus the army

With the Democrats out of the White House for the first time since the Depression and with right-wing McCarthyites in retreat, Eisenhower did indeed seem to be leading the nation on a course "right down the middle." Still, it is worth noting how much that sense of "middle" had changed.

Both the Great Depression and World War II made most Americans realize that the nation's economy was firmly tied to the international order. The crash in 1929, with its worldwide effects, illustrated the closeness of the links. The New Deal demonstrated that Americans were willing to give the federal government power to influence American society in major new ways. And the war led the government to intervene in the economy even more actively.

So when peace came in 1945, it became clear that the "middle road" did not mean a return to the laissez-faire economics of the 1920s or the isolationist politics of the 1930s. "Modern" Republicans supported social welfare programs such as Social Security and granted that the federal government had the power to lower unemployment, control inflation, and manage the economy in a variety of ways. Furthermore, the shift from war to peace demonstrated that it was no longer possible to make global war without making a global peace. Under the new balance of power in the postwar world, the United States and the Soviet Union stood alone as superpowers, with the potential capability to annihilate each other and the rest of the world.

chapter summary

In the postwar period, the cold war between the Soviet Union and the United States affected every aspect of American domestic and foreign policy and overshadowed American life.

- The cold war had roots in American suspicions of Soviet communism dating back to World War I, but Stalin's aggressive posture toward Eastern Europe and the Persian Gulf region raised new fears among American policy makers.

- In response, the Truman administration applied a policy of containment through the Truman Doctrine, the Marshall Plan, and NSC-68.

- The domestic transition from war to peace did not go smoothly because of inflation, labor unrest, and shortages of goods and housing, but the return of prosperity, fueled by consumer and government spending, eased the readjustment.

- Domestic fear of Communist subversion led the Truman administration to devise a government loyalty program and inspired the witch-hunts of Senator Joseph McCarthy.

- The Soviet detonation of an atomic bomb and the fall of China to the Communists, followed one year later by the Korean War, undermined the popularity of Harry Truman and the Democrats, opening the way for Dwight Eisenhower's victory in the 1952 presidential election.

interactive learning

The Primary Source Investigator CD-ROM offers the following materials related to this chapter:

- Interactive maps: **Election of 1948** (M7)

- A collection of primary sources exploring the onset of the cold war period, including the Marshall Plan, the treaty that created NATO, and the charter of the United Nations. Several documents illuminate fear and anxiety at the dawn of the nuclear age: a film clip of an early nuclear blast, students practicing "duck and cover" exercises, and images from the Korean War.

additional reading

On the cold war Daniel Yergin, *Shattered Peace* (2nd ed., 1989), is both readable and balanced, as are Thomas Paterson, *On Every Front* (3rd ed., 1996), and Walter LaFeber, *America, Russia, and the Cold War* (9th ed., 2002). David McCullough, *Truman* (1992), combines the best of good history and popular biography. Alonzo Hamby, *Liberalism and Its Challengers* (1992), and Donald Coy, *The Presidency of Harry S Truman* (1984), are useful on the Fair Deal.

Much of the domestic Red scare was fought out in and over the media. Stephen Whitfield, *The Culture of the Cold War* (1991), and John Diggins, *The Proud Decades* (1988),

both provide good introductions to the tensions between popular and intellectual culture and McCarthyism. James Gilbert, *A Cycle of Outrage: America's Reaction to Juvenile Delinquency in the 1950s* (1986), shows that some critics found other forms of subversion in comic books and movies aimed at teen audiences. The special problems of Hollywood are explored in Robert Sklar, *Movie Made America: A Cultural History of American Movies* (rev. ed., 1994); Nora Sayre, *Running Time: Films of the Cold War* (1982); and Peter Biskind, *Seeing Is Believing: How Hollywood Taught Us to Stop Worrying and Love the Fifties* (1983). Erik Barnouw, *Tube of Plenty: The Evolution of American Television* (1975), argues that the same cold war tensions inhibited television programming. For a most vivid dramatic view of the witch hunt in television, see the 1976 movie *The Front,* starring Woody Allen and Zero Mostel, a blacklist victim. For a fuller list of readings, see the Bibliography at www.mhhe.com/davidsonnation5.

significant events

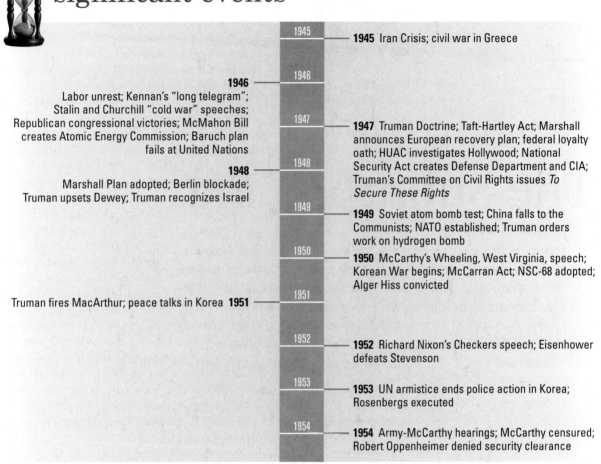

1945 Iran Crisis; civil war in Greece

1946 Labor unrest; Kennan's "long telegram"; Stalin and Churchill "cold war" speeches; Republican congressional victories; McMahon Bill creates Atomic Energy Commission; Baruch plan fails at United Nations

1947 Truman Doctrine; Taft-Hartley Act; Marshall announces European recovery plan; federal loyalty oath; HUAC investigates Hollywood; National Security Act creates Defense Department and CIA; Truman's Committee on Civil Rights issues *To Secure These Rights*

1948 Marshall Plan adopted; Berlin blockade; Truman upsets Dewey; Truman recognizes Israel

1949 Soviet atom bomb test; China falls to the Communists; NATO established; Truman orders work on hydrogen bomb

1950 McCarthy's Wheeling, West Virginia, speech; Korean War begins; McCarran Act; NSC-68 adopted; Alger Hiss convicted

1951 Truman fires MacArthur; peace talks in Korea

1952 Richard Nixon's Checkers speech; Eisenhower defeats Stevenson

1953 UN armistice ends police action in Korea; Rosenbergs executed

1954 Army-McCarthy hearings; McCarthy censured; Robert Oppenheimer denied security clearance

Chapter 28

No company epitomized the corporate culture of the 1950s more than General Motors. GM executives sought to blend in rather than to stand out. They chose their suits in drab colors—dark blue, dark gray, or light gray—to increase their anonymity. Not head car designer Harley Earl. Earl brought a touch of Hollywood into the world of corporate bureaucrats. He had a closet filled with colorful suits. His staff would marvel as he headed off to a board meeting dressed in white linen with a dark blue shirt and *blue suede shoes,* the same shoes that Elvis Presley sang so protectively about.

Mr. Earl—no one who worked for him ever called him Harley—could afford to be a maverick. He created the cars that brought customers into GM showrooms across the country. Before he came to Detroit, engineering sold cars. Advertising stressed mechanical virtues—the steady ride, reliable brakes, or, perhaps, power steering. Earl made style the distinctive feature. Unlike the boxy look other designers favored, an Earl car had a low, sleek look, suggesting motion even when the car stood still. No feature stood out more distinctively than the fins he first put on the 1948 Cadillac. By the

The Suburban Era

1945–1963

preview • The culture of the automobile in many ways defined America at midcentury. Superhighways encouraged newly prosperous Americans to move into suburban homes boasting green lawns and new televisions. The middle-class consensus of an American dream revolved around single-family homes, religious observance of some sort, and women who cared for the family at home. And the continuing cold war cast a long shadow culminating in a confrontation over Cuba in 1962 that skirted the edge of all-out nuclear war.

mid-1950s jet planes inspired Earl to design ever more outrageous fins, complemented by huge, shiny chrome grills and ornaments. These features served no mechanical purpose. Some critics dismissed Earl's designs as jukeboxes on wheels.

To Earl and GM that did not matter. Design sold cars. "It gave [customers] an extra receipt for their money in the form of visible prestige marking for an expensive car," Earl said. The "Big Three" auto manufacturers—General Motors, Ford, and Chrysler—raced one another to redesign their annual models, the more outrageous the better. Earl once joked, "I'd put smokestacks right in the middle of the sons of bitches if I thought I could sell more cars." In the lingo of the Detroit stylists, these designs were "gasaroony," an adjective *Popular Mechanics* magazine translated as "terrific, overpowering, weird." The goal was not a better car but what Earl called "dynamic obsolescence" or simply change for change's sake. "The 1957 Ford was great," its designer remarked, "but right away we had to bury it and start another." Even a successful style had to go within a year. "We would design a car to make a man unhappy with his 1957 Ford 'long about the end of 1958." Even though the mechanics of cars changed little from year to year, dynamic obsolescence persuaded Americans in the 1950s to buy new cars in record numbers.

Fins, roadside motels, "gaseterias," drive-in burger huts, interstate highways, shopping centers, and, of course, suburbs—all these were part of a culture of mobility in the 1950s. Americans continued their exodus from rural areas to cities and from the cities to the suburbs. African Americans left the South, heading for industrial centers in the Northeast, Midwest, and West Coast. Mexican Americans concentrated in southwestern cities, while Puerto Ricans came largely to New York. And for Americans in the Snow Belt, the climate of the West and South (at least when civilized by air-conditioning) made the Sun Belt irresistible to ever-larger numbers.

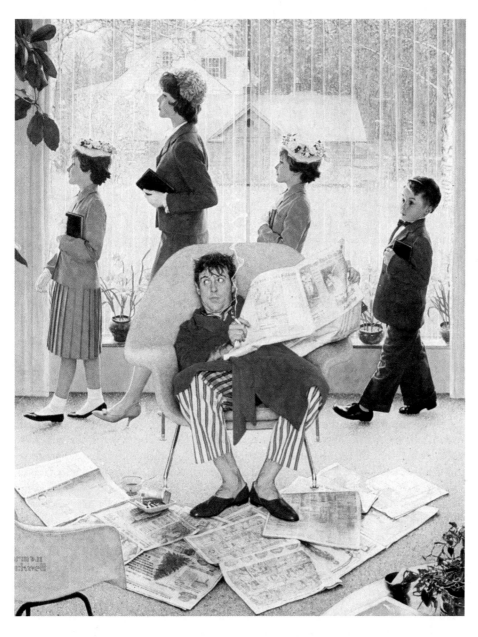

The mobility was social, too. As the economy continued to expand, the size of the American middle class grew. In an era of prosperity and peace, some commentators began to speak of a "consensus"—a general agreement in American culture, based on values of the broad middle class. In a positive light, consensus reflected the agreement among most Americans about fundamental democratic values. Most citizens embraced the material benefits of prosperity as evidence of the virtue of "the American way." And they opposed the spread of communism abroad.

But consensus had its dark side. Critics worried that consensus bred a mindless conformity. Were Americans becoming too homogenized? Was there a depressing sameness in the material goods they owned, in the places they lived, and in the values they held? Besides, wasn't any notion of consensus hollow as long as racism and segregation prevented African Americans and other minorities from fully sharing in American life?

Consensus in the 1950s

The baby boomers born into this era seldom agonized over such issues. In the White House President Eisenhower radiated a comforting sense that the affairs of the nation and the world were in capable hands. That left teenagers free to worry about what really mattered: a first date, a first kiss, a first job, a first choice for college, and whether or not to "go all the way" in the back seat of one of Harley Earl's fin-swept Buicks.

The Rise of the Suburbs

The lure of the suburbs was hardly new to Americans. From the mid–nineteenth century onward, suburbs had been growing up around cities as new modes of transportation made traveling to work easier. But suburban growth accelerated sharply at the end of World War II. During the 1950s suburbs grew 40 times faster than cities, so that by 1960 half the American people lived in them. Urbanites escaping the crowding of large cities were drawn to more pastoral communities with names like Park Forest or Pacific Palisades.

Other changes in postwar society shaped the character of suburban life. With the end of the war came a baby boom and a need for new housing. With the return of prosperity came a boom in automobiles that made the suburbs accessible. But the spurt in suburban growth took its toll on the cities, which suffered as the middle class fled urban areas.

A Boom in Babies and in Housing

The Depression forced many couples to delay beginning a family. In the 1930s birthrates had reached the low point of American history, about 18 to 19 per thousand. As prosperity returned during the war, birthrates began to rise. In 1946 Americans married in record numbers, twice as many as in 1932. The new brides were also younger, most in their peak years of fertility. In a 10-year period the American population increased by 30 million, giving the United States a rate of growth comparable to that of India. By 1952 the birthrate passed 25 live births per thousand, and it did not peak until 1957. Ten years later it had dropped to under 18.

The boom worldwide

Historians and demographers have been hard-pressed to explain this extraordinary population bulge. It was not limited to the United States. In several other industrialized nations fertility rates also soared, Australia, New Zealand, Britain, and West Germany prime among them. France and Czechoslovakia saw similar, shorter rises in the first few years after the war, but these increases seemed merely to have been a kind of catching up after the war's disruptions. Yet as the chart on the facing page indicates, the long-term trend in American fertility rates was downward, as it was in other industrialized nations. Fertility rates peaked in Australia and New Zealand in 1961, and three years later, in Great Britain and West Germany. Hence the baby boom stands as an anomaly, one that remains hard to explain.

Perhaps Americans were indeed "making up for lost time" after the war. Rising income allowed more people to afford marriage and children. But Americans should have caught up by the early 1950s, whereas the baby boom continued. Furthermore, rising standards of living do not always or even regularly go hand in hand with a baby boom. Worldwide, urbanization and higher living standards are linked to lower birthrates. In 1950 the most industrialized and urban nations had a birthrate of 21.8 per thousand, while in less developed and less densely settled sub-Saharan Africa the rate was 49.8. In South Asia it was 44.8.

Whatever factors contributed to the baby boom, it had both immediate and long-term consequences for American society. In the short run, it increased demand

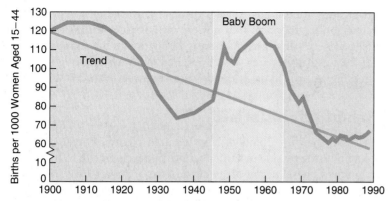

The United States Birthrate, 1900–1989 Despite periods of rapid rise and fall, the nation's birthrate has shown a steady downward trend. The Depression years showed an even sharper decline as financially strapped couples deferred child rearing. Younger marriages and postwar prosperity triggered the baby boom, but in general, affluence encourages lower birthrates.

for housing, food, consumer goods, and schools. In the long run, it made the children of the postwar era the largest population cohort in the nation. Their particular needs and expectations would have a major impact on social and political life.

Certainly, at war's end, five million American families were eagerly searching for housing, tired of living in doubled-up conditions with other families, in basements, or even in coal cellars. With the help of the GI Bill and the rising prosperity, the chance to own a house rather than rent became a reality for over half of American families. And it was the suburbs that offered the residence most idealized in American culture: a detached single-family house with a lawn and garden.

After World War II inexpensive, suburban housing became synonymous with the name of William Levitt. From building houses for war workers, Levitt learned how to use mass production techniques. In 1947 he began construction of a 17,000-house community in the New York City suburb of Hempstead. All the materials for a Levittown house were precut and assembled at a factory, then moved to the site for assembly. If all went according to schedule, a new house was erected on a cement slab every 16 minutes. Buoyed by his success in Hempstead, Levitt later built developments in Bucks County, Pennsylvania, and Willingboro, New Jersey.

The typical early Levitt house, a "Cape Codder," had a living room, kitchen, bath, and two bedrooms on the ground floor and an expansion attic, all for $7990. None had custom features, insulation, or any amenities that complicated construction. "The reason we have it so good in this country," Levitt said, "is that we can produce lots of things at low prices through mass production." Uniformity in house style extended to behavior as well. Levitt discouraged owners from changing colors or adding distinctive features to the house or yard. Buyers promised to cut the grass each week of the summer and not to hang out wash on weekends. African Americans were expressly excluded. Other suburban communities excluded Jews and ethnics through restrictive covenants that dictated who could take up residence.

In California, a state with three cars registered for every four residents, suburbs bloomed across the landscape. By 1962 it had become the nation's most populous

Levittown, U.S.A.

William Levitt and his "Cape Codder" tract homes

state. Growth was greatest around Los Angeles. In 1940 city planners began building a freeway system to lure shoppers into downtown Los Angeles. Instead, white Angelinos saw the road network as an opportunity to migrate to the suburbs. Eventually one-third of the Los Angeles area was covered by highways, parking lots, and interchanges, increasing to two-thirds in the downtown areas.

Cities and Suburbs Transformed

Single-family houses on their own plots of land required plenty of open land, unlike the row houses built side by side in earlier suburban developments. That meant Levitt and other builders chose vacant areas outside major urban areas. With the new houses farther away from factories, offices, and jobs, the automobile became more indispensible than ever.

Almost all suburban activities depended on the availability of cars, cheap gasoline, and accessible roads. Shopping centers, the predecessors of more elaborate malls, exemplified the new auto-centered life. At the end of World War II the United States had just eight of these retail complexes, their clusters of stores attracting customers with convenient parking. Even a few churches and funeral homes provided drive-in facilities to attract people committed to life behind the wheel. By 1960 more than 3840 shopping centers covered as much land as the nation's central business districts.

As the population shifted to suburbs, traffic choked old country roads. To ease this congestion, the Eisenhower administration proposed a 20-year plan to build a massive interstate highway system of some 41,000 miles. Eisenhower addressed cold war fears to build support, arguing that the new system would ease evacuation of cities in case of nuclear attack. In 1956 Congress passed the Interstate Highway Act, setting in motion the largest public works project in history. The federal

America's automobile culture and one special highway, Route 66

Interstate Highway Act of 1956

Like a freak of evolution run riot, automotive tailfins metamorphosed from the modest stubs of a 1948 Cadillac into the monstrous protrusions of the 1959 Cadillac. With a return of prosperity, the suburban era celebrated a culture of mobility.

Blacks

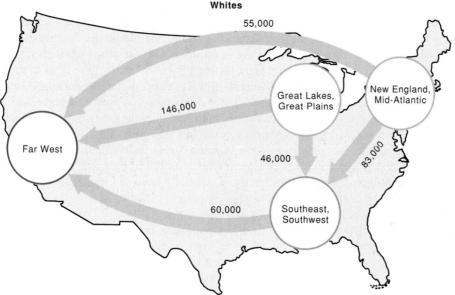

Whites

Average Annual Regional Migration, 1947–1960 In this period, African Americans were moving in significant numbers to urban centers in the Northeast, the Midwest, and the Far West. Whites were being drawn to the increasingly diversified economy of the South as well as to the new industries, stimulated by the war, in the Far West. By the 1970s, the trend had become known as the "Sun Belt" phenomenon.

government picked up 90 percent of the cost through a Highway Trust Fund, financed by special taxes on cars, gas, tires, lubricants, and auto parts.

The Interstate Highway Act had an enormous impact on American life. Average annual driving increased by 400 percent. Shopping centers, linked by the new roads, sprang up to provide suburbanites with an alternative to the longer trip downtown. Almost every community had at least one highway strip dotted with drive-in movies, stores, bowling alleys, gas stations, and fast-food joints.

For cities, the interstates created other problems. The new highway system featured beltways—ring roads around major urban areas. Instead of leading traffic downtown, the beltways allowed motorists to avoid the center city altogether. As people took to their cars, intercity rail service and mass transit declined. Seventy-

Declining cities

five percent of all government transportation dollars went to subsidize travel by car and truck; only one percent was earmarked for urban mass transit. At the same time that middle-class homeowners were moving to the suburbs, many low-paying, unskilled jobs disappeared from the cities. That forced the urban poor into reverse commuting, from city to suburb. All these trends made cities less attractive places to live or do business in. With fewer well-to-do taxpayers to draw on, city governments lacked the tax base to finance public services. A vicious cycle ensued that proved most damaging to the urban poor, who had few means of escape.

Much of the white population that moved to the suburbs was replaced by African Americans and Hispanics. They were part of larger migrations, especially of millions of black families leaving the South to search for work in urban centers. Most headed for the Middle Atlantic, Northeast, and Upper Midwest regions. While central cities lost 3.6 million white residents, they gained 4.5 million African Americans. Indeed, by 1960 half of all black Americans were living in central cities.

Earlier waves of European immigrants had been absorbed by the expanding urban economy. During the 1950s, however, the flight of jobs and middle-class taxpayers to the suburbs made it difficult for African Americans and Hispanics to follow the same path. In the cities fewer jobs awaited them, while declining school systems made it harder for newcomers to acculturate. In the hardest-hit urban areas, unemployment rose to over 40 percent.

Minorities and suburbs   In contrast, the suburbs remained beyond the reach of most minorities. Because few black or Hispanic families could afford the cost of suburban living, they accounted for less than 5 percent of the population there. The few black suburbs that existed dated from before the war and had little in common with the newer white "bedroom communities." Black suburbanites were poorer, held lower-status jobs, lived in more ramshackle housing, and had less education than urban African Americans.

Minorities who could afford the suburbs discovered that most real estate agents refused to show them houses; bankers would not provide mortgages. And many communities adopted either restrictive covenants or zoning regulations that kept out "undesirable" home buyers. One African American, William Myers, finally managed in 1957 to buy a house from a white family in Levittown, Pennsylvania, but the developers did not sell directly to African Americans until 1960.

The Culture of Suburbia

Suburban home ownership was popularly associated with the broad middle classes: those workers who held white- or blue-collar jobs and made enough income to afford the housing. Unlike many urban neighborhoods, where immigrant parents or grandparents might be living on the same block or even in the same apartment, single-family dwellers often left their relatives and in-laws behind. As a result, ethnic lifestyles were less pronounced in the suburbs. The restrictive immigration policies of the 1920s had also eroded ethnicity by reducing the number of newly arrived foreign-born Americans.

Class distinctions were more pronounced between suburban communities than within them. The upper middle class clustered in older developments, often centered around country clubs. Working-class suburbs sprouted on the outskirts of large manufacturing centers, where blue-collar families eagerly escaped the city to own their own homes. Within these suburbs, where differences of class and ethnicity blurred, a more homogeneous suburban culture evolved. "We see eye to eye on most things," commented one Levittown resident, "about raising kids, doing things together with your husband . . . we have practically the same identical background."

American Civil Religion

If the move to the suburbs gradually stripped many ethnics of their native customs and languages, it seldom forced them to abandon their religious identities. Religion continued to be a distinctive and segregating factor during the 1950s. Catholics, Protestants, and Jews generally married within their own faiths, and in the suburbs they kept their social distance as well.

Communities that showed no obvious class distinctions were sometimes deeply divided along religious lines. Catholics attended parochial rather than public schools, formed their own clubs, and generally did not socialize with their Protestant neighbors. Protestant and Catholic members of the same country club usually did not play golf or tennis in the same foursomes. As for Jews, social historian Richard Polenberg has remarked that whereas a gulf divided many Catholics and Protestants, Jews and Gentiles "seem to have lived on the opposite sides of a religious Grand Canyon." Even superficial signs of friendliness masked underlying mistrust and the persistence of old stereotypes.

The religious division

Although such religious boundaries remained distinct, religion was central to American life. Church membership rose to more than 50 percent for the first time in the twentieth century, and by 1957 the Census Bureau reported that 96 percent of the American people cited a specific affiliation when asked "What is your religion?" The religious upswing was supported in part by the prevailing cold war mood, because Communists were avowedly atheists. Cold war fervor led Congress in 1954 to add the phrase "under God" to the Pledge of Allegiance. With this phrase, commented one supporter, "we denounce the pagan doctrine of communism and declare 'under God' in favor of a free government and a free world."

Such patriotic and anticommunist themes were strong in the preaching of clergy who pioneered the use of television. Billy Graham, a Baptist revival preacher, warned Americans to repent, for God would not long abide the sin of materialism. Graham first attracted national attention at a tent meeting in Los Angeles in 1949. Following in the tradition of nineteenth-century revivalists like Charles Finney and Dwight Moody, he soon achieved an even wider impact by televising his meetings. Though no revivalist, the Roman Catholic bishop Fulton J. Sheen became one of television's most popular celebrities. In his weekly program he extolled traditional values and attacked communism.

The growing consensus among Americans was that *any* religious belief was better than none. President Eisenhower joined the chorus of those extolling this view. "Our government makes no sense unless it is founded on a deeply religious faith," he proclaimed, "—and I don't care what it is." Children got the message too. Every Friday afternoon kids watching *The Howdy Doody Show* were exhorted by Buffalo Bob to worship "at the church or synagogue of your choice."

Baptist Billy Graham led the revival of evangelical religion in American culture. While his message emphasized the traditional Fundamentalist themes of sin, redemption, and the Second Coming of Christ, his up-to-date methods took advantage of television, advertising, radio, and paperback books to reach the widest possible audience.

"Homemaking" Women in the Workaday World

The growth of a suburban culture revealed a contradiction in the lives of middle-class women. Never before were their traditional roles as housewives and mothers

Daily Lives

PUBLIC SPACE/ PRIVATE SPACE

The New Suburbia

When World War II ended, many Americans were happy to find housing of any kind. But prosperity in the 1950s brought a greater demand for houses that, like automobiles, reflected the status of those who owned them. No longer would William Levitt's standard 900-square-foot Cape Cod saltbox satisfy popular demand. Levitt's success inspired new designs, often created by builders rather than architects. Eager to please buyers rather than critics, they haphazardly mixed styles and colors.

Even so, suburban design did evolve from major architectural traditions. The most renowned of all suburban features, the picture window, traced its roots to architect Frank Lloyd Wright. Wright had come of age in the 1890s, at a time when "streetcar suburbs" were expanding around major urban areas. Wright's turn-of-the-century innovations combined open interior space, wide windows for natural lighting, and a horizontal, single-story layout. California architects translated Wright's ideas into the ranch house, where rooms flowed into each other and indoor spaces opened to the outdoors to take advantage of the mild climate. Houses with fewer walls and defined spaces discouraged formality and even privacy.

Developers across the country seized on the California "fantasy" style to conjure up dreams of informal living along with a touch of glamour. The use of picture windows allowed them to make small houses seem more spacious. Critics of suburban living suggested that the picture window was a means to ensure conformity. Why, after all, was the window most often placed looking onto the front yard, except to afford homeowners a means to keep an eye on neighbors who were watching them through their own picture windows? In truth, it made sense to have a picture window look onto the street in order to keep an eye on children. More important, the view provided about the only vantage point from which people could enjoy their front yards. Few suburbanites sat out front or actually used the lawn. But since front yards made an important statement about houses and their owners, families decorated and tended them with special care.

In the wake of the baby boom and a demand for new homes, mass-produced houses soon filled suburban developments all across the United States. By varying styles only slightly, developers were able to construct houses quickly at prices many young couples could afford.

so central to American society. Yet never before did more women join the workforce outside the home.

Most housewives found that suburban homes and growing families required increasing time and energy. With relatives and grandparents less likely to live nearby, mothering became full-time work. Dependence on automobiles made many a suburban housewife the chauffeur for her family. In the 1920s grocers or milkmen had commonly delivered their goods from door to door; by the 1950s delivery services were being replaced by housewives doing "errands."

Yet between 1940 and 1960 the percentage of wives working outside the home doubled, from 15 to 30 percent. Although some women took jobs simply to help

Working women

By 1955, economics forced developers to forsake the box shape of most suburban houses. Surveys showed that three-quarters of all would-be buyers wanted a single-story house. But with land prices rising and new zoning codes being enforced, builders could not fit enough floor space onto typical lots. To build a two-story house without seeming to, they hit upon the split-level, or "raised ranch": something, as one critic wryly noted, that "looked like a ranch-style house that had fallen out of the air and landed on something else." The front door opened onto a landing halfway between the upper and lower floors, creating an illusion that it was only half the distance from one floor to the next. The basic construction, two simple boxes side by side, was cheap to build. By placing half the living space—either the kitchen, dining, and family rooms or the bedrooms—in what would otherwise be a basement, the split level created more habitable living space at little additional cost.

Most of all, homeowners in the 1950s wanted family rooms and "live-in kitchens." One magazine described the family room as "the newest room in the house, but also the oldest," for the concept originated in the middle-class Victorian front parlor. Like it, the 1950s living room acquired more elegant furnishings for use during holidays or special entertaining. That led to the conversion of what often had been a basement "rumpus" room for the kids into a family room. Here, families sought a cozier feel with pine paneling and furniture designed for comfort and durability, with the television as the focus of the room.

The growing families of the late 1950s needed more space to prepare and eat meals. Earlier kitchens had normally been small and limited largely to food preparation. Meals were eaten in a combined living-dining area. The new, larger live-in kitchens were designed, one advertiser claimed, to make "mother a member of the family again." Everyone could gather while mom cooked. The same space would also hold appliances such as dishwashers, dual ovens, and televisions, which became common kitchen features.

Clearly, suburban houses were more than "Little boxes on the hillside / Little boxes all the same," as one folk-singing critic of the 1960s complained. To the people who flocked to suburbia, their homes represented a compromise between fantasy and practicality, fulfilling the American dream, "To own your own home."

make ends meet, often more than financial necessity was involved. Middle-class married women went to work as often as lower-class wives, and women with college degrees were the most likely to get a job. Two-income families were able to spend far more on extras: gifts, education, recreation, and household appliances. In addition, women found status and self-fulfillment in their jobs, as well as a chance for increased social contacts.

More women were going to college, too, but that increased education did not translate into economic equality. The percentage of women holding professional jobs actually dropped between 1950 and 1960. And the gap between men's and women's wages was greater than in any other industrial nation. In the United States, the median wage for women was less than half that for men.

To housewife and mother, many suburban women of the 1950s added the role of chauffeur. Husbands who once walked to work and children who walked to school now needed to be delivered and picked up. The average suburban woman spent one full working day each week driving and doing errands.

Media images of women

Despite women's wider roles in society, the modern media continued to portray women either as sex objects or as domesticated housewives and mothers. A typical article appearing in *Redbook* in 1957 made a heroine of Junior, a "little freckle-faced brunette" who had given up work. As the story closed, Junior nursed her baby at two in the morning, crooning "I'm glad, glad, glad I'm just a housewife." In 1950 Lynn White, the president of Mills College for women, advocated a curriculum that displaced traditional academic subjects with those that were "distinctly feminine," such as crafts or home economics.

The media trivialized women in other ways. Whereas the films of the 1930s and 1940s often starred independent, confident women, the heroines of the 1950s appeared more vulnerable. Marilyn Monroe's voluptuous sensuality, combined with a little-girl innocence, clearly appealed to male tastes. Similarly, women's fashions portrayed a male vision of femininity. In 1947 Christian Dior introduced his "new look": narrow waistlines emphasizing shapely hips and a full bosom, rarely achieved without constricting foundation garments. The heels on shoes became ever higher and the toes pointier. As historian Lois Banner concluded, "Not since the Victorian era had women's fashions been so confining."

A Revolution in Sexuality?

The suburbs themselves encouraged other changes in sexual attitudes, especially among the middle classes who lived there. Throughout the twentieth century, a trend had been under way deemphasizing the tradition that sex within marriage was primarily for the procreation of children—a duty (especially for women) to be endured rather than enjoyed. During the 1920s reformer Ben Lindsey promoted the idea of "companionate marriage," stressing personal happiness and satisfaction as primary goals. Such a marriage included the enjoyment of sex for both wife and husband. The suburban home of the 1950s encouraged such ideals, symbolizing as it did a place of relaxation and enjoyment. Unlike city apartments, where extended families often lived in crowded conditions, the suburban single-family houses provided greater privacy and more space for intimacy.

The increased willingness to see sexual pleasure as an integral part of marriage received additional attention in 1948 with the publication of an apparently dry scientific study, *Sexual Behavior in the Human Male.* Its author, Professor Alfred

The Kinsey Report

Kinsey, hardly expected the storm of publicity received by that study or its companion, *Sexual Behavior in the Human Female* (1953). Kinsey began his research career as a zoologist with a zest for classifying data. During the 1940s he turned to collecting information on sexual behavior. Based on more than 10,000 interviews, Kinsey reached conclusions that were unorthodox and even startling for his day. Masturbation and premarital petting, he reported, were widespread. Women did not just endure sex as a wifely duty; they enjoyed it in much the same way men did. Extramarital sex was common for both husbands and wives. About 10 percent of the population was homosexual.

Publicly, Kinsey maintained a posture of scientific objectivity. He argued that he had only published a report "on what people do" and wasn't concerned with "what they should do." But biographers of Kinsey have revealed that, in fact, he was as much interested in social change as in scientific research, believing that many behaviors treated as deviant should be placed within a normal range of sexual behavior. His personal attitudes influenced that conclusion, for sexual obsessions were central to Kinsey's private life. (He practiced masochism; and he, his wife, and members of his staff filmed themselves engaged in group sex.) Though the public remained unaware of his private life, Kinsey provoked intense controversy. Commentators called his report "the most talked-about book of the twentieth century." Social scientists objected that Kinsey's sample was too narrow to produce valid norms. (Most of his subjects were midwestern, middle class, and well educated.) Later studies challenged some of his figures—for example, the percentage of homosexuals in the population. His most severe critics called him "a menace to society." According to opinion polls, most Americans disagreed. The large majority took comfort (as he had hoped) that behaviors once condemned as sinful or perverse were widely practiced.

The Flickering Gray Screen

In the glow of postwar prosperity, most Americans found themselves with more leisure time and more income. In the suburbs, a yard to tend and a young family to raise determined that much of that free time would be spent around the house. The new medium of television fit perfectly into suburban lifestyles. It provided an ideal way to entertain families at home as well as sell them consumer goods.

Television viewership boomed after World War II. By 1949 Americans had bought a million sets. In only three years the figure jumped to 15 million, and by 1960, 46 million. Indeed, by then more Americans had television sets than had bathrooms. Home viewing transformed American entertainment habits, cutting sharply into pastimes like movies and professional sports. In cities around the country more than 4000 neighborhood theaters closed. Many were replaced in the suburbs by popular drive-ins, which allowed whole families to enjoy movies in the comfort of their cars.

In 1948 television began its involvement in politics, covering both the Democratic and Republican conventions. Two years later, it combined entertainment, politics, and news by televising a series of hearings on organized crime chaired by Senator Estes Kefauver. Some 30 million viewers watched senators grill mobster Frank Costello about his criminal organization and its ties to city governments. Millions more watched Senator Joseph McCarthy's ill-fated crusade against the army in 1954. Clearly, television demonstrated the potential to shape the political life of the nation. By the mid-1950s, however, controversy over news coverage of issues like McCarthyism led the networks to downgrade public affairs programs. As an alternative, the networks turned to Hollywood film studios, which provided

Television and politics

them with telefilm series. By selling time to advertisers, the networks, rather than the sponsors, gained ultimate control over program content. By 1959 live television was virtually a thing of the past. Westerns, detective and quiz shows, and old movies led the ratings.

The Politics of Calm

In presiding over these changes in American society, President Dwight David Eisenhower projected an aura of paternal calm. Pursuing "modern Republicanism," the new president sought consensus, not confrontation. No longer would die-hard conservatives like Herbert Hoover and Robert Taft dictate the Republican agenda. Eisenhower declared that he was "conservative when it comes to money and liberal when it comes to human beings."

Eisenhower's Modern Republicanism

Eisenhower had been raised in a large Kansas farm family. His parents, though poor, offered him a warm, caring home steeped in religious faith. In an era of organization men, Eisenhower succeeded by mastering the military's bureaucratic politics. A graduate of West Point, he was neither a scholar nor an aggressive general like George Patton. In the years between the two world wars, the skills "Ike" demonstrated at golf, poker, and bridge often proved as valuable as his military expertise. Yet these genial ways could not hide his ambition or his ability to judge character shrewdly. It took a gifted organizer to coordinate the D-Day invasion and to hold together the egocentric generals who pushed east to Berlin. Eisenhower was so widely respected that both parties had considered running him in the 1948 presidential race.

President Dwight D. Eisenhower

In pursuing his pragmatic course, Eisenhower resisted conservative demands to dismantle New Deal programs. He even agreed to increases in Social Security, unemployment insurance, and the minimum wage. He accepted a small public housing program and a modest federally supported medical insurance plan for the needy. But as a conservative, Eisenhower remained uncomfortable with big government. Thus he rejected more far-reaching liberal proposals on housing and universal health care through the Social Security system.

To make modern Republicanism successful, Eisenhower had to woo the newly prosperous Democratic voters joining the middle class. Success in that effort hinged on how well the administration managed the economy. The Democrats of the New Deal had established a tradition of activism. When the economy faltered, deficit spending and tax cuts were used to stimulate it. Eisenhower, in contrast, wanted to reduce federal spending and the government's role in the economy. When a recession struck in 1953–1954, the administration was concerned more with balancing the budget and holding inflation in line than with reducing unemployment through government spending.

But these policies worked poorly enough (and the voters expressed their resentment in midterm elections) so that when recessions hit again in 1957–1958 and 1960–1961 the administration spoke less of balancing the budget. Indeed, Eisenhower achieved that goal in only three of eight fiscal years, and in 1959 he faced what was then the largest peacetime deficit in history. The result was that although the economy grew during the Eisenhower years, that growth remained uneven. The poor of both urban and rural areas remained largely unaffected by economic expansion.

Eisenhower followed a similar pragmatic approach in other areas. When major projects called for federal leadership, as with the Highway Act, he supported the policy. In 1954 he signed the St. Lawrence Seaway Act, which joined the United States and Canada in an ambitious engineering project to open the Great Lakes to ocean shipping. Like the highway program, the Seaway was fiscally acceptable because the funding came from user tolls and taxes rather than from general revenues.

In farm policy Eisenhower's practical approach yielded scant results. Farmers made up a major Republican voting bloc. For the president to abolish the price supports established under the New Deal was to commit political suicide. On the other hand, crop surpluses continued to fill government silos with unwanted grain. Eisenhower's secretary of agriculture, Ezra Taft Benson, proposed a system of lower support payments designed to discourage farmers from overproducing basic commodities like corn, cotton, and wheat. Benson also established a soil bank program to pay farmers for taking land out of production.

Farm policy

In the end, however, modern technology made it difficult to limit agricultural production. Automated harvesters, fertilizers, and new varieties of plants increased farm outputs even though farmers were planting fewer acres. Pressure to maximize production and profit grew as more and more small farms were being replaced by large commercial farms called agribusinesses. Modern business farmers made ever more use of artificial pesticides, herbicides, and fertilizers. Runoff of these chemicals began to poison the nation's groundwater, lakes, and rivers, but the damage went largely unnoticed. Americans in the 1950s worried more about economic growth than the quality of their environment.

Despite occasional economic setbacks Eisenhower remained popular. Even after he suffered a major heart attack in 1955, voters gladly reelected him over Adlai Stevenson in 1956. But poor economic performance took its toll on the Republican party. In the wake of the 1954 recession the Democrats gained a 29-member majority in the House and a 1-vote edge in the Senate. Never again would Eisenhower work with a Republican majority in Congress. In 1958, when recession again dragged down the economy, the Democrats took a 68-seat majority in the House and a 12-vote advantage in the Senate. Modern Republicanism did not put down deep roots outside of Eisenhower's White House.

Eisenhower reelected

The Conglomerate World

Large corporations welcomed the administration's probusiness attitudes as well as the era's general prosperity. Wages for the average worker rose over 35 percent between 1950 and 1960. At the same time, the economic distress of the 1930s had led corporate executives to devise new ways to minimize the danger of economic downturns. Each of the approaches expanded the size of corporations in various ways in order to minimize shocks in specific markets.

General Electric emerged as one of the great conglomerate corporate enterprises of the postwar era. It produced consumer, military, and industrial goods. To shape its public image General Electric used former movie star and television celebrity (and later president) Ronald Reagan as its spokesperson.

One expansion strategy took the form of diversification. In the 1930s, a giant like General Electric had concentrated largely in one industrial area: equipment for generating electric power and light. When the Depression struck, GE found its markets evaporating. The company responded by entering markets for appliances, X-ray machines, and elevators—all products developed or enhanced by the company's research labs. In the postwar era General Electric diversified even further, into nuclear power, jet engines, and television. Diversification was most practical for large industrial firms, whose size allowed them to support extensive research and development.

Conglomeration often turned small companies into giants. Unlike earlier horizontal and vertical combinations, conglomerate mergers could join companies with seemingly unrelated products. Over a 20-year period International Telephone and Telegraph branched out from its basic communications business into baking, hotels and motels, car rental, home building, and insurance. Corporations also became multinational by expanding their overseas operations or buying out potential foreign competitors. Large integrated oil companies like Mobil and Standard Oil of New Jersey (Exxon) developed huge oil fields in the Middle East and markets around the free world.

One aid to managing these modern corporate giants was the advent of electronic data processing. In the early 1950s computers were virtually unknown in private industry. But banks and insurance companies saw these calculating machines as an answer to their need to manipulate huge quantities of records and statistical data. Manufacturers, especially in the petroleum, chemical, automotive, and electronics industries, began to use computers to monitor their production lines, quality control, and inventory.

Cracks in the Consensus

As corporations merged in order to increase their reach, power, and stability, corporate spokespeople praised the prosperity of business as a part of the emerging consensus over the American way. ("What was good for our country was good for General Motors.") Yet there were distinct cracks in the consensus. Intellectuals and social critics spoke out against the stifling features of a conformist corporate culture. At the fringes of American society, the beatniks rejected conformity, while the more mainstream rock and roll movement broadcast its own brand of youthful rebellion.

Critics of Mass Culture

In Levittown, New Jersey, a woman who had invited her neighbors to a cocktail party eagerly awaited them dressed in newly fashionable Capri pants—a tight-fitting calf-length style. Alas, one early-arriving couple glimpsed the woman through a window. What on earth was the hostess wearing? *Pajamas?* Who in their right mind would entertain in pajamas? The couple sneaked home, afraid they had made a mistake about the day of the party. They telephoned another neighbor, who anxiously called yet others on the guest list.

The neighbors finally mustered enough courage to attend the party. But when the hostess later learned of their misunderstanding, she put her Capri pants in the closet for good. Levittown was not ready for such a change in fashion.

Was America turning into a vast suburban wasteland, where the neighbors' worries over Capri pants would stifle all individuality? Many highbrow intellectuals worried openly about the homogenized lifestyle created by mass consumption, conformity, and mass media. Critics such as Dwight Macdonald sarcastically attacked the culture of the suburban middle classes: *Reader's Digest* Condensed Books, uplifting film spectacles such as *The Ten Commandments*, television dramas that pretended to be high art but in reality were little more than simplistic pontificating. "Midcult," Macdonald called it, which was his shorthand for middlebrow culture.

Other critics charged that the skyscrapers and factories of giant conglomerates housed an all-too-impersonal world. In large, increasingly automated workplaces, skilled laborers seemed little more than caretakers of machines. Large corporations required middle-level executives to submerge their personal goals in the processes and work routines of a large bureaucracy. David Riesman, a sociologist, condemned stifling conformity in *The Lonely Crowd* (1950). In nineteenth-century America, Riesman argued, Americans had been "inner directed." It was their own consciences that formed their values and drove them to seek success. In contrast, modern workers had developed a personality shaped not so much by inner convictions as by the opinions of their peers. The new "other-directed" society of suburbia preferred security to success. "Go along to get along" was its motto. In a bureaucratized economy, it was important to please others, to conform to the group, and to cooperate.

David Riesman's *The Lonely Crowd*

William Whyte carried Riesman's critique from the workplace to the suburb in *The Organization Man* (1956). Here he found rootless families, shifted from town to town by the demands of corporations. (IBM, according to one standard joke, stood for "I've Been Moved.") The typical organization man was sociable but not terribly ambitious. He sought primarily to keep up with the Joneses and the number of consumer goods they owned. He lived in a suburban "split-level trap," as one critic put it, one among millions of "haggard" men, "tense and anxious" women, and "the gimme kids," who, like the cartoon character Dennis the Menace, looked up from the litter under the Christmas tree to ask, "Is that all?"

William Whyte's *The Organization Man*

No doubt such portraits were overdrawn. (Where, after all, did Riesman's nineteenth-century inner-directed Americans get their values, if not from the society around them?) But such critiques indicated the problems of adjustment faced by people working within large bureaucratic organizations and living in suburbs that were decentralized and self-contained.

The Rebellion of Young America

Young Americans were among suburbia's sharpest critics. Dance crazes, outlandish clothing, strange jargon, rebelliousness toward parents, and sexual precociousness— all these behaviors challenged middle-class respectability. More than a few parents and public figures warned that America had spawned a generation of rebellious juvenile delinquents. Psychologist Frederic Wertheim told a group of doctors, "You cannot understand present-day juvenile delinquency if you do not take into account the pathogenic and pathoplastic [infectious] influence of comic books." Others laid the blame on films and the lyrics of popular music.

The center of the new teen culture was the high school. Whether in consolidated rural school districts, new suburban schools, or city systems, the large, comprehensive high schools of the 1950s were often miniature melting pots in which middle-class students were exposed to, and often adopted, the style of the lower classes. Alarmed school administrators complained of juvenile delinquents who wore jeans and T-shirts, challenged authority, and defiantly smoked cigarettes, much like the motorcycle gang leader portrayed by Marlon Brando in the film *The Wild One* (1954).

Juvenile delinquency

In many ways the argument about juvenile delinquency was an argument about social class and, to a lesser degree, race. Adults who complained that delinquent teenagers dressed poorly, lacked ambition, and were irresponsible and sexually promiscuous were voicing the same arguments traditionally used to denigrate other outsiders—immigrants, the poor, and African Americans. Nowhere were these racial and class undertones more evident than in the hue and cry greeting the arrival of rock and roll.

Before 1954 popular music had been divided into three major categories: pop, country and western, and rhythm and blues. A handful of major record companies with almost exclusively white singers dominated the pop charts. On one fringe of

The rise of rock and roll

the popular field was country and western, often split into cowboy musicians such as Roy Rogers and Gene Autry and the hillbilly style associated with Nashville. The music industry generally treated rhythm and blues as "race music," whose performers and audience were largely black. Each of these musical traditions grew out of regional cultures. As the West and the South merged into the national culture, so too were these musical subcultures gradually integrated into the national mainstream.

By the mid-1950s the distinctiveness of the three styles began to blur. Singers on the white pop charts recorded a few songs from country and from rhythm and

blues. The popularity of crossover songs such as "Sh-boom," "Tutti-Frutti," and "Earth Angel" indicated that a major shift in taste and market was under way. Lyrics still reflected the pop field's preoccupation with young love, marriage, and happiness, but the music now vibrated with the rawer, earthier style of rhythm and blues. Country and western singer Bill Haley brought the new blend to the fore in 1954 with "Shake, Rattle, and Roll," the first rock song to reach the top ten on the pop charts.

And then—calamity! Millions of middle-class roofs nearly blew off with the appearance in 1955 of the rhythmic and raucous Elvis Presley. By background, Elvis was a country boy whose musical style combined elements of gospel, country, and blues. But it was his hip-swinging, pelvis-plunging performances that electrified teenagers. To more conservative adults, Presley's long hair, sideburns, and tight jeans seemed menacingly delinquent, an expression of hostile rebellion. What they often resented but rarely admitted was that Elvis looked lower class, sounded black, and really could sing.

The King, Elvis Presley

The beat generation

Beyond the frenetic rhythms of rock and roll, and even farther beyond the pale of suburban culture, flourished a subculture known as the beat generation. In run-down urban neighborhoods and college towns this motley collection of artists, intellectuals, musicians, and middle-class students dropped out of mainstream society. In dress and behavior the beatniks self-consciously rejected what they viewed

as the excessive spiritual bankruptcy of America's middle-class culture. Cool urban hipsters—especially black jazz musicians like John Coltrane and Sonny Rollins—were their models. They read poetry, listened to jazz, explored Oriental philosophy, and experimented openly with drugs, mystical religions, and sex.

The "beats" viewed themselves as being driven to the margins of society, rejecting the culture of abundance, materialism, and conformity. "I saw the best minds of my generation destroyed by madness, starving hysterical naked," wrote Allen Ginsberg in his 1955 poem *Howl*. They had become "angelheaded hipsters . . . who in poverty and tatters and hollow-eyed and high sat up smoking in the supernatural darkness of cold-water flats floating across the tops of cities contemplating jazz." Jack Kerouac tapped the frenzied energy beneath the beatniks' cool facade in *On the Road* (1957), a novel based on his travels across the country with his friend Neal Cassady. Kerouac finished the novel in one frenetic three-week binge, feeding a 120-foot roll of paper through his typewriter and spilling out tales of pot, jazz, crazy sex, and all-night raps undertaken in a search for "IT"—the ultimate transcendental moment when mind and experience mesh.

The original manuscript of the novel *On the Road*. Jack Kerouac taped together ten 12-foot rolls of paper to use in typing out his manuscript.

Nationalism in an Age of Superpowers

Try as they might, the beats could not ignore the atomic menace that overshadowed American society at midcentury. Along the Iron Curtain of Eastern Europe and across the battle lines of northern Asia, Soviet-American rivalry had settled into a stalemate. The American public shared with most foreign policy makers a view of the globe as divided between the "free world" nations and the "communist bloc." Thus the Eisenhower administration sought ways to contain the Soviets: setting up security and trade agreements, employing covert action to install governments favorable to the United States, and using the threat of nuclear war, if need be.

Not all nations viewed the world in such bipolar terms. World War II had disrupted Europe's longstanding imperial relationships. As nationalists in the Middle East, Africa, and Southeast Asia fought to gain independence from their colonial masters, new nations like India proclaimed themselves "nonaligned," independent of the Soviet Union and the United States. Nonetheless the two superpowers competed for the allegiance of emerging nations. And as crises flared in one region or another, the risk was always present that a minor conflict might escalate into the ultimate nuclear confrontation between the superpowers.

To the Brink?

As a general who had fought in a global war and as commander of NATO, Eisenhower was no stranger to world politics. Still, he shared the conduct of foreign policy with his secretary of state, John Foster Dulles. Dulles approached his job with a somber enthusiasm. Coming from a family of missionaries and diplomats, he had within him a touch of both. He viewed the Soviet-American struggle in almost religious terms: a fight of good against evil between two irreconcilable superpowers. Admirers praised his global vision; detractors saw him as "the wooliest type of pontificating American." Certainly Dulles did not lack confidence. "With my understanding of the intricate relationship between the peoples of the world," he told Eisenhower, "and your sensitiveness to the political considerations, we will make the most successful team in history."

John Foster Dulles

The administration was determined to make Truman's containment strategy more forceful. Dulles, the more confrontational of the two men, wanted the United States to aid in liberating the "captive peoples" of Eastern Europe and other Communist nations. On the other hand, Eisenhower was equally determined to cut back military spending and troop levels in order to keep the budget balanced. The president, who understood well how the military services and their allies in defense industries competed for government money, was irked at the "fantastic programs" the Pentagon kept proposing. "If we demand too much in taxes in order to build planes and ships," he argued, "we will tend to dry up the accumulations of capital that are necessary to provide jobs for the million or more new workers that we must absorb each year."

So Eisenhower and Dulles hit on a more economical strategy. Rather than rely on conventional forces, they would contain Soviet aggression by using the threat of massive nuclear retaliation. Dulles insisted that Americans should not shrink from the threat of nuclear war: "If you are scared to go to the brink, you are lost." As Treasury Secretary George Humphrey put it, a nuclear strategy was much cheaper—"a bigger bang for the buck." Henceforth American foreign policy would have an aggressive "New Look." Behind the more militant rhetoric, however, lay an ongoing commitment to containment.

The New Look in foreign policy

Brinkmanship in Asia

Moving from talk of "brinkmanship" to concrete action did not prove easy. When Dulles announced American intentions to "unleash" Chiang Kai-shek to attack mainland China from his outpost on Taiwan (formerly Formosa), China threatened

Taiwan and mainland China

Asian Trouble Spots After the Geneva Accords divided Indochina into North and South Vietnam, Secretary of State Dulles organized the Southeast Asia Treaty Organization (SEATO) to resist Communist aggression in Southeast Asia. In addition to the conflict in Vietnam, tensions were fueled by the mutual hostility between mainland Communist China and Chiang Kai-shek's Taiwan as well as the offshore islands of Quemoy and Matsu.

to invade Taiwan. At that, Eisenhower ordered the Seventh Fleet into the area to protect rather than unleash Chiang. If the Communists attacked, he warned bluntly in 1955, "we'll have to use atomic weapons."

Nuclear weapons also figured in the American response to a crisis in Southeast Asia. There, Vietnamese forces led by Ho Chi Minh were fighting the French, who had returned to reestablish their own colonial rule. Between 1950 and 1954, the United States provided France with more than $1 billion in military aid in Vietnam. Eisenhower worried that if Vietnam fell to a Communist revolutionary like Ho, other nations of Southeast Asia would soon follow. "You have a row of dominoes set up," the president warned, "you knock over the first one. . . . You could have the beginning of a disintegration that would have the most profound influences."

Vietnamese victory at Dien Bien Phu

Worn down by a war they seemed unable to win, the French in 1954 tried to force a final showdown with Ho's forces at Dien Bien Phu. With Vietnamese and Chinese Communist troops holding the surrounding hilltops, the French garrison of 12,000 could not have chosen a worse place to do battle. Desperate, the French government pleaded for more American aid and the Joint Chiefs of Staff responded by volunteering to relieve the besieged French forces with a massive American air raid—including the use of tactical nuclear weapons, if necessary. Dulles too recommended an air strike, but Eisenhower pulled back. After Korea, the idea of American involvement in another Asian war aroused opposition from both allies and domestic political leaders.

United States backs Diem

Collapsing under the siege, the garrison at Dien Bien Phu surrendered in May 1954. At a peace conference held in Geneva, Switzerland, Ho Chi Minh agreed to withdraw his forces north of the 17th parallel, temporarily dividing the nation into North and South Vietnam. Because of Ho's widespread popularity, he could count on an easy victory in the elections that the peace conference agreed would be held within two years. Dulles, however, viewed any Communist victory as unacceptable, even if the election was democratic. He convinced Eisenhower to support a South Vietnamese government under Ngo Dinh Diem. Diem, Dulles insisted, was not bound by the agreement signed in Geneva to hold any election. The United States became further involved by sending a military mission to train an army to keep Diem in power.

The Covert Side of the New Look

In pursuing their aggressive New Look in foreign policy, Dulles and Eisenhower sometimes authorized the Central Intelligence Agency (CIA) to use covert operations against Communists or those they saw as sympathetic to Moscow. For example, in Iran in 1951 a nationalist government under Mohammed Mossadeq seized the assets of a giant British oil company. With the United States boycotting Iranian oil, Dulles worried that Mossadeq would turn to the neighboring Soviet Union for aid. Eisenhower approved a secret CIA operation to topple the Mossadeq government. Led by Teddy Roosevelt's grandson, Kermit Roosevelt, Operation Ajax recruited a mob to help Iranian armed forces drive Mossadeq from the country and return Iran's monarch, Shah Mohammad Reza Pahlavi, to his throne in August 1953.

Overthrowing Mossadeq

Seeing how cheaply American influence had been restored in Iran, Secretary Dulles looked for similar results in Guatemala. Unlike Iran, however, Guatemala had an elected democratic government under Colonel Jacobo Arbenz Guzmán. Arbenz was determined to reduce the poverty in his country by confiscating the idle farmland of rich landowners and giving it to the peasants. Guatemala's richest landowner was the Boston-based United Fruit Company. United Fruit had long supported conservative governments, paid few taxes, and shipped its profits back to the United States.

Crushing a democracy

When the Guatemalan government seized 400,000 acres from United Fruit, the company's agents branded Arbenz a Communist. The American ambassador to Guatemala knew that the label was not true but later explained "that the man thought like a communist and talked like a communist, and if not actually one, would do until one came along." After Communist Czechoslovakia sent Guatemala 1900 tons of small arms, Dulles ordered a CIA-trained band of Latin American mercenaries into the country, supported by American planes. Within a week the leader of the Guatemalan rebels, Carlos Castillo Armas, replaced the Arbenz democracy with a military dictatorship that quickly returned the expropriated lands to United Fruit.

Success in Iran and Guatemala greatly enhanced the reputation of the CIA. American policy makers developed a misplaced faith that covert operations could achieve dramatic results at low cost. But in overthrowing popular governments or defending unpopular ones, the United States gained a reputation in many Third World countries as a foe of national liberation, popular democracy, and social

The CIA secretly helped overthrow the Guatemalan government in 1954. One plan, apparently never carried out, called for the assassination of 58 Guatemalan officials. But the CIA's chilling "Conference Room Technique" survived, a four-step plan showing how "a room containing as many as a dozen subjects can be 'purified' in about 20 seconds" by two assassins. Step 4 was to "leave propaganda," making it seem as if Communists had carried out the massacre.

The Response to *Sputnik*

Castro's turn to the Soviets seemed all the more dangerous because the Soviet Union in 1957 stunned America by launching the first space satellite, dubbed *Sputnik*. By 1959, the Soviets had crash-landed a much larger payload on the moon. If the Russians could target the moon, surely they could launch nuclear missiles against America. In contrast, the American space program suffered so many delays and mishaps that rockets exploding on launch were nicknamed "flopniks" and "kaputniks."

How had the Soviets managed to catch up with American technology so quickly? Some analysts blamed U.S. schools, especially weak programs in science and math. In 1958 Eisenhower joined with Congress to enact a National Defense Education Act, designed to strengthen graduate education and the teaching of science, math, and foreign languages. At the same time, crash programs were undertaken to build basement fallout shelters to protect Americans in case of a nuclear attack. Democrats charged that the administration had allowed the United States to face an unacceptable "missile gap" (an accusation that was not borne out).

A missile gap?

Thaws and Freezes

Throughout this series of crises, each superpower found it difficult to interpret the other's motives. The Russians exploited nationalist revolutions where they could— less successfully in Egypt, more so in Cuba. "We will bury you," Khrushchev admonished Americans, though it was unclear whether he meant through peaceful competition or military confrontation. More menacingly, in November 1958 he demanded that the Western powers withdraw all troops from West Berlin within

Berlin crisis

Even before the launch of *Sputnik* in 1957, Americans had begun devising fallout shelters for protection from the effects of a nuclear attack. This one was exhibited in 1955.

six months. Berlin would then become a "free city," and the Western powers could negotiate further access to it only through East Germany, a government that the West had refused to recognize. When Eisenhower flatly rejected the ultimatum, Khrushchev backed away from his hard-line stance.

Rather than adopt a more belligerent course, Eisenhower determined to use the last 18 months of his presidency to improve Soviet-American relations. The shift in policy was made easier because the president knew from American intelligence (but could not admit publicly) that the missile gap was not real. Eisenhower, although willing to support some additional development of missile systems, also invited Khrushchev to visit the United States in September 1959. The Soviet premier undertook a picturesque tour across America, swapping comments about manure with Iowa farmers, reacting puritanically to movie cancan dancers, and grousing when his visit to the new capitalist marvel, Disneyland, was canceled for security reasons.

Eisenhower's plans for a return visit to the Soviet Union were abruptly canceled in 1960 after the Russians shot down a high-altitude U-2 American spy plane over Soviet territory. At first Eisenhower claimed that the plane had strayed off course while doing weather research, but Khrushchev sprang his trap: the CIA pilot, Gary Powers, had been captured alive. The president then admitted that for reasons of national security he had personally authorized the U-2 overflights.

The U-2 incident

That episode ended Eisenhower's hopes that his personal diplomacy might thaw cold war tensions. Yet a less mature president might have led the United States into more severe conflict or even war. Eisenhower was not readily impressed by the promises of new weapons systems or overheated talk about a missile gap between the United States and the Soviet Union. He left office with a warning that too much military spending would lead to "an unwarranted influence, whether sought or unsought" by the "military-industrial complex" at the expense of democratic institutions.

The 1960 election promised to bring the winds of change to Washington. The

The Cold War along a New Frontier

opponents—Vice President Richard Nixon and Senator John F. Kennedy of Massachusetts—were the first major presidential candidates born in the twentieth century. At the age of 43, Kennedy would be the youngest person ever elected to the presidency, and Nixon was only four years older. The nation needed to find new challenges and "new frontiers," Kennedy proclaimed. His rhetoric was noble, but the direction in which he would take the nation was far from clear.

The Election of 1960

Jack Kennedy's biggest hurdle to election was social as much as political. He was a Roman Catholic out of Irish Boston, and no Catholic had ever been elected president. Conservative Protestants, many concentrated in the heavily Democratic South, were convinced that a Catholic president would never be "free to exercise his own judgment" if the pope ordered otherwise. Kennedy chose to confront the issue head-on. In September he entered the lions' den, addressing an association of hostile Protestant ministers in Houston. The speech was the best of his campaign. "I believe in an America where the separation of church and state is absolute," he said, "—where no Catholic prelate would tell the President (should he be Catholic) how to act, and no Protestant minister would tell his parishioners how to vote." House Speaker Sam Rayburn, an old Texas pol, was astonished by Kennedy's bravura performance. "My God! . . . He's eating them blood raw."

The Catholic issue

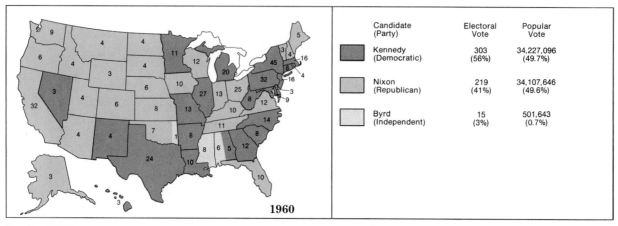

Candidate (Party)	Electoral Vote	Popular Vote
Kennedy (Democratic)	303 (56%)	34,227,096 (49.7%)
Nixon (Republican)	219 (41%)	34,107,646 (49.6%)
Byrd (Independent)	15 (3%)	501,643 (0.7%)

Election of 1960

Both candidates stressed cold war themes. Kennedy lamented the apparent "missile gap" and attacked Eisenhower and Nixon for not better managing tensions between Communist China and the nationalists on Formosa (Taiwan). Vice President Richard Nixon ran on his record as an experienced leader and staunch anti-Communist, but his campaign faltered in October as unemployment rose. Nixon agreed to a series of debates with Kennedy—the first to be televised nationally. Image proved more telling than issues. According to one poll, radio listeners believed Nixon won the debate; but television viewers saw a fatigued candidate with "five o'clock shadow," because Nixon had refused to use television makeup. A relaxed Kennedy convinced many viewers that he could handle the job.

In the end religion, ethnicity, and race played decisive roles in Kennedy's triumph. One voter was asked if he voted for Kennedy because he was a Catholic. "No, because *I* am," he answered; and in key states Catholic support made a difference. "Hyphenated" Americans—Hispanic, Jewish, Irish, Italian, Polish, and German—voted Democratic in record numbers, while much of the black vote that had gone to Eisenhower in 1956 returned to the Democratic fold. Indeed, when civil rights leader Martin Luther King was imprisoned during a protest in Georgia, Kennedy attracted the support of black Americans by telephoning his sympathy to Dr. King's wife. Interest in the election ran so high that 64 percent of voters turned out, the largest percentage in 50 years. Out of 68.8 million ballots cast, Kennedy won by a margin of just 119,000.

The Hard-Nosed Idealists of Camelot

Many observers compared the Kennedy White House to Camelot, King Arthur's magical court. A popular musical of 1960 pictured Camelot as a land where skies were fair, men brave, women pretty, and the days full of challenge and excitement. With similar vigor, Kennedy brought into his administration bright, energetic advisers. He and his stylish wife, Jacqueline, invited artists, musicians, and intellectuals to the White House. Impromptu touch football games on the White House lawn displayed a rough-and-tumble playfulness, akin to Arthur's jousting tournaments of old.

In truth, Kennedy was not a liberal by temperament. Handsome and intelligent, he possessed an ironic, self-deprecating humor. In Congress he had led an undistinguished career, supported Senator Joe McCarthy, and earned a reputation as a playboy. Once Kennedy set his sights on the White House, however, he revealed an astonishing capacity for political maneuvering and organization. To woo the liberals in his party, he surrounded himself with a distinguished group of intellectuals and academics.

The urbane and energetic John F. Kennedy (center) was associated with both King Arthur (left, played by Richard Burton in the 1960 musical) and the spy James Bond (played by Sean Connery, right). Kennedy and his advisers prided themselves on their pragmatic, hard-nosed idealism. But whereas Bond used advanced technology and covert operations to save the world, in real life such approaches had their downside, as the growing civil war in Vietnam would demonstrate.

Robert McNamara

Robert Strange McNamara typified the pragmatic, liberal bent of the new Kennedy team. Steely and brilliant, McNamara was one of the postwar breed of young executives known as the "whiz kids." As a Harvard Business School professor and later as president of Ford Motor Company, he specialized in using quantitative tools to streamline business. As the new secretary of defense, McNamara intended to find more flexible and efficient ways of conducting the cold war.

Kennedy liked men such as McNamara—witty, bright, intellectual—because they seemed comfortable with power and were not afraid to use it. The president's leisure reading reflected a similar adventurous taste: the popular James Bond spy novels. Agent 007, with his license to kill, was sophisticated, a cool womanizer (as Kennedy himself continued to be), and ready to use the latest technology to deal with Communist villains. Ironically, Bond demonstrated that there could be plenty of glamour in being hard-nosed and pragmatic. That illicit pleasure was the underside, perhaps, of Camelot's high ideals.

The (Somewhat) New Frontier at Home

Despite campaign promises for bold initiatives, the president's domestic legislative achievements were modest. Once in the White House, Kennedy found himself hemmed in by a Democratic Congress dominated by conservatives. The modest Area Redevelopment Act of 1961 provided financial aid to depressed industrial and rural areas, and Congress raised the minimum wage to $1.25. But on key issues, including aid to education and medical health insurance, Kennedy made no headway.

He wavered too on how best to manage the economy. The president's liberal economic advisers favored increased government spending to reduce unemployment, even if that spending meant a budget deficit. Similarly, they argued that tax cuts could be used to increase consumer spending and so stimulate the economy. Kennedy toyed with both remedies, but conservatives continued to push for a balanced budget. So Kennedy moved cautiously, relieved at first to discover that the economy was growing quite nicely without a tax cut. Only in 1963 did he send a tax proposal to Congress, which passed it the following year.

Always pragmatic, Kennedy hoped to work with, not against, the leaders of big business. He firmly believed that prosperity for large firms spelled growth for the whole nation. Thus the president asked Congress to ease antitrust restrictions and grant investment credits and tax breaks—all actions that perfectly suited corporate interests. But he did believe that the government should be able to limit wages and prices for large corporations and unions. If not, an inflationary spiral

Showdown with Big Steel

might result. Wage increases would be followed by price increases followed by even higher wage demands.

To prevent that, the Council of Economic Advisors proposed to stabilize prices by tying wage increases to improved productivity. In April 1962 the United Steel Workers, like most other major unions, agreed to a contract that followed those guidelines. The large steel corporations, however, broke their part of the informal bargain by raising steel prices substantially. Incensed, Kennedy called for investigations into price fixing, mounted antitrust proceedings, and shifted Pentagon purchases to smaller steel companies that had not raised prices. The intense pressure caused the big companies to drop the price hikes but soured relations between Kennedy and the business community.

Kennedy's Cold War

During the 1952 election, Republicans exploited the stalemate in Korea, the fall of China, and the fear of domestic communism to suggest that the Democrats could not protect the nation's security. During the 1960 race for the White House, Kennedy had pledged to fight the cold war with new vigor. Once elected, the new president was determined not to be seen as soft on communism. The cold war contest, Kennedy argued, had shifted from the traditional struggle over Europe to the developing nations in Asia, Africa, and Latin America. The United States should be armed with a more flexible range of military and economic options.

Alliance for Progress and Peace Corps

The "Alliance for Progress," announced in the spring of 1961, indicated the course Kennedy would follow. He promised to provide $20 billion in foreign aid to Latin America over 10 years—about four times what Truman and Eisenhower had provided. In return, Latin American nations would agree to reform unfair tax policies and begin agricultural land reforms. If successful, the alliance would discourage future Castro-style revolutions. With similar fanfare, the administration set up the Peace Corps. This program sent idealistic young men and women to Third World nations to provide technical, educational, and public health services. Under the alliance, a majority of Peace Corps volunteers were assigned to Latin America.

To give economic programs some military muscle, the Pentagon created jungle warfare schools in North Carolina and the Canal Zone. These schools trained Latin American police and paramilitary groups to fight guerrilla wars. They also trained American special forces such as the Green Berets in the arts of jungle warfare. If the Soviets or their allies promoted "wars of liberation," United States commandos would be ready to fight back.

Space program

Kennedy believed, too, that the Soviets had made space the final frontier of the cold war. Only a few months after the president's inauguration, a Russian cosmonaut orbited the world for the first time. In response, Kennedy challenged Congress to authorize a manned space mission to the moon that would land by the end of the decade. In February 1962 John Glenn circled the earth three times in a "fireball of a ride." Gradually, the American space program gained on the Russians. In July 1969, a lunar module from the *Apollo 11* spacecraft touched down on the moon. It was a showy triumph in the cold war rivalry.

Cold War Frustrations

In more down-to-earth ways, high ideals did not translate easily into practical results. Although Latin American governments eagerly accepted aid, few welcomed the intrusive Yankee diplomats who came from north of the border to inspect their programs and press for reform. Instability remained a problem, for in the first five years of the alliance, nine Latin American governments were overthrown by military coups. The Peace Corps, for its part, proved a tremendous public relations success and helped thousands of Third World farmers on a people-to-people basis. But individual Peace Corps workers could do little to change corrupt policies on a national level.

Nor did Kennedy succeed in countering revolutionary "wars of liberation." His prime target was Fidel Castro's Communist regime in Cuba. After breaking diplomatic relations in 1960, the Eisenhower administration had secretly authorized the CIA to organize an invasion of that nation. The CIA assured Kennedy that its 1400-member army of Cuban exiles could inspire their compatriots in Cuba to overthrow Castro. Eager to establish his own cold war credentials, the president approved an attack. But the invasion in April 1961 turned into a disaster. The poorly equipped rebel forces landed at the swampy Bay of Pigs with no protective cover for miles. Within two days Castro's army had rounded them up. Taking responsibility for the fiasco, Kennedy suffered a bitter humiliation whose sting goaded the administration to undertake further covert operations. The CIA secretly hatched plans to destabilize the Cuban government or even murder Castro.

Bay of Pigs invasion

Kennedy's advisers took a similar covert approach in South Vietnam. There, a civil war with religious overtones was under way. The autocratic Prime Minister Ngo Dinh Diem remained in power, although he was growing more unpopular by the month. South Vietnamese Communists, known as the Vietcong, waged a guerrilla war against Diem with support from North Vietnam. Buddhist elements backed the rebellion against Diem, who was a Catholic. In May 1961, a month after the Bay of Pigs invasion, Kennedy secretly ordered 500 Green Berets and military advisers to Vietnam to help Diem. By 1963 the number of "military advisers" had risen to more than 16,000 soldiers. Increasingly, they were being drawn into combat with the Vietcong.

Kennedy and Vietnam

Diem's corruption, police state tactics, and ruthless campaign against his Buddhist opposition increasingly isolated the regime. Worse yet, he was not winning the war. As the Kennedy administration lost faith in Diem, it tacitly encouraged a military coup by other South Vietnamese military officers. To the surprise of American officials, the coup plotters not only captured Diem but shot him in November 1963. Despite Kennedy's policy of pragmatic idealism, the United States found itself mired in a Vietnamese civil war, which it had no clear strategy for winning.

Diem falls

Confronting Khrushchev

Vietnam and Cuba were just two areas in the Third World where Kennedy sought to battle Communist forces. But the conflict between the United States and the Soviet Union soon overshadowed developments in Asia, Africa, and Latin America.

June 1961 was the president's first chance to take the measure of Nikita Khrushchev, at a summit meeting held in Vienna. For two long days, Khrushchev was brash and belligerent. East and West Germany must be reunited, he demanded. In the divided capital of Berlin, located deep within East Germany (see map, page 919), citizens from all across East Germany were crossing from the eastern sector of Berlin into the free western zone as a way of escaping Communist rule. This "problem" must be settled within six months, Khrushchev insisted. Kennedy tried to stand up to Khrushchev's bullying, but he left Vienna worried that the Soviet leader perceived him as weak and inexperienced. By August events in Berlin confirmed his fears. Under cover of night, the Soviets threw up a wall sealing off any entry into West Berlin. Despite American protests, the heavily guarded Berlin Wall stayed up.

The Berlin Wall

Tensions with the Soviet Union led the administration to rethink American nuclear strategy. Under the Dulles doctrine of massive retaliation, almost any incident threatened to trigger a launch of the full arsenal of nuclear missiles.

A flexible nuclear response

The World of the Superpowers
This map shows the extent of the cold war Soviet and American military buildup. The United States established a worldwide network of bases and alliances surrounding Soviet bloc nations that extended from Japan and South Korea, South Vietnam, Pakistan, and Turkey in Asia to the nations of the NATO alliance in Europe. Soviet efforts to expand its influence in the Third World led to the creation of an outpost in Cuba. Around these strategic perimeters, hot spots and centers of crisis continued to simmer.

Kennedy and McNamara sought to establish a "flexible response doctrine" that would limit the level of a first nuclear strike and therefore leave room for negotiation. In that case, however, conventional forces in Europe would have to be built up so that they could better deter aggression. McNamara proposed equipping them with smaller tactical nuclear weapons.

But what if the Soviets were tempted to launch a first-strike attack to knock out American missiles? McNamara's flexible response policy required that enough American missiles survive in order to retaliate. If the Soviets knew the United States could survive a first strike, they would then be less likely to launch a surprise attack. So McNamara began a program to place missile sites underground and to develop submarine-launched missiles. The new flexible response policies resulted in a 15 percent increase in the 1961 military budget, compared with only 2 percent increases during the last two years of Eisenhower's term. Under Kennedy, the military-industrial complex thrived.

The Missiles of October

The peril of nuclear confrontation became dramatically clear in the Cuban missile crisis of October 1962. President Kennedy had emphasized repeatedly that the United States would treat any attempt to place offensive weapons in Cuba as an unacceptable threat. Khrushchev had promised that the Soviet Union had no such intention but bristled privately at what he perceived as a gross inequality in the cold war. "The Americans had surrounded our country with military bases and threatened us with nuclear weapons," he told high Soviet officials in May 1962. In that month he convinced them to begin building a secret nuclear base in Cuba. "Now [the Americans] would learn just what it feels like to have enemy missiles pointing at you."

Throughout the summer the buildup went undetected by Americans. But by October 14, overflights of Cuba by U-2 spy planes had uncovered the offensive missile sites. Kennedy was outraged.

For a week, top American security advisers met in secret strategy sessions. Hawkish advisers urged air strikes against the missile sites, and at first Kennedy agreed. "We're certainly going to . . . take out these . . . missiles," he said. But others pointed out that the U-2 flights had not photographed all of Cuba. What if there were more concealed bases with missiles ready to fire? The Soviets could then launch an atomic attack on the United States despite the air strikes. Furthermore, if the United States attacked Cuba with no advance warning, the act would appear to the world uncomfortably like the Japanese surprise attack on Pearl Harbor in World War II.

A naval blockade

Although the Joint Chiefs of Staff continued to press for a large air attack, Kennedy finally chose the more restrained option. The United States would impose a naval blockade to intercept "all offensive military equipment under shipment to Cuba." On October 22, word of the confrontation began to leak out. "CAPITAL CRISIS AIR HINTS AT DEVELOPMENTS ON CUBA; KENNEDY TV TALK IS LIKELY," ran the *New York*

The discovery of Soviet offensive missile sites in Cuba, revealed by low-level American reconnaissance flights, led to the first nuclear showdown of the cold war. For several tense days in October 1962, President Kennedy met with his National Security Council to debate alternative responses.

Times headline. In Moscow, Soviet leaders awaited Kennedy's speech convinced that an American invasion of Cuba was likely. "The thing is we were not going to unleash war," a nervous Khrushchev complained to his colleagues. "We just wanted to intimidate them, to deter the anti-Cuban forces." Americans were stunned that evening by the president's television address.

Over the next few days, tensions mounted as a Soviet submarine approached the line of American ships. On October 25 the navy stopped an oil tanker. Several Soviet ships reversed course. In Cuba, Soviet general Issa Pliyev felt that he had to assume the worst—that despite all the talk of a blockade, an American invasion of Cuba was being prepared. Pliyev sent a coded message to Moscow that "in the opinion of the Cuban friends [i.e., the Castro government] the U.S. air strike on our installations in Cuba will occur in the night between October 26 and October 27 or at dawn on October 27." Equally ominously, he added, "We have taken measures to disperse 'techniki' [the nuclear warheads] in the zone of operations." In other words, Pliyev was making his nuclear missiles operational.

The morning of October 27, alarmed Soviet technicians detected a U-2 plane flying over Cuba. Was this the beginning of the expected attack? General Pliyev had issued strict instructions not to use force without his authorization, but when the air defense command looked to consult him, he could not be found, and the U-2 would leave Cuban airspace shortly. Soviet officers went ahead and shot it down, killing its pilot.

Meanwhile, Kennedy was making strenuous efforts to resolve the crisis through diplomatic channels. On October 26 he had received a rambling message from Khrushchev agreeing to remove the missiles in return for an American promise not to invade Cuba. The following day a second, more troubling message arrived with a new condition, that the United States must also dismantle its missile bases in Turkey, which bordered on the Soviet Union. As the president and his advisers debated, word came of the downed U-2. Kennedy was shocked. A policy had already been established that the United States would retaliate if the Soviets launched an attack from their Cuban bases. American planes were standing by on thirty-minute alert, ready to take off. Worried that events might quickly spiral out of control, the president put off that decision until the following morning.

Then he decided to ignore Khrushchev's second letter and accept the offer in the first: removal of Soviet missiles if the Americans pledged not to invade Cuba. Kennedy also gave private assurances that the missiles in Turkey would come out within half a year. In Moscow, Khrushchev agreed reluctantly to the deal, telling his advisers somberly that there were times to advance and times to retreat; and this time, "we found ourselves face to face with the danger of war and of nuclear catastrophe, with the possible result of destroying the human race." Thus the face-off ended on terms that saved either side from overt humiliation.

The nuclear showdown prompted Kennedy and his advisers to seek ways to control the nuclear arms race. "We all inhabit this small planet," he warned in June 1963. "We all breathe the same air. We all cherish our children's future. And we are all mortal." The administration negotiated a nuclear test ban with the Soviets, prohibiting all above-ground nuclear tests. Growing concern over radioactive fallout increased public support for the treaty. A telephone hot line was also installed, providing a direct communications link between the White House and the Kremlin for use in times of crisis. At the same time Kennedy's prestige soared for "standing up" to the Soviets.

Nuclear test ban treaty

The Cuban missile crisis was the closest the world had come to "destroying the human race," in Khrushchev's words, and it sobered both superpowers. It did not end the cold war, however; indeed, both nations endured long, drawn-out regional wars before scaling back their ambitions—the United States in Vietnam and the Soviet Union in Afghanistan. Yet the intensity of confrontation—with Eisenhower and Dulles's brinkmanship, Khrushchev's provocations, and Kennedy's cold war rhetoric—began to ease. The nuclear anxieties of the 1950s, so much a part of the suburban era, yielded to different concerns in the 1960s.

In large part, that change came about because the supposed consensus of the 1950s masked a profound *lack* of consensus concerning the state of equality in America. While the suburbs flourished, urban areas decayed. While more white Americans went to college, more African Americans found themselves out of work on southern farms or desperate for jobs in northern ghettos, and still in segregated schools. As Mexican American migrant workers picked crops in California or followed the harvest north from Texas, they saw their employers resist every attempt to unionize and improve their wages. To all these Americans, the long-accepted "consensus" about opportunity in American life was no longer acceptable. The 1950s sparked a movement pursued by ordinary Americans who acted, despite the reluctance of their leaders, to bring about a civil rights revolution.

chapter summary

At midcentury, during an era of peace and prosperity, the United States began to build a new social and political agenda.

- Automobiles and the culture of the highways helped bind Americans to one another in a "consensus" about what it meant to be an American.

  - Highways made possible rapid suburban growth.

  - Suburbs proved popular with the growing white-collar middle class.

  - Consensus in suburbs blurred class distinctions and promoted the notion of "civil religion."

- Suburban life nurtured the ideal of the woman who found fulfillment as a homemaker and a mother, even though more women began to work outside the home.

• President Eisenhower resisted the demands of conservatives to dismantle the New Deal and of liberals to extend it, in favor of moderate, or "middle of the road," Republicanism.

• Cracks in consensus appeared among discontented intellectuals and among teenagers who, through Elvis Presley and new teen idols, discovered the power of rock and roll.

• Efforts to more vigorously contain the U.S.S.R. and Communist China, through a policy of "brinkmanship," proved difficult to apply because of growing Third World nationalism.

- Eisenhower held back from using tactical nuclear weapons during crises in Vietnam and Taiwan.

- Successful CIA operations in Iran and Guatemala encouraged American policy makers to use covert operations more frequently.

- Post-colonial nationalism contributed to crises in Hungary, Egypt, and Cuba, where President Kennedy was embarrassed by the failure of an invasion attempt to overthrow Fidel Castro.

• Relations between the two superpowers thawed gradually but not without recurring confrontations between the United States and the Soviet Union.

- Under Eisenhower, the Soviet success with *Sputnik* increased fears that the United States was vulnerable to missile attacks, while the U-2 spy plane incident worsened relations.

- John F. Kennedy proved willing to use covert operations as well as diplomatic and economic initiatives like the Peace Corps and the Alliance for Progress.

- The construction of Soviet missile bases 90 miles from American shores triggered the Cuban missile crisis of 1962, the closest the United States and the Soviet Union ever came to nuclear war.

interactive learning

The Primary Source Investigator CD-ROM offers the following materials related to this chapter:

• Interactive map: **Election of 1960** (M7)

• A short documentary movie on America's automobile culture and one special highway, Route 66 (D16)

• A collection of primary sources exploring the growth of the suburbs in America during the 1950s: read the Interstate Highways Act, watch the comedy "A Housewife's Dream," and view images of suburban tract housing. Several other sources depict the continuing prominence of the American military and national security during the cold war.

additional reading

No modern president's reputation has risen more among historians than Dwight Eisenhower's. Contrast the dismissive view of Eric Goldman, *The Crucial Decade and After, 1945–1960* (1960),

with Stephen Ambrose, *Eisenhower: The President* (1984), or Fred Greenstein, *The Hidden Hand Presidency: Eisenhower as Leader* (1982). A similar revision has occurred in the treatment of his foreign policy, in which Eisenhower receives credit that once went to Dulles. See, for example, Robert Divine, *Eisenhower and the Cold War* (1981). On the other hand, John F. Kennedy's stock has fallen sharply since the heady days of Camelot. Contrast the reverential treatments of Kennedy in Arthur Schlesinger Jr., *The Thousand Days* (1965), and Theodore Sorenson, *Kennedy* (1965), with David Burner and Thomas West, *The Torch Is Passed: The Kennedy Brothers and American Liberalism* (1992), and Mark Stern, *Calculating Visions: Kennedy, Johnson, and Civil Rights* (1992).

For an overview of the era, see John Diggins, *The Proud Decades: America in War and Peace, 1941–1960* (1988), or the even more readable, but less analytical, David Halberstam, *The Fifties* (1993). The Cuban missile crisis is told with the aid of newly released Russian sources in Aleksandr Fursenko and Timothy Naftali, *"One Hell of a Gamble": Khrushchev, Castro, and Kennedy, 1958–1964* (1997), and the tape-recorded secret White House debates are published in Ernest R. May and Philip D. Zelikow, eds., *The Kennedy Tapes: Inside the White House during the Cuban Missile Crisis* (1997). For a fuller list of readings, see the Bibliography at www.mhhe.com/davidsonnation5.

significant events

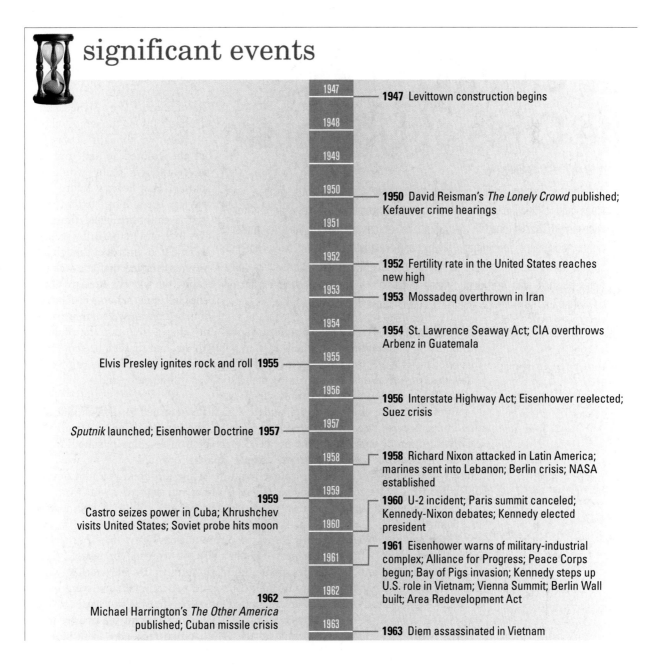

1947 Levittown construction begins

1950 David Reisman's *The Lonely Crowd* published; Kefauver crime hearings

1952 Fertility rate in the United States reaches new high

1953 Mossadeq overthrown in Iran

1954 St. Lawrence Seaway Act; CIA overthrows Arbenz in Guatemala

Elvis Presley ignites rock and roll **1955**

1956 Interstate Highway Act; Eisenhower reelected; Suez crisis

Sputnik launched; Eisenhower Doctrine **1957**

1958 Richard Nixon attacked in Latin America; marines sent into Lebanon; Berlin crisis; NASA established

1959
Castro seizes power in Cuba; Khrushchev visits United States; Soviet probe hits moon

1960 U-2 incident; Paris summit canceled; Kennedy-Nixon debates; Kennedy elected president

1961 Eisenhower warns of military-industrial complex; Alliance for Progress; Peace Corps begun; Bay of Pigs invasion; Kennedy steps up U.S. role in Vietnam; Vienna Summit; Berlin Wall built; Area Redevelopment Act

1962
Michael Harrington's *The Other America* published; Cuban missile crisis

1963 Diem assassinated in Vietnam

Chapter 29

Six-year-old Ruby knew the lessons. She was to look straight ahead—not to one side or the other—and especially not at *them*. She was to keep walking. Above all, she was not to look back once she'd passed, because that would encourage them. Ruby's parents had instructed her carefully, but she still struggled to keep her eyes straight. The first day of school, federal marshals were there along with her parents. So were hundreds of nasty white people who came near enough to yell things like "You little nigger, we'll get you and kill you." Then she was within the building's quiet halls and alone with her teacher. She was the only person in class: none of the white students had come. As the days went by during that autumn of 1960, the marshals stopped walking with her but the hecklers still waited. And once in a while Ruby couldn't help looking back, trying to see if she recognized the face of one woman in particular.

Ruby's parents were not social activists. They signed their daughter up for the white school because "we thought it was for all the colored to do, and we never thought Ruby would be alone." Her father's white employer fired him; letters and phone calls threatened the family's lives and home. Ruby seemed to take it all in stride, though her parents worried that she was not eating the way she used to. Often she left her school lunch untouched or refused anything other

Civil Rights & the Crisis of Liberalism

1947–1969

preview • Largely walled out from the prosperity of the 1950s, African Americans and Latinos campaigned to gain the freedoms denied them through widespread racism and, in the South, a system of segregation. As the civil rights movement blossomed, young and relatively affluent baby boomers spread the revolution to other areas of American life. Their radical goals sometimes clashed with President Lyndon Johnson's liberal strategy of using federal programs to alleviate inequality and create a Great Society.

than packaged food such as potato chips. It was only after a time that the problem was traced to the hecklers. "They tells me I'm going to die, and that it'll be soon. And that one lady tells me every morning I'm getting poisoned soon, when she can fix it." Ruby was convinced that the woman owned the variety store nearby and would carry out her threat by poisoning the family's food.

Over the course of a year, white students gradually returned to class and life settled into a new routine. By the time Ruby was 10, she had developed a remarkably clear perception of herself. "Maybe because of all the trouble going to school in the beginning I learned more about my people. Maybe I would have anyway; because when you get older you see yourself and the white kids; and you find out the difference. You try to forget it, and say there is none; and if there is you won't say what it be. Then you say it's my own people, and so I can be proud of them instead of ashamed."

If the new ways were hard for Ruby, they were not easy for white southerners either—even those who saw the need for change. One woman, for years a dedicated teacher in Atlanta, vividly recalled a traumatic summer 10 years earlier, when she went north to New York City to take courses in education. There were black students living in the dormitory, an integrated situation she was not used to. One day as she stepped from her shower, so did a black student from the nearby stall. "When I saw her I didn't know what to do," the woman recalled. "I felt sick all

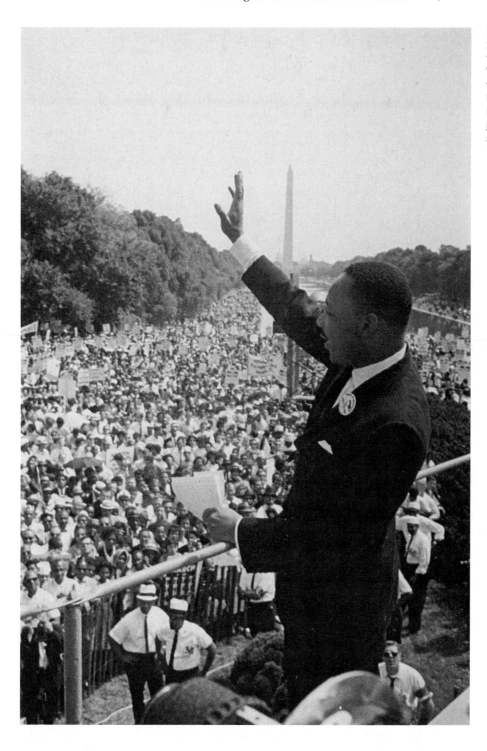

On August 28, 1963, more than 250,000 demonstrators joined the great civil rights march on Washington. The day belonged to the Reverend Martin Luther King Jr., who movingly called on black and white Americans to join together in a color-blind society.

over, and frightened. What I remember—I'll never forget it—is that horrible feeling of being caught in a terrible trap, and not knowing what to do about it. I thought of running out of the room and screaming, or screaming at the woman to get out, or running back into the shower. . . . My sense of propriety was with me, though—miraculously—and I didn't want to hurt the woman. It wasn't *her* that

When Ruby drew pictures for psychologist Robert Coles, her true feelings came out. Her white children had all their features carefully sketched. The black children had body parts missing. "When I draw a white girl, I know she'll be okay," Ruby explained, "but with the colored it's not okay."

was upsetting me. I knew that, even in that moment of sickness and panic." So she ducked back into the shower until the other woman left.

Summer was almost over before she felt comfortable eating with black students at the same table. And when she returned home, she told no one about her experiences. "At that time people would have thought one of two things: I was crazy (for being so upset and ashamed) or a fool who in a summer had become a dangerous 'race mixer.'" She continued to love the South and to speak up for its traditions of dignity, neighborliness, and honor, but she saw the need for change. And so in 1961 she volunteered to teach one of the first integrated high school classes in Atlanta, even though she had her doubts. By the end of two years she concluded that she had never spent a more exciting time teaching. "I've never felt so useful, so constantly useful, not just to the children but to our whole society. American as well as Southern. Those children, all of them, have given me more than I've given them."

For Americans in all walks of life, the upheavals that swept America in the 1960s were wrenching. From the schoolrooms and lunch counters of the South to the college campuses of the North, from eastern slums to western migrant labor camps, American society was in ferment.

On the face of it, such agitation seemed to be a dramatic reversal of the placid 1950s. Turbulence and change had overturned stability and consensus. Yet the events of the 1960s grew naturally out of the social conditions that preceded those years. The civil rights movement was brought about not by a group of farsighted leaders in government but by ordinary folk who sought change, often despite the reluctance or even fierce opposition of people in power. After World War II, grassroots organizations like the NAACP for blacks and the American GI Forum for Latinos acted with a new determination to achieve the equality of opportunity promised by the American creed.

Thus the 1950s were a seedbed for the more turbulent revolutions of the 1960s. The booming postwar economy held out the possibility of better lives for minorities; yet systematic discrimination and racism, long embedded in American life by custom and law, prevented prosperity from spreading equally. Time and again, activists challenged the political system to deal with what the 1950s had done—and what had been left undone. As one friend of Martin Luther King predicted in 1958, "If the young people are aroused from their lethargy through this fight, it will affect broad circles throughout the country."

The Civil Rights Movement

The struggle of African Americans for equality during the postwar era is filled with ironies. By the time barriers to legal segregation in the South began to fall, millions of black families were leaving for regions where discrimination was less easily challenged in court. The South they left behind was in the early stages of an economic boom. The cities where many migrated to had entered a period of decline. Yet, as if to close a circle, the rise of large black voting blocs in major cities created political pressures that helped force the nation to dismantle the worst legal and institutional barriers to racial equality.

The Changing South and African Americans

After World War II the southern economy began to grow significantly faster than the national economy. The remarkable about-face began during the New Deal with federal programs like the Tennessee Valley Authority. World War II brought even more federal dollars to build and maintain military bases and defense plants. And the South attracted new business because it offered a "clean slate." In contrast to the more mature economic regions of the Northeast and Upper Midwest, the South had few unions, little regulation and bureaucracy, and low wages and taxes. Finally, there was the matter of climate, which later caused the region to be nicknamed the Sun Belt. Especially with improvements in air-conditioning, the South grew more attractive to skilled professionals, corporate managers, and affluent retirees.

Before World War II, 80 percent of African Americans lived in the South. Most raised cotton as sharecroppers and tenant farmers. But the war created a labor shortage at home, as millions of workers went off to fight and others went to armament factories. This shortage gave cotton growers an incentive to mechanize cotton picking. In 1950 only 5 percent of the crop was picked mechanically; by 1960 at least half was. Farmers began to consolidate land into larger holdings. Tenant farmers, sharecroppers, and hired labor of both races, no longer in short supply, left the countryside for the city.

The national level of wages also profoundly affected southern labor. When federal minimum wage laws forced lumber or textile mills to raise their pay scales, the mills no longer expanded. In addition, steel and other industries with strong national unions and manufacturers with plants around the country set wages by national standards. Those changes brought southern wages close to the national average by the 1960s. As the southern economy grew, what had for many years been a distinct regional economy became more diversified and more integrated into the national economy.

Mechanized cotton farming

As wages rose and unskilled work disappeared, job opportunities for black southerners declined. Outside of cotton farming, the lumber industry provided the largest number of jobs for young black men. There, the number of black teenagers hired by lumber mills dropped 74 percent between 1950 and 1960. New high-wage jobs were reserved for white southerners, because outside industries arriving in the South made no effort to change local patterns of discrimination. So the ultimate irony arose. As per capita income rose and industrialization brought in new jobs, black laborers poured out of the region in search of work. They arrived in cities that showed scant tolerance for racial differences and little willingness or ability to hire unskilled black labor.

The NAACP and Civil Rights

In the postwar era the NAACP decided it would use the judicial system to attack Jim Crow laws. That stepped-up attack reflected the increased national political influence that African Americans achieved as they migrated in great numbers out of the South. No longer could northern politicians readily ignore the demands black leaders made for greater equality. The Swedish scholar Gunnar Myrdal had amply documented the black case in his landmark work *The American Dilemma* (1944), sponsored by the Carnegie Corporation. Presidents Roosevelt and Truman had taken small but significant steps to address the worst forms of legal and economic discrimination. And across the South black churches and colleges became centers for organized resistance to segregation.

Thurgood Marshall

Thurgood Marshall emerged as the NAACP's leading attorney. Marshall had attended law school in the 1930s at Howard University in Washington. There, the law school's dean, Charles Houston, was in the midst of revamping the school and

Overton Park Zoo in Memphis, Tennessee, was segregated like thousands of other public facilities throughout the South in the late 1950s. In the case of the zoo, Tuesdays were "colored" days, the only time when blacks could attend—except if the Fourth of July fell on a Tuesday. Then "colored" day was moved to Thursday.

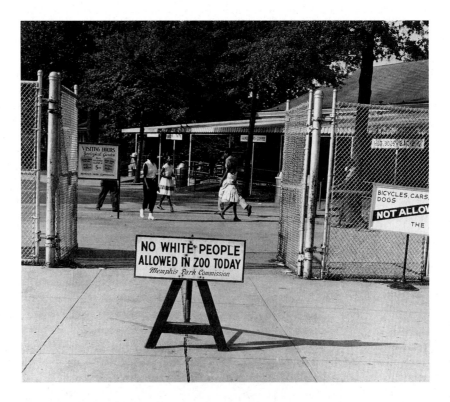

turning out sharp, dedicated lawyers. Marshall not only was sharp but had the common touch. "Before he came along," one observer noted,

> the principal black leaders—men like Du Bois and James Weldon Johnson and Charles Houston—didn't talk the language of the people. They were upper-class and upper-middle-class Negroes. Thurgood Marshall was *of* the people. . . . Out in Texas or Oklahoma or down the street here in Washington at the Baptist church, he would make these rousing speeches that would have 'em all jumping out of their seats. . . . "We ain't gettin' what we should," was what it came down to, and he made them see that.

During the late 1930s and early 1940s Marshall toured the South (in "a little old beat-up '29 Ford"), typing out legal briefs in the back seat, trying to get teachers to sue for equal pay, and defending blacks accused of murder in a Klan-infested county in Florida. He was friendly with whites, not shy, and black citizens who had never even considered the possibility that a member of their race might win a legal battle "would come for miles, some of them on muleback or horseback, to see 'the nigger lawyer' who stood up in white men's courtrooms."

For years NAACP lawyers had worked hard to organize local chapters, to support members of the community willing to risk their jobs, property, and lives in order to challenge segregation. But they waged a moderate, pragmatic campaign. They chose not to attack head-on the Supreme Court decision (*Plessy v. Ferguson*, 1896) that permitted "separate but equal" segregated facilities. They simply demonstrated that a black college or school might be separate, but it was hardly equal if it lacked a law school or even indoor plumbing.

The *Brown* Decision

In 1950 the NAACP changed tactics: it would now try to convince the Supreme Court to overturn the separate but equal doctrine itself. Oliver Brown was one of the people who provided a way. Brown was dissatisfied that his daughter Linda had to walk past an all-white school on her way to catch the bus to her segregated black school in Topeka, Kansas. A three-judge federal panel rejected Brown's suit because the schools in Topeka, while segregated, did meet the test of equality. But the NAACP had been making headway with other cases in other courts. After two years of arguments the Supreme Court in *Brown v. Board of Education of Topeka* (1954) overturned the lower court ruling.

Marshall and his colleagues succeeded in part because of a change in the Court itself. The year before, President Eisenhower had appointed Earl Warren, a liberal Republican from California, as chief justice. Warren, a forceful advocate, managed to persuade the last of his reluctant judicial colleagues that segregation as defined in *Plessy* rested on an untenable theory of racial supremacy. The Court thus ruled unanimously that separate facilities were inherently unequal. To keep black children segregated solely on the basis of race, it ruled, "generates a feeling of inferiority as to their status in the community that may affect their hearts and minds in a way unlikely ever to be undone."

Overturning Plessy

At the time of the *Brown* decision, 21 states and the District of Columbia operated segregated school systems. All of them had to decide, in some way, how to comply with the new ruling. The Court allowed a certain amount of leeway, handing down a second ruling in 1955 that required that desegregation be carried out "with all deliberate speed." Some border states reluctantly decided to comply, but in the Deep South, many citizens called for die-hard defiance. In 1956, a "Southern

Manifesto" was issued by 19 U.S. senators and 81 representatives; it declared their intent to use "all lawful means" to reestablish legalized segregation.

Latino Civil Rights

Mexican Americans also considered school desegregation as central to their campaign for civil rights. At the end of World War II, only 1 percent of children of Mexican descent in Texas graduated from high school. Both the American GI Forum (page 922) and the League of United Latin American Citizens (LULAC; pages 824–825) supported legal challenges to the system.

Delgado and segregated schools

In a 1947 case, *Mendez et al. v. Westminster School District of Orange County,* the courts had ordered several California school districts to integrate. LULAC saw a way to apply that ruling in Texas. The superintendent in the town of Bastrop had refused a request to enroll first-grader Minerva Delgado in a nearby all-white school. Civil rights lawyer and activist Gus Garcia, a legal adviser to both LULAC and the GI Forum, helped bring a case on Minerva's behalf against the school district. Before *Delgado et al. v. Bastrop et al.* went to trial, a Texas judge ordered an end to segregated schools beyond the first grade (based on the assumption that the youngest Mexican American children needed special classes to learn English). *Delgado* served notice that Mexicans would no longer accept second-class citizenship. It also served as a precedent in *Brown v. Board of Education* in 1954.

Two weeks before the Supreme Court made that landmark civil rights ruling, it also decided a case of great importance to Latinos. Unlike African Americans, Latinos did not face a Jim Crow system of laws imposing segregation. Throughout the Southwest the states recognized just two races: black and white. That left Mexican Americans in legal limbo. Though legally grouped with whites, they were by long-standing social custom barred from many public places, they could not serve on juries, and they faced widespread job discrimination. To remedy the situation, Mexican Americans had to establish themselves in the courts as a distinct class of people.

Hernández and desegregation

An opportunity arose in the case of Pete Hernández, who had been convicted of murder by an all-white jury in Jackson County, Texas. Indeed, as Mexican American lawyer Gus Garcia realized, no Mexican American had served on a Jackson jury in the previous 25 years. Garcia, one of the leaders of the American GI Forum,

Attorney Gus Garcia (left) was one of the key leaders of the American GI Forum, founded by Mexican American veterans to pursue their civil rights. He and his colleagues successfully appealed the conviction of Pete Hernández (center) before the Supreme Court in 1954.

saw in the tactics of Thurgood Marshall and the NAACP a way to use the Hernández case to extend to Mexicans the benefits of the Fourteenth Amendment's equal
protection clause.

The key to the case was ingenious but direct. The state argued that because
Mexicans were white, a jury without Mexicans was still a jury of peers. Yet the courthouse in which Hernández was tried had two men's rooms. One said simply, "MEN."
The other, labeled with a crudely hand-lettered sign, said "COLORED MEN" and below
that, in Spanish, "HOMBRES AQUI [MEN HERE]." As one of Gus Garcia's colleagues
recalled, "In the jury pool, Mexicans may have been white, but when it came to
nature's functions they were not." This and similar examples of discrimination persuaded the Supreme Court, in *Hernández v. Texas,* to throw out the state's argument.
Latinos in south Texas, like African Americans across the South, were held to be a
discrete group whose members deserved equal protection under the law. "The Fourteenth Amendment is not directed solely against discrimination due to a 'two-class
theory,' that is, based upon differences between 'white' and Negro," ruled Chief Justice Earl Warren. Warren's reasoning made it possible for Latinos to seek redress as a
group rather than as individuals. After *Hernández,* the Mexican American community
had both the legal basis and the leadership to broaden its attack against discrimination.

A New Civil Rights Strategy

Neither the *Brown* nor the *Hernández* decision ended segregation, but they combined with political and economic forces to usher in a new era of southern race
relations. In December 1955 Rosa Parks, a 43-year-old black civil rights activist,   Rosa Parks
was riding the bus home in Montgomery, Alabama. When the driver ordered her
to give up her seat for a white man, as Alabama Jim Crow laws required, she
refused. Police took her to jail and eventually fined her $14.

Determined to overturn the law, a number of women from the NAACP, friends
of Parks, met secretly at midnight to draft a letter of protest.

> Another Negro woman has been arrested and thrown into jail because she refused
> to get up out of her seat on the bus and give it to a white person. . . . Until we do
> something to stop these arrests, they will continue. The next time it may be you,
> or you or you. This woman's case will come up Monday. We are, therefore, asking
> every Negro to stay off the buses on Monday in protest of the arrest and trial.

Thousands of copies of the letter were distributed, and the Monday boycott was
such a success it was extended indefinitely. Buses wheeled around the city virtually empty, losing over 30,000 fares a day. The white community, in an effort to
halt the unprecedented black challenge, resorted to various forms of legal and physical intimidation. No local agent would insure cars used to carpool black workers.
A bomb exploded in the house of the Reverend Martin Luther King Jr., the key
boycott leader. And when that failed to provoke the violence that whites could use
to justify harsh reprisals, 90 black leaders were arrested for organizing an illegal
boycott. Still, the campaign continued until November 23, 1956, when the Supreme
Court ruled that bus segregation was illegal.

The triumph was especially sweet for Martin Luther King Jr., whose leader-   Martin Luther King Jr.
ship in Montgomery brought him national fame. Before becoming a minister at the
Dexter Street Baptist Church, King had little personal contact with the worst forms
of white racism. He had grown up in the relatively affluent middle-class black community of Atlanta, Georgia, the son of one of the city's most prominent black

ministers. He attended Morehouse College, an academically respected black school in Atlanta, and Crozer Theological Seminary in Philadelphia before entering the doctoral program in theology at Boston University. As a graduate student, King embraced the pacifism and nonviolence of the Indian leader Mohandas Gandhi and the activism of Christian reformers of the progressive era. King heeded the call to Dexter Street in 1954 with the idea of becoming a theologian after he served his active ministry and finished his dissertation.

As boycott leader it was King's responsibility to rally black support without triggering violence. Because local officials were all too eager for any excuse to use force, King's nonviolent approach was the ideal strategy. King offered his audience two visions. First, he reminded them of the many injustices they had been forced to endure. The boycott, he asserted, was a good way to seek redress. Then he counseled his followers to avoid the actions of their oppressors: "In our protest there will be no cross burnings. No white person will be taken from his home by a hooded Negro mob and brutally murdered." And he evoked the Christian and republican ideals that would become the themes of his civil rights crusade. "If we protest courageously, and yet with dignity and Christian love," he said, "when the future history books are written, somebody will have to say, 'There lived a race of people, of black people, of people who had the moral courage to stand up for their rights. And thereby they injected a new meaning into the history of civilization.'"

Indeed, the African Americans of Montgomery did set an example of moral courage that rewrote the pages of American race relations. Their firm stand caught the attention of the national news media. King and his colleagues were developing the tactics needed to launch a more aggressive phase of the civil rights movement.

Little Rock and the White Backlash

The civil rights spotlight moved the following year to Little Rock, Arkansas. White officials there had reluctantly adopted a plan to integrate the schools with a most deliberate lack of speed. Nine black students were scheduled to enroll in September 1957 at the all-white Central High School. Instead, the school board urged them to stay home. Governor Orval Faubus, generally a moderate on race relations, called out the Arkansas National Guard on the excuse of maintaining order. President Eisenhower tacitly supported Faubus in his defiance of court-ordered integration by remarking that "you cannot change people's hearts merely by laws."

Still, the Justice Department could not simply let Faubus defy the federal courts. It won an injunction against the governor, but when the nine blacks returned on September 23 a mob of 1000 abusive whites greeted them. So great was national attention on the crisis that President Eisenhower felt compelled to uphold the authority of the federal courts. He sent in federal troops and took control of the National Guard. For a year the Guard preserved order until Faubus, in a last-ditch maneuver, closed the schools. Only in 1959, under pressure of another federal court ruling, did Little Rock schools reopen and resume the plan for gradual integration.

In the face of such attitudes, King and other civil rights leaders recognized that the skirmishes of Montgomery and Little Rock were a beginning, not the end. In fact, segregationist resistance increased in the wake of King's Montgomery success. From 1955 to 1959 civil rights protesters endured over 200 acts of violence in the South. Legislatures and city councils passed scores of laws attempting either to outlaw the NAACP or prevent it from functioning. Black leaders were unable to achieve momentum on a national scale until 1960. Then, a series of spontaneous demonstrations by young people changed everything.

Angry white students, opposed to integration, menace black students during a recess at Little Rock's Central High. This civil rights crisis was the first covered by television; for weeks NBC correspondent John Chancellor took a chartered plane daily from Little Rock to Oklahoma City to deliver film footage for the nightly news program. Such national attention made people outside the South more sensitive to civil rights issues.

A Movement Becomes a Crusade

On January 31, 1960, Joseph McNeill got off the bus in Greensboro, North Carolina, a freshman on the way back to college. When he looked for something to eat at the lunch counter, the waitress gave the familiar reply. "We don't serve Negroes here."

It was a refrain repeated countless times and in countless places. Yet for some reason this rebuke particularly offended McNeill. He and his roommates had read a pamphlet describing the 1955 bus boycott in Montgomery, Alabama. They decided it was time to make their own protest against segregation. Proceeding the next day to the "whites only" lunch counter at a local store, they sat politely waiting for service. "The waitress looked at me as if I were from outer space," recalled one of the protesters. Rather than serve them, the manager closed the counter. Word of the action spread. A day later—Tuesday—the four students were joined by 27 more. Wednesday, the number jumped to 63, Thursday, to over 300. Come the weekend, 1600 students rallied to plan further action.

On Monday, February 8, sit-ins began in nearby Durham and Winston-Salem. Tuesday it was Charlotte. Thursday, High Point and Portsmouth, Virginia. A news broadcast reassured white residents in Raleigh that black students there would not follow Greensboro's example. In response, angry black students launched massive

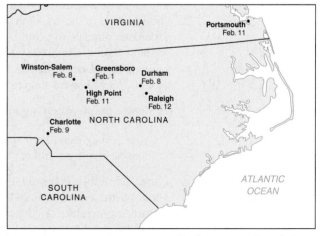

The Spontaneous Spread of Sit-ins, February 1960

sit-ins at variety stores in Raleigh. By Lincoln's birthday, the demonstrations had spread to Tennessee and Florida; by April, to 78 different southern and border communities. By September at least 70,000 African Americans as well as whites had participated. Thousands had been arrested and jailed.

The campaign for black civil rights gained momentum not so much by the power of national movements as through a host of individual decisions by local groups, churches, and citizens. When New Orleans schools were desegregated in 1960, young Ruby's parents had not intended to make a social statement. But once involved, they refused to back down. The students at Greensboro had not been approached by the NAACP, but acted on their own initiative.

Riding to Freedom

Newer civil rights organizations

Of course, organizations channeled these discontents and aspirations. But the new generation of younger activists also shaped and altered the organizations. Beginning in the 1960s, the push for desegregation moved from court actions launched by the NAACP and the Urban League to newer groups determined to take direct action. Since organizing the Montgomery boycott, Martin Luther King and his Southern Christian Leadership Conference (SCLC) had continued to advocate nonviolent protest: "To resist without bitterness; to be cursed and not reply; to be beaten and not hit back." A second key organization, the Congress of Racial Equality (CORE), was more willing than the SCLC to force confrontations with the segregationist system. Another group, the Student Non-Violent Coordinating Committee (SNCC, pronounced "Snick"), grew out of the Greensboro sit-in. SNCC represented the more militant, younger generation of black activists who grew increasingly impatient with the slow pace of reform.

In May 1961 CORE director James Farmer led a group of black and white "freedom riders" on a bus trip into the heart of the South. They hoped their trip from Washington to New Orleans would focus national attention on the inequality of segregated facilities. Violent southern mobs gave them the kind of attention they feared. In South Carolina, thugs beat divinity student John Lewis as he tried to enter an all-white waiting room. Mobs in Anniston and Birmingham, Alabama, assaulted the freedom riders as police ignored the violence. One of the buses was burned.

President Kennedy had sought to avoid forceful federal intervention in the South. When the freedom riders persisted in their plans, he tried to convince Alabama officials to protect the demonstrators so that he would not have to send federal forces. His hopes were dashed. From a phone booth outside the bus terminal, John Doar, a Justice Department official in Montgomery, relayed the horror to Attorney General Robert Kennedy, the president's brother:

> Now the passengers are coming off. They're standing on a corner of the platform. Oh, there are fists, punching! A bunch of men led by a guy with a bleeding face are beating them. There are no cops. It's terrible! It's terrible! There's not a cop in sight. People are yelling, "There those niggers are! Get 'em, get 'em!" It's awful.

Freedom riders attacked

Appalled, Robert Kennedy ordered in 400 federal marshals, who barely managed to hold off the crowd. Martin Luther King, addressing a meeting in town, phoned the attorney general to say that their church had been surrounded by an angry mob of several thousand—jeering, throwing rocks, and carrying firebombs. As Kennedy later recalled, "I said that we were doing the best that we could and that he'd be as dead as Kelsey's nuts if it hadn't been for the marshals and the efforts that we made."

Both Kennedys understood that civil rights was the most divisive issue the administration faced. For liberals, civil rights measured Kennedy's credentials as a reformer. Kennedy needed black and liberal votes to win reelection. Yet an active federal role threatened to drive white southerners from the Democratic party. It was for that reason that Kennedy had hedged on his promise to introduce major civil rights legislation. Through executive orders, he assured black leaders, he could eliminate discrimination in the government civil service and in businesses filling government contracts. He appointed several African Americans to high administrative positions and five, including Thurgood Marshall, to the federal courts. The Justice Department beefed up its civil rights enforcement procedures. But the freedom riders, by their bold actions, forced the Kennedys to do more.

Civil Rights at High Tide

By the fall of 1961 Robert Kennedy had persuaded SNCC to shift tactics to voter registration, which he assumed would stir less violence. Voting booths, Kennedy noted, were not like schools, where people would protest, "We don't want our little blond daughter going to school with a Negro."

As SNCC and CORE workers arrived in southern towns in the spring of 1962, they discovered that voting rights was not a peaceful issue. Over two years in Mississippi they registered only 4000 out of 394,000 black adults. Angry racists attacked with legal harassment, jailings, beatings, bombings, and murders. Terrorized workers who called on the administration for protection found it woefully lacking. FBI agents often stood by taking notes while SNCC workers were assaulted. Undaunted, SNCC workers made it clear that they intended to stay. They fanned out across the countryside to speak with farmers and sharecroppers who had never before dared to ask for a vote.

Confrontation increased when a federal court ordered the segregated University of Mississippi to admit James Meredith, a black applicant. When Governor Ross Barnett personally blocked Meredith's registration in September 1962, Kennedy faced the same crisis that had confronted Eisenhower at Little Rock in 1957. The president ordered several hundred federal marshals to escort Meredith into a university dormitory. Kennedy then announced on national television that the university had been integrated and asked students to follow the law of the land. Instead, a mob moved on campus, shooting out streetlights, commandeering a bulldozer, and throwing rocks and bottles. To save the marshals, Kennedy finally sent in federal troops, but not before 2 people were killed and 375 wounded.

James Meredith

In Mississippi, President Kennedy had begun to lose control of the civil rights issue. The House of Representatives, influenced by television coverage of the violence, introduced a number of civil rights measures. And Martin Luther King led a group to Birmingham, Alabama, to force a showdown against segregation. From a prison cell there, he produced one of the most eloquent documents of the civil rights movement, his "Letter from Birmingham Jail." Addressed to local ministers who had counseled an end to confrontation, King defended the use of civil disobedience. The choice, he warned, was not between obeying the law and nonviolently breaking it to bring about change; it was between his way and streets "flowing with blood," as restive black citizens turned toward more militant ideologies.

"Letter from Birmingham Jail"

Once freed, King led new demonstrations. Television cameras were on hand that May as Birmingham police chief "Bull" Connor, a man with a short fuse, unleashed attack dogs, club-wielding police, and fire hoses powerful enough to peel

In Birmingham, Alabama, firefighters used high-pressure hoses to disperse civil rights demonstrators. The force of the hoses was powerful enough to tear bark off trees. Pictures like this one aroused widespread sympathy for the civil rights movement.

the bark off trees. When segregationist bombs went off in African American neighborhoods, black mobs retaliated with their own riot, burning a number of shops and businesses owned by whites. In the following 10 weeks, more than 750 riots erupted in 186 cities and towns, both North and South. King's warning of streets "flowing with blood" no longer seemed far-fetched.

Kennedy sensed that he could no longer compromise on civil rights. In phrases that, like King's, drew heavily on Christian and republican rhetoric, he asked the nation, "If [an American with dark skin] cannot enjoy the full and free life all of us want, then who among us would be content to have the color of his skin changed and stand in his place? Who among us would then be content with counsels of patience and delay?" The president followed his words with support for a strong civil rights bill to end segregation and protect black voters. When King announced a massive march on Washington for August 1963, Kennedy objected that it would undermine support for his bill. "I have never engaged in any direct action movement which did not seem ill-timed," King replied. Faced with the inevitable, Kennedy convinced the organizers to use the event to promote the administration's bill, much to the disgust of militant CORE and SNCC factions.

The march on Washington

On August 28 some 250,000 people gathered at the Lincoln Memorial to march and sing in support of civil rights and racial harmony. Appropriately, the day belonged to King. In the powerful tones of a southern preacher, he reminded the crowd that the Declaration of Independence was a promise that applied to all people, black and white. "I have a dream," he told them, that one day "all of God's children, black men and white men, Jews and Gentiles, Protestants and Catholics, will be able to join hands and sing in the words of the old Negro spiritual, 'Free at last! Free at last! Thank God Almighty, we are free at last!'" Congress began deliberation of the civil rights bill, which was reported out of the Judiciary Committee on October 23.

The Fire Next Time

While liberals applauded Kennedy's stand on civil rights and appreciative African Americans rejoined the Democratic party, substantial numbers of southern whites and northern ethnics deserted. The president scheduled a trip to Texas to recoup some southern support. On November 22, 1963, the people of Dallas lined the streets for his motorcade. Suddenly, a sniper's rifle fired several times. Kennedy slumped into his wife's arms, fatally wounded. His assassin, Lee Harvey Oswald, was caught several hours later. Oswald seemed a mysterious figure: emotionally unstable, he had spent several years in the Soviet Union. But his actions were never fully explained, because only two days after his arrest—in full view of television cameras—he was gunned down by a disgruntled nightclub operator named Jack Ruby. An investigative commission headed by Chief Justice Earl Warren concluded that Oswald had acted alone, a conclusion with which historians generally agree. But the commission acted so hastily that a host of critics arose and rejected its conclusions in favor of theories placing Oswald as part of various conspiracies.

Tragedy in Dallas

In the face of the violence surrounding the civil rights campaign as well as the assassination of the president, many Americans came to doubt that programs of gradual reform could hold the nation together. A few black radicals believed that the Kennedy assassination was a payback to a system that had tolerated its own racial violence—the "chickens coming home to roost," as separatist Malcolm X put it. Many younger black leaders observed that civil rights received the greatest national coverage when white, not black, demonstrators were killed. They wondered, too, how Lyndon Johnson, a consummate southern politician, would approach the civil rights programs.

The new president, however, saw the need for action. Just as the Catholic issue had tested Kennedy's ability to lead, Johnson knew that without strong leadership on civil rights, "I'd be dead before I could ever begin." On November 23, his first day in office, he promised civil rights leaders that he would pass Kennedy's bill. Despite a southern filibuster in the Senate, the Civil Rights Act of 1964 became law the following summer. The bill marked one of the great moments in the history of American reform. It barred discrimination in public accommodations such as lunch counters, bus stations, and hotels; it authorized the attorney general to bring suit to desegregate schools, museums, and other public facilities; it outlawed discrimination in employment by race, color, religion, sex, or national origin; and it gave additional protection to voting rights.

LBJ and the Civil Rights Act of 1964

Still, the Civil Rights Act did not bar the techniques that southern registrars routinely used to prevent black citizens from voting. A coalition of idealistic young black and white protesters had continued the Mississippi voting drive in what they called "Freedom Summer." In 1965 Martin Luther King led a series of demonstrations, climaxed by a 54-mile walk from Selma to Montgomery, Alabama. As pressure mounted, Johnson sent Congress a strong Voting Rights Act, which was passed in August 1965. The act suspended literacy tests and authorized federal officials to supervise elections in many southern districts. With some justice Johnson called the act "one of the most monumental laws in the entire history of American freedom." Within a five-year period black registration in the South jumped from 35 to 65 percent.

Voting Rights Act of 1965

Black Power

The civil rights laws, as comprehensive as they were, did not strike at the de facto segregation found outside the South. These forms of segregation were not codified in law but practiced through unwritten custom. In large areas of America, African Americans were locked out of suburbs, kept out of decent schools, barred from exclusive clubs, and denied all but the most menial jobs. Nor did the Voting Rights Act deal with the sources of urban black poverty. The median income for urban black residents was approximately half that for white residents.

In such an atmosphere, militants sharply questioned the liberal goal of integration. Since the 1930s the Black Muslim religious sect, dedicated to complete separation from white society, had attracted as many as 100,000 members, mostly young men. During the early 1960s the sect drew even wider attention through the energetic efforts of Malcolm X. This charismatic leader had learned the language of the downtrodden from his own experience as a former hustler, gambler, and prison inmate. His militancy alarmed whites, though by 1965 Malcolm was in fact moving toward a more moderate position. He accepted integration but emphasized black community action. After he broke with the Black Muslims he was gunned down by rivals.

Malcolm X

But by 1965–1966, even CORE and SNCC had begun to give up working for nonviolent change. If black Americans were to liberate themselves fully, militants argued, they could not merely accept rights "given" to them by whites—they had to claim them. Some members began carrying guns to defend themselves. In 1966 Stokely Carmichael of SNCC gave the militants a slogan—"Black Power"—and the defiant symbol of a gloved fist raised in the air. In its moderate form, the black power movement encouraged African Americans to recover their cultural roots, their African heritage, and a new sense of identity. African clothes and natural hairstyles became popular. On college campuses black students pressed universities to hire black faculty, create black studies programs, and provide segregated social and residential space.

Black Panthers

For more militant factions like the Black Panther party of Oakland, California, violence became a revolutionary tool. Led by Huey P. Newton and Eldridge Cleaver, the Panthers called on the black community to arm. Because California law forbade carrying concealed weapons, Newton and his followers openly brandished shotguns and rifles as they patrolled the streets protecting blacks from police harassment. In February 1967 Newton found the showdown he had been looking for. "O.K., you big fat racist pig, draw your gun," he shouted while waving a shotgun. A gun battle with police left Newton wounded and in jail.

Eldridge Cleaver, who assumed leadership of the party, attracted the attention of whites with his searing autobiography, *Soul on Ice*. But even at the height of the Black Panthers' power, the group never counted more than 2000 members nationwide. Most African Americans remained committed to the goals defined by the civil rights movement: nonviolence, not armed confrontation; integration, not segregation.

A National Guardsman watches as flames consume large areas of the Watts section of Los Angeles during the 1965 riot. Often, a seemingly trivial event set off such scenes of violence, revealing the depth of explosive rage harbored within ghettos.

Violence in the Streets

No ideology shaped the reservoir of frustration and despair that existed in the ghettos. Often, a seemingly minor incident such as an arrest or an argument on the streets would trigger widespread violence. A mob would gather, and police cars and white-owned stores would be firebombed or looted. As police and the National

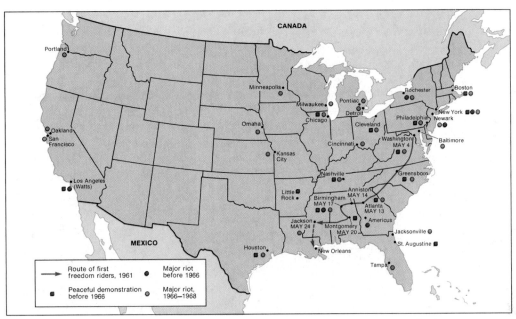

Civil Rights: Patterns of Protest and Unrest The first phase of the civil rights movement was confined largely to the South, where the freedom riders of 1961 dramatized the issue of segregation. Beginning in the summer of 1964, urban riots brought the issue of race and politics home to the entire nation. Severe rioting followed the murder of Martin Luther King Jr. in 1968, after which the worst violence subsided.

Guard were ordered in, the violence escalated. Riots broke out in Harlem and Rochester, New York, in 1964, the Watts area of Los Angeles in 1965, Chicago in 1966, and Newark and Detroit in 1967. In the riot at Watts, more than $200 million in property was destroyed and 34 people died, all of them black. It took nearly 5000 troops to end the bloodiest rioting in Detroit, where 40 died, 2000 were injured, and 5000 were left homeless.

To most whites the violence was unfathomable and inexcusable. Lyndon Johnson spoke for many when he argued that "neither old wrongs nor new fears can justify arson and murder." Martin Luther King, still pursuing the tactics of nonviolence, came to understand the anger behind it. Touring Watts only days after the riots, he was approached by a band of young blacks. "We won," they told him proudly. "How can you say you won," King countered, "when thirty-four Negroes are dead, your community is destroyed, and whites are using the riot as an excuse for inaction?" The youngsters were unmoved. "We won because we made them pay attention to us."

For Johnson, ghetto violence and black militance mocked his efforts to achieve racial progress. The Civil Rights and Voting Rights acts were essential parts of the Great Society he hoped to build. In that effort he had achieved a legislative record virtually unequaled by any other president in the nation's history. What Kennedy had promised, Johnson delivered. But the growing white backlash and the anger exploding in the nation's cities exposed serious flaws in the theory and practice of liberal reform.

Lyndon Johnson and the Great Society

Like the state he hailed from, Lyndon Baines Johnson was in all things bigger than life. His gifts were greater, his flaws more glaring. Insecurity was his Achilles heel and the engine that drove him. If Kennedy had been good as president, Johnson

Lyndon Johnson's powers of persuasion were legendary. He applied the "Johnson treatment" (as here, in 1957, to Senator Theodore Green) whenever he wanted people to see things his way. Few could say no, as he freely violated their personal space and reminded them who dominated the situation.

would be "the greatest of them all, the whole bunch of them." If FDR won in a landslide in 1936, Johnson would produce an even larger margin in 1964. And to anyone who displeased him, he could be ruthlessly cruel. His scatological language and preoccupation with barnyard sex amused few and offended many. He counted himself among history's great figures. A visiting head of state once asked Johnson if he was born in a log cabin. "No, no," the president responded. "You have me confused with Abe Lincoln. I was born in a manger." Yet Johnson could not understand why so few people genuinely liked him; one courageous diplomat, when pressed, found the nerve to respond, "Because, Mr. President, you are not a very likable man."

Johnson was born in Stonewall, Texas, in the hill country outside Austin, where the dry climate and rough terrain only grudgingly yielded up a living. Schooled in manners by his overbearing mother and in politics by his father and his cronies, Johnson arrived in Washington in 1932 as an ardent New Dealer who loved the political game. When he became majority leader of the Senate in 1954, he cultivated an image as a moderate conservative who knew what strings to pull or levers to jog to get the job done. Johnson knew what made his colleagues run. On an important bill, he latched onto the undecided votes until they succumbed to the famous "Johnson treatment," a combination of arguments, threats, emotional or patriotic appeals, and enticing rewards. Florida senator George Smathers likened Johnson to "a great overpowering thunderstorm that consumed you as it closed around you." Or as Ben Bradlee of the *Washington Post* recalled, "He never just shook hands with you. One hand was shaking your hand; the other was always someplace else, exploring you, examining you."

Despite his compulsion to control every person and situation, Johnson possessed certain bedrock strengths. No one was better at hammering out compromises among competing interest groups. To those who served him well he could be loyal and generous. As president, he cared sincerely about society's underdogs. His support for civil rights, aid to the poor, education, and the welfare of the elderly came from genuine conviction. He made the betterment of such people the goal of his administration.

The Origins of the Great Society

In the first months after the assassination, Johnson acted as the conservator of the Kennedy legacy. "Let us continue," he told a grief-stricken nation. Liberals who had dismissed Johnson as an unprincipled power broker grudgingly came to respect the energy he showed in steering reform through Congress. The Civil Rights Act and tax cut legislation were only two of the most conspicuous pieces of Kennedy business Johnson quickly finished. Kennedy's advisers believed tax cuts would create economic growth beneficial to the poor. Under Johnson, they did.

Kennedy had come to recognize that prosperity alone would not ease the plight of America's poor. In 1962 Michael Harrington's book *The Other America* brought attention to the widespread persistence of poverty despite the nation's affluence. Harrington focused attention on the hills of Appalachia that stretched from western Pennsylvania south to Alabama. In some counties a quarter of the population survived on a diet of flour and dried-milk paste supplied by federal surplus food programs. Under Kennedy Congress had passed a new food stamp program as well as laws designed to revive the economies of poor areas, replacing urban slums with newer housing and retraining the unemployed. Robert Kennedy also headed a presidential committee to fight juvenile delinquency in urban slums by involving the poor in "community action" programs. Direct participation, they hoped, would overcome "a sense of resignation and fatalism" that sociologist Oscar Lewis had found while studying the Puerto Rican community of New York City.

Discovering poverty

Such forces for change brought hope and energy to the liberal tradition. Like the New Dealers and the progressives before them, liberals of the 1960s did not wish to overturn capitalism. They looked primarily to tame its excesses, taking a pragmatic approach to reforming American society. Like Franklin Roosevelt, they believed that the government should play an active role in managing the economy in order to soften the boom-and-bust swings of capitalism. Like progressives from the turn of the century, liberals looked to improve society by applying the intelligence of "experts."

The liberal tradition

Liberals had confidence, at times bordering on arrogance, that poverty could be eliminated and the good society achieved. "The world seemed more plastic, more subject to human will," one liberal recalled. He and his fellow reformers believed that "the energy and commitment of multitudes could be linked to compel the enrichment of human life." That faith might prove naive, but during the 1960s such optimism was both infectious and energizing.

It fell to Lyndon Johnson to fight Kennedy's "war on poverty." By August 1964 this master politician had driven through Congress the most sweeping social welfare bill since the New Deal. The Economic Opportunity Act addressed almost every major cause of poverty. It included training programs such as the Job Corps, granted loans to rural families and urban small businesses as well as aid to migrant workers, and launched a domestic version of the Peace Corps, known as VISTA (Volunteers in Service to America). The price tag for these programs was high. Johnson committed almost $1 billion to Sargent Shriver, a Kennedy brother-in-law, who directed the new Office of Economic Opportunity (OEO). When Michael Harrington complained that even $1 billion could barely scratch the surface, Shriver tartly replied, "Maybe you've spent a billion dollars before, but this is my first time around."

The speed Johnson demanded led inevitably to confusion, conflict, and waste. Officials at OEO often found themselves in conflict with other cabinet departments as well as with state and local officials. For example, OEO workers organized voter registration drives in order to oust corrupt city officials. Others led rent strikes to force improvements in public housing. The director of city housing in Syracuse,

New York, reacted typically: "We are experiencing a class struggle in the traditional Karl Marx style in Syracuse, and I do not like it." Such battles for power and bureaucratic turf undermined federal poverty programs.

The Election of 1964

In 1964, however, these controversies had not yet surfaced. Johnson's political stock remained high. To an audience at the University of Michigan in May, he announced his ambition to forge a "Great Society," in which poverty and racial injustice no longer existed. The chance to fulfill his dreams seemed open to him, for the Republicans nominated Senator Barry Goldwater of Arizona as their presidential candidate. Ruggedly handsome, Goldwater was a true son of the West who held a narrow view of what government should do, for he was at heart a libertarian. Government, he argued, should not dispense welfare, subsidize farmers, tax incomes on a progressive basis, or aid public education. At the same time, Goldwater was so anti-Communist that he championed a large defense establishment.

Goldwater's extreme views allowed Johnson to portray himself as a moderate. He chose Minnesota's liberal Senator Hubert Humphrey to give regional balance to the ticket. Only the candidacy of Governor George Wallace of Alabama marred Johnson's election prospects. In Democratic primaries, Wallace's segregationist appeal won nearly a third or more of the votes in Wisconsin, Indiana, and Maryland—hardly the Deep South. He was persuaded, however, to drop out of the race.

The election produced the landslide Johnson craved. Carrying every state except Arizona and four in the Deep South, he received 61 percent of the vote. Democrats gained better than two-to-one majorities in the Senate and House. All the same, the election was probably more a repudiation of Goldwater than a mandate for Johnson. The president realized that he had to move rapidly to exploit the momentum of his 1964 majority.

The Great Society

In January 1965 Johnson announced a legislative vision that would extend welfare programs on a scale beyond Franklin Roosevelt's New Deal. By the end of 1965, 50 bills had been passed, many of them major pieces of legislation, with more on the agenda for the following year.

Programs in education

As a former teacher, Johnson made education the cornerstone of his Great Society. Stronger schools would compensate the poor for their disadvantaged homes, he believed. Under the Elementary and Secondary School Act, students in low-income school districts were to receive educational equipment, money for books, and enrichment programs like Project Head Start for nursery-school-age children. As schools scrambled to create programs that would tap federal money, they sometimes spent more to pay middle-class educational professionals than to teach lower-income students.

Medicare and Medicaid

President Johnson also pushed through the Medicare Act to provide the elderly with health insurance to cover hospital costs. Medicare targeted the elderly, because studies had shown that older people used hospitals three times more than other Americans and generally had incomes only half as large. Because Medicare made no provision for the poor who were not elderly, Congress also passed a program called Medicaid. Participating states would receive matching grants from the federal government to pay the medical expenses of those on welfare or too poor to afford medical care.

In many ways, Medicare and Medicaid worked. The poor and elderly received significantly more help when facing catastrophic illnesses. Over the next two decades, such aid helped to lower significantly the number of elderly poor. But as more patients used hospital services, Medicare budgets rose. In addition, nothing in the act restricted hospitals or doctors from raising their fees. The cost of the programs soared by more than 500 percent in the first 10 years.

Ten days after signing the Medicare bill, Johnson signed the Omnibus Housing Act, designed to subsidize rents for poor families unable to find adequate public housing. Four days later came the Voting Rights Act. Within two weeks Congress approved the creation of a new cabinet-level Department of Housing and Urban Development (HUD). To head it, Johnson named Robert Weaver, a former president of the NAACP. And in the tradition of the New Deal, which had patronized the arts under the WPA, Johnson created the National Foundation of the Arts and Humanities. Colleges and their students received support for scholarships and loans, research equipment, and libraries.

HUD

The Great Society also reformed immigration policy, in ways that reflected the drastic changes in global economics and culture since the last major immigration legislation was passed in 1924. Then, the National Origins Act (page 802) had embodied the deeply Eurocentric orientation of American society and its prejudices against people of color. Almost all the annual admissions quota of 154,000 went to Northern Europeans. Asians were barred almost entirely. By the 1960s American attitudes were changing, in terms of both race and region. American soldiers, after all, had fought wars to defend Korea, the Philippines, Vietnam, Taiwan, Japan, and other Asian nations. How could it justify discriminating against citizens from those countries? President Kennedy had challenged Congress to eliminate the national origins system, which he argued "satisfies neither national need nor accomplishes an international purpose."

Immigration reform

By 1965, with Asian economies growing, the war in Vietnam expanding, and civil rights sentiments at a peak, the need for reform took on special urgency. The Immigration Act of 1965 abolished the national origins system. It increased annual admissions to 170,000 people and put a cap of 20,000 on immigrants from any single nation. The law gave marked preference to reuniting families of those immigrants already in the United States—so much so that some observers nicknamed it the "brothers and sisters act." Asians and Eastern Europeans were among its prime beneficiaries.

The act's liberalization was offset, however, by prejudice toward Central Americans, especially Mexicans. The National Origins Act of 1924 had placed no limit on immigrants from the Americas. But by the 1960s many in Congress feared a massive influx of workers from south of the border. Widespread poverty in Latin American nations had left thousands unemployed and desperate to find work. Hence the new act capped arrivals from the Western Hemisphere at 120,000 annually. In that way immigration reform reflected the shifting balance of the global economy.

Booming economies took an increasing toll on the environment. By the mid-1960s many Americans had become increasingly concerned about acrid smog from factories and automobiles; about lakes and rivers polluted by detergents, pesticides, and industrial wastes; and about the disappearance of wildlife. Congress had already, in 1964, passed the National Wilderness Preservation System Act to set aside 9.1 million acres of wilderness as "forever wild." Lady Bird Johnson, the president's wife, campaigned to eliminate the garish billboards and junkyards along many of the nation's roads. Congress first established pollution standards for interstate waterways and a year later provided funds for sewage treatment and water purification. Legislation also tightened standards on air pollution. Environmental reform provoked

The environment

opposition from groups like mining companies, cattle-grazers, and the timber industry, who wanted to continue using the public domain for their own purposes. But the public accepted the benefits of the new regulation. Among other accomplishments, by the mid-1990s smog had declined nationwide by about a third and the number of rivers and lakes suitable for swimming and fishing had doubled.

For all he had done, Johnson wanted to do more. In 1966 he pushed through bills to raise the minimum wage, improve auto safety, aid mass transit, and develop "model cities." But in time opposition mounted. "Doesn't matter what kind of majority you come in with," Johnson had predicted early on. "You've got just one year when they treat you right, and before they start worrying about themselves." Yet as late as 1968 Johnson pushed major legislation through Congress to ban discrimination in housing (Fair Housing Act), to build public housing, to protect consumers from unfair credit practices (Truth-in-Lending Act), and to protect scenic rivers and expand the national park system.

Evaluating the Great Society

Historians have difficulty measuring the Great Society's impact. It produced more legislation and more reforms than the New Deal. It also carried a high price tag. Economic statistics suggested that general prosperity, accelerated by the tax cut bill, did more to fight poverty than all the OEO programs. And the inevitable scandals began to surface: Job Corps retrainees burglarizing homes in their off-hours, school equipment purchased that no one knew how to use. Conservatives and radicals alike objected that the liberal welfare state was intruding into too many areas of people's lives. Ethnic groups like Italian and Polish Americans objected to what they considered favoritism accorded black Americans and Latinos under many programs.

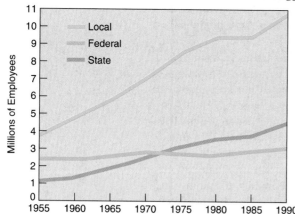

Growth of Government, 1955–1990 Government has been a major growth industry since World War II. Most people think of "big government" as federal government. But even during the Great Society, far more people worked in state and local government. Despite the antigovernment rhetoric, federal employment grew substantially in the Reagan-Bush era.

For all that, the Great Society established the high-water mark of interventionist government, a trend that began in the progressive era and flourished during the Great Depression and in World War II. Although Americans continued to pay lip service to the notion that government should remain small and interfere little in citizens' lives, no strong movement emerged to eliminate Medicare or Medicaid. Few Americans disputed the right of the government to regulate industrial pollution or to control the excesses of large corporations or powerful labor unions. Even conservatives of that era granted the government a role in managing the economy and providing citizens with a safety net of benefits in sickness and in old age. In this sense, the tradition of liberalism prevailed, whatever Johnson's failings.

The Reforms of the Warren Court

Although Lyndon Johnson and the Congress left the stamp of liberalism on federal power during the decade, the third branch of government played a role that, in the long run, proved equally significant. Supreme Court chief justice Earl Warren turned what was traditionally the least activist branch of government into a center of liberal reform. His political skills, compassion, and tact had been instrumental in bringing his colleagues to a unanimous ruling on school desegregation in *Brown v. Board*

> I was sentenced to the state Penitentiary by the Circuit Court of Bay County, State of Florida. The present proceeding was commenced on a writ petition for a writ of Habeus Corpus to the Supreme Court of the State of Florida to vacate the sentence, on the grounds that I was made to stand Trial without the aid of counsel, and, at all times of my incarseretion. The said Court refused to appoint counsel and therefore deprived me of Due process of law, and violate my rights in the Bill of Rights and the constitution of the United States.
>
> Clarence Earl Gideon
> 5th day of Jan 1962 Petitioner
>
> Lawrence C. Sunzza
> NOTARY PUBLIC
> Notary Public...
> My Comm..... ... 19, 1962
> Bonded by American Surety Co. of N.Y.

Gideon's Letter to the Supreme Court
John F. Davis, Clerk, Supreme Court of the United States

Clarence Earl Gideon (right) used this handwritten letter to bring his appeal to the attention of the Supreme Court. In the *Gideon* case the court ruled that even poor defendants have the right to legal counsel. Such incidents, while rare, restore faith in the idea of a government for the people.

of Education. And Warren continued to use these skills, until his retirement in 1969, to forge a liberal coalition of justices who handed down a series of landmark decisions in broad areas of civil liberties and civil rights.

In 1960 the rights of citizens accused of a crime but not yet convicted were often unclear. Those too poor to afford lawyers often faced trial without representation. The police and the courts seldom informed those accused of a crime of their rights guaranteed under the Constitution. In a series of decisions, the Court ruled that the Fourteenth Amendment provided broad guarantees of due process under the law. *Gideon v. Wainwright* (1963), an appeal launched by a Florida prisoner, made it clear that all citizens were entitled to legal counsel in any case involving a possible jail sentence. In *Escobedo v. Illinois* (1964) and *Miranda v. Arizona* (1966) the Court declared that individuals detained for a crime must be informed of the charges against them, of their right to remain silent, and of their right to have an attorney present during questioning. Though these decisions applied to all citizens, they were primarily intended to benefit the poor, who were most likely to be in trouble with the law and least likely to understand their rights.

Protecting due process

In *Engel v. Vitale* (1962), the Court issued a ruling that especially troubled conservative religious groups. The case involved a nonsectarian prayer written by the New York State Board of Regents that public school students were required to recite. Even if dissenting children could be excused, the Court ruled, they faced indirect pressure to recite the prayer. That violated the constitutional separation of church and state. The following year the Court extended the ban on school prayer to cover the reading of the Bible and the Lord's Prayer.

Banning school prayer

Other decisions promoted a more liberal social climate. In *Griswold v. Connecticut* (1964) the Warren Court overturned a nineteenth-century law banning the sale of contraceptives or providing medical advice about their use. The Court demonstrated its distaste for censorship by greatly narrowing the legal definition of obscenity. A book had to be "utterly without redeeming social value" to permit censorship. The combination of decisions reforming criminal rights, prayer, free speech, and morality angered conservatives of almost all social and political backgrounds. These issues would again become a political battleground in the 1980s and 1990s.

The Court's most far-reaching decision was probably one of its least controversial, though politically most sensitive. As cities and suburbs grew, few states redrew their legislative districts to reflect the change. Rural (and generally conservative) elements continued to dominate state legislatures. In *Baker v. Carr* (1962) and a series of later cases the Court ruled that the states must apportion seats not by "land or trees or pastures," but as closely as possible by the principle of "one person, one vote."

One person, one vote

The Counterculture

In 1964 some 800 students from Berkeley, Oberlin, and other colleges met in western Ohio to be trained for the voter registration campaign in the South. Middle-class students who had grown up in peaceful white suburbs found themselves being instructed for this "Mississippi Freedom Summer" by protest-hardened SNCC coordinators. The lessons were sobering. When beaten by police, the SNCC staff advised, assume the fetal position—hands protecting the neck, elbows covering the temples. That minimized injuries from nightsticks. A few days later, grimmer news arrived. A volunteer who had left for Mississippi two days earlier had already been arrested by local police. Now he and two others were reported "missing." Six weeks later, their mangled bodies were found, bulldozed into the earthworks of a freshly finished dam. That did not stop other sobered volunteers from heading to Mississippi.

By the mid-1960s dissatisfied members of the middle class—and especially the young—had launched a revolt against the conventions of society and politics as usual. The students who returned to campus from the voter registration campaign that summer of 1964 were the shock troops of a much larger movement. They included a curious mix of political activists and apolitical dropouts, labeled hippies.

Activists on the New Left

More than a few students had become disillusioned with the slow pace of reform. Since the "establishment"—whether it was liberal or conservative—blocked meaningful change, why not overthrow it? Tom Hayden, raised in a working-class family outside Detroit, went to college at the University of Michigan, then traveled to Berkeley, and soon joined civil rights workers in Mississippi. "At first, you thought, well, the southern system is some kind of historical vestige," he recalled. "Instead, we found out that the structure of power was very tied into the structure of power in the whole U.S. You'd find that Harvard was investing in Mississippi Power and Light, which was a company that economically dominated Mississippi."

SDS and Port Huron

Hayden, along with Al Haber, another student at the University of Michigan, was a driving force in forming the radical Students for a Democratic Society (SDS). SDS had little sympathy with an "old left" generation of radicals who grew up in the 1930s and still debated the merits of Marxism. Action was the route to change, Hayden argued: through sit-ins, protest marches, and direct confrontation. At a meeting in Port Huron, Michigan, in 1962 the group condemned the modern bureaucratic

Edie Black from Smith College was one of hundreds of middle-class students who volunteered during Freedom Summer of 1964. Here she teaches in a school at Mileston, Mississippi. Many students returned to their campuses in the fall radicalized, ready to convince others to join them in finding alternatives to "the system."

society exemplified by the organization man of the 1950s. The Port Huron Statement called for "participatory democracy," in which large organizations run by bureaucrats would be decentralized and turned into face-to-face communities in which individual participation mattered. The Port Huron Statement did not exactly revolutionize America; only 60,000 copies of it were ever sold. It did, however, anticipate the dramatic increase in political and cultural conflict that was spreading across the nation.

The Free Speech Movement at the University of California, Berkeley, was a case in point. To most liberals, Berkeley seemed the gem of the California state university system. Like so many other universities, it had educated a generation of GIs following World War II. But to people like Tom Hayden and the SDS, Berkeley was a bureaucratic monster, enrolling more than 30,000 students. Students at Berkeley, as at other large universities, filed into impersonal classrooms to hear lectures from remote professors. In the fall of 1964, Berkeley declared off-limits the one small area in which political organizations had been allowed to advertise their causes. When university police tried to remove a recruiter for CORE, thousands of angry students surrounded the police car for 32 hours. They were led by a student named Mario Savio.

The Free Speech Movement

Before traveling south to Freedom Summer in 1964, Savio had been an undistinguished graduate student in philosophy. Mississippi changed him. "There was this single-mindedness of purpose and moral certainty that pushed him," a fellow Berkeley volunteer commented. And not just Savio. Twelve of the 21 Freedom Summer veterans at Berkeley were arrested during the protest. "In our free-speech fight," Savio proclaimed, "we have come up against what may emerge as the greatest problem of our nation—depersonalized, unresponsive bureaucracy." When the university's president, Clark Kerr, threatened to expel Savio, 6000 students took control of the administration building, stopped classes with a strike, and convinced many faculty members to join them. Kerr backed down, placing no limits on free speech on campus except those that applied to society at large. But the lines between students and administrators had been drawn. The rebellious spirit spread to other major universities, such as Michigan, Yale, and Columbia, and then to campuses across the nation.

By no means were all students radicalized on college campuses. To the conservative members of Young Americans for Freedom (YAF), those behind the Free Speech Movement at Berkeley were a motley crowd of beatniks, liberals, and Communists. YAF had a far larger (though probably less visible) membership than leftist groups like SNCC or Students for a Democratic Society (SDS). These clean-cut young Americans seldom marched or demonstrated. They wanted instead to limit the power of the federal government that they believed threatened true freedom and liberty. Both Eisenhower's "middle of the road Republicanism" and Kennedy's liberalism, they charged, sapped the "moral and physical strength of the nation." YAF denounced the Peace Corps as "a grand exercise in self-denial and altruism, paid for by the American taxpayers and administered by the United Nations." Barry Goldwater embodied for YAF members the values they cherished. Although Goldwater went down to defeat, the ranks of the YAF would supply a new generation of conservative activists in the 1980s.

Vatican II and American Catholics

Many conservatives feared that the secular trends of modern life threatened the Christian faith as well. They worried that even the traditions of the Roman Catholic church seemed under siege when Pope John XXIII summoned church leaders to an ecumenical council, popularly known as Vatican II. It assembled in October 1962.

Racing against the cancer that would soon fell him, Pope John bade the council deal with issues of social change engaging the world in the 1960s, including poverty, nuclear war, atheism, and birth control. He wished, as well, to bring the church hierarchy more closely in touch with lay members and with the modern world around it. By the time the council concluded in 1965 Pope John had died, having been succeeded by Pope Paul VI, and the acts of the council had transformed the church. At a superficial level, many changes seemed small, though they affected the everyday lives of American Catholics. No longer was it a requirement to go without meat on "fish Fridays" or to say confession on Saturdays. More significant, during services American priests would now face the congregation rather than the altar and conduct the mass in English rather than Latin. Lay members would also have a greater role in implementing the faith. In addition, Vatican II encouraged a spirit of ecumenism, in which Catholics would seek greater understanding with other Christians.

The changes of Vatican II energized many Catholics and led them to embrace further reform within and without the church. Priests like Fathers Daniel and Philip Berrigan were active in the antipoverty and antiwar movements of the era. Many female Catholics sought a larger role for women in religious life. Yet even those who did not take to the streets or the pulpit felt the effects of Vatican II. As historian Garry Wills concluded, "Catholics live in a different world since the council."

The Rise of the Counterculture

Spiritual matters also aroused more secular rebels, who found their culture too materialistic and shallow. These alienated students, often from conservative backgrounds, began to grope toward spiritual, nonmaterial goals. "Turn on to the scene, tune in to what is happening, and drop out of high school, college, grad school, junior executive," advised Timothy Leary, a Harvard psychology professor who dropped out himself. People who heeded Leary's call to spiritual renewal rejected politics for a lifestyle of experimentation with music, sex, and drugs. Observers labeled their movement a "counterculture."

The counterculture of the 1960s had much in common with earlier religious revival and utopian movements. It admired the quirky individualism of Henry David Thoreau, and like Thoreau, it turned to Zen Buddhism and other Oriental philosophies. Like Brook Farm and other nineteenth-century utopian communities, the new hippie communes sought perfection along the fringes of society. Communards built geodesic domes based on the designs of architect Buckminster Fuller; they "learned how to scrounge materials, tear down abandoned buildings, use the unusable," as one member of the Drop City commune put it. Sexual freedom became a means to liberate them from the repressive inhibitions that distorted the lives of their "uptight" parents. Drugs appeared to open the inner mind to a higher state of consciousness or pleasure. No longer would people be bound by conventional relationships and the goals of a liberal, bourgeois society.

Communes

The early threads of the 1960s counterculture led back to the 1950s and the subculture of the beat generation (page 958). For the beats, unconventional drugs had long been a part of the scene, but now their use expanded dramatically. Timothy Leary began experimenting with hallucinogenic mushrooms in Mexico and soon moved on to LSD. The drug "blew his mind," as he described it, and he became so enthusiastic in making converts that Harvard blew him straight out of its hallowed doors.

Whereas Leary's approach to LSD was cool and contemplative, novelist Ken Kesey (*One Flew over the Cuckoo's Nest*) embraced it with antic frenzy. His ragtag company of druggies and freaks formed the "Merry Pranksters" at Kesey's home outside San Francisco. Writer Tom Wolfe chronicled their outrageous style in *The Electric Kool-Aid Acid Test,* a book that pioneered the "New Journalism." Wolfe dropped the rules of reporting that demanded objectivity and distance by taking himself and his readers on a psychedelic tour with Kesey and his fellow Pranksters. Their example inspired others to drop out.

The Rock Revolution

In the 1950s rock and roll defined a teen culture preoccupied with young love, cars, and adult pressures. One exception was the Kingston Trio, which in 1958 popularized folk music that appealed to young adult and college audiences. As the interest in folk music grew, the lyrics increasingly focused on social or political issues. Joan Baez helped define the folk style by dressing simply, wearing no makeup, and rejecting the commercialism of popular music. She joined folksinger Bob Dylan in the civil rights march on Washington in 1963, singing "We Shall Overcome" and "Blowin' in the Wind." Such folksingers reflected the activist side of the counterculture as they sought to provoke their audiences to political commitment.

Rock groups like the Grateful Dead were closely associated with the drug culture. LSD inspired the genre of psychedelic art that adorned album covers and posters with freaked-out lettering (the album is *American Beauty Rose*) that seemed to dazzle and dance even if the viewer had not inhaled or ingested.

Daily Lives

CLOTHING AND FASHION
The Politics of Dress

Three-piece suits, fur coats, berets, Grateful Dead T-shirts—clothing has always made a statement about the values of the wearer. In the 1950s that statement was conformity. The khaki slacks and brush-cut hair popular with middle-class boys hinted at military regimentation. Rock-and-rollers, lower-class kids, and farm boys often wore dungarees and T-shirts, perhaps with a cigarette pack tucked in the rolled-up sleeve. Beatniks advertised their nonconformity by adopting an exotic look: long hair, goatees, turtlenecks, and sandals.

During the 1960s nonconformity became the norm. The revolution began in earnest with the coming of the Beatles, four British rockers from working-class Liverpool. John, Paul, George, and Ringo hit the United States like a cultural tidal wave. Their longish hair, mod clothes, and zaniness defined a new masculine style. It was youthful rather than macho, irreverent without being overtly rebellious.

The ambiguity of this androgynous image, especially the long hair, disturbed many Americans.

While traditional men thought long hair was effeminate, rock stars saw it as sexy. And in the 1960s rock stars displaced movie stars as the public figures who most defined the male image. Mick Jagger of the Rolling Stones rejected the idea that "being masculine means looking clean, close-cropped, and ugly."

New fashions represented a desire to break social constraints in favor of greater sensuality and freedom of expression. Nowhere was that more evident than in the costuming of the counterculture. Middle-class students began to let their hair grow. African American men and women found an alternative way to make long hair into a cultural statement. They gave up wavy processing or short cuts that mirrored Anglo hair and let their hair grow into bushy Afros. Many whites with naturally kinky or curly hair imitated the Afro look.

Hippies added a more theatrical twist. They rejected commercial fashion, synthetic fabrics, and cosmetics in favor of a natural look. To express a return to nature, they adopted the Latino shawl and

The Beatles had a major impact on men's style as well as on popular music. This 1963 photo shows their "mod" look popular first in England. Later they adopted a hippie look.

The Beatles

In 1964 a new sound, imported from England, exploded on the American scene. Within a year the Beatles, four musicians from Liverpool, had generated more excitement than any previous phenomenon in popular music. Their concerts and appearances on television drove teen audiences into frenzies as the mod crooners sang "I Want to Hold Your Hand." Part of the Beatles' appeal came from their distinctly English style. With hair that was considered long in the 1960s, modish clothes, fresh faces, and irreverent wit, they looked and sounded like nothing young Americans had experienced before. Their boyish enthusiasm for life captured the Dionysian spirit of the new counterculture. But the Beatles' enormous commercial success also reflected the creativity of their music. Along with other English groups serape; the Indian fringed buckskin, beads, and moccasins; and the bright coloring of African, Indian, and Caribbean cotton fabrics. This costuming became standard wear at folk and rock music festivals and be-ins as well as at political demonstrations. Most of the clothing and accessories were handcrafted and sold largely through street vendors, medieval-style craft fairs, and small shops. Often these same shops, located in college towns and artsy urban neighborhoods, did a lively business selling paraphernalia of the drug culture: water pipes, "bongs," rolling papers, roach clips, strobe lights, posters, and Indian print bedspreads.

Fashion had become a function of politics and rebellion. Traditional Americans saw beads, long hair, sandals, drugs, radical politics, and rock and roll as elements of a revolution. To them, hippies and radicals were equally threatening. To restore order, they tried to censor and even outlaw the trappings of the counterculture. Schools expelled boys when their hair was too long and girls when their skirts were too short. It became indecent to desecrate the flag by sewing patches of red, white, and blue on torn blue jeans. Short-haired blue-collar workers harassed long-haired hippies and antiwar protesters. The personal fashions of the youth rebellion came to symbolize a "generation gap" between the young and their elders.

In time, however, that gap narrowed. Men especially broke with past tradition. Sideburns lengthened and mustaches and beards flourished as they had not since the nineteenth century. Men began to wear jewelry, furs, perfume, and shoulder-length hair. Subdued tweeds and narrow lapels gave way to bell-bottoms, broad floral ties, and wide-collared, sometimes psychedelic, shirts. By the early 1970s, commercial success, not legal repression, had signaled an end to the revolution in fashion. As formerly hostile blue-collar workers and GIs began to sport long hair and hip clothes, fashion no longer made such clear distinctions. Even middle-aged men and women donned boots, let their hair grow a bit fuller, and slipped into modified bell-bottoms. Feminists rejected the more extreme styles as an example of the male-dominated fashion world that treated women as sex objects. Hippie garb, which was impractical in the office, was replaced by knee-length skirts or pants suits. Before long, three-piece suits, khakis, and short hair were back for men, although the democratic and eclectic spirit of the 1960s persisted. Informality provided Americans of both sexes with a wider choice in fashions.

such as the Rolling Stones, the Beatles reconnected white American audiences with the rhythm-and-blues roots of rock and roll.

Until 1965 Bob Dylan was the quintessential folk artist, writing about nuclear weapons, pollution, and racism. He appeared at concerts with longish frizzy hair, working-class clothes, an unamplified guitar, and a harmonica suspended on a wire support. But then Dylan shocked his fans by donning a black leather jacket and shifting to a "folk-rock" style featuring an electric guitar. His new songs seemed to suggest that the old America was almost beyond redemption. The Beatles, too, transformed themselves. After a pilgrimage to India to study transcendental meditation, they returned to produce *Sergeant Pepper's Lonely Hearts Club Band*, possibly

Dylan

the most influential album of the decade. It blended sound effects with music, alluded to trips taken with "Lucy in the Sky with Diamonds" (LSD), and concluded, "I'd love to turn you on." Out in San Francisco, bands such as the Grateful Dead pioneered "acid rock" with long pieces aimed at echoing drug-induced states of mind.

Soul music

The debt of white rock musicians to rhythm and blues led to increased integration in the music world. Before the 1960s black rhythm-and-blues bands had played primarily to black audiences, in segregated clubs, or over black radio stations. The civil rights movement and a rising black social and political consciousness gave rise to "soul" music. One black disc jockey described soul as "the last to be hired, first to be fired, brown all year round, sit-in-the-back-of-the-bus feeling." Soul was the quality that expressed black pride and separatism: "You've got to live with us or you don't have it." Out of Detroit came the "Motown sound," which combined elements of gospel, blues, and big band jazz. Diana Ross and the Supremes, the Temptations, Stevie Wonder, and other groups under contract to Berry Gordy's Motown Record Company appealed to black and white audiences alike. Yet although soul music promoted black consciousness, it had little to offer by way of social commentary. It evoked the traditional blues themes of workday woes, unhappy marriages, and the troubles between men and women.

The West Coast Scene

For all its themes of alienation, rebellion, and utopian quest, the counterculture also signaled the increasing importance of the West Coast in American popular culture. In the 1950s the shift of television production from the stages of New York to the film lots of Hollywood helped establish Los Angeles as a communications center. San Francisco became notorious as a home of the beat movement.

Then in 1958 the unthinkable happened. The Brooklyn Dodgers and the New York Giants baseball teams fled the Big Apple for Los Angeles and San Francisco. When Alaska and Hawaii became states in 1959, the national center of gravity shifted westward. Richard Nixon, a Californian, narrowly missed being elected president in 1960. By 1963 the "surfing sound" of West Coast rock groups like the Beach Boys and Jan and Dean had made southern California's preoccupation with surfing and cars into a national fad.

The first Be-In

Before 1967 Americans were only vaguely aware of another West Coast phenomenon, the hippies. But in January a loose coalition of drug freaks, Zen cultists, and political activists banded together to hold the first well-publicized Be-In. The beat poet Allen Ginsberg was on hand to offer spiritual guidance. The Grateful Dead and Jefferson Airplane, acid rock groups based in San Francisco, provided entertainment. A mysterious group called the Diggers somehow managed to supply free food and drink, while the notorious Hell's Angels motorcycle gang policed the occasion. Drugs of all kinds were plentiful. And a crowd attired in a bizarre mix of Native American, circus, Oriental, army surplus, and other costumes came to enjoy it all.

The West Coast had long been a magnet for Americans seeking opportunity, escape, and alternative lifestyles; now the San Francisco Bay Area staked its claim as the spiritual center of the counterculture. The more politically conscious dropouts, or "fists," gravitated toward Berkeley; the apolitical "flower children" moved into Haight-Ashbury, a run-down San Francisco neighborhood of apartments, Victorian houses, and "head shops" selling drug paraphernalia, wall posters, Indian bedspreads, and other eccentric accessories. Similar dropout communities and communes sprang up across the country. Colleges became centers of hip culture, offering alternative courses, eliminating strict requirements, and tolerating the new sexual mores of their students.

In the summer of 1969 all the positive forces of the counterculture converged on Bethel, New York, in the Catskill Mountains resort area, to celebrate the promise of peace, love, and freedom. The Woodstock Music Festival attracted 400,000 people to the largest rock concert ever organized. For one long weekend the audience and performers joined to form an ephemeral community based on sex, drugs, and rock and roll. But even then, the counterculture was dying. Violence intruded on the laid-back urban communities that hippies had formed. Organized crime and drug pushers muscled in on the lucrative trade in LSD, amphetamines, and marijuana. Bad drugs and addiction took their toll. Urban slum dwellers turned hostile to the strange middle-class dropouts who, in ways the poor could not fathom, found poverty ennobling. Free sex often became an excuse for rape, exploitation, and loveless gratification.

Much that had once seemed outrageous in the hippie world was readily absorbed into the marketplace. Rock groups became big business enterprises commanding huge fees. Slick concerts with expensive tickets replaced communal dances with psychedelic light shows. Yogurt, granola, and herbal teas appeared on supermarket shelves. Ironically, much of the world that hippies forged was co-opted by the society they had rejected.

By the late 1960s most dreams of human betterment seemed shattered—whether those dreams emanated from the promise of the march on Washington, Lyndon Johnson's Great Society, or the communal society of the hippie counterculture. Recession and inflation brought an end to the easy affluence that made liberal reform programs and alternative lifestyles seem so easily affordable. Poverty and unemployment menaced even middle-class youth who had found havens in communes, colleges, and graduate schools. Racial tensions divided black militants and the white liberals of the civil rights movement into sometimes hostile camps.

But the Vietnam War more than any other single factor destroyed the promise of the Great Society and distracted from the campaign for civil rights. After 1965 the nation divided sharply as the American military role in Southeast Asia grew. Radicals on the left looked to rid America of a capitalist system that promoted race and class conflict at home and imperialism and military adventurism abroad. Conservatives who supported the war called for a return to more traditional values like law and order. Both the left and the right attacked the liberal center. Their combined opposition helped undermine the consensus Lyndon Johnson had worked so hard to build.

chapter summary

Largely excluded from the prosperity of the 1950s, African Americans and Latinos undertook a series of grass-roots efforts to gain the legal and social freedoms denied them by racism and, in the South, by an entrenched system of segregation.

- Early postwar campaigns focused on legal challenges to the system, culminating with victories in the Supreme Court decisions of *Brown v. Board of Education* and *Hernández v. Texas*.

- Later in the 1950s, Martin Luther King and other civil rights activists used new techniques of protest, such as the boycott, to desegregate the bus system in Montgomery, Alabama.

- Continued resistance by white southerners sparked a school integration dispute in Little Rock, Arkansas.

- Beginning in 1960, widespread grassroots efforts from African American churches, students, and political

- groups across the South accelerated the drive for an end to segregation.

- Violence against sit-ins, freedom rides, voter registration drives, and other forms of nonviolent protest made the nation sympathetic to the civil rights cause.

- In the wake of the assassination of President Kennedy, Lyndon Johnson persuaded Congress to adopt the Civil Rights Act of 1964 and the Voting Rights Act of 1965.

- The Supreme Court under Chief Justice Earl Warren expanded civil rights and liberties through its *Gideon*, *Escobedo*, and *Miranda* decisions, while also easing censorship, banning school prayer, and increasing voting rights.

- Lyndon Johnson delivered on the liberal promise of his Great Society through his 1964 tax cut, aid to education, Medicare and Medicaid, wilderness preservation, and urban redevelopment, and through the many programs of his war on poverty.

- Johnson's liberal reforms did not satisfy student radicals, minority dissidents, feminists, gays, and the counterculture whose members sought to transform America into a more just and less materialistic society.

interactive learning

The Primary Source Investigator CD-ROM offers the following materials related to this chapter:

- Interactive map: **Civil Rights: Patterns of Protest and Unrest** (M30)

- A collection of primary sources exploring the rise of the civil rights movement and the crisis of liberalism in America during the 1950s and 1960s: baseball legend Jackie Robinson's letter to President Eisenhower regarding civil rights, and an excerpt from *Rosa Parks: My Story*. Some sources reveal the legal aspects of the civil rights era, such as a transcript of *Brown v. Board of Education*.

additional reading

Among the many excellent studies of civil rights are Robert Weisbort, *Freedom Bound: A History of America's Civil Rights Movement* (1990); Harvard Sitkoff, *The Struggle for Black Equality* (1981); and Juan Williams, *Eyes on the Prize: America's Civil Rights Years, 1954–1964* (1987). Taylor Branch's study of Martin Luther King and the civil rights era begins with the eloquent *Parting the Waters: America in the King Years, 1954–63* (1988). *Pillar of Fire: America in the King Years, 1963–1965* (1998) is sometimes slower going. *The Autobiography of Malcolm X*, as told to Alex Haley (reissue, 1989), is a classic that provides sharp contrast to King's pacifism.

Good recent studies of the civil rights movement at the grassroots level include John Dittmer, *Local People: The Struggle for Civil Rights in Mississippi* (1994), and Stuart Burns, ed., *Daybreak of Freedom: The Montgomery Bus Boycott* (1997). Latino civil rights movements are covered in Henry A. J. Ramos, *American G.I. Forum* (1998), and F. Arturo Rosales, *Chicano! The History of the Mexican American Civil Rights Movement* (1997).

Lyndon Johnson receives a critical but evenhanded treatment in Doris Kearns, *Lyndon Johnson and the American Dream* (1976), and Robert Dallek, *Lyndon Johnson: Lone Star Rising* (1991), but is savaged in Robert Caro, *The Years of Lyndon Johnson: The Path to Power* (1982) and *Means of Ascent* (1990). On foreign policy under Kennedy and Johnson, see Walter LaFeber, *America, Russia, and the Cold War* (9th ed., 2002).

For surveys of the upheavals of the 1960s, see Allen Matusow, *The Unraveling of America* (1984), and Todd Gitlin, *The Sixties* (1987). The counterculture has received no balanced treatment yet, but Terry H. Anderson, *The Movement and the Sixties* (1995), and Edward P. Morgan, *The 60s Experience* (1991), offer much insight into political activism. For a fuller list of readings, see the Bibliography at www.mhhe.com/davidsonnation5.

significant events

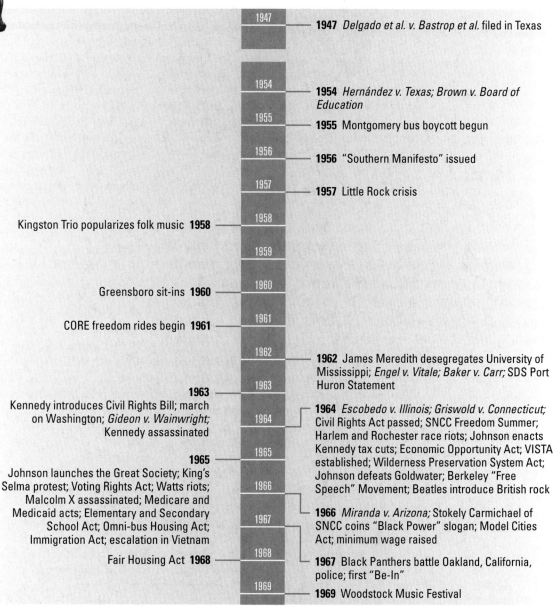

1947 *Delgado et al. v. Bastrop et al.* filed in Texas

1954 *Hernández v. Texas; Brown v. Board of Education*

1955 Montgomery bus boycott begun

1956 "Southern Manifesto" issued

1957 Little Rock crisis

Kingston Trio popularizes folk music **1958**

Greensboro sit-ins **1960**

CORE freedom rides begin **1961**

1962 James Meredith desegregates University of Mississippi; *Engel v. Vitale; Baker v. Carr;* SDS Port Huron Statement

1963
Kennedy introduces Civil Rights Bill; march on Washington; *Gideon v. Wainwright;* Kennedy assassinated

1964 *Escobedo v. Illinois; Griswold v. Connecticut;* Civil Rights Act passed; SNCC Freedom Summer; Harlem and Rochester race riots; Johnson enacts Kennedy tax cuts; Economic Opportunity Act; VISTA established; Wilderness Preservation System Act; Johnson defeats Goldwater; Berkeley "Free Speech" Movement; Beatles introduce British rock

1965
Johnson launches the Great Society; King's Selma protest; Voting Rights Act; Watts riots; Malcolm X assassinated; Medicare and Medicaid acts; Elementary and Secondary School Act; Omni-bus Housing Act; Immigration Act; escalation in Vietnam

1966 *Miranda v. Arizona;* Stokely Carmichael of SNCC coins "Black Power" slogan; Model Cities Act; minimum wage raised

Fair Housing Act **1968**

1967 Black Panthers battle Oakland, California, police; first "Be-In"

1969 Woodstock Music Festival

Chapter 30

Vietnam from afar: it looked almost like an emerald paradise. "I remember getting up on the flight deck and seeing one of the most beautiful visions I've ever seen in my life," recalled Thomas Bird, an army rifleman sent there in 1965: "A beautiful white beach with thick jungle background. The only thing missing was naked women running down the beach, waving and shouting 'Hello, hello, hello.'" Upon landing, Bird and his buddies were each issued a "Nine-Rule" card outlining proper behavior toward the Vietnamese. "Treat the women with respect, we are guests in this country and here to help these people."

But who were they helping and who were they fighting? When American troops sought to engage Vietcong forces, the VC generally disappeared into the jungle beyond the villages and rice fields. John Muir, a marine rifleman, walked into a typical hamlet with a Korean lieutenant. To Muir the place looked ordinary, but the Korean had been in Vietnam a while. "We have a little old lady and a little old man and two very small children," he pointed out. "According to them, the rest of the family has been spirited away . . . either been drafted into one army or the other. So there's only four of them and they have a pot of rice that's big enough to feed fifty people. And rice, once it's cooked, will not keep. They gotta be feeding the VC." Muir, whose only experience with rice till then had been Minute Rice or Uncle Ben's, watched as the lieutenant set the house on fire. The roof "started cooking off ammunition because all through the thatch they had ammunition stored."

GIs soon learned to walk down jungle trails with a cautious shuffle, looking for a wire or a piece of vine that seemed too straight. "We took more casualties from booby traps than we did from actual combat," recalled David Ross, a medic. "It was very frustrating because how do you fight back against a booby trap? You're just walking along and all of a sudden your buddy doesn't have a leg. Or you don't have a leg." Yet somehow the villagers would walk the same paths and never get hurt. Who was the enemy and who the friend?

Kent State

The same question was being asked half a globe away, on the campus of Kent State University in May 1970. By then the Vietnam War had dragged on for more than five years and had driven President Lyndon Johnson from office. And it had embroiled his successor, Richard Nixon, in controversy when he expanded the war into Cambodia. Kent State, just east of Akron, Ohio, was one of the many campuses that flourished in the 1950s and 1960s to accommodate the children of the baby boom. Opposition to the war had become so intense in this normally apolitical community that 300 students had torn the Constitution from a history text and, in a formal ceremony, buried it. "President Nixon has murdered it," they charged. That evening demonstrators spilled into the nearby town, smashed shop windows, and returned to campus to burn down an old army ROTC building. The panicked mayor declared a state of emergency, and Governor James Rhodes ordered in 750 of the National Guard. Student dissidents were the "worst type of people we harbor in America," he announced. "We are going to eradicate the problem."

The Vietnam Era
1963–1975

preview • Presidents from Truman to Nixon argued that communism in Southeast Asia threatened vital American interests. But it was Lyndon Johnson who began a massive bombing campaign and sent half a million American troops to intervene in Vietnam's civil war. Amid dissent at home and continued campaigns for equality by women, gays, Latinos, and Indians, Richard Nixon gradually withdrew U.S. forces from Vietnam, signaling limits to America's influence as a superpower.

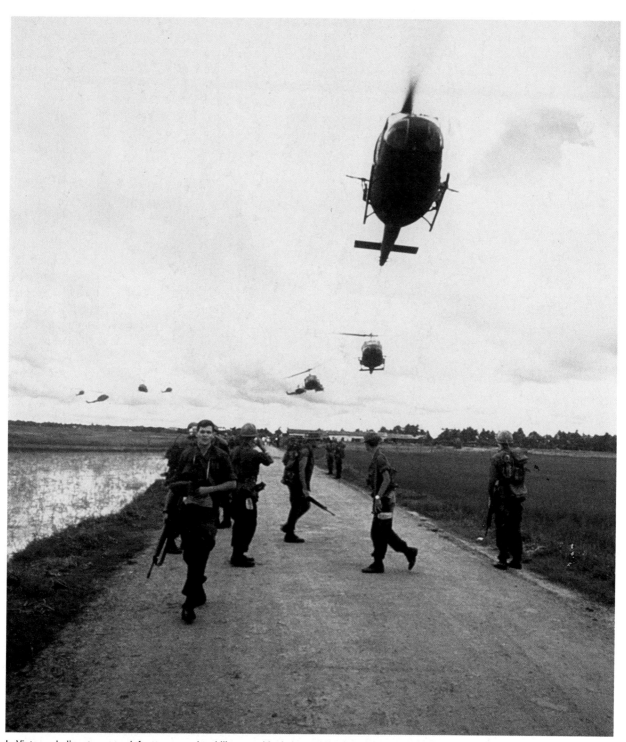

In Vietnam, helicopters gave infantry unusual mobility—a critical element in a war with no real front line, because troops could be quickly carried from one battle to another. These soldiers await a pickup amid rice paddies south of Saigon.

Death at Kent State: who was
the enemy, who was the friend?

By background and education, the National Guard troops were little different from the students they had come to police. Almost all were white, between 18 and 30, and from Ohio. But guard veterans who fought in World War II or Korea disdained students who evaded or openly rejected their military obligation or who openly criticized their country. As his troops arrived at Kent, Guard Commander General Robert Canterbury remarked that "these students are going to have to find out what law and order is all about."

When demonstrators assembled for a rally on the college commons, the Guard ordered them to disperse, though the troops' legal right to break up a peaceful demonstration was debatable. The protesters stood their ground. Then the guardsmen advanced, wearing full battle gear and armed with M-1 rifles, whose high-velocity bullets had a horizontal range of almost two miles. Some students scattered; a few picked up rocks and threw them. The guardsmen suddenly fired into the crowd, many of whom were students passing back and forth from classes. Incredulous, a young woman knelt over Jeffrey Miller; he was dead. By the time calm was restored, three other students had been killed and nine more wounded, some caught innocently in the Guard's indiscriminate fire.

Jackson State

News of the killings swept the nation. At Jackson State, a black college in Mississippi, antiwar protesters seized a women's dormitory. On May 14 state police surrounding the building opened fire without provocation, killing two more students and wounding a dozen. In both incidents the demonstrators had been unarmed. The events at Kent State and Jackson State turned sporadic protests against the American invasion of Cambodia into a nationwide student strike. Many students believed the ideals of the United States had been betrayed by those forces of law and order sworn to protect them.

Who was the friend and who the enemy? Time and again the war in Vietnam led Americans to ask that question. Not since the Civil War had the nation been so deeply divided. As the war dragged on, debate moved off college campuses and into the homes of middle Americans, where sons went off to fight and the war came home each night on the evening news. As no other war had, Vietnam seemed to stand the nation on its head. When American soldiers shot at Vietnamese "hostiles" who could not always be distinguished from "friendlies," or when National Guardsmen fired on their neighbors across a college green, who were the enemies and who were the friends?

The Road to Vietnam

"The enemy must fight his battles far from his home base for a long time," one Vietnamese strategist wrote. "We must further weaken him by drawing him into protracted campaigns. Once his initial dash is broken, it will be easier to destroy him." The enemy in question was not American soldiers or the French but the Mongol invaders of 1284 C.E. For several thousand years Vietnam had struggled periodically to fight off foreign invasions. Buddhist culture penetrated eastward from India. More often Indochina faced invasion and rule by the Chinese from the north. After 1856 the French entered as a colonial power, bringing with them a strong Catholic tradition.

Ho Chi Minh was one Vietnamese who hoped to throw off French influence as well as the Chinese. In 1912, at the age of 22, Ho gave up life as a poor schoolteacher and hired out as a mess boy on a French ocean liner. He was in France at the end of World War I, when President Wilson came to Versailles calling for self-determination for small nations. Ho bought a formal pinstriped suit at a secondhand

Ho Chi Minh

Nguyen Ai Quoc, who became Ho Chi Minh, once worked at London's posh Carlton Hotel in the pastry kitchen of the renowned French chef Escoffier. But he was soon swept up in socialist and nationalist politics, appearing at the Versailles Peace Conference (left) to plead for an independent Vietnam. By the time the United States was increasing its involvement in Vietnam, Ho had accumulated a lifetime of anti-colonialist and revolutionary activity and become a revered leader of his people. He died in 1969, six years before his dream of a united Vietnam became a reality.

store and attended the peace conference to petition for Vietnam. When the delegates ignored his plea, he became a Communist, taking the recent Russian Revolution as his model. Visits to Moscow followed, after which he returned to the Indochina region to organize revolutionary activity.

Once Japan was defeated in 1945, Ho seized the opportunity to unite Vietnam under a nationalist government. But France moved to recover control of its old colony. Some of Ho's colleagues suggested approaching the Chinese Communists for help. But Ho was foremost a nationalist. He worried that Chinese aid might lead to permanent domination. "I prefer to smell French dung for five years rather than Chinese dung for the rest of my life," he concluded, and he accepted the French return. Soon after, negotiations for independence broke down. Ho and his forces began eight years of guerrilla war against the French, which led to victory at Dien Bien Phu in 1954 (page 960). Ho's dream of an independent Vietnam seemed at hand. He agreed at the Geneva peace conference to withdraw his forces north of the 17th parallel in return for a promise to hold free elections in both the North and the South.

Ngo Dinh Diem

The United States, however, was determined to thwart Ho. Having supported the French in what they saw as a fight to contain communism, President Eisenhower helped install Ngo Dinh Diem and then supported Diem's decision not to hold elections. Frustrated South Vietnamese Communists—the Vietcong—began their guerrilla war once again. "I think the Americans greatly underestimate the determination of the Vietnamese people," Ho remarked in 1962, as President Kennedy was committing more American advisers to South Vietnam.

Lyndon Johnson's War

For Kennedy, Vietnam had been just one of many anti-Communist skirmishes his activist advisers wanted to fight. As attention focused increasingly on Vietnam, Kennedy accepted President Eisenhower's "domino theory": if the pro-Western Catholic government fell to the Communists, all the other nations of Southeast Asia would collapse in a row. Such an event would discredit Kennedy's effort to use counterinsurgency to fight the cold war with new vigor. But even 16,000 American "advisers" had been unable to help the unpopular Diem, who was overthrown by the military in November 1963. When Kennedy was assassinated in the same month as Diem, the problem of Vietnam was left to Lyndon Johnson.

The domino theory

Johnson's political instincts told him to keep the Vietnam War at arm's length. He felt like a catfish, he remarked, who had "just grabbed a big juicy worm with a right sharp hook in the middle of it." Johnson's heart was in his Great Society programs. Yet fear of the political costs of defeat in Vietnam led him steadily toward deeper American involvement. He shared the assumptions of Kennedy holdovers such as National Security Advisor McGeorge Bundy and Defense Secretary Robert McNamara that Vietnam was a key cold war test. And Republican presidential candidate Barry Goldwater raised the stakes by insisting on a "let's-win" policy of total military victory.

Always preferring the middle way, Johnson wanted a policy somewhere between total commitment and disengagement. Until August 1964 American advisers had focused on South Vietnam itself: guiding the South Vietnamese army in its struggle against the Vietcong. North Vietnam, for its part, had been infiltrating modest amounts of men and supplies along the Ho Chi Minh Trail, a primitive network of jungle routes threading through Laos and Cambodia into the highlands of South Vietnam. In the summer of 1964 North Vietnam began to modernize the trail so it could handle trucks in addition to the peasants who carried supplies on their backs or used modified bicycles. At the time American officials were unaware of the change, but they realized all too well that the Vietcong already controlled some 40 percent of South Vietnam. Johnson strategists decided to relieve the South by increasing pressure on North Vietnam itself.

American ships in the Gulf of Tonkin began to patrol the North Vietnamese coast and provide cover for secret South Vietnamese raids. On August 2, three North Vietnamese patrol boats exchanged fire with the American destroyer *Maddox*—neither side hurting the other—and then the Vietnamese boats fled. An angry Johnson chided several admirals. "You've got a whole fleet and all those airplanes, and you can't even sink three little ol' PT boats?" Two nights later, in inky blackness and a heavy thunderstorm, radar operators on the *C. Turner Joy* reported a torpedo attack. But a follow-up investigation could not establish whether enemy ships had even been near the scene. "The Gulf is a very funny place," explained one communications officer. "You get inversion layers there that will give you very solid radar contacts . . . that just aren't there. That may have happened to us." The president was not pleased. "For all I know our navy might have been shooting at whales out there," he remarked privately.

Whatever his doubts, the president called the incidents "open aggression on the high sea" and ordered retaliatory air raids on North Vietnam. He did not disclose that the navy and South Vietnamese forces had been conducting secret military operations at the time. Such deception would become standard practice. It allowed Johnson to ask Congress for authority to take "all necessary measures" to "repel any armed attack" on American forces and to "prevent future aggression." Congress overwhelmingly passed what became known as the Gulf of Tonkin resolution.

Senator Ernest Gruening of Alaska, one of the two lawmakers to object, sensed danger. The Tonkin Gulf resolution gave the president "a blank check" to declare war, a power the Constitution specifically reserved to Congress. Johnson insisted— no doubt sincerely at the time—that he had no such intention. But as pressure for an American victory increased, the president exploited the powers the resolution gave him.

Tonkin Gulf incident

Rolling Thunder

In January 1965 Johnson received a disturbing memorandum from McGeorge Bundy and Robert McNamara. "Both of us are now pretty well convinced that our present policy can lead only to disastrous defeat," they said. The United States should either increase its attack—*escalate* was the term coined in 1965—or simply withdraw. In theory escalation would increase military pressure to the point at which further resistance cost more than the enemy was willing to bear. By taking gradual steps, the United States would demonstrate its resolve to win while leaving the door open to negotiations.

Escalation

The theory that made so much sense in Washington did not work well in Vietnam. Each stage of American escalation only hardened the resolve of the Vietcong and North Vietnamese. When a Vietcong mortar attack in February killed seven Marines stationed at Pleiku airbase, Johnson ordered U.S. planes to begin bombing North Vietnam. The following month Operation Rolling Thunder was launched, a systematic bombing campaign aimed at bolstering confidence in South Vietnam and cutting the flow of supplies from the North.

Air strikes

But Rolling Thunder achieved none of its goals. American pilots could seldom spot the Ho Chi Minh Trail under its dense jungle canopy. Even when bombs hit, North Vietnamese crews kept the supplies moving by quickly filling the bomb craters or improvising pontoon bridges from woven bamboo stalks. Equally discouraging,

The War in Vietnam North Vietnam established the Ho Chi Minh Trail (red arrows) through central Laos in order to supply South Vietnam's Vietcong forces. In the earlier stages of the war, supplies were transported by foot, but by 1964 the North Vietnamese were building roads and bridges that could handle heavy trucks.

South Vietnamese leaders spent their energy on political intrigue. One military government after another proved equally inept. And Ho Chi Minh refused to negotiate unless the bombing stopped and American troops went home.

Once the Americans established bases from which to launch the new air strikes, these, too, became targets for guerrilla attacks. When General William Westmoreland, the chief of American military operations in Vietnam, requested combat troops to defend the bases, Johnson sent in 3500 marines, almost without considering the implication of his decision. Until then, only military "advisers" to the South Vietnamese had been sent. Once the crucial decision to commit combat troops had been taken, the urge to shore up and protect those already there became strong. Another 40,000 soldiers arrived in May and 50,000 more by July.

Johnson, as before, deliberately downplayed the escalation because he feared a political backlash. By the end of 1965 almost 185,000 American troops had landed—and still the call for more continued. In 1968, at the height of the war, 536,000 American troops were being supported with helicopters, jet aircraft, and other advanced military technologies. This conflict was "escalation" with a vengeance.

Social Consequences of the War

The impact of the war, naturally enough, fell hardest on the baby-boom generation of the 1950s. As these young people came of age, draft calls for the armed services were rising. At the same time, the civil rights movement and the growing counterculture were encouraging students to question the goals of establishment America. Whether they fought in Vietnam or protested at home, supported the government or demonstrated against it, eventually these baby boomers—as well as Americans of all ages—were forced to take a stand on Vietnam.

The Soldiers' War

The social structure determining which Americans would be required to fight and which would remain civilian was the draft. The system in place generally favored the middle and upper classes because college students and graduate students at first received deferments. Thus the Vietnam War increased male enrollment in colleges. As the war escalated, the draft was changed so that some students were called up through a lottery system. Still, those who knew the medical requirements might be able to produce a doctor's affidavit certifying a weak knee, flat feet, or bad eyes—all grounds for flunking the physical. About half the potential draftees flunked—two to three times the rejection rate of those called up by the NATO allies. Of the 1200 men in Harvard's class of 1970, only 56 served in the military, and only 2 of them in Vietnam.

The poorest and least educated were also likely to escape service, because the Armed Forces Qualification Test and the physical often screened them out. Thus the sons of blue-collar America were most likely to accept Uncle Sam's letter of induction, as were the sons of Latino and black Americans, who, having fewer skills, were more often assigned to combat duty. The draft also made it a relatively young man's war. The average soldier serving in Vietnam was 19, compared with 26 years old for World War II.

Most American soldiers came to Vietnam well trained and with high morale. But the physical and psychological hardships inevitably took their toll. In a war of continual small skirmishes, booby traps, and search-and-destroy missions, it was hard to relax. An American force would fight its way into a Communist-controlled hamlet, clear and burn it, and move on—only to be ordered back days or weeks

The Vietcong often fought in small groups, using the dense vegetation to cover their movements. These suspects faced a difficult interrogation as U.S. soldiers tried to learn more about the location of Vietcong units.

Body counts

later because the enemy had moved in again. Because success could not be measured in territory gained, the measure became the "body count": the number of Vietcong killed. Unable to tell who was friendly and who was hostile, GIs regularly took out their frustrations on innocent civilians. Their deaths helped inflate the numbers used to prove that the Americans were winning.

Other social factors affected the way soldiers fought. Only about one in nine soldiers was actually in combat; the rest supported them. Most new recruits went to Vietnam as individuals, not as part of a unit. When they joined units already in the field, combat veterans saw their inexperience as a liability. Ignorance got people killed. This departure from military tradition undermined the camaraderie critical to good morale. Combat veterans had even less sympathy for the rear echelon, or "REMF," soldiers who faced little danger while sorting supplies or lifeguarding at beaches near Da Nang. Paradoxically, the miracles of modern technology also made the war hard to cope with. Helicopters could whisk GIs from the front lines of a steaming jungle back to Saigon, where they could catch overnight flights to Hawaii or the mainland. The sudden shift from the hell of war to civilian peace could be wrenching.

Technology and its limits

To support a technological war, American forces built the shell of a modern society in South Vietnam. By 1967 a million tons of supplies arrived in Vietnam each month—an average of a hundred pounds a day for every American in the country. South Vietnam's airports soon handled more flight traffic than New York, Rome, Tokyo, or any other city in the world. No matter where they were, ground forces could count on air strikes to strafe or bomb suspected enemy positions. Because the Vietcong routinely mixed with the civilian population, the chances for deadly error increased. Bombs of napalm (jellied gasoline) and white phosphorus rained liquid fire from the skies, coating everything from village huts to the flesh of fleeing humans. Cluster bombs, designed to explode hundreds of pellets in midair, sprayed the enemy with high-velocity shrapnel. To clear jungle canopies and expose Vietcong camps and roads, American planes spread more than 100 million pounds of defoliants such as Agent Orange. ("Only You Can Prevent Forests" was the sardonic motto of one unit assigned to the task.) The destroyed forests totaled more than one-third of South Vietnam's timberlands—an area approximately the size of the state of Rhode Island. In many ways the ecological devastation was more severe than the military destruction.

By 1967 the war costs exceeded more than $2 billion a month. The United States dropped more bombs on Vietnam than it had during all of World War II. After one air attack on a Communist-held provincial capital, American troops walked into the remains, now mostly ruined buildings and rubble. "We had to destroy the town in order to save it," an officer explained. As the human and material costs of the war increased, that statement stuck in the minds of many observers. What sense was there in a war that saved people by burning their homes?

The War at Home

As the war dragged on, such questions provoked anguished debate among Americans, especially on college campuses. Faculty members held "teach-ins" to explain the issues to concerned students. Scholars familiar with Southeast Asia questioned every major assumption the president used to justify escalation. The United States and South Vietnam had brought on the war, they charged, by violating the Geneva Accords of 1954. Moreover, the Vietcong were an indigenous rebel force with legitimate grievances against Saigon's corrupt government. The war was a civil war among the Vietnamese, not an effort by Soviet or Chinese Communists to conquer Southeast Asia, as Eisenhower, Kennedy, and Johnson had claimed.

Hawks and doves

By 1966 national leaders had similarly divided into opposing camps of "hawks" and "doves." The hawks argued that America must win in Vietnam to save Southeast Asia from communism, to preserve the nation's prestige, and to protect the lives of American soldiers fighting the war. A large majority of the American people supported those views. The doves were a prominent minority. They included New Left radicals as well as respected editorialist Walter Lippmann; Senator J. William Fulbright, head of the Foreign Relations Committee; and Dr. Benjamin Spock, the physician whose child care manuals had raised the generation of baby boomers.

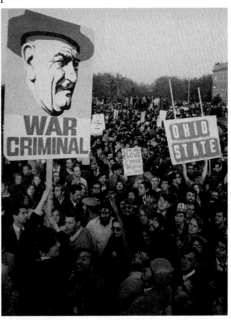

Despite the liberal achievements of the Great Society, anti-war protestors villified Lyndon Johnson as a fascist.

African Americans as a group were far less likely than white Americans to support the war. Some resented the diversion of Great Society resources from the cities to the war effort. Many black Americans' heightened sense of racial consciousness led them to identify with the Vietnamese people. Martin Luther King, SNCC, and CORE all opposed the war.

By 1967 college students and faculty turned out in crowds of thousands to express their outrage: "Hey, hey, LBJ, how many kids have you killed today?" More than 300,000 people attended the demonstration organized in April 1967 in New York City. Sixty college protesters organized by SDS leaders from Cornell University burned their draft cards in defiance of federal law. In the fall more violent protests erupted as antiwar radicals stormed a draft induction center in Oakland, California. The next day 55,000 protesters, including some prominent writers and artists, ringed the Pentagon in Washington. Mass arrests followed.

Student protests forced policy makers and citizens to take a sobering look at the justice of the war. But the guerrilla tactics of more radical elements alienated many. It would be hard to exaggerate the shock that university communities felt when radicals shut down Columbia University and clashed with police for a week in 1968. The following year black militant students—bandoliers draped across their shoulders, shotguns at their sides—seized the student union at Cornell. Even more shocking, a graduate student at the University of Wisconsin was killed in his lab when a bomb exploded there. The device had been planted by radicals protesting government-sponsored defense research.

On the other hand, key moderates both within and outside the government were convinced that the United States could not win the war. Senator Fulbright was among them. Having helped President Johnson push the Tonkin Gulf resolution through the Senate, Fulbright now held hearings sharply critical of American policy. Even the strongest supporters of the war felt the pressure. Secretary of State Dean Rusk, a hard-liner throughout, was dismayed to hear his relatives back home in Cherokee County, Georgia: "Dean, if you can't tell us when this war is going to end, well then, maybe we just ought to chuck it."

McNamara loses faith

Defense Secretary McNamara became the most dramatic defector. For years the statistically minded secretary had struggled to quantify the success of the war effort. General Westmoreland duly provided body counts, number of bombs dropped, and pacification reports. For a time McNamara remained confident that there was indeed a "light at the end of the tunnel." But by 1967 the secretary had become skeptical. "The picture of the world's greatest superpower killing or seriously injuring 1,000 non-combatants a week, while trying to pound a tiny, backward nation into submission on an issue whose merits are hotly disputed, is not a pretty one," he advised.

Johnson, however, thought of himself as a moderate on the war. He weighed doves like McNamara against hawks like Senator John Stennis of Mississippi and General Westmoreland, who pressed to escalate further. Because Johnson did not want to be remembered as the first American president who lost a war, he sided more with the hawks. And so McNamara resigned.

Inflation

As the war dragged on, it had one severe economic consequence: inflation. By 1967 the cost of the war had soared to more than $50 billion a year. Medicare, education, housing, and other Great Society programs raised the domestic budget sharply, too. Through it all Johnson refused to raise taxes, for fear of losing support for his domestic programs. From 1950 to 1960 the average rate of inflation hovered at about 2 percent a year. From 1965 to 1970, as the war escalated, it jumped to around 4 percent. The economy was headed for trouble.

The Unraveling

Almost all the forces dividing America seemed to converge in 1968. Until January of that year, most Americans had reason to believe General Westmoreland's estimate that the United States was winning the war. Johnson and his advisers, whatever their private doubts, in public painted an optimistic picture. With such optimism radiating from Washington, few Americans were prepared for the events of the night of January 30, 1968.

Tet Offensive

As the South Vietnamese began their celebration of Tet, the Vietnamese lunar new year, Vietcong guerrillas launched a series of concerted attacks. Assault targets included Saigon's major airport, the South Vietnamese presidential palace, and Hue, the ancient Vietnamese imperial capital. Perhaps most unnerving to Americans,

19 crack Vietcong commandos blasted a hole in the wall of the American embassy compound in Saigon and stormed in. They fought in the courtyard until all 19 lay dead.

Tet must rank as one of the great American intelligence failures, on a par with Pearl Harbor or China's intervention in Korea. For nearly half a year the North Vietnamese had lured American troops into pitched battles at remote outposts like Khe Sanh, Con Thien, Song Be, and Dak To. As American forces dispersed, the Vietcong infiltrated major population areas of Saigon and the delta region. A few audacious VC, disguised as South Vietnamese soldiers, even hitched rides on American jeeps and trucks.

Though surprised by the Tet offensive, American and South Vietnamese troops quickly counterattacked, repulsing most of the assaults. Appearing before the American press, General Westmoreland announced that the Vietcong had "very deceitfully" taken advantage of the Vietnamese holiday "to create maximum consternation" and that their "well-laid plans went afoul." In a narrow military sense, Westmoreland was right. The enemy had been driven back, sustaining perhaps 40,000 deaths. Only 1100 American and 2300 South Vietnamese soldiers had been killed—a ratio of more than 10 to 1 (though 12,500 civilians died).

But Americans at home received quite another message. Tet created a "credibility gap" between the administration's promises and the harsh reality. Westmoreland, Johnson, and other officials had repeatedly claimed that the Vietcong were on their last legs. Yet as Ho Chi Minh had coolly informed the French after World War II, "You can kill ten of my men for every one I kill of yours . . . even at those odds, you will lose and I will win." Highly respected CBS news anchor Walter Cronkite drew a gloomy lesson of Tet for his national audience: "To say that we are mired in stalemate seems the only realistic, yet unsatisfactory, conclusion."

Stalemate

Two months later, American forces remained edgy about Vietcong attacks. At the remote hamlet of My Lai, American troops under Lieutenant William Calley

My Lai

swept in, rounded up the villagers, and slaughtered more than 200 men, women, and children. The dead of My Lai would have been just more figures in the "body count," except that an army photographer had taken pictures and a helicopter pilot intervened. If returning veterans were to be believed, there had been hundreds of similar incidents, though perhaps few as bloody. On the Communist side, vengeance was at times even more severe. Before Hue could be retaken, the Vietcong had shot, clubbed to death, or buried alive perhaps 3000 civilians.

The Tet offensive sobered Lyndon Johnson as well as his new secretary of defense, Clark Clifford. Clifford was a stalwart believer in the war. But as he reviewed the American position in Vietnam, he could get no satisfactory answers from the Joint Chiefs of Staff, who had requested an additional 206,000 troops. "How long would it take to succeed in Vietnam?" Clifford recalled asking them.

Levels of U.S. Troops in Vietnam (at Year End) This graph suggests one reason why protest against the war increased after 1964, peaked by 1968, and largely ended after 1972.

They didn't know. How many more troops would it take? They couldn't say. Were two hundred thousand the answer? They weren't sure. Might they need more? Yes, they might need more. Could the enemy build up [their own troop strength] in exchange? Probably. So what was the plan to win the war? Well, the only plan was that attrition would wear out the Communists, and they would have had enough. Was there any indication that we've reached that point? No, there wasn't.

Clifford decided to build a case for deescalation. To review policy, he formed a panel of "wise men," respected pillars of the cold war establishment, that included Dean Acheson, Harry Truman's secretary of state; Henry Cabot Lodge, a Republican and former ambassador to South Vietnam; and several retired generals. Johnson's advisers had led him "down the garden path" on Vietnam, the wise men concluded. The war could not be won, and he should seek a negotiated settlement.

Meanwhile, the antiwar forces had found a political champion in Senator Eugene McCarthy from Minnesota. McCarthy was something of a senatorial maverick who wrote poetry in his spare time. He announced that no matter what the odds, he would challenge Johnson in the 1968 Democratic primaries. Idealistic college students got haircuts and shaves in order to look "clean for Gene." Thus transformed, they canvassed New Hampshire voters. Johnson had not formally entered the 1968 presidential race, but his supporters sponsored a write-in campaign, confident of a decisive win in this opening primary. When the votes were counted, McCarthy had lost by only 300 out of 50,000 votes cast. For the president, so slim a victory was a stunning defeat. To the outrage of McCarthy supporters, Robert Kennedy, John Kennedy's younger brother, now announced his own antiwar candidacy.

"I've got to get me a peace proposal," the president told Clifford. The White House speechwriters finally put together an announcement that bombing raids against North Vietnam would be halted, at least partially, in hopes that peace talks could begin. They were still trying to write an ending when Johnson told them, "Don't

"Clean for Gene"

"WHO? ? ?" taunts one poster behind the relatively unknown Senator Eugene McCarthy after his strong showing against President Johnson in the New Hampshire Democratic primary. College students were among McCarthy's most fervent supporters.

worry; I may have a little ending of my own." On March 31 he supplied it, announcing: "I have concluded that I should not permit the presidency to become involved in the partisan divisions that are developing in this political year. . . . Accordingly I shall not seek, and I will not accept, the nomination of my party for another term as your president."

LBJ withdraws

The Vietnam War had pulled down one of the savviest, most effective politicians of the modern era. North Vietnam, for its part, responded to the speech by sending delegates to a peace conference in Paris, where negotiations quickly bogged down. And American attention soon focused on the chaotic situation at home, where all the turbulence, discontent, and violence of the 1960s seemed to be coming together.

The Shocks of 1968

On April 4 Martin Luther King Jr. traveled to Memphis to support striking sanitation workers. He was relaxing on the balcony of his motel when James Earl Ray, an escaped convict, fatally shot him. King's campaign of nonviolence was overshadowed by the frustration and anger that greeted news of his death. Riots broke out that evening in ghetto areas of the nation's capital; by the end of the week, disturbances had rocked 125 more neighborhoods across the country. Almost before Americans could recover, a disgruntled Arab nationalist, Sirhan Sirhan, assassinated Robert Kennedy on the evening of June 5. Running in opposition to the war, Kennedy had just won a crucial primary victory in California.

The King and Kennedy assassinations

The deaths of King and Kennedy pained Americans deeply. In their own ways, both men exemplified the liberal tradition, which reached its high-water mark in the 1960s. King had retained his faith in a Christian theology of nonviolence. He sought change without resorting to the language of the fist and the gun. In the final years of his life, his campaign broadened to include the poor of all races.

Unlike his rival Eugene McCarthy, Robert Kennedy (left) felt comfortable reaching out to minorities and blue-collar workers. In March 1968, Kennedy traveled to California to join Mexican American labor activist Cezar Chavez (right), who was leading a hunger strike in support of a farm workers' union (see page 1031).

Robert Kennedy had begun his career as a pragmatic politician who, like his brother John, had not hesitated to use power ruthlessly. But Kennedy, like King, had come to reject the war his brother had supported, and he seemed genuinely to sympathize with the poor and minorities. At the same time, he was popular among traditional white ethnics and blue-collar workers. Would the liberal political tradition have flourished longer if these two charismatic figures had survived the turbulence of the 1960s?

Chicago

Once violence had claimed the clearest liberal voices, it became obvious that the Democrats would choose Hubert Humphrey when their convention met at Chicago in August. Humphrey had begun his career as a progressive and a strong supporter of civil rights. But as Johnson's loyal vice president he was intimately associated with the war and the old-style liberal reforms that could never satisfy radicals. Humphrey's impending nomination meant, too, that no major candidate would speak for Americans disillusioned with the war or the status quo. The Republicans had chosen Richard Nixon, a traditional anti-Communist (now reborn as the "new," more moderate Nixon). As much as radicals disliked Johnson, they abhorred any Nixon, "new" or old.

Chicago, where the Democrats met, was the fiefdom of Mayor Richard Daley, long the symbol of machine politics and backroom deals. Daley was determined that the radicals who poured into Chicago would not disrupt "his" Democratic convention. The radicals were equally determined that they would. For a week the police skirmished with demonstrators: police clubs, riot gear, and tear gas versus the demonstrators' eggs, rocks, and balloons filled with paint and urine. When Daley refused to allow a peaceful march past the convention site, the radicals marched anyway. With the mayor's blessing, the police turned on the crowd in what a federal commission later labeled a police riot. In one pitched battle, many officers took off their badges and waded into the crowd, nightsticks swinging, chanting, "Kill, kill, kill." Reporters, medics, and other innocent bystanders were injured; at 3:00 A.M. police invaded candidate Eugene McCarthy's hotel headquarters and pulled some of his assistants from their beds.

Convention mayhem

With feelings running so high, President Johnson did not dare appear at his own party's convention. Theodore White, a veteran journalist covering the assemblage, scribbled his verdict in a notebook as police chased hippies down Michigan Avenue. "The Democrats are finished," he wrote.

Revolutionary clashes worldwide

The clashes in Chicago seemed homegrown, but they reflected a growing willingness among students worldwide to use violence to press their revolutionary causes. In 1966 Chinese students were in the vanguard of Mao Zedong's Red Guards, formed to enforce a Cultural Revolution that was purging China of all bourgeois middle-class culture. Although that revolution persecuted millions among the educated classes and left China in economic shambles, Mao became a hero to student activists in Europe and America, who also lionized other armed revolutionaries: Fidel Castro and Che Guevara of Cuba and Ho Chi Minh.

Revolutionary targets varied. In Italy students denounced the official Marxism of the Soviet Union and the Italian Communist party. French students at the Sorbonne in Paris rebelled against the university's efforts to discipline student activists and protested their decrepit classrooms and dormitories. Students in Czechoslovakia launched a full-scale rebellion in the Prague Spring of 1968, which the Soviets eventually crushed. Although radical agendas varied from region to region, students showed remarkable unanimity in condemning one event on the world stage: the American war in Vietnam.

Whose Silent Majority?

Radicals were not the only Americans alienated from the political system in 1968. Governor George Wallace of Alabama sensed the frustration among the "average man on the street, this man in the textile mill, this man in the steel mill, this barber, this beautician, the policeman on the beat." In running for president, Wallace sought the support of blue-collar workers and the lower middle classes.

George Wallace

Wallace had first come to national attention as he stood at the door barring integration of the University of Alabama. Briefly, he pursued the Democratic presidential nomination in 1964. For the race in 1968 he formed his own American Independent party with the hawkish General Curtis LeMay as his running mate. (LeMay spoke belligerently of bombing North Vietnam "back to the stone age.") Wallace's enemies were the "liberals, intellectuals, and long hairs [who] have run this country for too long." Wallace did not simply appeal to law and order, militarism, and white backlash; he was too sharp for that. With roots in southern Populism, he called for federal job-training programs, stronger unemployment benefits, national health insurance, a higher minimum wage, and a further extension of union rights. Polls in September revealed that many Robert Kennedy voters had shifted to Wallace. A quarter of all union members backed him.

In fact, Wallace had tapped true discontent among the working class. Many blue-collar workers despised hippies and peace marchers yet wanted the United States out of Vietnam. And they were suspicious, as Wallace was, of the upper-class "establishment" that held power. Old-style radicals of the 1930s might have tried to tap such discontent, but the leaders of the New Left by and large had given up on traditional workers. They aimed their appeal at the newer minorities: students, Latinos, African Americans, and the unorganized poor.

Richard Nixon also sought to attract traditionally Democratic voters, especially disaffected southern Democrats, away from Wallace into the Republican party. The Republicans, of course, had been reviled by the Populists of old as representatives of the money power, monopoly, and the old-line establishment. But Nixon himself had modest roots. His parents owned a general store in Whittier, California, where he had worked to help the family out. His high school grades were good enough to earn him a scholarship to Harvard, but fearing the cost of traveling east, he turned it down in favor of nearby Whittier College. At Duke Law School he was so pinched for funds that he lived in an abandoned toolshed. If ever there had been a candidate who could claim to be self-made, it was Nixon. And he well understood the disdain ordinary laborers felt for "kids with the beards from the suburbs"—hippies who wore flags sewn to the seat of their pants—who seemed always to be insisting, protesting, *demanding*. Nixon believed himself a representative of the "silent majority," as he later described it, not a vocal minority.

Nixon's "silent majority"

He thus set two fundamental requirements for his campaign: to distance himself from President Johnson on Vietnam and to turn Wallace's "average Americans" into a Republican "silent majority." The Vietnam issue was delicate, because Nixon had generally supported the president's efforts to end the war. He told his aide Richard Whalen, "I've come to the conclusion that there's no way to win the war. But we can't say that, of course. In fact, we have to seem to say the opposite." For most of his campaign he hinted that he had a secret plan to end the war but steadfastly refused to disclose it. He pledged only to find an honorable solution, at the

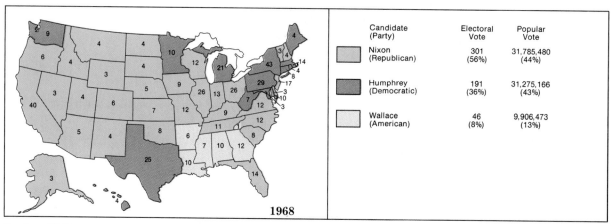

Candidate (Party)	Electoral Vote	Popular Vote
Nixon (Republican)	301 (56%)	31,785,480 (44%)
Humphrey (Democratic)	191 (36%)	31,275,166 (43%)
Wallace (American)	46 (8%)	9,906,473 (13%)

1968

Election of 1968

The election of 1968

same time promising to promote "law and order" while cracking down on "pot," pornography, protest, and permissiveness.

Hubert Humphrey had the more daunting task of surmounting the ruins of the Chicago convention. All through September antiwar protesters dogged his campaign with "Dump the Hump" posters. Finally the vice president distanced his position on Vietnam, however slightly, from that of his unpopular boss. The protests then faded, Humphrey picked up momentum, and traditional blue-collar Democrats began to return to the fold. By November his rallies were enthusiastic and well attended. But the late surge did not turn the tide. Nixon captured 43.4 percent of the popular vote to 42.7 percent for Humphrey and 13.5 percent for Wallace. More important, Nixon's "southern strategy" paid off; he and Wallace carried the entire southern tier of states except Texas. Some voters had punished the Democrats not just for the war but also for supporting civil rights. The majority of the American electorate seemed to have turned their backs on liberal reform.

Nixon's War

In Richard Nixon, Americans had elected two men to the presidency. On the public side, he appeared as the traditional small-town, middle-class conservative who cherished individual initiative, chamber-of-commerce capitalism, Fourth of July patriotism, and Victorian mores. The private Nixon was a troubled man. His language among intimates was caustic and profane. He waxed bitter toward those he saw as enemies. Never a natural public speaker, he was physically rather awkward—a White House aide once found toothmarks on a "childproof" aspirin cap the president had been unable to pry open. But Nixon seemed to search out challenges—"crises" to face and conquer.

The new president saw himself as a master of foreign policy. The Vietnam War stood in the way of his major goals. Hence, ending it became one of his first priorities. He found a congenial ally in National Security Adviser Henry Kissinger. Kissinger, like Nixon, had a global vision of foreign affairs. Like Nixon, he had a tendency to pursue his ends secretly, skirting the traditional channels of government such as the Department of State.

Henry Kissinger

Vietnamization—and Cambodia

To bring the Vietnam War to an end, Nixon and Kissinger wanted to negotiate a settlement that would bring American troops home, but they insisted on "peace with honor." That boiled down to preserving a pro-American South Vietnamese government. The strategy Nixon adopted was "Vietnamization," which involved a carrot and a stick. On its own initiative, the United States began gradually withdrawing troops as a way to advance the peace talks in Paris. The burden of fighting would shift to the South Vietnamese army, equipped now with massive amounts of American supplies. Critics likened this strategy to little more than "changing the color of the corpses." All the same, it helped reduce antiwar protests at home. Once the media shifted their focus from the war to the peace talks, the public had the impression that the war was winding down.

Carrot and stick approach

Using the stick, President Nixon hoped to drive the North Vietnamese into negotiating peace on American terms. Quite consciously, he traded on his reputation as a cold warrior who would stop at nothing. As he explained to his chief of staff, Robert Haldeman,

> I call it the Madman Theory, Bob. I want the North Vietnamese to believe that I've reached the point where I might do anything to stop the war. We'll just slip the word to them that, "for God's sake, you know Nixon is obsessed about Communists. We can't restrain him when he's angry—and he has his hand on the nuclear button"—and Ho Chi Minh himself will be in Paris in two days begging for peace.

To underline his point, Nixon in the spring of 1969 launched a series of bombing attacks against North Vietnamese supply depots inside neighboring Cambodia. Johnson had refused to widen the war in this manner, fearing domestic reaction. Nixon simply kept the raids secret.

The North Vietnamese refused to cave in to the bombing or the threats of the "Madman." Ho Chi Minh's death in 1969 changed nothing. His successors continued to reject any offer that did not end with complete American withdrawal and an abandonment of the South Vietnamese military government. Once again Nixon decided to turn up the heat. Over the opposition of his secretaries of defense and state, he ordered American troops into Cambodia to wipe out North Vietnamese bases there. This action was, to be sure, Johnson's old policy of escalation—precisely the opposite of the withdrawal Nixon had promised. But the Joint Chiefs argued that such an attack would buy time to strengthen the South Vietnamese army.

Invading Cambodia

Nixon recognized that a storm of protest would arise. (The administration was "going to get unshirted hell for doing this," he noted.) On April 30, 1970, he announced the "incursion" of American troops into Cambodia, proclaiming that he would not allow "the world's most powerful nation" to act "like a pitiful helpless giant." The wave of protests that followed included the Kent State tragedy as well as another march on Washington by 100,000 protesters. Even Congress was upset enough to repeal the Tonkin Gulf resolution, a symbolic rejection of Nixon's invasion. After two months American troops left Cambodia, having achieved little.

Fighting a No-Win War

For a time, Vietnamization seemed to be working. As more American troops went home, the South Vietnamese forces improved modestly. But for American GIs still in the country, morale became a serious problem. Obviously the United

A helicopter machine gunner: cigarette dangling, a knife and "jungle juice" insect repellent stuck in his helmet. Increasingly, there were few illusions about this no-win war.

States was gradually pulling out its forces. After Tet, it was clear there would be no victory. So why were the "grunts" in the field still being asked to put their lives on the line? The anger surfaced increasingly in incidents known as "fragging," in which GIs threw fragmentation grenades at officers who pursued the war too aggressively.

Nor could the army isolate itself from the trends dividing American society. Just as young Americans "turned on" to marijuana and hallucinogens, so soldiers in Vietnam used drugs. The Pentagon estimated that by 1971 nearly a third of American troops there had experimented with either opium or heroin, easily obtained in Southeast Asia. Nor did black GIs leave black power issues at home. Robert Rawls recalled that the brothers "used to make a shoestring that they braided up and tied around their wrist, and everywhere a whole lot of blacks used to go, they'd give a power sign." One white medic noticed that Muhammad Ali's refusal to be drafted caused the blacks in his unit "to question why they were fighting the Honky's war against other Third World people." Indeed, he said, "I saw very interesting relationships happening between your quick-talking, sharp-witted Northern blacks and your kind of easygoing, laid-back Southern blacks. . . . Many Southern blacks changed their entire point of view by the end of their tour and went home extremely angry."

The problem with morale only underlined the dilemma facing President Nixon. As the troops became restive, domestic opposition to the war grew. By repealing the Gulf of Tonkin resolution, Congress itself had put the president on notice that he would have to negotiate a settlement soon. Yet the North Vietnamese refused to yield, even after the American assaults in Cambodia.

The Move toward Détente

Despite Nixon's insistence on "peace with honor," Vietnam was not a war he had chosen to fight. Both Kissinger and Nixon recognized that the United States no longer had the strength to exercise unchallenged dominance across the globe. The Soviet Union, not Vietnam, remained their prime concern. Ever since Khrushchev had backed down at the Cuban missile crisis in 1962, the Soviets had steadily expanded their nuclear arsenal. Furthermore, the growing economies of Japan and Western Europe challenged American leadership in world trade. Continued instability in Southeast Asia, the Middle East, and other Third World areas threatened the strength of the non-Communist bloc. Thus Vietnam diverted valuable military and economic resources from more critical areas.

Nixon Doctrine

In what the White House labeled the new "Nixon Doctrine," the United States announced it would no longer expect to fight every battle, win every war, or draw every line to keep the global peace. Instead, Americans would shift some of the military burden for containment to such allies as Japan in the Pacific, the shah of Iran in the Middle East, Zaire in central Africa, and the apartheid government in South Africa. Over the next six years American foreign military sales jumped from

Upon seeing China's Great Wall, an ebullient Richard Nixon pronounced it a "great wall," built by a great people. Perhaps precisely because he had been so staunch an anti-Communist, Nixon appreciated the enormous departure his trip marked in Sino-American relations.

$1.8 billion to $15.2 billion. At the same time, Nixon and Kissinger looked for new ways to contain Soviet power not simply by the traditional threat of arms but through negotiations to ease tensions. This policy was named, from the French, détente.

To pursue détente Kissinger and Nixon used "linkages," a system of making progress on one issue by connecting it with another. They recognized, for example, how much the cold war arms race burdened the Soviet economy. To ease that pressure, they would make concessions to the Soviets on nuclear arms. The Soviets in return would have to limit their arms buildup and, in a linked concession, pressure North Vietnam to negotiate an end to the war. To add pressure, Nixon and Kissinger developed a "China card." The United States would stop treating Mao Zedong as an archenemy and, instead, open diplomatic relations with the Chinese. Fearful of a more powerful China, the Soviets would be more conciliatory toward the United States.

It took a shrewd diplomatist to sense an opportunity to shift traditional cold war policy. Conservative Republicans in particular had denounced the idea of ever recognizing Mao's government, even after 20 years. They believed that the Soviets responded only to force and that they were united with China in a monolithic Communist conspiracy. Now Richard Nixon, the man who had built a career fighting communism, made overtures to the Communist powers. Kissinger slipped off to China on a secret mission (he was nursing a stomachache, his aides assured the press) and then reappeared having arranged a week-long trip to China for the president. During that visit in early 1972, Nixon pledged to normalize relations, a move the public enthusiastically welcomed, although some conservative Republicans

Daily Lives

TIME AND TRAVEL
The Race to the Moon

In campaigning for the presidency in 1960 John F. Kennedy charged the Republicans with creating a missile gap. While the American space program limped along, the Soviet Union had launched *Sputnik*. Only a few months after Kennedy's inauguration, Russian cosmonaut Yuri Gagarin orbited the world in a five-ton spacecraft. The first American space flight on May 6, 1961, succeeded only in carrying Commander Alan Shepard into a suborbital flight of 300 miles. Kennedy feared that if it lost the space race, the United States might lose the cold war as well.

Thus Kennedy ordered his science advisers "to shift our efforts in space from low to high gear." He announced on national television that the United States would do something truly dramatic: land a man on the moon and bring him back alive "before the decade is out." No matter how great the cost, Kennedy believed the investment was sound. "This is not merely a race," he remarked in an allusion to the Soviets' success. "Space is open to us now; and our eagerness to share its meaning is not governed by the efforts of others. We must go into space because whatever mankind must undertake, free men must fully share."

There were skeptics, such as former President Eisenhower, who thought anyone was "nuts" to spend billions for a space spectacular that promised little in the way of scientific discoveries. Nor was it clear that NASA could achieve such a feat in so short a time. To many members of Congress, however, the space program was a huge pork barrel, so they voted to fund Kennedy's "great new American enterprise." From then on the space program achieved a string of triumphs. In February 1962 Colonel John Glenn successfully circled

Landing on the moon may have been one small step for a man, but NASA spent $25 billion on the project, over $2 billion for each of the 12 astronauts who took lunar walks.

were angered at the idea of betraying their old ally in Taiwan, Chiang Kai-shek. Only Nixon's impeccable anti-Communist credentials had allowed him to reverse the direction of America's China policy.

A new overture to the Soviet Union followed the China trip. Eager to acquire American grain and technology, Soviet premier Leonid Brezhnev invited Nixon to visit Moscow in May 1972. Nixon saw in the Soviet market a chance to ease the earth three times in "a fireball of a ride"; an unmanned satellite passed Venus later that year; and a Telstar communications satellite began relaying television broadcasts, launching an era of truly global mass communications.

One after another, the space spectaculars continued, much to the public's delight. In March 1965 American astronauts first maneuvered their capsule; in May Edward White took America's first space walk; the following year two vehicles met and docked for the first time. The Gemini program was followed by the Apollo missions, whose Saturn rockets powered their payloads into lunar orbit. From there, two astronauts planned to pilot a separate module to the moon's surface, while a third remained in the orbiting command module waiting for them and the return trip. By Christmas eve 1968 the *Apollo 8* mission was circling the moon. It seemed a "vast, lonely and forbidding sight," one astronaut remarked to hundreds of millions in a live telecast.

On July 20, 1969, the lunar module of *Apollo 11* at last touched down on the earth's closest neighbor. Commander Neil Armstrong, moving awkwardly in his bulky space suit, worked his way down a ladder to the white, chalky surface. He was not alone. Besides Edwin Aldrin, who followed him, and Michael Collins, orbiting in the command module, Armstrong brought along a quarter of the world's population, who monitored the moment live on television. "That's one small step for a man, one giant leap for mankind," he proclaimed.

For all its stunning success, the space program did not escape the political crosscurrents of the 1960s. Critics argued that those billions might better have been spent solving more earthly problems. And Richard Nixon turned *Apollo 11* into a public relations gold mine, even though Kennedy and Johnson had supported the space program against Republican attacks. "This is the greatest week in the history of the world since the Creation," Nixon told the astronauts after their capsule splashed down in the Pacific. Evangelist Billy Graham took exception to his friend's theological excess. What of Christ's birth, his death, and his resurrection, Graham wanted to know. "Tell Billy," Nixon wrote White House chief of staff H. R. Haldeman, "RN referred to a week not a day."

But *Apollo 11* marked the climax of a phase of exploration, not, like the Creation, a beginning. After *Apollo 17* and $25 billion in costs, Nixon predicted "this may be the last time in this century men will walk on the moon." Space travel since then has belonged largely to the space shuttles and to science fiction, where the crew of the starship *Enterprise* and their Kennedyesque captains like James T. Kirk and Jean Luc Picard, "boldly go where no one has gone before."

American trade deficits by selling grain surpluses. The two leaders struck a major wheat deal, but the most important benefit of the meeting was the signing of the first Strategic Arms Limitation Treaty (SALT I). In the agreement, both sides pledged not to develop a new system of antiballistic missiles, which would have accelerated the costly arms race. And they agreed to limit the number of intercontinental ballistic missiles each side would deploy.

SALT I

Both the China and Moscow visits strengthened Nixon's reputation as a global strategist. Americans were pleased at the prospect of lower cold war tensions. But it was not clear that the linkages achieved in Moscow and Beijing would help extricate the United States from Vietnam.

The New Identity Politics

During the 1968 campaign Richard Nixon had noticed a placard carried by a hopeful voter—"Bring Us Together." That phrase became his campaign theme. Yet in the divisive atmosphere of the 1960s, unity was an elusive goal. George Wallace had attracted a large bloc of voters fed up with protest and social unrest. If Nixon could add those discontented southerners and blue-collar workers to his traditional base of Republicans, his enlarged silent majority could easily return him to the White House in 1972.

Separate identities vs. assimilation

Nixon's effort to create among his followers the sense that they held the moral high ground played off a growing unease over the divided nature of American society. To the silent majority, it seemed as if the consensus of the 1950s was increasingly being ripped apart. In their campaign for civil rights, African Americans very often insisted that because they had *not* been treated equally, they therefore necessarily belonged to a separate, oppressed group. In the 1960s activists took pride in proclaiming black power or even, like the Nation of Islam, embracing a doctrine of separation. Latinos, American Indians, Asian Americans, feminists, and gay Americans all applied much of the same critique to their own situations. Out of this increased pride in each group's distinctive values and characteristics came a new political and social assertiveness. Whereas before, Latino civil rights groups such as LULAC and World War II veterans in the American GI Forum had sought assimilation into American society, now minorities began to forge identities in opposition to the prevailing culture.

Latino Activism

Part of the increased visibility of minorities resulted from a new wave of immigration from Mexico and Puerto Rico after World War II. That wave was augmented by Cubans, after the 1959 revolution that brought Fidel Castro to power. Historical, cultural, ethnic, and geographic differences made it difficult to develop a common political agenda among Latinos. Still, some activists did seek greater unity.

Puerto Ricans and Cubans

After World War II a weak island economy and the lure of prosperity on the mainland brought more than a million Puerto Ricans into New York City. As citizens of the United States, they could move freely to the mainland and back home again. That dual consciousness discouraged many from establishing deep roots stateside. Equally important, the newcomers were startled to discover that, whatever their status at home, on the mainland they were subject to racial discrimination and most often segregated into urban slums. In 1964 approximately half of all recent immigrants lived below the poverty level, according to the Puerto Rican Forum. Their unemployment was three times greater than for whites and 50 percent higher than for blacks. Light-skinned migrants escaped those conditions by blending into the middle class as "Latin Americans." The Puerto Rican community thereby lost some of the leadership it needed to assert its political rights.

Still, a shared island orientation preserved a strong group identity. By the 1960s the urban barrios had gained greater political consciousness, as groups such as Aspira adopted the strategies of civil rights activists and as organizations like the

Black and Puerto Rican Caucus linked with other minority groups. The Cubans who arrived in the United States after 1959—some 350,000 over the course of the decade—forged fewer ties with other Latinos. Most settled around Miami. An unusually large number came from Cuba's professional, business, and government class and were racially white and politically conservative.

Mexican Americans, on the other hand, constituted the largest segment of Latinos. Until the 1940s most were farmers and farm laborers in Texas, New Mexico, and California. But during the 1950s, the process of mechanization had affected them just as it had southern blacks. By 1969 about 85 percent of Mexican Americans had settled in cities. With urbanization came a slow improvement of the range and quality of jobs they held. A body of skilled workers, middle-class professionals, and entrepreneurs emerged.

Yet Mexican agricultural workers continued to face abysmally low wages and harsh working conditions. Previous attempts to unionize them had failed partly because workers migrated from job to job and strikebreakers were easily imported. In 1963 a soft-spoken but determined farmworker, Cesar Chavez, recruited fellow organizers Gil Padilla and Dolores Huerta to make another attempt. Their efforts over the next several years led to the formation of the United Farm Workers (UFW) labor union.

Cesar Chavez and the UFW

Chavez, like Martin Luther King, proclaimed an ethic of nonviolence. Also like King, he was guided by a deep religious faith (Roman Catholicism in the case of Chavez and most Mexican American farmworkers). When the union's meager financial resources made it difficult to sustain a strike of Mexican and Filipino grape workers that began in the summer of 1966, Chavez rallied supporters for a 250-mile march on Sacramento. "Dr. King had been very successful" with such marches, he noted. Seeking additional leverage, the union looked to use consumers as an economic weapon by organizing a boycott of grapes in supermarkets across the nation. Combined with a 24-day hunger strike by Chavez—a technique borrowed from Gandhi—the boycott forced growers to negotiate contracts with the UFW beginning in 1970.

Chavez's movement was rooted in the traditional issues of labor organizing. But just as Martin Luther King found his nonviolent approach challenged by more radical activists, a new generation of Mexican Americans forged a more aggressive brand of identity politics. Many began calling themselves Chicanos. Like blacks, Chicanos saw themselves as a people whose culture had been taken from them. Their heritage had been rejected, their labor exploited, and their opportunity for advancement denied. Of Chavez's generation, Reies Lopez Tijerina attracted wide attention as a charismatic leader. His movement in northern New Mexico ("La Alianza") organized armed bands to occupy federal lands that Hispanos in the region had once used for grazing livestock. In Denver, Rodolfo "Corky" Gonzales laid out a blueprint for a separatist Chicano society, with public housing set aside for Chicanos and the

Chicano activists

Most Mexican American migrant workers were devout Catholics. This farmworker's altar combines both religious symbols (the Crucifixion) and the UFW's red-and-black Aztec eagle (surrounded by the arms of workers of different races, showing solidarity) into designs signifying the strike and national grape boycott.

development of economically independent barrios in which a new cultural pride could flourish. "We are a Bronze People with a Bronze Culture," declared Gonzales. "We are a Nation. We are a union of free pueblos. We are Aztlán."

Recruits to the new activism came from both college and high school students. Like other members of the baby boom generation, Mexican Americans attended college in increasing numbers. In addition, Lyndon Johnson's Educational Opportunity Programs (EOP), part of his war on poverty, brought thousands more Latinos onto college campuses, especially in California. By 1968 some 50 Mexican American student organizations on college campuses counted at least 2000 to 3000 members among their ranks. In Los Angeles that year thousands of Chicano high school students walked out to protest substandard educational conditions. Two years later the new ethnic militancy led to the formation of La Raza Unida (The Race United). This third-party movement sought to gain power in communities in which Chicanos were a majority and to extract concessions from the Democrats and Republicans. The more militant "Brown Berets" adopted the paramilitary tactics and radical rhetoric of the Black Panthers.

La Raza Unida

The Choices of American Indians

Like African Americans and Latinos, Indians began to protest, yet the unique situation of Native Americans (as many had begun to call themselves) set them apart from other minorities. A largely hostile white culture had in past centuries sought either to exterminate or to assimilate American Indians. Ironically, the growing strength of the civil rights movement created another threat to Indian tribal identities. Liberals came to see the reservations not as oases of Indian culture but as rural ghettos. During the 1950s liberals joined conservatives (eager to repeal the New Deal) and western state politicians (eyeing tribal resources) in adopting a policy of "termination." The Bureau of Indian Affairs would reduce federal services, gradually sell off tribal lands, and push Indians into the "mainstream" of American life.

Termination

In 1890 the U.S. cavalry had killed 146 Indians at Wounded Knee, South Dakota. In 1973 these members of the American Indian Movement seized the hamlet of Wounded Knee, making it once again a symbol of conflict.

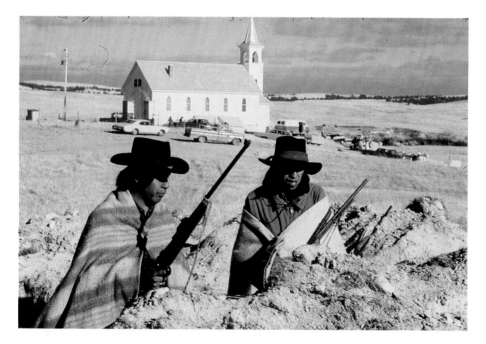

Although most full-blooded Indians objected to the policy, some mixed bloods and Indians already assimilated into white society supported the move. The resulting relocation of approximately 35,000 Indians accelerated a shift from rural areas to cities. The urban Indian population, which had been barely 30,000 in 1940, had reached more than 300,000 by the 1970s.

The social activism of the 1960s inspired Indian leaders to shape a new political agenda. In 1968 urban activists in Minneapolis created AIM, the American Indian Movement. A year later like-minded Indians living around San Francisco Bay formed Indians of All Tribes. Because the Bureau of Indian Affairs refused to address the problems of urban Indians, more militant members of the organization dramatized their dissatisfaction by seizing the abandoned federal prison on Alcatraz Island in San Francisco Bay.

American Indian Movement

The Alcatraz action inspired a national Pan-Indian rights movement. Richard Oakes, a Mohawk Indian from New York, declared that the Alcatraz protest was not "a movement to liberate the island, but to liberate ourselves." Then in 1973, AIM organizers Russell Means and Dennis Banks led a dramatic takeover of a trading post at Wounded Knee, on a Sioux reservation in South Dakota. Ever since white cavalry had gunned down over a hundred Sioux in 1890 (see pages 586–587), Wounded Knee had symbolized for Indians the betrayal of white promises and the bankruptcy of reservation policy. Even more, Wounded Knee now demonstrated the problems that Indian activists faced. When federal officers surrounded the trading post, militants discovered that other Indians did not support their tactics, and they were forced to leave. A Pan-Indian movement was difficult to achieve when so many tribes were determined to go their own ways as distinct, self-regulating communities. Thus even activists who supported the Pan-Indian movement found themselves splintering. During the 1970s more than 100 different organizations were formed to unite various tribes pursuing political and legal agendas at the local, state, and federal levels.

Wounded Knee

Asian Americans

In removing quotas that had discriminated against immigration from non-European nations (page 995), the 1965 Immigration Act removed one of the major affronts to Asian Americans. Further, it spurred a rapid increase in immigration from Asia to the United States. Asians, who in 1960 constituted just 1 percent of the American population (about a million people), were by 1985 2 percent (about five million). This new wave included many middle-class professionals, a lower percentage of Japanese, and far more newcomers from Southeast and South Asia. Civil rights reforms had already swept away legal barriers to full citizenship that had previously stigmatized Asians.

Many Americans treated these new immigrants as "model minorities." They brought skills in high demand, worked hard, were often Christians, and seldom protested. The 1970 census showed Japanese and Chinese Americans with incomes substantially above the median for white Americans. Such statistics hid significant fault lines within communities. Although many professionals assimilated into the American mainstream, agricultural laborers and sweatshop workers remained trapped in poverty. And no matter how much Anglos praised their industry, the distinguishing appearance of Asian Americans still amounted to what one sociologist defined as a "racial uniform." They were nonwhites in a white society.

Few Americans were aware of Asian involvement in identity politics. That was in part because the large majority of Asian Americans lived in just three states—Hawaii, California, and New York. Further, Asian Americans were less likely to join in the era's most vocal protests. Nonetheless, some Asian students on California campuses joined with African Americans, Chicanos, and Native Americans to advocate a "third world revolution" against the white establishment. Specifically, Asian activists called for a curriculum that recognized their particular histories and cultures. As the Asian population increased, so too would the demands of Asian Americans for recognition of their place in a multicultural society.

Gay Rights

In 1972, Black Panther leader Huey Newton observed that homosexuals "might be the most oppressed people" in American society. Certainly Newton was qualified to recognize oppression when he saw it. But by then a growing number of homosexuals had publicly declared their sexual identity. Growing political activism placed them among minorities demanding equal rights.

By the early 1970s gay Americans had a new sense of political awareness. "Coming out" by acknowledging one's sexual orientation was a key strategy for developing gay pride.

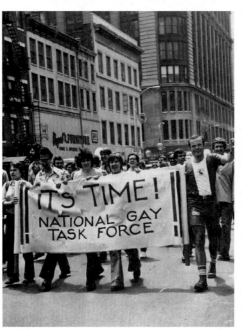

Even during the "conformist" 1950s, gay men founded the Mattachine Society (1951) to fight antihomosexual attacks and to press for a wider public acceptance of their lifestyle. Lesbians formed a similar organization, the Daughters of Bilitis, in 1955. Beginning in the mid-1960s, more radical gay and lesbian groups began organizing to raise individual consciousness and to establish a gay culture in which they felt free. One group called for "acceptance as full equals . . . basic rights and equality as citizens; our human dignity; . . . [our] right to love whom we wish."

Stonewall incident

The movement's defining moment came on Friday June 27, 1969, when New York City police raided the Stonewall Inn, a Greenwich Village bar. Such raids were common enough: gay bars were regularly harassed by the police in an attempt to control urban "vice." This time the patrons fought back, first with taunts and jeers, then with paving stones and parking meters. Increasingly, gay activists called on homosexuals to "come out of the closet" and publicly affirm their sexuality. In 1974 gays achieved a major symbolic victory when the American Psychiatric Association removed homosexuality from its list of mental disorders.

Feminism

The movement for women's rights and equality in the United States was not, of course, a creation of the 1960s. It began well before the Civil War, and the sustained political efforts of its supporters had won women the vote in 1920. But the women's movement of the 1960s and 1970s began to push for equality in broader, deeper ways.

Writer Betty Friedan was one of the first women to voice dissatisfaction with the cultural attitudes prevalent at midcentury. Even though more women were entering the job market, the media routinely glorified housewives and homemakers while discouraging those women who aspired to independent careers. In *The Feminine Mystique* (1963) Friedan identified the "problem that has no name," a dispiriting boredom or emptiness in the midst of affluent lives. "Our culture does not permit women to accept or gratify their basic need to grow and fulfill their potentialities as human beings."

The Feminine Mystique gave birth to a new women's rights movement. The Commission on the Status of Women appointed by President Kennedy proposed the 1963 Equal Pay Act and helped add gender to the forms of discrimination outlawed by the 1964 Civil Rights Act. Women also assumed an important role in both the civil rights and antiwar movements. They accounted for half the students who went south for the Freedom Summers in 1964 and 1965. Living with violence and assuming heavy responsibilities, these women discovered new freedom and self-confidence.

Movement women also realized that they were themselves victims of systematic discrimination. Male reformers often limited them to behind-the-scenes services such as cooking, laundry, and fulfilling sexual needs. Casey Hayden, a veteran of SDS and SNCC, confronted the male leadership. The "assumptions of male superiority are as widespread . . . and every bit as crippling to the woman as the assumptions of white superiority are to the Negro," she wrote. By 1966 activist women were less willing to see their grievances eclipsed by other political constituencies. Friedan joined a group of 24 women and 2 men who formed the National Organization for Women (NOW). The new feminists sought to force the Johnson administration to take bolder action to eliminate discrimination in such areas as jobs and pay. When feminists argued that "sexism" was not qualitatively different from racism, Johnson accepted the argument and in 1967 included women as well as African Americans, Hispanics, and other minorities as groups covered by federal affirmative action programs.

Broader social trends established a receptive climate for the feminist appeal. After 1957 the birthrate began a rapid decline; improved methods of contraception, such as the birth control pill, permitted more sexual freedom and smaller family size. By 1970 more than 40 percent of all women, an unprecedented number, were employed outside the home. Education also spurred the shift from home to the job market and increased consciousness of women's issues. Higher educational levels allowed women to enter an economy oriented increasingly to white-collar service industries rather than blue-collar manufacturing.

As much as women sought liberation from old restrictions, their new circumstances raised problems. Men did not readily share traditional family responsibilities with working women; obligations of a job were added to domestic routines. Because women often took part-time jobs or jobs treated as "female" work, they earned far less than men. And though greater sexual freedom implied more gender equality, the media continued to promote the image of women as sex objects.

By 1970 feminists had captured the media's attention. Fifty thousand women participated in NOW's Strike for Equality Parade down New York's Fifth Avenue. Television cameras zeroed in on signs with such slogans as "Don't Cook Dinner—Starve a Rat Today." Some newscasters reported that marchers had burned their bras to protest sexual stereotyping. "Bra burners" became the media's condescending

The Feminine Mystique

National Organization for Women

Ms. magazine, edited by feminist Gloria Steinem, gave the women's movement a means to reach a broader audience. The cover of the first issue, published in 1972, uses the image of a many-armed Hindu goddess to satirize the multiple roles of the modern housewife.

phrase used to deny credibility to militant feminists such as Kate Millett, whose *Sexual Politics* (1970) condemned a male-dominated "patriarchal" society.

Equal Rights and Abortion

With its influence growing, the feminist movement sought to translate women's grievances into a political agenda. NOW members could agree in 1967 to a "Bill of Rights" that called for maternity leave for working mothers, federally supported day-care facilities, child care tax deductions, and equal education and job training. But they divided on two other issues: the passage of an Equal Rights Amendment to the Constitution and a repeal of all state antiabortion laws.

At first, support seemed strong for an Equal Rights Amendment that would forbid all discrimination on the basis of gender. By the 1970s public opinion polls showed that even a majority of American men were sympathetic to the idea. In 1972 both the House and the Senate passed the Equal Rights Amendment (ERA) virtually without opposition. Within a year 28 of the necessary 38 states had approved the ERA. It seemed only a matter of time before 10 more state legislatures would complete its ratification.

Roe v. Wade

Many participants in the women's movement also applauded the Supreme Court's decision, in *Roe v. Wade* (1973), to strike down 46 state laws restricting a woman's access to abortion. In his opinion for the majority, Justice Harry Blackmun observed that a woman in the nineteenth century had "enjoyed a substantially broader right to terminate a pregnancy than she does in most states today." As legal abortion in the first three months of pregnancy became more readily available, the rate of maternal deaths from illegal operations, especially among minorities, declined.

But the early success of the ERA and the feminist triumph in *Roe v. Wade* masked underlying divisions among women's groups. *Roe v. Wade* triggered a sharp backlash from many Catholics, Protestant Fundamentalists, and socially conservative women. Their opposition inspired a crusade for a "right to life" amendment to the Constitution. A similar conservative reaction breathed new life into the "STOP ERA" crusade of Phyllis Schlafly, an Illinois political organizer. Although Schlafly was a professional working woman herself, she believed that women should embrace their traditional role as homemakers subordinate to their husbands. "Every change [that the ERA] requires will deprive women of a right, benefit, or exemption that they now enjoy," she argued.

In the middle ground stood women (and a considerable number of men) who wanted to use the political system, rather than a constitutional amendment, to correct the most glaring inequalities between the sexes. Within a year after Congress passed the ERA, the National Women's Political Caucus conceded that the momentum to ratify was waning. Although Congress in 1979 extended the deadline for state legislatures to act for another three years, it became clear that the amendment would fail.

The Legacy of Identity Politics

The identity politics of the late 1960s and early 1970s marked a beginning, not an end. Over the next decade, African Americans, Latinos, American Indians, Asian Americans, gays, and feminists would discover that many of the issues they raised remained unresolved. White males still earned more than women or minority men. A glass ceiling barred the path to the executive suites in most corporations, professions, and politics. Many laws and social customs favored white males. The military, for example, barred women from combat and gays altogether. Being labeled a feminist, a homosexual, or a social activist carried a stigma in many areas of American society. Conservatives continued to see identity politics as a threat to national unity.

All the same, political and social activism had brought a sense of empowerment to people who had long seen themselves as "other." By speaking up, they had demonstrated how traditional ways of presenting American history and culture excluded the experience of the majority of Americans. They had opened doors to jobs, careers, and avenues of success previously closed to them. An increasing number of women and minorities won election to political office. Beyond that, identity politics forced the nation to see itself, not as Eurocentric, but as a multicultural society—a nation of nations—that struggled to reconcile separate with common identities, as it had since its founding two centuries earlier.

The End of an Era

Just as identity politics revealed the divisions in American society, so did the continuing debate over Vietnam. President Nixon was particularly frustrated because a settlement there still eluded him. The North Vietnamese refused any peace agreement that left the South Vietnamese government of General Nguyen Van Thieu in power. Nixon wanted to subdue his opponents through force but recognized that it would be political suicide to send back American troops. Instead, he ordered Haiphong harbor mined and blockaded in May 1972, along with a sustained bombing campaign. Then on December 18 the president launched an even greater wave of attacks, as American planes dropped more bombs on the North in 12 days than they had during the entire campaign from 1969 to 1971.

Once again, Kissinger returned to Paris, hoping that the combination of threats and conciliation would bring a settlement. Ironically, the Americans' ally, General Thieu, threw up the most stumbling blocks, for he was rightly convinced that his regime would not last once the United States departed. But in January 1973 a treaty was finally arranged, smoothed by Kissinger's promise of aid to the North Vietnamese to help in postwar reconstruction, as well as a secret pledge to Thieu to send troops again if they were needed. By March the last American units were home.

Paris peace treaty

"The enemy must fight his battles . . . [in] protracted campaigns," wrote the Vietnamese strategist in 1284. For all concerned, the American phase of the Vietnam War had been a bloody, wearying conflict. Between 1961 and 1973 the war claimed 57,000 American lives and left more than 300,000 wounded. The cost to Southeast Asia in lives and destruction is almost impossible to calculate. More than a million Vietnamese soldiers and perhaps half a million civilians died. Some 6.5 million South Vietnamese became refugees, along with 3 million Cambodians and Laotians. Nixon claimed the "peace with honor" he had insisted on, but experienced observers predicted that South Vietnam's days were numbered. By any real measure of military success the Vietcong peasant guerrillas and their lightly armed North Vietnamese allies had held off—and in that sense defeated—the world's greatest military power. The fall of Saigon in 1975 would complete that defeat.

Truman may have started the United States down the road to Vietnam by promoting a doctrine of containment all around the globe. Certainly Eisenhower and Kennedy increased American involvement and Richard Nixon ended it. But fairly or not, Vietnam is remembered as Lyndon Johnson's war. He committed both the material and human resources of the United States to defeat communism in Southeast

Vietnam and the cold war

Asia. The decision to escalate eventually destroyed the political consensus that had unified Americans since the late 1940s. That consensus was built on two major assumptions. First, it assumed that the United States must bear the burden of containing communism around the world. Second, American leaders had believed that the prosperity generated by the American economy made it possible both to fight communism abroad and to solve major social problems at home.

Liberal dreams died with Vietnam, too. The war in Southeast Asia shattered the optimism of the early 1960s: the belief that the world could be remade with the help of enough brilliant intellectuals or enough federal programs. The war also eroded the prosperity upon which the optimism of the postwar era had rested. After 1973 the economy slid into a long recession that forced Americans to recognize they had entered an era of limits both at home and abroad. Lyndon Johnson, who sought to preserve both liberal dreams and the cold war consensus, died on January 22, 1973, one day before the American war in Vietnam ended.

chapter summary

Though presidents from Truman to Nixon sent American forces to Indochina, Vietnam was Lyndon Johnson's war, and the political divisions it caused ended both his presidency and his attempts to establish the Great Society.

- To force the North Vietnamese to negotiate a peace, Johnson escalated the American war effort in 1965. By 1966 American soldiers were doing most of the fighting and American warplanes subjected North Vietnam to heavy bombing.

- As the war dragged on into 1968 and as the nation divided into prowar hawks and antiwar doves, the Vietcong's Tet offensive so shocked Americans that Johnson almost lost the New Hampshire presidential primary to maverick senator Eugene McCarthy, leading the president to abandon his campaign for a second full term.

- In the wake of the assassinations of Martin Luther King and Robert Kennedy, Hubert Humphrey became the Democrats' presidential nominee. But riots at the Chicago convention so damaged Humphrey's candidacy that Richard Nixon won the election, promising a "peace with honor" in Vietnam.

- Despite Nixon's promise to "bring us together," the nation remained divided not only because of the war but also because a wide range of minorities—Latinos, Indians, Asian Americans, gays, and feminists—adopted newly assertive identity politics as a way to claim their full rights and opportunities as Americans.

  - Mexican American migrant workers led by Cesar Chavez successfully established a farmworkers' union, the UFW, while a rising generation of Latino students adopted more militant techniques for establishing a Chicano identity.

  - Though often divided by tribal diversity, militant Native Americans called attention to the discrimination faced by Indians in urban settings as well as on reservations.

  - Feminists campaigned for civil and political equality as well as to change deep-seated cultural attitudes of a "patriarchal" society.

interactive learning

The Primary Source Investigator CD-ROM offers the following materials related to this chapter:

- Interactive maps: **Election of 1968** (M7) and **Vietnam War** (M29)

- A collection of primary sources exploring the many facets of the Vietnam War era, including a poster depicting the insurgency in Vietnam, images of soldiers in the field, and the Gulf of Tonkin resolution. Several sources illustrate the growing counterculture, including an excerpt from Betty Friedan's *Feminist Mystique*. Other sources include a portion of the *Apollo 11* flightplan, a State Department report on American opinion on the war, and world reaction to the war.

additional reading

A number of questions have framed the debate about American involvement in Vietnam. Over the past few years, historians have paid particular attention to Lyndon Johnson's responsibility for escalating the war. Larry Berman, *LBJ's War* (1990), raised the issue, which has more recently been taken up by George Herring, *LBJ and Vietnam* (1995); Lloyd Gardner, *Pay Any Price: Lyndon Johnson and the Wars for Vietnam* (1995); and LBJ biographer Robert Dallek, *Lone Star Rising* (1991) and "Lyndon Johnson and Vietnam," *Diplomatic History* (Spring 1996).

For a broader view of the war see George Herring, *America's Longest War* (2nd ed., 1986), and Marilyn B. Young, *The Vietnam Wars* (1991), two good surveys. George Kahin, *Intervention* (1986), is useful to understand the road to escalation. Melvin Small, *Johnson, Nixon, and the Doves* (1988), explains how the antiwar movement impacted Washington, and Tom Wells, *The War Within: America's Battle over Vietnam* (1994), examines the full range of antiwar protest. On Richard Nixon and his administration, see Stephen Ambrose, *Nixon, the Triumph of a Politician, 1962–1972* (1989). For an introduction to identity politics see Stewart Burns, *Social Movements in the 1960s* (1990); on Latinos see F. Arturo Rosales, *Chicano! The History of the Mexican American Civil Rights Movement* (rev. ed. 1997), and Joan Moore and Harry Pachon, *Hispanics in the United States* (1985); for Asian Americans we recommend Sucheng Chan, *Asian Americans: An Interpretive History* (1991). Barry D. Adam, *The Rise of a Gay and Lesbian Movement* (1987); John D'Emilio, *Sexual Politics, Sexual Communities: The Making of a Homosexual Minority in the United States, 1940–1970* (1983); and Martin Duberman, *Stonewall* (1993), provide complementary perspectives on the emergence of gay and lesbian activism. John William Sayer, *Ghost Dancing the Law: The Wounded Knee Trials* (1997), recounts one of the most contested moments of Native American activism. Feminism and women's rights have produced a rich literature. A particularly readable and slightly irreverent work is Susan Douglas, *Where the Girls Are: Growing Up Female with the Mass Media* (1994). Sara Evans, *Personal Politics* (1980), links women's liberation to the civil rights movement and the New Left. For two other significant topics see Mary Frances Berry, *Why ERA Failed: Politics, Women's Rights, and the Amending Process of the Constitution* (1986), and Amy Erdman, *Yours in Sisterhood: Ms. Magazine and the Promise of Popular Feminism* (1998). For a fuller list of readings, see the Bibliography at www.mhhe.com/davidsonnation5.

significant events

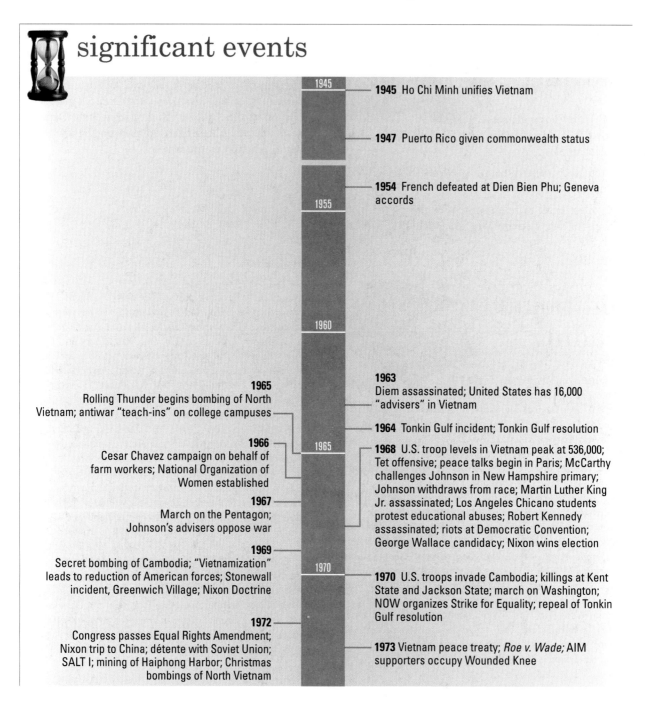

1945 Ho Chi Minh unifies Vietnam

1947 Puerto Rico given commonwealth status

1954 French defeated at Dien Bien Phu; Geneva accords

1965
Rolling Thunder begins bombing of North Vietnam; antiwar "teach-ins" on college campuses

1963
Diem assassinated; United States has 16,000 "advisers" in Vietnam

1964 Tonkin Gulf incident; Tonkin Gulf resolution

1966
Cesar Chavez campaign on behalf of farm workers; National Organization of Women established

1968 U.S. troop levels in Vietnam peak at 536,000; Tet offensive; peace talks begin in Paris; McCarthy challenges Johnson in New Hampshire primary; Johnson withdraws from race; Martin Luther King Jr. assassinated; Los Angeles Chicano students protest educational abuses; Robert Kennedy assassinated; riots at Democratic Convention; George Wallace candidacy; Nixon wins election

1967
March on the Pentagon; Johnson's advisers oppose war

1969
Secret bombing of Cambodia; "Vietnamization" leads to reduction of American forces; Stonewall incident, Greenwich Village; Nixon Doctrine

1970 U.S. troops invade Cambodia; killings at Kent State and Jackson State; march on Washington; NOW organizes Strike for Equality; repeal of Tonkin Gulf resolution

1972
Congress passes Equal Rights Amendment; Nixon trip to China; détente with Soviet Union; SALT I; mining of Haiphong Harbor; Christmas bombings of North Vietnam

1973 Vietnam peace treaty; *Roe v. Wade;* AIM supporters occupy Wounded Knee

Chapter 31

I n July 1969, tens of thousands of spectators gathered at Cape Kennedy to witness the launching of *Apollo 11*, the first manned space flight to the moon. Among the crowd was a mule-cart procession led by the Reverend Ralph Abernathy, a leader in the civil rights movement. Abernathy brought his Poor People's March to the moon launching to dramatize the problem of poverty. The *Saturn 5's* thunderous ignition and fiery rocket blast proved so awesome that Abernathy instead prayed for the safety of the crew. Days later, he, too, celebrated when astronauts Neil Armstrong and Buzz Aldrin walked across a lunar landscape.

The triumph had been epochal. And yet some uncertainty lingered over what it all meant. One scientist took comfort that after *Apollo* the human race could always go elsewhere, no matter how much a mess was made of the planet Earth. That was no small consideration given the increasing problems of smog, water pollution, and toxic wastes. There had been some dramatic warnings. In 1967 an oil tanker, the *Torrey Canyon,* spilled 100,000 tons of oil into the English Channel. Detergents used to clean up the spill left the area clean but without plant and animal life for years after.

THE AGE OF LIMITS

1965–1980

preview • Americans in the 1970s discovered painful limits to many aspects of their society: limits to economic growth sparked by a shortage of oil, limits on the environment due to pollution and overdevelopment. Richard Nixon met political limits, as he was forced from office by his role in campaign scandals. With the nation mired in an economic downturn, Presidents Ford and Carter steered a course that acknowledged the decline of American power.

Such dangers worried city officials in Santa Barbara, California, an outpost of paradise along the Pacific coast. In the channel stretching between there and Los Angeles, 90 miles to the south, oil companies had drilled some 925 wells in the coastal tidelands. State efforts to impose stringent regulations on federal oil leases offshore had failed. The Department of the Interior repeatedly assured local officials they had "nothing to fear." That changed on January 28, 1969, when Union Oil Company's well A-21 blew a billow of thick crude oil into the channel. Crews quickly capped the hole, only to discover that pressure had driven natural gas and oil through another hole. "It looked like a massive, inflamed abscess bursting with reddish-brown pus," one observer commented.

By February 1, an oil slick covered 5 miles of Santa Barbara's white beaches. In the 11 days it took workers to seal the leak, more than 200,000 barrels of oil left a slick extending for some 800 miles. Black, tarry goo coated beaches, boats, and wildlife as far south as San Diego. "Cormorants and grebes dived into the oily swells for fish, most never to surface alive. All along the mucky shoreline, birds lay dead or dying, unable to raise their oil-soaked feathers," one reporter wrote. Despite the efforts of environmentalists, thousands of shore birds perished, and detergents claimed the entire population of limpets, abalones, lobsters, sea urchins, mussels, clams, and some fish.

Santa Barbara, not *Apollo 11*, served as a portent of the coming decade. Having reached the moon, Americans discovered more pressing concerns closer to home. War erupted in the Middle East.

A sea bird, tarred by oil

On January 28, 1969, oil erupted from the seabed underneath a Union Oil drilling rig in the Santa Barbara channel. A gooey mess coated beaches and killed fish, shore birds, and sea mammals. Even as Americans put a man on the moon, environmental disasters underscored the dangers technology posed to nature.

Arab members of the Organization of Petroleum Exporting Countries (OPEC) announced that they would embargo oil shipments to Western nations. Growing concern over environmental deterioration, the shocking revelations of the Watergate scandals, and the continuing rise of inflation eroded the nation's optimism. Americans began to doubt that technological know-how could solve any problem or that economic growth was both inevitable and beneficial. Elliot Richardson, the Nixon administration's secretary of health, education and welfare, drew the appropriate lesson when he remarked, "We must recognize, as we have with both foreign affairs and natural resources, that resources we thought were boundless . . . are indeed severely limited." The United States had entered an era of limits.

The Limits of Reform

Like the space program, the reform movements of the early 1960s had sprung from an optimistic faith in the perfectibility of society. But as Vietnam dragged on, Americans had become more fragmented. America still seemed a nation in need of reforming, but as inflation dogged the economy and unemployment grew, Americans set their sights much lower. According to social observer Tom Wolfe, in the 1970s the self-obsessed "Me Generation" displaced the crusading New Left.

Amid frustrated hopes, some elements of the reform movement kept alive the idea of restructuring society. Environmentalists and consumer advocates used many of the same strategies of nonviolent protest and legal maneuver that had worked so effectively in the civil rights crusade. But unlike much of the radicalism of the 1960s, these movements each had long been associated with the American reform tradition. And though they often had radical goals, their leadership most frequently came from the political mainstream and won some major victories, even if they failed to achieve the transformation they sought.

Consumerism

In 1965 a thin, intense young man shocked the automotive world by publishing *Unsafe at Any Speed: The Designed-in Dangers of the American Automobile.* The author, Ralph Nader, argued that too many automobiles were unsafe even in minor accidents. Nader's particular target was the Chevrolet Corvair, a rear-engined small car built by General Motors. Crash reports indicated that the Corvair sometimes rolled over in routine turns and that drivers quickly lost control when the car skidded. Even more damning, Nader accused General Motors of being aware of the flaw from its own internal engineering studies.

Ralph Nader's dogged, ascetic style forced corporations like General Motors to examine more seriously issues of public safety in products they produced. Nader's organization, Public Citizen, expanded its efforts on behalf of consumers to a wide range of issues.

GM, the corporate Goliath, at first decided that rather than defend the Corvair, it would attack Nader, this countercultural David. It sent out private investigators to dig up dirt from his personal life. They discovered no hippie disguised in a suit but the hardworking son of Lebanese immigrants who had fulfilled the American dream. Nader had graduated from Princeton and Harvard Law School, wore his hair short, and never used drugs. And when he discovered GM's underhanded tactics against him, he sued.

GM's embarrassed president, James Roche, publicly apologized, but by then Nader was a hero and *Unsafe at Any Speed* a bestseller. In 1966 Congress passed the National Traffic and Motor Vehicle Safety Act and the Highway Safety Act, which for the first time required safety standards for cars, tires, and roads. Nader used $425,000 from his successful lawsuit to launch his Washington-based Center for the Study of Responsive Law (1969) with a staff of five lawyers and a hundred college volunteers. "Nader's Raiders," as the group soon became known, investigated a wide range of consumer and political issues, lobbying against water pollution, influence-peddling in Congress, and abuses in nursing homes and in favor of consumer-oriented government agencies.

Nader's Raiders were part of a diverse consumer movement of people who ranged from modest reformers to radicals. The radicals viewed the system of markets in which consumers bought goods to be deeply flawed. Only a thorough overhaul of the system, carried out by an active, interventionist government, could empower citizen-consumers. Nader suggested both the radicals' tone and their agenda when he called on corporations "to stop stealing, stop deceiving, stop corrupting politicians with money, stop monopolizing, stop poisoning the earth, air and water, stop selling dangerous products, stop exposing workers to cruel hazards." To pressure corporate America, Nader created the Public Interest Research Group, whose branches across the country lobbied for consumer protection.

More moderate reformers concentrated on making the existing market economy more open and efficient. To be better consumers, people needed better information. Reformers identified specific abuses: unsafe toys, dangerous food additives, the health consequences of smoking, and defective products dubbed "lemons." They brought suit against unethical marketing strategies such as "bait-and-switch advertising" and hidden credit costs that plagued the poor. Many consumer organizations concentrated on a single issue, such as auto safety, smoking, insurance costs, or health care.

Diversity of goals broadened the movement's appeal but also fragmented support. Consumerism often overlapped with other causes, such as environmentalism, civil rights, and women's rights. Nader was never able to establish consumerism as a mass political movement, finding supporters largely among the more affluent middle class. Furthermore, a weak economy created fears that more regulation would drive up consumer prices and thus add to inflation. Still, the consumer movement had placed its agenda in the mainstream of political debate, and powerful consumer groups continued to represent the public interest.

Environmentalism

The Santa Barbara oil spill was hardly the first warning that Americans were abusing the environment. As early as 1962 marine biologist Rachel Carson had warned in *Silent Spring* of the environmental damage done by the pesticide DDT. Though chemical companies tried to discredit her as a woman and a scientist, a presidential commission vindicated her work. Forty state legislatures passed laws restricting DDT. Certainly, anyone with a sense of irony couldn't help marveling that the oil-polluted Cuyahoga River running through Cleveland, Ohio, had burst into flames. Smog, nuclear fallout, dangerous pesticides, and polluted rivers were the not-so-hidden costs of a society wedded to technology and unbridled economic growth.

In some ways, the environmental movement echoed the concerns and approaches of both the traditional conservation movement associated with Teddy Roosevelt, Gifford Pinchot, and Harold Ickes and the preservationist philosophies of John Muir and the Sierra Club. Conservationists had always stressed the idea of proper *use* of both renewable and nonrenewable resources. Efficient use would ensure the nation's future prosperity. Engineers, lawyers, and economists shaped the conservation agenda. Preservationists shared the Romantics' vision of humankind's spiritual links to nature. They sought largely to save unique wilderness areas like Yellowstone, Yosemite, and the Grand Canyon from *any* development and commercial exploitation.

Conservation versus preservation

In addition the new environmental movement drew heavily on the field of ecology. Since the early twentieth century, this biological science had demonstrated how closely life processes throughout nature depend on one another. Barry Commoner in his book *The Closing Circle* (1971) argued that modern society courted disaster by trying to "improve on nature." American farmers, for example, had shifted from animal manures to artificial fertilizers to increase farm productivity. But the change also raised costs, left soil sterile, and poisoned nearby water sources. After laundry detergents artificially "whitened" clothes, they created foamy scum in lakes and rivers while nourishing deadly algae blooms. Industry profited in the short run, Commoner argued, but in the long run the environment was going bankrupt.

Barry Commoner and ecology

By the 1970s, environmentalists had organized to implement what biologist René Dubos had called a "new social ethic." They brought an unsuccessful lawsuit to block the plan of a consortium of oil companies to build an 800-mile pipeline across Alaska's fragile wilderness. In addition, they successfully lobbied in Congress to defeat a bill authorizing support for the supersonic transport plane, the SST, whose high-altitude flights threatened to deplete the earth's vital ozone layer. Similarly, environmental groups fought a proposed jet airport that threatened South Florida's water supply and the ecology of Everglades National Park.

Even President Nixon, normally a friend of business and real estate interests, responded to the call for more stringent environmental regulation. His administration banned the use of DDT (though not its sale abroad) and supported the National Environmental Policy Act of 1969. The act required environmental impact statements for most public projects and made the government responsible for representing the public interest. Nixon also established the Environmental Protection Agency to

EPA established

Daily Lives

FOOD/DRINK/ DRUGS

Fast-Food America

Before the 1960s, few Americans regularly ate food prepared outside the home. The rich, with access to servants, restaurants, and clubs, might regularly eat food prepared by a nonfamily member. So, too, might college students or the very poor who had to take their meals in prisons, soup kitchens, or other institutional settings. By the 1970s the consumption of prepared foods and meals had become common for most Americans. Fast-food chains, school and office cafeterias, vending machines, and other public facilities served up more than 40 percent of the meals Americans ate. Many home meals consisted of packaged foods like TV dinners or frozen entrées that required nothing but heating prior to consumption. Whether at home or away, the emphasis at mealtime was less on nutrition and more on speed, convenience, and economy.

As prepared foods became more popular, meals as social occasions for families became rarer. Common meals required the participants to foresake personal preferences and time schedules to share the same foods, served in the same order, at the same time. But in an age of fast-food chains and ethnic food takeouts, it became practical for individual family members to eat different foods at the same time or to break the "one-cook-to-one-family" pattern. In the process, eating became desocialized. The two most communal meals, breakfast and dinner, no longer brought families together. By the end of the 1970s some 75 percent of American families did not share breakfast, and the average family sat down to dinner fewer than three times a

Once limited largely to hamburgers, ice cream, and pancakes, during the 1970s fast-food chains increasingly allowed Americans to bolt down indifferently synthesized varieties of ethnic and regional foods as well.

enforce the law. Echoing Barry Commoner, he announced, "We must learn not how to master nature but how to master ourselves, our institutions, and our technology."

By the spring of 1970 a healthy environment had become a widely popular cause. Senator Gaylord Nelson of Wisconsin suggested a national "Earth Day" to celebrate this new consciousness. On April 22, 1970, for at least a few hours pedestrians reclaimed downtown city streets, millions of schoolchildren planted trees and picked up litter, college students demonstrated, and Congress adjourned. The enthusiasm reflected the movement's dual appeal: it combined the rationalism of science with a religious vision of life's organic unity. But at least one member of Congress recognized the movement's more radical implications: "The Establishment sees this as a great big anti-litter campaign. Wait until they find out what it really means . . . to clean up our earth."

Earth Day

week. The meal seldom lasted more than 20 minutes. As formal meals lost their importance, snacking became common. Individual family members ingested food in some fashion as often as 20 times a day. More and more often, people combined the consumption of food with activities other than meals: popcorn and movies, beer and TV sports, coffee and commuting.

As important as where and how people ate were nutritional trends. In earlier societies meals had consisted largely of a core complex carbohydrate (rice, bread, potatoes, or noodles), served up with a fringe complement of meats, vegetables, and fruits, and seasoned perhaps with a sauce. The core carbohydrate provided most nutrition, calories, and satisfaction; the fringe abetted the eating of the core. In modern Western society, including the United States, that pattern reversed over time. By the 1970s the bulk of Americans' calories came from protein foods like meat and eggs and even more from foods rich in sugars and fats.

As preoccupation with slimness grew, the direct consumption of sugar declined. But because most Americans ate more prepared and precooked foods, the indirect consumption of sugar and sweeteners increased. Food manufacturers discovered that sugars and dense fats like palm and coconut oil improved flavor, texture, taste, and shelf life. Thus they included sweeteners or fats in places where most people did not expect them: table salt, coatings for fried foods, peanut butter, and "health" foods like granola. By the late 1970s the average American consumed some 130 pounds of sugar and sweeteners per year and about 40 percent of all calories in the form of animal and vegetable fats. That led to a steady increase in obesity and diet-related heart diseases and cancers.

So eating patterns suggest some basic contradictions of the 1970s. While traditionalists called for family values, most families discarded the most traditional ritual, "breaking bread together." And as the American diet, like the population, became more diverse, the basic sources of food energy became less varied. Further, while medical technologies added to life expectancy, most doctors ignored dietary patterns responsible for life-threatening diseases. In this way, the patterns of daily life may be more revealing than the great events of the era.

Earth Day did not signal a consensus on an environmental ethic. President Nixon, for one, was unwilling to restrict economic development. In his own Earth Day speech he supported the oil industry's Alaskan pipeline project, which threatened huge caribou herds and the Arctic's fragile ecology. Despite a long series of court challenges construction began in 1973. "We are not going to allow the environmental issue . . . to destroy the system," he announced in 1972.

Nixon's political instincts were shrewd. Conflict between social classes underlay the environmental debate. To those he courted for his silent majority, the issue came down to jobs versus the environment. "Out of work? Hungry? Eat an environmentalist," declared one bumper sticker. During the 1960s many middle Americans came to resent the veterans of the counterculture, civil rights, and antiwar movements who now found an outlet in environmental activism. But as long as pollution threatened, the environmental movement would not go away. Whether Ducks Unlimited with its conservative hunters or the Wilderness Society with its mainstream nature lovers or radical groups like Greenpeace, numerous organizations continued the fight to protect the environment.

Watergate and the Politics of Resentment

As president, Richard Nixon saw himself as a global leader with a grand strategic vision. Domestic politics interested him far less. His instincts were often those of a pragmatist. He recognized that the popularity of issues like Social Security, consumer protection, and pollution control required compromise from the White House. All the same, as a conservative Republican he looked to scale back or eliminate many New Deal and Great Society programs. "After a third of a century of power flowing from the people and the states to Washington," he proclaimed, "it is time for a New Federalism in which power, funds, and responsibility will flow from Washington to the people."

Twenty-five years of cold war had given the presidency enormous power. One historian described the White House ascendance over Congress and the judiciary as an "imperial presidency." Nixon would use the power in his office both to assert American interests abroad and to destroy his enemies at home. Despite his pragmatism, he had never overcome his resentment of liberals, the media, and the eastern establishment that had often looked slightly askance at the awkward young man from Whittier, California. Such animosities led Nixon to see himself as embattled, surrounded by enemies who conspired against him and his administration. The line between the use and abuse of presidential power would prove a thin one. Crossing it led to a third-rate burglary at the Watergate office complex in Washington, D.C., and the political downfall of Richard Nixon.

Nixon's New Federalism

Revenue sharing

Nixon envisioned his New Federalism as a conservative counter to liberal policies that had depended on the federal government to implement. His new system proposed that Washington give money in block grants to state and local governments. Rather than receiving funds earmarked for specific purposes, localities could decide which problems needed attention and how best to attack them. Congress passed a revenue-sharing act in 1972 that distributed $30 billion over the subsequent five years. A similar approach influenced aid to individuals. Liberal programs from the New Deal to the Great Society often provided specific services to individuals: job retraining programs, Head Start programs for preschoolers, food supplement programs for nursing mothers. Republicans argued that such a "service strategy" too often assumed that federal bureaucrats best understood what the poor needed. Nixon favored an "income strategy" instead, which simply gave recipients money and allowed them to spend it as they saw fit. Such grants would encourage individual initiative, increase personal freedom, and reduce government bureaucracy.

Family Assistance Plan

In this spirit Nixon encouraged a maverick liberal academic, Daniel Patrick Moynihan, to develop a program to replace the welfare system. His "Family Assistance Plan" stressed "workfare," not welfare; it targeted the working poor, not the undeserving poor. Poor families would be guaranteed a minimum annual income of $1600. An emphasis on family would encourage fathers to live at home. The plan also required recipients to register for employment to satisfy conservative critics who believed that too many welfare recipients were able-bodied workers addicted to handouts and too lazy to work. Though Moynihan's proposals died in Congress, they defined the general terms in which poverty and assistance to the poor would be debated into the 1990s.

Even if Nixon was determined to reverse the liberalism of the 1960s, critics were wrong to dismiss him as a knee-jerk conservative. His appeal to local author-ity and individual initiative in some ways echoed the New Left's rhetoric of "power to the people." In 1970 he signed a bill establishing an Occupational Safety and Health Agency (OSHA) to enforce health and safety standards in the workplace. And although the president was no crusader for the environment, he did support a Clean Air Act to reduce car exhaust emissions as well as a Clean Water Act to make polluters liable for their negligence and to deal with disastrous oil spills.

Nixon reforms

Stagflation

Ironically, economic distress, aggravated by the Vietnam War, forced Nixon to adopt liberal remedies. By 1970 the nation had entered its first recession in a decade. Tra-ditionally a recession brought a decrease in demand for goods and a rise in unem-ployment as workers were laid off. Manufacturers then cut wages and prices in order to preserve profit margins and encourage demand for their goods. But in the recession of 1970, while unemployment rose as economists would have expected, wages and prices were also rising in an inflationary spiral. Americans were getting the worst of two worlds: a stagnant economy combined with rising prices—or "stagflation." Unfriendly Democrats labeled the phenomenon "Nixonomics," in which "all things that should go up—the stock market, corporate profits, real spendable income, productivity—go down, and all things that should go down—unemployment, prices, interest rates—go up."

To blame the recession on Nixon was hardly fair, because Lyndon Johnson had brought on inflation by refusing to raise taxes to pay for the war and Great Society social programs. In addition, wages continued their inflationary rise partly because powerful unions had negotiated automatic cost-of-living increases into their contracts. Similarly, in industries dominated by a few large corporations, like steel and oil, prices did not follow the market forces of a recession. So prices and wages continued to rise as demand and employment fell—as baby boomers flooded into the job markets.

Mindful that his own silent majority were the people most pinched by the slower economy, Nixon decided that unemployment posed a greater threat than inflation. Announcing "I am now a Keynesian," he adopted a deficit budget designed to stimulate the growth of jobs. More surprising, in August 1971 he announced that to provide short-term relief, wages and prices would be frozen for 90 days. For a Republican to advocate federal wage and price controls was near heresy, almost as heretical as Nixon's overtures to China. Yet the president did not hesitate. For another year federal wage and price boards enforced the ground rules for any increases; most controls were lifted in January 1973. As in foreign policy, Nixon had reversed long-cherished economic policies to achieve practical results.

Social Policies and the Court

Many of the blue-collar and southern Democratic voters Nixon also sought to attract resented the Supreme Court's use of school busing to achieve desegregation. Fifteen years after *Brown v. Board of Education* had ruled that racially separate school sys-tems must be desegregated, many localities still had not complied. Busing to achieve

School busing

racial balance aroused determined opposition from white neighborhoods. White parents resented having their children bused away from their neighborhood to more distant, formerly all-black schools. Black parents, although they worried about the reception their children might receive in hostile white neighborhoods, by and large supported busing as a means to better education.

Under President Nixon, federal policy on desegregation took a 180-degree turn. In 1969, when lawyers for Mississippi asked the Supreme Court to delay an integration plan, the Nixon Justice Department supported the state. The Court rejected that proposal, holding in *United States v. Jefferson County Board of Education* that all state systems, including Mississippi's, had an obligation "to terminate dual systems at once and to operate now and hereafter only unitary schools." Two years later, in *Swann v. Charlotte-Mecklenburg Board of Education* (1971), the Court further ruled that busing, balancing ratios, and redrawing school district lines were all acceptable ways to achieve integration.

Nixon and the Court

The Warren Court's liberal activism, in decisions such as *Brown v. Board of Education, Hernández v. Texas,* and *Baker v. Carr,* had encouraged minorities to seek redress through the courts. Nixon looked to create a more conservative judicial system. When Earl Warren resigned as chief justice in 1969, the president nominated Warren Burger, a jurist who accepted most of the Court's precedents but had no wish to break new ground. When another vacancy occurred in 1969, Nixon tried twice to appoint conservative southern judges. But because both nominees had reputations on the federal bench for opposing civil rights and labor unions, the Senate rejected them. In the end, Nixon chose Minnesotan Harry Blackmun, a moderate judge of unimpeachable integrity. In 1971 he made two additional appointments: Lewis Powell, a highly regarded Virginia lawyer, and William Rehnquist of Arizona, an extreme conservative.

The successive appointments of Burger, Blackmun, Powell, and Rehnquist effectively transformed the Court. No longer would it lead the fight for minority rights, as it had under Chief Justice Earl Warren. But neither would it reverse the achievements of the Warren Court.

Us versus Them

In so many of his battles, as in the struggle to shape the Supreme Court, Nixon portrayed those who opposed him as foes of traditional American values. Just as Nixon had tended to equate liberal reformers with Communist "pinkos" during the 1950s, now his administration blurred the lines between honest dissent and radical criminals. In doing so, it reflected the president's tendency to see issues in terms of "us against them."

Few organizations stood higher on the Nixon administration's enemies list than the Black Panthers. Government agencies infiltrated the Panthers and even provoked violence. In a raid that killed leader Fred Hampton, Chicago police riddled this door as he slept. Many on the left of the political spectrum called it an assassination.

With Nixon's consent (and Lyndon Johnson's before him), J. Edgar Hoover and the FBI conducted a covert and often illegal war against dissent. The CIA and military intelligence agencies also allowed themselves to be used. Attorney General John Mitchell and his Justice Department aggressively prosecuted civil rights activists, antiwar groups like Vietnam Veterans Against the War, socially conscious members of the Catholic clergy, the Black Panthers, SDS activists, and leaders of the peace movement. In its war on the drug culture of hippies and radicals, the administration proposed a bill that would allow police to stage "no-knock" raids and use "preventive detention" to keep suspected criminals in jail without bail. It also lobbied for permission to use more phone taps and other means of electronic surveillance.

In the political arena, Vice President Spiro Agnew launched an alliterative assault on the administration's enemies. He referred to the press and television news commentators as "nattering nabobs of negativism" and "troubadours of trouble" who contributed to the "creeping permissiveness that afflicted America." Antiwar demonstrators were "an effete corps of impudent snobs." In the campaign between "us" and "them," the national press corps was clearly "them," a hostile establishment that gave the news a liberal slant.

Triumph

As the election of 1972 approached, Nixon's majority seemed to be falling into place, especially as the antiwar candidacy of Senator George McGovern of South Dakota became unstoppable. Under the new rules of the Democratic party, which McGovern had helped write, the delegate selection process was open to all party members. Minorities, women, and young people all received proportional representation. No longer would party bosses handpick the delegates. McGovern's nomination gave Nixon the split between "us" and "them" he sought. The Democratic platform embraced all the activist causes that the silent majority resented. It called for immediate withdrawal from Vietnam, abolition of the draft, amnesty for war resisters, and a minimum guaranteed income for the poor. Those issues antagonized much of the traditional New Deal coalition of urban bosses, southerners, labor leaders, and white ethnic groups.

George McGovern

By November the only question to be settled was the size of Nixon's majority. An unsolved burglary at the Watergate complex in Washington, D.C., while vaguely linked to the White House, had not touched the president. He even captured some antiwar sentiment by announcing on election eve that peace in Vietnam was at hand. When the smoke cleared, only liberal Massachusetts and the heavily black District of Columbia gave McGovern a majority. Nixon received almost 61 percent of the popular vote. In the races for the Senate and governorships, however, the Democrats actually made gains, and they lost only 13 House seats. As one pollster concluded, "Richard Nixon's 'new American majority' was the creation of George McGovern."

Even this overwhelming victory did not bring peace to Richard Nixon. He still felt that he had scores to settle with his political opponents. "We have not used the power in the first four years, as you know," he remarked to Haldeman during the campaign. "We haven't used the Bureau [FBI] and we haven't used the Justice Department, but things are going to change now. And they are going to change and they're going to get it, right?" Haldeman could only agree.

The President's Enemies

In June 1971 the *New York Times* had published a secret, often highly critical military study of the Vietnam War, soon dubbed the Pentagon Papers. Nixon was so irate, he authorized his aide John Ehrlichman to organize a team known as "the plumbers" to find and plug security leaks. The government prosecuted Daniel Ellsberg, the disillusioned official who had leaked the Pentagon Papers. The

The plumbers

plumbers also went outside the law: they burglarized the office of Ellsberg's psychiatrist in hopes of finding personally damaging material.

Encouraged by his victory, Nixon determined to use the power of his office even more broadly. Members of his staff began compiling an "enemies list"—including popular television news correspondents and celebrity antiwar activists. Some on the list were targeted for audits by the Internal Revenue Service or similar harassment.

Impoundment

When Congress passed a number of programs Nixon opposed, he simply refused to spend the appropriated money. Some members of Congress claimed that the practice, called impoundment, violated the president's constitutional duty to execute the laws of the land. By 1973 Nixon had used impoundment to cut some $15 billion out of more than 100 federal programs. The courts eventually ruled that impoundment was illegal. But the president continued his campaign to consolidate power and reshape the more liberal social policies of Congress to his own liking.

Break-In

Nixon's fall began with what seemed a minor event. In June 1972 burglars had entered the Democratic National Committee headquarters, located in Washington's plush Watergate apartment complex. But the five burglars proved an unusual lot. They wore business suits, carried walkie-talkies as well as bugging devices and tear-gas guns, and had more than $2000 in crisp new hundred-dollar bills. One of the burglars had worked for the CIA. Another was carrying an address book whose phone numbers included that of a Howard Hunt at the "W. House." Nixon's press secretary dismissed the break-in as "a third rate burglary attempt" and warned that "certain elements may try to stretch this beyond what it is." In August, Nixon himself announced that White House counsel John Dean's own thorough investigation had concluded that "no one on the White House staff . . . was involved in this very bizarre incident. What really hurts in matters of this sort is not the fact that they occur," the president continued. "What really hurts is if you try to cover up."

Matters were not so easily settled, however. *Washington Post* reporters Bob Woodward and Carl Bernstein traced some of the burglars' money back to the Nixon reelection campaign, which had a secret "slush fund" to pay for projects to harass the Democrats. The dirty tricks included forged letters, false news leaks, and spying on Democratic campaign workers.

To the Oval Office

In January 1973 the five burglars plus former White House aides E. Howard Hunt Jr. and G. Gordon Liddy went on trial before Judge John Sirica. Sirica, a no-nonsense judge tagged with the nickname "Maximum John," was not satisfied with the defendants' guilty plea. He wanted to know whether anyone else had directed the burglars and why "these hundred dollar bills were floating around like coupons."

Facing a stiff jail sentence, one of the Watergate burglars cracked. He admitted that the defendants had been bribed to plead guilty and had perjured themselves to protect other government officials. The White House then announced on April 17 that all previous administration statements on the Watergate scandal had become "inoperative." Soon after, the president accepted the resignations of his two closest aides, H. R. Haldeman and John Ehrlichman. He also fired John Dean, his White House counsel, after Dean agreed to cooperate with prosecutors.

Senate hearings

Over the summer of 1973 a string of administration officials testified at televised Senate hearings. Attorney General John Mitchell, it became clear, had attended

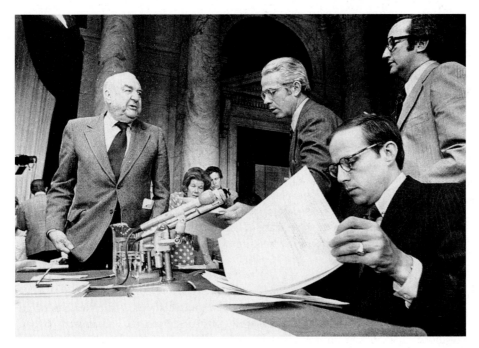

meetings in 1972 in which Gordon Liddy outlined preliminary plans for a campaign of dirty tricks. Liddy and others had also worked as the plumbers under the direction of Ehrlichman in the White House. Then White House counsel John Dean gave his testimony. Young, with a Boy Scout's face, Dean declared in a quiet monotone that the president had personally been involved in the cover-up as recently as April. The testimony stunned the nation. Still, it remained Dean's word against the president's—until Senate committee staff discovered, almost by chance, that Nixon had been secretly recording conversations and phone calls in the Oval Office. The reliability of Dean's testimony was no longer central, for the tapes could tell all.

Obtaining that evidence proved no easy task. In an effort to restore confidence in the White House, the president agreed to appoint a special prosecutor, Harvard law professor Archibald Cox, to investigate the new Watergate disclosures. When Cox subpoenaed the tapes, the president refused to turn them over, citing executive privilege and matters of national security.

As that battle raged and the astonished public wondered if matters could possibly get worse, they did. Evidence unrelated to Watergate revealed that Vice President Spiro Agnew had systematically solicited bribes, not just as governor of Maryland but while serving in Washington. To avoid jail, he agreed to resign the vice presidency in October and to plead no contest to a single charge of federal income tax evasion. Under provisions of the Twenty-fifth Amendment, Nixon appointed Representative Gerald R. Ford of Michigan to replace Agnew.

Agnew resigns

Meanwhile, when Special Prosecutor Cox demanded the tapes, the president offered to submit written summaries instead. Cox no longer had any reason to trust the president and rejected the offer. On Saturday night, October 20, Nixon fired Cox. Reaction to this "Saturday Night Massacre" was overwhelming. The president's own attorney general resigned in protest, 150,000 telegrams poured into Washington, and by the following Tuesday, 84 House members had sponsored 16 different bills of impeachment. The beleaguered president agreed to hand over the

Saturday Night Massacre

tapes. And he appointed Texas lawyer Leon Jaworski as a new special prosecutor. By April 1974, Jaworski's investigations led him to request additional tapes. Again the president refused, although he grudgingly supplied some 1200 pages of typed transcripts of the tapes.

Even the transcripts damaged the president's case. Littered with cynicism and profanity, they revealed Nixon talking with his counsel, John Dean, about how to "take care of the jackasses who are in jail." When Dean estimated it might take a million dollars to shut them up, Nixon replied, "We could get that. . . . You could get a million dollars. And you could get it in cash. I know where it could be gotten." When the matter of perjury came up, Nixon suggested a way out: "You can say, 'I don't remember.' You can say, 'I can't recall.'"

Even those devastating revelations did not produce the "smoking gun" demanded by the president's defenders. When Special Prosecutor Jaworski petitioned the Supreme Court to order the release of additional tapes, the Court in *United States v. Nixon* ruled unanimously in Jaworski's favor.

Resignation

The end came quickly. The House Judiciary Committee adopted three articles of impeachment, charging that Nixon had illegally obstructed justice, had abused his constitutional authority in improperly using federal agencies to harass citizens, and had hindered the committee's effort to investigate the cover-up.

The smoking gun

The tapes produced the smoking gun. Conversations with Haldeman on June 23, 1972, only a few days after the break-in, showed that Nixon knew the burglars were tied to the White House staff, knew that his attorney general had been involved, and knew that Mitchell had acted to limit an FBI investigation. Not willing to be the first president convicted in a Senate impeachment trial, Nixon resigned on August 8, 1974. The following day Gerald Ford became president. "The Constitution works," Ford told a relieved nation. "Our long national nightmare is over."

Had the system worked? In one sense, yes. The wheels of justice had turned, even if slowly. For the first time a president had been forced to leave office. Four cabinet officers, including Attorney General John Mitchell, the highest law officer in the nation, were convicted of crimes. Twenty-five Nixon aides eventually served prison terms ranging from 25 days to more than 4 years.

Yet what would have happened if Woodward and Bernstein had been less resourceful? With the exception of the *Washington Post* and one or two other newspapers, the media had accepted the administration's cover-up. Later abuses within the executive branch, such as the "Irangate" scandals under Ronald Reagan, have demonstrated that the imperial powers of the presidency are still largely unchecked.

Fair Campaign Practices Act

The Fair Campaign Practices Act was adopted in 1974 in an attempt to enforce greater financial accountability on campaigns. Yet special interest groups have circumvented the law by funneling money through political action committees. The system works, as the Founders understood, only when citizens and public servants respect the limits of government power.

A Ford, Not a Lincoln

Gerald Ford inherited a presidential office almost crippled by the Watergate scandals. As the first unelected president, he had no popular mandate. He was little known outside Washington and his home district around Grand Rapids, Michigan. Ford's success as the House minority leader came from personal popularity, political reliability, and party loyalty, qualities that suited a member of Congress better than an unelected president.

Ford respected the limits of government. His easy manner came as a relief after the mercurial styles of Johnson and Nixon. By all instincts a conservative, he was determined to continue Nixon's foreign policy of cautious détente and a domestic program of social and fiscal conservatism.

Kissinger and Foreign Policy

As Nixon's star fell, that of his secretary of state and national security adviser, Henry Kissinger, rapidly rose. Kissinger cultivated reporters, who relished his witty quips, intellectual breadth, and willingness to leak stories to the press. Kissinger viewed himself as a realist, a man for whom order and stability were more important than principle. In that way he offended idealists on the political left and right. Quoting the German writer Goethe, Kissinger acknowledged, "If I had to choose between justice and disorder, on the one hand, and injustice and order on the other, I would always choose the latter."

Kissinger had struggled to prevent Vietnam and Watergate from eroding the president's power to conduct foreign policy. He believed Congress was too sensitive to public opinion and special-interest groups to pursue consistent long-term policies. But after Vietnam congressional leaders were eager to curtail presidential powers. The War Powers Act of 1973 required the president to consult Congress whenever possible before committing troops, to send an explanation for his actions within 2 days, and to withdraw any troops after 60 days unless Congress voted to retain them. Such limits often led Kissinger to take a covert approach, as he did in an attempt to quell political ferment in Chile.

War Powers Act

In 1970 Chile ranked as one of South America's few viable democracies. When a coalition of Socialists, Communists, and radicals elected Salvador Allende Gossens as president, the Central Intelligence Agency determined that his victory created a danger to the United States. Kissinger pressed the CIA to bribe the Chilean Congress and to promote a military coup against Allende. When those attempts failed, Kissinger resorted to economic warfare between the United States and the Allende government. By 1973 a conservative Chilean coalition with CIA backing had driven the Socialists from power, attacked the presidential palace, and killed Allende. The United States immediately recognized the new government, which over the next decade deteriorated into a brutally repressive dictatorship. Kissinger argued that the United States had the right to destroy this democracy because Communists themselves threatened an even longer-term dictatorship.

Coup in Chile

Global Competition and the Limits of American Influence

Kissinger understood that the United States no longer had the economic strength to dominate the affairs of the non-Communist bloc of nations, even in areas such as Central America and the Middle East, where it had once prevailed. Soaring inflation was a major source of weakness. In addition, key American industries were crippled by inefficient production, products of poor quality, and high wages. They faced mounting competition from more efficient manufacturers in Europe and in nations along the Pacific Rim (Japan, South Korea, Taiwan, Hong Kong, Singapore, and the Philippines). Reacting to these changes, American-based multinational corporations moved high-wage jobs overseas to take advantage of lower costs and cheap labor. The bellwether industry of the American economy, automobile manufacturing,

GREECE

TURKEY
• Ankara

SOVIET UNION
▲

SOVIET UNION
▲

CASPIAN SEA

MEDITERRANEAN SEA

• Nicosia
CYPRUS

SYRIA

IRAQ
• Teheran

IRAN

Kabul •
AFGHANISTAN
1979—Soviets invade,
U.S. aids Muslim revolt
1989—Soviets pull out;
civil war continues

• Tripoli
GULF OF SIDRA

LEBANON • Beirut
ISRAEL • Damascus
Jerusalem
• Amman
JORDAN

Baghdad •
1980–1988—War with Iran
1988—Chemical attacks
on Kurds

KUWAIT

PERSIAN GULF

Straits of Hormuz

PAKISTAN

LIBYA
1969—Qaddafi takes power,
expels U.S. bases
1977—Border clashes with Egypt
1986—U.S. bombs Tripoli

Cairo •
EGYPT
1956—Suez crisis
1972—Soviet advisors expelled
1979—Peace treaty with Israel
1981—Sadat assassinated

SAUDI ARABIA

• Riyadh

BAHRAIN

QATAR

OMAN
Abu
Dhabi •

GULF OF OMAN

• Muscat

CHAD

SUDAN
1983—North-South war begins
1985—Pro-U.S. regime ousted

UNITED ARAB EMIRATES

OMAN

1980–1987—France, Libya
intervene in civil war

• Mecca
1979—Mecca Mosque battle

1951—Mossadegh nationalizes
foreign oil holdings
1953—U.S. helps oust
Mossadegh, return Shah
1979—Shah deposed
1979–1981—U.S. Embassy seized
1987–1988—U.S. naval clashes
in Gulf

YEMEN
• Sana

SOUTH YEMEN
1979—War with Yemen
1986—Pro-Soviet factions battle

ARABIAN SEA

DJIBOUTI
• Aden
GULF OF ADEN

SOMALIA

ETHIOPIA

EXPANSION OF ISRAEL

LEBANON • Beirut
1958—U.S. Marines
bolster government
1975—Civil war begins
1982—Israel invades
1983—U.S. marine
barracks bombed
1984—U.S. naval
shelling; pull-out

• Sidon
• Tyre

1976—Invasion
of Lebanon

• Damascus
SYRIA
GOLAN HEIGHTS

ISRAEL
1948—War of Independence
1956—Sinai War
1967—Six-Day War
1973—Yom Kippur War

WEST BANK

Tel •
Aviv
• Amman
• Jerusalem

Jordan R.

Dead Sea

MEDITERRANEAN SEA

GAZA STRIP

1987—Palestinian uprising begins
1988—PLO declares independence

Suez Canal

EGYPT

SINAI PENINSULA

JORDAN
1988—King Hussein gives
up West Bank claim

GULF OF SUEZ

GULF OF AQABA

• Eilat
• Aqaba

SAUDI ARABIA

RED SEA

0   50 Miles
0   50 Kilometers

Legend	
■ Israel, 1948	▨ Territory occupied, 1982–1986
■ Territory gained, 1949	⦂ Area of Israeli settlements
□ Territory occupied, 1967	□ OPEC member nations
⧄ Territory yielded, 1979–1982	▲ Major oil fields

OPEC: Organization of Petroleum Exporting Countries
(Members not shown are Nigeria, Algeria, Gabon,
Indonesia, Venezuela, and Ecuador)

PLO: Palestine Liberation Organization

0   250   500 Miles
0   250   500 Kilometers

MADAGASCAR

Oil and Conflict in the Middle East, 1948–1988 After World War II, the Middle East became a vital geopolitical region beset by big-power rivalry and complicated by local tribal, ethnic, and religious divisions and political instability. Much of the world's known oil reserves lie along the Persian Gulf. Proximity to the former Soviet Union and vital trade routes like the Suez Canal have defined the region's geographic importance. Revolutions in Iran and Afghanistan, intermittent warfare between Arabs and Jews, the unresolved questions of Israel's borders and a Palestinian homeland, the disintegration of Lebanon, and a long, bloody war between Iran and Iraq were among the conflicts that unsettled the region.

steadily lost sales to Japan and Germany. Speaking on behalf of its blue-collar workers, the AFL-CIO complained that the loss of high-wage manufacturing jobs would create "a nation of hamburger stands, a country stripped of industrial capacity . . . a nation of citizens busily buying and selling cheeseburgers and root beer floats."

The United States was particularly vulnerable because of its dependence on foreign oil—a dependence far greater than most Americans appreciated. With just 7 percent of the world's population, the United States consumed about 30 percent of its energy. The nation's postwar prosperity came in large part from the use of cheap energy. Inflation had already bedeviled the economy, but it would become a much more serious problem if a basic commodity such as oil rose dramatically in price.

That problem materialized the autumn of 1973, after Syria and Egypt launched a devastating surprise attack against Israel on the Jewish holy day of Yom Kippur. The Soviet Union airlifted supplies to the Arabs; the United States countered by resupplying Israel while pressing the two sides to accept a cease-fire. The seven Arab members of OPEC backed Egypt and Syria by imposing a boycott of oil sales to countries seen as friendly to Israel. The boycott from October 1973 until March 1974 staggered the economies of Western Europe and Japan, which imported 80 to 90 percent of their oil from the Middle East. And by November 1973 President Nixon was warning the nation that it faced "the most acute shortage of energy since World War II." As the price of petroleum-based plastics soared, everything from records to raincoats cost more. In some places motorists hoping to buy a few gallons of gas waited for hours in lines miles long. With the steep climb in oil prices, recession spread.

Yom Kippur War and the energy crisis

Shuttle Diplomacy

Kissinger believed that stability in the Middle East would ease pressures on the Western economies. He wanted the Arab states to view the United States as neutral in their conflict with Israel. That would make them less likely to resort to oil blackmail. And as American prestige rose, Kissinger could reduce Soviet influence in the region. From January to April 1974 Kissinger intermittently engaged in "shuttle diplomacy" between Sadat's government in Cairo and the Israeli government of Golda Meir in Jerusalem. Flying back and forth, Kissinger persuaded Israel to withdraw its troops from the west bank of the Suez Canal. He also arranged a disengagement between Israel and Syria in the Golan Heights.

Still, Kissinger's whirlwind efforts could not stem the erosion of American power everywhere. While the secretary of state struggled to restore order to the Middle East, the American client government in South Vietnam was nearing defeat by North Vietnam. President Ford asked Congress for $1 billion in aid to Vietnam, Cambodia, and Laos. This time, Congress refused to spend money on a lost cause. As North Vietnamese forces marched into Saigon in April 1975, hundreds of thousands of desperate South Vietnamese rushed to escape Communist retribution.

South Vietnam falls

Détente

Vietnam, Chile, and the Yom Kippur War indicated that the spirit of détente had not ended Soviet-American rivalry over the Third World. Seeking to ease tensions, Ford met with Soviet leader Leonid Brezhnev in November 1974. Since economic stagnation also dogged the Soviet Union, Brezhnev came to Vladivostok eager for more American trade; Ford and Kissinger wanted a limit on nuclear weapons that preserved the current American advantage. Though many issues could not be resolved, the two sides agreed in principle to a framework for a second SALT treaty.

After having won a Nobel Peace Prize in 1973 for his role in ending the Vietnam War, Henry Kissinger (left) entered the Ford administration as something of a hero. But his efforts to improve relations with the Soviet Union by strengthening détente aroused the ire of the Republican right wing, whereas liberals accused Kissinger of being too secretive and friendly to dictators. Here, he briefs President Ford (right) on a train on the way to a 1974 summit meeting in Vladivostok in the Soviet Union.

Helsinki summit   A similar hope to extend détente brought Ford and Brezhnev together with European leaders at Helsinki, Finland, in August 1975. There they agreed to recognize the political boundaries that had divided Eastern and Western Europe since 1945. For the first time the United States sent an ambassador to East Germany. In return Brezhnev eased restrictions on the right of Soviet Jews to emigrate.

The erosion of American power, symbolized by Kissinger's overtures to the Soviet Union, dismayed Republican conservatives. The 1976 presidential hopeful Ronald Reagan criticized Ford and Kissinger for selling out American interests and weakening the nation's power. In an effort to subdue the critics, Ford in 1976 stripped Kissinger of his post as national security adviser.

The Limits of a Post-Watergate President

At home, Gerald Ford found himself facing a Congress determined to restrain an "imperial presidency." Because Ford himself had served in Congress for many years, he enjoyed a brief honeymoon with the legislative branch. But after only a month in office the new president granted Richard Nixon a pardon for any crimes committed during the Watergate affair. In trying to put Watergate in the past, Ford only managed to reopen the wounds. Pardon meant no prosecution, leaving charges against Nixon unanswered and crimes unpunished. The move was especially controversial because at the same time President Ford refused to provide any similar full pardon to draft resisters from the Vietnam War for any wrongdoing. Instead, the president offered them conditional amnesty after review by a government panel.

If Ford was willing to forgive and forget presidential sins, Congress was not, especially after reports surfaced of misconduct by the nation's intelligence agencies. Senate investigations as well as a presidential commission appointed by Ford revealed that the CIA had routinely violated its charter by spying on American citizens at home. It had opened private mail, infiltrated domestic protest organizations—even conducted experiments on unwitting subjects using the hallucinogenic drug LSD. Abroad, the CIA had been involved in the assassination or attempted murder of foreign leaders in Cuba, Chile, South Vietnam, the Dominican Republic, and the Congo. The FBI had also used illegal means to infiltrate and disrupt domestic dissidents, including an attempt by J. Edgar Hoover to drive Martin Luther King to suicide. In an effort to bring the executive branch under control, the Senate created an oversight committee to monitor the intelligence agencies.

CIA and FBI abuses

Fighting Inflation

By the time Ford gave Congress his first State of the Union message in January 1975, he faced the twin scourges of inflation and recession. Inflation had climbed to almost 14 percent, and unemployment exceeded 7 percent. At the heart of the economic crisis lay the problem of rising energy costs. By 1976 oil consumption had returned to 1973 levels, even though domestic oil production had fallen by more than 1 million barrels per day. Before the Arab oil boycott, OPEC crude oil had been selling at around $2 to $3 a barrel. In a matter of months the price had tripled; by 1976 it was averaging $12 a barrel. (And the worst was yet to come: prices would peak in 1981 at nearly $35 a barrel.)

Congress responded in 1975 by passing the Energy Policy and Conservation Act. It authorized the Federal Energy Administration to order utilities to burn abundant coal rather than expensive oil. In addition, the act created a strategic petroleum reserve as a hedge against future boycotts and ordered the auto industry to improve the energy efficiency of the engines it produced. And as a final—but environmentally dangerous—stopgap measure, the government encouraged the rapid development of nuclear power plants.

The energy-driven recession struck hardest at the older industrial centers of the Northeast and Upper Midwest, which imported most of their energy. Housing and plants built in the days of cheap energy proved wasteful and inefficient. Nixon's and Ford's fiscal conservatism hurt, too. Cutbacks in federal spending fell hardest on major cities with shrinking tax bases, outmoded industries, and heavy social service costs. The crisis for "Rust Belt" cities came to a head in October 1975 when

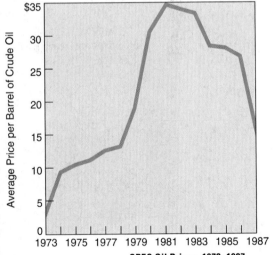

OPEC Oil Prices, 1973–1987
Prices fell even further than the chart shows after 1980 because the dollar was worth much less than in 1973. By the late 1980s gasoline was actually cheaper than in the 1950s.

New York City announced that it faced bankruptcy. New York's plight reflected the wrenching adjustments faced in an era of economic limits. A shrinking economic base could not support high wages and expensive public services.

The Election of 1976

In the 1976 presidential campaign the greatest debates occurred within rather than between the major parties. Ford's challenge came from former California governor, movie actor, and television pitchman Ronald Reagan. Once a supporter of Franklin Roosevelt, Reagan discovered true conservatism after his marriage to actress Nancy Davis. The polished Reagan won crowds with an uncompromising but amiable conservatism. "Under Messrs. Nixon and Ford this nation has become Number Two in military power," he would tell enthusiastic audiences. Ford barely eked out the nomination at the convention.

Jimmy Carter

Before 1976 few Democrats had ever heard of presidential hopeful James Earl (Jimmy) Carter. That allowed Carter, a peanut farmer and former governor of Georgia, to run as a Washington outsider. Carter managed to address controversial issues like abortion without offending large groups on either side. (He was "personally opposed to abortion" as a Christian but against a constitutional amendment overturning *Roe v. Wade*.) As a southerner and a "born-again" Christian he appealed to voters who had recently left the Democratic party.

Because both candidates rejected Great Society activism, party loyalty determined the outcome. Most voters (80 percent of Democrats and 90 percent of

In the 1976 election African American votes provided Jimmy Carter with the crucial margin for victory. Here Carter, a born-again Christian, worships with black leaders including (to his right) Coretta Scott King, widow of Martin Luther King Jr.

Republicans) backed their party's candidate, giving Carter 50.1 percent of the vote, a popular edge of almost 1.7 million votes. Carter's overwhelming margin among African Americans (90 percent) carried the South and offset Ford's margin among whites, especially in the western states, which all went Republican. Resounding Democratic majorities in Congress indicated more accurately than the presidential race how much the weak economy had hurt Ford's campaign.

Jimmy Carter: Restoring the Faith

Jimmy Carter looked to invest the White House with a new simplicity and directness. Rather than the usual Inauguration Day ride down Pennsylvania Avenue in the presidential limousine, the new president and his wife, Rosalynn, walked. Carter shunned the formal morning coat and tails for a business suit. But Congress too was determined to see that the executive branch would no longer be so imperial. Because the president and many of his staff were relative newcomers to Washington, Carter found it difficult to reach many of his goals.

The Search for Direction

Although the president possessed an ability to absorb tremendous amounts of information, too often he focused on details. His larger goals remained obscure. Carter's key appointments reflected this confusion. In foreign policy, a rivalry arose between National Security Adviser Zbigniew Brzezinski and Secretary of State Cyrus Vance. Brzezinski harbored the staunch cold warrior's preoccupation with containing the Communist menace. Vance believed negotiations with the Communist bloc were both possible and potentially profitable. Stronger economic ties would reduce the risk of superpower conflict. At different times, Carter gravitated in both directions.

The president found that it was no easy task to make government more efficient, responsive to the people, and ethical. His first push for efficiency—calling for the elimination of 19 expensive pork barrel water projects—angered many in Congress, including the leaders of his own party. They promptly threatened to bury his legislative program. Even the weather seemed to conspire against the Carter administration. The winter of 1977 was one of the most severe in modern history, as heavy snows and fierce cold forced many schools and factories to close. Supplies of heating fuels dwindled, and prices shot up. Like Ford, Carter preferred voluntary restraint to mandatory rules for conserving energy and controlling fuel costs. The nation should adopt energy conservation measures as the "moral equivalent of war," he announced in April 1977.

Carter correctly sensed that conservation was the cheapest and most practical way to reduce dependence on foreign oil. But homilies about "helping our neighbors" did not sell the president's program. Most controversial were new taxes to discourage wasteful consumption. The American way, as domestic oil producers were quick to argue, was to produce more, not live with less. Americans were too wedded to gas-guzzling cars, air conditioners, inefficient electrical appliances, and warm houses to accept limits as long as fuel was available. Although Congress did agree to establish a cabinet-level Department of Energy, it rejected most of Carter's energy taxes and proposals to encourage solar energy alternatives.

Department of Energy

By 1978 what Carter had called the "moral equivalent of war" was sounding more like its acronym: MEOW. Renewed administration efforts resulted in a weak National Energy Act, which provided tax credits for installation of energy-saving equipment, encouraged utility conversion to coal, and allowed prices to rise for newly discovered natural gas. As a result, the nation was ill prepared for the dislocation in international oil markets that followed the 1978 revolution against the shah of Iran. Renewed shortages allowed OPEC to raise prices steeply again. Carter could only complain that such hikes were unfair while asking Americans to lower thermostats to 65 degrees, take only essential car trips, and "drive 55."

Three Mile Island

The nuclear power industry had long touted its reactors as the best alternative to buying foreign oil. But on March 28, 1979, a valve stuck in the cooling system of the Three Mile Island nuclear power plant near Harrisburg, Pennsylvania. A cloud of radioactive gas floated into the atmosphere, and for a time, officials worried that they faced a meltdown of the reactor core. About a hundred thousand nearby residents fled their homes. The debate that followed revealed that public utilities had often constructed nuclear power plants before installing adequate safeguards or solving the problem of where to dispose of the nuclear radioactive wastes generated by the plant. Large construction cost overruns and concerns about safety inspired a growing antinuclear backlash. By the time of the accident at Three Mile Island, many energy experts believed that nuclear plants could be no more than a temporary response to the nation's long-term needs.

Three Mile Island gave President Carter another opportunity to press for his energy program, most of which Congress rejected. By May motorists once again faced long lines at the gas pumps. Not until spring 1980 did Congress pass a bill taxing some windfall profits of oil companies, regulating nuclear power more stringently, and establishing a solar-energy program. Carter had promoted sacrifice as a way to "seize control of our common destiny"; Congress preferred halfhearted measures that left America's energy future in OPEC's hands.

Oil shortages in the 1970s increased American dependence on nuclear power as an alternative energy source. The danger became evident in 1979 when an accident closed a nuclear power plant at Three Mile Island near Harrisburg, Pennsylvania. The large towers pictured on this *Time* magazine cover are part of the cooling system in which the accident occurred. Huge construction costs, the unsolved problem of nuclear waste disposal, and safety issues soon soured many Americans on nuclear energy.

A Sick Economy

Rapid OPEC price hikes dislocated an economy built on cheap energy. Inflation shot from just below 6 percent in 1976 to almost 14 percent by 1979. Federal policies added to these inflationary pressures. Government subsidies to farmers continued to keep prices artificially high, as did laws protecting key industries like steel from foreign competition. As prices rose, wages could not keep pace. Workers took home more dollars, but inflation guaranteed that those dollars, in real terms, were worth less.

Within factories, the news was no better. If workers' real income was declining, so too was their productivity. It was difficult to produce efficiently when so many industrial plants had become outdated and union rules blocked innovation. Furthermore, wage contracts with built-in cost-of-living adjustments (COLAs) lowered the competitive standing of American industry in world markets. Plants in Japan and other Pacific Rim nations were newer, labor costs were lower, and the products turned out were often better.

The Chrysler bailout

The plight of the automobile industry reflected this economic malaise. Americans had turned in increasing numbers to higher-quality and more fuel-efficient Japanese cars. By 1978 Chrysler Corporation, the nation's tenth largest business enterprise, stood on the brink of bankruptcy unless the government provided a billion-dollar tax credit. The threat of massive unemployment persuaded Congress to guarantee a $1.5 billion loan. New financing and concessions from union workers brought Chrysler off the critical list. Still, disgruntled liberals and conservatives laughed when folk singer Tom Paxton announced,

> I'm changing my name to Chrysler.
> I'll be waiting in that great receiving line.
> So when they hand a billion grand out,
> I'll be standing with my hand out;
> Mister I'll get by.

"Hard choices," not stopgap loans, were needed to place the economy back on a competitive footing, the *Wall Street Journal* argued. Those choices might mean higher taxes and cuts in popular programs like Social Security or subsidies to farmers. But Carter called only for voluntary restraints on prices and wages while seeking to restore the strength of the dollar in international trade. Meanwhile, high interest rates struck hardest at American consumers addicted to installment and credit-card buying. Before Carter's economic remedies could work, OPEC began another round of oil price hikes that increased energy costs almost 60 percent. Interest rates shot up to almost 20 percent. Such high rates discouraged American consumers who bought on credit. With the Federal Reserve determined to keep interest rates high in order to dampen inflation, recession seemed to doom Carter's political future.

Income Projections of Two-Income Families, 1967–1984 Had the economy maintained its earlier growth, family earnings (Projected Income line) would have continued to rise. In an age of limits, family income leveled off instead. It stayed relatively even, rather than falling, only because more wives entered the workforce. Wages for individual workers fell when calculated in real dollars.

Leadership, Not Hegemony

Presidents battered on the domestic front often find that a strong foreign policy can restore power and prestige. Carter approached foreign policy with a set of ambitious yet reasonable goals. Like Nixon and Kissinger, he accepted the fact that in a postcolonial world, American influence could not be heavy-handed. The United States should exert "leadership without hegemony," Carter announced. Unlike Nixon and Kissinger, Carter believed that a knee-jerk fear of Soviet power and disorder had led Americans to support too many right-wing dictators simply because they professed to be anti-Communist. Carter reasserted the nation's moral purpose by giving a higher priority to preserving human rights.

Human rights

Though this policy was often jeered at by foreign policy "realists," it did make a difference. At least one Argentinian Nobel Peace Prize winner, Adolfo Pérez Esquivel, claimed he owed his life to it. So did hundreds of others in countries like the Philippines, South Korea, Argentina, and Chile, where dissidents were routinely tortured and murdered. The Carter administration exerted economic pressure to promote more humane policies.

Debate over American influence in the Third World soon focused on the Panama Canal, long a symbol of American intervention in Latin America. Most Americans were under the impression that the United States owned the canal—or if it didn't, it at least deserved to. Senator S. I. Hayakawa of California spoke for defenders of the American imperial tradition when he quipped, "It's ours. We stole it fair and square." In reality the United States held sovereignty over a 10-mile-wide strip called the Canal Zone and administered the canal under a perpetual lease. Since the 1960s Panamanians had resented, and sometimes rioted against, the American presence. Secretary of State Vance believed conciliation would reduce anti-American sentiment in the region. He convinced Carter in 1977 to sign treaties that would return the canal to Panama by 1999. The United States did reserve the right to defend and use the waterway.

Brzezinski and Central America

From 1979 on, however, it was not Vance but Zbigniew Brzezinski who dominated the administration's foreign policy. Brzezinski was determined to reimpose a cold war framework, even in Latin America. Unrest troubled all the region's struggling nations, especially Nicaragua. Its dictator, Anastasio Somoza, had proved so venal and predatory that even the normally conservative propertied classes disliked him. Only the United States, at Brzezinski's urging, proved willing to support Somoza. With support from Nicaragua's business leaders, Marxist rebels called Sandinistas toppled him. They then rejected American aid in favor of a nonaligned status and friendliness toward Communist Cuba.

Revolution soon spread to neighboring El Salvador. The Carter administration also found it hard to make a case for the Salvadoran government, which had systematically murdered its own people as well as four American Catholic churchwomen. But hard-liners grew more alarmed when the Sandinistas began supplying the Salvadoran rebels. Worried about the spread of communism in Latin America, Carter agreed to assist El Salvador while encouraging the overthrow of the leftist government in Nicaragua.

The Wavering Spirit of Détente

The United States was not the only superpower with a flagging economy and problems in the Third World. The Soviet Union struggled with an aging leadership and an economy that produced guns but little butter. Even though the Russians led the world in oil production, income from rising oil prices was drained off by inefficient industries. Support for impoverished allies in Eastern Europe, Cuba, and Vietnam and attempts to extend Soviet influence in the Middle East and Africa proved costly.

Economic weakness made the Soviets receptive to greater cooperation with the United States. In that spirit President Carter and Soviet premier Leonid Brezhnev in 1977 issued a joint statement on a Middle East peace. But domestic opposition to any Soviet role as a peacemaker in the Middle East was immediate and powerful. Carter quickly rendered his understanding with Brezhnev inoperative. The Soviets then renewed arms shipments to Israel's archenemy, Syria. And in that troubled environment, Zbigniew Brzezinski flew off to Beijing to revive "the China card"—Kissinger's old hope of playing the two Communist superpowers against each other. The United States extended formal recognition to China in 1979, and trade doubled within a year.

Reviving the China card

For the Russians the China card was a blow to détente. A potential Japanese-Chinese-American alliance threatened their Asian border. In an attempt to save détente Brezhnev met Carter at Vienna in 1979. Following through on the summit with President Ford, their talks produced an arms control treaty—SALT II—to limit nuclear launchers and missiles with multiple warheads. But neither the Americans nor the Soviets would agree to scrap key weapons systems. Conservative critics saw the SALT agreements as another example of the bankruptcy of détente. Nuclear "parity" (an equal balance of weapons on the American and Soviet sides) was to them yet another insulting symbol of declining American power. They successfully blocked ratification of the treaty in the Senate.

SALT II

With détente under attack Carter turned to Brzezinski and his hard-line approach to the Soviet Union. Confrontation and a military buildup replaced the Vance policy of negotiation and accommodation. The president expanded the defense budget, built American bases in the Persian Gulf region, and sent aid to anti-Communist dictators whatever their record on human rights. The Soviet Union responded with similar hostility.

The Middle East: Hope and Hostages

Before World War I, the unstable Balkans had proved to be the spark setting off a larger conflict. For the superpowers in the 1970s and 1980s, the Middle East promised a similar threat. Oil and the Soviets' nearby southern border gave the area its geopolitical importance. Religious, tribal, national, and ethnic rivalries created chronic instability, dramatized by the wars between Israel and its Arab neighbors in 1948, 1956, 1967, and 1973. The United States had to balance its strong ties to oil-rich Saudi Arabia with its commitment to the survival of Israel.

Preservation of the peace was one key to American policy. As a result, Americans were greatly encouraged when President Anwar el-Sadat of Egypt made an unprecedented trip to Israel to meet with Prime Minister Menachem Begin. To encourage the peace process, Carter invited Begin and Sadat to Camp David in September 1978. For 13 days the talks waxed hot and cold, often breaking into argument and heated debate. When the marathon session ended, Carter had succeeded in helping the two long-standing rivals reach agreement. The 30-year state of war between Israel and Egypt finally ended. Israel accommodated Egypt by agreeing to withdraw from the Sinai peninsula, which it had occupied since 1967. Carter compensated Israel by offering $3 billion in military aid. Begin and Sadat shared a Nobel Peace Prize that might just as fairly have gone to Carter for pushing the two leaders to compromise. But even as the ink dried on the accords, Israeli and Egyptian militants began to undermine the terms. Assassins gunned down Sadat two years later.

Camp David Accords

The shah of Iran, with his American-equipped military forces, was another key to American hopes for stability in the Middle East. A strong Iran, after all, blocked Soviet access to the Persian Gulf and its oil. But in the autumn of 1978, the shah's regime was challenged by Iranian Islamic fundamentalists. They objected to the Western influences flooding their country, especially the tens of thousands of American advisers. Brzezinski urged Carter to support the shah with troops if

The Iranian revolution

It was at Camp David, in private talks sponsored by President Jimmy Carter (center), that Egyptian president Anwar el-Sadat (left) and Israeli prime minister Menachem Begin (right) hammered out a "Framework for Peace in the Middle East" as a first step toward ending decades of war and mistrust. For their efforts Begin and Sadat shared the Nobel Peace Prize of 1978, but the prize justifiably might have gone to Carter.

necessary; Vance recommended meetings with the revolutionary leaders, distance from the shah, and military restraint.

Carter waffled between the two approaches. He encouraged the shah to use force but ruled out any American participation. When the shah's regime collapsed in February 1979, fundamentalists established an Islamic republic led by a religious leader, the Ayatollah Ruhollah Khomeini. The new government was particularly outraged when Carter admitted the ailing shah to the United States for medical treatment. In November student revolutionaries stormed the American embassy in Teheran, occupying it and taking 53 Americans hostage. In the face of this insult the United States seemed helpless to act. Would Muslim Shiite fundamentalists spread their revolution to neighboring Arab states? Worse yet, would the Soviets prey on a weakened Iran?

The Soviet Union invades Afghanistan

In fact, the Soviets were equally worried that religious zeal might spread to their own restless minorities, especially to Muslims within their borders. In December 1979 Leonid Brezhnev ordered Soviet troops into neighboring Afghanistan to subdue anti-Communist Muslim guerrillas. President Carter condemned the invasion, but the actions he took to protest it were largely symbolic, especially the decision to withdraw the American team from the 1980 Olympic games in Moscow. And he announced a Carter Doctrine: the United States would intervene unilaterally if the Soviet Union threatened American interests in the Persian Gulf.

A President Held Hostage

The spectacle of "America held hostage" shown on nightly newscasts dimmed Carter's hopes for another term. It did not help that Iran's turmoil led to another round of OPEC price hikes and new inflationary pressures.

Once again Carter faced a test of his leadership. Even more than the 53 Americans in Teheran, Jimmy Carter had been taken hostage by events there. His ratings in national polls sank to record lows (77 percent negative). Carter responded by reviving the cold war rhetoric of the 1950s and accelerating the development of nuclear weapons. But where the CIA in 1953 had successfully overthrown an Iranian government, an airborne rescue mission launched in 1980 ended in disaster. Eight marines died when two helicopters and a plane collided in Iran's central desert. Cyrus Vance, a lonely voice of moderation, finally resigned.

Crisis of confidence

By 1980 the United States was mired in what Carter himself described as "a crisis of confidence." Visions of Vietnam, Central America, and the Middle East produced a nightmare of waning American power. Economic dislocations at home revived fears of a depression. None of these problems had begun with Jimmy Carter. The inflationary cycle and declining American productivity had their roots in the Vietnam era. And ironically, America's declining influence abroad reflected long-term success in bringing economic growth to Europe and the Pacific Rim.

In that sense, Carter's failure was largely symbolic. But the uneasiness of the late 1970s reflected a widespread disillusionment with liberal social programs and even with pragmatic engineers like Carter. Had the government become a drag on the American dream? Tom Wolfe's Me Generation seemed to be rejecting Carter's appeals to sacrifice. It turned instead to promoters of self-help therapy, Fundamentalist defenders of the faith, and staunch conservatives who promised both spiritual and material renewal for the 1980s.

chapter summary

In the aftermath of Vietnam, Watergate, the economic recession, and the energy crisis, the United States found itself mired in what President Jimmy Carter described as a "crisis of confidence."

- Despite the fragmentation of the Left in the 1970s, consumer advocates and environmentalists kept alive the spirit of reform.

- Unpopular domestic political strategies like impoundment and the secret activities of the plumbers made Richard Nixon vulnerable to political attacks that followed revelations of White House involvement in the Watergate break-in and subsequent cover-up.

- Following a Senate investigation and the discovery of White House tapes containing the smoking gun linking the president to the cover-up, Richard Nixon resigned rather than face inevitable impeachment.

- As the nation's first unelected president, Gerald Ford inherited an office weakened by scandal and the determination of Congress to rein in an "imperial presidency," and made his own decision to pardon Richard Nixon for his role in Watergate.

- Under Ford, Henry Kissinger became the real power in Washington as he pursued peace between Israel and its Arab neighbors, détente with the Soviet Union, and an easing of oil prices that burdened the American economy with high inflation.

- Jimmy Carter, unable to end the recession at home, pursued success abroad with a human rights policy and the negotiation of the Camp David Accords between Israel and Egypt—only to have the Soviet invasion of Afghanistan and the Iranian hostage crisis undermine his foreign policy.

interactive learning

The Primary Source Investigator CD-ROM offers the following materials related to this chapter:

- Interactive map: **The Middle East** (M28)

- A collection of primary sources exploring the age of limits that emerged in the wake of the Watergate scandal and the Vietnam War. Sources include Nixon's letter of resignation, a cartoon about the scandal, and an excerpt from Ford's speech after being sworn in. Other sources explore a new awareness of environmental problems, including the founding legislation of the Environmental Protection Agency.

additional reading

The 1970s have begun to attract more attention from historians. Bruce J. Shulman, *The Seventies: The Great Shift in American Culture, Society, and Politics* (2002), is one example. See also David Frum, *How We Got Here: The 70s* (2000); the editors of *Rolling Stone* have reprinted numerous articles from their magazine in *The 70s* (2000).

Historians have also engaged in the debate over environmental reform. The story began with Barry Commoner, *The Closing Circle* (1971), which introduced many Americans to the core ideas of ecology. Donald Worster, *Nature's Economy* (3rd ed., 1994), offers a rich history of the ideas informing environmentalism, and Samuel Hays, *Beauty, Health, and Permanence* (1987), surveys the postwar era. Charles Rubin, *The Green Crusade* (1994), challenges the methods and assumptions of some of the movement's central figures, including Rachel Carson and Commoner. Robert Gottlieb provides another critical perspective in *Forcing the Spring: The Transformation of the American Environmental Movement* (1996).

On consumerism see Robert Mayer, *The Consumer Movement* (1989). Among the books on Watergate are J. Anthony Lukas, *Nightmare* (2nd ed., 1988); Stanley Kutler, *The Wars of Watergate* (1990) and *The Abuse of Power* (1997); and Stephen Ambrose, *Nixon: The Triumph of a Politician* (1989). Kissinger's own memoirs, *The White House Years* (1979) and *Years of Upheaval* (1982), contrast with the more critical studies by Walter Isaacson, *Kissinger* (1992), and Robert Schulzinger, *Henry Kissinger: Doctor of Diplomacy* (1991). For foreign policy during the Carter years, see Gaddis Smith, *Morality, Reason, and Power* (1986). For a fuller list of readings, see the Bibliography at www.mhhe.com/davidsonnation5.

significant events

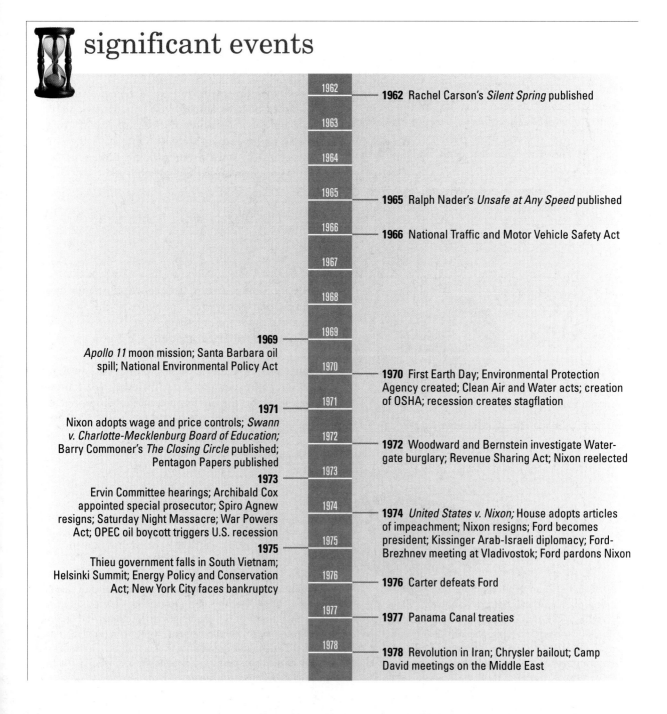

1962 Rachel Carson's *Silent Spring* published

1965 Ralph Nader's *Unsafe at Any Speed* published

1966 National Traffic and Motor Vehicle Safety Act

1969
Apollo 11 moon mission; Santa Barbara oil spill; National Environmental Policy Act

1970 First Earth Day; Environmental Protection Agency created; Clean Air and Water acts; creation of OSHA; recession creates stagflation

1971
Nixon adopts wage and price controls; *Swann v. Charlotte-Mecklenburg Board of Education;* Barry Commoner's *The Closing Circle* published; Pentagon Papers published

1972 Woodward and Bernstein investigate Watergate burglary; Revenue Sharing Act; Nixon reelected

1973
Ervin Committee hearings; Archibald Cox appointed special prosecutor; Spiro Agnew resigns; Saturday Night Massacre; War Powers Act; OPEC oil boycott triggers U.S. recession

1974 *United States v. Nixon;* House adopts articles of impeachment; Nixon resigns; Ford becomes president; Kissinger Arab-Israeli diplomacy; Ford-Brezhnev meeting at Vladivostok; Ford pardons Nixon

1975
Thieu government falls in South Vietnam; Helsinki Summit; Energy Policy and Conservation Act; New York City faces bankruptcy

1976 Carter defeats Ford

1977 Panama Canal treaties

1978 Revolution in Iran; Chrysler bailout; Camp David meetings on the Middle East

AFTER THE FACT
Historians Reconstruct the Past

The Contested Ground of Collective Memory

Perhaps the nation's most cherished commemorative space lies along the mall in Washington, D.C. On the south side of its grassy boulevards the Smithsonian Institution holds room after room of artifacts from the nation's past. Across the way is the National Gallery of Art. And the mall's western end is dominated by memorials to Washington and Lincoln.

As the mall makes clear, a culture defines itself by the history it elevates in public places. Such markers are hardly limited to Washington. Town squares boast statues; post office murals portray the deeds of forebears; even sports arenas hang honored jerseys from the rafters. As scholars of commemoration point out, all societies find visible ways to affirm their collective values.

For the historian, the Washington mall presents one singular puzzle. Today the most frequently visited and publicly acclaimed site also happens to be the least epic. Unlike Washington's 555-foot obelisk, this memorial does not soar. Unlike Lincoln's Greek temple, there are no columns evoking classical grandeur. In fact, at any reasonable distance the memorial cannot even be seen. It is simply a V of highly polished black granite incised into the ground—a V whose wide arms, each 247 feet long, converge 10 feet below the surface of the boulevard. This site is the Vietnam Veterans Memorial. Amid considerable controversy, the

memorial was built in the wake of what was not only the nation's longest war but a divisive one that the United States lost.

Why, in a mall that takes special care to burnish the nation's proudest memories, has this memorial moved so many Americans?

That question intrigues historians, who have been drawn in recent years to the study of collective memories. Their interest is not the traditional concern over whether this or that recollection is accurate. At issue instead is the *process* of memory making: "how people together searched for common memories to meet present needs, how they first recognized such a memory and then agreed, disagreed, or negotiated over its meaning." At first, the definition seems unnecessarily complex. But the process of forging a collective memory *is* complex and can take years or even decades.

For example, most people today take for granted commemorative statues honoring two sworn enemies, Ulysses S. Grant and Robert E. Lee. Yet the tradition that allows us to venerate *both* generals is possible only because of a collective memory that emphasizes the heroism of all Americans who fought. That memory began to take form in the 1880s, when northern and southern veterans started to hold joint reunions.

But for African Americans of that era, Confederate leaders such as Lee symbolized slavery, making this emerging collective memory difficult to endorse. Frederick Douglass, a former slave and prominent Republican, warned that monuments honoring Lee would only "reawaken the confederacy." He argued that emancipation, not martial valor, deserved the most emphasis. To that end, he supported efforts of African Americans to erect the Freedmen's Memorial Monument in Washington. The nation may "shut its eyes to the past . . . ," he warned, "but the colored people of this country are bound to keep the past in lively memory till justice shall be done them." Even today the collective memories of the Civil War remain contested ground.

The same can be said for the war in Vietnam. By the 1980s the vast majority of Americans, whether they had opposed or defended American involvement in Vietnam, agreed that the war had been a mistake. How, then, would a nation used to celebrating success find a way to remember failure?

Vietnam veteran Jan Scruggs took an approach that was consciously apolitical. Rather than celebrate the war, Scruggs proposed a monument honoring the veterans themselves. From 1959 to 1975 over three million American men and women had served in Vietnam, of whom 75,000 returned home permanently disabled. Yet many felt their sacrifices had been lost amid the debate over the war. To promote reconciliation Congress in 1980 set aside a two-acre site on the mall, almost equidistant from the Washington and Lincoln memorials.

In the competition to select a design for the memorial, over 1400 entries were submitted, all judged anonymously. The panel's unanimous choice came as a surprise: the entry of Maya Ying Lin, a Chinese American student at Yale University's School of Arts and Architecture. The idea for the design had occurred to her when she visited the projected site. "I thought about what

Maya Lin

death is . . . ," Lin recalled, "a sharp pain that lessens with time, but can never heal over. A scar. Take a knife and cut open the earth, and with time the grass would heal it."

To view the monument a visitor descends a gentle incline. Because there are no steps, the handicapped have easy access. The memorial's polished black granite sets a somber tone, yet the open sky and reflection of the sun dispel any sense that this is a tomb or mausoleum. A person beginning the descent at first sees only a few names carved into the granite, but as the wall deepens, so does the procession of names. Altogether, 70 panels enumerate over 54,000 Americans who died in Vietnam. As Lin insisted, "you cannot ever forget that war is not just a victory or loss. It's really about individual lives."

Despite his personal dislike of the statue (because the slave was kneeling rather than proudly standing) Frederick Douglass helped dedicate the Freedmen's Memorial Monument to Abraham Lincoln in 1876. Douglass believed emancipation was central to remembering the Civil War.

The design immediately aroused controversy. Some critics resented Lin's relative youth, her ethnicity, and the fact that she was a woman. Others objected to the memorial's abstract and decidedly unheroic character. Lin had rejected a traditional approach in favor of a more feminine and non-Western sensibility. "I didn't set out to conquer the earth, or to overpower it the way Western man usually does," she acknowledged. Ross Perot, a major financial supporter and later a presidential candidate, called the memorial a slap in the face to veterans. Others less politely described it as a public urinal. To them the black granite seemed a mark of shame and the descent below ground level an admission of wrongdoing.

So loud were these objections that in 1982 the secretary of the interior refused a construction permit until the memorial's sponsors agreed to add to the site a realistic sculpture by Frederick Hart. Hart, one of Lin's most outspoken critics, created three soldiers with an American flag, installed in 1984. This memorial provoked a female Vietnam veteran, Diane Carlson Evans, to lead a campaign for one additional monument, to honor the women of Vietnam. This third sculptural piece (also realistic) portrays three nurses, one holding a wounded soldier.

Who captured the contested terrain of Vietnam commemoration? For the historian, the evidence lies in the crowds who flock to Maya Lin's memorial. Often, visitors seek out the name of someone they knew and make a rubbing of it to take with them. So many have left flowers, flags, and personal objects, along with messages and poems, that the Park Service has created a museum for them. The messages vary wildly, from the hopeful and resolute to the sorrowful and disgusted:

> Thank you for having the courage to fight . . .
> You never would listen to anyone and you
>   finally screwed up . . .
> I am sorry Frankie, I know we left you,
>   I hope you did not suffer too much . . .

Given such diverse reactions, Lin's choice of polished black marble was inspired. "The point," she said, "is to see yourself reflected in the names." The reflective marble and the wall's abstract design allow people to find their own meaning in the memorial.

For the historian who passes by—even a century from now—the site will always bear witness to Vietnam's contested ground. As on a real battlefield, the opposing sides stand arrayed: heroic, realistic figures on one side, challenged and ultimately out-flanked by the wide embrace of that silent granite V. In aesthetic terms, traditional realism wars with abstract modernity. But that contrast only reflects a deeper cultural divide over the way we choose to remember war. Maya Lin's commemoration would have been unthinkable in 1946, when a triumphant United States was emerging as one of the world's superpowers. In an age of limits, when even super-powers falter, the gleam of black marble reflects faces that are less certain that martial valor can guar-antee a nation's immortality.

BIBLIOGRAPHY A useful introduction to the con-cept of collective memory is *Memory and American History* (1990), edited by David Thelen. Suzanne Vromen summarizes the controversy over Maya Lin's memorial in "The Vietnam Veterans Memorial, Washington, D.C.: Commemorating Ambivalence," *Focaal*, 25 (1995), 95–102. For more detail see Jan C. Scruggs and Joel T. Swerdlow, *To Heal a Nation* (1985); Brent Ashabranner, *Always to Remember: The Story of the Vietnam Veterans Memorial* (1988); and James Mayo's more interpretive *War Memorials as Political Landscapes* (1988). For Maya Ying Lin, see Peter Tauber, "Monument Maker," *New York Times Sunday Magazine*, February 24, 1991: 49–55, and a fine documentary film, *Maya Lin: A Strong, Clear Vision* (1995).

Chapter 32

In the early 1970s San Diego city officials looked out at a downtown that was growing seedier each year as stores and shoppers fled to the suburban malls that ringed the city. Nor was San Diego an exception. Across the nation many once-thriving downtown retail centers became virtual ghost towns at the close of the business day. But San Diego found a way to bounce back. The city launched a $3 billion redevelopment plan calling for a convention center, a marina, hotels, and apartment complexes.

At the core of the redevelopment plan was Horton Plaza, a mall with the look of an Italian hill town. Stores with stucco facades fronted twisting pedestrian thoroughfares where Renaissance arches lured customers to upscale stores like Banana Republic, to jewelers, and to sporting goods shops. Jugglers and clowns wandered the streets, while guitarists serenaded passersby. Horton Plaza soon ranked just behind the zoo and Sea World as San Diego's prime tourist attraction. By 1986 it drew more than 12 million shoppers and tourists.

THE CONSERVATIVE CHALLENGE

1980–1992

preview • As frustration mounted over an era of limits, conservatives pressed to restore traditional religious and social values. Ronald Reagan led the political charge with a program to reduce government regulations, raise military spending, and lower taxes. A newly conservative Supreme Court trimmed back more liberal rulings on civil rights, abortion, and the separation of church and state. But as the national debt rose sharply and a recession deepened, voters reined in the conservative movement.

For all its extravagance, Horton Plaza was hardly an innovation. The first enclosed mall, Southdale Center, had been completed nearly 20 years earlier in Edina, Minnesota, near Minneapolis. Edina had good reason for enclosure: with chilling winters and 100 days a year of rain, shopping conditions were hardly ideal for outdoor strollers. The mall's planners had approached Victor Gruen, an architect seeking ways to reclaim urban downtowns from what he saw as the tyranny of the automobile. Gruen contrasted the pedestrian-dominated streets and fountain-filled squares of European villages with the acres of sterile parking lots surrounding suburban shopping centers. As he noted in his manifesto, *The Tired Heart of Our Cities,* automobiles added pollution and congestion to the urban environment. Southdale provided an alternative: a climate-controlled marketplace where shoppers could browse or get a bite to eat at a café without dodging cars or inhaling exhaust fumes.

At first retailers feared that customers who couldn't drive by their stores or park in front wouldn't stop and shop. Success dispelled those fears. By 1985, when Horton Plaza opened, Southdale had expanded to a three-level, 144-store complex, spreading over 1.1 million square feet. Nationwide, there were more shopping centers (25,000) than either school districts or hospitals. Some 2800 were enclosed, like Southdale.

With their soaring atriums, lavish food courts, and splashing fountains, malls became the cathedrals of American material culture. Shopping on Sunday rivaled churchgoing as the weekly family ritual. Whereas American youth culture centered on the high school in the 1950s and on college campuses in the 1960s, in the 1970s and 1980s it gravitated toward mall fast-food stores and video amusement arcades. For single men and women, malls became a place to find a date. Older people in search of moderate exercise discovered that the controlled climate was ideal for "mall walking." Malls even had their counterculture—"mall rats" who hung out and diverted themselves by shoplifting.

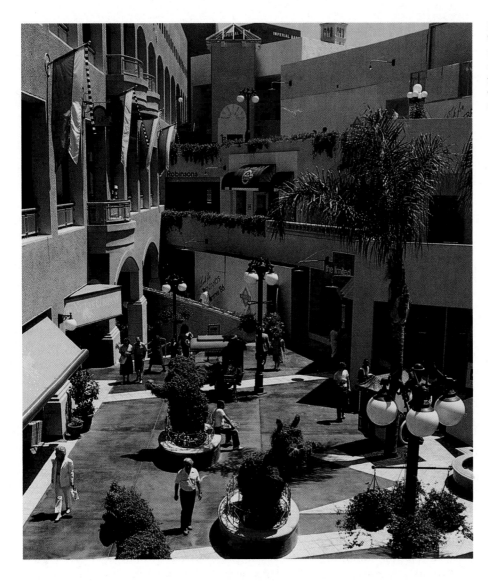

Bringing a touch of Disney World–style magic to urban redevelopment. San Diego succeeded in luring shoppers back to its downtown retail center with Horton Plaza, a replica of an Italian hill town.

Malls as cathedrals of consumption reflected a society turning away from social protest and crusades to more private paths of personal fulfillment. Some individuals adopted a consumerist or material path. Others chose a more spiritual direction. Evangelical religion offered them redemption in the prospect of being "born again." Still others extolled the virtues of traditional family values. Through private charity and volunteerism they proposed to replace the intrusive social policies of the modern welfare state. Along less orthodox paths, the "human potential movement" taught techniques such as yoga, Transcendental Meditation, and "biogenics" as means to find inner fulfillment.

Malls as symbols of an age

So it was not surprising, perhaps, that in 1980 Ronald Reagan chose to evoke Puritan John Winthrop's seventeenth-century vision of an American "city on a hill"—that city Winthrop hoped would inspire the rest of the world. For conservatives, the image carried strong religious overtones. The Puritans, after all, sought to create a Christian commonwealth that was both well ordered and moral. Reagan's vision updated the Puritans', embracing nineteenth-century ideals of "manifest destiny" as well. (America should "stand tall," he insisted, as the world's number one military power.) And Reagan affirmed the laissez-faire ideals of the late nineteenth century, encouraging citizens to promote the public good through the pursuit of private wealth. "Government is not the solution to our problem," he asserted. "Government is the problem."

Critics contended that Reagan could no more succeed with his revolution than John Winthrop had been able to impose his Puritan utopia on a disorderly world. History, they argued, had shown that private enterprise was unable to prevent or regulate the environmental damage caused by acid rain, oil spills, or toxic waste dumps. Furthermore, a severely limited federal government would prove unable to cope with declining schools, urban violence, or the AIDS epidemic. To liberals the Reagan agenda amounted to a flight from public responsibility into a fantasy world no more authentic than the Italian hill town nestled in downtown San Diego. John Winthrop's austere vision risked being transformed into a city on a hill with climate control, where the proprietors of Muzak-filled walkways banished all problems beyond the gates of the parking lots.

Throughout the 1980s Americans gravitated between the born-again vision of the conservative revolution and more secular, centrist politics. Ronald Reagan and his successor, George H. W. Bush, both championed the causes of social conservatives, such as abortion rights, the call to allow prayer in public schools, and an end to affirmative action. But in an increasingly secular society, those social causes received less attention than Reagan's economic and military agenda: to cut taxes and increase military spending.

The Conservative Rebellion

In 1964 conservative candidate Barry Goldwater had proclaimed on billboards across America: "In Your Heart You Know He's Right." Beneath one of the billboards an unknown Democratic wag unfurled his own banner: "Yes—Extreme Right." In 1964 most citizens voted with the wag, perceiving Goldwater's platform as too conservative, too extreme, too dangerous for the times.

By 1980 rising prices, energy shortages, and similar economic uncertainties fed a growing resistance to a liberal agenda. Hard-pressed workers resented increased competition from minorities, especially those supported by affirmative action quotas and government programs. Citizens resisted the demands for higher taxes to support social welfare spending. The traditional family, too, seemed under siege as divorce rates and births to single mothers soared. Increasingly the political agenda was determined by those who wanted to restore a strong family, traditional religious values, patriotism, and limited government.

The conservative tide worldwide

The United States was not the only nation to experience a resurgence of political conservatism, nationalism, and religious revival. The year before Ronald Reagan became president, Great Britain chose Margaret Thatcher as its first woman prime minister. Under her conservative leadership, "Thatcherism" became a synonym for cutting social programs, downsizing government, and privatizing state-controlled industries. Even within the Soviet bloc, rumblings could be felt as more citizens turned to religion after becoming disillusioned with the Communist system. In China, the successors to revolutionary leader Mao Zedong introduced market capitalism into the economy during the 1980s.

In some regions the conservative revival reflected a questioning of the liberal values that emerged from Europe's eighteenth-century Enlightenment. That era's faith in the rational spirit of science and technology had dominated Western thought for 200 years. Increasingly, Fundamentalists were demanding that traditional religion become the center of public life. The student radicals in Iran who seized the American embassy feared that Western ideas would destroy their Islamic faith. They saw the theocracy of the Ayatollah Khomeini as a way to rid Iran of Western secularism. In Israel, religious conservatives became a political force as they too resisted secular trends in their society. And as we shall see, leadership of the Roman Catholic Church fell to Pope John Paul II, who rejected calls to liberalize doctrine on such issues as birth control, abortion, and the acceptance of female priests.

Born Again

Thus the call for a revival of religion loomed large in the conservative rebellion. That call came most insistently from white Protestant evangelicals. Fundamentalist Protestants had since the 1920s increasingly separated themselves from the older, more liberal denominations. In the decades after World War II their membership grew dramatically—anywhere from 400 to 700 percent, compared with less than 90 percent for mainline denominations. By the 1980s they had become a significant third force in Christian America, after Roman Catholics and traditional Protestants. The election of Jimmy Carter, himself a born-again Christian, reflected their newfound visibility.

Like Fundamentalists of the 1920s, the evangelicals of the 1980s resisted the trend toward more secular values, especially in education. Some pressed states and the federal government to adopt a "school prayer" amendment allowing officially sanctioned prayer in classrooms. Others urged the teaching of "Creationism" as an acceptable alternative to Darwinian evolution. Frustrated with public schools, some parents created private Christian academies to insulate their children from the influence of "secular humanism." They condemned modernist notions of a materially

Evangelicals

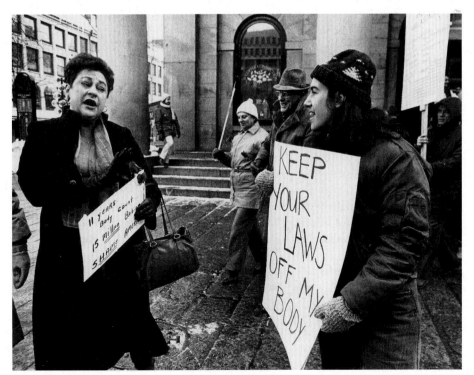

During the late 1970s and the 1980s conservatives increasingly spoke out against abortion and in favor of the right to life for an unborn fetus. Adopting the tactics of protest and civil disobedience once common to radicals in the 1960s, they clash here with pro-choice demonstrators outside Faneuil Hall in Boston.

determined world in which all truths were relative and in which circumstances rather than absolute moral precepts determined ethical behavior.

Like Aimee Semple McPherson in the 1920s (see pp. 784–785), evangelicals denounced the modern media as secular agencies, but they eagerly used broadcast technology to sell their message. Cable and satellite broadcasting allowed "tele-vangelists" to reach national audiences. The Reverend Pat Robertson, the son of a Virginia politician, introduced his *700 Club* over the Christian Broadcast Network from Virginia Beach, Virginia. His success inspired a *700 Club* regular, Jim Bakker, to launch a spin-off program called the *Praise the Lord Club—PTL* for short. Within a few years *PTL* had the largest audience of any daily show in the world. The content was Pentecostal in background: gospel singing, fervent sermons, faith healing, and speaking in tongues. The format, however, imitated that of sophisticated network "talk shows," including Bakker's Christian monologue, testimonials from celebrity guests, and musical entertainment.

It was the Reverend Jerry Falwell who first made the step from religious to political activism. In 1979 he formed the Moral Majority, Inc., an organization to attract campaign contributions and examine candidates around the country on issues important to Christians. America, Falwell proclaimed, possessed "more God-fearing citizens per capita than any other nation on earth." Using computerized mailing lists to identify donors and target audiences, the Moral Majority sent out more than a billion pieces of mail during the 1980 election.

The Catholic Conscience

American Catholics faced their own decisions about the lines between religion and politics. In the 1960s a social activist movement had arisen out of the church council known as Vatican II (1962–1965). Convened by Pope John XXIII and continued by his successor, Pope Paul VI, the council sought to revitalize the church and to reappraise its role in the modern world. The reforms of Vatican II reduced the amount of Latin in the mass, invited greater participation by ordinary church members, and encouraged closer ties to other Christians and to Jews.

Pope John Paul II

Disturbed by these currents, Catholic conservatives found support for their views when the magnetic John Paul II assumed the papacy in 1979. Pope John Paul reined in the modern trends inspired by Vatican II. He ruled against a wider role for women in the church hierarchy and stiffened church policy against birth control. That put him at odds with a majority of American Catholics. The American church also faced a crisis as fewer young men and women chose celibate lives as priests and nuns.

Though conservative Catholics and Protestant evangelicals were sometimes wary of one another, they shared certain views. Both groups lobbied for the government to provide federal aid to parochial schools and Fundamentalist academies. But it was the issue of abortion that attracted the greatest mutual support. Pope John Paul reaffirmed the church's teaching that all life begins at conception and that abortion amounts to murder of the unborn. Evangelicals, long suspicious of the power of secular technology and science, attacked abortion as another instance in which science had upset the natural moral order of life.

The Media as Battleground

Both evangelicals and political conservatives viewed the mass media as an establishment that was liberal in its politics and permissive in its tolerance of sex and violence.

Because film and television had come to occupy such a prominent place in American life, they became a battleground where conservatives and liberals clashed.

Topical sitcoms

By the late 1960s the film industry had left behind the strict standards of its Production Code, established in 1930 to police Hollywood's morals. Soft-core pornography with simulated sex and partial nudity had been exceeded in the 1970s by hard-core films. Even the traditionally inoffensive television programming became more topical. In 1971 producer Norman Lear introduced *All in the Family,* whose main character, Archie Bunker, was a rough-hewn blue-collar father. Archie treated his addlepated wife like a doormat, struggled to understand his modestly rebellious daughter, and shouted endless insults at his Polish American son-in-law. Americans were supposed to laugh at Archie's outrageous references to "Hebes," "Spics," and "Commie crapola," but many in the audience were not laughing. Some minority leaders charged that by making Archie lovable, the show legitimized the very prejudices it seemed to attack.

*M*A*S*H,* a popular television series launched in 1972, was more clearly liberal in its sympathies. Although the show was set in a medical unit during the Korean War, its real inspiration was Vietnam and the growing disillusionment with the war. *M*A*S*H* twitted bureaucracy, authority, pretense, bigotry, and snobbery. As newer liberal sensitivities emerged during the decade, the show adapted as well. "Hawkeye" Pierce and his fellow army doctors began as hard-drinking, womanizing foes of war and army life. Ten years later they still hated the army and war, but Hawkeye had become more vulnerable and respectful to women. "Hot Lips" Houlihan was transformed from an overly patriotic military martinet into Margaret Houlihan, a career woman struggling for respect. For conservatives, antiauthoritarian shows like *M*A*S*H* demonstrated how deeply liberal values pervaded American life. That same bias, they believed, affected newspaper and television reporters. For their part, feminists and minority groups complained that television portrayed them as stereotypes, when it bothered to portray them at all.

Perhaps inevitably, the wars for the soul of prime time spilled into the political arena. Norman Lear, Archie Bunker's creator, went on to form People for the American Way, a lobbying group that campaigned for more diversity in American life and attempted to counteract pressure groups like the Moral Majority. Conservatives, looking to make a stronger political impact, in 1980 embraced an amiable former movie actor who had long preached their gospel.

The Election of 1980

Jimmy Carter might have been born again, but Ronald Reagan spoke the language of true conservatism. "I think there is a hunger in this land for a spiritual revival, a return to a belief in moral absolutes," he told his followers. Such a commitment to Fundamentalist articles of faith was more important than the fact that Reagan actually had no church affiliation and seldom attended services.

The defection of many southern evangelical Protestants to the Republicans was just one of Jimmy Carter's problems. His rapid military buildup and cutbacks in social programs offended liberals, while rampant inflation and a weak economy alienated blue-collar voters. Preoccupied with the Iran hostage crisis, the president refrained from vigorous campaigning. When undecided voters saw Reagan as a candidate with the power to lead, the race turned into a landslide. Equally impressive, the Republicans won their first majority in the Senate since 1954. Reagan had splintered the New Deal Democratic coalition. Although his support was greatest among those who were over age 45, white, and earning more than $50,000 a year, he made

The Reverend Jerry Falwell's Moral Majority actively supported Ronald Reagan as well as other political candidates who shared the Moral Majority's social agenda.

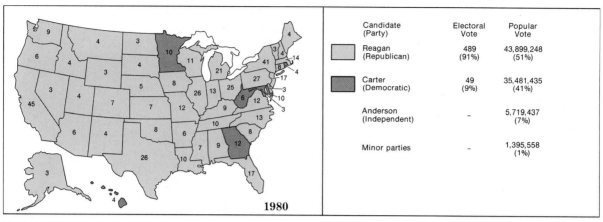

Candidate (Party)	Electoral Vote	Popular Vote
Reagan (Republican)	489 (91%)	43,899,248 (51%)
Carter (Democratic)	49 (9%)	35,481,435 (41%)
Anderson (Independent)	–	5,719,437 (7%)
Minor parties	–	1,395,558 (1%)

1980

Election of 1980

striking gains among union workers, southern white Protestants, Catholics, and Jews. For the next decade and beyond, conservatives would dominate the terms of debate in public policy.

Prime Time with Ronald Reagan

Ronald Reagan brought the bright lights of Hollywood to Washington. His managers staged one of the most extravagant inaugurations in the nation's history. Nancy Reagan became the most fashion-conscious first lady since Jackie Kennedy, while the new administration made the conspicuous display of wealth once again a sign of success and power.

The Great Communicator

Ronald Reagan came to Washington with a simple message. "It is time to reawaken the industrial giant, to get government back within its means, and to lighten our punitive tax burden," he announced on inauguration day. A strong national defense and a determined effort to revive the cold war crusade would reestablish the United States as the number one power in the world. Commentators began referring to the president as "the great communicator" because of his mastery of television and radio.

The Reagan style

Reagan's skill as an actor obscured contradictions between his rhetoric and reality. With his jaunty wave and jutting jaw, he projected physical vitality and the charismatic good looks of John Kennedy. Yet at age 69, he was the oldest president to take office, and none since Calvin Coolidge slept as soundly or as much. Reagan had begun his political life as a New Deal Democrat, but over the next two decades he moved increasingly to the right. By the 1950s he had become an ardent anti-Communist, earning a reputation among conservatives as an engaging after-dinner speaker. General Electric made him its corporate spokesperson. In 1966 he began two terms as governor of California with a promise to pare down government programs and balance budgets. In fact, spending jumped sharply during his term in office. Similarly, he continued to champion family values, although he was divorced and estranged from some of his children.

Similar inconsistencies marked Reagan's leadership as president. Outsiders applauded his "hands-off" style: less management, not more, was what the nation needed after a succession of activist presidents from Kennedy to Carter. Reagan set the tone and direction, letting his advisers take care of the details. On the other hand, many within the administration, such as Secretary of the Treasury Donald Regan, were shocked to find the new president remarkably ignorant of and uninterested in important matters of policy. "The Presidential mind was not cluttered with facts," Regan lamented.

Nancy Reagan (aided by an astrologer) often dictated the president's schedule, helped select his advisers, and sometimes even determined the major issues the president addressed. Yet the public believed that the president was firmly in charge and, until the Iran arms scandal in 1986, consistently approved his conduct. His capacity for deflecting responsibility for mistakes earned him a reputation as the "Teflon president," because no criticism seemed to stick.

In addition, Reagan was blessed by remarkable fortune: a number of events beyond his control broke in his favor. The deaths of three aging Soviet leaders, beginning with Leonid Brezhnev in 1982, compounded that country's economic weakness and reduced Russian influence abroad. Members of the OPEC oil cartel quarreled among themselves, exceeded production quotas, and thus forced oil prices lower. The lower oil prices removed a major inflationary pressure on the American economy. The day Reagan took office, the Iranians released the American hostages, relieving the president of his first major foreign policy crisis. And when a would-be assassin shot the president in the chest on March 30, 1981, the wound was not life-threatening. His courage in the face of death impressed even his critics.

Ronald Reagan's image as a plainspoken westerner helped build his reputation as "the great communicator."

The Reagan Agenda

Reagan set out with two major goals: to reestablish the prestige of a presidency battered by Watergate and to weaken big government. His budget would become an instrument to reduce bureaucracy and to undermine activist federal agencies in the areas of civil rights, environmental and consumer protection, poverty programs, urban renewal, transportation, the arts, and education. In essence, Reagan wanted to return government to the size and responsibility it possessed in the 1950s, before the reforms of Kennedy and Johnson.

At the heart of the Reagan revolution was a commitment to supply-side economics, a program that in many ways resembled the trickle-down economic theories of the Harding-Coolidge era. Supply-side theorists argued that high taxes and government regulation stifled enterprising businesses and economic expansion. The key to revival lay in a large tax cut—a politically popular, though economically controversial, proposal. Such a cut threatened to reduce revenues and increase an already large deficit. Not so, argued supply-side economist Arthur Laffer. The economy would be so stimulated that tax revenues would actually rise, even though the tax rate was cut.

Supply-side economics

The president's second target for action was inflation, the "silent thief" that had burdened the economy during the Ford and Carter years. Reagan resisted certain traditional cures for inflation: tight money, high interest rates, and wage and price controls. He preferred two approaches unpopular with Democrats: higher unemployment and weakened unions to reduce labor costs.

Fighting inflation

Lower public spending, a favorite Republican remedy, might have seemed one likely method of reducing inflation. But the third element of Reagan's agenda was a sharp rise in military outlays: a total of $1.5 trillion to be spent over five years. The American military would gain the strength to act unilaterally anywhere in the world

Military buildup

to beat back Communist threats. This goal was a remarkably expansive one: Presidents Nixon, Ford, and Carter had all looked to scale back American commitments, either through détente or by shifting burdens to allies in Western Europe. Reagan recognized no such limits. And rather than emphasize either nuclear defense or conventional weapons, Defense Secretary Caspar Weinberger lobbied Congress for both.

The Reagan Revolution in Practice

The administration soon found an opportunity to "hang tough" against unions when air traffic controllers went on strike, claiming that understaffing and long working hours threatened air safety. But because the controllers were civil service employees, the strike was technically illegal. Without addressing the merits of the controllers' complaints, Reagan simply fired them for violating their contract. The defeat of the air controllers signaled a broader attack on unions. When a recession enveloped the nation, major corporations wrung substantial concessions on wages and work rules. Organized labor witnessed a steady decline in membership and political power.

Environmental controversies

The president's war against government regulation took special aim at environmental rules. Conservatives, especially in the West, dismissed the environmental lobby as "nature lovers." Preservation of wild lands restricted mining, cattle grazing, farming, and real estate development—all powerful western industries. Reagan appointed westerner James Watt, an outspoken champion of this "sagebrush rebellion," to head the Interior Department. Watt, in turn, devoted himself to opening federal lands for private development, including lumbering and offshore oil drilling. A series of rash statements forced Watt to resign in 1983, but the administration continued to oppose most efforts to regulate or protect the environment. The president even refused to accept the conclusion of scientists that the smoke from coal-fired power plants in the Ohio valley was sending destructive acid rain over the lakes and forests of eastern Canada and the United States.

Tax cuts

Most important, by the summer of 1981 Reagan had pushed his supply-side legislation through Congress. The Economic Recovery Tax Act provided a 25 percent across-the-board reduction for all taxpayers. The president hailed it, along with recently passed budget cuts, as an antidote to "big government's" addiction to spending and a stimulus to the economy. Opponents pointed out that an "equal" cut of 25 percent for all taxpayers left far more dollars in the hands of the wealthy.

The Supply-Side Scorecard

The impact of Reagan's supply-side economics was mixed. By 1982 a recession had pushed unemployment above 10 percent. The Federal Reserve Board's tight money policies and high interest rates deepened the recession. But 1983 saw the beginning of an economic expansion that was to last through Reagan's presidency, thanks in part to increased federal spending and lowered interest rates. Then, too, falling energy costs and improved industrial productivity also contributed to renewed prosperity. Although many workers earned less per hour, the flow of women into the labor market kept family incomes from falling too much.

The transfer of wealth

Even so, the Reagan tax cut was one of a series of policy changes that brought about a substantial transfer of wealth from poor and lower-middle-class workers to the upper middle classes and the rich. For the wealthiest Americans, the 1980s were the best of times. The top 1 percent commanded a greater share of the nation's wealth (37 percent) than at any other time since 1929. Their earnings averaged

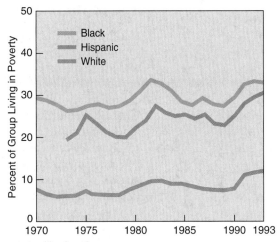

Poverty in America, 1970–1993 Social Security and other income supplements to older Americans reduced their rate of poverty. For all other traditionally impoverished groups the prosperity of the Reagan-Bush years left them slightly worse off than in 1980. The charts also indicate that poverty was most severe for unwed or divorced mothers and their children, and people of color.

about $560,000 per year as opposed to $20,000 or less for the bottom 40 percent. What counterculture hippies were to the 1960s, high-salaried "yuppies" (young, upwardly mobile professionals) were to the 1980s.

On the surface, the buoyant job market seemed to signal a more general prosperity as well. By the end of Reagan's term, more than 14.5 million jobs had been created for Americans. Yet these jobs were spread unevenly by region, class, and gender. More than 2 million were in finance, insurance, real estate, and law, all services used by the wealthy, not the poor. In highly paid "Wall Street" jobs—those involving financial services—more than 70 percent went to white males, only 2 percent to African Americans. New employment for women was concentrated in the areas of health, education, social services, and government, where approximately 3 million jobs opened, most dependent on government support. New jobs for the poor (more than 3 million) were largely restricted to minimum wage, part-time, dead-end jobs in hotels, fast-food restaurants, and retail stores.

Because Reaganomics preached the virtues of free markets and free trade, the administration did little to prevent high-wage blue-collar jobs from flowing to cheap labor markets in Mexico and Asia. Furthermore, Reagan aimed the sharpest edge of his budget ax at programs for the poor: food stamps, Aid to Families with Dependent Children, Medicaid, school lunches, and housing assistance. The programs trimmed back least were middle-class entitlements like Social Security and Medicare. Those programs affected Americans over age 65, who, as social activist Michael Harrington observed, as a general class "are not now, and for a long time have not been, poor."

As more income flowed toward the wealthy and as jobs were lost to overseas competitors, the percentage of Americans below the poverty level rose from 11.7 percent in 1980 to 15 percent by 1982. There the level remained into the 1990s. Reagan's successful war on inflation, which dropped to less than 2 percent by 1986, contributed to a rise in unemployment. Even during the recovery, the figure dropped below 6 percent of the workforce only in the months before the 1988 election. (In contrast, the highest rate under Jimmy Carter was 5.9 percent.) Thus the Reagan boom was an uneven one despite continued economic expansion.

The Military Buildup

Reagan described the Soviet Union as an "evil empire." To defeat Communism he supported a sharp rise in military spending. Outlays rose from less than $200 billion under Presidents Ford and Carter to almost $300 billion in 1985, when growing opposition led to some restraint. The largest increases were for expensive strategic nuclear weapons systems. The Reagan administration argued that a nuclear buildup would strengthen the position of American negotiators during arms reductions talks.

Huge costs were not the only source of criticism. When Reagan's tough-talking defense planners spoke about "winning" a nuclear exchange, they revived the antinuclear peace movement across Europe and America. The bishops of the American Catholic church felt moved to announce their opposition to nuclear war, and scientists

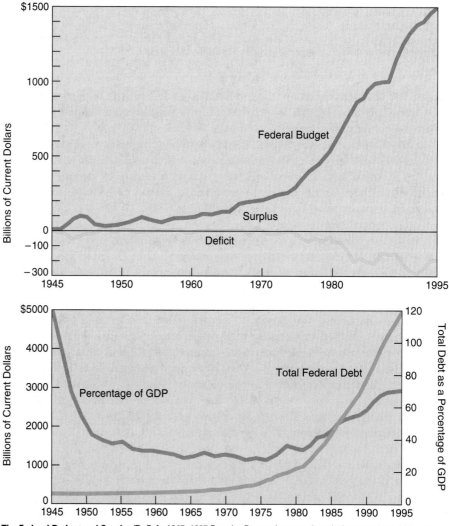

The Federal Budget and Surplus/Deficit, 1945–1995 Despite Reagan's campaign pledge to reduce federal spending, the federal deficit soared higher during his presidency than at any other time in the nation's history. During the presidency of George H. W. Bush the deficit continued to climb despite the restrictions of the Gramm-Rudman Act, passed in 1985.

warned that the debris in the atmosphere from an atomic exchange might create a "nuclear winter" fatal to all life on Earth. Equally vocal critics singled out the cost of the Pentagon's armament list. Stories of $600 toilet seats and $7000 coffeepots made headlines, but more serious were the failures of entire multibillion-dollar weapons systems. One of the president's favorite programs was the Strategic Defense Initiative, or SDI. Nicknamed "Star Wars" after a popular science fiction film, the program spent billions of dollars trying to establish a space-based missile system that would be merely "defensive." Most scientists contended that the project was as fantastic as the movie.

Star Wars

The combination of massive defense spending and substantial tax cuts left the federal government awash in red ink. Annual deficits soared to more than $200 billion. By the end of his term, Reagan had run up more debt within eight years than the federal government had accumulated in its entire 200-year history. Furthermore, with interest rates so high, the value of the dollar soared on world markets. The strong dollar pushed up the cost of American exports in foreign markets. As American exports declined, imports from abroad (such as Japanese autos) captured a larger market share in America. From the end of World War I until the beginning of the Reagan years, the United States had been the world's leading creditor nation. By 1986 it had become the world's largest debtor.

The spending excesses of the Reagan agenda would come to haunt his conservative successors. For the time being, however, Ronald Reagan's popularity seemed unassailable. In 1984 he easily won a second term, gaining 59 percent of the vote in his run against Democrat Walter Mondale of Minnesota. (Mondale's running mate, Geraldine Ferraro of New York, was the first female candidate for the vice presidency.) Reagan remained his sunny, unflappable self, seeming to enjoy the presidency immensely. "The 75-year-old man is hitting home runs," rhapsodized *Time* magazine at the beginning of his second term. In reality, Reagan would soon be tested by a series of crises arising out of his more aggressive stance toward foreign policy.

Standing Tall in a Chaotic World

Reagan brought to the conduct of foreign policy the same moral ardor that shaped his approach to domestic affairs. Reagan wanted the United States to stand tall: to adopt a policy that drew bold, clear lines as a means of restoring American prestige and defeating communism. But turmoil abroad demonstrated that bold policies were not always easy to carry out. And because the president remained indifferent to most day-to-day details, he was at the mercy of those officials who put into effect his aggressive anti-Communist foreign policy.

Terrorism in the Middle East

In the Middle East, the passions of religious factions demonstrated how difficult it was to impose order, even for a superpower like the United States. In 1982 President Reagan sent American Marines into Lebanon as part of a European-American peacekeeping force. His hope was to bring a measure of stability to a region torn by civil war. But in trying to mediate between Lebanon's religious and political sects, the American "peacekeepers" found themselves dragged into the fighting. Terrorists retaliated by blowing up a U.S. Marine barracks in October 1983, killing 239. The president then ordered American troops withdrawn.

Just as hostage-taking in Iran had frustrated the Carter administration, terrorist attacks by Islamic fundamentalists bedeviled Reagan. In 1985 terrorists took additional hostages in Lebanon; others hijacked American airline flights, killed an American hostage on a Mediterranean cruise ship, and bombed a nightclub where American soldiers met in West Germany. In such situations, the president's public response was always uncompromising: "Let terrorists beware: . . . our policy will be one of swift and effective retribution."

But against whom should the United States seek revenge? American intelligence agencies found it extremely difficult to collect reliable information on the many political and terrorist factions. In 1986 the president sent bombers to attack targets in Libya, whose anti-American leader, Colonel Muammar al-Qadhafi, had links to terrorists. But so did the more powerful states of Syria and Iran.

Mounting Frustrations in Central America

Grenada invasion

At first, a policy of standing tall seemed easier closer to home. In 1983, the administration launched an invasion of Grenada, a small Carribean island whose government was challenged by pro-Castro revolutionaries. U.S. forces crushed the rebels and succeeded in protecting several hundred American medical students attending school there. But the invasion was largely a symbolic gesture.

More frustrating to the president, Nicaragua's left-wing Sandinista government had established increasingly close ties with Cuba. In 1981 Reagan extended aid to the antigovernment "Contra" forces. When critics warned that Nicaragua could become another Vietnam, the president countered that the Contras were "freedom fighters," battling in the spirit of America's Founding Fathers. Although the Contras did include some moderate democrats and disillusioned Sandinistas, most of their leaders had served the brutal Somoza dictatorship that the Sandinistas had toppled in 1979.

Boland Amendment

Reagan might have sought a negotiated settlement between the Contras and the Sandinistas. Instead he allowed the CIA to help the Contras mine Nicaraguan harbors in hopes of overthrowing the Sandinistas outright. When some of the mines exploded, damaging foreign ships in violation of international law, even some conservative senators were dismayed. Congress adopted an amendment sponsored by Representative Edward Boland of Massachusetts, explicitly forbidding the CIA or "any other agency or entity involved in intelligence activities" to spend money to support the Contras "directly or indirectly." The president signed the Boland Amendment, though only grudgingly.

The Iran-Contra Connection

Thus by mid-1985 Reagan policy makers felt two major frustrations. First, Congress had forbidden any support of the Contras in Central America, and second, Iranian-backed terrorists continued to hold hostages in Lebanon. In the summer of 1985 a course of events was set in motion that eventually linked these two issues.

Arms for hostages deal

The president made it increasingly clear that he wanted to find a way to free the remaining hostages. National Security Adviser Robert McFarlane, eager to please, suggested opening a channel to "moderate factions" in the Iranian government. If the United States sold Iran a few weapons, the grateful moderates might use their influence in Lebanon to free the hostages. But an agreement to exchange arms for hostages would violate the president's often-repeated vow never to pay ransom to terrorists. Still, Reagan apparently approved the initiative. Over the following year, four secret arms shipments were made to Iran. One hostage was set free.

Central American Conflicts, 1974–1990 President Reagan's attempts to overthrow the Sandinista government in Nicaragua and to contain communism focused American attention on Latin America. So too did the staggering debts Latin countries owed to banks in America and elsewhere. Equally distorting to the hemisphere's social and economic fabric was the sharp rise in the drug trade organized by criminal syndicates. Most notorious was the Medellin cartel, which operated from a remote region in Colombia, shipping drugs through havens in Panama and the Bahamas into the United States while depositing its enormous profits in banks in Miami and offshore banking centers such as the Cayman Islands. The war on drugs led President Bush to invade Panama in December 1989 and bring its corrupt president, Manuel Noriega, to the United States for trial.

Reagan's secretaries of state and defense both had strongly opposed the notion of trading arms for hostages. "This is almost too absurd to comment on," Defense Secretary Weinberger remarked when he was first told of the proposal. Surprisingly, however, both men were kept largely uninformed of the shipments, precisely because their opposition was well known. McFarlane's successor as national security adviser, Admiral John Poindexter, had the president sign a secret intelligence "finding" that allowed him and his associates to pursue their mission without informing anyone in Congress or even the secretaries of defense and state. Because the president ignored the details of foreign policy, McFarlane, Poindexter, and their aides had assumed the power to act on their own.

Oliver North

The man most often pulling the strings seemed to be Lieutenant Colonel Oliver "Ollie" North, a junior officer under McFarlane and later Poindexter. A Vietnam veteran with a flair for the dramatic, North was impatient with bureaucratic procedures. He and McFarlane had already discovered a way to evade the Boland Amendment in order to secretly aid the Contras. McFarlane told Saudia Arabia and several other American allies that the Contras desperately needed funds. As a favor, the Saudis deposited at least $30 million in Swiss bank accounts set up to launder the money. North then used the cash to buy weapons that were delivered to Central America.

The two strands of the secret missions came together in January 1986, when North hit upon the idea that the profits made selling arms to Iran could be siphoned off to buy weapons for the Contras. The Iranian arms dealer who brokered the deal thought it a great idea. "I think this is now, Ollie, the best chance, because . . . we never get such good money out of this," he laughed, as he was recorded on a tape North himself made. "We do everything. We do hostages free of charge; we do all terrorists free of charge; Central America free of charge."

Cover Blown

Through the fall of 1986, both operations remained hidden from view. That changed abruptly when reports of the Iranian arms deal were leaked to a Lebanese newspaper. Astonished reporters besieged the administration, demanding to know how secret arms sales to a terrorist regime benefited the president's antiterrorist campaign. As the inquiry continued, the link between the arms sales and the Contras was discovered. Attorney General Edwin Meese moved so slowly to investigate that North and his secretary had time to shred crucial documents. Still, enough evidence remained to make the dimensions of the illegal operations clear.

Irangate

The press nicknamed the scandal "Irangate," comparing it to Richard Nixon's Watergate affair. But Irangate raised more troubling issues. Watergate sprang from political tricks that ran amok. The president had led the cover-up to save his own political skin. But the Iran-Contra congressional hearings, held during the summer of 1987, left the role of President Reagan unexplained. Poindexter testified that he had kept Reagan in ignorance "so that I could insulate him from the decision and provide some future deniability for the president if it ever leaked out. . . . On this whole issue, you know, the buck stops here, with me." In that way, Iran-Contra revealed a presidency out of control. An unelected segment within the government had taken upon itself the power to pursue its own policies beyond legal channels.

As one analyst noted, Reagan's ideological approach to foreign policy tended to give his aides an "absolute certainty of their own rightness." Because they were operating with "pure hearts," they found it all too easy to justify working with "dirty hands." In doing so, however, they subverted the constitutional system of checks and balances.

From Cold War to Glasnost

Because few members of Congress wanted to impeach a genial president, the hearings came to a sputtering end. Reagan's popularity returned, in part because of substantial improvement in Soviet-American relations. By the 1980s the Soviet Union was far weaker than American experts, including the CIA, had ever recognized. The Soviet economy stagnated; the Communist party was mired in corruption. The war in Afghanistan had become a Russian Vietnam. By accelerating the arms race, Reagan placed additional pressure on the Russians.

In 1985 a fresh spirit entered the Kremlin. Unlike the aged leaders who preceded him, Mikhail Gorbachev was young and saw the need for reform within the

Mikhail Gorbachev

Soviet premier Mikhail Gorbachev (right) used his summits with Ronald Reagan (left) to reduce Soviet-American tensions, although the spirit of glasnost did not ease the skirmishes between his wife, Raisa, and Nancy Reagan, who waged a quiet war over fashion and ideology. Gorbachev came to rival Reagan as a "great communicator," with many Americans applauding his efforts to reform Soviet society and to slow the arms race.

Soviet Union. Gorbachev's fundamental restructuring, or perestroika, set about improving relations with the United States. He reduced military commitments and adopted a policy of openness (glasnost) about problems in the Soviet Union. In October, the two leaders held their second summit in Reykjavík, Iceland. Gorbachev dangled the possibility of abolishing all nuclear weapons. Reagan seemed receptive to the idea, apparently unaware that if both sides eliminated all nuclear weapons, Soviet conventional forces would far outnumber NATO troops in Europe. In the end, the president refused to sacrifice his Star Wars system for so radical a proposal.

Despite the immediate impasse, negotiations continued after the summit. In December 1987 Reagan traveled to Moscow, where he signed the Intermediate Nuclear Force treaty, which eliminated an entire class of nuclear missiles with ranges of 600 to 3400 miles. Both sides agreed to allow on-site inspections of missile bases and the facilities where missiles would be destroyed.

The Election of 1988

Thus as the election of 1988 approached, the president could claim credit for improved relations with the Soviet Union. Loyalty to Ronald Reagan made Vice President George H. W. Bush the Republican heir apparent. Bush appealed most to party professionals, white Protestants, and the affluent middle class that had benefited from Reaganomics.

The Democratic challenger, Governor Michael Dukakis of Massachusetts, tried to call attention to weaknesses in the American economy. An alarming number of savings and loan institutions had failed, and Dukakis recognized that poor and even many middle-class Americans had lost ground during the 1980s. But Bush put the lackluster Dukakis on the defensive. With the economy reasonably robust, Bush won by a comfortable margin, taking 54 percent of the popular vote. The Reagan agenda remained on track.

An End to the Cold War

President George Herbert Walker Bush was born to both privilege and politics. The son of a Connecticut senator, he attended an exclusive boarding school and then the Ivy League Yale University. That background made him part of the East Coast establishment often scorned by more populist Republicans. Yet once the oil business lured Bush to Texas, he moved to the right, becoming a Goldwater Republican when he ran unsuccessfully for the Senate in 1964. Although he once supported Planned Parenthood and a woman's right to abortion, Bush eventually adopted the conservative right-to-life position. In truth, foreign policy interested him far more than domestic politics. But in the end, inattention to domestic issues proved his undoing as the economy slid into recession.

A Post–Cold War Foreign Policy

To the astonishment of most Western observers, Mikhail Gorbachev's reform policies led not only to the collapse of the Soviet empire but also to the breakup of the Soviet Union itself. In December 1988, Gorbachev spoke in the United Nations of a "new world order." To that end he began liquidating the Soviet cold war legacy, as the last Russian troops began leaving Afghanistan and then Eastern Europe.

The fall of communism

Throughout 1989 Eastern Europeans began to test their newfound freedom. In Poland, Hungary, Bulgaria, Czechoslovakia, and, most violently, Romania,

Communist dictators fell from power. Nothing more inspired the world than the stream of celebrating East Germans pouring through the Berlin Wall in November 1989. Within a year the wall, a symbol of Communist oppression, had been torn down and Germany reunified. Although Gorbachev struggled to keep together the 15 republics that made up the U.S.S.R., the forces of nationalism and reform pulled the Soviet Union apart. The Baltic republics—Lithuania, Latvia, and Estonia—declared their independence in 1991. Then in December, the Slavic republics of Ukraine, Belarus, and Russia formed a new Commonwealth of Independent States. By the end of December eight more of the former Soviet republics had joined the loose federation. Boris Yeltsin, the charismatic president of Russia, became the Commonwealth's dominant figure. With no Soviet Union left to preside over, Gorbachev resigned as president.

President Bush's response to these momentous changes was cautious: a policy of "status quo plus," one aide called it. Although the president increasingly supported Gorbachev's reforms, even if he had wished to aid Eastern Europe and the new Commonwealth states, soaring deficits at home limited his options. The administration seemed to support the status quo in Communist China, too. When in June 1989 China's aging leadership crushed students rallying for democratic reform in Beijing's Tiananmen Square, Bush muted American protests.

The fall of the Soviet Union signaled the end of a cold war that, more than once, had threatened a nuclear end to human history. At a series of summits with Russian leaders, the United States and its former rivals agreed to sharp reductions in their stockpiles of nuclear weapons. The Strategic Arms Reduction Treaty (or START), concluded in July 1991, far surpassed the limits negotiated in earlier SALT talks. By June 1992 Bush and Yeltsin had agreed to even sharper cuts.

The Berlin Wall had stood since August 1961 as a symbol of cold war tensions. Thus, Americans joined these Germans in celebrating the wall's destruction. At long last, the cold war seemed to have ended.

The Gulf War

With two superpowers no longer facing off against each other, what would the "new world order" look like? If anything, regional crises loomed larger. President Bush moved to project American power more forcefully in the Middle East. But civil wars in Eastern Europe and Africa demonstrated that a world order beyond the shadow of the cold war might be more chaotic and unpredictable than ever.

Instability in the Middle East brought Bush's greatest foreign policy challenge. From 1980 to 1988 Iran and Iraq had battered each other in a debilitating war. During those years the Reagan administration assisted Iraq with weapons and intelligence, until at last it won a narrow victory over Iran's fundamentalists. But Iraq's ruthless dictator, Saddam Hussein, had run up enormous debts. To ease his financial crisis, Hussein cast a covetous eye on his neighbor, the small oil-rich sheikdom of Kuwait. In August 1990, 120,000 Iraqi troops invaded and occupied Kuwait, catching the Bush administration off guard. Would Hussein stop there?

Saddam Hussein

"We committed a boner with regard to Iraq and our close friendship with Iraq," admitted Ronald Reagan. Embarrassed by having supported the pro-Iraqi policy, Bush was determined to thwart Hussein's invasion of Kuwait. The president successfully coordinated a United Nations–backed economic boycott. Increasing the pressure further, he deployed half a million American troops in Saudi Arabia and

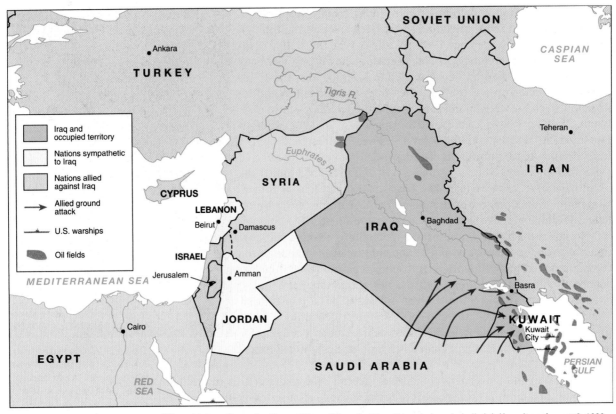

War with Iraq: Operation Desert Storm When Saddam Hussein invaded oil-rich Kuwait on August 2, 1990, the United States formed a coalition to force out the Iraqis. (Although Turkey was not a formal member, it allowed its airfields to be used. Israel remained uninvolved to avoid antagonizing Arab coalition members.) The coalition launched Operation Desert Storm in January 1991; land forces invaded on February 24 (Operation Desert Saber), routing Iraqi troops, who left Kuwait in ruin and its oil fields aflame.

the Persian Gulf. By November Bush had won a resolution from the Security Council permitting the use of military force if Hussein did not withdraw.

Operation Desert Storm

On January 17, 1991, planes from France, Italy, Britain, Saudi Arabia, and the United States began bombing Baghdad and Iraqi bases. Operation Desert Storm had begun. After weeks of merciless pounding from the air, ground operations shattered Hussein's vaunted Republican Guards in less than 100 hours. In an act of spite, Hussein resorted to ecoterrorism. His forces set Kuwait's oil fields ablaze and dumped huge quantities of crude oil into the rich Persian Gulf ecosystem. It did him no good: by the end of February Kuwait was liberated, and nothing stood between Allied forces and Iraq's capital, Baghdad. Bush was unwilling to advance that far—and most other nations in the coalition agreed. If Hussein were toppled, it was not clear who in Iraq would fill the vacuum of power. But long after the war ended, sanctions had still not driven the dictator from power. And with tensions still high between Israel and its Arab neighbors, the Middle East remained a volatile region.

Domestic Doldrums

Victory in the Gulf War so boosted the president's popularity that aides brushed aside the need for any bold domestic program. "Frankly, this president doesn't need another single piece of legislation, unless it's absolutely right," asserted John Sununu, his cocky chief of staff. "In fact, if Congress wants to come together, adjourn, and leave, it's all right with us." That attitude suggested a lack of direction that proved fatal to Bush's reelection hopes.

At first, Bush envisioned a domestic program that would soften the harsher edges of the Reagan revolution. He promised to create a "kinder, gentler" nation. Yet pressures from conservative Republicans kept the new president from straying too far in the direction of reform. Although he appointed a well-respected conservationist, William Reilly, to head the Environmental Protection Agency, Reilly often found his programs opposed by other members of the administration. When delegates from 178 nations met at an "Earth Summit" in Rio de Janeiro in 1992, the president opposed efforts to draft stricter rules to lessen the threat of global warming. Bush did sign into law the sweeping Clean Air Act passed by Congress in 1990. But soon after, Vice President Dan Quayle established a "Council on Competitiveness" to rewrite regulations that corporations found burdensome.

Environmental issues

Similarly, the president called for reform of an educational system whose quality had declined through the 1980s. But while he convened a well-publicized "Education Summit" in 1989, the delegates issued a modest set of goals only after the president was urged to do so by his cochair at the summit, Governor Bill Clinton of Arkansas. Secretary of Housing and Urban Development Jack Kemp searched for ways to improve the plight of the homeless and empower poor urban communities by promoting economic "free enterprise zones." But Kemp too found himself frustrated by the president's unwillingness to push hard for any of his programs.

The Conservative Court

Although Presidents Reagan and Bush both spoke out against abortion, affirmative action, the banning of prayer in public schools, and other conservative social issues,

Justice Clarence Thomas survived a bitter Senate battle during his Supreme Court confirmation hearings. Here, he is sworn in by Chief Justice William Rehnquist as Thomas's wife and President George Bush and Barbara Bush look on. Thomas's conservative views on abortion and affirmative action were later confirmed by the votes he cast as a justice.

Daily Lives

PUBLIC AND PRIVATE SPACE
Life in the Underclass

During the 1880s Jacob Riis "discovered" a class of people he described as invisible. They were "individuals who have lost connection with home life, or never had any, or whose homes had ceased to be sufficiently separated, decent, and desirable to afford what are regarded as ordinary wholesome influences of home and family." A century later investigators for the *Chicago Tribune* discovered in American cities "a lost society dwelling in enclaves of despair and chaos that infect and threaten the communities at large." This ghetto world of dilapidated housing, poverty, and despair was home to as many as 5 million Americans. Yet while many of its spaces and avenues were public, it too was invisible, except when its private behavior became so violent or criminal that the news forced the broad middle class to pay attention.

Like Riis the *Tribune* reporters portrayed this urban blight through the story of individual lives. Dorothy Sands was one. In 1957 Dorothy, her mother, Ora Streeter, and the rest of her family lived in a one-room shack in rural Mississippi. Conditions there had improved little since the days of Reconstruction. The shack had neither electricity nor indoor plumbing. Ora finally decided to escape the South, her job, and her abusive husband. She took six small children to Chicago, where her mother lived. For her daughter Dorothy, "It was something like going to a new world."

Life in Chicago imposed disappointments and cruelties of its own. For several years Streeter struggled to make a decent life for her family. Arthritis finally prevented her from working and forced her to sign up for public assistance. Dorothy, the oldest child, assumed responsibility for the household. With what little time she had for herself, she reached the ninth grade. But at age 15 her dream of a nursing career ended when she discovered she was pregnant. In 1965, after her mother died, Dorothy began a relationship with Carra Little, a man who promised he could not get her pregnant. Within a year, Dorothy had her second child. She asked the doctors to sterilize her, but they refused. And the children kept arriving—four more of them. "When you are young, you don't really think about the future," Dorothy recalled. "You say, 'If I have another baby, then I have another child.'"

After Little died suddenly of a heart attack in 1976, the household disintegrated. Dorothy's oldest

The bleak spaces of public housing in the "Chicago projects" and in other decaying urban areas made life difficult for residents.

neither made action a legislative priority. Even so, both presidents shaped social policy through their appointments to the Supreme Court. Reagan placed three members on the bench, including in 1981 Sandra Day O'Connor, the first woman to sit on the high court. Bush nominated two justices. As more liberal members of the Court retired (including William Brennan and Thurgood Marshall), the decisions handed down became distinctly more conservative.

On two occasions, the Senate challenged this trend. In 1987, it rejected Robert Bork, a nominee whose opposition to long-established Court policies on privacy and civil rights led even some Republicans to oppose him. But this fight proved so exhausting that the Senate quickly approved President Reagan's alternate choice, Antonin Scalia. In the end, Scalia proved to be the Court's most conservative member.

In 1991 the Senate also hotly debated President Bush's nomination of Clarence Thomas, an outspoken black conservative and former member of the Reagan

The Clarence Thomas hearings

daughter, Barbara, like her mother and grandmother before her, became pregnant at age 15. By 1985 Dorothy was suffering from chronic depression and considered suicide. She was a 37-year-old grandmother living in a three-room apartment with five of her six children, her daughter LaWanda's new boyfriend, two grandchildren ages 7 and 2, and two teenage runaways. In 20 years, the family had never been off welfare and no one in the household had held a regular job. Only one of her children attended school other than briefly.

With public assistance money Dorothy could afford only rooms in a dilapidated three-story building on Chicago's West Side. Each evening people pried open the building's front door to do "crack" or drink 100 percent grain alcohol. Sometime in 1985 the family stopped bathing because every time they turned on the water, plaster fell into the tub. The building manager reneged on his promise to make repairs. So the children just stood over the sink and washed their clothes by hand. An electrical wire attached to a bare bulb doubled as a clothesline. Only Dorothy had a room of her own. The girls slept on canvas cots in one room, while the boys took turns between cots and a mattress on the living room floor. Meals were irregular affairs, because money was scarce and no one liked to cook. For two weeks each month the family splurged on eggs for breakfast and Spam for dinner. More often they got by on hot dogs, rice, and beans.

Of the neighborhood's 61,500 people, more than half received some form of welfare. People lucky enough to find work quickly moved away. The social agencies that existed to help people in trouble had largely stopped trying. One government official described "a caste of people almost totally dependent on the state, with little hope of breaking free." By the late 1980s murders, drive-by shootings, and guns in school had become commonplace. For the rest of the American people, more fortunate in their circumstances, a question persisted: how could the problems of the largely invisible underclass be solved before the violence and desperation of their private world overwhelmed the city streets? As rioting swept Los Angeles in the spring of 1992 Americans had to wonder if that question had gone too long unanswered.

administration. The confirmation hearings became even more heated when Anita Hill, a woman who had worked for Thomas, testified that he had sexually harassed her. Because Hill was a professor of law and herself a Reagan conservative, her often graphic testimony riveted millions of television viewers. Suddenly the hearings raised new issues. Women's groups blasted the all-male Judiciary Committee for keeping Hill's allegations private until reporters uncovered the story. Thomas and his defenders accused his opponents of using a disgruntled woman to help conduct a latter-day lynching. In the end the Senate narrowly voted to confirm, and Thomas joined Scalia as one of the Court's most conservative members.

Evidence of the Court's changing stance came most clearly in its attitude toward affirmative action—those laws that gave preferred treatment to minority groups in order to remedy past discrimination. State and federal courts and legislatures had used techniques such as busing and the setting of quotas to overturn past injustices. As early as 1978, however, the Court began to set limits on affirmative action. In *Bakke v. Regents of the University of California* (1978), the majority ruled that college admissions staffs could not set fixed quotas, although they could still use race as a guiding factor in trying to create a more diverse student body. Increasingly, the Court made it easier for white citizens to challenge affirmative action programs. At the same time it set higher standards for those who wished to put forward a claim of discrimination. "An amorphous claim that there has been past discrimination in a particular industry cannot justify the use of an unyielding racial quota," wrote Justice O'Connor in 1989.

Court decisions on abortion and religion in public schools demonstrated a similar desire to set limits on the established precedents. *Planned Parenthood v. Casey* (1992) upheld a woman's constitutional right to an abortion, but it also allowed states to place new restrictions on the procedure. Other Court decisions let stand laws restricting abortions and even abortion counseling by clinics or hospitals receiving federal funds. And while the Court affirmed that religious teachings or prayer could have no official status in public schools, it allowed students to engage in voluntary prayer as well as to form religious clubs meeting after school.

Disillusionment and Anger

Ronald Reagan had given a sunny face to conservatism. He had assured voters that if taxes were cut, the economy would revive and deficits would fall. He promised that if "big government" could be scaled back, there would be a new "morning in America." Yet after a decade of conservative leadership, with its hands-off approach, the deficit had ballooned and state and local governments were larger than ever. A growing number of Americans felt that the institutions of government had come seriously off track. Indeed, such cynicism was fueled by the attacks on big government by Reagan and Bush.

S&L crisis

As the AIDS epidemic spread in the 1980s, quilts such as these expressed sorrow for lost friends and loved ones. The quilts also served to raise public awareness of the need for a more effective policy to aid the afflicted and fight the disease.

A series of longer-term crises contributed to this sense of disillusionment. One of the most threatening centered on the nation's savings and loan institutions. By the end of the decade these thrifts were failing at the highest rate since the Great Depression. To help increase bank profits, the Reagan administration and Congress had agreed to cut back federal regulations. That move allowed savings and loan institutions to invest their funds more speculatively. Few depositors noticed or cared, because their money was insured by the Federal Savings and Loan Insurance Corporation. The government, however, had to pay depositors if these banks failed. Reagan's advisers as well as members of Congress ignored the warnings that fraud and mismanagement were increasing sharply. Only during the Bush administration did it become clear that the cost of rebuilding the savings banks and paying off huge debts might run into hundreds of billions of dollars.

The late 1980s also brought a public health crisis. Americans were spending a higher percentage of their resources on medical care than were citizens in other nations, yet they were no healthier. New technologies that improved care also burdened the system with heavy expenses. Doctors complained of excessive paperwork. As medical costs soared, more than 30 million Americans had no health insurance. The crisis was worsened by a fatal disorder that physicians began diagnosing in the early 1980s: acquired immunodeficiency syndrome, or AIDS. With no cure available, the disease threatened to take on epidemic proportions not only in the United States but around the globe. Yet because the illness at first struck hardest at the male homosexual community and intravenous drug users, many groups in American society were hesitant to address the problem.

Bank failures, skyrocketing health costs, anger over poverty and discrimination—none of these problems by themselves had the power to derail the conservative rebellion. Still, the various crises demonstrated how pivotal government had become in providing social services and limiting the abuses of powerful private interests in a highly industrialized society. Neither the Reagan nor the Bush administration had developed a clear way to address such problems without the intervention of government—the sort of intervention envisioned by a more activist Republican, Teddy Roosevelt, at the turn of the century.

The Election of 1992

In the end, George Bush's inability to rein in soaring government deficits proved most damaging to his reelection prospects. "Read my lips! No new taxes," he had pledged to campaign audiences in 1988. But the president and Congress were at loggerheads over how to reach the holy grail of so many conservatives: a balanced budget. In 1985 Congress had passed the Gramm-Rudman Act, establishing a set of steadily increasing limits on federal spending. These limits were meant to force Congress and the president to make hard choices needed to reach a balanced budget. If they did not, automatic across-the-board cuts would go into effect. By 1990 the law's automatic procedures were threatening programs like Medicare, which Republicans and Democrats alike supported. Facing such unpopular cuts, Bush agreed to a package of new taxes along with budget cuts. Conservatives felt betrayed, and in the end, the deficit grew larger all the same.

Gramm-Rudman Act

As the election of 1992 approached, unemployment stood at more than 8 percent, penetrating to areas of the economy not affected by most recessions. Statistics showed that wages for middle-class families had not increased since the early 1970s and had actually declined during Bush's presidency. Many Reagan Democrats seemed ready to return to the party of Franklin Roosevelt, who had mobilized an activist government in a time of economic depression. Other disillusioned voters were drawn to the maverick candidacy of Texas computer billionaire H. Ross Perot. The blunt-talking, jug-eared Perot (he, too, made fun of his ears) demanded a government run

White-collar unemployment

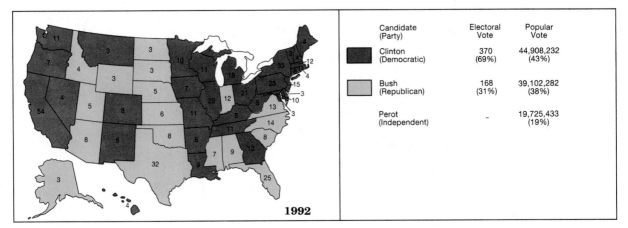

Candidate (Party)	Electoral Vote	Popular Vote
Clinton (Democratic)	370 (69%)	44,908,232 (43%)
Bush (Republican)	168 (31%)	39,102,282 (38%)
Perot (Independent)	-	19,725,433 (19%)

1992

Election of 1992

like a business but free of big-business lobbyists. He declared his willingness to administer the bitter medicine needed to lower the deficit.

Meanwhile, the Democrats gave their nomination to Governor Bill Clinton of Arkansas. Clinton had personal hurdles to surmount: he was dogged by reports of marital infidelity, by his lame admission that he had tried marijuana while a student (but had not inhaled), and by his youthful opposition to the war in Vietnam. Still, he gained ground by hammering away at Bush for failing to revive the economy.

"It's the economy . . ."

"It's the economy, stupid!" read the sign tacked up at his election headquarters to remind Clinton workers of the campaign's central theme. Clinton painted himself as a new kind of Democrat: moderate, willing to work with business, and not a creature of liberal interest groups.

The Bush campaign miscalculated by allowing the most conservative members of the party to dominate the Republican convention. Middle-of-the-road voters turned to Perot and Clinton. Clinton himself proved a resourceful campaigner, even willing to play his saxophone on MTV. On Election Day, he captured 43 percent of the popular vote (to Bush's 38 and Perot's 19) in the largest turnout—55 percent—in 20 years. The election of four women to the Senate, including the first African American woman, Carol Moseley Braun, indicated that gender had become an electoral factor.

The 1992 election left the fate of the conservative revolution unresolved. Under Reagan and Bush the economy had grown and inflation had subsided. Yet prosperity benefited mostly those at the upper end of the income scale. The majority of Americans saw their financial situation stagnate or grow worse. Reagan and Bush both had supported a conservative social agenda that sought to restrict abortion rights, return prayer to the schools, and end affirmative action, but neither had done much to put that agenda into action. Both presidents significantly weakened the capacity of the federal government to implement social programs. No longer did Americans expect Washington to solve all the issues of the day. How, then, would the nation meet the future needs of the increasing numbers of poor, minority, elderly, and immigrant Americans?

Reagan and Bush had also presided over the end of the cold war. Despite a growing isolationist sentiment among Democrats and Republicans, both presidents had shown a willingness to assert American power—in Libya, in Lebanon, in Nicaragua, in Panama, in Somalia, in the Persian Gulf—though these were situations in which no major conflict threatened. What role would the United States play in the post–cold war era, when it stood as the lone superpower in the world arena? That was a question for William Jefferson Clinton as he sought to lead the United States into the twenty-first century.

chapter summary

During the years of the Reagan and Bush administrations, the nation's political and social agenda was increasingly determined by a conservative movement, including newly politicized evangelical Christians, that sought to restore traditional religious and family values, patriotism, and a more limited role for government.

- Ronald Reagan led the conservative tide with a program to limit the power of labor unions, reduce government regulation, lower taxes, and sharply increase spending on the military.

- Despite a revived economy, Reaganomics had two undesirable outcomes: huge government budget deficits and a growing gap in income between the rich and poor.

- Conservative appointments to the federal judiciary and the Supreme Court led to decisions increasing limits on government intervention in the areas of civil rights, affirmative action, abortion rights, and the separation of church and state.

- Reagan's efforts to "stand tall" in foreign policy led to the Iran-Contra scandal, which revealed a broad pattern of illegal arms shipments to right-wing rebels in Nicaragua and the trading of arms to Iran in an unsuccessful attempt to win the release of hostages in Lebanon—actions for which the president was sharply criticized but not impeached.

- Both Reagan and George Bush welcomed reforms set in motion by Mikhail Gorbachev that led by 1991 to the breakup of the Soviet Union, reductions in nuclear arms, and an end to the cold war.

- In the post–cold war era, regional conflicts proved more troublesome as Iraq's invasion of Kuwait led Bush to form a UN coalition that routed the forces of Saddam Hussein in Operation Desert Storm.

- For George Bush, a continuing recession, high budget deficits, and high unemployment undermined his bid for reelection.

interactive learning

The Primary Source Investigator CD-ROM offers the following materials related to this chapter:

- Interactive maps: **Election of 1980** (M7); **Election of 1992** (M7); and **The United States in Latin America, 1895–1941** (M21)

- A collection of primary sources investigating the Reagan and Bush years in the 1980s and early 1990s, including President Reagan's "Evil Empire" speech, Reagan's Iceland summit address, and President Bush's diary during Desert Storm. Several other sources explore society in America, such as transcripts from the Clarence Thomas hearings. Other sources, such as a photo of a double-decker hamburger and one woman's story of her struggle with her weight, illustrate American culture.

additional reading

During Ronald Reagan's political career, the public knew little about the man or his inner thoughts. That remains true even after the publication of Edmund Morris, *Dutch* (1999), despite the author's unprecedented access to Reagan in the White House. Unable to penetrate Reagan's outer shell, Morris resorted to fiction to bring more light to his subject. Even less credible have been the efforts of Reagan's conservative supporters to turn him into a political giant. See, for example, Dinesh D'Souza, *Ronald Reagan* (1999). Haynes Johnson, *Sleep Walking through History: America in the Reagan Years* (1991); Jane Mayer and Doyle McManus, *Landslide: The Unmaking of the President, 1984–1988* (1988); and Gary Wills, *Reagan's America* (1987), still offer readers more insight, as does David Stockman's White House memoir, *The Triumph of Politics: The Inside Story of the Reagan Revolution* (1986). Godrey Hodgson, *The World Turned Right Side Up: A History of the Conservative Ascendancy in America* (1996), puts the conservatism of the 1980s into a wider perspective.

George Bush has inspired no major biography, but his *All the Best, George Bush: My Life and Other Writings* (1999) and, with Brent Scowcroft, *A World Transformed* (1999) give a picture of the person and his foreign policy. Thomas Friedman, *From Beirut to Jerusalem* (1988), offers many insights into Middle East politics, and Dilip Hiro, *Desert Shield to Desert Storm: The Second Gulf War* (1992), treats the war from a non-American perspective. Frank Levy, *The New Dollars and Dreams* (rev. ed. 1999), analyzes the patterns of income inequality. Racial currents of the decade are powerfully conveyed in Nicholas Lemann, *The Promised Land* (1991). For a fuller list of readings, see the Bibliography at www.mhhe.com/davidsonnation5.

significant events

1978   *Bakke v. Regents of the University of California*

1979   Moral Majority established; Sandinistas overthrow Somoza in Nicaragua

1980   Reagan defeats Carter

1981   Reagan breaks air traffic controllers' strike; recession sets in; Economic Recovery Tax Act; United States begins aiding Nicaraguan Contras

1982   Attack on U.S. Marine barracks in Lebanon

1983   Reagan proposes the Strategic Defense Initiative; invasion of Grenada

1984   Boland Amendment passed; Reagan defeats Mondale

1985   Gramm-Rudman Act sets in motion a plan to balance budget; United States begins secret arms-for-hostages negotiations with Iran

1986   Reykjavík summit; Iran-Contra scandal breaks

1988   Congress passes drug and welfare reform bills; Bush elected president

1989   Eastern Europe nations break with Soviet Union; China crushes revolt in Tiananmen Square; Berlin Wall taken down

1990   Iraq invades Kuwait; Clean Air Act; Bush agrees to higher taxes in budget agreement with Congress

1991
Operation Desert Storm launched; Strategic Arms Reduction Treaty (START) concluded; Clarence Thomas hearings; 11 former republics of the Soviet Union become the Commonwealth of Independent States

1992   *Planned Parenthood v. Casey* sets new restrictions on abortion; Clinton defeats Bush and Perot

Chapter 33

*J*uan Chanax had never been far from San Cristobal, a small village in the Guatemalan highlands. In that region, some two thousand years earlier, his Mayan ancestors had created one of the world's great civilizations. During the twentieth century, San Cristobal had escaped the political upheavals that disrupted much of Guatemala. Still, by the 1970s Chanax, a weaver, struggled to support his young family. Work at a nearby American textile factory brought steady wages, but scarcely enough to survive on. The coming of the factory alerted him to a larger world outside his mountain village. In 1978 he decided that the only way he could help his sick son and improve himself—to "*superarme,*" as he put it—was to go north. He told his wife "the United States was a place where people could work and make their own lives." So began a journey that changed the destiny of Juan Chanax, San Cristobal, and the multicultural community in America.

Reaching his destination was not easy. Several times Chanax was robbed. Twice border guards turned him away. On his third attempt he successfully eluded the border patrol and made his way to Houston, Texas, with little more than a letter introducing him to several Guatemalans. Through them he learned of a maintenance job at a Randall's supermarket.

In the late 1970s, high oil prices had brought a boom to Houston. And as the city grew, Randall's expanded with it. That expansion meant plenty of low-wage jobs for people like Chanax, even though he had almost no education and had entered the United States illegally. Randall's did not want just any low-wage

NATION OF NATIONS IN A GLOBAL COMMUNITY

1980–2000

preview • A renewed wave of immigration in the last decades of the century was only one way in which global ties increased both diversity in the United States and the nation's interdependence with the rest of the world. The rise of the Internet signaled a revolution in global communications and commerce as well. Amid the decade's robust economic expansion, the Clinton administration sparred with Republicans over how best to define the multicultural contours of a nation of nations.

workers. The chain specialized in high-priced goods in fancy suburban stores. Its upscale customers received valet parking, hassle-free shopping, and service from uniformed employees. Shortly before Chanax began working at Randall's, one of its managers had a falling out with several African American employees. When the manager criticized their work, they argued heatedly, until one employee finally threw a mop at the manager and quit.

That incident proved to be Chanax's opportunity. Unlike the worker who stormed out, Chanax was happy to do any job without complaint. The minimum wage was more than twice what he earned in Guatemala. Within several weeks he began to wire money home to his family. And when the manager said Randall's would soon need more workers, Chanax arranged for his brother-in-law and an uncle to come north. Over time Randall's began to hire Guatemalans exclusively. Shortly before a new store opened, the managers would tell Chanax how many maintenance people they needed. He would then recruit more Mayans from San Cristobal.

As the newcomers arrived, Chanax and the experienced Mayans prepared them for the job. Preparation meant more than learning to clean and stack. The recruits were also told to arrive on time, work hard, disrespect no one, and use proper manners. If a problem arose, they were to go not to a Randall's manager but to another Guatemalan. "That way," as Chanax observed, "if there was any problem, if a man

By 1995 over a quarter of a million laborers worked in Southern California's garment industry, many of them recently arrived immigrants from Mexico and Central America. "Very often we work until eight or nine at night the six days and then work a half day Sunday," commented one. Here Chicano artist Yolanda López celebrates the virtues of a hardworking seamstress by portraying her as the Virgin of Guadalupe, the traditional patron saint of Mexico.

was sick or had to leave work early or anything, we would solve it ourselves." As each store opened, the Guatemalans would have the entire maintenance department staffed and ready to work 24 hours a day, seven days a week.

Within five years after Chanax reached Houston, over a thousand Mayans from San Cristobal were working at Randall's. A single person had created what scholars call a migration chain. Through Chanax, Randall's had found access to a minimum-wage workforce who would perform willingly—in the company's words—as "cheerful servants." The Mayans, in turn, found opportunities unavailable in Guatemala. In the process Chanax and other early immigrants had become department managers and supervising assistants. Many of their wives worked as maids and servants in the homes of Houston's rapidly growing upper-income communities.

In many ways, Juan Chanax and his fellow Guatemalans mirrored the classic tale of immigrants realizing the American dream. In suburban Houston they formed

Migration chain

their own community in an area that came to be known as Las Americas. There, various Central American immigrant groups established churches and social clubs amid some 90 apartment complexes that a decade or two earlier had housed mostly young, single office workers. On weekends and evenings rival soccer teams played in the nearby park. (Juan, also the soccer league's president, helped new teams fill out the forms required by the parks department to use its fields.) The growth of Las Americas in the late twentieth century echoed the pattern of immigrants who had come to the United States at the century's opening.

Changes in the patterns of global immigration

Yet those patterns had changed in important ways, too. Although cities remained the mecca of most immigrants, Juan and many newcomers of the 1980s and 1990s settled in suburban areas, particularly in the West and Southwest. Industrial factories provided the lion's share of work in the 1890s, but a century later the service industries—grocery stores, fast-food chains, janitorial companies—absorbed many more of the new arrivals. Even the faces had changed, as European immigrants found themselves outnumbered by Latinos from Mexico and Central America as well as by Asians from the Philippines, China, Korea, Southeast Asia, and the Indian subcontinent, not to mention increasing numbers of Arabs from the Middle East and Africans. This broad geographic range reflected perhaps the most important shift in immigration: its truly global character. Transportation and communications networks tied immigrants to their home countries more strongly than in the past, allowing immigrants like Juan to keep regularly in touch with their former neighbors and relatives by phone as well as mail. Immigrants continued to participate in home-country politics more easily; they could wire money instantly to relatives and even build homes thousands of miles away where one day they planned to retire.

The global nature of immigration was only one aspect of an American society more tightly linked to the world community. For half a century the cold war had shaped American responses to the wider world. With the fall of the Soviet Union, attention shifted toward the need to manage regional conflicts. International economic ties linked the United States with the rest of the world in equally important ways, because the effects of a recession or financial collapse in Russia or Thailand could spread to other countries in a matter of weeks or months. Finally, the 1990s witnessed a communications revolution as the Internet tied together correspondents, consumers, manufacturers, and information systems. In short, the movement of people, financial capital, and data around the globe forced a nation of nations to adapt itself to an increasingly global community.

The New Immigration

The Immigration Act of 1965 (page 995) altered the face of American life—perhaps more significantly than any piece of legislation among Lyndon Johnson's Great Society programs. The lawmakers who passed the act did not expect such far-reaching changes, for they assumed that Europeans would continue to predominate among newcomers. Yet reform of the old quota system opened the way for a wave of immigrants unequaled since the beginning of the century.

Economic political causes of immigration

Turmoil abroad pushed many immigrants toward the United States, beginning in the 1960s with Fidel Castro's revolution in Cuba and unrest in the Dominican Republic. The war in Vietnam and its aftermath produced more than 500,000 refugees in the 15 years after 1975. Revolutionary conflicts in Central America during the 1980s launched new streams. Yet economic factors played as great a role as the terrors of war. Although some Filipinos fled the repressive regime of Ferdinand Marcos, many more came to the United States in a more straightforward search for economic prosperity. When Mexico suffered an economic downturn in the 1980s, emigration there rose sharply.

In all, about 7 million immigrants, both legal and illegal, arrived in the United States between 1975 and 1995. The nation's foreign-born population rose to 9 percent, the highest proportion since World War II. The tide rose even more sharply in the 1990s, with the Latino population increasing by over 35 percent to about 30.3 million by 1999. The Asian American population grew at an even faster rate, to about 10.8 million. Through the decade a steadily expanding economy made immigrants a welcome source of new labor. Prosperity, in turn, reduced—though it did not eliminate—conflict among long-standing residents, new immigrants, and people on the margin of the labor market.

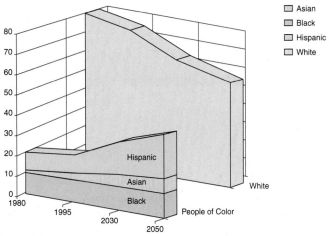

Projected Population Shifts, 1980–2050 The 6.5 million immigrants who arrived between 1990 and 1998 accounted for 32 percent of the increase in the total U.S. population. Census figures project an increasing racial and ethnic diversity. White population is projected to drop from 80 percent in 1980 to about 53 percent in 2050, with the nation's Latino population rising most sharply.

The New Look of America—Asian Americans

In 1970, 96 percent of Asian Americans were Japanese, Chinese, or Filipino. By the year 2000, those same three groups constituted only about half of all Asian Americans. As the diversity of Asian immigration increased, Asian Indians, Koreans, and Vietnamese came to outnumber Japanese Americans. The newcomers also varied dramatically in economic background, crowding both ends of the economic spectrum.

The higher end included many Chinese students who, beginning in the 1960s, sought out the United States for a college education, then found a job and stayed, eventually bringing in their families. "My brother-in-law left his wife in Taiwan and came here as a student to get his Ph.D. in engineering," explained Subi Lin Felipe. "After he received his degree, he got a job in San Jose. Then he brought in a sister and his wife, who brought over one of her brothers and me. And my brother's wife then came." Amy Tan, in her novel *The Joy Luck Club,* described the migration of upwardly mobile Chinese professionals to upscale urban and suburban neighborhoods. Asian Indians were even more acculturated upon arrival because about two-thirds entered the United States with college degrees already in hand. Indian engineers played a vital role in the computer and software industries. Similarly, Korean and Filipino professionals took skilled jobs, particularly in medical fields.

Prosperous newcomers

Yet Asian immigrants also included those on the lower rungs of the economic ladder. Among the new wave of Chinese immigrants, or *San Yi Man,* many blue-collar workers settled in the nation's Chinatowns, where they worked in restaurants or sewed in sweatshops. Without education and language skills, often in debt to labor contractors, most have remained trapped in Chinatown's ethnic economy. Refugees from war and revolution in Southeast Asia often made harrowing journeys. Vietnamese families crowded into barely seaworthy boats, sometimes only to be terrorized by pirates, other times nearly drowned in storms before reaching poorly equipped Thai refugee camps. By 1990 almost a million refugees had arrived in the United States, three-quarters of them from Vietnam, most of the others from

Blue-collar Asians

The Hmong people from Cambodia were among the many refugees fleeing Southeast Asia in the wake of the Vietnam War. While Chue and Nhia Thao Cha stayed in a refugee camp in Thailand, they stitched a traditional Hmong story cloth that, in this detail, shows refugees boarding a plane to come to the United States.

Laos or Cambodia. California and Texas absorbed the greatest number, with significant populations in Pennsylvania, Washington, and Minnesota. Among such populations, poor language skills and cultural differences locked workers into low-wage jobs and recurring cycles of unemployment.

Thus the profile of Asian immigration resembled an hourglass, with the most newcomers either relatively affluent or extremely poor. Even so, such statistics could be misleading. Although more Asian Americans made over $50,000 per year than any other racial or ethnic group, more than half of all Asian American families lived in just five metropolitan areas—Honolulu, Los Angeles, San Francisco, Chicago, and New York—where the cost of living ranked among the nation's highest. High prices meant real earnings were lower. On a per capita basis, only the Japanese and Indians among Asian Americans made above the national average in 1990.

Further, a close examination of employment patterns in those five cities showed that more Asians than whites worked in low-status, low-income jobs. Within professions like dentistry, nursing, and health technology where Asians found work, they often held the lower-paying positions. Those Asians who worked in sales were more often retail clerks than insurance agents or stockbrokers. A glass ceiling blocked many Asians from reaching the highest rungs in corporate management. As the *Wall Street Journal* reported, "the same companies that pursue them for technical jobs often shun them when filling managerial and executive positions."

Asian downward mobility

Finally, Asian Americans experienced two forms of downward mobility. First, highly educated Asian immigrants often found it difficult or impossible to land jobs in their professions. To American observers, Korean shopkeepers seemed examples of success, when in fact such owners often enough had been former professionals forced into the risky small-business world. One Filipino doctor noted that strict state licensing standards prevented him from opening up his own medical practice. Instead, he found himself working as a restaurant meat cutter, for employers who had no idea of his real occupation. "They thought I was very good at separating meat from the bone," he commented ironically. Second, schools reported significant numbers of Asian American students who were failing. This "lost generation" were most often the children of families who entered the United States with little education and few job skills.

The New Look of America—Latinos

Like Asian Americans, Latinos in the United States constituted a diverse mosaic, reflecting dozens of immigrant streams. Although the groups shared a language, they usually settled in distinct urban and suburban barrios across the United States. Such enclave communities provided support to newcomers and an economic foothold for newly established businesses. Money circulated within a community; the workers and owners of an ethnic grocery, for example, spent their wages at neighboring stores, whose profits fueled other immigrant businesses in a chain reaction.

Washington Heights, at the northern tip of New York City, followed that path as nearly a quarter of a million Dominicans settled there during the 1970s and 1980s. A hundred blocks to the south, Manhattan's downtown skyscrapers seemed distant; shopkeepers' stereos along the major thoroughfares boomed music of trumpets and congas, while peddlers pushed heavily loaded shopping carts through busy streets, crying "¡A peso! ¡A peso!" ("For a dollar!"). In addition, Dominican social clubs planned dances or hosted political discussions. Sports clubs competed actively. Similarly, in Miami and elsewhere in South Florida, Cuban Americans created their own self-sustaining enclaves. A large professional class and strong community leadership brought them prosperity and political influence.

The Dominicans of Washington Heights

Along the West Coast, Los Angeles was the urban magnet for many Latino (and Asian) immigrants. Mexican immigrants had long flocked to East Los Angeles, which in the 1990s remained convenient to the jobs in factories, warehouses, and railroad yards across the river. Many Mexican Americans now owned their own businesses and homes, whose neatly kept backyards were filled with blooming bougainvillea. But beginning in the mid-1980s and 1990s the neighborhood of MacArthur Park became the focal point for the newest immigrants from Mexico and Central America. MacArthur Park was less developed as a community, and many of its residents were transient, passing quickly to other neighborhoods or jobs. Vendors of pirated audiocassettes competed with the occasional evangelist preacher, while hand-lettered signs in windows offered services to parents working long hours: "SE CUIDAN BEBÉS" (babysitting).

East Los Angeles

As more factories and service industries became decentralized, locating themselves beyond urban downtowns, the barrios followed as well. Las Americas near Houston, where Juan Chanax lived, was one example; but suburban barrios could be found dotted all across the nation, from Rockville, Maryland, to Pacoima, California, near Burbank. Pacoima's well-kept bungalows housed working-class Mexican Americans who had lived in California for decades. But the front lawns of many residences were often paved over to hold the cars of additional workers or families, and the garages were converted to dormitories with a sink and toilet, where four or five newcomers from Central America could rent a spot to lay a bedroll on the cement floor.

Illegal Immigration

Because Mexico and the United States share such a long common border—and an equally long history of intermingling of peoples and cultures—many Mexicans entered the United States illegally. But the number of illegal immigrants increased

Daily Lives

TIME AND TRAVEL

Motels as an Ethnic Niche

For Americans who traveled by car in the 1950s, the end of the day meant a stop at a motel. These motels were mostly mom-and-pop businesses in rural towns or along highways into the nation's cities. Because the motel industry had no standards, a motorist never knew what to expect. A flashy sign might lure the unsuspecting tourist into a rattrap. Some motels catered to the hot sheet trade, offering privacy for a midday tryst. Still, the majority provided clean sheets, a decent bed, and a hot shower at an affordable price.

In the 1960s, with the completion of the main links of the interstate highway system, the motel business changed. The interstates brought drivers to major exchanges. There, large chains like Ramada, Sheraton, and Holiday Inn were ready to provide travelers with accommodations that were familiar whether they were in California or Maine. Holiday Inn's slogan was "At Holiday Inn the best surprise is no surprise." The rise of the major motel chains spelled financial disaster for the mom-and-pop operations, which were often built in older, less desirable locations that by the 1970s were showing signs of decay.

A ray of hope came from an unexpected source. For reasons that remain far from clear, immigrants from India began to go into the lodging business. One Indian motel owner cited an ancient Sanskrit phrase, *Atithi devo bhava*—the guest is God. "Hospitality is in our culture," he concluded. But there were other reasons, more practical. After the Immigration Reform Act of 1965 Indians, along with other Asians, came to the United States in large numbers. Newcomers of modest means saw motels as an attractive opportunity. Because many of the new Indians were professionals who did not "like working for other people," as one owner recalled, motels supplied an independent business. They also provided housing without the need to tie up capital in a home. Prejudice played a role too. More affluent Indians who approached the large chains learned quickly that "the big brands didn't really want us."

By the mid-1980s Indians owned 50 percent of all the non-chain motels in the country. Even more remarkable, 70 percent of those Indians shared the same name—Patel. A common joke among them was that "in some American small

Dinu Patel, the owner of a motel in Branford, Connecticut. By 1999 a little over 50 percent of all American non-chain motels were owned by people of Indian origin.

---

during the 1980s as Central Americans joined the northward flow, along with Mexicans escaping a sharp economic downturn in their own country. By 1985, the number of illegal immigrants in the United States was estimated at anywhere from 2 to 12 million.

Immigration and Control Act of 1986

Congress attempted to stem that flow by passing the Immigration and Control Act of 1986. Tightened border security was coupled with a new requirement that American employers bear the responsibility of certifying their workers as legal residents of the United States. At the same time, those illegal immigrants who had arrived before 1986 were granted amnesty and allowed to become legal residents. In the end, however, the terms of the law failed to create the clean slate Congress had hoped for. California's fruit and vegetable growers, who worried that they would not have enough laborers under the new rules, lobbied for exceptions to towns they think that 'Patel' is an Indian word for 'motel.'" In fact, the name identified them as the members of one of India's four principal castes—the *vaishyas,* or traders. Among Indians, Patel was as common a name as Smith was to Americans. When the many Patels emigrated to the United States, they brought their experience in commerce with them.

A closer look at the motel phenomenon makes the story a bit less unusual. Sociologists have defined such occupational clustering as a "nonlinear ethnic niche." After the early pioneers from a group discover the opportunities in a particular enterprise or profession, they attract fellow ethnics to it. What Indians did with motels, Arabs in greater Detroit did with gas stations, Koreans with groceries, and Vietnamese in Los Angeles with fingernail salons.

Once an ethnic group achieved dominance in a niche, other groups found it difficult to move in. Indians kept close track of any motel properties that came up for sale. Hotel brokers, in turn, learned that they were among the most reliable prospects. "If it's a motel with less than 60 rooms," one broker commented, "the likely buyers will be Indians 98 times out of 100. And why not? They run them better than anyone else." All that was needed, one owner recalled, was financing, which relatives and other Indians generally provided, and "the will to work long hours." One Indian who moved from London to Hickory, North Carolina, in 1990 bought a motel for $713,000. His father gave him $50,000 and his in-laws another $50,000 to cover the down payment. At first he thought Hickory was "Hicksville." "The whole town sat out on the porch in rocking chairs," he recalled. The culture shock soon wore off and Hickory became home. Careful management and shrewd investment paid large dividends. In 1999 the property was appraised at almost $2 million.

Among Indians this motel success story is more the norm than an exception. By the late 1990s Indian motels employed over 800,000 people and had property valued at close to $40 billion. In fact, Indians provided 37 percent of all the hotel rooms in America. Twenty five years ago, "the hotel establishment . . . didn't want to know about us," one owner remarked. "But now we are the establishment."

the rules, which allowed over 1.7 additional illegal immigrants to gain amnesty. Furthermore, the many immigrants who suddenly became legal under the terms of the law quickly sought to reunite their families, bringing in wives and children illegally. Reluctantly, the federal government decided it could not break up these families, and it allowed them to live illegally in the United States while they applied for visas. By 1995 the backlog in applications had soared to over 800,000 new submissions.

Thus by 1996, the illegal population of Latinos in the United States stood at about 5 million people—about the same number as in 1986, when the immigration reform act was passed. Thus legal immigrants continued to be intertwined with illegals in a host of different ways: as relatives helping loved ones make the transition to living in the United States, as landlords boarding newcomers until they could get on their feet, as links with communities in the home country—just as Juan Chanax continued to be after he received amnesty from the act in 1986.

Links with the Home Country

Because systems of communication and transportation drew the world closer, the new immigrants found it easier to maintain links with their points of origin. Chanax, we have seen, regularly wired money back to relatives in Guatemala, and he was hardly alone in the practice. Pacoima, the suburban barrio outside Burbank, California, boasted only a small town center. But along that half-mile stretch of Van Nuys Boulevard, 13 different currency exchanges were open for business to handle immigrant funds. By 1992, the amount of funds sent worldwide was so great that it was surpassed in volume only by the currency flows of the global oil trade.

And not just money traveled these routes. An immigrant entering La Curaçao, a furniture store in Los Angeles's MacArthur Park, could sign up to buy a bedroom suite on the installment plan. When the payments were completed, the furniture was released—not in Los Angeles but at a branch warehouse in El Salvador, where relatives could pick up the purchase. Cultural ties remained strong as well.

Banda music

Young Mexican immigrants flocked on Saturday night to popular dance halls like the Lido in Los Angeles to hear a variety of music known as *banda*. Women wore tight tank tops and jeans or skirts, while the men's cowboy outfits were distinguished by their *cuarta*, a small riding whip at the belt, and by a kerchief hanging from the right hip pocket, with the name of the wearer's native Mexican state embroidered proudly for all to see. State by state, the band leader would call out a welcome to *"nuestros amigos"* ("our friends") from the various states, such as Sinaloa or Jalisco. In return, each region's group of immigrants would cheer and stomp their approval.

Religious Diversity

The global nature of the new immigration also reshaped the religious faiths of America. During the 1950s, most Americans' sense of religious diversity encompassed the mainline Protestant churches, Roman Catholicism, and Judaism. But immigrants brought with them not only their own brands of Christianity and Judaism but also Buddhist, Hindu, and Islamic beliefs. By 1999 there were perhaps 5 to 6 million Muslims in the United States. Many had emigrated from Arab states, but adherents from South Asia made up an even greater number. Buddhists and Hindus numbered about a million each.

Mainline Protestants and Catholics changed as well. The Presbyterian Church (U.S.A.) increased its Korean-speaking congregations from about 20 in 1970 to over 350. In New York City, Episcopalian services were held in 14 different languages. And Catholic churches increasingly found themselves celebrating mass in both English and Spanish. Such arrangements took place not only in urban congregations such as the Church of the Nativity in South Central Los Angeles (where Latinos alternated services with African Americans) but increasingly even in rural areas like Columbus Junction, Iowa, whose Catholic church was energized by Mexican Americans working in a nearby meat-processing plant.

The religious and cultural diversity of the new immigrant streams broadened the ties between the United States and the rest of the world. Despite the end of the cold war, the future of that world remained as uncertain as ever. Regional conflict in

At Our Lady of Guadalupe Catholic Mission, a family in the growing Mexican and Central American community of Muscatine, Iowa, held a *quinceañera*—a celebration of a girl's 15th birthday. Even towns in rural southeastern Iowa reflected the growing diversity of immigrant religious life.

Vietnam, the Middle East, the former Yugoslavia, and elsewhere became an increasing source of unrest. Such political unrest had driven many immigrants to America. Economic pressures around the world had encouraged many more to come. The nation's newest immigrants often linked the United States to the conflicts that presented the greatest challenge to American leadership in the post–cold war world.

With the presidential inauguration of 1992, William Jefferson Clinton became the first baby boomer to occupy the

The Clinton Presidency: Managing a New Global Order

White House. His wife, Hillary Rodham Clinton, would be the most politically involved presidential wife since Eleanor Roosevelt. Like so many couples of their generation, the Clintons were a two-career family. Both trained as lawyers at Yale University during the tumultuous 1960s. Bill chose politics as his career, while Hillary mixed private practice with public service. Their marriage had not been easy. Revelations of Clinton's sexual affairs as governor of Arkansas almost ruined his campaign for the presidency. The first couple seemed, however, more intent on making public policy than in defending their private lives.

As a young man, Bill Clinton had met John Kennedy, an event that inspired him to enter politics. Like Kennedy, Clinton envisioned himself as an activist president, not a more detached leader like Reagan. But Clinton's desire for major legislative initiatives ran up against the election results of 1992. He had received just 43 percent of the popular vote, while the Republicans had narrowed the Democratic majorities in Congress. Still, Clinton believed that an activist executive could achieve much, "even a president without a majority mandate coming in, if the president has a disciplined, aggressive agenda."

Clinton: Ambitions and Character

Clinton agenda

Certainly, the agenda was ambitious. The new president pledged to revive the economy and rein in the federal deficit that had grown so enormously during the Reagan years. Beyond that, he called for systematic reform of the welfare and health care systems as well as measures to reduce the increasing violence that too often had turned urban neighborhoods like Las Americas into war zones.

What often seemed missing in the White House was the "disciplined, aggressive" approach needed to move legislation through Congress. As one of his first presidential acts, Clinton attempted to eliminate a rule that banned homosexuals from serving in the military, fulfilling a campaign pledge to the gay community.

Don't ask; don't tell

Resistance from conservatives and the military led Clinton to accept a compromise position satisfactory to no one: "Don't ask; don't tell." As long as gay soldiers kept their sexual orientation private, they could serve their country. Clinton had also promised to appoint a cabinet reflecting the gender and racial diversity of the nation. When several nominees provoked controversy, he withdrew his support.

These early failures could be set down partly to the stumbles of a newcomer learning his way around the office. But larger issues of character could not be dismissed. One observer shrewdly noted that there were two Bill Clintons—the idealistic young man from Hope, Arkansas (his hometown), and the boy from Hot Springs (his mother's home). The latter was a resort town associated with the seamier side of Arkansas high life. With increasing frequency, the leadership mustered by the idealistic politician from Hope seemed to be undermined by the character flaws of the boy from Hot Springs.

Although Clinton's conservative opponents disliked his politics, it was the president's moral lapses that they most deeply resented. Critics nicknamed him "Slick Willie" and sought continually to expose discreditable or illegal dealings from his past. Accusations were published that, when Clinton was governor in the early 1980s, both he and his wife had received special treatment from a failed real estate

Whitewater

venture known as Whitewater. An air of mystery deepened when Vince Foster, a White House adviser and close friend of Hillary Clinton's from Arkansas, committed suicide. (The Clintons' most vocal critics suggested that the verdict of suicide was merely a murder cover-up, although the best evidence suggested depression as a cause.) Rumors also abounded about Clinton's womanizing, fanned in 1994 when a former Arkansas state employee, Paula Jones, filed a sexual harassment suit against the president. Under pressure from congressional conservatives, Attorney General Janet Reno appointed former judge Kenneth Starr as a special prosecutor to investigate Whitewater. But during Clinton's first term, investigations by Starr as well as two Senate committees produced no evidence that the Clintons had acted illegally.

The New World Disorder

Determined to focus on domestic issues, Clinton hoped to pay less attention to foreign affairs. He discovered that the "new world order," hailed by both Mikhail Gorbachev and George Bush, seemed more like a world of regional disorders. The

Boris Yeltsin

United States depended heavily on Russian president Boris Yeltsin to bring order out of chaos, yet market reforms failed to revive Russia's stagnant economy. Although Yeltsin maintained his own grip on power, he suffered from chronic ill health and routinely dismissed rivals for power. Elsewhere in the world, rampant ethnic and nationalist movements provoked a number of regional crises. By using American power in a limited way, Clinton gained considerable public support.

In sub-Saharan Africa, corruption and one-party rule severely weakened most economies, tribal violence mounted, and AIDS became epidemic. Brutal civil wars broke out in both Somalia and Rwanda. As a presidential candidate, Clinton had supported President Bush's decision in December 1992 to send troops to aid famine-relief efforts in Somalia. But attempts to install a stable government proved difficult. Tragically, the United States as well as European nations failed to intervene in Rwanda before over a million people were massacred in 1994.

Instability in Haiti pushed the president to take a bolder approach closer to home. In 1991 Haitian military leaders had forced their country's elected president, Jean-Bertrand Aristide, into exile. The harsh rule that followed prompted over 35,000 refugees to flee toward the United States, often in homemade boats and rafts. When a UN-sponsored economic embargo failed to oust the military regime, the Security Council in 1994 approved an invasion of Haiti by a multinational force. American troops proved crucial in convincing the military to leave. A smaller UN force stayed on to maintain order as new elections returned Aristide to the presidency.

Americans in Haiti

Yugoslavian Turmoil

Europe's most intractable trouble spot proved to be Yugoslavia, a nation divided by ethnic rivalries within a number of provinces, including Serbia, Croatia, and Bosnia.

Conflicts in Bosnia and Croatia

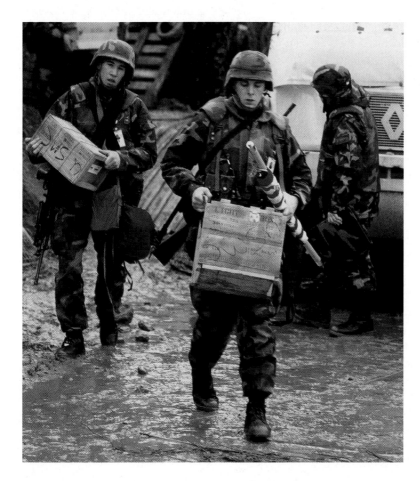

American troops were part of the NATO peacekeeping force sent to Bosnia after the Dayton Accords of 1995. These marines were among the first arrivals, who encountered chilly, wet weather.

After 1991 Bosnia and Croatia declared their independence from Yugoslavia, which was dominated by Serbia and its leader, Slobodan Milosevic. Milosevic urged the Serbian minorities within Bosnia and Croatia to take up arms, and he sent in Serbian troops to aid them. The Croats had sufficient military force to drive the Serbs out, but in Bosnia the population mix was more complex and resistance less organized. Serbs, Bosnians, and Muslims had lived side-by-side and intermarried for generations. After Bosnia became independent in 1992 both sides, but especially the Serbs, resorted to what was euphemistically referred to as "ethnic cleansing"—the massacre of rival populations—to secure control. Serbs even set up rape camps where they brutalized Muslim women.

The United States initially viewed the civil war in Yugoslavia as Europe's problem. But as the civilian death toll mounted to a quarter of a million, Nobel Peace Prize winner and Holocaust survivor Elie Wiesel beseeched President Clinton, "Stop the bloodshed. . . . Something, anything, must be done." Still, the ghosts of Vietnam loomed. Many members of Congress feared the prospect of American troops bogged down in a distant civil war. By 1995 Clinton had committed the United States to support NATO bombing of Serb forces, and when Bosnian and Croatian forces began to win back territory, the Serbs agreed to peace talks at a meeting in Dayton, Ohio. The Dayton Accords created separate Croatian, Bosnian, and Serbian nations. Some 60,000 NATO troops, including 20,000 Americans, moved into Bosnia to enforce the peace. Clinton had intervened successfully without the loss of American lives, though nearly ten years later U.S. troops remained in Bosnia.

Dayton Accords

Intervention in Kosovo

Having lost Croatia and Bosnia, Milosevic was determined not to lose Kosovo, a province in which the Serb minority ruled over a mostly Albanian population. In fighting Albanian rebels Serbian police and militia groups committed widespread atrocities against civilians. Hundreds of thousands of Albanian refugees poured into the surrounding countries. In the spring of 1999 Clinton committed U.S. forces to a NATO bombing campaign that hit targets in both Serbia and Kosovo. They destroyed much of Serbia's industrial, military, and transportation infrastructure. Without admitting defeat, Milosevic finally agreed to a NATO occupation of Kosovo. Once again, American troops entered as peacekeepers. The inclusion of troops from Russia, Serbia's traditional ally, helped prevent the revival of cold war tensions.

Middle East Peace

Steps forward in Haiti and the Balkans could not quiet fears of a new Middle East crisis. Sporadic protests and rioting by Palestinians in the Israeli-occupied territories of Gaza and the West Bank gave way in the 1990s to negotiations. At a ceremony hosted by President Clinton in 1993, Palestinian leader Yasir Arafat and Israeli prime minister Itzak Rabin signed a peace agreement permitting self-rule for Palestinians in the Gaza Strip and in Jericho on the West Bank. In 1995 Arafat became head of the West Bank Palestinian National Authority.

Middle East peace negotiations

Still, a full settlement remained elusive. As Clinton pursued negotiations, he found he had limited leverage to broker a lasting peace. The assassination of Prime Minister Rabin in 1995, by an angry Orthodox Jew, began a period of increased suspicion on both sides as extremists sought to derail the peace process. Clinton engaged in two marathon negotiating sessions with the two sides, in 1998 and in 2000 at Camp David, in hopes of hammering out an agreement that would allow for a separate Palestinian state alongside Israel. But the negotiations ended without agreement, and positions on both sides hardened. Whether in the Middle East, Eastern Europe, Africa, or the Caribbean, such regional crises demonstrated that a new global "world order" would be difficult to maintain.

Global Financial Disorder

Yet crises in such distant regions could not be ignored, because the world's political and economic systems had become so closely intertwined. The effects from a calamity in one area of the world rippled outward in unpredictable ways. In 1997 and 1998 a series of shocks nearly brought the world financial system to its knees.

The crisis began along the Pacific Rim. There the booming economies of Japan, South Korea, the Philippines, Thailand, and other East Asian nations faltered when the Japanese economy slid into a long recession that slowed growth throughout the world. Then the government of Thailand suddenly announced it was closing 56 of the nation's 58 banks. Quickly the Thai crisis spread to South Korea, Indonesia, and Hong Kong, causing foreign investors to withdraw their capital from the region. Prices of stocks on Asian exchanges fell precipitously. A popular sweatshirt announced its wearer "Formerly Rich."

Thai crisis sets off an Asian recession

Now Asian economies were no longer consuming large quantities of raw materials. As demand slackened for commodities such as oil, for example, prices fell, hurting exporting nations as diverse as Venezuela, Saudi Arabia, and Russia. Russia was especially hard hit, because the Yeltsin government had developed no effective system for collecting taxes, relying instead on the sale of commodities such as oil to finance its operations. To make up the deficit, the Russians borrowed heavily from foreign investors, offering attractive interest rates as high as 70 percent. In August 1998 the jerry-built Russian financial structure collapsed when the Yeltsin government defaulted on—refused to pay—much of its debt.

That default should not have had a severe effect on the global financial system—except that Russia's interest rates had been so tempting that many speculators had borrowed money to take advantage of them. To repay their creditors, these investors were forced to sell bonds they held from reasonably strong economies such as Israel, Egypt, Mexico, and Brazil. As those bonds lost value, other investors, worried that the chain reaction might continue, fled to the safe haven offered by U.S. Treasury bonds. Brazil's currency in particular was under severe pressure.

Hong Kong residents anxiously scan monitors displaying plummeting stock prices during the Asian recession of 1997 and 1998.

At first the United States had seemed insulated from these crises. But over the previous year, one respected investment fund, Long-Term Capital Management (LTCM), had bet an immense sum—about $120 billion—that the price of U.S. treasuries would fall and those of currencies in emerging markets like Russia's would rise. But the crisis that had spread from Thailand through Russia to Brazil sent prices and interest rates in exactly the opposite direction. LTCM suddenly faced bankruptcy—and many large American banks and investment firms had put large sums of their own money into LTCM. Fearing a financial crisis, Federal Reserve chair Alan Greenspan intervened. He arranged for LTCM's creditors to take over the embattled fund.

Financial crisis at home

Similarly the International Monetary Fund (IMF) organized loans and credits that pumped $115 billion into Asia, then $10.2 billion into Russia, $50 billion into Mexico (of which the United States supplied $20 billion), and yet another $41.5 billion for Brazil. Although Russia remained largely insolvent, Brazil recovered and the Asian economy began to turn around. But the resources of the IMF had been stretched dangerously thin in order to escape a full-blown world crisis. The fragile underpinnings of global financial markets had been exposed.

The Clinton Presidency on Trial

Throughout Clinton's presidency the nation experienced a powerful economic expansion. Despite low unemployment, there was little inflation. Prosperity allowed the president to eliminate the budget deficits that had soared during the 1980s. It also kept his popularity high despite recurring scandals. But soaring government revenues did not persuade Congress to support Clinton's reform agenda.

Recovery without Reform

Clinton program

In his first speech to Congress, Clinton proposed a program that began reducing the deficit but also provided investments to stimulate the economy and repair the nation's decaying public infrastructure. In contrast, Presidents Reagan and Bush had cut funds to rebuild schools, roads, dams, bridges, and other public structures. In August 1993 a compromise budget bill passed by only a single vote in the Senate, with Republicans blocking the stimulus portion of Clinton's program. Still, deficit reduction was a significant achievement. During the Reagan-Bush years deficits had risen sharply, despite conservative rhetoric about balancing the budget.

NAFTA

The victory in the budget battle provided Clinton with some momentum. In the fall he hammered together a bipartisan coalition to pass NAFTA, the North American Free Trade Agreement. With the promise of greater trade and more jobs, the pact linked the United States economy more closely with those of Canada and Mexico. The president also helped supporters of gun control overcome the powerful opposition of the National Rifle Association to pass the Brady Bill, which required a five-day waiting period on gun purchases. And with inner-city violence and drive-by shootings making headlines, the president pushed through a compromise crime bill in September 1994.

Health care reform

Health care reform topped Clinton's legislative agenda. A task force led by Hillary Rodham Clinton developed a plan to provide health coverage for all Americans, including the 37 million who in 1994 remained uninsured. The plan rejected a more sweeping single-payer system, in which the government would act as the central agency reimbursing medical expenses. At the same time, it proposed more far-reaching changes than did a Republican plan merely to reform insurance laws in order to make private medical coverage more readily available. But a host of interest groups attacked the proposal, especially small businesses that worried they would bear the brunt of the system's financing. Despite last-minute lobbying, even a compromise bill lacked the votes needed to win approval.

If the Clintons' plan had passed, the president and the Democratic majority in Congress might have staked their claim to a government that was actively responding to some of the long-term problems facing American society. But the failure of health care reform heightened the perception of an ill-organized administration and an entrenched Congress content with the status quo. Republicans, sensing the level

President Clinton's most ambitious attempt at reform was to overhaul the nation's health care system to provide all Americans with basic health care (along with a card to guarantee it). But medical interest groups defeated the proposal, arguing it would create yet another huge and inefficient bureaucracy. In 1996 Congress passed a more modest medical reform bill that made it easier for workers to retain health insurance if they lost or changed jobs.

of public frustration, stepped up their opposition to other Democratic legislation. The partisan battle only increased the sense of stalemate.

The Conservative Revolution Reborn

The 1994 midterm elections confirmed the public's anger over political gridlock. For the first time since the Eisenhower years, Republicans captured majorities in both the House and the Senate. The combative new Speaker of the House, Newt Gingrich of Georgia, proclaimed himself a "genuine revolutionary" and vowed to complete what Ronald Reagan had begun. Gingrich used the first hundred days of the new Congress to bring to a vote ten proposals from his campaign document "The Contract with America." The contract proposed a balanced budget amendment, tax cuts, and term limits for all members of Congress. To promote family values, its anticrime package included a broader death penalty and welfare restrictions aimed at reducing teen pregnancy. Although the term limits proposal did not survive, the other nine proposals were passed by the House.

The Contract with America

The whirlwind performance was impressive. "When you look back five years from now," enthused Republican governor Tommy Thompson of Wisconsin, "you're going to say 'they came, they, saw, they conquered.'" But the Senate was less eager to enact the House proposals. And as Republicans assembled a more comprehensive budget, it became clear that the public was increasingly worried about the Gingrich revolution. Fiscally, the Republicans set out to balance the federal budget in the year 2002 while still cutting taxes by $245 billion. To do that, they proposed scaling back Medicare expenditures by $270 billion and allowing Medicare premiums to double. Republicans also sought to roll back environmental legislation that had been passed over the previous quarter century. Their proposals reduced protection for endangered species, relaxed pollution controls set up by the Clean Water Act, and gave mining, ranching, and logging interests greater freedom to develop public lands.

"I am a genuine revolutionary," House Speaker Newt Gingrich proclaimed, and the newly elected Republican freshmen in Congress led the charge to complete the Reagan revolution. By clothing Newt's followers as stiff-armed, flag-waving militarists, illustrator Anita Kunz recalls Mussolini's overzealous Brown Shirts. Enough of the public agreed, forcing the Republicans to backpedal.

Government shutdown

When President Clinton threatened to veto the Republican budget, first-year Republicans (among Gingrich's most committed troops) pushed the Speaker toward confrontation. Rather than compromise, Republicans twice forced the federal government to shut down. The result was a disaster for the self-proclaimed revolutionaries. Most of the public viewed their stance as intransigent, and the Congress was forced to back down. At the same time, right-wing extremists were linked to the bombing of a federal building in Oklahoma City that killed 168 men, women, and children. The incident made Americans aware of the many right-wing militia groups operating on the fringes of American society. Though these groups ranged from religious cults to survivalists, anti-Semites, skinheads, and rabid nationalists, what did seem to unite them was a profound mistrust of the federal government.

At the same time, President Clinton moved steadily to preempt the Republican agenda. In his earlier efforts to reduce public debt, he had been willing to settle for a $200 billion annual budget deficit. (It had run as high as $290 billion under George H. W. Bush.) By 1995, he was proposing his own route toward a balanced budget by

Welfare reform

2002. Similarly, in 1996 the president signed into law a sweeping reform of welfare. The law owed as much to Republican ideas as it did to the president's. For the first time in 60 years, the social welfare policies of the liberal democratic state were being substantially reversed. The bill ended guarantees of federal aid to poor children, turning over such programs to the states. Food stamp spending was cut, and the law placed a five-year limit on payments to any family. Most adults receiving payments were required to find work within two years.

Thus as the election of 1996 approached, the Republican revolution had been either dampened or co-opted by the president. The Republicans nominated former senator Bob Dole, a party loyalist, to run for president. Dole sought to stir excitement with promises of a 15 percent tax cut. But the economy was robust, and skeptical voters doubted he could balance the budget and still deliver his tax cut. In November Bill Clinton became the first Democrat since Franklin Roosevelt to win a second term in the White House.

Conservatives and the Feminist Agenda

Conservatives aimed some of their most bitter barbs at Hillary Clinton. Throughout her career she had supported liberal causes disdained by most conservatives, including the Children's Defense Fund, the American Bar Association's commission on women, and educational reform in Arkansas. Hillary Clinton also used her influence to promote opportunity for women and to draw attention to feminist issues. Bill Clinton shared many of his wife's concerns. During the election he told voters that he had "learned that building up women does not diminish men." In that spirit he appointed Ruth Bader Ginsburg to the Supreme Court and three women to his cabinet, including Janet Reno as attorney general. In 1997 he named Madeleine Albright as the first female secretary of state.

Both Clintons had supported a woman's right to control her decisions on reproduction, an issue that remained hotly contested during the 1990s. Because antiabortion conservatives had been unable to secure the repeal of *Roe v. Wade,* they sought to limit its application as much as possible by proposing to make illegal a procedure they referred to as "partial birth" late-term abortion. Doctors seldom performed the procedure and did so only to save a mother's life. Twice President Clinton vetoed bills that would criminalize the procedure.

More problematic for feminists was the legacy of the Supreme Court decision in the 1991 case of *UAW v. Johnson Controls.* Since *Muller v. Oregon* in 1908 (page 716), the Court had declared laws constitutional that gave women special protection based on their biological differences from men. Using this standard, Johnson Controls had established a policy of not hiring women workers to manufacture batteries, because the lead fumes in the workplace might damage a pregnant woman's unborn fetus. The workers' union challenged the policy, noting that fertile men who faced reproductive risks in the workplace were not restricted. The Court agreed with the union, ruling that the emphasis on biological differences denied women an "equal employment opportunity." Justice Harry Blackmun wrote that a woman's decision as to whether her "reproductive role is more important to herself and her family than her economic role" was one for her to make on her own.

UAW v. Johnson Controls

Many feminists hailed the decision as a step toward workplace equality. Feminist scholar Cynthia Daniels saw it as more ambiguous. Should laws recognize biological difference, or should they uphold equality? As Daniels argued, "To ignore difference is to risk placing women in a workplace designed by and for men, with all of its hazards and lack of concern for the preservation of life and health." Yet rules that recognized difference had in the past reinforced "those assumptions and economic structures which form the foundation of women's inequality." Throughout the 1990s feminists struggled with how to balance gender neutrality with gender justice. "For some, feminism necessarily means the promotion of equality between men and women," historian Elizabeth Fox Genovese wrote. "For others, it just as necessarily means the celebration of differences between women and men."

Contrasting views of feminism

Scandal

Almost every two-term president has faced some crisis in his second term. Franklin Roosevelt squandered an enormous electoral mandate with his plan to pack the Supreme Court. Watergate brought down Richard Nixon, whereas the Iran-Contra controversy tarnished Reagan. Bill Clinton's scandal was in some ways more puzzling. At once smaller and more personal, it nonetheless threatened his presidency with the American political system's ultimate sanction: impeachment, conviction, and removal from office.

Four years into the Whitewater investigation, Special Prosecutor Kenneth Starr had spent $30 million and produced only the convictions of several of the president's former business partners. (The Watergate investigation during the Nixon years, in contrast, lasted just over two years.) Starr dismissed the grand jury in Arkansas

The Lewinsky affair

Special Prosecutor Kenneth Starr, holding a copy of the Constitution during House Judiciary hearings. Starr proved so zealous in his investigation that many people saw him as a partisan rather than an independent prosecutor.

Impeachment

Acquittal

without filing charges against either of the Clintons on Whitewater; still, he pursued several other investigations while the sexual harassment suit brought by Paula Jones kept alive allegations of Clinton's sexual misconduct. Then in January 1998, Starr hit what looked like the jackpot. Linda Tripp, a disgruntled federal employee with links to the Bush administration, produced audiotapes of phone conversations in which a 21-year-old White House intern, Monica Lewinsky, talked of an intimate relationship with the president.

Starr succeeded in preventing Clinton from learning of the tapes before the president and Lewinsky testified in depositions to Paula Jones's attorneys that they had not had "sexual relations." When word of the tapes leaked out several days later, the news media predicted ominously that the president must resign or face impeachment—if not for his personal conduct, at the very least for lying under oath. That summer Starr subpoenaed the president to appear before a Washington grand jury. Four hours of testimony was taken on videotape, and in September Starr recommended that the president be impeached on the grounds of perjury, obstruction of justice, and witness tampering.

To the astonishment of the news media, polling indicated that the public did not support the Republican calls for impeachment. Although Clinton had clearly engaged in behavior most Americans found inappropriate or even repugnant, they seemed to draw a line between public and private actions. Furthermore, Starr's report went into such lurid detail that many Americans questioned the special prosecutor's motives. Nonetheless, the Republicans pressed their attack. Along strict party lines, a majority in the House voted three articles of impeachment for lying to the grand jury, suborning perjury, and orchestrating a cover-up. In January 1999 the matter went to the Senate for trial, with Chief Justice of the United States William Rehnquist presiding.

In a month-long hearing, the House managers presented the case against the president. But unlike with the Watergate scandals, in which Richard Nixon resigned because a bipartisan consensus had determined that impeachment was necessary, the accusers and defenders of Bill Clinton had always divided along strongly partisan lines. The Senate voted to acquit, with five Republicans joining all 45 Senate Democrats in the decision.

The Politics of Surplus

The impeachment controversy left the president weakened, but hardly powerless. Throughout the political tempest the nation's economy had continued to grow. By 1999 the rate of unemployment had dropped to 4.1 percent, the lowest in nearly 30 years, while the stock market reached new highs. Furthermore, as the economy expanded, federal tax receipts grew with it. By 1998 Bill Clinton faced a situation that would have seemed improbable a few years previous—a budget surplus. By balancing the budget the president had appropriated a key Republican issue. Political debate shifted to what to do with the surplus.

Social Security crisis

Clinton sought to revive much of his initial agenda. He wanted the money spent on education, paying down the national debt, and protecting Social Security and Medicare funds from predicted future deficits. The deficits seemed sure to arise because an entire generation of graying baby boomers was heading toward retirement beginning around the year 2010. During the 1990s six workers paid taxes for each retiree collecting benefits; thus for years the government had been able to borrow excess revenues from the Social Security trust fund to help reduce annual deficits. But projections indicated that by around 2030, only three workers would be paying taxes for each person collecting benefits. That ratio threatened fiscal disaster. Clinton thus argued that the budget surplus could best be used to ensure the solvency of Social Security and Medicare.

As the presidential campaign of 2000 loomed, the Senate unexpectedly took up debate on a treaty banning underground nuclear testing by the 44 nations of the world considered to have nuclear capabilities. Clinton had signed the treaty in 1996, but Senate Republicans refused to ratify it, claiming that it could be neither verified nor enforced. Democrats pressed for a vote, underestimating the degree of opposition. The treaty was voted down in October 1999, coming far short of the two-thirds support needed to ratify. It was the first time a treaty of that magnitude had been rejected since the Senate voted down the Versailles agreement ending World War I. Although some Republicans known as internationalists opposed the treaty, others in the party reflected a long strain of isolationism. House Republican Dick Armey captured that spirit when he remarked, "I've been to Europe once. I don't have to go again."

Defeat of nuclear test ban treaty

Hanging by a Chad: The Election of 2000

The 2000 election campaign at first seemed little more than a contest about personality, as both the leading candidates strayed little from the center of the political spectrum. The Democratic candidate, Al Gore of Tennessee, had served loyally as President Clinton's vice president. He had written a significant book on the global environmental crisis, promoted federal support for the Internet, and taken a more active role in matters of policy than most vice presidents. But Gore's often wooden speaking style gave him the appearance of a policy wonk patronizing his uninformed audience. In contrast, the Republican candidate, George W. Bush (son of President George H. W. Bush) was usually affable and relaxed on the campaign trail. Bush's experience in foreign affairs was slight, and he had a checkered career in business before being elected governor of Texas.

The campaign was Gore's to lose, for polls gave him a substantial lead as the two candidates squared off. But Bush attacked the "integrity" of the Clinton administration, which led Gore to keep the president out of the day-to-day campaigning, even though Clinton's personal behavior seemed not to have dented his popularity. Gore's lead dissipated after lackluster performances in televised debates. One critic observed that everything the Democratic candidate said "seemed calculated"—"the calculations were often so transparent as to be embarrassing." By election night many pollsters predicted a race too close to call.

Still, they were not prepared for the debacle that ensued. Early exit polls seemed to give the race to Gore, but by 2 A.M. the actual results had shifted so strongly to Bush that Gore called to say he was prepared to concede defeat. An hour later he reversed himself. The election had come down to Florida, where two days after the election, Bush led by just 300 votes out of 6 million cast statewide. Nationally Gore led by half a million votes, but without Florida's 25 electoral votes neither candidate had a majority in the Electoral College. The 9000 votes that went to Green Party candidate Ralph Nader most likely cost Gore a clear victory in the state.

Determining Florida's actual vote proved daunting. Evidence immediately surfaced of voting irregularities. The ballots in some counties featured complicated and confusing layouts, in which it was easy to cast a vote for Reform Party candidate Pat Buchanan when the tally looked as if it was going to Gore. Other counties

Election officials in Broward County, Florida, examine a ballot for chads, punched paper from holes, in the hotly contested presidential election of 2000.

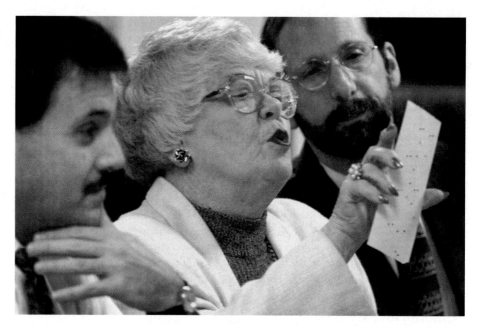

used punch-card machines that failed to fully perforate many ballots, leaving behind tiny punch-hole paper known as "hanging chads." Republicans alleged that Democratic election supervisors had not properly counted many military absentee ballots, while Democrats accused Republican officials of working to suppress voting in heavily African American counties.

After weeks of legal challenges, the Florida state supreme court ruled in favor of a Democratic request to have the contested votes manually recounted. Normally the U.S. Supreme Court would let stand election disputes decided by a state court. But when Republicans appealed the Florida court decision, the Supreme Court agreed to hear the case in *Bush v. Gore*. On December 12 the court's conservative majority (all Republican appointees) voted, outnumbering the minority 5 to 4, that the recount must end, leaving George Bush as the president-elect. Citing the Fourteenth Amendment's equal protection clause, the majority argued that because the recount procedure was limited to only three counties, it valued some votes more than others. "It becomes our unsought responsibility to resolve the federal and constitutional issues the judicial system has been forced to confront," concluded the majority. The minority protested. "Although we may never know with complete certainty the identity of the winner of this year's Presidential election, the identity of the loser is perfectly clear," wrote Justice John Paul Stevens. "It is the Nation's confidence in the judge as an impartial guardian of the rule of law."

Elections, to be sure, are among the most political acts in the life of a nation. In the election of 2000 even the Supreme Court seemed unable to escape politics. The more liberal justices supported their position by citing the states rights' principle usually advanced by conservatives—that "Federal courts defer to state high courts' interpretations of their state's own law." For their part, conservatives cited the equal protection clause (often used by liberal justices to expand federal power) to uphold their position. Regardless of who had the better argument, in the end the Supreme Court, not the American electorate, had made George W. Bush the president of the United States.

Bush v. Gore

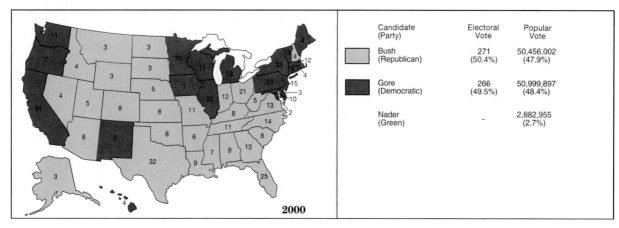

Candidate (Party)	Electoral Vote	Popular Vote
Bush (Republican)	271 (50.4%)	50,456,002 (47.9%)
Gore (Democratic)	266 (49.5%)	50,999,897 (48.4%)
Nader (Green)	–	2,882,955 (2.7%)

2000

Election of 2000

The United States in a Networked World

In 1988 economist Lawrence Summers was working on the presidential campaign of Michael Dukakis. At a meeting in Chicago, the staff assigned him a car with a telephone. Summers was so impressed, he recalled, that "I used it to call my wife to tell her I was in a car with a phone." A decade later as deputy treasury secretary in the Clinton administration, he visited the Ivory Coast in Africa to help launch an American-supported health project. One village on his itinerary could be reached only by dugout canoe. As Summers stepped into the canoe for his return trip, an aide handed him a cell phone. "Washington has a question for you," the aide said. The same man who once marveled at a phone in his car in Chicago ten years later expected one in his dugout canoe in the interior of Africa.

The Internet Revolution

Like Summers, Americans at the end of the twentieth century had become linked to a global communications network almost wherever they went. Computers, cell phones, pagers, and other electronic devices provided almost instant contact with the wider world. The process of connection had been driven by a revolution in microchip technologies.

Although the Internet communications revolution gained global momentum only after 1995, its roots could be traced to the early 1960s. In 1962 J. C. R. Licklider of the Massachusetts Institute of Technology wrote a series of memos laying out the concept of what he grandly termed a "Galactic Network": computers all across the world connected in order to share data and programs. But the technology for sending data efficiently along phone lines was still primitive. Computer technicians cobbled together a network between four host computers in 1969. Known as the ARPANET, it allowed university and Department of Defense researchers to share computer capacity more efficiently as well as to create a communications system that could survive a nuclear attack. Managers discovered that many of the researchers with access to the network used it to send personal messages. E-mail had been born.

The Galactic Network and ARPANET

A second phase of the revolution began in the 1970s when a Harvard dropout named Bill Gates helped write software to operate personal computers. Most computing was then done on what were called mainframes, massive and hugely expensive machines found only in large businesses, universities, and government agencies. Gates was among a growing group of technically minded visionaries who saw that the technologies of miniaturization would make personal computers useful in everyday life.

The personal computer

Most software writers made their work freely available to anyone wanting to use it. Gates perceived that software had commercial potential because it was a key to making computers accessible to a mass public. He created the Microsoft Corporation to exploit that promise. In 1980 International Business Machines Corporation (IBM) adopted Microsoft's program, MS-DOS, to operate IBM personal computers. MS-DOS became a standard for the computer industry. By the mid-1980s small businesses, homes, and schools were using personal computers for word processing, graphic design, and spreadsheets that tracked personal and financial data. Other manufacturers used microprocessors on silicon chips to operate complex mechanical systems ranging from watches to jet aircraft. By the 1990s desktop computers could boast more power than the mainframes of just forty years earlier.

The Internet (successor to the ARPANET) was growing too. By 1985 it linked about 1000 host computers. To help users connect, sites were given domain names instead of a faceless string of numbers. Taking the next step in the evolutionary process, British-born physicist Tim Berners-Lee wrote software that created the World Wide Web as a facet of the Internet. Berners-Lee saw the possibility for a universal system with access to anything that was information. He applied the hypertext link (http://) that allowed users to move freely from one site to sites of related interest, each with its own Web address, or URL (uniform resource locator).

The World Wide Web

Berners-Lee shared the democratic vision common among software programmers and Internet pioneers. They saw the Web as open and free to all. Users could communicate without restriction and find access to any form of information. Such openness was the bane of authoritarian governments, which found it difficult to control public opinion in a world in which information flowed freely. The unregulated format of the Web raised substantial legal, moral, and political questions in the United States as well. By 1999 five million Web sites were in operation—among them sites promoting pornography, hate speech, and even instructions on how to build atomic bombs. A number of politicians and civic groups called for the censorship of the more extreme Web content. But the system's openness, coupled with the opposition of a majority of Web users, made censorship extremely difficult to effect.

The Web's interactivity also gave it enormous commercial potential. With Web browsers, developed in the mid-1990s, seekers and finders increasingly became buyers and sellers. Early sites such as CDNow and The Onion tended to offer goods—music CDs, financial information, news, and games—favored by young, technically sophisticated Web surfers. After 1995 business on the Web, or e-commerce, grew at over 175 percent per year as more and more people went "online." By 1999 over 200 million people internationally and 100 million Americans had used the Web to buy over $300 billion in goods.

E-commerce

The revolution in microchip technologies contributed substantially to the economic expansion of the 1990s. In 1998 e-commerce alone generated some 482,000 jobs. Whereas in 1965 business committed just 3 percent of their spending to high technology, they committed 45 percent in 1996. That increase in spending contributed to a significant rise in labor productivity. Improved productivity in turn proved to be a critical factor behind economic growth.

Use of the Internet broadened sharply after 1995. As of 2000, the number of pieces of mail handled daily by the U.S. Postal Service was 668 million. The average number of e-mails sent daily was 10 billion. This graphic by Stephen G. Eick, of Bell Laboratories, plotted worldwide Internet traffic.

American Workers in a Two-Tiered Economy

The benefits of prosperity were not evenly distributed, however. Economists described the United States in the 1990s as a two-tiered labor market in which most increases in earning went to people at the top of the wage scale. Thus despite the computer revolution and the decade's prosperity, the median income of American families was barely higher in 1996 than in 1973. Indeed, the earnings of the average white male worker actually fell. Only because so many women entered the job market did the family standard of living remain the same. In the early 1970s some 37 percent of women worked outside the home; in 1999 about 57 percent did.

Education was a critical factor in determining winners in the computer economy. Families with college-educated parents were three times more likely to have home access to the Web than were those families in which parents' education ended with high school. Because average education levels were relatively lower among African Americans and Latinos (and relatively higher among Asian Americans), the computer divide took on a racial cast as well. But the implications went beyond mere access to the Web and its feast of information and commerce. More important, the high-wage sector of the computer economy required educated workers, and the demand for them drove up those workers' salaries.

In contrast, most semiskilled and unskilled workers saw little growth in earnings despite full employment. The choices facing the nation's half-million long-haul truck drivers was a case in point. Typically, drivers piloting these eighteen-wheel rigs—on the road for two to three weeks at a time—made as much as $35,000 a year in the mid-1990s, about the same as they had in the 1970s. To keep their earnings that high, drivers needed to log around 3000 hours a year—50 percent more than the average work-year in America. Because the motor freight business was so competitive, trucking firms did not grant wage increases that would have to be passed on to their customers. And because most drivers did not belong to a union, they could not bargain effectively for higher wages. (Membership in the Teamsters, which represented truck drivers, fell from 30 percent in the 1970s to 10 percent by 1999.) So rather than make less money or strike, the drivers stayed on the road longer. In 1998 they averaged 65 hours every seven days. To skirt regulations limiting the amount of time on the job, drivers logged loading and unloading time as rest periods. Accidents involving the big rigs increased.

Wage stagnation

If the hours were long and conditions grueling, why did so many truckers continue to drive? In essence, they had no appealing alternative. The highest-paid unskilled workers in the United States averaged 2000 hours per year at about $14 per hour, or $28,000 a year—an effective pay cut of $7000. "So there [was] a lot of movement between companies," one executive observed, but few drivers were willing to quit. Unlike computer programmers or corporate executives who were in high demand, low-skill workers like the truckers were not able to increase their earnings simply by switching jobs. Some economists concluded that "the most important economic division is not between races, or genders, or economic sectors, but between the college-educated and the noncollege-educated."

Effects of prosperity   The booming economy in the last three years of the twentieth century brought a small decrease in the inequality between the highest- and lowest-paid Americans. Wages rose slightly, boosting the median American income to $38,885 in 1998. The number of Americans living in poverty dropped by a million in 1998, to a decade low. Once again, earnings differences between white, black, and Latino males began to narrow. Governments showed new willingness to spend money on education and transportation, services most vital to the poor. Even the Republican Congress restored some spending cuts on housing, urban development, and social welfare, all programs that increased the well-being of the poorest Americans.

The prosperity of the late 1990s produced an interesting dilemma. On the one hand, it eased many social tensions that had long divided the nation. Inner-city crime rates fell; the poor began to experience a marked improvement in their economic situation; consumer confidence reached an all-time high. But over the longer term, the boom's statistics were not encouraging. Despite the decline in the poverty rate, it remained above the rate for any year in the 1970s. If the strongest economy in 30 years left the poverty rate higher than during the inflation-plagued years of the 1970s, what would happen if the economy faltered?

 Multiculturalism and Contested American Identity

No state more fully represented the multicultural and global complexion of late-twentieth-century America than California. More of the nation's recently arrived immigrants from Asia, Central America, and Mexico settled there than in any other state. By 1990, fully 33 percent of the residents of Los Angeles County were foreign-born, a figure rivaling the high-water mark of 40 percent set by New York City in 1910. Predictably, then, it was California that so often led the national debate over multiculturalism. Californians put forth election propositions challenging the policies of affirmative action, proposed to make English an official language, and sought to restrict welfare, education, and other social benefits for immigrants and aliens. A recession there sharpened the debate in the early 1990s, as did several explosive legal cases raising the issue of racism. The battles over race, immigration, and multiculturalism suggest that in an era of internationally linked economies and global migrations, the United States remains a nation of nations seeking to accommodate distinctive identities along lines of race, ethnicity, and national origin.

African Americans and the Persistence of the Racial Divide

In the 1990s the highest-paid celebrity in the world was an African American—Michael Jordan. Oprah Winfrey, also an African American, was the highest-paid woman in America. Both political parties eyed former general Colin Powell as a possible presidential candidate. Millions of white as well as black Americans expressed outrage when an all-white jury acquitted four Los Angeles police officers charged with beating Rodney King, a black American man. Yet when a largely black jury acquitted football star O. J. Simpson of murder in a 1994 trial, polls indicated that whites and blacks sharply disagreed over Simpson's guilt or innocence. Although the situation of African Americans had improved vastly compared with their position in the 1950s, race still mattered.

In 1991 Los Angeles police arrested a black motorist, Rodney King, for speeding and drunken driving. The police were all white; King was African American. As King lay on the ground, four officers proceeded to beat him with nightsticks more than 50 times. When blacks complained about such brutality at the hands of largely white police, public officials often dismissed their complaints. This case was different. A man in a nearby apartment videotaped the beating, which the news media repeatedly broadcast to the entire nation. But the following year, an all-white suburban jury acquitted the officers, concluding that King had been threatening and that the officers had acted within their authority.

Rodney King and the Los Angeles riots

The verdict enraged the African American community in Los Angeles, where widespread riots erupted for three days, making the violence the worst civil disturbance in Los Angeles history. By the time police and the National Guard restored order, nearly 2000 people had been injured, 40 people had died, over 4500 fires burned, and $500 million of property had been looted, damaged, or destroyed.

At first glance the riot appeared to be much like the one that had decimated Watts, a poor area of Los Angeles, in 1965. Poor African Americans had lashed out in frustration at white racism. In fact, the 1992 riots were multiracial in character, exposing divisions in Los Angeles's multicultural communities. Rioters, both black and Latino, damaged over 2000 small groceries, liquor stores, and other businesses run by Korean American immigrants. African Americans also attacked Latinos; and after the first day, Latinos also joined in the disturbances. But there was a revealing pattern. In the more established Latino communities of East Los Angeles, where families had more to lose, residents remained quiet or worked actively to maintain the peace. In contrast, fires and looting destroyed many businesses in the MacArthur

Complexity of the riots

The Los Angeles riots of 1992 revealed divisions in the city's multicultural communities of African Americans, Latinos, and Asian Americans.

Park area, where the newest Latino immigrants lived. "Everybody said, 'How can they destroy their neighborhoods, their jobs . . . ?'" commented a Latino demographer from UCLA. "Well, my answer is that they did not consider it to be their own." Thus the 1992 riots exposed tension and competition among ethnic groups.

The O. J. Simpson case

In quite another way the case of O. J. Simpson revealed the persistence of a racial divide. Born into a ghetto family, Simpson had become first a football legend, then a movie star and television personality. He seemed to defy all notions that race prejudice restricted African Americans. But in 1994 police charged Simpson with the brutal murders of his white ex-wife, Nicole, and her friend Ron Goldman. Millions of television viewers watched with rapt attention as Simpson's attorneys transformed what seemed to be a strong prosecution case into a trial of the Los Angeles police. Their client had been framed, his attorneys suggested, by racist police officers. Defense lawyers revealed that the lead officer in the case had lied on the stand about his own prejudice and about his use of racial slurs.

After a trial lasting almost a year, a jury of nine African Americans, two whites, and one Mexican American took just four hours to acquit Simpson. Regardless of his guilt or innocence, the verdict revealed a racial fault line dividing Americans. The vast majority of whites believed the evidence against Simpson allowed just one verdict—guilty. Most African Americans were equally persuaded that Simpson had been framed. Why? Both groups had watched the same trial; yet each brought to it significantly different personal experiences of the American system of justice. Black Americans who had all too often found themselves stopped arbitrarily by police or pulled over while driving in white neighborhoods disagreed fundamentally over whether that system applied equally to all people regardless of race.

African Americans in a Full-Employment Economy

In 1966 the African American community of North Lawndale, on Chicago's West Side, was one of the worst slums in America. At the time, Martin Luther King Jr. rented an apartment there, hoping to draw attention to its plight. When he was assassinated two years later, rioters burned down much of the neighborhood. Over the next 20 years half the population moved away from the crime, drug addiction, and violent gangs.

Inner-city renewal

By the late 1990s North Lawndale had undergone a rebirth. African American professionals had returned to the neighborhood. Homes that once stood deserted now sold for over $250,000. What happened in North Lawndale reflected new circumstances for many African Americans across the country during a decade of economic expansion. Home ownership reached 46 percent and employment increased from around 87 percent in 1980 to nearly 92 percent in 1998. African Americans in increasing numbers rose up the ladder in corporate America. Many started their own businesses. Test scores for reading and math proficiency also improved, and more African Americans, though fewer males, attended college.

Economic success brought new hope to the nation's inner cities. Crime and poverty decreased significantly, especially rates of murder and violence. Births to unwed mothers reached a postwar low. Fewer blacks lived below the poverty level and fewer were on welfare. The most hard-core block of the unemployed—males between 16 and 24—found many more jobs. The gap between wages for whites and blacks narrowed as well. Life expectancy increased substantially—from 63.8 years for African American males in 1980 to 66.1 in 1996 (70.7 and 73.8 for white males).

Yet many African Americans were reserved in their reaction to such statistics. "To the extent that you proclaim your success," one community leader remarked, "people forget about you." Furthermore, an economic downturn might reverse those gains, especially if employers resorted to the traditional practice of "last hired, first fired."

Civil rights leaders were most concerned about the continued assault on affirmative action. In 1996 California voters passed a ballot initiative, Proposition 209, that eliminated racial and gender preferences in hiring and college admissions. Ironically, the leading advocate for Proposition 209 was a conservative black businessman, Ward Connerly. Connerly argued that racial preferences demeaned black and other minority students by setting up a double standard that patronizingly assumed minorities could not compete on an equal basis. In any case, Proposition 209 had a striking effect. Enrollments of Latinos and blacks at the elite California university campuses and professional schools dropped sharply: down 57 percent for black students at Berkeley and 34 percent for Latinos. What remained was a student body that was only 3 percent black and 9 percent Latino, in a state in which African Americans constituted 7 percent and Latinos 29 percent of the population. A ballot initiative banning racial preference in admissions had a similar impact on the University of Washington. Enrollment for African Americans there dropped 40 percent and for Hispanics some 30 percent, while whites and Asians had small percentage increases. Major state universities in Texas and Michigan also experienced declines after passing similar laws.

Opponents of affirmative action pointed out that total enrollments for blacks, Native Americans, and Latinos remained almost constant within the California university system. Minority students flocked to California's second- and third-tier university campuses, where they could benefit from smaller class sizes and a less competitive environment. But defenders of affirmative action remained skeptical. "Students' aspirations are very much shaped by the aspirations of their peers," wrote Derek Bok, a former president of Harvard University. "When you go to a very selective school, you probably set your sights higher." Other critics added that the decline of minority students at the elite campuses reduced ethnic and cultural diversity there, to the detriment of other students' education.

Also in 1996 a federal circuit court had gone so far as to claim, in *Hopwood v. State of Texas et al.*, that race could not be used as a factor in college admissions. The Supreme Court did not fully address that issue until 2003, in the case of *Gratz v. Bollinger*, when the Bush administration pressed the Court to strike down the use of any racial preference in the admissions programs of the University of Michigan. Leading universities, retired military officers, and some corporate leaders supported Michigan's position. They argued that by encouraging diversity, affirmative action benefited their institutions. In deciding the case the justices did strike down a point system used by Michigan giving minorities preference in undergraduate admissions. However the Court approved, 5 to 4, a separate program used by the university's law school, which gave race less prominence in the admissions process. In so doing the justices left room for the nation's public universities as well as other public and private institutions to take race into account in less overt ways. In short, they narrowed, but left available, a basis for using affirmative action.

Although African Americans had made undoubted gains, the census figures still challenged the notion that the playing field had been leveled enough for blacks to compete equally. Although joblessness among young black males fell by nearly a third between 1985 and 1998, unemployment remained twice as high among blacks (8.9 percent in 1998) as among whites (3.9 percent). A remarkably high percentage of black males were, in the language of the street, on "some kind of paper"—meaning they were in jail, on parole, or on probation. Some 13 percent, or 1.4 million, could not vote because they had been convicted of a felony. Such

Proposition 209 against affirmative action

Persistent poverty

disparities suggested that even in the booming 1990s, race remained an evident dividing line along which inequalities persisted.

Global Pressures in a Multicultural America

Clearly the enormous changes wrought by immigration and the new global economy affected not just the immigrant enclaves but American culture as a whole. Salsa rhythms became part of the pop culture mainstream, and Latino foods competed with Indian curries, Japanese sushi, and Thai takeout for the loyalties of two-career families whose parents lacked the time to cook. In 1999 the first baseball player ever to hit over 60 home runs in two seasons was Sammy Sosa, a Dominican and only one of many Latino stars in the game.

But the mix of cultures was not always benign. Throughout the course of American history, when immigration flows increased, members of the dominant culture often reacted defensively. The Know-Nothings of the 1850s took as their slogan "Americans should rule America," and nativists of the early twentieth century succeeded in sharply restricting immigration. During the 1990s the debate continued over how diverse the United States could become without losing its central identity.

Proposition 187 and illegal aliens

Restriction again became a goal of those citizens worried about American identity. In 1916 Madison Grant had written *The Passing of the Great Race* to warn that unrestricted immigration might lead to racial suicide. In 1990 Lawrence Auster published *The Path to National Suicide,* in which he complained of the "browning of America." The new restrictionists in Congress proposed the Immigration and Stabilization Act of 1993, but neither the Democrats, who controlled Congress, nor President Clinton supported major changes in immigration policy. The following year, restrictionists used a different strategy in California. Their Proposition 187 ballot initiative denied health, education, and welfare benefits to illegal aliens. Despite the opposition of most major religious, ethnic, and educational organizations, the measure passed with a lopsided 59 percent of the vote. In the end, though, the proposition was not put into effect because a federal judge ruled unconstitutional the provision denying education to children of illegal aliens.

English as an official language

A movement to make English the official language of the United States received broader support. As early as 1981 California senator S. I. Hayakawa had urged Congress to adopt an English language amendment to the Constitution. The proposal forbade the use of foreign languages in government documents and sought to eliminate bilingual education from public schools. Speaking a native tongue in the privacy of the home was acceptable, one English-only supporter granted, but "English is the 'glue' that helps keep American culture vibrant and dynamic."

Unable to move Congress to act, Hayakawa lent his support to a voter initiative to make English California's official language. There, state forms were often printed in Spanish, and San Francisco printed ballots in three languages—Chinese, Spanish, and English. Asian and Latino organizations, along with the Democratic party and many state officials, opposed the proposition. They saw it as an attack on a liberal immigration policy and an effort to eliminate bilingual education. Nonetheless, in 1986 73 percent of Californians voted for the measure. Similarly, as a new wave of Cuban immigrants flooded southern Florida during the 1980s, voters of Dade County adopted an initiative making English the county's official language. Cubans resented the initiative as an attempt to restrict their culture and in 1993 they pressured county officials into repealing it. The same year, however,

Florida voters approved an English-only referendum for the state. By 1996 23 states had adopted either resolutions or laws declaring English their official language.

Traditionally, nativist conflicts pit the dominant majority culture against the minority cultures of more recent arrivals. But in a multicultural society, such polar opposites often break down. In 1998 yet another ballot initiative passed in California (Proposition 227), mandating that schools phase out all their bilingual education programs. Students would be granted only one year of English-language immersion courses before receiving all instruction in English. In this instance both white and Latino voters approved the proposition by nearly the same margin, within one or two points of 62 percent. And the measure itself had been proposed after a group of Spanish-speaking parents boycotted their elementary school until it agreed to teach their children to read and write in English.

The pressures of global migration also increased tensions between minorities, as the Los Angeles riots of 1992 demonstrated. As recently as 1980 blacks and Latinos seldom competed directly in California's economy. African Americans had made gains in older industries and in the public sector. Latinos were more likely to work in agriculture or the low-wage service sector. But those economic boundaries were always changing. In the 1980s, for example, a great many of the janitors working in the downtown office buildings of Los Angeles were African American. As union members, their wages and benefits came to more than $12.00 an hour. By 1990 most had been replaced by nonunion Latino immigrants, usually illegals, working for only about $5.00 an hour with no contract, no benefits or health insurance, and no vacation time. That same dynamic had caused Juan Chanax and his fellow villagers from Guatemala to replace African Americans at Randall's supermarkets in Houston.

For the time being, the prosperity of the late 1990s muted the tensions arising from such conflicts. High employment meant ample work for both blacks and Latinos, though often in low-paid and unskilled jobs. And even after the heavy influx of immigrants, foreign-born residents accounted for less than 10 percent of the total U.S. population. If prosperity continued to be fueled by the productivity sparked by the computer revolution and the interconnections of the Web, the benefits of the two-tier economy might spread.

Libertad by Ester Hernandez

Yet the long-term trend remains unchanged. Since the peoples of Europe, Africa, and Asia made contact with the Americas half a millennium ago, the cultures and economies of the world have been drawn ever more tightly together. With the arrival of an information superhighway and the acceleration of international migrations, the United States will necessarily remain what it has always been: a nation of nations whose political system continues to evolve new ways of democratically encompassing a diversity that now reflects the world.

November 1999: Outside the Food Emporium on New York City's West Side, Lillian Winston, a woman in her eighties, emerged with four grocery bags. A young man approached promptly, dressed in a crisp white shirt, tie, and brightly polished shoes—one of the store's delivery workers. He was not Guatemalan, like Juan Chanax. He came from the continent that, during the first three centuries after the arrival of Columbus in the Americas, supplied four times as many immigrants as any other land. His name was Gasel Lii and he hailed from the Congo. The number of sub-Saharan Africans such as Lii living in New York City had almost doubled, from 44,000 in 1990 to about 84,000 in 1999. Like earlier immigrants from Europe, Asia, and Latin America, these newcomers arrived willing to work for a better life. Lii was putting in 12 hours a day, six days a week, for pay that averaged out to $2.50 an hour, or $107 a week. He supported a wife and children who still lived in Africa. "We thought life in America was going to be easier," commented one of his fellow workers, from Gabon, who added sardonically, "Maybe we watched too much *Dynasty*." Gasel Lii picked up the grocery bags, two in each hand, and headed down the street.

chapter summary

During the 1990s the United States became increasingly tied to a worldwide network of economic, financial, and demographic relationships that increased both the nation's diversity and its interdependence.

- The Immigration Act of 1965 opened the United States to a new wave of immigration in the 1980s and 1990s, different from the influx earlier in the century because of its truly global diversity.

  - Immigrants from Asia—hailing from South and Southeast Asia as much as from China, Japan, and the Philippines—crowded both ends of the economic spectrum in an hourglass profile.

  - Both legal and illegal immigrants from Mexico, Cuba, and Central America contributed to the growing Latino population, settling in both urban and suburban barrios.

  - Many immigrants retained closer financial, political, and emotional ties with their home countries.

  - Immigration changed the shape of religion in America, adding an increased presence of Muslim, Buddhist, and Hindu faiths.

- During the Clinton presidency, regional conflicts in the Middle East, Eastern Europe, Africa, and the Caribbean replaced cold war rivalries as the central challenge of foreign policy.

  - The world financial crisis of 1997, spreading from Asia to Russia to Brazil and beyond, demonstrated how American and other world economies were closely linked.

- President Clinton's ambitious political agenda included rebuilding the nation's infrastructure, improving education, and reforming the health care system.

  - A divided and (after the elections of 1994) increasingly hostile Congress limited the president's legislative program.

  - The campaign of Republican congressional conservatives to impeach President Clinton ended when the Senate failed to adopt the three articles of impeachment.

  - The election of 2000, the most closely contested since that of 1876, was settled only after the Supreme Court ruled against a recount of disputed Florida ballots, giving George W. Bush the victory.

- The growth of the Internet, the World Wide Web, and e-commerce was part of a revolution in communications and information management made possible by advances in microchip and computer technology. But those advances also threatened to create a permanent two-tiered economy divided by levels of education and literacy.

- The political battles of the 1990s over race, immigration, and multiculturalism suggest that the United States will remain a nation in which distinctive identities along lines of race, ethnicity, social class, and religion continue to be a source of both strength and political conflict.

interactive learning

The Primary Source Investigator CD-ROM offers the following materials related to this chapter:

- Interactive maps: **Election of 1996** (M7)

- A collection of primary sources capturing the fall of communism, the end of the cold war, and the era of President Clinton, including a photo of President Clinton's first inauguration. Other sources include California Proposition 187 to prevent illegal aliens from receiving public benefits and services and a portrait of Katie Harman, Miss America 2002.

additional reading

To write on the recent past, historians must rely heavily on journalists, social scientists, and the memoirs of those who participated in the events. Often these accounts reflect the partisan spirit of those caught up in the battles of the era. For example, Hillary Rodham Clinton, *Living History* (2003), sheds little light on some of the most controversial episodes of her husband's presidency. On the other hand, Sidney Blumenthal, *The Clinton Wars* (2003), offers the perspective of an insider, but one who is an unabashed defender of the Clintons. In *Madam Secretary* (2003) Madeleine Albright reveals much about her personal road to political prominence. Robert Reich, author of *Locked in the Cabinet* (1997), served as Clinton's labor secretary, while George Stephanopoulos, author of *All Too Human: A Political Education* (1999), served as a spokesperson for the White House. Journalist Joe Klein, *The Natural: The Misunderstood Presidency of Bill Clinton* (2002), is the first of what will likely be numerous interpretations of the Clinton era. Dan Balz and Ronald Brownstein, *Storming the Gates: Protest Politics and the Republican Revival* (1996), in combination with Elizabeth Drew, *Showdown: The Struggle between Gingrich and the Clinton White House* (1996), covers the intensely partisan battles that beset Washington after the Republican congressional victories of 1994. Joe Conason and Gene Lyons, *The Hunting of the President: The Ten Year Campaign to Destroy Bill and Hillary Clinton* (2001), supports the liberal view of an orchestrated conservative crusade to overturn the 1992 election results. Finally, we must commend federal judge Richard Posner for books on two constitutional crises. In *An Affair of State: The Investigation and Trial of President Clinton* (1999), he analyzes the issues behind the campaign to impeach Clinton. His *Breaking the Deadlock: The 2000 Election, the Constitution, and the Courts* (2003) examines the issues raised by the Supreme Court's intervention in the Florida election results.

A useful portrait of the global economy in the Internet era is Thomas Friedman, *The Lexus and the Olive Tree* (1999). Michael Lewis takes readers inside the new world of the Internet and e-commerce in his readable *The New New Thing: A Silicon Valley Story* (1999). The problem of income inequality is carefully examined in Frank Levy, *The New Dollars and Dreams* (1999). For the debate over multiculturalism and diversity, see Lawrence Levine, *The Opening of the American Mind* (1996), and Alan Wolf, *One Nation, After All* (1998). Richard Alba and Victor Nee, *Remaking the American Mainstream: Assimilation and Contemporary Immigration* (2003), make a persuasive case that today's Latino, Asian, and other new immigrants are assimilating in much the same way earlier immigrants did. David Reimers, *Unwelcome Strangers: American Identity and the Turn against Immigration* (1999), places the recent debates on immigration in historical context. Roberto Suro provides a sensitive examination of Latino cultures in the 1990s in *Strangers among Us: How Latino Immigration Is Transforming America* (1998). For profiles of the new Asian immigration, see the final chapters of Ronald L. Takaki, *Strangers from a Different Shore* (rev. ed., 1998), and Sucheng Chan, *Asian Americans* (1991), as well as Gary Okihiro, *Margins and Mainstreams* (1995). Nicholas Lemann, *The Big Test* (1999), takes a broad historic look at the SATs and affirmative action. For a fuller list of readings, see the Bibliography at www.mhhe.com/davidsonnation5.

significant events

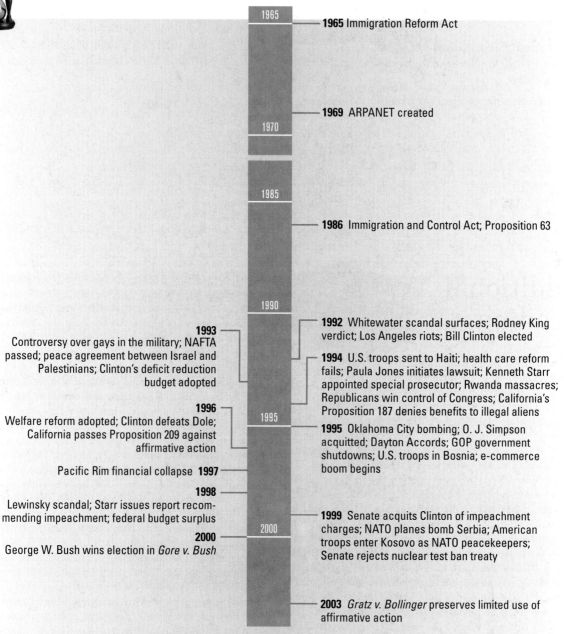

1965

1965 Immigration Reform Act

1969 ARPANET created

1970

1985

1986 Immigration and Control Act; Proposition 63

1990

1993
Controversy over gays in the military; NAFTA passed; peace agreement between Israel and Palestinians; Clinton's deficit reduction budget adopted

1992 Whitewater scandal surfaces; Rodney King verdict; Los Angeles riots; Bill Clinton elected

1994 U.S. troops sent to Haiti; health care reform fails; Paula Jones initiates lawsuit; Kenneth Starr appointed special prosecutor; Rwanda massacres; Republicans win control of Congress; California's Proposition 187 denies benefits to illegal aliens

1996
Welfare reform adopted; Clinton defeats Dole; California passes Proposition 209 against affirmative action

1995

1995 Oklahoma City bombing; O. J. Simpson acquitted; Dayton Accords; GOP government shutdowns; U.S. troops in Bosnia; e-commerce boom begins

Pacific Rim financial collapse **1997**

1998
Lewinsky scandal; Starr issues report recommending impeachment; federal budget surplus

2000
George W. Bush wins election in *Gore v. Bush*

2000

1999 Senate acquits Clinton of impeachment charges; NATO planes bomb Serbia; American troops enter Kosovo as NATO peacekeepers; Senate rejects nuclear test ban treaty

2003 *Gratz v. Bollinger* preserves limited use of affirmative action

Epilogue

A long the northeast coast of the United States, September 11, 2001, dawned bright and clear. One New Yorker on the way to work remembered that it was the day of the Democratic mayoral primary. He decided to vote before going to his job at the World Trade Center. There, at about the same time, Francis Ledesma was sitting in his office on the sixty-fourth floor of the South Tower when a friend suggested they go for coffee. Francis seldom took breaks that early, but he decided to make an exception. Almost everyone makes similar small choices every day. But this was no ordinary day, and the choices proved to be life-saving.

In the cafeteria Francis heard and felt a muffled explosion. He thought a boiler had burst, but then saw bricks and glass falling by the window. Although he intended to head back to his office for a nine o'clock meeting, his friend insisted they leave immediately. Out on the street Francis noticed the smoke and gaping hole where American Airlines Flight 11 had hit the North Tower. At that moment a huge fireball erupted as United Airlines Flight 175 hit their own South Tower. "We kept looking back," Francis recalled as they escaped the area, "and then all of a sudden our building, Tower 2, collapsed. I really thought that it was a mirage."

Both planes had left Boston's Logan Airport that morning carrying passengers—and a full load of jet fuel—for their flights to Los Angeles. Once the planes

FIGHTING TERRORISM IN A
GLOBAL AGE

2000–2003

preview • A world already connected in a thousand ways found those connections challenged and shattered by a terrorist movement that was itself global. The attack on the World Trade Center and the Pentagon reoriented American priorities, causing the Bush administration to wage a war on terror both at home and abroad. While an invasion of Afghanistan received widespread support, the decision to invade Iraq, without the support of the United Nations, signaled a more controversial, unilateralist foreign policy.

were aloft, terrorists commandeered their controls and turned them into lethal missiles. And that was only the beginning of the horror to follow. American Airlines Flight 77 to San Francisco left half an hour later from Dulles Airport. Shortly after takeoff it veered from its path and crashed into the Pentagon. News of the terrorist attacks began to spread. Several passengers on United Airlines Flight 93 from Newark to San Francisco heard the news over their cell phones. But hijackers seized that plane as well. Rather than allow another disaster, several passengers stormed the cockpit. Moments later the plane crashed into a wooded area of western Pennsylvania. The 38 passengers, 5 flight attendants, and 2 pilots, as well as the hijackers, all died instantly.

President George W. Bush was in Sarasota, Florida, that morning to promote educational reform. He learned about the attacks while reading to schoolchildren. Aides rushed him to Air Force One, which then flew to a secure area at Barksdale Air Force Base in Louisiana. There the president addressed a shaken nation. He called the crashes a "national tragedy" and condemned those responsible. "Freedom itself was attacked this morning by a faceless coward, and freedom will be defended," he assured the American people.

The attack on the World Trade Center left New York City in chaos. The airports shut down, tunnels and bridges closed, and masses of people struggled to leave lower Manhattan. Fearing a potentially staggering loss of life, 10,000 rescue workers swarmed to the scene, where as many as 50,000 people had worked.

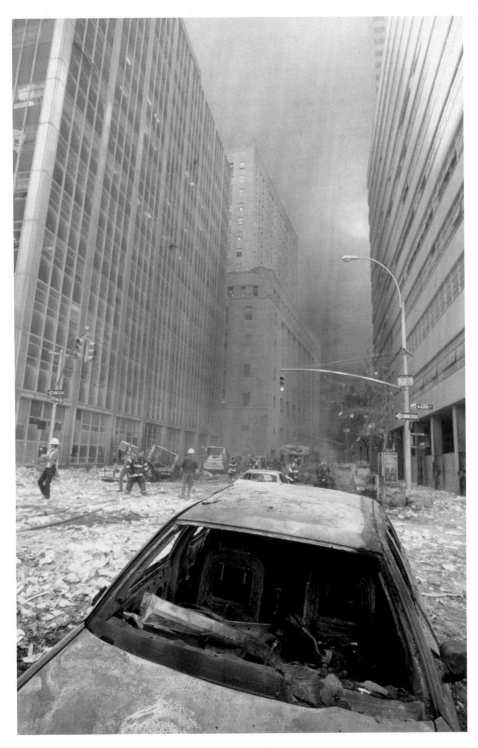

The cold war of the 1950s had imagined a Manhattan like this: debris everywhere, buildings in ruin, the city shrouded in smoke and fumes (see the movie poster on page 913). On September 11, 2001, however, disaster on such a large scale came not from confrontation with another superpower but through the actions of international terrorists. The attack made clear that in a post–cold war world, global threats could come from small groups as well as powerful nations.

Firefighters and police, arriving just after the explosions, did what they were trained to do with little regard for their personal safety. They rushed into the burning towers hoping to save as many people as they could. Some victims trapped on the top floors jumped to their deaths to escape the deadly flames. Then, with little warning, the two towers collapsed, one after the other, trapping inside thousands of office workers. With them died nearly 100 Port Authority and city police officers and some 343 fire personnel. At the Pentagon in Washington rescue workers struggled with similar heroism to evacuate victims and extinguish the intense flames. Eighty-four people died there along with the 64 people aboard Flight 77.

Global dimensions of the World Trade Center attack

In an age of instant global communications, the entire world watched as the tragedy unfolded. Three minutes after the first plane hit the World Trade Center's North Tower, Diane Sawyer of *ABC News* announced that an explosion had rocked the towers. British television was already covering the fire when the second plane reached its target at 9:03. Japanese networks were on the air with coverage of the Pentagon crash about an hour later, around midnight their time. TV Azteca in Mexico carried President Bush's statement from Barksdale Air Force Base, and China Central Television was not far behind. For this was, indeed, an international tragedy. The aptly named World Trade Center was a hub for global trade and finance. The citizens of more than 50 nations had died in the attack, hailing from states as diverse as Argentina and Belarus to Yemen and Zimbabwe. Expressions of sorrow flowed in from around the world. Paraguay, for example, issued a stamp memorializing the event, with the slogan "No to Terrorism" (left).

As for the United States, the events of September 11, 2001, changed it profoundly. Not since Pearl Harbor had the nation experienced such a devastating attack on its homeland. Most directly the tragedy claimed approximately 3,000 lives. Some 2,000 children lost a parent in the World Trade Center attack. More than 20,000 residents living nearby had to evacuate their homes. Officials estimated the cost to the New York City economy at over $83 billion.

Economic downturn

Before September 11 the booming economy of the 1990s had already shown serious signs of strain. Shares in many once high-flying dot-com Internet companies had plummeted, sending the stock market into a sharp decline. Telecommunications companies were among the biggest losers. Having spent vast sums on broadband connections for the Internet, they found themselves awash in debt they could not repay. Thus the disruptions of September 11 and its aftermath shocked an economy already sliding into recession.

Added to those economic worries were new fears for American security. The attacks seemed to be the work not of enemy nations but of an Arab terrorist group known as al Qaeda, led by a shadowy figure, Saudi national Osama bin Laden. Members of al Qaeda had moved freely around the United States for years, attended flight training schools, and found jobs. How many more undetected terrorist cells were preparing to commit acts of sabotage? Malls, high-rise buildings, and sports stadiums all loomed as possible targets.

What had also changed was the nature of the threat. Following World War II, the possibility of atomic war reduced American confidence that the United States could remain safely isolated from the great-power conflicts of the Old World. The attack on the World Trade Center proved that nations were no longer the only threat to national security. Smaller groups—subnational or international—possessed the capability of using weapons of mass destruction to make war against the most powerful nation on Earth.

The Bush Agenda

The burden of the World Trade crisis fell squarely on the shoulders of President George W. Bush, and that crisis energized him. Before September 11, the administration seemed somewhat unsure on its feet. Comedians liked to poke fun at the president's fractured use of the English language. Many observers considered his vice president, Richard Cheney, to be the person actually running the White House. Bush's claim to leadership was shaky partly because when he came to office in January 2001, a majority of the electorate had voted for his Democratic opponent, Al Gore. Among critics the president had a reputation for showing little mastery of complex domestic issues and almost none of foreign policy. Yet his easy self-assurance contrasted sharply with Bill Clinton's more frenetic style. The era of 20-hour workdays was over. Early on, Bush let his staff know that he wanted them home for dinner with their families. He seemed happier relaxing on his ranch in Texas than wielding power in Washington.

Still, as the president began his term he recognized a prime opportunity to advance his agenda, since the elections had given the Republicans control of both legislative branches. Even when the Democrats gained a temporary edge in the Senate, as Vermont senator James Jeffords defected from the Republicans to become an independent, Bush's political hand remained strong.

In his inaugural address the president vowed that his would be an inclusive administration. Prominent appointments of women, Latinos, and African Americans reinforced that promise. Condoleezza Rice, an African American academic from Stanford, became the first woman to serve as national security adviser. The highly respected former chair of the Joint Chiefs of Staff, Colin Powell (also an African American), became secretary of state. Bush drew heavily as well on those who had served his father's administration—not only Powell but also Vice President Richard Cheney and Secretary of Defense Donald Rumsfeld. Other appointments indicated that the president would still listen closely to the conservatives who formed the core of his support. His attorney general was former Missouri senator John Ashcroft, an outspoken abortion foe and critic of homosexual lifestyles and the gay rights movement.

Conservative Domestic Initiatives

In the first months of his administration Bush launched initiatives to cut taxes, meet the nation's future energy needs, reform the nation's schools, and improve national defense. Very often he spoke as a moderate; yet he acted as a conservative, judging by the details of his programs. When Vice President Cheney brought energy industry leaders together in the summer of 2001 to discuss policy, he

Energy policy

The Bush administration reversed a number of environmental rulings put in place during the Clinton era, including a gradual ban of snowmobiles in Yellowstone and Grand Teton National Parks. In general the new administration was more receptive to deregulation and voluntary standards as ways of addressing environmental problems.

included no one from the environmental community. The group recommended a course of action that stressed energy production rather than conservation. For example, they rejected tougher gas-mileage standards for popular sport utility vehicles and light trucks. Their proposal to drill for oil in the Alaska National Wildlife Refuge particularly angered environmentalists.

Education

To improve education, the administration pressed to make schools more accountable through the use of standardized tests. Liberal Democrats like Senator Ted Kennedy joined the president in January 2002 when he signed into law the "No Child Left Behind" initiative. Yet while the bill allowed for $18 billion in funding, the administration asked for only $12 billion, leaving much of the burden of implementing the ambitious new program to state and local governments, which were already strapped for funds. Evangelical Christians were pleased with the president's proposal for "faith-based initiatives" that would provide public funds to churches involved in education and social work. Critics complained that such aid blurred the line separating church and state.

Tax cuts

Tax cuts formed the cornerstone of the Bush agenda. Budget surpluses inherited from the Clinton administration seemed to justify some tax relief. Many conservatives wanted lower taxes in order to limit the government's ability to initiate new policies—a strategy referred to as "starving the beast." With the threat of recession looming, Bush also defended his tax proposals as a means to boost the economy. Lower taxes, he argued, would lead to new growth and more jobs. The Republican-controlled Congress supported the cuts, passing first the Economic Growth and Tax Reform Reconciliation Act of 2001 (EGTRRA) and then the Job Creation and Workers Assistance Act of 2002 (JCWA).

Size alone did not make these tax bills controversial. The cuts were not as large as Lyndon Johnson's in 1964 or Ronald Reagan's in 1981. Furthermore, many of the cuts were to be phased in gradually and then expire abruptly after 2010. (This juggling was designed to lessen the size of deficits over the long-term, although conservatives were soon campaigning to make the cuts permanent.) What critics objected to was how heavily the tax relief seemed targeted at the upper income brackets. Citizens for Tax Justice claimed that by 2010, when (and if) the Bush tax reductions were fully in place, 52 percent of the total tax relief would be going to the richest 1 percent of Americans—whose average 2010 income would be $1.5 million. That 1 percent made more money than the bottom 40 percent of all wage earners. Their tax windfall in 2010 alone would average $85,000. For the four out of five families and individuals making less than $73,000 in 2001, the savings came largely in the first year and averaged about $350.

Many economists argued that by making the top 1 percent the prime beneficiaries of tax relief, the cuts offered little economic stimulus. Further, ballooning deficits would likely destroy the opportunity to deal with other pressing problems: rising unemployment, future insolvency for the Social Security system, prescription drug benefits for elderly retirees, better schools, and state and local governments burdened by heavy debt. Even more controversial, EGTRRA phased out estate taxes, or what Republicans labeled "death taxes." Among its sharpest critics were some of the nation's richest people, including investors Warren Buffett and George Soros. They argued that the end of estate taxes would lower the incentive to give to charities and nonprofit organizations—by "between $3.6 billion and $6 billion per year," according to one economist. Whether or not the tax cut stimulus was worth its hefty price tag, the economy seemed on the upswing by the end of 2003.

Unilateralism in Foreign Affairs

Even before the events of September 11, in foreign affairs the president rejected the policy of multilateralism that had guided American presidents, including his father, since World War II. Bill Clinton had sent American troops on peacekeeping missions to Yugoslavia and Haiti. Bush opposed the use of American forces to settle local crises. "The vice president and I have a disagreement about the use of troops," he noted of Al Gore, during the presidential campaign debates of 2000. "He believes in nation-building. I would be very careful about using our troops as nation builders." This reluctance to commit American forces did not mean a policy of isolation so much as one of acting alone, if and when the policies of American allies conflicted with those of the United States. President Bush was determined that the United States would play an important role in global economic and political affairs, but largely on its own terms.

Soon after taking office the president announced plans to revive Ronald Reagan's Star Wars missile defense shield. Bush claimed that "rogue states" such as Iraq, Iran, and North Korea threatened the United States with nuclear weapons programs. But in order to build a national missile defense (or NMD), the United States would have to break the antiballistic missile treaty Richard Nixon had negotiated with the Soviet Union at the SALT talks of 1972. Like Europe's other leaders, Russian premier Vladimir Putin feared that the NMD program would trigger a renewed arms race. He refused to renegotiate the treaty.

Then, in a move that shocked many of America's allies, President Bush refused to sign the 1997 Kyoto Protocols on global warming subscribed to by 178 other nations. "We have no interest in implementing that treaty," announced Christie Whitman, head of the Environmental Protection Agency. Compliance would add an unfair burden on American energy producers, she argued. Environmentalists around the globe were dismayed. With only 4 percent of the world's population, the United States produced about 25 percent of Earth's greenhouse gas emissions (of carbon dioxide, methane, and other gases) thought by scientists to contribute to a warming of the world's climate.

Kyoto Protocols rejected

After seven months in office George Bush's conservative agenda and his unilateralism had not stirred widespread popular enthusiasm. Domestically, his approval ratings had dropped 10 points over six months. Abroad, one normally friendly British newspaper worried that the United States sought to "force everybody else to make concessions, while itself remaining impervious to change." Other Europeans cautioned that the United States itself "could become a rogue nation if it continues in refusing to cut climate pollution." Angry members of the United Nations removed the United States from the Commission on Human Rights.

But September 11 changed perspectives both at home and around the world.

Wars on Terrorism

"This is not only an attack on the United States but an attack on the civilised world," insisted German chancellor Gerhard Schroeder, while French prime minister Lionel Jospin expressed his feelings of "sadness and horror." Even normally hostile nations like Cuba and Libya conveyed their shock and regrets. At home the president seemed energized by the crisis. In a speech to the nation he vowed that "the United States will hunt down and punish those responsible for these cowardly acts." At the same time he was careful to note that Americans would wage war on terrorism, not Islam.

He distinguished between the majority of "peace loving" Muslims and "evil-doers" like Osama bin Laden. This war would produce no smashing victories nor a quick end, he warned, but the adversary's identity was clear: "Our enemy is a radical network of terrorists and every government that supports them." Other countries now had a simple choice: "Either you are with us or you are with the terrorists." The war would end only when terrorism no longer threatened the world.

But a war with so many shadowy opponents was not always easy to reduce to an *either/or* proposition, because it was not always easy to agree on which radical groups or even which nations threatened American security directly. The "radical network of terrorists" worked underground, communicated secretly, and was spread across dozens of nations. Even the states most hospitable to al Qaeda proved hard to single out. Afghanistan was an obvious target, as it had long been haven to bin Laden and the seat of the Taliban Islamic fundamentalists who ruled the country. Yet 15 of the 19 hijackers in the World Trade attacks hailed from Saudi Arabia, long an ally of the United States. Over the course of the next three years, as the administration widened its campaign to root out terrorism, there seemed to be not one war on terror but several—waged both abroad and at home.

The Roots of Terror

Before September 11 few Americans had paid much attention to terrorism or terrorist movements—that is, movements that used violent attacks against civilian populations to bring about change in the political and social order.* Indeed, few American radicals had resorted to terrorist tactics. During the Red scare following World War I anarchists exploded bombs, including one detonated on Wall Street in New York City (see pages 773–774). Thirty people died, but no other major incidents had followed. Incidents of terror became more frequent in the 1960s and 1970s. Radical groups such as the Weathermen and Symbionese Liberation Army planted bombs, robbed banks, and occasionally killed innocent bystanders. In 1995 Timothy McVeigh, a right-wing terrorist, exploded a bomb that killed 168 people in a federal building in Oklahoma City. Yet those events were shocking precisely because, in the United States, they were relatively rare.

Most twentieth-century terrorist attacks had taken place abroad. Radical Zionists used terrorism in Palestine after World War II, during their struggle to create the state of Israel. In Northern Ireland both Catholics and Protestants resorted to terror. In 1971 the Irish Republican Army (IRA) used bombs to avenge the murder of Catholic civil rights protestors by Protestant Unionists. Occasionally the IRA struck targets in England. The Unionists (or Orangemen) countered IRA efforts with their own bombs; and for over two decades a reign of terror gripped Northern Ireland. In 1972 members of the Palestinian "Black September" movement killed 11 Israeli athletes at the Munich Olympics. A suicide bomber had killed 241 U.S. Marines in Lebanon in 1983. Over the next seven years hijackers destroyed six large commercial aircraft.

Most of those terrorists had resorted to violence not because they were strong but because they were weak. By creating widespread fear they hoped to undermine the legitimacy of governments or force their enemies to recognize their grievances.

---

*The U.S. State Department's formal definition of terrorism is "Premeditated, politically motivated violence perpetrated against noncombatant targets by subnational groups or clandestine agents, usually intended to influence an audience."

For most of the twentieth century, Americans were accustomed to thinking of terrorism as a problem encountered abroad, as in Northern Ireland, where this IRA mural was painted on a wall (left) or in Israel, where Palestinian terrorists used bombings to campaign for their own independent state (center). In 1995 terrorism at home shocked Americans, when Timothy McVeigh (right) was arrested for bombing a federal building in Oklahoma City.

In both Northern Ireland and in Israel, for example, the ruling governments possessed far more power than the insurgents.

In the Middle East, conditions that fostered terrorist movements increased during the 1980s and 1990s, especially in Saudi Arabia. There, some 6,000 princes and their families controlled most of the vast oil revenue flowing into the country. They used much of it to live in luxury and in the 1980s had enough money left over essentially to guarantee every Saudi citizen a government job. But by 2000 the nation's population had soared to 19 million, nearly tripling from the 7 million of 1980. Per capita income fell from around $19,000 to $7300. Much of the Saudi population was young, educated, and without much hope for the future.

Pressures in Saudi Arabia

Most of these discontented young Saudis received their education in schools run by Wahabbi clerics, a sect of radical, Islamic fundamentalists. Funding for those schools came from the Saudi monarchy as part of an effort to deflect criticism of the regime. The Wahabbis viewed the United States and its Western values as the greatest threat to Islam. They used some of their government funds to support a growing network of terrorists who bitterly opposed American support for Israel and, after 1991, the presence of American troops in Saudi Arabia.

The anti-Americanism in Saudi Arabia was shared by much of the Muslim world. Even in Kuwait, which had been liberated in the Persian Gulf War by the American-led coalition, one business leader observed that "if the U.S. is on one side, everyone else wants to be on the other." High unemployment afflicted other Islamic nations besides Saudi Arabia. Throughout much of the Middle East 50 percent or more of the population was under 25 years of age. These discontented youth provided fundamentalist clerics with a receptive audience for anti-Americanism.

Afghanistan and al Qaeda

Social conditions in the Middle East were no doubt conducive to terrorist movements, but ironically it was the cold war—and, indirectly, the United States—which

Deciding who was an ally or enemy of terror was not always easy. Pakistan was an ally of the United States in the war on terror, but many Pakistanis supported al Qaeda and Osama bin Laden, as this demonstration in Karachi, Pakistan, in September 2001 indicated. The posters picture bin Laden.

provided terrorists with the training and the weapons that made them effective. During the early 1980s the Soviet Union was bogged down in its war in Afghanistan (see page 1066). To encourage resistance to the Soviets, the United States secretly provided thousands of shoulder-fired Stinger missiles to the Mujaheddin—the Afghan rebels. The CIA, with help from Pakistan, Saudi Arabia, and the United Kingdom, encouraged Muslims from all over the world to join in the fight. Between 1982 and 1992, approximately 35,000 radicals traveled to Afghanistan from over 40 Islamic nations in the Middle East, Africa, Central Asia, and the Far East. At the time, U.S. policy makers were delighted with the alliance they had helped forge. "What was more important in the world view of history?" recalled Zbigniew Brzezinski, national security adviser during the Carter administration. "A few stirred-up Muslims or the liberation of Central Europe and the end of the Cold War?"

One of the militants who had journeyed to Afghanistan was a lanky 6-foot, 5-inch Saudi who towered over most of his fellow rebels. Osama bin Laden came from a wealthy family (he was the 17th of 57 children of a construction magnate) and was devoted to Wahabbi teachings. During the 1980s he lived in Afghanistan and used millions from his family's fortune to help construct Mujaheddin tunnel complexes (also funded by the CIA) in the Afghan mountains. It was during these years that he founded al Qaeda as a broad-based alliance of Afghan and Arab rebels. After the Taliban came to power in Afghanistan, he returned to Saudi Arabia, where in 1991 he called upon that nation to mobilize and help Kuwait repel Iraq's invasion.

Saudi Arabia did mobilize. But to bin Laden's dismay, it allowed the United States to use its lands to invade Iraq—not the kind of holy war he had imagined. He believed that the 20,000 U.S. troops stationed in Saudi Arabia profaned the Muslim holy places in Mecca and Medina. Returning to the network of hidden camps in Afghanistan, bin Laden directed a worldwide terror network. By using the Internet and cell phone technology he was able to direct his far-flung network, including operatives in the United States.

Bin Laden's global terror strategy

Bin Laden's organization differed from previous movements in important ways. As historian Walter LaFeber has noted, earlier attacks came from nation-based groups, with nationalist objectives. The Irish Republican Army wanted a unified Ireland. Palestinians wanted an independent state of their own. Al Qaeda, in contrast, had no national home. Born out of the global alliance of radical Muslims who gathered in Afghanistan in the 1980s, its primary motivation was religious rather than nationalist. It operated in small, largely independent cells located around the world, but directed by bin Laden and his comrades. The followers of al Qaeda believed that the United States promoted the globalization of secular materialism "contrary to Islamic values"; and al Qaeda intended its counterattack to be global too.

Its anti-American terrorist campaign began with the bombing at the World Trade Center in 1993. That attack killed six people but did only minimal damage

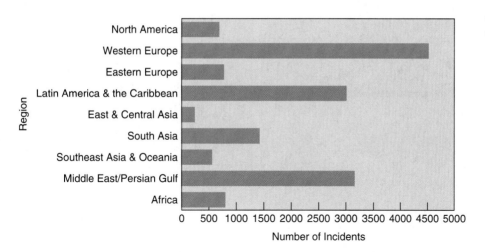

to the building. Americans remained unconcerned because authorities captured and convicted most of those directly responsible. But the attacks continued, in places far from the United States: 5 Americans dead in a training school bombing in Saudi Arabia (1995); 19 killed, 240 wounded from a truck bomb explosion at a U.S. Air Force base, also in Saudi Arabia (1996). In 1998 massive explosions hit American embassies in Kenya and Tanzania, leaving 224 people dead and thousands hurt. In 2000 a small boat approached the U.S. destroyer *Cole* at a dock in Yemen. Suddenly, a huge explosion ripped a hole in the side and killed 17 of the *Cole*'s crew.

Twice the Clinton administration retaliated against al Qaeda with missile attacks; once it narrowly missed killing bin Laden himself in one of his Afghan camps. President Clinton rejected the use of greater force, out of concern that it would provoke Muslim hostility. But the attacks of September 11 could not be ignored.

The War on Terror: First Phase

The American military campaign against terrorism began in early October 2001 with an offensive against Afghanistan. Despite intense pressure to deliver bin Laden "dead or alive," Taliban rulers had refused to expel him or other members of al Qaeda. The United States then launched sustained air attacks followed by an invasion of its special forces. The rugged Afghan mountains and deserts that had frustrated Soviet invaders in the 1980s did not stop the Americans. Using sophisticated new technology, they discovered a widespread network of hidden caves and destroyed underground bunkers. Under this deadly assault the Taliban government quickly collapsed. The United States established a coalition government in Kabul to help in the slow and expensive process of rebuilding Afghanistan.

Afghanistan

Although it became clear only months later that bin Laden had managed to escape the bombing campaign, this first stage of the war on terrorism went well. President Bush's approval ratings soared at home, and many Afghans celebrated the end of the restrictive Taliban rule, particularly women, whose rights and public roles had been severely restricted.

The War on Terror: Afghanistan and Iraq In Afghanistan al Qaeda forces were concentrated in the mountainous region along the border with Pakistan. Ethnic and religious divisions influenced allegiances in both wars. In Iraq the most severe resistance to American occupation occurred from around Baghdad to Fallujah in the west and Tikrit to the north. In this "Sunni triangle," Sunni Muslims had prospered more under Saddam Hussein than had Shia Muslims to the south.

Domestically the war on terrorism faced a daunting task. In an open society, where citizens traveled freely and valued their privacy, Americans debated how aggressively the government should act to prevent further terrorist incidents. A month after the World Trade attacks, American vulnerability was further exposed by the deaths of five people from letters tainted with anthrax bacillus sent through the postal system. Investigators eventually decided that evidence pointed to a domestic rather than foreign source of the bacillus, but widespread fears led the administration to propose the USA Patriot Act, which Congress passed so quickly that some members did not even have time to read the bill. The act broadly expanded government powers to monitor electronic communications, investigate bank transactions (to fight money laundering), and investigate people suspected of terrorist activities.

In addition, the Justice Department detained hundreds of aliens—mostly Muslims and Arabs—whom it suspected of terrorist connections. By November 5 over a thousand had been brought into custody; after that date the Justice Department refused to say how many more were being detained or to provide their names or even the location of detention. By May 2003 observers estimated that some 5000 aliens were being held, only 4 of whom had been charged with any terrorist activity. Two of those were acquitted. Critics charged that these detentions, as well as the broad powers of the Patriot Act, threatened the constitutional rights of Americans as well as the natural rights of aliens. Opponents of the measures also protested the treatment of over 650 prisoners taken in Afghanistan, who were being held indefinitely as "illegal combatants" in a camp at Guantanamo Bay, Cuba. Authorities refused to say when or if the prisoners would be tried or even accused of a crime. (A number claimed they were civilians caught up in the fighting due to the chaos of war.) Attorney General John Ashcroft responded that

Anthrax bacillus

USA Patriot Act

"those who scare peace-loving people with phantoms of lost liberty . . . only aid terrorists. . . . They give ammunition to America's enemies, and pause to America's friends."

Beyond locating and arresting terrorists, a massive effort was needed to secure vital systems of transportation, communication, and energy production. If terrorists had hijacked planes, they might also plant explosives at nuclear plants and bridges or smuggle in a low-level nuclear device via trucks or on incoming cargo freighters. In order to coordinate new security measures, Bush created the Office of Homeland Security, placing former Pennsylvania governor Tom Ridge in charge. In January 2003 it was converted into the cabinet-level Department of Homeland Security, to give it more effective power to coordinate security measures. As late-night comedians made fun of its color-coded threat-level announcements, the department struggled to impose change on bureaucracies unused to sudden transformations.

The Invasion of Iraq

For the war in Afghanistan, George Bush received widespread international support, including that of General Pervez Musharraf, the president of neighboring Pakistan; Prime Minister Tony Blair of the United Kingdom; and Premier Vladimir Putin of Russia. With Afghanistan conquered, however, Bush's focus shifted from Osama bin Laden to Iraq's brutal dictator, Saddam Hussein. Indeed, a decision to pursue the overthrow of Hussein was made in the first weekend after the September 11 attacks. The only question, Deputy Defense Secretary Paul Wolfowitz acknowledged, "was whether [invading Iraq] should be in the immediate response or whether you should concentrate simply on Afghanistan first."

Of course, it was Bush's father, George H. W. Bush, who had forged the coalition that humiliated Hussein in the Persian Gulf War of 1991. At that time, the senior Bush had made a controversial decision not to attack Baghdad and to leave Hussein in power. Bush's son seemed determined to finish the job his father had left undone. In September 2002 the president appeared before the UN General Assembly, challenging it to enforce its inspection program for weapons of mass destruction (WMD) in Iraq. Iraq had admitted, in 1995, to having manufactured chemical weapons, including VX and mustard gas, as well as to having undertaken a program to develop nuclear weapons. Hussein had agreed to destroy such materials, but beginning in 1998 he no longer allowed UN inspectors to verify the situation on the ground. "All the world now faces a test," concluded President Bush, "and the United Nations a difficult and defining moment. Are Security Council resolutions to be honored and enforced, or cast aside without consequence? Will the United Nations serve the purpose of its founding, or will it be irrelevant?"

The speech was well received; and under renewed pressure from the United Nations, Hussein allowed inspections to resume. But Bush also seemed impatient about letting the inspection process run its course. "If we know Saddam Hussein has dangerous weapons today—and we do—," he proclaimed, "does it make any sense for the world to wait . . . for the final proof, the smoking gun that could come in the form of a mushroom cloud?"

Earlier in the year, in fact, the president had laid the groundwork for a policy of not waiting, by asserting that the United States would be "ready for preemptive action when necessary to defend our liberty and to defend our lives." This doctrine of preemption—that the United States might attack before it was itself

Preemption vs. containment

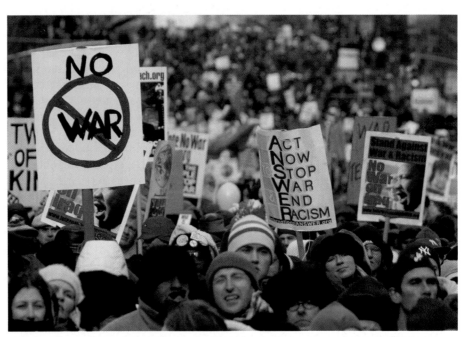

Almost forty years had passed since the United States escalated the war in Vietnam, but for many anti-war protestors the invasion of Iraq in 2003 revived painful memories of an unpopular war.

attacked—was a major departure from the policy of containment followed throughout the cold war. "A preventive war, to my mind, is an impossibility," President Eisenhower declared in 1954. "I don't believe there is such a thing, and frankly I wouldn't even listen to anyone seriously that came in and talked about such a thing." But Bush argued that, in a changed world where terrorists struck without warning, containment would no longer work.

The goal of a democratic Iraq

Furthermore, the administration was inclined to press for a "regime change" in Iraq in hopes of establishing a democracy. With a friendly government in Baghdad, the United States could use Iraq as its base of power in the Middle East. No longer would America have to depend on the increasingly vulnerable monarchy in Saudi Arabia. A democratic Iraq might also eventually inspire reform in other Muslim nations. With midterm elections looming in October 2002, the president persuaded Congress to pass a joint resolution giving him full authority to take military action if he deemed it necessary.

UN inspectors, however, reported that they could find no weapons of mass destruction nor any evidence of programs to build them. So Secretary of State Colin Powell returned to the United Nations in February 2003 to make the case that inspections would no longer suffice and that force was needed to compel Hussein's compliance. Much of the world community remained skeptical of American intentions. They were inclined to believe Hussein's charge that the Americans were inventing a pretext to seize Iraq's oil. Despite intensive negotiations, the Security Council refused to approve an American resolution giving the United States the authority to lead a UN-sponsored invasion. Only the United Kingdom, Spain, and Italy, among the major powers, were willing to join the United States. France and Germany balked (they were a part of "Old Europe," sniffed Secretary of Defense Rumsfeld), as did Russia.

On March 19, 2003, without a UN mandate, a "coalition of the willing" (about 30 nations) attacked Iraq, though the actual troops were virtually all American and British. The invasion was executed with remarkable speed and precision. Laser-guided weapons, unmanned drones, and "bunker buster" bombs shattered Iraq's defenses. Within days U.S. forces were halfway to Baghdad. On May 1 Bush announced an end to major combat operations. Coalition casualties (135 dead and 1511 wounded) were remarkably low. All the same, the ultimate prize eluded the victors. Saddam Hussein and many of his inner circle escaped.

Among the leaders of the major powers, only Prime Minister Tony Blair (left) of the United Kingdom unreservedly supported President Bush's war in Iraq. The two leaders met at the Azores several days before the invasion of Iraq, with the prime ministers of Spain and Portugal.

A Messy Aftermath

Although the large majority of Americans supported the invasion of Iraq, a vocal minority had opposed the war. Some believed that a doctrine of preemption was not only morally wrong but also dangerous. If the United States felt free to invade a country, what was to stop other nations from launching wars, justified by their own doctrines of preemption? Opponents also argued that no solid evidence linked the secular Saddam Hussein with the religious al Qaeda, a charge the president conceded, after the invasion was completed. Furthermore, a nation like North Korea—which publicly admitted that it was developing nuclear weapons—seemed a more dangerous and imminent threat than Iraq.

The administration dismissed such concerns but found it harder to ignore the practical problems arising out of swift victory. Ethnic and religious factions divided Iraq: Shiite Muslims in the southeast, Sunni Muslims around Baghdad, and Kurds in the north. Only Hussein's brutal tyranny had held the country together. Now the burden of peacekeeping fell to the American military. The United States set up an appointed governing council to consult with an American civil administrator, L. Paul Bremer III. But the governing council made slow progress toward drawing up a new constitution and holding elections. And as well trained as American troops were to fight a war, they were equipped to neither maintain public order as a police force nor rebuild Iraq's shattered economy. The United States sought both aid and troops from other nations, but most were reluctant to participate, angered by the American go-it-alone attitude toward the war. As the hot summer waned, the number of violent acts against the American occupation sharply increased. By the fall of 2003 more Americans had died preserving the peace than in winning the war. Adding insult to injury, the United States had spent over half a billion dollars searching for the weapons of mass destruction it claimed Iraq had stockpiled, without finding any. The lack of such evidence severely undermined the president's claim that Saddam Hussein had posed an imminent threat to U.S. security.

Postwar Iraq

The cost of the war rose as well. In September 2003 President Bush asked Congress for $87 billion in additional funds for Iraq. This request came as the federal government faced a deficit soon to exceed $550 billion dollars, created both by the tax cuts and by increased expenses arising out of the September 11 attacks.

The Bush administration predicted Iraqis would welcome American troops as liberators from the tyranny of Saddam Hussein. The reality proved far more complex as a drawn-out war with terrorists followed a sweeping military victory.

Some Americans asked why they should buy school buses for Iraq when their own schools were short of funds. In both Afghanistan and Iraq rebuilding war-torn economies promised to be slow and expensive—"a long, hard slog," as Secretary Rumsfeld admitted in a confidential memo.

At the end of 2003 the long-term effects of the war in Iraq remained unclear. Would that nation's instability subside, giving way to a democracy that would set a new tone in the region? Or would an American occupation lead to a destabilized Middle East, where the threat of terrorism had actually increased? Whatever the answer, in the short run unilateralism had extracted a heavy price from the United States and George Bush. Without help from the international community, U.S. troop strength was stretched to its limits. Over forty years earlier President John Kennedy had warned against a global mission that overreached the nation's powers. With only 6 percent of the world's population, the United States could not readily impose its will on the other 94 percent, he observed. Nor could it "right every wrong or reverse every adversity." In the end, "there cannot be an American solution to every world problem," he concluded. Only time would tell whether a nation of nations could act successfully to police an uncertain world.

chapter summary

The tragedy of September 11, 2001, changed the United States as much as any event since the bombing of Pearl Harbor.

- President George W. Bush began his term in 2001 with Republican majorities in both houses of Congress and a conservative agenda for lower taxes, education reform, and promotion of private energy development.

  - Major tax cuts favoring high-income Americans marked the Bush administration's major domestic success.

- Even before September 11, George Bush pursued a unilateral approach to foreign policy that led him to reject the Kyoto Protocols on global warming, withdraw from the SALT II agreements, and propose a national missile defense.

- The attacks of September 11 gave new stature to the Bush presidency as it declared war on Osama bin Laden and global terrorism.

  - Unemployed and discontented young people in the Islamic nations such as Saudi Arabia became a fertile source of recruits for Osama bin Laden and for global terrorism.

  - In October 2001 the Bush administration launched a devastating attack on Afghanistan that quickly toppled the Taliban, but bin Laden escaped.

- The new Homeland Security Department and USA Patriot Act limited civil rights and liberties in an effort to combat any domestic terrorist threat.

- In March 2003 George Bush persuaded Congress and popular opinion that Saddam Hussein's possession of weapons of mass destruction justified a preemptive American war on Iraq, but his unilateral approach offended most allies. Only the British provided major combat support.

- The combat phase of the war ended quickly as Hussein fled, but the Allies failed to find weapons of mass destruction.

- Occupation of Iraq threatened to be long and expensive when resistance among terrorists and Hussein loyalists kept Iraq in turmoil while claiming a steady toll of American lives.

additional reading

Historians lack the perspective to write effectively about the recent past. For example, the outcome and significance of the Iraq War remained much in doubt as we wrote this section. Journalists have nonetheless given us considerable insight into many issues. David Frum, *The Right Man: The Surprise Presidency of George W. Bush* (2003), draws a sympathetic portrait of the president. James Moore, *Bush's Brain: How Karl Rove Made George W. Bush Presidential* (2003), examines the political consultant most responsible for the president's political strategies. Bob Woodward, *Bush at War* (2003), gives an inside account of the Bush White House, the war in Afghanistan, and the argument over preemptive war. Todd S. Purdum, *A Time of Our Choosing: America's War in Iraq* (2003), covers the causes, conduct, and consequences of the war through August 2003. Williamson Murray and Robert H. Scales Jr., *The Iraq War: A Military History* (2003), should serve for many years as a definitive account of the military aspects of the war. Walter LaFeber, *America, Russia, and the Cold War 1945–2003*, 10th ed. (2003), contains an epilogue that looks at terrorism and the unilateralist foreign policy of George W. Bush. A number of social scientists have taken up some of the public policy issues we discuss. For a discussion of tax policy see Joel Slemrod and Jon Bakija, *Taxing Ourselves to Death: A Citizens' Guide to the Great Debate over Tax Reform* (2003). Jacob S. Hacker, *The Divided Welfare State: The Battle over Public and Private Benefits in the United States* (2003), shows how recent policy has scaled back the least generous social services among industrial nations.

To keep abreast of current history, we recommend a close reading of newspapers, journals, and social science. The *New York Review of Books*, though decidedly leftist in its point of view, covers major issues and ideas in great depth. Those who want a more conservative view might choose the *National Review*, while the *Economist* provides an international perspective. The Internet is another source for contemporary debate. Josh Marshall provides political discussions at http://talkingpointsmemo.com/index.html and Juan Cole, a history professor at the University of Michigan, follows Iraq developments at http://www.juancole.com/. Andrew Sullivan, http://www.andrewsullivan.com, has a conservative flavor. For a fuller list of readings, see the Bibliography at www.mhhe.com/davidsonnation5.

significant events

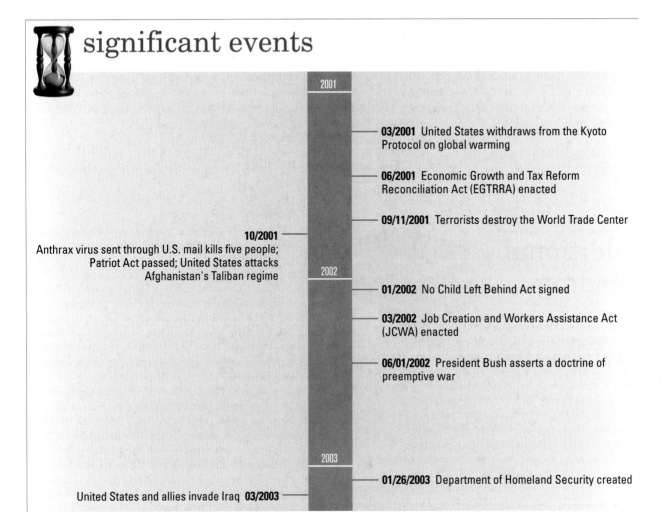

2001

03/2001 United States withdraws from the Kyoto Protocol on global warming

06/2001 Economic Growth and Tax Reform Reconciliation Act (EGTRRA) enacted

09/11/2001 Terrorists destroy the World Trade Center

10/2001
Anthrax virus sent through U.S. mail kills five people; Patriot Act passed; United States attacks Afghanistan's Taliban regime

2002

01/2002 No Child Left Behind Act signed

03/2002 Job Creation and Workers Assistance Act (JCWA) enacted

06/01/2002 President Bush asserts a doctrine of preemptive war

2003

01/26/2003 Department of Homeland Security created

United States and allies invade Iraq **03/2003**

The Declaration of Independence

In Congress, July 4, 1776,

THE UNANIMOUS DECLARATION OF THE THIRTEEN
UNITED STATES OF AMERICA

When, in the course of human events, it becomes necessary for one people to dissolve the political bands which have connected them with another, and to assume, among the powers of the earth, the separate and equal station to which the laws of nature and of nature's God entitle them, a decent respect to the opinions of mankind requires that they should declare the causes which impel them to the separation.

We hold these truths to be self-evident, that all men are created equal; that they are endowed by their Creator with certain unalienable rights; that among these, are life, liberty, and the pursuit of happiness. That, to secure these rights, governments are instituted among men, deriving their just powers from the consent of the governed; that, whenever any form of government becomes destructive of these ends, it is the right of the people to alter or to abolish it, and to institute a new government, laying its foundation on such principles, and organizing its powers in such form, as to them shall seem most likely to effect their safety and happiness. Prudence, indeed, will dictate that governments long established, should not be changed for light and transient causes; and, accordingly, all experience hath shown, that mankind are more disposed to suffer, while evils are sufferable, than to right themselves by abolishing the forms to which they are accustomed. But, when a long train of abuses and usurpations, pursuing invariably the same object, evinces a design to reduce them under absolute despotism, it is their right, it is their duty, to throw off such government and to provide new guards for their future security. Such has been the patient sufferance of these colonies, and such is now the necessity which constrains them to alter their former systems of government. The history of the present King of Great Britain is a history of repeated injuries and usurpations, all having, in direct object, the establishment of an absolute tyranny over these States. To prove this, let facts be submitted to a candid world:

He has refused his assent to laws the most wholesome and necessary for the public good.

He has forbidden his governors to pass laws of immediate and pressing importance, unless suspended in their operation till his assent should be obtained; and, when so suspended, he has utterly neglected to attend to them.

He has refused to pass other laws for the accommodation of large districts of people, unless those people would relinquish the right of representation in the legislature; a right inestimable to them, and formidable to tyrants only.

He has called together legislative bodies at places unusual, uncomfortable, and distant from the depository of their public records, for the sole purpose of fatiguing them into compliance with his measures.

He has dissolved representative houses repeatedly for opposing, with manly firmness, his invasions on the rights of the people.

He has refused, for a long time after such dissolutions, to cause others to be elected; whereby the legislative powers, incapable of annihilation, have returned to the people at large for their exercise; the state remaining, in the meantime, exposed to all the danger of invasion from without, and convulsions within.

He has endeavored to prevent the population of these States; for that purpose, obstructing the laws for naturalization of foreigners, refusing to pass others to encourage their migration hither, and raising the conditions of new appropriations of lands.

He had obstructed the administration of justice, by refusing his assent to laws for establishing judiciary powers.

He has made judges dependent on his will alone, for the tenure of their offices, and the amount and payment of their salaries.

He has erected a multitude of new offices, and sent hither swarms of officers to harass our people, and eat out their substance.

He has kept among us, in time of peace, standing armies, without the consent of our legislatures.

He has affected to render the military independent of, and superior to, the civil power.

He has combined, with others, to subject us to a jurisdiction foreign to our Constitution, and unacknowledged by our laws; giving his assent to their acts of pretended legislation:

For quartering large bodies of armed troops among us:

For protecting them by a mock trial, from punishment, for any murders which they should commit on the inhabitants of these States:

For cutting off our trade with all parts of the world:

For imposing taxes on us without our consent:

For depriving us, in many cases, of the benefit of trial by jury:

For transporting us beyond seas to be tried for pretended offences:

For abolishing the free system of English laws in a neighboring province, establishing therein an arbitrary government, and enlarging its boundaries, so as to render it at once an example and fit instrument for introducing the same absolute rule into these colonies:

For taking away our charters, abolishing our most valuable laws, and altering, fundamentally, the powers of our governments:

For suspending our own legislatures, and declaring themselves invested with power to legislate for us in all cases whatsoever.

He has abdicated government here, by declaring us out of his protection, and waging war against us.

He has plundered our seas, ravaged our coasts, burnt our towns, and destroyed the lives of our people.

He is, at this time, transporting large armies of foreign mercenaries to complete the works of death, desolation, and tyranny, already begun, with circumstances of cruelty and perfidy scarcely paralleled in the most barbarous ages, and totally unworthy the head of a civilized nation.

He has constrained our fellow citizens, taken captive on the high seas, to bear arms against their country, to become the executioners of their friends, and brethren, or to fall themselves by their hands.

He has excited domestic insurrections amongst us, and has endeavored to bring on the inhabitants of our frontiers, the merciless Indian savages, whose known rule of warfare is an undistinguished destruction of all ages, sexes, and conditions.

In every stage of these oppressions, we have petitioned for redress, in the most humble terms; our repeated petitions have been answered only by repeated injury. A prince, whose character is thus marked by every act which may define a tyrant, is unfit to be the ruler of a free people.

Nor have we been wanting in attention to our British brethren. We have warned them, from time to time, of attempts made by their legislature to extend an unwarrantable jurisdiction over us. We have reminded them of the circumstances of our emigration and settlement here. We have appealed to their native justice and magnanimity, and we have conjured them, by the ties of our common kindred, to disavow these usurpations, which would inevitably interrupt our connections and correspondence. They, too, have been deaf to the voice of justice and consanguinity. We must, therefore, acquiesce in the necessity which denounces our separation, and hold them as we hold the rest of mankind, enemies in war, in peace, friends.

We, therefore, the representatives of the United States of America, in general Congress assembled, appealing to the Supreme Judge of the world for the rectitude of our intentions, do, in the name, and by the authority of the good people of these colonies, solemnly publish and declare, that these united colonies are, and of right ought to be, free and independent states: that they are absolved from all allegiance to the British Crown, and that all political connection between them and the state of Great Britain is, and ought to be, totally dissolved; and that, as free and independent states, they have full power to levy war, conclude peace, contract alliances, establish commerce, and to do all other acts and things which independent states may of right do. And, for the support of this declaration, with a firm reliance on the protection of Divine Providence, we mutually pledge to each other our lives, our fortunes, and our sacred honor.

The foregoing Declaration was, by order of Congress, engrossed, and signed by the following members:

JOHN HANCOCK

New Hampshire	New York	Delaware	North Carolina
Josiah Bartlett	William Floyd	Caesar Rodney	William Hooper
William Whipple	Philip Livingston	George Read	Joseph Hewes
Matthew Thornton	Francis Lewis	Thomas M'Kean	John Penn
	Lewis Morris		

Massachusetts Bay	New Jersey	Maryland	South Carolina
Samuel Adams	Richard Stockton	Samuel Chase	Edward Rutledge
John Adams	John Witherspoon	William Paca	Thomas Heyward, Jr.
Robert Treat Paine	Francis Hopkinson	Thomas Stone	Thomas Lynch, Jr.
Elbridge Gerry	John Hart	Charles Carroll, of Carrollton	Arthur Middleton
	Abraham Clark		

Rhode Island
Stephen Hopkins
William Ellery

Connecticut
Roger Sherman
Samuel Huntington
William Williams
Oliver Wolcott

Pennsylvania
Robert Morris
Benjamin Rush
Benjamin Franklin
John Morton
George Clymer
James Smith
George Taylor
James Wilson
George Ross

Virginia
George Wythe
Richard Henry Lee
Thomas Jefferson
Benjamin Harrison
Thomas Nelson, Jr.
Francis Lightfoot Lee
Carter Braxton

Georgia
Button Gwinnett
Lyman Hall
George Walton

Resolved, That copies of the Declaration be sent to the several assemblies, conventions, and committees, or councils of safety, and to the several commanding officers of the continental troops; that it be proclaimed in each of the United States, at the head of the army.

The Constitution of the United States of America[1]

We the People of the United States, in Order to form a more perfect Union, establish Justice, insure domestic Tranquility, provide for the common defence, promote the general Welfare, and secure the Blessings of Liberty to ourselves and our Posterity, do ordain and establish this CONSTITUTION for the United States of America.

ARTICLE I

Section 1. All legislative Powers herein granted shall be vested in a Congress of the United States, which shall consist of a Senate and House of Representatives.

Section 2. The House of Representatives shall be composed of Members chosen every second Year by the People of the several States, and the Electors in each State shall have the Qualifications requisite for Electors of the most numerous Branch of the State Legislature.

No Person shall be a Representative who shall not have attained to the Age of twenty-five Years, and been seven Years a Citizen of the United States, and who shall not, when elected, be an Inhabitant of that State in which he shall be chosen.

[Representatives and direct Taxes[2] shall be apportioned among the several States which may be included within this Union, according to their respective Numbers, which shall be determined by adding to the whole Number of free Persons, including those bound to Service for a Term of Years, and excluding Indians not taxed, three fifths of all other Persons.][3] The actual Enumeration shall be made within three Years after the first Meeting of the Congress of the United States, and within every subsequent Term of ten Years, in such Manner as they shall by Law direct. The Number of Representatives shall not exceed one for every thirty Thousand, but each State shall have at Least one Representative; and until such enumeration shall be made, the State of New Hampshire shall be entitled to chuse three, Massachusetts eight, Rhode-Island and Providence Plantations one, Connecticut five, New York six, New Jersey four, Pennsylvania eight, Delaware one, Maryland six, Virginia ten, North Carolina five, South Carolina five, and Georgia three.

When vacancies happen in the Representation from any State, the Executive Authority thereof shall issue Writs of Election to fill such Vacancies.

The House of Representatives shall chuse their Speaker and other Officers; and shall have the sole Power of Impeachment.

Section 3. The Senate of the United States shall be composed of two Senators from each State, chosen by the Legislature thereof, for six Years; and each Senator shall have one Vote.

Immediately after they shall be assembled in Consequence of the first Election, they shall be divided as equally as may be into three Classes. The Seats of the Senators of the first Class shall be vacated at the Expiration of the second Year, of the second Class at the Expiration of the fourth Year, and of the third Class at the Expiration of the sixth Year, so that one-third may be chosen every second Year; and if Vacancies happen by Resignation, or otherwise, during the Recess of the Legislature of any State, the Executive thereof may make temporary Appointments until the next Meeting of the Legislature, which shall then fill such Vacancies.

No Person shall be a Senator who shall not have attained to the Age of thirty Years, and been nine Years a Citizen of the United States, and who shall not, when elected, be an Inhabitant of that State for which he shall be chosen.

The Vice President of the United States shall be President of the Senate, but shall have no vote, unless they be equally divided.

The Senate shall chuse their other Officers, and also a President pro tempore, in the absence of the Vice President, or when he shall exercise the Office of President of the United States.

The Senate shall have the sole Power to try all Impeachments. When sitting for that purpose they shall be on Oath or Affirmation. When the President of the United States is tried, the Chief Justice shall preside: And no person shall be convicted without the Concurrence of two thirds of the Members present.

Judgment in Cases of Impeachment shall not extend further than to removal from Office, and disqualification to hold and enjoy any Office of honor, Trust, or Profit under the United States: but the Party convicted shall nevertheless be liable and subject to Indictment, Trial, Judgment, and Punishment, according to Law.

Section 4. The Times, Places and Manner of holding Elections for Senators and Representatives, shall be prescribed in each State by the Legislature thereof; but the Congress may at any time by Law make or alter such Regulations, except as to the Places of Chusing Senators.

---

[1]This version follows the original Constitution in capitalization and spelling. It is adapted from the text published by the United States Department of the Interior, Office of Education.

[2]Altered by the Sixteenth Amendment.

[3]Negated by the Fourteenth Amendment.

The Congress shall assemble at least once in every Year, and such Meeting shall be on the first Monday in December, unless they shall by Law appoint a different Day.

Section 5. Each House shall be the Judge of the Elections, Returns and Qualifications of its own Members, and a Majority of each shall constitute a Quorum to do Business; but a smaller number may adjourn from day to day, and may be authorized to compel the Attendance of absent Members, in such Manner, and under such Penalties, as each House may provide.

Each House may determine the Rules of its Proceedings, punish its Members for disorderly Behaviour, and, with the Concurrence of two thirds, expel a Member.

Each House shall keep a Journal of its Proceedings, and from time to time publish the same, excepting such Parts as may in their Judgment require Secrecy; and the Yeas and Nays of the Members of either House on any question shall, at the Desire of one fifth of those Present, be entered on the Journal.

Neither House, during the Session of Congress, shall, without the Consent of the other, adjourn for more than three days, nor to any other Place than that in which the two Houses shall be sitting.

Section 6. The Senators and Representatives shall receive a Compensation for their Services, to be ascertained by Law, and paid out of the Treasury of the United States. They shall in all Cases, except Treason, Felony, and Breach of the Peace, be privileged from Arrest during their Attendance at the Session of their respective Houses, and in going to and returning from the same; and for any Speech or Debate in either House, they shall not be questioned in any other Place.

No Senator or Representative shall, during the Time for which he was elected, be appointed to any civil Office under the Authority of the United States, which shall have been created, or the Emoluments whereof shall have been increased, during such time; and no Person holding any Office under the United States shall be a Member of either House during his continuance in Office.

Section 7. All Bills for raising Revenue shall originate in the House of Representatives; but the Senate may propose or concur with Amendments as on other bills.

Every Bill which shall have passed the House of Representatives and the Senate, shall, before it become a Law, be presented to the President of the United States; If he approve he shall sign it, but if not he shall return it, with his Objections, to that House in which it shall have originated, who shall enter the Objections at large on their Journal, and proceed to reconsider it. If after such Reconsideration two thirds of that House shall agree to pass the bill, it shall be sent, together with the objections, to the other House, by which it shall likewise be reconsidered, and if approved by two thirds of that House, it shall become a Law. But in all such Cases the Votes of both Houses shall be determined by Yeas and Nays, and the Names of the Persons voting for and against the Bill shall be entered on the Journal of each House respectively. If any Bill shall not be returned by the President within ten Days (Sundays excepted) after it shall have been presented to him, the Same shall be a Law, in like Manner as if he had signed it, unless the Congress by their Adjournment prevent its Return, in which Case it shall not be a Law.

Every Order, Resolution, or Vote to which the Concurrence of the Senate and House of Representatives may be necessary (except on a question of Adjournment) shall be presented to the President of the United States; and before the Same shall take Effect, shall be approved by him, or being disapproved by him, shall be repassed by two thirds of the Senate and House of Representatives, according to the Rules and Limitations prescribed in the Case of a Bill.

Section 8. The Congress shall have Power To lay and collect Taxes, Duties, Imposts and Excises, to pay the Debts and provide for the common Defence and general Welfare of the United States; but all Duties, Imposts and Excises shall be uniform throughout the United States;

To borrow money on the credit of the United States;

To regulate Commerce with foreign Nations, and among the several States, and with the Indian Tribes;

To establish an uniform rule of Naturalization, and uniform Laws on the subject of Bankruptcies throughout the United States;

To coin Money, regulate the Value thereof, and of foreign Coin, and fix the Standard of Weights and Measures;

To provide for the Punishment of counterfeiting the Securities and current Coin of the United States;

To establish Post Offices and post Roads;

To promote the Progress of Science and useful Arts, by securing for limited Times to Authors and Inventors the exclusive Right to their respective Writings and Discoveries;

To constitute Tribunals inferior to the Supreme Court;

To define and punish Piracies and Felonies committed on the high Seas, and Offenses against the Law of Nations;

To declare War, grant Letters of Marque and Reprisal, and make Rules concerning Captures on Land and Water;

To raise and support Armies, but no Appropriation of Money to that Use shall be for a longer Term than two Years;

To provide and maintain a Navy;

To make Rules for the Government and Regulation of the land and naval forces;

To provide for calling forth the Militia to execute the Laws of the Union, suppress Insurrections and repel Invasions;

To provide for organizing, arming, and disciplining the Militia, and for government such Part of them as may be employed in the Service of the United States, reserving to the States respectively, the Appointment of the Officers, and the Authority of training the Militia according to the discipline prescribed by Congress;

To exercise exclusive Legislation in all Cases whatsoever, over such District (not exceeding ten Miles square) as may, by Cession of particular States, and the acceptance of Congress, become the Seat of the Government of the United States, and to exercise like Authority over all Places purchased by the Consent of the Legislature of the State in which the Same shall be, for the Erection of Forts, Magazines, Arsenals, Dock-yards, and other needful Buildings;—-And

To make all Laws which shall be necessary and proper for carrying into Execution the foregoing Powers, and all other Powers vested by this Constitution in the Government of the United States, or in any Department or Officer thereof.

Section 9. The Migration or Importation of such Persons as any of the States now existing shall think proper to admit, shall not be prohibited by the Congress prior to the Year one thousand eight hundred and eight, but a tax or duty may be imposed on such Importation, not exceeding ten dollars for each Person.

The privilege of the Writ of Habeas Corpus shall not be suspended, unless when in Cases of Rebellion or Invasion the public Safety may require it.

No bill of Attainder or ex post facto Law shall be passed.

No capitation, or other direct, Tax shall be laid unless in Proportion to the Census or Enumeration herein before directed to be taken.

No Tax or Duty shall be laid on Articles exported from any State.

No Preference shall be given by any Regulation of Commerce or Revenue to the Ports of one State over those of another: nor shall Vessels bound to, or from, one State, be obliged to enter, clear, or pay Duties in another.

No Money shall be drawn from the Treasury, but in Consequence of Appropriations made by Law; and a regular Statement and Account of the Receipts and Expenditures of all public Money shall be published from time to time.

No Title of Nobility shall be granted by the United States: And no Person holding any Office of Profit or Trust under them, shall, without the Consent of the Congress, accept of any present, Emolument, Office, or Title, of any kind whatever, from any King, Prince, or foreign State.

Section 10. No State shall enter into any Treaty, Alliance, or Confederation; grant Letters of Marque and Reprisal; coin Money; emit Bills of Credit; make any Thing but gold and silver Coin a Tender in Payment of Debts; pass any Bill of Attainder, ex post facto Law, or Law impairing the Obligation of Contracts, or grant any Title of Nobility.

No State shall, without the Consent of the Congress, lay any Imposts or Duties on Imports or Exports, except what may be absolutely necessary for executing its inspection Laws; and the net Produce of all Duties and Imposts, laid by any State on Imports or Exports, shall be for the use of the Treasury of the United States; and all such Laws shall be subject to the Revision and Control of the Congress.

No state shall, without the Consent of Congress, lay any duty of Tonnage, keep Troops, or Ships of War in time of Peace, enter into any Agreement or Compact with another State, or with a foreign Power, or engage in War, unless actually invaded, or in such imminent Danger as will not admit of delay.

ARTICLE II

Section 1. The executive Power shall be vested in a President of the United States of America. He shall hold his Office during the Term of four years, and, together with the Vice President, chosen for the same Term, be elected, as follows:

Each State shall appoint, in such Manner as the Legislature thereof may direct, a Number of Electors, equal to the whole Number of Senators and Representatives to which the State may be entitled in the Congress: but no Senator or Representative, or Person holding an Office of Trust or Profit under the United States, shall be appointed an Elector.

[The Electors shall meet in their respective States, and vote by Ballot for two persons, of whom one at least shall not be an Inhabitant of the same State with themselves. And they shall make a List of all the Persons voted for, and of the Number of Votes for each; which List they shall sign and certify, and transmit sealed to the Seat of the Government of the United States, directed to the President of the Senate. The President of the Senate shall, in the Presence of the Senate and House of Representatives, open all the Certificates, and the Votes shall then be counted. The Person having the greatest Number of Votes shall be the President, if such Number be a Majority of the whole Number of Electors appointed; and if there be more than one who have such Majority, and have an equal Number of Votes, then the House of Representatives shall immediately chuse by Ballot one of them for President; and if no Person have a Majority, then from the five highest on the List the said House shall in like Manner chuse the President. But in chusing the President, the Votes shall be taken by States, the Representation from each State having one Vote; a quorum for this Purpose shall consist of a Member or Members from two-thirds of the States, and a Majority of all the States shall be necessary to a Choice. In every Case, after the Choice of the President, the Person having the greatest Number of Votes of the Electors shall be the Vice President. But if there should remain two or more who have equal votes, the Senate shall chuse from them by Ballot the Vice President.][4]

The Congress may determine the Time of chusing the Electors, and the Day on which they shall give their Votes; which Day shall be the same throughout the United States.

No person except a natural-born Citizen, or a Citizen of the United States, at the time of the Adoption of this Constitution, shall be eligible to the Office of President; neither shall any Person be eligible to that Office who shall not have attained to the Age of thirty-five years, and been fourteen Years a Resident within the United States.

In Case of the Removal of the President from Office, or of his Death, Resignation, or Inability to discharge the Powers and

---

[4]Revised by the Twelfth Amendment.

Duties of the said Office, the same shall devolve on the Vice President, and the Congress may by Law provide for the Case of Removal, Death, Resignation, or Inability, both of the President and Vice President, declaring what Officer shall then act as President, and such Officer shall act accordingly, until the disability be removed, or a President shall be elected.

The President shall, at stated Times, receive for his Services a Compensation, which shall neither be increased nor diminished during the Period for which he shall have been elected, and he shall not receive within that Period any other Emolument from the United States, or any of them.

Before he enter on the execution of his Office, he shall take the following Oath or Affirmation:—"I do solemnly swear (or affirm) that I will faithfully execute the Office of President of the United States, and will, to the best of my Ability, preserve, protect, and defend the Constitution of the United States."

Section 2. The President shall be Commander in Chief of the Army and Navy of the United States, and of the Militia of the several States, when called into the actual Service of the United States; he may require the Opinion, in writing, of the principal Officer in each of the executive Departments, upon any subject relating to the Duties of their respective Offices, and he shall have Power to Grant Reprieves and Pardons for Offenses against the United States, except in Cases of Impeachment.

He shall have Power, by and with the Advice and Consent of the Senate, to make Treaties, provided two-thirds of the Senators present concur; and he shall nominate, and by and with the Advice and Consent of the Senate, shall appoint Ambassadors, other public Ministers and Consuls, Judges of the supreme Court, and all other Officers of the United States, whose Appointments are not herein otherwise provided for, and which shall be established by Law: but the Congress may by Law vest the Appointment of such inferior Officers, as they think proper, in the President alone, in the Courts of Law, or in the Heads of Departments.

The President shall have Power to fill up all Vacancies that may happen during the Recess of the Senate, by granting Commissions which shall expire at the End of their next Session.

Section 3. He shall from time to time give to the Congress Information of the State of the Union, and recommend to their Consideration such Measures as he shall judge necessary and expedient; he may, on extraordinary occasions, convene both Houses, or either of them, and in Case of Disagreement between them, with respect to the Time of Adjournment, he may adjourn them to such Time as he shall think proper; he shall receive Ambassadors and other public Ministers; he shall take care that the Laws be faithfully executed, and shall Commission all the Officers of the United States.

Section 4. The President, Vice President and all civil Officers of the United States, shall be removed from Office on Impeachment for, and Conviction of, Treason, Bribery, or other high Crimes and Misdemeanors.

ARTICLE III

Section 1. The judicial Power of the United States, shall be vested in one supreme Court, and in such inferior Courts as the Congress may from time to time ordain and establish. The Judges, both of the supreme and inferior Courts, shall hold their Offices during good Behaviour, and shall, at stated Times, receive for their Services, a Compensation, which shall not be diminished during their Continuance in Office.

Section 2. The judicial Power shall extend to all Cases, in Law and Equity, arising under this Constitution, the Laws of the United States, and Treaties made, or which shall be made, under their Authority;—to all Cases affecting ambassadors, other public ministers and consuls;—to all cases of admiralty and maritime Jurisdiction;—to Controversies to which the United States shall be a Party;—to Controversies between two or more States;—between a State and Citizens of another State;[5]—between Citizens of different States—between Citizens of the same State claiming Lands under Grants of different States, and between a State, or the Citizens thereof, and foreign States, Citizens, or Subjects.

In all Cases affecting Ambassadors, other public Ministers and Consuls, and those in which a State shall be Party, the supreme Court shall have original Jurisdiction. In all the other Cases before mentioned, the supreme Court shall have appellate Jurisdiction, both as to Law and Fact, with such Exceptions, and under such Regulations as the Congress shall make.

The trial of all Crimes, except in Cases of Impeachment, shall be by Jury; and such Trial shall be held in the State where the said Crimes shall have been committed; but when not committed within any State, the Trial shall be at such Place or Places as the Congress may by Law have directed.

Section 3. Treason against the United States, shall consist only in levying War against them, or in adhering to their Enemies, giving them Aid and Comfort. No Person shall be convicted of Treason unless on the Testimony of two Witnesses to the same overt Act, or on Confession in open Court.

The Congress shall have power to declare the Punishment of Treason, but no Attainder of Treason shall work Corruption of Blood, or Forfeiture except during the Life of the Person attainted.

ARTICLE IV

Section 1. Full Faith and Credit shall be given in each State to the public Acts, Records, and judicial Proceedings of every other State. And the Congress may by general Laws prescribe the Manner in which such Acts, Records and Proceedings shall be proved, and the Effect thereof.

---

[5]Qualified by the Eleventh Amendment.

Section 2. The Citizens of each State shall be entitled to all Privileges and Immunities of Citizens in the several States.

A Person charged in any State with Treason, Felony, or other Crime, who shall flee from Justice, and be found in another State, shall on demand of the executive Authority of the State from which he fled, be delivered up, to be removed to the State having Jurisdiction of the crime.

No Person held to Service or Labour in one State, under the Laws thereof, escaping into another, shall, in Consequence of any Law or Regulation therein, be discharged from such Service or Labour, but shall be delivered up on Claim of the Party to whom such Service or Labour may be due.

Section 3. New States may be admitted by the Congress into this Union; but no new State shall be formed or erected within the Jurisdiction of any other State; nor any State be formed by the Junction of two or more States, or parts of States, without the Consent of the Legislatures of the States concerned as well as of the Congress.

The Congress shall have Power to dispose of and make all needful Rules and Regulations respecting the Territory or other Property belonging to the United States; and nothing in this Constitution shall be so construed as to Prejudice any Claims of the United States, or of any particular State.

Section 4. The United States shall guarantee to every State in this Union a Republican Form of Government, and shall protect each of them against Invasion; and on Application of the Legislature, or of the Executive (when the Legislature cannot be convened) against domestic Violence.

ARTICLE V

The Congress, whenever two-thirds of both Houses shall deem it necessary, shall propose Amendments to this Constitution, or, on the Application of the Legislatures of two-thirds of the several States, shall call a Convention for proposing Amendments, which, in either Case, shall be valid to all Intents and Purposes, as part of this Constitution, when ratified by the Legislatures of three-fourths of the several States, or by Conventions in three-fourths thereof, as the one or the other Mode of Ratification may be proposed by the Congress; Provided that no Amendment which may be made prior to the Year One thousand eight hundred and eight shall in any Manner affect the first and fourth Clauses in the Ninth Section of the first Article; and that no State, without its Consent, shall be deprived of its equal Suffrage in the Senate.

ARTICLE VI

All Debts contracted and Engagements entered into, before the Adoption of this Constitution, shall be as valid against the United States under this Constitution, as under the Confederation.

This Constitution, and the Laws of the United States which shall be made in Pursuance thereof; and all Treaties made, or which shall be made, under the Authority of the United States, shall be the supreme Law of the Land; and the Judges in every State shall be bound thereby, any Thing in the Constitution or Laws of any State to the Contrary notwithstanding.

The Senators and Representatives before mentioned, and the Members of the several State Legislatures, and all executive and judicial Officers, both of the United States and of the several States, shall be bound by Oath or Affirmation to support this Constitution; but no religious Tests shall ever be required as a qualification to any Office or public Trust under the United States.

ARTICLE VII

The Ratification of the Conventions of nine States shall be sufficient for the Establishment of this Constitution between the States so ratifying the same.

Done in Convention by the Unanimous Consent of the States present the Seventeenth Day of September in the Year of our Lord one thousand seven hundred and Eighty seven, and of the Independence of the United States of America the Twelfth. In Witness whereof We have hereunto subscribed our Names.[6]

GEORGE WASHINGTON
PRESIDENT AND DEPUTY FROM VIRGINIA

New Hampshire	**New Jersey**	**Delaware**	**North Carolina**
John Langdon	William Livingston	George Read	William Blount
Nicholas Gilman	David Brearley	Gunning Bedford, Jr.	Richard Dobbs Spaight
	William Paterson	John Dickinson	Hugh Williamson
	Jonathan Dayton	Richard Bassett	
		Jacob Broom	

---

[6]These are the full names of the signers, which in some cases are not the signatures on the document.

Massachusetts	**Pennsylvania**	**Maryland**	**South Carolina**
Nathaniel Gorham	Benjamin Franklin	James McHenry	John Rutledge
Rufus King	Thomas Mifflin	Daniel of St. Thomas Jenifer	Charles Cotesworth Pinckney
	Robert Morris	Daniel Carroll	Charles Pinckney
Connecticut	George Clymer		Pierce Butler
William Samuel Johnson	Thomas FitzSimons	**Virginia**	
Roger Sherman	Jared Ingersoll	John Blair	**Georgia**
	James Wilson	James Madison, Jr.	William Few
New York	Gouverneur Morris		Abraham Baldwin
Alexander Hamilton			

Articles in Addition to, and Amendment of, the Constitution of the United States of America, Proposed by Congress, and Ratified by the Legislatures of the Several States, Pursuant to the Fifth Article of the Original Constitution[7]

[AMENDMENT I]

Congress shall make no law respecting an establishment of religion, or prohibiting the free exercise thereof; or abridging the freedom of speech, or of the press; or the right of the people peaceably to assemble, and to petition the Government for a redress of grievances.

[AMENDMENT II]

A well regulated Militia, being necessary to the security of a free State, the right of the people to keep and bear Arms shall not be infringed.

[AMENDMENT III]

No Soldier shall, in time of peace, be quartered in any house, without the consent of the Owner, nor in time of war, but in a manner to be prescribed by law.

[AMENDMENT IV]

The right of the people to be secure in their persons, houses, papers, and effects, against unreasonable searches and seizures, shall not be violated, and no Warrants shall issue, but upon probable cause, supported by Oath or affirmation, and particularly describing the place to be searched, and the persons or things to be seized.

[AMENDMENT V]

No person shall be held to answer for a capital or otherwise infamous crime, unless on a presentment or indictment of a Grand Jury, except in cases arising in the land or naval forces, or in the Militia, when in actual service in time of War or public danger; nor shall any person be subject for the same offence to be twice put in jeopardy of life or limb; nor shall be compelled in any criminal case to be a witness against himself, nor be deprived of life, liberty, or property, without due process of law; nor shall private property be taken for public use, without just compensation.

[AMENDMENT VI]

In all criminal prosecutions, the accused shall enjoy the right to a speedy and public trial, by an impartial jury of the State and district wherein the crime shall have been committed, which district shall have been previously ascertained by law, and to be informed of the nature and cause of the accusation; to be confronted with the witnesses against him; to have compulsory process for obtaining witnesses in his favour, and to have the Assistance of Counsel for his defence.

[AMENDMENT VII]

In suits at common law, where the value in controversy shall exceed twenty dollars, the right of trial by jury shall be preserved, and no fact tried by a jury, shall be otherwise reexamined in any Court of the United States, than according to the rules of the common law.

[AMENDMENT VIII]

Excessive bail shall not be required, nor excessive fines imposed, nor cruel and unusual punishments inflicted.

[AMENDMENT IX]

The enumeration of the Constitution, of certain rights, shall not be construed to deny or disparage others retained by the people.

[AMENDMENT X]

The powers not delegated to the United States by the Constitution, nor prohibited by it to the States, are reserved to the States respectively, or to the people.
[Amendments I-X, in force 1791.]

[AMENDMENT XI][8]

The Judicial power of the United States shall not be construed to extend to any suit in law or equity, commenced or

---

[7]This heading appears only in the joint resolution submitting the first ten amendments, known as the Bill of Rights.

[8]Adopted in 1798.

prosecuted against one of the United States by Citizens of another State, or by Citizens or Subjects of any Foreign State.

[AMENDMENT XII][9]

The Electors shall meet in their respective States and vote by ballot for President and Vice-President, one of whom, at least, shall not be an inhabitant of the same State with themselves; they shall name in their ballots the person voted for as President, and in distinct ballots the person voted for as Vice-President, and they shall make distinct lists of all persons voted for as President, and of all persons voted for as Vice-President, and of the number of votes for each, which lists they shall sign and certify, and transmit sealed to the seat of the government of the United States, directed to the President of the Senate;—The President of the Senate shall, in the presence of the Senate and House of Representatives, open all the certificates and the votes shall then be counted;—The person having the greatest number of votes for President, shall be the President, if such number be a majority of the whole number of Electors appointed; and if no person have such majority, then from the persons having the highest numbers not exceeding three on the list of those voted for as President, the House of Representatives shall choose immediately, by ballot, the President. But in choosing the President, the votes shall be taken by states, the representation from each state having one vote; a quorum for this purpose shall consist of a member or members from two-thirds of the states, and a majority of all the states shall be necessary to a choice. And if the House of Representatives shall not choose a President whenever the right of choice shall devolve upon them, before the fourth day of March next following, then the Vice-President shall act as President, as in the case of the death or other constitutional disability of the President.—The person having the greatest number of votes as Vice-President, shall be the Vice-President, if such number be a majority of the whole number of Electors appointed, and if no person have a majority, then from the two highest numbers on the list, the Senate shall choose the Vice-President; a quorum for the purpose shall consist of two-thirds of the whole number of Senators, and a majority of the whole number shall be necessary to a choice. But no person constitutionally ineligible to the office of President shall be eligible to that of Vice-President of the United States.

[AMENDMENT XIII][10]

Section 1. Neither slavery nor involuntary servitude, except as a punishment for crime whereof the party shall have been duly convicted, shall exist within the United States, or any place subject to their jurisdiction.

Section 2. Congress shall have power to enforce this article by appropriate legislation.

[9]Adopted in 1804.

[10]Adopted in 1865.

[AMENDMENT XIV][11]

Section 1. All persons born or naturalized in the United States, and subject to the jurisdiction thereof, are citizens of the United States and of the State wherein they reside. No State shall abridge the privileges or immunities of citizens of the United States; nor shall any State deprive any person of life, liberty, or property, without due process of law; nor deny to any person within its jurisdiction the equal protection of the laws.

Section 2. Representatives shall be apportioned among the several States according to their respective numbers, counting the whole number of persons in each State, excluding Indians not taxed. But when the right to vote at any election for the choice of electors for President and Vice-President of the United States, Representatives in Congress, the Executive and Judicial officers of a State, or the members of the Legislature thereof, is denied to any of the male inhabitants of such State, being twenty-one years of age, and citizens of the United States, or in any way abridged, except for participation in rebellion, or other crime, the basis of representation therein shall be reduced in the proportion which the number of such male citizens shall bear to the whole number of male citizens twenty-one years of age in such State.

Section 3. No person shall be a Senator or Representative in Congress, or elector of President and Vice-President, or hold any office, civil or military, under the United States, or under any State, who, having previously taken an oath, as a member of Congress, or as an officer of the United States, or as a member of any State legislature, or as an executive or judicial officer of any State, to support the Constitution of the United States, shall have engaged in insurrection or rebellion against the same, or given aid or comfort to the enemies thereof. But Congress may by a vote of two-thirds of each House, remove such disability.

Section 4. The validity of the public debt of the United States, authorized by law, including debts incurred for payment of pensions and bounties for services in suppressing insurrection or rebellion, shall not be questioned. But neither the United States nor any State shall assume or pay any debts or obligation incurred in aid of insurrection or rebellion against the United States, or any claim for the loss or emancipation of any slave; but all such debts, obligations, and claims shall be held illegal and void.

Section 5. The Congress shall have the power to enforce, by appropriate legislation, the provisions of this article.

[11]Adopted in 1868.

[AMENDMENT XV][12]

Section 1. The right of citizens of the United States to vote shall not be denied or abridged by the United States or by any State on account of race, color, or previous condition of servitude—

Section 2. The Congress shall have power to enforce this article by appropriate legislation.

[AMENDMENT XVI][13]

The Congress shall have power to lay and collect taxes on incomes, from whatever source derived, without apportionment among the several States, and without regard to any census or enumeration.

[AMENDMENT XVII][14]

The Senate of the United States shall be composed of two Senators from each State, elected by the people thereof, for six years; and each Senator shall have one vote. The electors in each State shall have the qualifications requisite for electors of the most numerous branch of the State legislatures.

When vacancies happen in the representation of any State in the Senate, the executive authority of such State shall issue writs of election to fill such vacancies: *Provided,* That the legislature of any State may empower the executive thereof to make temporary appointments until the people fill the vacancies by election as the legislature may direct.

This amendment shall not be so construed as to affect the election or term of any Senator chosen before it becomes valid as part of the Constitution.

[AMENDMENT XVIII][15]

Section 1. After one year from the ratification of this article the manufacture, sale, or transportation of intoxicating liquors within, the importation thereof into, or the exportation thereof from the United States and all territory subject to the jurisdiction thereof for beverage purposes is hereby prohibited.

Section 2. The Congress and the several States shall have concurrent power to enforce this article by appropriate legislation.

Section 3. This article shall be inoperative unless it shall have been ratified as an amendment to the Constitution by the legislatures of the several States, as provided in the Con-

stitution, within seven years from the date of the submission hereof to the States by the Congress.

[AMENDMENT XIX][16]

The right of citizens of the United States to vote shall not be denied or abridged by the United States or by any State on account of sex.

Congress shall have power to enforce this article by appropriate legislation.

[AMENDMENT XX][17]

Section 1. The terms of the President and Vice-President shall end at noon on the 20th day of January, and the terms of Senators and Representatives at noon on the 3d day of January, of the years in which such terms would have ended if this article had not been ratified; and the terms of their successors shall then begin.

Section 2. The Congress shall assemble at least once in every year, and such meeting shall begin at noon on the 3d day of January, unless they shall by law appoint a different day.

Section 3. If, at the time fixed for the beginning of the term of the President, the President elect shall have died, the Vice-President elect shall become President. If a President shall not have been chosen before the time fixed for the beginning of his term or if the President elect shall have failed to qualify, then the Vice-President elect shall act as President until a President shall have qualified; and the Congress may by law provide for the case wherein neither a President elect nor a Vice-President elect shall have qualified, declaring who shall then act as President, or the manner in which one who is to act shall be selected, and such person shall act accordingly until a President or Vice-President shall have qualified.

Section 4. The Congress may by law provide for the case of the death of any of the persons from whom the House of Representatives may choose a President whenever the right of choice shall have devolved upon them, and for the case of the death of any of the persons from whom the Senate may choose a Vice-President whenever the right of choice shall have devolved upon them.

Section 5. Sections 1 and 2 shall take effect on the 15th day of October following the ratification of this article.

Section 6. This article shall be inoperative unless it shall have been ratified as an amendment to the Constitution by the legislatures of three-fourths of the several States within seven years from the date of its submission.

---

[12]Adopted in 1870.
[13]Adopted in 1913.
[14]Adopted in 1913.
[15]Adopted in 1918.

---

[16]Adopted in 1920.
[17]Adopted in 1933.

[AMENDMENT XXI][18]

Section 1. The eighteenth article of amendment to the Constitution of the United States is hereby repealed.

Section 2. The transportation or importation into any State, Territory, or possession of the United States for delivery or use therein of intoxicating liquors, in violation of the laws thereof, is hereby prohibited.

Section 3. This article shall be inoperative unless it shall have been ratified as an amendment to the Constitution by conventions in the several States, as provided in the Constitution, within seven years from the date of the submission hereof to the States by the Congress.

[AMENDMENT XXII][19]

No person shall be elected to the office of the President more than twice, and no person who has held the office of President, or acted as President, for more than two years of a term to which some other person was elected President shall be elected to the office of the President more than once.

But this Article shall not apply to any person holding the office of President when this Article was proposed by the Congress, and shall not prevent any person who may be holding the office of President, or acting as President, during the term within which this Article becomes operative from holding the office of President or acting as President during the remainder of such term.

This article shall be inoperative unless it shall have been ratified as an amendment to the Constitution by the legislatures of three-fourths of the several states within seven years from the date of its submission to the states by the Congress.

[AMENDMENT XXIII][20]

Section 1. The District constituting the seat of Government of the United States shall appoint in such manner as the Congress may direct:

A number of electors of President and Vice-President equal to the whole number of Senators and Representatives in Congress to which the District would be entitled if it were a State, but in no event more than the least populous State; they shall be in addition to those appointed by the States, but they shall be considered, for the purpose of the election of President and Vice-President, to be electors appointed by a State; and they shall meet in the District and perform such duties as provided by the twelfth article of amendment.

Section 2. The Congress shall have power to enforce this article by appropriate legislation.

[AMENDMENT XXIV][21]

Section 1. The right of citizens of the United States to vote in any primary or other election for President or Vice-President, for electors for President or Vice-President, or for Senator or Representative in Congress, shall not be denied or abridged by the United States or any state by reason of failure to pay any poll tax or other tax.

Section 2. The Congress shall have the power to enforce this article by appropriate legislation.

[AMENDMENT XXV][22]

Section 1. In case of the removal of the President from office or of his death or resignation, the Vice-President shall become President.

Section 2. Whenever there is a vacancy in the office of the Vice President, the President shall nominate a Vice President who shall take office upon confirmation by a majority vote of both Houses of Congress.

Section 3. Whenever the President transmits to the President Pro Tempore of the Senate and the Speaker of the House of Representatives his written declaration that he is unable to discharge the powers and duties of his office, and until he transmits to them a written declaration to the contrary, such powers and duties shall be discharged by the Vice-President as Acting President.

Section 4. Whenever the Vice-President and a majority of either the principal officers of the executive departments or of such other body as Congress may by law provide, transmit to the President Pro Tempore of the Senate and the Speaker of the House of Representatives their written declaration that the President is unable to discharge the powers and duties of his office, the Vice President shall immediately assume the powers and duties of the office as Acting President.

Thereafter, when the President transmits to the President Pro Tempore of the Senate and the Speaker of the House of Representatives his written declaration that no inability exists, he shall resume the powers and duties of his office unless the Vice President and a majority of either the principal officers of the executive departments or of such other body as Congress may by law provide,

---

[18]Adopted in 1933.
[19]Adopted in 1951.
[20]Adopted in 1961.

[21]Adopted in 1964.
[22]Adopted in 1967.

transmit within four days to the President Pro Tempore of the Senate and the Speaker of the House of Representatives their written declaration that the President is unable to discharge the powers and duties of his office. Thereupon Congress shall decide the issue, assembling within forty-eight hours for that purpose if not in session. If the Congress, within twenty-one days after receipt of the latter written declaration, or, if Congress is not in session, within twenty-one days after Congress is required to assemble, determines by two-thirds vote of both Houses that the President is unable to discharge the powers and duties of his office, the Vice President shall continue to discharge the same as Acting President; otherwise, the President shall resume the powers and duties of his office.

[AMENDMENT XXVI][23]

Section 1. The right of citizens of the United States, who are eighteen years of age or older, to vote shall not be de-

nied or abridged by the United States or by any State on account of age.

Section 2. The Congress shall have power to enforce this article by appropriate legislation.

[AMENDMENT XXVII][24]

No law, varying the compensation for the services of the Senators and Representatives, shall take effect, until an election of Representatives shall have intervened.

---

[23]Adopted in 1971.

[24]Adopted in 1992.

Presidential Elections

Year	Candidates	Parties	Popular Vote	% of Popular Vote	Electoral Vote	% Voter Participation
1789	**George Washington**				69	
	John Adams				34	
	Other candidates				35	
1792	**George Washington**				132	
	John Adams				77	
	George Clinton				50	
	Other candidates				5	
1796	**John Adams**	Federalist			71	
	Thomas Jefferson	Dem.-Rep.			68	
	Thomas Pinckney	Federalist			59	
	Aaron Burr	Dem.-Rep.			30	
	Other candidates				48	
1800	**Thomas Jefferson**	Dem.-Rep.			73	
	Aaron Burr	Dem.-Rep.			73	
	John Adams	Federalist			65	
	Charles C. Pinckney	Federalist			64	
	John Jay	Federalist			1	
1804	**Thomas Jefferson**	Dem.-Rep.			162	
	Charles C. Pinckney	Federalist			14	
1808	**James Madison**	Dem.-Rep.			122	
	Charles C. Pinckney	Federalist			47	
	George Clinton	Dem.-Rep.			6	
1812	**James Madison**	Dem.-Rep.			128	
	DeWitt Clinton	Federalist			89	
1816	**James Monroe**	Dem.-Rep.			183	
	Rufus King	Federalist			34	
1820	**James Monroe**	Dem.-Rep.			231	
	John Quincy Adams	Indep.-Rep.			1	
1824	**John Quincy Adams**	Dem.-Rep.	108,740	31.0	84	26.9
	Andrew Jackson	Dem.-Rep.	153,544	43.0	99	
	Henry Clay	Dem.-Rep.	47,136	13.0	37	
	William H. Crawford	Dem.-Rep.	46,618	13.0	41	
1828	**Andrew Jackson**	Democratic	647,286	56.0	178	57.6
	John Quincy Adams	National Republican	508,064	44.0	83	
1832	**Andrew Jackson**	Democratic	688,242	54.5	219	55.4
	Henry Clay	National Republican	473,462	37.5	49	
	William Wirt	Anti-Masonic	101,051	8.0	7	
	John Floyd	Democratic			11	
1836	**Martin Van Buren**	Democratic	765,483	50.9	170	57.8
	William H. Harrison	Whig			73	
	Hugh L. White	Whig	739,795	49.1	26	
	Daniel Webster	Whig			14	
	W. P. Mangum	Whig			11	

Year	Candidates	Parties	Popular Vote	% of Popular Vote	Electoral Vote	% Voter Participation
1840	**William H. Harrison**	Whig	1,275,016	53.0	234	80.2
	Martin Van Buren	Democratic	1,129,102	47.0	60	
1844	**James K. Polk**	Democratic	1,338,464	49.6	170	78.9
	Henry Clay	Whig	1,300,097	48.1	105	
	James G. Birney	Liberty	62,300	2.3		
1848	**Zachary Taylor**	Whig	1,360,967	47.4	163	72.7
	Lewis Cass	Democratic	1,222,342	42.5	127	
	Martin Van Buren	Free Soil	291,263	10.1		
1852	**Franklin Pierce**	Democratic	1,601,117	50.9	254	69.6
	Winfield Scott	Whig	1,385,453	44.1	42	
	John P. Hale	Free Soil	155,825	5.0		
1856	**James Buchanan**	Democratic	1,832,955	45.3	174	78.9
	John C. Fremont	Republican	1,339,932	33.1	114	
	Millard Fillmore	American	871,731	21.6	8	
1860	**Abraham Lincoln**	Republican	1,866,452	39.8	180	81.2
	Stephen A. Douglas	Democratic	1,375,157	29.5	12	
	John C. Breckinridge	Democratic	847,953	18.1	72	
	John Bell	Constitutional Union	590,631	12.6	39	
1864	**Abraham Lincoln**	Republican	2,206,938	55.0	212	73.8
	George B. McClellan	Democratic	1,803,787	45.0	21	
1868	**Ulysses S. Grant**	Republican	3,013,421	52.7	214	78.1
	Horatio Seymour	Democratic	2,706,829	47.3	80	
1872	**Ulysses S. Grant**	Republican	3,596,745	55.6	286	71.3
	Horace Greeley	Democratic	2,843,446	43.9	66	
1876	**Rutherford B. Hayes**	Republican	4,036,298	48.0	185	81.8
	Samuel J. Tilden	Democratic	4,300,590	51.0	184	
1880	**James A. Garfield**	Republican	4,453,295	48.5	214	79.4
	Winfield S. Hancock	Democratic	4,414,082	48.1	155	
	James B. Weaver	Greenback-Labor	308,578	3.4		
1884	**Grover Cleveland**	Democratic	4,879,507	48.5	219	77.5
	James G. Blaine	Republican	4,850,293	48.2	182	
	Benjamin F. Butler	Greenback-Labor	175,370	1.8		
	John P. St. John	Prohibition	150,369	1.5		
1888	**Benjamin Harrison**	Republican	5,477,129	47.9	233	79.3
	Grover Cleveland	Democratic	5,537,857	48.6	168	
	Clinton B. Fisk	Prohibition	249,506	2.2		
	Anson J. Streeter	Union Labor	146,935	1.3		
1892	**Grover Cleveland**	Democratic	5,555,426	46.1	277	74.7
	Benjamin Harrison	Republican	5,182,690	43.0	145	
	James B. Weaver	People's	1,029,846	8.5	22	
	John Bidwell	Prohibition	264,133	2.2		
1896	**William McKinley**	Republican	7,104,779	52.0	271	79.3
	William J. Bryan	Democratic	6,502,925	48.0	176	
1900	**William McKinley**	Republican	7,218,491	51.7	292	73.2
	William J. Bryan	Democratic; Populist	6,356,734	45.5	155	
	John C. Wooley	Prohibition	208,914	1.5		

Year	Candidates	Parties	Popular Vote	% of Popular Vote	Electoral Vote	% Voter Participation
1904	**Theodore Roosevelt**	Republican	7,628,461	57.4	336	65.2
	Alton B. Parker	Democratic	5,084,223	37.6	140	
	Eugene V. Debs	Socialist	402,283	3.0		
	Silas C. Swallow	Prohibition	258,536	1.9		
1908	**William H. Taft**	Republican	7,675,320	51.6	321	65.4
	William J. Bryan	Democratic	6,412,294	43.1	162	
	Eugene V. Debs	Socialist	420,793	2.8		
	Eugene W. Chafin	Prohibition	253,840	1.7		
1912	**Woodrow Wilson**	Democratic	6,293,454	42.0	435	58.8
	Theodore Roosevelt	Progressive	4,119,538	28.0	88	
	William H. Taft	Republican	3,484,980	24.0	8	
	Eugene V. Debs	Socialist	900,672	6.0		
	Eugene W. Chafin	Prohibition	206,275	1.4		
1916	**Woodrow Wilson**	Democratic	9,129,606	49.4	277	61.6
	Charles E. Hughes	Republican	8,538,221	46.2	254	
	A. L. Benson	Socialist	585,113	3.2		
	J. Frank Hanly	Prohibition	220,506	1.2		
1920	**Warren G. Harding**	Republican	16,143,407	60.4	404	49.2
	James M. Cox	Democratic	9,130,328	34.2	127	
	Eugene V. Debs	Socialist	919,799	3.4		
	P. P. Christensen	Farmer-Labor	265,411	1.0		
1924	**Calvin Coolidge**	Republican	15,718,211	54.0	382	48.9
	John W. Davis	Democratic	8,385,283	28.8	136	
	Robert M. La Follette	Progressive	4,831,289	16.6	13	
1928	**Herbert C. Hoover**	Republican	21,391,381	58.2	444	56.9
	Alfred E. Smith	Democratic	15,016,443	40.9	87	
1932	**Franklin D. Roosevelt**	Democratic	22,821,857	57.4	472	56.9
	Herbert C. Hoover	Republican	15,761,841	39.7	59	
	Norman Thomas	Socialist	881,951	2.2		
1936	**Franklin D. Roosevelt**	Democratic	27,751,597	60.8	523	61.0
	Alfred M. Landon	Republican	16,679,583	36.5	8	
	William Lemke	Union	882,479	1.9		
1940	**Franklin D. Roosevelt**	Democratic	27,307,819	54.8	449	62.5
	Wendell L. Wilkie	Republican	22,321,018	44.8	82	
1944	**Franklin D. Roosevelt**	Democratic	25,606,585	53.5	432	55.9
	Thomas E. Dewey	Republican	22,014,745	46.0	99	
1948	**Harry S Truman**	Democratic	24,105,812	50.0	303	53.0
	Thomas E. Dewey	Republican	21,970,065	46.0	189	
	J. Strom Thurmond	States' Rights	1,169,021	2.0	39	
	Henry A. Wallace	Progressive	1,157,172	2.0		
1952	**Dwight D. Eisenhower**	Republican	33,936,234	55.1	442	63.3
	Adlai E. Stevenson	Democratic	27,314,992	44.4	89	
1956	**Dwight D. Eisenhower**	Republican	35,590,472	57.6	457	60.6
	Adlai E. Stevenson	Democratic	26,022,752	42.1	73	
1960	**John F. Kennedy**	Democratic	34,227,096	49.7	303	62.8
	Richard M. Nixon	Republican	34,107,646	49.6	219	
	Harry F. Byrd	Independent	501,643		15	
1964	**Lyndon B. Johnson**	Democratic	43,129,566	61.1	486	61.7
	Barry M. Goldwater	Republican	27,178,188	38.5	52	

Year	Candidates	Parties	Popular Vote	% of Popular Vote	Electoral Vote	% Voter Participation
1968	**Richard M. Nixon**	Republican	31,785,480	44.0	301	60.6
	Hubert H. Humphrey	Democratic	31,275,166	42.7	191	
	George C. Wallace	American Independent	9,906,473	13.5	46	
1972	**Richard M. Nixon**	Republican	47,169,911	60.7	520	55.2
	George S. McGovern	Democratic	29,170,383	37.5	17	
	John G. Schmitz	American	1,099,482	1.4		
1976	**Jimmy Carter**	Democratic	40,830,763	50.1	297	53.5
	Gerald R. Ford	Republican	39,147,793	48.0	240	
1980	**Ronald Reagan**	Republican	43,899,248	51.0	489	52.6
	Jimmy Carter	Democratic	35,481,432	41.0	49	
	John B. Anderson	Independent	5,719,437	7.0	0	
	Ed Clark	Libertarian	920,859	1.0	0	
1984	**Ronald Reagan**	Republican	54,451,521	58.8	525	53.3
	Walter Mondale	Democratic	37,565,334	40.5	13	
1988	**George Bush**	Republican	48,881,221	53.9	426	48.6
	Michael Dukakis	Democratic	41,805,422	46.1	111	
1992	**William J. Clinton**	Democratic	44,908,254	43.0	370	55.9
	George H. Bush	Republican	39,102,343	37.4	168	
	H. Ross Perot	Independent	19,741,065	18.9	0	
1996	**William J. Clinton**	Democratic	47,401,185	49.3	379	49
	Robert Dole	Republican	39,197,469	40.7	159	
	H. Ross Perot	Reform	8,085,294	8.4	0	
2000	**George W. Bush**	Republican	50,455,156	47.9	271	51.2
	Al Gore	Democratic	50,992,335	48.4	266	
	Ralph Nader	Green	2,882,737	2.7	0	

Presidential Administrations

The Washington Administration (1789–1797)

Vice President	John Adams	1789–1797
Secretary of State	Thomas Jefferson	1789–1793
	Edmund Randolph	1794–1795
	Timothy Pickering	1795–1797
Secretary of Treasury	Alexander Hamilton	1789–1795
	Oliver Wolcott	1795–1797
Secretary of War	Henry Knox	1789–1794
	Timothy Pickering	1795–1796
	James McHenry	1796–1797
Attorney General	Edmund Randolph	1789–1793
	William Bradford	1794–1795
	Charles Lee	1795–1797
Postmaster General	Samuel Osgood	1789–1791
	Timothy Pickering	1791–1794
	Joseph Habersham	1795–1797

The John Adams Administration (1797–1801)

Vice President	Thomas Jefferson	1797–1801
Secretary of State	Timothy Pickering	1797–1800
	John Marshall	1800–1801
Secretary of Treasury	Oliver Wolcott	1797–1800
	Samuel Dexter	1800–1801
Secretary of War	James McHenry	1797–1800
	Samuel Dexter	1800–1801
Attorney General	Charles Lee	1797–1801
Postmaster General	Joseph Habersham	1797–1801
Secretary of Navy	Benjamin Stoddert	1798–1801

The Jefferson Administration (1801–1809)

Vice President	Aaron Burr	1801–1805
	George Clinton	1805–1809
Secretary of State	James Madison	1801–1809
Secretary of Treasury	Samuel Dexter	1801
	Albert Gallatin	1801–1809
Secretary of War	Henry Dearborn	1801–1809
Attorney General	Levi Lincoln	1801–1805
	Robert Smith	1805
	John Breckinridge	1805–1806
	Caesar Rodney	1807–1809
Postmaster General	Joseph Habersham	1801
	Gideon Granger	1801–1809
Secretary of Navy	Robert Smith	1801–1809

The Madison Administration (1809–1817)

Vice President	George Clinton	1809–1813
	Elbridge Gerry	1813–1817
Secretary of State	Robert Smith	1809–1811
	James Monroe	1811–1817
Secretary of Treasury	Albert Gallatin	1809–1813
	George Campbell	1814
	Alexander Dallas	1814–1816
	William Crawford	1816–1817
Secretary of War	William Eustis	1809–1812
	John Armstrong	1813–1814
	James Monroe	1814–1815
	William Crawford	1815–1817
Attorney General	Caesar Rodney	1809–1811
	William Pinkney	1811–1814
	Richard Rush	1814–1817
Postmaster General	Gideon Granger	1809–1814
	Return Meigs	1814–1817
Secretary of Navy	Paul Hamilton	1809–1813
	William Jones	1813–1814
	Benjamin Crowninshield	1814–1817

The Monroe Administration (1817–1825)

Vice President	Daniel Tompkins	1817–1825
Secretary of State	John Quincy Adams	1817–1825
Secretary of Treasury	William Crawford	1817–1825
Secretary of War	George Graham	1817
	John C. Calhoun	1817–1825
Attorney General	Richard Rush	1817
	William Wirt	1817–1825
Postmaster General	Return Meigs	1817–1823
	John McLean	1823–1825

Secretary of Navy	Benjamin Crowninshield	1817–1818
	Smith Thompson	1818–1823
	Samuel Southard	1823–1825

The John Quincy Adams Administration (1825–1829)

Vice President	John C. Calhoun	1825–1829
Secretary of State	Henry Clay	1825–1829
Secretary of Treasury	Richard Rush	1825–1829
Secretary of War	James Barbour	1825–1828
	Peter Porter	1828–1829
Attorney General	William Wirt	1825–1829
Postmaster General	John McLean	1825–1829
Secretary of Navy	Samuel Southard	1825–1829

The Jackson Administration (1829–1837)

Vice President	John C. Calhoun	1829–1833
	Martin Van Buren	1833–1837
Secretary of State	Martin Van Buren	1829–1831
	Edward Livingston	1831–1833
	Louis McLane	1833–1834
	John Forsyth	1834–1837
Secretary of Treasury	Samuel Ingham	1829–1831
	Louis McLane	1831–1833
	William Duane	1833
	Roger B. Taney	1833–1834
	Levi Woodbury	1834–1837
Secretary of War	John H. Eaton	1829–1831
	Lewis Cass	1831–1837
	Benjamin Butler	1837
Attorney General	John M. Berrien	1829–1831
	Roger B. Taney	1831–1833
	Benjamin Butler	1833–1837
Postmaster General	William Barry	1829–1835
	Amos Kendall	1835–1837
Secretary of Navy	John Branch	1829–1831
	Levi Woodbury	1831–1834
	Mahlon Dickerson	1834–1837

The Van Buren Administration (1837–1841)

Vice President	Richard M. Johnson	1837–1841
Secretary of State	John Forsyth	1837–1841
Secretary of Treasury	Levi Woodbury	1837–1841
Secretary of War	Joel Poinsett	1837–1841
Attorney General	Benjamin Butler	1837–1838
	Felix Grundy	1838–1840
	Henry D. Gilpin	1840–1841
Postmaster General	Amos Kendall	1837–1840
	John M. Niles	1840–1841
Secretary of Navy	Mahlon Dickerson	1837–1838
	James Paulding	1838–1841

The William Harrison Administration (1841)

Vice President	John Tyler	1841
Secretary of State	Daniel Webster	1841
Secretary of Treasury	Thomas Ewing	1841
Secretary of War	John Bell	1841
Attorney General	John J. Crittenden	1841
Postmaster General	Francis Granger	1841
Secretary of Navy	George Badger	1841

The Tyler Administration (1841–1845)

Vice President	None	
Secretary of State	Daniel Webster	1841–1843
	Hugh S. Legaré	1843
	Abel P. Upshur	1843–1844
	John C. Calhoun	1844–1845
Secretary of Treasury	Thomas Ewing	1841
	Walter Forward	1841–1843
	John C. Spencer	1843–1844
	George Bibb	1844–1845
Secretary of War	John Bell	1841
	John C. Spencer	1841–1843
	James M. Porter	1843–1844
	William Wilkins	1844–1845
Attorney General	John J. Crittenden	1841
	Hugh S. Legaré	1841–1843
	John Nelson	1843–1845
Postmaster General	Francis Granger	1841
	Charles Wickliffe	1841–1845
Secretary of Navy	George Badger	1841
	Abel P. Upshur	1841
	David Henshaw	1843–1844
	Thomas Gilmer	1844
	John Y. Mason	1844–1845

The Polk Administration (1845–1849)

Vice President	George M. Dallas	1845–1849
Secretary of State	James Buchanan	1845–1849
Secretary of Treasury	Robert J. Walker	1845–1849
Secretary of War	William L. Marcy	1845–1849
Attorney General	John Y. Mason Nathan Clifford Isaac Toucey	1845–1846 1846–1848 1848–1849
Postmaster General	Cave Johnson	1845–1849
Secretary of Navy	George Bancroft John Y. Mason	1845–1846 1846–1849

The Taylor Administration (1849–1850)

Vice President	Millard Fillmore	1849–1850
Secretary of State	John M. Clayton	1849–1850
Secretary of Treasury	William Meredith	1849–1850
Secretary of War	George Crawford	1849–1850
Attorney General	Reverdy Johnson	1849–1850
Postmaster General	Jacob Collamer	1849–1850
Secretary of Navy	William Preston	1849–1850
Secretary of Interior	Thomas Ewing	1849–1850

The Fillmore Administration (1850–1853)

Vice President	None	
Secretary of State	Daniel Webster Edward Everett	1850–1852 1852–1853
Secretary of Treasury	Thomas Corwin	1850–1853
Secretary of War	Charles Conrad	1850–1853
Attorney General	John J. Crittenden	1850–1853
Postmaster General	Nathan Hall Sam D. Hubbard	1850–1852 1852–1853
Secretary of Navy	William A. Graham John P. Kennedy	1850–1852 1852–1853
Secretary of Interior	Thomas McKennan Alexander Stuart	1850 1850–1853

The Pierce Administration (1853–1857)

Vice President	William R. King	1853–1857
Secretary of State	William L. Marcy	1853–1857
Secretary of Treasury	James Guthrie	1853–1857
Secretary of War	Jefferson Davis	1853–1857
Attorney General	Caleb Cushing	1853–1857
Postmaster General	James Campbell	1853–1857
Secretary of Navy	James C. Dobbin	1853–1857
Secretary of Interior	Robert McClelland	1853–1857

The Buchanan Administration (1857–1861)

Vice President	John C. Breckinridge	1857–1861
Secretary of State	Lewis Cass Jeremiah S. Black	1857–1860 1860–1861
Secretary of Treasury	Howell Cobb Philip Thomas John A. Dix	1857–1860 1860–1861 1861
Secretary of War	John B. Floyd Joseph Holt	1857–1861 1861
Attorney General	Jeremiah S. Black Edwin M. Stanton	1857–1860 1860–1861
Postmaster General	Aaron V. Brown Joseph Holt Horatio King	1857–1859 1859–1861 1861
Secretary of Navy	Isaac Toucey	1857–1861
Secretary of Interior	Jacob Thompson	1857–1861

The Lincoln Administration (1861–1865)

Vice President	Hannibal Hamlin Andrew Johnson	1861–1865 1865
Secretary of State	William H. Seward	1861–1865
Secretary of Treasury	Samuel P. Chase William P. Fessenden Hugh McCulloch	1861–1864 1864–1865 1865
Secretary of War	Simon Cameron Edwin M. Stanton	1861–1862 1862–1865
Attorney General	Edward Bates James Speed	1861–1864 1864–1865

Postmaster General	Horatio King	1861
	Montgomery Blair	1861–1864
	William Dennison	1864–1865
Secretary of Navy	Gideon Welles	1861–1865
Secretary of Interior	Caleb B. Smith	1861–1863
	John P. Usher	1863–1865

The Andrew Johnson Administration (1865–1869)

Vice President	None	
Secretary of State	William H. Seward	1865–1869
Secretary of Treasury	Hugh McCulloch	1865–1869
Secretary of War	Edwin M. Stanton	1865–1867
	Ulysses S. Grant	1867–1868
	Lorenzo Thomas	1868
	John M. Schofield	1868–1869
Attorney General	James Speed	1865–1866
	Henry Stanbery	1866–1868
	William M. Evarts	1868–1869
Postmaster General	William Dennison	1865–1866
	Alexander Randall	1866–1869
Secretary of Navy	Gideon Welles	1865–1869
Secretary of Interior	John P. Usher	1865
	James Harlan	1865–1866
	Orville H. Browning	1866–1869

The Grant Administration (1869–1877)

Vice President	Schuyler Colfax	1869–1873
	Henry Wilson	1873–1877
Secretary of State	Elihu B. Washburne	1869
	Hamilton Fish	1869–1877
Secretary of Treasury	George S. Boutwell	1869–1873
	William Richardson	1873–1874
	Benjamin Bristow	1874–1876
	Lot M. Morrill	1876–1877
Secretary of War	John A. Rawlins	1869
	William T. Sherman	1869
	William W. Belknap	1869–1876
	Alphonso Taft	1876
	James D. Cameron	1876–1877

Attorney General	Ebenezer Hoar	1869–1870
	Amos T. Ackerman	1870–1871
	G. H. Williams	1871–1875
	Edwards Pierrepont	1875–1876
	Alphonso Taft	1876–1877
Postmaster General	John A. J. Creswell	1869–1874
	James W. Marshall	1874
	Marshall Jewell	1874–1876
	James N. Tyner	1876–1877
Secretary of Navy	Adolph E. Borie	1869
	George M. Robeson	1869–1877
Secretary of Interior	Jacob D. Cox	1869–1870
	Columbus Delano	1870–1875
	Zachariah Chandler	1875–1877

The Hayes Administration (1877–1881)

Vice President	William A. Wheeler	1877–1881
Secretary of State	William M. Evarts	1877–1881
Secretary of Treasury	John Sherman	1877–1881
Secretary of War	George W. McCrary	1877–1879
	Alex Ramsey	1879–1881
Attorney General	Charles Devens	1877–1881
Postmaster General	David M. Key	1877–1880
	Horace Maynard	1880–1881
Secretary of Navy	Richard W. Thompson	1877–1880
	Nathan Goff Jr.	1881
Secretary of Interior	Carl Schurz	1877–1881

The Garfield Administration (1881)

Vice President	Chester A. Arthur	1881
Secretary of State	James G. Blaine	1881
Secretary of Treasury	William Windom	1881
Secretary of War	Robert T. Lincoln	1881
Attorney General	Wayne MacVeagh	1881
Postmaster General	Thomas L. James	1881

Secretary of Navy	William H. Hunt	1881
Secretary of Interior	Samuel J. Kirkwood	1881

The Arthur Administration (1881–1885)

Vice President	None	
Secretary of State	F. T. Frelinghuysen	1881–1885
Secretary of Treasury	Charles J. Folger	1881–1884
	Walter Q. Gresham	1884
	Hugh McCulloch	1884–1885
Secretary of War	Robert T. Lincoln	1881–1885
Attorney General	Benjamin H. Brewster	1881–1885
Postmaster General	Timothy O. Howe	1881–1883
	Walter Q. Gresham	1883–1884
	Frank Hatton	1884–1885
Secretary of Navy	William H. Hunt	1881–1882
	William E. Chandler	1882–1885
Secretary of Interior	Samuel J. Kirkwood	1881–1882
	Henry M. Teller	1882–1885

The Cleveland Administration (1885–1889)

Vice President	Thomas A. Hendricks	1885–1889
Secretary of State	Thomas F. Bayard	1885–1889
Secretary of Treasury	Daniel Manning	1885–1887
	Charles S. Fairchild	1887–1889
Secretary of War	William C. Endicott	1885–1889
Attorney General	Augustus H. Garland	1885–1889
Postmaster General	William F. Vilas	1885–1888
	Don M. Dickinson	1888–1889
Secretary of Navy	William C. Whitney	1885–1889
Secretary of Interior	Lucius Q. C. Lamar	1885–1888
	William F. Vilas	1888–1889
Secretary of Agriculture	Norman J. Colman	1889

The Benjamin Harrison Administration (1889–1893)

Vice President	Levi P. Morton	1889–1893
Secretary of State	James G. Blaine	1889–1892
	John W. Foster	1892–1893
Secretary of Treasury	William Windom	1889–1891
	Charles Foster	1891–1893
Secretary of War	Redfield Proctor	1889–1891
	Stephen B. Elkins	1891–1893
Attorney General	William H. H. Miller	1889–1893
Postmaster General	John Wanamaker	1889–1893
Secretary of Navy	Benjamin F. Tracy	1889–1893
Secretary of Interior	John W. Noble	1889–1893
Secretary of Agriculture	Jeremiah M. Rusk	1889–1893

The Cleveland Administration (1893–1897)

Vice President	Adlai E. Stevenson	1893–1897
Secretary of State	Walter Q. Gresham	1893–1895
	Richard Olney	1895–1897
Secretary of Treasury	John G. Carlisle	1893–1897
Secretary of War	Daniel S. Lamont	1893–1897
Attorney General	Richard Olney	1893–1895
	James Harmon	1895–1897
Postmaster General	Wilson S. Bissell	1893–1895
	William L. Wilson	1895–1897
Secretary of Navy	Hilary A. Herbert	1893–1897
Secretary of Interior	Hoke Smith	1893–1896
	David R. Francis	1896–1897
Secretary of Agriculture	Julius S. Morton	1893–1897

The McKinley Administration (1897–1901)

Vice President	Garret A. Hobart	1897–1901
	Theodore Roosevelt	1901
Secretary of State	John Sherman	1897–1898
	William R. Day	1898
	John Hay	1898–1901
Secretary of Treasury	Lyman J. Gage	1897–1901

Secretary of War	Russell A. Alger	1897–1899
	Elihu Root	1899–1901
Attorney General	Joseph McKenna	1897–1898
	John W. Griggs	1898–1901
	Philander C. Knox	1901
Postmaster General	James A. Gary	1897–1898
	Charles E. Smith	1898–1901
Secretary of Navy	John D. Long	1897–1901
Secretary of Interior	Cornelius N. Bliss	1897–1899
	Ethan A. Hitchcock	1899–1901
Secretary of Agriculture	James Wilson	1897–1901

The Theodore Roosevelt Administration (1901–1909)

Vice President	Charles Fairbanks	1905–1909
Secretary of State	John Hay	1901–1905
	Elihu Root	1905–1909
	Robert Bacon	1909
Secretary of Treasury	Lyman J. Gage	1901–1902
	Leslie M. Shaw	1902–1907
	George B. Cortelyou	1907–1909
Secretary of War	Elihu Root	1901–1904
	William H. Taft	1904–1908
	Luke E. Wright	1908–1909
Attorney General	Philander C. Knox	1901–1904
	William H. Moody	1904–1906
	Charles J. Bonaparte	1906–1909
Postmaster General	Charles E. Smith	1901–1902
	Henry C. Payne	1902–1904
	Robert J. Wynne	1904–1905
	George B. Cortelyou	1905–1907
	George von L. Meyer	1907–1909
Secretary of Navy	John D. Long	1901–1902
	William H. Moody	1902–1904
	Paul Morton	1904–1905
	Charles J. Bonaparte	1905–1906
	Victor H. Metcalf	1906–1908
	Truman H. Newberry	1908–1909
Secretary of Interior	Ethan A. Hitchcock	1901–1907
	James R. Garfield	1907–1909
Secretary of Agriculture	James Wilson	1901–1909

Secretary of Labor and Commerce	George B. Cortelyou	1903–1904
	Victor H. Metcalf	1904–1906
	Oscar S. Straus	1906–1909
	Charles Nagel	1909

The Taft Administration (1909–1913)

Vice President	James S. Sherman	1909–1913
Secretary of State	Philander C. Knox	1909–1913
Secretary of Treasury	Franklin MacVeagh	1909–1913
Secretary of War	Jacob M. Dickinson	1909–1911
	Henry L. Stimson	1911–1913
Attorney General	George W. Wickersham	1909–1913
Postmaster General	Frank H. Hitchcock	1909–1913
Secretary of Navy	George von L. Meyer	1909–1913
Secretary of Interior	Richard A. Ballinger	1909–1911
	Walter L. Fisher	1911–1913
Secretary of Agriculture	James Wilson	1909–1913
Secretary of Labor and Commerce	Charles Nagel	1909–1913

The Wilson Administration (1913–1921)

Vice President	Thomas R. Marshall	1913–1921
Secretary of State	William J. Bryan	1913–1915
	Robert Lansing	1915–1920
	Bainbridge Colby	1920–1921
Secretary of Treasury	William G. McAdoo	1913–1918
	Carter Glass	1918–1920
	David F. Houston	1920–1921
Secretary of War	Lindley M. Garrison	1913–1916
	Newton D. Baker	1916–1921
Attorney General	James C. McReynolds	1913–1914
	Thomas W. Gregory	1914–1919
	A. Mitchell Palmer	1919–1921
Postmaster General	Albert S. Burleson	1913–1921
Secretary of Navy	Josephus Daniels	1913–1921

Secretary of Interior	Franklin K. Lane	1913–1920
	John B. Payne	1920–1921
Secretary of Agriculture	David F. Houston	1913–1920
	Edwin T. Meredith	1920–1921
Secretary of Commerce	William C. Redfield	1913–1919
	Joshua W. Alexander	1919–1921
Secretary of Labor	William B. Wilson	1913–1921

The Harding Administration (1921–1923)

Vice President	Calvin Coolidge	1921–1923
Secretary of State	Charles E. Hughes	1921–1923
Secretary of Treasury	Andrew Mellon	1921–1923
Secretary of War	John W. Weeks	1921–1923
Attorney General	Harry M. Daugherty	1921–1923
Postmaster General	Will H. Hays	1921–1922
	Hubert Work	1922–1923
	Harry S. New	1923
Secretary of Navy	Edwin Denby	1921–1923
Secretary of Interior	Albert B. Fall	1921–1923
	Hubert Work	1923
Secretary of Agriculture	Henry C. Wallace	1921–1923
Secretary of Commerce	Herbert C. Hoover	1921–1923
Secretary of Labor	James J. Davis	1921–1923

The Coolidge Administration (1923–1929)

Vice President	Charles G. Dawes	1925–1929
Secretary of State	Charles E. Hughes	1923–1925
	Frank B. Kellogg	1925–1929
Secretary of Treasury	Andrew Mellon	1923–1929
Secretary of War	John W. Weeks	1923–1925
	Dwight F. Davis	1925–1929
Attorney General	Henry M. Daugherty	1923–1924
	Harlan F. Stone	1924–1925
	John G. Sargent	1925–1929
Postmaster General	Harry S. New	1923–1929
Secretary of Navy	Edwin Derby	1923–1924
	Curtis D. Wilbur	1924–1929

Secretary of Interior	Hubert Work	1923–1928
	Roy O. West	1928–1929
Secretary of Agriculture	Henry C. Wallace	1923–1924
	Howard M. Gore	1924–1925
	William M. Jardine	1925–1929
Secretary of Commerce	Herbert C. Hoover	1923–1928
	William F. Whiting	1928–1929
Secretary of Labor	James J. Davis	1923–1929

The Hoover Administration (1929–1933)

Vice President	Charles Curtis	1929–1933
Secretary of State	Henry L. Stimson	1929–1933
Secretary of Treasury	Andrew Mellon	1929–1932
	Ogden L. Mills	1932–1933
Secretary of War	James W. Good	1929
	Patrick J. Hurley	1929–1933
Attorney General	William D. Mitchell	1929–1933
Postmaster General	Walter F. Brown	1929–1933
Secretary of Navy	Charles F. Adams	1929–1933
Secretary of Interior	Ray L. Wilbur	1929–1933
Secretary of Agriculture	Arthur M. Hyde	1929–1933
Secretary of Commerce	Robert P. Lamont	1929–1932
	Roy D. Chapin	1932–1933
Secretary of Labor	James J. Davis	1929–1930
	William N. Doak	1930–1933

The Franklin D. Roosevelt Administration (1933–1945)

Vice President	John Nance Garner	1933–1941
	Henry A. Wallace	1941–1945
	Harry S Truman	1945
Secretary of State	Cordell Hull	1933–1944
	Edward R. Stettinius Jr.	1944–1945
Secretary of Treasury	William H. Woodin	1933–1934
	Henry Morgenthau Jr.	1934–1945
Secretary of War	George H. Dern	1933–1936
	Henry A. Woodring	1936–1940
	Henry L. Stimson	1940–1945

Attorney General	Homer S. Cummings	1933–1939
	Frank Murphy	1939–1940
	Robert H. Jackson	1940–1941
	Francis Biddle	1941–1945
Postmaster General	James A. Farley	1933–1940
	Frank C. Walker	1940–1945
Secretary of Navy	Claude A. Swanson	1933–1940
	Charles Edison	1940
	Frank Knox	1940–1944
	James V. Forrestal	1944–1945
Secretary of Interior	Harold L. Ickes	1933–1945
Secretary of Agriculture	Henry A. Wallace	1933–1940
	Claude R. Wickard	1940–1945
Secretary of Commerce	Daniel C. Roper	1933–1939
	Harry L. Hopkins	1939–1940
	Jesse Jones	1940–1945
	Henry A. Wallace	1945
Secretary of Labor	Frances Perkins	1933–1945

The Truman Administration (1945–1953)

Vice President	Alben W. Barkley	1949–1953
Secretary of State	Edward R. Stettinius Jr.	1945
	James F. Byrnes	1945–1947
	George C. Marshall	1947–1949
	Dean G. Acheson	1949–1953
Secretary of Treasury	Fred M. Vinson	1945–1946
	John W. Snyder	1946–1953
Secretary of War	Robert P. Patterson	1945–1947
	Kenneth C. Royall	1947
Attorney General	Tom C. Clark	1945–1949
	J. Howard McGrath	1949–1952
	James P. McGranery	1952–1953
Postmaster General	Frank C. Walker	1945
	Robert E. Hannegan	1945–1947
	Jesse M. Donaldson	1947–1953
Secretary of Navy	James V. Forrestal	1945–1947
Secretary of Interior	Harold L. Ickes	1945–1946
	Julius A. Krug	1946–1949
	Oscar L. Chapman	1949–1953

Secretary of Agriculture	Clinton P. Anderson	1945–1948
	Charles F. Brannan	1948–1953
Secretary of Commerce	Henry A. Wallace	1945–1946
	W. Averell Harriman	1946–1948
	Charles W. Sawyer	1948–1953
Secretary of Labor	Lewis B. Schwellenbach	1945–1948
	Maurice J. Tobin	1948–1953
Secretary of Defense	James V. Forrestal	1947–1949
	Louis A. Johnson	1949–1950
	George C. Marshall	1950–1951
	Robert A. Lovett	1951–1953

The Eisenhower Administration (1953–1961)

Vice President	Richard M. Nixon	1953–1961
Secretary of State	John Foster Dulles	1953–1959
	Christian A. Herter	1959–1961
Secretary of Treasury	George M. Humphrey	1953–1957
	Robert B. Anderson	1957–1961
Attorney General	Herbert Brownell Jr.	1953–1958
	William P. Rogers	1958–1961
Postmaster General	Arthur E. Summerfield	1953–1961
Secretary of Interior	Douglas McKay	1953–1956
	Fred A. Seaton	1956–1961
Secretary of Agriculture	Ezra T. Benson	1953–1961
Secretary of Commerce	Sinclair Weeks	1953–1958
	Lewis L. Strauss	1958–1959
	Frederick H. Mueller	1959–1961
Secretary of Labor	Martin P. Durkin	1953
	James P. Mitchell	1953–1961
Secretary of Defense	Charles E. Wilson	1953–1957
	Neil H. McElroy	1957–1959
	Thomas S. Gates Jr.	1959–1961
Secretary of Health, Education, and Welfare	Oveta Culp Hobby	1953–1955
	Marion B. Folsom	1955–1958
	Arthur S. Flemming	1958–1961

The Kennedy Administration (1961–1963)

Vice President	Lyndon B. Johnson	1961–1963
Secretary of State	Dean Rusk	1961–1963
Secretary of Treasury	C. Douglas Dillon	1961–1963
Attorney General	Robert F. Kennedy	1961–1963
Postmaster General	J. Edward Day	1961–1963
	John A. Gronouski	1963
Secretary of Interior	Stewart L. Udall	1961–1963
Secretary of Agriculture	Orville L. Freeman	1961–1963
Secretary of Commerce	Luther H. Hodges	1961–1963
Secretary of Labor	Arthur J. Goldberg	1961–1962
	W. Willard Wirtz	1962–1963
Secretary of Defense	Robert S. McNamara	1961–1963
Secretary of Health, Education, and Welfare	Abraham A. Ribicoff	1961–1962
	Anthony J. Celebrezze	1962–1963

The Lyndon Johnson Administration (1963–1969)

Vice President	Hubert H. Humphrey	1965–1969
Secretary of State	Dean Rusk	1963–1969
Secretary of Treasury	C. Douglas Dillon	1963–1965
	Henry H. Fowler	1965–1969
Attorney General	Robert F. Kennedy	1963–1964
	Nicholas Katzenbach	1965–1966
	Ramsey Clark	1967–1969
Postmaster General	John A. Gronouski	1963–1965
	Lawrence F. O'Brien	1965–1968
	Marvin Watson	1968–1969
Secretary of Interior	Stewart L. Udall	1963–1969
Secretary of Agriculture	Orville L. Freeman	1963–1969
Secretary of Commerce	Luther H. Hodges	1963–1964
	John T. Connor	1964–1967
	Alexander B. Trowbridge	1967–1968
	Cyrus R. Smith	1968–1969

Secretary of Labor	W. Willard Wirtz	1963–1969
Secretary of Defense	Robert F. McNamara	1963–1968
	Clark Clifford	1968–1969
Secretary of Health, Education, and Welfare	Anthony J. Celebrezze	1963–1965
	John W. Gardner	1965–1968
	Wilbur J. Cohen	1968–1969
Secretary of Housing and Urban Development	Robert C. Weaver	1966–1969
	Robert C. Wood	1969
Secretary of Transportation	Alan S. Boyd	1967–1969

The Nixon Administration (1969–1974)

Vice President	Spiro T. Agnew	1969–1973
	Gerald R. Ford	1973–1974
Secretary of State	William P. Rogers	1969–1973
	Henry A. Kissinger	1973–1974
Secretary of Treasury	David M. Kennedy	1969–1970
	John B. Connally	1971–1972
	George P. Shultz	1972–1974
	William E. Simon	1974
Attorney General	John N. Mitchell	1969–1972
	Richard G. Kleindienst	1972–1973
	Elliot L. Richardson	1973
	William B. Saxbe	1973–1974
Postmaster General	Winton M. Blount	1969–1971
Secretary of Interior	Walter J. Hickel	1969–1970
	Rogers Morton	1971–1974
Secretary of Agriculture	Clifford M. Hardin	1969–1971
	Earl L. Butz	1971–1974
Secretary of Commerce	Maurice H. Stans	1969–1972
	Peter G. Peterson	1972–1973
	Frederick B. Dent	1973–1974
Secretary of Labor	George P. Shultz	1969–1970
	James D. Hodgson	1970–1973
	Peter J. Brennan	1973–1974
Secretary of Defense	Melvin R. Laird	1969–1973
	Elliot L. Richardson	1973
	James R. Schlesinger	1973–1974
Secretary of Health, Education, and Welfare	Robert H. Finch	1969–1970
	Elliot L. Richardson	1970–1973
	Caspar W. Weinberger	1973–1974

Secretary of Housing and Urban Development	George Romney James T. Lynn	1969–1973 1973–1974
Secretary of Transportation	John A. Volpe Claude S. Brinegar	1969–1973 1973–1974

The Ford Administration (1974–1977)

Vice President	Nelson A. Rockefeller	1974–1977
Secretary of State	Henry A. Kissinger	1974–1977
Secretary of Treasury	William E. Simon	1974–1977
Attorney General	William Saxbe Edward Levi	1974–1975 1975–1977
Secretary of Interior	Rogers Morton Stanley K. Hathaway Thomas Kleppe	1974–1975 1975 1975–1977
Secretary of Agriculture	Earl L. Butz John A. Knebel	1974–1976 1976–1977
Secretary of Commerce	Frederick B. Dent Rogers Morton Elliot L. Richardson	1975–1976 1975–1976 1976–1977
Secretary of Labor	Peter J. Brennan John T. Dunlop W. J. Usery	1974–1975 1975–1976 1976–1977
Secretary of Defense	James R. Schlesinger Donald Rumsfeld	1974–1975 1975–1977
Secretary of Health, Education, and Welfare	Caspar Weinberger Forrest D. Mathews	1974–1975 1975–1977
Secretary of Housing and Urban Development	James T. Lynn Carla A. Hills	1974–1975 1975–1977
Secretary of Transportation	Claude Brinegar William T. Coleman	1974–1975 1975–1977

The Carter Administration (1977–1981)

Vice President	Walter F. Mondale	1977–1981
Secretary of State	Cyrus R. Vance Edmund Muskie	1977–1980 1980–1981
Secretary of Treasury	W. Michael Blumenthal G. William Miller	1977–1979 1979–1981
Attorney General	Griffin Bell Benjamin R. Civiletti	1977–1979 1979–1981

Secretary of Interior	Cecil D. Andrus	1977–1981
Secretary of Agriculture	Robert Bergland	1977–1981
Secretary of Commerce	Juanita M. Kreps Philip M. Klutznick	1977–1979 1979–1981
Secretary of Labor	F. Ray Marshall	1977–1981
Secretary of Defense	Harold Brown	1977–1981
Secretary of Health, Education, and Welfare	Joseph A. Califano Patricia R. Harris	1977–1979 1979
Secretary of Health and Human Services	Patricia R. Harris	1979–1981
Secretary of Education	Shirley M. Hufstedler	1979–1981
Secretary of Housing and Urban Development	Patricia R. Harris Moon Landrieu	1977–1979 1979–1981
Secretary of Transportation	Brock Adams Neil E. Goldschmidt	1977–1979 1979–1981
Secretary of Energy	James R. Schlesinger Charles W. Duncan	1977–1979 1979–1981

The Reagan Administration (1981–1989)

Vice President	George Bush	1981–1989
Secretary of State	Alexander M. Haig George P. Shultz	1981–1982 1982–1989
Secretary of Treasury	Donald Regan James A. Baker III Nicholas Brady	1981–1985 1985–1988 1988–1989
Attorney General	William F. Smith Edwin A. Meese III Richard Thornburgh	1981–1985 1985–1988 1988–1989
Secretary of Interior	James Watt William P. Clark Jr. Donald P. Hodel	1981–1983 1983–1985 1985–1989
Secretary of Agriculture	John Block Richard E. Lyng	1981–1986 1986–1989

Secretary of Commerce	Malcolm Baldrige	1981–1987
	C. William Verity Jr.	1987–1989
Secretary of Labor	Raymond Donovan	1981–1985
	William E. Brock	1985–1987
	Ann D. McLaughlin	1987–1989
Secretary of Defense	Caspar Weinberger	1981–1987
	Frank Carlucci	1987–1989
Secretary of Health and Human Services	Richard Schweiker	1981–1983
	Margaret Heckler	1983–1985
	Otis R. Bowen	1985–1989
Secretary of Education	Terrel H. Bell	1981–1985
	William J. Bennett	1985–1988
	Lauro F. Cavazos	1988–1989
Secretary of Housing and Urban Development	Samuel Pierce	1981–1989
Secretary of Transportation	Drew Lewis	1981–1983
	Elizabeth Dole	1983–1987
	James H. Burnley	1987–1989
Secretary of Energy	James Edwards	1981–1982
	Donald P. Hodel	1982–1985
	John S. Herrington	1985–1989

The George H. W. Bush Administration (1989–1993)

Vice President	J. Danforth Quayle	1989–1993
Secretary of State	James A. Baker III	1989–1992
Secretary of Treasury	Nicholas Brady	1989–1993
Attorney General	Richard Thornburgh	1989–1991
	William P. Barr	1991–1993
Secretary of Interior	Manuel Lujan	1989–1993
Secretary of Agriculture	Clayton K. Yeutter	1989–1991
	Edward Madigan	1991–1993
Secretary of Commerce	Robert Mosbacher	1989–1992
	Barbara Franklin	1992–1993
Secretary of Labor	Elizabeth Dole	1989–1991
	Lynn Martin	1991–1993
Secretary of Defense	Richard Cheney	1989–1993
Secretary of Health and Human Services	Louis W. Sullivan	1989–1993
Secretary of Education	Lauro F. Cavazos	1989–1991
	Lamar Alexander	1991–1993

Secretary of Housing and Urban Development	Jack F. Kemp	1989–1993
Secretary of Transportation	Samuel K. Skinner	1989–1992
	Andrew H. Card Jr.	1992–1993
Secretary of Energy	James D. Watkins	1989–1993
Secretary of Veterans Affairs	Edward J. Derwinski	1989–1993

The Clinton Administration (1993–2001)

Vice President	Albert Gore	1993–2001
Secretary of State	Warren Christopher	1993–1997
	Madeleine Albright	1997–2001
Secretary of Treasury	Lloyd Bentsen	1993–1995
	Robert E. Rubin	1995–1999
	Lawrence H. Summers	1999–2001
Attorney General	Janet Reno	1993–2001
Secretary of Interior	Bruce Babbitt	1993–2001
Secretary of Agriculture	Michael Espy	1993–1995
	Dan Glickman	1995–2001
Secretary of Commerce	Ronald Brown	1993–1996
	Mickey Kantor	1996
	William Daley	1997
	Norman Mineta	1997–2001
Secretary of Labor	Robert B. Reich	1993–1997
	Alexis Herman	1997–2001
Secretary of Defense	Les Aspin	1993–1994
	William J. Perry	1994–1997
	William Cohen	1997–2001
Secretary of Health and Human Services	Donna Shalala	1993–2001
Secretary of Housing and Urban Development	Henry G. Cisneros	1993–1997
	Andrew Cuomo	1997–2001
Secretary of Education	Richard W. Riley	1993–2001
Secretary of Transportation	Federico Peña	1993–1997
	Rodney Slater	1997–2001
Secretary of Energy	Hazel R. O'Leary	1993–1997
	Federico Peña	1997
	Bill Richardson	1998–2001
Secretary of Veterans Affairs	Jesse Brown	1993–1998
	Togo D. West Jr.	1998–2001

The George W. Bush Administration (2001–)

Vice President	Richard B. Cheney	2001–
Secretary of State	Colin Powell	2001–
Secretary of Treasury	Paul H. O'Neill	2001–2002
	John Snow	2003–
Attorney General	John Ashcroft	2001–
Secretary of Interior	Gale Norton	2001–
Secretary of Agriculture	Ann M. Veneman	2001–
Secretary of Commerce	Don Evans	2001–
Secretary of Labor	Elaine Chao	2001–
Secretary of Defense	Donald Rumsfeld	2001–
Secretary of Health and Human Services	Tommy G. Thompson	2001–
Secretary of Housing and Urban Development	Melquiades Rafael Martinez	2001–
Secretary of Education	Rod Paige	2001–
Secretary of Transportation	Norman Mineta	2001–
Secretary of Energy	Spencer Abraham	2001–
Secretary of Veterans Affairs	Anthony Principi	2001–
Secretary of Homeland Security	Tom Ridge	2003–

Justices of the Supreme Court

	Term of Service	Years of Service	Life Span
John Jay	1789–1795	5	1745–1829
John Rutledge	1789–1791	1	1739–1800
William Cushing	1789–1810	20	1732–1810
James Wilson	1789–1798	8	1742–1798
John Blair	1789–1796	6	1732–1800
Robert H. Harrison	1789–1790	—	1745–1790
James Iredell	1790–1799	9	1751–1799
Thomas Johnson	1791–1793	1	1732–1819
William Paterson	1793–1806	13	1745–1806
*John Rutledge**	1795	—	1739–1800
Samuel Chase	1796–1811	15	1741–1811
Oliver Ellsworth	1796–1800	4	1745–1807
Bushrod Washington	1798–1829	31	1762–1829
Alfred Moore	1799–1804	4	1755–1810
John Marshall	1801–1835	34	1755–1835
William Johnson	1804–1834	30	1771–1834
H. Brockholst Livingston	1806–1823	16	1757–1823
Thomas Todd	1807–1826	18	1765–1826
Joseph Story	1811–1845	33	1779–1845
Gabriel Duval	1811–1835	24	1752–1844
Smith Thompson	1823–1843	20	1768–1843
Robert Trimble	1826–1828	2	1777–1828
John McLean	1829–1861	32	1785–1861
Henry Baldwin	1830–1844	14	1780–1844
James M. Wayne	1835–1867	32	1790–1867
Roger B. Taney	1836–1864	28	1777–1864
Philip P. Barbour	1836–1841	4	1783–1841
John Catron	1837–1865	28	1786–1865
John McKinley	1837–1852	15	1780–1852
Peter V. Daniel	1841–1860	19	1784–1860
Samuel Nelson	1845–1872	27	1792–1873
Levi Woodbury	1845–1851	5	1789–1851
Robert C. Grier	1846–1870	23	1794–1870
Benjamin R. Curtis	1851–1857	6	1809–1874
John A. Campbell	1853–1861	8	1811–1889
Nathan Clifford	1858–1881	23	1803–1881
Noah H. Swayne	1862–1881	18	1804–1884
Samuel F. Miller	1862–1890	28	1816–1890
David Davis	1862–1877	14	1815–1886
Stephen J. Field	1863–1897	34	1816–1899
Salmon P. Chase	1864–1873	8	1808–1873
William Strong	1870–1880	10	1808–1895
Joseph P. Bradley	1870–1892	22	1813–1892
Ward Hunt	1873–1882	9	1810–1886
Morrison R. Waite	1874–1888	14	1816–1888
John M. Harlan	1877–1911	34	1833–1911
William B. Woods	1880–1887	7	1824–1887
Stanley Matthews	1881–1889	7	1824–1889
Horace Gray	1882–1902	20	1828–1902
Samuel Blatchford	1882–1893	11	1820–1893
Lucius Q. C. Lamar	1888–1893	5	1825–1893
Melville W. Fuller	1888–1910	21	1833–1910
David J. Brewer	1890–1910	20	1837–1910
Henry B. Brown	1890–1906	16	1836–1913
George Shiras Jr.	1892–1903	10	1832–1924
Howell E. Jackson	1893–1895	2	1832–1895
Edward D. White	1894–1910	16	1845–1921
Rufus W. Peckham	1895–1909	14	1838–1909
Joseph McKenna	1898–1925	26	1843–1926
Oliver W. Holmes	1902–1932	30	1841–1935
William R. Day	1903–1922	19	1849–1923
William H. Moody	1906–1910	3	1853–1917
Horace H. Lurton	1909–1914	4	1844–1914
Charles E. Hughes	1910–1916	5	1862–1948
Edward D. White	1910–1921	11	1845–1921
Willis Van Devanter	1911–1937	26	1859–1941
Joseph R. Lamar	1911–1916	5	1857–1916
Mahlon Pitney	1912–1922	10	1858–1924
James C. McReynolds	1914–1941	26	1862–1946
Louis D. Brandeis	1916–1939	22	1856–1941
John H. Clarke	1916–1922	6	1857–1945
William H. Taft	1921–1930	8	1857–1930
George Sutherland	1922–1938	15	1862–1942
Pierce Butler	1922–1939	16	1866–1939
Edward T. Sanford	1923–1930	7	1865–1930
Harlan F. Stone	1925–1941	16	1872–1946
Charles E. Hughes	1930–1941	11	1862–1948
Owen J. Roberts	1930–1945	15	1875–1955
Benjamin N. Cardozo	1932–1938	6	1870–1938
Hugo L. Black	1937–1971	34	1886–1971
Stanley F. Reed	1938–1957	19	1884–1980
Felix Frankfurter	1939–1962	23	1882–1965
William O. Douglas	1939–1975	36	1898–1980
Frank Murphy	1940–1949	9	1890–1949
Harlan F. Stone	1941–1946	5	1872–1946
James F. Byrnes	1941–1942	1	1879–1972
Robert H. Jackson	1941–1954	13	1892–1954
Wiley B. Rutledge	1943–1949	6	1894–1949
Harold H. Burton	1945–1958	13	1888–1964
Fred M. Vinson	1946–1953	7	1890–1953
Tom C. Clark	1949–1967	18	1899–1977
Sherman Minton	1949–1956	7	1890–1965
Earl Warren	1953–1969	16	1891–1974

*Appointed and served one term, but not confirmed by the Senate.

Note: Chief justices are in italics.

A-30

	Term of Service	Years of Service	Life Span
John Marshall Harlan	1955–1971	16	1899–1971
William J. Brennan Jr.	1956–1990	33	1906–1997
Charles E. Whittaker	1957–1962	5	1901–1973
Potter Stewart	1958–1981	23	1915–1985
Bryon R. White	1962–1993	31	1917–2002
Arthur J. Goldberg	1962–1965	3	1908–1990
Abe Fortas	1965–1969	4	1910–1982
Thurgood Marshall	1967–1991	24	1908–1992
Warren C. Burger	1969–1986	17	1907–1995
Harry A. Blackmun	1970–1994	24	1908–1999
Lewis F. Powell Jr.	1972–1987	15	1907–1998

	Term of Service	Years of Service	Life Span
William H. Rehnquist	1972–1986	14	1924–
John P. Stevens III	1975–	—	1920–
Sandra Day O'Connor	1981–	—	1930–
William H. Rehnquist	1986–	—	1924–
Antonin Scalia	1986–	—	1936–
Anthony M. Kennedy	1988–	—	1936–
David H. Souter	1990–	—	1939–
Clarence Thomas	1991–	—	1948–
Ruth Bader Ginsburg	1993–	—	1933–
Stephen Breyer	1994–	—	1938–

A Social Profile
of the American Republic

Year	Population	Percent Increase	Population per Square Mile	Population Percent Urban/ Rural	Percent Male/ Female	Percent White/ Nonwhite	Persons per Household	Median Age
1790	3,929,214		4.5	5.1/94.9	NA/NA	80.7/19.3	5.79	NA
1800	5,308,483	35.1	6.1	6.1/93.9	NA/NA	81.1/18.9	NA	NA
1810	7,239,881	36.4	4.3	7.3/92.7	NA/NA	81.0/19.0	NA	NA
1820	9,638,453	33.1	5.5	7.2/92.8	50.8/49.2	81.6/18.4	NA	16.7
1830	12,866,020	33.5	7.4	8.8/91.2	50.8/49.2	81.9/18.1	NA	17.2
1840	17,069,453	32.7	9.8	10.8/89.2	50.9/49.1	83.2/16.8	NA	17.8
1850	23,191,876	35.9	7.9	15.3/84.7	51.0/49.0	84.3/15.7	5.55	18.9
1860	31,443,321	35.6	10.6	19.8/80.2	51.2/48.8	85.6/14.4	5.28	19.4
1870	39,818,449	26.6	13.4	25.7/74.3	50.6/49.4	86.2/13.8	5.09	20.2
1880	50,155,783	26.0	16.9	28.2/71.8	50.9/49.1	86.5/13.5	5.04	20.9
1890	62,947,714	25.5	21.2	35.1/64.9	51.2/48.8	87.5/12.5	4.93	22.0
1900	75,994,575	20.7	25.6	39.6/60.4	51.1/48.9	87.9/12.1	4.76	22.9
1910	91,972,266	21.0	31.0	45.6/54.4	51.5/48.5	88.9/11.1	4.54	24.1
1920	105,710,620	14.9	35.6	51.2/48.8	51.0/49.0	89.7/10.3	4.34	25.3
1930	122,775,046	16.1	41.2	56.1/43.9	50.6/49.4	89.8/10.2	4.11	26.4
1940	131,669,275	7.2	44.2	56.5/43.5	50.2/49.8	89.8/10.2	3.67	29.0
1950	150,697,361	14.5	50.7	64.0/36.0	49.7/50.3	89.5/10.5	3.37	30.2
1960	179,323,175	18.5	50.6	69.9/30.1	49.3/50.7	88.6/11.4	3.33	29.5
1970	203,302,031	13.4	57.4	73.5/26.5	48.7/51.3	87.6/12.4	3.14	28.0
1980	226,545,805	11.4	64.0	73.7/26.3	48.6/51.4	86.0/14.0	2.76	30.0
1990	248,709,873	9.8	70.3	75.2/24.8	48.7/51.3	80.3/19.7	2.63	32.9
2000	281,422,426	13.1	79.6	79.0/21.0	49.0/51.0	81.0/19.0	2.59	35.4

NA = Not available.

		Vital Statistics (rates per thousand)				
Year	Births	Year	Births	Deaths*	Marriages*	Divorces*
1800	55.0	1900	32.3	17.2	NA	NA
1810	54.3	1910	30.1	14.7	NA	NA
1820	55.2	1920	27.7	13.0	12.0	1.6
1830	51.4	1930	21.3	11.3	9.2	1.6
1840	51.8	1940	19.4	10.8	12.1	2.0
1850	43.3	1950	24.1	9.6	11.1	2.6
1860	44.3	1960	23.7	9.5	8.5	2.2
1870	38.3	1970	18.4	9.5	10.6	3.5
1880	39.8	1980	15.9	8.8	10.6	5.2
1890	31.5	1990	16.7	8.6	9.8	4.6
		2000	14.7	8.7	8.5	4.2

NA = Not available.

*Data not available before 1900.

| Year | Total Population | Life Expectancy (in years) | | White Males | Nonwhite Males |
		White Females	Nonwhite Females		
1900	47.3	48.7	33.5	46.6	32.5
1910	50.1	52.0	37.5	48.6	33.8
1920	54.1	55.6	45.2	54.4	45.5
1930	59.7	63.5	49.2	59.7	47.3
1940	62.9	66.6	54.9	62.1	51.5
1950	68.2	72.2	62.9	66.5	59.1
1960	69.7	74.1	66.3	67.4	61.1
1970	70.9	75.6	69.4	68.0	61.3
1980	73.7	78.1	73.6	70.7	65.3
1990	75.4	79.3	76.3	72.6	68.4
2000	76.9	80.0	NA	74.8	NA

The Changing Age Structure

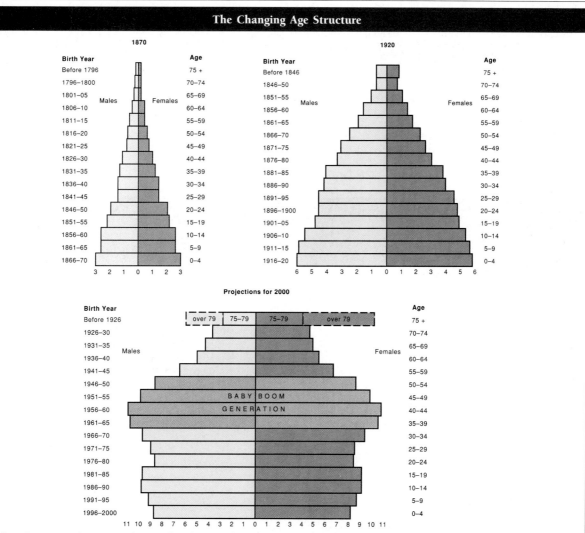

Before the twentieth century, the age distribution of Americans could be charted roughly as a pyramid, as seen in the figures for 1870 and 1920. High birthrates create a broad base at the bottom, while mortality rates winnow the population to a small tip of elderly. But by the year 2000, the pyramid has been transformed more nearly into a cylinder. Over the past two centuries fertility rates have undergone a steady decline, pulling in the base of the pyramid, while higher living standards have allowed Americans to live longer, broadening the top. Only the temporary bulge of the baby boom distorts the shape.

Years	Total Number of Immigrants	Regional Origin of Immigrants (percent) EUROPE				Western Hemisphere	Asia
		Total Europe	North and West	East and Central	South and Other		
1821–1830	143,389	69.2	67.1	—	2.1	8.4	—
1831–1840	599,125	82.8	81.8	—	1.0	5.5	—
1841–1850	1,713,251	93.8	92.9	0.1	0.3	3.6	—
1851–1860	2,598,214	94.4	93.6	0.1	0.8	2.9	1.6
1861–1870	2,314,824	89.2	87.8	0.5	0.9	7.2	2.8
1871–1880	2,812,191	80.8	73.6	4.5	2.7	14.4	4.4
1881–1890	5,246,13	90.3	72.0	11.9	6.3	8.1	1.3
1891–1900	3,687,546	96.5	44.5	32.8	19.1	1.1	1.9
1901–1910	8,795,386	92.5	21.7	44.5	6.3	4.1	2.8
1911–1920	5,735,811	76.3	17.4	33.4	25.5	19.9	3.4
1921–1930	4,107,209	60.3	31.7	14.4	14.3	36.9	2.4
1931–1940	528,431	65.9	38.8	11.0	16.1	30.3	2.8
1941–1950	1,035,039	60.1	47.5	4.6	7.9	34.3	3.1
1951–1960	2,515,479	52.8	17.7	24.3	10.8	39.6	6.0
1961–1970	3,321,677	33.8	11.7	9.4	12.9	51.7	12.9
1971–1980	4,493,300	17.8	4.3	5.6	8.4	44.3	35.2
1981–1990	7,338,000	10.4	5.9	4.8	1.1	49.3	37.3
1991–2000	9,095,417	14.9	4.8	8.6	1.6	49.3	30.7

Dash indicates less than 0.1 percent.

Recent Trends in Immigration (in thousands)					PERCENT		
	1961–1970	1971–1980	1981–1990	1991–2000	1971–1980	1981–1990	1991–2000
All countries	3,321.7	4,493.3	7,338.1	9095.4	100.0	100.0	100.0
Europe	1,123.5	800.4	761.5	1359.7	17.8	10.4	14.9
Austria	20.6	9.5	18.3	15.5	0.2	0.3	0.2
Belgium	9.2	5.3	7.0	7.0	0.1	0.1	0.1
Czechoslovakia	3.3	6.0	7.2	9.8	0.1	0.1	0.1
Denmark	9.2	4.4	5.3	6.0	0.1	0.1	0.1
France	45.2	25.1	22.4	35.8	0.6	1.3	0.4
Germany	190.8	74.4	91.6	92.6	1.7	2.2	1.0
Greece	86.0	92.4	38.3	26.7	2.1	0.4	0.3
Hungary	5.4	6.6	6.5	9.3	0.1	0.1	0.1
Ireland	33.0	11.5	31.9	56.9	0.3	0.9	0.6
Italy	214.1	129.4	67.2	62.7	2.9	0.2	0.7
Netherlands	30.6	10.5	12.2	13.3	0.2	0.1	0.1
Norway	15.5	3.9	4.2	5.1	0.1	1.1	0.5
Poland	53.5	37.2	83.3	163.7	0.8	0.5	1.8
Portugal	76.1	101.7	40.4	22.9	2.3	0.3	0.3
Spain	44.7	39.1	20.4	17.1	0.9	0.2	0.2
Sweden	17.1	6.5	11.0	12.7	0.1	0.1	0.1
Switzerland	18.5	8.2	8.8	11.8	0.2	0.1	0.1
United Kingdom	213.8	137.4	159.2	151.8	3.1	2.2	1.7
USSR	2.5	39.0	57.7	462.8	0.9	0.3	5.1
Yugoslavia	20.4	30.5	18.8	66.5	0.7	0.5	0.7
Other Europe	9.1	18.9	8.2	57.7	0.2	0.0	0.6

Recent Trends in Immigration (in thousands)				PERCENT		
	1961–1970	1971–1980	1981–1990	1991–2000	1971–1980	1981–1990	1991–2000

	1961–1970	1971–1980	1981–1990	1991–2000	1971–1980	1981–1990	1991–2000
Asia	427.6	1588.2	2738.1	2795.6	35.2	37.3	30.7
China	34.8	124.3	298.9	419.1	2.8	4.1	4.6
Hong Kong	75.0	113.5	98.2	109.8	2.5	1.3	1.2
India	27.2	164.1	250.7	363.1	3.7	3.4	4.0
Iran	10.3	45.1	116.0	69.0	1.0	1.6	0.8
Israel	29.6	37.7	44.2	39.4	0.8	0.6	0.4
Japan	40.0	49.8	47.0	67.9	1.1	0.6	0.7
Korea	34.5	267.6	333.8	164.2	6.0	4.5	1.8
Philippines	98.4	355.0	548.7	503.9	7.9	7.5	5.5
Turkey	10.1	13.4	23.4	38.2	0.3	0.3	0.4
Vietnam	4.3	172.8	281.0	286.1	3.8	3.8	3.1
Other Asia	36.5	176.1	631.4	735.4	3.8	8.6	8.0
America	1716.4	1982.5	3615.6	4486.8	44.3	49.3	49.3
Argentina	49.7	29.9	27.3	26.6	0.7	0.4	0.3
Canada	413.3	169.9	158.0	192.0	3.8	2.2	2.1
Colombia	72.0	77.3	122.9	128.5	1.7	1.7	1.4
Cuba	208.5	264.9	144.6	169.3	5.9	2.0	1.9
Dominican Rep.	93.3	148.1	252.0	335.3	3.3	3.4	3.7
Ecuador	36.8	50.1	56.2	76.5	1.1	0.8	0.8
El Salvador	15.0	34.4	213.5	215.7	0.8	2.9	2.4
Haiti	34.5	56.3	138.4	179.6	1.3	1.9	2.0
Jamaica	74.9	137.6	208.1	169.2	3.1	2.8	1.9
Mexico	453.9	640.3	1655.7	2249.4	14.3	22.6	24.7
Other America	264.4	373.8	639.3	744.3	8.3	8.7	8.2
Africa	29.0	80.8	176.8	355.0	1.8	2.4	3.9
Oceania	25.1	41.2	45.2	55.8	0.9	0.6	0.6

Figures may not add to total due to rounding.

American Workers and Farmers						
Year	Total Number of Workers (thousands)	Percent of Workers Male/Female	Percent of Female Workers Married	Percent of Workers in Female Population	Percent of Workers in Labor Unions	Farm Population (thousands)	Farm Population as Percent of Total Population
1870	12,506	85/15	NA	NA	NA	NA	NA
1880	17,392	85/15	NA	NA	NA	21,973	43.8
1890	23,318	83/17	13.9	18.9	NA	24,771	42.3
1900	29,073	82/18	15.4	20.6	3	29,875	41.9
1910	38,167	79/21	24.7	25.4	6	32,077	34.9
1920	41,614	79/21	23.0	23.7	12	31,974	30.1
1930	48,830	78/22	28.9	24.8	7	30,529	24.9
1940	53,011	76/24	36.4	27.4	27	30,547	23.2
1950	59,643	72/28	52.1	31.4	25	23,048	15.3
1960	69,877	68/32	59.9	37.7	26	15,635	8.7
1970	82,049	63/37	63.4	43.4	25	9712	4.8
1980	108,544	58/42	59.7	51.5	23	6051	2.7
1990	117,914	55/45	58.4	44.3	16	3871	1.6
2000	135,208	54/46	61.3	45.7	15	3305	1.1

| Year | Gross National Product (GNP) (in billions)* | FOREIGN TRADE (in millions) | | | Federal Budget (in billions) | Federal Surplus/Deficit (in billions) | Federal Debt (in billions) |
		Exports	Imports	Balance of Trade			
1790	NA	$20	$23	$−3	$0.004	$+0.00015	$0.076
1800	NA	71	91	−20	0.011	+0.0006	0.083
1810	NA	67	85	−18	0.008	+0.0012	0.053
1820	NA	70	74	−4	0.018	−0.0004	0.091
1830	NA	74	71	+3	0.015	+0.100	0.049
1840	NA	132	107	+25	0.024	−0.005	0.004
1850	NA	152	178	−26	0.040	+0.004	0.064
1860	NA	400	362	−38	0.063	−0.01	0.065
1870	$7.4	451	462	−11	0.310	+0.10	2.4
1880	11.2	853	761	+92	0.268	+0.07	2.1
1890	13.1	910	823	+87	0.318	+0.09	1.2
1900	18.7	1499	930	+569	0.521	+0.05	1.2
1910	35.3	1919	1646	+273	0.694	−0.02	1.1
1920	91.5	8664	5784	+2880	6.357	+0.3	24.3
1930	90.7	4013	3500	+513	3.320	+0.7	16.3
1940	100.0	4030	7433	−3403	9.6	−2.7	43.0
1950	286.5	10,816	9125	+1691	43.1	−2.2	257.4
1960	506.5	19,600	15,046	+4556	92.2	+0.3	286.3
1970	992.7	42,700	40,189	+2511	195.6	−2.8	371.0
1980	2631.7	220,783	244,871	+24,088	590.9	−73.8	907.7
1990	5803.2	394,030	495,042	−101,012	1253.1	−220.5	3206.6
2000	9872.9	1,102,900	1,466,900	−364,000	1788.8	+236.4	5629.0

The Economy and Federal Spending

*For 1990 and after, gross domestic product (GDP) is given.

	U.S. Military Personnel (thousands)	American Wars Personnel as % of Population	U.S. Deaths	U.S. Wounds	Direct Cost 1990 dollars (millions)
American Revolution Apr. 1775–Sept. 1783	184–250	9–12	4004	6004	$100–140
War of 1812 June 1812–Feb. 1815	286	3	1950	4000	87
Mexican War May 1846–Feb. 1848	116	0.5	13,271	4102	82
Civil War: Union	3393	14	360,222	275,175	2302
Civil War: Confederacy Apr. 1861–Apr. 1865	1034	11	258,000	NA	1032
Spanish-American War Apr. 1898–Aug. 1898	307	0.4	2446	1662	270
World War I Apr. 1917–Nov. 1918	4714	5	116,516	204,002	32,740
World War II Dec. 1941–Aug. 1945	16,354	12	405,399	670,846	360,000
Korean War June 1950–June 1953	5764	4	54,246	103,284	50,000
Vietnam War Aug. 1964–June 1973	8400	4	47,704	219,573	140,644
Persian Gulf War Jan. 1991–Feb. 1991	467	0.1	293	467	20,163*

*Amount paid by United States. Total cost of war calculated to be $61.1 billion.

Credits

Index